NEW COMPARAT ... R
OF GREEK AN ...

NEW COMPARATIVE GRAMMAR OF GREEK AND LATIN

Andrew L. Sihler

OXFORD
UNIVERSITY PRESS

OXFORD
UNIVERSITY PRESS

Oxford University Press, Inc., publishes works that further
Oxford University's objective of excellence
in research, scholarship, and education.

Oxford New York
Auckland Cape Town Dar es Salaam Hong Kong Karachi
Kuala Lumpur Madrid Melbourne Mexico City Nairobi
New Delhi Shanghai Taipei Toronto

With offices in
Argentina Austria Brazil Chile Czech Republic France Greece
Guatemala Hungary Italy Japan Poland Portugal Singapore
South Korea Switzerland Thailand Turkey Ukraine Vietnam

Published by Oxford University Press, Inc.,
198 Madison Avenue, New York, New York 10016-4314

www.oup.com

First issued as an Oxford University Press paperback, 2008

Library of Congress Cataloging-in-Publication Data
Sihler, Andrew L.
New comparative grammar of Greek and Latin / Andrew L. Sihler.
p. cm.
ISBN 978-0-19-508345-3; 978-0-19-537336-3 (pbk.)
1. Greek language—Grammar, Comparative—Latin. 2. Latin language—Grammar,
Comparative—Greek. I. Title.
PA111.S54 1994
485—dc20 93-38929

11 13 15 17 19 18 16 14 12
Printed in the United States of America
on acid-free paper

In memory of

Warren Crawford Cowgill

1929 – 1985

PREFACE

Historical linguistics does not change as rapidly as some disciplines. Even though 60 years have elapsed since the appearance of Carl Darling Buck's Comparative grammar of Greek and Latin, its value has endured, both as a reference work and as a handbook for students in the classical languages. However, with time there have accumulated many small changes along with a few large ones in Proto-Indo-European reconstruction, and concomitantly in how the historical developments of the daughter languages are best accounted for. Substantial as its virtues are, therefore, except for experts Buck's Comparative grammar is no longer serviceable.

For this reason in 1986 I set out to prepare a revised edition. I imagined that revisions would be extensive only in certain areas—laryngeal phonology, and a necessarily very different approach to the Indo-European verb, for instance. However, as work progressed the retrenching became so extensive that it was no longer appropriate to think of the results as a 'revision'.

Nevertheless, owing to the genesis of this book, readers familiar with Buck will often be reminded of that work, which provides the robust underpinnings for what follows. The layout is similar, for one thing, especially in the phonology. Throughout there are phrases, sentences, even whole paragraphs, reproduced from Buck with little or no change, for example in the treatment of the Greek aorist (504–7, cf. Buck 396–400), though even here a few differences in detail as well will be noted. At the opposite extreme, remnants of Buck surrounded by largely new material may be seen in the treatment of vowel contraction in Latin (88, Buck 105), the Greek palatalizations (197-207, Buck 181-8), and passim in the discussions of the mediopassive and the PIE stative ('perfect'). An example of the most usual state of affairs—much retained while much is changed—would be the treatment of syllabic resonants (93ff, cf. Buck 113ff).

Mere updating would not require such a wide departure from Buck's model, however, and in fact the greatest differences between the books stem from two other factors. One is the difference in the scope of the two works. It has always seemed to me that a demerit of Buck's Comparative grammar is its uniformly oracular presentation. It is of course unnecessary (not to say impossible) to motivate every detail of Proto-Indo-European reconstruction de novo, but it seemed to me worthwhile to treat the reconstruction of the features of an ancestral language as an object of study itself. Throughout, therefore, I have included discussions of why this or that is reconstructed, or why one explanation is more satisfactory than another, and, where no clear choice is evident among competing theories, have set out briefly the merits and demerits of the options. The resulting changes are pervasive, but may be assessed in the discussion of ablaut (166-83)—it is not only different from Buck's in the linguistics (laryngeals have seen to that); it is very different in scope and aim.

Secondly, explaining the rationale of reconstruction inevitably changes the scope of the work in another way: it requires presenting the facts of the Indo-European languages apart from Greek and Latin more amply than Buck needed to. The result may serve as a vade-mecum to a study of Indo-European linguistics; but the added material will I hope nourish whatever curiosity readers—even those classicists who are concerned with the details of Greek and Latin alone—might have about the backdrop before which the classical forms are displayed.

Widening the aims of the book in these ways not only required departure from the original in detail, it has increased its size. To compensate, the discussion of word formation (Buck 441-530) has been omitted. It would require a good deal of refinement in any case, and informative material can nowadays be found in the specialized handbooks. For reasons of size, too, it has not been possible to retain the introductory discussion of the fundamentals of historical linguistics (35-63). This is the more regrettable loss, as in the view of many users it was one of the book's signal assets; and since it cannot be presumed that students of Classics or of other ancient languages will have much background in historical and comparative linguistics, I hope to publish something along the lines of this introductory material separately.

I make no claim to the originality of any ideas in this work. That is not to say that none are original, only that intellectual paternity is claimed for none. However, whenever an idea is presented with a value judgment, either approbative or the reverse (*a better analysis* . . ., or *this implausible concept* . . ., and the like), the reader may be certain that the idea at stake is not the author's.

The most important influence on both the content and the manner of this work is the teaching and thinking of the late Warren Cowgill. John Aubrey's brief life of John Selden quotes, from a source unknown to Aubrey himself, the observation that *when a learned man dies, there dyes a great deale of learning with him.* This dismaying truism is particularly hard to contemplate in Cowgill's case, as his publications represent a very incomplete record of his thinking on Indo-European linguistics. And given Cowgill's age when death claimed him, a second remark of Aubrey's regarding Selden is even harder to contemplate without a heightened sense of loss: *if Learning could have kept a man alive our Brother had not dyed.*

As one of the few who had the luck to study with Warren Cowgill, it is one of my aims in this work to get at least a little more of his thinking into general circulation, however fragmentarily and inadequately. It must be understood that no claim is made for any excellence of the product on that account, however; and more, this is not in any way an intellectual mausoleum in the vein of the Cours de linguistique générale, by means of which Bally and Sechehaye endeavored to present Ferdinand de Saussure's teaching entire, without addition, subtraction, or change. Warren Cowgill's teaching, that is to say, is not simply reproduced here. There is too much of his thought that is unknown to me, and besides, his ideas changed over the years. And even a Cowgill is capable of hasty or insecurely-grounded opinions—and it is precisely in classroom discussions (my chief insider source) that a provisional idea that would never deserve to see print might well surface.

Hardly less important than Cowgill's contributions, and more visible, as they are entirely from published sources, are the theories of Oswald Szemerényi. These are perhaps most obvious in the discussions of numerals (386-99) and the present participle (556-8) but they are in fact pervasive.

The influence of the work of many other scholars is evident on these pages. Those who are now or until recently were still alive include (in alphabetical order): David Anthony, Raimo Anttila, Françoise Bader, Philip Baldi, Alfred Bammesberger, Robert Beekes, Madison Beeler, Emile Benveniste, Thomas Burrow, George Cardona, N.E. Collinge, Bernard Comrie, James Dishington, E. David Francis, Marija Gimbutas, Eric Hamp, E. Adelaide Hahn, Rolf Hiersche, Hans Hock, Henry Hoenigwald, Karl Hoffman, Franklyn Horowitz, Martin Huld, Stanley Insler, Stephanie Jamison, Jay Jasanoff, Carol F. Justus, Paul Kiparsky, Jared Klein, Frederik H.H. Kortlandt, F.B.J. Kuiper, Jerzy Kuryłowicz, W.P. Lehmann, Michel Lejeune, Frederik Otto Lindeman, Gordon Fairbanks, Sarah Kimball, James Mallory, Thomas Markey, Manfred Mayrhofer, Wolfgang Meid, C. Gerhard Meiser, Craig Melchert, Denise Meyer, Anna Morpurgo Davies, Johanna Narten, Alan Nussbaum, Martti Nyman, Angel Pariente, Martin Peters, Edgar Polomé, Jaan Puhvel, C.J. Ruijgh, Donald Ringe, Helmut Rix, Hartmut Scharfe, Jochem Schindler, Hans Schmeja, Rüdiger Schmitt, Elmar Seebold, Klaus Strunk, Paul Tedesco, Brent Vine, F.M.J. Waanders, Rudolf Wachter, Calvert Watkins, Werner Winter, William Wyatt, Kazuhiko Yoshida, and Valdis Zeps.

ACKNOWLEDGEMENTS

Grants from the Graduate School Research Committee of the University of Wisconsin have been crucial to this enterprise: first in 1986 for the purchase of Greek-speaking word processing software, without which it would have been unthinkable to tackle such a project; in 1989 a generous grant of a semester's salary excused me from teaching duties; and lastly in

1992 the Committee provided a Project Assistant's salary to aid in the preparation of indexes.

Over the years I have been trying out parts of the book on students in courses, who as informed end-users were in the best position to judge such matters as the intelligibility and consistency of the whole. Particular thanks are due to Denise Meyer, Geoffrey Koby, George Hall, Stephen Israel, Gregory Hanson, Bradley Holtman, Charles Schleicher, Bożena Tieszen, and Polly Hoover. Improvements to the text were not all that was provided: association with these smart and funny people has confirmed the observation that the best part of teaching is the students.

I am also indebted to my colleagues: Jeffrey Wills bravely volunteered his students in his course on the Comparative Grammar of Greek and Latin for guinea pigs, using a preliminary draft of the ms. as a text, and relayed comments and suggestions back to me; Valdis Zeps was kind enough to read and comment on large sections of an earlier draft, and later vetted the work for the accuracy of Baltic and Slavic citations; and Raimo Anttila carefully read a late draft and made many useful suggestions. Most particular and especial gratitude is due Brent Vine, who recommended countless improvements touching on organization as well as content. The handling of Old Latin and Italic evidence in particular was greatly improved by his advice, but the beneficial effects of Vine's attention are ubiquitous. Thanks to his careful attention, a large number of defects (including a hair-raising blunder or two) have been corrected.

I would also like to thank two anonymous referees for the Oxford University Press, who in 1988 read drafts of the introduction and phonology sections with care and pointed out many matters that would profit from closer attention.

As for the defects of fact or judgment which have resisted or eluded the efforts of my colleagues, I naturally take full responsibility.

I am grateful also for the family, friends, students, colleagues, publishers, former teachers, and even some total strangers, who have been generous with their encouragement.

Finally, I owe special and personal gratitude to John Tallman, whose many lovely qualities do not include knowledge of, or an interest in, historical linguistics. But without him this never would have been written.

MADISON, WISCONSIN A.L.S.
MAY 1994

CONTENTS

PART III: Declension

Abbreviations

1 first person
2 second person
3 third person
abl. ablative
abs. absolute
acc. accusative
act. active voice
adj. adjective, adjectival
adv. adverb(ial)
Aeol. Aeolic
Akk. Akkadian
Alb. Albanian
aor. aorist
ἅπ.λεγ. once attested
App.Prob. Appendix Probi
Arc. Arcadian
arch. archaic
Arg. Argolic
Arm. Armenian
athem. athematic
Att. Attic
Att.-Ion. Attic-Ionic
AV Atharvaveda
Av. Avestan
Boeot. Boeotian
Brāh. Brāhmaṇas; Brāhmaṇical Sanskrit
BS Baltic and Slavic Assemblage
c. common (gender)
caus. causative
Celt. Celtic
Cic. Cicero
class. classical
conj. conjugation
cpd(s). compound(s)
Cyp. Cypriot
dat. dative
decl. declension
dep. deponent
desid. desiderative
dial. dialect(s), dialectal
dim. diminutive
Dor. Doric
Du. Dutch
du. dual
du.tant. dual only
dub. dubious
EGmc. East Germanic
El. Elean
encl. enclitic
Ep. Epic
Epid. Epidaurus
esp. especially
Etr. Etruscan
etym. etymology; etymological(ly)
Eur. Euripides
f. feminine
Falisc. Faliscan
Fam. Ad Familiares
fem. feminine
fn. footnote
Fr. French
freq(uent). frequentative
fut. future tense
G Greek
Gaul. Gaulish
GAv. Gāthic Avestan
gen. genitive
ger. gerund
Gmc. Germanic
Go. Gothic
gramm. grammarians
Hdt. Herodotus
Heracl. Heraclean
Hes. Hesiod
Hesych. Hesychius
Hitt. Hittite
Hom. Homer(ic)
imper(at). imperative
imperf. imperfect tense
indecl. indeclinable
indef. indefinite
indic(at). indicative
inf(in). infinitive
InIr. Indo-Iranian
inj. injunctive
inscr. epigraphic
inst. instrumental
intens. intensive
intr(ans). intransitive
Ion. Ionic
It. Italian
it.-dur. iterative-durative
Ital. Italic
L Latin
Lac. Laconian, Lacedemonian
Latv. Latvian
Lesb. Lesbic
lit. literally
Lith. Lithuanian
LL Late Latin
loc. locative
Luv. Luvian
lw. loan word
m. masculine
masc. masculine
ME Middle English
Mess. Messenian
midd. middle voice
MIr. Middle Irish
Mon.Ancyr. Monumentum Acyranum
Myc. Mycenaean
MW Widdle Welsh
n. neuter
NE Modern English
neut. neuter
NG Modern Greek
NGmc. North Germanic
NHG Modern German
nom. nominative
nom.act. nomen actionis
NT New Testament
O Oscan
obl. oblique
OCS Old Church Slavic
OE Old English
OFr. Old French
OHG Old High German
OIc. Old Icelandic
OIr. Old Irish
OL Old Latin
ON Old Norse
OP(ers.) Old Persian

OPr. Old Prussian
opt. optative
Or. De Oratore
orig. original(ly)
ORu. Old Russian
OU Osco-Umbrian
Paelig. Paelignian
Pamph. Pamphylian
pass. passive voice
Paul.Fest. Paulus-Festus
PCelt. Proto-Celtic
perf. perfect tense
PG Proto-Greek
PGmc. Proto-Germanic
Ph. Phoenician
Pind. Pindar
PInIr. Proto-Indo-Iranian
PItal. Proto-Italic
pl. plural
pl.tant. plural only
Plaut. Plautus
plpf. pluperfect
poet. poetic(al)
Port. Portuguese
pple. participle
Prāk. Prākrit
PreG Pre-Greek
PreGmc. Pre-Germanic
PreL Pre-Latin
pres. present tense
pret. preterite
pret.-pres. preterite-present
prim. primary
pron. pronounced
prn. pronoun, pronominal
PRom. Proto-Romance
PSem. Proto-Semitic
PWGmc. Proto-West-Germanic
redup(l). reduplicated
rel. relative
Rom. Romanian
RV Rigveda, Rigvedic
Sab. Sabellian
SC de Bacch. Senatusconsultum de Bacchanalibus (186 BC)
sec. secondary
sg. singular
Skt. Sanskrit
Sp. Spanish
SPic. South Picenian
subj. subjunctive
suppl. suppletive
Ter. Terence
Thess. Thessalian
tr(ans). transitive
transl. translation of
U Umbrian
Ved. Vedic Sanskrit
VL Vulgar Latin
voc. vocative
W Welsh
WG West Greek
WGmc. West Germanic

NEW COMPARATIVE GRAMMAR OF GREEK AND LATIN

INTRODUCTION

1. THE INDO-EUROPEAN FAMILY OF LANGUAGES. Similarities will always be found between any two languages. Some of these similarities are due to pure chance, such as the resemblance between L *deus*, G θεός, and Aztec *teotl* all 'god', or between NE *whole* and G ὅλος, or between Fr. *le* and Samoan *le* both 'the', or between G στῦλος 'pillar' and L *stilus* 'stake'.[1] And of course human languages are generally similar by virtue of being human languages.

Two remaining kinds of similarity, however, are the direct result of the histories of the languages in question. One of these is diffusion, that is, a language takes over traits (vocabulary or other details of structure) from another language. The familiar term for this phenomenon is *borrowing*. By far, the most frequently borrowed elements are words, but in fact any component of linguistic structure might be borrowed.

The other kind of similarity with historical significance is a pervasive PATTERN of similarities (and differences) in the most BASIC VOCABULARY. Since basic vocabulary is largely immune to changes of fashion, it is highly persistent through time; that means it is least likely to be replaced as time passes, either by borrowing or by disuse. And where PATTERNS are noted, the odds against chance resemblance, as an explanation for the similarity, increase exponentially. Recurring correspondences in basic vocabulary are best explained by assuming that the languages showing such patterns are descended from a common ancestor; less figuratively, THEY WERE ONCE THE SAME LANGUAGE. This ancestor is called a *proto-language*.

Languages which are changed later forms of a proto-language are said to belong to a *language family*. There are many such families; Greek and Latin are members of one of the earliest discovered, largest, and best understood language families: *Indo-European*. At the dawn of recorded history, IE languages were being spoken in Chinese Turkestan and Ireland (Tocharian and Old Irish, respectively), and over vast regions in between; since then its worldwide distribution has actually increased, as IE languages have come to be spoken by the majority of the populace of the New World and by many inhabitants of Africa, the Philippines, Japan, and elsewhere.

a. The term *Indo-European* (IE) dates from 1813, and for a long time was applied both to the language family and to the proto-language; for the latter the term *Proto-Indo-*

---

[1] 'Chance resemblances', that is words of similar meaning with coincidentally similar form, are abundant within a single lexicon too: NE *ill* and *ailment* have no historical connection, neither do *miniature* and *diminutive*, nor G ὕδωρ 'water' and ἱδρώς 'sweat', nor G δύο and δεύτερος, nor L *sūmen* 'sow, pig' and *sūs* 'swine', nor *cubus* and *cubiculum*.

Please see **28-35** for an explanation of citation conventions.

European (PIE) is preferable. This terminology is mirrored in most European languages (Fr. *indo-européen* and the like). The exception is German *Indogermanisch* (= IE) and *Urindogermanisch* (= PIE). This is the source of the *Indo-Germanic* of some English works. The term *Aryan* is also used in the same sense, but more by historians and ethnologists than by linguists—though in fact the term is obsolete, having been contaminated by its association with homicidal social theories. The term is encountered among linguists, though rarely these days, as an alternative designation for the Iranian group of the Indo-Iranian branch of IE (4).

2. BRANCHES OF INDO-EUROPEAN. Members of a language family show greatly varying degrees of similarity. Special similarity can be the basis for collecting certain members of a language family together in *branches*, such as Germanic (8) or Celtic (7). A branch can be thought of as being traceable to an intermediate proto-language (Proto-Germanic or Proto-Celtic, in the case of these examples), which evolved as single daughters of PIE until the point where each ramified into various daughters of its own.

In the infancy of our science, scholars thought of Greek and Latin in terms of special similarity—a branch, or at the very least a subgroup; but this was an error, promoted by cultural considerations. In fact, the most evident linguistic similarities between these languages are conservative features. Taking these to add up to a special similarity is a serious blunder, as it is INNOVATIONS that define both branches and subgroups. Greek and Latin have little in common beyond their descent from a single proto-language. Accordingly, a 'comparative grammar' of Greek and Latin means starting from the very beginning and recounting perhaps 3,000 years of virtually independent lines of development. A comparative grammar of, say, Sanskrit and Greek would be very much more revealing, as those two languages have much in common in addition to what they inherited from PIE.

3. ANATOLIAN. In Anatolia (roughly equivalent to Asia Minor) were anciently spoken several languages related to the familiar IE languages. The best attested is *Hittite*.[1] Hittite was the language of administration of the Hatti empire, whose capital city Hattusas was at the site of the present-day Turkish village of Boğazköy, within the great bend of the Halys (modern Kızıl-Irmak) River; this is also the source of the major part of our Hittite texts. The clay tablets on which the texts are written in cuneiform script range in date from about 2000 to 1200 BC. There are significant differences in the language of the earlier and later texts.

4. INDO-IRANIAN. *Indic*, *Iranian*, and *Dardic* languages are descendants of Proto-Indo-Iranian. The early forms of these languages rank among the most important sources of information about PIE, and in fact were somewhat overvalued in that connection—in the early days of IE studies, Sanskrit was taken to be little but a dialect of PIE.

---

[1] The name *Hittite* is derived from the pre-Hittite name of the empire and its capital Hattusas; our Hittites seem to have called themselves *Nesis*.

The earliest form of *Indic* is found in the Vedic texts of the Hindu religion. Of these the oldest is the Rigveda, a collection of hymns in bulk slightly less than the Iliad and Odyssey together. The language of this and the other collections of hymns, with the prose commentaries attached to them, is known as *Vedic (Sanskrit)*. Vedic differs considerably from the later *Epic* and *Classical Sanskrit*, much as Homeric differs from Attic Greek.

Iranian extended over the Persian Empire east of Mesopotamia and Elam, namely from Media and Persia in the west to Bactria and Sogdiana in the northeast. There is evidence (largely indirect) suggesting that Iranian speech communities were spread over a vast area, though how well organized politically these regions were, and how uniform ethnically and linguistically, cannot be told. Two ancient Iranian languages are known. The earlier, and the more important for linguistic historians, is *Avestan* (formerly sometimes called *Zend* by a misunderstanding). This is the language of the Avesta, a fragmentary collection of Zoroastrian rites, myths, hymns, and prayers. In this text, certain hymns known as the Gāthās show a particularly early form of the language; their dates are disputed but lie somewhere between 1000 and 600 BC. The rest of the Avesta was composed at various later times, and may be taken as reflecting the language of say 500-300 BC. The extant text, which is preserved by the Parsees of India (8th century Iranian refugees from Islam), is only a small part of the original.

Old Persian, from a later period, is known from the cuneiform inscriptions of the Achaemenid kings, mainly of Darius I (dārayavahuš) and Xerxes (χšayāršа). It is presumably based on the speech of their homeland, Persia proper, but being a language of administration it is well attested elsewhere, for example in Susa (an old Elamite center) and Persepolis. The longest Old Persian inscription, a document of outstanding importance for historians as well as linguists, is the huge bas-relief and inscription of Darius I on a cliff face at Behistun (Bihistun, Bisutun), the ancient Βαγίσταvov ὄρος, southwest of Ecbatana.

a. *Dardic* was not known before modern times; it is little more than a term of convenience to designate some twenty Indo-Iranian vernaculars which it appears cannot be easily traced either to Proto-Indic or Proto-Iranian. Chief among these in terms of numbers of speakers is *Kashmiri*.

5. ARMENIAN. The Armenians of IE speech were relative latecomers in Armenia (now eastern Turkey and adjacent parts of the former Soviet Union), which is known to have been occupied about 950-650 BC by a people which left records in a non-IE language. The earliest Armenian texts are from the 5th century AD. Much of the early literature consists of translations from Greek, including one of the earliest translations of NT texts (5th century). A noteworthy feature of Armenian is that it shows a consonant shift very similar to that of the Germanic languages (**8**).

6. ALBANIAN is the language of Albania on the Adriatic coast, though there are sizable communities of speakers in adjacent polities. There are

also Albanian colonies dating from the 15th century AD in Greece, southern Italy, and Sicily.

Except for some meager records of the 16th and 17th centuries, the language is known only from recent times. There was no standardized written language until the promulgation of a national orthography, based upon Latin characters, in 1909.

a. Identification of modern Albanian with ancient Thracian or Illyrian has been proposed. Each alternative has its partisans; and as is often the case, the nearly complete blank in our knowledge of both of those ancient languages has stimulated rather than hobbled the controversy.

7. CELTIC speech, now restricted to three or four small areas, was in ancient times spread over a vast territory. Celtic-speaking tribes occupied the British Isles, Gaul, part of Spain, and central Europe, extending through Bohemia (which takes its name from the Boii, a Celtic group) and Austria, while the Galatians passed over into Asia Minor. Upper Italy (Gallia Cisalpina) was mainly Celtic in 400 BC. Almost all of the ancient Celtic territories are now occupied by Germanic, Slavic, and Romance languages.

The old continental Celtic is conventionally known as *Gaulish*. It is paltry in its attestation. Most remains are short—brief votary inscriptions, epitaphs, and so on. There are a number of longer texts inscribed on lead panels, and their probable purposes (cures, curses, and other kinds of magic) go far to render them incomprehensible.

The better known languages fall into two groups, *Gaelic* (Goidelic) and *Britannic* (Brythonic), with *Irish* and *Welsh* the chief representatives of each, respectively.

Primitive Irish is the language of the Ogam stones, chiefly epitaphs, dating from around 400-600 AD. *Old Irish* is known from the 8th century AD, consisting of one short prose work, glosses inserted in Latin texts by Irish monks on the Continent, and a few poems. Even the earliest attestations of OIr. exhibit a language so transformed that in the early days of comparative linguistics it was doubted that Irish could be IE at all.

A little *Old Welsh* dates from the 8th century AD; there is a large *Middle Welsh* (1100 - 1500) literature. A close relative of Welsh, *Cornish*, became extinct at the end of the 18th century.

Breton, in the French province of Brittany, is not a relic of the old continental Gaulish, but was brought by immigrants from southern England after the Anglo-Saxon invasion; it is closely related to Cornish. Similarly, *Scots Gaelic*, spoken in parts of Scotland is not a relic of an indigenous language, but was imported from Ireland.

Celtic languages are traditionally divided into '*P*-Celtic' (Welsh, Gaulish) and '*Q*-Celtic' (Irish), according to their reflexes of PIE $*k^w$ (155).

8. GERMANIC, formerly sometimes called *Teutonic*, is a branch of IE characterized by a number of striking innovations; but much of the remaining structure of Germanic is notably conservative. During the first millennium BC, Germanic tribes lived in southern Scandinavia and northern Germany. For unknown reasons, some tribes began pressing south in the 4th

century BC. This was the beginning of a period of Germanic migration that strongly influenced the course of early European history. It seems to have been the ultimate cause of the Celtic incursions into Italy in the 4th century BC, for instance.

On the basis of certain shared innovations, the Germanic languages are conventionally subdivided into *East*, *North*, and *West*.

East Germanic. Except for brief and often obscure Runic inscriptions, the earliest record of Germanic speech is the (fragmentary) Bible translation of Bishop Wulfilas, who lived in the 4th century AD and wrote in *Gothic*. The other remains of Gothic and of other East Germanic dialects, *Gepid*, *Vandal*, and others, are of minimal account. There are no descendents of East Germanic speech in modern times; the last reliable trace of the branch is notice of a band living in the Crimea in the 16th century.

North Germanic. *Old Norse*, representing this branch, is known from runic inscriptions and the extensive *Old Icelandic* literature. By gradual differentiation arose the present Scandinavian languages: *Swedish*, *Danish*, *Norwegian*, *Icelandic*, and *Faroese*. (The 'dialects' within these languages in some cases differ more from one another than the official forms do, which in the case of Norwegian, Swedish, and Danish are mutually intelligible.)

West Germanic is the most questionable of the Germanic subdivisions. The differences between *Old English* and the Continental languages (*Dutch*, *High German*, and *Saxon*) are considerable; and the points of similarity between OE and North Germanic are striking. *Old High German*, in various dialects, is known from the 8th century on. *Old Low German* is represented chiefly by the *Old Saxon* of the Hêliand, a long 9th century poem on the life of Christ. New High German (NHG), in common parlance simply *German*, is based mainly on East Franconian dialects. There are many local High German dialects, among them *Yiddish*. *Low German* (*Plattdeutsch*) of northern Germany is not in linguistic fact a dialect of German; it was the language of the Hanseatic League, and during the Middle Ages was vigorous and prestigious. But shortly after the Reformation it yielded its status to High German.

The history of *English* is one with the history of Britain. The peoples speaking the ancestor of OE once occupied the coast region from the mouth of the Scheldt to Schleswig-Holstein. Exactly how and why these continental Germanic tribes were transplanted is obscure. But given the success of the English language in Britain, we must surmise the involvement of family groups in the process, and in non-trivial numbers too.

Later, Scandinavian invasion and occupation of the land north of the Saxon domain, a region known for a long period as the Danelaw, introduced a related Germanic element. This resulted in a permanent mixture of both language and customs. The number of English words which reflect a Scandinavian rather than the true English form is large, and includes much basic vocabulary (1).

The earliest OE literary remains are poems, the oldest dating from before the 7th century AD. Though few in number (thanks to a fire in a major collection of mss), the artistic quality of the poetry is very high. The longest, and most famous, is the heroic tale of Bêowulf, identified in the text as a Dane. The earliest prose works, from several centuries later, are mainly products of the sponsorship of King Alfred the Great (849-901). English was the first language other than Latin to be used as a language of administration in western Europe.

9. BALTIC AND SLAVIC: THE BALTIC ASSEMBLAGE. *Lithuanian* and *Latvian* (formerly sometimes called Lettish) together constitute East Baltic; the only representative of the more conservative West Baltic—*Old Prussian*—is attested slightly earlier but has been extinct since the 17th century. The numerous *Slavic* vernaculars are all descended from a form of speech very nearly identical to *Old Church Slav(on)ic*.

Of the languages traditionally called *Baltic* the most important for a linguistic historian is *Lithuanian*, spoken in Lithuania and the USA (where perhaps a tenth of the speakers are found). Between the 11th and 14th centuries AD Lithuanian princes conquered much Russian territory, and the old Grand Duchy of Lithuania once extended from the Baltic to the Black Sea. But Lithuanian was not then employed as a written language; the earliest records of the language are from the 16th century AD, and are meager until a later period. Lithuanian is remarkable among IE languages for its conservatism, and despite the late date of attestation it is of great importance in IE comparative grammar.

Latvian, spoken principally in Latvia but widely by émigré communities in the USA, Canada, and Australia, as well, is known from about the same period. It too is conservative, but significantly less so than Lithuanian.

Old Prussian, once spoken in what is now East Prussia but extinct since about 1700, is known only from meager remains, mainly a catechism of the 16th century and some word lists transcribed by agents who had only the haziest knowledge of the language. It is remarkable for conservative details of structure of great interest for the Indo-Europeanist.

Slavic. By the time of the Roman writers, the Venedi of Tacitus and Pliny occupied the region west of the Vistula and south of the Baltic Sea. Hence they spread northeast, east, and south. These migrations occurred between 200 and 600 AD, after the great Germanic migrations. Those moving to the south came into contact with Greco-Roman civilization, and among them arose the earliest Slavic states and the earliest form of written Slavic.

Old Church Slavic, formerly sometimes called *Old Bulgarian*, is based on a direct ancestor of modern Macedonian. It is first attested in connection with the 9th century missionary work of the Apostles to the Slavs, the brothers Constantine (Cyril) and Methodius. OCS is not merely the earliest recorded form of Slavic; for a long time it was the only written or literary language among the Slavs, for whom it held the same position as Latin in the West. Moreover, while not identical with Proto-Slavic, it is so nearly so that it serves as the main representative of Slavic in the comparative grammar of the IE languages.

10. TOCHARIAN is the conventional name for two languages that have come to light in Chinese Turkestan (Sinkiang, now usually Xinjiang) dating from the 7th and 8th centuries AD, preserved in texts containing for the most part translations of Buddhist scriptures and commentaries. The two

forms, known as *Tocharian A* and *Tocharian B* (occasionally referred to as Turfanian and Kuchean, respectively), are commonly called dialects but are really different languages.

a. The name Tocharian was attached to the languages soon after their discovery on the surmise that the speakers were the Bactrian Τοχαροί of Strabo. This view is no longer held, but it is not known what the Tocharians called themselves or by what name (if any) they were known to classical geographers. As if the wrong name for a language were something unusual, some scholars call the languages *'Tocharian'*, with antiseptic quotation marks, or *so-called Tocharian.*

11. CENTUM AND SATEM LANGUAGES. In the early years of IE comparative linguistics it was discovered that Indo-Iranian, Baltic, and Slavic reflect three PIE stops as sibilants, while Greek, Italic, and Germanic keep them as stops or otherwise treat them differently. These two groups are known as the 'Satem' and 'Centum' languages, respectively (see 152-3), the tags being the Avestan (*satəm*) and Latin (*centum*) reflexes of PIE **ḱm̥tom* 'hundred'.[1]

The idea of a sound law dividing a whole language family into two great groups was riveting, and before methodological refinements could put its significance in proper perspective, a serious interpretive blunder became established which lingers to this day: namely taking the two moieties of IE as coordinate branches. While membership in a language FAMILY (1) is established by a pattern of SHARED RETENTIONS, membership in a proper SUBGROUP of a family is established by a pattern of SHARED INNOVATIONS. It cannot be too strongly emphasized, therefore, that ONLY the satem languages make up a subgroup. The centum languages are not a subgroup, having nothing in common beyond the fact of their descent from PIE (a property shared fully by the satem languages). An analogy may make this clear. Members of a club have something common—they joined the club; but the people in the community who are not members of the club do not constitute a second de facto club. Just so, certain IE languages figuratively joined the satem club, but that does not make the remaining languages members of a centum club.

GREEK

12. OUTLINES OF THE EXTERNAL HISTORY. *The* external history *of a language is an account of the speakers of the language, their political, material, and artistic culture, and geographical distribution. Though the subject of this book is internal history—that is, an account of the changes in the language through time—a sketch of the external histories of Greek and Latin is appropriate in this Introduction.*

---

[1] Armenian, Albanian, and Celtic were largely out of the picture at that stage. In time, the first two were recognized as Satem, the last as Centum.

Archeology has provided a history of Greek lands which far antedates any written records and (at least in the usual view) long before the arrival of the historical Greeks of IE speech. Refinements in archeological techniques in general and in dating techniques in particular continue to appear; augmented by new finds, these have given us an increasingly detailed picture of the pre-Greek civilizations of the area and of the IE incursions which overwhelmed them. The subject is complex, and continues to unfold; only the barest notice can be given here.

The inhabitants of neolithic Greece were a component of the Old European (Paleo-European) society which did not, despite its name, cover all of Europe by any means. Furthermore, far from being homogeneous, it was made up of several similar culture complexes, dating from the 7th millennium BC; as of say 5000 BC the Greek peninsula and islands (including Crete) were occupied by peoples belonging to one of these subvarieties, known as the Aegean. Their closest cultural kin occupied the Danube and Dnieper valleys, the southern half of Italy, and Sicily. These neolithic cultures reached a high level of sophistication and complexity, as demonstrated by their sizable agricultural villages and towns (containing as many as a thousand structures) with multi-room, two- to four-storey dwellings, painted walls, and furniture; the remarkable variety of shapes and designs of their pottery, with elegant decorations in polychrome and other techniques; rich male and female ritual attire; copper, bronze, and gold metallurgy; craft specialization; prominent female deities; and so on.

This civilization collapsed in the 4th millennium BC. No natural disaster, even an insidious one such as gradual desiccation of the climate, can be associated with this cultural revolution. On the other hand, it coincides with the first appearance of Kurgan Culture elements in the region, most revealingly with Kurgan burial practices.[1] The significance of this is that material objects typical of Kurgan society might find their way into Aegean archaeological sites as a result of trade, but when the graves themselves agree in the minutest particulars with the structure and arrangement of late Kurgan graves, we are certainly dealing with Kurgan peoples themselves.

[1] *Kurgán* is the Russian word for 'mound'. In the steppes of Russia, in a region to the north of the Caspian and Black Seas, was a culture complex characterized by small settlements made up of small numbers of rather crude dwellings crowded together behind a rampart. (Few of these permanent and more or less fortified settlements are known to archaeology; this fits with the presumption that we are dealing with a nomadic or seminomadic society.) Round and about was a necropolis, a collection of low mounds covering characteristic graves. The economy was pastoral-agricultural; though based on cattle, its most salient feature is domestication of the horse and, at least a millennium later, the invention of wheeled wagons and carts. The pottery is heavy and crude.

This complex is known to archeologists as the Kurgan Culture; it appears on various grounds to be the source of Indo-European speaking peoples.

Three separate Kurgan incursions into Europe have been proposed; which of these (or what combination of them) is directly reflected as 'Greek' is not clear. It is however evident that the Mycenaean culture of Greece of the 2nd millennium BC, which we now know to have been Greek-speaking, was an amalgam of Old European (specifically Minoan) and Kurgan components. The latter is the source of male-oriented warrior values, wheeled vehicles, and the horse. The former is presumed to be the source of obviously non-IE architecture, terms for plants and animals indigenous to the Mediterranean basin, nautical terms, and many place names. The unsuitability of the Linear B writing system (26) for the representation of Greek strongly implies that it was first contrived for some other language and adapted for Greek; and Linear A, which has some similarities with Linear B, is apparently used to write non- (presumably pre-) Greek speech.

The decipherment of Linear B was first announced in 1952, followed by more formal accounts in the following year. The discovery that the language of the some 4,000 clay tablets found in Mycenae, Thebes, Pylos, and Cnossos was a form of Greek put our knowledge of the period on a different footing. Conventional wisdom had generally assumed a pre-Greek language for the inscriptions.[1] The Greek Linear B texts date from about 1250-1150 BC, or as some think as early as 1400 BC, in any case well before the likely dates of the Homeric lays. The texts themselves offer many difficulties of interpretation and are disappointing in some ways—there are few finite verb forms in them, for example, and upwards of three quarters of the words are names—but they have proved invaluable for our understanding of pre-Homeric language, and of Proto-Greek.

Later, as the Greeks themselves tell us, there was a wave of invasion from the north by the Dorians, themselves obviously Greek but speaking a notably different family of dialects and different enough in culture and even physique to cause comment.

13. From the time of the earliest records Greek appears, not as a unified language, but in numerous dialects. The differentiation of the larger

---

[1] With the reassignment of Linear B inscriptions to Greek, non-Greek records in the area become unexpectedly sparse—if the writing system is in fact pre-Greek, we might have expected a fair amount of pre-Greek writing in the script. But non-Greek remains are truly meager: a number of tablets and inscriptions on artifacts in Linear A, several 'Eteocretan' inscriptions from eastern Crete written in the Greek alphabet—two of them as late as the 4th century BC; and what appears to be an archaic form of Etruscan in an inscription on Lemnos.

There is however a plausible explanation for the dearth of pre-Greek texts, namely the purpose of the texts themselves—bookkeeping records. Old files were presumably cleaned out from time to time, and ledgers in Paleo-European cannot have been of much interest to later bookkeepers in any case.

dialect groups probably goes back to a remote period, before the Greeks had entered Greece. Nevertheless there are many distinctive features common to all the Greek dialects; some of these are likely to postdate the appearance of dialect divisions (including some of the more striking developments, as in the treatment of the labiovelars, 161–4); but some date from a period of a relatively unified Proto-Greek (PG) branch of IE. Most of the innovations of the earliest period are peculiarly Greek, but some—for example the treatment of syllabic resonants (95)—have parallels elsewhere.

14. Dialects. The Greeks of the heroic age, the period portrayed in Homer, were speakers of the 'Old Hellenic' dialects representing the Attic-Ionic, the Aeolic, and the Arcado-Cypriot groups, of which the last two have important characteristics in common and very probably represent divisions of a larger group coordinate with the first. The assignment of these groups to a particular series of waves of migration is somewhat speculative. But there are some grounds for guessing that the first wave of Greeks is reflected in the Arcado-Cypriot dialects, of which Mycenaean Greek seems to be a representative. (Even apart from the evidence of Mycenaean, the geographic distribution of the later Arcado-Cypriot dialects points to relic status.) That was followed by a wave of Ionic, covering Attica and the shores of the Saronic Gulf, and perhaps considerable parts of central Greece and the Peloponnesus. Whatever the prehistory, the situation in the period preceding the Doric invasion was as follows:

As indicated by tradition, Mycenaean archaeology, and linguistic evidence, northern Greece beyond Attica except in the far northwest was Aeolic—not only Thessaly and Boeotia, which remained Aeolic in speech with some West Greek admixture, but also Locris, Phocis, and southern Aetolia. Aeolic speech was carried to Lesbos and the adjacent coast of Asia Minor, where it survived in its purest form.

Most of the Peloponnesus at that point was occupied by those whose speech, later, would survive the Doric invasion only in the inland Arcadia. Before the Doric incursions Greeks from the eastern Peloponnesus colonized Cyprus; as Doric speech never reached Cyprus, the dialects of Cyprus and Arcadia remained closely akin despite the geographic distance. (Closely related groups had migrated also to Pamphylia, where the language has a more mixed form; and to Rhodes, Crete, Thera, and elsewhere, where but scattered traces of it survived in the Doric which later became dominant there. There are also some survivals of it in the Doric of Laconia and Argolis.)

The West Greek speaking tribes were entirely out of the picture in the heroic age, and presumably located in the northwest. The Doric invasion was part of a general West Greek expansion, which affected northern Greece scarcely less than the Peloponnesus, and brought about a greatly changed distribution of dialects—the one we know in the historical period.

Phocis, Locris, and Aetolia became West Greek; and there is a strong West Greek admixture in Boeotian and Thessalian, so that these dialects share in some of the important West Greek characteristics (notably δίδωτι = δίδωσι, 148–9, a conservative trait), while retaining distinctive Aeolic characteristics. The West Greek influence is greater in Boeotian than in Thessalian. In the Peloponnesus the dialects of Elis and Achaea are nearest to the Northwest Greek dialects of Locris and Phocis. Megara, Corinth, Argolis, Laconia, and Messenia became Doric. Doric speech was carried from Argolis and Laconia to Rhodes, Thera, Crete, and other places including the southern part of Asia Minor; from Corinth to Corcyra and the Acarnanian coast, to Sicily, etc.

The relationship between the Doric and the 'Northwest Greek' dialects is very close. In fact, the defining characteristics of the Doric dialects as a whole are common also to the Northwest Greek, which in other words are really West Greek.

We know these dialects mainly from thousands of inscriptions, which incidentally reveal that 'literature' as such gives no idea of the actual linguistic diversity of Greek —Greece was as decentralized in language as in politics. As there was no unified Greece as a state, but only a number of city states and shifting leagues, so there was no standard Greek language, but only a series of local dialects. Not only in early times, but also, in most parts of Greece, long after Attic had become the norm of literary prose, each state employed its own dialect not only for private monuments of internal concern but not infrequently for records of a more external or even interstate character such as decrees in honor of foreigners, decisions of interstate arbitration, and communications between different states. Many of the dialects remained in common written use down to about 200 BC, and some till the beginning of our era, though more or less mixed with Attic. How long they may have survived in spoken form, especially in remote districts, no one can say. Eventually they were replaced by the κοινή—'common Greek'—both as the written and spoken language, and from this is descended Modern Greek. The only clear exception is the present Tsakonian dialect, spoken in a small portion of Laconia, which is in part the offspring of ancient Laconian (Spartan); see 187a. Less clear is the status of Graecanic (16, end).

15. THE GREEK LITERARY DIALECTS are regional or archaic dialects which came to be characteristic of certain classes of literature; and once their role had been established, the choice of one or another usually depended on what might be called belles-lettristic factors rather than on the native dialect of the author.

The language of Homer is Old Ionic, but with an admixture of unmistakably Aeolic forms. These can most easily be explained as survivals from earlier Aeolic lays (though elaborate theories of an Aeolic original which was imperfectly translated into Ionic are unnecessary). There was to be sure a transition zone in the region near the border of Aeolic and Ionic, as in Chios; but the mixture in Homer cannot possibly be any natural dialect.

The Homeric language was closely imitated in all later epic poetry; it was followed by Hesiod and by the elegiac and iambic poets like the

Ionian Archilochus, the Athenian Solon and the Megarian Theognis; and to some extent it influenced all Greek poetry.

Alcaeus and Sappho employed their native Lesbic, with some traces of epic forms. Their language was imitated by Theocritus in three of his idylls, and certain of their Lesbic forms were used by other lyric poets and even in the choral lyric.

Doric was seemingly obligatory for choral lyric, whether written by a Boeotian like Pindar or by Ionians like Simonides and Bacchylides. This Doric, however, is not any specific Doric dialect. It is rather a conventionalized Doric, an artificial composite, showing many general Doric characteristics with some admixture of epic and Lesbic forms, with the occasional outright fabrication. The language of Alcman, by contrast, is more nearly the local Laconian. A Sicilian literary Doric appears in the scanty fragments of Epicharmus and Sophron, and later in Theocritus. There are fragments of Doric prose by writers of Magna Graecia in southern Italy. Corinna of Tanagra, whose fame was scarcely more than local, used her native Boeotian unalloyed. Boeotian, Megarian, and Laconian dialects appear in crude caricature in Aristophanes.

The earliest prose writers were the Ionic philosophers and historians of the 6th century BC; by the 5th century not only Herodotus, but Hippocrates of Cos, a Dorian, were writing in Ionic. Meantime, with the political and intellectual supremacy of Athens, Attic had become the recognized language of the drama, and before the end of the 5th century was employed ever more widely in prose. The earlier prose writers such as Thucydides, like the tragedians, avoided certain Attic peculiarities which must have been felt as provincial, such as the native *-ττ-* and *-ρρ-* (*πρᾱ́ττω*, 199, and *ἄρρην*, 229) for which they substituted the *-σσ-* and *-ρσ-* of Ionic and the majority of dialects. Later Athenian writers were less shy about such Atticisms.

a. Greek was cultivated by Roman upper classes, among whom it enjoyed high prestige. At the same time, and to an increasing degree as time went on, Greek was also widely found among the lower orders in Rome and other urban centers of the late Republic and Empire. These were native speakers of the language, however, mainly freed Greek slaves and Greek artisans. The result was a socially-stratified value system of unusual character: Greek was a high-prestige language among the Roman upper crust, and at the same time it was a low-prestige language among the many. Whatever its lowly status, however, it influenced the Romance languages profoundly.

LATIN AND THE ITALIC LANGUAGES

16. THE LANGUAGES OF ITALY. In contrast to Greece, which in the historical period was a country of one language though many dialects, Italy was a land of many languages: non-IE, IE but not of the Italic branch, and those that were sister languages to Latin but not in any sense dialects of it.

Etruscan, the language of that people which had the most profound influence upon early Roman civilization, is not obviously IE, though there may be some remote connection. The tradition of the Anatolian (specifically Lydian) origin of the Etruscans (Hdt. 1.94) may be substantially true. In fact, a recent idea takes Etruscan to be a close relative of Hittite, but there are difficulties with this as with all other Etruscan theories.

Epigraphic evidence for the ancient languages of Italy (Old Latin included) is very scanty; and, worse, in the 19th century forgeries of archaic Italic materials were produced in abundance. The consequences of this are still being sorted out.

Ligurian, once spoken along the Gulf of Genoa, is believed by some to be an IE language intermediate between Italic and Celtic. However, the linguistic material is very scanty—local and tribal names. The 'Lepontic' inscriptions, from the region of the North Italian lakes, are better regarded as Celtic in fact—an archaic form of Gaulish (appropriately so for 550–150 BC) and more or less dating from the Celtic invasion, vid.inf.

There are nearly three hundred short Venetic inscriptions from the land of the Veneti (not to be confused with the Slavic Venedi) at the head of the Adriatic, and about two hundred of Messapian from Calabria. Both are IE, and for a long time were thought to belong with Illyrian (itself poorly attested). The bracketing of Illyrian and Messapian is still generally accepted, but Venetic seems—with due caution owing to the highly speculative interpretation of the inscriptions—to show strong similarities to the Italic languages. The chief controversy is over whether Venetic is simply an Italic language, like Sabellian or Latin, or belongs to a separate IE branch.

Celtic tribes, which poured in from the north and sacked Rome itself in the early 4th century BC, settled in northern Italy (Gallia Cisalpina). Greek colonies occupied nearly the entire southern portion of Italy, along the coasts especially, and this 'Magna Graecia' remained Greek in speech until late times. Indeed, a form of Greek known as *Graecanic*, distinct in many particulars from the forms of modern Greek which directly continue the *κοινή*, is said to maintain a precarious existence in southern Italy.

17. The languages that constitute the traditional Italic branch of the IE family fall into two distinct groups, Sabellian (whose best-attested components are Oscan and Umbrian) and Latin-Faliscan. There are so many differences between the two in structure and lexicon that a case can be made that the notion of an Italic Branch is an error, a distortion of the linguistic analysis to justify a subgroup based more on geography than linguistic evidence. The alternative is to take Latin-Faliscan as representing an earlier incursion of IE peoples into Italy, while Sabellian speakers are a later-arrived and unrelated group, whose incursion was survived by a small pocket of Latin-Faliscan dialects in the region of the Tiber. If the notion

of an Italic branch is valid, its internal differentiation is without question extreme by comparison to the more or less contemporaneous Greek, or any other contemporaneous IE branch.

The Sabellian group includes Oscan and Umbrian (and is sometimes known as Osco-Umbrian), but also includes a number of poorly-attested languages of central Italy. These 'dialects', as they are traditionally but improperly known, include Paelignian, Marrucinian, Vestinian, Volscian, Marsian, Sabine, Southern Picenian, and Aequian. Though all of these languages, Oscan and Umbrian included, are very poorly understood, they appear to form a classic *dialect continuum* (like the modern-day Romance languages). So for example Volscian, like Paelignian and Marrucinian, shows the distinctively O feature of a perf. in *-t-*, but also the distinctively U traits of *i* < **ū* (50b) and *-f* < **-ns* (237.5).

Oscan, though the name comes from the Campanian Oscans, was the language of all the Samnites. (In one of the Samnite wars the Roman consul sent out spies acquainted with the Oscan language.) The Oscan inscriptions, over two hundred in number, are from Campania, Samnium, northern Apulia, Lucania, Bruttium, and some written by the Campanian Mamertines in Messana. Most of them date between 200 BC and the social war in 90–89 BC.

Umbrian is known mainly from the Iguvinian Tables, seven bronze tablets from Gubbio (ancient Iguvium). They contain an account of the ceremonies of the Atiedian Brothers, similar in general character to the Roman Acta Arvalium. There are many difficulties of interpretation; the ritual nature of the texts contributes to the difficulty.

Most Oscan and Umbrian inscriptions are written in the native Oscan and Umbrian alphabets, derived from the Etruscan (though there are some difficulties about the details); some are written in the ordinary Latin alphabet. See 34 for an explanation of how these different sources are indicated in transcription. A few Oscan inscriptions are in the Greek alphabet. (See also 25a.)

18. Those who classify Sabellian and Latin-Faliscan as belonging to the same IE branch find much that points to a period of common Italic development. The inflectional system is substantially the same in broad outlines and in many details, though to the degree that these are conservative features they say nothing about common development. Formerly, for example, the *r*-endings of the medio-passive in Italic were taken as innovations, and perplexing ones at that, and as such they were a highly salient branch trait. Now that they are recognized as conservative features (435a), they lose all value for defining an Italic branch. In addition, the agreement between Sabellian and Latin types of declension and conjugation discerned by some authorities has been dismissed as the forcible wedging of the forms of Sabellian into Latin-Faliscan categories.

Nevertheless, there are some shared innovations: in morphology, the extension of the ablative singular in *-d* from the *o*-stems to other declensions (263.6, 306.7); partial fusion of *i*-stems and consonant stems (308); fusion of the aorist and the perfect (522–31); the formation of imperfect indicative (498) and imperfect subjunctive (544); the gerundive (567-8). In phonology, the change of the voiced aspirated stops to voiceless fricatives and the merging of PItal. **f* and **θ* as *f* (135, 147.1). In vocabulary, L *dīcō*, O *deicum* 'say' (in other IE languages 'point (out)', with different words for 'say'); and 'law' from the root **leg-* 'gather' as in L *lēx*, O *ligud.* What remains to be settled is whether these details must be traced to a common ancestor or can be accounted for by borrowing (1).

19. The earliest Latin inscriptions are meager indeed compared to what we have for Greek in the same period. For perhaps the past hundred years, the oldest sample of Latin known was an inscription on a gold fibula from Praeneste, dated about 600 BC: MANIOS:MED:FHE⋮FHAKED:NVMASIOI 'Manius made me for Numerius'. A number of otherwise hypothetical features of early L are on display here, but the text is interpretable with absolute confidence—a bonus, as most early Italic inscriptions are more or less enigmatic. Doubts were in fact voiced as soon as the inscription was published, but soon its authenticity came to be taken for granted, and for several generations of scholarship there were few qualms on that score. Recently, however, a succession of thorough investigations have pointed to modern forgery.

The Duenos inscription of the 6th–7th century BC is more characteristic of very old Latin inscriptions. The difficulties are twofold. First, it is a string of about 125 letters with no separation between the words; second, evidence[1] suggests it is a blessing or a curse, and such forms of discourse are peculiar and enigmatic to start with.

The Forum inscription of about 550 BC is so fragmentary that only a few words are certain. From around 500 BC comes the Castor-Pollux dedication, a small bronze tablet found at the site of Lavinium (the capital of Latium) inscribed in two lines CASTOREI:PODLOVQVEIQVE QVROIS 'To Castor and Pollux the [Dios]kouroi'. It shows many details antedating Latin sound laws, or apparently does; but much about the inscription is strange, even after blame is lavishly thrown upon the competence of the inscriber.

From roughly the same period may be mentioned the Lapis Satricanus, from a temple foundation at the site of Satricum (30 miles east of Rome); the Corcolle (near Tivoli) altar fragments; and an inscribed dish and five short altar inscriptions found in the vicinity of Ardea. The Tibur (modern Tivoli) pedestal inscription dates from the late 5th century.

There are many short inscriptions, the Scipio epitaphs and so on, of the 3rd century BC. The earliest inscription of any length, and a very im-

---

[1] It is incised around the lip of a vessel of unique design, somewhat like three small cone-shaped pots joined at the mouth. The inscription is written from right to left, and runs in a sort of spiral (making one and a half circuits), so oriented that it is right-side up when the vessel is held mouth-down.

portant one for Early Latin, is the Senatusconsultum de Bacchanalibus (SC de Bacch.) of 186 BC. Latin from these sources is distinguished as Old Latin.

The literary remains of early Latin chiefly comprise the fragments of Livius Andronicus, Naevius, and Ennius, the prose of the elder Cato, and the comedies of Plautus and Terence.

20. THE EXPANSION OF LATIN. The spread of the Latin language followed, at longer or shorter intervals, the advance of Roman power. It first displaced the local dialects of the rest of Latium and those of the neighboring Sabines (several of the hills of Rome itself originally had Sabine settlements on them), Aequians, Marsians, Volscians, and others; and later, further from Rome or declining in power, the Umbrian, Etruscan, Venetic, Celtic, and others. By 100 BC Italy was mainly of Latin speech, except for Oscan and Greek. But even before this Latin had been carried beyond Italy by the Roman conquests—to Spain, southern Gaul, Illyria. In these, as in the lands occupied later, Latin displaced the native languages. In the East, Greek with its old prestige held its own, even while Latin was the official language of administration of the Eastern Empire.

21. VULGAR LATIN.[1] Latin had the normal degree of socio-educational and regional variation, and the Latin spoken over this vast Romanized territory was not the formal Latin of the classical writers. The more colloquial or popular ('vulgar') Latin shows itself to some extent in Plautus and Terence and, after being submerged in the classical period, reappears in Petronius, who exhibits it intentionally, and in various writers of the early Christian centuries, who reveal it inadvertantly. The comparative method, when applied to the Romance Languages, recovers features of Vulgar Latin which happen not to be attested otherwise.

Among the more important of the postclassical texts are: some of the early Christian Fathers, as Tertullian; the Latin versions of the Bible (the so-called Itala) preceding Jerome's Vulgate; a veterinary treatise, the Mulomedicina Chironis; the Peregrinatio ad loca sancta of the nun Aetheria, written in the late 4th century AD (or, some think, the 6th); the Historia Francorum of Gregory of Tours; and various chronicles and documents of the Merovingian period in France.

The authors of these works did not deliberately choose to write in colloquial rather than classical Latin. To the contrary: they were writing as good a Latin as they could, sometimes actually saying as much (indirectly) by way of apologizing for ignorance of correct Latin. There is therefore

[1] *Vulgar Latin* is not synonymous with *Late Latin* (LL). Late Latin is a chronological term as much as a stylistic one, referring to post-Augustan Latin, whereas Vulgar Latin refers to a register or style of speech. Of course, the later the Latin text, the more features of a non-classical nature it is likely to show.

no document before the emergence of French, Italian, and the rest, which can be trusted as a full and faithful representation of contemporary speech. The latter merely shows through, like a wallpaper pattern through paint: confusion of spelling discloses changes in pronunciation; the main skeleton of Latin structure remains, but cases are often confused, prepositional phrases encroach on the old genitive, dative, and ablative, and periphrastic expressions for tenses and moods begin to appear, as do characteristically Romance semantics: for example *mittō* 'send' now 'throw, put' (Fr. *mettre*, It. *mettere*) and *demoror* 'delay, tarry' now 'dwell' (Fr. *demeurer*, It. *dimorare*).

In the time of Charlemagne knowledge of literary Latin was revived, and from this time on, written Latin, though different in many important ways from classical, is much less instructive for vulgar Latin than texts of the preceding period.

a. Some scholars have proposed that regional features of Romance languages are traceable to the fact that the countries were Romanized at widely different periods, so that the Latin first carried to Spain was different from that carried to other regions by the later conquests. But this only transfers the site of innovations from the regions back to Rome—not impossible, but without obvious theoretical advantage. Other scholars, who for some reason are unable to appreciate the fact that language change is incessant, attach significance to the fact that the indigenous peoples of the different countries of the Roman empire spoke various languages: it is reasoned that the structural features of these 'substratum' languages account for the ramification of the Romance languages—first they turned Latin from its proper course and then influenced its subsequent development. This theory seems to start from the mistaken impression that Romance languages are discrete; it is hard to imagine how it might explain the Romance dialect continuum. In any case there is little concrete evidence to support either notion. Indeed, it appears rather that, owing to the extensive intercourse between all parts of the empire and the centralizing influence of the Roman organization, the language remained fairly uniform during the first centuries of our era—that is, at exactly the period when 'substratum influence' should have been strongest.

THE GREEK AND LATIN SIGNARIES

22. The study of writing systems in general, and of the histories of the Greek and Latin alphabets in particular, are matters for specialists. And although certain facts are pretty solidly established, for example that the ultimate origin of these alphabets is the Phoenician signary, there continues to be much discussion of the details. The dating of many inscriptions crucial to the debate is uncertain. Indeed, some long-standing views about relative dates are being questioned, such as the too-ready assumption that inscriptions using simpler signaries (lacking the supplementary characters, for example) are primitive prima facie, and therefore necessarily earlier than inscriptions in more elaborate signaries. Newly-discovered inscriptions have been challenging settled opinion about the age or route of diffusion of this or that detail. Those interested in a proper discussion of the histories of the amphimediterranean signaries should consult specialized treatments of these matters.

23. THE PHOENICIAN-BASED ALPHABETS. The Greek alphabet is in reality a collection of similar signaries differing in such matters as their inventories of signs, the shapes of the letters, and even in the values of the letters. These differences are partly regional and partly chronological. The Latin alphabet—technically rather the Latin ABC, but the term *alphabet* is too well established to be dislodged by puristic qualms—belongs to a family of signaries known as Italic, which include the alphabets used to write Oscan, Umbrian, Etruscan, and most other Italic languages (17-8). The Italic alphabets are plainly related to the Greek, and closely. Beyond that point of agreement it is hard to go. Even what used to be thought certain—that they were surely DERIVED FROM Greek—has been challenged by evidence that Italic scripts might rather have the SAME SOURCE AS the Greek. And there have always been uncertainties about the genealogical interrelations of the various strains of Italic writing.

The starting point of both the Greek and Italic signaries was the Phoenician consonantal script, known from before the first millennium BC. Its paternity is proved by the shapes and values of the symbols, and by the names for the letters in Greek: the words ἄλφα, βῆτα, and so on, are meaningless in G, but they are clearly based on Semitic forms which are ordinary nouns—the Phoenician names for the letters are unknown, but their names in Hebrew are quite close enough to the G (*'alef* 'ox', *bayit* 'house', and so on).

An innovation of immense significance in the adaptation of this signary to the writing of Greek was the use of certain of the symbols to represent VOWELS. Now, a similar practice is widely found in Semitic writing conventions from earliest times: certain letters are used to indicate /ā/, /ī/, and /ū/. But the use of these *matres lectionis*, as they are known, differs from the Greek practice in two vital ways. First, the employment of a mater lectionis is always optional. Second, in all cases the normal value of the mater lectionis symbol is for a consonant segment. In Greek, by contrast, the symbol ancestral to A always and only stands for a vowel, or two different vowels to be exact (/a/ and /ā/), and its use is just as fixed as the use of B or Γ. It is this systematic assignment of a symbol to EVERY segment of the spoken word which demarcates true alphabets from the Semitic consonant-only system (which might be called rather *alphasyllabic*).

24. VARIATION IN THE USE OF SYMBOLS. The question of the value of the signs used in writing an ancient language resolves itself into two quite different issues. The more straightforward matter is the observation, say, that at different times and places in the ancient Greek world the symbols Π, ΠΗ, and Φ could have equivalent value. A more demanding question is

what exactly that value was. (On the comparatively few occasions in the discussion of the historical phonologies of G and L, when the actual values of the letters are at issue, the questions will be discussed in situ.)

There are three main types of variability seen in the meanings of the symbols of the Greek alphabets. (There are also interesting and significant differences in their FORMS, but while a discussion of these matters would be vital for understanding G epigraphy, they are tangential to our purpose.)

1. Phoenician, like any Semitic language, had an inventory of sibilant sounds and other fricatives unlike anything in G, and the Ph. signary had signs for them. These were to begin with retained in the G signary, and unsurprisingly there was much variability in their application to G sounds, and even in the names for them. Thus, depending on locality, either M or Σ was the preferred sign for /s/;[1] the names for the two, σάν and σῖγμα, respectively, are not directly derivable from any Semitic name (cf. the names for the Hebrew sibilant letters: *zayin*, *samex*, *ṣade*, and *šin*). Two other sibilant characters were I (Ph. /z/) and Ɪ (Ph. /s/). The former retains its ancient shape in West Greek signaries (and also in Italic types) but in Ionic evolves into the familiar Z (see 201), in which form it was at a late date borrowed into the Latin signary. Ɪ is absent altogether from the early Attic signary but is the ancestor of Ionic Ξ /ks/. It is sometimes found in the same function as I, as in Thera ƗEYM 'ζευς'.

2. It is the communis opinio that the most primitive form of the G signary had only the five vowel signs—A E I O and Y—and this is also essentially the inventory for the Italic signaries (with a different evolution of the shape of the last character and the absence of O in Etruscan, Oscan, and Umbrian). For all varieties of G this inventory is UNDERDIFFERENTIATED, as vowel length is not represented; and in virtually all forms of G there were more contrasts in the mid vowels than could be shown in this system: G /e ę̄ ẹ̄/ all were necessarily written E, and /o ǭ ọ̄/ all as O. In Ionic there appeared two additions to the basic inventory, which partially address the deficiencies of this system: a new letter Ω (= /ǭ/), apparently a modification of O;[2] and the use of H for a long front vocoid. At first the new use of H was applied only to the Ionic development of ᾱ (54). The long mid front vowels continuing PG *ē and the spurious diphthong (from various sources; 76) were all written with E. Later, presumably when the Att.-Ion. reflex of ᾱ had in fact merged with the reflex of PG *ē (54-6), H was naturally used for both. Regional practice varied with regard to the treatment of /ẹ̄/ (the spurious diphthong, 76)—ει in our texts, but often epigraphically E in inscriptions, as TPEΣ 'τρε̄ς' (τρεῖς).

---

[1] At this stage there was no possible confusion between σάν and μῦ. The latter had five strokes, the initial down-stroke considerably longer than the other strokes.

[2] Other forms are known locally, for example ⊙ rather than Ω.

Originally, the symbol Η (early 𐌇) stood for /h/, the spiritus asper of G (174). Its reassessment in Ionic is the result of the loss of /h/ in East Ionic. Greeks who still had /h/ were presented with an obvious problem when they adopted the Ionic signary. It was usually not so much dealt with as ignored: /h/ was simply left unrepresented in writing (so epig. Attic ΕΠΤΑ 'seven' for earlier ΗΕΠΤΑ). But in some areas alternative shapes of the letter were functionally differentiated, as Η for /ę̄/ and 𐌇 for /h/. Possibly another example of the same principle is the sign ⊢ in the value /h/, which occurs in the Heraclean Tables and other inscriptions. The Greeks regarded it as a 'halved Η'; whether or not that is the true story, it explains the logic behind the later invention of the otiose sign ⊣ in manuscript practice to indicate smooth breathing (that is, no breathing at all). These two signs were often used in the manner of a diacritic, whence the evolved shapes ˪ and ˩, the immediate source of the 'breathings' (ʽ and ʼ).

3. Of the G symbols for the voiceless aspirated stops, Φ, Θ, Χ (136) only one is directly from the Phoenician signary: Ph. ⊗ /ṭ/ is evidently the source of early G ⊕, whose variant ⊖ is the prototype of G Θ. Depending on the time and place, the remaining two aspirated stops were represented as ΠΗ, ΚΗ, or even by Π, Κ alone. The source of the special letters Φ for /p^h/ and of Ψ (Ѵ) or Χ—depending on the region—for /k^h/ is unknown. It is to be noted that the use of the latter two signs varies in other ways, as in the generally West Greek use of Χ for /ks/ (hence the Italic usage, as in Roman *x* = /ks/), while in eastern (Ionic) writing Ψ was used for /ps/, and is the source of familiar Ψ. Old Attic has neither Ξ nor Ψ. In Ionic it is Ξ, the prototype of the letter Ξ, that has the value /ks/. West G alphabets, furthermore, use Ψ in the value /k^h/.

25. The italic alphabets. From very early times there were West Greek colonies in southern Italy, and it used to be assumed that the Romans got their alphabet from them directly. But given the cultural and political importance of the Etruscans in the first millennium BC, and also certain details of the Italic signaries generally, it is more likely that an Etruscan adaptation of Greek letters[1] is the proximate source of the various Italic alphabets. The use of both K and C—early form ⟨ (which aligns with G gamma in both form and location in the alphabet)—for /k/ in Latin and Etruscan can hardly be a coincidence. On the other hand, Umbrian lacks the symbols corresponding to C and D altogether, while Oscan uses ⟨ for /g/. The Oscan and Umbrian 8 for /f/ can only be from the Etruscan sign

[1] It has been pointed out that a Greek source for Etruscan letters has serious difficulties. Certain archaic details of Etruscan (such as right to left writing) contrast oddly with the presence in the signary of the 'supplemental' letters *ϕ* and *χ*, not to mention that the latter is in its non-west value of a dorsal stop rather than /ks/. It has been ably argued, therefore, that it is easier to trace Etruscan and Greek letters to a common source.

of the same shape and value, which, remarkably, agrees in form and function with a letter found in Lydian inscriptions from the eastern end of the Mediterranean. There can be little doubt that Roman F is in some sense the reflex of the G letter ϝ known in G as the *digamma* (187), but it differs notably in both form and function from the corresponding Sab. character, Ϲ, which stands for /w/. This may suggest that L F owes something of both its form and function to Etr. 8.[1]

In the earliest Old Latin epigraphy, the symbols C (〈), K and Q (Ϙ) were all employed for both /k/ and /g/, the choice of symbol being determined by the vowel following: Q stood before rounded vowels (EQO 'ego'), C before front vowels and consonants (FECED 'fecit', CRATIA 'gratia'), and K before A. This last detail is continued into the classical period in the few forms where *k* is retained, chiefly *Kalendae* 'the Kalends'. Otherwise, the use of C spread at the expense of the other two letters. The persistence of Q in its single environment is hard to explain (as is the ouster, a thousand years later, of the straightforward English spelling *cw* by the Anglo-Norman preciosity *qu*).

How (or why) the Latin and Umbrian alphabets ended up with signaries unable to represent voiced and voiceless stops consistently is unknown, but the fact itself points away from any proximate Greek source of the Italic signaries. In Latin the underdifferentiation was limited to the dorsal stops, and was eventually repaired. The invention of the letter G, historically nothing but C with a diacritic (and even in relatively late times sometimes found epigraphically as C̵), is ascribed by Plutarch to the freedman Spurius Carvilius Ruga, a noted schoolmaster of the early third century BC. Others have been named for the honor, and in truth schoolmasters are not often found at the leading edge of innovation.

In Latin writing of all periods long vowels are indicated only haphazardly, and by inconsistent means. The usual diacritic, called the *apex*, looks like a lopsided circumflex, sometimes little more than an acute accent: epig. MÂTER, MÁTER. For /ī/ specifically there was a special sign, *i longa*, literally an elongated letter I: LIBER. The least-used method is geminatio vocalium, as in Oscan and (occasionally) Umbrian: PAASTORES. The present-day scholastic use of macrons has no direct counterpart in Roman scribal practice.

[1] Possibly Etr. 8 and L F have a common origin. The idea is that /f/, for which the G signary had no remotely suitable equivalent, was represented by the digraph FB (with G ϝ (digamma) /w/—in effect /wh/), and that both Etr. and L simplified the orthography by dropping one of the letters: 8 is the second symbol used alone with the value of the digraph, and F is the first symbol ditto. However, the sole attestation in Latin epigraphy of FB for /f/ is the inscription on the Praeneste fibula, now exposed as a forgery (19). And the existence of 8 /f/ in Lydia (above) makes the derivation of Etr. 8 from FB or the like hard to maintain.

a. Oscan orthography is as fixed as Latin, which is to say somewhat variable. By contrast Umbrian spelling is highly variable. Paradoxically, variable orthography reveals more about the structural details of a language than a consistent one.

26. PRE-PHOENICIAN GREEK SCRIPTS. There are two dialects of Greek that are written with SYLLABARIES rather than alphabets: Cypriot and Mycenaean. Of these the latter, being much older, is of greater importance for the historian.

Unlike an alphabet, in which each sound of the language is represented by a sign, in a syllabary the signs represent a SEQUENCE of sounds always including a vowel. To write Greek unambiguously in a syllabary, a form like τίκτω 'I beget' might be written *ti-ik-to-o* or *ti-ik-tō* or, if the inventory of signs allowed it, *tik-to-o*, and so on. (In transcription, each sequence of letters demarcated by a hyphen stands for a single sign in the syllabary.) Such a signary is best suited for phonologies with few sequences (clusters) of consonants. With its large array of syllable types, if Greek were to be written accurately by such a means the number of signs needed would be enormous. Most syllabaries are simpler, and the Mycenaean and Cypriot syllabaries are in fact of the very simplest kind, consisting almost entirely of signs for consonant plus vowel and a number of signs for vowels alone.

It follows from the preceding discussion that such a sign-system necessarily writes Greek very ambiguously, as it must either leave out consonants or else interlard consonant clusters with nonexistent vowels. The Mycenaean syllabary does both.

The Mycenaean syllabary includes signs for the following syllables (the equivalents in the usual Greek alphabet are appended at the right):

MYCENAEAN VALUES					GREEK EQUIVALENTS
a	e	i	o	u	α, ᾱ, ε, η, etc.
ja	je	–	jo	–	
wa	we	wi	wo	–	ϝ
pa	pe	pi	po	pu	π, φ, β
ta	te	ti	to	tu	τ, θ
da	de	di	do	du	δ
ka	ke	ki	ko	ku	κ, χ, γ
qa	qe	qi	qo	–	(PIE *k^w, *g^wh, *g^w; 161-4)
ma	me	mi	mo	mu	μ
na	ne	ni	no	nu	ν
ra	re	ri	ro	ru	λ, ρ
sa	se	si	so	su	σ
za	ze	–	zo	–	(various affricates)

1. There are six gaps in this array. Of these, the signs for *-*ji*-, *-*qu*-, and *-*wu*-, are probably not so much unattested as nonoccurring.

2. *-ja-*, *-je-*, and so on stand for [ya], [ye], and so on.
3. For the most part, the three Greek series of stops—plain voiceless, aspirated voiceless, and voiced—are represented by a single series of signs; the sole exception is a set of five signs expressly for the Myc. equivalent of G δ, as against another set for τ and θ.
4. Greek has three points of articulation in the stop system, exemplified by π, τ, and κ, but the Myc. syllabary represents four, exemplified by *-pa-*, *-ta-*, *-ka-*, and *-qa-*; the last continues PIE labiovelar consonants (161-4).
5. Neither vowel length nor accent are written; and there is no means of representing *h*, except possibly *-ha-* (*-a₂-*, see 6a below). There is no distinction between *r* and *l*; a syncretism between the two liquids in the vein of Indo-Iranian is remotely possible, and has been endorsed by some authorities; but a much likelier surmise is a defect, one of many, in the writing system itself.
6. In addition to the above signs there are several of less certain value:

(a) Some signs seem to be used with special meanings:
-a₂-[1] stands for *ha*; *-a₃-* = *ai*; *-a₄-* = *au*; all these values are also represented by *-a₁-* alone.
-pu₂- = *pʰu*, though this value is also written *-pu₁-*.
-ra₃- = *lai*, *rai*, which are often written with *-ra₁-*.
(b) Less clear are signs that may stand for syllables beginning with consonant clusters, which are alternatively written in other ways: *-dwe-*, *-dwo-*, *-nwa-*, *-pte-*, *-tja-* (*-ta₂-*), *-rja-* (*-ra₂-*), and others. As this partial list hints, there is little system to the phonetics of the additional signs. But with the exception of *-pte-*, the second consonant in all of them is *y* or *w*.
7. The CYPRIOT syllabary's 50-odd signs have a puzzlingly intermittent formal similarity to the Myc. signary. Like the Myc. it has CV and V signs only. The chief differences are: the voiced, voiceless, and aspirated stops are NOWHERE distinguished; there is no *q*-series (and no need for one, 154-5); there is nothing corresponding to the Myc. *z*-series (except for *zo* and maybe *za*); *l* and *r* are distinguished. In transcription, the *y*-series is romanized *ya, ye, . . .* ; the *w*-series as *va, ve, . . .* (cf. the table above).

27. The Mycenaean scribes dealt in two ways with consonants at the ends of syllables and (what amounts to the same problem) in consonant clusters:

1. A dummy vowel is written: *po-ti-ni-ja* (potniya) 'mistress', *te-ko-to-ne* (tektones) 'carpenters, craftsmen', *wi-ri-za* (wriǰa) 'root'. The dummy vowel typically matches the next following real vowel, as seen in these examples. Dummy vowels in final syllables, which are relatively uncommon, copy the preceding vowel, as *wa-na-ka* (wanaks) 'lord'; this detail is sporadically carried over into longer forms, as in *wa-na-ka-te-ro* (rather than the usual *wa-na-ke-te-ro*) (wanakteron) 'royal'. Before *w*, a dummy *u* competes with the usual vowel, as in *pa-ra-ku-we* next to *pa-ra-ke-we* (dat. or instr. of a *u*-stem adjective, of unknown meaning).

2. One or more of the consonants is not written. This is the invariable method for dealing with word-final *-s*, *-r*, and *-n*, as in *te-ko-to-ne*, above; *ki-to* (kʰitōn) 'tunic'; and *pa-te* (patēr) 'father'. Myc. *pe-ma* (sperma) 'seed'

---

[1] Unmarked transcriptions are primary, so for example the sign shown as *-a-* in the table above is *-a₁-* in effect, in contrast to the *-a₂-*, *-a₃-*, and so on, discussed here.

shows omission of both the first consonant of the initial cluster and the postvocalic *-r-* medially.

NOTES ON CITATION AND ON THE TRANSCRIPTION OF WORDS IN IE LANGUAGES.

28. SANSKRIT. Various transcription systems have been used to romanize Skt.; the system used here is in accord with current practice. The Skt. short vowels are *a* (pronounced [ə]), *i*, and *u*; the long counterparts are *ā*, *ī*, and *ū*, respectively. The symbols *r̥* and *l̥* (the latter only occurring in a few forms from a single root) are syllabic liquids, and are short vowels in the Skt. grammatical tradition; *r̥̄*, which is of secondary origin in Indic, is to *r̥* as *ā* is to *a*. The letters *e* and *o* stand for syllabics which the native grammarians call diphthongs; they reflect PInIr. **ay* and **aw*, respectively, and although not marked as such they are always LONG as to literal duration (but they are nevertheless at the same time 'short diphthongs'). In Ved. *devī́* nom.sg. 'goddess' < PInIr. **daywī* < PIE **deyw-iH₂* both syllabics are long, even though only one letter carries a macron. The 'long diphthongs' (63-4) corresponding to *e* and *o* are are written *āi* and *āu*, respectively.

Many of the letters used in transcribing consonants are self-explanatory, such as *m*, *r*, *p*. The sound system of Indic, though complex, is highly patterned; the following is the scheme of the native grammarians, and is incidentally the order of the letters of the Devanāgarī writing system (read across):

	voiceless plain	voiceless aspirated	voiced plain	voiced aspirated	nasal
Dorsal:	k	kh	g	gh	ṅ
Palatal:	c	cch	j	jh	ñ
Retroflex:	ṭ	ṭh	ḍ (=ḷ)	ḍh (=ḷh)	ṇ
Dental:	t	th	d	dh	n
Labial:	p	ph	b	bh	m

Palatals: the letter *c* is a palatal stop, vaguely like English *ch* in *each*; the voiced counterpart *j* is a sound vaguely like the *j* of Eng. *just.* Aspirated stops, voiced and voiceless alike, are single consonants (that is, phonetic units). The unique exception is *cch*, which always behaves like a long consonant. Its peculiar status results from its history: it is a reflex of PInIr. consonant clusters, either **sś* or **tś*, and is phonetically in effect [cś] or [t͡ś]. (In a similar way, manuscripts sometimes write *kś* for proper *khy*, thereby giving an indication of what both *khy* and *ś* actually sounded like.)

The sound *jh* is exceedingly rare in Skt. (153d). There is but a single occurrence of it in the RV; in later periods, the sound is not much commoner. It occurs in words of obscure and presumably non-Indic origin.

Retroflexes (also known as *cacuminals*, *domals*, or—a calque of the Indic term—*cerebrals*): the consonants transcribed with a subscript dot are apicodomal in articulation, that is, the tip of the tongue contacts the roof of the mouth behind the alveolar ridge.

The sound *ṇ* is the only nasal found adjacent to a retroflex stop, as in *ā́ṇḍa-* 'egg', but also (and more commonly) is the modification of *n* by a preceding retroflex consonant or *r*, either adjacent, as in *pūrṇá-* 'full', or at a distance, as *brā́hmaṇa-* 'pious'. Affixes containing *-n-*, therefore, have two forms depending on the presence of a preceding retroflex or *r* in the stem, such as the gen.pl. ending of the *a*-stems, *-ānām* and *-āṇām*, as in *devānām* 'of gods' vs. *vṛkāṇām* 'of wolves', *iṣṭāṇām* 'of desires'. An intervening palatal or apical stop blocks the retroflexing influence, thus *vratānām* 'of commands' (not ˣ*vratāṇām*).

Retroflexes are also found in words of uncertain etymology, as in Ved. *gaṇá-* 'troop', *kū́ṭa-* 'horn'; such words are rare in the oldest parts of the RV. —The Rigveda uses special symbols, transcribed as *ḷ(h)*, in place of *ḍ(h)* intervocalically: *ī́ḷé* 'I praise', *réḷhi* 'licks' are equivalent to Skt. *īḍe* and *leḍhi* (PIE **leyǵh-ti*).

Semivowels: y, r, l, and *v.* The last is [v] initially and between vowels: *vedaḥ* [ve:dəh] 'knowledge', *gāvam* acc.sg. [ga:vəm] 'cow'; but it is [w] (or a very lenis [β]) after consonants: *svasā* nom.sg. [swəsa:] 'sister', *vidvāṃs* [vidwā:s] 'knowing'.

Fricatives are *ś* (palatal), *ṣ* (retroflex), and *s* (dental). They are always voiceless.[1] The retroflex fricative *ṣ* in place of *s* originally occurred only after a high vowel (*ĭ̄, ŭ̄*), any diphthong, *r*, or *k*, but the distribution vis-à-vis high vowels was much disturbed by analogy. The sound also results from **ḱ* before **t*, as **oḱtōw* 'eight' (389.8) > PInIr. **aśtāu* > Ved. *aṣṭā́(u)*.

The remaining sounds are *h*, which is a VOICED (or murmured) sound; it reflects Proto-Indic **jh* (regularly) and *bh, dh, gh* (occasionally); *ḥ* (called *visarga*), is the development of syllable-final *s*, and was phonetically [h]; *ṃ* (called *anusvāra*), is the development of ordinary nasal consonants in certain environments, chiefly before fricatives. (The actual employment of anusvāra varies greatly from ms to ms.)

Accent. The rules of accentuation in post-Vedic Skt. are essentially those of L (247). For Vedic, whose accent system was totally different (242), tonic vowels are indicated with an acute: *á, ā́.*

29. AVESTAN. The symbols used to transcribe Avestan are as follows: *a, ā, e, ē, ə, ə̄, o, ō, å, ą, i, ī, u, ū, k, g, χ, γ, č, ǰ, t, d, θ, δ, ṯ, p, b, f, ŋ, n, m, y, v, r, s, z, š, ž, h, χ^v.*

Diphthongs: *aē* (also written *ōi*, particularly in the Gāthās, 4), *ao, əu, āi,* and *āu.*

Av. *əe* is not a diphthong, but the reflex of **-ayay*. Av. *ai* and *yei* are not real diphthongs, but result from epenthesis of a following *-i-* or *-y-* on PInIr. **a*, **ya* respectively: Av. *baraiti* 'carries' (= Ved. *bhárati*); Av. *spasyeiti*

---

[1] Prehistoric **ź* fell together with **ǰ*; prehistoric **ẓ* and **z* dropped, with compensatory lengthening of a preceding vowel, as **nisdos* 'nest' > **niẓḍas* > *nīḍaḥ*.

'looks at' < **spaśyati* (L *-spiciō*). Some authorities indicate their spurious nature by writing them raised, as *bara*^{i}*ti*, *spasye*^{i}*ti.*

Av. *å* and *ą* are different kinds of *ā*. Vowel length is inconsistently indicated in Avestan; in particular, *ī* and *ū* often stand for *i*, *u*, but long vowels are rarely written short. Vowels in final syllables are regularly written long: *paitīm* = Ved. *patím* acc.sg. 'lord'; Av. *-bīš* = Ved. *-bhis* ending of the instr.pl.; Av. *kahyā* = Ved. *kásya* gen.sg. 'of whom?'.

The Greek letters used in transcribing Avestan are fricatives: β, δ, γ voiced, θ, χ, χ^v voiceless. Some authorities use the letter *w* instead of β, and *þ* instead of θ.

Av. χ^v is a labialized χ. The letter *t̰* continues PInIr. **t* in certain environments. Its original value is uncertain; in scholastic Avestan it is pronounced [θ] before a voiceless sound, as in *at̰ča*, and [ð] before a voiced one, as *t̰bištō.*

30. GERMANIC.

Most of the symbols used in representing PROTO-GERMANIC are self-explanatory. A raised *n* denotes a nasalized vowel, as in **fōtu*^{n} acc.sg. 'foot' [fo:tũ]; *j* = [y]; and *b̶*, *d̶*, *g* stand for what would more conveniently be written [β ð γ] (but the usual custom will be followed here).

1. GOTHIC. The Gothic texts are written in a special alphabet designed expressly for the language by Bishop Wulfila around 345, in connection with his translation of Christian scriptures into Gothic.

Vowels. The vowel signs *i*, *ai*, and *au* (transcriptions of Wulfila's symbols) stand for short vowels, /i/, /e/, and /o/, respectively. When *ai* and *au* continue PGmc. diphthongs, their interpretation continues to be discussed. It is indisputable that *ai*, *au* stand for short vowels at least some of the time, as shown by the treatment of loanwords: Go. *Pauntius** for *Pontius*, *praufetes* for προφήτης, *Aifaisium* dat.pl. 'to the Ephesians' (G Ἐφέσιος). Other items, like *Pawlus* (G Παῦλος), furthermore indicate that whatever its value the Go. sequence *-au-* was not a suitable equivalent for G -αυ-. Many authorities write *aí*, *aú* for Go. vowels that continue short vowels, *ái*, *áu* for those that continue PGmc. diphthongs; thus: Go. *haúrn* 'horn' < PGmc. **hurna*^{n} (L *cornu*), next to *áukan* 'grow' < PGmc. **aukana*^{n} (L *augeō*), and the like. This distinction corresponds to nothing in the texts themselves.

The signs *e* and *o* stand for long vowels, /ē, ō/. The digraph *ei* stands for /ī/. The signs *a* and *u* are ambiguous as to length: it is likely that *ă*, *ŭ* contrasted with *ā*, *ū* in Go. (in *brahta* /brāχta/ 'brought', for example); actual marks of length on these two vowels are in all cases the opinion of a scholar, not an attestation.

The pronunciation of *iu* (from PGmc. **iu* and **iwu*) is disputed. Most assume it was just what it looks like, but some argue for a front rounded, or a back unrounded, or a central vowel.

To summarize: short vowels *i, ai, a, au, u*; long vowels *ei, e,* and *o*, and probably also *a, u.*

CONSONANTS. The symbol *þ* is a voiceless interdental fricative like the initial consonant in NE *thin.* The letters transcribed *q* and h^w stand for labiovelar articulation, probably [k^w] and [χ^w], continuing PIE *g^w and *k^w respectively. The corresponding voiced stop is for some reason written with two letters in the Gothic alphabet, *gw.* In imitation of Greek practice, the letter *g* additionally stands for a velar nasal before another velar stop, so *drigkan* [driŋkan] 'to drink', *sagq* [saŋk^w] 'sank'. The letters *w* and *j* are glides: *satjan* [satyan] 'to set'. The letters *b, d, g* are thought to have been voiced stops initially, after nasals, and perhaps after liquids; and voiced fricatives between vowels: *bindan* [bindan] 'to bind', but *silubr* [siluvr] (or [siluβr]) 'silver', *fadar* [faðar] voc. 'father', *ogan* [o:γan] 'to be afraid'.

2. OLD ENGLISH. Long vowels are indicated with an acute accent: *á* /ā/, *ó* /ō/, and so on. The vowel *æ* is low front unrounded (as in NE *bad*) and the vowel *y* is high front rounded (as in NHG *dünn* or Fr. *plus*). In very archaic texts, the digraph *œ* stands for mid front rounded vowels [ö ö:], which by the time of most OE sources had merged with *ē̆* and are so written. —The phonetic interpretation of such sequences as *eo, ie,* and *ea,* which reflect earlier short vowels, is disputed; the usual interpretation takes them as complex (gliding) nuclei, that is, the result of changes which added offglides to previously simple sounds. The long complexes, *éo, ío, íe, éa* have a different history from their short counterparts, being for the most part old diphthongs: PGmc. **au* > OE *éa*, PGmc. **iu* > OE *éo*, and so on; see the vowel table below (36).

The OE fricatives *f, þ, s* were VOICED between resonants, and VOICELESS initially, finally, and adjacent to an obstruent; so, to take *f* for a model: *fæder* [fæder] 'father', *lufu* [luvu] 'love', *wulf* [wulf] 'wolf', nom.pl. *wulfas* [wulvas]. —It is uncertain whether initial *h-*, as in *hæft* 'prisoner', had much the value that it now has or was still a fricative, [χ]. In final position, as *furh* 'furrow', *sealh* 'willow', and *fáh* 'hostile' it is generally agreed that the value was [χ], which has since disappeared (*furrow, sallow, foe*) except in dialects. —In OE scribal practice, *ð* and *þ* (called *edh* and *thorn*) were used interchangeably, so that *oþþe* 'or' is wholly equivalent to *oððe, oþðe,* and *oðþe.*

OE *c* was /k/ except as follows. Before ORIGINAL front vowels, it stood for /č/, as in *céosan* /čēǫsan/ 'choose', *cése* /čēse/ 'cheese'. In some cases the triggering vowel was subsequently lost, as in *persoc* /persoč/ 'peach', *crycc* /krütč/ 'crutch'. (Some authorities indicate /č/ as *ć* or *ċ*, so *líc* /līč/ 'body' but *píc* /pīk/ 'pike'; this is not a feature of the texts themselves.) Note that before front vowels resulting from umlaut the sound was /k/, as in *céne* 'eager' (NE *keen*) < **kö:nja* < PGmc. **kōnjaz* (cf. NHG *kühn*). Additionally, *c* has special value in certain combinations: *sc* was /š/: *scip* /šip/ 'ship', *fisc* /fiš/ 'fish'; and, somewhat oversimplified, *cg* stood for /ǰ/ (or

/dǰ/) before a front vowel or finally, for /gg/ before a back vowel: *brycge* /brüdǰe/ 'bridge', but *frocga* /frogga/ 'frog'.

The letter *g* stood for a glide before or after front vowels: *geolu* /yeə̯lu/ 'yellow', *nægl* /næyl/ 'nail', *clæg* /klæy/ 'clay'. In some cases of *ge*, the vowel was a purely graphic sign to show the glide value of the *g*, as in *geoc* /yok/ 'yoke'. Initially before cons. and back vowels, the sound was /g/, as *gnagan* [gnaγan] 'to chew' (NE *gnaw*), *gán* [ga:n] 'to go', *gúþ* [gu:θ] 'battle'. Medially between back vowels, *g* was a fricative, [γ]: *slógon* [slo:γon] pl. 'struck, smote', *fugol* [fuγol] 'bird' (NE *fowl*), and *gnagan* above.

3. OLD HIGH GERMAN. The scribal practices of OHG mss vary greatly with period, region, and (apparently) the training of the individual scribe. Few forms therefore are known in only one shape, and strict observance of philological principles in citing an OHG form would necessitate a veritable index variorum. Therefore most scholars cite more or less normalized spellings except where the details of attestation are pertinent. The preferred normalizations, however, differ slightly from scholar to scholar.

In OHG, many letters are used with more or less self-evident values, as *g* = /g/, *uu* (followed by a vowel) = /w/. Orthography such as *uo* and *ei* evidently represented pronounciations more or less directly, unlike say NHG where *ei* is /ay/ and *ie* is /ī/. Vowel length is sporadically indicated in the mss with an apex, and some scholars use that sign for OHG long vowels; in this work the apex is reserved for vowels so attested, a macron indicates vowels known or surmised to be long but not by chance actually attested so marked. —In certain environments *u* stood not only for /u/ and /ū/, but also for /ü ǖ/; *o* for /ȫ/ as well as /o/ and /ō/; and *uo* for /üö/ as well as /uo/. Conversely, *e* continues both PWGmc. **e* and PWGmc. **ă* before a high front vocoid, thus OHG *nest* 'nest' < PWGmc. **nest* < PGmc. **nistaz*; and on the other hand OHG *nezzi* 'net' < PWGmc. **natja* (OE *nett*) < PGmc. **natja*^{n}. Some scholars distinguish between *ë* for original **e* and *e* for umlauted **a*, as in *nëst* vs. *nezzi*, a distinction never made in the OHG mss themselves.

CONSONANTS. In OHG, *h* has two functions. First, it stands for a consonant, [h] or [χ], as in *horn* 'horn', *slahta* 'slaughter', or *huual* 'whale'. Second, it was also used as a consonantal diacritic: *th*, found only in the earliest mss, was [θ] or [ð] (the latter sometimes actually spelled *dh*). *Ch*, *kh* are equivalent, and originally stood for /k^x/, but postvocalically this early became /χ/ (as in NHG *Bach*) and alternates with *hh*, *h*, and, rarely, *chch*. Similarly *p(p)h* (OHG *kempfo*, *kempho*, *chenfo*, all /k^{x}emp^{f}o/, later /kemp^{f}o/ 'warrior', cf. NHG *Kämpfer*). Before back vowels, the letter *c* was used interchangeably with *k*; though *c* predominates in in the mss, most authorities prefer normalized *k* for citation. Before front vowels, *c* occasionally is used in place of *z*. In OHG mss, *z* and *zz* represent affricates /t^s/ and /tt^s/, respectively, continuing PWGmc. **t* and **tt*.

31. HITTITE. GENERALITIES. Hittite was written on clay tablets in a cuneiform script. Though borrowed ultimately from the Akkadian scribal practice, the pervasive differences in ductus and even in the values of the symbols (the interchangeability of the voiced and voiceless stops, for example; vid.inf.) indicate that standard Akkadian was not the proximal source.

In cuneiform writing the relationship between symbol and language is remarkably complicated. One component of the system was a sizable set of symbols making up a syllabary. These included signs for individual vowels; for CV sequences (C = any consonant, V = any vowel) such as *-ma-*, *-te-*, *-šu-*; for VC sequences such as *-um-*, *-aš*, *-ir-*; and (fewest in number) for CVC sequences such as *-tum-*, *-ḫar-*, *-pat-*. Many symbols have more than one value; a choice from these is presented silently in the transcription of cited forms. For example, the character transcribed *-tar* in *wa-a-tar* 'water' (**290a**) occasionally has the value *-ḫaš-* in Hittite texts, a fact which is passed over in silence in the transcription of *wa-a-tar*.

Conversely, several different signs may have the same value. One of the objects of a system of transcription is to indicate unambiguously what actually stands in the original text. *-Šu-*, above, in fact stands for only one of several homophonous signs. A second sign thought to have the same reading value is transcribed *-šú-*. The acute accent is a shorthand way of writing *-šu*$_2$*-*, and accordingly *-šu-* is in reality shorthand for *-šu*$_1$*-*. In a similar vein, a grave accent stands for subscript '3' (*-tàš-* = *-taš*$_3$*-*). After that, the subscripts are written (*-tu*$_4$*-*).

VOWELS. The inventory of syllabic signs indicates four vowels, transcribed *a, i, e, u.* The set of signs for indicating syllables with *e* contained a relatively small number of signs, and in fact is defective; the scribes fell back on signs from the *i*-series: there being no sign for *ke*, they write *ki-e* [ke(:)] 'these'. On top of this there appears to have been a degree of coalescence of Proto-Anatolian **i* and **e* (and, in some environments, also with the outcome of the diphthongs **ay*, **oy*, and **ey*). Thus while *ki-e* is the usual writing for 'these' in earlier texts, and common at all periods, in later Hitt. *ki-i* occurs frequently, as well as peculiar compilations such as *ki-e-i* or *ki-i-e*.

The significance of extra ('plene') vowels, which are extremely regular in some forms and haphazard in others, is debated. Some think there is no significance; others think they represent long vowels; others think they represent accented syllables. In forms where an intervocalic *-y-* has dropped, one supposes the resulting vowel to be long: *šu-ul-la-a-aš* gen.sg. 'big' (an *i*-stem, and occasionally actually written *šu-ul-la-ya-aš*) was almost certainly /sulās/ or /sullās/.

CONSONANTS. The writing system had signs for two series of stops in accord with their Akkadian values, *-ta-* and *-da-*; *-ka-* and *-ga-*; and so on. These are used interchangeably in writing Hitt., however, so that *du-um-me-ni* and *tu-um-me-ni* 'we take' are equivalent. Nevertheless scribes show definite preferences, so that *ḫu-u-ma-an-da-aš* gen.sg. 'all' occurs much more often than *ḫu-u-ma-an-ta-aš*; but both occur. (They write only *ḫu-u-ma-an-te-eš* nom.pl., but for a quite different reason: there is no sign for *-de-* in the signary.)

In regard to postvocalic stops, as in *-uk-*, *-at-*, the system as used in Akkadian had no contrast like that between *-ka-* and *-ga-*: there was just one series. They are traditionally transcribed to match the following stop, however, such that in the cuneiform text the first sign of what are transcribed *-ug-ga-* and *-uk-ka-* is actually the same. Where the sign is followed by some other kind of sound, the choice of how to transcribe is the scholar's; Hitt. *ut-ne-e* n. 'country' and *ud-ne-e* are equivalent.

DOUBLE CONSONANTS. Scribal practice is fairly consistent in the 'doubling' of intervocalic consonants via the use of -(C)VC- signs. Some forms are typically written with a single consonant sign, like *a-ki* 'dies'; others are consistently written like *da-a-ak-ki* 'corresponds to, resembles'. The distinction is possible only medially, and convenient only intervocalically. Nevertheless, the hesitation between *iš-tar-ak-ta*, *iš-tar-ak-ki-it*, and *iš-tar-ki-it* 3sg. pret. 'it went badly' (the reading was probably something like /starkt/) indicates a determination to be explicit about whatever *-kk-* represented, even against odds.

The significance of this orthography is debated. Formerly some influential scholars doubted that the choice of writing reflected any feature of the language, but most authorities nowadays take the orthography as significant. It is noteworthy that the single writing occurs in words of secure etymology which reflect the PIE plain voiced and voiced aspirated series (133), whereas the double writing seems to correspond to PIE voiceless stops. (This correlation is known as *Sturtevant's Law*.) So Hitt. *ne-pí-iš* 'sky' (**nebh-*: G νέφος, OCS *nebo*, L *nebula*, 143); *a-da-an-zi* 'they eat' (PIE **ed-*: G ἔδω, L *edō*, Ved. *adanti* 'they eat', 146), vs. *pa-at-tar* nom., *pa-ad-da-na-aš* gen.sg. 'wing' ? /patnas/ (PIE **pet-* 'fly': Ved. *pátra-*, G πτερόν, L *penna* 'feather' < **petneH₂*, 222.1). There are perplexing exceptions, however, like the simple writing of the affix *-tar* < PIE **-ter*, **-tr̥* (as in L *iter* 'way') where one would expect *-tt-*.

Some authorities suppose the orthography is trying to represent some such contrast as voiced vs. voiceless stops; others imagine such things as plain vs. aspirated stops or tense vs. lax stops; still others, pointing to the many inconsistencies, doubt that any systematic distinction was being attempted at all, only an orthographic differentiation parallel to NE *rode* vs. *road* (both from OE *rád*). The scribes are at least as consistent in the double writing of liquids, nasals, and *-šš-* vs. *-š-*. Here too the evidence is inconsistent: in a form like *ap-pa-an-na-aš* 'of taking' (< **-tn-os*) the *-nn-* might, like NE *keenness*, be spelled as sounded. But one is reminded of such English whimsies as *canon* vs. *cannon*, and it is hardly conceivable that the very frequent spelling of, say, the Hitt. 1pl. ending as *-um-me-ni* (427, end) represents a long consonant.

The transliteration *-ḫ-* in Akkadian stands for a sound corresponding to Semitic *x* (something like the sound of *ch* in Ger. *Bach*). How it was pronounced in Hitt. is unknown. The great majority of Hitt. words containing *-ḫ-* are of unknown etymology. In forms whose etymology is understood they represent the sound or sounds that continue the laryngeals **H_2* (165) and (less conclusively) **H_3*, as in *ḫa-aš-ta-a-i* 'bone' < ? **H_3estoH₁*.

The transliteration *-š-* stands for presumed /š/ in Akkadian, where there were in addition two other sibilant series, *-s-* and *-ṣ-* (velarized; the so-called 'emphatic *s*'). These latter are found in Hitt. texts only when writing forms from Akkadian. The Hitt. sound transcribed *-š-* was probably an ordinary [s].

The signs transliterated with *-z-* stood for /z/ in Akkadian, but in Hitt. stood for /ts/. In forms of known IE origin, the sequence continues **t* before **i*, so *e-eš-zi* 'is' < **H₁es-ti* (Ved. *ásti*, G ἐστί, L *est*); the Hitt. pronunciation was something like /estsi/. The *z*-series also writes the sequence *-t-s-*, as in *a-da-an-za*, that is *adant-s* nom.sg. 'having eaten' (554) and *ḫu-u-ma-an-za*, that is *ḫomant-s* nom.sg. 'all'.

DUMMY VOWELS. The syllabic writing system creates problems for writing certain kinds of Hitt. consonant clusters. The only cluster in the Hitt. signary was /ts/ (the Akk. *z*-series); the result is that in most clusters dummy vowels had to be written if all the component consonants were to be indicated. The surest evidence that a vowel written was not pronounced is orthographic hesitation, as in the three different versions of the same word /starkt/ cited above. Furthermore, spoken vowels usually are represented with signs reading V, CV, or CVC (where C = any consonant, V = any vowel). Therefore a spelling like *kar-ap-zi* 'he raises', especially if anything like consistent, points to a dummy second vowel, that is /karptsi/. In some other cases our knowledge of the morphology and phonology is enough to provide the correct interpretation: the root *spand-* 'pour an oblation' (G σπένδω, L *spondeō*) occurs with the iterative/frequentative affix *-sk^e/a-* (PIE **-sḱ^e/o-*); the 1sg. pres. is written *ši-pa-an-za-ki-mi*, presumably *spant-sk-i-mi*. Many vowels written at the ends of words were dummies. Here too hesitation is evidence for dummy vowel orthography, as in *iš-tar-ak-ta*, *iš-tar-ki-it*, cited above. In the nom.sg. of *nt*-stems (participles mostly, but some others as well, such as *ḫu-u-ma-an-za* cited above), there is little orthographic hesitation, but knowledge of the morphology is sufficient to establish *-ants* as the probable reading.

32. LITHUANIAN AND OLD CHURCH SLAVIC. The PIE contrasts of length are faithfully preserved in Lithuanian, where however the representation is inconsistent. Lith. *ū* and *ų* are allographs for /ū/; *ė* is /ē/, *y* is /ī/. Lith. *ie* and *uo* are reflexes of long mid vowels under certain circumstances. The diacritics ´, `, and ˜ are scholarly indications of intonation and length; they are not a feature of standard Lithuanian orthography.

In Slavic, it seems likely that *a*, *ě*, *i*, *u*, and *y* were at least for a time in fact long vowels, next to short *o*, *e*, *ĭ*, *ŭ*; but, perhaps aided by significant differences in the phonetics of long vs. short vowels, the length distinction disappeared in OCS. In Slavic, *y* is a high back unrounded vowel, the reflex of earlier **ū*. OCS *ě* reflects **ē* and most **oy* and **ay*; it was pronounced something like [yæ].

OCS *ę* and *ǫ* are nasalized vowels reflecting various sequences of vowel plus **n*.

33. OLD IRISH. The spelling system of Old Irish bears a very complex relationship, albeit a tolerably regular one, to what are surmised to have been the features of the spoken language. So *p t c* in initial position stand for voiceless stops, in medial position for voiced ones. OIr. *b d g* in initial position stand for voiced stops, in medial position for voiced fricatives (which is sometimes also the value initially). The voiceless fricatives are unambiguously written *ph th ch*, respectively. The pairs represented in transcription with Greek and Roman letters (/χ k/, /θ t/, /δ d/, /β b/, and the like) are respectively *lenited* and *unlenited* sounds,[1] and in fact all consonants were found in these two states. The lenited sounds will be indicated in transcription by Greek letters, as orthographic *ath(a)ir* = /aθəρ'/.

As an additional complexity, most consonants in OIr. may be palatalized or rounded as well as plain. The orthography indicates these details by the vowels, using various strategies somewhat vacillatingly. A spelling like *athair* 'father' alternating with *athir* (summarized in the *ath(a)ir* of scholars) indicates only that the *th* is plain and the *r* is palatal. In tonic syllables, *-i-* and *-u-* after another vowel indicate the quality of the following consonant, as *daur* /$daρ^w$/ nom.sg. 'oak' (= G δόρυ); *daire* gen.pl. /daρ'e/; *daird(a)e* /dar'δe/ 'oaken'—here the optionally-written *a* before the invariably-written *e* signals that the preceding consonant is plain. (In transcription palatalized consonants are indicated by /'/, rounded by /^{w}/.)

The acute accent indicates long vowels; but written on the second of two vowel letters indicates a (true) diphthong, as in *roída* /royδa/ gen.sg. 'great wood' < **pro-wid-* (nom.sg. *ruud* /rūδ/); cf. *cóic* /kōg'/ 'five' where the *-i-* is a diacritic.

Owing to its complexity, OIr. orthography will not be further described here. Instead, whenever OIr. forms are cited an explanatory transcription will be supplied.

34. SABELLIAN. In quoting Oscan and Umbrian inscriptions the forms written in the native alphabets are distinguished from those written in the Latin alphabet by bold face and italic type, respectively. For example, native O **fakiiad** 'faciat', but in Latin letters *factud* 'facito'. Citations from inscriptions in Greek characters are transcribed as such. The signs in native scripts transcribed **í** and **ú**, as in O **píd** 'quid', **púd** 'quod', stand for vowels which were lower, evidently, than **i** and **u**. Vowel length is indicated only

---

[1] *Lenition* is a lessening in duration or closure of a consonant, as when a stop becomes a spirant, or a nasal becomes an approximant, or a glide disappears altogether. In Welsh the lenition of voiceless stops yields voiced ones, however, which is not a 'lessening' of anything; in OIr., *s* lenites to /h/, which fits the general definition, but **sw* lenites to /f/, which hardly does.

sporadically, by such means as gemination (25, end), postvocalic *h* (U *stahmei* dat.sg. 'station'), intervocalic *h* (*traha(f)* 'trans'), and occasionally in combination (O **saahtúm**, cf. U *sahatam*). It is not the custom to supply marks of quantity in transcription, even where the length of the vowel is beyond question as is the case with O gen.sg. /-ās/ in *eituas* 'money', or gen.pl. /-āzom/ in *egmazum* 'of things' (L *-ārum*).

In native Umbrian a symbol **d** stands for a special development of PItal. **k*; in U inscriptions in Latin characters the equivalent sign is **Ś**, and ś is commonly used to transliterate the U symbol in modern technical literature; it is here transcribed ś. (Earlier authorities sometimes use the symbol ç.) Its likeliest value was [č].

35. THE CITATION-FORMS OF WORDS IN IE LANGUAGES. Except where there is some specific reason for deviating from the norm, Greek and Latin forms are cited in accord with the usual practices—verbs in the 1sg., nouns in the nom.sg., and so on. Vedic (Sanskrit) nouns and adjectives are cited in the stem form, as indicated by the hyphen; the customary citation form for verbs is the 3sg., usually the pres. For the Vedic language, when the usual citation form is unattested, actually attested forms are cited. OIr. verbs are similarly cited in the 3sg. where attestation allows. Germanic verbs are cited in the infinitive, Baltic and Slavic verbs in the 1sg. Hitt. forms are cited as attested.

For all citations the following style will be observed: The cited form (usually preceded by an abbreviation identifying the language) is in italics, and as a rule it is followed by a gloss without punctuation other than single quote-marks. Such glosses are tags for convenience only and must not be imagined to give a trustworthy idea of the true meaning of a form. Pertinent grammatical or morphological tags for details like case or person may come between the cited form and its gloss, but occasionally precede the citation. Cited forms from all languages are treated thus, except of course modern English (NE) forms usually do not need a gloss. NB: *A word is cited without a gloss when there is substantial agreement in meaning between it and the immediately preceding form, or if it has already been glossed within a paragraph or two preceding the citation.* The colon is used as a sign of comparison, to be interpreted as 'to be compared with' or 'being cognate with'. (In many cases the comparanda are by no means identical in all details of formation.) Examples:

(1) L *ālium* n. 'garlic'.
(2) NHG *Teig* 'dough', OE *dág*, NE *dough*.
(3) U **vitluf** acc.pl. 'calves'.
(4) G ἄλλος 'another', L *alius* : Ved. *anyá-*.

Englished: (1) The Latin neuter noun *ālium*, meaning 'garlic'. (2) Modern German *Teig*, meaning 'dough', cognate with Old English *dág* and English *dough*, of the same meaning. (3) Umbrian **vitluf** (as written in the native alphabet) is an accusative plural noun meaning 'calves'. (4) The Greek word ἄλλος and the Latin word *alius* are cognate, as is also the Vedic stem *anyá-*; all three mean roughly 'another'.

UNATTESTED FORMS. There are several categories of forms that might be *cited* even though not anywhere actually *attested*:

An asterisk (*) identifies a form which is *reconstructed*, not actually attested—usually a form thought to predate the attested forms. Such reconstructions may be merely for the sake of the argument or may be serious hypotheses. The same mark may be used for hypothetical MEANINGS, as: L *carō* 'meat' (*'a cut').

The sign × before a form also means that it is unattested, but unattested because it is thought NOT ever to have existed in the history of the language. (The asterisk is used when the validity of a reconstructed form is irrelevant or unknown.)

Very occasionally it is desirable to identify unattested but confidently surmised contemporary forms ('accidental gaps' in paradigms) with a FOLLOWING asterisk. For example, various cases of the Gothic word for 'dog' are attested, but the normal citation form, the nominative singular, happens not to be among them and for strict accuracy would be written *hunds**.

A form preceded by two asterisks is a form predating what can be reached by the comparative method strictly speaking. Thus Hom. βῶν acc. sg. 'cow', Ved. *gā́m* point to PIE *g^wōm*. But it can be argued that behind this *g^wōm* is a still earlier form, not reachable by the comparative method but suggested by other kinds of reasoning. This earlier form, **g^wŏwm* (324), is marked with two asterisks.

The signs > and < mean 'becomes' and 'comes from', respectively. The diachronic relationship in question can be semantic or formal; show the action of a single sound law or of many; and encompass a mixture of phonological and analogical innovations. Thus: 'PreL **honōses* "of worth" > L *honōris*' would be an appropriate way of demonstrating the phonological development of *s* to *r* between vowels (173), even though the example simultaneously exhibits the regular change of *-e-* to *-i-* in final syllables (71.3). 'PIE **sek^{w}otor* > G ἕπεται "follows"' states a diachronic development which entails an assortment of phonological and analogical replacements acting over a considerable span of time; the formula simply means: 'PIE **sek^{w}otor* becomes (by various developments) G ἕπεται'. However, when an analogical change is SPECIFICALLY under discussion, the signs → and ← will be used for 'is analogically remodeled as' and 'is the result of analogical remodeling acting on', respectively. Thus, 'OL *honōs* → L *honor*' would be unpacked as: 'the final *-s* in OL *honōs* becomes L *-r* by an analogical, not a phonological, change'. (Of course, most of the diachronic relationships seen in the two forms—the shortening of the *-ō-* (83.3), the preservation of other sounds unchanged—are regular phonological developments.)

PHONOLOGY

VOWELS AND DIPHTHONGS

36. The normal correspondences of the vowels and short diphthongs may be surveyed in the accompanying table. The long diphthongs (63-4), and the syllabic liquids (93-8), nasals (99-100), and laryngeals (101-2) are treated separately.

PIE	G	L	Skt.	Lith.	OCS	Go.	OE
i	ι	i	i	i	ĭ	i, ai	e, i
u	υ	u	u	u	ŭ	u, au	u, o
e	ε	e	a	e	e	i, ai	e, i
o	o	o	a	a	o	a	æ
a	α	a	a	a	o	a	æ
ī	ῑ	ī	ī	y	i	ei	í
ū	ῡ	ū	ū	ū	y	u (?ū)	ú
ē	η	ē	ā	ė	ě	e	ǽ
ō	ω	ō	ā	uo	a	o	ó
ā	ᾱ, η	ā	ā	ō	a	o	ó
ey	ει	ī (ei)	e	ei, ie	i	ei	í
oy	οι	ū, oe (oi)	e	ai, ie	ě	ai	á
ay	αι	ae	e	ai, ie	ě	ai	á
ew	ευ	ū (ou)	o	au	u	iu	éo
ow	ου	ū (ou)	o	au	u	au	éa
aw	αυ	au	o	au	u	au	éa

Notes to the table.

1. PIE LONG VOWELS and sequences of SHORT VOWELS PLUS LARYNGEAL with few exceptions (mostly in G, 49-50) have identical reflexes in the IE languages. As a consequence it is not always possible to determine whether a given long vowel, for example the *ū* of L *mūs* 'mouse', continues PIE **ū* or **uH*.

2. GREEK. The Greek vowels and diphthongs reflect most nearly those of the parent speech, though the system is not as conservative as used to be taught. The most obvious innovations are Attic-Ionic rather than generally Greek, namely the change of **ā* to η (54-6), and the (purely phonetic) change of **u* and **ū* to front rounded vowels /ü ǖ/ (38a). There are in addition a number of pan-Greek metatheses, syncopes, and assimilations, and a variety of conditioned lengthening and shortening.

The conservatism of G vowels ended with the classical period. Since then there has been a wholesale and radical shift in the pronunciation of vowels and diphthongs, and the loss of contrastive vowel length: no fewer than eleven Classical vowels and diphthongs are reflected in NG as the phoneme /i/. NG orthography is prevailingly etymological, however, so these far-reaching innovations are not apparent in written Greek.

3. Latin. (These correspondences are for initial syllables only.) The principal restructuring of the PIE vowel system in Latin, at least as it appears in this table, is the merging of diphthongs apart from **ay* and **aw* with long vowels; in PItal. and early Latin (the forms in parentheses in the table) all the diphthongs were still diphthongal. Vowels in Latin have undergone a large number of changes under special conditions, to the extent that there are three sets of sound laws for Latin vowels: for initial syllables (shown here); for medial syllables (65–70); and for final syllables (71, 75).

4. Sanskrit. The outstanding feature of the Indo-Iranian vowel system is the merger of all non-high vowels into *a* and *ā*; this applies to the diphthongs as well as to the independent vowels. The result is a triangular vowel system: *i, u, a*; *ī, ū, ā*; *ai, au*. In Sanskrit, however, PInIr. **ai*, **au* smoothed to monophthongal /ē, ō/; see 28.

By Brugmann's Law, *o*-grade vowels in open syllables are reflected in InIr. as *ā*, not *a*: **swesorm̥* acc. 'sister' > Ved. *svásāram*, **memore* 'is dead' > Ved. *mamā́ra*. Cf. *pitáram* < **pH̥$_2$term̥* acc. 'father'. A form like Ved. *dadarśa* < **dedorḱe* 'sees' shows the reflex before a consonant cluster, and Ved. *páti-* 'master' reflects the non-ablauting vowel of **poti-*.

5. Lithuanian and Old church slavic. See 32.

6. Gothic and Old english. In PGmc. the PIE vowel system was reorganized in two ways. The distinction between *o-* and *a*-vowels was lost, with results more in agreement with Lithuanian than with OCS, phonetically speaking, namely the remaining short vowel was *a*-like and the long one was *ō*-like. Additionally, PIE **i* and **e* coalesced (it is still being debated whether the merger was complete or partial). —Diphthongs were preserved, with the exception of the merger of **ey* and **ī* (from all sources) as PGmc. **ī*.

In *Gothic*, PIE **e* and **i* coalesce completely, as Pre-Go. **i*, which becomes *ai* (that is, /e/) before *h*, *r*, and h^w (a single letter in Gothic), and remains *i* elsewhere. Analogously, PGmc. **u* splits in Gothic, becoming *au* (that is, /o/) before *h*, *r*, and h^w, and remaining *u* elsewhere.

Old English. Only developments in initial syllables are shown here, and not all of them by any means. The secondary changes of OE are very complicated, in part because of umlaut (changes brought about by the vowels in following syllables). The correspondences shown in the table are for non-umlauted vowels, except for one detail: the short high vowels corresponding to PGmc. **i*, **u* become *e*, *o* when followed by PGmc. **a* or **ō* in the next syllable. For example, PGmc. **i* is reflected as follows: PIE **wid-mé* 'we know' > PGmc. **witum* > OE *witon* (= Go. *witum*); but PIE **ni-sd-ós* 'nest' > PGmc. **nistaz* > OE *nest* (= Go. *nists*). Note that the crucial conditions have been effaced in the OE words themselves.

SHORT VOWELS

i[1]

37. PIE *k^w*id* 'what' > G τί, L *quid* : Ved. *cit* indef. particle.
PIE **sti-steH₂-* 'stand' > G ἵστημι, L *sistō* : Ved. *tiṣṭhati.*
PIE **wid-me* 'we know' (zero grade of **weyd-*) > Hom. ἴδμεν : Ved. *vidmá,* Go. *witum,* OE *witon,* cf. NE *wit.*
PIE **wid-* 'see' (zero grade of **weyd-*)[2] > G ἰδεῖν (Hom. ἰδέειν), 2nd aor. infin. of εἶδον, L *videō.*

a. In L **i* > *e* (as **u* > *o*, **38b**) before *r* arising from *s* (173):
PIE **si-sH₁-* redup. pres. of **seH₁-* 'sow' > L *serō*; L *cinis* 'ash', gen. *cineris* < **kinises*; L *Faleriī* < **falisioy* (cf. *Faliscus*). Cf. **i* before original **r*: **wiros* 'man' > L *vir.* —The failure of this lowering in *pirum* 'pear' < **pisom* (cf. G ἄπιον) is unexplained.

u

38. PIE **yug-ó-* n. 'yoke' (zero grade of **yewg-* 'join') > G ζυγόν, L *iugum* : Ved. *yugá-,* Go. *juk,* OE *geoc* /yok/.
PIE **rewdh-* 'red': zero grade **rudh-* (various suffixes) > G ἐρυθρός, L *ruber* : Ved. *rudhirá-* 'bloody' (Skt. 'blood'), OE *rudig* 'reddish'. Full grades of the same root are seen in Ved. *róhita-* 'red', L *rūfus* 'red-haired', and OE *réad.*

a. G υ and ῡ retained the inherited phonetic value of high, back, and rounded in many dialects. But in Attic they became front, while remaining high and round, like Fr. *u* /ü/ from PRom. **u* (L *ū*). In late times (1st century AD and later, according to locality) these sounds unrounded and fell together with ĭ̄.

In early loanwords from G, υ is manifested as *u* in L, as in *cubus* 'cube' < G κύβος. But in the L of the 1st century BC the letter *y* was introduced to represent the then-current Attic sounds. Just as in vernacular G, and probably under the influence of the large émigré Greek population of Roman urban centers, in VL the sound thus written became unrounded; *y* and *i* were then merely variant spellings of the same sound, and *y* was often introduced into loanwords which did not have υ in G, as *ydolon* (from εἴδωλον 'image'), and even into words not of G origin at all, as *stylus* 'stick; stylus' (unrelated to G στῦλος 'pillar') and *sylva* 'forest'. Some of these solecisms have remained in present-day English spelling, as for example *stylus* and *sylvan.*

---

[1] This and similar headings refer to the PIE reconstructions. PIE sequences of short vowel followed by a laryngeal followed in turn by a consonant or a word boundary are, with one exception in the phonology of Greek (maybe two), indistinguishable from PIE long vowels. Accordingly in 49-53 they will be treated together with long vowel reflexes. For other details regarding laryngeal phonology, see 101-9 (lengthening of preceding syllabics) and 165-7 (a discussion of laryngeals as such).

[2] Most authorities think PIE **weyd-* 'see' and **weyd-* 'know' are the same root, with the meaning 'know' derived from 'see' ('has seen' = 'know'). But such a view does not fit the strikingly archaic-looking morphology of the 'know' forms, namely, a perfect without reduplication (512). Furthermore, if the view of the PIE perfect as a stative (410, 509) is correct, **woyde* from a root 'see' should mean 'has in sight, is looking at', not 'has seen'. Mere homophony is credible here, given the uncommonly large number of homophonous roots beginning with **w* in PIE (142a).

b. In L, *u > o before r arising from s (173), cf. the change of *i > e (37a). OL *forem* from **fusēm* (archaic impf. subj.) with **fu-* as in *futūrus* etc. Unexpectedly, PIE **snusos* 'daughter-in-law' > L *nurus* (*u*-stem); but PRom. **nora* (Sp. *nuera* for example) proves that in some forms of Roman speech the expected form was current. See 77 for a summary of Romance vowel phonology.

39. Some see evidence for a special development of **Hu-* in G. In word-initial position only, *H_1*u-* > εὐ-, *H_2*u-* > αὐ-. (There are no examples for *H_3*u-*.) Thus *H_1*uru-* 'wide' > G εὐρύς : Ved. *urú-*. *H_2*ug-s-* 'grow, strengthen' > G αὔξω : Ved. *ukṣ-*.

The obvious problem is how to distinguish between this development and reflexes of ordinary full grades (111-5). For the PIE root 'grow', for example, an initial *H_2- is indicated by G ἀ(ϝ)έξω < *H_2*weg-* (though that exhausts the evidence), and an unambiguous full grade *H_2*ewg-* is well-attested in L *augustus* 'majestic, dignified', Go. *aukan* 'grow', Ved. *ójas-* n. 'strength', and so on. The weight of G αὔξω as evidence for αὐ- < *H_2*u-* depends on the confidence with which it can be aligned precisely with Ved. *ukṣ-*. The latter however appears to be a secondary form: it has no Iranian counterpart; in the RV it occurs only in late hymns; besides, a full grade (though equally suspect) is twice attested in the aor. stem *ā́ukṣ-*. And some have suggested that G αὔξω itself is a syncopated (80) doublet of ἀ(ϝ)έξω.

G εὐρύς is not an inherited full grade, on the evidence of Ved. *várīyas* adv. (based on the comparative) 'more widely' and *váras-* n. 'breadth'. But a comparison of εὐρύς with Ved. *urú-* is an error. Ved. *urú-* and Av. *vouru-* continue PInIr. **wr̥rú-*; Ved. evidence (fem. *urvī́-*, not ˣ*ūrvī́-*) disallows *wr̥Hu-*; and the shape **(H)urú-* with or without initial H_1- would be unique to G. The conventional explanation for the G forms is metathesis of expected *ϝερ-. The weakness of an appeal to metathesis is partially offset by the extreme unlikeliness of either zero grade *H_1*ur-* or a full grade *H_1*ewr-* in the etymon of the *s*-stem neut. εὖρος (= Ved. *váras-*) ? < **weros*.

a. G σῠ́, τῠ́, for those who reconstruct PIE **tuH* 'thou' rather than **tū̆*, are cases of a syllabic plus laryngeal in final position giving a short vowel (next to L *tū*, OE *þú*, and others). In some instances such a development is plausible (53a). Here, however, there is no actual evidence for a laryngeal in the first place, and the likelier explanation is that in PIE (as in several of its daughters) monosyllables ending with a vowel alternated between a tonic form with a long vowel and an atonic short, thus **tū́/tŭ*. Although most languages generalized one or the other, some maintained the ancestral alternation. WGmc., for example, maintained such an arrangement; in a development parallel to the analysis endorsed here, NE *thou* reflects the long/tonic alternant and NHG *du* the short/atonic. In this interpretation, Hom. τῡ́νη—as the accent suggests—is a formation based on original **tū́*.

e, H_1e

40. PIE *H_1*e* is never distinct from **e*. This makes it hard to know whether forms traditionally reconstructed with an initial **e-* might have been *H_1*e-* instead. The problem cases include roots like **ed-* 'eat', **es-* 'be', and pron. **e-* 'this', as well as forms like the augment **e-* (441) and the preposition **en-* 'in' (406.3). Given the elusiveness of the evidence, a reconstruction like H_1*ed-* 'eat' is usually based on nothing more than principle. Data pointing to *H_1*e-* is however cogent for *H_1*es-* 'be' (491-3).

In L, PIE **e* and the *em, en* that arise from PIE **m̥* and **n̥* (99–100) develop identically.
PIE **bher-* 'carry' > G φέρω, L *ferō* : Ved. *bhárati*, Go. *bairan*, OE *beran*, OIr. *berith*.
PIE **ǵenH₁-* 'beget', **ǵenH₁os-* 'race, kind' > G γένος, L *genus* : Ved. *jánas-*.
PIE **egṓ* (or **egoH*) 'I' > G ἐγώ, L *ego* : Ved. *ahám* (< ?**eǵH-óm*), OLith. *eš*, Go. *ik*. See 360.

a. In G, some etymologies suggest that in a strongly labial environment, *-*e*- must have become **o* and hence eventually -υ- in accord with 44:
PIE **kʷékʷlom, kʷekʷlóm* 'wheel, circle' > G κύκλα 'wheels'. All cognates attest *e*-grade in the first syllable, as Ved. *cakrá-*, OE *hwéol* and *hweowol* (the OE doublets result from different IE accentuation).
PIE **gʷenH₂-* n. 'woman' (311a), reassigned to various feminine declensions in the daughter languages and variously remodeled: G γυνή : Ved. *jánī* (1×), OIr. *ben* (**gʷenā*), Go. *qino* (*n*-stem), OCS *žena* (*ā*-stem). (PIE **o* would regularly > G υ here (44), but no evidence points to *o*-grade forms.)
PIE **swépnos* 'sleep' > G ὕπνος : Ved. *svápna-*, OE *swefn* 'dream'. This is the most doubtful example, as PIE **supno-* would give both ὕπνος and OCS *sŭnŭ*.

41. **e* > L *i*:

1. Before dorsal nasal (ŋ), that is, *n* plus *g, gu, c,* and *qu*, and before *gn* (220a).
PIE **teng-* 'soak, dip' > L *tingō* : G τέγγω.
PIE **dn̥ǵhweH₂-* 'tongue' > **dengwā* (100) > L *dingua* (Fest.), *lingua* (151) : OE *tunge*.
PIE **penkʷe* 'five' > PItal. **kʷenkʷe* (141a) > L **quinque* > *quīnque* (*ī* from *quīnctus*, 81.2) : G πέντε, Ved. *páñca*.
PIE **leǵ-* 'gather': **leǵ-no-* 'firewood' > L *lignum*.
PIE **deḱ-* 'conform (to societal norms)' **deḱ-no-* 'fitting' > **deŋnos* (220) > L *dignus* (cf. L *decet* 'is fitting').

The raising of mid vowels before nasals in general, and before [ŋ] in particular, is met with in the histories of many languages. It happened in PGmc., and then some time after the 12th century a similar development occurred in English: *þencan* > *think*; *enke* > *ink*; and NB the pronunciation of *England* and *English*.

a. In G mid-vowels are unchanged (so τέγγω). However, ἴγνυς f. 'back of the knee and thigh' can be traced to **en-ǵnu-* (cf. γόνυ 'knee') if it is thinkable that prefixal **en-* 'in' did at least sometimes become ἰγ- /iŋ/-.

2. MISCELLANEOUS.

The factors involved include assimilation and proclitic or enclitic weakening (analogous to medial weakening, 65–75), but true generalizations cannot be framed. The majority of the cases involve **e* followed by *m, l, n,* and in most cases there is a high vowel (*i* or *u*) in the following syllable.

Preposition *in* and verbal prefix *in-* < PIE **en-*: G ἐν.
Privative prefix *in-* < **en-* < PIE **n̥-* (100).

nihil 'nothing' < **ne-hilom* (cf. *nefās* '(is) unholy', *nesciō* 'I don't know').
mihi 'to me', *tibi* 'to you' < *mihī*, *tibī* < **mehei*, **tebei* (75, 84).
tilia 'linden' : G πτελέα.
sinister 'left' if from **senisteros* (but its etymology is very uncertain).
similis 'resembling', *simul* (SEMOL) 'at the same time as', *simplex* 'simple'; but perhaps because of the following non-high vowel, no such change is seen in *semel* 'once' < **semēlom* < **sm̥-meH₁-lo-* and *semper* 'always'; all from PIE **sem-*, **sm̥-* 'same, one' (389.1 and 1B).
PIE **weǵ-* 'be vigorous' (Ved. *vā́ja-* 'strength') underlies both *vigil* 'alert', *vigeō* 'am lively', on the one hand, and *vegetus* 'vigorous' on the other. (For *vegeō* 'stir up' see 46.1.)
vitulus 'calf' : G ετάλον (Cos) 'yearling', U *vitluf* acc.pl.; ultimately from PIE **wet-* 'year' (G ϝετος/ἔτος 'year').
L *Minerva* for OL MENERVA.

Nihil, *mihi* may be distracted forms of the very frequent *nīl*, *mī*, and *tibi* for **tebi* may be influenced by *mihi*.

a. Proclitic weakening in initial syllables must POSTDATE the period of L word-initial accent (65, 246). Accordingly some analogical force must explain disyllables like *indō* 'put in', *impos* 'powerless', *infit* 'begins', and the like. A few forms with *en-* 'in' are attested in OL: ENDO, ENFITIARE 'to deny', though this may be nothing more than the hesitation between E and I which is common in OL epigraphy.

42. **e* > L *o* before *w*, after *w* (mostly consonant plus *w*), or before *l* pinguis (176a), but subject to further conditions only partly understood (the vowel of the following syllable apparently being a factor). The main facts are as follows.

1. **ew* > **ow*, whether or not followed by a vowel.

PIE **newos* 'new' > L *novus* : G νέ(ϝ)ος, Ved. *náva-*, Hitt. *ne-e-u-it* inst.sg.
PIE **newn̥* 'nine' > L *novem* : G ἐννέα, Ved. *náva*, Go. *niun*.
PIE **dewk-* 'lead' > OL *douc-* > L *dūcō* : Go. *tiuhan* (61).

a. This development is pan-Italic, and something similar is found in Celtic and BS: U **nuvis** 'more recent' (= L *novius*), OCS *novŭ* 'new', Lith. *naũjas*, OIr. *náue* < **nóue*. Some Gaulish inscriptions still show *eu*, alternating with *ou* in several cases; this might mean that the Celtic innovation was later than the others and unconnected with them, except that the attestations in *eu* are generally later than those in *ou*, and are best taken as a development FROM *ou* (or even *ō*; cf. British [ɛw] in *go* and *show*). Some similar explanation is likely for OL forms like NEVNA dat. (Nōnae), which are much too late—4th or 3rd century BC—to be unaltered reflexes of **ew*. In Proto-Germanic, **ew* and **ow* do not fall together, becoming **iw* and **aw* respectively, as Go. *niujis* 'new' = Lith. *naũjas*.

b. In *levis* 'light', *brevis* 'short', the *ew* is not from PIE **ew* but from **egʷh* and **éghw*, respectively (163, 160).

2. **swe-* > **swo-*, hence (183) *so-*.

PIE **swépnos* 'sleep' > L *somnus* : Ved. *svápna-*, OE *swefn* 'dream'.
PIE **swésor-* 'sister' > L *soror* : Ved. *svásar-*, OE *sweoster*.
PIE **swéḱuro-* 'husband's father', **sweḱrú-* 'husband's mother' > L *socer*, *socrus*

: G ἑκυρός, ἑκυρᾱ́ (ἑ- from *σϝε-, 171); Ved. *śváśura-*, *śvaśrū́-*; OE *swéor*, *sweger*.
PIE **swe-dhH₁-* '(our) custom' > OL SVODALES > L *sodālēs* 'usual companions'.

3. **dwe- > dwo-* whence (185.1) *bo-*.
OL DVENOS 'good' (dubious etymology but securely attested in OL from the 6th century BC), whence DVO(NORO) (Scipio epitaphs), L *bonus*.

a. In three forms **dwe-* unexpectedly > *be-*. L *bene* < **dwenēd* is unexplained. L *bellum* 'war' < **dwellom* (epigr. DVELLOM; ultimate makeup much debated) and *bellus* 'handsome' < **dwenelo-*, may be explained by the following *l* exilis (176a).

4. Evidence for **we* > L *wo* in other environments is scanty and suspect. PIE **pekʷō* > PItal. **kʷekʷō* > L *coquō* 'cook' is the only apparent example of **kʷe* > *quo* next to better-attested **kʷe* > *que*. *E*-grade is to be sure expected in the verb; but in this same root *o*-grade is well-attested in other unexpected places such as **pokʷtos* (where zero grade is the norm—128.3) 'ripe; cooked' > L *coctus*, W *poeth* 'hot'. Although *coquere* is not evidently a denominative verb, the noun *coquus* 'cook', which is a proper *o*-grade formation, may have influenced details of its form.

A better case can be made for PIE **wemH₁-* 'vomit' > L *vomō* (Ved. *avamīt* imperf., G (ϝ)εμέω, Lith. *vémti*). Elsewhere **we- > vo-* only before *l* pinguis (5, below, and 176a), and some think that *vomō* might be simply the *o*-grade of the root; but the original root-class inflection (479.2) for PIE **wem-* is well-attested and calls for *e*-grade. Certainly the environment of the **e* here, flanked by labial consonants, would be a potent one for backing and rounding, given that **e* is seen to do just that, with less reason (ITEMS 5 and 6, below.)

5. Before a velarized *l* (that is, '*l* pinguis', 176a):
**welō* (orig. athem.), **welti* 'I, he wants' > L *volō*, *volt* (later *vult*), in contrast to **welīt* subj. > L *velit*; **wel-(e)si* inf. > L *velle*.
**kʷelō* 'till' > **quolō* > L *colō* (183), cf. **en-kʷel-īno-* > L *inquilīnus* 'tenant, lodger' (with regular weakening of *e*, 66.2).
L *olīva* 'olive' (the tree) was borrowed from G ελαιϝᾱ́ or Aegean **elaywā* directly: **elaywā* > **olaywā* > L *olīva* (70.2); note that **e > o* must predate the change of medial **ay* to *ī*.

a. Most exceptions are only apparent, though the correct explanation in many cases is uncertain. Some hold that in initial syllables **e* between a dorsal obstruent and an *l* pinguis remains unchanged, thus *celsus* 'upright', *helvus* 'yellow' (**χel-*), *celer* 'fast' (**keles-*) and *celōx* 'fast ship', *gelu* 'frost'. However, such conditioning is phonetically suspect, and special explanations can be found for each of these, thus *celsus* < **cellsos* (*l* exilis) < **keld-so-*; *helvus* < **hellwo-* < **ghels-wo-* (= Lith. *gel̃svas* a horse color—'? palomino'); leveling explains *gelu*, cf. *gelidus* 'freezing' in which the *e* is before *l* exilis; *celōx* may be either a borrowing from G κέλης 'yacht' (NB Dor. κέληξ) or else formed from *celer* 'speedy'.

L *vel* 'or (else)' is from **vell* < **wels* < **wel-si* 'you wish' (484.1).

6. L *homō* 'man' is from earlier *hemō* (PIE **dhǵhm̥mon-*), quoted in Paul.

Fest. and vouchsafed—if only weakly—by *nēmō* 'no one' < **ne hemō* (**99**). Similarly, the family of words exemplified by *domō* 'tame' and its nomen agentis *domitor* have *-o-* where original *e*-grade is a certainty. These changes are unexplained—cf. unaltered *emō* 'take, buy'.

o, H_3e

43. PIE **o* (**H_1o*, **H_3o*), and **H_3e* fall together in G and L.
PIE **potis* 'master' > G πόσις 'husband', L *potis est* (in early L pronounced **potist*, whence usual *potest* by contamination with *est*) 'is able' : Ved. *páti-*, Go. *-faþ-* in *hundafaþs* 'centurion'.
PIE **oktōw* 'eight' (**389.8**) > G ὀκτώ, L *octō* : Ved. *aṣṭā́(u)*, Go. *ahtau*.
PIE **g^werH_3-* 'swallow', *o*-grade **g^worH_3-* > L *vorāre* 'devour' iter.-dur. to **g^worH_3-* (**456.2B**) : G βορᾱ́ 'food'.
PIE **H_3ek^w-* 'eye' > G ὄψομαι fut. of ὁράω 'see', L *oculus* 'eye'. PIE **H_3ek^w-iH_1* n.du. 'eyes' > Hom. ὄσσε (**199**); **H_3ek^w-mn̥* > ὄμμα (**219**) 'eye'. The initial laryngeal is guaranteed by lengthening in Indic compounds such as Ved. *ánīka-* 'face' < **enĭ-$H_3$$k^w$-o-*.

44. COWGILL'S LAW: **o* from any source > υ in Greek between a labial and a resonant.
PIE **nok^wt-* 'night' > G νύξ : L *nox*, RV *nák* nom.sg. (< **nakts*), Go. *nahts*, OIr. *innocht* /inoχt/ 'tonight'.
PIE **bholyom* 'leaf' > G φύλλον : L *folium*.
PIE **mol-eH_2-* 'mill' > G μύλη : L *molīna*.
PIE **H_3nog^wh-* 'nail' > PG **onok^wh-* (**90**) > **onuk^wh-* > G ὄνυξ, stem ὄνυχ- (**154.1**): OE *nægl*.
The PIE *n*-infix present stems to roots ending in **H_3*, like **sterH_3-* 'spread, scatter': zero grade stem **str̥-n-H̥$_3$-*; from **-nH̥$_3$-* came first PG **-no-* (**101a, 102**) then *-νυ-*: στόρνυμεν (**454A.3, 472.3**).
G γυμνός 'naked' and μύρμηξ 'ant' ultimately reflect PIE **nog^wno-* and **morwo-/mormo-* respectively; though many other details are obscure, the development of υ from **o* in these words is evident.

The derivation of πρυμνός from **pro-mno-* would fit here and is so accepted by some, but its meaning (the back or underside of anything, so δόρυ πρυμνόν 'the socket of a spear-point', πρύμνη 'the stern of a boat; the foot of a mountain') is hard to connect with **pro(H)-* 'forth'.

a. The development of -υ- is sometimes obscured by vowel assimilations (**91**), which though early postdate Cowgill's Law. Thus in the outcomes of PIE **nomn̥* 'name' > PG **onuma* > Att. ὄνομα; unaltered ὄνυμα is attested as such in Aeolic, Doric, and in νώνυμ(ν)ος (later ἀνώνυμος) 'nameless, inglorious'.[1] The relative chronology of assimilation

[1] For the possibility of an initial laryngeal in this reconstruction, cf. **90, 108**. The reconstruction **H_3neH_3mn-* endorsed by some is unlikely. The medial laryngeal would explain the long vowel of one or two West Germanic denominative formations, which for

vis-à-vis Cowgill's Law explains why G κολοφών 'summit' is not ˣκολυφών: the second -ο- is not original, being assimilated from original α in *κολαφον- < *koln̥- 'hill'; cf. *kl̥ni- > L *collis* and OE *hyll*.

b. The proper interpretation of the reflexes of PIE *k^wetwores* m. 'four' is hampered by its complicated PIE and PG paradigm and the leveling it has undergone in the various G dialects (389.4); but the -συρ- of Lesb. πέσυρες, Hom. πίσυρες probably continues PIE *-*twor*- (190.4).

c. G πολύς 'many, much' and combining form πολυ- are usually traced to PIE *$polH_1u$-. However, PIE *u*-stem adjectives of this type almost invariably take zero grade of the root (128.3), so *pl̥Hú- (> Ved. *purú*-), and the same is true of combining forms. In any case, the root was *$pleH_1$- 'fill', so that any full grade vowel before the *l would have to be secondary; and the only certain such full-grades have *e*-grade, like Go. *filu* 'much', OIr. *il*. Added to these problems is the one raised by Cowgill's Law, namely that PreG *polús should have given G ˣπυλύς, not πολύς.

The expected G forms would be *παλύς = Ved. *purú*-, or (rather less likely) *πελύς = Go. *filu*-; but see 106.2a for a more radical solution.

45. *o > *u* in Latin:

1\. Before nasals, esp. nasal + cons.; and before *l* plus cons. (except another *l*).

PItal. *χom-ke* 'this' acc.sg.m. > OL *honc* (73) > L *hunc*.

Early L *mol(c)tā* 'fine, levy' > L *multa*.

PIE *H_3emeso-* (or, less likely, *omeso-*; 117.2a) 'arm, shoulder' > L *umerus* : U *onse* loc.sg. 'on the shoulder', Go. *amsans* acc.pl., Ved. *áṃsa*-. (L *humerus* is an unetymological form; see 159.)

PIE *nem-* 'take', *o*-grade *nomo-* > L *numerus* 'number' : G νόμος 'custom, law'.

PIE *dhǵhomo-* adj. 'pertaining to the earth' > L *humus* and derivatives (for *homō* see 42.6) : U *hondra* 'below', G χθον- 'earth'.

a. This development applies to L *oNC* < *eNC < *n̥C (where *N* = any nasal and *C* = any cons. not *c* or *g*):

PIE *nebh-/*nobh-/*n̥bh-* 'navel' (various suffixes): *n̥bh-on- > *embon- > *ombon- > L *umbō* 'shield boss'; *m̥bhl̥- > *umbilīcus* 'navel'. (G ὀμφαλός is not exactly parallel, reflecting an *o*-grade: *nobhl̥- > *onophal- (*o*- prothetic, 89) > *ὀνυφαλός (44) > ὀμφαλός (80). (This root has also been reconstructed *H_3n̥ebh-* and so forth, with development parallel to *H_3nog^wh-; 90, 100b.)

b. There are several unexplained exceptions to this rule: L *longus* 'long', *onus* 'burden', *domus* 'house', and *omnis* 'all' (the etymology of the last is in any case obscure).

2\. Obscure, perhaps dialectal, is the patternless change of *o* > L *u* before *r* + cons. in some words, as *furnus* 'oven' (*fornus* rare), beside *fornāx* 'furnace' (*furnāx* rare); also in loanwords like *purpura* 'purple (dye)' < G πορφύρα. This has the nature of a regular sound law in Sab., but in L for

---

now have no obvious explanation. But it is necessary for nothing else; difficult for Gmc. *namōⁿ and G ὄνομα and most other forms (the syllabification it requires, *HnH̥men-, would be unexampled); and impossible for OIr. *ainm*.

the most part *or* + cons. remains unaffected, and this is assumed to be the proper development for urban Latin.

46. Other changes of *o* in L.

1. Initial *vo* > *ve* except before labials, *r* + vowel, and *l* pinguis (42.5, 45.1). This development is late (about 150 BC) and forms predating the change are well-attested.

Early *vortō* 'turn', *vorsus* 'a turning', *vorrō* 'sweep', *voster* 'your', *votō* 'forbid' > later *vertō, versus, verrō, vester, vetō.*

PIE **wr̥mi-* 'worm' > OL **vormis* > L *vermis* : OE *wyrm.*

PIE **wobhseH₂* > **wospa* > L *vespa* 'wasp' : OE *wæps.*

Dialect borrowing may explain the persistence of *vortex* 'whirlpool' alongside expected *vertex* 'crown of the head', with semantic differentiation.

PIE **woǵ-eyᵉ/o-* (caus. of **weǵ-*) > **wogeō* > L *vegeō* 'stir up, invigorate'.

a. In many words *vo-* > *va-*: *Valerius* cf. *Volesus, vocāre*~ *vacāre* both meaning 'call' and 'be empty', *vastus* 'empty', and several others. The forms in *vo-* are in most cases earlier attested, and some authorities take its development to *va-* except before apicals to be the regular one. (The vowels of as *vegeō*, above, and persistent *vŏc-* next to *vac-* seen in *vocō* 'call' and forms derived from it, such as *vocābulum*, can be traced to contamination.)

2. *ov* (of any origin) sporadically becomes *av*:

L *cavus* 'hollow' (VL also *covus*) : G *κόοι* 'hollows' (Hesych.).

PIE **kew(H)-* 'take note', from which *o*-grade **kow(H)-eyᵉ/o-* iter.-dur. L *caveō* 'am on guard', G *κο(ϝ)έω* 'take note' : **kowHi-* > Ved. *kaví-* 'wise' (*k-* points to *o*-grade, *ă* points to a closed syllable).

L *faveō* 'cherish' orig. *'keep warm' next to earlier *foveō*, cf. L *favilla* 'ashes', all < **dhogʷh-*.

PIE **lewH₃-* 'wash' > **low-* (42.1) > L *lavō* : G λο(ϝ)έω (the latter from **lewo-* as in Myc. *re-wo-te-re-jo* 'for bathing').

In many words of clear etymology, like *novem* 'nine' and *novus* 'new', this fails to happen. The sporadic nature of the development suggests an analogy rather than a sound law, and an analogical explanation has been proposed. According to it, the real sound law applied to LONG vowels, that is, **ōw* > *āv* as in L *octāvus* 'eighth' next to *octō*, and perfects *fāvī, cāvī, lāvī* from **-ōvī*. The root vowels of *faveō, caveō, lavō* are thereby the result of leveling on the pattern of these perfects. A weakness in this elegant explanation is that all but one of the crucial starting points, **fōvī* and the rest, are themselves not only hypothetical but would have to be secondary; the exception is *lāvī* which beyond reasonable doubt presupposes **lōwai* (88.3) < **lo(w)awai* (from either **lewH̥₁-*, 42.1, or **lowH̥₁-*; 184.3, 525.3).

L *ōvum* 'egg' is not a counter-example, as it probably reflects **ōom* < **ōyom* < **ōwyom* < **oH₂wyom* (based on **H₂ewi-* 'bird').

a, H₂e

47. PIE **a* and **H₂e* fall together in G and L. In any case there are relatively few cases of undoubted **a* in PIE; the clearest instances are found in underived nouns:

PIE **sal-* 'salt' > L *sāl* 'salt', G ἅλς : OE *sealt.*

PIE **kapro-* 'stud' > L *caper* 'male goat' (74.4), G κάπρος 'boar' : Ved. *kápr̥th-* 'penis'.
PIE **H₂eǵ-* (or **aǵ-*) 'drive' > G ἄγω, L *agō* : Ved. *ájati.*
PIE **H₂eǵro-* 'field' (possibly derived from the preceding—but probably not) > G ἀγρός, L *ager* : Ved. *ájra-*, Go. *akrs.*
PIE **H₂erǵ-* 'bright white' > G ἀργός, G ἄργυρος 'silver', L *argentum* : Ved. *árjuna-* 'bright, white', Hitt. *ḫar-ki-iš*, Toch. B *arkwi.*
PIE **apo* (or **H₂epo*) 'away' > G ἀπό, L *ab* : Ved. *ápa*, Go. *af*, NE *off* and *of.* (Hitt. *ap-pa* 'back, again', usually quoted in this context, corresponds to G ὀπ- in ὄπισθε(ν) 'behind, back', the *o*-grade of ἐπί, and is unrelated to the 'away' forms.)

a. PIE **a* cuts a very small figure; its peripheral status in the vowel system is typologically very odd. G α and L *a* are proportionately much more prominent in their languages; they come from various sources, of which PIE **a* is the least significant.

b. VERBAL ROOTS with medial **a* typically have clear and convincing reflexes only in adjacent IE languages, suggesting diffusion rather than genuine PIE origin. They show no ablaut. Thus **kan-* 'sing' (the only form of the root) is clearly seen in L *canō* and derivatives, and OIr. *canim* /kavəμ'/ 'I sing'; Gmc. forms meaning 'cock', for example Go. *hana*, NHG *Hahn*, are plausible cognates; but alleged G cognates, such as καναχή 'clang, loud sharp sound', have both semantic and formal problems. Similarly PIE **kap-* 'sieze, hold' is exuberantly attested in Germanic and Italic, and perh. in OIr. *cúan* 'port' < **kōno-* < **kawno-* < **kapno-*. (The OIr. form is isolated in Celt. but 'harbor' is one of the common developments of the root elsewhere—cf. NE *haven*—and the phonology is impeccable.) Beyond that, most possible cognates have obscurities of both form and meaning; typical is G κώπη 'handle (of an oar); oar', plausible semantically but not formally, as an *ō*-grade in the root is inexplicable. (Formally G κώπη superimposes on Lith. *kuopà* 'troop, band' —and the comparison is commonly made, despite the questionable semantics.)

For verb roots in **-a-*, PIE **kan-* and **kap-* are exceptionally clear.

Although the secure NOMINAL ROOTS in **a* have generally wider distribution, like PIE **sal-* 'salt' and **ǵhans-* 'goose', many more show the same limited distribution as the verbal roots. Thus **laḱs-* 'salmon' is certainly reflected only in Gmc. and BS; **mak-* 'pouch' is seen in one Celtic derivative, some Gmc. words meaning 'stomach', and in some BS words meaning things like 'purse'.

H_2o

48. The proper development of PIE **H₂o* in G and L (that is, in those languages which distinguish between /a/ and /o/) has been much discussed. The debate results from the difficulty of pinning down which etyma for G and L forms most probably contained **H₂* followed by an *o*-grade vowel.

One view holds that the laryngeal was without effect, as in G ὄκρις 'jagged peak', L *ocris*, also G ὀξύς 'sharp', which can be explained as reflecting **H₂oḱ-* next to the **H₂eḱ-* seen in G ἄκρις 'hill-top', ἀκρο- (a combining form with the general sense of the point or end of a thing), L *acūtus* 'sharp', *acus* f. 'needle', *acētum* 'vinegar', and many other forms. The G and L forms in ἀ- and *a-* could equally well be zero grade; Ved. *áśri-* 'edge' must however be full grade, though which full grade is not apparent. A stronger example, because *o*-grade is expected in the root of a nomen actionis in *-*mo-* (and there is no such expectation in the previous example), is G ὄγμος 'furrow, line' < *H_2*oǵ-mo-*.

The other view holds that the outcome of *$H_2 o$ was identical to that of *$H_2 e$, as seen in G ἄνεμος 'wind', L *animus* 'breath, spirit'. Now, these are usually traced to PIE *H_2*enH̥*$_1$*-mo-*, a derivative of the root *H_2*enH*$_1$- 'breathe'; but as nomina actionis in *-*mo-* are typically in *o*-grade (as G στολμός 'equipment, gear' to στέλλω), the likely etymon for ἄνεμος is *H_2*onH̥*$_1$*-mo-*, not *H_2*enH̥*$_1$*-mo-*.

In the system of endings, the middle voice is marked with a vowel after the person-marker (433, 435). The formal patterns in this system of endings are clearest if the 1sg.midd. (L *-ar* and G -μαι) can reflect *-H_2-*o*-.

Both interpretations encounter difficulties, but the view endorsed here is that *$H_2 o$ > G α, L *a*. Most supposed cases of G ο, L *o* from *$H_2 o$ are more vulnerable than generally recognized. G ὄκρις, L *ocris*, above, for example, are traced to etyma in *$H_2 o$—not because an *o*-grade is expected there, but because the reconstruction will (in one view) yield the attested forms. This leaves G ὄγμος as the only plausible datum. But even this form is in fact quite problematic.[1]

LONG VOWELS AND VOWEL + LARYNGEAL

ī, iH

49. Certain examples of PIE *ī (in contrast to *iH) are few, if indeed there are any. PIE *iH > ī in all IE languages except G, as follows:

1. *iH_1 > G ῑ before a consonant, but apparently *-*ye* in final position.
PIE *weyH- 'rush': *wiH-s- 'force, vehemence' > G ἶς, L *vīs*.
PIE *H_1*s-i*H_1*-me* 1pl. opt. of *H_1*es-* 'be' > G εἶμεν (via *ehīme), L *sīmus*. See also 540.
PIE *-iH_1 cons. stem nom./acc.du.neut.: *H_3*ek*^{w}*-i*H_1 'the two eyes' > *ok^{w}ye > Hom. ὄσσε (199) : Ved. *akṣī́*, OCS *oči*. (The same ending is seen generally in the Ved. nom./acc.du. ending of cons. stems.) Hom. ὄσσε exhausts the evidence, but the development is parallel to that of *-iH_2, next.

2. PIE *iH_2 > PG *yă after stop plus resonant (all positions); *yă in final position; and—perhaps (the evidence is slim)— *-yā- medially, analogous to the nasals and liquids, as -νᾱ- < *-nH_2- (107).

---

[1] Neither ἄγω nor its direct cognates are attested as having any connection with plowing. The other Homeric meaning of ὄγμος, 'swath' (that is, the space covered by the sweep of a scythe), is not easy to relate either to 'furrow' or to *H_2*eǵ-*. —The connection of PIE *ágros or *H_2*égros* 'field' with *H_2*eǵ-*, though standard and by implication endorsing the plowing idea, is not self-validating (the word may actually have meant 'pasture').

PIE *tri-H_2 neut. 'three' > G τρία : Ved. *trī́*. (Archaic OIr. *tre* and L *tria* are from *$tri\bar{a}$*, that is *$tr\bar{i}$ < *$triH_2$ with the *-*ā* of the *o*-stem neut.pl. added to the inherited form; 307.3.)
PIE *$k^w riH_2$- 'buy' > G πρίασθαι : Ved. *krītá-* pple., OIr. *críth* /kρīθ/ (ἅπ. λεγ.) 'payment, price'.
PIE *$potniH_2$ > G πότνια 'mistress' (f. of **potis* 'master') : Ved. *patnī́-*.
PIE *-iH_2 fem. suff. > PG *-*yă* with subsequent changes just as for PIE **y* (195–207): *bheront-iH_2 > PG **pherontya* > G φέρουσα f. 'carrying' : Ved. *bhárantī*.

G δίζημαι < PIE *di-diH_2- 'seek' is the only example of medial *-*yā-* < *iH_2-. This is too bad, as its root *$deyH_2$- or *$dyeH_2$- is recoverable only on the basis of G evidence.

3. PIE *iH_3. There are no cases of final *-iH_3. In medial position, *-iH_3- appears to give PreG *-*yō-*, similar to the outcomes of liquids and nasals, as -ρω- < -$\textit{r̥}H_3$- (103–8), and *-iH_2- above:
PIE *$g^w iH_3$-wo- 'alive' > PreG *$g^w y\bar{o}wos$ > PG **ǰōwos* > G ζω(ϝ)ός (201), L *vīvus* : Ved. *jīvá-*, Lith. *gývas*.
PIE *proti-$H_3 k^w$- > *$proty\bar{o}k^w$- > G πρόσωπον 'face' : Ved. *prátīka-* n. 'front; face'.

A competing datum pointing instead to G -ῑ- < *-iH_3- is Hom. ὀπῑπεύω 'look around, regard'. This formation has been explained in two different ways, both involving *-iH_3-. (1) *$H_3 k^w i$-$H_3 k^w$- (or *$H_3 ek^w i$-$H_3 k^w$-), an intensive built ultimately to *$H_3 ek^w$- 'eye', seen in verbal use in G ὄπωπα (perf. to ὁράω). The semantics are fine, but there are formal difficulties. (2) A denominative built to an unattested *ὀπῑ́πη 'a long look' < *opi-$H_3 k^w$-eH_2, containing the zero grade of *$H_3 ek^w$- 'eye'. The evidence for *-*yō-* < *-iH_3- seems much clearer.

a. Before a vowel, *-iH_3- shows no special development, so *$g^w iH_3$-etos 'life' > G βίοτος (-o- from *$H_3 e$) : L *vīta* (probably: *(g)wiotā > *wietā (66.3) > *wiita, vīta; 88.1). (G βίος 'life', in Hom. only in the Odyssey and rarely there—three times, including a repetition—is probably a syncopated form of this βίοτος.)

ū, uH

50. 1. In all IE languages the reflexes of PIE **ū* and *uH (assuming there was such a thing as PIE **ū*) in medial position appear to be the same.
PIE **mūs-* (or *$muHs$-) 'mouse' > G μῦς, L *mūs* : Ved. *mū́ṣ-*, OE *mús*.
PIE *$dhuH$-mo- (or **dhū-mo-*) 'smoke' > G θῡμός, L *fūmus*, Ved. *dhūmá-*, Lith. *dúmai*, OCS *dymŭ*, all meaning 'smoke, vapor' except θῡμός 'soul, spirit, anger', presumably from *'vapor' > *'breath' > 'soul', the rest of the semantics following from this. This is reminiscent of the semantic relationship between L *animus* 'soul, spirit, courage, anger' and G ἄνεμος 'wind'.

2. In final position, *-uH > -*ū* (or its reflex) in most IE languages. Some hold that in G *-uH_2 > *-*wa*. Evidence for this is limited to one mor-

phological category, the nom./acc./voc.pl. of neuter *u*-stems, seen in γοῦνα 'knees' < **gonwa* < **ǵonuH₂*. (Indic m.f. *u*-stem du. in *-ū*, as *vásū* 'good', points to PIE **-uH₁*; this would perhaps have given G -υε, -ϝε; however, G ἡδεῖ nom./acc.du.m. (spurious diphthong) < ἡδέε < **hwādewe* < **sweH₂dewH̥₁* points instead to full grade of the stem.)

a. It is possible that G γοῦνα 'knees', δοῦρα 'shafts', and the like are analogical for *γονῦ, *δορῦ much as δοῦρε nom./acc./voc.du. is analogical for δορῦ (? the du. of *u*-stems is uncertain) < **doruH₁*. One datum might support this view: if Hom. πολλάκι (later πολλάκις) 'many times; for the most part' is parallel to Ved. *purū́ cit* 'much, often, very' < **pl̥H₁u-H₂ kʷid*, then an underlying **polū-kʷi* is necessary to account for the delabialization of the **kʷ* (154.1). But **pl̥H₁u-H₂ kʷid* was probably a single word, phonologically, and if the change of **-uH₂* to **-wa* was proper to word-final position, we would not find it here in any case. (In favor of the idea that **-uH₂* regularly became **-wa* in final position is the early and complete abandonment of the original inflection of neut. *u*-stems in G for an unvarying oblique stem γονϝ-: an in herited **gonwa* < **ǵonuH₂* would provide the very forms crucial for such a remodeling.) G πολλ- does not continue πολϝ-; see 341.

b. In Umbrian, PItal. **ū* > *-i-*, as *pir* 'fire' (G πῦρ), **sim** acc.sg. and **sif** acc.pl. < **sūm*, **sūms* 'pig', **trefi** *u*-stem abl.sg. 'populace' (cf. **trifu** acc.sg.).

c. For the phonetics of G ῠ̄ see **38a**.

ē, eH₁

51. Most cases of η in G and *ē* in L in root syllables are reflexes of **eH₁* and other forms of compensatory lengthening.
PIE **sēmi-* 'half' (or **seH₁mi-*) > G ἡμι-, L *sēmi-* : OE *sám-*, OHG *sāmi-*.
PIE **mē* conditional negative > G μή : Ved. *mā́*.
PIE **dheH₁-* 'put' > G τί-θη-μι, L *fēcī* (= G ἔθηκα aor.) 'made' : Ved. *dá-dhā-mi*, Go. *ga-deþs* 'deed', OE *dǽd*.
PIE **pleH₁-* 'fill', secondary full grade **pelH₁-* (various suffixes) 'full': G πλήρης (probably; see **106a**), L *plēnus* : Ved. *a-prā-t* (aor. of *pr̥ṇā́ti* 'fills').
PIE **seH₁-* 'sow' > L *sēmen* 'seed', *sēvī* (aor. stem; pres. *serō* is an old redup. stem **si-sH₁-*): Lith. *sė́ti* 'to sow', OE *sǽd* 'seed', OIr. *síl* /s'īλ'/.

a. Att.-Ion. η reflects PG **ā* as well as **ē* (54). Phonetically, this η was a lower-mid front vowel, [ɛ:] or the like, which in Hellenistic times raised to [e:] as revealed by confusion in spelling between η and ει.

b. For a handful of words, etymologies have been proposed which require a development of L *-ī-* < **-ē-*: *fīlius* 'son', *suspīciō* 'regard intently', *convīcium* 'outcry', *subtīlis* 'of fine consistency', *dēlīniō* doublet of the much commoner *dēlēniō* 'soothe, charm'. The value of these is very uneven. Some of the semantic fits are excellent, as **speḱ-* 'look at', **wekʷ-* 'voice, call', others are weaker (*tēla* 'cloth' < **tekslā* is impeccable but its connection with *subtīlis* is questionable—*subtexō* in L means 'veil, obscure', not 'weave sheer cloth'). On the formal side, the lengthened *e*-grades called for in **spēḱ-* and **wēkʷ-* are morphologically incomprehensible. Alternative etymologies or other explanations have been proposed for most of these; the strongest cases for such a development are probably *fīlius* and *vīlis* 'price' (Plt.) later 'cheap; degraded' < **wes-li-* < **wes-*; cf. *vēnum* 'sale' < **wes-no-* = RV *vasná-* 'price'; Hitt. *wa-a-ši* 'buys'). Together they hint at a regular change of **-ēli-* to *-īli-*, which is plausible on its face; but there are many apparent exceptions.

ō, oH, eH$_3$

52. 'Long *o*' has three sources: (1) PIE **ō*; (2) PIE **ŏ* followed by any laryngeal; and (3) PIE **e* followed by **H₃*.

1. The lengthened grade of **o* occurs in particular morphological categories, such as the nom.sg. of certain consonant stem nouns: G κύων (gen. κυνός) 'dog'; χθών (gen. χθονός) 'earth'; εὐπάτωρ, -τορος 'well-born' (*'having a good father'); and in L *homō* (gen. *hominis*) < *hemō*, **hemones* (42.6). From here it has often been leveled through whole paradigms, in the uniform long-vowel stems of PGmc. **fōt-* 'foot', L *vōc-* 'voice/ speak', G φωρ- 'thief'. (Latin and Germanic are particularly partial to this kind of leveling.)

2. PIE **oH₁* in **dhoH₁-*, *o*-grade of **dheH₁-* 'put', G θωμός 'heap', L *sacerdōt-* 'priest', Hitt. *dai-* as in *da-a-it-ti* 'you put' < **dhoH₁-tH₂e-(i)*.
PIE **oH₁s-* 'mouth' > L *ōs*, *ōris* : Hitt. *a-i-iš* neut., Ved. *ā́s** 'face' (inferrable from *anā́sas* acc.pl. 'faceless' and fossilized cases with adverbial function, for example *āsā́* inst. 'in (one's) presence').
PIE **-o-H₁* nom./acc.du. of the *o*-stems: **H₂embhoH₁* 'both' > G ἄμφω, L *ambō* : Ved. *ubhā́*.
PIE **-o-H₂* 1sg. ending of thematic verbs (424), thus G φέρω, L *ferō* : Av. *spasyā* 'I see' (from the older parts of the text; in the usual Av. form *barā-mi* 'I carry' and Ved. *bhárā-mi*, the athem. ending *-mi* has been added to *-ā* < **-oH₂*), Go. *baira*, OIr. *·biur* /biρ^w/ < **berū*.

3. PIE **eH₃*: PIE **ǵneH₃-* 'know' > G γνωτός 'known', L *nōtus* (cf. *ignōtus* 'unknown', 220) : Ved. *jñātá-*. (Note: the pple. in **-tó-* normally requires zero grade of the root, as do presents in **-ske/o-*. Therefore PIE **ǵneH₃-ské/o-* and **ǵneH₃-tó-*, reflected in L *nōscō*, *nōtus*, and Ved. *jñātá-* indicate that the root was abnormal in having no zero grade.)
PIE **deH₃-* 'give': *e*-grade doubtless in G δίδωμι, but **doH₃-* is possible in **doH₃-ro-*, **doH₃-no-* 'gift' > G δῶρον 'gift', L *dōnum* : OIr. *dán*, Ved. *dā́na-*, OCS *darŭ*.

a. Long vowels are very stable in L, but in monosyllables **ō* > *ū* before *r*: L *fūr* 'thief' = G φώρ (from **bher-* 'carry') and *cūr* 'why' from earlier *quōr*.

b. For **ōw* > L *āv*: **oktōwos* 'eighth' > L *octāvus*, see 46.2.

ā, eH$_2$

53. There are few certain cases of PIE **ā*, fewer even than of **ē* and **ō*. In both G and L, *ā* of known origin mostly come from *ă* by compensatory lengthening; from PIE **eH₂*; and from long syllabic resonants (104-7).

All these give L *ā*, Att.-Ion. η (per 54, below), and ᾱ in Doric. (In this summary, 'Doric' stands for all dialects apart from the innovative Attic-Ionic.)
PIE **gār-* 'make noise' > Dor. γᾶρυς, Att.-Ion. γῆρυς 'voice', L *garriō* (for

**gāriō*, 234) 'chatter' : OIr. *do·gair* /do'gaρ'/ 'calls', *ad·gair* /aδ'gaρ'/ 'bewails'. (The symbol /'/ marks the onset of stress.)
PIE **steH₂*- 'stand' in **sti-steH₂-mi* > Dor. ἵστᾱμι, Att.-Ion. ἵστημι : Ved. root *sthā*-. (Ital. forms, incl. *stāre* 'to stand', reflect only **stă*-, that is, the zero grade **stH̥₂*-; see 475.5.)
PIE **má-H₂ter*- 'mother' > Dor. μᾱ́τηρ, Att.-Ion. μήτηρ, L *māter* : Ved. *mātár*-, OE *módor*.
PIE **bheH₂*- 'declare' > Dor. φᾱ́μᾱ, Att.-Ion. φήμη 'announcement, news', L *fāma* : OE *bén* 'petition, request' < PGmc. **bōni*-, OE *bóg(i)an* /bōγan/ 'to boast'.
PIE **sweH₂du*- 'sweet' > Dor. ἁ̄δύς, Att.-Ion. ἡδύς, L *suāvis* : Ved. *svādú*-, OE *swéte*, OHG *suozi* (NHG *süß*).

a. Sometimes *-*eH₂* > -ᾰ. The distribution is statable in morphological terms: *-*eH₂*, nom./voc.sg of the *eH₂*-stems (263.1), which yields -η, -ᾱ in the nom.sg. but gives -ᾰ (archaic, 263.2, 267.3) in the voc.sg. But the explanation is phonological after all, having to do with whether a word ending with a vowel + laryngeal was in close construction with a following form. Vocatives typically are not in any syntactic relationship with any other word in an utterance; in languages that can be directly observed, vocatives often are followed (as well as preceded) by a pause, even in rapid and casual speech.

54. ATTIC-IONIC η FROM **ā*. In Greek words in their familiar (that is, Attic-Ionic) form, we have to distinguish between the special Att.-Ion. η < PG **ā* and the general G η from PG **ē*. (The latter was written E until the introduction of the Ionic alphabet.) Thus in 'mother', cited above, the discrepancy between Att.-Ion. η and Doric ᾱ in the first syllable points to PG **ā*. The history of a given Att.-Ion. η may be determined from (1) the forms of other dialects, (2) cognates in other IE languages, (3) from paradigmatic patterns within Attic-Ionic, for example the participles στᾰτός 'stood' and θετός 'put' (102), which reveal the different historical status of the -η- in ἵστημι and τίθημι.

This statement of the Attic-Ionic innovation requires two important qualifications.

In East Ionic, the change to η was uniform, affecting all **ā* current in the language at the time. It is thus in Homer. The single exception is that in the sequence **āē*- (for all practical purposes reflecting PG **āwē*-), **ā* > ᾱ even in East Ionic: **āwēr* nom. 'air' > Hom. ἀ̄ήρ but gen. **āweros* > ἠέρος. (Late Ion. ἠήρ is the result of leveling.)

In Attic, there are three more environments where ᾱ remained, namely when ᾱ immediately followed ε, ι, or ρ. Thus Att. γενεᾱ́ 'race, generation', καρδίᾱ, 'heart', πρᾱ́σσω 'achieve'. This is the origin of the Att. division of the 1st declension into the τῑμή 'honor' and χώρᾱ 'place' types (262), the latter having ε, ι, and ρ before the endings. It also accounts for discrepancies between Homeric and Attic forms, such as Hom. χώρη = Att. χώρᾱ.

The change of ᾱ to η was a gradual one in the sense that there was a period, revealed in some inscriptions of the Ionic islands, during which old *ā was moving forward but had not yet merged with η. In Cycladic inscriptions, for example, original -ē- is written E, the vowel which results from original *-ā- (presumably something like /ǣ/) is written H, while new -ā- (as in πᾶς 'all') is written A. In Attic, however, the inadequate inventory of symbols was deployed differently: H was used for both /ǣ/ and /ē/, and it is clear that *ā did not merge with *ē in Attic until the end of the 5th century BC. Only at that time do confusions arise between the inflection of s-stems and masc. η-stems (so Ἱπποκράτην on the one hand, Αἰσχίνους on the other; see 300). At the same time, 'hyperdoric' forms (for example πᾱδός 'blade of an oar' for genuine Dor. πηδός) start to appear in choral lyric passages of plays. Previously, Doric ᾱ was used with a correctness which is easy to explain if it were merely a matter of replacing Att. /ǣ/ with Dor. /ā/; once Att. /ǣ/ and η actually merged, only memory could supply correct Doric /ā/ or /ē/ corresponding to Attic forms in η, and the confusions of the 4th century and later are only to be expected.

55. ATTIC REVERSION. There has been much discussion about whether all *ā first became /ǣ/ in Att. (as it did in Ion.), with subsequent REVERSION of /ǣ/ to /ā/ after ι, ε, and ρ; or whether the change of *ā to /ǣ/ was so to say blocked in these environments. Att. παρειᾱ 'cheek' and Ἰέωνες 'Ionians' establish that the first (and more probable) scheme is the correct one. PG **parawsā* > **parāwā* (attested in Myc. *pa-ra-wa-jo* nom.du. 'cheek-pieces') > pre-Att. **parǣwǣ*, **parǣǣ*; with the shortening of the long vowel before another vowel (79.3), shortened *ǣ* merged with *e* (it could have become a distinct phoneme, but did not). The resulting **pareǣ* subsequently reverted to παρεᾱ. If *ā had remained unaltered after *r*, the Att. form would have been ˣπαράη < ˣ*paraǣ* < ˣ*parā(w)ǣ*. Similarly **iyāwones* 'Ionians' > **iāwones* > **iǣwones* > **iǣones* > Ἰέωνες (quantitative metathesis, 79.3, with the same development of shortened *ǣ* to ε as above), later Ἴωνες.

The chronology then is as follows:

1. PG *ā > Att.-Ion. *ǣ*.
2. Loss of intervocalic ϝ (187, 189).
3. Shortening of long vowels in various environments (79).
4. ᾰ > ᾱ (about 800 BC; before -νς and secondary νσ, 228.2, 228.4).
5. In Att., *ǣ* after ι, ε, ρ reverted to ᾱ.
6. Remaining *ǣ* fell together with η (end of 5th century BC).
7. Loss of postconsonantal ϝ: κορϝη > Att. κόρη 'girl'.

Only later, in a deceptively similar but unrelated development, Att.-Ion. εα contracted to η except after ι, ε, where the outcome was ᾱ (86.4); so ὑγιᾶ < ὑγιέα acc.sg. 'healthy' and ἐνδεᾶ nom./acc.pl.n. 'lacking', but πλήρη nom.acc.pl.n. 'full' < πλήρεα and γένη nom./acc.pl. 'races' < γένεα.

56. The *ā which undergoes the Att.-Ion. change to η has various origins: reflexes of PIE *ā; of PIE **eH₂*; of PIE **R̥H₂* (> PG **Rā* > Dor. *Rā*,

Att.-Ion. *R*η. where *R* = any resonant NOT ρ); and **ă* before ORIGINAL INTERVOCALIC -*ns*-, -*sn*- (228.1). Thus the examples above, and such things as: **ep*ʰ*ansa* > **ep*ʰ*āna* > ἔφηνα, aor. of φαίνω (**p*ʰ*an-yō*) 'make clear'; PIE **g*ʷ*hn̥H₂*- (elaborated from **g*ʷ*hen*- 'strike down, kill') in **g*ʷ*hn̥H₂-tó*- > PG **t*ʰ*nātó*- (for **p*ʰ*nāto*-, 154.1) > Att.-Ion. θνητός 'mortal'.

Later-arising ᾱ, for instance before SECONDARY intervocalic -νσ- (228.2), final -νς (228.4), or by contraction, all remain in Att.-Ion.: **pantyă* f. 'all' > **pansa* > πᾶσα; τάνς acc.pl.f. > τᾱ́ς; τῑμάεται > τῑμᾶται.

a. Apparent exceptions to the Attic rule are due to various causes. Some are the result of analogy, as when the form of χορηγός 'chorus-leader' was influenced by στρατηγός 'general' (87)(the expected χορᾱγός actually occurs in Attic). Some are the result of dialect borrowing: Att. λοχᾱγός 'company commander' is a loanword from Spartan.

Much more important is a class of forms attributable to the effects of relative chronology, namely, that the change of **ā* all the way to η in Att. predated the loss of postconsonantal ϝ and σ. Thus **wrā* > ρϝη > ρη and ρσᾱ > ρση > ρρη. This accounts for such forms as κόρη 'girl' and κόρρη 'side of the forehead', from κόρϝᾱ and κόρσᾱ respectively.

Note however PG **newā* f. 'new' > G νέϝᾱ > Att.-Ion. νέᾱ, and PG **genehā* 'race, generation' > Att. γενεᾱ́, in contrast to the above-discussed development of κόρϝᾱ > κόρη. The simplest hypothesis is that -ϝ- between vowels disappeared prior to the Attic reversion of *ǣ* to ᾱ after ε, thus **ewā* > **ewǣ* > **eǣ* > εᾱ; but when **w* was preceded by a consonant it disappeared only after the Att. innovation. Perhaps **ehǣ* likewise became *eǣ*, whence εᾱ; but it is just as likely that the intervening [h] (however long it lasted) was simply transparent to the influence of ε on the following *ǣ*.

DIPHTHONGS

ey

57. PIE **ey* > G ει, PItal. **ey* > OL *ei* > L *ī*.

PIE **deyḱ*- 'point (out)' > G δείκνῡμι 'show', OL *deicō* 'say' > L *dīcō* : O *deicum* 'dicere', Ved. *dídeśati* redup.pres. (thematized) 'points', Go. *ga-teihan* 'announce'.

PIE **ey*- 'go' > G εἶμι, L *īs* 2sg. : Ved. *émi*.

PIE **bheydh*- 'be persuaded, be confident' (trans. 'convince') > G πείθω, L *fīdō* 'trust'. (Many authorities trace Gmc. forms like Go. *beidan* 'wait' and OE *bídan*, NE *bide* from this root. Such an etymology is impeccable formally but semantically problematic.)

1. In G, as early as the 5th century BC, the diphthong had become a monophthong [eː], that is, a long higher-mid vowel in contrast to the lower η [ɛː] (76). But the SPELLING ει was unchanged, and ει thus came also to be used to write the [eː] which had never been a diphthong (76). Thus φέρει 'carries' < φέρ-ε-ι next to φέρειν infin. < φέρ-ε-εν.

a. In Roman times ει (spurious and legitimate alike) changed further and became identical with ῑ; but the spelling persisted, and was sometimes used for original ῑ as in τειμή = τῑμή. It is from such confusions of spelling that we learn of phonological mergers of originally distinct elements.

2. L *ei* was a real diphthong in the earliest period. In Plautus and Terence it reflects PItal. **ey*, and also was the sound resulting from **ay* in medial syllables (70.2) and **oy* in final syllables (75.2). The spelling for all three was *ei*, occasionally *e*, as in the SC de Bacch. DEICERENT, INCEIDERETIS, nom.pl. FOIDERATEI (never *i* in such forms, and conversely never *ei* for original *ī*, as later). Also during this period, *ei* is occasionally used for proper *ē* and even for *ĕ*. By the middle of the 2nd century BC, however, the sound had become identical with *ī*, the spelling for which fluctuated between *ei* and *i*; and the former, being now merely a sign for *ī*, was also used for L *ī* which had never been a diphthong (AVDEIRE). This spelling *ei* is frequent in inscriptions down to the time of Cicero, and even in the Augustan period was not wholly obsolete.

a. Evidence that *ei* first became a long monophthong intermediate between *ē* and *ī* is not rigorous: the occasional epigraphic use of *e* (but never *i*) for *ei* (and the converse use of *ei* for *ē̆*) at least allows for this interpretation, with the ancillary argument that the Romans' familiarity with the Greek use of ει for a monophthong (76) provided a model for the convention of using *ei* for a monophthong. Additionally, the hypothesis of a long monophthong not yet identical to *ī* serves to explain *deus* next to *dīvus* (both from OL *deivos*) 'god' from **deyw-o-*, 183a.

b. *Seu* 'or if; whether' next to *sīve* (< **sey-(i)we*), *ceu* 'as, like' < **ḱe-iwe*, and *neu* 'nor' < **ne-iwe* (**i-we* = Ved. *iva* 'as, like') are often stated to exhibit the apocope of the final vowel just at the stage when orig. **ey* had monophthongized but not yet merged with *ī*. This is chronologically implausible, as apocope of these final short vowels is prehistoric in L and the smoothing of diphthongs occurs within the historical period. It is more likely that we are here dealing with reflexes of something like **seyw*, **keyw*, **neyw*.

(H)oy, H_3ey

58. PIE **oy* > G οι, OL *oi*, *oe* whence L *ū* (but *oe* remained in some words, 59).

PIE **oy-no-* 'one' > G οἴνη, οἶνος 'ace' (on dice), L *ūnus* 'one', early *oinos*, *oenus* : Go. *ains*, OE *án*, OIr. *óen* /oyν/.

L *cūrō* 'take care of': prehistoric etym. unknown but early *coiravere*, Paelig. COISATENS guarantee the relevance of the form.

PIE **H_3eyd-* 'swell' > G οἶδος n. 'a swelling' (*e*-grade is expected in *s*-stem neuters) : Arm. *aitnum* 'I swell'; presumably *o*-grade (PIE **H_3oyd-o-*) in OCS *jadŭ* m. 'poison'.

a. Ital. **oy* > L *ī* after *v*.

PIE **woyḱ-o-* 'village, clan' > OL VECOS, VEICVS > L *vīcus* : G (ϝ)οἶκος. (PIE **weyḱ-* would likewise give L *vīc-*, and is unambiguously attested in Go. *weihs* 'village'; but the latter is a neut. *s*-stem, where *e*-grade is expected (128.1), whereas the L and G *o*-stems presuppose the *o*-grade form of the root.)

Aegean **woyn-o-* 'wine' > L *vīnum* : G ϝοῖνος/οἶνος.

b. Ital. **oy* > L *ī* between *l* and a following labial.

L *lībāre* 'pour a libation' built to an unattested **lība* 'drink offering' < **loybā* = G λοιβή. (L *lībāre* might instead be a causative, **loyb-eH_2y^e/o-*, 456.2; the point is the same.)

PIE **ley-* 'slimy, wet': **loy-mo-* 'mud' > L *līmus* = OHG *leim* > NHG *Lehm*, OE *lám* > NE *loam*. (L *līmus* admits of other explanations, **225.1c**.)
PIE **ḱley-* 'lean, slope' in **ḱloy-wo-* 'slope, rise' > L *clīvus* : Go. *hlaiw* neut. 'grave' (*'mound').

Note that **loy-* before non-labials becomes L *lū-*, so OL *loidos* > *lūdus* 'game'.

c. It is probable that monophthongization in *ūnus* and the others had already taken place by the time of Plautus, as hinted by punning on *Lȳdus* and *lūdus*, though the earliest inscriptional examples of the spelling *u* are somewhat later (VTIER 'uti' in a Scipio epitaph, precise date uncertain; VSVRA 'interest' 146 BC). The old spelling *oe* remains frequent in inscriptions until about the middle of the 1st century BC, and Cicero in the laws for his ideal state purposely wrote such forms as *oenus* and *coerari*.

Since *ū* also comes from *ou* (61), archaizing spellings sometimes mistakenly write *ū* as *ou* in place of etymological *oe*, as COVRAVERVNT.

59. LATIN *-oe-*. Nine words together with most of their derivatives retain *oe* (about as in NE *coin* presumably), instead of showing the usual change to *ū*. The explanation for this is disputed. In all such forms, the *oe* is between a labial and an apical consonant (*proelium* 'battle' is at most a partial exception); this is unlikely to be a coincidence. Some authorities set store by the circumstance that some of the words with *oe* have a palpably technical or literary flavor. Thus *foedus* 'treaty' and *poena* 'penalty' (legal terms), whereas *pūniō*, which was less technical, and the commonplace *impūne* 'safely, with impunity' show the usual development. *Poenus* is the old official title for a Carthaginian (a sobriquet for Hannibal in particular), and persisted, whereas the common term *poenicus* became *pūnicus*, as in *mālum pūnicum* 'pomegranate'. *Moenia* 'walls' has been explained as retaining *oe* to avoid homophony with *mūnia* 'duties' (which seems unlikely); it is at all events somewhat archaic, and the more general term for wall, orig. *moeros*, did become *mūrus*. However, the appeal to the special character of the affected vocabulary as an explanation for the retention of *oe* is obviously shaky: in the case of **moyn-* giving both *moenia* 'walls' and *mūnia* 'duties', the latter would seem to be the technical term, not the former, and *foedus* 'foul' and *foeteō* 'have a bad smell' can hardly have been 'technical or literary'. (They might be euphemistic distortions, of course, like NE /tiyt/ *teat* for phonologically regular /tit/, or *crouch* for *crotch*).

In words like *poena* the diphthongal pronunciation of *oe* was probably maintained in educated speech until a late period. But eventually it monophthongized, this time falling together with *ē*. Hence the frequent confusion in spelling, in late inscriptions and in manuscripts, between *oe*, *ae*, and *e*. And accordingly, Romance reflexes of L *oe* are indistinguishable from those of *i* and *ē* (see 77 for L vowels in Romance). Curiously, the slightly later smoothing of the diphthong *ae* fell together with a SHORT vowel, *ĕ* (77).

a. MISCELLANEA. L *coepī* 'began' is from *coēpī* (sometimes so spelled in early L), formed from *ēpī*, aor. to *apiō* 'snag, snare' (Paul.Fest.). The change from *oē* to *oe* is unlikely to be phonological; rather, it shows the influence of the pple. *coeptus* < **co-apto-* (**66.1**, and see **81.3**).

L *oboediō* 'obey', according to Paul.Fest., is derived from *ob-audiō*. There is little reason to doubt the truth of this, but the phonological development is unexpected (70.3). —In *oboediō* and L *amoenus* 'pleasant' the *-oe-* is between a labial and an apical consonant, which is in accord with the normal rules, but in a non-initial syllable, which is not.

L *nōn* is from earlier *noenum* (-*ōe*-) < **ne oynom* (NE *none* and *no*—the adj.—have the same history as L *nōn*; and for the semantics cf. NE *not*, the atonic doublet of *naught* from OE *ná-wiht* lit. 'no-thing'). In the absence of counterexamples, the development of **ōy* to *ō* in open syllables may be accepted as regular. (Cf. the outcome of *o*-stem dat. *-*ōy* and the different outcome of **ōy* in original closed syllables, 63.)

ay, H_2ey

60. PIE **ay* is found in few verbal roots. In initial position, most roots with traditionally-reconstructed **ay* probably had *H_2*ey* in fact. For a number of nominal roots, however, generally denoting figure faults, there is no reason for supposing anything but PIE **ay*. Such roots show no ablaut phenomena (see also 117.1). Some exceptions, like L *maeror* 'grieve, am sad' and *maestus* 'mournful, dolorous' next to what looks like a zero grade in *miser* 'wretched', are hard to assess, as they have no IE etymology. Others, like the ordinary-looking ablaut of Ved. *edh-/idh-* 'kindle' seen below, may be the leveling of an originally non-alternating form rather than anything very old; zero-grades to the root **aydh-* (or *H_2*eydh-*) free of suspicion can hardly be said to exist.

PIE *H_2*eydh-* 'be hot' > G αἴθω 'kindle', L *aestus*, *-ūs* 'heat', *aedēs* 'room; temple' (orig. 'hearth'; cf. NE *stove* = NHG *Stube* '(heated) room') : Ved. *édhas-* 'firewood', OIr. *áed* /ayδ/ 'fire'.

PIE *H_2*eyu-* 'life(time)' > Hom. αἰεί 'for ever' < *H_2*eywesi* (*s*-stem dat./loc. sg.), L *aevum* 'life(time)', *aetās* 'age' < *aevitas* (XII Tab.) : Go. *aiws* 'time', *ni aiw* 'never'.

PIE **laywo-* 'left handed' > G λαιός, L *laevus* : OCS *lěvŭ*.

PIE **skaywo-* 'left hand' > G σκαιός, L *scaevus* (this word and the preceding were early replaced by *sinister*).

PIE **kayko-* 'visually blighted' > L *caecus* 'blind' : Go. *haihs* 'one-eyed', OIr. *cáech* /kayχ/, Skt. *kekara-* 'squinting'.

a. The L spelling *ae*, which replaced *ai* early in the 2nd century BC, indicates that the second element of the diphthong was lower than *i* in other positions; the phonetics of the NE diphthong in words like *ride* (for many dialects, at least) are similar. The same holds for *oe* in place of *oi* (59).

b. L *ae* remained a diphthong in educated urban speech down to imperial times, as appears from statements of the grammarians and from early loanwords like Proto-WGmc. **kaysar-* (OHG *keisur* 'emperor', OE *cásere*) from L *Caesar*. But smoothing to a monophthong took place earlier in colloquial speech, and eventually prevailed, with resulting confusion of spelling between *ae* and *e*. Romance language reflexes of L *ae* are identical to those of L *ĕ*. This is hardly comprehensible, since a long monophthong would be the expected result of a smoothened diphthong. The simplest explanation is that the smoothing postdated the Romance loss of the length contrast (77), which is thereby seen to have been quite early.[1] If this reasoning is correct, the smoothing seen already in *prĕhendō* (PRom. **prendere*) from *prae* and **hendō* is just a case of vowel shortening in accord with **85**. Furthermore, the late Imperial and Romance smoothing is not a continuation of the much earlier phenomenon vouchsafed by spelling confusions (E for AI, AE) as early as the 2nd century BC, as E must here mean *ē*.

ew; ow, H_3ew

61. PIE *ew* > G ευ, **ow* and **H_3ew* > G ου; all three > PItal. **ow* > OL *ou* > L *ū*.

PIE *yewg-* 'join' > G ζεῦγος 'span' (of oxen and the like), L *iūmentum* 'packhorse' (OL IOVXMENTA, **231.1** fn.).

PIE **lewk-* 'be light' > G λευκός 'white', L *lūx* 'light', *lūna* < **lowksnā* < **lewk-sneH_2-* : Av. *raoχšnā* 'lantern', Ved. *rocati* 'shines', OE *léoht* 'light'.

PIE **(H_1)ews-* 'burn' > PG **ewhō* > G εὕω 'singe' (**172c**), L *ūrō* 'burn' : Ved. *óṣati.*

PIE *dewk-* 'lead' > OL *douco* (*e*-grade), L *dūcō* : Go. *tiuhan.*

PIE **spewd-* > G σπεύδω 'hasten', **spowd-* > G σπουδή 'haste'.

1. In G the two diphthongs are kept distinct at all periods. But as early as the 5th century BC ου fell together with 'secondary long *o*' (**76**). This development is usually presented as the smoothing of the original diphthong, and that is the most likely development—it is parallel to the later merging of ει and [e:], for one thing. But it is not the only possibility. Diphthongization of 'secondary long *o*' is nearly as plausible in terms of phonetic norms. Whatever the intermediate stages, the ultimate development in Att.-Ion., as revealed by loan-words among other things, was to /ū/, NG /u/.

a. G **wew* became ϝει by dissimilation. This change predated the familiar G development of the PIE labiovelars (**154.1**). Thus εἶπον < ἔϝειπον (= Ved. *ávocam*), redup. aor. of **wek^w-* 'speak' < **e-we-yk^w-om* < **e-we-wk^w-om*; and ἀείδω 'sing' < **awe-ud-* < PIE **H_2we-H_2ud-*, a (thematized) redup. present, built to *H_2wed-* (cf. Ved. *vāvadīti* 'declares' from full grade **H_2we-H_2wed-*).

2. The prehistoric Italic development of *ow* from *ew* before consonants is of a piece with the same development before vowels as seen in *novus* (**42.1**). This *ow* is preserved in OL (as in Oscan), but had fallen together with *ū* by about 200 BC. The spelling OV, however, still appears in the SC de Bacch. of 186 BC, and often later.

a. L *ū* also comes from *-ovi-*, *-ove-*, with syncope of the second vowel, as *prūdēns* 'judicious, knowing' from **prŏ-vident-* (*videō*); *nūndinae* 'market day' (NOVNDINVM in SC de Bacch.) from **noven-dināy* (*novem*); *nūntiō* 'announce (news)' from **noventiō* (*novus*); *nūdus* 'naked' from **novedos* < **nog^wodhos* or the like : Go. *naqaþs*, NE *naked.*

---

[1] The Gmc. words for 'Greeks'—OE *Crécas*, OHG *Chreachi*, and Go. *Kreks*—despite appearances are not evidence for a L smoothing of *ae* to *ē*. These words reflect PGmc. **$ē_2$*, a vowel found in a handful of words and thought to continue somehow an earlier diphthong. In any case, the notion of a very early borrowing indeed is supported by the PGmc. **k-* for the voiced stop of L *Graecae.*

But a different development is seen in _mōtus_ 'moved', _vōtus_ 'vowed' from *_movetos_, *_vovetos_,[1] _nōnus_ 'ninth' from *_novenos_ (_novem_ 'nine'), _cōntiō_ 'assembly' from *_coventiō_, and some others. The most plausible explanation for the difference is as follows, and starts from the observation that syncope of medial vowels in L (73-4) is unpredictable (_dexter_ but _maximus_, for example). Early syncope of the second vowel, whereby _-ove-_ fell together with _-ou-_ and shared its development to _-ū-_, would explain the development of _-ove-_ to _-ū-_. In some words, the structure was maintained: *_movetos_, *_vovetos_ were presumably propped up by the influence of _monetos_ and the like; and any tendency for *_nowenos_ to go to *_nownos_ would have been counteracted by the cardinal *_nowen_ (whereas the semantically remote *_nowendināy_ would be less subject to this influence). Whatever the explanation for its persistence in particular cases, _ove/ovi_ eventually became _ō_, except of course when recomposed (as in _prōvidentia_ next to undisturbed _prūdentia_). —The chief difficulty with this interpretation is that IOVESTOD, IOVESAT persisted late enough to be actually attested, but we nevertheless find _iūstus_ 'just' and _iūrat_ rather than expected ˣ_iōstus_, ˣ_iōrat_. There are similar difficulties with all other explanations offered, however.

b. L _Līber_ god of increase, early LEIBERO and LEBRO dat.sg. < PIE *_lewdh-_ 'increase', cognate with O **lúvfreís** gen.sg. 'Liberi', G ἐλεύθερος 'free', shows a dissimilatory change (*_ow_ > *_oy_) between _l_ and _b_ analogous to that seen in _libet_ from _lubet_.

c. L _eu_ never represents PIE _ew_, but is always of secondary origin, as in _seu_ 'or if', _ceu_ 'as' from *_sey-we_, *_key-we_ (57.2**b**). _Neuter_ 'neither' is a compound (*_ne-utros_), and remained trisyllabic till a late period.

aw, H_2ew

62. PIE *_aw_ and *_H_2ew_ > G αυ, L _au_.

PIE *_sawso-_ (**_sH_2ews-_; *_H_ drops in PIE after _s_) 'dry' > Hom. αὖος, Att. αὗος : Skt. (Epic) _śoṣa-_ (with _ś-_ for expected _s-_; more straightforward is Av. _haoš-_ 'wither away'), OE _séar_, Lith. _saũsas_. Cf. L _sūdus_ 'dry' (of weather) < *_s(H)us-d(h)o-_.

PIE *_kawl-_ 'stalk' > G καυλός 'shaft, stalk', L _caulis_ 'stalk' : MIr. _cuaille_ 'arrow' /kuə̯l'e/.

PIE *_H_2ewg-_ (often *_H_2ewk-s-_) 'increase' > G αὔξω, L _augeō_, _auxilium_ 'help' (orig. *'reinforcements') : Ved. _ójas-_ n. 'strength', Go. _aukan_ 'increase'.

PIE *_H_2ew-_ pron. stem: *_H_2ewti_ 'on the other hand' > G αὖ, αὖτε (altered from *αὖτι by contamination with -τε 'and' < *_-k^we_; the original *αὖτι was elaborated with what looks like a genitive/adverbial marker in Ion. αὖτις), L _aut_ < *_awti_, _autem_ < *_awtim_ (71.1).

a. The pronunciation _ō_ for _au_, as _Clōdius_ for _Claudius_, was current in certain varieties of L (according to contemporary accounts it was 'rustic') and figures in the punch line of a well-known anecdote in Suetonius's life of Vespasian. The Romance developments guarantee the persistence of diphthongal _au_ as the normal pronunciation into the PRom. period; in Italian, for example, L _ŏ_, _ō_, and _au_ all have different reflexes (see 77). Nevertheless, specific items do show up in Romance languages with reflexes of *_ō_ rather than a diphthong: Sp. _pobre_ 'poor' < *_pōperum_ (_pauper_; the medial stop would not voice after the diphthong), Rom. _ureche_ 'ear' < *_ōric(u)la_ (_auriculum_; cf. _oricla_ in the App.Prob.).

[1] PItal. *_mowatos_, *_wowatos_; formation like _monitus_ < *_monatos_ to _moneō_.

63. LONG DIPHTHONGS. The existence of PIE long diphthongs, *_ēy_, *_ēw_, *_ōy_, and *_ōw_, is most clearly indicated by Indo-Iranian, where *_āi_ and *_āu_ were distinct from *_ai_, *_au_:

PIE	PInIr.	Vedic	PIE	PInIr.	Vedic
ey			ēy		
oy	ai	e	ōy	āi	āi
ay			āy		
ew			ēw		
ow	au	o	ōw	āu	āu
aw			āw		

Skt. _āi_, _āu_ (in the transcription followed here—others are met with) were in phonetic fact the commonplace diphthongs _ai_, _au_, and they are frequently so transcribed; but they were always distinct from InIr. *_ai_, *_au_, which had become Indic _e_, _o_ (36.4).

1. In PIE, such diphthongs have three origins. (1) Crasis, as when dat. sg. ending *_-ey_ combines with the _o_-stem vowel to make *_-ōy_ (259.6). (2) Secondary lengthening, as in PIE *_g_^{w}_ōws_ nom.sg. 'cow' with _-ō-_ imported from acc. *_g_^{w}_ōm_ (< **_g_^{w}_owm_; 324). (3) PIE lengthened grade (126)—probably at bottom analogical—in diphthongs.

2. OSTHOFF'S LAW. Indo-Iranian provides not merely the best evidence for types (2) and (3); it provides well-nigh the only evidence. The reason for this is that in most IE languages, long diphthongs merged with ordinary diphthongs. This phenomenon is known as _Osthoff's Law_, which more specifically states that long vowels become short when followed by a resonant (that is, any glide, nasal, or liquid) followed in turn by another consonant. Thus not only does PIE *_dyēws_ 'sky (god)' (Ved. _dyā́us_) show up with an ordinary diphthong in G Ζεύς, but similarly *_tāms_ fem.acc.pl. > _τᾰνς_ (whence _τᾱ́ς_, 228.4). OE _cú_ 'cow' and OHG _chuo_ support *_g_^{w}_ōws_ (324), as *_g_^{w}_ŏws_ would have given something like OE ×_céa_, OHG ×_chōr_.

3. In final position, *_-ōy_ lost the glide element in prehistoric L; in G, several centuries later, all long diphthongs in _-y_ (see 64) lost the glide. The dat.sgs. of _o-_ and _ā_-stems show up in both languages: PIE *_-o-ey_ > *_-ōy_ > G _-ωι_ > _-ω_ (embellished with iota subscript in writing), O _-oi_, L _-ō_. Contrast the _o_-stem inst.pl. *_-ōys_ (exact prehistory unknown) which undergoes Osthoff's Law in both G and L, hence dat.pl. _-οις_, _-īs_ (OL _-eis_) respectively (cf. O **-úís**, _-ois_). In G, the nom.sg. of the type Σαπφώ (not written with iota subscript) < *Σαπφώι, a noun type (322) not retained in L, shows the same development.

In L, final *_-āy_ > _-ae_, as in the 1st decl. dat.sg. (= G _-ᾱι_, _-ηι_, which later became _-ᾱ_, _-η_, but written with iota subscript).

a. The only epigraphic evidence for OL _-oi_ in the dat.sg. of _o_-stems is NVMASIOI

'Numeriō' on the Praeneste Fibula. Since this is now thought to be a forgery (19), our evidence is limited to the citation of *populoi Romanoi* by a grammarian, which is probably legitimate enough, though *populoi* for expected *popoloi* or *poploi* is not reassuring. Some early inscriptions in Faliscan seemingly still show *-oi*.

b. PIE nouns traditionally reconstructed **nāws* 'ship' and **rēys* 'valuables' did not in fact contain long diphthongs; for the correct interpretation see 328-9.

c. The term 'Osthoff's Law' applies properly to the phenomenon in G, which manifestly was independent of similar developments in L and other IE languages. However, the term is loosely used to refer to all shortening of long diphthongs in closed syllables.

64. Except for the word-final *-ᾱι, -ηι, -ωι* discussed in the preceding section, the Greek long diphthongs are of secondary origin: the result of contraction, as Ion. *κληΐς* 'bolt, latch' from *κλη(ϝ)ῑ́ς* < *κλᾱ(ϝ)ῑδ-* (cf. L *clāvis*); the result of crasis, as Ion., Dor. *ωὑτός* 'the same' masc. from *ὁ αὐτός*; analogical, as the augmented forms of the type *ἥιτησα* (to *αἰτέω* 'ask'), *ὥικησα* (to *οἰκέω* 'inhabit'), and *ηὔξησα* (to *αὐξάνω* 'augment'); and subjunctives, also analogical, of the type *λέγηις* 2sg., *λέγηι* 3sg. (to *λέγω*; 536).

In Attic long diphthongs lost the offglide in two unrelated processes. The earlier development, which might have been predicted on the basis of the phonetics alone, involved *-ηι-* specifically. As early as the 4th century BC this became ē̜, written *ει*, as *κλείς* 'latch' < *κληϝῖδ-* < *κλᾱϝῖδ-*. So too in the augmental forms, in the dat.sg., and in the subj., the spelling *ει* prevailed for a time—in 3rd century Att. inscriptions EI is more than twice as common as HI; but in those three categories *ηι* was restored by analogy: *χώρα* : *τῑμή* :: *χώρας* : *τῑμῆς* :: *χώρᾱι* :: *X*, where *X* = *τῑμῆι*.

Some two centuries later a new weakening, different in detail, began to affect the *ι* of *ᾱι, ωι*, and restored *ηι*; by 100 BC the spelling of Attic inscriptions is fluctuating between AI and A, HI and H, ΩI and Ω. (Note that in this round, the smoothed *-ηι* fell together with *-η* rather than with the spurious diphthong.) The spelling of such vowels with iota subscript, as *κλῄς*, *ᾔτησα*, *λέγῃ*, which is usual in our editions, is a late Byzantine device for indicating vowels which had once been distinct from *ᾱ*, *η*, and *ω*, but no longer were. (In this work, long diphthongs are written *ᾱι, ηι, ωι*, but with breathings and accents on the FIRST vowel; thus *ἥιει* 'he went' rather than either *ηἵει* or *ᾔει*.)

a. The difference between the earlier and later value of the G long diphthongs is reflected in L words borrowed at different periods, as early *tragoedus* 'tragic actor' from *τραγωιδός*, but later *rapsōdia* 'rhapsody' from *ῥαψῳδία* (*ῥαψωδία* in effect).

VOWELS IN MEDIAL AND FINAL SYLLABLES IN LATIN

65. In initial syllables L preserves the quality and quantity of PIE vowels reasonably intact, likewise the diphthongs **ay* and **aw*; but in medial and final syllables short vowels undergo far-reaching coalescences and even loss, and some PItal. diphthongs have different reflexes depending

on their position in the word. The traditional term for these phenomena, especially as they apply to the changes in the short vowels, is *weakening*.

Reduction in contrast between vowels, or their complete loss, is generally a concomitant of weak stress in languages in which different syllables are pronounced with significant differences in prominence. In L, however, the location of the stress in the historical period—familiar from school grammars of the language and vouchsafed by the location of the accent in the Romance languages—has no bearing on the sound laws governing the weakening of L vowels. That is, in *factus* and *refectus* the PItal. **a* of the root shows two different reflexes, even though the root vowel has the tonic stress in both L forms. If it is true that vowels weaken chiefly in unstressed syllables, then we must infer that in a prehistorical phase of L the system of word accent was different from the historically attested one, namely, that it always fell on the initial syllable of the word. During this period, vowels in the initial (stressed) syllables remained more or less unchanged, but short vowels in the then-posttonic syllables underwent the weakenings we see in the language as attested. Subsequently the scheme of accentuation familiar from historical Latin replaced this hypothetical first-syllable accentuation.

Something very similar is seen in English: in NE *revise* and *revision* the accent falls on the same syllable (etymologically speaking), but the accented vowels are pronounced very differently. These syllables were once identical, and the development of the vowel in one of them to /ay/ and in the other to /i/ is to be explained by the location of the word-accent in English at the time of the pertinent vowel changes (15th century). In words of the type *revise*, the accent was where it is now; but in *revision* the accent was on the last syllable. Subsequent to the vowel changes, tonic stress more than two syllables from the beginning of the word was retracted two syllables (suffixes in *-ion* were still disyllabic at the time), thus *revīsión* > *revĭsión* > *revĭ́sion* /re'vizion/ > /rə'vižən/.

The hypothetical first-syllable accent of Italic, or at least Pre-Latin, was not itself an inheritance from PIE; it replaced the PIE accentual system (242). Interestingly, the selfsame retraction of PIE accent to initial syllables is seen also in Proto-Germanic and Proto-Celtic, and the three developments are conceivably a single innovation. If Sab. underwent the same innovation, the matter would be clearer; but as nothing is known of the location of the accent in any Italic language except L, the point remains in doubt.

66. SHORT VOWELS IN MEDIAL SYLLABLES.[1] PItal. **e*, **o*, **a*, and **u* merge nearly completely. The result at first was **e*, which remained when followed by two or more consonants, but before a single consonant it became

---

[1] PItal. **e*, **a*, **o* and **u* have a variety of indigenous as well as PIE histories, and additionally all five short vowels appear in very early loan words from Greek and other sources. The sound laws in 66–9 apply to PItal. vowels of whatever origin.

i. There are three qualifications to this general statement: (1) the intermediate **e* became *o*—and then *u*—before *l*-pinguis (176a) and *w*;[1] (2) it remained *e* before *r* of any origin; (3) it became *i* before [ŋ] in accord with 41.1. PItal. **o* (item 3, below, and 67) requires special discussion; and see item 4, below regarding PItal. **i*.

The inputs to the following changes somewhat postdate PItal., as the changes affect loan words from G.

1. PItal. **a*:

**re-fakyō* 'make anew' > **refakiō* (193) > **refekiō* > *reficiō*; **refaktos* > *refectus*.
**in-armis* 'unarmed' (*arma*) > *inermis*.
**talantom* 'talent' (lw. from G *τάλαντον*) > *talentum*.
Lat.-Falisc. **ke-kad-ay* > L *cecidī* 'fell' (*cadō*).
Lat.-Falisc. **pe-par-ay* (attested as Falisc. PE:PARAI̯) > *peperī* 'I brought forth'.
**ad-tangō* 'arrive' > **attengō* > *attingō* (41.1).
**en-saltō* 'leap on' > **inseltō* > *īnsoltō* (81.2) > *īnsultō*.
**ad-alēskō* 'grow up' (*alō*) > **adelēskō* > *adolēscō* > *adulēscō*.

2. PItal. **e*:

**ad-tenēyō* > *attineō* 'concern'; **ad-tentos* > *attentus*.
**kom-regō* > *corrigō* 'set right'.
**ad-sedēyō* > *assideō* 'sit beside'; **ad-sed-tos* > *assessus* (212).
**kom-premō* > *comprimō* 'press together'.
G Σικελία 'Sicily' > L *Sicilia* (cf. *Siculus*, below).
**kom-gesō* > *congerō* 'collect'; **kom-gestos* > *congestus*.
**re-ferō* > *referō* 'carry back'.
**ob-kelō* > *occulō* 'conceal'.
G Σικελός 'a Sicilian' > **sikolos* > L *Siculus*.

3. PItal. **o*:

PIE **me-mon-H_2e* > Lat.-Falisc. **me-mon-ay* 'have in mind' > *meminī* 'remember'.
**nowotāts* (PIE **newo-*, 42.1) > *novitās* 'newness'.
**en stlokōd* 'on the spot' > L *īlicō* 'immediately'.
G Περσεφόνη > L *Proserpina* (the first syllable somewhat Latinized).
G ἀγχόνη 'throttling' > L *angina* 'quinsy' (later *angīna* under the influence of the multitude of L words in *-īnus*, *-a*, *-um*).
PIE **-foro-* (in compounds) 'carrying' (= G -φόρος) > *-fero-*, as in *furcifer* 'gallows-bird' (lit. '*furca*-carrier').
**te-tol-ay* > L *tetulī* 'I carried'.
PIE **peH₃-tlo-* > **pō-klo-* > *pōcolom* > L *pōculum* 'cup'.
**kom-solō* > L *cōnsulō* 'deliberate'.
PIE **-kl̥d-to-* > **-kolsso-* > L *perculsus* pple. 'beaten down' (98; 212).

---

[1] This must be distinguished from the similar but unrelated development of medial short vowels in labial environment, 69.

a. Orig. *o* before *l* pinguis remained after a vowel, *fīliolus* dim. 'son', *alveolus* 'trough'. Cf. *medietās* **68**.

b. PItal. **o* > L *u* medially before two consonants.
**legontor* > L *leguntur* 'they gather'.
**eyontes* pple. gen.sg. > L *euntis* 'going' : G ἰόντος.
**rōbos-to-* > L *rōbustus* 'oaken' (cf. *rōbur* < **rōbos*).
PIE *H_2*enǵhos-to-* > L *angustus* 'narrow' : Ved. *áṃhas-* 'narrowness, distress'.

c. The change to *u* before *l* pinguis (**176a**) or two consonants, and in final syllables (**71.6**) took place within the historical period. The earlier *o* appears regularly in inscriptions down to about 200 BC. So HONC, MOLTA, PRAIFECTOS, SACROM, DONOM, POCOLOM, COSENTIONT. The SC de Bacch. of 186 BC (**19**) has -VS, -VM, -VNT, -TVR, but *o* before *l* in TABOLAM, CONSOLVERVNT, COSOLERETVR.

4. Before *r*, PItal. **i* and **u* become *e*; before any other consonant, they developed as above; before two consonants, *i* remains:
**kom-itāyō* 'accompany' > *comitō*.
**kornu-kan-* > *cornicen* 'trumpeter' (*cornu*).
Epigraphic TREBIBOS for *tribubus* dat./abl.pl. (*tribus* 'tribe').
**kaputes* gen.sg. 'head' > *capitis* (*caput*).
**re-likʷtos* 'left (behind)' > *relictus*.
**sub-ruptos* 'filched' > *surreptus*.
**kinis* 'ash' gen.sg. **kinises* > L *cinis*, *cineris*.
Ital. **falisioy* (cf. *Faliscus*) > L *Faleriī*.
PIE **swekuro-* 'father-in-law' > OL **sokeros* > *socer*, *-erī* (**74.4**).

a. In the course of the development of short vowels to *e* before *r*, it is unknown whether (a) all the vowels first became **i* and subsequently shared the fate of original **i*, or (b) their progress to *i* was arrested at *e* when they were followed by an *r*.

5. PItal. **i*, **e*, **a*, and **o* become *u* before **w*. In normal L spelling the resulting /uw/ before another vowel is written *u*:
**doma-way* > **domeway* > L *domuī* 'I tamed'. (PIE **dom*$\underset{\circ}{H}_2$*-*; cf. pple. *domitus* < PItal. **domatos* as if < PIE **dom*$\underset{\circ}{H}_2$*-to-*.)
eks-lawō* > L *ēluō* (231.1**) 'wash away' (*lavō*).
mon-i-way* 'I warned' > *monuī* (see **528c).
**tris-diw-om* > L *trīduom* later *trīduum* 'period of three days'.
**dē nowōd* > L *dēnuō* 'anew'.

6. Complexes coined after the action of these sound laws do not show their effects, nor do forms altered by recomposition: *dētrahō* 'take down', *irrepertus* 'undiscovered', *irruptus* 'burst into'. Such forms are very numerous. It is rarely possible to say whether chronology or recomposition is the correct explanation for a given form.

67. Remarkably, the expected development of *-i-* from **-o-* in medial syllables is limited to isolated or derivationally opaque forms, such as *meminī* and *angina*, above. The persistence of compounds in *-fer* (**66.3**) from **-foros* results from the similarity of the phonologically regular outcome to the *e*-grade simplexes, such as *ferō*.

Transparent compounds based on simplexes with *o* always had the *o* restored by analogy: L *inhorrēscō* 'begin to bristle', *inhonestus* 'dishonorable', *dissonus* 'discordant', and so on.

Neut. *s*-stems in *-er-*, like *genus, generis*, reflect *-*es*- (**296**); *s*-stems in *-or-* like *temporis* to *tempus* are secondary hypercorrect forms (**297.4a**), and provide clear (if indirect) evidence of a period when *e* and *o* were in alternation in accord with **66.3**. That is, a creation like *tempora* is possible only if Romans could think that the stem-vowel *-e-* of intermediate **tempera* was a weakened form of the vowel seen in the nom. **tempos*.

68. Given the above principles, one would anticipate that **ie*, **io*, and **ia* would become **ie* before two consonants or *r*, and **ii* before a single consonant; this latter would then become *ī*. However, there are only a very few instances which seem to show the last development. At least two cases seem clear: **tībia-kan-* 'flute-player' > **tībiikan-* > L *tībīcen* (**71.4**), and *$g^w iH_3 eteH_2$ 'life' (cf. G βίοτος) > **wiotā* > **wietā* > **wiita* > *vīta*. Something similar seems to be seen in *$H_1 s$-iH_1-*ent* 3pl.opt. 'they may be' > OL *sient*[1] > **siint* > **sīnt* whence *sint* by **82**, though of course **sīnt* could owe its shape to analogy with *sīmus, sītis*. L *merīdiēs* 'noon' < **merie-diēs* < **merio-* < **medio-* (by dissimilation) < **meθyo-* (cf. *medius*) would appear to be an example, though its value may be discounted by the appeal to dissimilation. (Of course, the disfigurement of the first element accounts for its escape from remodeling as ˣ*mediediēs* or the like.)

In the majority of cases however, *i* plus vowel > L *ie* in all environments except before *l* pinguis: **sokiotāts* > *societās* 'fellowship', **wariogāyesi* > *variegāre* 'to make diverse', **mediotāts* > *medietās* 'the mean'; cf. *fīliolus*, **66.3a**, above. On the assumption that the most altered and the least transparent formations are likeliest to be the original ones (cf. **209**), we must take *tībīcen* and *vīta* as the regular outcome, and ascribe the usual *-ie-* to analogical effects.

69. Medially before a labial consonant (*p, b, f, m*), there is confusion between *i*—both original and as the product of **66**—and *u*.

From the root *cap-* (*capiō*): *occupō* 'seize' beside *occipiō* 'begin' and *anticipiō* 'anticipate'; *aucupis* gen. of *auceps* 'bird catcher' beside *prīncipis* gen. of *prīnceps* 'chief'; and *mancupium* 'purchase' alternating with (later) *mancipium*.

contubernālis 'messmate, comrade' (cf. *taberna*).

surrupuit 'filches', later *surripuit* (*rapiō*).

proxumus 'nearest', *optumus* 'best', *maxumus* 'biggest' beside later *-imus*, all from *-*emos* (**358**).

possumus 'we can', *volumus* 'we want' beside the thematic type *legimus* 'we gather', all from *-*omos*.

aurufex 'goldsmith', *pontufex* 'pontiff', later *aurifex, pontifex*.

---

[1] For simplicity this derivation ignores the probable change of final *-*nt* to *-*ns* (**237.5**) and its subsequent replacement by the primary ending *-nt*.

Some see the *u* development to be associated particularly with rounded vowels in adjacent syllables, but there are many exceptions. Some of these are attributable to analogy. In the 1pl. ending, *-imus* was supported by the 2pl. *-itis*; the persistence of *-umus* in the paradigms of *volō* (and derivatives) and *possum* neatly accords with the lack of a 2pl. in *-itis* in just those verbs. Such an explanation leaves *edimus* 'we eat' (2pl. *estis*, ? *ēstis*) unaccounted for, however. Forms like *surripuit* for earlier *surrupuit* are perhaps analogical, having been drawn into the dominant *i*~*e* pattern of the *reficiō* : *refectus* type through forms like *surreptus*, namely *refectus* : *reficiō* :: *surreptus* : *X*, where *X* = *surripiō*. Plautine *surruptus* may have its vowel from a fancied association with *ruptus* (*rumpō* 'break').

a. The superlative suffix *-umus* is the prevalent spelling in early inscriptions; the earliest epigraphic instance of *-imus* is seen in the word *minimus*. In later inscriptions, and in mss of the early playwrights, there is fluctuation between *u* and *i*; by imperial times the spelling with *i* is standard. Exceptions like *postumus* 'last' and the gens name *Postumus*, which never were dislodged by *-imus*, are hard to explain.

b. Quintilian and others state that the sound in question was intermediate between *u* and *i*, and the emperor Claudius is said to have proposed adding a letter to the alphabet in order to write the sound unambiguously. During the period of orthographic hesitation the vowel in question was in all likelihood a schwa (that is, a central or back unrounded vowel), not unlike the second vowel of NE *maximum*. This might well have been true for other periods too, and conceivably the shift from *u* to *i* was a change in orthographic vogue only, like changes in the use of the letters *u* and *v* in the history of written English. The possibility cannot be ruled out, however, that in the earlier period *u* was simply [u], and later *i* was simply [i].

70. DIPHTHONGS IN MEDIAL SYLLABLES.

1. PItal. **ey* > L *ī*; **ow* and **oy* > *ū* in medial syllables, just as they do in initial syllables (57-8):

**en-deykō* > L *indīcō* (*dīcō*);

**en-dewkō* > **indoucō* > L *indūcō* 'draw over, cover' (*dūcō*);

**n̥-poyni* 'with impunity' > L *impūne* (cf. *poena*). (Some think this is a calque on G νη-ποινεί; the principle is the same in any case.)

2. PItal. **ay* > *ei* > *ī*:

**ke-kayd-a(y)* perf. 'I cut' > L *cecīdī* (*caedō*).

**en-kaydō* 'cut into' > OL *inceido* > L *incīdō*.

**elaywā* 'olive (tree)' (lw., either from G ἐλαί(ϝ)ᾱ or directly from the same source as the G word) > L *olīva* (42.5).

3. PItal. **aw* > *ū*:

**en-klawdō* 'enclose' > *inclūdō* (*claudō*).

a. The numerous instances of L *ae* or *au* in medial syllables—*inaequālis* 'uneven' (*aequor*), and *incautus* 'heedless' (*cautus*)—are in formations that either postdate the pertinent sound laws or have been modified by recomposition.

b. L *oboediō* 'listen to', if from *ob-* + *audiō* (59a), uniquely shows a change of medial **-aw-* to **-oy-*.

71. SHORT VOWELS IN FINAL SYLLABLES. The rounded vowels **o*, **u* fall together as *u* before any consonant; the unrounded vowels **i*, **e*, **a* fall together as *e*, which then becomes *i* before any single non-nasal consonant. In final position all short vowels become *-e*, though for *-*a* and *-*u* evidence is doubtful.

1. PItal **i* remains in final syllables, with two exceptions:

(1) Word-final *-*i*, when not lost (74.1-2), becomes *-e*.

PIE *H_2*enti* 'in front of, facing' > L *ante* : G ἀντί, Ved. *ánti*.

PIE **mori* 'sea' > L *mare*, and similarly other neut. *i*-stems.

a. L *-ĭ* is always from *-ī* by iambic shortening (84), as *quasi* < *quasī*.

b. Note that the PIE *-*i* in certain primary verb endings, such as L *legit* < **legeti* 'gathers', is out of the picture at this point; its apocope is PItal. (if not Italo-Celtic).

(2) PItal. *-*im* > *-em*:

PIE **kʷim* acc. 'whom' > L *quem*.

PIE *i*-stem acc.sg. *-*im* > L *-em*: PIE **mn̥tim* 'mind' > L *mentem*.

a. A difficulty with this view is the adverb suffix *-(t)im*, as in *partim* 'in part', which is usually explained as an accusative of a *ti*-stem (see 306.3), with the corollary that the usual *i*-stem acc.sg. in *-em* is imported from the consonant stems (308). The evidence of *quem* is weighty, however, and *autem* appears to be an elaboration of **awti* (the source of L *aut*). If this is the correct view, then the productive adverbs in *-tim* are left isolated and unexplained, beyond the likelihood that they continue earlier *-*tīm*.

2. PItal. **e* remains word-finally and before a final nasal.

PIE *nomn̥* > L *nōmen* 'name, word' (the *ō*, and the *g* of *cognōmen*, by contamination with reflexes of **ǵneH₃*- like *ignōtus* and *nōbilis*).

PIE **deḱm̥t* > L *decem* 'ten'. (L *ūndecim* 'eleven' and the other teens by metathesis: **ūndicem* < **oyno-dekem*.)

PIE *o*-stem voc.sg. *-*e* > L *-e*, L *lupe* 'O wolf' : G λύκε, OCS *vlĭče*, Ved. *vr̥ka*.

PIE *-*e* 2sg. themat. imperat. and *-*te* 2pl. > L *-e*, *-te*: *age*, *agite* 'do!' : G ἄγε, ἄγετε, Ved. *-a*, *-ata*.

3. Before a single final consonant not a nasal, *-*e*- > *-i*-.

Cons. stem gen.sg. *-is* from *-*es* (276.7).

2sg. *legis*, 3sg. *legit* from *-*esi*, *-*eti* (74.2, 425-6).

a. Cases of final *-ĕs* in L are always from *-*ets*, either original as in *mīles* 'soldier' (stem *mīlet-*), or via syncope (74.5) as in **hosti-potis* > **hostpetis* > **hospets* > *hospes* 'stranger/guest'. Thus also L *ades* 'you are present' if from *adess* (required by Plautine scansion, like simplex *ess*); but this form could easily be analogical.

4. PItal. **a* > L *e* in final syllables before consonant sequences or a nasal:

**prīsmo-kap-s* > *prīnceps* 'first, chief' (*capiō*); see 74.5.

**kornu-kan-(?s)* > *cornicen* 'trumpeter' (*canō*).

**tībia-kan-(?s)* > *tībīcen* 'piper'.

PItal **a* in final position or before a single word-final consonant is not generally recognized; but there are several strong candidates for such. The 3rd conj. endings of compounds of *dō, dare*, as 2sg. *reddis*, 3sg. *reddit* must continue **rededas*, *-*at* < *-*dedH̥₃*- (488.B). The root of L *condere* 'found', *condidī, conditus*, and five other compounds of the same form (as *ab-, ad-, ob-, per-*, and *sub-dere*) is perhaps traceable through PItal. *-*θa-* to PIE **dhH̥₁-*, zero grade of **dheH₁-* 'put'. If this analysis is correct, then L *condis, condit* from PItal. **komθas(i)*, **komθat(i)* show L *i* < **a* < **H̥₂* before single non-nasal consonants in final position. Similarly, but very much more tenuous because the form might be simply analogical, the imperatives of these verbs (e.g. *perde* 'destroy!') if from *-*da*, would show that PItal. **a* in absolute final position became *-e*.

Several other verb stems in L can be convincingly explained thus, as *tollis* 2sg. 'carry' < **tolnas(i)* < **tl̥nH̥₂-* (479.4B); *womis* 2sg. 'vomit' < **womas(i)* < **wemH̥₁-si* (479.2).

5. PItal. **o* in word-final position gives L *-e*.

PIE *-*so* 2sg. mid. imper. (550.1) > L *-re* : G *-(σ)o*, less certainly Ved. *-sva* (for *-*sa*, contaminated by the reflexive pronoun *sva-* with help from the pl. ending *-dhvam*).

Endingless masc. pronouns of the type L *iste* 'that' from **is-to*.

a. L *-ŏ* is always from *-ō(d)* via iambic shortening and its sequelae (84): *cedo* 'gimme', *modo* 'just, only'.

6. Before all final consonants, PItal. **o* > L *u*:

PIE *-*os* nom.sg. *o*-stems, *-*om* acc.sg., *-*os* neut. *s*-stem > L *-us, -um, -us*.

PIE **H₂elyod* neut. 'another' > L *aliud* : G ἄλλο, Ved. *anyát*.

PIE *-*onti* 3pl. thematic > L *-unt* : Dor. -οντι, Att. -ουσι, Ved. *-anti*, Go. *-and*.

PIE *-*tor* 3sg. pres. mid. > L *-tur* : Hitt. *-tari*.

a. This applies to **ō* that became short prior to the time of the sound law, thus *-*ōm* gen.pl. > *-*om* already in PItal., hence L *-um*. But the shortening of long vowels before final *-r* postdates the innovation, hence **swesōr* 'sister' > L *soror*, not ˣ*sorur*.

b. L *quod, tot, quot* next to *illud* and *aliud*, shows the change does not affect monosyllables. However, as might be expected from 45.1, PItal. **o* does become L *u* when before *-m* even in monosyllables: **kʷom* 'when, since' > *quom* > *cum* (= Ved. *kám*), **tom* 'then' > *tum* (= G τόν, Ved. *tám*).

c. After *u, v*, or *qu* the change of *o* to *u* did not take place until considerably later than in other environments. The forms of Plautus and Terence were *dolus, dōnum, legunt*, on the one hand, and, on the other, *volt* 'wants', *volnus* 'wound', *mortuos* 'dead', *servos* 'slave', *relinquont* 'they leave', *sequontur* 'they follow', *quom* conj. 'cum'. This spelling persisted until about the middle of the 1st century BC, though probably the pronunciation changed sooner, as guaranteed by the bogus spelling of *cum* 'with' as *quom*—something that is thinkable only after *quom* 'as' had become homophonous with the preposition (notwithstanding their difference in the usual spelling at that period). And Quintilian, writing around 95 AD—long after the change in pronunciation was certainly complete—remarks that his teachers still wrote *servos, cervos*. The earliest example of *u* in such cases is SVVM beside SVOM in an inscription of 45 BC, and the spelling *o* is often found much later, especially in *volt* and *volnus*.

When at last *o* > *u* even after *u/v*, the glide component of *qu* was lost before this new *u*, so that *equos, relinquont, sequontur, quom* became *ecus, relincunt, secuntur, cum*, which are the proper forms of the Augustan period. Later, in paradigms, *qu* and *gu* were restored by leveling analogy, hence *equus* after inflected forms like *equī*, and *relinquunt* after *relinquit*. But isolated *cum* remained. (*Quum* conj. is a late, pseudoarchaic spelling.)

7. PIE **u* remains unchanged before a final consonant: PIE *u*-stem **-tus* nom., **-tum* acc. > L *-tus*, *-tum*.

In word-final position, **-u* might be expected to become L *-e*, like all other short vowels, but there are no certain examples. Thinkably *nōnne* 'is it not?' has this history; it corresponds in function, and very nearly in form, to Ved. *nanú*, PIE **ne-nŭ*. The neut. *u*-stems, such as *genu* 'knee' and *cornu* 'horn' (cf. Ved. *jā́nu-*, *o*-grade), apparent counter-examples, are often *-ū* in poetry; the alternative *-ŭ* can be attributed to shortening.

72. ASSIMILATION AND LEVELING. The action of the sound laws discussed in the preceding sections may be disturbed by leveling analogies and assimilation to vowels in adjacent syllables. The frequent—and phonologically regular—interchange of *i* and *e* in *prīnceps*, *prīncipis* (**-a-*), *mīles*, *mīlitis* (**-e-*), and especially compounds in *-fex*, *-ficis* (**-a-*) led to the remodeling of **iūdix*, **indix*, *-dicis* (root *dĭc-*, zero grade of **deyḱ-*) to the familiar *iūdex*, *index*, *-dicis*.[1] Within paradigms there is sometimes cross-pollination. Compounds of *gradior* 'step' show *-gredior* instead of expected **-gridior*, perhaps leveled from the compound pple. in *-gressus*. This form is certainly the source of the simplex *gressus*, for expected **grassus* (pple. of *gradior*). A mixture of influences is seen in: *fessus* for **fassus* (*fatīscor* 'weary'), its vowel imported from *dēfessus*, whose presents, in turn—*dēfetīscor* and *dēfatīscor*—are neither one of them phonologically regular.[2]

Assimilation is thought to account for *vegetus* 'lively'; *segetis* (nom. *seges* 'standing crops'); *alacer* 'quick'; *anatis* (*anas* 'duck'; expected vocalism in Plt. *anitēs* and continued in various Romance forms); *tegetis* (nom. *teges* 'mat, covering', from *tegō*); *ēlegāns* 'select, choice' (*legō*); *cinis* 'ash' from **cenis* (cf. ordinary *o*-grade in G κόνις); and many others.

As is often the case when dealing with sporadic processes, there can be more than one plausible explanation for a given form. Some of the forms just mentioned could have arisen via leveling from the nom.sg. The *-e-* of L *iuvenis* 'young (man)' was propped up on one side by *sen-* 'old' (as in *senēs* 'old (men)') and on the other by the perfectly regular vowels of

---

[1] This is the opinion endorsed by tradition, but it is likelier that *-dex* < **-diks* is phonologically regular. Until the shortening rules (82-5) reintroduced all five short vowels into final syllables, the L final-syllable sound laws exhibited in 71 had effectively boiled down short vowel contrast in final syllables to a single axis: front (*i* or *e* depending on environment) vs. back (*u* or *o*). Late OL **ioudix* vs. **aurofex* or the like would presuppose a unique contrast between /i/ and /e/ in final syllables, which seems less likely than an interpretation whereby all non-rounded short vowels in final syllables followed by two obstruents became *e*.

[2] Appealing to a compilation of phonologically inconsistent features in a single word is undeniably ad hoc, but there is no shortage of clear examples of such compilations: NE *thatch* as noun and verb supplants both the expected noun *thack* (OE *þæc* = NHG *Dach* 'roof') and the expected verb *thetch* (OE *þeċċan* = NHG *decken* 'cover'), and is a composite of details proper to both.

iuventūs, *iuventās*. *Vehemēns* 'violent' (and derivatives) has been explained as assimilation, in contrast to *vehiculum* 'conveyance' (**weǵhetlo-*); but it is as well or better explained as a fanciful spelling of **vē-menti-* (*menti-* 'mind') with the same first element as *vēsānus* 'raving mad' (also known in the whimsical spelling *vaesānus*), *vēgrandis* 'runty', *vēcors*, *-cordis* 'insane'.

a. *Integer* 'whole' (from *tag-*: cf. *tangō* 'touch') is actually the phonologically regular outcome of the earlier form of the nom.sg. **entagros* (66.1).

b. In reduplicated perfects (523), the inherited **e* of the reduplication syllable often assimilates to a following *o* or *u*, more rarely to a following *i*: so classical *poposcī* 'demanded', *spopondī* 'pledged', *pupugī* 'stabbed', *cucurrī* 'ran', for which Gellius cites OL *peposcī*, *spepondī*, *pepugī*, *cecurrī*.

73. SYNCOPE AND APOCOPE. The limiting case of weakening is *loss*, namely syncope and apocope.[1] Short vowels are not infrequently lost altogether in medial and final syllables in L. These losses occurred at various periods in the history of the language. Vowel loss is sometimes regular; but it is more commonly a sporadic phenomenon. The latter is largely the case for the history of L; some generalizations can be framed, however, and will be found in 74.

Sometimes both the truncated and the longer form remained in use, often with a differentiation in meaning; but usually the older form was displaced by the truncated form, as in the earliest examples of syncope.

1. Syncope occurred most extensively in the prehistoric period of word-inital accent (65); these rarely leave any trace of competing unsyncopated forms.

k^wi̯nk^{w}e-dekem > *quīndecim* '15' (via **quīndicem*; 390).
**deḱsiteros* 'right' > L *dexter* : G δεξιτερός.
OL *balineum* 'bath' > L *balneum* : G βαλανεῖον.
**formo-kap-* 'hot-holder' > L *forceps* 'tongs'.
**hosti-potis* > **hostpet(i)s* > *hospes* 'stranger, guest'.
**falisinos* > *Falernus* (cf. *Faliscī*).
**θak-li-tāt-s* > **fakltāts* > L *facultās* 'power' (cf. L *facilis* < **fak-li-s*).
PIE **ḱe-d$\underset{\circ}{H}_3$-te* (root **deH_3-*) 'give here' pl. > PItal. **kedate* > L *cette*, pl. of *cedo*.
**re-tetol-e(y)* 'he carried back' > L *rettulit*.
Nom.sg. **partis* 'part', **mentis* 'mind' > L *pars*, *mēns*. (Syncope of the *-*i*- is regular after *-nt-*, *-rt-*; 309).
In view of 74.3-4, the final-syllable syncope in **feres* 'you carry', **feret* 'he carries' > L *fers*, *fert*, may be seen as regular. (It seems to be the only 3rd conj. verb whose root ends in *-r*.)
Similarly the apocopated thematic imperative *fer*, and also *dīc*, *dūc*, *fac*,

---

[1] A third type, *aphaeresis* (loss of a word-initial vowel), is practically unknown in the classical languages, though it plays a role in the evolution of Romance.

usual from Plt. on, for scantily-attested *dīce, dūce, face* (NB not *faci*). For the last three see 547.1a.
Vocatives *vir* 'man', *puer* 'boy' in Plaut. and Ter.
PIE **eti* > L *et* : G ἔτι 'further', Ved. *áti* 'beyond, over'.
Final vowels were also lost in *ab, sub, post,* cf. G ἀπό, ὑπό, OL *poste.*

a. Note that in some cases the syncopated vowel would have had tonic accent if it had survived into the period of historical L accentuation; once **rétetole(y)* had become ˣ*retítulīt,* in accord with the usual rules of L accentuation, the attested syncope of the second vowel would have been unlikely.

2. When the original structure persists alongside the truncated form we are generally dealing with syncopations of later date than the foregoing. There are two sorts.

(a) Different adventures of related words: *superus* 'upper' but *suprā* 'above' and *suprēmus* 'uppermost' (regular from **superisemos,* 358); *īnferus* 'lower' but *īnfrā* 'below' (earlier **inferā* additionally guaranteed by the development of *-f-* < **dh*: original **n̥dhro-* must have given ˣ*imbrā* by 147.2); *validus* 'strong' but *valdē* 'very' (still *validē* in Plt.).

(b) Different forms of the same word: *cal(i)dus* 'hot', *sol(i)dus* 'solid', *sur(ri)gō* 'raise up' (syncope regular in forms like *surgimus* < tetrasyllabic **surregemos*), *neque* and *nec* 'nor', *atque* and *ac* 'but'; in Plt. also *nemp* for *nempe* 'forsooth', and others.

74. As remarked above, the facts of L vowel loss resist generalization, but there are perhaps six valid observations:

1. The stem vowel of neut. *i*-stems is lost in neuter NOUNS of more than two syllables: *animal* 'animal', OL *animāle* (gramm.), *lupānar* 'brothel', pls. *animālia, lupānāria.* Note that neuter adjectives retain this vowel: *dēbile* 'weak', *facile* 'easy'. But later *celere* 'speedy' for earlier *celer* indicates that forms like *dēbile* are to be understood as the result of leveling on the basis of disyllablic *i*-stems such as *ācre* 'sharp'.

2. Primary verb endings **-si, *-ti, *-nti* > Ital. **-s, *-t, *-nt* > L *-is, -it, -unt.* This is apparently a kind of quasi-morphological rather than a phonological change, shared by O and U and, evidently, Celtic. But NB the 3pl. perf. *-ēre* < **-ēr-i* (514.4, 530.6A); the survival of the vowel here is perplexing because it should have been prone to loss owing to the *-r-* preceding the at-risk vowel (items 3, 4, and 6, below).

3. Ital. **ri* > L *er* before apical cons. This can be taken as a metathesis but in light of item 4, below, it is probably syncope followed by anaptyxis: **ākris* 'sharp' > **ākrs* > **ākers* > L *ācer.*

A remarkable feature of this vowel loss is that it affects stressed syllables (including monosyllables) as well as unstressed ones:
PIE **tris* 'thrice' > OL *terr* (so scanned in Plt.) > L *ter* : Ved. *trís,* G τρίς.
PIE **krey-H₁-* 'sift, sort' (cf. L *crībrum* 'sieve') builds *n*-infix present **kri-ne-H₁-* > PItal. **krin-* > L *cernō,* cf. perf. *crēvī.*

The original shape is preserved in other environments, whence preservation of the original shape in forms like *tribus* 'tribe' and the mixture of compounds in *ter-* and *tri-* 'three-' (389.3).

4. OL *-ro-s* (nom.sg.masc. of *o*-stems in *r*) > L *-er* after consonants, *-r* after vowels: **agros* > L *ager* 'field', OL SAKROS (Forum inscription) > L *sacer* 'sacred', Ἀλέξανδρος > L *Alexander*, **alteros* 'the other' > *alter*, **wiros* 'man' > *vir*. Medially: *sacerdōs* 'priest' < **sakro-θōts*, *mātertera* 'mother's sister' < **mātro-terā*. If this does not apply to L *-ros* < *-sos*, then *umerus*, *numerus* are phonologically regular. L *merus* 'unmixed' and *ferus* 'wild' have not been explained.

5. *Exon's Law* (as it was once more generally known) holds that in a PItal. tetrasyllable with two light medial syllables (schematically x$\breve{\text{x}}\breve{\text{x}}$x) the second vowel regularly syncopates.[1] In some cases it is vital to consider the whole paradigm. The syncope rule seems not to work correctly in words like *prīnceps* 'chief, leader' from **prīsmokaps*,[2] *auceps* 'fowler' from **awikaps* (cf. unaltered *avidus* 'greedy'), and *forceps* 'tongs' from **formokaps* 'hot-holder'; but note that the nom.sg. is the only case-form not satisfying the input conditions of Exon's Law, which correctly predicts the outcome of **prīsmocapem* acc., **awikapem*, and so on. Two additional points: short vowels arising from anaptyxis (as in *nōbilitās* 'fame' < **gnōθlitāts*, or *comitia* pl. 'assembly' < **komityā*) do not count, which means that they arose after the round of second-syllable syncope. Second, a cross-current arises from the especial readiness of short vowels following *l* and *r* to syncopate (item 6, below). Accordingly when the consonant between two medial short vowels is a liquid, the short vowel following the liquid—the third syllable—usually syncopates rather than the second syllable: **ussurupā-* 'to break *ūsus* (enjoyment)' > *ūsurpāre* (not ˣ*ūstripāre*); **sepelitos* > *sepultus* 'interred' (pple. of *sepeliō*); **koselinos* (cf. NE *hazel*) 'made of hazel wood' > **korelnos* > **corulnus* > *colurnus* (metathesis); and many others. *Falernus* < **falisinos* indicates that this principle applies to *-r-* < *-s-*.

6. Medial and final vowels following *r* (especially original **r*) and, in lesser degree, *l*, are liable to syncope. This is seen in various guises in the preceding five sections. Perhaps its most striking manifestation is the inflection of *ferō* 'carry' (*fers*, *fert* for expected **feris*, **ferit*).

75. DIPHTHONGS IN FINAL SYLLABLES.

1. PIE **ey* > OL *ei* > L *ī* in the cons. stem. dat.sg. **-ey*: **maH₂tr-ey* 'to mother' > L *mātrī*.

---

[1] In Sab. a similar rule seems to delete the third vowel instead.

[2] The development of **prīsemo-* (398.1, end) into **prīsmo-* or **prīmo-* must be assumed prior to the creation of this form; an original **prīsemokaps* and **prīsemokapes* would fail to give the expected outcome; the development expected of the still earlier **pri-isemokaps*, **priisemokapes* would be hard to judge.

2. PIE **oy* > PItal. **oy* > OL *ei* (SC de Bacch. FOEDERATEI) > L *ī* in the *o*-stem nom.pl., an ending imported from the pronouns (as in G also, but not O and U): *vīcī aliī* 'other villages' = G οἶκοι ἄλλοι (260.1).
wirōys* inst.pl. 'by means of men' > **wirŏys* (Osthoff's Law, 63.2) > L *virīs* dat.pl. : O **-úís, G -οις, Ved. *-āis*.

This change in seen in monosyllables in *hī, quī* nom.pl. This is somewhat unexpected, and might be analogical to forms like *istī* and *illī*, except that the very same outcome is seen also in the relative pronoun **kʷoy* > OL *quoi* > L *quī* (O **pui**), for which, it being nom. SINGULAR, there is no pattern for an analogy. A somewhat speculative explanation for the development is that the environment was equivalent to non-initial position because the pronouns are more or less atonic.

3. PIE **-ew-s* or **-ow-s* gen.sg. of *u*-stems, so L *manūs* : Ved. *-os*, Go. *-aus* (the only evidence pointing specifically to **-ows*), O *-ous*, Umbr. *-or*.

4. Lat.-Falisc. *-ay* > L *-ī*, in the 1sg. perf.: Falisc. PEPARAꟾ (the last letter doubtful) 'I brought forth' = L *peperī*. In monosyllables **ay* > L *ae*, as in *prae* : G παραί, both prob. from PIE **pr̥H₂-ey*.

5. The loc.sg. of *i*- and *u*-stem nouns (302, 312) was **-ēy* and **-ēw*; it is thinkable that the L endings *-ī* (306.5) and *-ū* (abl.)(314.6) include these among their etyma.

PHONETICS OF LONG AND SHORT VOWELS

76. SPURIOUS DIPHTHONGS (Greek secondary ē̩ and ō̩). In many dialects, including Att.-Ion., Greek ε and ο differed in tongue height from η and ω. This is unremarkable in itself, indeed it is the norm. But for mid and high vowels, most commonly, the long vowels are HIGHER than the corresponding short ones, such as was the case in L for instance, whereas in Greek it is evident that the inherited long mid vowels written η and ω were LOWER than the short ones. The long vowels which came from ε and ο by contraction with a like vowel (86.1) or by compensatory lengthening (79.1) retained in some dialects the tongue position of the short vowels, and therefore did not merge with η and ω. In Attic and the κοινή these new long vowels were written ει and ου. In the former case, for a time, the diphthong [ey] and the long mid front vowel higher than η (ē̩ in effect) remained distinct, but eventually they merged. In the case of the back vowel, the inherited diphthong ου and the new higher mid long vowel quite a bit earlier fell together (61.1), and the result soon became [u:].

Eventually, once the new long vowels and the original diphthongs had fallen together, they were both written ει and ου. The new long mid vowels, written like diphthongs, are traditionally if infelicitously called *spurious diphthongs*.

PIE **treyes* 'three' nom.pl. masc. > τρεες (Cret.) > G τρεῖς [tre:s] (**y* lost per 192).

PIE *H_1*es-mi* 'I am' > PG **esmi* > εἰμί [e:mi] (**227.2**).
PIE *-*osyo* gen.sg. > Hom. - οιο, -οο > G -ου first [o:] then [u:] (**61.1, 86.1, 259.8**).
PIE *-*oms* acc.pl. masc. > PG -*ons* > G -ους first [o:s] then [u:s] (**228.4**).

a. In Att. and Ion. inscriptions the usual spelling is Ε and Ο until about 400 BC, though occasional examples of ΕΙ (especially ΕΙΜΙ 'am') and ΟΥ are much earlier.

b. In many dialects secondary ē̜ and ō̜ apparently did merge with η and ω; at any rate they are so written: τρῆς, ἠμί, gen.sg. -ω, acc.pl. -ως.

c. Whether ει or ου in any given case is a genuine diphthong or 'spurious' is discoverable in various ways. In the infinitive λείπειν 'to leave' < **leykʷ-e-sen*, that the first ει is a genuine diphthong and the second is spurious is shown by:

1) The early spelling ΛΕΙΠΕΝ

2) Dialectal λείπην.

3) Pres. λείπω, perf. λέλοιπα, and aor. ἔλιπον, which exhibit the alternation pattern **ey*, **oy*, **i* (111), in which the *e*-grade is necessarily a genuine diphthong. Compare the forms of φθείρω 'ruin', perf. ἔφθορα, aor. ἐφθάρην, exhibiting the alternation ερ, ορ, αρ, that is, reflexes of the PIE pattern **er*, **or*, **r̥*. This discloses that the ει of φθείρω is a spurious diphthong (in this case from **pʰtʰer-yō*, 203.1).

4) In contract verbs, spurious diphthongs have no iota in the infinitive ending, in contrast to the contractions of genuine diphthongs: compare τῑμᾷ 3sg. with τῑμᾶν infin., from τῑμάει (genuine diphthong) and τῑμάειν (spurious diphthong), respectively.

The last test is dependent on the preceding three, not independent of them. The iota subscript is written promiscuously in mss, with at best a statistical inclination toward the etymologically correct use. In modern printed editions they are written where they belong, but that determination is made via the first three criteria.

d. An early change of ē̜ to ī occurs in a few Attic words: **ǵhesliyoy* > χῑ́λιοι = Ion. χείλιοι '1000' (227.2), ῑ̔μάτιον 'cloak' beside εἵματα 'clothes' (PIE **wes-mn̥-*). These are reminiscent of νῑ́φει 'is snowing' for expected νείφει (163), where, however, the ī occurs in place of a genuine diphthong. (No satisfactory explanation has been offered for either development.)

77. IN LATIN there were also differences between long and short vowels with regard to tongue height, except for *a*/*ā*. But unlike G, the phonetic relationship was the more typical one, namely the long vowels were higher than the short ones. This is known from statements of Roman authorities, from spelling mistakes in inscriptions (*e* for *ĭ*, *i* for *ē*), and from the reflexes of the vowels in the Romance languages, as diagrammed below. In VL, length contrasts between vowels disappeared. In one small branch of Romance (Sardo) the result was a straightforward coalescence of pairs of vowels originally distinguished by length: L *i*, *ī* became *i*; L *e*, *ē* became *e*; and so on. In the majority of Romance languages, however, the differences in tongue height between long and short vowels in L led to a skewed pattern of merger, such that originally LONG MID vowels fall together with SHORT HIGH vowels, as shown in the following tabulation.

Note that (1) The developments shown here apply to tonic syllables only. (2) The vowels traditionally written ẹ, ọ in Romance philology are [e o], and ę, ǫ stand for [ɛ ɔ]. (3) The 'breaking' of the lower mid vowels in stressed syllables seen in Italian is a

Latin		PWR[1]	Italian	Latin		PWR[1]	Italian
ī	quī	i	chi	ū	lūna	u	luna
i	quid	ẹ	che	u	suprā	ọ	sopra [o]
ē	fēcī	ẹ	feci	ō	dōnum	ọ	dono [o]
oe	poena	ẹ	pena	o	bonus	ǫ	buono
e	decem	ę	diece	au	cauda	au	coda [ɔ]
ae	laetus	ę	lieto	a	casa	a	casa 'house'
				ā	cāsus	a	caso 'event'

1. PWR is Proto-Western-Romance.

widespread feature of Western Romance languages. (4) Note that in VL, L *oe* merges with L *ē*, whereas *ae* merges with L *ĕ*; and *au* merges with neither L *ŏ* nor *ō*. The monophthongization of *ae* therefore apparently postdates the disappearance of the L contrast between long and short vowels.

78. Which L vowels were long and which were short is known from six kinds of contemporaneous evidence. (1) Epigraphy—the use of the apex, *i* longa, and geminatio vocalium to indicate long vowels: CÓNSVLES, INFRA, IÝNCTA, EXÁCTVS, PAASTORES (see **25**). (2) Vowel length in words borrowed into European languages which preserve vowel length, such as Irish or Germanic. Thus the following: OE *strǣt* (NE *street*), OHG *strāz(z)a* from L *(via) strata* (*ā*) 'paved [road]' next to OE *catt*, NE *cat*, OHG *cazza* from L *cattus* (*ă*). (3) Direct statements by ancient authorities, such as one of Cicero stating that *in-* and *con-* were pronounced with a long vowel when compounded with words beginning with *s* or *f* (**81.2**), e.g. *cōnservō*, *cōnferō*, and statements of various grammarians regarding forms like *amāns* and *dēns*. (4) Lack of weakening in medial syllables: *exāctus*, *intāctus* next to *refectus* < **refăctos* (**66.1**). (5) As *ss* becomes short after a long vowel (as in *fūsus* 'poured' < **fūssus*, in accord with **232.2**), its survival in such forms as *passum* and *fissus* establishes that the root vowels in such forms are short. (6) The use of words in poetry in which rules of scansion were partly dependent on differences in vowel length.

a. There are inconsistencies and lacunae in all of these forms of evidence. The most copious and reliable is poetry; but poetry is useless in the case of 'hidden quantity', that is, syllables which would scan the same whether they contained a long or a short vowel. These would be syllables ending in certain sequences of consonants: *dictus* and *scrīptus* scan alike.

Evidence for the length of such vowels can often be gleaned from a seventh sort of evidence, namely the reflexes of Romance languages. In Romance, the reflexes seen in the above table are valid for all tonic syllables (subject to various conditions which are immaterial here), so that the difference between It. *detto* from L *dĭctus* and It. *scritto* from L *scrīptus* illustrates Romance evidence for L quantity, hidden though it is. Sp. *mes*, Fr. *mois*, and It. *mese* 'month' < PRom. **mẹse-* confirm L *mēnsis*.

b. The same phonetic relation between long and short vowels as in L obtained in Oscan and Umbrian, on the evidence that Oscan *ē*, *ō* were regularly written *i*, *u* in inscriptions which used the Roman alphabet, for example O *licitud* = L *licētō* 'let it be permitted'.

LENGTHENING AND SHORTENING OF VOWELS IN GREEK

79. 1. The simplification of various consonant groups containing a nasal or liquid is attended by lengthening of the preceding vowel; for these see the treatment of consonant groups (203, 227–8).

2. Long vowels were shortened in prehistoric G before a nasal or liquid plus consonant (a corollary of Osthoff's Law), so regularly before *ντ*, as in pple. *γνόντες* 'knowing' nom.pl. from **γνω-ντες*, or Dor. *ἔγνον* 'they understand' 3pl.aor. from **e-gnō-nt*.[1] But long vowels arising later by contraction or analogy were not affected, such as *τιμῶντες* contract pple., *φέρωνται* 3pl.subj.mid.

3. A long vowel becomes short before another vowel in various dialects. This does not apply to all vowels, and most commonly affects *η* before *ο* or *ω* in Att.-Ion. So *βασιλέων* 'of kings' gen. pl. from *βασιλήων* (as still in Hom.), Att. *ἕως* 'dawn' from an earlier form something like Hom. *ἠώς*. When the second vowel is short it may be lengthened, resulting in what is known as *quantitative metathesis*. This is peculiar to Att.-Ion., and most uniformly manifested in Att.: *νεώς* gen. of *ναῦς* 'ship' (cf. Hom. *νηός*); *νεώς* 'temple' (cf. Hom. *νηός*, Dor. *νᾱός*); λεώς 'people' < λησς (Hom. has the non-Ion. λᾱός); *βασιλέως* from *βασιλῆος* gen.sg. (Hom.). The shortening without metathesis appears to be seen in later Ion. *βασιλέος*, and similarly acc.sg. *βασιλέᾰ* from *βασιλῆα*. (Similar forms in Homer are evident in names, such as Πελέος, which may have a different explanation; see 320.5.) However, forms like *βασιλέος*, *-έᾰ* can be explained differently as analogical replacements of expected *-έως*, *-έᾱ*, on some such model as *πεδῶν* : *βασιλέων* :: *πεδός* : *X*, where *X* = *βασιλέος*. The best evidence in favor of this view is that the metathesis is dependable in non-paradigmatic forms, as Ion. *τέως* < *τῆος* < **tāwos* 'meantime, while'. Significantly, in Hom., conservative forms like *βασιλῆος*, *βασιλήων*, and so on, are prevailingly found in formulae. The formulaic nature of the art-form does not explain their occurrence in Hdt. so well, however.

a. The 'Attic declension' (259.1a)—λεώς, λεώ, λεώι, λεών. These are ordinary o-stem nouns which have been deformed by quantitative metathesis. The details of these forms incidentally confirm the evidence of Ion. *τέως*, above, that quantitative metathesis postdates the Att.-Ion. development of *ᾱ* to *η*, thus λᾱϝο- > ληϝο- > ληο- > λεω-.

b. Quantitative metathesis also postdates the fixing of the rules for regressive word accent in G (243–4). Thus, in *i*-stem forms built to a frozen stem alternant in *-*ēy*-, we find first *πόληος* 'city' gen.sg., whose accent is unexceptionable, giving Att. *πόλεως*, with the accent now in an illegal location. Strange to say, analogical changes took the form of

[1] Laryngeal theory, 117–24, somewhat complicates such analyses. There is room for question about the historical status of a reconstruction like **γνώντες*; but the central point remains, namely, that a form like *γνόντες* cannot be the unaltered reflex of any thinkable etymon.

EXTENDING the type of πόλεως rather than of bringing πόλεως into line with the usual rules: thus gen.pl. πόλεων for πολέων from original πολήων.

SYNCOPE IN GREEK

80. Syncope is not a conspicuous feature of G historical phonology, unlike its role in L (73-4), but there are more than a dozen clear cases of it. For example:

PIE **lewdh-* 'go' gives G forms which are suppletive to ἔρχομαι: fut. ἐλεύσομαι, 'Attic perfect' ἐλήλυθα (**444**). The expected aor. would be ἤλυθον, infin. ἐλυθεῖν; these occur, but are sparsely attested next to syncopated ἦλθον and ἐλθεῖν.

PIE **ḱuno-H₁dont-es* (or else, within the history of G, **kuno-odont-es*) 'dog-teeth' (the two projections at the base of the point of a hunting spear) > G κνώδοντες.

PG **ess^e/o-* fut. of **es-* 'be' shows expected G froms like ἔσομαι 1sg., ἐσόμεθα 1pl., but 3sg. ἔσται takes the place of expected ἔσεται. (The latter actually occurs in Hom.)

3sg. οἴεται 'has the opinion' has syncopation in 1sg. οἶμαι for οἴομαι. The reasons for syncopation in any particular word in G are obscure, but in this case we can plausibly surmise that the insertion of 'in my view' into remarks reduced the verb to little more than a particle, phonologically; cf. NE *I s'pose*, *pro(b)'ly*, and *mem'ry* next to the never-syncopated *supposition*, *probable*, and *memorize*.

G ὀμφαλός 'navel' < **onupʰalos* < **H₃nobh-* (cf. Ved. *nábhya-*); 45.1A.

LENGTHENING OF VOWELS IN LATIN

81. 1. Certain consonant groups, such as medial *sn* and *sd* and final *ns*, simplify with lengthening of the preceding vowel (225.1).

2. Vowels were regularly lengthened before a nasal plus a fricative (*ns*, *nf*), and before *nct*, as in *cōnsul*, *īnfrā*, *iūnctus*. Similar lengthening before *nx* is but vaguely attested; on the one hand there is the epigraphic evidence of forms like CONIV́NXIT, while on the other hand Priscian expressly states that the first vowel of *vinxī* is short.

Lengthening before *mpt*, while plausible because of the exact parallel of lengthening before *nct*, is effectively limited to derivatives of just one root: *emō* 'take' (*ēmptus*, *ēmptiō*, *sūmptus*, and so on).

3. LACHMANN'S RULE. As Roman authorities themselves point out, in some few verbs the past participle (and similar forms, like action nouns in *-tiō*) had a long vowel when the pres. stem had a short one; and that this phenomenon was typical of roots ending in a voiced stop. Thus to roots ending in *g*: *lēctus*, *rēctus*, *tēctus*, *āctus*, *tāctus*, *pāctus* but pres. *legō*, *regō*, *tangō*, *agō*, *tegō*, *pangō*; and to those ending in *d*, *vīsus*, *fūsus*, *ēsus*, *cāsum*, but *videō*, *fundō*, *edō*, *cadō*. This antique rule of thumb has latterly been promoted to

a phonological principle, whereby the lengthening is regarded as resulting from the change of the voiced root-final voiced consonant to a voiceless one. However, lengthening is not invariable with devoicing, as is proved by *strictus* (*stringō*), *passum* (*pandō*), *fissus* (*findō*), *scissus* (*scindō*), *sessum* (*sīdō*), *ingressus* (*ingredior*), and others.

The crux of the explanation is the vowel length of the perfect ACTIVE stems. In L these sometimes have short vowels, and sometimes long ones of various origins (including analogy; see 525). Vowel lengthening in the perf.pple. is found when there is BOTH devoicing of the root-final stop AND a long vowel, of whatever origin, in the perf. act. Since, therefore, *fūdī* 'I poured' and *fidī* 'I split' had generalized different grades of the old aorist stem (524), the full and zero grades respectively, their pples. were correspondingly different: *fūsus* (< **fūssus* < **fŭd-to-*) and *fissus* < **fid-to-*. The role of the pple. in the formation of the passive of the perfect—*fūsus est* next to *fūdit*, and *fissus est* next to *fidit*—accounts for the influence of the perf. act. on the past pple. Thus *strictus* (**strinxī*), *fissus* (*fidī*), *scissus* (*scicidī*, later *scidī*), *passum* (*pandī*). The short vowel of *strictus* shows that the lengthening in *strīnxī* per 2, above, postdates Lachmann's Rule.

Only *tāctus* (*tangō*, *tetigī*) and *cāsum* (*cadō*, *cecidī*) remain problematic.

A consequence of the crucial role of the perfect active form is that part of the conditioning is in effect morphological: the paradigm must be active and transitive. Intransitive verbs (which can hardly be said to have passive forms) like *sīdō* 'take a seat, sit down' and *sedeō* 'am seated' do not show lengthening (supine *sessum*, derivatives like *sessitō* 'sit much', and so on), despite perf. *sēdī*.

Deponent verbs, having no perfect active stem at all, do not show Lachmannian lengthening. (*Gradior* 'step', and its derivatives, may be the only case.)

4. There was a tendency in some quarters to lengthen a vowel before *r* + consonant, and this seems to have been the accepted pronunciation of a few words such as *fōrma*, *ōrdō*, *ōrnō*, as attested in inscriptions with the apex or with gemination, as in AARMI-. The etymologies of many of these words are uncertain, but complexes like *inermis* 'unarmed' < **inărmis* at least establish that the *-a-* was short to begin with and was still short at the time of the changes in short vowels in medial syllables (66.1). And Romance reflexes vouchsafe many exceptions like *fīrmus* 'sturdy', whose *-ĭ-* is revealed by It. *fermo*, Fr. *ferme* (77).

a. In *quārtus* 'fourth' and *Mārs* the long vowel is unconnected with the foregoing. PIE **kʷ(e)twr̥to-* loses the first **t* in both Germanic and Italic, whence OE *féorþa*, and PItal. **kʷaworto-* gives > L *quārtus* (88.3). Similarly, whatever the remoter details, L *Mārs* continues **măort-* from OL *Māvort-*.

5. Priscian states that words ending in *-gnus*, *-gna*, *-gnum* had a long vowel in the penult; cf. epigraphic *i* longa in SIGNVM 'sign', DIGNVS 'worthy', IGNIS 'fire', and PRIVIGNVS 'step-son', all of which certainly had an etymologically short *i*. But this seems to have been a local or socially

restricted tendency, as the Romance evidence points to short vowels in these words, and most words of the right shape show no evidence at all for a long vowel: *magnus*, with all its great frequency in inscriptions, never appears with the apex. (In *rēgnum* 'kingdom' the long vowel is original, reflecting PIE **re*H_1*ǵ-*.)

6. The cluster **-gdhl-* > L *-gul-* with lengthening of the preceding vowel: **reǵ-dhle*H_2*-* 'rule, measure' > L *rēgula* (*regō*); **teg-dhle*H_2*-* > L *tēgula* 'roofing tile' (*tegō*); *H_2*eǵ-dhlo-* (or **aǵ-dhlo-*) > L *coāgulum* 'rennet'. —All these formations embody **-dhl-*, a form of the PIE 'tool' suffix.

a. The L phenomenon known as 'muta cum liquida' is misrepresented as a question of vowel length when the forms involved are cited—as some authorities do—as *pā̆tria* 'fatherland', *dū̆plex* 'twofold', and so on. What is at stake here is scansion and syllable weight rather than vowel length; in such forms the vowel is always phonetically short, but in poetry sometimes scanned as 'long by position' (better, 'heavy by position'), like the first syllables of *captus* and *omnis*, whose first syllables are always metrically heavy but contain vowels that are phonetically short. The vacillation in L scansion of such forms as *duplex* seems to be imitation of G rules of scansion. In early L, such as Plautus, and unlike G and Indic, 'muta cum liquida' never makes a preceding short vowel metrically heavy; even in later periods metrically heavy scansion is erratic.

Scansion of *tenebrae* 'darkness' and *volucrēs* 'birds' as *tene-brae* and *volu-crēs* (⏑⏑–), implied by Plautine and later scansion, must however be an innovation: short vowels in medial syllables develop differently before one vs. two consonants (**66**), which latter category invariably includes muta cum liquida (*tenebrae*, not $^{\times}$*tenibrae*, from **temabrāi*); and the fixing of the L accent likewise: *tenébrae* (proved by Romance reflexes) like *reféctus*. These facts suggest that the change of **teneb-rae* to *tené-brae* took place after the weakening of medial short vowels and the fixing of the L accent, but before the time of Plautus. (Romance etyma like **tenébrae* are not self-validating, and are treated by some as a replacement of earlier *ténebrae* such as must have happened in **fenéstra* 'window' (**247d**); but it is just as likely that in the type of Roman speech underlying Romance the change of earlier *tenébrae* to classical *ténebrae* had never taken place to begin with.)

SHORTENING OF VOWELS IN LATIN

82. Long vowels were shortened in prehistoric times before a resonant plus consonant. Apart from one evident case of **-ōys* > **-ŏys* (below, and **260.4**), the shortening is practically limited to position before *nt* or *nd*; for example, from stems *amā-* 'love' and *vidē-* 'see': pres. pple. stem *amant-*, *vident-* (the long vowels of *amāns*, *vidēns* nom.sg. are lengthenings, per **81.2**); and gerundive *amandus*, *videndus*. The zero grade of the PIE opt. of *H_1*es-* 'be', namely *H_1*s-i*H_1*-*, underlies PItal. **sīmos* 1pl., **sītes* 2pl., **sīnt* 3pl. (< *sient*, **68**), whence L *sīmus*, *sītis*, but *sĭnt*.

This development looks like Osthoff's Law (**63.2**), but the G and L shortenings are independent rather than shared innovations. Evidence pointing to a relatively late date for the L shortening is as follows. The rule applies to sequences that arose within the history of L, as **lawdāyonti* 'they praise' > **laudānt* (**88.3**) > L *laudănt*, and **moneyonti* 'they cause to think' > **monēnt* (**88.3**) > *monĕnt* 'they warn'. L *talentum*, early borrowed from

G τάλαντον, shows that medial *-ănt-* > L *-ent-* in accord with **66.1**; this indicates that the shortening of the stem vowel of **amāntem* and the like postdates the L changes in **66.1**, which would have given ˣ*amēns*, ˣ*amentem*.

In final syllables, the shortening of the *o*-stem ending **-ōys* (**260.4**) to **-ŏys* must have taken place prior to the development of **-ōy-* to *-ō-*, and early enough for the development of **-oys* > **-eys* > L *-īs* abl.pl. (**75.2**).

a. Some think that the vowel shortenings in question did in fact predate the medial syllable weakening of *talentum*, and that *amant-* is leveled from **ament-*. Evidence for this interpretation is limited to a single form, *Kalendae* 'the first day of the month'—if this is from **kaland-*; and if the latter is in fact from **kalānd-*; and if the last is in fact from *calāre* 'call, summon'. (Such an explanation is found in Varro.) The connection of *Kalendae* with *calāre* is doubted by most authorities; and in any case *amănt-* for **ament-* is hardly likely—the expected form would have been ˣ*amānt-*, because the only vowel other than *-e-* in the whole paradigm would have been nom.sg. *amāns*.

b. Changes during the historical period led to the reappearance of long vowels in this position, as *cōntiō* from *coventiō* (**61.2a**); **nowenti-* > *nūntiō* 'announce (news)'; **oyno-dekem* > *ūndecim* 'eleven'; **prīmo-kaps-* > *prīnceps* 'leader'. Evidence for the length of these vowels, however, is conflicting. Since their quantity for purposes of scansion is 'hidden' (**78a**), we are dependent on less direct evidence. Grammarians tell us that *ūndecim* 'eleven', for example, begins with a long vowel, and It. *undeci* confirms that (cf. *onda* 'wave' < *ŭnda*). But Fr. *onze, once,* and *annoncer* reflect **ŭndecim, ŭncia,* and *nŭnt-*. Roman grammarians say that *cōntiō* and *prīnceps* have short vowels; such a short vowel is confirmed by archaic It. *prence*, contradicted by the arch. It. doublet *prince* and It. *principe*.

c. Shortening of long vowels before *rt* and *rc*, hypothesized by some, is parallel to the development before nasal clusters. However, the occasional lengthening of originally short vowels before *r* + consonant (**81.4**) confuses the evidence.

83. 1. Long vowels were regularly shortened before final *-m*. PIE **-ōm* gen.pl. (the internal structure of the PIE suffix is not known more exactly; **257.15**) > PItal. **-ŏm* > OL *-om* > L *-um*, Osc. *-om*, **-úm**. Since this shortening is also seen in Celtic and Slavic, it is apparently a very early change. This poses a problem for the interpretation of the two L endings in *-ăm* < **-ām*, the acc.sg. of *ā*-stems (1st decl.) and the 1sg. imperf.: should not genuinely antique **-am* < **-ām*, undisturbed by analogy, give L ˣ*-em* (**71.4**)? In the case of the 1st decl., the elimination of all such forms by leveling analogy would be unremarkable; it is less a matter of course, but still reasonable, that leveling would also have eliminated a 1sg. ending in ˣ*-em*. No leveling at all is required if the regular outcome of **-ăm* was *-am* in the first place—but that would be very much unlike the behavior of short vowels in final syllables generally.

2. Relatively late in the history of L, PItal. **-ā* > *-ă*, thus the nom.sg.f. of *fēmina* (**263.1**), and the nom.acc.n.pl., as in *iuga* (**260.3**). From a theoretical standpoint, the notion that a particular vowel would uniquely undergo shortening is suspect, but the facts seem clear.[1] The shortening predated the

---

[1] Cf. the vowel-specific shortening which much later attacked only *-ō*, **84a**.

loss of final *-d* (237.4), hence 1st decl. abl. *-ā* < *-ād*. The *-ā* in the 1st conj. imperat. (as for example *portā* 'carry!') is an ordinary example of leveling. It is a little surprising that no such leveling acted on nom.sg. of the type *fēmina*. (The neut.pl. *-ă*, 260.3, would not have been subject to leveling in any case.)

3. Much later than the foregoing, long vowels were regularly shortened before final *t* and, except in monosyllables, before final *r* and *l*. (Put differently, long vowels before a final consonant survive as such only before *-s*.) Long vowels before final *t* and *r* are regularly still preserved in Plaut.—except in iambs, see **84**; and forms like *vidēt* and *amōr* are found even in later poetry.

a. The words for the decads in *-gintā* (*trīgintā* '30' and so on) are apparent exceptions to this analysis. The likeliest source for this *-ā* is analogy; **391**.

b. No shortening of PItal. **-ā* is seen in Sab., as revealed by the characteristic (if inconsistent) rounding of *-ā in final position: *ā*-stem nom.sg., O **víú** 'street', *touto* 'people', U **mutu** 'much'; neuter nom.acc.pl., O **prúftú** 'placed', U **iuku** 'prayers' (*o*-stems), and U **triiu-per** 'thrice' (*i*-stem).

c. The shortening of vowels in certain final syllables as described above accounts for such features of L as: (1) The ragged distribution of length in verb paradigms like *legăm, legās, legăt, legāmus, legātis, legănt*, all from a uniform stem **legā-*; *veniō, venīs, venĭt*, from *venī-*, next to *capiō, capis, capit*, from (in effect) *capi-* (480-1); (2) PIE *r*-stem nom.sg. in **-ēr, *-ōr* > L *-ĕr, -ŏr*: L *patĕr, mātĕr* = G πατήρ, μήτηρ; L *victŏr, -ōris* = G -τωρ (282); similarly *s*-stems like *amŏr, -ōris* (299); (3) Nom./acc.sg. neut.: *animăl, -ālis*; *exemplăr, -āris*; (4) L imperf. **-bā-* > 1sg. pass. *amābăr*, 2sg. *-bāris*, and so on.

84. IAMBIC SHORTENING. Early L very often shortens a long vowel in the second syllable of a disyllabic word with a light first syllable; in other words, iambic forms are converted into pyrrhic ones. This was presumably a feature of the spoken language, but of course is best attested in poetry. In the early playwrights it is found—optionally—in words of all types, as *bonīs* abl.pl., *bonī* gen.sg., *amō* 1sg. It is uncertain what the phonetics were of *bonīs* pronounced to scan ⏑⏑, in part because such phenomena do not survive in later periods for which both attestation and commentary are richer. In the classical period, the effects of this tendency are limited—with the qualifications mentioned below—to isolated (non-paradigmatic) words ending in a vowel; in them the vowel is simply short: **dwenēd, *malēd, *modōd, *kitōd* > *bene* 'well', *male* 'ill', *modo* 'just, merely', *cito* 'quickly'; cf. unaltered spondees of like morphology: *altē* 'on high', *prīmō* adv. 'first'.

PIE **du(w)ō* 'two' > L *duo*, G δύο (Epic G δύω, Ved. *d(u)vā́*); L *ego* = G ἐγώ. Cf. spondee *octō* = G ὀκτώ, Ved. *aṣṭā́(u)* 'eight'.

PIE **ḱe-deH₃* > **ke-dō* > L *cedo* 'gimme'.

OL *ne sei* 'unless', *qua sei* 'as if' > *nisī, quasī* > *nisi, quasi*.

Likewise *mihi, tibi, sibi, ibi, ubi*, though here the poets continued to use the older forms such as *mihī* as well.

a. In paradigmatic categories, there is next to nothing to be seen of this in Republican Latin: *amō*, not *amo*; *homō*, not *homo*; *lupō* abl. not *lupo*; and note the paradigmatic abl.sg. of *modus*, *modō*, which is etymologically identical to the adv. *modo*. This is the result of leveling in favor of the long vowel alternants of these endings. Only in a few imperatives that were isolated by their interjectional use, such as *ave*, *cave*, *puta*, did the phonologically regular short vowel persevere. —It is not to be imagined that long vowels were favored in this process by reason of their etymological correctness: rather, it is characteristic of L to favor the long vowel alternants in ANY leveling of a long/short alternation.

In the later Republican period forms like *homŏ*, *volŏ* are employed by poets only occasionally and are more or less artificial; but from Ovid onward such *-ŏ* becomes more and more frequent. That this is unrelated to the earlier iambic shortening is revealed (a) by the virtual limitation of the phenomenon to *-ō*, and (b) by its occurrence in non-iambic words too (*esto*, *ergo*, *octo*). Finally, by the 4th century AD the grammarians recognized *-ō* only in the dat. and abl.sg., and in the monosyllabic verbs *dō* and *stō*.

85. Long vowels were generally shortened before another vowel (*vocalis ante vocalem corripitur*). So *pius* from *pīus* 'true'; *fuit* from *fūit* 'was'; gen.sg. *reī* 'thing', *fideī* 'trust' from *-ēī* (which was however retained after *i*, as in *diēī* 'day', *faciēī* 'external form', 331.1); *deesse* 'to be wanting' from *dē-*. Intervening *h* does not prevent such shortening, thus *dehinc* 'from here', *dehīscō* 'split open'. Even diphthongs before another vowel shorten: **praehendō* > *prehendō* 'seize' and *praeeō* 'precede' (*praeīre*, *praeeunt-*) regularly scan with a light first syllable, as if *prĕ-*.

In evident contradiction of this rule, *ī* is found before another vowel in some forms of *fīō* 'become' (see 489). Only slightly less puzzling is the pronominal genitive in *-īus*: as in *illīus*, *ūnīus*. The source of the *-ī-* is debated (375.1), but it is clear that this is the form in Plaut., and it was regarded by Roman authorities as correct. But *illĭus*, *ūnĭus* were also familiar, as proved by their frequent occurrence in poetry.

Contraction of Vowels in Greek

86. The Greek loss of intervocalic **y* (192) and **h* (from **s*, 172), and the much later loss of intervocalic **w* (in those dialects which lost it, 189) produced every sort of vowel sequence. The readiness of these sequences to contract varied: contraction was most extensive in the sequences resulting from the loss of **y* and **s*. There are dialectal and chronological differences, however, which were furthermore crosscut by levelings and distractions at all periods. The complications are discussed in Greek grammars, descriptive as well as historical, and need not be repeated in detail here.

There seem to have been four discernable periods of vowel contraction, with different rules. The earliest, of PIE date, favors the first vowel, so ***-o-es* nom.pl. of *o*-stems, and **-o-ey* dat.sg. ditto > PIE **-ōs*, **-ōy*. This does not concern us here. The remaining three are, in chronological order: Wackernagel's Law (87); the usual Attic (and other mostly post-Homeric) contractions (items 1-5); and 'grammatical contraction' (item 6).

1. In Homer there is not much contraction. In Attic, contraction of sequences stemming from *-*VsV*- (172) and *-*VyV*- (192; V = any vowel) is the norm, but not from *-*VwV*- (187), except where the now-adjacent vowels were similar: thus **genehos* gen.sg. 'race' > Hom. γένεος, Att. γένους; **hwādewos* 'sweet' gen. > Hom., Att. ἡδέος; but **hwādewes* nom.pl. > trisyllabic Hom. ἡδέες, disyllabic Att. ἡδεῖς. Taken together, these principles account for the similarities and differences in the Attic paradigms reflecting PG **de-y*^{e}/*o*- 'bind' (PIE **d*$\underset{\circ}{H}_1$-) and **dew*-^{e}/*o*- 'require, lack':

*deyō	δῶ 'I bind'	*dewō	δέω 'I lack'
*deyesi	δεῖς	*dewesi	δεῖς
*deyei	δεῖ	*dewei	δεῖ
*deyomen	δοῦμεν *etc.*	*dewomen	δέομεν *etc.*

In disyllabic nouns, even in Att., εο and εα do not normally contract, so θεός 'god', of uncertain etymology, and ἔαρ 'spring' < **wes*$\underset{\circ}{r}$ (though contracted ἦρ is attested).

2. ι and υ unite with a preceding vowel to form a diphthong, as 2sg. εἶ < **ehi* < **H_1esi* 'you are', εὐ- 'well-' < **ehu*- < **H_1su*-. On the other hand, nothing happens to ι and υ before another vowel: μῆνις 'rage', denom. μηνίω 'be furious with' < **māni-yō*, βραδίων 'slower' < **g*^{w}*radihō(n)*, νυός 'daughter-in-law' < **snusos*.

3. As a rule of thumb, in the combination of an *o*-vowel with an *a*- or *e*-vowel, the *o*-quality prevails: ο + ε > ου; ο + α > ω; ω + anything > ω. However, the contraction of ε + ο to ου is Attic only. In other dialects εο remains uncontracted, or falls together with ευ.

4. In Attic, in sequences of *a*-vowels plus *e*-vowels, the quality of the first prevails: τιμάετε > τιμᾶτε, γένεα n.pl. > γένη. In Doric, by contrast, either sequence results in η.

a. Even in Attic, ᾱ rather than η is the product of εα when it is preceded by ε or ι (54-5). Thus in the acc.sg. of adjectives built to κλέϝος 'fame': *-*kleweha* > -κλέεα > -κλέᾱ; ὑγιέ(*h*)α acc.sg. 'healthy' > Ion. ὑγιέα, Att. ὑγιᾶ. (See 300, 344a.)

5. Note that the Att.-Ion. sound law ᾱ > η (more accurately ǣ, 54) PRECEDED these contractions; thus ᾱω first > ηω then > εω (79.3) > ω; ᾱε > ηε > εη (79.3) > η. In other dialects the result of any contraction of ᾱ was ᾱ, as in the 1st decl.gen.pl. -ᾱ́ων > most G -ᾶν, in contrast to Att. -ῶν.

6. Nom./acc.n.pl. of the type ὀστέα 'bones', ἁπλόα 'single' give ὀστᾶ and ἁπλᾶ instead of ˣὀστῆ and ˣἁπλῶ. This has been traced to the influence of the -ᾰ of the cons. and *o*-stem nom./acc.pl.neut. This is reasonable on its face, except for the problem that the comparative adj. ending -ω < -οα experienced no such influence from the selfsame -α, even though it was in active competition with -ονα (354.4). A better explanation relies on chronology: -ᾶ is in fact purely phonological, but is the product of a later, different contraction of εα and οα, seen also in 'grammatical contraction'

whereby *οα* becomes *ᾱ* even in Att. (as *ὁ ἀνήρ* > *ἁνήρ*; **239.4**). Underlying the forms *ὀστᾶ* and *ἁπλᾶ* therefore are forms distracted from -*ῆ* and -*ῶ*. The cons. stem ending -*α* was without doubt the catalyst for the distraction, but could hardly have CAUSED -*ῆ* and -*ῶ* to become -*ᾶ*. —The same contraction of relatively late date accounts for Dor. *πρᾶτος* 'first' < *πρόατος* (created on the pattern of *ὕπατος* 'highest', either de novo or by way of an unetymological distraction of *πρῶτος*; **106.1a**, **398.1**).

a. Homeric forms like *ὁρόω* 'see', *ὁράασθαι* are thought by some to represent an intermediate state between original *ὁράω*, *ὁράεσθαι* and contracted *ὁρῶ*, *ὁρᾶσθαι*; that is, one in which the vowels were assimilated but not yet contracted. This is a reasonable notion, but no such forms are attested in the inscriptions of any dialect. The more probable view is that with the exception of a very few forms, most notably *ἀρόω* 'plow' < **$H_2 er H_3$-y^e/o*-, forms in -*όω* are artificial (**468.3**). Many contracted forms would not scan in traditional poetry; after the contracted forms had become standard, the necessary metrical value was restored in poetic texts by a purely mechanical distraction of *ᾱ* to *αᾱ̆*, *ω* to *οω*, and so on, which were sometimes (but only by chance) the same as the genuine uncontracted forms. Some such procedure must explain the Homeric monstrosity *κραιαίνω* 'accomplish'. The sound laws would have worked as follows: **ḱr̥H_2sn̥-yoH_2* *'bring to a head' > **krāhan-yō* (**106.1**, **99a**, **172**) > **κρᾱαίνω* (**203.2**). Eventually this yields the familiar Att. *κραίν*-, which will not do for the two heavy syllables required for Homeric scansion. Now, redactors who replaced received *αι* with *αιαι* to meet this emergency would have had no qualms about creating unetymological *οω* out of *ω* and *αᾱ̆* out of *ᾱ*.

87. WACKERNAGEL'S LAW.[1] In some compounds the second ingredient begins with a vowel; in a majority of compounds the first ingredient ends with a vowel as well. In G, when either vowel in such a sequence is high, the development is the same as given above, with the proviso that in transparent compounds (say, those beginning with *πολυ*- 'many-'), the vowel is preserved, while in opaque ones it becomes a glide (as in *σήμερον* 'today' < **ki-āmer*-; **199c**). Rigvedic evidence suggests that the loss of syllabicity this way is a post-PIE development.

When neither vowel is high the first vowel is without effect and the second is replaced by its long counterpart. So *στρατο*- + *αγος* (or *στρατε*- + *αγος*) > *στρατᾱγός* 'general', rather than ˣ*στρατωγός* (**86.3**) or ˣ*στρατηγός* (**86.4**). Similarly, *ὠμο*- 'raw' + *εστο*- (**ed-to*-) 'eating' > *ὠμηστής* 'eater of raw flesh', rather than ˣ*ὠμουστής* (**86.3**). This is an early development indeed, as -*ε*- and -*ο*- lengthen to -*η*-, -*ω*-, respectively (rather than to spurious diphthongs, **76**.)

At some point in the development of G the relationship between the two elements was reinterpreted as the truncation of the first vowel and the lengthening of the vowel at the beginning of the second element. Analogous lengthening is therefore found when the second element of a compound begins with a vowel even when the first element does not end with one: *δυσ-ώνυμος* 'ill-omened' (*ὄνυμα*), *δυσ-ώδης* 'evil-smelling' (*ὄζω*), *τρι-ήρης*

---

[1] Another phenomenon known by this name denotes a rule of PIE syntax, namely that enclitic sentential particles always occur second in the clause.

'trireme' (ἐρετμόν 'oar'), παν-ήγυρις '(festal) assembly' (παν(τ)-, ἀγ-). This phenomenon, being analogical, is inconsistent; thus Παναθήναια 'the Panathenaea'.

CONTRACTION OF VOWELS IN LATIN

88. The principal source of vowel sequences for contraction was the loss of intervocalic **-y-* (192), but **-h-* and **-w-* were sometimes lost between like vowels. Some compounds of *dē-*, *pro-*, and *co-* built to words beginning with a vowel show contraction.

1. LIKE VOWELS contract to the corresponding long vowel. So L *trēs* 'three' < **treyes* (G τρεῖς, Ved. *tráyas*); *cōpia* 'abundance' < **ko-opiā*; *nēmō* 'no one' < **nehemō*; *nīl* beside *nihil* (but see 159). The diphthong *ae* absorbs a following *e* or *i*: **pray-emiom* (*emō*) > *praemium* 'gain'; **pray-χafēyō* (*habeō*) > **praehibeō* > *praebeō* 'hold out to, offer'. (Earlier disappearance of the *h* would have given ˣ*prayabeō* > ˣ*prābeō*.)

2. UNLIKE VOWELS. L *i*, *u* do not contract before a following unlike vowel: **tenwis* 'thin' > *tenuis* (three syll.); **mone-way* > *monuī* 'I warned' (66.5). Likewise **fīni-yō* 'limit' (denom. to *fīnis*) > *fīniō* (three syll.). But *bīgae* pl.tant. 'team (of horses)' < **biugā-* < **dwi-yugā-*, and the matters discussed in 68, suggest that forms like *fīniunt* and perhaps even *fīniō* are analogical distractions.

3. REGULAR CONTRACTION. The following contractions are reconstructable with reasonable confidence. Note that they invariably show the quality of the first vowel in the sequence prevailing:

āe > *ā*: **lawdāyesi* > **lawdāes* > *laudās* 'you praise'.

āo > *ā*: **mag-welō* 'wish more' > **magwolō* > *māvolō* > **māolō* > *mālō* 'would rather'.

ao > *ā*: **k*ʷ*awortos* 'fourth' (398.4) > **quaortos* > *quārtus*.

ēa > *ē*: **dē-agō* 'spend time' > *dēgō*.

ēi > *ē*: **dē-habēyō* 'have from, owe' > *dēhibeō* (Plt.) > *dēbeō*. (But *dēinde* 'thereupon' > *deinde*, an artificial spelling: the word scans as two syllables, and is found epigraphically as DENDE, that is *dēnde*, the expected form.)

ea > *ē*: **e-aga(y)* (redupl. perf.; 525.1) 'I drove' > *ēgī* (but perhaps *ēgī* is analogical to *fēcī*). **KreyH̥-* > **krea-wa(y)* > *crēvī*, perf. of *cernō* 'sort'.

oa > *ō*: **ko-agō* > *cōgō* 'drive together'.

oe > *ō*: **ko-emō* > *cōmō* 'arrange'.

iu > *ī*: **dwi-yugāi* (pl.tant.) > **biugai* > *bīgae* 'span (of horses)'.

But *ĕŏ* generally remain: **mon-eyō* 'warn' caus. of **men-* 'have in mind' > L *moneō*; **dē-worssom* (root **wert-*) 'downwards' > *deorsum*, and **sē-worssom* 'apart' > *seorsum* (183, 85).

a. L *nōlō* 'not want' is sometimes cited as a contraction from **ne-wol-*, but the immediate ancestor of *nōl-* is rather **newl-*, with a secondary diphthong **-ew-* from syncope in the thematized forms of the verb (such as **newelō*; see 484.2).

b. The 1sg. of the first conj., as in *laudō* 'I praise', is from **-āyō*, and therefore most authorities teach that **āō* contracts to *ō*. On the basis of the other contractions, however, where the quality of the first vowel always prevails, we would expect *ā* from **āō*. 1sg. **laudā* would have been identical with the imperative (< **lawdāye*), however, and would have been odd for a 1sg. verb besides. On both accounts it would have been an obvious target for leveling to attested *-ō*.

Similarly, 1st conj. subjunctives in *-ē-*, like *laudēs*, are usually traced to some such sequence as **-ā-ē-* < **-ā-yē-*, containing the element seen in subj. (originally opt.) *siēs* 'you may be' < *H_1*s-ye*H_1*-s*. But even while conceding that the origin of the *ē*-subjunctive (543.2) is obscure, it is enough for now to comment that an ATHEMATIC opt. marker is implausible here, which compromises the idea that *-āē-* > **-ē-*.

c. L *sōl* m. 'sun' is a puzzle, one of whose cruces is vowel contraction. The word is a reflex of a PIE nominal root whose existence is certain, but the details of its original form, such as the distribution of ablaut grades, are difficult to work out. Some nom.sg. forms, like Ved. *súvar* n. 'sun' point to **suHel*, albeit with unexpected accent. Other forms, like G **hāwelios* (Hom. ἠέλιος, Att. ἥλιος, Aeol. ἀϝέλιος), point to **se*H_2*wel-* with the addition of a derivational affix. Zero grade **suHl-* is seen in OIr. *súil* /sūλ'/ 'eye' (an ordinary *i*-stem), and in oblique cases of the Ved. root noun *súvar-* (for example Ved. *sūré* < **suHl-ey* dat.). Note that among these etyma even the order of the **H* and the **w* is inconsistent. (In this discussion, *n*-stem forms, 292.2, are ignored.)

L *sōl* m. has usually been taken as superimposable on G **hāwel(ios)*, that is something like **sāwel* > **sāwol* (42.5) > **sāol* > *sōl*. There are two problems with this. First, since the shape **se*H_2*wel-* is otherwise seen only in derived forms, its appearance in a root formation is unexpected. Second, the prevailing pattern of L contractions makes such a development unlikely on its face: **sāwol* must have given L ˣ*sāl*, like **laudānt* < **-āyonti*.

Now, the most original form of the root noun nom. was certainly **su*H_2*el* (= Ved. *súvar*), whence PItal. **suwal* > OL **suwol* (66.1), **suol* (183). The subsequent contraction to L *sōl* is reminiscent of the change of **swo-* to *so-* in for example *soror* and *somnus* (183). The difference in length between **swo-* > *sŏ-* and **suo-* > *sō-* correlates with the difference between *wo* (one mora) and *uo* (two). L of course has examples of *suo-*, but these come from **ewo*: *suos* (*suus*) 'own' orig. *sovos* < **sew-* (Osc. **súvad** abl.).[1]

d. L **ayos*, **ayesis* 'copper' should have given **aos*, **aeses* whence ˣ*ās*, ˣ*āris*; *aēnus* adj. 'bronze' and derivatives seem to reflect PItal. **ayes-(i)no-*, but PreL. **aē-* should have become L *ā-*, like *stā-* 'stand' < **staē-* (475.5). The persistence of *aēnus* is perhaps traceable to 'inconvenient'—not to say embarrassing—homophony: the expected contraction would have resulted in L ˣ*ānus*, homophonous with *ānus* 'anus'. 'Inconvenient homophony' as a factor influencing language change was freely, indeed frivolously, invoked once upon a time. It is not completely certain that language change ever works that way. (This is a different matter altogether from after-the-fact tabuistic deformations, such as pronouncing *con(e)y* to rime with *bony* instead of *honey*, or in minced oaths such as Fr. *par bleu* and NE *dog-gone*.) The conservative pronunciation of *aēnus* might in any case have been available from rustic dialects—something very like it is actually attested in U **ahesnes**. As for monosyllabic *aes*, there is some slight reason for thinking it might reflect an archaic form of the *s*-stem nom.sg. with zero grade of the ending, so **ays* (*H_2*eys*) or

---

[1] A heterodox proposal has traced *sōl* to a PIE **swōl*. Phonologically, this would develop into the L form unproblematically, apart from the question of the whereabouts of the laryngeal in such a reconstruction; but formally, **swōl* resembles nothing in the cognate languages, though it might be defended in connection with the shift from the original neut. to masc. inflection (nom.sg. ***swŏl-s*, along the lines of 126.1).

the like (which would give L *aes* regularly); cf. OL AIRID abl.sg., and even more clearly O AIZNIΩ 'aenea'; see 297.1.

e. Vowel sequences as seen in *coalēscō, coemō, praeesse, deesse,* are found in late compositions or recompositions (*praeesse* after *praesum,* and so on).

PROTHETIC VOWELS IN GREEK

89. In G, a vowel, usually ἐ- but sometimes ἀ- or ὀ-, appears before resonant consonants in word-initial position. Such a vowel invariably develops before an original initial **r*-; less commonly before **l*-, **m*-, **n*-, and **w*-; and never before **y*-. (For the special behavior of **y*-, see 191.) The term *prothetic vowel* is reserved for vowels that have no self-evident PIE source, either in ablaut alternations or as a morphological prefix. Some of them are now generally agreed to reflect word-initial laryngeals (90).

PIE **rudh*- 'red' (zero grade of **rewdh*-; various suffixes) > G ἐρυθρός : L *ruber,* Ved. *rudhirá*- 'bloody', OE *rudig* 'ruddy'.

PIE **reg^w os* neut. 'darkness' > G ἔρεβος : Go. *riqis,* Ved. *rájas*-.

PIE **reǵ*- 'send/go/arrange in a straight line' > G ὀρέγω : Ved *r̥ñjáti,* L *regō.*

PIE **lewdh*- 'increase' > G ἐλεύθερος 'free' : L *līber,* Go. *liudan* 'increase'.

PIE **l̥ng^w h*- 'light' (various grades and suffixes) > G ἐλαχύς 'little' = Ved. *raghú*- 'light' : L *levis* from *n*-less **leg^w hu-i*-; OHG *līhti,* Go. *leihts,* OE *léoht* from **leng^w h-to*-.

PIE **melǵ*- 'milk' > G ἀμέλγω 'milk' trans. : L *mulgeō,* OE *meolcian,* Lith. *mélžu.*

PIE **nomn̥* 'name' > G ὄνομα (Aeol. ὄνυμα) : L *nōmen,* Hitt. *la-a-ma-an,* Ved. *nā́man*-, Go. *namo.*

PIE **wīk̑m̥ti* 'twenty' > G *ἐϝῑκατι > Hom. ἐείκοσι (incorrect distraction for orig. *ἔίκοσι; cf. **86.6a**), Att. εἴκοσι beside Dor. ϝικατι (ϝί-) : L *vīgintī,* Av. *vīsaiti,* OIr. *fiche* /fiχ'e/ (gen. *fichet* /fiχ'əd/).

a. A similar phenomenon is seen in Armenian: *erek* 'evening' (cf. ἔρεβος); *anun* 'name'.

b. There are a few instances of what look like prothetic vowels before obstruents. PIE **dhǵhūs* 'fish' gives G ἰχθῦς for expected ˣχθῦς. More interesting is the following. PIE **dn̥t*-/**dont*- 'tooth' gives L *dent*-, PGmc. **tanþ*- (> OE *tóþ*), Ved. *dant*-, W *dant,* but G ὀδόντ- and Arm. *atamn.* The initial vowels can be explained if PIE 'tooth' is taken to be a participle, built to the zero grade of **ed*- 'eat', and if, additionally, this root is redrawn as **H₁ed*- (see 90). Thus PIE **H₁dont*-, whence the Aeol. form ἔδοντ-, representing the original G shape, while the more familiar G ὀδοντ- is an assimilation from this per 91. A problem with this explanation is that L appears to show *a*- from word-initial **H*- before a stop, as in *apiō* (Paul.Fest.) 'snag' if < **H₁p*-, zero grade of **eH₁p*- (as in *co-ēpī,* Hitt. *e-ip-zi* 'takes').

PIE **bhruH*- '(eye)brow' (a root noun): Ved. *bhrū́*-, OE *brú,* but G ὀφρῦς. OCS has both *brŭvĭ* and *obrŭvĭ,* however, and OIr. *brái* du. 'brows' contrasts with MIr. *abrait* /aβρəd'/ < **abrantī* 'eyelids'. It is easier to say what this fugitive vowel is not than to say what it is: it is hardly a laryngeal reflex. Nevertheless, some authorities reconstruct **H₃bhruH*- (see next).

90. LARYNGALS AND PROTHETIC VOWELS. A number of G prothetic vowels are the presumably regular outcomes of word-initial laryngeals rather than spontaneously generated within G. For example, G ἄ(ϝ)ησι 'blows' was traditionally traced to PIE **wē-* (that is, **weH₁-*) 'blow' with prothetic ἀ-. But now Hitt. *ḫu-u-wa-an-te-eš* 'winds' < **H₂uH₁-ont-* (556) requires instead **H₂weH₁-*, such that G ἀϝ- is seen to come from **H₂w-*.

G ἀείδω 'speak' and Ved. *vāvadīti* 'declares' together point to a reduplicated pres. (451A) **H₂we-H₂wed-* (Indic), **H₂we-H₂ud-* (G), from a root **H₂wed-* (Indic *ā* < **-eH-*; G ϝει < **wew*, 61.1a).[1] Similarly, PIE **nogʷh-/*ongʷh-* 'nail, hoof' (100b); this, the traditional reconstruction, supposes implausibly elaborate ablaut for an underived form, and can be replaced to advantage by **H₃nogʷh-*, whence PG **onoks* > G ὄνυξ (44), L *unguis* (100b). Such an etymon also accounts elegantly for μώνυξ 'single-hooved' (107).

G ἐγείρω 'wake up, rouse', perf. ἐγρήγορα (for *ἤγορα) 'is awake' (**H₁e-H₁gor-H₂e*, a perfectly regular perf. formation, 509, 512), νήγρετος 'unwaking' (**n̥-H₁gr-*), Ved. *jāgā́ra* 'is awake' (for **āgā́ra* < **H₁e-H₁gor-e*), amount to a considerable weight of evidence in favor of a root **H₁ger-*. Such a root is odd-looking from the point of view of normal PIE root structure, however, and some data apparently from the same root are better explained without a laryngeal. L *expergīscor* intr. 'awaken' is generally traced to **eks-pro-grīskᵉ/ₒ-*, a development which **prōgrīsk-* from **pro-H₁grīsk-* would render impossible. And Av. *fraγrīsəmnō* midd.pple. 'awakening' also points away from **pro-Hgr-*.

A laryngeal explanation for this or that particular prothetic vowel in G is however more or less circular when (as commonly) there is little or no corroborative evidence. For example, G ἀνήρ (Ved. *nár-* (*nā́rī-* 'lady'), W *ner* 'hero', L *Nerō*) has been traced to **H₂ner-*. There is no objection to such a reconstruction on its face, but the actual evidence for the initial laryngeal—which is strong evidence, as such things go—is as follows:

1. The G prothetic vowel, as likewise Arm. *air* (89a).

2. The Vedic compound *viśvā́-nara-* '[pertaining to] all men', interpreted as the regular reflex of **wiḱwo-Hner-* with the final vowel of expected *viśva-* 'all' lengthened by the following laryngeal. This evidence is undercut, however, by the existence of other Ved. compounds in *viśvā-*, such as *viśvā-bhū́-* 'omnipresent', whose second element (here **bhuH-* or **bhū-*) certainly did not begin with a laryngeal. (Of course, the combining form *viśvā-* had to come from somewhere, and *viśvā-nara-* is a far from implausible source for it.)

3. GAv. *kamnā-nar-* 'having few men' (cf. *kamnă-fšva-* 'having few cattle'), accounted for by the same developments as in RV *viśvā́nara-*.

---

[1] A troublesome detail in this reconstruction is G **wew*, where the laryngeal should have given **waw* instead.

4. Other Vedic formations supposedly pointing to **Hner-*, but in fact of very doubtful relevance, are *sūnára-*, *sūnṛ̥ta-*, and several forms derived from *sūnar-*. If relevant, these compounds should mean something like 'having good/true/handsome men'; but *sūnára-* and *sūnṛ̥ta-* mean 'glad, joyous, merry'. These are used once in the RV of riches, and several times of Uṣās, the dawn-goddess; but they usually refer TO young men. It is thus hard to believe that these forms have anything to do with PIE **(H₂)ner-* 'man'.

On balance, the reconstruction **H₂ner-* is plausible, and is endorsed here; but the evidence for it is not overwhelming.

For some other forms, a laryngeal source for G prothetic vowels is implausible or even impossible. For example, where some G reflexes of a form have a prothetic vowel and others do not, it is hardly likely that a laryngeal is the source of the vowel. Thus G ἔρση (Att.) next to ἐέρση (Hom.) 'dew, rain-drops', cf. Ved. *varṣá-* 'rain' (and RV *abhrá-varṣa-* 'raining from clouds', not ˣ*abhrā-*). Similarly G ἀμαλδῡ́νω 'soften' with prothetic vowel, next to βλαδύς 'soft' and μέλδω 'melt', all from **meld-* 'soften'.

Positing a laryngeal origin for a given prothetic vowel can create problems faster than it solves them. The reconstruction **H₃nomn-* 'name' is commonly met with, on the basis of G ὄνομα and Arm. *anun*. But this etymon is unsuitable for Hitt. *la-a-ma-an* (a laryngeal would presumably result in an initial *al-* or *ḫal-*), and there is no lengthening in any of the InIr. compounds of **nāman-* (for example RV *saptá-nāman-* 'having seven names'). On the other side may be adduced the old G negative νώνυμνος 'nameless, inglorious' (later ἀνώνυμος), which would be regular from **n̥-H₃nomn-*. But even though this TYPE of formation (see 108) surely arose in forms with word-initial laryngeals, it palpably spread within G. For example νή-κερως 'hornless' is based on the abundantly-attested element **ḱer(H)-* 'head' which nowhere else shows any indication of an initial laryngeal: G κέρας 'horn', Arm. *sar* 'peak'. Since in fact most G privatives with this form of the prefix are like νή-κερως, it follows that no given G example of the formation can be taken as trustworthy evidence for an initial laryngeal. Indeed, even in the case of ὄνομα, some authorities see in the different form *ενυμα 'name', implied by the Lac. name Ενυμακαρτιδας, as well as in the initial *ñ-* in Toch. A *ñem*, B *ñom*, evidence for a different reconstruction, **H₁nomn-*. But in exchange for a simple explanation of *ενυμα this reconstruction has a heavy price: a complicated treatment indeed of the other G forms.[1] That is, we now must suppose that in most parts of the Proto-Greek

---

[1] Arm. *anun* is a problem for this reconstruction: the PIE parallel for **H₁nomn-* is **H₁newn̥* 'nine', whence G ἐννέα, Toch. *ñu*—but Arm. *inn*. If *inn* is the reflex of **H₁n-*, then Arm. *anun* is more consistent with a reconstruction **H₃nomn-*. That can be dealt with (though hardly neutralized) by more or less elaborate additional theories, such as postulating both **H₃neH₃men-* AND a dissimilated form **H₁n̥H₃men-*, as mentioned below.

speech community **enoma* assimilated (91) to **onoma*, and then the privative adj. **nōnomnos* was substituted for **nēnomnos* (which disappeared); the subsequent action of Cowgill's Law (44) yielded ἐνυμα/ὄνυμα/νώνυμνος, with later assimilation back to -*o*- in ὄνομα. This sequence is not impossible, but the great age of Cowgill's Law presents problems. Further embellishments of the etymon (such as **H_3neH$_3$men-*, **H_3nēH$_3$men-*, and by dissimilation also **H_1n̥H$_3$men-*) to explain this or that detail entail more or less great departures from PIE phonological and morphological norms. (See **108a**.)

a. As for the possibility that some of the vowels in question simply grew spontaneously out of nothing, there are well-attested sporadic (as opposed to rule-governed) phenomena in other languages of a like nature: in Welsh, a number of words beginning with *n*- borrowed from L—but not all such words—acquire an unetymological vowel: W *ynifer* (*numerus*), *Aneurin* (earlier and more correctly *Aneirin*) lw. from Lat. *Nerōn*-. And of course there is the well-known case of the systematic growth of prothetic vowels in Western Romance in developments like Sp. *escuela* 'school' < PRom. **scǫla*, *espada* 'sword' < **spata*, and so on.

Some scholars however are inclined to take a prothetic vowel or a long-vowel privative (108) in G as ipso facto proof of a PIE laryngeal, and so reconstruct **H_1legʷh*- 'light', **H_2melǵ*- 'milk' **H_3reǵ*- 'make straight', and so on, despite the lack of corroborating evidence or, as in the case of **H_3nomn*- and **H_1ed*- 'eat' (**108a**), despite difficult inconsistencies in the evidence.

b. Some have seen in the uniform development of a prothetic vowel before PIE **r*- in G reflexes, together with the absence of word-initial *r*- in Hittite, to be evidence that all PIE roots normally reconstructed with word-initial **r*- actually began with a cluster **Hr*-. But if that is so, the extremely high percentage of **H_1*- and the rarity of **H_2*- in such clusters, compared to the preponderance of **H_2* among laryngeals elsewhere in our reconstructions, would be odd. In fact, the spontaneous development of a vocoid element before an initial tap or trill is unremarkable, and in the absence of similar developments before the other resonants would not call for comment. (The relevance of the Hittite matter is unclear in any case: no Hittite reflex of ANY PIE form hitherto reconstructed with initial **r*- has been discovered, with or without evidence for an initial laryngeal.)

c. See also temporal augment, **442**.

VOWEL ASSIMILATION IN GREEK

91. Stable as the vowels of G are by comparison with those of L, the short vowels of G are subject to assimilation to the phonetics of SHORT vowels in adjacent syllables. A resonant (ρ, λ, μ, ν) is almost invariably the intervening consonant, but there are secure instances of assimilation across obstruents.

There are two kinds of evidence for assuming assimilation in a given word. First, the word may be attested in two forms, one with matching vowels and one with different ones; these are sometimes found in different dialects, but occasionally are different chronologically. In these cases, it is generally prudent to assume that the form showing a sequence of different vowels is more original. The second kind of argument rests upon our understanding of the distribution of ablaut grades in PIE (and hence G) morphology. Both kinds of argument are demonstrated by Att. μέγεθος, Ion. μέγαθος 'magnitude'. The certain etymology of the first part of the formation is **meǵH̥$_2$-* (cf. Ved. complexes like *mahitvá-* and *mahimán-* 'greatness', *mahiṣá-* 'great', all from **meǵH̥$_2$-*, with *-h-* < **-ǵH$_2$-* just as in *duhitár-* 'daughter' < **dhugH̥$_2$ter-*) which would give G μεγα-. —G ταναός 'thin' is a case where only ablaut patterns point to assimilation. The form is manifestly a thematization of PIE **tn̥nú-* (100; cf. G τανυ-, combining form), built to a full grade of the stem. This would be either **tn̥newo-* or **tn̥nowo-*, probably the former, giving in the first place G **tanewos*. The inference is that the original *ε (or *ο) has assimilated to the α preceding it. (See also **94b**.)

1. Assimilation over obstruents.

Att. μέγεθος for orig. (Ion.) μέγαθος < **meǵH̥$_2$-*.

Hom. ἐγένοντο 3pl.mid.aor., if from **e-ǵn̥H$_1$-onto*, is assimilated from *ἐγανοντο.

Given Aeol. ἐδοντ- 'tooth' next to the usual G ὀδοντ-, there are two possible analyses. First, if ἐδοντ- is archaic, the usual G ὀδοντ- would be a case of assimilation. If ὀδοντ- is archaic (and Arm. *atamn* and G νωδός 'toothless' hint that it might be), the Aeol. change of ὀδ- to ἐδ- must be traced to some other source, say by ἔδω 'eat'.

Hom. πλαταμών 'flat stone' < *πλεταμών (= Ved. *prathimán-* 'wideness'). (**Pl̥tH̥$_2$mon-* would give the G form directly, but *men*-stems usually take full grade of the root, 128.1.)

2. Assimilation over resonants.

Orig. ὄνυμα (seen in Aeol.) 'name' < PIE **nomn̥* assimilates to familiar ὄνομα; cf. unassimilated (ἀ)νώνυμ(ν)ος 'nameless'.

PIE **temH̥$_2$-* 'cut off' > τεμα-, whence both G τέμαχος 'slice' (unassimilated) and τέμενος 'a piece of land resulting from some partition' (assimilated).

PG **og^{w}elo-* > Cret., Arc. οδελος, Att.-Ion. ὀβελός, later Att. ὀβολός 'obol'; here, in addition to the test of matching vs. different vowels, the originality of the medial ε is vouchsafed by the Cret. development of **g^{w}e* > δε (154.1), and the detail that orig. **og^{w}olos* would probably have given ˣὀγυλός (44, 154.1).

PIE **demH$_2$-* 'tame', **e-demH̥$_2$-* in aor. ἐδάμασ(σ)α < *ἐδεμασσα (δάμνημι).

G τανα(ϝ)ός 'thin' < **tanewos* is discussed above.

In the case of ἕβδομος, ἕβδεμος 'seventh' both the -ε- and the -ο- are secondary developments within the history of G (the PIE etymon was **sptmós*, 398.7). Since an assimilation across -μ- is more likely than one across the cluster -βδ-, it is probable that ἕβδομος is the product of assimilation. (But the case is further complicated by ὄγδο(ϝ)ος 'eighth' in which the -ο- is original; this raises the possibility that ἕβδομος owes its shape to contamination, 387.)

ANAPTYXIS IN LATIN

92. In L an anaptyctic vowel develops regularly within intervocalic *-cl-* of whatever source, and *-bl-*, *-pl-*: it is *i* before *l* exilis and *o* (later *u*) before *l* pinguis (**176a**).
PIE **peH*$_3$*-tlo-* 'drinking utensil' > PItal. **pōtlom* > **pōclom* (**223.2**) > *pōcolom*, *pōculum* 'drinking cup'.
**fak-li-s* > L *facilis* 'easy'; cf. *facul* 'easily' < **fakl* < **fak-li* and *facultās* 'capacity, power' < **fakltāt-* < **fak-li-tāt-*.
OL HERCLE—that is, **Herclēs*—nom.sg. (lw. from G Ἡρακλέης, probably via Etruscan) > **Hercolēs* > *Herculēs*.
PItal. **sta-θlom* 'place of abode', **sta-θlis* 'firm' (**stH̥*$_2$*-*, zero grade of **steH*$_2$*-*) > **stabl-* > L *stabulum*, *stabilis* : Osc. **staflatas** nom.pl. 'statutae'.
PIE **s(y)uH-dhleH*$_2$*-* 'sewing tool' (**193a**) > PItal. **sūθlā* > **sūblā* > L *sūbula* 'shoemaker's awl'.
Habilis 'handy; skillful', *nūbilis* 'marriageable', and similar forms built to verb roots ending in *-b-* are formed like *amābilis* 'lovable', *flēbilis* 'lamentable; weeping'; but expected **habi-bilis* and **nūbi-bilis* undergo haplology.
OL POPLO- > *populus* 'people'. (But NB *templum* < **templo-*, and the given name *Publius*, OL POPLIVS.)

a. Some think L *coclēs* 'one-eyed' owes its lack of anaptyxis to the fact that it is a lw. from G Κύκλωψ 'Cyclops' via Etruscan. As the development of *Herculēs* shows, however, borrowing cannot by itself account for failure to develop anaptyxis. (Nor would we expect it to.)

b. Vowels appear between other consonant sequences on occasion; these sometimes become established, as in *specimen* 'mark (of recognition), token' apparently from **spek-mn̥*. But most are ephemeral, such as *iūgulāns* 'walnut' Paul.Fest. for usual *iūglāns*.

c. Anaptyxis is very rare in G. It explains ἕβδομος, dial. ἕβδεμος 'seventh' (the more original form, **398.7**) < PIE **s(e)ptmos* seen in OPr. *septmas*, OLith. *sēkmas*. (The survival of the cluster **-ptm-* as late as PG is necessary to explain the voicing of the stops, **219**, but see especially **221**.)

SYLLABIC CONSONANTS

93. Liquids and nasals are sounds of such sonority that while they usually function as consonants they may also function as vowels. That is, they may be pronounced so as to form a distinct syllable in the absence of an adjacent vocoid. This is the case in many languages, and not uncommon in NE in the case of *l* and *n*, for example the unaccented syllables of words like *bottle* and *hidden*, in which the vowels appearing in the spelling correspond to no spoken sound.

Such sounds, transcribed **r̥*, **l̥*, **m̥*, and **n̥*, were found in PIE. Together with with **i* and **u* they form a natural class, called the PIE *resonants* or *semivowels*. All six pattern as follows:

(a) They all are related to the consonants **r*, **l*, **m*, **n*, **y*, and **w* in the same way, namely, the consonantal forms occur adjacent to a vowel, the syllabic forms elsewhere. Thus the PIE acc.sg. ending was *_-m_ after a vowel, *_-m̥_ after a cons., just as the loc.sg. ending (257.11) was *_-y_ after a vowel, *_-i_ after a cons.

(b) They alternate with full grades, *^{e}/_or_, *^{e}/_ol_, *^{e}/_om_, *^{e}/_on_, *^{e}/_oy_, and *^{e}/_ow_, respectively, as will be made clear in the discussion of ablaut (110–29).

A more exact account of the distribution of the SYLLABIC FORMS of the resonants (*_r̥_, *_l̥_, *_m̥_, *_n̥_, *_i_, and *_u_) is as follows:

1. between two obstruents, or between a word boundary and an obstruent: *_(d)ḱm̥tóm_ 'hundred'; *_podm̥_ acc.sg. 'foot'; *_n̥-podos_ 'footless'.

2. Between a resonant and a following obstruent, laryngeal, or word boundary: *_wl̥kʷos_ 'wolf'; *_likʷtós_ 'left (over)'; *_wl̥H$_2$no-_ 'wool'; *_bheroym̥_ 1sg. opt. 'I would carry'; *_nomeni_ (or better *_n̥meni_) 'name' loc.sg.; *_piHwr̥_ 'fat'.

The relative sonority of two resonants between two non-resonants is immaterial; the second is always the syllabic, hence *_ym̥_ rather than ×_im_, *_wr̥_ rather than ×_ur_. There are however two exceptions to this rule, or rather classes of exceptions: (a) the acc.sg. and pl. of _i-_ and _u_-stems are *_-im_, *_-ims_; *_-um_, *_-ums_ (rather than regular *_-ym̥_, *_-wm̥_); and (b) zero grades of _n_-infix presents, wherein the _-n-_ is exclusively consonantal: so *_pl̥nH$_1$-_ 'fill', *_yung-_ 'yoke', *_linkʷ-_ 'leave', *_H$_2$indh-_ 'kindle' (instead of ×_pln̥H$_1$-_, ×_iwn̥g-_, ×_l̥yn̥kʷ-_, ×_H$_2$yn̥dh-_, as required by the usual rules).

3. Between a word boundary and a following obstruent or laryngeal: *_ukʷtós_, pple. of *_wekʷ-_ 'utter'; *_r̥Hǵ-_ zero grade of *_reH$_1$ǵ-_ 'be strong' (RV _ūrj-_); *_n̥Hwe(-óm)_ acc.du. 'us two' (Ved. _āvā́m_).

4. Between a laryngeal and an obstruent or a word boundary, thus: *_pl̥H$_1$u-_ 'many', *_Hr̥ḱo-_ 'bear', *_ḱr̥Hsron-_ 'hornet', *_gʷl̥Hen-_ 'acorn'.

94. When syllabic liquids and nasals occur before vowels they show reflexes indistinguishable from *_r̥r_, *_l̥l_, *_n̥n_. Thus PIE *_ten-_ 'stretch' underlies both *_tn̥nú-_ (or *_tn̥ú-_) 'thin' and the _new_-suffix pres. *_tn̥-new-_ 'stretch'; these give Ved. _tanú-_ adj., _tanute_ 3sg.mid.; and G τανυ- combining form, Hom. τάνυται respectively. L _semel_ < *_semēl_ < *_sm̥-meH$_1$lom_ 'one time' shows the same thing. Additionally, the development of the PIE ordinals reveals that **_tri-ó-_ 'third' was at some level of reality *_triyó-_, the source of the element *_-yó-_ (by metanalysis) that played a role in the further development of the ordinal system (397).

Such morpheme shapes as *_tn̥nu-_ and *_gʷr̥ru-_ 'heavy' are the result of leveling analogy (of PIE date) from forms where the syllabic resonant is phonologically proper, as in the feminine stems *_tn̥w-iH$_2$-_ and *_gʷr̥w-iH$_2$-_. (For a different, and less tenable, explanation see 179–80.) However, in most cases of what superficially looks like a syllabic resonant before a vowel, the real explanation is the presence of a laryngeal between the syllabic resonant and the following vowel, as in two of the examples in 93.4, above.

a. The choice of *_-n̥no-_, say, vs. *_-n̥o-_ is purely notational. The latter would have the trifling advantage of underlining the distinction at the morphological level between say the simplex *tn̥u- vs. the verb *tn̥-new-; but there is never any such difference at the phonological level. In this work the notation of the type *-n̥no- is favored for all purposes, as being parallel to the glide sequences *-iyo-, *-uwo-.

b. Some authorities avoid all prevocalic syllabic resonants by proposing *tn̥Hu- and *g^wr̥Hu-, for example; but while these reconstructions may serve to explain the prevocalic syllabic resonants, they create serious problems elsewhere. L *tenuis* is if anything harder to explain from such a basis (*tn̥HwiH_2- should have given ×*nāvis*); Ved. *tanomi* < *tn̥-new-, Skt. *tanvī-* f. 'thin', *tántu-* 'thread', *tántra-* 'warp' (on a loom), and pple. *tatá-* < *tn̥-tó- are impossible from a root *tenH-. The chief secondary benefit of such a construct would be the slender one that G ταναϝός could be traced directly to *tn̥H_2ewo-.

Evidence bearing on *g^wr̥Hu- is meager by comparison, but the evidence against a laryngeal is better than the evidence in favor of one.

95. TABLE OF CORRESPONDENCES OF SYLLABIC LIQUIDS AND NASALS.

PIE	Att.-Ion.	Myc., Aeol. Arc.-Cyp., etc.	L	Ved.	Lith.	PGmc.
*r̥C	αρ, ρα	ορ, ρο	or	r̥	ir	*ur
*r̥(H)V	αρ	ορ	r(a)	ir, ur	ir	*ur
*l̥C	αλ, λα	ολ, λο	ol	r̥	il	*ul
*l̥(H)V	αλ	ολ	l	ir, ur	il	*ul
*m̥C	α	α	em	a	im	*um
*m̥(H)V	αμ	αμ	em	am	im	*um
*n̥C	α	α	en	a	in	*un
*n̥(H)V	αν	αν	en	an	in	*un

(V = any vowel; C = any consonant NOT A LARYNGEAL; see 103-9.)

1. The conditions governing the appearance in Greek of αλ and αρ vs. λα and ρα have not been determined. In some words the difference is dialectal, but not in most. The following generalizations seem to be valid:

The development in final position is -αρ (there are no examples of *-l̥).

Before another resonant the regular form is -αρ-, -αλ-, as in ἀρν- 'lamb' < *wr̥n-.

Medially before stops, in isolated forms the vowel grows after the liquid, so πλατύς 'broad'. But where full-grade vowels stand before the liquid, it has been claimed that the zero grade vowel will usually be found there too, as καρδίᾱ 'heart', old nom.sg. κῆρ (whence the adv. κῆρι 'heartily'). In these instances there is often competition between forms, as Hom. κραδίη next to later καρδ-. This explanation is not always wholly convincing, however: it is hard to credit the rare θέρσος n. 'audacity' (full grade forms of this root are rare in IE generally) with the replacement of θρασ- by θαρσ- in all but a few forms.

The same trend to replace -ρα- with -αρ- is seen in roots with prevocalic syllabic resonants, as *der(H)- 'flay': Hom. has once δρατός 'flayed', early replaced by δαρτός under the influence of aor. ἐδάρην, perf. δέδαρμαι as well as of pres. δέρω.

2. In Indo-Iranian a vowel grows in front of a PIE syllabic resonant before a vowel—that is, a PInIr. vowel; these stem from sequences like *n̥HV and *n̥-nV as well as *n̥V (where V = any vowel).

The vowel is *a* before nasals (and therefore masquerades as a full grade). For the liquids, excrescent *i* is the neutral development, but *u* is found in the environments of

PInIr.—not PIE—labials. So *g^wr̥Hi-* 'mountain' > Proto-Satem **gr̥Hi-* > *girí-*, **tr̥H*$_2$*-enti* 3pl. 'attain' > Ved. *tiranti* (cf. **tr̥H*$_2$*-nó-* pple. > Ved. *tīrṇá-*). Cf. **wr̥rú-* 'broad' > PInIr. **wurú-* > Ved. *urú-*, **g^wr̥rú-* 'heavy' > Ved. *gurú-* (the crucial labial environment follows, here; NB *girí-* < **g^wr̥Hi-*, above), **pl̥H-es* n.pl. 'cities' > Ved. *púras* (cf. **pl̥Hs* nom.sg. > Ved. *pū́r*).

3. Note that the G and InIr. developments overall are far more similar to one another than to any group beside.

Some authorities feel that in reflexes of **R̥HV* in G (where **R̥* = any syllabic resonant), the vowel that grows before the resonant is determined by the laryngeal following, so **-l̥H*$_1$*e-* would give -ελε-, **-l̥H*$_3$*e-* would give -ολο-, and so on. Some etymologies seem to support this, as ἔμολον 'came' (aor. of βλώσκω; see **106.2**) < **(e-)ml̥H*$_3$*-*^{e}*/o-*. But more significant are such forms as καλέω < **kl̥H*$_1$*-ey*^{e}*/o-*, πάρος 'before' < **pr̥H*$_3$*es* or **pr̥H*$_3$*os* (**pr̥H*$_2$*os* or **pr̥H*$_2$*es* would have given ×πάρας, 48), and γαλέη 'weasel' < **gl̥H*$_1$*-* (98), which combine to suggest that forms of the ἔμολον type arose via assimilation or analogy. Also, see **106.2A**, below.)

4. In Baltic, Slavic, and Germanic, the more familiar dialects of Greek, and for prevocalic **r̥*, **l̥* in Indic, the vowel that grows adjacent to the syllabic resonant is distinct from the PIE ablauting vowels (110); here reflexes of syllabic resonants and full grades can easily be told apart.[1] In L, however, the *e* and *o* from the syllabic nasals and liquids, respectively, counterfeit the *e-* and *o*-grades of PIE ablaut. The only way to tell whether a given L *en*, say, continues an *e*-grade or a zero grade is by comparison with unambiguous cognate forms in other languages, together with consideration of the usual distribution of ablaut grades in particular formations.

EXAMPLES. In L *genus*, the equivalence in form and meaning with the unambiguous *e*-grade of G γένος points to an original *e*-grade here, as does the morphology (*e*-grade is the norm for roots in neut. *s*-stems). For L *centum* 'hundred', G ἑκατόν, Ved. *śatám*, OE *hund*, Lith. *šim̃tas* point unambiguously to a syllabic nasal (**m̥* in this case) rather than a full grade in the first syllable, and the principle of parsimony leads us to trace the cognate L *en* to the same source.

The case of PIE 'tooth' demands subtler reasoning, as the cognates include: unambiguous *o*-grades (G ὀδοντ-); unambiguous zero grades (Go. *tunþus*); forms that might be either *e-* or *o*-grade (Ved. *dántam* acc.). But L *dent-* might be *e-* or zero grade. The simplest explanation for all this is an original root noun paradigm with alternation between *o-* and zero grade forms, say **donts* or **dōnts* nom.sg., **dontm̥* acc.sg., **dn̥tos* gen./abl., and so on. Except for Indo-Iranian and Proto-Germanic, each language generalized one of the two stem forms. If this line of reasoning is valid the etymon of L *dent-* can only be **dn̥t-*.

---

[1] Note that the developments of Baltic, Slavic, and Germanic are closely parallel, namely the growth of a uniform high vowel before all syllabic liquids and nasals, and furthermore differ from the developments of all other IE branches.

In Baltic, reflexes *-ur-*, *-ul-*, and so on (with parallel details in Slavic) are also found. No proposal for the factors determining whether the anaptyctic vowel will be front or back has won general approval.

5. Two of the numerous special developments of short vowels in West Germanic are: **u* (the original vowel in the reflexes of all syllabic liquids and nasals) becomes **o* before **a* or **ō* in the following syllable; and becomes *ü* (variously written) before *ī* or *y* after a following consonant. Thus PGmc. **fullaz* > OHG *fol(l)* 'full', but **fullyana*^{n} 'fill' trans. > OE *fyllan*, OHG *fullen* (NHG *füllen*).

96. PIE **r̥* before consonants and finally:
PIE **ḱr̥d-* 'heart' (root **ḱerd-*) > G καρδίᾱ, κραδίη (Pamphylian κορζια), L *cor* (< **kord*, 237.7), gen. *cordis* : OIr. *cride*, Lith. *širdìs*. (The Gmc. forms, such as OE *heorte*, have *e*-grade.)
PIE **tr̥s-* 'be dry' (root **ters-*): **tr̥s-to-* > L **torstos* > *tostus* 'dried out' (231.3) : Ved. *tr̥ṣitá-* pple. of *tŕ̥ṣyati* 'thirsts', OE *þurst*.
PIE **dhr̥s-* 'dare, be brave' (root **dhers-*) > G θάρσος, θράσος 'courage', θρασύς, θαρσύς 'bold' (Lesb. θορσέως 'boldly') : Ved. *dhr̥ṣ-* 'dare', OE *dorste* pret. of *durran* 'dare'.
PIE **pr̥ḱ-sḱ*^{e}*/o-* 'ask' (root **preḱ-*) > **porskō* > L *poscō* : Ved. *pr̥cchati* (NHG *forschen* 'search, inquire, investigate' is a denominative, but is ultimately related).
PIE **H*$_{2}$*ŕ̥tḱo-* (or **ŕ̥tḱo-*) 'bear' > G ἄρκτος, L *ursus* (< **ortk-*, but with problems; see 235.1) : Ved. *ŕ̥kṣa-*, W *arth*, and perhaps Hitt. *har-ta-ag-ga-* (it occurs in a list of beasts of prey; its meaning not more certainly known, but formally at least it is an excellent fit; see 235.1).
PIE *yek*^{w}*r̥(t)* 'liver' > G ἧπαρ (ἡ- for ἐ- unexplained), L *iecur* (via **-or*) : Ved. *yakŕ̥t*.

Before vowels:
PIE **g*^{w}*r̥rú-* 'heavy' > G βαρύς : Ved. *gurú-*, Go. *kaurus* (PGmc. **k*^{w}*urus*). See **94b**.
PIE **pr̥H*$_{2}$*ey* or **pr̥H*$_{3}$*ey* 'before' (dat. of a root noun?) > L *prae*, OIr. *ar*^{L}, Go. *faura*.[1]
PIE **pr̥H*$_{3}$*os* or **pr̥H*$_{3}$*es* gen./abl. 'in front' > G πάρος : Ved. *purás*.

a. Myc. shows a mixture of reflexes of syllabic liquids, now agreeing with the relic dialects of Aeolic and Arcado-Cypriot (**14**) in showing *or* from **r̥*: *a-no-* (*anor-*) as the first element in male names = ἀνδρα- (both from **H*$_{2}$*nr̥-*); *to-pe-za* (*torpeźa*) 'table' (= τράπεζα), now showing *ar*: *tu-ka-ta-si* (*t*^{h}*ugatarsi*) 'to daughters' (= θυγατράσι).

97. L reflexes of prevocalic **r̥* are disputed. Some see evidence for *-ar-*, some for *-or-* (as in preconsonantal position).

1. Evidence for *-ar-*: L *pariō* 'give birth' (full grade in Lith. *periù* 'brood,

---

[1] G παραί is a perfect formal fit, but the semantics—'beside', essentially—are inappropriate. OIr. *ar* is slightly problematical in this context. Its early and regular attestation is *air*, that is /aρ'/, agreeing with Gaul. *are-*; the latter might be *arē-* < PCelt. **arai-*, though the syncope already evident in Caesar's *Armoricī* (cf. *Aremorica*) is easiest to understand if the vowel was originally short.

hatch') and *carō*, gen. *carnis* 'meat' orig. 'cut' (G *κείρω* 'cut off' of hair, 'shear'; aor. pass. *ἐκάρην*).

2. Evidence for *-or-*: L *morior* 'die' (= Ved. *mriyase* 2sg. < **mr̥-ye-*).[1]

Now, regarding *pariō*, a zero grade is not expected in a transitive **-y^e/o*-stem in the first place (NB the Lith. cognate). The whole discussion is beside the point, however: if there was **r̥* in the picture, it was followed by **y*, not a vowel. The same is true of *morior*.

The **r̥* of *carō* MIGHT have been prevocalic in certain cases (of which, in L, only the nom.sg. survives); elsewhere it was preconsonantal, and if leveling were to disturb the inherited paradigm **karō* nom.sg., **kornes* gen.sg., (? acc.sg. **kronem*) analogy should have favored the *-or-* of the oblique stems (one imagines that the word was relatively rarely the subject of a verb, for example).

In fact, the critical data are none of the above forms; they are L *prae* (vid.sup.), and *gravis* 'heavy', which must somehow continue the PIE **gʷr̥ru-* (remodeled in Italic, as were all *u*-stem adjectives, into an *i*-stem, 342). If the above alternatives were valid, the expected L reflex of **gʷr̥ru(i)-* would be ˣ*vor(u)vis* or (less likely) ˣ*var(u)vis* (154.2; the cluster **gʷrV-* must be fairly old to give L *gr-*). The details of the formation of the rest of the word are obscure, but the obvious inference is that **gʷr̥-* before a vowel gives L *gra-*.

Another, more uncertain, datum is L *trāns* 'across', U *tra(f)*, *traha(f)* /trāf/, usually interpreted as a participle; among IE languages a pres. participle would be remarkable as the source of a preposition, but the chief demerit is that the supposed participle is from a verb **trāō* < **tr̥H₂-y^e/o-* (root **terH₂-* 'cross') unattested in Italic or in any other IE language.[2] In Ved. *tirás* 'through, across' we have the functional equivalent of L *trāns*, also from the root **terH₂-*, but formally much more appropriate, namely the abl. or gen. of a noun (or so it appears; the acc.pl. is also a possibility, and **tr̥Hm̥s* would give L *trāns* and Ved. *tirás* alike by the operation of sound laws). The details remain uncertain, but an attested form like Ved. *tirás* < **tr̥H₂ós* or the like is the proper starting point, rather than a hypothetical verb-stem, and PItal. **tra-* from prevocalic **tr̥-* is a likely component of the history of L *trāns*.

98. PIE **l̥* before consonants:

PIE **ml̥dú-* 'soft' > G *βλαδύς* (224.1), *ἀμαλδύνω* 'soften' (*ἀ-* prothetic, 89), L *mollis* < **molwis* (185.2) < **moldwi-* : Ved. *mr̥dú-*, NE *molten*.

PIE **pl̥tH₂ú-* 'broad, flat' > G *πλατύς* : Ved. *pr̥thú-* (fem. *pr̥thivī́-* < **pl̥tH₂w-iH₂-* specifically 'earth, ground'[3] = G *Πλαταιαί* 'Plataea' (in Boeotia), W *lladaw* 'Brittany').

PIE **telH₂-* 'carry' zero grade in *n*-infix present **tl̥-ne-H₂-* > L *tollō* (thematized) 'lift'. G cognates in *ταλα-* from this root that are not wholly secondary formations are nearly all assimilated from **τελα-*. A possible

---

[1] Ved. *-riy-* is the normal reflex of PInIr. **-r̥y-*.

[2] L *intrāre* 'to enter', sometimes cited as evidence for **trāō*, has been alternatively explained as a denominative based on *intrā*, like such forms as *iterāre* 'repeat' from *iterum*, *superāre* 'to rise above' from *super*.

[3] The fem. of the adjective is for some reason actually transmitted as *pr̥thvī́-* in the Rigveda; but analysis of the meter reveals that it usually must be scanned *pr̥thivī́-*, and always can be.

exception is *τάλαντον* if a thematization of the aor. pple. **tl̥*H_2*-ont-* (48).

Before vowels (including **H* plus vowel).
There is a measure of difficulty about all of the examples. The interpretation favored here is that **l̥* before vowels became L *l*:
PIE **ǵl̥Howo-* or **ǵl̥Hewo-* 'husband's unmarried sister' > G *γάλοως* (see 321.3a), L *glōs* : Slav. **zŭly*.
PIE ***g^w*l̥*H_2*en-* 'acorn' > G *βάλανος*, L *glāns*, st. *gland-* : Lith. *gìlė*.
PIE **gl̥*H_1*ey-* 'small rodent' > G *γαλέη* 'weasel, marten', L *glīs*, *glīris* 'dormouse' : Skt. *girí-* 'mouse' (only in Skt. lexical materials).
PIE **dl̥*H_2^{e}*/okt-* 'milk' > **dlakt-* > *lac*, *lactis*; cf. G *γάλα*, *γάλακτος*. (The difficult 'milk' words have been variously explained.)

Against this view is L *palma* 'palm (hollow) of the hand', G *παλάμη*, in which *palma* is taken as a syncope of an earlier **palamā* as a reflex of **pl̥*H_2*eme*H_2*-* or **pl̥*H_2*ome*H_2*-* and therefore directly superimposable on G *παλάμη*. The supposed syncope is reasonable, but OHG, OS *folma* 'hand', OE *folm*, OIr. *lám* point to **pl̥HmeH*$_2$*-*, not **pl̥*H_2*eme*H_2*-*, which should have given OHG $^{\times}$*folama* or the like and OIr. $^{\times}$*ilam*. If the L form is not simply a borrowing from G, Ital. **palamā* constitutes the only evidence for L *-alV-* < **-l̥HV-*. See also **112a**.

99. PIE **m̥* before consonants and finally:
PIE **dékm̥t* 'ten' (389.10) > G *δέκα*, L *decem* : Ved. *dáśa*, Go. *taihun*, Lith. *dẽšimt*.
PIE **(d)ḱm̥tóm* 'hundred' > G *ἑ-κατόν*, L *centum* : Ved. *śatám*, Go. *hunda* (pl.), Lith. *šim̃tas*.
PIE ***g^w*m̥-* (zero grade of ***g^w*em-* 'set out') in ***g^w*m̥-y*^{e}*/o-* > G *βαίνω* (< ***g^w*an̥yō*, 203.2), L *veniō*.
PIE ***g^w*m̥-ti-* 'step; point of departure' > G *βάσις*, L *(con)ventiō* : Ved. *gáti-* 'gait', Go. *ga-qumþs* 'con-ventiō'.
PIE **-m̥* acc.sg. > G *-α*, L *-em* in *πόδα*, *pedem* : PGmc. **-u*^{n}.
PIE **-m̥s* acc.pl. > G *-ας*, L **-ens* > *-ēs* : Ved. *-as*, Go. *-uns*.

Before vowels:
PIE **dhǵhm̥mon-* 'earthling' (235.1) > OL *hemō* 'man' Paul.Fest. (*homō* 42.6), **ne-hemō* > *nēmō* 'no one' : Go. *guma*, OLith. *žmuo*.
PIE **sm̥-me*H_1*lom* 'one time' > **semēl* > *semel* (83.3).
PIE **dhǵhm̥m-ey* dat. > G **χαμεί* > *χαμαί* (91.2) 'on the ground'.

a. In G, as in Indo-Iranian, **m̥* or **n̥* followed by another resonant generally yields G *αμ/αν*, not *α*: PIE **ḱm̥-ne-H-*, *n*-infix pres. of **ḱemH-* 'work (hard)' > G *κάμνω*, not $^{\times}$*κάνω*; and **ḱm̥n*H_2*-* > Skt. *śamnīte* not $^{\times}$*śanīte*. PIE ***g^w*m̥-y*^{e}*/o-*, pres. of ***g^w*em-* 'set out' > ***g^w*amyō* > ***g^w*anyō* > G *βαίνω*. PIE **nomn̥-y*^{e}*/o-* 'name, call' > PG **onoman-y*^{e}*/o-* > G *ὀνομαίνω*.

b. In derived feminine stems in **-e*H_2*-* (262-6) and **-ye*H_2*-/*-i*H_2*-* (268-9), according to the usual behavior of resonants, the forms of the acc.sg. should have been **-e*H_2*m̥* and **-i*H_2*m̥* respectively, likewise acc.pl. **-e*H_2*m̥s*, **-i*H_2*m̥s*. There is not a particle of evidence in IE languages for such a configuration, however: all attested forms imply *-H_2m rather than *-H_2m̥. This may be the result of leveling, though it would be unusual for such a process to leave no traces anywhere of the expected outcomes; and besides, the discrepancies between the endings of the 'long vowel' stems and the o-stems, the most obvious source of influence, provide few or no patterns for the needed analogical proportion. Some authorities have therefore proposed that the equivalent of *-ām is simply the regular reflex of *-eH_2m̥ in all IE languages; but that is no more probable. (One remembers for example that opt. *bheroym̥ > PGmc. *beraju^n > Go. bairau; the failure of say *tewteH_2m̥ to become Go. ˣþiudau instead of attested þiuda is hard to understand.)

It is likely that in fact the forms were **-eH_2m, **-iH_2m and the like to begin with, and the histories of PIE *dyēm acc.sg. 'sky' < **dyewm and *g^wōm 'cow' acc.sg. < **g^wowm (324) point to a period in the prehistory of PIE when the syllabicity of resonants was somewhat different from 'classical' PIE (93).

100. PIE *n̥ before consonants and finally:

PIE *-n̥to 3pl.mid. endings after consonants (beside *-nto after vowels) > Hom., Hdt. -αται, -ατο, as for example φεροίατο 'may they carry for themselves'.

PIE *nomn̥ 'name' > G ὄνομα, L nōmen : Ved. nā́ma n.sg., OIr. ainm /an'm'/ < *anmen < PCelt. *anman (as if from ˣn̥mn̥, that is, with zero grade of stem leveled from, say, the gen.sg. *n̥men-s). Hitt. la-a-ma-an. (L ō by folk etymology with (g)nō- 'know', NB cognōmen with likewise unetymological -g-; Skt. ā < *o is regular, 36.4; Hitt. l for n by dissimilation.)

PIE *tn̥-tó- pple. of *ten- 'stretch' > G τατός, L tentus (older than tēnsus as vouchsafed by iterat. tentāre) : Ved. tatá-.

Before vowels:

PIE *tn̥nú- 'thin' (from *ten- 'stretch') full grade *tn̥new- thematized as *τανεϝός > G τανα(ϝ)ός (91.2) 'long (and thin)', L tenuis 'thin' : Ved. tanú-, OE þynne (*þunwi-), OCS tĭnŭkŭ.

a. Some evidence suggests that in G, a syllabic liquid or nasal following a laryngeal develops into -ερ-, -αλ-, -ομ-, and the like, depending on the laryngeal: *H_1r̥-sḱ^e/o- > G ἔρχεται 'goes', Hitt. a-ar-aš-ki-iz-zi /arskitsi, -etsi/, Ved. r̥cchánti 3pl. 'encounter'. Similarly *H_3n̥bh-l̥- 'nave(l)' > G ὀμφαλός; and G ἄρκτος 'bear' (see 235.1) might confirm the etymon *H_2r̥tḱ- rather than *H_1r̥tḱ- or *H_3r̥tḱ-.

This suggestion is particularly attractive for ἔρχομαι: the suffix *-sḱ^e/o- calls for zero grade of the root, and the Hitt. a-ar- might confirm a root-initial laryngeal. But if G ὀρχέομαι 'dance' is a cognate intensive (456.3), then ἐρχ- is presumably a root. Cognate languages support—weakly—just such a root *ergh- (as seen in OIr. eirg 'go!' ? < *erghe), which provides an alternative etymology for ἔρχομαι.

b. PIE *ong^{w}h- (or *H_3eng^{w}h-) 'nail, hoof' is commonly cited as the etymon for L unguis (45.1); but elsewhere the evidence points to zero grade *n̥g^{w}h- (OIr. ingen) or full grade *nog^{w}h- (OE nægl 'nail', OCS noga 'foot', Lith. nãgas 'nail, claw'). G ὄνυξ shows the latter, with prothetic ὀ- probably from *H_3- (90, and NB μώνυχες 'single-hooved' < *sm̥-H_3nog^{w}h-, 107.1); for -υ- < *-o- see 44.

As for unguis < *H_3^{e}/ong^{w}h-, two different full grades in an underived noun are unexpected. Skt. áṅghri- 'foot', often cited in this connection, is immaterial: the original meaning of the word is 'root'. The likeliest source for L unguis therefore is a zero grade form, but *n̥ before a dorsal consonant should first give *en and then *in (41.1), as in L *inguen* 'groin' < **enguen* < **n̥g*^{w}- (cf. G ἀδήν 'gland'). L *unguis* has therefore been differently explained as the regular outcome of **H*$_3$*n̥g*^{w}*h*-.

c. It is disputed whether **n̥* before vowels becomes L *en* (as before consonants) or *an*. Proponents of the latter view take L *maneō* 'remain' from **mn̥*- (full grade **men*- in G μένω); and they see L *canis* 'dog' (PIE **ḱwon*-) as somehow traceable to a prevocalic **n̥*. However, (a) prevocalic **n̥* was not a part of the PIE paradigm for 'dog', and (b) *canis* is too odd in too many ways to be used as evidence for anything. *Maneō* too is poor evidence. First, there are many verbs in L with unexpected -*ă*- vocalism (*tangō* and *frangō*, for example). More to the point, the *ē*-stem statives in L (**452**, **477.2**) form a class well-defined in form and meaning, in which *a*-vocalism is very general: *habeō, pateō, iaceō, placeō, candeō*, and so on, which may have influenced expected **meneō*. By comparison, both the morphology and phonology of OL *hemō* (> *homō*) and L *tenuis* are straightforward.

d. The original outcome of **N̥* in PG seems not to have been identical to PG **a* straightaway. At any rate it did not uniformly fall together with it. In Myc. the normal reflex is *a*, as in other varieties of G: *a-ki-ti-to* 'untilled' (Hom. ἄκτιτος), *a*$_2$-*te-ro* (hateros) 'next, following, other' < **sm̥-teros*. But after a labial the reflex is usually *o*: *pe-mo* 'seed' < **sper-mn̥* n. (= σπέρμα), only occasionally *pe-ma*. This outcome is reminiscent of Arc. δεκο 'ten', ἑκοτον '100' for usual δέκα, ἑκατόν, < **dekm̥t*, **(d)km̥tom*, and even in Att. εἴκοσι '20' (cf. εἰκάς '20th day' and Dor. ϝῖκατι).

101. SYLLABIC LARYNGEALS. Much like the resonants, the PIE laryngeals (**165-7**) occurred in both consonantal and syllabic form. The syllabic form was found:

1. Between obstruents, and between an obstruent and a word boundary: **pH̥*$_2$*tēr* 'father'; **dhH̥*$_1$-*tó*- pple. of **dheH*$_1$-'put'; **meǵH̥*$_2$ 'big' nom.sg.neut.; *-*mosdhH̥*$_2$ 1pl. mid.

After a resonant or **s*, a word-final laryngeal dropped, with compensatory lengthening of the preceding vowel. Thus **-*osH*$_2$ *s*-stem nom./acc.pl.n. > *-*ōs* (**297.3**); **-*onH*$_2$ *n*-stem nom./acc.pl.n., **-*onH*$_1$ nom./acc.du.m.f. both > *-*ōn* (**282a**).

2. Between a consonant and a following (consonantal) resonant: **dm̥nH̥*$_2$*mós* 'we tame' (**demH*$_2$-); **pl̥tH̥*$_2$*w*-*íH*$_2$- f. 'broad'.

Whatever their phonetic features were, laryngeals must have been less sonorant than any resonant: in sequences of a resonant and a laryngeal between two consonants, it is always the resonant that is syllabic. (Cf. the different rule for sequences of resonants, **93.2**.) Thus the fem. of **pl̥H*$_1$*ú*- 'many' is **pl̥H*$_1$*wíH*$_2$-, not $^\times$*plH̥*$_1$*wíH*$_2$-; the pple. of **ǵenH*$_1$- 'beget' is **ǵn̥H*$_1$*tó*-, not $^\times$*ǵnH̥*$_1$*tó*-. This is one of the sharpest departures of the laryngeal theory from the theory that PIE schwa belonged to the class of vowels: reconstructions of the type **plə*- and **ǵnə*- were not merely possible in the systems that included the vowel *ə; they seemed to explain certain facts well. Such constructs cannot be converted into laryngeal terms by replacing *ə with **H̥*, however, because **plH̥*$_1$- and **ǵnH̥*$_1$- are impossible (with one limited exception; **a**, below). Data seeming to point to such etyma, when not resulting from misinterpretation, are the result of secondary developments (leveling, back formation, and the like) within the histories of the daughter languages. Thus G πίμπλαμεν 'we fill' to πίμπλημι is not actually from **pi-plə-mos* (still less from *pi-plH̥-mos*), but arose within G by analogy with such genuinely inherited paradigms as ἵστημι : ἵσταμεν (including earlier stages of paradigms that were later remodeled, such as expected PG **kamnāmi*, **kamnamen* < **ḱm̥-ne-H$_2$-mi*, **ḱm̥-n-H̥$_2$-mos*, replaced by thematized κάμνω). The original form replaced by πίμπλαμεν would have been *πί(μ)πλημεν < **pi-pl̥H$_1$-mos* (or perhaps even *πι(μ)πόλιμεν, per **106.2a**).

a. The *n*-infix pres. stems to roots ending in a laryngeal are an exception to the rule against **RH̥*. The *n*-infix is always consonantal, hence **plnH$_1$-mós* 'we fill' (root **pleH$_1$-*) would be syllabified **pl̥nH̥$_1$-mós*. Normally the *RR̥* principle (**93.2**) and the relatively lesser sonority of laryngeals would have agreed on an outcome ×*pln̥H$_1$-mós*.

102. In G, *H̥$_1$ > ε, *H̥$_2$ > α, *H̥$_3$ > ο. In L, all syllabic *H̥ becomes in the first instance **a*; this is subject to the usual weakenings and syncope set forth in **65-75**.

PIE **dhH̥$_1$-tó-* pple. of **dheH$_1$-* > G θετός, L *factus* (PItal. **θak-* for **θa-*) : Ved. *hitá-* (from **dhitá-*, **144.3**). From the same root form are for example L *refectus*; without the analogical *-c-*, *con-di-tus* 'founded' and similar forms (**479.2**), from *-θa- < **-dhH̥$_1$-*.

**ǵenH̥$_1$-tor-* 'begetter' > G γενέτωρ Hdt., L *genitor* (via **genatōr*) : Ved. *janitár-*.

PIE **H$_2$onH̥$_1$-mo-* 'breath' from **H$_2$enH$_1$-* 'breathe' > G ἄνεμος, L *animus* (via **anamos*) : Skt. *anitum* infin. of *an-* 'breathe'.

PIE **H$_3$estH̥$_1$* 'bone' > G ὀστέ-ον, perhaps L *osseus* adj. 'bony' < **ossa-yo-* < **H$_3$estH̥$_1$* : AV *ásthi*; Hitt. *ḫa-aš-ta-(a-)i* < **H$_3$estoH$_1$*.

PIE **stH̥$_2$-tí-* 'a standing' (from **steH$_2$-*) > G στάσις, L *statiō* : Brāh. *sthití-*, OHG *stat*, OE *stede*.

PIE **pH̥$_2$tḗr* 'father' > G πατήρ, L *pater* : Ved. *pitā́*, OE *fæder*.

PIE **pl̥tH̥$_2$w-iH$_2$* 'broad' fem. > G Πλαταιαί 'Plataea' : Ved. *pr̥thivī́-* 'Earth' (**98**, and see fn. 3 on p. 95).

PIE **meǵH̥$_2$* 'big' nom./acc.sg.n. > G μέγα : Ved. *máhi*, Hitt. *me-ik-ki-i*.[1]

PIE **H$_2$erH̥$_3$-tro-* 'plow' > G ἄροτρον, L *arātrum* for **arătrum*, with *ā* imported from *arāre*, *arātum* : W *aradr*, ON *arðr*, Lith. *árklas*. (The loss of syllabic laryngeals in medial syllables in Gmc. and BS is seen here; the intonation of the first syllable of *árklas*, however, reveals the previous existence of an element between the *r* and the *k*.)

PIE **dH̥$_3$-tó-* pple. of **deH$_3$-* 'give' > G δοτός, L *dătus* : Ved. *ditá-*.

a. G is the only IE language to have distinct reflexes for each of the three syllabic

---

[1] PIE **meǵH$_2$-* 'big' is guaranteed for InIr. and G and perhaps Hitt. But Celtic and Italic—for example, L *magnus* 'big'—uniformly reflect an etymon **mag-*: though the number of forms involved is large, not one shows a trace of *-H$_2$-, or *e*-grade, or any morphological details similar to those of **meǵH$_2$-*. This **mag-* is nevertheless generally presumed to be somehow connected with **meǵH$_2$-*. The similarities between the two—and NE *big*—are unlikely to be anything more than chance resemblance.

laryngeals. Otherwise, the nearly universal reflex is *a*, as in L. InIr. departs from this generalization: the usual Indic reflex is *i*, as the above examples reveal, and *ī* in some environments (but most *ī* are analogical). In Iranian the vowel in question is lost altogether medially, so Av. nom. *ptā, tā* = Ved. *pitā́*. The G data presented here have been explained as the product of analogy rather than different reflexes from different laryngeals; but the better arguments favor the latter. For example, in the isolated forms ἄροτρον and ἄνεμος neither analogy nor assimilation are possible explanations, whereas the theory of separate reflexes easily accounts for the facts.

b. The behavior of laryngeals in initial position before a consonant is much debated. Some prothetic vowels in G (or, according to some authorities, all of them) arise from word-initial **H*-, the particular vowel being determined by the particular laryngeal (89-90). In L there is no good evidence for any special reflex of a laryngeal before consonantal resonants or **s*; but *apiō* (Paul.Fest.) 'snare' is a plausible reflex of **H̥*$_1$*p*-, zero grade of **eH*$_1$*p*- (103.1).

103. COMPENSATORY LENGTHENING OF PIE SYLLABICS. Systematic compensatory lengthening in IE languages took place when syllabics were followed by a laryngeal (165-7) plus a consonant. (A laryngeal in word final position seems usually to lengthen a preceding syllabic, but not invariably; 53a.) Unless disturbed by leveling, contamination, and the like, a PIE syllabic—any syllabic—in this position behaves in such IE branches as G, L, InIr., and Celt. as though it had become long. In Hitt., of course, many laryngeals survive, and probably do not affect the length of preceding elements. In Germanic and BS such lengthening phenomena are overt only for the vowels. In BS the reflexes of syllabic liquids and nasals were different depending on whether a laryngeal originally followed (105.4), but the distinction seems not to have been one of length.

1. Compensatory lengthening before laryngeals.

PIE **dheH*$_1$- 'put' > G τί-θη-μι, L *fēcī*; PIE **deH*$_3$- 'give' > G δί-δω-μι, L *dōnum*; PIE **eH*$_1$*p*- 'take' > L *co-ēpī*, Hitt. *e-ip*-. Cf. Ved. *āpnóti* 'attains' and desid. *ī́psate* < **H*$_1$*i-H*$_1$*p-s*-. —L *ēp*- is evidently the orig. aor. of **H̥*$_1$*p-yoH*$_2$ > *apiō* 'snare, snag', Paul.Fest., though a transitive *-*y*^{e}/*o*- stem built to the zero grade of a root is out of order for a genuinely antique formation.[1]

PIE -*o-H*$_2$ 1sg.pres. thematic active > G -ω, L -*ō*, etc: **bheroH*$_2$ 'I carry' > G φέρω, L *ferō*. (Here *-*o*- is the theme vowel, *-*H*$_2$ is the person marker, which is also seen in the stative (perf.), 513-4.)

a. PIE **iH*$_1$ > PG **ī* medially but **ye* finally (49.1); **iH*$_2$ > **yā* medially after a single consonant, otherwise **ya* (49.2); and **iH*$_3$ > **yō* (49.3).

2. Lengthening also is seen in PIE in acc.sg. **dyēm* 'sky' and **g*^{w}*ōm* 'cow' from earlier ***dyewm*, ***g*^{w}*owm* (325, 324).

3. Original **-*ons*, **-*ens* in the nom.sg. of *n*-stems > PIE *-*ō*, *-*ē* (282).

---

[1] G ἅπτω 'fasten, bind' is traditionally taken to match this OL *apiō* (-πτ- < *-*py*-, 202), but this is unlikely. The initial *h*- is troublesome; the meaning is only passably suitable; and, most significantly, **H̥*$_1$*p*- would give G ×επ- not απ-; 102.

According to some scholars, these long vowels were different in some way from the usual PIE long vowels, as is manifested by their reflexes in Gmc. and BS, but in G and L they coalesce with ordinary long vowels. Thus L *homō* 'man', *cardō* 'hinge'; in G, the long-gone stem-final nasal was re-imported into the nom.sg. from the oblique cases: *τέκτων* 'carpenter', *ἄρσην* 'a male'.

4. In the PIE compounds for decads, any syllabic at the end of the first element lengthens: (as traditionally reconstructed) **trī-ḱn̥tə* '30' (**tri-*), *penkʷē-ḱn̥tə* '50' (**penkʷe*), **septm̥̄-ḱn̥tə* '70' (**septm̥*). Compensatory lengthening here is the result of the loss of **-*d*- in **-*dkm̥t*, a zero grade derivative of **deḱm̥t* 'ten'. (See 391.)

a. A similar phenomenon is seen in PIE **ḱēr* nom.sg. 'heart' < ***ḱerd*, as reflected in Ved. *hā́rdi* (the -*d* restored, with the aid of prop-vowel -*i*), Hom. *κῆρ*, Hitt. šÀ-*ir*—that is, as it were, HEART-*ir*—and OPr. *seyr*. Likewise the nom.sg. of *s*-stems in *-*ēs* and *-*ōs* < **-*ess*, **-*oss*; and certain other cases mentioned in the discussion of the morphology.

104. LONG SYLLABIC LIQUIDS AND NASALS. Where ordinary vowels are involved, the phonetics of compensatory lengthening are straightforward: a vowel of such-and-such phonetic features is simply prolonged, and commonly coalesces with a long vowel already present in the language. A corresponding lengthening of syllabic liquids and nasals is straightforward in theory, but less obvious as regards the phonetic details of their reflexes. They are posited for forms where syllabic resonants (that is, zero grades) would be predicted by the usual morphology of PIE, but the actual reflexes are very different from ordinary syllabic liquids and nasals. Thus for the PIE root **ster*- (to cite it in its pre-laryngeal garb) 'spread, scatter', derivatives where the zero grade is expected are attested as G *στρωτός*, L *strātus*, Ved. *stīrṇá*-. The etymon underlying these things obviously had neither an ordinary full grade vowel nor a syllabic resonant of the kind discussed in 93-100. The same correspondences show up in derivationally opaque forms: G *λῆνος* 'wool' (*η* < **ā*, 54), L *lāna*, Ved. *ū́rṇā*-, Go. *wulla*, Lith. *vìlna* 'strand of wool', pl. 'wool' (the normal reflex of **l̥* in Lith. is -*il̃*-). Before the advent of the laryngeal theory the syllabics in question were reconstructed as long syllabic liquids and nasals, bearing the same relationship to **r̥*, **l̥*, **m̥*, **n̥* as **ē* bears to **e*, **ō* to **o*, and so on. Thus, for the examples here, PIE **str̥̄-tó*-, *-*nó*- 'scattered' and **wl̥̄nā*-, *-*no*- 'wool'. However, there was no explanation for WHY a feature of length should appear in the zero grade of **ster*-, as above, but not in the same grade of say **bher*- 'carry'.

Current thinking takes long syllabic liquids and nasals to be ordinary (short) syllabic resonants that have undergone compensatory lengthening, exactly like **ē* from orig. **ĕ* in **e*H_1.

In the case of an isolated form like PIE 'wool' reconstructing **wl̥*H_2*no*- in place of **wl̥̄no*- has the virtues of economy and consistency: economy because laryngeals are necessary anyhow (and **l̥̄* is not), and consistency because the correspondences among the IE languages here are identical to the correspondences seen in forms whose structure is more transparent. A reconstruction of the type *str̥H_3-tó- (full grade *sterH_3-) 'scatter' adds to these virtues the satisfactory explanation of many other details of the morphology of the attested forms. For example, Ved. *ástr̥ṇāt* 'spread' 3sg.impf., G στόρνῡμι are seen to be ordinary *n*-infix presents: PIE *str̥-ne-H_3- to *sterH_3-, exactly like *yu-ne-g- to *yewg- 'join' (453). Additionally, Ved. *upa-stíre* inf. to *upa-str̥ṇāti* 'spreads over' is formally the dat.sg. of a root noun, but *-stire* (rather than *-stre*) is explained by the structure of the etymon, *-str̥H_3-ey. A gratifying datum is the reflex of the laryngeal itself in forms like Ved. *stárīman-* 'a strewing' < *ster$H̥_3$-men- (*ī* for *i* is secondary).

105. The principal correspondences of the 'long' syllabic liquids and nasals may be surveyed in the following table:

PIE	r̥̄	l̥̄	m̥̄	n̥̄
Skt	īr, ūr	īr, ūr	āṃ	ā
G (Dor.)	ρη, ρᾱ, ρω	λη, λᾱ, λω	μᾱ, μω	νη (νᾱ)
L	rā	lā	mā	nā
Go.	aur	ul	um	un
Lith.	ìr	ìl	ìm	ìn

1. The growth of a vowel in front of the resonant in some daughter languages and after it in others forestalls the reconstruction of any actual vowel segment in these etyma in PIE.

2. Indic *ūr* is typical of labial environments, with *īr* elsewhere; thus Ved. *pūrṇá-* 'filled' < *pl̥H_1-nó-, but *stīrṇá-* 'strewn'.

3. The correct interpretation of the G facts is complicated by the variety of vowels seen growing after the consonant. Prior to the discovery of laryngeals, long liquids and nasals were of necessity believed to develop a uniform vowel in G (usually assumed to be ᾱ, Att.-Ion. η), other vowels arising from time to time via dialect differences and leveling. A significantly more economical interpretation traces the vowel colors of the long vowels that appear in G directly to the particular laryngeal that originally followed the syllabic liquid or nasal. In this view, μᾱ, νᾱ, λᾱ, and ρᾱ reflect PIE *m̥H_2, *n̥H_2, *l̥H_2, and *r̥H_2 specifically; *n̥H_1, *r̥H_1, *l̥H_1 > G νη, ρη, λη; and *l̥H_3, *m̥H_3, *r̥H_3 > λω, μω, ρω respectively. (Examples below. Some possible sequences, *m̥H_1 and *n̥H_3, are unattested.)

G ἑβδομήκοντα '70' ultimately reflects an *m̥̄ not derived from a following laryngeal. In the absence of a Dor. form it is not apparent whether pre-laryngeal *m̥̄ gave PG -μᾱ- or -μη-.

4. Note that the Germanic reflexes of *R̥̄ are identical in every way with the reflexes of ordinary *R̥. In Lith. there is a difference: *R̥̄ > *ìr, ìl, ìm,* and *ìn*, whereas ordinary *R̥ > *ir̃, iñ* and so on.

106. Examples. Liquids:

1. *r̥̄.

PIE *terH_1- 'rub, bore', full grade *terH̥$_1$-tro- > G τέρετρον 'gimlet' (cf. τείρω), zero grade in pple. *tr̥H_1-tó- > G τρητός 'with holes; drilled'. (L *trītus*, pple. of *terō* 'bore, rub', and perf. *trīvī*, are not derivable from the root *terH_1-; their explanation is uncertain.)

PIE *ǵr̥H_2-no- (adj. or pple. to *ǵerH_2- 'soften; ripen') > L *grānum* 'grain' : Ved. *jīrṇá-* 'soft(ened); old', Go. *kaurn* 'grain, seed', NE *corn* 'wheat, maize' (the original meaning still in NE *peppercorn*), Lith. *žìrnis* 'pea'. —A different derivative of the same root in Att. γραῦς, gen. γρᾱός, dat. γρᾱΐ, 'old woman' < *ǵr̥H_2u-s, gen. *ǵr̥H_2w-os, dat. *ǵr̥H_2w-i. (This inflection is therefore exactly like that of *neH_2u- 'boat', **328**.) The laryngeal is followed by a vowel in the nom., and by a cons. in the gen. (Hom. γρηῦς, γρῆϋς for *γρᾱ́ϋς —and before that, *γάρυς—with leveling from the oblique cases, γρηός and so on). Much is obscure about the historical details, but the widely-encountered reconstruction *γρᾱϊϝ-, parallel to *πρᾱϊϝ- 'tender'—which may have influenced some of the details of the inflection of γρῆϋς—is not justified by the evidence or by morphological considerations.

PIE *str̥H_3-tó- pple. of *sterH_3- 'scatter, spread' > G στρωτός, L *strātus* (*sternō*) : Ved. *stīrṇá-*.

a. Dor. πρᾶτος, standard G πρῶτος 'first' is a crux in the debate over the sound laws for long syllabic resonants in G. A number of cognates point to *pr̥H-, the *H probably specifically *H_3 on the basis of the pervasive *o*-vocalism (G πρό, L *prō*). Thus PIE *pr̥H_3es or *pr̥H_3os gen.sg. of a root noun explains G πάρος 'formerly' and Ved. *purás*; PIE *pr̥H_3-wo-, *pr̥H_3-mo- 'first' > Ved. *pū́rva-*, OCS *prĭvŭ*, Lith. *pìrmas*, OE *forma* (the last an *n*-stem). For those who reconstruct something like PIE *pr̥H_3-to-, G πρῶτος is the regular reflex and Dor. πρᾶτος is a problem. In the opposing view, πρᾶτος is the regular outcome of *pr̥$H_3$to-, and πρῶτος is analogical. For further discussion see 398.1.

2. *l̥̄.

PIE *pleH_1- 'fill', zero grade *pl̥H_1-to 3sg.mid.aor. > Hom. πλῆτο. The usual morphology would call for zero grade, but cognates point unambiguously to full grade (*pleH_1-) in certain other formations which normally take zero grade, as L *plēnus* 'full' and Ved. *prātá-* adj., next to more typical *pūrṇá-* pple. 'filled'; and *ple$H_1$to may be the etymon of πλῆτο as well.

PIE *kl̥H_1- 'hail, call' > G καλέω 'call' (orig. athem. like ἐμέω 'vomit'), pple. κλητός, κλῆσις 'a calling', κικλήσκω 'call' (poet.). Thess. συνκλειτος 'assembly' shows Att.-Ion. η is not from ᾱ.

The homophonous full grade from PIE *kleH_1- is seen in Hom. κλήτωρ 'herald' (128.1); the doublet καλήτωρ arose by contamination from καλέω; G κελαδ- 'make a loud noise' (rushing water, say), at best a different extension of a basic *kel-, is probably unrelated.

PIE *wl̥H-neH_2-, *-no- 'wool' (on the G evidence probably *wl̥H_2- specifically) > Att. λῆνος (54), L *lāna*. Evidence for an initial laryngeal is suggested by Hitt. *ḫulana-* and *ḫuliya-* both (apparently) 'wool'; but *lH_2

seems to remain in Hitt. in *pa-al-ḫi-iš* 'broad', cf. L *plānus* 'plain (of terrain)', and *ḫul-* here is better seen as a metathesis of **ulḫ-*.

L *plānus* 'level, flat', just mentioned, Hitt. *pal-ḫi-iš* 'broad', *pal-ḫa-a-tar* 'breadth' point to an etymon **pl̥H₂-no-*.

PIE **tl̥H₂-to-* pple. of **telH₂-* 'pick up' > Dor. τλᾱτός, Att. τλητός 'patient, steadfast', L *lātus* < **tlātos* (pple. of *ferō*).

The following G forms have no convincing IE cognates: pres. βλώσκω 'go, come', fut. μολοῦμαι, infin. μολεῖν, perf. μέμβλωκα. Even in the absence of cognates, these forms point to an etymon **melH₃-*, a root of normal PIE shape. A knowledge of PIE verbal morphology together with G sound laws treating laryngeal sequences enables us to explain the apparently diverse G paradigm as follows.

PIE **-sḱ-* pres. presupposes zero grade of the root, **ml̥H₃-sḱe/o-*, whence regularly βλώσκω < *μλωσκω (224.1).

The expected fut. would have been full grade *μελό(σ)ομαι ~ μελοῦμαι < **melH̥₃-(H₁)se/o-* (457B); attested μολοῦμαι results from a regular metathesis to *μολέομαι (109 fn.), whence μολοῦμαι. An orig. **mol-*, from any source, would have given ˣμυλ-, 44, and anyhow *o*-grade is out of order for a future stem.

The aor. μολ- was presumably a root inflection to begin with, and therefore would have had three stem forms: *μελ(ο)- in 3sg. *μελο < **melH̥₃-t*; *βλω- in the 1,2pl., *βλωτε < **ml̥H₃-te*; and μαλ- in the 3pl. μαλον < **ml̥H₃-ent*. The regular metathesis (109 fn.) of the first stem type to *μολες 2sg., *μολε 3sg. would have laid the groundwork both for the observed form of the root in the aor. and for a thematic inflection.

The perf. paradigm was at first *μεμολα (or *μεμυλα) 1sg., *μεμβλωμεν 1pl.—odd-looking but phonologically regular from **me-ml̥H₃-me*. With help from the pres. βλώσκω the stem μεμβλω- was generalized, reworked as a (productive) κ-perf. (518).

a. G δολιχός 'long', ἐνδελεχής 'continuous, perpetual', Ved. *dīrghá-* 'long', *drā́ghīyas-* 'longer' plainly continue a root **dleH₁gh-*, but the history of δολιχός has long been a mystery. It has recently been suggested that the troublesome -ολι- is simply the regular reflex of **-l̥H₁-*. Against this idea are the phonetic implausibility of it, and the seeming contradiction of the much more straightforward reflexes as shown above. In favor of the idea are its simplicity—the likeliest etymon is unquestionably **dl̥H₁ghós*—and the remarkable (prevocalic) parallel of G πολυ- 'many', somehow from **pl̥H₁u-* and likewise difficult to account for by better-grounded means. A third example might be G πόλις 'city' if exactly superimposable on Ved. *pū́r* < **pl̥Hs* (though here **H₁* specifically is a surmise). The very clarity of **-l̥H₁-* > G -λη- makes an analogical creation easier to defend; certainly, no remotely plausible analogy has ever been discovered for δολιχός or πολυ-. (The failure of πολυ- to become ˣπυλυ- (44c) is no less mysterious in terms of this theory, however.)

107. EXAMPLES. Nasals:

1. **m̥̄*.

PIE **dm̥H₂-to-* pple. of **demH₂-* 'build' > G νεόδμητος 'new-built', Dor. (Pindar) νεόδμᾱτος.

PIE **dm̥H₂-tó-* (zero grade pple. of **demH₂-* 'tame', perhaps orig. the same as the preceding): **n̥-dm̥H₂-to-* > G ἄδμητος 'untamed' : Skt. *a-dāmta-*. (**H₂* is vouchsafed by ἀδάματος.)

PIE **ḱm̥H$_2$-* (zero grade of **ḱemH$_2$-* 'work, toil, get tired'): **ḱe-ḱm̥H$_2$-wōs* perf. pple. > **kekmāwōs* > Hom. κεκμηώς 'being weary' : Ved. *śāṃtá-* 'calm(ed); appeased'.[1]

PIE **sm̥-H$_3$nogʷh-* 'single-hooved' (an epithet of horses) > Hom. μώνυχες nom.pl. (389.1B, 171, 44; cf. ὄνυξ < **H$_3$nogʷh-*, 90).

a. PIE **m̥H$_1$* seems not to be attested in G.

b. Examples of **m̥̄* in L are elusive. L *māteries* 'building supplies, timber' perhaps reflects PItal. **dmāto-* < **dm̥H$_2$-to-*, root **demH$_2$-* 'build'; cf. G νεόδμητος 'new-built', above. (Since the semantics of *māteriēs* are peculiar for a form based on a past passive pple., a better starting point from the morphological point of view would be a nomen actionis **dm̥H$_2$-ti-*; such a formation works for all the sound changes required, but is unattested anywhere.) More certain, even though disturbed by a dissimilation, is PIE **septm̥̄-ḱn̥tH$_2$* '70' > **septmāgintā*, **septumāgintā* > L *septuāgintā* (cf. G ἑβδομήκοντα, and see 391 for a discussion of the formation of decads).

2. **n̥̄*.

PIE **ǵn̥H$_1$-* (full grade **ǵenH$_1$-* 'beget' seen in **ǵenH̥$_1$-tor-* 'begetter' > G γενέτωρ): pple. **ǵn̥H$_1$-to-* > G διόγνητος 'born of Zeus', κασίγνητος 'brother' (Thess., Cyp., and others attest original η) = L *(g)nātus*, Ved. *jātá-*. G γνήσιος 'belonging to the race' is often taken as a secondary full-grade **ǵneH$_1$-*, but it is much more likely to be the usual zero-grade *tí*-stem nomen actionis formation **ǵn̥H$_1$-tí-* seen unambiguously in OE *cynd* (NE *kind*) and L *nātiō*.

a. There are no certain examples of **n̥H$_2$* in G. The morphophonemics of θνήσκω 'die' however, correspond generally to what would be expected of a root ending in *-*n̥H$_2$-*: G θνητός (Dor. θνᾱτός) 'mortal', θνήσκω (Dor. θνᾱ́σκω) 'die'.

b. There are no certain instances of **n̥H$_3$* in G. The root **ǵneH$_3$-* 'know', well attested in G, apparently had no zero grade in PIE: significantly, unambiguous full grade of the root is found in formations normally REQUIRING zero grade, as Ved. *jñātá-* 'known' = L *nōtus*. Even if it did have a zero grade, its reflex in G would be indistinguishable from those of the full grades. —None of the attested privatives in νω- (see 108) are clearly traceable to **n̥-* before roots beginning with **H$_3$C-*, for all the likelihood that that is the ultimate origin of the type.

108. PRIVATIVE ADJECTIVES IN **n̥̄-*. The G privative adjectives ('characterized by lacking such-and-such') are built from nouns by means of an element ἀ-, ἀν- (before consonants and vowels, respectively, these being the regular developments of PIE **n̥-*, 100): ἄ-λογος 'without speech; without reason', ἀν-όστεος 'boneless'. This distribution is to some extent generalized within G, as ἀν- is found before *h-* < **s-*, so ἀν-όμοιος 'dissimilar', whereas the correct reflex of **n̥-somo-* would have been *ἀόμοιος. Such a configura-

[1] In Vedic the root *śam-* still has the inherited sense 'work, toil, exert oneself' and, fleetingly, the obvious derived sense 'be weary [from labors]'; but the somewhat different derived sense of 'relax, be at rest' (as the aftermath of exertions) is more prominent, and is the meaning that endures.

tion is in fact found occasionally, as ἄοπλος 'without heavy arms' (ὅπλα 'weapons'), ἀόρᾱτος 'unseen' (ὁράω); it is of course regular when the base word began with *w-, as ἄοικος 'homeless', ἄοινος 'without wine, sober', from *awoyk-, *awoyn-.

This much is uncontroversial. In some instances, however, the privative prefix is νη-, νᾱ- (which of course fall together in Att.-Ion., 54-6) or νω-, as Hom. νήγρετος 'unwaking', νήνεμος 'calm, without wind' (*νᾱ́νεμος), νωδός 'toothless'.

The explanation that once found most favor is that they somehow continue compounds in *ne-, that is, with full grade of the negative particle. Such formations would be morphologically very strange, however, as the only certain combining form of the element in question is *n̥-; and the necessary vowel contractions (-ᾱ- < *-εα-; -ω- < *-εο-), while not unthinkable, are not supported by much.

Laryngeals provide a more appealing explanation, as such formations would be the regular result of *n̥- combining with a word-initial laryngeal in the base word, as *n̥-H_1ǵr- 'unwaking' > νήγρετος. Some scholars take such formations as positive evidence for a laryngeal, as if νώνυμ(ν)ος 'nameless/inglorious' established the PIE form for 'name' as *H_3nomn- rather than *nomn-. Though it is probably the wrong analysis in this case, it is at least supported by the possibility that the ὀ- of G ὄνομα is also a trace of an original *H_3- (90). In many such cases, however, there is no independent evidence for a laryngeal, and in some of them a laryngeal (or the right laryngeal) is an impossibility, or there are other difficulties. So νήπιος 'infans' if from ἔπος (ϝεπος) cannot continue any *n̥H-, as a root-initial laryngeal is out of the question. And while *ed- 'eat' may well have begun with a laryngeal, that laryngeal would have to have been *H_1-, which cannot be the source of νωδός (or of the initial vowel of ὀδοντ- 'tooth'), though it might be the explanation for νῆστις 'not eating, fasting' < *n̥-H_1d-ti- (212). On the other hand, PIE *H_2enH_1- 'breathe' begins with a laryngeal, and the right one too, but a zero-grade form rather than *n̥-H_2on$\underline{H}_1$-mo- is not likely on the formal level; and, if it did exist, the syllabification *n̥H_2n̥$\underline{H}_1$mo- necessary to generate νᾱ́νεμος is implausible. Similarly unlikely on morphological grounds would be *n̥-$H_3$$k^w$-, thought by some to underlie νώψ 'half blind'; but the form is known only from Hesych. and is possibly a blunder for something like *ἀνόψ (cf. RV anák nom.sg. 'blind' < *n̥-H_3ek^{w}s, with expected full grade of the root).

Privatives in *n̥-H- must have existed, of course, and the observed shapes in G (νᾱ-, νη-, νω-) would be the expected results of such formations. But it is plain that by the time of our earliest literary records they were simply in competition with the more usual privative formation built to roots beginning with a vowel, that is, with prefix ἀν-. Indeed, since it is certain that most such formations in G do not continue *n̥H-, such formations are not useful evidence for root-initial largyngeals (90).

a. No other IE language has formations that clearly parallel the G ones. Of course, in BS and Gmc. there would be no difference in any case, but neither L nor OIr. has privatives in nā-; and Ved. evidence is limited to three formations. The text has two instances of ā́sant- 'untrue; nonexistent', which would be appropriate from *n̥-H_1s-ont-, and a root-shape *H_1es-/*H_1s- is indicated by other evidence. But both are found in the LATEST stratum of the RV, where a genuinely ancient relic is unexpected, and the form in earlier passages is ásant- (5×). The text writes ávr̥ta- 'unimpeded' in all six of its occurrences, but the meter favors ā́vr̥ta- in all of them, and all occur in passages of respectable age. But as the word is of doubtful meaning it is also necessarily of doubtful etymology.[1] Finally, Ved. *ā́deva-* 'godless', which occurs three times next to 30-odd instances of *ádeva-*, is built from the root of G Ζεύς, for which an initial laryngeal is out of the question.

109. REDUCED GRADE REFLEXES IN GREEK. The foregoing reflexes are clear-cut. In addition there are forms which do not fit this scheme; being much less transparent, they have been explained in a number of different ways. These forms apparently do not contain full grades of roots but do not obviously reflect zero grades of the **R̥H* (**R̥̄*) sort either. Generally similar things are found occasionally in all IE languages, but they are abundant in G: next to the regular zero grades presented above—(Δίο)γνητος, τλᾱτός, δμᾱτός, θνᾱτός, βλώσκω—are such forms as γένεσις, τάλαντον, ἐδάμασσα, θάνατος, and ἔμολον. Over the years these have been dealt with in a variety of ways. One analysis posits PIE **r̥ə*, **l̥ə*, **m̥ə*, **n̥ə* for γένεσις, τάλαντον, and so on, alongside **r̥̄, l̥̄, m̥̄, n̥̄* for forms like -γνητος and τλᾱτός. In effect, this supposes two different types of zero grade: one in which the *ə retains independent existence adjacent to a syllabic resonant, and the other in which it disappears and the syllabic resonant is long. An alternative hypothesis (in fact a notational variant merely) postulates an ablaut grade, 'reduced' (112a), which is intermediate between full and zero, thus **ьrə*, **ьlə*, **ьmə*, **ьnə* (and, for ἔμολον and the like, shapes like with a different reduced grade, **ъlə*). The demerits of theories of reduced grades are discussed below (124); but the real defect (which applies equally to the idea of **r̥ə* vs. **r̥̄*) is that the supposed distinction in the parent language itself is unconditioned and unexplained, and is therefore no improvement on supposing an unconditioned and unexplained development of an original **ǵn̥̄-* to both G γνη- and γενε-.

A recent theory takes the G reflexes to be conditioned phonological developments of the usual type: the *-RV̄-* reflexes (where *R* = any resonant, *V* = any vowel) reflect atonic **R̥̄*, while *-VRV-* reflects long syllabic resonants which somehow acquired tonic accent (secondarily, in all or almost all cases): **ǵn̥̄tós* > G -γνητος, whereas **ǵn̥̄́tis* > γένεσις. (The color of the vowels depends on the laryngeal, so $*\acute{\text{n̥}}H_1$ > -ενε-, $*\acute{\text{n̥}}H_2$ > -ανα-, and so on.) From the point of view of phonetic plausibility, such a theory has much to recommend it. However, tonic accent correlates with full grade, and it is likely therefore that some or most cases of G forms in *-VRV-* reflect ordinary full grades with subsequent assimilation of vowels: aor. **e-telH̥₂-s-* 'fetched' > *ἐ-τέλα-σα > ἐτάλασσα.[2] The reasoning is as follows:

---

[1] It is an epithet of Indra; like many other words known only thus, that is where the context provides few clues, the supposed meaning is a guess based on the form.

[2] There are some reasons for suspecting that metathesis played a role in the development of the type ἐτάλασσα from *ἐτέλασσα. This may seem like a gratuitous com-

1. The accentual theory accounts for the FORMS more plausibly than the functions. The semantics of the forms with 'secondary tonic stress' differ greatly from those of the forms from which they are necessarily derived, and with which they were once formally identical, ex hypothese: κάματος 'toil' hardly bears a derivational relationship to κμᾱτός 'worn out'.

2. The tendency for stems in *-VRV-* to show up in futures and aorists, specifically, a conspicuous feature of G morphology (vid. inf. 3**b**), accords poorly with any theory of accentual distribution, secondary or otherwise.

3. Doublets like βάραθρον and βέρεθρον (the latter Ionic) 'pit, chasm' are awkward for such a theory, but are what one would expect from phenomena like metathesis and assimilation, which are inherently sporadic. In the same vein, τέμαχος n. 'slice' is interpreted as the unassimilated reflex of **témH̥₂-* next to the assimilated τέμενος n. 'allotted land, fief, demesne'; ditto τελαμών (**telH̥₂-*) 'shield-strap' next to ἐτάλασσα (*ἐτάλεσα < *ἐτελασα) aor.

a. That is not to say that assimilation is the explanation for all *-VRV-* forms of G. G τάλαντον for example probably can be traced directly to **tl̥H₂-ont-* (aor.pple.). Similarly θάνατος formed exactly like βίοτος 'life' < **gʷiH₃-eto-*. (The accent is a problem for both theories.) —G γένεσις 'birth, origin' is a *ti*-stem nomen actionis of a type which normally takes zero grade of the root with accent on the suffix, but which has many representatives in G with secondary root accent: βάσις 'a stepping' < **gʷm̥-tí-* (βαίνω), θέσις 'a placing' < **dhH̥₁-ti-* (τίθημι); and also clear cases of actual full-grade *ti*-stems with root accent: ζεῦξις 'a yoking', μῆτις 'counsel, an advising'. Finally, δμῆσις 'a taming' and βρῶσις 'meat; an eating' plainly are from **dm̥H₂-ti-* and **gʷr̥H₃-ti-*, and the secondary root-accent should have yielded G ˣδάμασις and ˣβόροσις according to the accentual theory. Similarly τλήμων (τλᾱ́μων) 'patient, enduring'. There are many such forms.

b. However the *-VRV-* forms of G arose, and however they align with cognate forms in IE languages, they have acquired a strongly functional alignment within G itself: they are commonplace in futures like βαλέω 'will throw' (500.2), and aorists like ἔβαλον, ἐκάλεσα 'called', and ἐδάμασα 'tamed' (505.3). Contrariwise, *-RV̄-* forms are notably productive in various other tenses of the verb (root aorists and perfects) and derivatives, as, for example, ἔβλητο 3sg.aor.midd., βέβληκα 1sg.perf., βλητέος 'for putting', βλῆμα 'a throw'.

Vowel Gradation – Ablaut

110. The term *ablaut* is German for 'sound variety' or the like. The purely English synonym *gradation* was once more common than it is nowadays (though the prevailing terminology still speaks of ablaut *grades*). *Apophony* (Fr. *apophonie*) has never been favored by more than a few important scholars writing in English. All three terms refer to the same feature

---

plication, but metathesis cannot be avoided in any case: note the unassimilated metathesized forms in Hom. λοετρόν 'bath' < **lewo-tro-* < **lewH̥₃-tro-*; and ἐστόρεσα 'I scattered' < **stero-s-* < **sterH̥₃-s-*. This process seems to be very general in the case of sequences of -ε*Co*-, where *C* = any consonant. Furthermore, metathesis would mean that all such assimilations could be traced to a uniform assimilation of an atonic vowel to a tonic one, and helps explain a form like βάραθρον (< metathesized *βάρεθρον) next to βέρεθρον (< original *βέραθρον), item 3, below.

of PIE phonology and its reflexes in the IE daughter languages, namely a pattern of vowel alternations.

Ablaut is conspicuous in the interrelations of Greek forms such as πέτομαι 'fly', ποτή 'flight', πτερόν 'wing' (root *pet-) and also in Sanskrit, Baltic and Slavic, and the Germanic languages (where such things as NE *drive, drove, driven*; *skim, scum*; and *white, wheat* are traceable to it). In Greek the inherited patterns have been analogically extended, leveled, and otherwise confused; in Latin such disturbances were likewise very extensive, and moreover were coupled with regular sound laws which effaced the original patterns. Thus, for example, the PIE alternation **ew*~**ow*~**u* is a transparent embodiment of the basic alternating framework (**e*~**o*~∅) when followed by **w*. This remains transparent in Greek ευ~ου~υ and Go. *iu*~*au*~*u*, but in Latin the pattern was first denatured by an Italic sound law (61) into **ow, *ow, *u*, and by a later L sound law (61.2) further to *ū, ū, ŭ*, in which no similarity to the basic pattern *e*~*o*~∅ can be detected. Amid this ruin, L established alternations of its own invention. For example, from a number of sources—regular ablaut being only a small part of the picture—L had acquired an array of perfect stems (most of them etymologically aorists in fact, 524-5) whose long root vowels contrasted with short vowels in the root in the present: *agō, ēgī*; *faciō, fēcī*; *fundō, fūdī*; *pangō, pānxī*; *sedeō, sēdī*; and so on. This pattern of vowel alternation was extended to such perfect stems as *vēnī* and *cēpī*, which are therefore at best only indirectly connected with PIE ablaut (525.6).

a. Vowel alternations result from commonplace kinds of sound change. English has vowel alternations which arose at various times from various causes. Thus the alternations seen in NE *drink, drank, drunk*; *meet, met*; *blood, bleed*; *wise, wisdom*; *revise, revision*; *efficient, effective* represent six unrelated patterns, that is, they arose via six different historical developments. In addition, accidents (such as borrowing or chance resemblance) on occasion create an appearance of alternation: *cat, kitten*; *ill, ailing*; *choose, choice*; *bed, boudoir*; *strap, strop*; *whole, hale*. The term ablaut might fairly be used for any or all of these phenomena; but in the context of historical linguistics it usually refers to a particular feature of the PIE proto-language, and its continuation in the IE languages; in this book the term will always and only be used in these two senses. (Of the above forms, only *drink, drank, drunk* is a case of ablaut thus defined.)

III. GRADES. The individual items in ablaut are called *grades*. These are the different vowels, and absence of a vowel, that are found in PIE roots and affixes identifiable as 'the same' because they have the same meaning and the same consonants. For example PIE 'foot' (see 116.1) is normally cited as **ped-*. But this is actually just one grade of the root, specifically *e-grade*. In addition there are etyma in **pod-* (*o-grade*), **pd-* (*zero grade*), **pēd-* (*ē-grade*), and **pōd-* (*ō-grade*). The *e*-grade is attested in the L stem *ped-* 'foot', G πεζός 'afoot'. The *o*-grade **pod-* is seen in G ποδ- (the obl. stem of πούς), Lith. *pãdas* 'sole (of the foot)', and in Ved. *pādam* acc.sg. 'foot' < **podm̥* (-*ā*- < **-o-* via 36.4). A zero grade is manifest in Av. *frabda-* 'instep' (lit. 'forefoot'), and indirectly in Ved. _padás_ gen./abl.sg. 'foot', a remodeling (of very early date) of _*pd-os._ The _ē_-grade is apparently seen in L _pēs_ < _*pēds_; the _ō_-grade is manifest in PGmc _*fōt-_.

In roots and affixes alike, _e-_, _o-_, and zero grades are the most frequently encountered, by a wide margin. Lengthened grades are uncommon in the parent language; but they were already extending their range in PIE, and by various means became prominent in several daughter languages.

In principle, ablaut as introduced above is simple. The details of the full working out of vowel alternations in what might be called the traditional analysis of PIE are very complex, however, requiring: (1) three patterns, or 'series', of SHORT vowels—only one of which, the '_e_-series', is sketched above; each of the three series has, in theory, five grades; (2) three series of LONG vowels each with three grades; and (3) an array of 'disyllabic' alternations (whose patterns are much less clear-cut but in most accounts there are about twenty of them; see 112 and 117-20).

112. The traditional framework of PIE ablaut:

	Grades:	Full	Zero/Weak	Lengthened	Reduced
'e-series':		e, o	∅	ē, ō	ь, ъ[1]
'a-series':		a, o	∅	ā, ō	ь, ъ[1]
'o-series':		o, o	∅	ō, ō	ь, ъ[1]
'ē-series':		ē, ō	ə	_(lengthened and reduced grades do not apply)_	
'ā-series':		ā, ō	ə		
'ō-series':		ō, ō	ə		

The raw materials of these alternations were as follows: three short vowels (_*e, *a, *o_) and three long (_*ē, *ā, *ō_); total absence of a vowel (zero grade); six short (93-100) and six long (104-7) syllabic resonants—another manifestation of zero grade; and a sixth short vowel *ə (PIE _schwa primum_, usually _schwa_ for short), which shows up mainly in the long vowel (118) and disyllabic (121-3) patterns, but occasionally is an independent element (as in the 1pl.midd.sec. ending _*-medhə_ > G -μεθα, Ved. _-mahi_; or in PIE _*pətér-_ 'father' > G πατήρ, L _pater_, Ved. _pitár-_).

a. Reduced grades. Not even twenty-odd elements arranged in some thirty patterns were adequate to account for everything—particularly the details of disyllabic roots (121-3), but other things as well—so a majority of scholars have worked with one or more _reduced grades_, that is, items in the short-vowel series which were intermediate between the full grades and zero. They are therefore reminiscent of the relationship between long vowels and *ə, as explained below (118-20), but different from *ə in showing a complete lack of phonological or morphological patterning of the type discussed in 127-9. For example, both G τάλαντον 'talent' (the weight), τλητός 'patient' (Dor. τλᾱτός) are supposedly 'weak' grades of _*telH_$_2$_-_ 'fetch, heft'. The latter shows the outcome of an ordinary

[1] 'Schwa secundum' (*ə is 'schwa primum'). These reduced vowels are variously symbolized: ь, ĭ, ^{e}, $_{e}$ all stand for a reduced vowel with generally front vowel reflexes or _a_; ъ, ŭ, ^{o}, $_{o}$ all stand for a reduced vowel with generally back vocoid reflexes.

zero-grade form of the root in a suffix-accented derivation, **tl̥H-tó-*; the former is traced to a **tъlH̥-nto-*, a not-quite-zero grade form (the basis for the difference between zero and not-quite-zero being left unexplained).

The G forms of the τλᾱ-/ταλα-, γνη-/γενε- type at least have the appearance of a pattern. A more typical role of reduced grades is tying up loose ends in what might be called etymological messes. The following is typical: starting with a root **pelH-* 'flat' (Hitt. *pa-al-ḫi-iš* 'broad') such words as G παλάμη 'palm' (of the hand), L *palma*, OIr. *lám* /lāμ/, OHG *folma* (all f. eH_2-stems); L *planta* 'sole' (of the foot); G πλάνος 'leading astray; wandering', Ved. *pāṇí-* m. (?< **parṇí-*) 'hand; hoof'; L *palpō* 'touch gently'; and L *plānus* 'flat'. (There is a semantic problem here: παλάμη, *palma* and the others refer not to the hand open flat, but to the cupped hand as a sort of utensil.) One understands the wish to make sense out of such things by any means, but no defensible theory of ablaut can do so. OIr. *lám* and the cognate Gmc. words attest a zero-grade *$*pl̥H\text{-}meH_2$-* straightforwardly, and likewise—with a different meaning in accord with its different formation —L *plānus* (106.2). Why the etymon for G παλάμη and L *palma* (say, **pъlH̥mo-*) should have 'reduced' rather than zero grades in what otherwise looks like the identical formation is unexplained; no better (for the same reason) is *$*pl̥H_2emo$-*. A similar question is provoked by such reconstructions as **pl̥Hnó-* for L *plānus* but **pъlHní-* for Ved. *pāṇí-* and *$*plъHnteH_2$-* for L *planta*.

It would be preferable to recognize that a word like *palma* is readily borrowed, as confirmed by its adoption by English (via OFr.), and take L *palma* (**palamā*) as a borrowing from G, and G παλάμᾱ (< *πάλαμᾱ by 244) < *πύλαμᾱ < **polH̥-*.[1] G πλάνος, L *palpō*, L *planta*, and Indic **parṇi-* are unlikely to have any connection with the others or with one another.[2] This account leaves much unexplained, but its virtue is that its loose ends are fully apparent. 'Reduced grades', by contrast, merely restate the raw facts, and therefore lack any predictive or explanatory power. There will be no further discussion of this theory of PIE ablaut here; more or less complete expositions of it will be found in any IE historical handbook published until very recently.

113. The view of PIE ablaut endorsed here is significantly leaner. It works with a SINGLE pattern of alternation, **e*~**o*~∅ (plus the marginal **ē* and **ō*, 126). PIE **m̥̄*, **n̥̄*, **r̥̄*, **l̥̄*, most cases of **ī* and **ū*, and also *ə, are subtracted from the inventory of PIE vowels. This economy is achieved by a complication elsewhere in the system: in place of the thirty-odd patterns and sub-patterns of alternation, PIE *ə, and the long syllabic liquids and nasals, we need three new consonants of obscure phonetics, the PIE *laryngeals* (165–7): $*H_1$, $*H_2$, and $*H_3$; and also of course a number of sound laws applying to them. These questions will be discussed below, 117–20.

The net result is simplification and clarification. For example, it is not merely the case that traditional accounts of PIE ablaut use a larger number of units and a much larger number of patterns and sub-patterns; the distribution and frequency of occurrence of the sub-patterns was strikingly

---

[1] *O*-grade is suggested here because nouns in *-mo-* typically have *o*-grade of the root. Adjectives in *-mo-* take zero grade, however, and the Gmc. and Celt. forms, above, could be a nominalization of an original adjective.

[2] It is perhaps worth noting that in the scheme of L phonology endorsed here (98), a proto-form **pl̥H-ent-* or **pl̥H-ont-* would in fact regularly give L *plant-*.

uneven. In roots, one of the six alternating sets, the *e*-series (see the table above), made up more than nine tenths of the whole; and it was the only series that figured in affixes, with perhaps three exceptions (opt. **-yē-/-ī-* (539.1), stative -ə-/-*ē-* (452), and fem. **-yā-/-ī-* (268-9)). The long-vowel series were not only virtually confined to roots, they were peculiar to roots of one shape, namely those ending in a long vowel: **dhē-* 'put', **stā-* 'stand', and **dō-* 'give'. There are only a few roots like **bhāǵhú-* '(fore)arm' and **ēs-* 'is sitting'; and none at all of the type *×bhēm-* or *×pār-*, that is, where a vowel of a long series is followed by a resonant. (A form like **sēmi-* 'half' shows no alternation, so it is not possible to tell whether it is the full grade of the *ē*-series or the lengthened grade of the *e*-series.)

These lopsided distributions, and gaps in distributions, were inexplicable in terms of traditional notions of ablaut. They were simply peculiarities of the language, like the absence of good evidence for PIE **b* (142). With laryngeals, however, the *e*-series is promoted from being the principal series to being the ONLY series. And when the '*a*-series' is analyzed into the usual *e*-series vowels preceded by **H_2*, the 'comparative rarity' of the *a*-series becomes nothing more than the fact that only so many roots in PIE began with **H_2e-*, just as only so many began with **se-* or **dhe-* or **le-*. Roots possibly beginning **H_2e-*, such as **H_2eǵ-* 'drive', **H_2el-* 'other' (**al-*), or **H_2eyos-* 'metal' (**ayos-*) are not in fact rare, being more common than roots beginning with some long-familiar members of the PIE consonant inventory—three or four times more numerous than roots beginning with **g^whe-*, as in **g^when-* 'strike' and **g^wher-* 'warm'.

a. The prominence in PIE phonology of the mid vowels **e* and **o* and the marginal status of **a* are extremely odd from the standpoint of the structural norms of languages. The laryngeal theory, which renders **a* even more marginal by reinterpreting many occurrences of traditional **a* as **H_2e*, actually aggravates the eccentricity. Nevertheless there can be no question that, whatever else was true of their phonetics, the full grade vowels differed by being FRONT and BACK: in Indo-Iranian, where they coalesce phonetically, the erstwhile **e* palatalized PIE labiovelars (as did **i*) whereas **o* did not: to the root **k^weyt-* 'notice', **k^weyt-eti* pres. 'takes notice' > Ved. *cétati*; **k^we-k^woyt-e* perf. 'is aware of' > *ciketa* (for **caketa*); pple. **k^wit-tó-* > *cittá-*. PIE **penk^{w}e* 'five' > Ved. *páñca*; **k^wos* 'which' > Ved. *kás* 'who' (153d).[1]

b. Not all syllables ablauted in PIE. To be fastidious, terms like 'full grade' and 'zero grade' should be confined to elements as they relate to other degrees in a SYSTEM OF ALTERNATION. However, it is universal practice to refer to any SYLLABLE containing **e* as '*e*-grade'. Such 'grades without alternation' are not especially rare; for example PIE **ǵneH$_3$-* 'know', **eǵoH* 'I', and nom. pl **-es* have only *e*-grade forms; **bhod-* 'dig' has only *o*-grade (unless the *e*-grade forms of Lith. are old, which is unlikely); and fixed 'zero

---

[1] These examples have been selected to demonstrate the point. In reality the action of this sound law in Indo-Iranian was much disturbed by analogical leveling, especially in Indic. In part for this reason, the 'Law of Palatals' was recognized late in the early history of IE linguistics (around 1875). It caused a sensation.

grades' are seen in the first syllables of PIE **wl̥kʷos* 'wolf', PIE **ukʷsen-* 'ox', and PIE **pH̥₂ter-* 'father'; and in the second syllables of PIE **septm̥* 'seven', **meǵH̥₂* 'big' nom.sg. neut., and **H₃ewis* 'sheep'. One might classify traditional **sēmi-* 'half' and **ēs-* 'sit' as having either lengthened grades or **eH₁*; either way, they show no alternation.

Some orphaned ablaut grades are doubtless nothing but limitations in our knowledge, and on occasion gaps in that knowledge are filled. For most of the history of IE studies, PIE **nokʷt-* 'night' was known only in the *o*-grade (as in G *νύξ*, L *noct-*, OHG *naht*) and possibly as a zero grade in Ved. *aktā́-* 'Night' (the goddess) if from **n̥kʷt-éH₂-*. However, Hitt. *ne-ku-(uz-)zi* /nekʷtsi/ 'becomes evening', a root-inflected verb (447), and *ne-ku-uz (me-ḫur)* /nekʷts/ 'at eventide', reveal actual *e*-grades for this root, and of great antiquity. Toch. B *nekcīye* 'in the evening' reflects *o*-grade, but its meaning at least supports the theory that real meaning of PIE **nᵉ/okʷ-t-* to have been 'evening', not 'night', with the further implication that the root **nekʷ-* originally meant something like 'get dark'. It does not follow from such episodes, however, that we are entitled to assume, as some authorities do, that all syllables in PIE were originally full grade, whereby **wl̥kʷos* and **septm̥* are presumed without further ado to continue earlier ***welkʷos* and ***septem* (if not indeed ***welekʷos* and ***sepetem*).

114. 1. The ablaut grades in their simplest aspect are as follows:

Full Grades		Zero Grade	Lengthened Grades	
e	o	–	ē	ō
ey	oy	i	ēy	ōy
ew	ow	u	ēw	ōw
er	or	r̥	ēr	ōr
el	ol	l̥	ēl	ōl
em	om	m̥	ēm	ōm
en	on	n̥	ēn	ōn
eH₁	oH₁	H̥₁	ēH₁	ōH₁
eH₂	oH₂	H̥₂	ēH₂	ōH₂
eH₃	oH₃	H̥₃	ēH₃	ōH₃

2. The same array occurs with the ablauting vowel FOLLOWING the resonant or laryngeal, at least in theory: in fact, zero grades for this type are scantily attested (probably as a result of analogical disturbances).

Full Grades		Zero Grade	Lengthened Grades		
ye	yo	i	yē	yō	
we	wo	u	wē	wō	
re	ro	r̥	rē	rō	
le	lo	l̥	lē	lō	*etc.*
⋮	⋮	⋮	⋮	⋮	
H₁e	H₁o	H̥₁	H₁ē	H₁ō	*etc.*

Note that full grades in *re* and *er* have the same zero grade, *r̥*. That is, a zero grade **pr̥ḱ-* (the Skt. term *samprasāraṇa* is used by some authorities) alternating with **preḱ-* looks exactly like **dr̥ḱ-* to **derḱ-* 'see'. Native speakers usually keep partially similar alternating patterns straight, naturally, but any ambiguity is an invitation to at least an occasional blunder. Cf. English *lean, lent, lent* 'lend' (cf. *loan*), which was remodeled as *lend, lent* on the pattern of *bend, bent*; *send, sent*, and so on. Here *lent* plays the pivotal role that zero grades **pr̥ḱ-*, **pl̥*H_1- played in the evolution of novel full grades like **perḱ-* and **pel*H_1- for original **preḱ-* and **ple*H_1-. The occurrence of more than one full grade, as in **preḱ-* ~ **perḱ-* 'ask', **ple*H_1- ~ **pel*H_1- 'fill', is called *Schwebeablaut* 'floating ablaut'. In each case, one of the full grade forms is original—it is not always clear which—and the other has arisen by analogy (for instance **dm̥*H_2- : **dem*H_2- :: **pl̥*H_1- : *X*, where *X* = **pel*H_1-).

3. The array in 1, above, occurs with resonants or laryngeals on both sides of the ablauting vowel: **yem*, **yeH*, **Hem*, and so on. Sequences with following resonants and following laryngeals differ only in the zero grades: in a sequence of two resonants before a consonant, the FIRST is the consonant and the SECOND is the vowel, thus **ym̥*, **mr̥*, **mu* (there are two classes of exceptions to this generalization, 93.2); in a sequence of a resonant and a laryngeal, the resonant is ALWAYS the vowel regardless of the relative order, thus **r̥H*, **Hr̥*. A syllabic followed by a laryngeal becomes a long syllabic in the history or prehistory of a majority of IE languages (103-7).

4. DISYLLABIC BASES. What were traditionally known as *disyllabic bases* (or *roots*; see 121 for a full discussion) are actually roots ending with a cluster of a consonant (usually a resonant) followed by a laryngeal, for example **ǵen*H_1- 'beget'. Applying the principles seen in the preceding tables mechanically we get the following. Traditional reconstructions are added in parentheses (a more complete discussion follows):

	Before a Vowel		Before a Consonant	
Full grades:	*ǵenH_1-	(= *ǵen-)	*ǵenH̥$_1$-	(= *ǵenə-)
	*ǵonH_1-	(= *ǵon-)	*ǵonH̥$_1$-	(= *ǵonə-)
Zero Grade:	*ǵn̥H_1-	(= *ǵn̥n-)	*ǵn̥H_1-	(= *ǵn̥̄-)

a. Roots of the shape **petH-* 'fly' (an elaboration of basic **pet-*) or **ghrebhH-* 'seize', with an obstruent rather than a resonant before the root-final laryngeal, were not particularly unusual in PIE. They are no less 'disyllabic' than **ǵen*H_1- and the like, but the reflexes of their phonological and morphological behavior are less complex than the roots with a resonant consonant before the root-final laryngeal. Thus Ved. *gr̥bhṇā́ti* 'seizes' points to **ghr̥bh-ne-H-* (an ordinary *n*-infix present), pple. *gr̥bhītá-* < **ghr̥bhH̥-tó-*. Less transparently, Ved. *grábha-* masc. 'a taking possession' < **ghrobhH-o-* confirms the **-bhH-* cluster, as **ghrobho-* would have given Ved. ˣ*grā̆(b)ha-* by the action of Brugmann's Law (36.4) on **o* in an open syllable.

115. EXAMPLES OF ABLAUT GRADES. The most commonly occurring are the *e*, *o*, and zero grades.

These roots do not contain laryngeals. See 117 for the laryngeal equivalent of the traditional a- and o-series; see 118-20 for the long-vowel series; see 121-3 for the 'disyllabic bases'.

e-Grade	*o*-Grade	Zero Grade
1. **PIE **e* between stops:**		
Root **pet-* 'fly, fall':		
G πέτομαι 'fly'	ποτή 'flight'	ἐπτόμην aor.midd.
	ποτέομαι 'fly about'	πτερόν 'wing'

e-Grade	*o*-Grade	Zero Grade
L *penna* 'feather' < *pet-nēH$_2$		
Ved. *patati* 'flies'	*pātayati* 'makes fly'	*apaptat* redup.aor.
Root *sek^{w}- 'see', in middle 'follow':		
G ἕπομαι		ἑσπόμην aor. (/h-/ from pres.)
L *sequor*		
Ved. *sácate*	*abhi-ṣācam* acc.sg. 'accompanying'	*saścus-* perf.pple.
Root *deḱ- 'be fitting; conform':		
Ion. δέκομαι 'accept'	δοκεῖ 'seems (good)'	
L *decet* 'is fitting'	*doceō* 'teach' *didicī* perf.	*discō* 'learn' < *di-dḱ-sḱ^{e}/$_{o}$-)
2. PIE *ey, *ye:		
Root *bheydh- 'be convinced/persuade':		
G πείθω	πέποιθα perf.	ἔπιθον aor.
L *fīdō*	*foedus*[1] n. 'treaty' Go. *baidjan* 'compel' (caus.)	*fidēs* 'trust'
Root *deyḱ- 'show, point out':		
G δείκνῡμι[2]		δίκη 'justice'
L *dīcō* 'say'		*dictus* pple.
Ved. *dídeṣṭu* redup.pres. 3sg.imperat.		*díś-* 'direction'
Root *leyk^{w}- 'leave':		
G λείπω (orig. aor.)	λέλοιπα perf. λοιπός 'remainder'	ἔλιπον aor. -λιμπάνω[3]
L *līquī* perf. (orig. aor.)		L *relictus*
Root *steyǵh- 'stride':		
G στείχω 'go in order'	στοῖχος 'order'	ἔστιχον aor.
Go. *steigan* 'climb'	*staig* 3sg.pret.	*stigun* 3pl.pret.
Suffix *-yes- (adjective suffix, 349–53):		
L *māiestās*[4] 'grandeur'	*māius* 'bigger' neut.	*magis* 'rather'
Skt. *návyasi* 'newer', loc.sg.	*návyāṃsam* acc.	*náviṣṭha-* superl.
3. PIE *ew, *we:		
Root *bhewdh- 'become aware':		
G πεύθομαι 'hear of'		ἐπυθόμην aor.
Ved. *bódhati* 'notices'	*bodhayati* caus. 'wakes'	*buddhá-* pple.
OE *béodan* 'request'	*béad* pret.sg.	*budon* pret.pl.

---

1 As a neut. *s*-stem, this should be *e*-grade rather than *o*-grade; the more original form of the root is seen in Enn. *fīdus*. *Foedus* is possibly a false archaism.

2 Zero grade is required for *new*-presents (455). Here the *e*-grade is probably genuine enough; it is the *new*-present that is late and secondary.

3 Lesb. -λιμπάνω is only found with preverbs; it is middle in force, though active in form. This, the original pres., corresponds to Ved. *riṇákti*, L *linquō*, Go. *leih^{w}an*.

4 From *mag-yes-, *mag-yos (194). —*Māiestās*, *māius* are more properly *maiiestās*, *maiius* (194c; 352–3).

e-Grade	*o*-Grade	Zero Grade
Root **dewk*- 'lead':		
L *dūcō*		*ductus* 'drawing'
		dux 'leader'
Root **spewd*- 'push':		
G σπεύδω 'hasten'	σπουδή 'haste'	
Root **ǵhew-d*- 'pour':		
G χέϝω	χο(ϝ)ή 'libation'	κέχυται perf.midd.
L *fūdī* orig. aor.		*fundō* *n*-infix
OHG *giozan*	*gōz* 1sg.pret	*guzzum* 1pl.
4. PIE *er, *re:		
Root **derḱ*- 'see':		
G δέρκομαι	δέδορκα perf.	ἔδρακον aor.
Ved. *ádarśam* root aor.	*dadárśa* perf.	*ádr̥śan* 3pl.aor.
Root **der*- 'flay, split':		
G δέρω 'flay'	δορᾱ́ 'hide'	δέδαρμαι perf.midd.
Ved. *dárt* 3sg.aor.	*dadā́ra* 3sg.perf	*dardr̥hi* intens.imper.
OE *teran* 'tear'	*tær* pret.	*torn* 'anger'
Root **preḱ*- 'ask':		
L *precor*	*procus* 'suitor'	*poscō*[1]
Ved. *praśná*- 'a question'		*pr̥cchati*[1]
OE *frignan*	*frægn* pret.sg.	OHG *forscōn*[1]
5. PIE *el, *le:		
Root **stel*- 'put':		
G στέλλω 'equip'	στόλος 'equipment'	ἔσταλκα perf.
Root **pletH*$_2$- 'flat(en)':		
G πλαταμών 'flat stone' (**91.1**)	πλατύς 'broad'	
Ved. *prathimán*- 'wideness'	*prathaya*- 'make flat' caus. to *práthate*	*pr̥thú*-
W *lledu* 'spread out' trans.		*llydan* 'broad'
6. PIE *en, em:		
Root **ten*- 'stretch':		
G τείνω (**tenyō*)	τόνος 'a stretching'	τάσις (**tn̥-ti*-)
		τατός
		τάνυται (**tn̥-nu*-)
Ved. *tántra*- 'warp' (weaving)	*tatā́na* 3sg.perf.	*tatá*- pple.
L *tenor* 'course'	OL *tetinī* perf. of *teneō*	*tentus* orig. pple. of *tendō* (**218**)

[1] These verb forms in the zero-grade of this root are from PIE **pr̥ḱ-sḱ*^{e}/*o*-. OHG *forscōn* is a denominative formation. OHG *fergōn* 'ask', Lith. *peršù* 'woo' are examples of secondary full grades built on zero grades (cf. Lith. zero grade *piřšti* 'woo' inf.) mentioned above, **114.2**.

e-Grade	*o*-Grade	Zero Grade
Root *g^{w}*hen-* 'strike (dead)':		
G θείνω (*t^{h}*enyō*)	φόνος 'murder'	Hom. πέφαται perf. ἔπεφνον aor.
L *(dē)fendō* 'drive away' < *g^{w}*henyō* (= G θείνω; **218**)		*(dē)fēnsus*
Ved. *hánti* 3sg. 'strikes dead'	*jaghā́na* 3sg. perf.	*ghnánti* 3pl. *hatá-* pple.
Hitt. *ku-en-zi* 3sg. 'kills'		*ku-na-an-zi* 3pl.
Root **men-* 'remain':		
G μένω	μονή 'a waiting'	μίμνω (thematized redup. pres.)
Root **sem-* 'one, same'		
G ἕν n. (**sem*)	ὁμός 'same'	ἅπαξ 'once' (**sm̥-*)
	Go. *sama* 'same'	μία 'one' f. (*$smiH_2$) L *semel* 'once' (**sm̥-mēlom*, **99**, **389.1Bb.3**)

116. Further examples, including the *ē*- and *ō*-grades:

1. Root *ped- 'foot':

e-grade: L *ped-* 'foot', G πεζός 'on foot', (**ped-yo-*), Ved. *padí* loc.sg. 'foot' (root noun);

o-grade: G πόδα acc.sg. (root noun = Ved. *pā́dam*), Ved. *pā́da-* 'foot' < **podo-*, L *tripudium* a kind of sacred dance; G (Hom.) τριπός 'tripod';

zero grade: Av. *fra-bda-* 'instep', Ved. *upa-bdá-* 'a trampling';

ē-grade: L *pēs*;

ō-grade: Gmc. **fōts* as in Go. *fotus*, OE *fót*; 'Dor. πώς'.

Some scholars doubt whether the paradigm of a root like **ped-* really contained totally vowelless zero grades of the type **pdós* gen. 'of a foot'. But such zero grades are securely attested: Ved. *turī́ya-* 'fourth', Av. *ā-χtūirīm* 'up to the fourth (time)' < *k^{w}*turyo-* (ordinal to *k^{w}*etwor-* 'four'); Av. *fšūmant-* 'wealthy; having cattle' < **pku-* (**peku-* '(movable) property') and, possibly, G Κύκλωψ if as seems likely the word reflects *πκυ-κλωπ- 'cattle-thief'. G πτερόν 'wing' is from **pet(H)-* 'fly' (cf. πέτομαι). Obviously there is nothing remarkable about zero grades with obstruents of the type **pd-ós* gen. But with rare exceptions these have been dislodged by analogical full grades (so gen.sg. **pdós* or **pdés* yield to G ποδός, L *pedis*, Ved. *padás*).

Ved. *pā́t* nom.sg., might be **ē* or **ō*, but is probably the latter, as *pā́dam* acc.sg. points to *o*-grade (**pódm̥*) per 36.4. The RV hapax *pādú-* 'foot' superimposes exactly on Go. *fotus*, but a PIE **pōdu-* is unlikely. The other Gmc. languages have a root noun, presumably original except for the unvarying stem *fōt-*. Go. *fotus*, like a number of *u*-stems based on root nouns, is an innovation, based on the homophony of the acc. *-u^{n}, **-uns* (the regular outcomes of both *u*-stem **-um*, **-ums* and cons. stem **-m̥*, **-m̥s*; 255; 257.3, 257.14).

G πούς is not from **pod-s*, which must underlie Hom. τριπός 'tripod', nor from **pōd-s*, which would give ˣπώς. The latter is widely cited in the literature as Doric; in fact the attestation consists of an entry in Hesych. that reads: πῶς · πὸς ὑπὸ Δωριέων. But since there is no such word as 'πός' the true meaning of this entry is enigmatic. Nevertheless, there can be little doubt that a G *πώς (= Ved. *pā́t*) was the starting point for πούς. The replacement of ω by ου has yet to be explained.

2. Root $^*wek^w$- 'utter':

e-grade:	G ἔπος (ϝέπος) 'word', Ved. *vácas-*; Ved. *vívakti*;
o-grade:	G ὄψ*, ὀπός 'voice' (sg. obl. cases only), L *vocō* (? but perhaps < $^*wek^w$-), OIr. *foccul* /fokkʷəlʷ/ 'word' < $^*wok^w$-*tlo-* (? = Skt. *vaktra-* 'mouth'), Ved. *uvā́ca* perf.;
zero grade:	G εἶπον < **e-we-wk*ʷ- (redup. aor., **61.1a**, **506**) = Ved. *ávocam*; Ved. pple. *uktá-*;
ō-grade:	Ved. *vā́k* 'speech', L *vōx* 'voice, word', OE *wóma* 'uproar, outcry' < **wōh*ʷ*man-*.

No likely *ē*-grade forms are known from this root (see **51b**). Ved. *vā́k* 'speech' could equally well reflect **wēk*ʷ*s* or **wōk*ʷ*s*, but the latter is the likely etymon: as in L *vōc-*, the Ved. paradigm of this word has a stem with an unvarying long vowel, *vāc-*. In L, the explanation for this is the generalization of the vowel of the nom.sg. not only through the paradigm but also to most derivatives. Indic, unlike L, rarely (never?) generalizes long vowels in this way; the Vedic forms are from **ŏ* in open syllable via Brugmann's Law: **wok*ʷ*m̥* acc.sg., **wok*ʷ*es* n.pl. > Ved. *vā́cam*, *vā́cas* regularly (apart from the generalization of *c* at the expense of *k*). If **wok*ʷ- was the stem apart from the nom.sg., then the latter was **wōk*ʷ*s*, not **wēk*ʷ*s*.

3. Suffix *-H_2*ter-* **'kinsman'**, for example in **pH̥₂tér-* 'father':

e-grade:	G πατέρα acc.sg. = Ved. *pitáram*;
o-grade:	G ἀπάτορα acc.sg. 'fatherless', ? Skt. *tvátpitāras* (ἅπ.λεγ.) nom.pl. 'having thee as father' (**36.4**; see **129a**)
zero grade:	G πατρός gen.sg., πατράσι dat.pl. (*-r̥su*); L *patris*, *patrī*; G πάτρως, L *patruus* 'father's brother'; Ved. *pitré* dat.sg., *pitṛ́ṣu* loc.pl. (= G πατράσι; **284A.1**); L *mātertera* 'mother's sister' < **mātro-terā* (**74.4**);
ē-grade:	G πατήρ, L *pater*, Ved. *pitā́*, all nom.sg.;
ō-grade:	G ἀπάτωρ.

The *o*-grades are derivative in this stem: simplex forms are *e*- or zero grade. Note that in the *o*-stem paradigms G has only full and lengthened grades (so ἀπάτορος gen.sg. next to πατρός). The PIE acc.sg. had full grade of the stem; case forms like L *patrem* acc.sg. might with equal justice be taken as either a syncope of the full-grade stem vowel or a generalization of the zero grade stem, which is proper to the gen.sg. among other cases. —In all of Skt. literature there is only the one, fairly late, form pointing to an *o*-grade in such stems (**129a**); any earlier evidence has been erased by levelings.

117. LARYNGEALS AND THE ABLAUT SERIES. Without the three laryngeal consonants, in addition to the *e*~*o*~∅ alternation described above there are two more short vowel series (*a*~*o*~∅ and *o*~*o*~∅), and three long vowel series (*ē*~*ō*~ə, *ā*~*ō*~ə, and *ō*~*ō*~ə). The identification of the first element in each triad as equivalent to *e* in the *e*/*o*/zero series, the second with *o* in that series, and so on, is possible only because of the *morphologization* of the ablaut grades as discussed below (**125**; **127–9**). The reasoning works like this:

for Ved. *ájati* 'drives', G ἄγει, L *agit*, W *aeth* 'goes' we reconstruct PIE **ágeti*. But *e*-grade is the proper form for a root in a thematic present, and the root in question has no reflexes pointing to **eǵ-*; therefore, the inference is that in some structural sense **aǵ-* IS the *e*-grade of this root. In a similar way an aorist like PIE **e-dō-t* 'he gave' should have an *e*-grade in the root; **dō-* 'give' has no *e*-grade form as such; the inference is that in some sense *dō-* IS the *e*-grade of the root 'give'.

With the addition of laryngeals, the 'in some sense' qualification can be dispensed with, as *H_2eǵ-* (in place of **aǵ-*) is simply an *e*-grade. Likewise, when we rewrite traditional **dō-* 'give' as **deH₃-*, we see that aor. **e-deH₃-t* is not merely analogous to, but indistinguishable from, the type of the root aor. exemplified by **e-g^w em-t* built from the '*e*-series' root **g^w em-* 'set out'.

1. Examples of the '*a*-series' are as follows:

PIE *H_2eǵ- 'drive' is a well-attested root, widely cited as showing '*a*-series' ablaut: G ἄγω, L *agit* : Ved. *ájati*. —Many think that PIE *H_2oǵ- is seen in G ὄγμος 'furrow'; however, that is unlikely (see 48 fn.). G ἀγωγή 'a carrying' (with 'Attic reduplication', 444) seems to show an *o*-grade, but it is unlikely to be genuinely inherited from PIE. L *ēgī* perf. could be from either PItal. **e-ag-ay* or **e-og-ay*. But in fact neither could be of PIE date: a root of this meaning could not have had a perfect stem in PIE in any case (410, 509); and if one were to be made up at a time when laryngeals still existed it would have been *H_2e-H_2oǵ-, which would have given Ital. **a-ag-*, L ˣ*āgī*; and the zero grade of the same stem, *H_2e-H_2ǵ-, would have given the same thing. (If ˣ*āgī* had ever existed in L, it is hard to believe that it would have been dislodged by attested *ēgī*.) —As is usually the case with roots in *a* (*H_2e), there seems to be no evidence for a zero grade of the root. —L *ambāgēs* (pl.tant. except for a singular case form used adverbially) 'a leading about, a winding' is thought by some to be evidence for PIE *H_2ēǵ-, the lengthened grade.

G ἀγός 'leader' aligns with Ved. *ajá-*. Functionally these are agent nouns and so morphologically they should be *o*-grade *o*-stems, but *H_2oǵ-o- should give Ved. ˣ*ājá-*, and the etymon that best accounts for the facts is therefore *H_2eǵ-ó- (48) if not **aǵ-ó-*.

PIE *H_2ek- 'sharp' > G ἀκμή 'point, edge', L *aciēs* 'keenness', *acus* (*u*-stem) 'needle' : Ved. *áśri-* 'edge, point'. —Many authorities see PIE *H_2ok- in G ὀξύς 'sharp', and perhaps in L *ocris* 'jagged mountain', though there is no reason to expect *o*-grade in either formation,[1] and *H_2o probably gives G α, L *a* (48). —What looks like *H_2ēk- appears in L *ācer* 'sharp' < **ācris*, but lengthened grade is not expected in an adj. in *-*ri*-.

[1] In fact, the formal relationship between PIE *H_2eḱ- and G ὀξ- is obscure; -*s*- is not an adjective stem-building element.

Some scholars attempt to derive G ὠκύς 'swift', Hom. ὠκύπτερος 'hawk' (lit. 'quick-winged'), Ved. *āśú-* from the same root. But these actually reflect *$*eH_3\acute{k}u$-*, whose zero grade combining-form *$*\underset{\circ}{H}_3\acute{k}u$-* is seen in L *acu-pedius* 'fleet of foot' and *accipiter* 'hawk' (**acu-petr-* 'quick-winged'; expected **acipiter* was contaminated by *accipere* *'take; receive'). These latter are also commonly confused with the 'sharp' words—by the Greeks themselves, not just by historians: NB G ὀξύπους 'quick-footed' (hardly 'sharp-'), ὀξύπτερος for Hom. ὠκύπτερος 'quick-winged'.

PIE *$*H_2eydh$-* 'burn' > G αἴθω 'kindle', L *aedēs* 'room, temple', pl. 'house' (< *'hearth') : Ved. *édhas-* n. 'fuel'. PIE *$*H_2oydh$-o-* certainly in Ved. *édha-* m. 'fuel'. —PIE *$*H_2idh$-* perhaps in Ved. *iddhá-* pple.

As previously remarked, PIE roots in **a* often show no ablaut. Although the present example seems to be an ordinary ablauting root, *$*H_2eydh$-*, the evidence is of uncertain value: the patterns this root shows are so productive in Indic that such forms as the zero grade *iddhá-* would have readily been created. The Ved. *n*-infix *inddhé* (depon.) 'kindles' < *$*H_2i$-n-dh-toy* is likelier to be inherited, but not certainly so.

PIE *$*sH_2ews$-* 'dry' > G αὖος (Att. αὗος) : Lith. *saũsas*, OE *séar*. Certain zero grade in L *sūdus* 'dry' (of weather) < *$*s(H_2)uz$-d(h)o-*. Ved. forms in *śoṣ-*, *śuṣya-* and their derivatives are plausibly explained as assimilations of expected **soṣ-* and **suṣ-*; Av. *huška-* (PInIr. **suš-ka-*; cf. Ved. *śúṣka-* 'dry').

PIE *$*H_2eyu$-* 'age, life(time)' > G αἰ(ϝ)ών, αιϝει 'ever, always' > αἰεί, L *aevum*, *aetās* 'age' < OL *aevitās* < **aywotāt-* : Go. *ni aiw* 'never', NHG *nie*. —PIE *$*H_2oyu$-* has been seen in G οὐ 'not' < 'ever', like Fr. *jamais* 'never' from *ne jamais* 'not ever' (< L *(nōn) iam magis*). The semantics are fine, but this attractive etymology conflicts with the view endorsed here regarding the outcome of *$*H_2o$* (48). A likelier specimen is Ved. *ā́yu-* 'life(time), vitality', with *ā* < **o* by Brugmann's Law, 36.4. —Zero grade perhaps underlies Go. *ajukdu*þ*s* 'eternity', OE *éce* 'eternal' (= *ajuk-*) < *$*\underset{\circ}{H}_2yu$-*.

This noun was proterokinetic (272.2), *$*H_2oyu$-* ~ *$*H_2yew$-*, like **doru-* 'tree', gen. **drew-s*; the stem *$*H_2yew$-* is attested in Av. *yaoš* gen., *yavaē* dat.

2. Examples of the *o*-series are as follows:

$*H_3e$ and *$*H_3o$* fall together in all IE languages except InIr., where evidence for *o*-grade forms would be provided by the action of Brugmann's Law on **o* in open syllables (36.4). But such evidence is virtually non-existent:

PIE *$*H_3ek^w$-* 'see' > G (Hom.) ὄσσε du. 'eyes' (*$*H_3ek^wi$-e* or *$*H_3ek^w$-iH_1*), ὄψομαι (fut. of ὁράω), L *oculus* 'eye' : Ved. *ákṣi* (*-i* not an inherited element, but a prop-vowel for would-be **ákṣ*; obl. stem *akṣn̥-*). —There is no evidence for an *o*-grade. —Zero grade in Ved. *prā́k-* 'facing; east; forward' < *$*pro$-H_3k^w$-*, *prācā́is* adv. (inst.pl.) 'forward'; *prátīka-* 'face', G πρόσωπον < *$*proti$-H_3k^w$-* (49.3); and other similar forms. (The long vowels of the Indic forms give away the root-initial laryngeal.) G ὤψ (Hom. acc. ὦπα) 'face' probably from lengthened grade *$*H_3\bar{e}k^ws$* or *$*H_3\bar{o}k^ws$* nom.sg. with the long vowel generalized (as it is in φώρ, φωρός 'thief'), though a secondary full grade *$*^e/_oH_3k^w$-* is thinkable.

Other examples of such roots are *H_3ed- 'smell' (G ὄζω 'smell', L *odor* and *oleō*, 151); *H_3eyd- 'swell' (G οἶδος n. 'a swelling'); and *H_3ep- 'work' (L *opus*, O **úpsannam** 'to be done' Ved. *ápas-*).[1]

a. Some forms traditionally reconstructed with an *o-, *-o-, as *oktṓ(w) 'eight', *owi- 'sheep', *omeso- 'shoulder', *ost(ə)- 'bone', *poti- 'master', and the verbal root *bhod- 'dig' (L *fodiō*) do not strictly speaking belong to an *o*-series, for in fact they show no ablaut at all. Some of those with word-initial *o-* surely had a word-initial *H_3-, which is actually confirmed for *H_3estH_1- 'bone' by Hitt. *ḫa-aš-da-a-i* n. and *H_3ewi- 'sheep' by Luv. *ḫawi-*. A PIE *pH_3eti- is unlikely in place of *poti-, however, and a verbal root *bhH_3ed- is scarcely thinkable in place of *bhod-. In the latter case it is more likely that we are here dealing with an irregular root, namely, one that lacks an *e*-grade in the same sense that *ǵneH_3- 'know' lacks a zero grade and *bhū- 'become' lacks any full grade. (Both L *fodiō* and OCS *bodǫ* 'pierce' belong to abundantly-attested types in which an *e*-grade is normally required in the root.)

118. POSTVOCALIC LARYNGEALS AND THE LONG VOWEL ABLAUT SERIES. Traditional accounts of the PIE ablaut system recognize three patterns of LONG VOWEL alternation parallel to the *e*/*o*/zero pattern:

Categories (*see* 127):

	e-Grade	*o*-Grade	Zero-grade
ē-*series:*	ē	ō	ə
ō-*series:*	ō	ō	ə
ā-*series:*	ā	ō	ə

Taking the *ē*-series for example, the lineup between ordinary gradation and the long vowel series was traditionally conceived of as follows:

	Short Vowel Ablaut	Long Vowel Ablaut
Full grades	*sed- 'sit'	*dhē- 'put'
	*sod-	*dhō-
Zero grade	*sd-	*dhə-/*dh-

(The two forms of the zero grade of *dhē- are preconsonantal and prevocalic, respectively.)

The equivalence of *ə and zero grade made good sense phonetically: conditions which cause a short vowel to drop might reasonably make a long vowel shrink but not disappear altogether; the *ə was in effect a sort of residue. And finally, the total disappearance of such a residue when followed by another vowel is also reasonable.

The laryngeal theory reanalyzes *ə as a CONSONANT, or more accurately several different consonants. (In fact, what is now usually known as the laryngeal theory is also known as the 'theory of consonantal schwa'.) The laryngeals are somewhat like the familiar PIE resonants in the sense that they function as syllabics as well as consonants (93-5), and what was

---

[1] Ved. *ā́pas-* n. 'religious ceremony' would be welcome evidence for *H_3opes-, via Brugmann's Law, but an *o*-grade is out of place in a neut. *s*-stem.

traditionally reconstructed as *ə is now taken to be the syllabic form of the laryngeals—*H̥$_1$ and the like, just like *r̥, *m̥ and the like. This means that the bracketing of *dhē- with *sed-, *dhə- with *sd-, in the table above, is a misprision: the short-vowel pattern that most closely parallels the long vowel patterns is not to be sought in roots like *sed-, with two non-syllabics, but in roots like *ten- 'stretch', zero grades *tn̥- (before consonants), *tn- (before vowels). That is, *ə (or rather *H̥) is not a residue, but is an element that is physically present in all forms of the root:

	Short Vowel Root	Long Vowel Root
Full grades	*ten- 'stretch'	*dheH$_1$- 'put'
	*ton-	*dhoH$_1$-
Zero grade	*tn̥-/*tn-	*dhH̥$_1$-/*dhH$_1$-

119. Examples of long vowel (laryngeal) ablaut.

1. PIE *eH$_1$:

PIE root *dheH$_1$- 'put' (traditionally *dhē-) is seen in G *τίθημι*, L *fēcī* 'made' (orig. a root aor. = G *ἔθηκα*), Ved. *dádhāmi*. —PIE *dhoH$_1$- in G *θωμός* 'heap', perhaps in L *sacerdōs* 'priest' < *sakro-θōts < *-dhoH$_1$-, and clearly in Hitt. *da-a-it-ti* 'you put' < *day-ta-y < *dhoH$_1$-tH$_2$e (PIE *oH$_1$ > Hitt. *ay*). —Zero grade *dhH̥$_1$-tó- pple. > G *θετός* (and also the pres.pl. stem as in *τίθεμεν*), L *factus* (PItal. *θakto- remodeled from *θato-) : Ved. *hitá-*. Reflexes of *dhH$_1$- have been eliminated by analogical leveling in G, for example *τιθέᾱσι* 3pl. for expected ˣ*τίθασι* = Ved. *dádhati* < *dhé-dhH$_1$-n̥ti. A similar leveling is seen in Vedic, but working in the opposite direction: on the basis of 3pl. *dádhati* inherited stems in *dadhi-* < *dhedhH̥$_1$- have been almost totally replaced by a uniform *dadh-, so for example *dádhmas(i)* 1pl. in place of *dádhimas(i).[1]

PIE root *yeH$_1$- 'travel' (traditionally *yē-). Full grade in redup. pres. *yi-yeH$_1$-mi > G *ἵημι* 'set in motion' (191.1), L *iēcī* 'threw' (orig. a root aor., like *fēcī*). —*O*-grade in Dor. *ἕωκα* perf.

Forms traditionally described as zero grade are G *εἶναι* aor.inf. < *ἑεναι, G *ἵεμεν* 1pl., L *iactus* (presumably remodeled from *iatos), and Ved. *yayivás-* perf.pple. But the proper zero grade of *yeH$_1$- would be *iH$_1$-, and such a root form in appropriate formations would have given G ˣ*ἵ̄μεν* ˣ*ἵεναι*, L ˣ*ī(c)tus*, Ved. ˣ*yaīvás-*. But even in the most archaic Indic there is no trace of expected zero grade forms like *īmás 1pl., *ītá- pple.; instead one everywhere finds the full grade *yā-*: *yāmás*, *yātá-*. The absence of zero grade forms in this root makes it hard to believe that such a grade actually existed. L *iactus* presumably replaces *iēctus (if it replaces anything), on the analogy of *fēcī/factus*.

PIE root *eH$_1$p- 'grasp, take' is not attested in G but underlies Ved. *ā́pat* aor. 'obtains' < *eH$_1$p-et, also seen in L *coēpī* perf. (aor., 525.5), Hitt. *e-*

---

[1] This development is found in present-tense stems. In the perf., contrariwise, *dadhimá* 1pl. not only retains the proper zero grade of the root, but the ending in *-ima* spreads to properly aniṭ (121) forms, so *saścima* 'we follow(ed)'.

ip-mi 'I take'. —*O*-grade underlies Ved. *ā́pa* 3sg.perf. < *e-oH$_1$p-e. (L *cōpula* 'rope, bond, connection' is probably from zero-grade *co-apulā by regular contraction (88.3), and therefore despite appearances not an example of *o*-grade). —Zero grade in L *aptus* 'fastened to' < *H̥$_1$p-to- and *apīscor* 'grasp' as well as in the obsolete *apiō* 'snare' (Paul.Fest.) and *cōpula*, above; cf. Hitt. *ap-pa-an-zi* 3pl. of *e-ip-me*, above, though here the form of the root *ap-* is probably analogical, as *H$_1$- seems normally to leave no trace. Indic shows analogical full grade forms in place of zero grade, as *āpnóti* 'obtains', *āptá-* pple. (cf. L *aptus* above); zero grade is found only in desid. *ī́psate* AV 'strives to obtain' < *i-H$_1$p-s- (457A).

2. PIE *eH$_2$:

PIE root *bheH$_2$- 'utter' (traditionally *bhā-) root pres. *bheH$_2$-mi > G φημί (Dor. φᾱμί), L *fārī.* —The *o*-grade clearly seen in G φωνή 'voice' is welcome; since in most IE languages *ā and *ō fall together, evidence for *o*-grades in roots of this shape is scanty. —Zero grade in G φᾰμέν 3pl., φατός pple., L *fateor* 'confess'.

PIE root *steH$_2$- 'stand' (trad. *stā-), redup. pres. *sti-steH$_2$-mi > G ἵστημι (Dor. ἵστᾱμι); the Ved. reflex of the redup. pres. was thematized in prehistoric times, but the original state of affairs is seen in the root aor. *ásthāt* < *e-steH$_2$-t. —Though the root is abundantly attested, there are no unambiguous *o*-grade forms. Presumably Vedic compounds of the type *rathe-ṣṭhā́-* adj. 'standing in a chariot' (in effect 'a chariot warrior') reflect formations in *-stoH$_2$-, like *-bhor-o- 'carrying' in *muṣká-bhāra-* 'having testicles' (of Indra) and abundantly attested in G, for example χοηφόρος 'libation-bearing'. —Zero grades in pple. *stH̥$_2$-tó- > G στατός, L *status*, Ved. *sthitá-*, likewise in G ἵσταμεν. Disguised zero grades in L *stō, stās, stāmus* < *sta-ē(y^e/o)- (475.5).

3. PIE *eH$_3$:

PIE root *deH$_3$- 'give' (trad. *dō-), redup. pres. *de-deH$_3$-mi > G δίδωμι, Ved. *dádāmi*; perhaps *deH$_3$- plus *-ro- or *-no- 'gift' > G δῶρον, L *dōnum*, Ved. *dā́na-*, OIr. *dán*; aor. imper. *ḱe-deH$_3$ 'gimme' > PItal. *kedō > L *cedo* (with iambic shortening; an original *-ŏ would have given L *-e*.). —No self-evident *o*-grades are known, but the 'gift' words, above, may well be from *doH$_3$-ro- and *-no-; and in accord with item 2, above, Ved. compounds of the type *sahasra-dā́-* 'giving thousands' probably reflect *-doH$_3$-. —Zero grades are clearly seen in G δοτός 'given', L *datus*, Ved. *ditá-*; G δίδομεν 1pl., L *damus*, Skt. (Brāh.) *adita* 3sg.aor.midd. 'took'.

120. G alternations of α with ᾱ (Att.-Ion. η) are by no means invariably valid reflexes of *eH$_2$/*H̥$_2$ as discussed above. They often do not express PIE forms so much as G reflexes of PIE patterns (or fragments of such patterns) which have spread beyond the original sites. The alternations in the following verbs, presented here as examples of a very extensive phenomenon, only mimic various inherited patterns (the details of the problems are explained below): G ἁνδάνω 'gratify, please', perf. Hom. ἕᾱδε; λαμβάνω 'grasp' (root *$sleg^w$-), fut. λήψομαι, perf. εἴληφα; λανθάνω 'escape notice', fut. λήσω, perf. λέληθα.

THE PARTICULARS: G ἁνδάνω 'please, gratify' would supposedly be the regular outcome from PIE *$sw\underset{\circ}{H}_2nd$-, the expected zero-grade form of a nasal-infix stem (453-4) formed from *$sweH_2d$- 'sweet' seen as such in *$sweH_2du$-, G ἡδύς, L *suāvis*. The somewhat peculiar pattern of syllabification starts from the rule that the *-*n*- of the nasal infix is never syllabic (93.2), and ˣsuH_2nd- is not a possible sequence. Nevertheless, though the equation 'works', there is reason for doubting that such a form ever existed; no other *n*-infix formation has two (potentially) syllabic consonants before the infix, the few that have three consonants before the infix being things like *$spreH$- 'kick away' (L *spernō*). But *$sweH_2d$- would probably not have made an *n*-infix present in any case. First, it appears to be adjectival rather than verbal (*n*-infix presents are primary formations only). Second, true *n*-infix presents are built to inherently aoristic roots (413), and 'be pleasing' is not obviously aoristic. The two objections have a common basis: adjectives are hardly aoristic in essence, being more stative than otherwise, and ἁνδ- may well be some kind of secondary creation starting from the Hom. perf. (stative) ἕᾱδε, itself a replacement of expected *ἕωδε < *hehwōde < PIE *$se\text{-}swoH_2d\text{-}e$. (Most expected perfects in -ω- < *-oH_2- have been replaced by -ᾱ-.)

G λαμβάνω 'grasp' could, like the above, reflect *$sl\underset{\circ}{H}_2ng^w$-, but the history of the form is obscured by a lack of IE cognates; the jumble of vowels in its various stem forms in G is unlikely to continue any genuinely ancient paradigm straightforwardly. In any case, the zero grade to a root like *$sleH_2g^w$-, that is *$s\underset{\circ}{l}H_2g^w$-, would have given G λᾱβ- (Att.-Ion. ληβ-), indistinguishable from the *e*-grade.

G λανθάνω 'escape (notice)' is a creation within G; the exact starting point is unobvious, but a genuinely original *n*-infix built to a root of the shape *leH_2dh- (or as traditionally written *lādh-) is very unlikely.

a. The ubiquity of ᾱ for expected ω has led to the suggestion that at least under some circumstances ᾱ from *oH_2 is a phonologically regular development. A development peculiar to a single morphological category is usually to be taken as analogical at bottom, though just what the analogy is, for the G perfects in -ᾱ-, is unobvious. At all events, Ved. *svádāmi* 'I please', pple. *svaditá*- shed no light on the history of ἁνδάνω, as the genuine forms from this root would be ˣ*svād*-/ˣ*sūd*-; the pple. *svaditá*- is neither original nor explicable as a replacement of earlier (regular) **sūttá*- or **sūnná*-.

DISYLLABIC ROOTS

121. TERMINOLOGY. The term *disyllabic root* (sometimes *disyllabic base*) reflects the long-held view that roots like **ǵenə*- 'beget' or **temə*- 'cut' (as then written) had two vowels, unlike the typical PIE root. Although the term is still used, it has been rendered inappropriate by the reanalysis of *ə as a syllabic consonant—a root like *$\acute{g}enH_r$- being no more 'disyllabic' than a root like **serp*- 'creep'.

Seṭ and *aniṭ*. The Sanskrit grammarian Pāṇini treated verb roots as falling into two classes, those to which certain suffixes were attached directly and those with a linking vowel -*i*- between the root and the suffix. Thus, using Pāṇini's analysis: the agent noun built to *han*- 'strike down' is *han*-

tar-, whereas to *jan-* 'beget' the same formation is *jan-i-tar-*. In Pāṇini's nomenclature, roots of the type of *han-* are *aniṭ* lit. '*i*-less', and roots of the type of *jan-* were *seṭ* lit. 'with an *-i-*'. These terms are widely used in IE historical linguistics, though not in quite the sense that Pāṇini intended. As is now seen, the 'linking vowel' is neither a link nor a vowel, but the root-final laryngeal consonant: **ǵenH̥*$_1$*-ter-* 'begetter' > *jani-tar-*.

Roots with long vowels are sometimes called *heavy bases* (or *roots*); these include roots like **dhē-*, now interpreted as **dheH*$_1$*-*, and also the seṭ or disyllabic roots, because the zero grades of the latter have long vowels in Sanskrit (**122a**): the zero grades of seṭ roots *jan-* 'beget', *dam-* 'master', *tar-* 'cross' are *jā-*, *dām̥-*, and *tīr-*, for example, in contrast to the 'light' zero grades of aniṭ roots like *han-* 'strike down', *yam-* 'reach', *bhar-* 'carry', namely *ha-*, *ya-*, and *bhr̥-*, respectively.

122. A property of seṭ roots which is enigmatic without the aid of the laryngeal theory is exemplified by **ǵn̥̄-to-* 'born', with a long syllabic resonant in formations corresponding to the zero grades of ordinary roots (**sed-* 'sit', **leykʷ-* 'leave'), or the reduced grades of long vowel roots (**dhē-* ~ **dhə-*). But this is something which follows straightforwardly from the normal workings of ablaut: since a following laryngeal lengthens a preceding syllabic, in most IE languages the reflexes of (zero grade) **-i-* or **-u-* followed by a laryngeal would be *-ī-* and *-ū-*, and when the root contained a liquid or a nasal the result would be what has traditionally been represented as **-r̥̄-*, **-m̥̄-* and the like. (**104-8**). In a scheme of reconstruction that posits laryngeals, there is nothing special about such forms:

	e-Grade	*o*-Grade	Zero Grade	
as:	*bher-	*bhor-	*bhr̥-/*bhr-	'carry'
	*leykʷ-	*loykʷ-	*likʷ-	'leave'
	*dheH$_1$-	*dhoH$_1$-	*dhH̥$_1$-/*dhH$_1$-	'put'
	*gʷhen-	*gʷhon-	*gʷhn̥-/*gʷhn-	'strike down'
so:	*temH̥$_2$-/*temH$_2$-	*tomH̥$_2$-/*tomH$_2$-	*tm̥H$_2$-	'cut'
	*ǵenH̥$_1$-/*ǵenH$_1$-	*ǵonH̥$_1$-/*ǵonH$_1$-	*ǵn̥H$_1$-	'beget'
	*ǵhewH̥-/*ǵhewH-	*ǵhowH̥-/*ǵhowH-	*ǵhuH-	'invoke'

Where two forms are given separated by a solidus, the first is the PRECONSONANTAL alternant and the second is the PREVOCALIC alternant: thus **bhr̥-*, **gʷhn̥-* **dhH̥*$_1$*-*, and **ǵenH̥*$_1$*-* when a consonant follows; **bhr-*, **gʷhn-*, **dhH*$_1$*-*, and **ǵenH*$_1$*-* when a vowel follows. As the table shows, the syllabicity of resonants and laryngeals comes and goes in FULL grade forms when roots end in a resonant + laryngeal cluster, but in the ZERO grade forms when roots end in a single resonant or a laryngeal. In zero grade forms of disyllabic roots, the parent language had a uniform root shape before vowels and consonants, for example **e-ǵhuH-ent* 'they invoked', **ǵhuH-to-* 'invoked'. But in the daughter languages, if **R̥H* develops differently depending on whether it is followed by a consonant or a vowel, the result is a radical deviation from the usual ablaut patterns. Thus in Vedic (roots given in the same order as in the preceding table; as before, forms given before a solidus are preconsonantal, those following a solidus are prevocalic):

	Full Grade	Zero Grade
aniṭ roots:	bhar-	bhr̥-/bhr-
	rec-	ric-
	han-	ha-/ghn-
	dhā-	dhi-/dh-
seṭ roots:	tari-/tar	tīr-/tir- 'pass, cross'
	jani-/jan-	jā-/jan-
	havi-/hav-	hū/huv-

a. In Indo-Iranian and Lithuanian the original patterns are tolerably clear. In fact they have undergone analogical extension, and date of attestation is of great importance for the evidential value of a form. The infinitive *jánitos* to the root *jan-* 'beget' is Rigvedic, and agrees with an assortment of other antique Indic forms pointing to **ǵenH*$_1$*-* (pple. *jātá-* < **ǵn̥H*$_1$*-tó-*, agent noun *jánitrī-* 'mother' < **ǵenH̥*$_1$*-triH*$_2$*-*, *jána-* m. 'man, race' < **ǵonH*$_1$*-o-*, caus. *janáyati* < **ǵonH*$_1$*eyeti* (NB the short vowel in both these forms, 36.4), and *jániman-* 'birth' < **ǵenH̥*$_1$*-men-*). By contrast, the infinitive *hanitum*, to the root *han-* 'strike down' does NOT vouchsafe a root **g*^{w}*henH-*. It first appears in the Classical period, perhaps a thousand years after the Rigveda; the Vedic infin. moreover is *hántum*, which agrees with all other crucial forms from the oldest periods in pointing specifically to an anit root. Compare the following RIGVEDIC forms of the roots *han-* and *jan-*:

ROOT:	*han-* (aniṭ)	*jan-* (seṭ)
infin.:	hántum	jánitos
pple.:	hatá-	jātá-
nomen agentis:	hantár-	janitár-
nomen actionis:	hánman- 'a blow'	jániman- 'birth'

Sometimes there is conflicting evidence, that is, forms showing both seṭ and aniṭ traits will be found side by side even in the Rigveda. It is usually possible to tell whether these are early analogical formations (no language, Vedic Sanskrit included, is immune to the effects of analogical innovation) or point to two different forms of the same root: a shorter one (aniṭ) and a form of the root with a *root extension*,[1] in this case a laryngeal, which explains the seṭ forms.

123. The following are examples of various grades of seṭ roots as they are reflected in G and L:

1. PIE **pleH*$_1$*-* 'fill' (aoristic and intransitive; traditionally **plē-*, **pelə-*)

[1] Many PIE roots are attested in two or more forms identical in meaning, so far as can be told: **ǵhew-* and **ǵhewd-* 'pour'; **yew-*, **yewH-*, and **yewg-* 'join'; **pet-*, **petH*$_1$*-*, **petH*$_2$*-* 'fly'; **ley-*, **leyH-*, **leyk*^{w}*-* 'leave (behind), put by'. These additional consonants are known as *root extensions*, though they are probably ancient morphemes—too ancient to be reconstructable as structural elements.

> G πίμπλημι, (for expected *πίπλημι, like τίθημι), L *plēnus* 'full', *(im)pleō* (**-plēyō*, **192**, **85**), *-plēvī* perf. (orig. aor.) : Ved. *aprās* 2sg.aor.

Zero grade *pl̥H$_1$- before a cons. in G πλῆτο mid. aor. (but see **106.2**), Ved. *pūrṇá-* pple., Lith. *pìlnas*, Go. *fulls*, NE *full*, all < *pl̥H$_1$-no-. (L *-plētus* pple. of *-pleō* likely to be a remodeling of *plātus (*plH$_1$-to-, **106.2**) on the influence of regular perf. act. *-plēvī*.)

Zero grade *pl̥H$_1$- before a vowel is certainly seen in Ved. *purú-* 'many', and possibly in G πολύς—whether this is a remodeling of *παλύς or a direct development (as discussed in **106.2a**). Already in PIE a secondary full grade *pelH$_1$- had arisen, which explains Go. *filu* 'much, very' (*e*-grade). A secondary full grade is seen in Ved. *píparti* 'fills', which, being aniṭ, must postdate the loss of laryngeals; to it was added aniṭ zero grades, Ved. *pipr̥tām* 3du., prevocalic *píprati* 3pl. (as if from *pi-pl-n̥ti*). Just as these must have been created within the history of Indic, G πίμπλαμεν 1pl. within the history of G replaced *πί(μ)πλημεν < *pi-pl̥H$_1$-me*; the model for this pattern of secondary ablaut (which is very vigorous in G) is inherited paradigms like ἵστημι : ἵσταμεν.

2. PIE *telH$_2$- 'fetch, pick up' (aoristic; traditionally *tel-, *telə-) > τελαμών 'carrying strap', Hom. aor. ἐτάλασσα 'submitted' (assimilated from *ἐτέλασσα < *e-telH̥$_2$-s-), ταλασί-φρων 'patient of mind' (if from *τελα-).

O-grade perhaps in G τόλμα f. 'courage' (**269a**), L *tetulī* < *te-tolH$_2$-, (but *tetulī* could also be zero grade, as next; **98**).

Zero grades appear in the *n*-infix present seen in L *tollō* remade from *tollām < *tl̥-ne-H$_2$-mi (**223.1**; **479.4B**). Behavior more saliently peculiar to disyllabic roots is seen in *tl̥H$_2$-tó- pple. > G τλᾱτός, Att.-Ion. τλητός, PItal. *tlātos > L *lātus*.

Zero grade before a vowel is perhaps seen in L *tetulī*, if from *te-tl̥H$_2$-V- (but *o*-grade, as mentioned above, would serve as well). G τάλαντον 'talent' (the weight) perhaps < *tl̥H$_2$-ont- (athem. aor. pple.). Go. *þulan* 'endure', definitely shows prevocalic zero grades; ditto other, more elaborately derived, forms with the same meaning, like OE *þolian* and OHG *dolēn*.

G τέτλᾰμεν 1pl.perf. is a secondary weak grade (for orig. *τέτλᾱ-), like πίμπλαμεν, above.

3. PIE *ǵenH$_1$- (traditionally *ǵen-, *ǵenə-) 'beget': *ǵenH̥$_1$-tor- 'begetter' > G γενέτωρ (γενέτης), L *genitor* = Ved. *janitár-*. Before a vowel: *ǵenH$_1$os- 'birth, race' > G γένος, L *genus* = Ved. *jánas-*.

O-grade in *o*-stems G γόνος 'offspring' = Ved. *jána-* 'man(kind)'. —Zero grade *ǵn̥H$_1$-; before cons.: pple. *ǵn̥H$_1$-tó- > G -γνητός 'born' (κασίγνητος 'brother'), L *(g)nātus* (etymological *g-* indirectly visible in *cognātus* 'related by birth', **220a**) = Ved. *jātá-*. Zero grade before vowel in RV *jajanúr* 3pl.perf. (*ǵe-ǵn̥H$_1$-r̥); the usual forms are somewhat remodeled, but this *jajanúr* is both in an old part of the text and the expected form. G ἐγένοντο 3pl.midd. assimilated from (or just a remodeling of) *ἐγανοντο < *eǵn̥H$_1$-onto.

A very few reflexes of this root seem to be aniṭ; some are perhaps of PIE date but most can be developments within the daughter languages, and compared to the copious evidence for a seṭ root, convincingly antique aniṭ reflexes are few indeed: Ved. *jantú-* 'offspring', *jánman-* 'birth' (with the same meaning as seṭ *jániman-*; in the Rigveda both are common), L *gēns, gentis* < **ǵn̥-ti-* (309; cf. the seṭ zero grade **ǵn̥H₁-ti-* in L *nātiōn-* and *cognātus*), and L *germen* 'seed' (= *jánman-*) < **ǵenmn̥*. Much less clear is Hom. γέγα- perf. (for example γέγαα 1sg.) < ? **ǵe-ǵn̥-*. But *o*-grade is the expected form of the root here; and even if for the sake of the argument **ǵegn̥-wōs* is posited for γεγαώς pple., it should have given G ˣγεγαν(ϝ)ώς. —Seemingly aniṭ formations like G γίγνομαι and Ved. perf. *jajñúr* (the normal form for the unique *jajanúr*, cited above) are probably developments within the histories of the various languages.

4. PIE **demH₂-* (trad. **dem-*, **demə-*) 'tame, master': *n*-infix **dm̥-ne-H₂-* > G δάμνημι; aor. **edemH̥₂sm̥* 1sg. > G ἐδάμασ(σ)α (assimilated from **dema-*), nom. agentis fem. **demH̥₂-ter-iH₂-* > G δαμάτειρα (from **dematerya*, 203.1); masc. **demH̥₂-ter-* > Ved. *damitár-*.

O-grade in Ved. *damáyant-* caus. pple. < **domH₂-eyont-* (*ă* indicates that PIE **o* was in a closed syllable), perhaps L *dominus* 'master', if not a derivative directly from *domus*. (The *o*-vocalism of L *domitor* 'tamer', *domō* 'tame', *domitus, -ūs* 'a taming' is unexpected, as *e*-grade of the root would be more typical of the formations. But the *o* may be a purely phonological development from **dema-*, like *homō* and *vomō* from *hemō*, **wemō*, 42.6, 42.4.)

Zero grade in G δμῆσις 'a taming' < **dm̥H₂-ti-*; ἄδμητος 'untamed' = Skt. *adāmta-* < **n̥-dm̥H₂-to-*. A remote possibility: L *immānis* generally 'enormous' earlier 'fierce, inhuman' (the derivative *immānitās* only 'savageness, fierceness, cruelty'), which might reflect PItal. **en-dmāno-* < **n̥-dm̥H₂-no-* 'untamed'. (The usual derivation from OL *mānus* 'good' (Varro) is straightforward formally but dubious semantically.)

REDUCED GRADES

124. As alluded to in 112, in addition to the full and zero grades discussed here, many scholars posit two or more reduced grades, that is, vowels somehow intermediate between full and zero grades. To such grades were traced all sorts of things: the first vowels of G γυνή 'woman', κύκλος 'circle', θάνατος 'death', ἴσθι 'be' (imperat.), L *frangō* 'break', *maneō* 'remain', *in-* 'un-', *canis* 'dog', *simul* 'at once', and many others. Theories requiring reduced grades were once the norm, but are less in vogue now; and in fact there have been objections to such constructs from their first appearance. One serious reproach, which has never been squarely faced by proponents of reduced grades, is that once one starts subdividing the distinction between PRESENCE and ABSENCE (in other words, full vs. zero grade), it is in principle possible to insert as many intermediate degrees as one wishes. That is, the number and kind of such intermediate vowels is open-ended and unconstrained, which is a serious demerit from the standpoint of methodology and theory. A different and possibly even graver objection is that

no generalizations can be made in regard to their distribution, in terms of either phonology or morphology. In this regard the theory is unlike ablaut. See 112A, especially ad fin.

CONDITIONS AND CAUSES OF PIE ABLAUT

125. Ex hypothese, all patterned alternations are the result of conditioned sound change. However, since vowel gradation was already a feature of PIE, it must be the outcome of processes which took place well back in its history, and it is natural that the conditions and causes of these remote developments should be involved in obscurity.

Only one matter is reasonably clear, namely the relation of the full grade to the zero grade forms: there is an association between full grade (especially *e*-grade) and the tonic accent, while zero grades of roots and affixes occur in formations when the tonic accent is elsewhere. In Vedic, where the position of the PIE accent is best preserved, this relation between accent and gradation is most apparent: thus *ás-ti* 'is' but *s-ánti* 'they are'. To the root **yewg-* 'join': **yuk-tó-* > Ved. *yuktá-* pple.; *n*-infix pres. **yu-né-g-mi* 'I yoke' > *yunájmi* (for **yunágmi*, by leveling); **yu-n-g-énti* 3pl. > *yuñjánti*; add to this **yéwg-mn̥* > G ζεῦγμα 'a joining' vs. **yug-óm* 'yoke' > G ζυγόν (= Ved. *yugá-*). Germanic, through the indirect medium of Verner's Law (139), corroborates the main outlines of the Vedic system: to the root **wert-* 'turn, roll', PGmc. **werþ-* pres. and **warþ-* pret.sg. match root-accented Ved. *várt-* pres. and *vavárt-* perf.sg., whereas PGmc. **wurđ-* pret. pl. and **wurđana-* pple. agree with Ved. *vavr̥t(-má)* (1pl.)perf. and *vr̥t-tá-* pple., whose accents are elsewhere.

Even at the most elementary level, however, this scheme is anything but rigorous. PIE **wóyd-e* 'knows' has two full grades, and the tonic accent is on *o* rather than *e*; from the root **yewg-* again, **yug-óm* 'yoke' (Ved. *yugám*, G ζυγόν, L *iugum*) has no *e*-grade syllable. A very common type of noun is the *o*-grade *o*-stem with root accent, such as **yówg-o-* (> Ved. *yóga-* 'a joining'); an agent noun is identically formed but with ending accent (**yowg-ó-*); and there are crass violations of even the most basic principles: **septḿ̥* 'seven' and **wĺ̥kʷos* 'wolf'. Such forms are certainly secondary of course, albeit already PIE. The same thing is true of another kind of anomaly, thematic forms like **bhérete* 'you (pl.) carry', with an abundance of *e*-grades in the same form. These are certainly less ancient than athematic (eventive) verb inflection, whose primitiveness is in part vouchsafed by the virtual limitation of full grade syllables to one per form. Even at that, for all the obvious antiqueness of the perfect stem, for example, its inflection hardly shows a close relation between accent and grade: **me-món-e* 'has in mind' has three full grades, two of them *e*-grades, but neither of them has the tonic accent. Equally primitive—that is, not explicable as a reworking of something better in accord with the general correlation of full grade and accent—is PIE *$*pénk^we$* 'five', with two *e*-grades; and NB the conjunction **-k^we* 'and', certainly enclitic (and atonic) from very ancient times, but with *e*-grade nevertheless.

Thus, the alternation between full and zero grade is at best only approximately correlated with the tonic accent; but the mere fact that we can recognize a form like **septḿ̥* as aberrant proves that the correlation is salient. By contrast, the phonological basis for the relation between *e*- and *o*-grade is profoundly enigmatic. Accent can play no role here; identical accentuation is seen in *s*-stems like **ǵénH₁-os* nom.sg.'type, race' (to **ǵenH₁-*) and *o*-grade *o*-stems like **ǵónH₁-o-s* 'a begetting, offspring, child' with no hint as to which, if either, is the more original type. The only generalizations that can be made are MORPHOLOGICAL (127); that is, that certain FORMATIONS take *e*-grade of the root, certain take *o*-grade, certain take zero grade, and so on. This is discussed in greater detail below.

Lengthened Grades

126. The lengthened grades, although a feature of the parent language, are clearly secondary. They are particularly associated with three morphological categories: the nom.sg. of consonant stems; the root vowel of *s*-aorist verbs; and semantically derivative forms.

1. *Nominative singulars.* A long vowel in the nom.sg. of consonant stems is seen in InIr., L, and G (though in L particularly the original distribution was obscured by the tendency of such long vowels to be leveled through whole paradigms). These long vowels arose by compensatory lengthening in the nom.sg. of various stem types. These included isolated forms like **ḱēr* 'heart' < ***ḱerd* nom./acc.neut. More important were the non-neuter *r*- and *n*-stems (***pH̥₂ters* 'father' > PIE **pH̥₂tēr*, ***dhǵhm̥mons* 'earthling' > PIE **dhǵhm̥mō*), and the trait was transplanted from there to other forms like PIE **pōts* 'foot' for ***pots*, and **dyēws* 'sky' for ***dyews*. (The last was additionally influenced by acc.sg. **dyēm* < ***dyewm*, 325.)

2. s-*Aorists* (459). Osthoff's Law (63.2) obscures the evidence for lengthened grade in the root vowel of *s*-aorists outside of InIr. (and even in that group there are a number of *s*-aorists with full grade of the root rather than lengthened grade). To **bher-* 'carry', PIE **ebhērsm̥* 1sg., **ebhērss* 2sg., **ebhērst* 3sg. give Ved. *abhārṣam, abhār, abhār.* Vedic carries the lengthened grade through the dual and plural in this type, evidently an innovation (in Skt. the athematic aorist types have retrenched the ablaut of the root vowel generally).

These long vowels are probably ultimately also the results of compensatory lengthening, as ***bherss* and ***bherst* first became **bhērs* (if not **bhēr* for both), reconstituted as **bhērss* and the like, from which a stem **bhērs-* was abstracted.

3. *Secondary Derivations* (adjectives based on nouns, for example). Lengthened grade in derivatives was perhaps a feature of PIE, the best evi-

dence for it being found in patronymics and metaphorical extensions thereof. Thus to **swékuro-* (OHG *suuehur*, NHG *Schwäher*) 'husband's father' was built PIE **swēḱuró-* 'brother-in-law' (lit. 'son of a father-in-law'), as seen in OHG *suuāger* (NHG *Schwager*—the different developments of **ḱ* in OHG result from Verner's Law, 139). Clearer in form than in function is PIE **swe-dhH₁-* 'custom, "our own" matter' (a compound of **swe-* 'own' and seemingly **dheH₁-* 'put') next to **swēdhH₁-*; the former is evident in G ἔθος 'custom', L *sod-ālis* 'accustomed companion', Ved. *svadhā́-* 'custom, native way' next to the seemingly isofunctional G ἦθος, Ved. *svā́ha-* 'oblation, consecration' (but later merely an ejaculation, like *amen*).

In Indic of even the earliest periods, lengthened grade (*vr̥ddhi*) in a word's first syllable (whatever its etymology or functional role) as a marker of derivation was exploited, becoming the norm for adjectives derived from nouns and vice versa. Thus RV *āmitrá-* 'hostile' from noun *a-mítra-* 'enemy', and RV *sā́ubhaga-* 'happiness, prosperity', from adj. *su-bhága-* 'generous'. By the earliest Vedic texts it is already found in syllables to which ablaut is inapplicable, as is the case with both of these examples: the *a-* of *amítra-* (lit. 'nonfriend') is the PIE prefix **n̥-* (108); and the full grade of PIE **H₁su-* 'well-' is not **H₁sew-* but **H₁esu-*, as seen in Hitt. *a-aš-šu-uš* 'good'. (Lengthening has various antecedents; the inherited Indo-European trait seems to have been quite limited, and probably more important is the *-ā-* from *o*-grades in open syllables (Brugmann's Law, 36.4).)

DISTRIBUTION OF PIE ABLAUT GRADES

127. Even though the origins of ablaut (125-6) were necessarily phonological, by the earliest period reachable by the comparative method the distribution of different ablaut grades in PIE had been MORPHOLOGIZED, that is, a given form or class of forms was associated with a certain grade in PIE. This is particularly true of the distribution of *e-* vs. *o*-grades, since the distribution of full vs. zero grades was still to some extent phonological. As is to be expected when phonological alternations are captured by morphology, the system was never completely regular; indeed, it tended with time to became more regular rather than less, where the patterns remained clear at any rate. Thus, evidence points to a non-ablauting root **bhū-* or **bhuH-* 'become'; but various IE languages introduced full grades into the root in accord with the prevailing ablaut patterns: so Skt. *bhavati* 'becomes'.

No list of the morphological categories of the grades can be exhaustive or even completely accurate, since PIE was a language like any other and had forms that stood apart from the general patterns: aor. **ebhūt* or **ebhuHt* 'became' should have had a full grade in the root, but as mentioned above, it did not: G ἔφῡ, Ved. *ábhūt*. Pple. **ǵneH₃-tó-* 'known' should have had a zero grade in the root, but did not: L *nōtus*, Ved. *jñātá-*. PIE **H₂eǵ-* 'drive' seems to have been stuck in *e*-grade, so to speak, as that is seen even in formations that nearly universally embody *o*-grade of the root, such as the PIE *o*-grade *o*-stem ending-accented agent noun; but all evidence points to **H₂eǵ-ó-* 'driver' (and none to expected **H₂oǵ-ó-*). Thus for example Ved. *ajá-*, as normally-formed *H_2ogó- would have given Ved. ˣ*ājá-*. The norms for all of these formal categories were potent enough to engender, eventually, 'regular' forms in place of these irregular ones: OE *cúþ* 'known' < PGmc. ***kunþa-*** as if < PIE **ǵn̥H₃-tó-*, Vedic *bhávati* '(will) be' mentioned above, and so on. There were probably many such oddities of PIE morphology we know nothing about, owing to their early and complete replacement by forms in better agreement with the dominant patterns.

128. Ablaut grades in roots:

1. *E*-grade:

Simple (root-accented) thematic verbs: **bhér-e-ti* 'carries'.

Singular active indicative of root presents: **H₁és-mi* 'I am'; reduplicated presents: **de-deH₃-mi* 'I give'; root aorists: **e-gʷem-t* 'set out'.

Subjunctive, all numbers and voices: **H₁es-et(i)*, **de-deH₃-et(i)*, **gʷem-et(i)*.

Neut. *s*-stems: **ǵenH₁-os* 'birth, race', obl. **ǵenH₁-es-*.

Neut. *men*-stems: **yewg-men-*, **ǵenH̥₁-men-*.

Root-accented *tu*-stems (nomina actionis, generally masc.): **ǵénH̥₁-tu-* 'a begetting', **démH̥₂-tu-* 'a taming'. Cf. the ending-accented *ti*-stems, section 3, below.

Root-accented agent nouns in **-ter-/-tor-*: **ǵénH̥₁-tor-* 'begetter'.

'Tool' derivatives in **-tro-/-tlo-/-dhro-/-dhlo-*, typically neut., but not unusually fem. (originally collective): **speḱ-tlo-* 'mirror' (root **speḱ-* 'see').

Nom./acc. sg. of certain proterokinetic (**272.2**) *u*-stem neuter nouns: **péḱu* 'property', *médhu* 'sweet drink'. (See also under *o*-grade.)

Some root nouns, and the loc.sg. of all root nouns: **reH₁ǵ-* 'king', **leg-* 'a gathering'; loc.sg. **pedi* to **pod-* (prevailingly *o*-grade) 'foot'.

A small number of primary *u*-stem adjectives have full grade of the 'root': **sweH₂du-* 'sweet', **H₂enǵhu-* 'narrow', **eH₃ḱu-* 'swift', **H₂eḱu-* 'sharp'. Whether it is significant or not, these all have a laryngeal; cf. the forms mentioned in 3 (zero grade), below.

2. *O*-grade:

Singular of perfect: **me-mon-e* 'has in mind', **woyd-e* 'knows'.

Causative/frequentative verbs in **-éyᵉ/ₒ-* and **-eH₂-y-*: **mon-éyeti* 'reminds, warns', **sod-éyeti* 'sets', **bhor-éyeti* 'carries around', **molǵ-éyeti* 'strokes repeatedly; milks'; **domH₂-eH₂-yeti* 'dwells'. Derivatives from same, such as **mon-i-tor-* 'reminder, warner'.

Certain root-nouns seem to be mainly *o*-grade: **wokʷ-* 'voice', perhaps **dom-* 'house', **gʷow-* 'cow' (but for the latter two see **272.1**).

O-stem nouns: these are prominent as the last element of compounds, like G χο(ϝ)η-φόρος 'libation-bearing'. In simplex formations, there are two types. (1) Root-accented masculine nomina actionis: **bhór-o-* 'a carrying'; (2) ending-accented nomina agentis: **bhor-ó-* 'a carrier'. (Neuter *o*-stems are unpredictable in regard to both meaning and ablaut: typical neuters are **yugó-* 'yoke' to **yewg-* 'join', and **werǵó-* 'work' from **werǵ-*.)

Nomina actionis in **-mó-* (**-meH₂-*), as **gʷhor-mo-* 'heat', **pot-mo-* 'a falling, fate', **bhor-mó-* 'a carrying', **dhoH₁-mó-* 'heap'. (Cf. zero-grade adj., below.)

Nom.sg. of certain proterokinetic (**272.2**) neuter nouns: **dóru-* 'tree/wood', **ǵónu-* 'knee', **H₂óyu-* 'age, life(time)'. (These are mostly *u*-stems, but belonging here is the *n*-stem **nomn̥* 'name', gen. **n̥men-s*, **311a**; for a more conventional discussion see **288**.)

3. Zero grade:

All persons, numbers, and voices of:

_n_-infix (453) and _new_-suffix (455) present stems: _*yu-né-g-mi_ 'I yoke', _*yungmós_ 'we yoke'; _*gʷl̥-né-_H_1_-mi_ 'I throw', _*gʷl̥n_$H̥_1$_mós_ 'we throw'; _*tn̥-néw-mi_ 'I stretch', _*tn̥numós_ 'we stretch' (_*yewg-_, _*gʷel_H_1_-_, _*ten-_).

_*-sḱ_^{e}/$_o$_-_ suffix thematic present stems (456.3): _*gʷm̥-sḱe-ti_ 'sets out', _*pr̥ḱ-sḱe-ti_ 'asks'. This includes the subtype with reduplication.

Suffix-accented thematic verbs in _*-y_^{é}/$_{ó}$_-_ (typically intransitive and often middle, 456.1A): _*mr̥-yé-tor_ 'dies', _*gʷm̥-yé-ti_ 'sets out'.

All root and athematic reduplicated verbs (which includes perfects) with the accent on any affix (namely the person ending in the dual and plural indicative active, and in all middle forms): _*_H_1_s-wós_ 'we two are', _*_H_1_s-mós_ 'we (pl.) are', _*likʷ-mé_ (aor.) 'we leave', _*me-mn̥-mé_ perf. 'we have in mind', _*ǵhs-tór_ 'swallows'. The Narten roots, note **a** below, are an exception regarding athem. middle inflection.

Optatives built to roots (see 533): _*_H_1_s-yé_H_1_-m̥_ 'may I be', _*_H_1_s-i_H_1_-mé_ 'may we be', _*likʷ-yé_H_1_-m̥_ 'may I leave', _*likʷ-i_H_1_-mé_ 'may we leave'. The Narten roots, note **a** below, show full grade in these forms.

Perf. stem for pple. in _*-wos-/-us-_: _*me-mn̥-wṓs_ 'having in mind', acc. _*me-mn̥-wós-m̥_, dat. _*me-mn-us-éy_ (root _*men-_).

Verbal adjectives in _*-tó-_ and _*-nó-_ (564-6, 569): _*likʷ-tó-_ 'left over', _*ǵn̥_H_1_-tó-_ 'begotten', _*yuk-tó-_ 'yoked', _*pl̥_H_2_-nó-_ 'flat'.

Adjectives in _-mó-_, as _*gʷhr̥-mó-_ 'warm', _*(s)tig-mó-_ 'sharp', _*pr̥_H_3_-mó-_ 'first'. Cf. _o_-grade nouns in _-mó-_, above.

_u_-stem adjectives (typically of tangible physical property):[1] _*ḱr̥tú-_ 'strong', _*tn̥nú-_ 'thin', _*ln̥gʷhú-_ 'light', _*gʷr̥rú-_ 'heavy', _*pl̥t_H_2_ú-_ 'broad', _*bhn̥ǵhú-_ 'thick'.

Stem-accented _ti_-stems (fem. nomina actionis): _*gʷm̥-tí-_ 'a setting out', _*mn̥-tí-_ 'a thought', _*dh_$H̥_1$_-tí-_ 'a placing', _*sru-tí-_ 'a flowing' (_*gʷem-_, _*men-_, _*dhe_H_1_-_, _*srew-_). Cf. the root-accented _tu_-stems, above.

The 'weak' cases of hysterokinetic (272.3) root nouns, such as _*pd-éy_ dat., _*pd-ós_ gen./abl., to _*pod-_ 'foot'.

The oblique stem of proterokinetic (272.2) neut. _u_-stems (see _e-_ and _o_-grade examples above): genitives _*pkéw-s_ (_*péku-_), _*dréw-s_ (_*dóru-_), _*_H_2_yéw-s_ (_*_H_2_óyu-_), _*gʷné_H_2_-s_ (_*gʷén_H_2_-_), _*n̥men-s_ (_*nomn-_).

The first element of a bahuvrīhi (adjective) compound was originally in zero grade; so the numerals (_*tri-_ 'three-' for example), _*_H_1_su-_ 'well-', _*pl̥_H_1_u-_ 'many-', _*m̥ǵ_$H̥_2$_-_ 'great(ly)-', _*sm̥-_ 'having-the-same', _*n̥-_ privative adj.

Many zero grades in roots are not norms of PIE morphology so much as artifacts of other processes. For example, thematic present stems created in this or that IE language from original athematic formations like _n_-infix and reduplicated presents use the zero grade of the original stem: L _linquō_ 'leave' and G (Sappho) -λιμπάνω (_*leykʷ-_), L _serō_ 'sow' (_*se-s_H_1_-_), Ved. _r̥ñjáse_ 'make straight, arrange' 2sg. (_*reǵ-_), _tíṣṭhati_ 'stands' (_*ste_H_2_-_).

a. NARTEN ROOTS. There are roots that occur in verb categories given above as normally taking zero grade of the root (because the tonic accent is on a suffix or ending), which nevertheless have FULL GRADE of the root. Vedic reveals furthermore that in the

---

[1] The few exceptions in having _e_-grade, noted above, are widely-attested and though aberrant are presumably old.

middle paradigm the tonic accent is on the root, instead of being on the ending as in the usual athem. middles:
From root *$\acute{k}$*ey*-, G κεῖται 'lies', Ved. *śáye* (a *t*-less 3sg., 426), Av. *saētē*; 3pl. κεῖνται, AV *śére*, Av. *sōire*; opt. RV *śáyīta* 3sg. (The Hitt. paradigm, for example *ki-it-ta* 3sg., *ki-ya-an-ta-ri* 3pl., is ambiguous on the point in question.)
From root **wes-* 'dress', Hom. εἶμαι, ἕσσαι, imperf. ἕστο, Ved. *váste*, Av. *vastē*, Ved. *vásate* 3pl. = Hitt. *ú-e-eš-ša-an-ta*.
The same phenomenon underlies G ἧσται 'sits', Ved. *ā́ste*, Av. *āste*, Hitt. *e-ša*, *e-ša-(a-)ri*, from PIE **eH₁s-* 'is sitting'; here the lengthening effect of the laryngeal (103.1) disguises the underlying short (full grade) vowel. (NB: this stem has also been analyzed quite differently, namely as **H₁e-H₁s-*, an ordinarily-formed reduplicated present exactly parallel to **dhe-dhH₁-* and, more to the point, to **ste-stH₂-*.)

Given the degree of lexical and formal alignment between InIr., G, and Hitt., and in such inherently conservative vocabulary, the type must be old; but its relationship to the usual pattern is enigmatic.

129. Ablaut grades in affixes.

Many PIE affixes of all descriptions are attested in two or more ablaut grades. Thus, the stem affix of *n*-stem nouns is found as **-on-*, **-en-*, and **-n̥-/-n-*; the ending of the genitive singular is either **-es*, **-os*, or **-s*. The stem marker of the PIE *r*-stems is attested in all five grades, the 'comparative' suffix is certainly seen in **-yōs*, **-yos-*, **-is-*, and probably **-yes-* (L *māiestās*, 115.2). Other affixes, however, are seen in only one form, such as the acc.sg., which is only **-m̥* or **-m*, depending on whether it follows a consonant or a vowel. Some affixes alternate just like roots: the *n*-infix and *new*-suffix presents are tonic and full grade (**-né-*, **-néw-*) in the singular active indicative, but zero grade and atonic (**-n-*, **-nu-*) where the accent is on a suffix, as in the dual and plural indicative, and all numbers of the middle. The athematic optative marker is similar: **-yéH₁-* in the singular active, **-iH₁-* in the dual and plural, and all numbers of the middle.

The clarity of these forms is exceptional, however. The behavior of ablaut in affixes is generally more obscure, for two reasons. The first is the vexed question of the relationship between different elements: **-es*, **-os*, and **-s* are transparently the usual three grades of the same marker (gen.sg.); but are **-i* loc.sg. and **-ey* dat.sg. thus related? Are **-s* nom.sg. and **-es* nom.pl.? Authorities disagree.

The second problem is that in affixes the correlation between stress, grade, and function generally has been so much disturbed by leveling in attested languages as to be far less recoverable than is the case of the distribution of grades in roots. Thus, in defiance of the usual correlations, in PIE times the *i*-stems and *u*-stems seem to have inflected identically as to the distribution of gradation of the stem suffix, without regard to the grade of the root to which they were built, or where the tonic accent happened to be in any given form (304.2a, 312, 272.2a).

A peculiarity of the parent language was that for some suffixes one full grade vowel greatly preponderated but was nevertheless not exclusive. Thus, the vast majority of *n*-stem nouns had full grade in *-o-* (280), as reflected in the disproportion between *on-* and *en-*stems in L and Gmc., and the preponderance of full-grade stems in *-ān-* in Indic, reflecting **-on-* in open syllables (36.4). PIE *n*-stem nouns with full grades in **-en-* were very few in number—absolutely, not just by comparison: only one or two are securely attested for the parent language, most confidently **ukʷsen-* 'steer, ox'. (The abundance of *en*-stems in G is a secondary proliferation in that language, not an inheritance; **280** especially **a**, and **286.3**.) On the other hand, in the *s*-stems it was *e*-grade in the full grade stem that greatly preponderated (except of course for nom./acc.sg.). Once again there are a handful of exceptions in **-os-*: securely attested is **H₂usos-* f. 'dawn', **H₂usosm̥* acc.sg. > Ved. *uṣā́sam*.[1] Perhaps the *os*-type was originally more prominent, because in L, non-neut. stems in *-ōs-* are very much commoner than those in *-ēs-* (of which there are seemingly just two, *mulier* 'woman' and *Cerēs*, **299a**). The two *s*-stem adjective types heavily favor *o*-grade: the 'comparative' suffix in **-yos-/-is-* (**348-50**; data pointing to **-yes-* like L *māiestās* being in general isolated and enigmatic), and the perfect participle in **-wos-/-us-* (**561**; **-wes-* perhaps occurred in the loc.sg.) The significance of these skewed distributions of *e-* and *o*-grade vowels in affixes is unknown.

a. In G consonant stems, a *polarization* of ablaut grades is seen: if a basic form has *e*-grades, many derivatives will have *o*-grades. Whether this is an ancient trait or a Greek innovation is much debated. Skt., for example, has many compounds which are generally analogous to G ἀπάτωρ 'fatherless', like Ved. *a-bhrātáras* nom.pl. 'brotherless'; but in these, as in the quoted form, the short stem vowel points to original **e*, like the simplex noun, not **o*. A single form, *tvátpitāras* nom.pl.m. 'having thee as father' occurs in one of the later Vedic collections; its *-ā-* perhaps points to **-o-*, but is far from compelling evidence. It would not be daring to suggest that Greek-like patterns existed but were leveled in InIr.: Skt. shows little or nothing pointing to **-ter-* in the nomen agentis suffix, for example, while copiously confirming agent forms in **-tor-* (thanks to the agency of Brugmann's Law)—and here there can be no question about the ancient status of *e*-grades.

CONSONANTS

130. TABLE OF PIE CONSONANTS.

Points of Articulation:		labial	apical	palatal	velar	labiovelar
Manners of Articulation:						
STOPS:	voiceless:	p	t	ḱ	k	k^w
	voiced:	(b)	d	ǵ	g	g^w
	voiced aspirated:	bh	dh	ǵh	gh	g^wh
RESONANTS:	glides:	w		y		
	nasals:	m	n			
	liquids:		l, r			
FRICATIVE:			s			

LARYNGEALS *(points of articulation unknown)*: H_1 H_2 H_3

[1] There is some evidence that in this noun the root vowel as well as the stem vowel alternated in the paradigm, but the details of such an alternation are speculative.

The PIE consonants fell into four natural classes, according to *manner of articulation*: STOPS, RESONANTS, the single FRICATIVE *s, and LARYNGEALS.

Of these the *stops* (131-64) comprise the most complex system.

The *resonants* (175-207; known interchangeably as the *semivowels*) are the six elements that are sometimes syllabic and sometimes consonantal. The syllabic forms *i, *u, *r̥, *l̥, *m̥, and *n̥, have been discussed under vowels, above (37-9, 93-109); the consonantal forms *y, *w, *r, *l, *m and *n will be treated here.

The PIE consonant system has an oddly meager ration of *fricatives* (168-74) in view of its overall elaborateness. English, for example, has some 24 consonants, of which eight are fricatives and two are affricates; a ninth fricative /χ/ was only recently lost. By contrast, PIE had some 25 consonants, more or less (the extreme views range from 20 to about 50), but only a single fricative and no affricates.

Owing to the indirect nature of most of the evidence, the number, occurrence, and phonetic properties of the *larynageals* (165-7) are still the subject of debate. There are almost as many 'laryngeal theories' as there are Indo-Europeanists, though there are of course schools of thought.

STOPS

131. Three SERIES of stops are reconstructed for PIE: *voiceless*, *voiced*, and what are conventionally known as *voiced aspirated* (*bh, *dh, and so on). The phonetics of the first two types are tolerably certain, but the voiced aspirated series will require some discussion. Recently, in fact, a number of suggestions have been made for rethinking the whole system (133).

The status of a fourth series of stops in PIE, a *voiceless aspirated* series (*ph, *th, and so on), is an ongoing question. There are several lines of argument for reconstructing this series, all of them valueless.

132. Although five distinct POINTS OF ARTICULATION are shown here, including three dorsals (taking the voiceless series *ḱ, *k, and *kʷ by way of example), no more than two of the latter are required from the standpoint of G and L, or of any single IE language. The literal truth of a three-place system (plain velar stops in addition to palatal and labiovelar stops) for the sound inventory of the parent speech may be questioned on its face. The evidence for the *k ('plain velar') series is mostly of two kinds:

One involves etyma in which the plain velar is adjacent to an *r, *ă, or high back rounded vocoids (*ŭ and *w). Since there are many fewer instances of the palatal series in these same environments than one might expect, the inference is that our 'plain velars' were once originally members of the palatal series (or rather, what eventually became the palatal series; 152-3). But there are too many palpable exceptions to this generalization for it to be more than a springboard for glottogonic speculation.

The other main body of evidence is forms whose cognates among the satem languages are limited to Baltic and Slavic, where dorsal stops correspond to dorsal stops in the centum cognates. For example, G κολωνός 'hill', L *collis* and OE *hyll* (both < **kl̥-ni-*), MIr. *coll* 'chief, leader', are apparently cognate with Lith. *kálnas* 'hill' and OCS *čelo* 'forehead'. These outcomes indicate PIE **kel-* 'stick up, stick out', not **ḱel-* or **kʷel-*. But the BS forms are the only satem witnesses, and their evidence on exactly this point is compromised by the certainty that the Baltic Assemblage, while preponderantly satem, did not belong wholly to the satem group. To be sure the known languages are all from the satem side of the isogloss, but there was much dialect borrowing from the centum side. Thus, Ved. *áśman-* 'stone', Av. *asman-*, Lith. *ãšmens* (pl.tant.) 'blade' all show that the dorsal stop of PIE **H_2ekmon-* 'stone' was necessarily **ḱ*, and not **k*. But there are also Lith. *akmuõ* 'stone', OCS *kamy*. Accordingly, the BS attestations cannot be trusted all by themselves to contraindicate a reconstuction with a palatal stop, as here PIE **ḱel-* 'stick up/out'.

That said, the use of plain velar stops in reconstructing PIE forms is inescapable. One must have an unambiguous way of representing the forms in which satem stops (as attested outside of BS) correspond to stops in the more conservative groups; see 153.

133. In the following pages, PIE stops will be grouped under headings according to POINT of articulation, and the reflexes of the each of the three MANNERS—voiceless, voiced, and voiced aspirated—will be given under the point headings. But certain matters touching on the manners of articulation in general will be mentioned here.

VOICED ASPIRATED STOPS (**bh*, **dh*, and so on). The term *voiced aspirated* is one of convenience only. Reflexes of this series are: voiced aspirated stops in early Indic; voiceless aspirated stops in G; and fricatives in Italic (which were evidently voiceless at one time). Elsewhere they became voiced stops,[1] though with two different consequences: in Celtic, BS, and Iranian—three seemingly independent innovations—these fell together with the PIE voiced series, but in Germanic and Armenian they remained distinct from the PIE voiced stops, which became voiceless stops.

From such variety it is impossible to infer the phonetic value of the antecedent sounds in the parent speech with confidence. The term 'voiced aspirated', and the customary notation that goes with it, are holdovers from an earlier period in the history of IE studies, when the features of Sanskrit were too trustingly assumed to reflect PIE more or less directly.

In recent times there has been a rekindling of interest in the phonetics

[1] The outcomes of voiced stops in Tocharian and Anatolian cannot be confidently ascertained, thanks to obscurities in their writing systems.

of the PIE stop system. The main problem is not the voiced aspirated stops (which can be dealt with by refusing to reconstruct any particular phonetic features). The problem is the PLAIN VOICED stops as traditionally defined. Experience with living languages suggests that the distribution of voiced stops should be only relatively mildly constrained; that is, there should not be too many environments where other types of sounds occur but voiced stops do not (apart from commonplaces like word-final position). But in PIE there are a number of strong constraints on the distribution of the voiced series. For example, there is only one even tolerably certain instance of a voiced stop in the whole system of PIE endings (the pronominal nom./acc.sg.n. marker **-d*, as in L *id*, NE *it*). And remarkably, no solidly-attested PIE root contains two voiced stops. By contrast the other two series occur abundantly in endings and primary and secondary suffixes, and there are many cases of two of them together in the same root, for example **pet-* 'fly' and *dheg^{w}h-* 'be hot'.

One means of correcting such oddities is a wholesale reassignment of phonetic values, such as taking the voiced aspirated series as having actually been (plain) voiced, and the traditional voiced series as something else—say glottalized, or (voiceless) aspirated. However, the redesigned PIE stop systems proposed to date create as many problems as they solve. For example, as mentioned above, what are traditionally set up as the PIE **d* and **dh* series merge, independently, in several branches of IE; redefining **d* as **t^h* (or **t'*, that is, glottalized), and **dh* as **d*, makes the widespread IE merging of the two series less rather than more comprehensible; and the failure of the redefined **t^h* (or **t'*) series to merge with the **t* series in any IE language at all is difficult to fathom. Finally, and a point which seems to be generally overlooked in such proposals, a system of contrasts redefined as **t*, **t^h*, **d* (or **t*, **t'*, **d*) in place of traditional **t*, **d*, and **dh* succeeds if anything too well in attaining typological normality: such systems are not only very widely observed in the world's languages, they also exhibit a diachronic stability which is inconsistent with the IE family history, in which not a single language preserves the original structure (as thus redefined) intact.

Apart from observing that it seems unlikely that the PIE 'voiced aspirates' were literally voiced and aspirated, we will not attempt here to revise either the reconstructed system of PIE stops or the traditional notation.

a. Interestingly, the range of reflexes of the ancient Indic voiced aspirated stops in modern Indic vernaculars is quite as various as the IE reflexes of PIE 'voiced aspirates': they remain as such in Lahnda, (some) Panjabi, West Pahari, Assamese, Bengali, Oṛiya, Bihāri, Bhojpuri, Hindi, Gujarati, Marāṭhi, and many others; they become plain voiced stops in nearly as many groups (Palestinian Gypsy, Ḍumāki, Dameli, Pašaī, Woṭapuri, Savi, Shina, Kashmiri, and Siṃhalese, among others); and they actually become voiceless aspirated stops in two dialects of Gypsy (Armenian and European)—cf. the G and L reflexes of PIE **bh* and the like (135-6).

134. THE VOICELESS STOPS are the most persistent. They remain as such except in Germanic, where they become fricatives; and in Armenian they change to the extent of adding the feature of aspiration (generally thought to have been the first phonetic stage in the evolution of this series in Germanic too). In later forms of IE languages—Romance and Indic vernaculars for instance—they suffer extensive weakening and loss in medial and final position, but in the ancient languages they persist except in certain consonant clusters and in final position.

The VOICED STOPS also remain as such in most IE languages, including classical G and L. But *β*, *δ*, *γ* eventually became voiced fricatives, as they are in Modern Greek. This change took place at an early period in some dialects, but in standard Attic and the *κοινή* probably not until the 1st century AD or later. —L *b* also became a fricative in the early centuries AD, and in some Romance languages, most conspicuously Spanish, there is no difference at all between the reflexes of PRom. **b* and **v*. In the others, the two sounds remained distinct initially but coalesced postvocalically. Thus in It. *Gubbio*, ancient *Iguvium*; and *rabbia* 'rage' < PRom. **rabya*, in contrast to the maintenance of the distinction in It. *bile* 'bile' < L *bīlis*, vs. *vile* 'low, vile' < L *vīlis* 'cheap'; cf. 186).

135. THE PIE VOICED ASPIRATES IN ITALIC. The voiced aspirated stops, so-called (133), became voiceless aspirates in Prehistoric G and Italic.

They remained such in classical Greek, only later becoming fricatives (136). But in Italic a change to fricatives took place—at least in initial position (and probably elsewhere)—in prehistoric times; likewise prehistoric was the change of the apical fricative [θ] to *f*, and a weakening of the dorsal fricative [χ] to *h* (which sometimes then vanished). For the history of both Latin-Faliscan and Sabine we assume the following prehistoric steps for WORD-INITIAL position:

bh	>	p^h	>	f	>	f
dh	>	t^h	>	θ	>	f
gh	>	k^h	>	χ	>	h

In MEDIAL POSITION, where we also find *f* in Sab. but *b* or *d* in L, the steps leading to the L reflexes are disputed. But probably these too passed through the stage of the fricatives *f*, *θ*, *χ*. G λίτρα, name of a Sicilian coin, appears to confirm a prehistoric Italic **līθrā*, etymon of L *lībra* 'pound'.[1] Another kind of evidence for early **θ* is the change **sr* > L *br* (225.2), as in *fūnebris* 'funereal' < **fowVnes-ri-* (cf. *fūnestus* 'mournful'). This superficially startling change is easily explained if **sr* first changed to **θr*, which fol-

[1] Had the source of the borrowing still been at the **līt*ʰ*rā* stage, the G form would have been ˣλιθρα with a voiceless aspirated stop.

lowed the usual development of *θ to *b* adjacent to *r*. The Umbrian development of *-(n)f* from **-ns* (as in the acc.pl.) implies that in Sab., as well, **s* in certain environments fell together with *θ.

The crux of the problem of the common Italic development of these sounds is the voicing of the intervocalic reflexes in the history of L and their subsequent coalescence with voiced stops. One cannot have BOTH a common Italic coalescence of **f* and *θ AND a Latin voicing of intervocalic reflexes of these things, as *θ and **f* do not completely fall together in medial position in Latin. In other words, if **f* and *θ had totally coalesced in common Italic, they could not behave as they do in L (where intervocalic **f* and *θ fall together only when the *θ is adjacent to *r*, *l*, or a *ŭ̄*). And if the voicing of **f* and *θ was already a feature of PItal., the Sab. outcome *-f-* between vowels is impossible.[1]

At the center of this dispute is the assumption, which for generations has been conventional wisdom, that the intervocalic sound written *-f-* in Sab. was voiceless. But if intervocalic *-f-* was in fact [β] or [v], then [f] and [β,v] were in complementary distribution in Sab.—were the same sound, from the point of view of structure—and would have been written with the same letter as a matter of course (just as in English we write [p] and [pʰ] with the same letter). Even when writing their languages in the Latin alphabet, it would be expected that native speakers of Oscan and Umbrian would follow their custom of using the same letter for both sounds when writing a word like *fufans* 'they were'. The L alphabet had no means of representing [β] or [v] in any case.

The intervocalic *-f-* in L words which are assumed (doubtless correctly) to be of Oscan origin, such as *scrōfa* 'sow', *rūfus* 'red (haired)', and the family name *Afer*, was certainly voiceless in L; but that is not conclusive evidence for its pronunciation in Oscan. Recently evidence for a voiced value for Sab. *-f-* has been found in such correspondences as O MEBITHI ~ ME8ITHI (the characters being Greek except for the 8 '*f*'), and also—ancillary but pertinent—that the letter 8 in Etr. was voiced medially. But one can go further: L itself provides evidence for this view. If for the sake of argument medial *-f-* in Sab. stood for a voiced fricative, words containing such a sound when borrowed into L would have to be modified to fit L phonology.

Now, the same problem faced speakers of OE when borrowing Late Latin or Romance words beginning with *v-*, as OE had no [v] in word-ini-

---

[1] If medial *θ became **f* adjacent to liquids and high back vocoids as early as PItal., their developments in L would be unchanged from the usual view; but in that case Sab. requires a subsequent merger of the remaining *θ with **f*. This is not impossible, only over-elaborate; in any case, the communis opinio is that the partial merger of medial *θ and **f* was a specifically Latin-Faliscan development.

tial position. When such words were borrowed, the usual substitute was *f-*: *fers* 'verse' (L *versum*), *fann* 'winnowing fan' (L *vannus*). But in OE several different sounds were substituted, in fact; for example, *b-* rather than *f-* was occasionally substituted for LL *v-*, as in OE *berbena* < L *verbena* 'vervain'. With this in mind, it might be objected that Latin speakers would be unlikely to hit upon *-f-* as the substitute for every single instance of [β, v] in words borrowed from Sab. But if *b* were the makeshift for a Sab. borrowing into L it would be well-nigh impossible to recognize the form as a borrowing, because *b* is the intervocalic reflex of PItal. **f* in native L words. In other words, L *rūfus* 'red-haired' and *ruber* 'red' might BOTH be borrowings from Sab., one with *f* substituted for the sound, the other with *b*; but only the former is recognizable as a borrowing. Only when the expected L reflex would have been *d*, or when there is something else un-Latin about the form of the word, would the L substitution of *b* for Sab. *f* be revealed. A likely example of exactly that is L *rōbus*, reportedly (Paul.Fest.) a 'rustic' form of *rūfus*. Since *ō* is not the L reflex for **ow*, **ew*, but is the regular U reflex (cf. U **tota** acc., O *touto* nom. 'people'; cf. also South Picenian **tútas**), a plausible interpretation of *rōbus* and its congeners such as *rōbīgō* 'rust', the disease of plants, is that these are loan words showing the substitution of L *b* for source-dialect voiced fricative. Another likely example is L *lumbī* 'loins', PIE **londh-*, which in native L would have been **lundī*.

a. INTERCHANGE OF H- AND F-. Roman grammarians and antiquaries cite a number of forms with initial *h-* or *f-* for classical forms beginning with *f-* or *h-*, respectively, identifying them as dialectal or ascribing them vaguely to 'the ancients'. The conflicting forms reflect PIE **dh-* and **ǵh-* and, less certainly, **bh-*: *fordeum* 'barley' for L *hordeum* (PIE **ǵh-*), *hebris* for L *febris* 'fever' (PIE **dh-*). Similar forms are vouchsafed by inscriptions, like Falisc. HILEO = L *fīlius* 'son' (**dh-*). Such discrepancies are also found in words of probably non-IE ancestry like L *arēna* 'sand' next to 'Sabine' *fasēna* (Varro).

The explanation for most of these is unknown. But where dial. *f-* corresponds to what was necessarily an original [h], we can hazard a surmise. The phenomenon is found in G names, chiefly in the Praeneste area: FERCLES for Ἡρακλῆς, FELENA for Ἑλένᾱ. A similar phenomenon in Praenestine is attested in the Etruscan name FORATIA (cf. L *Horātia*). Here we may assume a SUBSTITUTION in a language which had no [h] (or [χ], depending on what the target sound was). Similar substitutions account for OFr. *froc* (NE *frock*) 'cowl' from OHG *hroc* (= NHG *Rock* 'coat, skirt'), and OFr. *flanc* (NE *flank*) from OHG *hlanca* 'hip'.

Another possibility is a sound law, for which there is actually evidence in Faliscan, whereby initial *f-* > *h-* followed by restoration of the original sound. This kind of succession of events is well-attested in various languages, and inevitably results in both hypercorrections (like L *humerus* for *umerus*) and missed items (like L *ānser*), which would account for the conflicting evidence of the inscriptions.

136. GREEK ASPIRATED STOPS. G φ, θ, χ were voiceless stops followed by a distinct aspiration, as in the initial consonants of NE *pill*, *till*, and *kill* —though probably the G stops were more strongly aspirated than those of English. (In observable languages with a contrast between plain and aspirated stops, such as Thai, Xhosa, or Hindi, the aspiration is quite strong.) In archaic G inscriptions before the introduction of the sign for χ, for example, its equivalent expression is ΓΗ, ΚΗ, or ϘΗ. The Romans rendered the G aspirates first as *p*, *t*, *c*, later more exactly as *ph*, *th*, *ch*. In the case of G θ and χ this conveys no particular information: since L in the historical period certainly had neither [θ] nor [χ], Romans would have been at sea over how to represent such sounds had they existed in G. But the rendition of G ϕ by L *p* rather than *f* is clear evidence that the G sounds were still stops at the time the Romans started to write them *ph*, *th*, *ch*.

Eventually ϕ, θ, χ did become fricatives, as they are in Modern Greek. There are indications that this change took place at an early period in some dialects, for example in Laconian where [θ] (if not indeed [s]) for θ is to be inferred from its representation by σ. But in standard Attic and the κοινή, pronunciation as fricatives did not prevail until sometime in the early centuries AD. The telltale transcription of ϕ by L *f* instead of *ph* is not found till the 1st century AD, and is not usual till the 4th.

137. LATIN ASPIRATED STOPS. As long as G ϕ, θ, χ in proper nouns and other loanwords were represented epigraphically by P, T, C it is not certain how they were actually pronounced. But after about 150 BC they were represented by PH, TH, CH; this and other evidence point to a Greek-like pronunciation of the sounds. The correct pronunciation of the aspirates was so highly esteemed in polite circles, in fact, that aspirated stops were introduced into a number of native Latin words—presumably on account of a fancied G origin. Cicero states that he yielded to popular usage against his own better judgment in the case of *pulcher* 'handsome', *triumphus* 'parade', and a few others, but he steadfastly endorsed the etymologically correct pronunciation of *sepulcrum* 'grave', *corōna* 'wreath', and *lacrima* 'tear', among others. A generation later, Quintilian disparages the improper use of aspirates in (for example) *chorona*, *praecho* 'herald, crier', and *chenturio*. Inscriptions and manuscripts show many examples of these blunders, most frequently *pulcher*—which was no longer a blunder, really, once it was established as the approved spelling.

Something similar is found in English. At the time that *th*—both the spelling and its pronunciation /θ/—was reintroduced into words of G origin which had been borrowed via L such as *theater*, *throne*, and *Bartholomew*, it was extended to some words which were indeed of classical origin but had no *th* in L or θ in G, for instance *anthem* (G ἀντίφωνα n.pl., earlier borrowed as OE *antefn*) and *author* from OFr. *autor*, L *auctor*. In American English that fate has befallen *Anthony* from L *Antōnius*, whereas in British English it retains the etymological pronunciation /t/ despite the whimsical spelling. For *Thomas*, ironically, whose spelling IS etymologically correct (G Θωμᾶς), the NE pronunciation is universally /t/.

138. DISSIMILATION OF ASPIRATES IN GREEK (GRASSMANN'S LAW). Voiced aspirated stops in successive syllables were commonplace in reconstructed PIE; but in G (and also in Indic) such sequences virtually disappeared, via dissimilation: almost invariably the first aspirate becomes a plain stop, but

in G there is a category or two where the second aspirated stop loses its aspiration instead.

This development is most consistent in reduplicated forms of roots beginning with aspirates, as *τί-θημι*, *τέ-θηκα*, *πέ-φευγα*. But the first aspirate remains unchanged when the second has lost its aspiration because followed by **s* (213a) or **y* (198), thus *θρίξ* 'hair', gen. *τριχός*, from **t^{h}rik$^{(h)}$s*, **t^{h}rik^{h}os*; *ταχύς* 'fast', comparative *θᾶττων*, both from **t^{h}ak^h-* (199a); *τρέφω*, fut. *θρέψω*, both from **t^{h}rep^h-*.

Spiritus asper from PIE **s-* (170) shows the effects of Grassmann's Law: from **seǵh-* 'possess' pres. **seǵhoH$_2$* > **hek^{h}ō* > dissimilated *ἔχω*; but fut. **seǵh-s-* > **seks-* > **heksō* which remains *ἕξω*. There are no clear cases of spiritus asper from PIE **y-* (191.1) occurring before an aspirate. G *ἵημι* 'throw' < **yi-yeH$_1$-* is from **hi-yē-*, with the simple disappearance of the medial **-y-*.

PIE **bhewdh-* 'become aware' > G *πεύθομαι* : Ved. *bódhati*, OE *béodan* 'offer; announce', *béad* < **baudaz* 'prayer'.[1]

PIE **bheydh-* 'be persuaded' > G *πείθω*, L *fīdō* : Go. *baidjan* < **bhoydh-ey^e/o-* caus. 'force, compel' (456.2).

PIE **dheyǵh-* 'smear, model' > G *τεῖχος* *s*-stem 'wall' (cf. Ved. *dehī́-* 'wall'), L *fingō* 'model' : Skt. *dehmi* 'I smear', Go. *daigs* 'dough' (= OHG *teig*, OE *dág*).

PIE **dheg^{w}h-* 'be hot' > G *τέφρᾱ* 'ashes', L *foveō* 'cherish' (caus./freq. **dhog^{w}h-ey^e/o-* 'keep warm') : Ved. *dáhati* 'burns', *dhakṣyánt-* fut.pple., Av. *dažaiti*, *daχša-* 'torch', Lith. *degù* 'burn'.

There are many exceptions, apparently the result of leveling.

1. Labials and dorsals show the effects of Grassmann's Law regularly only in reduplicated forms (as in perf. *πέφευγα*, above). In roots originally containing two aspirates, the dissimilated *π-*, *κ-* is generalized: PIE **bhn̥ǵhu-* > G *παχύς* 'thick' in accord with the Law; but comp. *πάσσων* has replaced **φάσσων*—cf. *ταχύς*, *θᾶσσων*, above. Similarly fut. *πεύσομαι* (for **φεύσομαι*) to *πυνθάνομαι* 'find out by asking', from PIE **bhewdh-*.

Contrariwise, in forms like the aor.pass. in *-θη-* and the imperative in *-θι*, a root-initial aspirate is retained under the analogical influence of other forms, as in *ἐχύθην*, *ἐφάνθην*, *φάθι*, *τέθναθι*.

2. By contrast with the behavior of labials and dorsals, *θ/τ* (from **g^{w}h* as well as from **dh*) can be depended upon to alternate according to the rules, as exhibited above. Thus even in forms in *-θη-* and *-θι*, dissimilation is observed: *ἐτέθην* (*τίθημι*), *ἐτύθην* (*θύω* 'offer up'). In the case of the aor. pass.imperat., such as *σώθητι* (*σώω* 'save') for **σώ-θη-θι*, dissimilation also

[1] The reflexes of three PIE roots, **bheydh-*, **bhewdh-*, and **g^{w}hedh-* (OIr. *guidid* /guδ'əθ'/ 'prays', G *ποθέω*, OE *biddan* 'ask'), became more or less confused in Gmc., both formally and semantically.

occurs, but it affects the SECOND aspirate. (Such forms as ἐτέθην, which are wholly in accord with Grassmann's Law, point strongly to analogical remodeling as the source of forms like ἐχύθην.) —The frequent Vedic form *jahí* 'slay!' (PIE root *g^w*hen-*), though remodeled in various details, confirms the ancient dissimilation of **jh-* (for **gh-*) before the *-dhi* of the 2sg.imperat.

a. Grassmann's Law applies to Indic, as seen in the examples above.

b. In L there appears to be no such dissimilation, though it has been suggested as an explanation for certain forms. For example, L *gradior* 'step' and *glaber* 'hairless', from original **gh . . . dh-*, might show dissimilation of the initial **gh* to **g*. But *fīdō*, *fingō*, *foveō*, and other forms establish that in L sequences of aspirates retain their proper identities. Cases that seem to point to dissimilation have other explanations; *gradior* and *glaber* for example are better explained as changes of the initial clusters **ghr-* and **ghl-* to L *gr-*, *gl-*, though the development of initial **gh-* before a liquid in the history of L is not open and shut (158A); and for *frendō* 'grind the teeth' < *g^w*hr-* see 163A.

139. STOPS IN GERMANIC: GRIMM'S LAW, VERNER'S LAW. The notable differences between the stops and fricatives of G and L and those of their English cognates are the result of a wholesale change in the phonetics of the Germanic obstruents. Such systematic innovations are familiarly known as *shifts*. The Germanic consonant shift is often referred to briefly as *Grimm's Law*. It took place in the prehistoric period of Germanic and therefore is characteristic of all the languages of this group. Further changes in the histories of the individual languages sometimes obscure the effects of the shift, especially in the case of High German, which experienced a second consonant shift (much later than the pan-Germanic shift and very different from it in detail). And there is a complication in Grimm's Law, which is known as *Verner's Law*: the pre-Germanic voiceless fricatives—reflexes of PIE **s* and of the voiceless stops **p*, **t*, **k*, and *k^w—split into voiced and voiceless counterparts: voiceless fricatives persisted in initial position and in certain consonant clusters, and elsewhere when the immediately preceding vowel had the PIE accent; otherwise, the fricatives became voiced, falling together with the Germanic reflexes of PIE **bh*, **dh*, and so on. Thus, Go. *fadar*, OE *fæder*, and NHG *Vater* 'father' show the outcome of PIE **t* preceded by an unaccented vowel (PIE *$p\underset{\circ}{H}_2$*tér-*, PGmc. **fađer-*; and parenthetically, note the voiceless reflex of **p* in initial position) whereas Go. *broþar*, OE *bróþor* (*þ* between vowels is [ð]), NHG *Bruder* show PIE **t* after a stressed vowel (PIE **bhráH₂ter-*, PGmc. **brōþer-*). —Subsequent to these changes, the PIE accent was replaced by a uniform first-syllable accent, as still seen in NE *father*, *brother*, NHG *Vater*, *Bruder*.

Shorn of these and many other complications, the principal correspondences are as follows:

PIE stops	p	t	ḱ	k^w	(b)	d	ǵ	g^w	bh	dh	ǵh	g^wh
PGmc.	f	þ	x	x^w	(p)	t	k	k^w	b	d	g	w
English	f	θ	h	(h)w	p	t	k	kw	b	d	g, y	w

The English reflexes are given in phonemic transcription. The proliferation of orthographies for /k/ in NE (including *qu* for /kw/) is the handiwork of Anglo-Norman scribes, as is the substitution of *wh-* for *hw-*. For OE *c* and *g* see 30.2, end.

BILABIAL STOPS

140. The normal representation of the bilabial stops:

PIE	G	L	Sab.	Indic	BS	OIr.	NE
p	π	p	p	p	p	–	f, v
(b)	β	b	b	b	b	b	p
bh	φ, π	f, b	f	bh, b, h	b	b	b, v

1. G π, Indic *b* from **bh* are via Grassmann's Law (138).
2. PIE **bh* gives L *f* in initial position; *b* is the reflex medially, but *f* is frequently restored medially by analogy.
3. In Indic, bilabial voiced aspirates occasionally lose their occlusion.[1] Thus *grah-* 'seize' is found side by side with more conservative *grabh-*. By the Middle Indic period this process became general, thus Skt. *bhavati* 'is' > Hindi *he*.
4. The NE *v* reflexes of **p* and **bh* occur in medial position.
5. PIE **p* disappears in Celtic, one of the defining traits of the branch. Traces of an intermediate **h* or **w* are seen in certain consonant clusters: OIr. *secht* /s′eχt/ 'seven' < **septm̥*; OIr. *cúan* 'harbor' < **kōn-* < PCelt. **kawno-* < **kap-no-*.

141. PIE *p.

PIE **pH̥₂tér-* 'father' > G πατήρ, L *pater* : Ved. *pitár-*, OE *fæder*, OIr. *ath(a)ir* /aθəρ′/.

PIE **ped-/pod-* 'foot' > G πούς, L *pēs* : Ved. *pā́d-*, OE *fót*.

PIE **apo* (or **H₂epo*) 'away' > G ἀπό, L *ap-* in *aperiō* 'uncover' (the prep. *ab* seems to be the same form; its *-b* perhaps arose before voiced consonants and was later generalized) : Ved. *ápa*, Go. *af*, OE *of*, OHG *aba*, NHG *ab*.

a. A striking innovation shared by Italic and Celtic is the assimilation of **p* to a following **kʷ*. This development obviously predates the Celtic loss of **p*:
**penkʷe* 'five' > L *quīnque* (for *ī* see 81.2): G πέντε 'five', πέμπτος 'fifth', Ved. *páñca* 'five', Av. *panča*, Lith. *penkì*; OIr. *cóic* /kōg′/, W *pimp*.
PIE **pekʷ-* 'ripen; cook' intrans. > L *coquō* (either denom. from, or contaminated by, *coquos* 'cook' < **pokʷ-o-*), *coctus*, *coquīna* 'kitchen'; *popīna* (lw. from a *p*-dialect, 155) 'cookshop' : G πέσσω (*yᵉ/o*-stem), **pekʷ-s-* > πέψω fut., **pekʷ-to-* > πεπτός pple.; Ved. *pac-*, pple. *pacatá-* and *pakvá-* (**pekʷ-wo-*); NB W *poeth* (*p* < **kʷ*) 'hot', MW *pobwries* 'baker'.
PIE **perkʷu-* 'oak' > L *quercus*, possibly the Goidelic ethnonym *Querni*.

L *cūnctus* 'all, whole' was of unknown etymology before the emergence of Hitt. *pa-an-ku-uš* 'all, whole; senate' and the *r/n*-stem (290-2) *pa-an-kur, pa-an-ku-na-aš* 'family, relations'; evidence from the two languages taken together point to **ponkʷu-*, and in addition have prompted a reinterpretation of U **puntes**, which occurs several times in the Iguvinian Tables. Hitherto it has been rendered 'groups of five' but makes far better sense as 'all': **inumek sakre uvem urtas puntes fratrum upetuta** 'then let the brothers all decide on a sacrifical sheep' (lit. 'the wholes of the brothers') is quite a bit more intelligible than 'let the brothers in groups of five . . .'.

---

[1] Cf. Proto-Indic **ǰh*, which INVARIABLY becomes *h* in Skt. (153d).

Hercynia silva, the forested region of Thuringia, was for a long time little more than a name to the ancients—which name appears to be the Celtic treatment of **perkun-* (a delabialization of **perk*^{w}*un-* prior to the assimilation).

142. **PIE **b*** is virtually unreconstructable. An example of forms which might point to **b* is the following array: L *labia, labea, labium, labrum* all 'lip'; OE *lippa*, MDu. *lippe* (NHG *Lippe* a loan from Low German). The following observations are true not only of these forms, they are typical of sets seeming to point to **b*: (1) **b* is found in nominal forms (rather than verbal roots), which are (2) usually shared only by two or three (usually adjacent) languages; and (3) there are many problems about the details of the forms: in the case of the 'lip' example, L *-a-* cannot be brought into accord with Gmc. *-i-*, and the variability within L itself is patternless and eccentric. Such sets of words are probably not in fact PIE, but come from such sources as slang and regional loan-words from non-IE sources.

For all that, there can be little doubt that the language we call PIE had a **b*, at least in a few loan-words, perhaps the clearest being **kan(n)abis* 'hemp' > G κάνναβις, OE *hænep*, MHG *hanef*. (L *cannabis*, whence VL *canabum*, is a lw. from G.) All the things that are true of *lip* above are true of this comparison, but there can be little serious doubt that we are dealing here with an actual item of (Western) PIE vocabulary; and it is equally evident that it is a loan word from some non-IE language. That is probably the story with most instances of **b* in PIE, but it is manifestly so in the case of the name of a plant which was probably not native to the PIE world.

a. Many languages have *gaps* in their system of sounds; most often [p] or [g] is the lacking stop, however. The absence of [b] in the core system of PIE as usually reconstructed is one of the stimuli for rethinking the whole PIE stop system, as mentioned in 133: the new proposals make **p*^{h} (or **p'*) the missing sound, which is typologically much more reasonable. However, there is an elegant explanation which is valid for the system as usually reconstructed. It proposes that in Pre-PIE, ***b* (whatever its actual phonetics) did not actually disappear, like PIE **p* in Celtic. Rather, it fell together with ***w*. There are three reasons for thinking so. 1. PIE **w* is the only PIE resonant that occurs in root-initial clusters with other resonants (**wr-*, **wl-*, **wy-*); it is always the first element in the cluster. Clusters of a stop plus a resonant were commonplace in PIE, and if ***b* became **w* in ***br-*, ***bl-*, and ***by-*, the anomaly is explained. (Note that this is not to say that all cases of PIE *w-* before another resonant are ipso facto guaranteed to be original ***b*; once such a cluster became a part of the repertory of the language, its numbers could be added to from other sources.[1]) 2. PIE has a remarkably large number of homophonic roots beginning with **w-*. Some of these actually began with **H*$_1$*w-*, **H*$_2$*w-*, and **H*$_3$*w-*, probably; but that still leaves a large tally of homophonous roots in a language which on the evidence had a low tolerance for homophony. If some of the roots with initial **w* in PIE had once begun with a different consonant altogether, ***b*, the swollen number of homophonous roots in **w-* would be partly explained. 3. Somewhat on the same head: rare as convincing

[1] For example, /š/ first arose in OE as a reflex of PGmc **sk*; but it is far from the case that all, or even most, NE /š/ continue PGmc. **sk*.

cases of PIE *b are, they almost never involve word-initial *b. (The best is the comparison of Ved. *balín-* 'strong', G βελτίων 'better', and L *dēbilis* 'weak'.)

Similar arguments have been advanced for **b > *m. For one thing, there do seem to be a few cases of *mR clusters, such as **mreǵh-yos-* 'very short' (349-50) > L *brevior*. And in fact, while there are a number of instances of *m* ~ *w* alternation in affixes (pronominal **-we/*-me*, 366.3-4; chime-stems in **-mer/*-men* and **-wer/*-wen*), on the other hand there is no remotely GENERAL *m* ~ *w* alternation in PIE; such facts may perhaps be most convincingly explained by the theory that Pre-IE **b merged now with *m, now with *w, under conditions yet to be explained.

See also 451B fn. re PIE Ved. *pibati*, L *bibō*, OIr. *ibid* 'drink'.

143. PIE *bh.

PIE **bher-* 'carry' > G φέρω, L *ferō* : Ved. *bhárati*, OE *beran*, OIr. *berith* /beρ'əθ'/.

PIE **bhráH₂ter-* 'brother' > G φρᾱ́τηρ 'member of a phratry', L *frāter* 'brother' : Ved. *bhrā́tar-*, OE *bróþor*, OIr. *bráth(a)ir* /brāθəρ'/.

PIE **e-bhū-t* (or **e-bhuH-t*) aor. 'became' > G ἔφῡ, L *fuit* : Ved. *abhū́t*; OE *béon*, NE *be*.

PIE **nebh-* (various stems) 'cloud, mist' > G νεφέλη, νέφος, L *nebula* : Ved. *nábhas-* (= νέφος), OHG *nebul*, NHG *Nebel*, Hitt. *ne-pí-iš* n. *s*-stem.

PIE **H₂elbh-o-* 'white' > G ἀλφός 'whiteness', L *albus* 'white', *alba* 'dawn' : U *alfer* dat./abl.pl. < **-ōys*.

PIE **lewbh-* 'please' (various grades) > L *lubet*, *libet* (cf. 58B?) 'pleases', *libīdō*, *lubīdō* 'longing, infatuation' : O *loufir* 'or' (semantics? but cf. the various meanings of NE *rather*, and cf. OE *léofre* *e*-grade 'preferable'), OCS *ljubŭ* 'dear'; zero grade in OE *lufu*, NE *love*.

APICAL STOPS

144. The normal representation of the apical stops:

PIE	G	L	Sab.	Indic	BS	OIr.	NE
t	τ	t	t	t	t	t	θ, d
d	δ	d	d	d	d	d	t
dh	θ, τ	f, b, d	f	dh, d, h	d	d	d

1. G τ and Indic *d* from *dh are the product of Grassmann's Law (138).
2. L *f-* is the outcome in initial position; medially, the outcome is *b* adjacent to *r*, *l*, or *ŭ̄*; *d* elsewhere (147.2-3). But medial *-f-* via recomposition is commonplace, as in *referō*.
3. As with the loss of occlusion in *bh* (140.3), the Indic development of *h* from *dh is general in the Middle Indic period, but is found sporadically as early as the Rigveda: *hitá-* pple. of root *dhā-*; *-hi* and *-dhi* are both 2sg. imperat. for athem. stems (= G -θι).
4. PIE *t > NE *d* results from Verner's Law: in accord with the conditions given in 139, PreGmc. *þ > PGmc. *đ > PWGmc. *d*).

145. PIE *t.

PIE **tréyes* 'three' nom.pl. masc. > G τρεῖς (spurious diphthong, 76), L *trēs* : Ved. *tráyas*, OIr. *trí*, NE *three*.

PIE **tn̥nú-* 'thin' L *tenuis* : Ved. *tanú-*, PGmc. **þunwijaz* > NHG *dünn*, OE

þynne, NE *thin*. G ταναός 'thin' (like a stick) continues stem full grade with assimilation (91.2): **tn̥newo-* > **tanewo-* > **tanawo-*.
PIE **pH̥₂ter-* 'father' > G πατήρ, L *pater* : Ved. *pitár-*, OIr. *ath(a)ir* /aθəρ'/, OE *fæder*.

146. PIE **d*.

PIE **déḱm̥t* 'ten' > G δέκα, L *decem* : Ved. *dáśa*, OIr. *deich* /deχ'/, Go. *taihun*, OE *tíon*, NE *ten*.
PIE **ed-* (or **H₁ed-*) 'eat' > G ἔδω, L *edō* : Ved. root *ad-*, 3sg. *átti* (= L *ēst*, W *ys* < PIE **H₁ed-ti* 212), Go. *itan*, OE *etan*, NE *eat*, NHG *essen*.

147. PIE **dh*.

1. Initial position:
PIE **dheH₁-* 'put' in G τίθημι, aor. ἔθηκα, L *fēcī* : Ved. *dádhāti*, OCS *děti* infin., OE *dón*, NE *do*.
PIE **dhū-mo-* (**dhuH-*?) 'smoke' > G θῡμός 'spirit, pluck' (see 50.1 for the semantics), L *fūmus* 'smoke' : Ved. *dhūmá-*, OCS *dymŭ*.
PIE **dhwor-* 'door' (originally du.tant.) > G θύρᾱ, L *foris* (back-formed from orig. *forēs* pl.tant. 'leaves of a door') : OIr. *dorus*, OE *dor*, Lith. *durìs* acc.pl. (Ved. has *dvā́rāu* du.tant. 'door' for expected ˣ*dhvā́rāu*, contaminated by *dvá(u)* 'two'.) A fossilized dual, having been reanalyzed as a singular, is seen in G θυρών 'antechamber' like Go. *daurons* pl.tant. 'door': PrePIE *n*-stem nom.du. ***-on-H* > PIE **-ōn*, whence G -ων, Ved.*-ā*, Av. *-ą̄n* (cf. 286.5).

a. The fate of PIE **dhr-* in L is uncertain. There are two competing data. PIE **dhragh-* 'draw, pull' may underlie L *trahō* 'drag' and a Gmc. family of words (Go. *ga-dragan* 'gather together', OHG *tragan* 'pull', OE *dragan*, NE *draw*) unattested elsewhere. The development of *tr-* rather than *fr-* would be unexpected, but it is not implausible. (Cf. the L development of *-tr-* < **-dr-*, 223.5.) But expected *fr-* may be seen in L *fraus*, *-dis* 'deceit' < **frawχ-ri-* < PIE **dhrewǵh-* 'swindle, deceive', cf. Ved. *drugdhá-* 'hurtful, malicious', Av. *družaiti* 'deceives', OHG *triogan* (NHG *trügen*). The latter has the merits of conforming to phonological expectation, and would reflect a root of impeccable PIE pedigree. Its demerits include a dissimilation (albeit one with known parallels, 151B), and L *-au-* < **-ᵉ/ₒw-* is most dubious. It is not clear moreover that the word is even an *i*-stem: both *fraudum* and *fraudium* occur in respectable sources.

2. Medially adjacent to *r*, *l*, or *ŭ̄*:
PIE **rewdh-* (various grades) 'red' > G ἐρυθρός (89), L *ruber*, *rubeō* 'am red' (*rūfus* 'red haired' is a lw. from an *f*-dialect, as is *rōbīgō* 'rust'; see 135 end) : Ved. *róhita-*, OHG *rōt*, OE *réad* (both *o*-grade, like Lith. *raũdas*), OE *réod* (*e*-grade).
PIE **werdho-* 'name, word' > L *verbum* : Lith. *var̃das* (*o*-grade) 'name', Go. *waurd* (transl. ῥῆμα), OE *word*, NE *word*.
PIE **steH₂-* 'stand' in **stH̥₂-dhlo-*, **-dhli-* > L *stabulum* 'abode', *stabilis* 'firm'; cf. U *staflarem* acc.sg. ?'pen'.
PIE **krey(H)-dhro-* 'sifting tool' > L *crībrum* 'sieve' (cf. *cernō* 'sort') : OIr. *críathar* /krīḁθəρ/, OHG *rītera*, OE *hríder* (NE *rider* 'coarse sieve').

L *iubeō* 'command' (*ŭ*; cf. SC de Bacch. IOVBEATIS), perf. (orig. aor.) *iussī*, and pple. *iussus* add up to an etymon **yewdh-* (aor. **yewdh-s-* (215), pple. *yudh-to-* (212)).[1] However, PIE connections are uncertain. Ved. *yudh-* 'fight', Lith. *judù* intrans. 'move around', caus. *jùdinu* 'set in motion, shake' agree with L *iubeō* better in form than in meaning.

3. Medially elsewhere:

PIE **H_2eydh-* 'be on fire' > G αἴθω 'blaze', L *aedēs* sg. 'temple', pl. 'house' : Ved. *édhas-* n., *édha-* m. (= G αἶθος) both 'fuel', OE *ád* 'pyre'.

PIE **medhyo-* 'middle' > G μέσ(σ)ος, L *medius*, O **mefiaí** : Ved. *mádhya-*, Go. *midjis*.

PIE **widhéwo-* '(?) deprived; (?) single', nominalized fem. 'widow' > L *viduus*, *vidua* 'widow' (also 'unmarried woman'); note that **dh* must > L *d* prior to the change of **ew* (> **ow*) to *u(v)*, 61, 66.5; otherwise the outcome would have been L ˣ*vibuus* : Ved. *vidhávа-* 'widowed', OIr. *fedb* [feδβ] 'widow', OCS *vĭdova*, OE *widewe*, NE *widow*, perhaps G ἠΐθεος (**ēwit^hewos*) 'unmarried' (whose η- however is without explanation).

148. ASSIBILATION – GREEK. G τ alternates with σ before ι in large classes of words.[2] But τ may also remain unchanged before ι; this has the appearance of a sound law whose conditions have been disturbed beyond recovery by analogical leveling. Significantly, the few generalizations that can be made are for the most part morphological rather than phonological:

1. τ remains: initially, thus τίκτω 'beget', τίθημι 'put', τῖφος 'marsh'; when preceded by σ, as in ἐστί 'is', πίστις 'faith'; before the feminine suffix -ιδ- (πολῖτις, -ῖτιδος f. 'citizen'); before the adj. suffix -ικο- (πολῖτικός 'civic'); and before the denominative suff. -ιζω (πλουτίζω 'enrich').

a. The unaltered τ of ἔτι, ἀντί has no explanation. Cf. πρός vs. Hom. προτί.

2. τ becomes σ in most of the nouns formed with the suffix **-ti-*, as βάσις 'a step' (= Ved. *gatí-* 'gait'), στάσις 'a standing' (= Skt. *sthiti-*), λύσις 'a releasing', θέσις 'a putting' (= Ved. *-dhiti-*). Forms in -στ-ις like πίστις 'faith' are covered in 1, above; genuinely unexplained are a few words like μῆτις 'wisdom' and (of unexpected meaning for a *ti*-stem noun) μάντις 'seer'. The change is seen in most adjectives in -ιος and nouns in -ίᾱ derived from stems containing τ, as πλούσιος 'wealthy' (πλοῦτος), ἀμβρόσιος 'ambrosial', ἀμβροσίᾱ (ἄμβροτος 'immortal'), ἐργασίᾱ 'labor' (ἐργάτης).

3. In certain forms, τ becomes σ in Att.-Ion., Lesb., and Arc.-Cyp., but remains unchanged in Doric: 3sg. Att. τίθησι, δίδωσι but Dor. τίθητι, δίδωτι;

---

[1] L *iubeō* and *iussī* have imported the short root vowel from the pple., where it is proper; OL (as in the pres. quoted here, and perf. IOVSIT, where S = *ss*) shows the original state of affairs with full grade of the root in the pres. and aor. stems.

[2] Note that **k^wi* (161) never becomes σι: τίς 'who' < **k^wis*, ὅ (τ)τι 'why' < **yod k^wid*; τῑμή 'honor', ἀτίετος 'unhonored' < **k^wiH_r-*. The time during which **t* was assibilating predates the change of **k^wi* to τι.

3pl. Att. φέρουσι, τιθέᾱσι, εἰσί, but Dor. φέροντι, τίθεντι, ἐντί; Att. εἴκοσι '20', διᾱκόσιοι '200', τριᾱκόσιοι '300', but Dor. ϝῑκατι, διᾱκάτιοι. This development is found in Myc., as in *e-ko-si* (*ek^honsi*) 'ἔχουσι'.

a. A similar dialectal variation is seen in a few other forms, such as Ἀρτεμίσιος ~ Αρταμιτιος 'a temple of Artemis'; Ἀφροδῑσιος ~ Αφροδιτιος 'pertaining to Aphrodite'.

b. A structural consequence of this development is the reintroduction of intervocalic /s/, following its PG loss per 172.

149. The other apical stops in G show little or no parallel behavior. PG **d* of whatever origin never assibilates before ι. PG *t^hi > σι, but under a constraint that verges on the bizarre: the change occurs only in adjectives in -ιος based on place names in -ινθος and -υνθος: Προβαλῑ́σιος 'from Probalinth', Τρικορῡ́σιος 'from Tricorynth'. Mycenaean attests this, and incidentally confirms the suspicion that forms like G Κορίνθιος 'from Corinth' are levelings of the expected *Κορῑ́σιος attested in Myc. *ko-ri-si-jo.* —Such place names are generally thought to be non-Greek in origin, which at least raises the possibility that the adjectives in -σιος are not actually G developments but were borrowed as such, much as in the case of the /k/ ~ /s/ alternation in NE *Greek*/*Greece*, which is not a native development. Myc. attests an additional form, *-ko-ru-si-jo* '-helmeted', connected with G κόρυς, κόρυθος; but this too is apparently a foreign word.

a. The developments discussed in 148-9 must not be confused with changes in G consonants before **y*, 195-207.

150. Assibilation – Latin (Iotacism). No later than the 3rd century AD, L medial *t* and *d* assibilated when immediately followed by *i* before another vowel: *cantiō* 'song', *merīdiēs* 'noon' pronounced [kant^{s}io:], [meri:d^{z}ie:s]. This development is reflected in all the Romance languages (LL *cantionem*: Fr. *chanson*, It. *canzone*, Sp. *canzon*). But it is additionally vouchsafed by grammarians, who supply the technical term for it and seem to endorse it as standard; by inscriptions (MARSIA⟨NENSES⟩ for *Martia-*, 3rd century); and by loanwords such as 6th century Go. *kawtsjo*, from L *cautiō* '(pre)caution'.

a. Somewhat earlier, in a development that was never standard but which is faithfully reflected in Romance, *di* and *de* before a following vowel came to be pronounced [y], and to share in the Romance developments of L 'consonantal *i*': Fr. *jour*, It. *giorno* 'day' reflect **iurnus*, not L *diurnus* (cf. Fr. *dieu*, It. *dio* < PRom. **diu* < *deus* 'god'). Medially, It. *mezzo* reflects standard *medius* 'middle', next to *raggio* < **raiius* (standard *radius*) 'spoke', cf. It. *maggiore* 'bigger' < L *maiiōrem* (194).

151. PItal. **d* > L *l* in several words. The data are characteristic of dialect borrowing. It is not axiomatic that in the source dialect **d* had merged with **l*; all that is necessary is that its reflex sounded like *l* to the Latin ear.

Lacrima 'tear' from *dacrima* : G δάκρυ, NE *tear*.[1]

[1] The surmise that L *lacrima, lacruma* f. is a borrowing from G δάκρῡμα n. is unlikely

Lingua 'tongue' from *dingua* (Paul.Fest.): OE *tunge*, NE *tongue*.
Oleō 'have an odor' beside noun *odor* : G ὄζω, ὄδωδα.
Solium 'throne' (and perhaps *cōnsulēs* *'having the same seat') from **sed-* 'sit' in *sedeō*.
Levir for **laever* 'husband's brother' (first attested in 6th century AD) : Ved. *devár-*, G δᾱήρ (207), OE *tácor*.
Capitōlium one of the hills of Rome, for orig. *Capitod-*.
Impelimenta (Paul.Fest.) for *impedīmenta* 'baggage'.

The question of whether L *Ulixēs* vs. G Ὀδυσσεύς 'Ulysses' is an example of this phenomenon is confused by the existence of variant G forms of the name already containing λ: Ολυττευς, Ωλιξης.)

a. Ancient authorities were aware of the phenomenon (they supply such forms as *dacrima*, *dingua*, *Capitodium*, and *impelimenta* which are not otherwise attested). Since the late 19th century it has been customary to identify Sabine (that is, Oscan) as the source of these *l*'s; but in Oscan, and all other known Italic languages near Rome, reflexes of **d* and **l* everywhere remain distinct. However, the allegedly Sabine origin of this phenomenon may help explain a peculiarity of the native Oscan alphabet: the symbol whose shape corresponds most closely to **R** stands for the sound /d/, while letter **D** stands for /r/. Evidently there was in fact something about the phonetics of the Sabine reflex of **d* (a flap perhaps) which, though always distinct in O from both *r* and *l*, confused whoever adapted the alphabet for writing Oscan; and the same phonetics may have on occasion led to O forms being taken over in L with *l* for *d*.

b. Perhaps somehow related to the foregoing, in early L *r* is also found for *d*: ARFVISE, ARVORSVM (SC de Bacch.), APVRFINEM (*apud fīnem*). Possibly this was a regular change of *d* before *f* or *v* (with some extension to other cases) which was later leveled in favor of the usual *ad* and *apud*. —L *merīdiēs* 'noon' from **medīdiēs* is a case of anticipatory dissimilation. L *crūdus* 'raw' is perhaps from **krūros* (*cruor*, cf. Ved. *krūrá-* 'slaughter, atrocity') by lag dissimilation; cf. It. *rado* 'scarce' < L *rārus*.

DORSAL STOPS

152. The PIE dorsal stops were as follows (for a survey of the usual reflexes see 154):

	Palatal	(Plain) Velar	Labiovelar
voiceless	ḱ	k	k^w
voiced	ǵ	g	g^w
voiced aspirated	ǵh	gh	g^wh

In considering the relations of the PIE dorsals—the general term for all kinds of *k*-sounds—it is necessary to distinguish two main series and, as regards their reflexes, to divide the IE languages into two groups (11).

One series, known as the *palatals* and denoted here by **ḱ*, **ǵ*, and **ǵh*

in view of: the discrepancy in gender; the discrepancy in the length of the second vowel; and the L development of *l-*. Besides, δάκρῡμα is a poetical, high-flown, and rare word—altogether unlikely as a source for a borrowing. As if these considerations were not enough, 'tear' is among the 15-odd lexical items known to be most resistant to borrowing.

—other notations are met with—is represented by simple dorsals in the more conservative IE languages. These are the western group (Greek, Italic, Celtic, and Germanic, and unattested strains of BS); Tocharian in the extreme east of the range; and Anatolian in the extreme south of it. In the innovative ('satem') subgroup, the palatals are reflected as sibilants; these languages are Armenian, Albanian, Indo-Iranian, and the historically attested members of BS (132).

The other series, the *labiovelars*, are denoted here by $*k^w$, $*g^w$, and $*g^wh$; other notations are common, especially in the older literature. In the satem languages these stops reveal no trace of a labial coarticulation. Instead, they split into affricated or palatal articulation before front vowels (PIE front vowels, that is), while remaining dorsal stops elsewhere. The 'centum languages' without exception attest to labialized articulation, though it is manifested in various ways (cf. 155, below, on *P-* and *Q-*dialects).

A contrast between plain dorsals and labialized dorsals is widespread among the world's languages; but so is a constrast between plain dorsal stops and palatal stops. Typology thus is no guide in framing the best hypothesis for the PIE dorsal system. The universal development of sibilants in satem languages from the first group of stops mentioned above implies a saliently palatal articulation, but of this there is no trace in the 'centum languages'. Two possibilities might account for this: (1) The 'centum languages' RETRACTED two series of stops—palatal and plain—converting them into plain and labialized, respectively; or else (2) the satem group FRONTED plain velar stops (whose aboriginal phonetics are faithfully reflected in the 'centum languages'), with the concomitant loss of rounding in the aboriginal labiovelar series.

The latter must be the correct view, for at least three reasons. First, in view of the diachronic instability of palatal stops, if palatal articulation was a feature of the parent language, the total lack of evidence pointing to specifically palatal articulation of **ḱ*, **ǵ*, and **ǵh* in ANY 'centum language' is nothing short of phenomenal. Second, the distribution of the two branches—satem languages in a central area flanked by 'centum languages' on three sides—is a classic one in dialect geography: the peripheral languages are the relics of an earlier state of affairs, cut off from one another by a centrally-located area of innovation. Finally, shifts of point of articulation typically move from back to front, so that diachronic norms favor the originality of velar articulation over palatal for the PIE **ḱ*-series. Linguistic norms are a rocking foundation which cannot sustain arguments of much weight, but in this case the structure is sufficiently sturdy. Starting from an ORIGINAL series **ḱ*, **ǵ* **ǵh*, the called-for development is not merely rare; there seem to be NO cases of palatal[1] stops developing into velar shops in

[1] For this discussion the distinction between the concepts PALATAL and PALATALIZED is

the course of the known history of any language—and the PIE *ḱ-series would have to have become 'centum plain velars' not once but at least three different times, namely to the east, west, and south of the putatively conservative satem group. The simultaneous and independent evolution of coarticulated labialization in *k^w and so on would be less incredible but still remarkable.

The history of the IE stops, then, is as follows. In a very early period, the stops had four points of articulation [p t k k^w] (to use the voiceless series to stand for all three series). The [k] series was of the normal velar sort, and the [k^w] series had a definite labial component, manifest in all non-satem languages without exception; that it was also articulated farther back on the velum than [k] is likely, as [k^w] seems to have been distinct from [kw]—though that may have been a matter of timing only (like the Polish contrast between [$t^š$] and [tš] in *czy* vs. *trzy*). This system remained unchanged in the early history of the 'centum' (better, non-satem) languages.

At a still very early period, a group of Proto-Indo-European speakers shifted both velars forward phonetically, such that [k] became [ḱ] and [k^w] became [k]. However, in certain environments (before *r, after *w and *ŭ, before *a), original *k usually failed to front, thereby falling together with the fronted and delabialized developments of [k^w].

	Archaic PIE (= Proto-Centum)	Pre-Satem	Proto-Satem
palatal:	–	ḱ	ś
velar:	k	k	k *and* ḱ (or č)
labio-velar:	k^w	–	–
apical:	t	t	t
bilabial:	p	p	p

Examples of unshifted stops:
PIE *$krewH_2$- > Ved. *kravís-* 'gore', G κρέας, L *cruor*, MIr. *crú* 'blood', Lith. *kraũjas*.
PIE *yugom* 'yoke' > G ζυγόν, L *iugum* : Ved. *yugá-*, OCS *igo*.
PIE *gras-* 'graze' > Ved. *grásate* 'eat' (of horses and cows), G γράω 'nibble', Cypriot γρασθι imperat., L *grāmen* < *grasmn̥* 'grass' orig. *'fodder'. (The Gmc. *grass* words are a chance resemblance.)
PIE *ghrem-* 'growl, make a menacing noise' > G χρόμος 'racket, whinnying' : Go. *gramjan* 'to anger', Lith. *gruménti* 'to thunder'.

---

crucial. The former is a point of articulation, involving the front or dorsum of the tongue and a region of the hard palate just behind the alveolar ridge. The latter is the coarticulation of a high front tongue body position, which may occur simultaneously with any point of articulation. (Thus, despite the occasional statement to the contrary, bilabial palatalized articulation is not only possible, it is more straightforward, mechanically, than some other combinations.) Now, DEPALATALIZATION—that is, the loss of this coarticulation—is a commonplace historical development (as in 198); it is the retraction of a PALATAL POINT OF ARTICULATION to a (dorso-)velar point of articulation that strains credulity.

153. THE PLAIN VELAR STOPS. Why, then, do we not reconstruct according to the list of sounds under 'Archaic PIE'? Because the conditions given above for the merger of Archaic **k* and **kʷ* into Pre-Satem **k* are approximations only; there are incontrovertible exceptions:

PIE **ḱr̥Hsron-* 'hornet' > L *crābro*, OLith. *širšuo*.
PIE **ǵr̥Hno-* 'grain' > L *grānum*, OE *corn*, Slovene *zŕno*.
PIE *ǵhans-* 'goose' G χην-, OHG *gans*, OE *gós*, NE *goose*, Ved. *haṃsá-*, Lith. *žąsìs*.
PIE **steygh-* > G στείχω 'march', Go. *steigan* 'climb', Ved. *stigh-*.

Thus we have in fact three partly-similar correspondence sets, *kʷ* = *k*, *k* = *k*, and *k* = *ḱ*, all strictly speaking in contrastive distribution, which leaves us no choice except the familiar 'Classical PIE' **kʷ*, **k*, and **ḱ*. However, this is an artifact of the method, not a picture of the early history of PIE: there never was a variety of PIE with three dorsal stops.

a. Some hold that Albanian and Armenian reflect the three reconstructed dorsal series directly, and more recently similar claims have been advanced for Anatolian. But the crucial evidence in Armenian and Anatolian seems to hinge upon especially difficult or vague or otherwise dubious etymologies, which is not surprising considering the languages involved and the fundamental improbability of the proposition. The Albanian evidence is of better quality, but can be accounted for (and easily) without recourse to a threefold system of dorsals.

b. In cases where cognates are known only from non-satem languages, such that it cannot be told whether we are dealing with a palatal or a plain velar, it is the custom to write the plain velar in the reconstruction. For example, G κνήμη (Dor. κνᾱ́μᾱ) 'shin', κνημῖδες 'greaves', OIr. *cnáim* /knāμ'/ 'bone', OHG *hamma* 'shank, ham', OE *hamm*, are reconstructed as PIE **kn̥H₂mo-* (G and Celt.) and **konH₂mo-* (Gmc.). This custom exaggerates the tally of plain velars for PIE, at least on paper. That is a small demerit; a much more important one is that it turns the comparative method on its head to assume that we should reconstruct a palatal stop only if we have definite evidence for it. The **ḱ*-series of stops was manifestly the unmarked PIE dorsal series, and in the ABSENCE of evidence to the contrary we should write **ḱn̥H₂mo-*. The usual convention will nevertheless be followed here.

c. It is sometimes implied (or even insisted upon) that the defining innovation of the satem group is the COALESCENCE of the PIE **k* and **kʷ* series, NOT the development of a sibilant from the **ḱ* series. But both components of this view are questionable. First, if the three-way contrast in the dorsal stop system is an artifact of the method to begin with, it follows that the putative coalescence is also an artifact. This objection is vulnerable to the charge of circularity; the second objection therefore is the sturdier: that is, the implausibility of the notion that each satem branch independently developed sibilants, and only sibilants, from original proto-satem **ḱ*, **ǵ* and **ǵh*. In all cases where palatalization phenomena are directly observable, such as in the histories of Romance, Slavic, and Chinese, stops of palatalized and palatal articulation evolve very diversely, even in closely related dialects. It is furthermore the case that while the developments thus observed do include sibilants, sibilants are among the less common outcomes and generally evolve from affricates. Accordingly, we must assume that the development of sibilant consonants from the pre-satem palatal stops took place only once and was ancestral to the whole satem group.

d. INDO-IRANIAN. The stops classed as *palatals* in Sanskrit grammar must not be confused with the PIE palatals, with which they have no connection. Skt. palatal *c* (pronounced something like [č]) and Av. *č* are the result of secondary palatalization, namely they are reflexes of PIE **k^w* or **k* when followed by a PIE front vowel. PIE palatal **ḱ* typically gives Indic *ś* (a palatal sibilant). In PInIr., there were three distinct series of obstruents from the pre-Satem inventory of two series:

	Pre-Satem	Satem	PInIr.	Skt.	Avest.
	ḱ	ś	ś	ś	s
	ǵ	ź	ź	j	z
	ǵh	źh	źh	h	z
Before front vowels:	k^w, k	k, č	č	c	č
	g^w, g	g, ǰ	ǰ	j	ǰ
	g^wh, gh	gh, ǰh	ǰh	h	ǰ
Elsewhere:	k^w, k	k	k	k	k, χ
	g^w, g	g	g	g	g, γ
	g^wh, gh	gh	gh	gh	g, γ

From this array, two important differences between Indic and Iranian are evident. 1. In Indic, three manners of articulation remain distinct (voiceless, plain voiced, and voiced aspirated) whereas in Iranian the two voiced series coalesce. 2. In Iranian, the reflexes of the PIE palatals and the Indo-Iranian secondary palatalization remain distinct, whereas in Indic the reflexes of the voiced (plain and aspirated) palatals fall together with the voiced palatalized stops. Thus Indic (Ved.) *jātá-* 'born' might continue either PIE **ǵ* or palatalized **$g^{(w)}$*; the Iranian (Av.) cognate *zāta-* might continue either PIE **ǵ* or **ǵh*. Taken together, however, the Indic and Iranian cognates point unambiguously to PIE **ǵ* as the initial consonant of this word, as that is the only item among the alternatives which will yield the attested reflexes in both branches.

Even wholly within Indic, patterns of alternation may reveal the etymological identity of Skt. *j* or *h*. Thus Skt. *yaj-* 'offer' and *vij-* 'tremble' have many similar forms (such as Ved. pres. *yájate, vijáte* and caus. *yājayati, vejayati*), but the participles *iṣṭá-* vs. *viktá-* reveal that in PInIr. the roots were **yaź-* and **wayg-/wayǰ-*, respectively.

154. The normal reflexes of the PALATALS and, in G, Italic, and Gmc., of the PLAIN VELARS may be summarized as follows:

PIE	G	Latin	Sab.	NE	Indic	Lith.	OCS
ḱ	κ	c	k	h	ś	š	s
ǵ	γ	g	g	k	j	ž	z
ǵh	χ, κ	f *before ŭ*	f	g, y[1]	h	ž	z
		g *before/after cons.*					
		h (or ∅) *elsewh.*					

1. PGmc. **g* > OE *y*, written *g*, before original front vowels; see 30.2.

The normal reflexes of the LABIOVELARS (and, in the satem languages, of the plain velars) are more complicated, but may be summarized as follows:

PIE	Greek	Latin	Sab.	NE	Indic	Lith.	OCS
k^w	π, τ, κ	qu, c	p	wh, f	k, c	k	k, č, c
g^w	β, δ, γ	v, gu, g	b	qu, c	g, j	g	g, ž, z
g^wh	φ, θ, χ	f, gu, v	f	w, g	gh, h	g	g, ž, z

1. GREEK. In late Proto-G the labiovelars fell together with the plain velars before **y*; see **199-201**. In all varieties of G including Myc., the labial element of the remaining labiovelars was lost when the cons. was adjacent to ῠ̄ or ϝ: Myc. *qo-u-ko-ro*, G βουκόλος < PG **g^w ow-k^w olos* 'cowherd' vs. *a-pi-qo-ro*, G ἀμφίπολος 'attendant' (see **161-4** for further examples). The syncretism of the remaining labiovelars and the labial and apical stops is not seen in Mycenaean, in which the labiovelar series remains separate from the other three. In all other dialects, the GENERAL pattern is that a labiovelar stop becomes an apical stop when it is followed by a front vowel; and becomes a labial stop elsewhere, as shown in **161-4**, especially **164A**.

a. Myc. evidence sometimes sheds light on the history of G forms; for example, Myc. *a-to-ro-qo* 'man' shows that in the etymology of G ἄνθρωπος 'man', whatever it might turn out to be, π continues a **k^w* rather than a **p*.

2. LATIN. All labiovelars lose the labial element when followed by any consonant. Otherwise, PIE **g^w* regularly becomes L *v*, except that **-ng^w-* > L *-ngu-*. PIE **g^wh* becomes *f-* initially, *-v-* intervocalically, and like **-ng^w-* becomes *-gu-* after an *n*.

This development contrasts with G, where labiovelars followed by a consonant (other than **y*, **199-200**) fall together with labial stops, as **k^w riH₂to* midd.aor. > G πρίατο 'bought' (cf. Myc. *qi-ri-ja-to*).

3. In GERMANIC the normal reflex of **k^w* is *hw*, written in Go. with a special letter here transcribed *h^w*, in early OHG *huu*, NE *wh* (written *hw* in OE); but it sporadically becomes *f*, as seen in NE *wolf*, Go. *wulfs* < **wl̥k^w os* (**155**). PIE **g^w* > Gmc. **k* (OE *c*) before rounded vowels: **g^w ōws* 'cow' > OE *cú*, NE *cow*.

4. INDO-IRANIAN reflexes, with their secondary palatalization, have been discussed above (**153d**); in SLAVIC also there was such a palatalization—a succession of palatalizations, in fact. The earliest two produce *č*, *ž* before original front vowel (OCS *vlĭče* 'O wolf' < **wl̥k^w e*; *žena* 'woman' < **g^w eneH₂*); but the dorsals give *c* and *(d)z* before a front vowel developing from **oy* and **ay* (*vlĭci* nom.pl. < **vlĭkī* < **wl̥k^w oy*, *lędzěte* 2pl. imperat. (old opt.) < **lęgěte* < **lengoyte*).

155. P-DIALECTS AND Q-DIALECTS. 'Centum languages' may be classified in two categories, defined by the fate of the labiovelars, which become (1) DORSAL obstruents with a more or less prominent labial satellite articulation, (2) LABIAL obstruents (in G apical obstruents as well). These are sometimes known as *Q-dialects* and *P-dialects*, respectively. Old Irish among the Celtic languages, and Latin-Faliscan in Italic, are *Q*-dialects; Welsh, Gaulish, Oscan, and Umbrian were *P*-dialects.[1] It is unclear whether the treatment

---

[1] In the Celtic branch, the difference between *P-* and *Q*-groups is limited to the development of **k^w*. In Proto-Celtic, PIE **g^w* > **b* and (apparently) **g^wh* >̇ **g^w*.

of the labiovelars in Mycenaean vs. later forms of Greek reveals the existence of *Q* and *P* strains of Greek, or is purely a matter of chronology.

No literary variety of Germanic belongs to a *P*-dialect, but scattered through the Gmc. lexicon there are a good number of PGmc. labials from PIE labiovelars. The distinction is chiefly evident in reflexes of PIE $^*k^w$ which, in mainstream Germanic, becomes PGmc. $^*\chi^w$ and (by Verner's Law) $^*g^w$. But there are a number of words where it shows up as *f*, PGmc. **wulfaz* 'wolf' < PIE **wĺ̥kʷos* for example. There is at least one clear form for each of the other two labiovelars: PGmc **skēp-* 'sheep' (OE *scéap*, OHG *scāf*) and Ved. *chā́ga-* 'goat' point to PIE **sḱēgʷ-* or **sḱeH₁gʷ-*. PIE **gʷhen-* 'strike dead' is the likely etymon of OE *bana*, OHG *bano* 'killer', Go. *banja*, OE *benn* 'wound' and such compounds as OE *brōþorbana* 'slayer of [someone else's] brother' (cf. Hom. πατροφονεύς 'slayer of [someone else's] father'). Such forms do not necessarily show up in all three Germanic branches uniformly, as in OE *ofen*, OHG *oven* 'oven', but a dorsal in NGmc. (Swedish *ugn* for example); here the WGmc. forms point to **uχʷna-* < **úkʷno-*, the NGmc. to **ugna-* < **ugʷna-* < **ukʷnó-*. Much effort has been devoted to trying to discover the conditions under which $^*k^w$ > *f* might be a regular Germanic development, but without success. The probable explanation is that these forms are dialect borrowings from an otherwise unattested *P*-dialect of Germanic.

In the innovative satem group, as mentioned above, the labial component of the labiovelars disappears without a trace. It follows from this that in satem languages, as in the parent language, there is a distinction between reflexes of $^*k^w$ and **ḱw* (Archaic PIE ***kw*), that is, between a labialized velar stop and a palatal stop followed by a glide. In the conservative ('centum') languages, *P* and *Q* strains alike, these two coalesce more or less completely. (For more detailed remarks see 160.)

PALATAL STOPS

156. PIE *ḱ.

PIE **déḱm̥t* 'ten' > G δέκα, L *decem* : Ved. *dáśa*, Av. *dasa*, Lith. *dẽšimt*, OCS *desętĭ*, Go. *taihun*, NE *ten*.

PIE **ḱm̥tóm* 'hundred' > G ἑκατόν, L *centum* : Ved. *śatám*, Av. *satəm*, Lith. *šim̃tas*, OCS *sŭto*, Go. *hunda* (pl.), NE *hund(red)*. (This **ḱm̥tóm* is probably a derivative from the preceding, which is to say ***dḱm̥tóm*; the only actual evidence for the initial consonant, however, is the lengthening of the vowels in the decads, as in **trī-ḱm̥t-* from **trĭ-* 'three'; see 391.)

PIE **woyḱo-* 'settlement' > G οἶκος 'house(hold)', L *vīcus* 'village' : Go. *weihs* 'country' (opposite of 'city', *in weihsa* transl. G εἰς ἀγρούς), Ved. *viś-* 'clan; homestead', Av. *vis-*, Lith. *viẽš-pats* (archaic *viẽšpatis*) 'master'.

PIE **deyḱ-* 'point (out)' > G δείκνῡμι, L *dīcō* 'say' : Ved. root *diś-* (*diśánt-* pres.pple.; cf. pple. *diṣṭá-*, 3sg. imperat. *dídeṣṭu*).

157. PIE *ǵ.

PIE **ǵenH*$_1$*-* 'beget' in G γένος, L *genus* : Ved. *jánas*, Av. *zanō*, OE *cynn* (**ǵn̥H*$_1$*-yo-*), NE *kin.*
PIE **ǵneH*$_3$*-* 'know' > G γιγνώσκω, L *(g)nōscō* : Ved. root *jñā-*, OE *cnáwan*, NE *know*, OCS *znati.* Cf. L *cognōscō* 'become acquainted with' < **kom-gnōskō.*
PIE **ǵews-* 'taste' > G γεύω; **ǵus-tu-* > L *gustus* : **ǵows-o-* > Ved. *jóṣa-* 'enjoyment' (root *juṣ-*) = Av. *zaoša-*; Go. *kiusan* 'test', OE *ċéosan*, NE *choose.*

158. PIE *ǵh.

PIE *ǵhans-* 'goose' (const. stem) > *χανσ- > χᾱν- > G χην- (nom. χήν for expected *χᾱ́ς by leveling; see **228**), L *ānser* (for **hānser*, **159**) : OHG *gans*, OE *gós*, NE *goose*, Ved. *haṃsá-*, Lith. *žąsìs.*
PIE **weǵh-* 'convey': G ὀχέω 'lead' (? caus. **woǵh-ey*^{e}*/o-*); Myc. *wo-ka* (ϝοχᾱ) 'wagon', Hom. τὰ ὄχεα n.pl. 'chariot' (wrong root grade for an *s*-stem, perhaps influenced by ὄχος m. 'wagon' < **woǵh-o-*), L *vehō* : OE *wegan* (NE *weigh*), OE *wægn* (NE *wain*—*wag(g)on* is a lw. from Du.); Ved. *váhati*, pple. *ūḷhá-* < PInIr. **uždha-* < **uǵh-to-*, Av. root *vaz-*, Lith. *vežù*, OCS *vezǫ.*
PIE **leyǵh-* 'lick' > G λείχω, L *lingō* : Ved. *lih-*, Lith. *liežiù*, OCS *lizatĭ.*[1]
PIE **dheyǵh-* 'smear, model' > G τεῖχος 'wall', O **feíhúss** acc.pl., L *fingō* 'model' (*figulus* 'potter' and *figūra* 'shape' have *-g-* from *fingō*) : Ved. *dih-* 'smear', *dehī́-* 'wall', Av. *pairi-daēza-* 'garden' ('surrounded by a wall', the source of G παράδεισος), Go. *digan* 'model', OE *dág* 'dough', OHG *teig.*
PIE **ǵhew-d-* 'pour' > G χέω, L *fundō*, *fūdī* (the one example of **ǵhu-* > L *fu-*) : Ved. root *hu-*, pres. *juhóti* < **źha-źhaw-ti*, *hótar-* 'priest', Av. *zaotar-*; Go. *giutan*, 'pour' OHG *giozan*, NHG *giessen.*

a. The outcome of initial **ǵhr-*, **ǵhl-* in L is uncertain:

Some L forms suggest *gr-*, *gl-*, as *grāmen* 'fodder' (p. 153); PIE **ghredh-* 'walk' > *gradior* 'step' (cf. Go. *grid* acc.sg. of a presumed fem. *i*-st. *griþs** 'a step', OCS *grędǫ* 'come'); and *glaber* 'hairless' (**ghladh-ro-*, cf. OHG *glat* 'smooth, shiny', OCS *gladŭkŭ*).

In several good-looking etymologies, however, **ghr-* seems to give L *r-*: *rūdus* 'rubble, gravel' < **ghrewd-*, cf. OE *gréot* 'sand' (= NHG *Grieß*), OE *grytt* 'grit' (= NHG *Grütze*); and *rāvus* 'grayish-yellow' < **ǵhrōwo-* (**46.2**), cf. OHG *grāo*, OE *grǽg*, NE *grey*). Perhaps the most persuasive evidence for this particular development comes from forms which are without satisfactory outside connections: on the one hand, L *congruō* 'run together' and *ingruō* 'fall upon violently' imply a simplex **gruō*, though no such form occurs. On the other hand, there is a *ruō* 'rush; collapse violently'; formally and semantically appropriate, it itself occurs in no straightforward compounds, and therefore might be the element in *congruō*, *ingruō.*

159. LATIN *h.* The sound written *h* in L was faintly sounded, and probably absent in colloquial speech from an early period. This is shown by the

---

[1] L *lingō* is probably not the *n*-infix present stem (**453**) it looks like: other evidence strongly supports a PIE root present. Perhaps *lingō* was influenced by *lambō* 'lick' and the unrelated *lingua.*

Despite appearances, NE *lick*, NHG *lecken* are unrelated to these forms.

fact that *h-* does not interfere with: (1) elision; (2) shortening of vowels before another vowel (85, cf. *dĕhinc* from *dē-*); (3) the change of intervocalic *s* to *r* (173, if *diribeō* is in fact from **dis-habeō*;[1] or (4) the contraction of like vowels (88.1, cf. *nīl* from *nihil*, though *nīl* might as well stand for **nehil* via **neil*, 57). Furthermore, there was confusion of spelling in many words, as *humerus* 'arm' beside correct *umerus* < **omesos* (45.1), and the correct use of initial *h-* was much discussed by the grammarians. Generally the approved spelling, which we still follow, was the historically correct one—but not always: the best usage endorsed unetymological *humerus*, *ānser* 'goose', and *arēna* 'sand'. (The etym. of the last is unknown, but *harēna* is vouchsafed by 'Sabine' *fasena* quoted by Varro; and *hānser* and *umerus* are guaranteed by comparative evidence, 158, 45.1.)

The letter *h* was sometimes used as a sign of hiatus, as in AHENVS beside AENVS (*aēnus* 'made of bronze'), where the H stands for no consonant and is used merely to distinguish *aē* from the diphthong *ae* in writing. Such a use proves that [h] was pronounced sporadically at best, since otherwise the letter *h* would have been no more suitable than any other consonant—*s*, say—for indicating hiatus.

160. PALATAL STOPS + **w*. PIE **ḱw* and **ǵhw* show a development in centum languages closely parallel to that of PIE *k^w and *g^wh. But in G the two distinct sounds **ḱw* give a double consonant medially, while the unitary *k^w gives a single consonant. It is thinkable that until an early L innovation adjusted the syllable boundary between a stop and a resonant (81.6a), a form like *aqua* 'water' (*k^w) had a light first syllable while *equos* 'horse' (**ḱw*) had a heavy one. But in all periods of attested L these words scan the same.

PIE **eḱwo-* 'horse' > G ἵππος, Myc. *i-qo*, L *equos* : Ved. *áśva-*, Av. *aspa-*. Cf. PIE *k^w in **sek^w-* 'follow' > G ἕπομαι, L *sequitur* : Ved. *sácate*, Av. *hačaitē*.

PIE **ǵhwēr-* 'wild animal' (cons. stem) > G θήρ, Lesb. φήρ (164A.2), L *fēra* : Lith. *žvėrìs*, OCS *zvěrĭ*. (L *ferus* adj. back-formed from *fera*. —Either all extra-Latin attestations have independently generalized *ē*-grade or L *ĕ* requires explaining.) Cf. PIE *g^wh in **g^wher-* 'warm' > G θερμός 'warm', θέρος n. 'summertime' (formally = Ved. *háras-* 'flame'), L *fornus* 'oven' (form = Ved. *ghr̥ṇá-* 'heat') : Ved. *gharmá-* 'warm', OPr. *gorme* 'heat', OCS *goritŭ* 'burn'.

There are no certain instances of PIE **ǵw*, but on the evidence of L *mālō* 'prefer' < **mag-wel-* (484.3), Ital. **gw* and *g^w (162) fall together, just as **kw* and *k^w do.

a. Greek is the only centum language (so called, 11) attesting a contrast between reflexes of **ḱw* and *k^w. Although the notion that **ḱw* > G ππ distinct from *k^w > π is reasonable on its face, the only obvious evidence for it is G ἵππος, whose peculiarities

[1] *dir-* for **der-* is unexpected on two grounds (see 37a), and its meaning, 'sort ballots', is semantically unobvious as a derivative of 'have'.

however—the unexplained rough breathing and the unexplained ι- from PIE *e- —do not inspire confidence. Myc. *i-qo* at least underwrites the ι, but raises another question: where *-kw-* occurs elsewhere it is written differently, as *te-tu-ko-wo-a*$_2$ (*tetuk*^{h}*woha*) 'wrought' perf. pple. of τεύχω. Perhaps a monomorphemic /(h)ikwos/ was different (phonetically? or just graphically?) from formations with an analyzable suffix beginning with *w*. But the writing *i-qo* may mean that the -ππ- of ἵππος is just one more odd thing about the word, and not a straightforward reflex of *ḱw.

Even slenderer evidence is afforded by in Boeot. πᾶμα 'possessions', on account of such epigraphic attestations as τα-ππαματα 'possessions', θιο-ππαστος ?'belonging to the god'. But the supposed cognate, Ved. *śvātrá-*, is a word of uncertain meaning used only of soma. An etymon *ḱweH$_2$- would account for all forms, Boeot. -ππ- and all; but the absence of semantic controls would enjoin extreme caution even without the discouraging evidence of the Homeric hapax πολυ-πᾶμονος gen.sg. 'exceedingly wealthy', which must scan πολῡ-. (This accords with the usual treatment of the initial, as in the aor. ἐπᾱσάμην 'get, acquire', and many others.)

b. Clusters of dorsal stop + *w* arising from affixes such as -ϝως perf.pple. (561-2) do not show labial development: δεδορκώς 'having in sight'.

LABIOVELAR STOPS

161. PIE *k^w.

PIE *k^{w}i-/*k^{w}e-, *k^{w}o- pron. stems 'who' and the like > G ποῦ 'where', πόθεν 'whence', τίς 'who', ὅ (τ)τι 'why' (= Myc. *jo-ti*) < *yod k^{w}id, L *quī*, *quod*, *quis*, *quid*, O *pod*, **píd** : Ved. *kás*, *cit*, Hitt. *ku-iš*, *ku-it*, Go. *h*^{w}*as*, *h*^{w}*a*, OE *hwá*, *hwæt*,[1] NE *who*, *what*, Lith. *kàs*, OCS *kŭto*, *čĭto*.

PIE *-k^{w}e enclit. 'and' (perhaps ultimately related to the preceding) > G τε, Myc. *-qe*, L *-que* : Ved. *-ca*, Av. *-ča*, Go. *-uh*.

PIE *penk^{w}e 'five' > G πέντε, πεμπάς, -δος 'group of five', πέμπτος 'fifth', Hom. πεμπάζω 'count on the fingers', L *quīnque* (141a, 81.2); *quīncu-plex* 'fivefold', *quīncūnx* 'five twelfths' : Ved. *páñca*, Av. *panča*, Lith. *penkì*; Gmc. forms (Go. *fimf*, OE *fíf*, NE *five*) show *f < PIE *k^w, 155.

PIE *k^{w}etwor- 'four' (with complex and only partly understood ablaut; 389.4) > G τέσσαρες, τέτταρες, Myc. *qe-to-ro-*, L *quattuor* : Ved. *catvā́ras* nom.pl.m., Lith. *keturì*; Gmc. forms (Go. *fidwor*, OE *féower*, NE *four*) show *f* < *k^w (155).

PIE *leyk^w- 'leave' > G λείπω, Myc. pple. *re-qo-me-no*, old *n*-infix pres. -λιμπάνω (Sappho) = L *linquō*, *līquī* (= λείπω), pple. *relictus* : Ved. *riṇákti* 'gives up', *ricyate* 'is emptied', *ririk-vás-* perf. pple., *rekú-* 'deserted', Lith. *liekù* 'leave', Go. *leih*^{w}*an* 'lend' (transl. δανείζω), *o*-grade in OE *lán*, NE *loan*. —OE *lǽfan*, NE *leave* and the like point to PGmc. *laiƀija-*, as if from *loyk^w-éy^e/o-, the caus. of this root, with *b (via Verner's Law, 139) from PIE *k^w (155), but other explanations are possible.

PIE *sek^w- 'see', in midd. 'follow' > G ἕπομαι, L *sequor*, *secundus* < *sek^{w}uon-

---

[1] WGmc. *-t* in 'what' is either imported from *þæt* = Go. *þata* < PIE *tod-ōm, or else WGmc. *hwat continues a PreGmc. etymon with an enclitic, *k^{w}od-ōm, different from Go. *h*^{w}*a* < PGmc. *hwa < *k^{w}od.

dos, **183** : Ved. *sacate*, OIr. *sechithir* /šeχ'əθ'əρ'/. L pple. *secūtus* is secondary; the intensive *sectārī* 'follow eagerly' proves the prior existence of the expected pple. **sectus*. The model for *secūtus* is prob. *volvitur* : *volūtus* :: *solvitur* : *solūtus* :: *sequitur* : *X*, where *X* = *secūtus*.

PIE **pek*^{w}- 'ripen; cook' intrans., **pek*^{w}*-y*^{e}*/o-* > G πέσσω (**199**), **pek*^{w}*-s-* > πέψω fut., **pek*^{w}*-to-* > πεπτός pple., L *coquō* (either denom. or contaminated by *coquos* 'cook' < **pok*^{w}*o-*, **141a**), *coctus*, *coquīna* 'kitchen', *popīna* (lw. from a *p*-dialect) 'cookshop' : Ved. *pac-*, pple. *pacatá-* and *pakvá-* (**pek*^{w}*-wo-*)—neither is regular in formation—W *poeth* (*p* < **k*^{w}) 'hot', Lith. *kepù* (with metathesis) 'bake, roast'; BS shows orig. *pek*^{w}- mainly in transferred senses, like OCS *potŭ* 'sweat' (< **pok*^{w}*-to-*).

PIE **k*^{w}*ey(H*$_1$*)-* 'take notice of' (with semantic development to chiefly unfavorable notice) > G τῑ́νω 'pay' (a price, a penalty), Myc. *qe-te-o* verbal adj., τῑ́μη 'honor', ποινή 'penalty' (whence L *poena*) : Ved. root *ci-* 'note, gather', *cetár-* 'avenger', Av. *kaēnā-* 'penalty', OCS *cěna* 'price'.

PIE **k*^{w}*ek*^{w}*lo-* 'wheel' > **k*^{w}*uk*^{w}*l-* (**40a**) > G κύκλος 'circle', κύκλα pl. 'wheels' : Ved. *cakrá-*, OE *hwéol*, NE *wheel* (see **40a**).

PIE **wl̥k*^{w}*os* 'wolf', metathesized **lúk*^{w}*os* > G λύκος, L *lupus* (lw. from a *P*-dialect, **155**); original sequence in Ved. *vŕ̥ka-*, Av. *vəhrka-*, Go. *wulfs*, OE *wulf* m., *wylf* f., Lith. *vil̃kas*.

162. PIE *g^w**.**

PIE **g*^{w}*em-* 'set out', pres. **g*^{w}*m̥-yoH*$_2$ > G βαίνω, L *veniō*; other stems in Sab. *ben-*, Ved. *gamati* aor.subj., Go. *qiman*, OE *cuman*, NE *come*. Stem **g*^{w}*m̥-sk*^{e}*/o-* in Ved. *gácchati* 'goes', G βάσκε imper. 'get going!'.

PIE **g*^{w}*erH*$_3$*-* 'devour': **g*^{w}*r̥H*$_3$*-* > G βιβρώσκω; L *vorō* (intens./caus. **g*^{w}*orH*$_3$*-eH*$_2$*y*^{e}*/o-*, **456.2B**) : Ved. *girati*, Lith. *geriù* 'drink'.

PIE **g*^{w}*ow-* 'cow' (**324**) > G βοῦς, βουκόλος 'cowherd' = Myc. *qo-u-ko-ro* (and OIr. *búachaill* /būəχəl'/) : Ved. *gāu-/go-* 'cow', OIr. *bó*, Latv. *gùovs*, OE *cú*. (L *bōs* is a lw. from a *P*-dialect; **155**).

PIE **g*^{w}*r̥rú-* 'heavy' > G βαρύς, L *gravis* : Ved. *gurú-*, Go. *kaurus*.

PIE **sm̥-g*^{w}*elbh-* (various stem forms) 'brother' lit. 'having the same womb' > Hom. ἀδελφεός, Att. ἀδελφός (both from *ἀ-, **170a**) : Skt. *sagarbhya-* 'full brother', Ved. *gárbha-* 'womb' < **g*^{w}*olbho-*;[1] G δελφύς f. *u*-stem, cf. Av. *gərəbuš-* n. Hom. ἀδελφεός is probably a thematized full grade, **g*^{w}*elbhewo-*, originally an adj. (like NE *relative* 'kinsman' orig. 'related').

PIE **g*^{w}*iH*$_3$*-* (various suffixes) 'life': **g*^{w}*iH*$_3$*-eto-* 'life' > Hom. βίοτος (**154.1**), L *vīta* (**88.3**); **g*^{w}*iH*$_3$*-wo-* 'alive' > G ζωός (**49.3**), L *vīvus* : Ved. *jīvá-*, Go. *qius*, OE *cwic*, NE *quick*, Lith *gývas*.

---

[1] Skt. *sagarbha-* 'pregnant', often cited in this connection, cannot be relevant: it has a late, peculiarly Indic, development of the meaning of the prefix *sa-* (**389.1** fn.).

PIE *H_3*eng*^{w}- 'anoint': *n*-stem in L *unguen* 'salve', OHG *anc(h)o* 'butter'; *i*-stem in Ved. *añjí-* orig. adj. 'anointing' then noun 'ointment'.
PIE **n̥g*^{w}*en-* 'bulge' > G ἀδήν, -ένος f. (later m.) 'gland', L *inguen* n. 'groin' : OIc. *økkr* 'swelling'.
PIE **g*^{w}*enH*$_2$, obl. **g*^{w}*neH*$_2$-/**g*^{w}*n̥H*$_2$- 'woman' (orig. neut., as still uniquely in arch. OIr. *bé*; much remodeled in the daughter languages) > G γυνή (40A), Boeot. βανα (**g*^{w}*n̥H*$_2$-) : Ved. *jani-* (**g*^{w}*enH̥*$_2$-) 'goddess' (more accurately, consort of a deity), *gnā́s* gen.sg. (**g*^{w}*neH*$_2$*-s*, = OIr. *mná*) in *gnā́s páti-* 'husband of a divine wife'; n.pl *gnā́s* disyll. (*gnáas* < **g*^{w}*néH*$_2$*-es*); OIr. *ben* f. < **g*^{w}*enā*, *bé* n. (legal, poetic) < **g*^{w}*enH*$_2$; *ā*-stem OCS *žena* 'woman' (an independent innovation); PGmc. **k*^{w}*enōn-* > Go. *qino*, OE *cwene*, NE *quean*.
PIE **neyg*^{w}- 'wash', zero grade **nig*^{w}- in G ἄνιπτος 'unwashed', χέρ-νιψ 'water for washing the hands', gen. χέρνιβος, vb. χερνίπτομαι 'wash the hands', Myc. *ke-ni-qe-te-we* nom.pl. 'hand-washers' (presumably **k*^{h}*ernik*^{w}*tēwes* to **k*^{h}*er-nik*^{w}*-teus*) : Ved. *niktá-* pple. 'washed', OIr. *nigid* /niγ'əθ'/ 'washes'. (For G νίζω < **nig*^{w}*-y*^{e}*/o-*, 200).

PIE *(*H*$_1$)*su-g*^{w}*iH*$_3$*ēs* lit. 'having a good life' > G ὑγιής 'healthy' (implying an unattested neut. *s*-stem *βίος 'life' < **g*^{w}*iH*$_3$*-os-*. This etymology, though attractive and generally accepted, has a number of difficulties. The necessary *s*-stem is not found anywhere; and ὑ- rather than εὐ- is a problem for those who hold that initial laryngeals become prothetic vowels in G and trace the usual form of the prefix to PIE **H*$_1$*su-*.) Cf. G βίοτος above and Skt. *su-jīvita-* 'living happily'.

G βάλλω 'throw' and G βούλομαι 'wish' are words of uncertain outside connections, but the correspondence of Att.-Ion. β- with δ- in Arc. δελλω and Locr. δειλομαι points to PG **g*^{w}![1]

163. PIE *g^{w}h.

PIE **g*^{w}*her-* 'be warm': two regular formations in *-*mo-*, a noun **g*^{w}*hór-mo-* 'heat', and adj. **g*^{w}*hr̥-mó-* 'warm', variously conflated. G θερμός 'warm' (for *θαρμός), L *formus* (Paul. Fest.) : OE *wearm* 'warm' (as if from **g*^{w}*hormo-*; Go. *warmjan* 'to warm' shows denominative stem **g*^{w}*horme-y*^{e}*/o-*), Ved. *gharmá-* 'heat' (**g*^{w}*hor-mo-*, only with accent proper to the adj.). A regularly-formed *s*-stem is seen in Ved. *háras-* n. 'flame' (*g*^{w}*her*^{e}*/os-*, formally = G θέρος 'summer').

PIE **g*^{w}*hen-* 'strike down, slay': **g*^{w}*henyō* > G θείνω, L **fendō* (only in *dē-*, *offendō*; 218); *o*-grade *o*-stem in G φόνος 'a slaying', Ved. *ghaná-* 'destroyer, slayer' (evidently **g*^{w}*honH-ó-*) : Ved. *hán-ti* 'slays' 3sg. (= Hitt. *ku-*

---

[1] There seems to be no satisfactory explanation of G βούλομαι; to G βάλλω there is a scattering of doubtful etymologies seeming to confirm the reconstruction **g*^{w}*elH*$_1$- arrived at from the G evidence. The best of these, W *blif* /bliv/ 'catapult' as if from PCelt. **blīmo-* < PIE **g*^{w}*leH*$_1$*-mo-*, is isolated not only in Welsh but in Celtic generally, and on historical and cultural grounds is very much more likely to be a borrowing from G than a native term. Morever, apart from W *blif*, all forms can be accounted for by an ablauting root with full grade **g*^{w}*elH*$_1$-.

(e-)en-zi /g^wen-tsi/), *ghn-ánti* 3pl. (= Hitt. *ku-na-an-zi* ?/g^wnantsi/). With a labial reflex of **g^wh* (155) this yields the Gmc. words exemplified by OE *bana* 'slayer' (NE *bane*) and OIc. *bani* 'a slaying'.

PIE **sneyg*^{w}*h*- 'snow': root noun **snig*^{w}*h*- > G *νίφα* acc.sg. (Hes., ἅπ. λεγ.), L *nix, nivis*; *n*-infix *ninguit* 'it is snowing' = Lith. *sniñga*; *d*-stem G *νιφάς* 'snowflake'; *e*-grade G *νείφει* 'ninguit' (usually *νῑφει*, an unexplained development, **76d**); *νείφει* for expected **νείθει* is from the fut. *νείψει* and aor. *ἔνιψε*; OHG *snīuuan*, NHG *schneien*, OE *sníwan* 'to snow' (the expected NE verb *snew* replaced by a denom. built to the following); *o*-grade *o*-stem noun in Go. *snaiws*, OE *snáw*, NE *snow*. (The Ved. root *snih*-, occurring in Skt. *o*-grade *o*-stem *sneha*- and a sizable family of derivatives, reconstructs flawlessly to a root **sneyg*^{w}*h*-. But the meanings—'be sticky, viscid; feel affection for', *sneha*-, 'greasiness; love(!)'—are hard to reconcile with 'snow'. Nevertheless, given the quality of the formal fit, the connection would be likely however improbable the semantics; and besides there are actual InIr. attestations of the usual 'snow' sort in Av. *snaēža*- vb., Prāk. *siṇeha* n.)

PIE **H_3eg*^{w}*hi*- (or, less likely, **og*^{w}*hi*-, as that should give Ved. ×*ā́hi*-) 'snake, monster' > G *ὄφις* 'snake' : Ved. *áhi*-, Av. *aži*-. (G *ἔχις* 'adder', L *anguis* 'snake' and other cognates point to **eǵhi*- and **ang*^{w}*(h)i*-, which cannot be reconciled either to one another or to **H_3eg*^{w}*hi*-/**og*^{w}*hi*-, but seem too similar not to be ultimately somehow related.)

PIE **l̥ng*^{w}*h*- 'light' (various suffixes): zero grade evidently in G *ἐλαχύς* 'small', *ἐλαφρός* 'nimble, light', Ved. *raghú*- 'quick', dial. *laghú*- 'light' (first in the AV), OE *lungre* 'quickly', and probably OCS *lĭgŭkŭ* (via **lingu*-), though there are problems with all interpretations of this form; *e*-grade in Lith. *leñgvas* 'light', PreGmc. **leng*^{w}*h-to*- > PGmc. **linχto*-, **līχto*- Go. *leihts*, OE *léoht*, NE *light*. L *levis* is usually explained as coming from an *n*-less form of the root, **leg*^{w}*hu*-, apparently also seen in Ved. *r̥hánt*- 'small, weak', as if from **l̥g*^{w}*h-ent*-. But *r̥hánt*- is not itself old, being an Indic creation patterned on the antonym *br̥hánt*- 'tall, strong', the *a* of *raghú*- having been reinterpreted as a full grade (whereas it is the reflex of **n̥*). The L form too is best taken as the result of contamination, but this time by a form of similar rather than antonymic meaning: PItal. **mreχwis* 'short' (etymon of L *brevis*, 223.4) led to a remodeling of **lenχwis* 'light' (from either **leng*^{w}*hu*- or **l̥ng*^{w}*hu*-, probably the latter) as **leχwis*.

PIE **kneyg*^{w}*h*- 'bend', not really a root because it contains both a voiceless and a voiced aspirated stop, is thought to underlie Gmc. and Ital. forms. Ital. **kom-knoyχweyō* (caus.) > **kongneyw*- (231.4) > L *cōnīveō* 'close [the eyes]', hence 'overlook, pretend not to see', perf. (aor.) *cōnīxī*; also *nictō* 'wink'; and perhaps *nītor* 'rest on'. Go. *hneiwan* 'bow', OHG *hnīgan*, NHG *neigen*, *o*-grade Go. *hnaiws* 'lowly'. (For developments of **g*^{w}*ht*, **ǵht* see 211.)

a. If L *frendō* 'grind the teeth' is cognate with OE *grindan* 'grind' and Lith. *gréndžiu* 'rub'—all these forms have been plausibly explained in other ways—a possible etymon would be PIE *g^w*hrendh*-. L *fr-* is not wholly expected from *g^w*hr*-, however, as the labial element of labiovelars is regularly lost in L before a consonant, and in other similar shapes voiced aspirates become voiced stops in L (so *glaber* 'smooth, bald' 158a), but there are no stronger competing etymologies. Furthermore, the same retention of a labial element in *g^w*hr* is attested, more securely, in medial position in L *febris* 'fever' < PIE **dheg*^{w}*h*- 'be hot' (164B.3).

164. REMARKS ON THE REFLEXES OF LABIOVELARS.

A. GREEK. Although most of the examples in 161-3 comply with the general rule given in the notes to the table in 154, there are a number of causes for deviation from the norm.

1. There is much leveling in favor of the labial reflexes. Thus the π of λείπω, ἕπομαι, ἔπος (= Ved. *vácas-*) regardless of the following vowel: λείπει, ἕπεται, ἔπεος. Interchange within an inflectional paradigm (as *λείτει next to λείπω) is unknown, the closest thing being in principal parts like θείνω aor. ἔπεφνον—though the principal parts of G verbs routinely are so chaotic (from the synchronic point of view) that the Greeks themselves were probably unaware of the true relation between these stems, as seems definitely to have been the case for groups like τίς/ποῦ, τῑμή/ποινή, θείνω/φόνος. (Even our modern dictionaries do not list ἔπεφνον as a form of θείνω, but accommodate it under the imaginary present stem ×φένω.)

Leveling does sometimes occur in groups of cognates when the semantics are transparent, as βέλος 'missile', βέλεμνον 'javelin' after βάλλω 'throw' (the regular δ before ε only in Arc. δελλω). For G νείφει 'it is snowing' the usual explanation won't quite do, since phonologically regular forms of the type νείφω, νείφομεν, νείφουσι 'I, we, they snow' can scarcely have existed; νείφει must therefore get its φ from another source, probably aor. ἔνιψε and fut. νείψει.

2. It is a notable characteristic of the Aeolic dialects that even before a front vowel the labial is found in some basic words, as Lesb., Thess. πεμπε = πέντε 'five'; Lesb. πέσυρες, Hom. πίσυρες, Boeot. πετταρες, all = τέσσερες 'four'; Lesb. πήλυι = Att. τηλοῦ (Hom. τῆλε) 'from afar'. But τίς 'who' and τε 'and' are the forms even in Aeol.

3. Contrariwise, there are some dialect forms with κ for usual π and τ in the pronouns: Ion. (Hdt.) κῶς = πῶς 'how'; Thess. κις = τίς 'whoever'.

4. In Att.-Ion. the normal development of *g^w and *g^w*h* before *i*, as before α and ο, is β and φ, as in βίος and ὄφις; the development to δ, θ is seen only before *ē̆. There is no obvious explanation for the discrepancy between the behavior of *k^w and the other two labiovelars. Dor. (Heracl.) perf. pple. ενδεδιωκοτα, if equivalent to standard ἐμβεβιωκότα, might show *g^w*i* > δι (and is generally so interpreted), but might merely show a leveling which is the reverse of the Att. development, both starting from *(εν)δεβιω-.

B. LATIN. 1. Beside *qu* from *k^w, we should expect *gu* from *g^w, corresponding to the parallelism in Sab. *p* : *b* or G π : β : φ. But *gu* remains only after a nasal, as in *unguen*, *ninguit*. Otherwise before a vowel the *g* is lost, hence *veniō*, *nivis*. Phonologically speaking, there is nothing remarkable about this: [gw] and [w] are closely related articulatorily, differing mainly in a very small adjustment of the height of the dorsum, and they readily interchange both diachronically and in the sound-substitutions connected with borrowing. PIE **w* regularly became W *gw*, as in PIE **weǵh-no-* 'conveyance' > W *gwain* (= OIr. *fén*; cf. OE *wægn*). Parallel to L *v* from *g^w, PIE *g^wh > PGmc. **w* rather than expected **gw*, as in *g^w*hermo-* > OE *wearm*, NE *warm* (cf. 163). —In loan-words, Germanic *w* was adapted as [gw] in Romance, for example PRom. **guerra* 'war'.

2. In L the *w*-element of labiovelars was lost before all consonants. So from *k^w, L *quīn(c)tus* 'fifth', *coctus* 'cooked' in contrast to G πέμπτος, πεπτός. The plain dorsal stop arising in this position was sometimes generalized. So from *vōx* not only in other case forms (*vōcis*, *vōcem*, and so on), but also in derivatives therefrom (*vocō*, *vōcālis*, and so on), such that there is no trace anywhere in L of a form with *qu*, in contrast to G ἔπος and εἶπον.

The appeal to leveling—from a single form—as an explanation for the absence of *qu* in this family of words is mildly troubling, as leveling rarely is quite so total. Conceivably the real explanation is a dissimilatory change of *k^w to **k* after the **w*-, with phonologically regular **wōks* < **wōk*^{w}*s* playing only a supporting role.

3. In general accord with this principle, PIE *g^w*r-* > L *gr-*, as in *gravis*, *grātus* (Osc. gen.sg. *brateis*); but the development of *g^w*hr* unexpectedly retains a labial element, hence initially *frendō*, medially *febris* 'fever' < **dheg*^{w}*h-ri-* (163a).

4. The *w* element of the labiovelars was lost before *u* and *o*, though often restored by analogy (*sequor*, *linquunt*); cf. more or less isolated forms like *secundus* 'following', *cum* 'since', 183.

5. Some L forms are plainly loanwords from neighboring *P*-dialects (155). Native forms continue alongside some, like *coquīna* 'kitchen' and the given name *Quīnctius* next to borrowed *popīna* 'cookshop' and *Pontius* (O **púntiis**); some, like *bōs* 'cow', *lupus* 'wolf', are known only in the dialect form. —L *poena* 'penalty' (the basis of several derivatives) is thought to be a lw. from G ποινή.

LARYNGEALS

165. The laryngeals are the latest addition to the PIE inventory of sounds. Their reconstruction dates back to the suggestion by the Swiss linguist Ferdinand de Saussure in 1879[1] (a period when the system of recon-

---

[1] To be precise, he mooted the theory in larval form two years earlier. —It must be noted that Saussure's main thesis was the establishment of **a* and **o* (as we would now put it) as separate PIE vowels, and in this he was successful.

structed PIE sounds was undergoing general rethinking) that the alternation of **ē*, **ō*, and **ā* with *ə, as they are traditionally written, was not analogous to the alternation of **ĕ* and *ŏ* with zero. Rather, they were better seen as parallel to the alternations of **ey* with **i*, or **en* with **n̥*. That is, the *ə was not a residue of the long vowel, but an element in its own right (118).

As there were three kinds of long vowels in the categories normally calling for *e*-grade (127-8), three varieties of *ə were entailed: $*ə_1$, which simply lengthened a preceding **e*; $*ə_2$ which both lengthened a preceding **e*-grade vowel and colored it, resulting in **ā*; and $*ə_3$, which lengthened a preceding **e* and colored it to **ō*. There was little basis for assigning any particular phonetic value to these elements, and Saussure labeled them *resonant coefficients* (coefficients sonantiques)—the same term that he used for glides, liquids, and nasals. In any case his analysis of the long vowel series along such lines, though generally admired for its ingenuity, had little immediate consequence.

The first serious effort to grasp the implications of the new analysis was a line of inquiry orthogonal to the main interests of IE linguistics, but it explains the designation 'laryngeals' by which the elements are nearly always known nowadays: it was the attempt to trace PIE and Proto-Semitic to a common ancestor. This has been widely recognized as a plausible avenue of research, but it is seriously hampered at the outset by the lack of resemblance between the inventories of PIE and PSem. consonants, as they are usually worked out. Two consonant systems could hardly be less alike; it is hard to know even where to begin probing tentatively for correspondences. The chief discrepancies are the abundance of fricatives in PSem. vs. the solitary PIE **s*, and the 'laryngeal' consonants in PSem. (as in the attested Semitic languages generally), namely consonants like the glottal stop, the voiceless pharyngeal fricative [ḥ], and its voiced counterpart usually known as *ʕayin* (after the name for the letter representing it in the Arabic alphabet). These 'laryngeal' consonants share two properties with the 'resonant coefficients' of PIE: they influence the phonetic features of neighboring vowels; and they are prone to merge, either with one another or with oral obstruents, or to disappear altogether (as in Maltese). It was in the service of facilitating comparison between PIE and PSem. that the 'resonant coefficients' were rechristened 'laryngeals'. The term has stuck, and is used even by authorities who have no opinions about the phonetics of the consonants in question, or who actually doubt (or deny) that they were laryngeals in the Semitic sense at all. There is nothing questionable about this; after all, the morbid effects of the parasite *Plasmodium* are still known as *malaria* to physicians and laymen alike, without any implied endorsement of prescientific notions of the cause of the disease. In any case, efforts to replace the term *laryngeal* with some less question-begging term, while doubtless laudable, have met with no success.

In time, the idea that these elements were essentially consonantal in nature was established, and the reinterpretation of the role of *ə in the PIE system of sounds is sometimes called *the theory of consonantal schwa*. (Incidentally, the word *theory* in expressions like *laryngeal theory* or *theory of consonantal schwa* should not be misconstrued as implying diffidence, as in the value-laden dismissal of something as *only a theory*. The whole of Indo-European linguistics—the idea of PIE itself, and the sound laws connecting it with the attested IE languages—are theories in exactly the same sense that the laryngeal theory is a theory.)

166. Once the existence of the elements was established in a general way, there ensued a search for their effects and their distribution, in order to establish their inventory in PIE. All these things are elusive, because most of the evidence is indirect: lengthening here, failure of lengthening there, aspiration of voiceless stops, and so on. The nature of the evidence makes dispute inevitable as to both the inventory of the laryngeals in PIE and their reflexes. In Anatolian there is clear and direct attestation of the consonants, or rather of some of them, as such. In Hitt., PIE $*H_2$ and $*H_3$ are reflected (under certain circumstances) as *ḫ*, and the sequence $*oH_1$ is reflected as *ay*, as in the Hitt. stem *da-a-i-* 'put' < $*dhoH_1$-. At one time or another, however, every unexpected consonant in every IE language has been traced to laryngeals—the κ of G perfects, and of aorists like ἔθηκα; the *v* of the L perfects of the type *amāvī*; the *-*đ* of the Gmc. dental preterites; the *k* of assorted Gmc. forms like MHG *spucken* 'to spit'; the *-c-* in L *senex* 'old' and in the L fem. agent suffix *-trīc-*; the *p* of Skt. causatives like *vāpaya-* 'fan' (root *vā-* 'blow'); the *-y-* of certain *ā*-stem cases in InIr. such as *senayā* inst. 'with an army', and many other things of a similar nature, namely things which cannot be readily explained by tracing them to a more straightforward source. In principle, such explorations are perfectly legitimate, and many of these suggestions have been made by able scholars; but most suffer from demerits too serious to ignore.

As to how many laryngeals there were in the PIE sound system there is no settled opinion. Some authorities work with a single item, usually written **h*. (This theory retains a three-series ablaut scheme (112), though the erstwhile long vowel ablaut series (118) are typically gathered up under the three short vowel series plus **h*.) At the other extreme, there are scholars who have proposed eight or more of the things. Interestingly, the theories positing elaborate inventories are characterized by a high degree of specificity about the phonetic details of the reconstructions—several plain laryngeals of various types (voiced and voiceless, for example; see **451B** fn. and **398.8a**) together with palatalized ones (alongside palatal ones), labialized ones, labialized palatal ones, and so on. However, most laryngealists work with a much smaller array, and worry little about the phonetics, having given them up as all but unrecoverable.

167. THE MAINSTREAM THEORIES, insofar as anything can be so characterized, work with three laryngeals, corresponding to the three 'consonantal schwas' of 165; an important subvariety of these theories adds a fourth, different from $*H_2$ only in dropping in Hitt. instead of becoming *ḫ*.

The following observations are widely accepted as valid.

The chief effects of the laryngeals are on adjacent vowels, namely coloring some and lengthening others. As a consequence the place to discuss laryngeal reconstruction is in connection with vowel developments, as has been done above in the discussion of ablaut (113-4 and 117-22) and the vowels (36-56). The effects of laryngeals on vowels are clearer in G and L than in most IE languages, because these two maintained the PIE distinction between *ă̄*- and *ŏ̄*-vowels.

In many languages are to be seen the effects of a laryngeal occurring between a syllabic semivowel and a following vowel, of the type **pl̥H₁ú*- 'full, many'. Without the laryngeal intervening, a resonant before a vowel would be non-syllabic under most normal circumstances, thus ˣ*plú*- rather than **pl̥H₂ú*-. (Not all such shapes involve laryngeals, however. PIE **gʷr̥ru*- 'heavy', for example, on the evidence of Skt. *gurvī́*- fem. < **gʷr̥w-iH₂*-, had no laryngeal in its makeup; cf. Ved. *pūrvī́*- fem. 'many' < **pl̥H₁w-iH₂*, 105-6.)

Specifically in InIr., *H_2 (the evidence for *H_1 and *H_3 is less clear) makes a preceding voiceless stop into an aspirate, thus **sti-stH_2-enti* 'they stand' (root **steH_2*-) > Ved. *tiṣṭhanti*; and they count as a consonant for purposes of Brugmann's Law (36.4), thus **te-top-H_2e* 'I burn' > Ved. *tatápa* 'I suffer' (expected **tatápha* leveled), vs. 3sg. **te-top-e* > Ved. *tatā́pa* 'he suffers' (root **tep*- as in L *tepidus* 'warm'). On the other hand, in neither G nor Indic scansion do laryngeals ever make a preceding short vowel heavy 'by position' (as, say, G ϝ still does in Homeric scansion).

Possibly **Hw* yields PGmc. **kw* in **kʷikwaz* 'alive' < **gʷiH_3-wo*- (= L *vīvus*); likewise the Gmc. 1du. stem **unkw*- < **n̥H_1we* (cf. Ved. *āvā́m* acc.du. < **āva-ám*); and OE *tácor* 'husband's brother' (if from **dayHwer*- rather than **daywer*-). But all of these are more or less controversial.

a. An early component of the laryngeal theory was the assumption that, as regards the development of the familiar IE languages, the laryngeals had totally disappeared very early indeed; in fact, according to one interpretation, the loss of the laryngeals as consonants had already taken place in PIE, and was one of the innovations which defined PIE as a branch of the Proto-Indo-Hittite language family (Proto-Anatolian being the other, conservative, branch). But there are many reasons for thinking that the laryngeals persisted as separate elements well into the individual histories of some IE branches. Discussion of such matters lies outside the scope of this work, however. —A subvariety of the early-disappearance theory holds that all laryngeals, however many there were, merged into a single sound in 'western' IE languages (Italic, Germanic, BS, Celtic). The explanation of L *unguis* 'hoof, nail' endorsed above (100b) would not work if the notion of 'western' laryngeal merger is valid.

PIE **s*

168. PIE **s* has diverse conditioned outcomes in most IE languages. For G and L the changes will be given in detail below, but the most striking innovations can be previewed here. (1) In G, **s* > **h* before a vowel, except when preceded by certain consonants. In most dialects this **h* survives as such in initial position, where it is known as the πνεῦμα δασύ (*spiritus asper*)—the term identifies an ordinary consonant phoneme, /h/, about which there is nothing unusual apart from the awkward fact that in the Athenian (Ionic) alphabet it was not represented by an actual letter. Intervocalically, PG **h* disappears in all varieties of G except (apparently—

172c) Myc. (2) In L, *s between vowels merges with r, a change known as *rhotacism* (173). Between a vowel and most voiced consonants *s drops, with compensatory lengthening of the preceding vowel (225.1).

a. In Indo-Iranian, *s becomes *š (Indic ṣ) after r, ī̆, ū̆; any diphthong (which of course all end in *y or *w); and k (including kṣ from *gs and *ghs). In Indic the innovation spread to iṣ < *H̥s. This development, known by an anagram of the environments as the RUKI *rule*, is partly shared with BS.

Beyond the scope of this work are the many outcomes of word-final *-s in Indic, as determined partly by the vowel that precedes it and by the sound that begins the following word. As a result of these changes, an actual -s is found as such only when the next word begins with t- or th-. Our citation forms, for example *jánas* 'race', *ágacchas* imperf. 'you arrived', and *pitáras* nom.pl. 'fathers', are unknown in Sanskrit grammatical tradition; indeed, they would be literally unpronounceable. In Sanskrit such words would be cited as *jánaḥ*, *ágacchaḥ*, and *pitáraḥ*, in which -ḥ (phonetically [h]) is the reflex of *-s in final position before pause. A few western authorities follow this convention.

b. In Germanic, PIE *s split into *s and *z in accord with the provisions of Verner's Law (139). These remain as such in Gothic, when not disturbed by leveling analogies; but in North and West Germanic *z merges with *r, resulting in such alternations as NE *lose/forlorn*, *was/were*, NHG *frieren* 'freeze' but *Frost* 'frost'.

c. PIE *s is very stable in Baltic languages; in Slavic, it is lost finally, and becomes š and χ in the RUKI environments (**a**, above).

d. s-MOVABLE. Many PIE roots are attested in two forms, with and without initial *s-: L *speciō* 'look at', G σκέπτομαι (with metathesis), OHG *spehōn*, Av. *spasyeiti*, all pointing to *spek̑-; but Ved. *páśyati* 'sees' points instead to *pek̑-. This is thought to result from a structural ambiguity: many of the nom. and acc. endings of PIE nouns ended in *-s (255), and when one of these (or a word with any other ending in *-s) stood before a form beginning *sC-, the pronunciation was the same as if it stood before plain *C-: **wl̥kʷoms spek̑yont* 'they saw the wolves' (root *spek̑-) was pronounced: [wl̥kʷomspekyont], while **wl̥kʷoms pek̑ent* 'they groomed the wolves'—a characteristic IE task (root *pek̑-)—was pronounced: [wl̥kʷomspekent]. Native speakers of a language usually keep ambiguous sequences straight, as they know what the components are, but ambiguity at least opens the way to confusion, namely the abstraction of a new root-shape *pek̑- 'see'.

In fact, as very little is known of PIE phonotactics this reasoning is circular (the phenomenon to be explained is the only evidence for the explanation). Still, typologically speaking, the assumed phonotactics are not exotic. The only unreasonable thing about the theory is that if it is valid, given the ubiquity of final *-s in PIE, a contrast between initial *sC- and *C- must have been close to nonexistent; nevertheless most roots are attested without any variation in form: *pleH₁- 'fill', *prek̑- 'ask', *ten- 'stretch', and many others, have no by-forms in *s-.

169. PIE *s remains unchanged in both G and L before or after a voiceless stop, and when final.

PIE *H₁esti 'is' > G ἐστί, L *est* : Ved. *ásti*, Go. *ist*, Hitt. *e-eš-zi*.
PIE *deyk̑-s- aor. of *deyk̑- 'point' > G ἔδειξα, L *dīxī* : Ved. *adikṣi* 1sg.mid.
PIE *ĝenH₁os 'race, kind' > G γένος, L *genus* : Ved. *jánas*.
PIE *seĝh-s- desid. of *seĝh- 'control' > G ἕξω fut. of ἔχω : Ved. *sīkṣant-* (from *sī-ḍẓhant- < *si-ẓḍẓhant- < *si-sĝh-s-) pres.pple. of desid. of *sahate*.

a. For -s in final position in L, see also 237.2.

170. Initial *s before vowels remains in L, but in G becomes /h/.[1] The change to /h/ is already complete in Myc., and therefore predates 1200 BC; it was probably a feature of Proto-Greek.

PIE *$septm̥$ 'seven' > G ἑπτά, L *septem* : Ved. *saptá*, OE *seofon*, NE *seven*.

PIE **si-sd-* (redup. pres. of root **sed-*) 'sit down' > G ἵζω, L *sīdō* : Ved. *sī́dati* (*d* for expected *ḍ* by leveling).

PIE **sēmi-* (or *seH_1mi-) 'half-' > G ἡμι-, L *sēmi-* : PGmc. **sēm-* in OE *sám-cwic* 'half dead' and *sám-soden* 'half boiled'.

PIE **so* m. *seH_2 f., nom.sg. 'that' (remaining forms built to stems **to-*/*teH_2-; 376.1) > G ὁ, ἡ : Ved. *sá*, *sā́*; Av. *ha*, *hā*; OE *se*, *séo*.

PIE *sek^w- midd. 'follow' > G ἕπομαι, L *sequor* : Ved. *sacate*, OIr. *sechithir*.

a. This G *h-* shows the effects of Grassmann's Law (138): from **seǵh-* 'prevail, control': **seǵhō* > PreG *$hek^h\bar{o}$ > G ἔχω, but **seǵh-s-* > **seks-* (214) > fut. ἕξω (the root is seen whole in the zero-grade aor. **e-sǵh-* > ἔσχον); cf. θρίξ, τριχός (138). —Many forms with ἀ- for ἁ- < *$sm̥$-, like ἀδελφός 'brother' (*'having the same womb'), ἄλοχος 'spouse' (*'having the same bed'), ἀθρόος 'in a bunch', may be so explained, though in some of them the second aspirate is separated from **h-* by intervening consonants. Unexpectedly, however, ἁθρόος occurs very commonly instead of ἀθρόος.

b. In Hellenistic G initial /h/ remained until the 2nd century AD, when its less and less consistent indication in texts points to its disappearance from the language. The breathing marks were until recently retained in NG, well over a millennium after the sound itself was last pronounced, as a distinction of spelling only. In the *psilotic dialects* of G (East Ionic, Lesbian, and some others), rough breathing was lost very much earlier; the many *h*-less forms in Hom. are importations from such dialects.

c. A change of initial **s-* to *h-* is seen in two IE languages adjacent to G (roughly speaking), Iranian and Armenian, though apparently affecting them at a later date. Later too, and separated geographically as well and so indisputably independent, was the change of *s-* to *h-* in Welsh, as MW *hebu* 'I speak' < *sek^w-, *halen* 'salt' < **sal-*. At all events, [h] from sibilants is a commonplace development, seen in languages as diverse as Finnish, Hawaiian, and Caribbean Spanish.

171. The same change of **s* to *h* in G took place in the INITIAL sequences **sw-*, **sr-*, **sl-*, **sm-*, and **sn-* (see 227 for the development of such clusters medially), which evidently passed through a stage of being pronounced as voiceless resonants (usually written [w̥, r̥, l̥, m̥, n̥] by phoneticians). This is the probable significance of the representation in very early inscriptions, namely FH, PH, ΛH, and so on, as literal [hw], [hr], and [hl] would probably have been spelled HF, HP, and HΛ, and so on. These developed diversely: FH became /h/, PH became ῥ-, and the remaining ones fell together with plain λ-, μ-, ν-. Compounds and augmented or reduplicated forms of words with original **sr-*, **sl-*, and so on, regularly have -ρρ-, and

---

[1] The curious analysis of the classical grammarians treats initial /h/ as a trait of vowels, called πνεῦμα δασύ 'rough breathing' or *spiritus asper*. It is to be presumed that had the sound been represented by a regular letter in the Ionic alphabet, it would have been regarded as just one more letter. See 24.2.

in Hom. frequently -λλ-, -μμ-, and -νν- as well; for these last three, later attestations generally have just -λ-, -μ-, -ν-.

PIE **swe* refl. > Pamph. ϝhε, Att. ἕ (poet.) : Ved. *sva-* in compounds.

PIE **srew-* 'flow', G ῥέ(ϝ)ω : Ved. *srávanti* 3pl. PIE **srowos* m. 'stream, current' > Hom. ῥόος, Cyp. *ro-vo* acc. of **(h)rowos*. PIE **sroweH₂* > PG **hrowā* > Att. ῥοή 'stream', Corfu inscr. PHOFAIΣI dat.pl. : Ved. *saṃsrāvá-* 'a flowing together' (root *sru-*), NE *stream*. Cf. G καταρρέω 'flow down', Hom. ἔρρεον aor. of ῥέω.

PIE **slagʷ-* 'grasp' (or 'squeeze') is hardly attested outside of G, but the root is reconstructable from G evidence alone: λαμβάνω, Hom. λάζομαι: Corfu ΛΗΑΒΩΝ (H = /h/) aor.pple.; Hom. aor. ἔλλαβε, later ἔλαβε (the regular medial development of **-esl-* is -ειλ-, 227.2).

PIE **smey-d-* 'smile' > G μειδιάω, Hom. φιλο-μμειδής 'smile-loving' (epithet of Aphrodite) : Ved. *smayate*, Latv. *smeju* 'laugh', Toch. A *smi-*.

PIE **sneygʷh-* 'snow' > G νείφει 'snows' but ἀγά-ννιφος 'very snowy' : NE *snow*, Lith. *sniñga*.

a. There are many G words of unknown etymology beginning with σ-, and a number more have σ- from **tw-* (190.4) and **ky-* (199c). But there are several with σ- from **s-*. These typically occur side by side with the expected outcome, as σῦς (next to ὗς) 'swine' < PIE **sūs* or **suHs*; σμῑκρός 'small' (beside μῑκρός); σμύρνη 'myrrh' (beside Aeol. μύρρᾱ). Tracing these forms to dialect borrowing would be a guess rather than an explanation, but that is the most likely possibility.

172. Intervocalic **s* is lost in G (via **h*); and becomes *r* in L.

Gen.sg. of *s*-stems: PIE **ǵenH₁esos, -es* > PG **genehos* > Hom. γένεος, Att. γένους, L *generis* : Skt. *janasas*, Av. *zanāŋhō*.

PIE **-eH₂sōm* gen.pl. of pron. ā-stems (imported into noun inflection in G and Italic): Hom. -ᾱ́ων (Att. -ῶν), L *-ārum*, O *-azum*, U *-aru(m)* : Ved. *-āsām* (only in pronominal paradigms).

PIE **H₁es-* 'be': pres.subj. **H₁esōH₂* > ἔω (Att. ὦ), L fut. *erō*.

L *gerō* 'do', of obscure etym. but transparently **ges-*, cf. pple. *gestus* < **ges-tos*. Similarly obscure as to remoter connections but clear as to immediate history is L *cūra* 'solicitude' < **koysā*, cf. Paelig. COISATENS 'curaverunt'.

a. Unexpectedly, as there is no obvious phonetic basis for such a thing, **s* remained unchanged in G after **-n̥-* and **-r̥-*:

G δασύς 'thick, rough, shaggy', L *dēnsus* (*o*-stem) 'thick, close' < **dn̥s-*.

G ἄσις 'mud, slime' : Ved. *ásita-* 'dark, black' and (with greater effort) Ved. *así-* 'knife', L *ēnsis* poet. '(iron) sword'—these latter taking 'dark, black' to be a metonym of 'iron'.[1]

Hom. -ασι dat.pl. of neut. *n*-stems < **-n̥si*: ὀνόμασι (ὄνομα).

G θρασύς (earlier than θαρσέω, 95.1) 'daring' < PIE **dhr̥su-*, cf. Ved. *dhr̥ṣṇú-* 'bold', Go. *gadaursan* 'dare'.

---

[1] Iron is in fact often so called, as Skt. *śyāmá-* 'black', and in Hom. and elsewhere, as when a leather shield is called μελάνδετος 'black-bound' (that is, iron-rimmed). And cf. English *blacksmith*.

b. In certain morphological categories, G -σ- was reestablished intervocalically by leveling. This explains aorists like ἔλῡσα 'loosed' and ἐφίλησα 'began to love', after the analogy of forms like ἔδειξα 'pointed out' in which the -σ- was not subject to loss; in *o*-stem dat.pl. -οισι, after the analogy of -σι in cons. stems (with some help from -οις, originally the inst.pl.). In 2sg. forms like τίθεσαι and ἐτίθεσο -σ- is restored after the analogy of γέγραψαι, ἐγέγραψο (in contrast to thematic φέρεαι, ἐφέρεο; see 425). This explanation is the generally accepted one, but it offers no hint as to how and why such an analogy acted on 2sg. *τίθεαι, *τίθεο and the like but not on φέρεαι, ἐφέρεο, which appear to be equally eligible.

In most cases, intervocalic -σ- in G represents an earlier group of consonants, such as -σσ- of whatever origin and -τσ- (215).

c. As fits the assumption that **s* > **h* at an early date, evidence for intervocalic *-*h*- in G is scanty and indirect; but it is clear nevertheless:

Such a stage is required to account for the words in which medial *-*h*- wicked through to the beginning of the word, as εὕω 'singe' < **ewhō* < **(H₁)ewsoH₂* (L *ūrō*); or ἱερός 'superhuman, mighty' (Hom.) < **isH̥₁ro*- (Ved. *iṣirá*- 'flourishing, vigorous').

Slightly more direct evidence comes from Mycenaean: there is some reason to think that one of the Linear B characters for /a/, namely a_2 (26.6), was used to write *ha* particularly (though not consistently); if so, an *s*-stem form like *pa-we-a₂* 'pieces of cloth' (= φάρεα < **pʰarweha*) actually attests /pʰarweha/.

173. LATIN RHOTACISM, as the change of *s* to *r* is often called, was doubtless through the medium of [z]; and in O the change did not go beyond this stage, as seen in the gen.pl. -*azum* = L -*ārum*. There is no direct evidence for [z] in L itself, but that is in accord with expectations: Romans would inevitably have continued to write [z] with the letter *s* until they switched to *r*, and that could not have happened until some time after [z] merged with [r]. The change to *r* was complete in the 4th century BC, but the grammarians and other authorities quote many old forms with -*s*-, as *Lases* (*Lārēs*) in the Carmen Arvale, and *arbosem* (*arborem*). These are confirmed epigraphically (VALESIOSIO 'Valerii' on the Lapis Satricanus, IOVESAT 'iurat' in the Duenos inscription, 19), and L. Papirius Crassus lives in history for a reason he himself would hardly have selected, namely that he was the first member of the Papirian gens to respell *Papisios* with an *r*.

For a sound law affecting such a large number of forms, L rhotacism is unusually dependable. The apparent exceptions to it, namely -*s*- between vowels (*rosa*, *nisi*, *causa*), or -*r* from -*s* in final position (*arbor*, *rōbur*), all have obvious explanations—borrowing after the change took place (*rosa*), leveling (*rōbur* 297.1b, *arbor* 299), and relative chronology (*nisi* was still a phrase at the time of the sound law, *causa* was still *caussa*, 232.2).

a. When the next syllable begins with *r*, the change of *s* to *r* is blocked, so *caesariēs* 'bushy-haired', *miser* 'wretched' (cf. *maestus* 'grief', *maeror* 'mourn'), *disertus* 'eloquent', OL *aser* 'blood'. The change does take place in *soror* 'sister' < **swesōr* and *aurōra* 'dawn' < **awsōsā*, however. Given the fewness of the forms involved, there is little basis for choosing between possible explanations for these two forms.

b. A change of *s* to *r* may appear extreme, phonetically, but is observed in many languages; cf. the development of PGmc. **z* in WGmc. and NGmc. to *r*, as in NE *better* and OIc. *betre* next to Go. *batiza* < PIE comp. suff. *-*is*- (349); and in fragments like NE *were* next to *was*; and *forlorn*, which is related to *lose*. The Eretrian dialect of Ionic shows the regular change of intervocalic (Ionic) *s* to ρ, as in ΟΠΟΡΑΙ (= ὁπόσ(σ)αι) 'quantae'. In final position after a high vowel, Skt. *-*s* > -*r* before a word beginning with a vowel: what is componentially *upapadnas guṇāis iṣṭāis* 'endowed with desirable qualities' surfaces as *upapanno guṇāir iṣṭāiḥ*.

174. REMARKS ON THE GREEK SPIRITUS ASPER. The regular source of G initial /h/ is PIE **s* (170). But it occurs also by analogy (item 3, below); or in words originally beginning with **y* or **w* (treated in **191** and **188**, respectively). Some instances are of wholly enigmatic origin, for example G ἵππος 'horse': its cognates—L *equus*, Ved. *áśva*-, OE *eoh*, Gaul. *Epona*, and so on—point unambiguously to a word-initial **e*- (or *H_1*e*-, which for present purposes is the same thing); and even in G itself compounds such as the name Ἄλκ-ιππος, with unaspirated κ, are inconsistent with the rough breathing of the simplex.

The explanation for individual cases is often doubtful, but some generalizations may be noted:

1. Initial ῠ̄-, of whatever history, always has spiritus asper. How this state of affairs came about is unknown.

2. Initial /h/ sometimes results from the anticipation of an intervocalic /h/ from -*s*- (172c). In a similar development, there are several cases of aspirated φρο- from προ- in compounds, for example φρουρᾱ́ 'a watch' < *προ-ὁρᾱ́, or φροῦδος 'quite gone' < *προ-ὁδός. But φρο- is probably the result of a loosely analogical process rather than a phonological one, by imitation of καθ- ~ κατα- and ἐφ- ~ ἐπι-.

3. Initial /h/ sometimes is imported from some other form via analogy, as in ἡμεῖς 'us' after regular ὑμεῖς 'you' pl.; Heracl. *hοκτω* 'eight' after regular ἑπτά 'seven'; late ἕτος for ἔτος 'year' perhaps after ἡμέρα 'day'.

LIQUIDS, NASALS, AND GLIDES.

175. TABLE OF CORRESPONDENCES.

PIE	G	L	Indic	NE
*r	ρ	r	r, l	r
*l	λ	l	r, l	l
*m	μ, ν	m	m	m
*n	ν	n	n	n
*w	ϝ, h, ∅	v, ∅	v	w
*y	h, ζ, ∅	i, ∅	y	y

1. GREEK. The loss of PIE **y* and **w* between vowels in G leaves few traces. However, because the loss of **y* was earlier than the loss of **w*, there are differences in the details of the contraction of the resulting vowel sequences, as set forth in **86**. When immediately following a consonant, **y* precipitated wholesale palatalizations, in the course of which the glide as such disappeared (195–207).

2. LATIN. In L, PIE **y* and **w* survive initially, and *w* ('consonantal *u*', herein anachronistically written *v*) remained a glide, phonetically, until early in the Romance period. L orthography obscures the facts of intervocalic *w*—before which all short vowels became *u* (66.5)—by shunning the sequence -*uu*- (-vv-), so usual *fuī*, *minuō*, *monuī* instead

of the more accurate *fuvī, minuvō, monuvī.* Italian *vedova, Genova* as reflexes of L *vidua* 'widow' (PIE **widheweH₂*) and *Genua* are revealing.

3. In Indo-Iranian, PIE **r* and **l* merge. The resulting liquid was *r*-like in Iranian and the western dialects of Indic, but *l*-like in eastern Indic. The bulk of our Skt. texts are from *r*-dialects. Dialect borrowing from eastern dialects, scanty in the Rigveda but increasing markedly already in the later Vedic texts, results in doublets in Sanskrit, such as *rabh-* and *labh-* both 'seize'. These are often differentiated semantically, however, as in *laghú-* 'light' vs. *raghú-* 'speedy' (both from **l̥ngʷhú-*; **95**, **163**). But most cases of *l* in Indic are in words borrowed from Dravidian and other non-Indic languages.

4. In PIE, as in IE languages generally, there were other phonetic varieties of nasals in addition to *m* and *n*, but they were found only in consonant clusters. See **216**.

LIQUIDS AND NASALS

176. PIE **r* and **l* are unchanged in both G and L.

PIE **rewdh-* (various grades and suffixes) 'red' > G ἐρυθρός (ἐ- prothetic, **89**), L *ruber* : Ved. *róhita-* and *lóhita-* (*dh* sporadically > Skt. *h*, **144.3**), OE *réad*, Lith. *raũdas.*

PIE **bher-* 'carry' > G φέρω, L *ferō* : Ved. *bhárati*, NE *bear*, OIr. *berith* /beρ'əθ'/.

PIE **ḱlew-* 'hear'; **ḱlu-tó-* 'famous' > G κλυτός, L *inclutus* : Ved. *śrutá-*, OE *hlysnan* 'listen'; full grade in OCS *slava* 'glory'.

PIE **plew-* 'flow, float' (a commonplace polysemy) > G πλέ(ϝ)ω 'swim', L *pluit* 'is raining' : Ved. *pravanta* 3pl. aor. midd. 'they swim' (the usual Epic and Classical form of the root is *plu-*, **175.3**), NE *flow, flood.*

a. In L there were two allophones of *l*, which influence the development of adjacent vowels (**42.5**, **66**). Perhaps because they differed from anything in G, they attracted the attention of Roman grammarians, who term them *l exilis* 'thin *l*' and *l pinguis* 'fat *l*'. These are plainly sounds pronounced with relatively high front and high back tongue-body, respectively, what in more recent times are sometimes called *bright l* and *dark l* (a terminology which is no improvement on *thin* and *fat*). The distribution was as follows: *l* exilis was found before the vowels *-i-* and *-ī-*, and before another *-l-*; *l* pinguis occurred before any other vowel; before any consonant EXCEPT *l*; and in word-final position. On the evidence of the vowel changes, **484.1**, *l* pinguis actually had two degrees of avoirdupois, being fatter before a consonant than before a vowel, such that **welō* > *volō* but **weltes* > *voltis* > *vultis.*

177. PIE **m* and **n.*

PIE **néwo-* 'new' > G νέ(ϝ)ος, L *novus* : Hitt. *ne-e-u-it* inst.sg., OLith. *navas*, Ved. *náva-* (in Skt. later usually *náv(ī)yas-* orig. 'rather new'); PIE **newyo-* in Ion. νεῖος, Lith. *naũjas*, OE *ní(e)we*, NE *new*, NHG *neu.*

PIE **má-H₂ter-* 'mother' > G μήτηρ, Dor. μᾱ́τηρ, L *māter* : Ved. *mātár-*, OE *módor*, OIr. *máth(a)ir* /māθəρ'/ (the G accent is inherited, that of Gmc. and Ved. has been influenced by **pH̥₂tér-*).

PIE **(H)nomn̥* 'name' > G ὄνομα, ὄνυμα (ὀ- prothetic, but see **90**), L *nōmen* (*ō* by contamination with *(g)nōtus*) : Ved *nāman-* (*ā* by Brugmann's Law, **36.4**), OE *nama*, NE *name*, Hitt. *la-a-ma-an.*

a. In L, *n immediately followed by *m dissimilates to -r- in *carmen* 'song' < **kan-mn̥* (cf. *canō*) and *germen* 'seed' < **gen(H̥)mn̥*. The latter is either an example of an aniṭ form of the root very much better attested as **ǵenH$_1$-* (123.3), or is the result of Exon's Law (74.5) acting on oblique forms such as gen.sg. **genamenes*.

GLIDES

178. SIEVERS' LAW. The PIE glides are **y* and **w*. They occur as such adjacent to a syllabic (usually a full grade vowel), and via ablaut interchange with **i* and **u* respectively, as discussed in 110–29. In Greek, Latin, Germanic, and Indo-Iranian there is evidence for a different kind of alternation—between **iy* and **y*, and perhaps between **uw* and **w*. Unlike ablaut alternations, whose conditions are unrecoverable, the distribution of these alternants is transparent: PIE **iy* occurred after a *heavy syllable*, namely a syllable containing a diphthong, a long vowel, or ending in two or more consonants; **y* occurred elsewhere. (Note that all syllabics count as vowels equally: **wr̥ǵ-* has the same weight as **ped-*.) Thus the adjective-forming suffix usually cited as *-*yo-* would actually have had two forms, *-*yo-* and *-*iyo-*: to **ped-* 'foot', **ped-yo-* (whence G πεζός 'afoot', Ved. *pádya-* 'pedal' adj.); to **reH$_1$ǵ-* 'king', **reH$_1$ǵ-iyo-* (whence L *rēgius* 'regal'—not ×*rēius* < ×*reH$_1$ǵyos*—and Ved. *rājiyá-*). Indic evidence is limited to the oldest Vedic texts; later, a Sanskrit sound law converts most inherited *-iy-* and *-uv-* from any source to *-y-* and *-v-*, and in fact the latter are what actually stand in the Vedic texts as transmitted: *rājyá-*, *dyā́us* 'sky', *svá-* 'own', and some dozen others. The readings *rājiyá-*, *diyā́us*, *suvá-*, and so on, in place of what stands in the text are justified by the metrics of the particular line.

This alternation goes by the name *Sievers' Law*. As originally framed by Eduard Sievers it applied to **y* in medial position in Germanic, with some corroborating evidence from Rigvedic Sanskrit and a few remarks about **w*.

Following Sievers, scholars looked for and found evidence for the same alternation in G and L, and also—though the supporting facts are significantly less clear—for the parallel alternation between **w* and **uw*.[1] Later still, the alternation was proclaimed for the remaining four semivowels (**n̥n* vs. **n*, and so on), though for these the evidence is poor indeed. For example, the great majority of formations in *-*tro-*/*-*tlo-*/*-*dhro-*/*-*dhlo-* (the four 'tool'-suffixes) occurred in environments where *-*tr̥ro-*, *-*dhl̥lo-*, etc. would be demanded by Sievers' Law. Among the RV formations in *-tra-*, however, although there are some 50 in which Sievers' Law would require ×*-tira-* < *-*tr̥ro-*/*-*tl̥lo-* (as in *yantrá-* 'bond, restraint' from the root *yam-*), there is not a single instance of the anticipated ×*-tira-*, or evidence that any forms transmitted as *-tra-* should actually be scanned with an additional syllable; nor are there comparable reflexes in G, Ital., or any other IE

---

[1] Forms suggesting that the distribution of **(u)w* did not follow the rules for **(i)y* include RV *ūrdhvá-* 'upright; elevated' (never ×*ūrdhuvá-*; cf. G ὀρθός 'straight' < *-*t^{h}w-*); and L *suāvis* 'sweet' < PItal. **swādwi-* (185.2).

branch. For *-*n*- similarly many secure etymologies contradict the principle, as G τέχνη 'art, skill' < **teks-neH₂-*, not ˣτέξανη < ˣ*teksn̥neH₂-*.

a. Even for the alternations between **y* and **iy*, as originally formulated, there are such important differences in detail from one IE language to another that it is unlikely that the alternation could have been inherited from the parent language. The development of [iy] into [y] in certain environments, or conversely of [y] into [iy], is the kind of thing that might easily arise independently in different languages. Whether inherited or not, however, it is possible that in both G and L some such principle governed the distribution of original **y* and **iy*, AT LEAST IN SOME AFFIXES.

b. Some apparent exceptions can be accounted for by the hypothesis that the syllabic resonants only occurred after sequences including a resonant, so *-*ntuwo*- but *-*stwo*- (as in G ἀστός 'oppidan' < *ϝαστϝο- (ϝάστυ 'town')). This is phonologically improbable, and accounts for only a small number of exceptions in any case.

179. EDGERTON'S LAW is the name commonly used for the most ambitious of the elaborations of Sievers' Law: namely that its provisions governed all six semivowels in all positions in the word. Thus, in initial sequences, forms traditionally cited as **yeseti* 'bubbles, foams', **reǵeti* 'sends/goes/arranges in a straight line', and **newos* 'new' would have been pronounced as such only after a pause, or when preceded by a word ending in a short vowel, a short diphthong, or a single consonant preceded by a short vowel. Immediately following anything else—a word ending in a long diphthong, or a diphthong or long vowel plus a consonant, or any two consonants—they would have been pronounced with a syllabic initial, namely **iyeseti*, **r̥reǵeti*, and **n̥newos*. For words beginning with a consonant cluster, the environments are the same, once you take into account the permanent presence of one more consonant in the sequence: **dyēws* 'sky', **preH₃* 'forth', and **snoygʷhos* 'snowing' would therefore have been pronounced as such in only one environment—when the preceding word ended in a short vowel; in any other position, easily four-fifths of the total, they would have been pronounced with an additional syllable: **diyēws*, **pr̥reH₃*, and **sn̥noygʷhos*.

180. THE CONVERSE OF SIEVERS' LAW. According to Edgerton's Law, semivowel sequences resulting from combination obey the same rules: **n̥dhi-yenti* 'they go down' and **n̥-nikʷtos* 'unwashed' (**neygʷ*-), have sequences of a syllabic and a non-syllabic semivowel over a morpheme boundary; their syllabification would follow the rules given previously: the former would have alternated between **n̥dhyenti* and (following a word ending in a vowel) **ndhiyenti*; and **n̥-nikʷtos* and its antonym **nikʷtos* would have been homophonous in all environments (**n̥nikʷtos* after heavy syllables, **nikʷtos* elsewhere). This theory is sometimes briefly called *Edgerton's Converse*.

a. Athough nothing remotely approaching such a system is evident in any attested IE language, those who endorse this theory hold that the patterns of alternation lasted in Indic to a period not too long before the creation of the poetry of the Rigveda, such that in Rigvedic scansion the remnants of the original distribution are clear enough to support the theory. The reasoning is analogous to that for the restoration of digamma in Homeric texts, 189.

Although Edgerton's Law has enjoyed general acceptance, those few who have searched systematically for themselves have found the evidence for it often to be different from what has been reported in scholarly literature—in fact, inadequate to support the theory erected upon it.

181. LINDEMAN'S LAW is an attempt to bring the theory of semivowel syllabification into better accord with the Rigvedic facts. Its contribution is to limit Sievers syllabification in word-initial sequences to those words whose short form was monosyllabic. Thus of the forms cited in this connection above, only **dyēws* and **preH₃* would have alternated, with **diyēws* and **pr̥reH₃* respectively.

In the Rigveda there actually are forms which show two different shapes, as *dyā́us* 'sky' next to *diyā́us*, *svá-* 'own' next to *suvá-*. The great preponderance are, as Lindeman's Law holds, monosyllabic; the exceptions are easily explained as paradigmatic leveling (*suvásya* gen.sg. for what should be invariant *svásya*). But against these seemingly straightforward facts must be set four other things which are true of the observed distributions but do not follow in any way from the hypothesis: (1) Alternation is never observed in the text itself apart from glides.[1] The form *prá* is required by Lindeman's Law to scan in two syllables more than a thousand times in the RV, but a mere three instances reasonably allow for such a scansion and none require it. (2) Given random distribution, shapes of the *diyā́us* type should preponderate over the *dyā́us* type by a sizable ratio, about five to one; but for all alternating forms—except one—the short form preponderates. Typical is *dyā́us* itself (50×) vs. *diyā́us* (26×). (The single exception is the numeral *d(u)vá-* 'two'; see 389.2.) (3) Only the *diyā́us*/*suvá-* shapes actually favor the phonological environment predicted by the Law; the distribution of the *dyā́us*/*svá-* shapes is random. (4) The long form often has strong distributional preferences which the Law neither predicts nor accounts for. All but one occurrence of *diyā́us*, for example, is found in line-initial position.

There is a second kind of evidence, which is indirect. The reasoning runs as follows: owing to the formulaic nature of Vedic diction, even a form showing no alternation in the RV could provide indirect but cogent evidence for an original alternation if it showed a statistically significant tendency to occur in the environment originally appro-

---

[1] Lindeman includes a single non-glide among his likely cases: the gen.pl. of 'woman', **gʷnōm* ~ **gʷn̥nōm*; the disyllabic phase is reflected directly by OIr. *ban* gen.pl., indirectly by Boeot. βανᾶ. But the gen.pl. (despite Lindeman's arguments to the contrary) was actually **gʷn̥H₂-ōm* (272.2, 311a); this accounts for OIr. *ban* directly and is one of the forms providing the raw materials for βανᾶ, but it is no longer a Lindeman form. On the other hand, the gen.sg. **gʷneH₂s* (OIr. *mná*) is a Lindeman form; it shows no evidence of alternation.

priate for that form. When one alternant became obsolete, the formulae and collocations in which it typically occurred would necessarily become obsolete as well, leaving behind half a distributional pattern, as it were. Edgerton cited much of such indirect evidence. It is not seen to be statistically significant when the facts are stated accurately and when appropriate statistical controls are used.

These theories have been successful—in the sense that they are widely embraced, not in the sense that they rest on persuasive evidence. In practical terms, Edgerton's or Lindeman's Law is for the historian a source of convenient alternative forms for explaining the details of particular attestations, taking its place among the other ad hoc explanatory devices of leveling, contamination, back-formation, and so on. So for example even an acknowledged master of our field has rejected a reconstruction like **s(e)ptmós* '7th', for which there is evidence (398.7), on the grounds that it is 'impossible under the terms of Edgerton's Law', while on the same page accepting without comment the equally impossible reconstructions **triyós* '3rd' (398.3) and **newn̥nós* '9th' (398.9).

PIE *w

182. PIE **w* remained in L as 'consonantal *u*' (the graphic distinction between *v* and *u* develops only much later); and in G as ϝ, which was lost at an early period in Att.-Ion.

PIE **weyd-*, **wid-* 'see' > L *videō*, G ϝιδεῖν, ἰδεῖν : Ved. *vid-*.

PIE **wekʷ-*, **wokʷ-* 'speak' > L *vōx* 'voice', G ϝέπος, ἔπος 'word' : Ved. *vácas-*.

PIE **woyḱo-* 'settlement' > L *vīcus* 'district, village', G ϝοῖκος, οἶκος 'house(hold)' : Ved. *viś-* 'tribe, homestead', *e*-grade Go. *weihs* 'country(side)'. (OE *wíc* 'village; villa' is a lw. from L; it survives in *baili-wick* and place names such as *War-wick* and *Sand-wich*.)

PIE **newos* 'new' > L *novus*, G νέ(ϝ)ος : Ved. *náva-*, *náv(ī)yas-*, OCS *novŭ*, OE *ní(e)we* (< **new-yo-*), NE *new*.

PIE **H₃ewi-* 'sheep' > L *ovis*, G ὄϝις, Hom. ὄϊς : Ved. *ávi-*, Luv. *ḫa-wi-*, OE *eow*, fem. *eowu*, NE *ewe*.

LATIN V

183. Loss of **w* and the labial component of PIE **kʷ* took place in prehistoric times before *o*. This applies to all **kʷ*, but **w-* in initial position is unaffected.

L *deus* 'god' < **dęos* (57.2) < **deywos* : Ved. *devá-*, Lith. *diẽvas*, OPr. *deiws*.

L *deorsum* 'downwards', *seorsum* 'apart' < **dē-vorsom*, *sē-vorsom*.

L *secundus* 'following' < **secondos* < **sequondos* (*sequor*).

L *cottīdiē* 'daily' < **kʷotitei diē* (cf. *quot* 'how many').

L *colō* 'cultivate' < **quolō* < **kʷelō* : L *inquilīnus* 'tenant', G πόλος 'plowed land' (if cognate. The semantics are fine, exactly paralleled by the development of NE *tillage*; but from **kʷolos* we would expect rather ˣκύλος by 44).

L *so-* from **swo-*, **swe-* (**42.2**) in *somnus* 'dream' (**219**) and *sodālis*.
L *coquō* 'cook' from **quoquō* (**42.4**).
L *iecur* 'liver' < **iecor* < **iequor* < PIE **yekʷr̥(t)* : G ἧπαρ, Ved. *yakŕ̥t*. (L *iecinoris, iocinoris* by leveling.)

In fact, this change is observed in relatively few of the words where it should be found. In the great majority, the *v* or *qu* was restored on the analogy of closely connected forms in which the *v* or *qu* was followed by a different vowel, and so was retained. Cf. NE *swore*, once pronounced *sore* but now with /w/ reimported from *swear*. (Contrast the isolated *sword*, which having lost its /w/ stayed that way.) Thus L *servos* 'slave' for *seros* after *servī*, *quod* for *cod* after *quī* within the same paradigm, and also the paradigmatically removed (but still semantically transparent) *quot* 'how many' for **cot(e)*; but note that the semantically remote *cottīdiē*, above, persists. The sometimes zigzag nature of the interaction between sound laws and analogy is demonstrated by **equos* 'horse' and **sequontor* 'they follow': these first became **ecos*, **secontor* per this sound law; having been restored to *equos, sequontor*, the later passage of *-o-* to *-u-* (**71.6**) resulted in *ecus, secuntur* by a much later sound law of the same character; and then finally these latter were once again refashioned into familiar *equus, sequuntur* by another round of leveling.

a. A single original paradigm underlies both L *deus, deī* and *dīvus, dīvī*, which result from leveling in opposite directions from a paradigm that looked something like:

	With **w*:		Without **w*:
gen.sg.	*dẹ̄wī	*nom.sg.*	*dẹ̄os
nom.pl.	*dẹ̄wẹ̄	*acc.sg.*	*dẹ̄om
	etc.		*etc.*

Based on the shapes retaining **w*, such as the gen. and nom.pl., newly created nom.sg. **dẹ̄wos*, acc.sg. **dẹ̄wom*, and the rest were created, yielding a uniform paradigm (*dīvus, dīvī*). Based on the shapes seen in the nom. and acc.sg., newly created nom.pl. **dẹ̄ī*, and the rest, yielded another uniform paradigm (*deus, deī*[1]). (In an analogous case, NE *staff, staffs* and *stave, staves* evolved from the same original paradigm, with the difference that here the original alternation remains intact in *staff, staves*.)

184. LOSS OF PIE **w* also occurs in L:

1. Initially before *r* and *l*. The majority of such sequences in L words arose within Italic, via such developments as Ital. **wlā-* from PIE **wl̥H-*:
PIE **wr̥H₂d(-īk)-* 'root' > **wrād-īk-* > L *rādīx*, G ῥᾱδιξ : cf. **wr̥H₂di-* (*i*-stem) in Go *waurts* 'plant, herb', OE *wyrt*, NE *wort* in plant names like *figwort*. —The G and L forms might equally well continue the full grade **wreH₂d-* seen in OIc. *rót* (borrowed in NE as *root*).
PIE **wl̥H₂n-eH₂-*, **-o-* 'wool' > **wlānā* (**106.2**) > L *lāna*, G λῆνος, Dor. λᾶνος : OE *wull*, Lith. *vìlna*.

2. After the labials *p* or *f*, whether the latter is from **bh* or **dh*:
PIE **wer-* 'cover': **ap-weryō* 'uncover' > L *aperiō* : Ved. *apa-vr̥-*, Lith. *àtveriu*.
PIE **op-wer-tlo-* lit. 'utensil for covering' > L *operculum* 'lid' (**92**).

---

[1] A later loss of **w* between like vowels (**184.3**) resulted in nom.pl. **dẹ̄ẹ̄*, whence the irregular form *dī* of classical L.

Future in *-bit*, imperfect in *-bat*, probably < **-bweti*, **-bwāt* respectively (**bhū-* **498**, **501.3**), though the details are obscure.
PIE **dhworom* 'dooryard' or the like > L *forum* 'public square, market' : OCS *dvorŭ* 'court' (cf. **147.1**).

3. Sporadically between like vowels:
L *aetās* 'age' < **aywitāt-*; cf. L *aevum*, Go. *aiwins* 'for ever'.
L *lātrīna* beside *lavātrīna* 'privy; drain' orig. 'washing place' (*lavāre*); and perf. *lāvī* < **lawaway*.
L *dīs*, *dītis* 'rich' beside *dīves*, *dīvitis*.
OL (but also later writers such as Cicero) *sīs* for *sī vīs* 'if you will'.

a. A number of perfects, originally formed regularly in the *vī*-paradigm, are sometimes put under this rule: **mowaway* (*moveō*) > **moaway* > *mōvī* (**525.3**). Contraction of **moaway* to **mōway* would be proper and expected (**88.3**), but the loss of the *-*w*- between unlike vowels is suspect. Given the regular development of short vowels medially before *-*w*- to -*u*- (**66.5**), we can refine the interpretation of these forms: in all probability an intermediate stage in the development of *-*a*- to -*u*- was *-*o*-, thus **mowaway* > **mowoway*, whence regularly **mooway* and then **mōway*. (Of course, it is always possible that the medial vowel simply syncopated, and that the first syllable of the resulting **mowway* underwent the *nōnus* development, **61.2a**.)

185. PIE POSTCONSONANTAL **w* IN LATIN.

1. Initial **dw-* > L *b-*:
PIE **dwis* 'twice', (combining form **dwi-*) > OL *duis* (Paul. Fest.) > L *bis*, *bi-* : G δίς, δι-, Ved. *dvís*, *dvi-*, OE *twi-* as in *twi-wyrdig* 'contradictory'.
OL DVENOS (6th/7th century BC); DVONORO gen.pl. (3rd century BC, showing the change of **we* to *wo*; and see **237.1**) whence L *bonus* 'good'. (Prior history unknown.)
L *bellum* 'war', OL DVELLOM; SC de Bacch. DVELONAI 'Bellonae' (a goddess). None of the etymologies proposed are satisfactory, but the OL forms make the development clear even so. The doublet *duellum* is disyllabic in Plaut; but as an archaistic form employed by later poets it is trisyllabic. This might be either the result of folk etym. from *duo* or a regular development.

2. Medial **dw* > *w*:
PIE **sweH₂du-* 'sweet' > Ital. **swādwi-* > L *suāvis* : G ἡδύς, Ved. *svādú-*, NE *sweet*.
PIE **mḷdu-* 'soft' > Ital. **moldwi-* > **molwi-* > L *mollis* (see 3, next) : G βλαδύς, Ved. *mṛdú-*.

a. The development of PItal **gw* everywhere agrees with **gʷ*; **χw* likewise agrees with **χʷ* (**154.2**): **mag-welō* 'prefer' > *māwolō* > **māolō* (**183**) > *mālō* (**88.3**).
PIE **mreǵhu-i-* 'brief' (much remodeled, **350**) > **breχwi-* > *brevis*.

3. Intervocalic **lw* > *ll*, as in *mollis* above and PIE **solwo-* 'all, whole' > OL *sollum* 'osce "totum"' (Fest.), L *sollers* (stem *soll-ert-*) 'skillful' ("'possessing the whole of an art') : O **sullus** n.pl.masc. 'omnes', G ὅλος (Hom. οὖλος, **190.1**), Ved. *sárva-*.

a. L *mollis* might show *-ll-* < **-ld-*, as in *sallō* 'salt' (**223.1**); but that would mean the loss of **-w-* from the resulting **mollwis*, which would be unexampled.

b. L *lv* comes from a variety of sources, chiefly the syncope of an intervening vowel: *salvus* 'healthy' < **salowos*, and (perh.) *solvō* 'loosen' (**se-luō* < **se-lewō*). Others result from formerly more complex clusters: *helvus* 'tawny' < **hellwos* < **ghelswos* = Lith. *gel̃svas* a horse-color term ('palomino'? 'Isabella'?).

In imperial times the cluster often appears as *lb* in inscriptions, as for example SALBVS 'healthy'.

4. Following a stressed vowel **tw* > L *ttu*, PRom. **tt*. (Examples below.) The lengthening of a consonant before a glide or resonant is widely encountered in phonology, and is found in a number of IE languages. In West Gmc., all consonants except **r* preceded by a stressed short vowel and followed by **y* lengthened. Thus PGmc. **satyanaⁿ* caus. of 'sit' > PWGmc. **sattyan* > OE *settan*, OHG *sezzen*, OS *settian*. Somewhat differently, in Skt. there was evidently no difference in pronunciation between the medial clusters of Ved. *cit-rá-* 'shining' (root *cit-* plus suff. *-ra-*) and *pat-tra-* 'wing' (lit. 'flying implement', root *pat-* plus suffix *-tra-*). Some Skt. mss distinguish between morphological *-tr-* and *-ttr-*, but not a few write all with one *t*, or all with two, or write both indifferently.

Such lengthening of consonants is far from rare in epigraphic L. It occurs before various consonants (so DEFVNCCTO, AVGVSSTI) but is mostly found before a resonant, as PVBBLICO, IANNVARIO, ACQVA, FILLIVS, LICINNIANVS. That these spellings genuinely represent pronunciation is supported by Romance forms, particularly Italian: *acqua* 'water' as above, *pozzo* 'well' < PRom. **puttˢyu-* < L *puteus*; *sappia* 'he might know' < L *sapiat* (subj. of *sapiō*); *rabbia* 'rage' < **rabia*.

In literary L, on the evidence of early poetry, in such clusters the syllable boundary retracted, so that in *patris* the first syllable was *pa-* and the second was *-tris* (see **247d**, **81.6a**). However, there is evidence that prior to this development, **t* lengthened before a following **w*.

PIE **kʷetwor-* 'four' has complicated and puzzling ablaut, but the old neut. pl. **kʷetwōr* > Ital. **kʷattwōr* > L *quattuor* (trisyllabic; *-a-* in L is unexplained). PRom. attests only **quattor*.

Similarly, all Romance reflexes of L *futuere* 'fuck' point to PRom. **futtere*, those of L *batuere* 'beat' to **battere*. This relates to the development of **tw* as follows. A few forms would have been accented on the second syllable: *futúere*, *futúimus*. But very frequently occurring were those accented on other syllables, such that **tu* > **tw* > *ttw*: **fúttwō*, **fúttwit*, **fúttwont*, **fúttwī*. In the kind of L underlying the written language, the stems *futu-*, *batu-* and the like were generalized, and the stems **futtw-* and **battw-* disappeared; since *quattuor* < **quáttwōr* had only one form, there was no opportunity for leveling along the lines of *futuō* and *batuō*. However, in the kind of L underlying PRom., the stems **futtw-*, **battw-* were generalized, becoming PRom. **futt-*, **batt-*, just like PRom. **quatt-*, above.

a. L *mortuus* 'dead', OCS *mrĭtvŭ* point to **mr̥two-*, and shows that **t* following a consonant does not lengthen before **w*; in Romance (for example It. *morto*) the -*w*- is lost, as it is after -*tt*-.

b. Since initial **dw*- > L *b*- (1, above), we would expect L *p*- from **tw*-. However, etymologies supporting such a development are few and doubtful. The best is L *paries* 'wall' (of a house): Lith. *tveriù* 'fence in', *tvorà* 'palisade', in which the semantics are no better than suggestive.

186. THE PRONUNCIATION OF LATIN *v*. A variety of consistent evidence points to [w] as the pronunciation of L *v*. This phonetic value obtained into the early imperial period, on the evidence of borrowings into Germanic languages (in initial position, PGmc. **wīna*ⁿ, whence OE *wín*, NE *wine*, from L *vīnum*; in medial position, PGmc. **pawaz* from L *pavō*, whence OE *péa*, NE *peacock*, NHG *Pfau*). In the early centuries AD the pronunciation changed to one with more friction. But as late as the 5th century AD the grammarian Consentius attests to the persistence of the value [w], or at any rate that is assumed to be the pronunciation which he disparages as *exilius* ('too thin'). Meantime, intervocalic -*b*- also became a fricative, hence the frequent confusion in spelling between *v* and *b* in late inscriptions and in mss.

In some languages, such as High German, [w] underwent an unconditioned change to some kind of fricative. In Romance, however, [w] remained a glide after *k* and *s*, hence It. *quando* 'when', *soave* 'sweet, gentle' (L *quandō*, *suāvis*). In some IE languages, similarly, the development of [w] to [v] was general but not universal; among present-day IE languages this is true of Latvian and many of the Indic vernaculars.

GREEK ϝ

187. The letter F (ϝαυ)[1] is of frequent occurrence in inscriptions of most G dialects except for Attic-Ionic and Lesbian. It disappeared first in consonant clusters, where it is preserved only in the earliest inscriptions of a few dialects; next between vowels; and lastly in initial position before a vowel, where it survived in some dialects as late as the 2nd century BC, and even to the present day in the isolated relic of Laconian (Lacedaemonian) known as Tsakonian.

The chronology just recited is based on epigraphic evidence. In Attic, where the letter was lost much earlier, relative chronology deduced from

---

[1] The name by which this letter is usually known, δίγαμμα, is a result of the disappearance of both [w] and the letter for writing it (even as the symbol for 'six' in the G system of numerals) from the dialects in which are transmitted the bulk of our G texts. Names of G letters that are descriptive, like 'simple *e*' and 'big *o*', are all late. In the case of 'double γάμμα', the name reflects ignorance as well as lateness—if our sources had known its real name, they presumably would have used it rather than the makeshift δίγαμμα. The Roman grammarian Cassiodorus, quoting (a little obtusely, on the face of it) a lost passage in Varro, gives the name of the letter as *va*, which is manifestly a garble for *vau*, that is to say G *ϝαῦ. (Cassiodorus 7.148.)

the ordering of sound laws necessary to account for the attested forms (particularly Attic Reversion, 55) seems to require a different sequence for the loss of ϝ in different positions. Att. κόρη 'girl' from κόρϝᾱ next to νέᾱ 'new' f. < νεϝᾱ, requires that in the history of Attic, at least, ϝ had dropped intervocalically BEFORE PG *ā > η, whereas ρϝ > ρ(ρ) only AFTER that change. However, as remarked in 55, a different interpretation of the same facts is consistent with the possibility that the loss of ϝ in consonant clusters in Att. was in fact earlier than its loss intervocalically.

a. G ϝ stood for [w], similar to NE *w* and L *v*. In later inscriptions it is often represented as β, for example Elean βοικιαρ (< **woykiās*) = Att. οἰκίᾱς gen.sg. 'dwelling', βεκατεροι = ϝεκατεροι, Att. ἑκάτερος (**swe*-) 'each of two'. This spelling points to a fricative pronunciation, [v] or [β]. But, contrary to the usual observations on this point, such a change of original [w] would not, all by itself, have affected the spelling. Indeed, it could not have. The confusion of ϝ- and β- in inscriptions requires that original ϝ- and β- FELL TOGETHER; the actual change might be in either sound, or in both. (The coalescence of [b] and [w] is commonplace; it is observed also in the histories of some Romance languages, and in Indic.) Had nothing but the pronunciation of ϝ- changed, speakers of such dialects would necessarily have gone right on using the letter ϝ- exactly as they had always used it. As a parallel, the change of L [w] to Romance [v], and a like change in the history of High German, had no effect on orthography—nor would we expect it to.

The case is different with manuscript sources such as Hesychius, where ϝ is replaced by ρ and γ as well as β: ρ and γ are nothing but scribal blunders resulting from unfamiliarity with the letter ϝ in the source documents, and some cases of Hesychian β doubtless are too.

The ultimate extinction of most dialects retaining ϝ makes the matter of its later pronunciation hypothetical, but in Tsakonian [v] is the current pronunciation: Tsak. [vanne] 'lamb' (formally akin to Att. ἀρνίον 'sheepskin' < ϝαρν- < **wr̥n*-).

188. In a number of forms, PIE **w* in initial position is reflected as G spiritus asper.

PIE **wid-tor*- 'knower' (the zero grade of the root is unexpected) > G ἵστωρ 'wise man'; but **w*- does not become spiritus asper in the numerous other forms traceable to ϝ(ο)ιδ-.[1]

PIE **wespero*- 'evening' > G ἕσπερος, ἑσπέρᾱ and derivatives : L *vesper*.

PIE **wes*- 'clothe' > G ἕννῡμι (**wes-new*-), fut. ἕσ(σ)ω; Att. εἷμα 'garb' = Dor. ϝῆμα = Lesb. ϝέμμα (= Ved. *vás-man*- 'a cloth') and other derivatives : L *vestis* 'garb', Go. *wasti*, Hitt. *wa-aš-še-iz-zi* 'clothes', Ved. *vas*-.

PIE **wes-ti*- 'abode' (from **wes*- 'spend the night, abide'—perhaps; determining the makeup of **westi*- is complicated by the sheer number of PIE roots **wes*- of very diverse meaning) > G ἑστίᾱ 'hearth' (and derivatives) : L *Vesta* 'goddess of hearths' (cf. Ἑστίᾱ, Ion. Ἱστίη).

---

[1] Owing to its unsuitable meaning—its early attestations mean 'inquire, seek', and only much later 'recount, explain'—the family of ἱστορέω has been ably argued to continue a different root, **H₂eys*- 'seek', with spiritus asper imported from ἵστωρ by folk etymology.

PIE **weḱ-* 'desire' > G ἑκών (old participle) 'willing' : Ved *vaś-* 'be willing, be obedient' (Ved. *vāvaśānā-* perf.midd.pple. 'willing'), Hitt. *ú-e-ik-zi* 'asks'. PIE **wedh-* (**wed-* before nasals) 'take home; marry (a woman)' > G ἕδνα pl. 'wedding gifts' (to the bride) : Ved. *vadhū́-* 'bride'.

There is general agreement that this phenomenon is not comparable to the twofold G word-initial reflexes of PIE **y* (191).[1] A few scholars have entertained the idea that laryngeals might account for the developments of PIE **w* in G, but the problems with such an approach are obvious. For one thing, it could not account for both ἰ- and (ϝ)ι- from the same PIE root **wid-*; for another, more is to be gained by tracing certain prothetic vowels (90) to PIE **Hw-* clusters.

Nearly all cases of PIE **w-* appearing as spiritus asper in G are followed by -σ- (as can be verified by the above citations). It is unlikely to be nothing but a coincidence, but hitherto no phonetic mechanism has been advanced which plausibly explains how *h-* might develop from *w-* in such a position. As for the few exceptions, they have more or less plausible ad hoc explanations. The suggestion that the isolated ἑκών 'willing' was influenced by folk-etymology involving the reflexive prn. ἕ < **swe* is a reasonable guess. Less plausible, in fact verging on the far-fetched, is the idea that the development of ἕδνα was similarly influenced by ἡδύς 'sweet, pleasant'. (However, the Greeks themselves seem to have thought that there was an etymological connection between these two words, so the idea cannot be dismissed outright.) —A contrary case is the smooth breathing of ἄστυ 'town' < ϝαστυ, a word of vexed etymology but whose ϝ- is attested. Among the suggestions made as to details of its form are contamination by its antonym ἀγρός 'country(side)', and loss by dissimilation of the ϝ- in ϝαστϝος (ἀστός) 'townsman', whence ἄστυ by back formation.

189. Whatever the exact details of relative chronology, ϝ was lost in Attic-Ionic at such an early date that there are scant traces of it even in the earliest inscriptions. But Homeric prosody furnishes ample evidence of its former existence. Words which originally began with ϝ- frequently (1) make position, (2) prevent elision, (3) prevent shortening of a preceding diphthong or long vowel. To be sure, such words often fail to show these traits, and, conversely, the absence of elision or of vowel shortening is not confined to cases where a ϝ- once was pronounced. But it is especially in the prevention of elision where this is otherwise to be expected, as in Ἀτρεΐδης τε ἄναξ—though the word is without etymology, FANAΞ 'prince' is widely attested in dialect inscriptions, and now of course in Myc.—that the proportion of effectiveness is overwhelming. The correlations of historical ϝ- with the other two effects, if not so striking, are statistically significant.

The ϝ had no doubt disappeared from the spoken Ionic before the time of the final constitution of our Homeric text, hence the discrepancies.

---

[1] For example, the development of **wid-* 'know' to ἰσ- in one form (and its derivatives) but not in other reflexes of the root is quite unlike the behavior of **y-*. There are no instances of a root in **y-* sometimes giving ζ- and sometimes giving *h-*.

But the text still reflects in very large measure the habits of prosody of a period when the ϝ was still pronounced.

190. Examples of initial and intervocalic ϝ have been given above (182). The treatment of ϝ in consonant groups is as follows:

1. Intervocalic νϝ, ρϝ, λϝ (there are no examples of μϝ) are preserved in the earliest inscriptions of some dialects. Otherwise the ϝ is lost, with lengthening of the preceding vowel in one group of dialects including Ionic, and without such lengthening in another group which includes Attic:

Doric	Ionic (Homer)	Attic	Early Dialect Forms	
ξηνος	ξεῖνος	ξένος	ξενϝος	'stranger'
κωρα	κούρη	κόρη	κορϝα	'girl'
ωρος	οὖρος	ὅρος	(ϝ)ορϝος	'boundary'
	κᾱλός	καλός	καλϝος	'beautiful'

There are other cases in which the forms with -νϝ- and the like are not quotable but are confidently inferred from the relations between the Ionic and Attic forms (in some cases additional confirmation comes from comparative evidence):

Ionic (Homer)	Attic	Proto-Forms	
μοῦνος	μόνος	**monwos*	'alone'
(cf. μᾱνός	μανός	**mn̥wo-*	'sparse')
οὖλος	ὅλος	**solwos*	'all' (cf. Ved. *sárva-*)

a. In view of these facts, forms in -λλ- in the paradigm of πολύς 'many'—fem. πολλή, nom./acc.n. πολλά—cannot represent *πολϝ-ᾱ. See further 341.

b. Doric indisputably shows long vowels before a cons. + lost ϝ, but it is by no means indisputable that Hom. μοῦνος, ξεῖνος, and so on, were really pronounced as spelled. Possibly they are a purely editorial device for the scansion required by original μονϝος, ξενϝος, and so on.

c. In Myc. texts, G -ρϝ- is represented differently from -νϝ-. Thus Myc. *ko-wa* 'girl' (κορϝᾱ) and *wo-wo* 'boundaries' (ϝορϝοι) show the omission of *r* before *w*; by contrast, ξενϝος 'stranger' is written *ke-se-nu-wo*. This difference is thought to be one of written representation only.

2. A similar relation is seen in Ion. ἶσος, Att. ἴσος, dial. ϝισϝος 'same'; and Ion. νοῦσος, Att. νόσος *νοσϝος 'disease'. Though the etymologies of these forms are uncertain, all that have been proposed take σϝ to be secondary, that is, from earlier clusters like **tsw* or **t^{h}sw*. Significantly, ORIGINAL intervocalic σϝ behaves differently, and goes parallel to original intervocalic σμ (227.2). Thus **naswos* 'cella' became first **nawwos* (probably via **nahwo-*), whence Lesb. ναῦος (cf. Lesb. ἄμμε 'us' acc.pl. < PG **asme* < PIE **n̥s-me*, 172); but elsewhere νᾱϝός, hence Dor. νᾱ(ϝ)ός (cf. Dor. ʽᾱμε < **n̥sme*), Hom. νηός, Att. νεώς (79.3). For initial σϝ, see 171.

3. δϝ is preserved in a proper noun in Corinth. Δϝενιας (ε̄, ᾱ) = Δεινίου, and is indirectly attested in Hom. δείδια perf. 'I fear', as if from

dedwia* (actually δείδω < **dedwoya* is the real 1sg.perf., **516), δείδιμεν 1pl.; and ἔδεισε aor. with first syllable long (so written ἔδδεισε in some mss), that is, *ἔδϝεισε; the root is **dwey-*, cf. Av. *dvaēθā* 'menace'.

PIE **dwis* 'twice', combining form **dwi-* (Ved. *dvís*, *dvi-*, L *bis*, *bi-*) > G δίς, δι- as in δίπους 'two-footed'.

This development is strangely unlike that of *τϝ-, next.

4. Apart from Doric, τϝ appears initially as σ-, medially as -σσ- or -ττ- depending on dialect.

Initially:

σέ 'you' acc.sg., Dor. τέ, τϝέ (not directly attested but unmistakable in the entry τρέ in Hesych.).

σείω 'brandish' < **tweysō* : Ved. root *tviṣ-* 'be stirred up', in *tveṣás-* 'energy, impulse' for example.

σάκος '[oxhide] shield' : Ved. *tvak-* '(cow)hide'.

Medially, the picture is confused. It is commonly stated that the outcomes of medial **tw* coincide with those of **k*$^{(w)}$*y* (**199**), namely: -ττ- in Att. and Boeot., -σσ- in most other dial. The evidence does not fully cooperate with this opinion. In accord with the usual formulation are Hom. ἐπισσείω 'shake at', Hes. φερεσσακής 'shield-bearing', Dor. ημισσον n. 'half' (< **sēmi-two-*, thematization of the *tu*-stem **sēmi-tu-*), and some of the dialect forms for 'four' (PIE **k*^{w}*etwores*, with ablaut): Ion. τέσσερες, next to Att. τέτταρες, Boeot. πετταρες. However, Att. ἐπισείω (not ˣἐπιττείω) 'shake at', and Hom. πίσυρες, Lesb. πέσυρες, Dor. τέτορες 'four' are NOT in accord. Furthermore, although Dor. τέτορες accords well with Dor. τέ < τϝέ (emended from τρε, **187a**), Dor. ημισσον exhibits a contradictory development.

5. θϝ appears to lose the ϝ; the only tolerably clear example is PIE **dhwr̥-yo-*, orig. an adj. derived from **dhwer-* 'door' > G θαιρός 'vestibule' (**96**, **203.2**). In accord with this, but obscurer as to detail, is G ὀρθός 'straight, plumb' < **wort*^{h}*wos* (cf. Dor. βορθο-, Ved. *ūrdhvá-*).

6. ϝρ is preserved in some dialect forms, as Elean ϝρᾱτρᾱ 'covenant' = ῥήτρᾱ, Arg. ϝε-ϝρē-μενα perf. pple. = εἰρημένα 'saying' (cf. also βρήτωρ 'speaker' in texts of the Lesb. poets), from ϝρη- beside ϝερ- in ἐρέω 'say', PIE **werH*$_{1}$*-*, **wreH*$_{1}$*-*. (Elean ᾱ < η is regular.)

7. In compounds, augmented, or reduplicated forms, whose simplexes have initial ϝρ, the ϝ occasionally unites with the preceding vowel to form a diphthong: Hom. ταλαύρῑνος 'having a shield of bull's hide' < *ταλα-ϝρῑνος; Lesb. εὐράγη aor. pass. 'broke' < *ἐ-ϝραγη(ν) (Att. ἐρράγην); and some others. But generally the result is -ρρ-, as in Att. ἐρρήθη aor. pass. 'was said' and ἐρράγην, ἀναρρήγνῡμι 'break up'.

a. The ει- of εἴρηκα perf. 'I said' is often explained as analogical to forms where ει- is regular, like εἴληφα < **he-hlap*^{h}*-*, perf. of λαμβάνω (**227.2**; **517.2**). Patterns do contaminate one another that way—the -η- of this self-same εἴληφα, for example, is imported from such forms as εἴρηκα, where it is etymological. But the first syllable of εἴρηκα needs no special explanation: *ϝειρη- is the regular outcome of the reduplicated stem *we-wrē- (*we-wr̥H₁-), per 61.1a.

PIE *y

191. In initial position, PIE *y remains in L as consonantal *i.* In G there are two outcomes: spiritus asper (which is sometimes then lost, **170b**) and ζ- (**201**).

1. PIE **yĕkʷr̥(t)* 'liver' > G ἧπαρ, L *iecur* : Ved. *yakŕ̥t*, Av. *yākarə* (with *ā* < **ē* as in G?).
PIE **yos* nom.sg.m., demonstrative prn. (the etymon of the rel. prn. in G and InIr.) > G ὅς : Ved. *yás.*
PIE **yoH₁-ro-* 'year, summer' > G ὥρᾱ 'time, period' (L *hōra* is a G lw.), ὧρος 'year' : Av. *yārə* n. 'year', Go. *jer*, OE *géar*, OHG *jār*, NE *year* (Gmc. forms from *e*-grade **yeH₁-ro-*).

2. PIE **yugom* 'yoke' > G ζυγόν, L *iugum* : Ved. *yugá-*, OE *geoc*, NE *yoke.*
PIE **yeH₃s-* (or **yōs-*?; the root shows no ablaut) 'gird, belt' > G ζώννῡμι; ζώνη 'belt' (< *ζωσνᾱ); ζωστός pple. 'belted' : Av. *yāsta-*.
PIE **yes-* 'bubble up' > G ζέω, ζεστός pple. : Ved. *yas-* 'boil', OHG *jesan* 'to foam', OE *giest* 'foam, yeast', NE *yeast.*

Showing the L reflex: PIE **yuHn̥-*/**yuHn-* 'young' > L *iuvenis* : Ved. *yúvan-*, *yū́n-*, NE *young.*

The number of good etymologies in ζ- and *h-* is nearly equal, about six items (or roots) apiece. The usual mark of dialect mixture—a variety of outcomes from the same root—is nowhere to be seen. A given root will have only ζ-, or else only *h-*, in all its forms. Brugmann dealt with the problem by positing two different consonants in PIE (in initial position only, or anyhow detectable only there) which fall together in all IE languages except G, where one gives spiritus asper and the other gives ζ-. This proposal, though methodologically correct, has rarely been endorsed. More recently it has been suggested that the two different G outcomes might reflect PIE word-initial **y-* vs. **Hy-*. (Or they might result from clusters of different laryngeals and **y*). The laryngeal suggestion fits with the failure of any prothetic vowels (**90**) to develop in G before **y-*, but beyond that there is little but speculation. The sum of the evidence is as follows:

PIE **(H)yewg-* 'yoke, link, join' (whence G ζυγόν 'yoke', and the rest, above): evidence for an initial laryngeal consists of two occurrences of augmented forms in the Rigveda in *ā-* for expected (and liberally-attested) *ă-*: *āyunak* 3sg.imperf., in a very late hymn, and *ā́yukta* 3sg.aor.midd. in an early one. Otherwise, reduplicated and compound forms show nothing out of the ordinary (so *aśva-yúj-* 'horse-harnessing', *áśva-yoga-* 'with harnessed horses', and so on).

PIE **(H?)yew-iH₂* > Hom. ζειαί pl.tant. 'fodder' : Ved. *yáva-* m. 'barley', Av. *yava-* 'grain', Lith. *jāvas.* Evidence for **H-* is limited to a derivative of *yávasa-* n. 'grass, pasture': RV *sū-yávasa-* 'having grassy pastures'; and variations on the theme (*sūyavasín-* and so on).

Now, the preverb *ā-* is common with the root *yuj-* in Vedic, and that might be the real explanation for the aorists in *āyuj-*. And, while 'metrical lengthening' is a weak explanation, it is at least worth pointing out that forms like **sŭyávasas* nom.sg., **sŭyavasiní* loc.sg., and **sŭyavasat-* ('battening on good pasture') have metrically inconvenient sequences of light syllables.

a. A distinction between the two G reflexes of **y-* is already evident in Mycenaean. One type is seen in Myc. *ze-u-ke-si* (dat.pl. of ζεῦγος). However, corresponding to the familiar G rough breathing reflex we find two representations, typically side by side for the same word: the relative stem, for example, is attested more than a dozen times as *o-*, and about half that often as *jo-*. The clear implication is that whatever underlies G ζ- had become an obstruent by the PG period, whereas the change of *y-* (? **hy-*) to *h-* was still underway at the time of the Myc. texts.

b. Some authorities assume that INTERVOCALIC **y* passed through [h] on its way to being lost in G (192). No such assumption is necessary, and besides it is unlikely on phonetic grounds.

c. It has been observed that **y-* > ζ- before **-ew-/-ŭ-* and before a following **-s-*. As a sound law, this suffers from the demerit of unnaturalness, but it is arguably no worse than the Attic reversion of **-ǣ-* to -ᾱ- following ρ and front vowels (55), where the first condition is phonologically unrelated to the second. Similarly, it has been observed that **y-* > *h-* when a stop immediately follows the vowel. But this too is phonetically implausible, and not just because it necessitates taking *H_1 as in **yeH₁-* 'year' as a stop. In any case there is one major exception in each list (**yewg-* in this scheme should give ×εὐγ-/×ὑγ-, and **yo-* 'who' should give ×ζο-).

192. LOSS OF **y*. Intervocalic **y* was lost in prehistoric L, arguably in PItal. In G the loss of **y* in most positions predates all literary and epigraphic texts, and therefore was long thought to date from Proto-Greek. It is still attested intervocalically in Myc., however, at least after short vowels, though even there it alternates (in the script at any rate) with zero.

PIE *treyes* 'three' m. > G τρεῖς (spurious diphthong; dial. τρης, τρεες), L *trēs* : Ved. *tráyas*, OIr. *trí* (< PCelt. **trīs* < **trēs*).

PIE adj. in **-eyo-*, for example *e-re-pa-te-jo* 'of ivory'; but *e-re-pa-te-o* occasionally occurs. (Some 50 such adjectives of substance are attested in Myc.; only five forms are missing the intervocalic glide.)

Causative/frequentatives formed with the suffix **-ey^e/o-* (Ved. *-áya-*): PIE **potH₁-ey^e/o-* 'fly about' > Hom. ποτέομαι (Ved. *patayati*); PIE **mon-ey^e/o-* 'warn' (orig. 'make think') > L *moneō*.

a. Some instances of Myc. *-j-* appear to be parasitic glides after a front vowel, as *i-je-re-u* 'priest' (ἱερεύς) < **ierēws* or **iherēws* < **isH̥₁re-*.

b. Apparent exceptions to the G development are not from intervocalic **-y-* but from the clusters **-wy-*, **-yy-*, and **-sy-* (205–7).

POSTCONSONANTAL *y IN LATIN

193. Postconsonantal **y* becomes vowel *i*.

PIE **medhyos* 'middle' > L *medius* : Ved. *mádhya-*, Go. *midjis*.

PIE *H_2*elyo-* '(an)other' > L *alius* : G ἄλλος, Go. *aljis*, OE *elles* 'otherwise', NE *else.*
**g*^{w}*m̥yoH*$_2$ 'I come' > L *veniō* : G βαίνω.
L *et* + *iam* (two monosyllables) > *etiam* (trisyllabic); ditto **quom* + *iam* > *quoniam.* Cf. the disyllabic phrase *nōn iam* 'no longer'.
Initial **sy* > *si*, as in **H*$_1$*s-yeH*$_1$*-t* opt. of **H*$_1$*es-* 'be' > OL *siet* : Ved. *syā́t.*

a. These forms of the verb 'be' in *siē̆-*, though convincing, exhaust the evidence. The difference in outcome between **syuH-dhleH*$_2$*-* > L *sūbula* 'awl', *sūtus* 'sewn' (root **syuH-* 'sew') and **H*$_1$*syeH*$_1$*t* > *siet* can be variously explained. Some take the former from **sy-*, the latter from **H*$_1$*siy-* via Lindeman's Law (181). More likely is that *siet* shows the regular outcome of **sy-*, whereas *sūbula* reflects ancient **sū-*: hesitation between **syuH-* and **suH-* in this root is attested in other languages, so for example next to Ved. root *syū-* (pple. *syūtá-*) we find *sū́tra-* 'thread' and *sūcī-* 'needle'.

194. Initial and medial **dy*, and medial **gy* and **sy* become consonant *i* (medial *ii*). (There are no certain cases of initial **gy-*.)
PIE **dyew-pH̥*$_2$*ter* 'sky-father' (voc.) > L *Iuppiter* : G Ζεῦ; **dyewos, -es* gen.sg. > OL DIOVOS, L *Iovis* : G Ζεύς, Ved. *dyā́us* nom.sg.
**pedyōs* 'worse' > L *pēior.*[1]
**magyōs* 'bigger' > *māior.* Cf. *magnus*; *magis* 'more', *maximus* < **mag-isṃmos* = O *maimas* gen.sg.f.
**k*^{w}*osyo* 'of whom' > L *cūius* : Ved. *kásya*, G ποῦ < PG **k*^{w}*ohyo.*

a. Many apparent exceptions are explained by Sievers' Law (178), such as L *rēgius* 'royal' reflects **reH*$_1$*ǵ-iyo-* with the expected Sievers alternant **-iyo-*.

b. The *-d-* of L *hodie* 'today' was imported from *diēs*; Falisc. FOIED 'hodie' shows the expected outcome of **dy*, and some Romance forms (It. *oggi* 'today'; cf. It. *maggiore*, and see **c**, below) reflect **(h)oiē*, or more exactly **(h)oiiē*, which is thereby seen to have survived in Roman speech concurrently with the remodeled *hodiē.* —Perhaps a similar importation of *d-* from *diēs* 'day' explains *diū* 'by day; for a long time', *sub diū* 'outdoors', which continue the PIE locative **dyewi*, Ved. *dyávi*; and similarly *nudiustertius* 'day before yesterday'. But the survival of the *d-* of L *diēs* is itself a puzzle. Some authorities suggest dialect borrowing to explain the survival of *d-* in this word, a plausible idea but a shot in the dark. Others appeal to an etymon **diyew-* via Lindeman's Law (181).

c. In L *eius, cuius, maior, peior* the first syllable of each form is heavy, but 'long by position' rather than 'long by nature'. That is, the forms are really *eiius* and the like, not *ēius*, and are in fact frequently so written in mss and inscriptions. Furthermore, It. *maggiore* 'bigger' points directly to a PRom. **mayyōrem.*

POSTCONSONANTAL **y* IN GREEK

195. THE GREEK PALATALIZATIONS. Postconsonantal **y* in G combines with all preceding consonants to form a complete series of PG palatalized

---

[1] An alternative reconstruction **pesyōs* is sometimes suggested. But the superlative *pessimus* is the key here: its structure must be parallel to that of its antonym *optimus*, namely **ped-tṃmo-* via 212, since all other instances of the suffix **-tṃmo-* in Ital. involve pairs of words of opposite meaning (356, 358). And it reasonable to assume that *peiior* is built to the same root as *pessimus.*

consonants (see 152 fn.), whose ultimate reflexes vary according to the class of the consonant. As **y* was very common in PIE, and prominent in the makeup of suffixes, these developments notably reshaped G morphology. In particular there are three large morphological classes in which these palatalizations are observed:

1. Presents of the iota (*-*y*^{e}/*o*-) classes (456.1, 460-2, 464-5).
2. Nouns of the first declension with nom.sg. in -ᾰ < *-*ya* (PIE *-*iH*$_2$, 268-9).
3. Comparatives in -ων, orig. *-*yōn* (PIE *-*yōs*, 348-51, 354).

None of these categories show the effects of Sievers' Law (178).

a. The two rounds of palatalization detailed below had the effect of eliminating all postconsonantal *-*y*- from G. However, there is clear albeit inconsistent evidence for the recreation of -*Cy*- sequences (where *C* = any consonant) via the synizesis of a front vowel before a back vowel, as -εα > -*y*α; -ῐα > -*y*α. When the accent lay on the lost vowel it shifted to the next mora to the right, thus Att. Βορρᾶς 'north wind' < *Βορ*y*ᾶς < Βορέᾱς. As this example also shows, such sequences in turn underwent futher development, for which see 233.

196. The development of postconsonantal **y* clusters in G took place in two distinct stages, both fully complete prehistorically.

THE FIRST GREEK PALATALIZATION. The first stage was the evolution of a category of assibilated APICAL STOPS only.[1] This is reflected in the special behavior of **ty* and **t*^{h}*y* (< **dhy*) in ISOLATED or otherwise MORPHOLOGICALLY OPAQUE formations, and in initial position (a special case of opaque formation, in effect):

1. From PIE **yo*- (prn. stem) the adv. **yoti*, from which PreG **yotyos* 'that much' > **hotsos* > Att. ὅσος, Hom. ὅσος and ὅσσος (similarly τόσος 'as much', πόσος 'how much?', and so on): Ved. *táti* 'so many', L *tot* < **tote* < PIE **toti*.

PIE **medhyos* 'middle' > Early Pre-Greek **met*^{h}*yos* > Late Pre-Greek **metsos* > Att. μέσος, Hom. μέσος and μέσσος, dial. μεσος, Boeot. μεττος : Ved. *mádhya*-, L *medius*.

a. Note that these reflexes and their distribution among dialects are the same as for *-*ts*- (the common result of *-*t*-, *-*d*-, and *-*t*^{h}- plus *-*s*-):

Hom. -σ- after long vowel, vacillation between -σ- and -σσ- after short: τάπησι dat.pl. (stem τάπητ- 'rug'), ποσσί(ν)/ποσί(ν) dat.pl. (ποδ- 'foot');
in Att.-Ion. generally, -σ-;
in Lesb., Thess., and WG, -σσ-;
in Boeot., -ττ-: εψαφιτταто (presumably εψᾱ-; cf. Att. ἐψηφισάμην 'vote (with a pebble)').

2. Initial **ty*-, **t*^{h}*y*- (from PIE **dhy*-) > σ- in all dialects. This is in

[1] The resulting affricates apparently showed no contrast of plain vs. aspirated articulation, which is surprising; many languages have the plain/aspirated contrast in affricate as well as stop consonants.

effect the development for unrestored clusters (196-7)—there being no basis for restorative leveling in the case of word-initial sequences:
PIE *$tyeg^w$- 'avoid' > G σέβομαι 'worship, be respectful', σεμνός (219) 'awesome' : Ved. *tyaj-* 'flee'.
PIE *$dhyeH_2$- 'notice' > Dor. σᾶμα, Att. σῆμα 'sign, token' : Ved. *dhyā́-* 'thought, contemplation'. —NB the different development of initial *$k^{(h)}y$- in the second round of palatalization, below.

3. In the cluster **nty*, the **ty* gives *s* in all dialects:
PIE *$bheront$-iH_2 f. 'carrying' > PreG *$p^herontya$ > PG *$p^herontsa$, *$p^heronsa$ > Att. φέρουσα.
PreG **pantya* f. 'all' (?*$pant$-iH_2, but the etymology is uncertain) > PG **pantsa*, **pansa* > Att. πᾶσα, Thess. πανσα, Lesb. παῖσα.

Note that the treatment of **ns* < **nty* and **nti* (148) is unlike that of original (PIE) **ns*, in which the **s* appears to have assimilated to the nasal (228.1).

197. IN PRODUCTIVE OR OTHERWISE MORPHOLOGICALLY TRANSPARENT formations, except for a few very common forms like **pantsa* fem. < **pantyă*, the **y* which had been lost in this first round of palatalization was reintroduced and, during the subsequent round, the resulting cluster[1] developed differently from original *$t^{(h)}y$, that is, it coalesced with the phonetics of **ky* and *k^hy, as shown in the following paragraphs. Thus, presumably, for **kretyōs* 'stronger; better' (vid.inf.) the development was as follows: **kretyōs* > *$kret^s ōs$ → *$kret^{(s)}yōn$ > **kreččōn* > κρέσσων, Att. κρείττων. (The replacement of inherited *-*s* by -*n* (354) is immaterial to the point.)

a. The scenario of an early palatalization affecting only apical stops, followed by a later and more general palatalization, is reminiscent of the history of palatalization in Romance. There, a late L development (3rd century AD, 150) affected only *ti* and *di* before a vowel; this change is reflected in all varieties of Romance. Then, in a later PRom. development, which is reflected in most Romance branches but not in Sardo, dorsals (and only dorsals) palatalized before any front vowel: **kentu* '100' > It. *cento* /čento/, Fr. *cent* /sã/, Sp. *ciento* /θiento/, /siento/, but Sardo *kent.*

b. Myc. *pa-sa* f. (= πᾶσα) and similar forms confirm that the assibilation of *$t^{(h)}$ predates 1200 BC, but thanks to the writing system (26) it remains unknowable whether *n* was still pronounced in such forms. Myc. writes the outcomes of PreG *$k^{(h)}y$ differently, as in *ka-zo-e* n.pl. 'worse' < **kakyoses*; but, curiously, there is no difference between the representations of 'original' *$t^{(h)}y$ and 'restored' *$t^s y$. There are a number of plausible interpretations of these facts. The simplest is that 'restoration' did not take place in the branch of G underlying Myc., though Myc. evidence is otherwise in accord with the notion that there were two separate rounds of palatalization, both pan-Greek.

c. It is unknown whether **dy* followed a course similar to *$t^{(h)}y$, as there is no difference in the outcomes of original **dy* and restored *$d^z y$. It is reasonable to suppose that the voiced and voiceless apicals developed in a parallel fashion at first. The history

[1] Whether the result of the restoration was **ty*/*t^hy or something more like a uniform *$t^s y$ cannot be determined.

of Indic (153d) includes a suggestively similar instance of a development in which voiced and voiceless stops run parallel at first and then diverge.

198. THE SECOND GREEK PALATALIZATION. Some time after the restoration of *y as sketched above, there arose an entire complement of palatalized consonants (152 fn.) in place of consonants followed by *y. These palatalized consonants were all phonetically long, and included all consonant types—nasals, glides, and liquids, as well as stops. The resonants appear to have been simply long and palatalized; but all the stops thus affected acquired some degree of assibilation as well.

PIE	Early Pre-Greek	Late Pre-Greek	Proto-Greek
ḱy, $k^{(w)}y$	$k^{(w)}y$	ky	čč
ǵhy, $g^{(w)}hy$	$k^{h(w)}y$	$k^{h}y$	čč
py	py	py	pč
bhy	$p^{h}y$	$p^{h}y$	pč
ty	t^{s} (196)	$t^{s}y$ (restored)	čč
dhy	t^{s} (196)	$t^{s}y$ (restored)	čč
dy	(d^{z}? 196)	$d^{z}y$ (?restored)	ǰǰ
ǵy, $g^{(w)}y$	$g^{(w)}y$	gy	ǰǰ
my		ny	ññ
ny		ny	ññ
ly		ly	l̃l̃
ry		ry	r̃r̃
wy		wy	ẅẅ[1]
sy		hy	yy

Prior to the historical period, there was a general and therefore presumably very early depalatalization. Another indication of its early date is the high degree of uniformity of the reflexes in the various dialects, which would be implausible if they had been developing independently along such lines for any period of time.[2] The only dialectal division to speak of is seen in the treatment of PG *$\check{c}\check{c}$ (of whatever source): the result is -ττ- in Attic and Boeotian, as well as the West Ionic of Eretria and Oropos, but -σσ- in all other dialects. In some early Ionic inscriptions a special sign is used instead of -σσ-; this suggests some distinctive sound, but some authorities hold that it was merely an attempt to find a use for the superfluous sibilant symbols of the early G signary. A few scholars have argued that the

[1] The symbol [ẅ] (IPA [ɥ]) stands for a high front rounded glide, that is [y] with lip rounding, as in Fr. *puis* [pẅi] 'then'.

[2] Where such matters can be directly observed, the evolution of palatalized affricates is a highly individual matter; for instance, PWRom. *$\check{c}$ yields [s] in French, Portuguese, and some dialects of Spanish; [θ] in other dialects of Spanish; [č] in Italian, [š] in Engadine, [t^{s}] in Friulan, and so on.

familiar spellings -σσ- and -ττ- were themselves attempts to render [č(č)], but that is unlikely.

a. In an interesting parallel, in the development of Spanish there once was a large inventory of palatalized and assibilated sounds; of these in modern Spanish only /č/, /ñ/, and /l̃/ are still palatal consonants (and in the New World the last has fallen together with /y/). Likewise for G it appears that /čč/ remained as the last of the distinctively palatalized consonants, as it manifestly survived into the dialectal period. Even so its reflexes are only triflingly divergent.

199. Voiceless dorsal and restored voiceless apical stops.

G φυλάσσω, -ττω 'I guard' < *p^hulak-yō* : G φύλαξ 'guard'.

G πέσσω, -ττω 'cook, ripen' < *pek^w-yō* : fut. πέψω, Ved. *pácyate.* (G πέπτω is a back-formation from fut. πέψω, aor. ἔπεψα, by analogy to inherited patterns like σκέπτομαι 'inspect' < *skep-y^e/o- **202**, fut. σκέψομαι < *skep-s^e/o-, **500.1**.)

G γλῶσσα, -ττα f. 'tongue' < *glōk^h-yă* (a word of disputed etymology, but the point is the same whether the word is connected with G γλωχῖς 'arrowhead' or δολιχός 'long').

G θᾱ́σσων, -ττων 'quicker' < *t^{h}ak^h-yōn* : G ταχύς < PIE *dhn̥gh-*. (For ᾱ see **354.4c**.)

G μέλισσα, -ττα f. 'bee' < *meli-lik^h-yă* 'honey-licker'.[1]

G ἐλάσσων, Att. ἐλᾱ́ττων 'smaller' < *elak^{wh}yōn* < PIE *l̥ng^{w}h-* : G ἐλαχύς 'small', ἐλαφρός 'nimble', Ved. *raghú-* 'quick'.

G ἐρέσσω, -ττω 'row' < *eret-yō*, cf. G ἐρέτης 'oarsman', ἐρετμόν 'oar', from *erH$_1$-* 'row' (**465.2**).

G κρέσσων, Att. κρείττων (for -ει- see **354.4c**) 'better' < *kret-yōs* : G κρατύς 'strong' < *kr̥tu-*.

G πλάσσω, -ττω 'model' < *plat^h-yō*, as is clear from Att. κοροπλάθος 'maker of figurines'; but outside connections of this *plat^h-* are obscure.

a. Note that θᾱ́σσων, above, and θάπτω (**202**, below) establish that aspirated stops in G became *čč, *pč and the like PRIOR to the dissimilation of aspirates (Grassmann's Law, **138**).

b. As mentioned above, -ττ- is the Attic form, unlike almost all other dialects. The -σσ- of the tragedians and Thucydides must be due to the literary influence of the earlier established Ionic prose, as the primogeniture of -ττ- is shown by Attic inscriptions from the earliest times. Even in literature, from Aristophanes on -ττ- prevails in literary Attic. In the κοινή the non-Attic -σσ- generally prevails (as in NE *thalassemia, glossary*), but there is fluctuation, as is reflected in G borrowings in modern languages (NE *glottis*).

c. Exactly parallel to the development of medial clusters of *k$^{(h)}$y* and restored *t^{s}y*, initial *ky-* > Att. τ- but general G σ-. Note the difference from *ty-*, which gives σ- in all dialects (**196.2**):

---

[1] G μέλισσα is usually taken from *melit-yă*, derived directly from μελιτ- seen in G μέλι (**236.1**), μέλιτος 'honey'. Formally there is no difficulty, but there is the semantic problem that a bee is not a female honey. The derivation preferred here traces the G form to a haplology (possibly of PIE date) from a compound *meli-liǵh-iH$_2$-*.

PreG **ki-āmerom* 'today' (exact derivational history obscure, but certainly including the deictic **ḱi-* seen in L *cis*, *citrā* 'on this side of', NE *hither*, Lith. *šìs* 'this') > **kyāmerom* > PG **čāmeron* > Dor. σᾱμερον, Ion. σήμερον, but Att. τήμερον.

Similarly, PreG **kyā-wetes* 'this year' > Att. τῆτες, Ion. σῆτες, Myc. *za-we-te*. (Myc. *za* regularly corresponds to G ζα, 200-1, and here presumably stands for the voiceless counterpart of that sound.)

200. VOICED APICAL AND DORSAL STOPS (including labiovelars) plus **y* give ζ in Att.-Ion., δδ in some dialects, *z* in Myc.

G ἅζομαι 'stand in awe' < **hag-y^e/o-* (ἅγιος 'sacred').

G νίζω 'wash' < PIE **nig^{w}yoH$_2$* : G νίψω fut.; χέρ-νιβον 'basin for washing hands', OIr. *nigid* /niγ'əθ'/ 'washes', Ved. *niktá-* 'washed'.

G πεζός 'afoot' < **pedyos* : G πούς, ποδός 'foot', Myc. *to-pe-za* 'table' (cf. G τράπεζα); Ved. *pádya-* adj. 'pedal'.

G ἐλπίζω 'hope for' < **elpid-yō* : G ἐλπίς, -ίδος 'hope'.

G Ζεύς < PIE **dyēws* (82) : Ved. *dyā̃us* (cf. Διϝός gen. = Ved. *divás*).

a. The development of G ζ- < PIE **y-* (191.2), as in G ζυγόν 'yoke', Myc,. *ze-u-ke-si* dat.pl. < **yug-/*yewg-*, points to an early coalescence of **dy-*, **gy-*, and plain **y-*. The history of Romance languages is similar, as L consonantal *i-* merges with palatalized *g-*: L *Iānus* > It. *Giano* 'Janus', just as L *Genua* > It. *Genova* /ǰénova/ 'Genoa'.

201. REMARKS ON GREEK ZETA. G ζ chiefly represents the combinations **g$^{(w)}$y* and **dy*. A number are from PIE initial **y-*, **191.2**. A few are from PIE **sd*, as in G ὄζος 'branch' < PIE **H$_3$esdos* or **osdos* (= NHG *Ast*), and G ἵζω 'take a seat' < **si-sd-* (= Ved. *sī́dati*, L *sīdō*; root **sed-*); or from a similar combination within the history of G as in Ἀθήναζε 'to Athens' < **-ans-de* (acc.pl.), **228.3**.

G ζ had the value of [zd] in the best period of Att.-Ion., but in late times became simple [z], as it still is in NG. Evidence for [zd] is as follows:

1. Statements of the ancient grammarians that the three 'diphthongs' ξ, ψ, and ζ were composed of κσ, πσ, and σδ, respectively.
2. Inscriptions and glosses that corroborate 1, like Lesb. ΣΔΕΥΣ nom., ΣΔΕΥ voc. = Ζεύς, Ζεῦ < **δy-* (200).
3. Transcriptions like Ὠρομάζης for OPers. *Auramazda*.
4. Loss of a nasal before -ζ- precisely as before -στ-, -σπ-, and -σκ-, as for example συν- 'together' in G σύ-ζυγος 'yoked' just like σύ-στασις 'a putting together' and συ-σπεύδω 'assist zealously'.

This evidence is cogent. From the purely phonetic point of view, however, the most straightforward reflex of [dy] and [gy] would have been something like [dž] or [dz], and such a pronunciation must in fact have been current in some parts; it was with this value that the letter Ι was carried to Italy, where it was used to represent [ts], for example Osc. **húrz** [horts] 'garden' < **χortos*. A development of stop + sibilant to sibilant + stop is not unprecedented: in several Slavic languages for example the presence vs. absence of such a metathesis is a distinguishing trait of dialect groups.

202. PreG **py* and **p^{h}y* become G ττ, presumably by way of **pč*, or (less likely) **pś* or something similar:

PreG **skep-y^e/o-* 'look at' > G σκέπτομαι.

PIE **ḱlep-y*^{e}*/o-* 'steal' > G κλέπτω.
G θάπτω 'honor with funeral rites' < **t*^{h}*ap*^{h}*yō* (**199a**): G τάφος 'funeral'.
(There are no instances of **by*.)

This development might surprise, but it is securely established: closely related forms and cognates make it plain that these roots end in labial stops (σκέψομαι fut.; κλέμμα 'a theft', L *clepō* 'steal'; τάφος), and, while there is no PIE present-stem formant in **t*, there are both primary and secondary formants in **y*. Note that a similar development is seen in some Romance languages, where **py* > *č* and **by* > *ǰ*.

203. **my* and **ny* fall together as PG **ñ̃*; and **ry* becomes PG **r̃r̃*. In Att. these not only depalatalize but shorten to ν and ρ respectively, with lengthening of a preceding short vowel. Additionally, an ο or α lengthened in this process diphthongizes.

1. Simple lengthening:
κρῑ́νω 'pick out' < **krĭnyō* : Lesb. κρῐ́ννω.
τείνω 'stretch' < **tenyō* : L *tendō* (**218**).
οἰκτῑ́ρω 'feel pity' < **oiktiryō* : Lesb. οἰκτίρρω, Att. οἰκτιρμός 'pity'.
εὐθῡ́νω 'steer straight' < **eut*^{h}*unyō*, cf. fut. εὐθῠνῶ.
γέφῡρα 'weir' < **gep*^{h}*uryă* (a word of obscure origin, but obviously a fem. in *-*yă* < *-*iH*$_2$).
φθείρω 'ruin' < **p*^{h}*t*^{h}*eryō* : fut. φθερῶ.

2. Diphthongization:
βαίνω 'go (along)' < **g*^{w}*anyō* < PIE **g*^{w}*m̥yoH*$_2$: L *veniō*.
φαίνω 'appear' < **p*^{h}*anyō* : fut. φανέω, -ῶ.
χαίρω 'take delight in' < **k*^{h}*aryō* : χαρᾱ́ 'delight'.
Hom. ἀγκοίναι pl.tant. 'arms' < **ankonya-* : ἀγκών 'elbow'.
μοῖρα 'portion' < **morya* : μόρος 'fate'.

a. Note that forms like τείνω and φθείρω contain 'spurious diphthongs' (**76**), that is, they are lengthened ε; this is revealed by such spellings as Arc. φθηρω = Att.-Ion. φθείρω.

204. **ly* > PG **l̃l̃*, which depalatalizes to become G λλ. This is the only member of the PG palatalized series to remain a long consonant in Att.-Ion.; but note from the forms quoted above (**203**) that in Lesb. and (apparently) in Thess. the regular outcome of **ny* and **ry*, also, is νν, ρρ.
PIE **H*$_2$*elyos* 'other' > G ἄλλος : L *alius*.
PIE **stelyoH*$_2$ 'place' > G στέλλω : fut. στελῶ.

205. **wy* > PG **ẅẅ* > *-*yy*- > G -*y*-.
G ἡδεῖα (*u*-stem fem.)'sweet' < **hwēdeyya* < **hwādeẅẅa* < **swādewyă* (**sweH*$_2$*dew-iH*$_2$).
Myc. *i-je-re-ja* 'priestess' (Att. ἱερεῖα) from **ihereyya* < **ihereẅẅa* < **iherewya* < **iherēwyă* (**63.2**, Osthoff's Law) < *-*ēw-iH*$_2$ (**319**), indicates that the development of *-*wy*- to -*y(y)*- had taken place already by Myc. times.

a. Some authorities teach that *-*iwy*- > -ῑ-, as in δῖος 'divine' < **diw-yo-*. This phenomenon seems to be limited to this form, and a better explanation is available: Ved. *diviyá-* 'heavenly', the usual Rigvedic scansion of this very common adj., implies that the G etymon was **diwiyo-* (**diwiHo-* ?) in the first place. This is not incompatible with the Myc., which vacillates between *di-u-jo* and *di-wi-jo* 'sanctuary of Zeus', *di-wi-ja* (name of a goddess), and would give G δῖο- < **diio-* via the usual sound laws.

b. On the basis of Myc. *di-u-jo/di-wi-jo*, mentioned in **a**, and the well-attested Myc. form *me-u-jo*, *me-wi-jo* 'less', some scholars doubt the PG development of *y* < **yy* < **wy*, and take Myc. *ke-ra-me-ja* 'female potter' and *i-je-re-ja* 'priestess' (above) next to *di-wi-jo* as evidence that *i-je-re-ja* had no *w* in the first place. But the makeup of fem. derivatives from υ-stem adjectives (340) and nouns of the βασιλεύς type (319-20) is well-understood, whereas there are various questions about the competing evidence. Myc. *di-u-jo* has been dealt with above. Myc. *me-u-jo* is evidently the same as G μείων, -ον, but the labial glide of Myc. is not expected, and awaits satisfactory explanation; it is hardly capable of overturning the clear evidence of ἡδεῖα 'sweet' and ἱερεῖα (= Myc. *i-je-re-ja*).

206. The development of -ι- from original **sy* in G presupposes the loss of sibilant pronunciation, via **hy* or the like, prior to the PG wave of palatalizations. An obstruent cluster like **sy* must have developed very differently from the observed outcome:

G ναίω 'dwell' < **nahyō* < **nasyō* (cf. aor. ἔνασσα).

G κεραίᾱ 'horn-like object' < **kerahyā* < adj. **kerH̥₂s-yo-* (cf. κέρας, Hom. gen. κέραος); Myc. *ke-ra-i-ja-pi* (more commonly written *ke-ra-ja-pi*) 'with κεραίαι'. G εἴην opt. 'may I be' < **ehyēn* < **esyēm* < PIE **H_1s-yeH_1-m* = Ved. *syā́m* and L *siem*).

G ἀλήθεια 'truth' < **alētʰehya* (ἀληθής 'true').

Perf. pple. fem. in -υῖα < **-uhya* < PIE **-us-iH_2* (562).

Hom. τελείω 'accomplish' < **telehyō* (τέλος).

Hom. ἐμεῖο 'of me' < **emehyo* (see **259.8A**, **367.2**).

a. Such Hom. scansions as ἀληθεΐᾱ 'truth' are difficult to explain. A suffix **-iyeH_2* is the wrong Sievers' alternant (178), and a devī-suffix '**-iyă*' (268) merely substitutes a morphological mystery for a phonological one.

207. For many of the forms cited in the preceding two sections there are doublets in which the intervocalic -ι- is seen in earlier attestations but later disappears: Hom. τελέω, Att. τελῶ; Hom. ἐμέο, ἐμεῦ, Att. ἐμοῦ; Hom. gen.sg. -οιο, -ου, Att. -ου. Cf. also Att. Ἀθηναίᾱ 'Athene' next to later Ἀθηνάᾱ, Ἀθηνᾶ; υἱός next to ὑός; ποιέω next to ποιῶ and ποῶ (so inscriptions of many dialects); αἰεί 'always' (from αἰϝεί) next to ᾱ̓εί; καίω 'burn' (**kawyō*, cf. aor. ἔκαυ-σα) next to κᾱ́ω; κλαίω 'lament' (**klawyō*) next to κλᾱ́ω. The conditions that govern the loss of ι in some cases and its persistence in others—if there are conditions—are obscure.

Changes in Groups of Consonants

208. The majority of changes in groups of consonants fall under the head of *assimilation*. The assimilation may be of the first consonant to the second (anticipatory assimilation, also called regressive), as in L *accipiō* 'receive' from **ad-kapiō*; or of the second to the first (lag assimilation, also called progressive), as in L *ferre* 'to carry' from **fer-si*. It may be in the features of voicing and aspiration only, as in L *strictus* 'drawn together' from **strig-to-* (*stringō*) or G ἐπλέχ-θην 'was plaited' (aor.pass. of πλέκω); or it may involve point of articulation, as in L *aggredior* 'approach' from **ad-grad-*; or it may involve both, as in *accipiō*. In G and L, as was also the case in PIE, voicing and aspiration adjustments in clusters are routine, unlike changes in point of articulation. And as in all languages, anticipatory assimilation is far more general than lag assimilation. However, in certain combinations a particular consonant may dominate regardless of relative position. Thus **dl*, **ld* both give L *ll*, as do **nl* and **ln* (223.1).

In groups of consonants which result from composition the developments do not always conform to that which is observed in the same groups in other situations. Often this results from a basic fact of language change: sound laws operating at different times in the history of a language affect the same clusters differently. So L *sessor* 'one who sits' (hence 'inhabitant') < PIE **sed-tor-* shows the outcome of a cluster of two apicals of PIE date, and the change in question reaches right back to the proto-language, 212; but identical sequences of later date, as in **ke-dte* 'gimme' pl. (syncopated from **ke-date*), undergo nothing more dramatic than a voicing adjustment: *cette*. Another important factor to be reckoned with in assimilation phenomena is *recomposition*, wherein the effects of regular sound laws in compounds are modified by leveling (the importation of elements from other, usually clearer, formations) and, because the sound laws that caused the changes in the first place are no longer operative, the recomposed forms remain unaltered. Thus L *adsum* 'am present' and *conlocō* 'locate' are so spelled in inscriptions and mss until a very late period, though the expected pronunciations (that is, the products of regular L sound laws) *assum* and *collocō* are attested for colloquial speech by puns in Plautus. In the conflict between the purely phonetic tendency and the influence of the uncompounded forms, parallel compounds may differ in the forms favored, for example L *conlocō* vs. *colligō* 'collect', both from **kom-l-*. Conversely, in some cases assimilation in compounds alters groups of consonants which normally are not assimilated: L *arripiō* 'seize', *surripiō* 'filch' < **ad-*, **sub-rep-* (cf. *crībrum* 'sieve', *quadrus* 'square', and NB the normal development of **-dr-* to L *-tr-*, 223.5). (These phenomena must be distinguished from artificially conservative spelling—*Manlius* for example, which evidence suggests was actually pronounced *Mallius*, 223.1a.)

On occasion, original and recomposed forms, differentiated in meaning, will be found side by side. So in L, earlier *sustineō* 'hold up, prop up' next to later *subteneō* 'hold under'. (The different age of the two compounds is corroborated by the different treatments of **e* in medial syllables before a single consonant, 66.) In a similar vein, by regular sound law Ved. *su-*

várṇa- lit. 'having a beautiful color' should be represented in Classical Skt. by *svarṇa-*. And so it is; but this *svarṇa-* means 'gold' (the metal). Skt. compounds which mean literally 'having a good so-and-so' all show the effects of recomposition: *svarṇa-* 'gold' and *suvarṇa-* 'having a beautiful color; brilliant' occur side by side in Skt.

209. METHODOLOGY. Many of the changes discussed in the following sections are clear as regards both the ingredients and their developments, but for some clusters the regular development is uncertain. Particularly in L, phonological complexities (both of the original clusters and of the changes they undergo) necessitate rather more speculation about sound change than is tolerable under more favorable circumstances. For example, L *flāmen* '(high) priest' might be cognate with Ved. *bráhman-* n. 'formulation, prayer' (see **287.3b**) from PIE **bhlagh(s)men-* (PItal. **flaχmen-* or **flaksmen-*; the version with an **-s-* would not do for the Ved. form). But in the alternative, it has been connected with Go. *blotan* 'to worship' via PIE **bhlād(s)men-*. As a matter of principle, neighboring language groups are expected to show important similarities, which would here favor the Gmc. association; but that is balanced in this case by the observation that Ital. and InIr. share many archaic details in their religious and legal lexicons. That such cases are strictly speaking undecidable, so far from calming debate, has seemed to stimulate bickering in the scholarly literature.

The technique for determining the history of groups of consonants is something like the following. First, one surmises by whatever means what the original structures probably were; then, if there is more than one apparent outcome, one decides which of them is original and which have been disturbed by analogy, recomposition, and the like. Sheer numbers count for little: examples of analogical or recomposed clusters may outnumber the cases of the genuine outcome. Sometimes a basis for deciding can be found in the behavior of clusters of similar makeup, since phonetically parallel clusters often change in a parallel manner. A rule of thumb is that the most shortened or otherwise transfigured outcome is likely to be the original development.

The following discussion of the development of **-kst-* (**231.1**) in L provides an example of the kinds of evidence to be had, and the kinds of arguments that apply:

1. L *lustrō* 'make light' is certainly from **lowkstrō* or **lukstrō*. The gens name *Sestius*, being a name, cannot be etymologized with quite the same confidence; but given the other forms derived from numbers in L gentilicia, and taken together with an alternative form of the name, *Sextius*, it is reasonable to reconstruct an original cluster **-kst-* derived from *sex* 'six'.

2. The doublet *Sextius* is not the only form apparently showing original **-kst-* unchanged: there are *sextus* 'sixth'; *textus* 'woven' (and many words of the same family); compounds like *extenuō* 'reduce'; and so on—more forms altogether than those showing

the presumably regular outcome *-st-* < **-kst-*. But these cases of *-xt-* are probably the result of analogy (specifically, recomposition).

3. Another group with unaltered *-xt-* includes *dexter* 'right', *iuxtā* 'next to' and some others. These cannot result from leveling, and must owe the survival of their clusters to relative chronology: AFTER the operation of the sound law on original **-kst-* clusters, the syncope of an earlier short vowel created these cases of *-xt-*: **deksiteros* is a certainty (cf. G δεξιτερός), **yugistād* is more hypothetical.

This example exemplifies yet another hazard: the most certain examples of L *-st-* from **-kst-* reflect **-kstr-*, not just **-kst-*, and in addition both *lustrō* and *illustris* probably contained *-ū-* before the cluster. Perhaps therefore the loss of **k* occurred only before **str*, not before **st*; or perhaps it occurred only after long vowels; or perhaps both conditions were necessary. The verdict turns entirely upon *Sestius* which, being a proper noun, cannot be etymologized with confidence. Even the byform *Sextius* is not quite clinching evidence, as it might owe its form to folk etymology, that is, it might be a counterfeit recomposition based on a *Sestius* whose history has nothing to do with *sex* 'six' or with any other original **-kst-* cluster. However, the simplest interpretation in this case is that *Sestius* continues **sekstios*, and that is also the most probable one.

210. SEQUENCES OF STOP + STOP. A stop is regularly assimilated to the voicing and aspiration of the FOLLOWING stop. As regards point of articulation, there is no change in G; in L the labials and dorsals remain as such before apicals, while apicals are assimilated to dorsals or labials, and labials to dorsals.

The groups in which the second stop is an apical are the most important, since apical stops are the most common stops in endings and derivative suffixes. The other sequences are mostly confined to compounds, and in G also to apocopated forms of prepositions in Homer and the dialects.

Greek

Ingredients	Result	Examples
β+τ, φ+τ	πτ	τέτριπται (perf.midd. of τρῑ́βω 'rub')
		γέγραπται (γράφω 'scratch')
π+θ, β+θ	φθ	ἐπέμφθην (aor.pass. of πέμπω 'lead')
		ἐτρῑ́φθην (τρῑ́βω)
π+δ, φ+δ	βδ	κρύβδην (adv. built to κρύπτω 'hide')
		γράβδην (γράφω)
γ+τ, χ+τ	κτ	λέλεκται (λέγω 'gather')
		βέβρεκται (βρέχω 'get wet')
κ+θ, γ+θ	χθ	ἐπλέχθην (πλέκω 'plait')
		ἐλέχθην (λέγω)
κ+δ, χ+δ	γδ	πλέγδην (πλέκω)
		σπέργδην (σπέρχω 'hasten')
τ+κ	κκ	Hom. καккείοντες (pple. of κατά-κειμαι)
τ+π	ππ	Hom. κάππεσε (aor. of κατα-πίπτω)

Latin

Ingredients	Result	Examples
b+t	pt	*scrīptus* (*scrībō* 'scratch')
g+t, h+t	ct	*āctus* (*agō* 'drive')
		vectus (*vehō* 'convey')
qu+t, gu+t	ct	*coctus* (*coquō* 'cook'; **164B.2**)
		ūnctus (*unguō* 'anoint')
t+c, d+c	cc	*siccus* 'dry' (**sitikos* cf. *sitis* 'thirst')
		accipiō (**ad-kapiō*) 'receive'
d+qu	cqu	*acquīrō* (**ad-kʷaysō*) 'add to, acquire'
d+g	gg	*aggerō* (**ad-gesō*) 'bring to'
d+p	pp	*quippe* (**kʷid-pe*) 'indeed'
b+c	cc	*occīdō* (**ob-kaydō*) 'knock down'
b+g	gg	*suggerō* (**sub-gesō*) 'put under'

a. Myc. spellings like *po-pi* 'with feet' have been interpreted as ποπφι, namely, with assimilation of the stem-final stop to the point of articulation of the ending. The reasoning is that heterorganic clusters are written in such forms as *te-ko-to-ne* (*tektones* nom.pl.) 'craftsmen', *wa-na-ka-to* (*wanaktos* gen.sg.) 'prince'. But it is thinkable that *po-pi* and the like simply stood for *potpʰi* or *potʰpʰi*, parallel to *pe-mo* 'seed' for *spermo*, *wa-tu* 'city' for *wastu*. The crucial forms are in any case very few in number.

b. Etymological spellings like *obtineō* (**ob-ten-*) 'possess', for *opt-*, have influenced the English pronunciation of such forms. But all evidence points to the actual pronunciation /pt/ and the like. (1) Spellings of the type *apsolutus* 'complete' are common; though they are most characteristic of older sources, they occur at all periods. (2) Romance attests no distinction between the treatment of sequences which were differentiated in the approved classical spelling as *-bt-* and *-pt-*: *subtus* 'beneath' and *septem* 'seven' become It. *sotto* and *sette*, respectively. (This quirky use of *b* to mean /p/ began in the sequence *bs*, **213b**.)

c. The combinations given in the tables occur in formations that in many cases greatly postdate the PIE period (the G aorist passive and perfect middle, for instance), but the testimony of all evidence points to the VOICING ADJUSTMENTS here demonstrated for G and L, and it was certainly a feature of PIE.

211. ASPIRATION ADJUSTMENT: BARTHOLOMAE'S LAW. In Indic, any obstruent consonant cluster with a voiced aspirate as an ingredient becomes VOICED AND ASPIRATED throughout: hence *-gh+t-*, *-gh+th-*, and *-k+dh-* all become *-gdh-* (*-ghdh-*). This phenomenon is known as *Bartholomae's Law.* There is no unambiguous trace of Bartholomae's Law in G and L, and it has been proposed that in PIE the treatment of such clusters was more like that of G and L than of Indic. Apparently ancient derivatives of **legh-* 'lie (down)', for example, show deaspiration and devoicing of the **gh*: **legh-tro-* > G λέκτρον 'bed', **legh-to-* > L *lectus* 'couch'. (This particular datum is especially significant because the root itself does not survive in L apart from this form, so *lectus* cannot well be the product of leveling or recombination.)

But there are facts of G and L which are hard to account for except by something like Bartholomae's Law in the prehistory of both G and L. Specifically, both languages continue the four versions of the PIE 'tool'-

suffix, *-*tro*-, *-*tlo*-, *-*dhro*-, and *-*dhlo*-. Of these the varieties in **t* are assumed to be the more original, and if so the only remotely plausible explanation for the origin of the forms in **dh* is something like Bartholomae's Law. This explanation, which is the usual one, has its weaknesses, admittedly: it is incomprehensible that G and L agree in preserving Bartholomae alternants in this suffix and not in any of the numerous other suffixes beginning with PIE **t*. Furthermore, the one place where the reflexes of *-*dhlo*- and *-*dhro*- are NOT found in G and L is in formations built to roots ending in a voiced aspirated stop—G λέκτρον, cited above, is precisely the kind of form where we could expect to find *-*dhro*-, not *-*tro*-. The obvious alternative, that the suffix was actually originally *-*dhro*-/*-*dhlo*- and underwent deaspiration creates as many problems as it solves, and severs any connection between these affixes and the agentive affixes *-*tor*-/*-*tol*-.

a. In the historical period of Indic, an apparent exception to Bartholomae's Law is aspirate + *s*, which yields plain voiceless stop + *s*: -*dh*+*s*-, for example, yields -*ts*-, as to *rādh*- 'succeed', Ved. *rātsyati* 'will succeed' < **rādh-sya*-. This is often presented as the PIE rule as well. Whether it was or wasn't, there is evidence that to begin with in Indic clusters including *s* were in full accord with Bartholomae's Law, that is, the whole cluster became voiced and aspirated. This accounts for such things as RV *gdha* 3sg.midd.aor. of *ghas*- 'swallow', etymologically **ghs-ta*. Had the familiar deaspiration and devoicing rule obtained, the result would have been ˣ*kṭa* < **kṣṭa*; attested *gdha* points rather to intermediate **gzdha*, that is, an aspirated cluster in which all elements were voiced. Similarly Ved. *sī́kṣant*- 'wishing to possess' (cited in 169) comes from **sīḍẓhant*- < **si-ẓḍẓhant*- (**si-sźh-s*-: root *sah*- < PInIr. **saźh*- < PIE **seǵh*-) by sound laws alone: the usual rules affecting voiced sibilants (loss with compensatory lengthing, deaspiration, and devoicing) give attested *sī́kṣant*-.

b. Much has been written about the plausibility of constructs like -*ghdh*-, the debate hinging on the phonetic details of the obstruents in question. If their 'aspiration' was purely a release feature, a sequence of stops would probably have had only one release; if so, -*gdha*- would be a good representation (and that is the usual style of writing such clusters in devanāgarī script). Nevertheless in G, evidence suggests that all (voiceless) aspirated stops in a sequence were released when there was a shift in point of articulation, so ἄχθος 'burden' and ἄφθιτος 'imperishable' but Σαπφώ; so perhaps a construct like -*ghdh*- is not implausible. According to some phonetic theories, the aspiration of voiced stops is not the defining feature anyway, but an artifact of the true distinction, which is one of phonation—'voiced aspirated' being neither voiced nor aspirated, but *murmured* (a discrete phonational state, also sometimes called *breathy voice*). In that case, assuming that sequences of stops agree in phonation, a representation like **dhǵhom*- 'earth', rather than **dǵhom*-, or PInIr. **ghzhdha* 'you swallowed', above, would only be intended to indicate explicitly (if clumsily) that both stops share the distinguishing phonetics, whatever they were, of that series of stops.

212. APICAL STOP + APICAL STOP SEQUENCES are a special case. It is apparent that in such stop sequences in PIE there arose a sibilant between the stops, perhaps from rearticulation of the second apical: PIE **sed-to*- 'set' pple. was something like **set^s tos* (variously transcribed). The sequence becomes -*ss*- in L and also Celt. and Gmc., and -*st*$^{(h)}$- in G and Iranian.

In Indic the excrescent **s* simply drops: PIE **ed-ti* 'eats', or rather **et^{s}ti*, gives Ved. *átti*. Cf. in composition: *ud-* 'up' plus *stambh-* 'fix' gives Ved. *úttabhitā* 'erected'. Hitt. is at the opposite extreme: prior to the discovery of Hitt., the **-t^{s}t-* cluster was a purely hypothetical construct, but in Hitt. it actually survived as such: **et^{s}ti* 'eats' > Hitt. *e-iz-za-az-zi* (the closest the writing system can come to representing /etstsi/ 31; the PIE 3sg. ending **-ti* > Hitt. /tsi/, written *-zi*); **t^{s}te(ne)* 2pl. > Hitt. *az-za-aš-te-ni* /atsteni/.

Apical + apical clusters become σ + apical in G; that is, the outcomes are indistinguishable from original **st$^{(h)}$* clusters. (More to the point, the development is exactly that of any **-s-* between two stops of the same point of articulation (**230.3**), which at least leaves open the possibility that **-tst-* was still present as such in PG.)

**H$_2$eyeri-d-to-* (containing the zero grade of **ed-* 'eat') > **ayeri-tsto-* > Hom. ˝ἄριστον 'breakfast'. This development is not explicitly written in Myc. but can be inferred: Myc. *e-pi-da-to* 'divided up' would be the way επιδαστος would be written; cf. G ἄδαστος 'undivided', δατέομαι.

In L to begin with apical + apical clusters become *-ss-*, indistinguishable from the outcome of **ts* clusters (**215**); see note **a**, below. It becomes *-st-* before *-r-*.

Thus the usual account; but NB note **b**, below, in conjunction with the following examples.

Ingredients	Result	Examples
τ+τ, δ+τ, θ+τ	στ	ἀνυστός 'practicable' (ἀνύτω 'accomplish')
		ἴστε (2pl. of οἶδα 'know')
		πέπεισται (perf. mid of πείθω 'persuade')
τ+θ, δ+θ, θ+θ	σθ	ἠνύσθην (aor. pass. of ἀνύτω)
		οἶσθα (2sg. of οἶδα)
		ἐπείσθην (aor. pass. of πείθω)
t+t, d+t, dh+t	*ss*	*passus* (*patior* 'undergo')
		sessum (*sedeō* 'am sitting')
		iussus (*iubeō* 'order', **147.2**)
	s	*versus* (*vertō* 'turn')
		salsus (*sallō* < **sald-* 'salt')
		rāsus (*rādō* 'scrape')
		fūsus (< **fūssus* secondary for original **fŭssus*, **232.2**; cf. *fundō* 'pour')
		ūsus[1] (*ūtor*, 'use' **oyt-*)
		clausus (*claudō* 'close')
	str	*rōstrum* 'beak' (**rōd-tro-*, cf. *rōdō* 'gnaw')
		tōnstrīx (**tond-trī-*; *tondeō* 'shave'; cf. *tōnsor* 'barber' < **tond-tōr*)

a. L *ss* (from any source) shortens after a consonant, diphthong or long vowel

---

[1] For expected **issus*. Full grade is not original in a pple.; **ūssus* (whence *ūsus* by **232.2**) owes its vowel to *ūtī* perf.act.

(232.2): _*lowd-s-a(y)_ 'I played' > _*lowtsay_ > _*lūssī_ > _lūsī_ (_lūdō_); _*χays-s-a(y)_ 'I stuck to' > _*haessī_ > _haesī_ (_haereō_); _*ard-s-a(y)_ 'I burned' > _*artsay_ > _*arssī_ > _arsī_ (_ardeō_). Note that L _s_ < _ss_ of whatever source never undergoes rhotacism (173), and the shortening of _*ss_ must therefore postdate that development.

b. The regular L development of _*dh+t_ is uncertain. Three different outcomes are generally recognized; evidence is fully satisfactory only for the first:

1. _-ss-_. Participles in _*-to-_ to roots in _*-dh-_ always attest _-ss-_ (unless shortened in accord with **a**): _fīsus_ 'trusted' (_fīdō_, PIE _*bheydh-_), _gressus_ 'stepped' (_gradior_, PIE _*ghredh-_).

2. _-st-_. PIE _*_H_2_eydh-tu-_ 'heat' > L _aestus_, _*_H_2_eydh-tāt-_ > L _aestās_ 'summer'. This exhausts the evidence for this development. However, there is at least one attestation of L _-st-_ from _*-d-t-_, in defiance of the usual (and securely-attested) development to _-ss-_, namely _comēstus_ 'eaten up' < _*ed-to-_.

3. _*-zd-_. PIE _*ḱred-dhe_H_1_-_ 'believe' ('heart' + 'put') somehow > _*krezdō_ > L _crēdō_; cf. Skt. _śraddhā-_. (This is not a case of original _*-dh-t-_; but it is generally accepted, though not free from doubt, that PIE sequences of _*-dh-t-_ and _*-d-dh-_ would have been pronounced the same, 211.)

c. The L developments shown here apply only to original sequences, and formations patterned after them (for example _tēnsus_; note **d**, below). Clusters of later origin undergo voicing adjustment and nothing more: _cette_ < _*cedite_ < _*kedate_ < _*ḱe-dH̥_$_3$_-te_ (pl. of _cedo_, 488A) 'gimme'; _attingō_ 'reach' < _*ad-tangō_; _rettudī_ 'beat back' < _*re-tetudī_ (_retundō_), _reddō_ 'give back'.

d. L _tentus_ < _*tn̥to-_ (= Ved. _tatá-_) is the original pple. of _tendō_ 'stretch'—the _d_ is not part of the root, _nd_ being from _*ny_ (218).[1] This _tentus_ was displaced by _tēnsus_ as if from _×tn̥d-to-_, in imitation of the pattern seen in such forms as _prandeō_ 'dine', _prānsus_ and _tondeō_ 'cut hair', _tōnsus_. The importation of the _d_ into the perfect _tetendī_ is just like the spread of the _n_-infix (479.4A) from the present stem in _pānxī_ 'agreed' (_pangō_) and _iūnxī_ 'linked' (_iungō_). _Pānsum_ (to _pandō_ 'extend') is a different analogy: the _-n-_ was imported into original _passum_ from _pandō_ (root _*pat-_, 222.2).

STOP + _s_

213. LABIAL STOPS + _*s_ give G _ψ_, L _ps_ (_bs_).
G _γράψω_ fut. of _γράφω_ 'scratch'; _φλέψ_ 'vein' (gen. _φλεβός_).
L _scrīpsī_ (perf. of _scrībō_ 'scratch'); _nūpsī_ (perf. of _nūbō_ 'marry').

a. Here, and likewise in the case of apical and dorsal stops + _s_, the general rule holds that before _s_ a voiced stop becomes voiceless and a G aspirate becomes unaspirated. But in early Att. inscriptions, before the introduction of the Ion. alphabet, _ψ_ and _ξ_ were commonly denoted, not by ΠΣ, ΚΣ, but by ΦΣ, ΧΣ, as ΦΣΕΦΙΣΜΑ (= _ψήφισμα_ 'motion carried'), ΕΔΟΧΣΕΝ (= _ἔδοξεν_ 'it met with approval', aor. of _δοκέω_), implying that the _-σ-_ had some secondary aspirating effect on the preceding stop. Cf. also developments of the type _τέχνη_ 'craft' < _*teksnā_ (230a).

b. In words like _urbs_, _abs_, _observō_, _bs_ stands for /ps/, and in early inscriptions was usually so written. The spelling with _b_ was imported from other cases (_urbis_ and so on),

---

[1] _Tendō_ 'stretch' is sometimes compared to Ved. _tandate_ 'is relaxed', _átandra-_ 'unwearied', Lith. _tandus_ 'lazy'. Scholars are divided on the cogency of the comparison, as the semantic connection is less direct than with _tanóti_ 'stretch'. It seems clear that in Indic and Baltic the _-d-_ is part of the root, which therefore disagrees with L _tentus_ < _*tn̥-to-_ (exactly superimposable on Ved. _tatá-_ formally and functionally).

and the uncombined *ab*, *ob*. Perhaps in some circles the actual pronunciation under the influence of this spelling was /b/, as indeed it is in current English (210b).

Of the voiced stops *b*, *d*, *g*, the letter *b* alone received this kind of treatment in L orthography. The explanation for this is clear: any contest between *gs* and *cs* was obviated by the spelling *x*, and both *d* and *t* before *s* are lost altogether (215). That is, orthographic patterns like *rēx*, *rēgis* and *pēs*, *pedis* provided no inspiration for artificial creations like ×*rēgs* and ×*pēds* parallel to *urbs*.

214. DORSAL STOPS + *s*. Any palatal or plain velar stop + **s* gives G ξ, L *x* (that is, κσ and *cs*, respectively).

G δείξω fut. of δείκνῡμι 'point out'; G λέξω fut. of λέγω 'gather'; βρέξω fut. of βρέχω 'get wet'; θρίξ 'hair', gen. τριχός, 138.

L *dīxī* perf. of *dīcō* 'say'; L *rēxī* perf. of *regō* 'send, arrange in a straight line'; *vēxī* perf. of *vehō* 'convey'; *rēx* 'king', gen. *rēgis*.

Before -*s*-, as before all consonants except **y* (199-200), labiovelar stops behave like labials in G, and like dorsals in L: G πέψω (fut. of πεπ- 'cook' < **pek*^{w}-), L *ūnxī* (perf. of *unguō* 'anoint').

a. Under dorsal stops are included of course PIE **ǵh* which gives L *h* between vowels (158), and PIE **g*^{w}*(h)* which gives L -*v*- between vowels (154.2, 163). This accounts for such relations as L *vēxī* to *vehō* (**ǵh*); *unguō* 'anoint', *ūnxī* (**g*^{w}); and *nix* 'snow' gen. *nivis* (**g*^{w}*h*). Such patterns were even extended to forms where they do not belong etymologically, as *vīxī* perf. of *vīvō* 'live' < PItal. **g*^{w}*īwō*.

215. APICAL STOPS + *s*. In both G and L, an apical stop + **s* is assimilated to *ss*, which is further simplified to *s* after a consonant, diphthong, or long vowel (232), and, within the historical period, when final. After a short vowel we have *ss* in L, and G σσ in many dialects, but regularly σ in Attic and later Ionic. Homer has both σσ and σ.

G pres.pple. dat.pl. **p*^{h}*eront-si* > **p*^{h}*eronssi* > φέρονσι > φέρουσι.

PIE **knīdos*- *s*-stem 'the smell of roasting meat', **knīd-s-eH*$_2$ > Hom. κνῑ́ση (Att. κνῖσα is unlikely to be < **knīds-iH*$_2$ directly); cf. L *nīdor* < **knīdōs*.

Hom. ποσσί, ποσί, Att. ποσί from **pod-si* dat.pl. of πούς 'foot'.

Hom. ἐκόμισσα, -ισα, Att. -ισα, from **ekomid-sa* aor. of κομίζω 'take care of'; cf. Il. κομιδή 'care [bestowed on horses]'.

G κλείς 'key' < **klāwid-s* (gen. κλειδός), and all the numerous G forms in -ας, -αδος; -ῑς, -ῑδος.

G ἄναξ 'prince' < **wanakts* (gen. ἄνακτος).

Hom. θέμις 'custom' < **t*^{h}*emists* (gen. θέμιστος).

G Ἄτλᾱς < **atlants* (gen. Ἄτλαντος).

Of uncertain etymology, but showing the expected developments are κόρυς, -υθος 'helmet', ὄρνῑς, -ῑθος 'bird', and others.

L *quassī* < **quat-sī* perf. of *quatiō* 'shake'.

L *iussī* < **yudh-s*- perf. of *iubeō* 'order', 147.2.

L *lūsī* < **lowd-sī* perf. of *lūdō* 'play'.

L *clausī* < **klawd-s*- perf. of *claudō* 'shut'.

L *pēs* < **pēd-s* 'foot'.

L *mīles* 'soldier' < *mīless* Plaut. < **mīlets*, cf. gen. *mīlitis*.

a. The simplification of final *-ss* is a feature of classical L. In OL, however, as revealed by Plautine scansion, there was still a distinction between final *-ss*, from any source, and *-s*, for example *ess* 'you are' < **-ss* and *mīless* 'soldier'.

b. In L and in most G dialects the result of the assimilation is identical with orig. **ss*, and its subsequent simplification to *s* is the same. But this convergence must postdate G of the earliest periods: in two dialects, Boeotian and Cretan, which show orig. *σσ* unchanged, **τσ* gives *ττ*, just as do original PreG **ty* and **tʰy* (196). Thus Boeot. aor. *εκομιττα* = Hom. *ἐκόμισσα*, above, and also Boeot. *μεττος* = *μέσ(σ)ος* 'middle'. Even Boeotian agrees with all other dialects in the development of **-ts* to *-ς* in final position: Boeot. *παῖς* = Att. *παῖς* 'boy' (**pawit-s*).

NASAL + CONSONANT

216. NASAL + STOP. A nasal is assimilated to the point of articulation of a following stop. There was no special letter for the dorsal nasal [ŋ] (as in NE *sing*) in the G alphabets or those derived from them; the sound was indicated in G by *γ* and in L by *n* (or in special cases *g*; **220a**).[1] The same thing is true of our PIE reconstructions: what we write as PIE **penkʷe* 'five' was phonetically [peŋkʷe] if not [peŋʷkʷe]. The phonetics of the nasal remained unchanged in L *quīnque* [kʷiːŋkʷe]; in the reflexes in other IE languages, the PIE *[ŋ⁽ʷ⁾] changed in accordance with the changes in the following **kʷ*: G *πέντε* and *πέμπε*, Ved. *páñca*, Go. *fimf*, W *pimp*.
From *συν-*: G *συμβαίνω* 'come together', *συγγενής* 'congenital', *συγχέω* 'pour together'.
PIE **(d)k̑m̥tóm* 'hundred' > L *centum* 'hundred' : Lith. *šim̃tas*. (This and certain other forms indicates that sequences like **mt* and **ms* were possible in PIE.)
PItal. **eom-dVm* > L *eundem* 'same' acc.sg.m.; PreL **pri-isemo-kap-s* > L *prīnceps* 'chief'.
PIE **n̥-ǵneH₃-to-* 'unknown' > L *ignōtus* /iŋnōtus/ (**220a**).

a. In L *ēmptus* 'taken', *sūmptus* 'employed', survival of the *-m-* (for ˣ*entus* and so on) is irregular, and to be explained as an importation from other forms, such as *emō* and *sūmō*, with the development of an excrescent *-p-* between *-m-* and *-t-*. (The same analogical retention of *-m-* with excrescence of *-p-* is seen in perf. *sūmpsī* < **-msay*; see **226.2**.)

217. PIE **my* > L *ny*, PreG **ny*, PG **ññ* (**198**, **203**):
PIE **gʷm̥yoH₂* 'set out' (Ved. *gam-*, NE *come*) > PreG **gʷanyō* > PG **gʷaññō* > G *βαίνω*, L *veniō* (originally disyllabic; **193**). However, L *gremium* 'armload, embrace' (whence *gremia* pl. 'sheaf') shows *my* < **my* instead. If this is the regular development, then the *n* of *veniō* needs explanation. It might reflect an Italic dissimilation of **gʷem-* to **gʷen-*, a dissimilation nourished by phonologically regular forms like PItal. supine **gʷentum*. This

[1] Epigraphically, Ν rather than Γ before Κ, Γ, Χ, Ξ is commonly encountered.

view would help explain the presence of *n* throughout the paradigm (in Sab. as well as L), rather than just in the present stem and in derivatives in *-nt-* like *ventum*, and *conventiō*. But the etymologies of *veniō* and *gremium* are on very different footings—the former is certain, the latter more than ordinarily conjectural. In addition, the usual interpretation of *veniō* seems to accord with *quoniam* (trisyllabic) 'since' < **k^wom yām*, as well as compounds with *com-*, for example *coniūrō* 'conspire'.

218. In G, **ny*, including the outcome of **my*, participates in the wave of palatalizations and their sequelae discussed in **198-207**. In L the outcome of (original) **ny* is controversial. The evidence best supports the view that **ny* > L *nd*, though such a change is phonetically unexpected, and is rejected by some authorities. (Note that *ny* from **my* does not participate in this change—hence *veniō*—and so must postdate it.)

PIE **ten-y^e/o-* > L *tendō* 'stretch', G τείνω; L *tentus* pple. supports original **ten-* rather than **tend-*. (L *tēnsus* is a later, analogical structure, **212d.**)

L *offendō, dēfendō* if (as most think) < PIE **g^when-* 'strike (down)', like G θείνω < **t^henyō* : Arm. *ǰnǰem* 'destroy'; Alb. *gjanj* 'hunt'; Lith. *geniù* 'lop off (branches)', all < PIE **g^whenyō*. The pples *dēfēnsus* and *offēnsus*, and *īnfēnsus* 'hostile' (which looks like a participle to an unattested **īnfendō*, see **458.3**) can be held to be like *tēnsus*, though the absence of derivatives in **-fen-t-* even in such isolated forms as *īnfēnsus* argues for a genuine **d* here rather than L *nd* < **ny*. But the pres. stem **g^when-y^e/o-* is a well-attested PIE form, whereas the root-extended form **g^whend-* would be unique to L.[1]

For L gerundives in *-ndo-* (Sab. *-nn-*, O **sakrannas** 'sacrandae' for example) < **-nyo-* see **568.2**.

a. A parallel suggestion is that **ly* > L *ld* (whence *ll*, **223.1**). This can be easily dismissed on the grounds of such secure counter-examples as PIE **H_2el-yo-* 'other' > L *alius*. In the case of *nd* < **ny* the best competing evidence is L *senior* 'elder' < **senyōs* (**353.1**). However, if *tendō* and *-fendō* do not continue **-ny-*, then (a) L has no *y^e/o*-stems built to roots ending in **n*, and, (b) at the same time, exactly where we would expect such formations on the basis of comparative evidence, we find instead a questionable present-stem formant in **d* (see **458.3**).

Stop + Nasal

219. Labial stop + nasal. Before either *-m-* or *-n-* a labial stop becomes *-m-* in L; in G, a parallel assimilation occurs when any labial (or labiovelar) stop is followed by -μ-, but does not affect -φ- and -π- before -ν-. That these developments in G and L are independent innovations is

[1] Evidence for a present-stem formative in **-d-*, though it is sometimes proposed (**458.3**), is doubtful. In the case of L *-fendō*, the isolated form *īnfēnsus* is equally inconvenient for a theoretical present-stem marker in **d* and for the idea that the present-stem in **fend-* continues **g^when-y-*.

shown by the fact that the change of *g^w and *k^w to G β, π predates the nasal assimilation, and by other differences in detail:

Latin

	m	n
p	mm	mn
b	mm	mn

Greek

	μ	ν
π	μμ	πν
φ	μμ	φν
β	μμ	μν

L _summus_ 'highest' < *_supmos_ : U _somo_; cf. L _super_, G ὑπό.
Att. ὄμμα 'eye' < *_opma_ < *_ok^{w}ma_ < *_H_3ek^w-mn̥_ : L _oculus_, G ὤψ 'face'.
G 1sg.midd. perfects λέλειμμαι, τέτριμμαι, γέγραμμαι (pres. λείπω 'leave', τρῑ́βω 'rub', γράφω 'scratch').
L _somnus_ 'sleep' < *_swepnos_ : Ved. _svápna-_, G ὕπνος.
G ἀφνειός 'wealthy' : ἄφενος n. 'riches'.
L _summittō_, _summoveō_ from _sub-_ and _mittō_, _moveō_.
L _Samnium_ < *_sabniom_ < *_sabh-_ : O **safinim**, cf. L. _Sabīnī_.
G σεμνός 'revered' < *_sebno-_ (σέβομαι 'honor') < *_seg^{w}no-_ < PIE _tyeg^w-_ (**196.2, 162**).
G ἀμνος 'lamb' : L _agnus_, PIE *_H_2eg^w-no-_.

a. L _ommovēre_ Cato (= _obmovēre_), OMMVTVERVN inscr. (= _obmūtuērunt_), _amnuit_ gl. (= _abnuit_), and AMNEGAVERIT inscr. (= _abnegāverit_) indicate that _obmoveō_, _abnegō_, and so on, familiar from our texts, are recompositions.

220. DORSAL STOP + NASAL. The pronunciation of -γμ- from orig. [gm] was apparently [ŋm], as indicated by ἄγμα, the special name according to Priscian for the letter γ when it stands for a nasal before γ, κ, χ. It may be assumed also that -γν- was pronounced [ŋn] in, say, ἄγνος 'awed' (cf. ἄγιος 'sacred'), though this is less certain.

G κ and χ normally remain unchanged when followed by a nasal, as in ἀκμή 'point', δραχμή 'drachma', τέκνον 'child', τέχνη 'art'. But in perfect and aorist middle forms, κμ and χμ are regularly replaced by γμ [ŋm], as in πέπλεγμαι and πεπλεγμένος (from πλέκω 'braid'), βέβρεγμαι (βρέχω 'get wet'). The explanation for these forms is uncertain. It is precisely in morphologically transparent formations that one expects to see the restorative effects of recomposition, not more extensive changes. For that reason, one suspects some sort of analogy as the source of forms like πέπλεγμαι. (On the other hand, forms like δράγμα n. 'handful', apparently dialectal for proper ˣδράχμα (cf. δραχμή), raise the possibility that some kind of dialect mixture may have been the starting point.)

L *_km_, *_kn_ become _gm_, _gn_. Initial _gn-_, whether original or from *_kn-_, is attested in early L, but subsequently the _g-_ drops (cf. the same kind of change in NE _knight_ < OE _cniht_; _gnat_ < OE _gnætt_).
L _dignus_ 'worthy, fitting' < *_dek-no-_ (_decet_ 'is fitting').
L _segmentum_ 'piece [cut off]' < *_sek-mn̥to-_ (_secō_ 'cut off').

L *nōscō* 'understand', early *gnōscō* : G γιγνώσκω, Ved. *jñā-*, OE *cnáwan*, and L *cognōscō*, *ignōtus* 'unknown' (see **a**, below).
L *nātus* 'born; son', early *gnātus* < PIE **ǵn̥H₁-to-* : L *gignō* 'beget', *cognātus* 'related by birth' (see below), G κασίγνητος 'brother', Ved. *jātá-*.
L *nīxus*, early *gnixus* (Paul.Fest.) pple. of *nītor* 'lean on' < PIE **kneygʷh-* : Go. *hneiwan* 'incline, bow' and cf. L *cōnnīveō* 'close the eyes'.
L *lignum* '[fire-]wood' < **leg-no-* (*legō* 'gather').
L *tignum* 'timber' < **teg-no-* (**teg-* 'cover, roof', cf. L *tēctum* 'roof', *tēgula* 'roofing tile', *tēctor* 'plasterer', *toga*).
L *īlignus* 'oaken' (*īlex, -icis* 'holm-oak').

a. There are clear indications that L *gn* was once pronounced [ŋn], that is, with a change of *-g-* and *-k-* before *-n-* to a dorsal nasal, parallel to the changes of **-p-* and **-f-* to *-m-* (219), and of apical stops to *n* (222). Such are: (1) the omission of *-n-* in *ignōtus* 'unknown', *cognātus* 'related by birth', from **in-gnō-*, **kom-gnā-*; (2) spellings in inscriptions like SINNV 'signum' and SINGNIFER 'signifer', showing two kinds of revealing deviation from the standard spelling; (3) the change of **e* to *i* before *gn* just as before *n* + dorsal (*dignus, lignum, tignum* like *lingua* and *tingō*); (4) in Romanian, L *gn* is reflected as *mn*: Rom. *lemn* 'wood' < *lignum*. If the L starting point was [ŋn], this development is exactly parallel to Rom. *pt* < *ct*: *faptu* < L *factus*; and Rom. *bd* < *gd*, *răbda* 'be patient' perh. < **rig(i)dare*. In other words, if we assume original [ŋn] we can simply say that ALL homorganic sequences of dorsal + apical become Rom. labial + apical. (The more familiar Romance development of [ñ:] from L *gn*, as in Italian (so *legno* 'wood' [lɛñ:o]), is also pertinent, being easiest to understand if traced to an original [ŋn]. However, it admits of other explanations. The Romanian development is more salient.)

On the other hand, the complete silence of the L grammarians and of writers like Cicero and Quintilian regarding any such pronunciation makes it unlikely that it was usual in their time among educated speakers. The probable explanation is that the retention of *g* in the spelling reacted on the pronunciation and that this spelling pronunciation wholly prevailed in cultivated speech. (The Romance developments cited above would in any case be better evidence for 'colloquial' than for cultivated speech.)

b. The reason for different behavior of **-ngn-* (as in *cognātus*) and **-nkn-* (as in *cōnnīveō*) can only be guessed, as there seems to be only the one example of the latter.

221. APICAL STOP + NASAL. G τμ, δμ, θμ, τν, δν, θν normally remain unchanged, as in πότμος 'destiny', ἀριθμός 'number', ἔθνος 'a people'. So also in Hom. (ϝ)ίδμεν 'we know', κεκορυθμένος 'furnishing with a helmet' (κορύσσω, from **korutʰ-yō*), Hes. πεφραδμένος 'declaring' (φράζω), Pind. κεκαδμένος 'excelling' (perf. to καίνυμαι). Later forms with -σμ- are not a phonological development, but have been remodeled after other forms in the paradigm which have -στ- from apical + apical (212): ἴσμεν after ἴστε, κέκασμαι, πέπεισμαι, πεπεισμένος (πείθω 'persuade'), after πέπεισται, ἐπείσθην, and so on. So sometimes in nouns too, as ὀσμή 'smell' for Hom. ὀδμή (cf. L *odor*); θεσμός 'law' for τεθμός (Pind.).

222. In L there are apparently two different outcomes of an apical stop and a following **n*: *-nn-* and *-nd-*. What might be the explanation for the diverse reflexes is unobvious.

1. Since assimilation of the stop to the nasal is straightforwardly parallel to the behavior of *-*pn*- and *-*kn*-, -*nn*- qualifies as the expected outcome. It is attested in:
PIE **atnos* (or *H_2*etnos*) > L *annus* 'year' : Go. *aþna*-.
PIE **pet-neH*$_2$- > L *penna* 'feather' : G πέτομαι 'fly', Ved. root *pat*- (OIr. *én* /ēn/ 'bird' reflects **pet-no*-).
L *mercēnnārius* 'soldier' < **mercēdin*- (from unattested **mercēdō, -dinis* *'hire', seen also in *mercedonius* 'paymaster' Paul.Fest.; cf. *mercēdula* 'low wages, paltry fee'). Similarly in compounds like *annuō* 'signal assent, nod' < **ad-nuō*.
2. Unexpected but well-attested is L -*nd*-:
L *pandō* 'extend' < **pat-nā*- : O **patensíns** (? if for **patnesēnt* 'panderent'), G πίτνημι 'spread out' (Att. πετάννυμι).
L gerund in -*ndo*- from *-*tn*-, oblique stem of *r/n*-stem *-*ter*, obl. *-*tn*-, seen in L *iter* 'way' built to *i*- 'go' : Hitt. *i-tar* 'way', gen. *in-na-aš*, functioning in Hitt. as a productive verbal noun (290a, 568.3).
L *unda* 'wave' : Hom. ἁλοσ-ύδνη 'billow', oblique stem of the PIE *r/n*-stem (290-2) **wodr̥*, **udn*- 'water', as seen in Ved. *udnás* gen.sg. 'water', Hitt. *ú-i-te-na-aš* gen. of *wa-a-tar* (n.pl. *ú-i-da-a-ar* = G ὕδωρ), and (indirectly) in G ὑδατός < **udn̥*- (100).
L *fundus* 'bottom' < **bhudh-no*- : Ved. *budhná*-, OE *bodan*, NHG *Boden*.
Forms pointing to **tm* are lacking; **dm* > L *mm*:
L *ammīror* = *admīror*.

a. L *mm* and *nn* shorten after a diphthong or long vowel: later *mercēnārius* from *mercēnnārius*, above; L *glūma* 'chaff' (Varro) < **glūmma* < **glewbmā*-, cf. *glūbō* 'hull'. L *rāmus* 'branch' < **rāmmos* if from **wrād-mo*- with the same element as that seen in *rādīx* 'root' (**wr̥Hd*-); L *caementum* 'quarry stone' < **caemmentom* < **kayd-ment*- if from the root of *caedere* 'hew'.

Sporadically, long nasals shorten after a SHORT vowel, with compensatory lengthening of the vowel (cf. 232.2b): *cōnīveō* (earlier *connīveō*, above; 231.4), *āmentum* 'strap' (earlier *ammentum* from either **H̥*$_1$*p*- (root **eH*$_1$*p*-) or *H_2*em*- 'grasp').

GROUPS CONTAINING A LIQUID

223. LATIN.

1. **dl*, **ld*, **nl*, **ln*, **rl*, **ls* become L *ll*. Most such sequences result in the first place from the syncope of medial short vowels (73-4).
L *sella* 'stool' < **sed-lā* (*sedeō*) : Go. *sitls* 'seat', NE *settle* (noun).
L *sallō* 'salt' < **saldō* : *-*d*- clearly attested in Gmc., such as NE *salt*, and an apical stop is indicated by L *salsus* 'salty' < **salsso*- < **sald-to*- (212).
L *corōlla* 'wreath' < **korōnlā* < **korōnelā* (dim. of *corōna*).
L *collis* 'hill' < **kolnis* < PIE **kl̥-ni*- : OE *hyll* (= L *collis*), Lith. *kálnas* 'hill' < **kolno*-.
L *agellus* 'little field' < **agerlo*- < **agro-lo*- (*ager*).
L *puella* 'girl' < **puerla* < **puero-lā* (*puer*).
L *velle* 'to want' < **welsi* < **wel-esi* (553.1).

a. *Colligō* 'fasten together' from **conlegō* < **kom-legō* accords with this development, but in most compounds the unassimilated forms, as *conlocō* 'place' and *inlūstris* 'bright', prevail until a late period (**208**). The masculine name *Mānlius* owes its retention of the *-nl-* sequence to a different cause, namely the peculiarly conservative SPELLINGS of L names; the G transliteration ΜΑΛΛΙΟΣ reveals the real pronunciation. (The purely orthographic conservatism of *Mānlius* is paralleled by the given names *Cnaeus* and *Caius*: the initial *Cn-*, the use of *-ai-* for *-ae-*, and the use of *C-* for /g/ (**25**).

b. Forms like L *agellus* < **agrolo-* indicate that these assimilations are relatively late, at all events postdating L innovations like the development of *-er-* from *-ro-* (**74.4**).

c. Initial **dl-* evidently > L *l-* in *longus* 'long'; evidence for the initial stop is found in Ved. *dīrghá-*, superl. *drāghiṣṭha-*, Hitt. *da-lu-uk-ki* nom.sg.neut., and G δολιχός, despite the puzzling details of the last form. Germanic shows a similar development (for example **dlongh-* > Go. *laggs*, NE *long*).

Slightly less clear is L *lact-* 'milk' (cf. G γάλακτ-) if from something like **dl̥H₂ekt-*, via **dlakt-*; cf. *gland-* 'acorn' < **gʷl̥Hen-* **98**.

d. OL epigraphic PODLOVQVEI (**19**, ultimately from Πολυδεύκης), underlying later *Pollux*, might be taken as evidence that **-ld-* first metathesized to *-dl-* and only then became *-ll-*. A similar (if converse) metathesis is seen, albeit sporadically, in the development of **-tn-* (**222**).

2. Medial **-tl-* became Ital. **-kl-*, *-cl-*, followed by the development of an anaptytic vowel: *pōculum* 'drinking cup' < *pōcolom* < *pōclom* (often so scanned in Plaut., as were many words normally *-culum*, *-cula* at a later date), this from **peH₃-tlo-*. This development is mainly connected with the 'tool' suffix **-tlo-*, including such unobvious items as *saeculum* 'clan; age' = W *hoedl*, originally *'bond, cord' < PIE **sH₂ey-tlom* < **sH₂ey-* 'bind'. O **puklum** acc. 'son' superimposes precisely on Ved. *putrá-*, Av. *puθra-* (cf. Latv. *putns* 'bird' < ? *'chick'; cf. L *pullus*, **c** below). —A similar development is seen in Baltic, as Lith. *árklas* 'plow' < **arəkla-* < **H₂erH₃-tlo-*. But Finnish *kantele* (a kind of musical instrument), a lw. from PBalt. **kantlaⁿ* (as in Latv. *kuokle*, Lith. *kañklės*) proves that the original cluster still remained at the time of Baltic and Finnic contact. A complication is considered in **c**, below.

a. When the usual shape of a word—*saeculō* for example—was metrically impossible in dactylic hexameter, many poets of the classical period (Lucretius for example) substituted forms like *saeclō*. The presence of several such forms on the Monumentum Ancyranum (14 AD), must have a different explanation, however, namely the self-conscious archaizing so often evident in formal epigraphic Latin.

b. Initial **tl-*, like **dl-* (**223.1c**), loses the stop:
L *lātus* 'carried' from **tlātos* < **tl̥H₂-to-* : G τλητός 'endured'; cf. L *tollō* < **tl̥-ne-H₂-*.
PIE **tlokʷ-* 'speak' > L *loquitur* : OIr *du·ttluchur* /du'tluxʷəρʷ/ 1sg. 'ask', *a(d)·tluchedar* /a'tlux'əδəρ/ 3sg. 'gives thanks'.

c. A number of L forms, clearest among which is *pullus* 'the young of any animal; chick(en)' < **put-lo-* (vid.sup.), seem to point to a development of *-ll-* from **-tl-*. It has been proposed that this assimilation occurs across a morpheme boundary (as here), whereas the dissimilation to **-kl-* takes place when there is no boundary. This suggestion has met with some favor, and indeed it reminds one of the development of *dr*, *br*, *mr*, and so on, which assimilate to *-rr-* only across morpheme boundaries (items 4 and 5, below).

Still, though the relevance of O **puklum** (cited above) is open to dispute, it might be seen as a problem for this view.

d. The App.Prob. cites *veclus* and *viclus* as incorrect for *vetulus* 'somewhat old' and *vitulus* 'calf'. These merely show that the change of /tl/ (apparently here the sequence results from syncope) to /kl/ is unremarkable—NB the parallel but independent change seen in Baltic, as exhibited above.

3. **rs* becomes *rr*, simplified to *-r* in final position (237.8).
L *ferre* 'to carry' < **fer-se* < **fer-esi* (553.1; cf. *esse*, *velle*).
L *torreō* 'dry out' < **tors-eyō*, caus. of **ters-* = Brāh. *tarṣáyati* : cf. L *terra* '[dry] land', G τέρσομαι 'dry up'.
L *far*, *farris* 'spelt' < **fars*, **farses* (n. *s*-stem) : U *farsio* 'farrea'.
L *fūr*, *fūris* 'thief' (**fōrs* to **fer-*, carry; **52.3a**) : G φώρ.

a. Historical L *rs* evolves from other clusters, **rss* (215) and **rtt* (e.g. *versus*, 212 and 231.3a); or from syncope, as in *fers* 'you carry' < **feres* (485). These remain.

4. In compounds, **-mr-* becomes *-rr-*: *corrumpō* 'destroy' < **kom-rumpō*. The expected development would be *-mbr-*, which some authorities see in *September* < **septem-ri-*, orig. an adj. 'belonging to the 7th [month]'; but these names of months in *-mber* are better explained otherwise (225.2). A still more problematic development to *-br-* is detected by some in L *hībernus* 'wintry' if from **χeym-eri-no-* parallel to G χειμερινός 'in winter'. But against this view, the thematic stem **ǵheym-^{e}/o-* is not otherwise attested in L, and the loss of **m* from the expected *-mbr-* is troublesome. A better explanation starts with **hiemērnos*, formed from *hiems* 'winter' on the model of **wērnos* 'vernal'; in this form, **m* > **f* (that is, [v]) by dissimilation from the following *-n-*, whence *-b-* (135(**b**)).[1] Cf. L *formīca* 'ant' (if cognate to G μύρμηξ), and, with a less drastic dissimilatory treatment of **m*, L *tenebrae* 'darkness' < **temabrāy* (225.2) < **temH̥-sr-*, cf. Ved. *támisrā-*, Lith. *témti* 'to grow dim' < **temH̥-*.

Initial **mr-* becomes *br-*:
L *brevis* 'short' < **mreχwi-* < **mreǵhu-*. (The zero grade of this adj., **mr̥ǵhú-*, is better attested: G βραχύς, Av. *mərəzu-*, Go. *maurgjan* 'shorten', OE *myrge* 'pleasant' < PGmc. **murgwi-*.)

5. **nr* and **dr* become *rr* in some compounds, while in others the unassimilated form prevails. Thus *irrigō* 'direct water to a place' < **in-regō*, and *arripiō* 'seize' < **ad-rapiō*; but also *inrumpō* 'rush in' (later *irrumpō*), and *adrogō* 'misappropriate' (later *arrogō*).

Elsewhere, **dr* regularly becomes L *tr*:
L *taeter* (< **taetros*) 'foul' : *taedet* 'irks, disgusts'.

---

[1] The appeal to dissimilation is a demerit. Still, in addition to the L examples here, a similar change is known in Low WGmc., for example OE *heofon* 'heaven' and OS *heƀan*; cf. Go. *himins*, NHG *Himmel* (the last showing a different dissimilation, namely of the following *n* to *l*).

L *uter* *i*-st. (< **utris*) 'water-skin' (*ŭ*- confirmed by It. *otre* 'goatskin bottle') continues **ud-ri-* with the root of G ὕδωρ, NE *water*; cf. G ὑδρία 'water pitcher'. Less well known is the analysis of L *vitrum* 'glass' as **wedr-o-* lit. 'water-like'—for the semantics there are a number of parallels. (See **41.2** for *vi-* < **we-*.) These are all medial; no example of PIE **dr-* is known to be reflected in L.

a. The development of *tr* < **dr* is not only unexpected, but seems to contradict the development of **-tr-* to *-dr-* seen in L *quadr-* 'four-' in *quadrupēs* 'animal' and *quadra* 'square' (389.4).

224. GREEK.

1. **mr*, **ml*, **nr* medially become μβρ, μβλ, νδρ; initially βρ-, βλ-, δρ-.
G ἄμβροτος 'immortal', βροτός 'mortal' < **(a-)mrotos* < **(n̥-)mr̥-to-* : Ved. *amŕ̥ta-*, *mr̥tá-*, L *mortuus*, NE *murder*.
G μέμβλωκα perf., βλώσκω pres. 'move' < **mlō-* < **ml̥H₃-* (cf. aor. ἔμολον, and see **106.2**).
G βραχύς 'short' : L *brevis*, Av. *mərəzu-*, PIE **mr̥ǵhu-*.
G ἀνδρός gen.sg. of ἀνήρ 'man' < **anros*. —The only supposed case of initial δρ- < **nr-* is from the same root, namely the entry in Hesychius: δρώψ · ἄνθρωπος. However, whether the etymon of ἀνήρ is **H₂nēr* or **nēr*, the zero grade would be **(H₂)n̥ro-H₃(e)kʷ-*, which would have given G ×ανδρωψ or ×αρωψ, not δρώψ. How the Hesychian form fits into this is unclear.

a. In some compounds νρ becomes ρρ, as συρρέω 'flow together' < **(k)sun-hrewō*, παρρησίᾱ 'openness' < παν-ρησίᾱ lit. 'saying everything'. So ἔρρυθμος beside ἔνρυθμος, though in compounds ἐν- before ρ remains unassimilated, as ἐνράπτω 'sew up'. A difference between the treatment of συν- and ἐν- is observed also in other combinations (σύστασις 'a putting together' but ἔν-στασις 'a beginning'.) The lateness of such assimilations is implied not only by the survival of ἐν- for the most part unchanged, but also by the participation, in the assimilation, of secondary παν- for original παντ-.

b. From inherited *νλ we would expect νδλ parallel to these developments, but there are no examples. For assimilation in compounds, see 2, next.

2. δλ, νλ, and sometimes λν, become λλ.
G ἐλλᾱ́ (Hesych., said to be Laconian) 'chair' < **hed-lā* = L *sella* **223.1**; cf. G ἕδρᾱ, all from **sed-* 'sit'.
G σύλλογος < **(k)sun-logos* 'assembly' (parallel to συρρέω, note **a** above).
G ὄλλῡμι 'destroy' < **olnōmi* (formation as in δείκνῡμι, **472.3**).

a. In πίλναμαι 'draw near', -ν- is restored on the analogy of the type seen in δύναμαι 'am able', σκίδναμαι 'scatter'.

b. There are a number of G forms of obscure[1] or ambiguous etymology in which there is -λλ- in Lesb. and Thess., but elsewhere -λ- with lengthening of a preceding short

[1] For example, Hom. οὖλος 'curly' as if < **wolnos*, that is, a cognate of L *lāna*, OE *wull*, and the rest, 'wool'. The semantics are imaginative, and the form (which must be rewritten **wol̥H₂no-*) can be justified only by means of two questionable sound laws: the one at hand, and the theory that laryngeals drop after resonants in *o*-grade roots.

vowel. Mutatis mutandis, this looks exactly like the behavior of such sequences as inherited σλ, σν, νσ (227.2, 228.1). A widely-held view, however, is that these continue original *-*ln*-, particularly in formally opaque formations (hence not subject to recomposition). In fact, the few forms thus analyzed that are not profoundly obscure admit of better explanations. One of the clearer among the latter is G στήλη 'block, slab', Dor. στᾱ́λᾱ, Lesb. στάλλᾱ, conventionally traced to **stalnā* < **stl̥-neH₂-*, from PIE **stel-* (the root seen in στέλλω 'put in order'). However, on both formal and semantic grounds the form is better taken as a noun in *-*sleH₂*- from a different root, **steH₂-* 'stand': **stH̥₂-sleH₂-* > PG **sta-slā*, the remaining details per 227.2.

GROUPS CONTAINING **s*

LATIN

225. 1. An *s* is lost before most voiced consonants (in compounds before all such); and a preceding vowel, if short, is lengthened (see also 231.3).

L *īdem* nom.sg.m. 'the same' < **is-dem*.

L *iūdex* 'judge' < **yowos-dik-* (72 fn.).

L *nīdus* 'nest' < PIE **ni-sd-o-* (**sed-* 'sit' and **ni-* 'down') : Go. *nists*, OE *nest*, Ved. *nīḍá-* 'resting-place, nest'.

L *bīnī* 'two each' < **dwisnoy* (*bis*, *duo*).

L *aēnus* (often spelled *ahenus*, cf. U **ahesnes**) < **ayesnos* 'brazen' (L *aes* 'bronze' : Ved. *áyas-* n. 'metal', Go. *aiza-smiþa* 'smith'); **88.3d**.

L *prēlum* 'oil press' < **pres-lo-* (though the root in question is obscure: of the principal parts, *premō*, *pressī*, *pressus*, only the second can continue **pres-* directly, though *pressus* could be a replacement of **prestus* on the basis of *pressī*).

L *dīligō* 'pick out, put aside as choice' < **dis-leg-*.

a. Unexpectedly, medial *-*sg*- > L -*rg*- in L *mergō* 'dip', *mergus* 'gull' : Lith. *mazgóti* 'wash', Ved. *majj-* 'sink'. Although this root **mesg-* exhausts the evidence, it seems sound. Across morpheme boundaries, the development is more in accord with expectations: *-*sg*- > L -*g*- with lengthening of the preceding vowel: L *dī-gerō*, 'separate' like *dī-rigō* 'send/make straight' < *dis-*. The idea that a consonant cluster might change more across a morpheme boundary than within a morphologically opaque form, though not without precedent, is peculiar; clusters are more likely to be restored at morpheme boundaries. Perhaps in fact *dīgerō* is merely analogical (to *dī-dō*, *dī-moveō* and the like), rather than the result of a sound law. But *iūglāns* 'walnut' appears to reflect **iovis glāns* (or more accurately **dyowes glands*), namely an ancient calque on G Διὸς βάλανος. If this etymology (from Varro) is correct, a morpheme boundary is after all, contrary to reasonable expectations, a condition for the loss of **s* before *g*. But it is at least as likely that the etymon of *iūglāns* already lacked an -*s* on the first element, in accord with the early tendency for final -*s* to weaken in L (and *deus* is one of the items in which final -*s* is lost with especial frequency, 237.2).

b. L *eōsdem*, *eāsdem* next to *īdem* have had the form of the acc.pl. restored on the basis of the simplex (377.2).

c. As in G (171), initial **sm-*, **sn-*, **sl-* lose the **s-*, though the evidence for all except **sn-* is meager; and for **sr-* see 2, below:

PIE *$sneyg^wh$- (various grades) 'snow' > L *nix*, G νείφει : NE *snow*, Lith. *sniñga*, OIr. *snigid* /sniγ'əθ'/.
PIE *$sneH_2$- > L *nō*, *nāre* 'swim', G νάω 'flow' : U *snata* 'moist', Ved. *snā*- 'get wet, bathe'.
? PIE *smey- > L *mīror* 'wonder' : NE *smile*, Ved. root *smi*- 'smile, blush, become radiant', Latv. *smeju* 'laugh'. (This is the best example for *sm-; the variations in root shape are excessive, and the semantics are only marginally convincing.)
? PIE *sley-mo- > L *līmus* 'mud, mire' : Gmc. *slīm- > NE *slime*, NHG *Schleim*. This is the best example of *sl-, but it is at most a possibility: an equally convincing etymology connects L *līmus* with OE *lám*, NE *loam*, NHG *Lehm*, all from *s*-less *loymo- (**58b**).

2. Medial *sr becomes L -*br*-:
L *fūnebris* 'funereal' < **fūnes-ri*- (*fūnus* n. *s*-stem 'funeral'; cf. *fūnes-tus* 'mournful', *fūner-eus* 'funereal', **173**).
L *cōnsobrīnus*, -*a* 'cousin' (on the mother's side, in fact *'mother's sister's child') < **kom-swesr-īno*- with zero grade of **swesor*- 'sister' (L *soror*).
L *muliebris* 'womanly' < **mulies-ri*-, an adjective from *mulier* (apparently an *s*-stem; see **299a**).
L *September* < **septemembris* (by haplology) < **septem-mens-ri*- 'pertaining to the seventh month (*mēnsis*). Similarly *November* and *December*; *Octōber* is an analogical creation (as is the **oktembrem* of various Romance languages).
L *tenebrae* pl.tant. 'darkness', with *n* by dissimilation < **temabrā*- **temasrā*- < PIE *$tem\underset{\circ}{H}sreH_2$- : Ved. *támisrās* pl.tant.

a. This seemingly surprising development has a simple explanation, if *s first became *θ before *r and thereby fell together with PItal. *θ < PIE *dh (**135**). Thereafter, all *θ became L *b* before *r*, per **147.2**.

b. Patterning would lead us to expect that initial *sr- > PItal. *θr- > L *fr*-, but there are no unproblematic examples:
L *frīgus* 'cold' (and derivatives) : G ῥῖγος 'frost', ῥῑγόω 'am cold'. The forms agree closely (< *srīg-?), but there are no other cognates.
PIE *srew- 'flow' is by contrast a widely-attested root (cf. OE *stréam*, G ῥέ(ϝ)ω 'flow', Ved. *srávanti* 3pl.). It seemingly is not found in L, unless L *fluō* 'flow', *flūmen* 'river' are a contamination of expected **fruwō*, **frūmen* (= OE *stréam*) by the synonymous **pluwō* (source of L *pluit* 'rains') < PIE *plew- 'flow, float'.
L *frāgum* 'strawberry' is a tantalizing datum; it might be connected with G ῥᾱ́ξ, ῥᾱγός (also ῥώξ, ῥωγός) 'grape' (Mediterranean *srāg-? PIE *$sreH_2g$-/*$sroH_2g$-?), and perhaps OE *stréa-wise* 'strawberry'. The OE word, which is not paralleled elsewhere in Gmc., agrees semantically with L better than G ῥᾱ́ξ does, but the G form agrees better formally; OE *stréa* requires PGmc. **strawa*-, which could be got from something like *$srag^wh$- or *sraghu-, which are incompatible with the L forms.

226. NASAL + *s*.

1. L *ns* in medial position, from all sources (*-*nts*-, *-*ntt*-, *-*ns*-) lasted into the period of written records and remained the normal spelling. But its frequent omission in inscriptions (the very common COSVL is a prime example) and lengthening of the preceding vowel (**81.2**) indicate that it was lost in common speech even at an early period; this agrees with Romance evidence, where there is no trace of an -*n*- in words reflecting classical L -*ns*-: L *mēnsis* 'month' but It. *mese*, Sp. *mes*, Fr. *mois*. The App.Prob. dispar-

ages *mesa* 'table' and *asa* 'handle'. But spelling without etymological *-n-* was more or less accepted in certain categories, notably the adverbs *totiē(n)s* 'so often', *deciē(n)s* 'ten times', and the like; adjectives in *-ē(n)sis*; and stray forms such as *sēmestris* (*sēmēnstris*) 'half-yearly'.

a. The fluctuation of spelling (and of pronunciation) of *-ns-* led to the introduction of spurious *n* into some words: *thēnsaurus* for *thēsaurus*, lw. from G θησαυρός 'treasury', and the App.Prob. lists *occansio* 'opportunity' among the errors of the vulgar. Later evidence of the same phenomenon is afforded by Spanish *prensa* '(printing) press'.

b. The suffix *-ōsus* is thought by some to be from **-onso-* < **-wonsso-* < **-wont-to-* (incorporating two well-established PIE suffixes); but this theory depends on a loss of the **n* so early that it leaves no orthographic trace, which is implausible. The same reservations about chronology apply to L *sēs-* 'half' in *sēsqui-* 'one and a half' and *sēstertius* 'half-denarius' (lit. 'two and a half [asses]'), possibly from **sēms-* by syncope of the form seen independently as L *sēmis* 'half' (noun). One might salvage this explanation of *sēs-* if it is plausible that the loss of a nasal after an ORIGINALLY long vowel (in contradistinction to the secondarily lengthened vowels of the *totiēns* and *mēnsa* sort, **81.2**) was significantly earlier than its similar loss after originally short vowels. And in that case *-ōsus* might reflect **-ōns(s)us*, though an original **ō* (rather than **ŏ*) in this form would be hard to explain.

c. Possibly in forms like COSVL ~ *cōnsul* the vowel before the etymological nasal was nasalized. But that would not explain the omission of the -N-: regardless of the phonetic details of the contrast, there would still BE a contrast, between [o:s] and [õ:s].[1] Nor is there any actual evidence for it, such as remarks by grammarians or rhetoricians. Probably nothing more was involved than a hesitation between omitting the *-n-* in casual speech and pronouncing it plainly (as before any other consonant) in careful or refined speech. At an earlier period, pronouncing an /n/ was merely conservative; later on it would have amounted to a spelling pronunciation, like the /h/ sometimes heard in *forehead* and *vehicle*.

2. **ms*. The development of **-ms-* in L is seen in *altrin-secus* 'on the other side', *intrin-secus* 'inwardly' with *-ĩn-s-*, containing the **-im-* seen in *utrimque* 'from both sides'. Similarly, **kom-* before **s* > *cōn-* (*cōnsul*, *cōnstō* 'stand still'); and *ānsa* 'handle' probably reflects **am-* (seen also in *amplus* 'comprehensive' < **am-lo-*, root **H₂em-* 'grasp'). For L *membrum* 'limb' < **mēmsrom* see **225.2**. The retention of *-m-* with excrescence of *-p-* seen in perf. *sūmpsī* < **-msay* is analogical.

In L, final *-ms* was restored in final position by leveling analogy in *hiems* 'winter' (obl. stem *hiem-*).

3. Word-final Ital. **-ns* loses the nasal, with lengthening of a preceding short vowel: acc.pls. *-ōs* < PItal. **-ons*; *-ēs* < PreL **-ens* < ***-m̥s*; *-ūs* < **-uns*; *-ās* < **-ams*. See also **237.5**.

GREEK

227. 1. σδ (IE **sd* **[zd]*) is represented by ζ, pronounced [zd] in Att.-Ion. (**201**).

---

[1] In most varieties of American English, *can't* is phonetically [kʰæ̃t], that is, it has no [n]. But it is hard to believe that even a beginning speller would decide on that account that *cat* and *can't* should be spelled alike.

PIE **osdo-* or **H_3esdo-* > G ὄζος 'branch' : Go. *asts*, Arm. *ost.*
Ἀθήναζε 'to Athens' < **at^h^ēnans-de*(228.3) acc.pl. (cf. Hom. οἶκόν-δε 'homewards').

2. Intervocalic σρ, σλ, σμ, and σν lose σ; but what else happens depends on the dialect:

In Att. a preceding short vowel is lengthened; ε, ο become ει, ου (spurious diphthongs). The lengthening is prior to the Att.-Ion. change of ᾱ to η (54), so ἄσν (for example) > ην.

Lengthening also occurs in Dor., but there the mid vowels fall together with original **ē*, **ō.*

In Aeol. (Thess., Lesb.) and often in Hom., the resonant is lengthened—ρρ, λλ, μμ, νν—while preceding vowel is unchanged.

Att. τρήρων 'timorous' < **trasrōn* (this much-cited form is not without problems; the existence of a root **tres-/*tr̥s-* 'tremble' is certain, but **-ron-* is not a legitimate adjective suffix; furthermore, ρᾱ should not become Att. ρη, 54, NB Att. ῥᾱχίᾱ next to Ion. ῥηχίη 'surf').

Att. χῑλιοι 'thousand' (ῑ enigmatic; **76d**, 396), Ion. χειλιοι, Lesb., Thess. χελλιοι, all < **k^h^eslioi* < PIE **ǵhesliyo-* : Ved. *sa-hásra-*, Pers. *hazar.*

PIE **H_1es-mi* 'I am' > G εἰμί, Dor. ἠμί, Lesb. ἔμμι (cf. Hom. inf. ἔμμεναι) : Ved. *ásmi*, OE *eom.*

G σελήνη 'moon', Dor. σελᾱ́νᾱ, Lesb. σελάννᾱ are from **selas-nā.* This σέλας n. 'bright light' has uncertain outside connections; the usual etymon, PIE **swelH-* 'gleam', is well attested, but G σ- < **sw-* is hard to accept, cf. 171.

a. Compounds and augmented or reduplicated forms of words with initial ῥ-, λ-, μ-, ν- from original **sr-* and so on (171) only rarely show this normal development of intervocalic **sr* and so on, such as Att. εἴληφα < **he-slāp^h^a* (perf. of λαμβάνω 'seize'; see 517.2), εἵμαρται 'is allotted' < **he-smartai* (perf. pass. of μείρομαι 'get one's share'). Most Att. forms are like those seen in 171; that is, forms like ἀναλάμβανω 'take up' are manifestly the result of imitation of such models as ἀναλέγω 'gather up' (root **leg-*), and such patterns as provided by μέμονα (**men-*) 'yearn for' and ἔλιπον (**leykʷ-*) 'left over', namely formations whose details are not complicated by changes in consonant clusters.

b. In Att. ἐσμέν 'we are' (for expected εἰμέν < PIE **H_1s-men*, a form actually attested in Hom.), the shape εσ- was restored under the influence of ἐστί and ἐστέ; similarly in τετέλεσμαι after τετέλεσται, pluperf. of τελέω 'attain'; πέπεισμαι after πέπεισται, perf.pass. of πείθω 'persuade', 212.

c. Any -σν- which arose by composition in the historical period or by analogical restoration of σ became -νν-, as in Πελοπόννησος, etymologically the phrase Πέλοπος νῆσος 'island of Pelops', or Att. ἕννῡμι 'clothe' from *ἕσνῡμι with σ restored from aor. ἕσσα (Hom.) and similar forms, all < PIE **wes-* (see 472.2); Ion. εἵνῡμι shows the undisturbed development of **-sn-*.

228. G **ns.* 1. ORIGINAL intervocalic **-ns-* gives the same result as **-sn-* (227.2 above).

G ἔκρῑνα 'picked out', Lesb. ἔκριννα < **ekrin-sa* aor. of κρῑ́νω < **krin-yō* (203.1).

G ἔφηνα 'appeared', Dor. ἐφᾱνα < **ep^h^an-sa* aor. of φαίνω < **p^h^an-yō* (203.2).

2. SECONDARY INTERVOCALIC νσ, in which σ comes from **ky*, **ty* (**199**), apical stop + σ (**215**), or τ before ι (**148**), remains unchanged in some dialects. But in most dialects the ν is lost, with lengthening of the preceding vowel in Att.-Ion. and some others, but with diphthongization in Lesb. These developments, then, unlike original **ns*, postdate the change of **ā* to Att.-Ion. η.

PreG **pant-yă* 'all' fem. > Thess. πανσα, πᾶσα, Lesb. παῖσα.

Dat.pl. **pʰeront-si* 'carrying' > φέρονσι, φέρουσι, Lesb. φέροισι.

3pl. φέροντι 'they carry' > φέρονσι, φέρουσι, Lesb. φέροισι.

a. A third generation of νσ is seen in Att. abstracts in -σις like ὕφανσις 'weaving' (ὑφαίνω). These were formed later than either of the preceding, either de novo or by recomposition, and retain νσ unchanged.

3. νσ + consonant (which includes νζ [nzd]; see **201**) loses the ν WITHOUT lengthening of the preceding vowel.

G κεστός 'embroidered' from **kenstos* < *κεντ-το- (κεντέω 'stick, stitch').

G σύστασις 'putting together' < **(k)sun-statis* (ἵστημι).

G σύζυγος 'yoked together' < **(k)sun-zdugos* (ζυγόν).

G δεσπότης 'master of the house(hold)' < **denspotis* < PIE **dems potis* (**272.1**). The G stem was remodeled in the process; but the development of *-*ns*- shows that the phrase had become a phonological word by the time of the change. Cf. Ved. *dámpati*- (occasionally *pátir dán*).

G Ἀθήναζε 'to Athens' = Ἀθηνασ-δε (**201**) < **atʰēnans-de*.

a. In compounds of ἐν-, ν is restored by analogy, as ἔνστασις 'a beginning' (cf. **224.1a**).

4. FINAL -νς shows two developments. In close combination with a word beginning with a consonant it was subject to the loss of ν without vowel lengthening, in accord with 3, above. Otherwise it had the same history as the secondary intervocalic -νσ-.

Acc.pl.fem. *-*āns* (> *-*ăns* per Osthoff's Law, **63.2**) > -ᾱς.

In Cretan we find actual doublets, as acc.pl. τος καδεστανς and τονς ελευθερονς, but in most dialects one type or the other was generalized. The alternant usually favored was the original τονς, τανς, which however later became τούς/τώς, τᾱ́ς (Lesb. τοίς, ταίς) per 6, below.

5. The different results of νσ described above may be surveyed below:

	**epʰansa*	**pantyă*	**pʰeronti*	**kenstos*	**tons*
Lesb.	ἔφαννα	πανσα (Arc.)	φέρονσι	κέστος	τόνς, τός
Dor.	ἔφᾱνα			κεστός	τόνς
Att.	ἔφηνα	πᾶσα	φέρουσι	κεστός	τούς, τώς, τοίς

6. In G, final *-*ms* first became -νς, then (in Att.-Ion.) -ς, with compensatory lengthening of a preceding short vowel: PIE **sem-s* 'one' nom.sg. m. (cf. L *semel*) > G ἑνς (Cret.), εἷς. This ἑνς, together with ἕν nom./acc.n. < **sem* (**389.1B**), was the basis for the replacement of medial *-*m*- through-

out the paradigm: ἑνός, ἑνί, ἕνα for expected ×ἑμός and the like. The same remodeling is seen in G χθών, χθονός 'earth' < PIE *dhǵhōms (Ved. kṣā́s), gen. *dhǵhom-os. But the nom.sg. should not be a fulcrum for any such remodeling, and it is noteworthy that the genuine outcome from *dhǵhōms would have been ×χθούς (parallel to εἶς) < *k^ht^hons < *k^ht^hōns. A look at χθών reveals the real nature of the remodeling, namely the absorption of the unusual m-stems into the commonplace n-stem pattern (286)—total in the case of χθών, partial in the case of εἶς. (If 'one' had coalesced with the n-stems, the nom.sg.m. would have been ×ἤν, like ποιμήν 'herdsman'.)

229. λσ, ρσ show a double treatment.

1. λσ, ρσ remain (with the detail that ρσ becomes ρρ in Att.).
G ἄλσος 'grove', τέλσον 'end of a furrow', ἔκελσα aor. of κέλλω 'drive on', ὦρσα aor. of ὄρνῡμι 'stir up'.
Ion κόρση 'the side of the head, temple', Att. κόρρη; G ἄρσην 'man' (cf. Ved. vṛ́ṣan- 'bull', L verrēs 'boar'), Att. ἄρρην; G θάρσος 'courage', Att. θάρρος (cf. G θρασύς 'bold').

2. λσ, ρσ become Aeol. λλ, ρρ, but in the remaining dialects become λ, ρ with compensatory lengthening of the preceding vowel. This development parallels the behavior of νσ (228).
G ἔστειλα, Lesb., Thess. ἔστελλα < *e-stel-sa, aor. of στέλλω 'put'.
G ἔφθειρα, Lesb. ἔφθερρα* < *ἔφθερ-σα, aor. of φθείρω 'spoil'.

a. The earliest Attic inscriptions exhibit the θάρρος development, and forms like θάρσος in early Attic writers, like -σσ- for native -ττ- (199b), are due to Ionic influence. Even so, Att. θηρσί dat.pl. of θήρ 'wild animal', κάθαρσις abstract noun in -σις built to καθαίρω 'cleanse', probably admit of a different explanation, namely leveling analogy. Analogy is sometimes mooted as the explanation for surviving λσ (item 1), but the forms cited above are typical: G ἄλσος has no even remotely certain etymology; and although G τέλσον might continue PIE *k^wel- 'turn', a *-so- formation is hardly self-explanatory. The only genuinely lucid forms, ἔκελσα and ὦρσα, are aorists and hence members of a form class in which etymological -σ- was widely reimported into forms where it had been lost via sound laws.

GROUPS OF THREE OR MORE CONSONANTS

230. GREEK. Many groups which are simplified in L (231) remain unchanged in G, as ρκτ, λκτ, ρξ, λξ. The more important changes are in groups containing σ.

1. Apical stop + σ becomes σ before or after another consonant.
G πάσχω, with transfer of aspiration, from *pat^h-skō (cf. ἔπαθον).
Dat.pl. φέρονσι (Att.-Ion. φέρουσι) from *p^herontsi.
G νύξ 'night', dat.pl. νυξί, from *nukt-s, *nukt-si < *nok^wt- (gen.sg. νυκτός).

2. σ is lost between two consonants in most groups.
Middle infinitives in -σθαι:
G γεγράφθαι from *$gegrap^h$-st^hai 'scratch'; ἐστάλθαι from *estal-st^hai 'place'; λελέχθαι from *lelek-st^hai (λέγω 'gather'); ἐσπάρθαι from *estar-st^hai (σπείρω

'sow'). So also πεφάνθαι for expected **pep^{h}ast^{h}ai* (228.3), with -ν- restored by analogy with forms such as πέφανται.

Note that the development of σδ, written ζ, is the same: to PIE **werǵ-* 'work' are built G ἕρδω 'do, make', fut. ἕρξω, and a doublet ῥέζω of the same meaning. The starting point was the PIE stem **wr̥ǵ-y^e/o-*, a formation reflected in Av. *vərəzyeiti*, Go. *waurkeiþ*. The first stage, PreG **wragyō* and **wargyō*, became PG **wreǰō* and **werǰō* per 200 (somewhere along the line the vocalism of both was altered, partly owing to the prevailing pattern of thematic presents but probably also influenced by specific forms like **wergon* 'work'). Thus straightforwardly ῥέζω; but as ζ stood for [zd] (201), **werzdō* > ϝερδω, ἕρδω in accord with the sound law governing σ between consonants.

a. In the groups **ksn*, **ksm*, **ksl* the **s* was lost, with aspiration of the **k*:
G λύχνος 'lantern' < **luksnos* : L *lūna* 'moon' < **lowksneH$_2$* = Av. *raoxšnā-* 'lantern'.
G τέχνη 'art, skill, science' < **teksnā* (cf. L *texō* 'weave', Ved. *tákṣan-* 'craftsman'; cf. 235.1a).
G πλοχμός 'braid' < **ploksmos* (πλέκω 'plait').

Similarly, in groups like **pst*, **kst* the **s* was lost with aspiration of both stops:
G ἑφθός (Hdt.) 'boiled' < **hepstos* (ἕψω 'boil').
NWG ἐχτός < **ekstos*. The usual G ἐκτός is from an ancient, already *s*-less form; the NWG form must be a recomposition based on ἐξ.

These developments were often imagined to be related somehow to the development of spiritus asper from **s*. But that development significantly does not take place after stops, and besides the clusters in question seem to be attested as such in Myc., if a form like *a$_3$-ka-sa-ma* acc.pl. is for *aiksmans* 'spear points' (cf. Hom. αἰχμή). The correct explanation is hinted at by the early Att. epigraphic evidence for /k^{h}s/ and /p^{h}s/ (ΧΣ, ΦΣ), as in ΕΔΟΧΣΕ for ἔδοξε (213a). This seems to have been a temporary state of affairs—neither the grammarians nor the reflexes of NG point to anything but plain stops before /s/—but if the loss of interconsonantal **-s-* took place during a time when preceding stops were regularly aspirated as well as voiceless, then the results would be as seen: **ksm* > **k^{h}sm* > χμ.

3. When **s* stood between stops of the same point of articulation, the first stop was lost by dissimilation.
G λάσκω 'make a loud noise' < **lak-skō* (aor. ἔλακον).
G βλάσφημος 'evil-speaking' < **blaps-p^{h}āmos* (βλάβος n. 'harm, damage').

Note that the sound law thus formulated accounts for the G reflexes of apical + apical clusters, 212.

a. The preposition ἐξ would normally become ἐκ before most consonants (per 2), and ἐς before a dorsal stop (per 3). But leveling effaced the original distribution: ἐκ was generalized before all consonants in Att.-Ion, ἐς was similarly generalized in some of the other dialects.

231. LATIN. Consonant clusters were considerably more transformed in L than in G. Out of the great variety of changes the more important may be grouped as follows.[1]

---

[1] The ingredients for the changes shown below are in most cases based on etymological reasoning, but there are actual attestations of unreduced forms: epigraphic (IOVXMENTA = *iūmenta* 'pack-horses', LOSNA = *lūna* 'moon'), textual (OL *ferctum* 'a kind of sacrificial cake' next to *fertum*), and in the grammarians (Fest. *cesna* = *cēna* 'dinner').

1. Stop + *s* becomes *s* before another consonant; and if the latter is voiced the *s* drops too, with compensatory lengthening of the preceding vowel (in accord with **225.1**).
L *inlūstris*, *illūstris* 'brilliant' < **in-lowkstris* (cf. **209**).
L *lūna* 'moon' < **lowksnā* : Av. *raoχšnā-* 'lantern'.
L *suspendō* 'hang up', *suscipiō* 'take up', *sustineō* 'hold up' from **sups-pendō*, **-kap-*, **-ten-*.
L *sūmō* 'take, buy' < **susmō* < **sups-(e)mō*.
L *ēdūcō* 'draw out' < **esdewkō* < **eks-dewkō*.
L *asportō* 'carry off' < **aps-portō*.
L *ostendō* 'exhibit' < **ops-tendō*.
L *ēveniō* 'come forth' < **esweniō* < **eks-wenyō*.
L *sēvirī* 'committee of six' < **seswiroy* < **seks-wiroy*; similarly *sēdecim* 'sixteen' < **sesdikem* (**71.2**, **390**) < **seks-dekem*.

a. The same development applies to *ns*: L *trādūcō* next to *trānsdūcō* 'lead over'.

b. In prepositional compounds recomposition is very frequent. So *subscrībō*, *abstineō*, *abscīdō*, *obstō*; and *ex-* (restored) was regular before a voiceless stop in contrast to *ē-* before voiced consonants, hence *extendō*, *expono*. For letter *-b-* in place of expected *-p-*, see **210b**.

c. Sequences arising later through the effects of syncope are hardly changed. Thus *xt* in *dexter* 'right' < **dexiteros* (but even here cf. Sab. *destr-*). L *mixtus* perhaps reflects **miscitos* via metathesis (since expected *mistus* < *-*skt-* also occurs). L *textus*, *-ī* 'woven' and *textus*, *-ūs* 'fabric' have reimported *x* from *texō*, *tēxī*; similar reimportation explains *sextus* 'sixth' (from *sex*). The gens name *Sextius* next to *Sestius* is probably a genuine old spelling (which affected the pronunciation, like the usual pronunciation of the NE names spelled *St Clair* and *St Leger* next to genuine—that is, phonologically regular—*Sinclair* and *Salenger*). See **209**.

2. A stop is lost between a liquid and another consonant in most such groups. So in *rkt*, *rtk*, *lkt* (but *rpt*, *lpt* remain[1]), *rdn*, *rkn*, *rkm*, *rpm*, *lkm*, *lgm*, *lpm*, and also *rks* and *lks* (though these remain when final, spelled *-rx*, *-lx*); apparently also in *rts*, *lts*, but these were considered under **215**.
L *tortus* 'twisted' < **tork^{w}tos*, *torsī* perf. < **tork^{w}say*, *tormentum* 'windlass, winch' < **tork^{w}mentom* (root in *torqueō* 'twist').
L *Mārcus* (= O *mamercus* (Fest.)) < **mārtkos* < **māwort(V)-ko-*.
L *quernus* 'oaken' < **k^{w}erkno-* (*quercus* 'oak', PIE **perk^w-*).
L *ultus* 'avenged' < **olktos*, pple. of *ulcīscor*.
L *ornāre* 'adorn' < **ordnāre* (a doublet of *ordināre*).
L *mulsī* 'stroked' < **molksay*, perf. of *mulceō*. (But the pple. *mulsus* continues no ancient cluster; it is analogical to *mulsī*.)
L *sarmen* (*sarmentum*) 'twigs, loppings' < **sarpmen-*; cf. *sarptus* 'pruned', *sarpō* 'prune'.

---

[1] Hence *carptim* 'in pieces', *serptum* 'to creep' (supine of *serpō*), *scalptor* 'engraver'. But *p* seems to have been lost in common speech even here, on the evidence of epigraphic forms like SCVLTVS 'carved'.

L *fulmen* 'lightning', *fulsit* 'it lightened' < **folgmen, *folksīt* cf. *fulgit* 'lightens', *fulgur* 'lightning'.
L *pulmentum* 'victuals' < **pelpmentom* (cf. *pulpa* 'flesh' < **pelpā* via **42.5**; cf. U *pelmner* gen.sg. 'food').

a. The expected outcomes were sometimes disturbed by leveling. So *mulctus* 'milked' (*mulgeō*) and *mulctrum* 'milking pail' were as it were reassembled from components of **multus* < **molktos* and **mulcrum* < **molk-trom*. This may be the real explanation of *carptim* and the other forms mentioned in the footnote on p. 220.

But the survival of isolated *mulctō* 'punish' denom. based on *mulcta* 'punishment', alongside expected *multō*, *multa*, where leveling cannot be the explanation, may result from spelling pronunciations of conservatively-written legal terms.

3. In the groups *rst*, *rsk*, the liquid is lost; in similar clusters where the *s* is before a voiced consonant, as in *rsd* and *rsn*, the *s* is lost instead, probably via **-rzd-*, **-rzn-*.
L *tostus* 'dried' < **torstos* (? < **torsitos*, pple. of *torreō* < **torseyoH₂*, **456.2A**).
L *poscō* 'ask' < **porskō* < **porkskō* < **pr̥k-sḱe/o-* : Ved. *pr̥cchati*, OHG *forscōn* (cf. L *precor* 'entreat', *procus* 'suitor').
L *hordeum* 'barley' < **horsdeyom* < **ghorsd-* : NHG *Gerste*.
L *perna* 'ham' < **persnā* : Ved. *pā́rṣṇi-* 'heel', Go. *fairzna*, NHG *Ferse*.

a. As in *rst*, *rsk*, so also in *rss* (from **-rtᵗt-* from PIE **-rt-t-*, **212**) the *r* was lost. But in most words it was restored by analogy; the resulting *rss* then became *rs*, as in *vorsus* and compounds replacing **vossus* < PIE **wr̥t-to-*. The original outcome is attested in: *dossum* 'back' (the PRom. form, Fr. *dos*, It. *dosso*) beside *dorsum*; *rūsus* (for **rūssus*, **232.2**) 'backward' beside *rursus*; and notably *prōsa*, in the specialized use *prōsa ōrātiō* 'prose', beside *prōrsa* 'straightforward'.

b. The group *rtsn* occurs in **kertsnā* from **kert-* 'cut'; this ultimately yields L *cēna* 'dinner' < *cesna* (Fest.) < **kessnā* < **kerssnā* (something like the last actually seen in O **kersnu**). Contrast *perna* 'ham' < **persnā*, above.

4. *nkt*, *nkn*, *ngn*. L *quīntus* 'fifth' from *quīnctus*, the two forms surviving side by side. But forms showing analogical restoration, like *sānctus* 'holy' and *iūnctus* 'joined', ousted the regular forms. To be sure, forms like *santus* are attested—but only late, and they are better ascribed to a later round of simplification.

Leveling cannot account for *cūnctus* 'whole' or *cūnctor* 'delay' (and derivatives), both of which were synchronically opaque. It is notable that in no case is the dorsal stop lost after a back vowel, and that may have been a condition of the change. If so, *iūnctus*, *sānctus* and so on would be the regular forms, not analogical recreations.

L *quīnī* 'five apiece' < **kʷinkʷnoy* (*quīnque*), with vowel lengthening as before *nct*, *nx* (**81.2**).
L *cōnīveō* (**cōnn-*, **222.2a**) 'lower (the eyelids); overlook' from **kom-kneyweyō* : Go. *hneiwan* 'bow'.
L *ignōscō*, 'overlook' *cognōscō* 'become acquainted with' from *in-*, *com-* plus **gnōskō* (**220a**).

a. L *inquit* 'says' (**490.2**) is generally etymologized as **in-skʷet(i)* (root **sekʷ-* 'say'), but this derivation has been questioned from time to time: as untidy as the development of various clusters is in L, there is just enough pattern to hint that **isquit* or **īsquit* would be likelier outcomes of **insk*$^{(w)}$-. See **490.2a** for further discussion.

SHORTENING OF LONG ('DOUBLE') CONSONANTS

232. 1. G σσ, whether original or from apical stop + σ or from **ty*, **t*^{h}*y* (per the first palatalization, **196**), was simplified after a consonant, a diphthong, or a long vowel, and when final. Between vowels -σσ- remains in many dialects, but becomes -σ- in Att. and later Ion., Homer having both σσ and σ. See also **215** and, for original σσ, cf. dat.pl. γένεσ-σι, Hom. -εσσι and -εσι, Att. -εσι.

2. L long consonants, whether original or the result of assimilation or other changes, shorten after a diphthong or long vowel. This is of particular significance in the case of *ss*: whether original, from apical stop + *s* (**215**), or from apical stop + apical stop (**212**), *ss* > *s* after a consonant, diphthong, or long vowel, and when final. As an example of original -*ss*-: *hausī* 'I drew out' from **haussay* (perf. to *hauriō* from **hausiō*) in contrast to *gessī* 'I did' from **gessay* (*gerō* from **gesō*).

After a long vowel or diphthong the shortening was late, -*ss*- surviving into the Augustan period. Quintilian states that *caussa* and *cāssus* were the spellings of Cicero's time. The Monumentum Ancyranum of Augustus has CLAVSVM beside CAVSSA and CLAVSSVM suggesting that by that date the pronunciation -*ss*- was obsolete or old-fashioned.

Note that because this shortening postdates L rhotacism (**173**), the resulting intervocalic -*s*- remains unaltered.

a. The -*ss*- persisted in the perf.act.infin. -*āsse*, -*īsse* under the supporting influence of the fuller form in -*āvisse*, -*īvisse* and functional equivalents like *monuisse*.

b. In a number of cases, etymological -*ss*- > -*s*- after an originally short vowel, with lengthening of the vowel. This is mainly seen in verbs whose participle has been influenced by the vowels of the present and, more importantly, the perfect stems; so to *fundō* 'pour' and *ūtor* 'use' (**oyt*-) the expected pples **fussus* and **issus* have been dislodged by *fūsus*, *ūsus* (whether or not via **fūssos*, **ūssos*) under the influence of *fūdī*, *ūtī* (**81.3**).

3. Alone among long consonants in L, -*ll*- remains even after a diphthong or a long vowel, as *mīlle*, *nūllus*. But even here, a late shortening occurs in *mīlia* 'thousands' from *mīllia* (which is still the spelling of the Mon. Ancyr.), and *paulum* from *paullum* 'a little'. Cf. also *vīlicus* 'steward' beside *vīlla* 'estate'. The explanation for these scattered exceptions to the general rule is unknown.

4. For shortening of -*NN*- after a diphthong or long vowel, see **222.2a**.

5. In L, a long consonant shortens without other effect after a short vowel in a number of words: *mamilla* 'breast' (dim. of *mamma*), *canālis* 'channel' (*canna* 'reed'), *farīna* 'meal, flour' (*farr*- < **fars*- 'spelt'), *omittō* 'lay aside' (*om-mittō* from *ob*-), *curūlis* 'relating to a chariot' (*currus*), *ofella* 'morsel' (dim. of *offa*), *polenta* 'barley-groats' (*pollen* 'fine flour'), and some others. Theories

about the conditions for this shortening are all undermined by counter-examples, or fail to account for more than a few of the forms. More than one phenomenon may be at stake here.

LENGTHENING OF CONSONANTS

This phenomenon is often referred to as gemination *or* doubling; *such terms are inspired by the usual written representation (G* ἄλλος *'other', for example) of what are in phonetic fact* LONG *consonants.*

233. GREEK. The second G palatalization (198–207) included among its effects a lengthening of the consonant preceding the **y*. In one case, -λλ- < **-ly-* (204), the length remained after depalatalization. A feature of length also persisted, though the phonetics were much altered, in the sounds -*ττ*- and -*σσ*- which continue **-k$^{(w)(h)}$y-* and **-t$^{(h)}$y-* (199).

SYNIZESIS. Sporadically, in a development particularly characteristic of Aeolic dialects but also found in Homer, Attic, and (most significantly) Mycenaean, a short front vowel before a back vowel lost its syllabicity and became [y]. Such a synizesis is sometimes revealed in Homeric scansion: *σῡκέαι* 'fig-trees' is scanned in two syllables (*σῡκyαῖ*), and the combining element *χαλκεο-* 'brazen-' is scanned likewise (*χαλκyο-*). This new post-consonantal *y* proved no more durable than its predecessors, but the resulting clusters develop differently from the earlier palatalizations (195–207). When the sound preceding the newly-arisen *-y-* was a resonant or *-σ-*, the consonant was lengthened and the glide lost. (This is reminiscent of the West Germanic consonant gemination.) Thus Hom. *πολλάκι(ς)* 'often' and the thematic forms of *πολυ-* (*πολλο-*, *πολλᾱ-*), as explained in 341. So also epigraphic Thess. *κυρρον* (= *κῡ́ριον* 'master') and *μνασσα* (= Μνασέα); and Lesb. (Sapph.) *πέρροχος* 'superior' (= *περίοχος*). Thess. inscriptions sometimes show gemination and the glide together, as *πανσαννιαιος*.

The clearest examples in Att. are *στερρός* (= *στερεός* 'stiff'); and Βορρᾶς 'north wind' corresponding to Βορέᾱς via *Βορyᾶς. Less widely recognized is *πολλό-* 'many' < **πολyό-* < **poleo-* < **polewo-* (341). Most interesting are the words in *γενν-*, as *γεννῆται* 'heads of families', *γεννητός* 'begotten', which ultimately all grew from a formation **geneā-* via **γενyᾱ-*. These show that the developments in question—both the change of **e* to *y* and its eventual loss—must have been very early, as it predates the Attic reversion of **eǣ* to *εᾱ* (55). (Note that Βορρᾶς < Βορέᾱς is not a problem for this view: the -*ᾱ*- was always in a 'reversion environment' no matter when *ε* became *y* or the latter coalesced with the preceding *ρ*.)

The Myc. attestations confirm that these developments are of some antiquity. Given the ambiguities of the Myc. writing system, gemination in the manner of Βορρᾶς would be hard to detect, but assibilation phenomena are patent. So Myc. *su-za* 'fig trees' (*sūčai* or the like) < **sūkyā-* (*σῡκέᾱ-*) and *ka-za* 'brazen' (*k^{h}alčā* or the like) < **k^{h}alkyā-* < **k^{h}alke(y)ā-*). These forms have long been recognized, but the stems in question have been assigned to the devī-type (268), that is, **sūkyă*, **kʰalkyă*. Such an analysis accounts for the palatalization, but not only are there are no forms corresponding to devī-derivatives for either of these stems in any other G dialect, there is no evidence otherwise for devī-type fem. stems in G built to *o*-stem adjectives (χαλκός 'copper'). It is better to connect the Myc. forms with the disyllabic scansion vouchsafed in Hom., noted above, of σῦκέαι and χαλκεο-.

234. Latin. Certain L words show lengthening of a consonant, with shortening of the preceding vowel if long.

L *Iuppiter* (the approved spelling) from *Iūpiter* < **dyew-pH̥₂ter* voc. 'sky-father' (327).

L *littera* for etym. *lītera*, OL *leitera* < **leyt-* 'scratch'.

L *mittō* 'send' for **mītō* ?

a. In several cases, a long-consonant form is known from inscriptions or graffiti, next to literary forms with a short one (LITTVS 'shore' once for usual *lītus*, SVCCVS 'thick fluid' for usual *sūcus*). The grammarian Consentius (5th century AD) faults *tottus* for *tōtus*. This pattern of attestation suggests that the long-consonant versions were low class, but interestingly the Romance reflexes generally point to the etymologically correct version with long vowel and short consonant.

b. For **tw* > **ttw* in *quattuor* 'four', PRom. **battere* 'strike', and epigraphic forms like ACQVA and FILLIVS, see 185.4.

c. Long consonants not resulting from morphological combination are commonly found in two classes of words, which are often spoken of as if connected somehow: more or less abusive epithets, and affectionate or hypocoristic forms of names. Most of these forms are in any case of very uncertain etymology, so perhaps the term 'lengthening' pretends to more knowledge than we have.

In the first category are *cuppes* 'sweet-toothed', *lippus* 'blear-eyed', *suppus* 'on all fours' (also as a sexual term), *gibber* 'hunch-backed', νάννος 'dwarf', ψελλός 'lisping, unable to pronounce certain letters', σάκκος 'a coarse beard', σίλλος 'squint-eyed'; in the latter category are *Acca* and *Appius*, ἄττα a salutation used for elders (orig. 'father'), Boeot. Μέννει (Μένης), Ἀγαθθώ (ἀγαθός), τιτθός 'nipple', *mamma* 'breast', *bucca* 'cheek', *pappāre* 'eat' (of children). Some have wondered if G ἵππος 'horse' (174) might owe one or more of the unexpected details of its form to hypocorism; that is unknowable (but unlikely).

Assimilation and Dissimilation of Non-Contiguous Consonants. Metathesis.

235. Most changes falling under these heads occur only sporadically, or under conditions too complex, obscure, or idiosyncratic to allow generalizations. For the most part these things are 'slips of the tongue' (and in writing as 'slips of the pen') which rarely become permanent. Being as a rule patternless and sporadic, most such changes are details in the history of specific words, as in G λύκος and L *lupus* 'wolf' < **lukʷos* < **wl̥kʷos*, but sometimes they are systematic—sound laws in fact. Perhaps unexpectedly, there is more of this sort of thing in G than in L.

1. Metathesis.

In L, the development of *-nd-* from **-dn-* and **-tn-* has been noticed (222.2). Less certain is the change of **-ld-* to **-dl-* (223.1d).

In literary G there was a metathesis of *-eCo-* to *-oCe-*: **stero-* 'spread' (**sterH₃-*), **lewo-* 'wash' (**lewH₃-*) yield στορέω fut. and λο(ϝ)ετρόν 'bath'. (This development is not seen in Myc., hence *re-wo-te-re-jo* 'for bathing'.)

In G there was a regular metathesis of stops, such that apical + dorsal became dorsal + apical:

G τίκτω < **titkō* redup. pres. of **tek-* 'beget', cf. τέκνον 'child'.

G χθών 'earth' < PIE **dhǵhom-* : Toch. A *tkaṃ*, gen. *tkanis*; Hitt. *te-(e-)kán*, gen. *ták-na-(a-)aš*. —Most IE languages simplify such initial clusters. A dorsal obstruent (or its outcome) is seen in Italic, Gmc., and BS, as for instance in L *homō* 'man', OE *guma*, 'man', and Lith. *žẽmė* 'earth'. In others the result is an apical, so OIr. *duine* /duν'e/, W *dyn* 'man'. The Indic development of *kṣ* from **tḱ* and **dhǵh* (for example *kṣam-*) starts with PInIr. **tś*, **dźh* and proceeds by stages (all being regular sound laws) through **ṭṣ* to *kṣ*; no metathesis is involved.

G κτίζω 'I people, I found' < **tḱey-* : Ved. *kṣéti* 'dwells'.

G ἄρκτος 'bear' < PIE **(H₂)r̥tḱo-* : Ved. *ŕ̥kṣa-*, MIr. *art*, and perh. Hitt. *ḫa-ar-ta-ag-ga-aš*. —L *ursus* certainly belongs here, but the details are difficult. The word belongs to a kind of vocabulary in which 'tabuistic distortions' are common, and its unexpected form has been attributed to that effect. (Cf. the distortion of L *ursus* itself in Aragonese *honso*.) But since *ur-* < **or-* (**r̥-*) is not a native L development in any case (96), like *lupus* the word might be a borrowing, from some dialect in which **ty* > *s* (such as Bantine: cf. *Bansae* loc.sg. 'in Bantium'). The starting point in such a case would be **orsos* < **ortyos* orig. 'ursine'. The semantic development envisioned is on display in Gmc. **suHīnaz* orig. *'porcine' > OE *swín* 'swine', NHG *Schwein*.

a. G τέκτων 'craftsman, adept', Myc. *te-ko-to-ne*, Ved. *tákṣan-* are usually included among such forms. It might reflect the root **tek-* 'make, beget' mentioned above, specifically an *on*-stem derivative of a reduplicated stem **te-tk-* (cf. **ti-tk-*, above). However, a PIE root for 'fashion skilfully' is pretty generally attested, and with the solitary exception of G τέκτων it is apparently **teks-*: G τέχνη < **teksneH₂-* (230.2a, though to be sure **-sneH₂-* is sometimes a suffix in its own right), OIr. *tál* /tāl/ 'axe' < **tokslo-*, OHG *dehsa* 'axe' < **tekseH₂*, L *texō* and derivatives 'weave', occasionally 'build', Hitt. *takš-* 'join, fit together' (and possibly Hitt. *ta-ak-ša-an* n. 'middle; half'). To these can be confidently added Ved. *tákṣati* 3pl. 'fashion' and its derivatives.

The problem, then, is how to explain G τέκτων. It is best taken as a conflation of two different inherited forms of similar meaning: *τεξων < **teḱs-on-* = Ved. *tákṣan-*, an agentive derivation of a type which is obsolete in both languages and therefore certainly inherited; and *τεκτωρ < **teḱs-tor-* (= Ved. *táṣṭar-*; cf. pple. *taṣṭá-* < **takṣṭá-*); for the development of the consonant cluster, cf. ἑκτός 'sixth' < **hweks-to-* (398.6).

b. Another form often cited in this connection is G χθές 'yesterday': Ved. *hyás* (always scanned *hiyás*), L *heri* (cf. *hesternus* 'relating to yesterday'), OE *géostra*, plus some more uncertain forms: Elean σερός (Hesych.), OIr. *in-dé* /in'd'ē/. The history of these forms is however different. The etymon, something like **ǵhd(h)iyes*, is the deictic root **ǵh-* (as in L *hic* (377.3) together with some remnant of **dyew-* 'day', probably ***diwes* abl./gen.; that must remain a surmise, in view of the irregular nature of changes found in more or less atonic and frozen phrases meaning things like 'today' and 'yesterday'. The same difficulty prevents more than a speculative treatment of details such as the apparent loss of **y* without a trace in χθές and *heri* and the apparent loss of **d* in Indic.

c. The G metathesis here described dates from PG. Thus it is evident in the Myc. cognate of κτίζω: *ki-ti-me-no* midd.pple. 'founding', *a-ki-ti-to* 'uninhabited' (or 'untilled'), and predates the characteristic development of labiovelars in G; hence PIE **dhg*^{w}*hey*- 'perish' and **dhg*^{w}*heyH*$_1$- 'destroy' underlie G φθίνω 'perish, wane' (root φθι- < PG **k*^{wh}*t*^{h}*i*-), Ved. *kṣiṇāti* 'destroys', Hom. φθῑσί-μβροτος 'men-destroying'. (In G the seṭ and aniṭ forms of the root seem to have become thoroughly confused.)

d. These correspondences have traditionally been dealt with in one of two ways. The less widely-held view reconstructs a whole series of PrePIE assibilated stops, ***k*^{s}, ***p*^{s}, ***g*^{z}*h*, and so on, which are distinctive only in InIr. and G and are but faintly attested even there. The more widely accepted reconstruction is a special PIE consonant, **þ* (**ð* next to a voiced consonant), called *thorn*, which is found only immediately following a dorsal stop. In one sense there is little real difference between **ḱþ* and **k*^{s}, apart from the fact that the latter approach adds several items to the list of ancient sounds and the former adds only one (which, however, has the structural demerit of occurring in two environments only). The sole purpose of both theories is to account for the words cited above where Indic has *kṣ* corresponding to G κτ, χθ, and φθ and a miscellany of uninformative single stops in other languages. As such, both reconstructions are best regarded as methodological strategems to some degree, rather than bona fide surmises about the structure of the proto-language.

In fact, most of the words involved can be dealt with wholly within the usual inventory of PIE stops, requiring only (a) the metathesis in G proposed in **235.1** and (b) a rethinking of Indic sound laws. A full explanation of the Indic details would take us too far afield, but the G metathesis is directly visible in τίκτω < **ti-tk-ō* and χθών, and is likely for many of the remaining data traditionally explained by 'PIE thorn'.

It would be too bold to say that all difficulties connected with these items vanish with this analysis, but few genuine problems remain. Fewer still remain if one abandons potential cognate sets whose semantics fall short of compelling. For example, InIr. **akš*- 'eye', **kšay*- 'rule, prevail', Ved. *kṣatrá*-, Av. *xšaθra*- 'dominion, government', and G κτάομαι 'acquire' are best regarded as unrelated. (The last two InIr. words in any case have been well explained as going with G σχέτλιος, in Hom. something like 'heedless, stubborn', from PIE **sǵhetlo*- 'doughty', and superimposable on Ved. *kṣatríya*- 'sovereign'.) Similarly L *situs*, -*ūs* 'place, situation' and Ved. *kṣi*- 'inhabit, settle' do not require explanation, as they are probably unrelated.

2. DISSIMILATION. G, like Indic, shows the dissimilation of aspirates (Grassmann's Law), treated in **138**. There is in addition a miscellany of sporadic phenomena, for example L *merīdiēs* 'noon, south' < **medyo-diyēs*, *tenebrae* 'darkness' < **temasr*- (**225.2**), G ϝει- < **wew*- (**61.1a**), L *crūdus* < **krowros* (**151b**).

FINAL CONSONANTS

236. GREEK.

1. A final stop is lost.

Voc.sg.: παῖ 'O boy' from **pawid* (stem visible in gen. παιδός); γύναι 'O woman' from **g*^{w}*enayk* (cf. gen. γυναικός); ἄνα 'O prince' from **wanakt* (cf. gen. ἄνακτος).

Adv. ὑπόδρα (ἰδών) '(looking) askance' < *-drak < *-dr̥k̑, cf. Ved. compounds
kī́dr̥ś- 'like what?', tā́dr̥ś- 'like that' (orig. *"looking like what/that', respectively); cf. δέρκομαι, root *derk̑- 'see'.
Nom./acc.sg.n. of pronouns: τό = Ved. tát (Go. þata, OE þæt reflect *tod-ŏ̄m);
τί = L quid, Ved. cit 'indef.'; ἄλλο = L aliud (in both languages the pronominal neuter -d, -t is probably secondary for original *H₂elyom; 374.2).
3pl. forms like ἔφερον 'they carried' < *ebheront, and likewise perhaps 3sg.
ἔφερε < *ebheret unless the form was t-less from the beginning (426, 429).

   a. The word-final stops in ἐκ, οὐκ, κατ, ἀπ are only apparent exceptions, as these
forms are proclitic upon the following word; phonologically speaking, that is, the stops
in question are medial, not final.
   b. Perhaps the solitary relic of word-final stops is preserved in Hom. ὅ ττι 'why' if
from *yod kʷid, in which the survival of the ending of the first pronoun (at least for a
time; NB Att. ὅ τι) reveals that the expression had become a phonological word before the
time of the dropping of final stops.

   2. Final *-m becomes -ν. Acc.sg. *-m > G -ν = L -m, Skt. -m (257.3):
*wl̥kʷom > λύκον, lupum, vr̥kam. Likewise 1sg. secondary *-m > G -ν, L -m
(in the fut. and subj.), Skt. -m, as in ἔφερον = Ved. ábharam 'I carried' (424).
PIE *sem nom.sg.n. 'one' > G ἕν. (The -ν was generalized, 228.6.)

   237. LATIN.
   1. Final -m remains in L, but there is some uncertainty about what
sound was actually pronounced. In poetry it does not interfere with elision
when the next word begins with a vowel, but on the other hand it 'makes
position', like any other consonant, when the next word begins with a consonant. The letter itself is frequently omitted in early inscriptions (even
carefully carved ones). In addition to these facts evident in the texts themselves, there are comments by the ancients. Roman authorities bequeathe
to us a special term, mytacism (variously spelled), denoting an objectionable
mispronunciation of final -m; and there are stray remarks by Romans, more
tantalizing than informative, such as Cicero's statement that 'with us' is
nōbīscum because cum nōbīs would be obscene.
   The ablest analysis of the question pins down the phonetics of -m as
a nasalized [w] in careful speech, which in poetry behaved like a final glide
and in casual speech styles seems to have dropped altogether. In certain
fossilized phrases the complete loss of m with elision of the preceding vowel was established even in careful speech: animadvertō 'notice' (animum advertō) or vēneō 'go for sale' (vēnum eō), 241.
   Mytacism, then, seems to denote the mistake of pronouncing -m as an
actual [m]; before a vowel, for the Roman ear, such an [m] had to belong
to the FOLLOWING word: so partem agis 'you play the part', if pronounced
[partemagis], could only be understood as parte magis 'in part rather'.
   2. Final -s weakened in early L, as shown by its frequent omission in
early inscriptions and by the fact that it often fails to make position in

early poetry. But it had regained its value by the time of Cicero, who remarks that the omission of final *-s* (when not followed by a vowel) had formerly been good usage but no longer was, 'quod iam subrusticum videtur'. Perhaps significantly, among the Romance languages Italian—and more specifically the forms of Italian geographically closest to Rome—are the only ones which from early times show no trace of *-s*, by some authorities taken as a persistence of the ancient loss, however 'subrustic'.

Even in early inscriptions the omission of *-s* is inconsistent, but the conditions for its loss have defied analysis. A recent study reveals why: it shows that the absence of *-s* in early L is frequent in specific words (*deus* for example) and rare in others. That is, it seems not to have been a phonological rule properly speaking.

3. PIE **-t* became PItal. **-d*, as in the 3sg. secondary ending: Duenos inscr. perf. FECED, opt. SIED; cf. *-t* < **-ti* in pres. IOVESAT, MITAT. In Sab. the original distribution was retained (so O **deded** 'dedit', **kúmbened** 'convenit'). In L that distribution is found only in the earliest inscriptions; later, as part of the general spread of primary endings at the expense of secondary ones (419-30), the *-t* from the primary ending **-ti* ousted *-d* from **-t*.

4. PItal. *-d* after a long vowel was lost toward the end of the 3rd century BC, as seen in the ablatives singular in *-ā*, *-ō*, *-ī*, *-ū*, and the imperative in *-tō*; in early inscriptions (and in Sab.) these appear as -AD, -OD, -ID, -VD, and -TOD. The monosyllabic pronouns *mēd*, *tēd* survived somewhat longer and occur before vowels in Plautus. A telling detail in the SC de Bacch. is the occurrence of SENTENTIAD, PREIVATOD, MAGISTRATVD and the like consistently in the legal text itself, while in the subjoined instructions for publishing the decree we find the phrase IN AGRO TEVRANO. That is, the *-d* was already lost in more or less contemporaneous speech, while still being written (and possibly even pronounced) in conservative legal style.[1]

a. The *o*-stem abl. ending seen in Italic languages as *-d* (in L only in early inscriptions) and in Skt. as *-t* could be from either PIE **-t* or **-d*: the outcomes of the two consonants fall together in both Indic and Italic. The case is different with the pronominal marker of the nom./acc.n. (L *quid*, Ved. *cit*, and so on) where other evidence is available: next to ambiguous L *id*, *quid* and Skt. *cit*, *tát* we have Ved. *idám* 'it' indicating PIE **-d*, with confirmation from Go. *ita*, NHG *es*, and other Germanic neuters. (NE *it* reflects the same ending, but is from a different stem: OE *hit*, Go. *hita* < PIE **ḱid-ōm*.)

b. Like the primary 3sg. ending *-t*, the L words *et*, *ut* and some others originally had a short vowel following the stop. Such an explanation is unlikely for *caput* 'head': although an apocopated vowel like that of *animal* and *exemplar* might be considered, *caput* is a proper consonant stem (so pl. *capita*, not ˣ*capitia*). Leveling after the oblique stem is presumably the explanation.

---

[1] Some think the appendix which includes the phrase IN AGRO TEVRANO is a later addition. But the anachronistic archaizing of the main text, though carried out with impressive consistency, is betrayed by such fabrications as OQVOLTOD = *occultō[d]*, where the etymon is certainly **kel-* 'hide, cover' (*celāre*, etc.).

The preservation of *-d* in *sed* 'but' < *sēd* 'without, except for' (? with proclitic shortening) is unexpected and unexplained.

5. PIE *-*nt* > Sab. -*ns*, as in the 3pl. secondary (430.1) ending in O *deicans* 'dicant', **fufens** 'fuerunt', U *dirsans* 'dent'; the same change is seen in Paelig. COISATENS 'curaverunt'. —The other source of Sab. -*ns* is syncope, as in O **humuns** nom.pl. 'men' < *χ*emōnĕs*. —Final -*nt* in Italic languages is from *-*nti*, the primary 3pl. ending, via 74.2. In L this -*nt* was generalized at the expense of the secondary ending *-*ns* < *-*nt*, 430.1-2 (which is nowhere attested), but in O and U -*nt* < *-*nti* and -*ns* < *-*nt* maintain the original distribution, like 3sg. -*t* and -*d*, item 3, above.

Such a development in L would account for the numerical adverbs of the type *quotiēns* < *-*ent* < *-*n̥t* (the latter exactly paralleled by Ved. *kíyat* nom.sg.n. 'how many', stem *kíyant*-), and the otherwise very puzzling appearance of -*s* on the neuter of the present participle—which is no longer puzzling if *ferēns* n. (homophonous with *ferēns* m. < **ferents*) is a regular development from **ferent* < **bhern̥t* (556-7). The participles are then the source of the other 3rd decl. adjectives with -*s* in all three genders, such as *ferōx*, 347.

Relative chronology, however, appears to raise the following difficulty for this view. The Sab. and L developments of ORIGINAL *-*ns* differed from one another, yielding O -*ss*, U -*f*, L -*s* (vid. inf.). In U, -*f* is apparently also the outcome of *-*nts*. (There are no certain forms reflecting *-*nts* attested for O.) Since -*ns* < *-*nt* shows none of these developments, it necessarily must have postdated them, and thereby might appear of necessity to have postdated any Proto-Italic period as well.

There are a number of plausible scenarios, however, for the development *-*nt* > -*ns* endorsed here.

The weakest of them would take the chronology at face value, and assume that the innovation of -*ns* < *-*nt* did indeed take place after O, U, and L had become different languages, much as the diphthongizing of *ī*, *ū*, and *ǖ* in ME, Dutch, and MHG postdated by many centuries their split into different languages. There are clear cases of just such a thing in the Italic sphere too, such as the development *dy*- > *y*- in L and Sab., which is traceable within the written histories of L and O; that is, it took place at a time when L and O were mutually unintelligible languages. Something similar may have happened in the case of Ital. *-*nt*.

But it is more likely that original *-*nts*[1] was merely more conservative in L than in Sab. In this analysis, in the variety of PItal. underlying Sab., inherited *-*ns* and *-*nts* fell together, while remaining distinct in PreL. Only after the syncretism of *-*ns* and *-*nts* in the family of dialects from which O and U emerged this did original *-*nt* develop an affricated pronunciation

[1] Such original *-*nts* apart from the pres. pple. was limited to the nom.sg. of a very small number of nouns, *frōns*, *frontis* 'brow', *frōns*, *frondis* 'leaf', and *glāns* 'acorn' < **glandis*.

throughout Italic. In L, this new *-nt^s < *-*nt* fell together with inherited *-*nts*, whereby the m. and n. nom.sg. forms of the present pple. became the same. In time, per regular sound law (215) the *t* disappeared from these forms, hence L *ferēns*, *totiēns*; prior to that, however, original *-*ns*, in effect limited to the acc.pl., lost the **n* with lengthening of the preceding vowel. These developments are summarized in the following chart.

PItal.	PreSab.	O	U
*-ns } *-nts }	*-ns	-ss	-f
*-nt	*-nts	-ns	–

PItal.	PreL	L
*-ns	*-ns	-s
*-nts } *-nt }	*-nts	-ns

6. In the prehistory of PIE, final **-*ns* (as in the nom.sg. of the m. and f. *n*-stems, 282) had dropped, with lengthening of the preceding vowel. Some authorities hold that the resulting vowel was longer than, or otherwise somehow different from, an ordinary long vowel, but that is not apparent in L and G: *n*-stem nom.sg. PrePIE **-*ons* > PIE *-*ō*, whence L *homō* 'man' (stem *homin-*), Go., OE *guma* (*guman-*), Ved. *rā́jā* 'king' (*rā́jan-*). But the corresponding G ending -ων has imported the -ν- from the oblique stems, on the analogy of *r*-stems, say πατέρες : πατήρ :: τέκτονες : *X*, where *X* = τέκτων. (For medial *-*ns*- in G, see 228.1; in L, 226.1.)

If this account is correct, the acc.pl. in *-*ns* familiar in traditional treatments must have had a different source, most probably PrePIE **-*ms*, whether actually derived from acc.sg. *-*m* or only influenced by it.

7. The final consonant of certain groups was lost: *cor* 'heart' from **cord* (gen. *cordis*), *lac* 'milk' from **dlakt* (gen. *lactis*), probably *mel* 'honey' < **meld* (item 8, below). Certain other groups were first assimilated and then simplified (see the following).

8. Final long consonants were shortened, as in:
2sg. *es* 'you are' < *ess* (so scanning in Plaut.)—not an inheritance but a remodeling of expected **es* < PIE *H_1*esi* (492).
Nom.sg. *mīles* 'soldier' < *mīless* (so scanning in Plaut.) < **mīlets* (gen. *mīlitis*).
Adv. *ter* 'thrice' < *terr* (so scanning in Plaut.) < **ters* < **tris*; similarly the nom.sg. in -*er* of *ri*-stem adjectives like *ācer* 'sharp' (cf. n. *ācre* < **ācri*). 74.3, 223.3.
L *o*-stem Nom.sg. in -*er*, such as *ager* < **agers* < **agrs* < **agros* (74.6, 223.3).
L *fūr* 'thief' <**fūrr* < **fūrs* (gen. *fūris*).
Nom.sg. *hoc* < *hocc* < **hod-ce* (377.3).
Monosyllabic neuters, for example L *far* n. 'spelt' < **farr* < **fars* (stem orig. **far(e)s*-, 74.6, 297.1a). Differently, *fel* 'gall' (stem *fell-* < **ǵheln-*).

However, the similar-looking L *mel, mellis* 'honey' does not reflect inherited **mell(-)*. The usual analysis takes **melis* and the like as the original oblique forms, which were then contaminated by *fel, fellis*. This is possible. More likely is an original paradigm **melid* (item 3, above), **melites*, as indicated by Go. *miliþ* 'honey', G μέλι, μέλιτος, Hitt. *mi-li-it*. Syncope of the second vowel would give **meld* (**mell*), with a remodeling of obl. **mel(i)tes* as **mel(i)des*, whence **melles*. The theory that *mell-* incorporates an apical stop is supported by *mulsus* 'sweet drink, mead' < **molssos* (98) < **m̥lt-to-* (42.5, 212).

a. Long final consonants are pretty much limited to early poetry and the playwrights; but *hoc* is regularly heavy even in the classical period, and the grammarians expressly state that the pronunciation was *hocc* before a vowel, in effect *hocc erat.* The parallel scansion of the nom.sg.masc. *hic* as heavy before a vowel, that is *hicc*, is assumed to be analogical to *hocc*.

b. L *sāl* 'salt', *par* 'equal', and *vel* 'or' are from **sall*, **parr*, and **vell* (from original **sals* (= G ἅλς), **pars*, **welsi* (the original 2sg. of *volō*; see 484.1). The pronunciation **vell* must have been current at the time that **e* > *o* before *l* pinguis (42.5). The Difference between the length of the vowel in *sāl* and the other two is unexplained.

SANDHI – CHANGES IN EXTERNAL COMBINATION

238. Changes in external combination, that is, those depending upon the relation of a word to adjacent words, are common in actual speech, but few such changes are represented in the written norms of most literary languages. In G certain of the changes belonging under this head—the familiar elision, crasis, and so on—are observed in our literary texts; but many others, common in inscriptions (and humdrum in substance), are disregarded. In L literary texts there is even less of such matters. But in both languages there are some recognized doublets, parallel in nature and extent to NE *a an*, as G ἐξ ἐκ and L *ex ē*, *ab abs ā*.

Written Sanskrit of all periods is unusual among the world's languages in indicating such changes in detail. Thus the form customarily cited as *tát* 'that' actually is written five different ways in the texts, depending on the initial sound of the following word: *tát*, *tád*, *tán*, *tác*, and *táj*. The general term in descriptive linguistics for the phenomenon, *sandhi*, is taken over from Sanskrit. grammar (*saṃdhi* 'combination', lit. 'putting together').

Several matters touching on sandhi have been mentioned already in connection with particular initial or final sounds, as for example the history of final **-ns* in G (228.4), and other finals (236-7).

Traditional terms of long standing, *euphony* and *euphonious combination*, are rarely met with nowadays.

239. GREEK.

1. Elision of a final short vowel (also -αι of verbal endings, and sometimes -οι) before a word beginning with a vowel, subject to certain restrictions, was probably a consistent feature of Greek speech; but the ancients were highly inconsistent in representing it in mss and inscriptions, even in metrical texts. (The current term for the phenomenon is *truncation*.)

Hiatus (that is, the absence of elision) in Homer is often due to the earlier presence of initial ϝ- in the following word, but is by no means confined to such cases.

In the case of αι and οι, elision presupposes the change of ι to [y], which was lost between vowels (192).

2. A long vowel shortens before a vowel per **79.3**. When a long vowel or diphthong in word-final position is followed by a word beginning with a vowel, shortening is observed in Homeric scansion, and is occasionally indicated in the spelling of inscriptions.

3. Aphaeresis, or inverse elision, mostly after *μή* or *ἤ*, as for example *ἤ'μέ*, occurs in poetry and occasionally in inscriptions. In reality, this is probably simple contraction (crasis, item 4, below), though called by a different name.

4. Crasis, in a closely connected group of words, is commonest when *καί* 'and' or forms of the article are followed by a word beginning with a vowel. It occurs in poetry and prose, and examples occur as well in early inscriptions of all dialects.

Crasis, which is simply a special name for vowel contraction, generally follows the rules of internal contraction. But in Att. there are some differences, as when the vowel of the second or principal word determines the quality of the contracted vowel: *ᾱνήρ* < *ὁ ἀνήρ*, in contrast to Ion. *ὡνήρ* showing the normal (internal) contraction of *ο* + *α* to *ω* (**86.3**; cf. Att. and Ion. *θᾶσσω* acc.sg. 'faster' < *θᾱσσοα*).

5. Apocope—the loss of a final vowel—commonly occurs in prepositions before a consonant in Homer and in many dialects. In some dialects it is more extensive than in Homer, so in Thess. even *ἀπ*, *ἐπ*, *ὑπ*. But in Att.-Ion. it is almost unknown.

6. Assimilation of a final consonant to the initial consonant of the following word is seen in Homer and in many dialects in the case of apocopated prepositions: *ἂμ πεδίον*, *κὰπ πεδίον*, *κὰρ ῥόον*. Very much more of such assimilation is to be seen in inscriptions, including Att. These are most evident in earlier attestations, though forms showing simple assimilation of point of articulation, as ΤΟΜ ΠΟΛΕΜΟΝ, ΤΗΜ ΒΟΥΛΗΝ, ΤΟΓ ΚΗΡΥΚΑ, are common even in late Attic inscriptions and in papyri, and have persisted in actual speech down to the present day. The more radical assimilations, as in ΤΟΛ ΛΟΓΟΝ, ΤΟΥΝ ΝΟΜΟΥΣ, are found only in the earlier inscriptions. Not uncommonly the article, which is in fact proclitic, is written solid: ΤΟΙΛΑΚΕΔΑΙΜΟΝΙΟΙΣ (phonologically a single word, and so governed by **227.2**). Neither sort appears in our current editions.

240. Greek *ν*-movable. The word-final -*ν* in forms like *λέγουσι(ν)* and *εἶπε(ν)* is an added element which, except for a few examples of dat.pl. -*σιν* in other dialects, is peculiar to Att.-Ion. Here however it is found from the earliest inscriptions, though increasing in frequency with time; and it occurs before both vowels and consonants. In Att. it came ultimately to be used mostly before a vowel or before a pause, though never with absolute consistency. It cannot be a purely phonetic addition, but must have its basis in analogical extension from certain forms in which the -*ν* was inherited. The clearest source, though hardly the only one, is the pronominal dative as seen in Att. ἡμῖν, Lesb. ἄμμιν ~ ἄμμι. Cf. Ved. *yásmin, tásmin* loc.sg., whose *-n* is some sort of optional element (it is missing in Av., and even in many Rigvedic passages the meter runs better with restored *yásmi, tásmi*). From here it passed first to the nouns' dat.pl. *-σι*, as *φύλαξι(ν)*, then to 3pl. *λέγουσι(ν)*, thence to 3sg. *τίθησι(ν)*; and again from 3sg. *ἦεν, ἦν* (493A) to *οἶδε(ν), ἔθηκε(ν)*.

a. There was in G a weakening and omission of inherited *-ν* generally (for example Att. epig. ΘΑΝΟΤΟΙ dat./gen.du. aor. pple. for *θανόντοιν* 5th century BC), though this appears to be a different (and somewhat later) development, on the grounds that it is particularly evident in dialects in which *ν*-movable is not attested, Cyp. and Pamph.

241. LATIN. In graffiti and the more carelessly written inscriptions we have evidence of how Latin was actually spoken: IM BALNEVM 'into the bath', CVN SVIS 'with their [own]', CVN CONIVGI 'with a spouse', QVAN NVNC 'than now'. Such traits are tolerably abundant in inscriptions (where in fact the prep. is often written solid with what follows), but L literary texts show even less of such matters than G. Even the elision required by poetic scansion was not written in mss, and aphaeresis (such as *cōpiast* for *cōpia est*) only occasionally.

Elision was doubtless common in actual speech, though in the approved spelling it is indicated only in set phrases: *magnopere* 'exceedingly' < **magnō opere*, *animadvertō* 'take notice of' < **animum advertō*, *potest* 'is able' ← *potist* < **potis est*; and NB especially the history of the paradigm of *sum* (492). Proto-Romance confirms inter alia the elision of the vowel of *de* before another vowel. But elision in Latin poetry is thought to go beyond its probable incidence in ordinary speech. Certain statements of Roman authorities imply that L poetry was read with slurring of the vowel rather than with elision. If that is so, it was probably an artificial compromise between the elided and the full form, an attempt to retain something of a vowel without giving it the value of a syllable. —For words ending with *-m*, see also 237.1.

ACCENT

242. In many languages particular syllables have special *prominence* relative to others. This prominence, which is the result of variations of amplitude or pitch of voiced phones (or spans of phones), goes by the name *accent*. Traditionally one speaks of two species of accent: *stress accent* and *pitch accent* (alternatively, *musical accent*), depending on which element is thought to be the more conspicuous in distinguishing *tonic* (more prominent) from *atonic* (less prominent) syllables.

But the phonetics of accent are not adequately captured in this scheme. For example, although it is widely taken as obvious that English has a stress accent, in fact the word accent of English is phonetically complex: the two most important marks of tonic syllables are (1) sharply changing pitch (usually but not invariably downward)—thus pitch, more specifically pitch change, is central to this supposed 'stress accent'; and (2) a notable lengthening of the tonic vowel. Prolongation of tonic vowels is notoriously associated with a corresponding reduction or loss of unaccented (short) vowels. An opinion sanctified by tradition is that stress accent CAUSES such reductions and losses; but Finnish, Hungarian, and Czech, for example, all have a strong stress accent on the first syllable of a word but maintain a full array of vowel contrasts in posttonic syllables, which shows that vowel weakening is not an inevitable concomitant of stress accent. The converse is probably more nearly true, namely that accent defined by pitch changes alone is not likely to result in phonetic differences between atonic and tonic vowels.

In Ved. and G, the two earliest-attested IE languages which afford any information on the point, the tonic syllable seems to have been distinguished from its neighbors by a difference in pitch, and it is a reasonable inference that this was the character of the PIE accent in the last period of the parent speech. But no doubt at an earlier period of the parent speech, the tonic accent was different, or at any rate one which resulted in the PIE zero grade through the loss of many atonic vowels (125).

A distinction of simple and compound accent, that is of acute and circumflex, to adopt the familiar terms applied to G, is thought by some to have existed in the parent speech, at least in final syllables. The evidence for this is seen in such comparisons as G τῑμή, gen. τῑμῆς, Lith. *mergà*, gen. *mergõs*; or G καλοί nom.pl. next to gen.pl. καλῶν, dat.pl. καλοῖς (< instr. **-ōys*) with Lith. *gerì* next to gen.pl. *gerų̃*, inst.pl. *geraĩs*. However, the points of similarity in Baltic and G, though impressive on the face of it, have been shown to be coincidental—the result of independent developments in the two branches.

Vedic Sanskrit had a *free accent* as opposed to a *fixed accent*. (The latter term is used both of accent which is absolutely fixed, as, for example, in Finnish and Czech, where all words are accented on the first syllable; and also of accent which is merely limited in some way, as in G and L, where the accent is confined to certain syllables of a word.) In Vedic the accent may stand on the first, last, or any intermediate syllable, regardless of the number of syllables or the quantity of the vowels.[1] —The Vedic accent agrees with the accent to be inferred from certain consonant changes in Germanic (Verner's Law, 139), and is thought to preserve the inherited PIE accent tolerably intact. (NB that the classical Skt. accent is wholly different. It is a recessive system practically the same as the Latin one.)

An exhaustive comparative grammar of G and L accent could be stated in sixteen words: There is little of the PIE system in Greek, and no trace of it in Latin. *However, the histories of the G and L accents are not without interest, and will be briefly discussed.*

---

[1] Students of classical languages may be particularly amazed by such Rigvedic forms as *páritakmiyāyām* loc.sg.f. 'unsteady'; *tigmámūrdhānas* nom.pl.m. 'sharp-headed' (that is, 'pointed'), *parivatsaré* loc.sg. 'in an entire year'.

GREEK

243. In the discussion that follows, 'Greek' must be understood to mean Athenian as described and codified by Alexandrian scholars. From such sources we also have information on Homeric accent. Of the dialects, only for Lesbic do we have reliable information. The habit of generations of Hellenists of inventing accents for dialect forms (which is not followed in this book) cannot be defended in principle, and seems particularly incautious in view of the fact that in Lesbic, the only dialect for which we do have reliable information, the accentual system differs in important ways from the Attic.

The G tonic syllable, as indicated above, was distinguished from its atonic neighbors by having a higher pitch. This is clear from its description by G writers, and from the metaphors that underlie the terminology they employ: the whole system of accentuation is *προσωιδίᾱ*, lit. 'a song sung to music'; the feature of prominence, *τόνος*, is lit. 'stretching' esp. tuning the strings of a musical instrument (the term *τάσις* < **tn̥-ti-* is synonymous on both counts). Similarly the names for the different kinds of syllables: *ὀξεῖα* (acute) lit. 'piercing, sharp', that is, 'shrill' of sounds; *βαρεῖα* (grave) lit. 'heavy'; of voice, 'deep'. Of special note is *βαρεῖα* (*τάσις*): 'heavy' is an appropriate metaphor for atonic syllables if their characteristic is 'low' pitch, whereas had the accent been one of stress, *βαρεῖα* would have been intelligible only as the term for the 'heavy' stress of the TONIC syllable.

Other facts point in the same direction: the rarity of vowel syncope and other phenomena which are associated with stress accent, and the independence of tonic accent and verse ictus. In NG, on the other hand, the accent retains its old position but is one of stress. The course of the change is unknown; the beginning of accentual verse in the 4th century AD establishes that as a terminus post quem, though a good two centuries earlier mistakes in versification regarding vowel quantity are frequent enough to suggest interference from a stress accent, and some scholars have claimed to see evidence of stress accent in colloquial and dialectal speech earlier still.

Tonic short vowels (acute accent) were of higher pitch than the neighboring atonic vowels (grave accent). On diphthongs or long vowels, however, higher pitch might either begin on the first mora and fall during the course of the syllable; or else begin later in the syllable, such that the pitch would rise more or less over the duration of the syllable. If the tonic accent started on the first mora, it was marked with the circumflex accent. (The mark itself is historically a combination of an acute immediately followed by a grave, that is *παῖς* 'child' = *πάὶς*, or *πῦρ* 'fire' = *πύὺρ*.) If the raised pitch occurred later in the syllable, the syllable is marked with an ordinary acute accent (as it were, *Ζεύς* = *Ζὲύς*). The actual PHONETIC difference was one of falling pitch ('circumflex') and rising pitch ('acute').

a. All syllables not having the acute or the circumflex, that is, what we call the atonic syllables, were regarded as grave, and were sometimes so marked (Μὲνέλὰὸς). A different scheme marked just the syllables preceding the tonic syllable (ἒπὲσσεύοντο); yet another scheme marked just the one immediately preceding (κρατὲρός). Sometimes, indeed, the tonic vowel was not marked at all, as γυνή 'woman' might be written γὺνη.

The only use of the grave accent sign in our current texts, namely in place of the acute on the final before another word, reflects (as do some other peculiarities in the use of the accent signs) a Byzantine convention, which is at variance with the practice of the Alexandrian period as observed in the papyri. In certain cases the sign may be understood as a survival of its original use on atonic syllables. Thus in τὸν πόλεμον the τὸν was really proclitic just as much as the ὁ of ὁ πόλεμος; and also in prepositional phrases (ἀνὰ λόγον, ἀπὸ δείπνου) the prepositions were as proclitic as ἐν, εἰς, ἐκ, ἐξ (sometimes in fact written ἒν, ἒκ in papyri). The practice finally established was the purely mechanical one that the grave accent was not written on proclitic vowels which also had a breathing sign, thus ἀπὸ but εἰς; and τὸν but ὁ, ἡ.

b. For polysyllables the significance of the grave accent in place of the acute on final syllables is harder to interpret. Some modern authorities believe that the distinction is graphic only, and some ancient descriptions seem to be driving at something similar. But why—not to mention how—such a distinction without a difference might have arisen is a mystery. Ancient authorities have also left us confusing discussions of intermediate accents, which might refer to a lowering of the tonic pitch on final syllables but not its complete disappearance; and some such reduction in prominence might be what one ancient authority meant by saying that in such a position the acute is 'put to sleep'. Sensible as this theory is, the fact remains that any tonic accent, even one altered phonetically, should by rights have been marked the same way as other TONIC syllables, not the same way as ATONIC syllables.

244. In G the PIE system of accent was altered in two different ways. First, the free accent was replaced in NOUNS and ADJECTIVES (including verbals) by one in which the accent must fall within the last three syllables; and if the ultima was long, within the last two. Or, expressed in terms of morae (a short vowel = one mora), the accent could stand on the fourth mora from the end in a case like ἄνθρωπος 'man' with a short ultima, otherwise not farther back than the third mora from the end. Hence the circumflex (in effect acute + grave) was excluded from the antepenult, and might occur on the penult only when the ultima was short.

If the etymological accent of a word stood too far from the end of the word to be in conformity with these rules, it moved to the leftmost mora within the required limits. Thus in middle participles, the root accent seen in Ved. *bháramāṇas* n.sg. 'obtaining', *bháramāṇasya* gen.sg. is pulled away from the root in G φερόμενος, and one syllable further in φερομένου (< φερομένοιο).

If on the other hand the PIE accent stood within the limits which came to be prescribed in G, it might remain unchanged. Thus G πούς nom.sg. 'foot', ποδός gen., ποδί dat., πόδα acc. like Ved. *pā́t*, *padás*, *padí* loc., *pā́dam*; πατήρ nom.sg. 'father', πατέρας acc.pl., πατράσι dat.pl. like Ved. *pitā́*, *pitáras*, *pitṛ́ṣu* loc.pl.; ὕστερος 'latter' like Ved. *úttara-* 'upper' (PIE **úd-tero-*). (Of course, some of the agreement between the two languages is the result of parallel innovation. The forms of the parent language for the four cited cases of 'foot' were something like **pōts* (or **póts*), **pdós*, **pedí*, and **pódm̥* —whence Ved. *pā́dam* by Brugmann's Law; see 274.)

But there have also been changes of accent in particular words and classes of words due to various causes, some obscure, some obvious. Contamination is reasonably transparent in say θυγάτηρ 'daughter' for expected *θυγατήρ (cf. Ved. *duhitár-*), which can be traced to the influence of μά́τηρ. A few have the character of sound laws, though they have many exceptions. Note that all of them entail a retreat of the accent to the left:

WHEELER'S LAW: end-accented dactyls retract the accent one syllable: x̄x̆x̆́ > x̄x̆́x̆. Thus PIE **poyḱeló-* 'mottled' > Ved. *peśalá-* but G ποικίλος; similarly ἡδύλος 'sweetish', στωμύλος 'mouthy'. Cf. similarly-formed non-dactylic adjectives which retain the original -λός, as παχυλός 'thickish', ὑψηλός 'lofty'. (Wheeler's accentuation was generalized through the paradigm, thus gen. ποικίλου on the basis of ποικίλος, ποικίλον, and the rest, in place of phonologically regular *ποικιλοῦ.)

VENDRYÈS' LAW: common Greek x̆x̄̂x̆ > late Attic x̆́x̄x̆. Thus common G ἑτοῖμος 'at hand, ready' > Att. ἕτοιμος.

In a parallel innovation, there was a pronounced tendency in words of (x̆)x̄́x̆ prosody (where x̄́ stands for an acute diphthong or long vowel) for the acute to become a circumflex, as τιθεῖσα 'putting' for what must have been *τιθείσα < **titʰénsa* (196.3; 559.2). This started in disyllables, in the interplay between acute and circumflex conditioned by the length of the ultima: οἶνος 'wine' but gen. οἴνου. From this, δῶρον 'gift' in place of δώρον (οἴνου : δώρου :: οἶνος : *X*, where *X* = δῶρον), and further the unetymological circumflex of μῆτερ voc. (See **a**.)

a. There is a long-standing debate in specialists' circles over whether the G contrast between acute and circumflex accent was inherited or arose within the history of G. The latter view is endorsed here: the original source of the circumflex accent is vowel contraction, as when **tréyes* 'three' > PG **tré(y)es* > τρέες whence (76) τρεῖς (that is, /trēs/ with circumflex). Compensatory lengthening, from any cause, normally results in a long acute, as χήν 'goose' < **kʰans-*, χείρ 'hand' < **kʰesr-*. As mentioned above, however, there was much replacement of acutes by circumflexes before a short vowel, so pl. χῆρες, χεῖρες, Ζῆνα acc.sg. 'Zeus' < **zdḗna* ← **zdḗn* < **dyēm* (326). (The accentuation of εἷς 'one' < **séms*, παῖς (πάϊς) 'boy', earlier παίς < **pawíts*, and πᾶς 'all' < **pánts* must be analogical.) The retreat of tonic accent to the first allowable mora in verbs, a G innovation, results in οἶδα, and a reinterpretation of the rule for the accentuation of vocatives, originally a matter of accent on the first vowel (257.2), as accent on the first MORA, resulted in such forms as μῆτερ.

245. RECESSIVE ACCENT IN VERBS. The second way in which PIE accent was transformed in G applies only to verbs.[1] The accent of the G verb is regularly RECESSIVE in the finite forms, with the exception of some imperatives like ἰδέ and ἐλθέ. Thus we have G εἶμι 1sg. 'go', ἴμεν 1pl., although the original accentuation was that of Ved. *émi*, *imás* (PIE **éy-mi*, **imós*); or

[1] That is, in Att.-Ion. and Doric; in Lesbic a uniformly recessive accent applies to all forms in the language—much as in L, though of course following G rules.

δέδορκα 1sg.perf. 'I saw', δεδόρκαμεν 1pl. in contrast to Ved. *dadárśa, dadr̥śimá* (PIE **de-dórḱ-H₂e*, **de-dr̥ḱ-mé*). (The accentuation of contract verb forms like τῑμᾶι is only an apparent exception to the general rule: the recessive accent was fixed prior to the vowel contraction, so τῑμᾶι reflects a perfectly regular τῑμάει.) The explanation for how a recessive accent peculiar to verbs arose is as follows:

In independent clauses, the finite verb in Vedic was regularly atonic (enclitic, in effect) except when standing at the beginning of a verse. This is manifestly not aboriginal: since the relationship between full grades and tonic accent is clearest in the verbs, verbs must have had accented syllables to begin with. But there is also the axiom that when dependent and independent clauses differ in morphology or syntax, the DEPENDENT clauses will show the more conservative state of affairs. The antiquity of the Vedic patterns may not therefore be very great, but there are so many shared innovations in G and InIr. that the enclitic treatment of verbs in independent clauses could easily have been a feature of the stock of parent speech which immediately underlies Greek and Indo-Iranian.

The original state of affairs in G was like that in Vedic, namely, the verb was sometimes accented and sometimes atonic—that is, enclitic. In G, when it came to pass that no more than two syllables could be unaccented at the end of a word, and enclitics of more than two syllables were therefore impossible, the erstwhile enclitic forms of the verb would have to acquire an accent. And this accent would be in the earliest (that is, leftmost) possible position, just as in the case of all words whose accent was originally farther back and was moved forward to come within the required limits (244). Just as *φέρομενος became φερόμενος, so enclitic -δεδορκα became δέδορκα. That is to say, G δέδορκα, δεδόρκαμεν are alterations of forms corresponding to Vedic *dadarśa, dadr̥śima* (atonic), not of forms corresponding to accented *dadárśa, dadr̥śimá*.

In fact, G actually preserves a couple of enclitic verbs, εἰμί 'am' and φημί 'I say', albeit they are enclitic in all circumstances, unlike the Vedic situation. The special status of these two in part reflects the specially conservative behavior of very common forms; but it is of crucial importance that, being so short, their (unaltered) forms fell within the limits possible for enclitics, such that the obligatory accent lies on the preceding word, as βασιλεύς ἐστι, ἄνθρωπός ἐστι, Ἀθηναῖός ἐστι.

Where the accented forms of the parent language were the same as the G forms, without adjustment, as in πεύθεται (PIE **bhéwdhetor*), or could be derived from parent forms by mechanically shifting the accent rightward such as must have happened in nouns, as in πευθόμεθα (PIE *bhéwdhomosdhH̥₂*), the G forms can be taken as continuations of such parental tonic forms. This is unnecessary. The circumstances outlined above are wholly sufficient to account for the attested facts; it would be a violation of the principle of

Occam's Razor to invoke additional mechanisms. One might go further: if tonic verb forms had in fact played any material role in the development of the G accentual system, it is hard to understand how ending-accented forms (which outside of thematic stems made up the bulk of verb forms) could have disappeared without a trace.

LATIN

246. Latin is the only Italic language for which we have any information regarding accent, and the occurrence of tonic syllables in L is unrelated to PIE accentuation. Furthermore, it appears that between the PIE system of free accent and the historical L accent there intervened a period when all words were stressed on the first syllable; see 65. It was during this interim accentual system that most of the syncope and weakening of vowels described in 65–75 took place. In numerous cases, like *dexter* from **deksiteros* or *perfectus* from **perfaktos*, the vowels affected by weakening stand in what under the historical system would have been the accented syllables. The older system must have prevailed when such G forms as τάλαντον 'scales; talent', ἐλαιϝᾱ 'olive' (42.5), (Dor.) μᾱχανᾱ́ 'machine', and the place name Ἀκράγᾱς, -αντος were borrowed, as these developed into L *talentum, olīva, māchina*, and *Agrigentum*.

a. Plautine scansion of words like *facilius* and *mulieribus*, which are generally so placed that the verse ictus falls on the first syllable, is open to different interpretations. One takes it to be a last survival of the otherwise hypothetical prehistoric initial-syllable accent. The other takes it rather to be part and parcel of the historical L system of accent, but a rule which subsequently was superceded by the antepenult rule. Interestingly, in post-Vedic Sanskrit, which has a Latin-type accentuation, the paṇḍits prescribe *fácilius* type accentuation: *gámayati* 'causes to go'.

247. The historical L accent resembled the G in that it could not stand farther back than the third syllable from the end of the word, but beyond this general restriction the resemblances cease. In L the penult (a syllable which plays almost no role in the G system) determined the position within these limits; in G the governing syllable was the ultima (a syllable which plays no role in the L system). The L accent, moreover, was uniformly recessive, while in G it was recessive only in the verb. Moreover, the ruling variable in L was the WEIGHT of the penult, while the LENGTH of the vowel in the ultima is operative in G: the L accent fell on the antepenult unless the penult was HEAVY (to borrow a term from Sanskrit grammarians), namely contained a diphthong or a long vowel or was followed by more than one consonant. In such a case, the accent fell on the heavy penult: *pércitus* 'aroused' but *perféctus* 'completed', *percússus* 'a knocking', and *percī́dō* 'I beat to pieces'. This system is described by contemporaneous grammarians, and agrees with the evidence provided by the Romance languages. Most exceptions are only apparent, being due to loss

of a final syllable by syncope or contraction, as *illī́c* 'at that place' < *illī́ce*, *audī́t* 3sg.perf. from *audī́vit* (**529**), *Vergílī* gen.sg. from *Vergíliī* (**259.8Ba**), *animál* < **animāle* (**74.1**).

a. There were apparently various exceptions to this rule, however. Our information for most of these is limited to statements by ancient authorities to the effect that *Camillus*, *fenestra* (see **d**, below), *trīgintā* and some others were accented on the first syllable. Romance evidence confirms some of this, for example It. *Bríndisi* (*Brúndisium*) and *Pésaro* (*Písaurum*). The two sources of information do not always agree, however. Romance unanimously attests PRom. **fenéstra* 'window'; and It. *trenta* 'thirty' seems to point to *trīgíntā* 'thirty', but something like *quadrā́gintā* 'forty' for expected *quadrāgíntā* does seem to be required for It. *quaranta*.[1]

b. Ancient authorities also plainly say that disyllabic prepositions were ending-accented (*suprā́*, *circúm*) in contrast to normally-accented adverbs (*súprā*) and nouns (*círcum* acc.sg.). This seems unlikely on its face and there is no Romance evidence for it, but it is hard to believe that something so straightforward could be totally imaginary. Perhaps in normal utterances the prepositions were more or less proclitic (and therefore atonic), and the end-accent described in the grammatical literature was an artifact of isolated pronunciation—something like the artificial citation form of the NE article *a* as /ey/, a pronunciation which rarely if ever actually occurs in unselfconscious connected speech.

c. ENCLITICS. Roman grammarians imply that words ending with the enclitics *-que*, *-ve*, *-ne*, *-ce* were accented in accord with the rules for whole words, so *bonús-que*, *bonī́-que*. This is surprising; it is furthermore contradicted by various kinds of evidence such as forms like *vidĕ́n* < *vidēs-ne*, *sátĭn* < *satis-ne*, in which not only the location of the tonic accent is known but also the forms have undergone iambic shortening (**84**). More surprising still are statements by late Roman authorities that ALL forms with enclitics were accented on the syllable preceding the enclitic, even when this was light (namely consisted of a short vowel): *bonắque*, *līminắque*. Both observations are commonly qualified as 'contra usum Latinum', 'improprie', and the like, though in individual cases it is not always clear whether the authority thinks *bonúsque* or *bónusque* is correct. Some have wondered about some sort of secondary accent here, either before the enclitic (as in *géneràque*) or in place of the original tonic accent (so *gènerápque* for original *géneraque*); and others have suggested a phenomenon, either real or fancied, parallel to or in imitation of the G treatment of enclitics as in ἄνθρωπός τις and Ἀθηναῖός ἐστι (thus *génerápque*). Modern authorities have endorsed no fewer than six different interpretations of the accentuation of a form like *generaque*: *géneraque* (accent anaesthetic to the enclitic), *genéraque* (accented as a whole word), *generáque* (in accord with the supposed enclitic attraction rule), *génerápque*, *génerà que*, and *gènerápque* (various kinds of compound accentuation).

d. Clear statements by grammarians indicate that 'muta cum liquida' does not 'make position': a word like *volucrēs* 'flying [creatures], birds' has a light penult and accordingly the tonic accent falls on the antepenult: *vólucrēs*. This however accords neither with L prehistory (in which all consonant sequences whatsoever affect short vowels in medial syllables identically, **66**) nor with subsequent developments revealed in the accentuation of the Romance languages, which treats all consonant sequences alike. See **81.6a**.

---

[1] In the case of the decads, by the usual rules of accent the numerator would have invariably been pretonic. The shift of the accent to the pars propria on occasion might be nothing more exotic than the shift to the pars propria in the pupillary chant *amó, amás, amát, amámus, amátis, amánt*.

Romance evidence is not completely trustworthy, however. Plautine *fenstra* (*fēstra*) 'window' confirms the statement in Paul.Fest. that the accent of *fenestra* fell on the first syllable—the second *-e-* is anaptyctic, and postdates the codification of the L accentual pattern—yet all Romance languages attest **fenéstra.*

248. PHONETICS OF THE LATIN ACCENT. Although Romance languages agree both with one another and (largely) with the rules ascribed to L as to the location of tonic syllables, they differ among themselves as to the phonetic details of the accent, and hence provide little evidence for the phonetics of the Proto-Romance accent. Roman grammarians, down to the 4th cent AD, describe L accent in terms appropriate only for a pitch accent. Scholars have been wary of taking this as cogent, however, as not only is the terminology of Roman grammarians taken over entire from Greek, their statements are often cribbed from G sources. Some scholars protest, however, that ancient authorities could hardly have thus identified G and L accent had there not been at least an appreciable element of pitch in the latter. But as we have seen (242), pitch features are in fact a prominent ingredient of tonic accent even in English, whose accent system is the type and model of 'stess-accent'. If English grammarians were to gaze fixedly and confidingly upon a descriptive tradition that spoke only of pitch, it is likely that they too would have little trouble finding that element in English tonic syllables—not least because pitch features are in fact there. The familiarity of educated Romans with G accent in both practice and theory probably would not have caused them to adopt an element of accent wholly irrelevant for their natural speech, but it could have made them more conscious of an existing element of pitch, and even to a studied enhancement of it—Latin with a Greek accent, if you will—in oratory or recitations of poety.

a. The Roman adaptation of G scansion is seen by some as evidence that L accent was not of the stress variety, it being held that under a system of stress accent the strict observance of quantity in the unaccented syllables would have been remarkable if not impossible, and the frequent conflict between accent and verse ictus intolerable. (There are countless words like *amant, animōs,* and *ingenium* which can be got into a hexameter line only with the ictus on an unaccented syllable.) The first point is nonfactual, and the second underrates the degree to which poetry might comfortably be unlike natural speech.

Besides, a clear relationship between verse ictus and tonic accent in L verse has been demonstrated:— (1) the Roman poets relegated to the early part of the verse words in which harmony between stress and verse ictus is impossible. (2) There is in fact a pretty good alignment of accent and ictus overall in Plautus and Terence, and in the surviving hexameters of early poets like Ennius the alignment is considerably closer than in later poets. Indeed, later taste faulted early poetry on exactly that score, regarding it as inartistic and pedestrian by comparison to the sophisticated dissonances of accent and ictus in the poetry of a more refined age. (3) For the last two feet in hexameter of all periods there is harmony which is apparently greater than could be accidental—99 percent or better in Catullus, Cicero, Vergil, Ovid, and many others—and, whether or not the attention of the poets to the matter was conscious, the observed distribution easily allows for a fairly vigorous stress accent in L even if one accepts the view that the clash of ictus and stress was a problem.

But despite the remarkable-looking statistics, chance is probably a large part of the explanation: the L rules for stress accent automatically ensure a high degree of congruence between stress and ictus in the last three feet of a hexameter line (not just the last two). Taking the two line-end metrical skeletons (. . . x̄x̆x̆|x̄x̆x̆|x̄x̄̆ and . . . x̄x̄|x̄x̆x̆|x̄x̄̆) and inserting metrically compatible words at random, it will be found that only the occasional combination results in a mismatch between ictus and accent, such as: . . . x̄ *míni|mō* x̆x̆|x̄x̄̆. Nevertheless, it is likely that poets—the high art poets especially (the facts are significantly otherwise for the satirists)—purposefully strove to improve upon chance, because for Virgil and some others the alignment of tonic accent and ictus in the last two feet is practically 100 percent, which chance unaided can hardly account for.

DECLENSION

The Parts of Speech

249. The familiar classification of the *parts of speech* is based on a description worked out over time by Greek philosophers and grammarians, from whom it was borrowed by Roman grammarians; and still later it provided the framework for the grammatical analysis of most European languages. But the longevity of Greek grammatical theory is no warranty of fundamental truth. It was based upon a hodge-podge of criteria—a word's meaning, its form (case markers as part of the definition of *noun*), its relation to other words, or even mere location (thus *πρόθεσις/praepositio*—though thanks to a shift to a vaguely functional notion of the term, we may speak without real absurdity of a postpositive preposition). Partly owing to the mixture of criteria, there are difficulties of precise definition—for the category *pronoun*, for example—which increase when the analysis is applied to languages of different structure from the one it was devised for. It is a very poor framework for describing English, for example. But with all its defects it is a fairly workable system, and other classifications have never attained currency.

250. The Greek and Roman classification is as follows:

Greek	Roman	English
ὄνομα	nomen	noun, adjective
ῥῆμα	verbum	verb
μετοχή	participium	participle
ἄρθρον		article
ἀντωνυμία	pronomen	pronoun
πρόθεσις	praepositio	preposition
ἐπίρρημα	adverbium	adverb
σύνδεσμος	coniunctio	conjunction
	interiectio	interjection

It has been argued of late that Roman grammarians did not imitate Greek models as slavishly as commonly asserted (or as the pervasive calquing in the above table would suggest); but manifestly the Roman grammarians followed the basic scheme very closely, and some of the changes they made to it are not distinguished. For example, it is reported that the L category *interiectio* was added for no better reason than the desire to have the same number of categories in L as in G, there being nothing in L corresponding to ἄρθρον.

The category *ἐπίρρημα/adverbium*, no less than English *adverb*, is not actually a genuine 'part of speech', and its constituents are definable in mostly negative terms. The items (quite heterogeneous in nature) included in it have in common only that they are not happily at home in any other category.

Both the Greeks and Romans included under *ὄνομα/nomen* what we now distinguish as *noun* (or *(noun) substantive*) and *adjective*. The classical grammarians made numerous subdivisions of the noun; and among many other such, Priscian uses *adiectivum* of a word added to other appellatives, hence the modern terminology. (For the older IE languages such as G and L, the real distinction between 'noun' and 'adjective' is that nouns HAVE a gender whereas adjectives assume—'agree with'—the gender of the noun they are in construction with. But such a definition is useless for English and many other languages.)

By *μετοχή/participium* the ancients meant much the same as our *verbal*, namely formations which have some of the categorical properties of verbs such as tense, but which in FORM are more or less nominal, and which have verb-like syntax. Thus infinitives have subjects and objects and, in some IE languages, tense and voice; but they lack such basic verb traits as markers of person, number, and mood, and like nouns can act as subject of a verb. Such morphosyntactic hybrids had a largely separate evolution in G and L, so they agree only to a limited extent in form and function.

A puzzling detail is that the Greeks included under pronouns only the personal pronouns and possessives. So also some of the Roman authorities, while others included forms like *ūnus*, *ūllus*, and *alius* or were in doubt about them. Certainly words meaning 'any', 'all', 'other' have a number of semantic traits similar to indubitable pronouns, and in inflected languages outward evidence of this is their susceptibility to pronominal morphology: L *tōtus* 'all' has the pronominal gen.sg. *tōtīus* but adjectival *tōtum* nom./acc.sg. neut., in constrast to *aliud* neut. 'other', with its pronoun ending. (But the inflection of *omnis* 'all' shows no pronominal traits at all.)

THE INDO-EUROPEAN NOMINALS

251. GENDER. The distinction of three genders (masculine, feminine, and neuter) is characteristic of G and L, together with most of the other IE languages. This is *grammatical gender*, that is, a purely formal and syntactic system of morphology and concord. The IE languages vary in the degree to which the *natural gender* of beings aligns with grammatical gender. Of course, words for most objects and abstractions are 'masculine' and 'feminine' rather than neuter, and it is commonplace for words for babies to be neuter. But in, say, German there is the additional peculiarity that personal nouns like *Weib* 'woman' and *Mädchen* 'young lady' are grammatically neuter, *Hoheit* 'Highness' is feminine, and cats and dogs are grammatically feminine and masculine, respectively, regardless of reproductive details. In G and L there is an accommodation of the grammatical gender of animate nouns to natural gender by means of epicene nouns, that is, nouns that are both masculine and feminine like L *fēlis* 'cat' and *canis* 'dog', ditto G *αἴλουρος* and *κύων*.

In nouns, overt (formal) indications of gender in PIE were few. For most form-classes, PIE masculine and feminine nouns inflected identically, and neuter differed from them only in the nominative and accusative cases. This is true also of *i*-stem adjectives (a common type) and interrogative/indefinite pronouns, though as a general rule adjectives and pronouns are more completely marked for gender than nouns are. Personal pronouns however have no gender in PIE (361) and in most daughter languages.

There is one stem-class which is prevailingly masculine and neuter, the *o*-stems (258-61); and two which are prevailingly feminine, the *eH_2*-stems (that is, *ā*-stems, 262-6) and the *$^*iH_2/yeH_2$*-stems (that is, *ī/yā*-stems, 268-9; note a, below). In both G and L, but unique to them among IE groups, there are a fair number of feminine *o*-stems, not formally different from *o*-stem masculines in any way; and in G a new and productive type of masculine ᾱ-stems grew up, with distinctive forms for a few cases (267). The antiquity of these cross-gender types is disputed. Indic, for example, has no feminine *a*-stems (= the *o*-stems of G and L) or masculine *ā*-stems at all; and of the seven masculine nouns in *-ī* (268) which occur in the RV, five are names. In any case, in all IE languages the reflexes of *$^*eH_2$*- and *$^*yeH_2$*-stem ADJECTIVES are purely feminine.

The paucity of distinctively feminine noun types, and the fact that all share the element *$^*H_2$*, make it appear that the feminine as a category is derivative, and not coeval with the masculine and neuter. The fact that Hittite lacks the feminine noun types (and feminine concord altogether) accords with this view, but other interpretations are possible. In any case, in the forms of speech underlying G and L and all IE languages apart from Anatolian, the three-gender system is well established in both concord and morphology. The origin of IE gender has always fascinated scholars, but most ideas on the question are necessarily very speculative.

a. The two distinctively feminine stems are commonly known as the senā type (262-6) and the devī type (268-70), from the Skt. stock examples of inflection (Ved. *sénā-* 'army' and *devī́-* 'goddess'). Both types make feminine nouns more or less transparently derived from masculines. In InIr., both types also build feminine stems to *o*-stem adjectives, whereas in the European IE languages only the senā type fills that office. There is better agreement among IE languages in the remaining functions of the devī type (see 268). In G, the devī type remains distinct from the senā type, but in only a single case form, the nom.sg. (The persistence of such a trifling formal distinction is remarkable.) In L (270) the devī type disappears as a type, merging with the originally quite different *i*-stems (306-9).

252. NUMBER. Besides singular and plural, the parent speech possessed a dual, denoting 'two' or 'a pair'. 'Plural' in such a system therefore means 'three or more', not 'more than one'. The dual occurs in the earliest stages of several IE languages in all categories (verbs, pronouns, nouns), and though generally tending to disappear did occasionally put forth new formations (370c). But in the historical period the use of the dual steadily waned, and it eventually disappeared from nearly all IE languages. In G it occurs through the classical period, in the inscriptions of many dialects as well as in literature. It does not occur in Hellenistic G—the New Testament for example—or in contemporary G. In L and the other Italic languages it had disappeared as a category in prehistoric times, though certain L forms are remnants of dual forms, chiefly *ambō* 'both' = G ἀμφώ (261, 257.16).

The dual is still found in Lithuanian, Slovenian, Sorbian, and Icelandic (where, however, in the colloquial language the dual forms have assumed the function of plural and the old plural forms are reserved for formal occasions); and such forms as *both* and *(n)either* in NE are relics of dual morphosyntax. Interestingly, there is no dual in Hittite. Its absence in Anatolian is customarily treated as loss, but there is no clear evidence that it ever existed in that group.

a. Some scholars have thought to recognize in Latin a survival of the dual in the form of the gentile following two praenomina in a few early inscriptions, as M.C. POMPLIO. But this is merely the nom.sg. with final *-s* omitted, as is often found, 237.2. A better case can be made for tracing L *-tis* 2pl. to a PIE dual ending (428).

b. The early withering of the dual was a trait of western European IE languages. In the ancient Gmc. languages the dual had shrunk to the first and second person pronouns and verbs, and the latter are attested only in Go.; OE and ON have the du. personal pronouns, but in even the earliest OHG the whole category is quite gone. In Celt. the dual is limited to a few noun forms.

253. CASE. The parent speech is usually spoken of as having eight cases, the six that are known in L together with the locative and the instrumental, whose names and uses, at least, are familiar to students of L syntax. This roster owes much to InIr. morphology, and the discovery of Hittite with its large but very different inventory of case markers has stimulated some rethinking of the PIE case system. For now it is enough to suggest that the usual reconstruction of the eight Sanskrit-style cases misrepresents the actual speech of the PIE period. A more accurate picture would be a case-system in which certain endings and functions were well established—nominative, accusative, genitive/ablative, dative, and locative—whereas much of the remainder was less a case system than a collection of markers more or less in flux—which inter alia might explain why the endings of the pronouns are in many details different from the endings seen in nouns. The G marker -φι seen in ναῦφι 'aboard ship' is obviously an ingredient in the Ved. markers *-bhis* inst.pl., *-bhyas* dat./abl.pl., *-bhyām* dat./abl./inst.du.; OIr. *-b* /β'/ dat.pl. (palatalized, hence from *-*bi*- or *-*by*-, and ending with some consonant not a nasal, though further details are obscure); less obviously L *-bus* dat./abl.pl.; and Gaul. MATPEBO 'to the mothers' (evidently) seems to attest an ending more similar to L *-bus* than to OIr. *-b* or InIr. *-*bhis*. Sab. *-*fs* is ambiguous. And though the composite endings mentioned here are all non-singular, and the same is largely true of Myc., the literary G form is indifferent to number; and PIE **tebhi* 'to you'—obviously a very ancient form, reflected by L *tibī*, Ved. *túbhyam*, Av. *taibyā*, OCS *tebě* (367.3)—is specifically SINGULAR. This looks like an evolving system rather than a well-defined ending (or set of endings).

It is instructive to compare the evidence for endings in *-*bhi(-)* to evidence for PIE *-*tos*, an ending familiar from adverbs such as G -τος in ἐντός 'within', ἐκτός 'outside', and L *-tus* in *funditus* 'from the ground', *intus* 'within'. Similar remnants are to be found in Skt., as *agratás* 'in front' (*ágra-* 'point, beginning'). But in the most archaic Indic *-tas* also functions as nothing less than an ablative case marker; and it is seen by some as the source of the Classical Arm. ablative in *-ē*. In sum, **-tos* is straightforward in form but somewhat limited in distribution, while the **-bh-* cases have bafflingly protean forms which, however, are widespread, and are paradigmatic in several mainstream IE branches, preeminently InIr. The reason for the canonization of PIE **-bhis*, **-bh(y)os*, and the like as 'endings', but not **-tos*, seems to have less to do with methodology than with the fact that in InIr. the former but not the latter happens to be a fully paradigmatic element. Put differently, if *-tas* had become established in InIr. as an abl. suffix, it can be taken for granted that historical grammars would treat **-tos* as a case-marker lost from the paradigms of Gmc., Celt., and others, and surviving in fossils like L *funditus* (much as in **257.11**, below). As it is, **-tos* simply goes without mention in rehearsals of IE case endings.

254. Eight cases are found in Indo-Iranian; seven in the Baltic Assemblage (where gen. and abl. are merged); seven in Sab.; six in L (albeit the voc. is marginal; it is effectively a five-case system); five in literary G (but with one or two more still seen in Myc.; and the remark about the L vocative applies to G as well); four in NG, where the dat. is obsolete in the spoken language; five in the earliest Celt. and Gmc., though as in L the voc. is distinct only in a single form class; two (for the noun) in NE; one (for the noun) in French, Italian, and Spanish.

The merging of two or more cases in one, which has already taken place to some extent in G and L but has gone much further in most of the modern European languages, is known as case *syncretism*. It is due to a variety of factors, such as:

Overlapping of areas of usage. —To take prepositions as surrogates for cases: one may drink from or out of a bottle; carry something in the hand or with the hand; compare something with or to something else; lean on a tree or against a tree; write about history or on history.

Phonetic changes resulting in loss of formal difference. —In VL the loss of final *-m* and of the contrast between long and short vowels led to formal identity of acc. and abl. in the singular of all noun types. In Finnish, the change of **-m* and **-ñ* to *-n* resulted in the formal identity of the old acc. and dat./gen. (respectively). In L the *o*-stem dat./abl. pl. *-īs* might be traced to either PIE inst.pl. **-ōys* or loc.pl. **-oysu* (**260.4**). In Gothic, an *a*-stem form like *wulfa* 'wolf', officially the dat.sg., would indeed be the expected reflex of the PIE dat. **-ōy*; but it could equally well continue PIE **-ē/*-ō* (inst.), **-oy* (loc.), and **-ōt* or **-āt* (abl.). Such purely phonological changes go hand in hand with semantic and syntactic restructuring, obviously, but it is a process in which causes and effects are difficult to disentangle.

Increasing use of prepositional phrases which express all that the case forms express, making the latter dispensable. —In PIE (and conservative languages like Vedic Sanskrit and Hittite) there were comparatively few elements functioning like the familiar prepositions of G, L, and NE. But in L and G prepositional phrases had encroached largely on the pure case uses, and in later times this went still further. This too is a chicken-and-egg problem: does the increasing use of prepositions cause the decay of the endings, or does the withering of distinctions in the endings stimulate the use of prepositions? In any case, note that once such a process starts, prepositional elements do not necessarily keep proliferating: in French, a great array of diverse functions are gathered up under the two forms *à* and *de*, which are no more explicit than the L ablatives-of-this, and datives-of-that, familiar from the grammars.

Declension of Nouns

255. Table of proto-indo-european case endings.

Singular

Stems:	Cons.	*o*-stems	*eH*$_2$-stems	*i*-stems	*u*-stems
Nom.	-s, -ø	-o-s	-eH$_2$-ø	-i-s	-u-s
Voc.	-ø	-e-ø	-eH$_2$-ø	-ey-ø	-ew-ø
Acc.	-m̥	-o-m	-eH$_2$-m	-i-m	-u-m
neut.	-ø	-o-m	—	-i-ø	-u-ø
Instr.	-bhi, -mi	-o-H$_1$, -e-H$_1$	-eH$_2$-bhi,	-i-bhi	-u-bhi,
	-(e)H$_1$		-eH$_2$-eH$_1$?	-i-H$_1$	-u-H$_1$
Dat.	-ey	-ōy	-eH$_2$-ey	-ey-ey	-ew-ey
Gen.	-s,	-ī, -osyo	-eH$_2$-es,	-oy-s	-ow-s
	-os, -es		-eH$_2$-os		
Abl.	= Gen.	-ōt, -āt	= Gen.	= Gen.	= Gen.
Loc.	-i, -ø	-o-y, -e-y	-eH$_2$-i	-ēy-ø	-ēw-ø

Plural

Stems:	Cons.	*o*-stems	*eH*$_2$-stems	*i*-stems	*u*-stems
Nom./Voc.	-es	-ōs	-eH$_2$-es	-ey-es	-ew-es
(pron.)		-oy			
Acc.	-m̥s	-o-ms	-eH$_2$-ms	-i-ms	-u-ms
neut.	-H̥$_2$	-e-H$_2$	—	-i-H$_2$	-u-H$_2$
Instr.	-bhis,	-ōys	-eH$_2$-bhis,	-i-bhis,	-u-bhis,
	-mī̆s	-o-mī̆s (?)	-eH$_2$-mī̆s	-i-mī̆s	-u-mī̆s
Gen.	-om (?)	-ōm	-eH$_2$-om	-y-om	-w-om
(pron.)		-oysōm	-eH$_2$sōm		
Dat./Abl.	-bhos,	-o-bhos,	-eH$_2$-bhos,	-i-bhos,	-u-bhos,
	-mos	-o-mos	-eH$_2$-mos	-i-mos	-u-mos
Loc.	-su	(-o-su?)	-eH$_2$-su	-i-su	-u-su
(pron.)		-oysu			

Here, and in tables below, the label neut. *stands for* nominative/accusative neuter.

256. Notes on the preceding table. Further details will be found under discussion of the particular stems.

1. The table gives a survey of the singular and plural case endings that are indicated for the parent speech by combined evidence (subject to the proviso in 253). The inflections of many IE languages have been influenced by pronominal endings, particularly in the *o*-stems. Those that bear on G

and L noun inflection are included in the table with the distinguishing label *pron.*

2. Under vowel stems the stem vowel is included, while under consonant stems only the endings proper are given; in both situations, when there is no overt element marking case function, this is indicated by -ø (zero). Stem markers are divided from case markers proper (or zero) by hyphens, except when the stem and the case marker were united by contraction or some other development. For example the nom.pl. of *o*-stems can be assumed to include the stem vowel *-*o*- and the ending *-*es* evident in other paradigms, such that PIE *-*ōs* nom.pl. can with perfect confidence be resolved into **-*o-es*; but the actual historical evidence takes us back only to *-*ōs*.

3. There is better agreement among the IE languages for the singular markers than for the plural ones. For most cases there is little connection between the forms of the singular and plural. Those that show the strongest formal resemblance appear to be late additions to the system; for instance, in one possible reconstruction there was an inst. *-*bhi* (in Gmc. and BS *-*mi*), either singular or (more likely) indifferent to number, whose pl. was *-*bhis* (*-*mis*).

4. STEM ABLAUT. The *o*-stems are more exactly $^{e}/o$-stems, parallel to the stem vowel -$^{e}/o$- in thematic verbs (**439**). The *o*-grade predominates, but the *e*-grade is obvious in the voc.sg. (the bare stem) and in alternative forms of another case or two; and *e*-grade likewise occurs in the feminine paradigm derived from *o*-stems by the addition of *-H_2- (traditionally, the *ā*-stems, **262-6**); as the first element in the most archaic kind of compounds; and in denominative verbs.

Similarly, the *i*- and *u*-stems, as they are usually called, are actually stems in -*i*/-*ey*/-*oy*/-*ēy* and -*u*/-*ew*/-*ow*/-*ēw*, respectively. This array of stem-forms is paralleled in the *n*- and *r*-stems (**279-89**); but the distribution of grades in the *i*- and *u*-stems is quite unlike that of the *r*- and *n*-stems, or of consonant stems generally (**274-8**).

5. Besides *e*H_2-stems (that is, feminines in -H_2- derived from *o*-stems), there are also *i*H_2- and *u*H_2-stems, not included in the table. (They are sometimes known as the vr̥kīs stems and tanūs stems, respectively, from the Skt. words for 'she-wolf' and 'body', the standard paradigmatic examples of these form classes.) These inflect as consonant stems. Thus Ved. *dhīs* nom. sg. 'thought, concentration', *dhiyás* gen.sg., *dhíyas* nom.pl., *dhībhís* inst.pl.; analogously, *bhrū́s* nom.sg. 'brow', *bhruvás* gen.sg., *bhrúvas* nom.pl., from **dhiH*- and **bhruH*- respectively; cf. G ὀφρῦς nom.sg., ὀφρύος gen.sg., ὀφρύες nom.pl., and so on (**317-8**).

Another type not included in the table is the ablauting *i*H_2/*ye*H_2-stems (the devī inflection, **251a**), for which see **268-9**.

All three of these types are poorly attested outside of InIr., though thanks to its strong functional distribution, the devī type can be traced in Gmc. and L even though lost as a distinct stem class.

257. Remarks on the specific cases.

1. Nominative sg. The marker of the nom.sg. in masc. and fem. paradigms is *-*s*. (This ending is not seen in the devī (268) and senā (262–3) types, the personal pronouns (360–3), and certain other pronominals (374.3–4); for the *r*- and *n*-stems see 282.) The neut. forms are unmarked in the nouns except for one form class, the *o*-stems, where the ending is *-*m*; and in certain pronouns the ending is *-*d*.

2. The vocative sg. was endingless.[1] The voc.pl. had the same form as the nom.pl., except for accent: vocative forms were atonic in PIE except when they occurred at the beginning of an utterance or at the beginning of a line of verse, in which case the accent fell automatically on the first vowel of the word. In nouns normally accented on the first vowel anyway there would consequently be no difference between the nom.pl. and the tonic voc.pl. A Vedic tonic voc.pl. like *rā́jānas* is indistinguishable from the nom.pl., but in some other nouns there would always be a difference between nom. and voc.: Ved. nom.pl. *pitáras* 'fathers' is distinct from the voc. pl., whether atonic (*pitaras*) or tonic (*pítaras*).

3. The accusative sg. in masc. and fem. nouns and pronouns is marked with *-*m* (which is automatically *-*m̥* after a consonant; 93.1–2; 99). The acc. of the neut. is always the same as the nom., as set forth under item 1, above.

4. For the genitive sg. the common element is -*s* (the *o*-stem ending is a special problem; 259.8). In cons. stems the ending is usually *-*es* or *-*os*, rarely *-*s*. In the *i*- and *u*-stems, however, the case was marked by *-*s* appended to the full grade of the stem.

Such an *-*s* gen.sg. was once more general in PIE morphology, but is attested too sketchily to reveal much of its original distribution. It certainly occurred in ablauting (*proterokinetic*, 272.2) resonant stem neuters, as **dóru* 'tree' gen. **dréw-s* (as seen in RV *dā́ru, drós)* and **nómn̥* 'name' gen. **n̥méns* (as seen in OIr. *ainm* /an′m/, gen. *anme* < **n̥mens*). InIr. puzzlingly reflects a double zero grade *-*r̥-s* in *r*-stem nouns (283.2, corroborated by a few OE forms).

Two other very ancient genitives in *-*s* are seen in (1) the archaic collocation **dem-s potis* 'master of the house' (G δεσπότης, Av. *dəŋ paiti*-, Ved. *dámpati*-), a remnant of what is manifestly a very ancient root-noun (whose inflection is however attested only in fragments; see 272.1); and (2) in Hitt. *ne-ku-uz me-ḫur* '(at the) time of evening' (see 113b) < **nek*^{w}*t-s*.

5. The ablative has a distinctive marker only in the singular of the *o*-stems, *-*t* (? or *-*d*) preceded by a long vowel; the same marker, with a

[1] That is, in PIE **wl̥k*^{w}*e* 'O wolf', we have no ending, only the bare stem (259.2). It is fair, however, to decribe G λύκε, L *lupe* as having a 'vocative ending', once the original scheme of stem + ending had been lost sight of.

short vowel, occurs in both the singular and plural of certain pronouns. Since the pronouns have manifestly influenced *o*-stem inflection (**258-61**) in many ways, perhaps the distinctive *o*-stem abl. marker is an import from the pronouns, of very ancient date to be sure. But as it is axiomatic, or nearly so, that pronouns have more elaborate paradigms than nouns, that would mean, paradoxically, that the distinctive abl. ending in **-t* is a pronominal remnant of an ancient ending, probably identical with Hitt. inst. *-at* and abl. *-az(a)* (< **-ati*).

In all other form classes in PIE the abl.sg. is always identical to the gen.sg.; the abl.pl. is identical to the dat.pl. in InIr. and Italic, and that may have been the state of affairs in PIE. In Sab., the distinctive *o*-stem/pronominal abl.sg. in **-ōd* (***-o-Vt*) was the basis for a complete set of endings made up of lengthened stem-vowel plus *-d*. The result of this innovation is a systematic contrast between abl. and gen. sg. which is unparalleled in the familiar IE languages.

a. In Hittite the endings for ablative, genitive, and dative are everywhere distinct from one another; but the abl. is unmarked for number. See **259** and **260**.

6. In G the trifling differences between the old GENITIVE and ABLATIVE SINGULAR are effaced, the genitive markers everywhere prevailing; and the genitive plural, acquiring ablative function by analogy with the singular, ousted whatever the old abl. marker was. The dative, locative, and instrumental, still distinct in Myc. (at least to some degree), merge functionally; the actual markers in literary G continue a mixture of dat., loc., and instr. endings.

7. For the DATIVE SINGULAR of cons. stems Ved. *-e* and OL *-ei* (L *-ī*) point to a diphthong which might be IE **-ey*, **-oy*, or **-ay*. The literary G dat., being of loc. origin rather than a genuine dat. (ποδί matches Ved. *padí* loc.sg., not Ved. *padé* dat.sg.), does not help decide. Certain G dialect forms such as διϝει-φιλος 'dear to Zeus', Myc. *tu-ka-te-re* (*tʰugaterei*) 'to the daughter', *po-de* (*podei*) dat.sg. 'foot', and O forms in -eí, point to PIE **-ey*. Evidence for an alternant **-oy* is limited to a single category: the encl. dat.sg. of the 1st and 2nd person and reflexive pronouns (**363** and **367.3**), **moy*, **toy*, **soy*, which appear to be roots **m-*, **t-*, **s-* with ending **-oy*.

That would seem to settle the matter, but the Homeric athem. infinitives in -εναι, -ϝεναι, -μεναι (and also aor. -σαι, midd. -σθαι; see **552B**) are taken by some scholars to be equivalent to Ved. infinitives in *-mane* and *-vane*, and to be dative singulars in origin. There are better explanations for G -αι in the infinitives; but even if there were not, **-ay* cannot be related to **-ey*, **-oy*, by any theory of ablaut.

8. **Bh*~**m*. Next to the endings containing **bh*—probably, as stated above (**253**), they are all elaborations of a single basic element—there is a parallel set of endings beginning with **m* instead of **bh*. These are limited to Germanic and the Baltic Assemblage where, conversely, forms in **bh* are nowhere to be found apart from two OCS forms of the 2sg. pron. (**363**,

367.3). (Anatolian languages have no forms of either type in paradigms; but Hitt. *ku-wa-pí* 'where, when', is thought by some to superimpose on L *ubī*.[1])

The *bh languages are Celtic, Italic, and InIr., with a sprinkling of forms in post-Homeric literary G (virtually adverbs): βίηφι 'by force', θύρηφι 'at the door(s)', ὄρεσφι 'on the mountains', ἀπὸ ναῦφι 'from aboard ship'. The suffix is more liberally attested in Myc., *po-pi* (*pot^{h}p^{h}i*) 'with feet', *ko-ru-pi* (*korut^{h}p^{h}i*) 'with helmet(s)', *po-ni-ki-pi* (*p^{h}oinik^{h}p^{h}i* < **p^{h}oinik-*) 'with purple', *e-re-pa-te-ja-pi* (*elep^{h}anteyap^{h}i*) f. 'with ivory'. In other words, the PG element which is no more than a remnant in the usual G lexicon here looks like a fully paradigmatic case marker. In literary G the ending is indifferent to number;[2] In BS, too, cognate forms (with *-m-*) occur in both the singular and plural paradigms; but in Myc., as elsewhere (Celt., Gmc., Ital., InIr.) it is a component of specifically plural or dual endings only. Homeric is more conservative than Mycenaean: aboriginal indifference to number is guaranteed by the PIE singular personal pronouns **mébhi* 'to me', **tébhi* 'to you' dat.sg. (367.3), which are very ancient.

a. It has seemed likely to most observers that the forms in **bh* and **m* are somehow at bottom the same, but nowhere else in IE is there any evidence for interchange between nasals and voiced aspirated stops. Besides, the forms are not exactly parallel in any case. BS evidence points to inst.sg. *-*mi*, pl. *-*mīs*; the latter corresponds to nothing, exactly, in the *bh* set. In Gmc. a dat.pl. in *-*mis* is needed to explain North Germanic (runic) -*mʀ*, but Go. *wulfam* dat.pl. probably does not continue **wl̥k^{w}omis*, and *þaim* 'to them' (rather than ˣ*þaims*—NB *haims* 'village' < **ḱoymis*) cannot very well continue **toymis* parallel to Ved. *tébhis* inst.pl.; these Go. forms seem to vouchsafe *s*-less **wl̥k^{w}omi* and **toymi* closer to the BS inst.sg. than to any other pl. ending. In any case, OCS *tebě* dat.sg. 'you' (and the secondary gen. *tebe*) establish that the element *-*bhi* played some sort of paradigmatic role in the prehistory of BS and presumably also of Germanic. It is therefore unlikely that there is any historical connection between the two families of endings.

9. In G and L the instrumental singular in *-*(e)H₁* is not represented in any of the regular paradigms, but is preserved in some adverbs. Exactly how far back in the history of Italic the affix ceased functioning as a regular part of the paradigm is unclear; see 10, next, and **276.6a**. It appears (though there is some disagreement about this) to have still been playing a paradigmatic role in Myc., as in forms like *e-re-pa-te* 'with ivory'. Whether we are dealing here with *elep^{h}ante* (*-*H̥₁*) or *elep^{h}antē* (*-*eH₁*) cannot be determined, but either way *-*H₁* is indicated.

10. In L the functions of old ablative, locative, and instrumental are merged. The resulting case is called the ablative; but depending on

---

[1] This equation is not inevitable: L *ubī*, U **pufe** and related forms can be quite satisfactorily connected instead with Ved. *kúha*, Av. *kudā* < **k^{w}u-dh-*; see 381.3.

[2] The usual description, that it is used for both singular and plural, is not saying the same thing in different words: taking ναῦφι as a kind of plural is like taking NE *on foot* or *to bed* in the sentence *The villagers had already gone to bed* as a kind of plural.

stem-class and number, the actual endings may come from any of the three categories. Such case syncretisms are commonplace (254), but the merging of the ablative and the locative is puzzling: the notions 'at, in, on' are functionally remote from '(away) from, with', as discussed in **276.6a**.

11. The LOCATIVE must have survived in PItal., as it seems to be attested as a paradigmatic case in Sab. (so O **eísei tereí** 'in eo territorio'; see **263.8a**). But in L it is seen only in isolated forms that function as adverbs, like *humī* 'on the ground', *rūre* 'in the country'.

For the loc.sg. of cons. stems, beside the usual type with ending *-*i* there was also the bare stem without ending. Unmarked ('flat') locatives are widely encountered in languages, as NE *next door*, *last Friday*, and *home*. In IE languages, endingless locatives are well-attested in the *n*-stems (283), thus Ved. forms in -*(m)an* beside -*(m)ani*, to which correspond the G infinitives in -μεν, like δόμεν 'to give'. OIr. similarly attests *n*-stem dat.sg. forms (etymologically loc.sg) with and without the final vowel: *toimte* /toμ'd'e/ 'opinion' continues **to-mantyon* (or *-*yen*), while the synonymous *toimtin* /toμ'd'əν'/ continues **to-mantyoni* (or *-*yeni*). Evidence apart from the *n*-stems is scanty; but that endingless locatives were once more general is hinted by various data: old-looking root-noun forms in Av.: *dvarə* 'at the door' < **dhwer*, *dąm* 'at home' < **dem(H₂)*.[1] Similarly in early Hitt., É-*ir* 'at home' (classical É-*ni* = *pa-ar-ni*), *ta-ga-(a-)an* 'on/at the ground' (PIE **dhĝhom*), *ne-pí-iš* 'in the sky' (PIE **nebhes*), *ki-eš-šar-ta* 'in your hand' (PIE **ĝheser*). The OCS cons.-stem loc.sg. -*e* is said to be a particle 'on, in' added to the endingless stem (though possibly it is historically the gen.sg. ending).

In the singular, DATIVE *-*ey* and LOCATIVE *-*i* appear to be different ablaut grades of the same ending, and the meanings are closely related. But if they are in fact a single ending etymologically, the functional distinction between them was already established in PIE. —It is likely that, aboriginally, the dative (like the Hitt. abl.) was unmarked for number; cf. NE *to bed*. If special endings for the dat.pl. were created separately in each IE dialect, that would help explain their differences in detail.

12. In the LOCATIVE PLURAL there is evidence for *-*su* (InIr. and BS) and *-*si* (G); the latter is a remodeling of the former under the influence of the singular *-*i*. The *o*-stem form *-*oy-su*, seen in Ved. -*eṣu*, OCS -*ěchŭ*, G -οισι and (perhaps) L -*īs*, is ultimately of pronominal origin. The expected nominal form would have been *-*osu*, and just such a form is indicated by Hitt. -*aš*, as in dat.pl. *an-tu-uḫ-ša-aš* 'to men', from *-*osu* with apocope of the final vowel. No other language, however, points to the expected *-*o-su*, which therefore may already have been eliminated in the form of the parent language that underlies the familiar IE languages.

---

[1] This may be the explanation for Skt. *parút* 'last year' (PIE **wet-* 'year'), known only from grammatical treatises; the usual locative formation is seen in G πέρυσι, Dor. πέρυτι. (In both languages the grade of the stem is wrong for a loc.sg.)

13. The NOMINATIVE PLURAL ending for all masc. and fem. nouns is a uniform **-es*. Some pronouns have a different termination, **-y*, though this is less a case-marker than a stem-forming element; see **260.1** and **374.4-6**. In neuters the nom./acc. ending is **-H₂* (**-H̥₂* after cons., **101.1**).

14. The ACCUSATIVE PLURAL of masc. and fem. nouns and pronouns is ***-ms*; ***-m̥s* after consonants (**93.1-2**). This becomes **-ns*/**-n̥s* in attested languages. The outcomes of most of these are straightforward products of the sound laws, but the acc.pl. of the *eH₂*-stems (**265.2**) pose a problem: the InIr., BS, and Go. forms point to a form without a nasal before the final *-s*, but the G and Ital. forms show a nasal. In the days when the stem in question was reconstructed as **-ā-* this was a dilemma: did **-ns*, or rather ***-ms*, lose the nasal after a long vowel in the parent language already (which would make the Ital. and G forms the result of analogical leveling)? Or was the nasal lost after long vowels in the various branches independently? The general feeling has been that the former is more plausible, even though the fact G and L lost their restored nasals again within the historical period proved independent loss to be a realistic possibility. However, now that the stem is reconstructed as **-eH₂-*, there is no longer a special environment ('preceded by a long vowel') in the parent language.[1] As for the daughter languages, there is nothing implausible about the independent loss of a nasal after a long vowel before *-s* even in languages which preserve *-ns* after a short one: *o*-stem acc.pl. in Go. *wulfans*, Ved. *vr̥̥kān(s)* (PInIr. **wr̥kans*), next to *eH₂*-stem acc.pl. Go. *gibos*, Ved. *sénās*.

15. For the GENITIVE PLURAL the InIr., Lith., and G forms point to uniform **-ōm*. The Celt. and Ital. forms may be derived from either **-ōm* or **-ŏm*, as in both groups long vowels shortened before final **-m*; archaic Hitt. gen.pl. *-an* is likewise ambiguous, though might be held to favor **-ŏm* on the grounds that **-ōm* would have given *-un*. The OCS forms point to **-ŏm*, as do two pronoun forms in InIr., *asmā́kam* 'of us' and *yuṣmā́kam* 'of you pl.' (though the latter are hard to interpret owing to poorly understood elaborations of the forms—and may in fact have nothing to do with the question). One final datum: in the Vedas, the gen.pl. ending *-ām* must have two syllables perhaps a third of the time. Evidence favors *-aám* rather than *-aām* for the correct reading, but only faintly: all but a very few of the instances are metrically ambiguous.

It is tempting to try to account for these data by starting with an ending **-om*, which contracted with the stem vowel of the *o*-stems to make forms like **wl̥kʷōm* 'of wolves'. Perhaps the pronominal endings **-oysōm* m.n. and **-eH₂sōm* f., though enigmatic in detail, result from a similar contrac-

[1] A new problem in place of the old one is the lack of evidence for the shape **-eH₂m̥s*, with a syllabic nasal. A kind of parallel is afforded by the *i*- and *u*-stem forms, which are **-ims* and **-ums* for 'required' **-ym̥s*, **-wm̥s*.

tion. The survival of *-aam* in Vedic might mean that this contraction was to some extent optional in the parent language, but other interpretations are possible. In any case, this distribution was everywhere disturbed, with one or the other form eliminating its competition. In OCS and perhaps in Celt. and Ital. the ending **-ŏm* replaced expected long-vowel forms in the descendants of the *o*-stems, while in some branches (also possibly including Sab. and Celt.) the *o*-stem complex **-ōm* spread to other stems.[1]

For all its simplicity, this scenario has a serious flaw: the supposed original distribution was so straightforward, and aligned so well with other facts of the language, that it is not easy to understand how it could have been vulnerable to leveling even once or twice, let alone universally. On the other hand, it appears that the gen.pl. was for some reason much subject to remodeling in the daughter languages. For some of the innovations the model is clear, as in the Ital. importation of pronominal **-āsōm* into the *ā*-stem nouns; for some, like InIr. *-ānām* m.n., the correct explanation is in doubt; for some, such as the Germanic gen.pl. forms overall, the historical development is a profound enigma.

16. NOMINATIVE/ACCUSATIVE DUAL. The evidence for the dual case-markers in general is of poor quality. Many IE languages have no dual category at all; and even when they do, they provide fragmentary, ambiguous, or otherwise unsatisfactory evidence.

The best-attested case is the nom./acc.m./f., but its forms lead to incompatable reconstructions:

The vowel stems show lengthening alone: so *o*-stems in G λύκω, Ved. *devā́* 'two gods'; *i*-stem inflection in Ved. *pátī* 'two lords', OCS *gosti* 'two guests'; *u*-stem in Ved. *sūnū́* 'two sons' = OCS *syny*. A suffix **-e* is indicated in consonant stems: G πατέρε, φερόντε; the same is found in OLith. (*du žmune* 'two persons'), and OIr. attests an ending consisting of a front vowel: *carait*ᴸ /kaɸəd'/ 'two friends' continues **karont-* plus **-ĕ̄* or **-ĭ̄*. In InIr. the *o*-stem form has invaded the consonant stems, so Ved. *pā́dā* 'the two feet'. Evidence for an earlier state of affairs has been seen in the dvandva compound *mātara-pitarā* 'parents' (Pāṇini). Now, this is neither a Vedic dvandva, that is with both components marked with the usual dual cases (as in RV *mātárā-pitárā* 'parents'), nor is it either of the two later types—with the first element in stem form (*bhrātr̥-bhaginī* 'brother and sister') or in the nom.sg. (*pitā-putrā́u* 'father and son'). Since the first element of a dvandva was originally in an overtly dual case, it is probable that *mātara-* here is the original nom./acc.du. that was supplanted by the *a*-stem ending *-ā(u)*.

The Ved. *-ă* thus slenderly attested, the *-e* of OLith., and the front vowel of OIr. can be gathered up under PIE **-e*. On the other hand, the lengthening of the vocalic stems is most easily accounted for by a final

[1] In Indic the original gen.pl. ending of the *a*-stem nouns is displaced by *-ānām*, though in the RV there are four instances of the fossilized collocation *devā́ñ jánman-* 'race of gods', in which the original *o*-stem gen.pl. in *-ām* < **-ōm* is uniquely preserved. In none of the four is the distracted reading *-aam* possible.

laryngeal. The G forms in -ε, which might reflect either *-*e* or *-$\underset{\circ}{H}_1$, are ambiguous. Likewise ambiguous is the *o*-stem dual, as either *-*o*H_1 or **-*oe* will give the same outcome in all IE languages (cf. nom.pl. *-*ōs* < **-*oes*, 260.1). The Indic, Lith., and OIr. cons. stem forms cannot reflect *-$\underset{\circ}{H}_1$, nor can the *i*- and *u*-stem forms readily continue **-*ie*, **-*ue*. Nevertheless, each of the two possibilities has its proponents among modern scholars as the sole etymon.

a. For what it is worth, an ending *-*e* would be unique among nominal case markers in containing no consonant at all, which might support amalgamating the two candidates for the ending into ablaut variants of a single ending, *-H_1e and *-H_1.

b. Indic evidence for original -*a* is perhaps slightly stronger than it first appears: the importation of the *a*-stem ending -*ā* into the cons. stems would have been facilitated if the original ending were -*a* < *-(H_1)*e*, rather than *-*i* < *-$\underset{\circ}{H}_1$, as it would mean nothing more complicated than lengthening a vowel.

c. There is some slender evidence (370a) that the marker of the *o*-stem and pronominal dual was actually *-H_3, not *-H_1. If accepted, this would of course forestall the speculation floated in note **a**, above.

o-STEMS. THE GREEK AND LATIN SECOND DECLENSION

258. The *o*- and *ā*-stems of G and L influenced one another and were both influenced by pronoun inflections. The *o*-stems will be taken up first, as they are more basic: the *ā*-stems were derived from them; were more influenced by the *o*-stems than conversely; and have certain complexities unlike anything in *o*-stems.

A Note on citation. The Oscan, Umbrian, Vedic, and Hittite forms cited here and in other tables below are those actually quotable. For the other languages, 'typical' paradigms are given (apart from somehow notable forms quoted from texts).

259. THE SINGULAR CASES OF *o*-STEMS (see table opposite).

1. Nom.sg. PIE *-*o-s*, G -ος, PItal *-*os*, OL -*os*, whence usual -*us* (71.6). For L *puer*, *vir*, *ager*, see 74.4. Regular syncope of the *o* is seen in Sab., as O **húrz** 'garden' (z = [ts]; cf. L *hortus*), *bantins* = L *bantīnus* 'of Bantia'.

a. 'ATTIC INFLECTION'. Nouns like νεώς, νεώ 'temple', λεώς, λεώ 'people', and λαγῶς, λαγῶ (earlier -ώς,-ώ) 'hare' show what is called 'Attic inflection'. These are ordinary *o*-stems in origin. Some are the results of quantitative metathesis (79.3, esp. note **a**), so νεώς λεώς < νηός ληός < **nāwos*, **lāwos*. Others, like λαγῶς, result from contraction: λαγωός, λαγωόο (λαγωοῦ) > λαγώς, λαγώ, and so on.

2. Voc.sg. PIE -*e*, not an ending per se but the bare stem in the *e*-grade, is seen as such in BS, G -ε, and PItal. *-*e*, whence L -*e*. But L *puer* 'O boy' (*puere* in Plaut.), *vir* 'O man' are identical to the nom.sg. This is probably a phonological development, as short vowels seem to be especially prone to drop after *r* (74.6). —From words in -*ius* a few early forms in -*ie* are quotable, as *fīlie* 'O son'; but the form is regularly *fīlī*, *Valerī*.

a. The accent of a form like the last was seemingly *Váleri*, in contrast to gen.sg. *Valérī* (see 8, below). This might be the result of relative chronology: contraction of the

The singular cases of *o*-stems

	Greek	Myc.	Latin	Oscan	Vedic	Hittite	Gothic	OCS	Lith.
Nom.	λύκος[1]	do-e-ro[2]	lupus[1]	**húrz**[3]	devás[4]	at-ta-aš[5]	wulfs[1]	vlĭkŭ[1]	vil̃kas[1]
Voc.	λύκε		lupe	U tefre[6]	déva	iš-ḫa-mi[7]	wulf	vlĭče	vilkè
Acc.	λύκον	do-so-mo[8]	lupum	dolom[9]	devám	at-ta-an	wulf	vlĭkŭ	vil̃ką
neut.	ζυγόν[10]	ri-no[11]	iugum[10]	**sakaraklúm**[12]	yugám[10]	i-ú-kán[10]	waurd[13]	igo[10]	
Inst.	τη-δε[14]	i-qo ?[15]			yajñā́[16] devéna[18]	te-eš-ḫi-it[17]	wulfaꝰ	vlĭkomĭ	vilkù
Dat.	λύκωι	do-e-ro	lupō	**húrtúí**	devā́ya	an-na(-i)[19]	wulfaꝰ	vlĭku	vil̃kui
Abl.	(*h*)οπω[20]		lupō(d)	dolud	vṛ́kāt[1]	te-eš-ḫa-az[21]	OHG tagu[22]	vlĭka	vil̃ko
Gen.	λύκοιο, λύκου	do-e-ro-jo	(cuius) lupī	**sakarakleís**	devásya	at-ta-aš	wulfis	(česo[23])	
Loc.	οἴκοι[24] ἐκεῖ[27]		humī[25]	**tereí**[26]	devé	at-ti	wulfaꝰ	vlĭčě	vilkè

1. 'Wolf'.
2. 'Slave' (= δοῦλος).
3. 'Garden'.
4. 'God'.
5. 'Father'.
6. 'O Tefer' (a deity).
7. 'O my lord': *iš-ḫa(-a)* with enclitic poss. prn. *-mi-*.
8. 'Delivery, receipt'.
9. 'Fraud'.
10. 'Yoke'.
11. 'Linen' (= λίνον).
12. 'Temple'.
13. 'Word'.
14. Thera 'in this way'.
15. 'Horse' (cf. ἵππος). The existence of a Myc. instrumental case in *-o* (i.e. *-ō*) is disputed.
16. 'By means of a rite'. This *-ā*, the original ending, is preserved in only a dozen forms in the RV. The usual ending, even in the RV, is *-enā̆*, imported from the pronominal inflection.
17. 'By means of a dream', stem *te-eš-ḫa-*.
18. In some twenty instances in the RV and two or three in the AV, the ending is *-enā*.
19. 'Mother'; the endings shown are archaic Hittite (where already the *an-na-i* type is rare). The 'classical' forms are the locatives *an-ni*, *at-ti*.
20. Locr. 'from where'.
21. The ending is occasionally *-za*, as in *an-na-za* next to *an-na-az*.
22. 'Day': this OHG case, which is rare, is traditionally called the instrumental; but most historians trace it to the abl. **-ōd* (**-ād*). —The Go. 'dative' in *-a* probably includes the PIE ablative and instrumental among its sources.
23. In nouns, reflexes of the PIE abl.sg. function as gen. in BS. This pronominal form, 'of which' neuter, is the sole remnant of a distinctive genitive singular ending.
24. 'At home'.
25. 'On the ground'.
26. 'in [that] region'.
27. 'In that place'.

final syllable in the voc. predated the fixing of classical L accent, and contraction in the gen. postdated it. It is more likely however that *Váleri̅* continues original **Válerie*, with first-syllable accent characteristic of words consisting wholly of light syllables (the type of *fácilius* 'easier', **246a**). See also item 8a, below.

3. Acc.sg. PIE **-o-m*: G *-ον* (**236.2**), PItal. **-om* whence Sab. *-om*, **-úm**, OL *-om*, whence in turn the usual L *-um* (**71.6**).

4. Nom./acc.sg.neut. PIE **-o-m*, with the same history in G and L as the preceding. See **257.1**.

5. Inst.sg. Both PIE **-e-H_1* or **-o-H_1* are hinted at by forms in various daughter languages; but the ending is unmistakably attested only in InIr., whose *-ā* is ambiguous as to grade. The instrumental as a category is not a regular case in either G or L, but is recognized in some adverbial formations. No *o*-stem form is quotable from Myc. (See abl.sg., 7, below.)

6. Dat.sg. PIE **-ōy* < ***-o-ey*: G *-ωι*, with the *-ι* eventually lost in the historical period (**63.3**); PItal. **-ōy*, preserved as *-oi* (**-úí**) in Sab. but *-ō* in L. It is uncertain when the final glide was lost (**63.3**). Antique forms in *-oe*, *-oi* are rare and difficult: DVENOI in the Duenos inscr. is probably one, but that exhausts the L epigraphic evidence if NVMASIOI from the Praeneste Fibula is bogus (**19**).

a. Hitt. *-a* as a paradigmatic case is found in early texts, and is conventionally explained as the regular development of **-ōy*. This may be half right; in any case only the *a*-stems have a by-form *-a-i*, which possibly preserves the final glide.

However, the ending *-a* is found in all stem types, and the inconsequential status of thematic inflection in Hitt. makes it unlikely that the ending could have spread from there. Furthermore, it typically signifies the goal of a motion: *ne-pí-ša s*-stem 'to the sky', *ták-na-a n*-stem 'to the earth', *a-ru-na a*-stem 'to the sea'. While even in this use it became obsolete in 'classical' Hittite, it remained in purpose infinitives in *-nna* < **-tna* (built to *r/n*-stems), as *a-da-an-na* 'to eat', cf. *a-da-tar* 'an eating'. All these facts are easily accommodated in a new case, 'directive' or the like.

This case, once its form and function had been perceived, explained a number of G and L adverbs: G ἄνω 'upwards', κάτω 'downwards', ὀπίσ(σ)ω 'backwards'; L *quō* 'whither', *eō* 'to that place'. Further, it might well underlie InIr. **ā* 'to, at' (a preverb and preposition without known cognates hitherto), and also provide insight into the Indic dat.sg. of the *a*-stems, *-āya*, long supposed to be for **-āyā* with the element *ā* 'to' just mentioned, but possibly a conflation of the true dative in **-ōy* and the directive case. An ending **-ō*, that is probably **-eH_3*, would furthermore provide a morphological function for *H_3, hitherto not known in suffixes and endings.

7. Abl.sg. PIE **-ōt*. One of the ingredients in the long vowel is the stem vowel, and Ved. prn. forms like *mát* 'from me', *tvát* 'from you (sg.)' indicate that the ending proper was **-ot* or **-et* rather than something with a laryngeal in it. The resulting **-ōt* is directly attested in Ital., thus O *-ud*, **-úd**, OL *-ōd*, whence the usual L *-ō* (**237.4**). Moreover, endings on the plan 'abl.sg. = long stem vowel plus *-d*' spread to all other vowel-stem noun types in Ital.

Though not a proper case form in G, the ending survives in Dor.

adverbs of place-from-which, like ὄπω 'whence' (functionally but not formally equivalent to Att. ὁπόθεν). Often quoted in this connection is Delph. ϝοικω 'at [one's] own expense' (? lit. 'from the house', ϝοικο- 'house'). Similar adverbial use is seen in L *prīmō* 'at first', *tūtō* 'safely' (lit. 'in one piece'), and—with iambic shortening, 84—*modo* 'only, but'.

a. L adverbs in *-ē* seem to have lost a final *-d*, on the basis of forms like FACILVMED (SC de Bacch.; equivalent to L *facillimē*) and Sab. forms like O *amprufid* = L *improbē* 'wickedly'. These have been interpreted as a remnant of a PIE abl.sg. built to the *e*-grade of the stem rather than the better-attested *o*-grade, but they are more plausibly taken as the PIE inst. in **-eH₁* (cf. 5 sup.) which became contaminated with the abl. *-d* during the period when the abl. marker was expanding its territory in Italic. Some of the adverb type in *-ō* mentioned in 6a, above, may likewise continue inst. **-oH₁* rather than **-ōt*.

b. A more curious datum is that Lith. *vil̃ko* abl.sg. cannot reflect **-ōt*, and points rather to **-āt*. (OCS *vlĭka* gen.sg. is ambiguous.) See 263.6a.

8. Gen.sg. The IE languages show only partial agreement in the *o*-stem gen.sg. ending, which however everywhere differs significantly from the gen.sg. markers in all other form classes of nouns, and instead aligns with those of certain pronouns.

Type A. PIE **-osyo*, PG **-ohyo*, **-oyyo* (206), earliest G *-οιο* preserved in Hom. and Thess. This yields Thess. *-οι* by apocope, but elsewhere with loss of *ι* (207) the outcome was first *-οο* then *-ου* or *-ω* (depending on dialect, 76). This ending was seemingly lost in L nouns, though Falisc. KAISIOSIO and one or two later inscriptions apparently show the expected form (albeit remodeled; 375.1). Clearer evidence is found in the 5th century BC inscription known as the Lapis Satricanus: POPLIOSIO VALESIOSIO SVODALES 'the accustomed associates of Publius Valerius'. Whether or not this is really Latin—it certainly appears to be—it is at all events Italic.

The PIE ending **-osyo* is attested as such in InIr. (Ved. *-asya* in both pronouns and *a*-stem nouns). Gmc. and BS seem to continue **-e-so* (pronouns), and Gmc. nouns perhaps reflected **-oso* rather than **-osyo*. By this interpretation, which is the usual one, the PGmc. loss of final short vowels rendered the nom.sg. **wulfaz* homophonous with the gen.sg.; the attested gen.sg. forms, for example Go. *wulfis*, ON *ulfs*, and OE *wulfes* (< arch. *-æs*), reestablished a formal contrast by adopting the form of the pronouns **þes*, **hwes*.

In fact, however, this scenario cannot be accurate, as PGmc. **h^wes* gen.sg. develops differently in West and North Germanic from what should have been the homphonous nom.sg.: OHG *huuer* nom. but *huues* gen.; OE *hwa* but *hwæs*; ON *hver* but *hves*. Similarly cf. OE *wulf* nom.sg. < **wulfaz* vs. *wulfas* gen.sg. < ?? **wulfes*. It has therefore been argued that, obscure as the details of development are, we must posit **-osyo* for the Germanic paradigm as well. The only remaining example of putative **-eso*, then, is OCS *česo* 'of what'. Its history is obscure, but can be provisionally seen as contamination by the animate *kogo* 'of whom', *togo* 'of that'. Such an explanation is ad hoc of course, but the manifestly conflated forms *česogo* and *čĭsogo* are suggestive.

In line with the traditional view of an ancient distinction between **-osyo* and **-oso*, some think that the Homeric endings *-οιο* and *-ου* (that is, *-οο*) continue the two different PIE endings. Owing to the indisputable loss of intervocalic *-y-* evident in Homer and already under way in Myc. (192, 205-7), there is no necessity to invoke two etyma; but in support of the theory is a striking fact of Homeric distribution. While in nouns the ending *-οιο* shows a slight preponderance, the ratio of *-οιο* to *-ου* in the pronouns is a mere one to five. This would be explained if there were an original distinction between a nominal ending **-osyo* and a pronominal ending **-oso*. But in view of the difficulties of maintaining the existence of PIE **-oso* in the first place, a purely G explanation is more likely, such as the vulnerability of *-y-* in the article to proclitic reduction.

Type B. L and Celt. agree instead on the ending **-ī* with no trace of the stem vowel, overtly attested in L, Gaulish SEGOMARI, and in Prim.Ir. (MAQ(Q)I 'of the son'), and indirectly in OIr. *maicc* /mak'/. Venetic seems to agree. In inscriptions which predate the confusion of *ī* and *ei* (57.2), the L gen.sg. *-ī* is uniformly -I; only later, when I and EI are used promiscuously to represent *ī*, does a gen.sg. spelled -EI crop up.

Authorities are divided on whether this *-ī* is connected with the Type A suffix in **-(y)^e/os(y)o*. The communis opinio is that it cannot be, but some important scholars persist in the feeling that it somehow must be. The chief obstacle to all proposed derivations from *-^{e}/*osyo* is the earliness and uniformity of the the attestation of simple *-ī*, in both L and Celtic, while the 5th century attestation of L -IOSIO (see Type A, above) leaves very little time for such a bulky form to reduce to *-ī*.

a. In L nouns in *-ius* and *-ium* the gen.sg. *-iī* was regularly contracted to *-ī*, as *consilī* 'council', *imperī* 'command, authority', but with the position of accent faithfully reflecting the uncontracted shape, thus *impérī* as if **impériī*. This was the normal form down through the Augustan period, but it later was replaced by *-iī*, with *-i-* restored after the analogy of the other cases. In proper nouns the older form was more persistent, as *Vergilī* alongside *consiliī*. Note that the nom.pl. in *-iī* < **-i-oy* (260.1) does not thus contract at any period. (These facts are another obstacle to the notion that L *-ī* somehow continues **-(i)yosyo*. The idea that this might have regularly become *-ī* prior to the 4th century BC while **-iyoi* nom.pl. reduced no further than *-iī* is implausible on its face.)

9. Loc.sg. PIE **-ey*, **-oy* (that is, *-^{e}/*o-i*). These forms are not a part of any attested G paradigm (there is but a single doubtful form in Myc.), but are preserved in adverbs: *οἴκοι* 'at home', *ἐκεῖ* 'in that place', Dor. *ὅπει* 'where' (Att. *ὅποι*). Italic is ambiguous: **-oy* or **-ey* would equally well account for the attested forms, O **eísei tereí** 'in eo territorio', L *-ī* in *domī* 'at home', *humī* 'on the ground'. The L forms, like the G, are in effect adverbs. (See **263.8a.**)

a. 'The loc.sg. has the same form as the gen.sg.' is a convenient rule of thumb for L, especially as it serves for both the first and the second declensions. But it has no historical basis and does not hold for early L (*o*-stem gen. *-ī*, but loc. *-ei*).

b. Since *e*-grade is typical of PIE loc.sg. in consonant stems, the twofold form of the *o*-stem ending poses the question of whether **-oy* is original and **-ey* a secondary creation; or **-ey* is original (in accord with the norm for the loc.sg.) and **-oy* results from leveling on the prevailing vocalism of the *o*-stems. The only data actually requiring **-ey* are non-paradigmatic scraps: a handful of G adverbs like *ἐκεῖ*; perhaps L *hīc* 'here' < **ǵhey-ke* (next to *hūc* 'hither' < ? **ǵhoy-ke*); and perhaps the archaic so-called dative ending *-i* in OE (in contrast with the genuine archaic dat.sg. in *-æ* < **-oy*). The G forms in *-οι*, the absence of palatalization in Avestan, OCS loc. *vlĭcě* instead of the ˣ*vlĭči* that would come from **-ey*, and possibly the Go. dat.sg. *wulfa*, all point to **-oy*. Attestation in remnants, non-paradigmatic forms, and in peripheral areas, is the hallmark of relics; but since it would be remarkable for the well-nigh universal **-oy* to have arisen by independent innovations, a move in favor of **-oy* must have been underway in late PIE.

260. THE PLURAL CASES OF *o*-STEMS.

The table of plural case forms is on page 262.

1. Nom.pl. PIE **-ōs* in *o*-stem nouns, **-oy* in pronouns (ultimately ***-o-es* and ***-o-i*, 374.5). The original distribution is preserved in InIr. and Gmc. only, hence Skt. *te vṛkās*, Go. *þai wulfos* nom.pl. 'the wolves'; and, with some sort of remodeling of the noun ending, in Hitt.: *ki-e* nom.pl. /kĕ/ 'these', but *at-te-eš* nom.pl. 'fathers' (nom.sg. *at-ta-aš*).

In the remaining IE languages the original distribution was disturbed. In G, L, BS, and OIr., the pronominal form was generalized to the *o*-stem nouns. This is self-evident in G λύκοι, and in OL *poploe* quoted by Fest. (with an anachronistic spelling for the presumed *-oi* of the original), from the Carmen Saliare; otherwise in L, even early, the form has progressed to *-ei* (75.2), whence the usual *-ī*. The PIE system manifestly had lasted into the PItal. period, however, because in Sab. the noun form was generalized to pronouns (a unique development in the IE languages), hence O *iusc* 'they' (**iyōs-ke*), **pús** nom.pl. 'who', like nominal **núvlanús** 'Nolani'.

a. L inscriptions, most of them from the 2nd century BC, show some *o*-stem nom.pl. forms in *-eis*, *-īs*, as MAGISTRE(I)S and HEIS (in pronouns also in Plaut. *hīsce* for example), in which *-s* has somehow been added to the pronominal ending—the exact source of the analogy or confusion or whatever it is has so far eluded convincing explanation. Possibly significant is that literary attestations of this feature are limited to the pronouns, leading to the suspicion that epigraphic -s in nouns (which parenthetically is practically limited to personal nouns, that is, names and titles) might be artificial.

b. From *deus* the normal form was *dī*, similarly dat./abl. *dīs*, resulting from a contraction that took place at an intermediate stage in the development of the diphthongs. That is, **deywoy*, **deywoys* became **deywey(s)* (75.2), then **dẹ̄wẹ̄(s)* (57.2), then per 183a **dẹ̄ẹ̄(s)*, and finally **dẹ̄(s)*, whence *dī*, *dīs* (57.2). The spelling in inscriptions is usually DI, DIS; *dii* and *diis*, more frequent in mss, are an artificial compromise. Real disyllabic *deī*, *deīs*, in later poets, are transparently an analogical reconstitution of a stem *de-* on the basis of other cases.

c. In OIr. the **-oy* imported into the *o*-stems from the pronouns served as nom.pl.; remarkably, the reflex of **-ōs* continued in the original role of voc.pl. Thus *fir* nom.pl. 'men' < **wiroy* but *firu* 'O men' < **wirōs*.

d. In the RV the nom.pl. of *a*-stems is usually *-ās* < **-ōs*, as in later Skt., but in fully a third of the RV occurrences the ending is *-āsas*. Analogous forms occur in Av., and are necessary to account for the *-s* plural of English and other Low WGmc. languages (but do not figure in the history of Go. and NGmc., and perh. OHG). They are the usual nom.pl. ending **-ōs* with a second application of the plural ending. The key is the relationship between the nom.sg. and the nom.pl. in nouns generally: in all other form classes the nom.pl. is a syllable longer than the nom.sg., such that inherited nom.pl. (Ved. *vṛ́kās*, PGmc. **wulfōz*) would have seemed truncated. (There are no neat proportional analogies leading directly to such formations; but cf. *herring boxes without topses* in the Carmen Clementinae, and hypocoristic *shoeses* for *shoes*).

The plural cases of *o*-stems

	Greek	Mycenaean	Latin	Oscan	Vedic	Hittite	Gothic	OCS	Lith.
Nom.									
(noun)		?do-e-ro[1]		**núvlanús**[2]	devā́s(as)[3]	at-te-eš[4]	wulfos		
				(**pús**[5])					
(prn.)	λύκοι	?do-e-ro[1]	lupī		(té[6])	(a-pí-e[7])	(þai[6])	vlĭci	vilkaĩ
Acc.	λύκους,	si-a₂-ro[8]	lupōs	**feíhúss**[9]	devā́n̐(s)	ad-du-uš[10]	wulfans	vlĭky	vilkùs
	ελευθερονς[11]								
neut.	ζυγά	do-ra[12]	iuga	comono[13]	yugā́(ni)[3]	dan-na-at-ta[14]	waurda	iga	
Inst.	λύκοις	do-e-ro-i[17]	lupīs	zicolois[15]	devā́is	ŠU.ḪI.A-it[16]		vlĭky	vilkaĩs
		de-so-mo[17]							
		o-mo-pi[18]			devébhis[3]				
Dat.		do-e-ro-i[17]			devébhyas	ad-da-aš	wulfam	vlĭkomŭ	vilkáms
Abl.					devébhyas	*-az(a)[19]			
Gen.	λύκων		deum[20]	zicolom	devā́m[3]	ši-ú-na-an[21]	wulfe	vlĭkŭ	vilkų̃
			deōrum[20]		devā́nām	ad-da-aš			
Loc.	λύκοισι	do-e-ro-i[17]			devéṣu	ad-da-aš		vlĭcěxŭ	vilkuosè

1. It cannot be told whether Myc. *-o* stands for the ending seen in G *-οι*, or for *-ōs* < PIE **-ōs*.
2. 'Citizens of Nola'.
3. Vedic forms. Classical Skt. has only *devās*, *yugāni*, *devāis*, and *devānām*.
4. The same ending is sometimes written differently, as in *an-ni-iš*. In later texts the acc. pl. *-uš* is promiscuously substituted for the orig. nom.pl. ending *-eš*.
5. 'Who'.
6. 'The/these' masc.
7. 'Those' common gender, the ending < **-oy*, as in L *quī*, G *οἱ*.
8. 'Hogs' (*sibalons* = G *σίαλους*).
9. 'Walls'.
10. In later texts, the ending proper to the nom.pl. is found in place of the original acc.pl. ending (but acc. *-uš* for nom. *-eš*, as in note 4, is more common).
11. Cret. 'free'.
12. 'Gifts'.
13. 'Assembly', pl.tant.; *-o* < PItal. **-ā*.
14. Adj. *dan-na-at-ta-* 'empty'.
15. 'Days'.
16. 'With the hands' (i.e. **ki-eš-ši-ri-it*). The inst.pl. is formally identical with the inst.sg., and therefore usually ambiguous; but in this one attestation the ending is appended to an explicitly plural logogram.
17. The interpretation of these forms is unclear without definite knowledge of the case SYSTEM of Mycenaean.

18. Meaning uncertain, beyond the fact that it is something (decorative?) on a chariot. If 'with garlands' then perh. the reading is *hormopʰi*, cf. G ὅρμος 'wreath, garland, chaplet'.
19. Unattested in *a*-stems, but the few certain ablative plurals in other form classes are all identical to the ablative singular.
20. The ending *-ōrum* is imported from the pronouns. The original *o*-stem ending is seen in certain specific nouns (as *deum*) or categories of noun.
21. 'Of gods'. The gen.pl. *-an* in later texts is limited to animate nouns in certain set phrases; elsewhere the ending is *-aš*, *ad-da-aš*, *ši-ú-na-aš*.

---

2. Acc.pl. PIE **-ons* < ***-o-ms*: G -ονς preserved in Cret. and Arg., whence, according to dialect, -ως, -ος, -οις, -ους (**228.4**); O **-úss**, L *-ōs* (**226.3**). See also **237.5**.

3. Nom./acc.pl.neut. PIE **-e-H₂*, whence PG and Ital. **-ā*, identical in form with the nom.sg. of *eH₂*-stems and probably the point of departure for the creation of that stem (**262**). The similarity between G -α and L *-a* in this ending is deceptive: they have different histories. All that the two languages have in common is the elimination of the distinction between the cons. stem ending **-ă* < **-H̥₂* (**277.3**) and the *o*-stem form **-ā* < **-eH₂*: in G the cons. stem -ᾰ replaced the *o*-stem ending *-ᾱ; in Ital. however, where long vowel alternants prevail over short, it was **-ā* that was generalized. This is directly visible in O *comono* 'assembly' (pl.tant. like L *comitia*), **prúftú** pple. 'placed', with the characteristic Sab. raising and rounding of Ital, **-ā* as in the *ā*-stem nom.sg. O **víú** 'via', *touto* 'city', U **mutu** 'much' (**263.1**). Later this neut. **-ā* > *-a* in L (**83.2**), just like the nom.sg. of the fem. *ā*-stems. (An original **-a*, corresponding to the G ending, would leave the Sab. forms unaccounted for and would have given L ˣ*-e*; **71.4**.)

4. Dat.(-abl.)pl. The PIE ending **-ōys*, whose internal structure is enigmatic, was the form of the inst.pl. peculiar to *o*-stems and pronouns. It is seen substantially unchanged in Ved. *-āis*. In G -οις and PItal. **-oys* the diphthong shortened by Osthoff's Law (**63.2**), whence O *-ois*, **-úís**; and OL *poplois* quoted from the Carmen Saliare, *ab oloes* 'ab illis' Fest., and other glosses. Epigraphic QVROIS (**19**) might be a genuine attestion of OL *-oys*, but some suspect that it is an outright importation of G κούροις. Otherwise in early OL *-eis* is well attested, whence usual *-īs*.

Ion., Lesb., and early Att. -οισι is a different ending altogether, namely the loc.pl. **-ŏysu* (pronominal pl. stem **-oy-* plus the usual loc.pl. **-su*), as in Ved. *-eṣu*; but in G the final **-u* was replaced by the **-i* of the loc.sg. Myc. distinguishes between an instr.pl. in *-o*, that is -οις, as in *de-so-mo* (? *desmois* 'with bindings'—or something; the meaning is uncertain), and a dat./loc. in *-o-i*, that is *-oihi* < **-oisi*, as in *te-o-i* (*tʰe(h)oihi* 'to the gods'). Att. inscriptions have both -ΟΙΣΙ and -ΟΙΣ down to about 440 BC, then -ΟΙΣ. Most of the dialects have -οις from the earliest times. The intervocalic -σ-in *-οισι* was restored (assuming it had been lost everywhere as in Myc.) in part owing to the *-σι* in cons. stems (for example *θριξί*, and also the *r-* and *n-* stems with *-ρασι*, *-ασι* regularly < *-*r̥su*, *-*n̥su*, **172a**), but more to the point because the ending must have been perceived as literally *-οις* plus *-ι*.

a. In Vedic, the inst.pl. ending *-ebhis* is nearly as frequent as the ending in *-āis*; by the AV the ratio is one to five; the ending *-ebhis* vanishes from the *a*-stems thereafter. Like the rarely-attested Myc. forms in *-o-pi* (*e-re-pa-te-jo-pi* 'with ivory' 2×, and a few others), Ved. *-ebhis* is an innovation, not a relic.

b. Given the nearly complete lack of functional tangency, the notion that the PIE inst.pl. could become dat./loc. would be remarkable if it happened once; the possibility that it might happen twice, in both G and L, is a puzzle which is rarely raised, let alone solved. The explanation is probably formal. Myc. appears to continue a distinction between the old inst. and dat.(loc), and in all likelihood PItal. did too. But Osthoff's Law would have converted the inst.pl. to *-*ŏys*, and the apocope of *-*oysu* to *-*oys*, while not a regular Ital. development, at least fits with the sporadic loss of final short vowels (**74.1-2**). The formal equivalence of the abl.(inst.) and dat. plurals elsewhere in the system would have paved the way for an acceptance of *-*oys* as both dat. and abl. In G the course of events is not so evident, but there too it appears that *-*ois* (< *-*ōys*) and *-*oibi* ~ *-*oisi* came to be regarded as formal alternatives for the same function. —The loss of 'adverbial' function (in effect, the equivalent of the abl.) for the ending in G is surprising.

5. Gen.pl. PIE *-*ōm* (see **257.15** for internal structure), G *-ων* (**236.2**); PItal. *-*om*, Sab. *-um*, *-om*, OL *-om* (**83.1**), later L *-um* (**71.6**). This last is well attested in L in earlier periods but in literature survives in only two classes of forms:

A. WORDS CONSTRUING WITH MASS NOUNS. The type mainly consists of words for measures (including coins), hence by analogy *passum* 'of paces' (for *passuum*, a *u*-stem). The real structure of these formations became obscure even to the Romans: many were reinterpreted as neuter singular, whence *sēstertia* pl. as if *sēstertium* were nom.sg.neut., rather than the archaic gen.pl. of *sēstertius*, a silver coin.

B. STEREOTYPED EXPRESSIONS: *duumvirum* (sc. *consilium* or the like) '[committee] of two men', whence by back formation *duumvir*, *-ī* 'member of such a committee'; *praefectus fabrum* 'commander of engineers'.

(There are in addition such forms attested for stray individual words, including *socium* 'of allies', *līberum* 'of children', *deum* 'of the gods'; occasionally in poetry *virum* 'of men'; and others.)

6. LATIN *-ōrum*.

The usual L ending, *-ōrum*, is a specifically L formation. Most remarkably, it was created on the model of gen.pl.fem. *-ārum* (**265.4**), itself a pronominal ending imported into the nouns. (It is rare for masculine paradigms to be influenced by feminines, but that is the case here.) The genuine masc./neut. pronominal ending parallel to fem. *-*eH₂sōm* was *-*oysōm*, which would have given L ×-*ūrum*. If the early history of the gen.pl. in L started with the pronominal ending, the absence of any trace of the expected vocalism (or earlier *-EIROM) would be strange, particularly as the remnants of the original *o*-stem ending *-um* are abundant enough to suggest that it was supplanted relatively late in the development of L. Accordingly the consensus is that *-ōrum* is a late form patterned directly on the f. in *-ārum*.

261. THE DUAL CASES OF *o*-STEMS

	G	L	Vedic	Lith.	OCS
nom./acc./voc.	λύκω	ambō	devā́	vil̃ku	vlĭka
gen./dat.	λύκοιιν		deváyos		vlĭku

1. Nom./acc./voc. PIE masc. **-o-H₁* or ***-o-(H₁)e* (257.16), whence **-ō*: Ved. *vṛ́kā* 'two wolves', Lith. *vil̃ku*, OCS *vlĭka*, G λύκω. The dual is lost as a paradigmatic category in L but its form is preserved in isolated forms such as *ambō* 'both' and, with iambic shortening (84), *duo* 'two'. The old neut. was **-o-yH₁* (or, less likely, **-o-y*) whence Ved. *-e*, OCS *-ě*. Exactly what this would have given in G is uncertain, but probably not the form seen in ζυγώ 'two yokes', which appears to be the m. ending.

a. In Skt. the normal ending of the *o*-stem du. is *-āu*, which spread to other stem types; in the RV, however, this form cuts a small figure: it accounts for a mere one seventh of the total (the balance being *-ā*), and is most frequent in the chronologically later portions of the text. Its rise is rapid: there are twice as many occurrences of *-āu* in the AV as in the RV, and only a little later *-ā* disappears altogether. This pattern of attestation makes it clear that the form *-āu* is an innovation within Indic. Nevertheless, one often sees **-ōw*, based on the Skt. form, given as the PIE ending.

b. The PIE word for 'eight' is multiply ambiguous in form (see 389.8), but together with its reflexes, Ved. *aṣṭā́(u)*, G ὀκτώ, L *octō*, it has almost from the first beginnings of our science been taken as a dual. But among the objections to this analysis is that the distribution of *-āu* vs. *-ā* in the RV is different, occurring in a ratio of three to one (rather than one to seven as in the duals). See 389.8 fn.

2. Gen./dat.du. Hom. -οιιν, usual -οιν. This cannot be identified fully with dual forms elsewhere. It has the general look of something originally proper to the *o*-stems; if so, it was extended from there to cons. stems and all others of the third declension. Arc. has -οιυν, also (to ᾱ-stems) -αιυν.

Ved. gen./loc. *-ayos* points to PIE **-eyows* or **-eyews*, and OCS *-oju* (in pronouns) to PIE **-oyow(s)* or **-oyō(s)*. Av. seems to distinguish between a gen. *-ayō* and a loc. *-ayå*; the former points to **-eyow(s)* in agreement with Ved. *-ayos*, though it could equally easily reflect **-eyos* or **-eyes* (cf. Av. *θrayō* 'three' nom.pl.masc. < **treyes*); the latter to an **-eyōs* (or the like) which is not exactly like anything in Indic but could go with OCS. The **-oy-* or **-ey-* component of all these is a mystery. (Pronominal stems in **-oy-* appear to have been saliently PLURAL.)

The similarity between these satem endings and G -οιιν is suggestive, but any attempt to be specific about the relationship encounters phonological problems, particularly the survival of medial **-y-* in G.

eH₂-STEMS. THE GREEK AND LATIN FIRST DECLENSION

262. The 'first declensions' of G and L continue the PIE *eH₂*-stems, sometimes known as the senā type (**251a**).

In L as in PIE there was only one form-class so built, but the G first declension has five subtypes. One subtype, with nominative in -ᾰ (θάλασσα 'sea' for example), is historically unrelated to the others; it will be discussed in **268-9**. The other four types all evolved from the single *eH₂*-stem formation that underlies the L first declension.

The difference, limited to Att., between the fem. χώρᾱ and τῑμή types is phonological in origin (**54-5**), a result of the Att. change of ᾱ to η except after ε, ι, and ρ, whence the χώρᾱ subclass.

The second major division in G is between the foregoing and the masculine -ης/-ᾱς nouns (**267**). The subdivision into -ης and -ᾱς types has the same basis as the fem. τῑμή and χώρᾱ types, above. The features peculiar to this paradigm arose wholly within G.

The *eH₂*-stems are found in all IE languages except Hitt., in which there is no trace of any distinctively feminine inflection in either nouns or pronouns. But in all other IE languages there is a close association between *o*-stems and what are traditionally known as *ā*-stems. A suggestive similarity between the nom./acc.pl. of the *o*-stem NEUTERS in *-ā* (**-eH₂*) and the nom. sg. of the *ā*-stem feminines has long been remarked, a connection particularly suggestive because of the otherwise puzzling lack of an overt case marker **-s* on the nom.sg. of the *eH₂*-stems.

A historical connection between *o*-stem neuter plurals and the feminine *eH₂*-stems was made easier when it was discovered that in Hitt., as in G, the 'plural' of the neuter was in a very real sense singular, as it construes with 3sg. verbs. Before that discovery, there was room for debate over whether G syntax of the πάντα ῥεῖ 'all things flow' type was an innovation. But now it is clear that it can only be an ancient trait. The reinterpretation of a neut.pl. as some kind of derivative (collective) singular is thinkable if **kʷekʷleH₂* (to **kʷekʷlom* 'wheel') was not so much 'wheels' as something like 'wheelage', or perhaps indifferently one or the other. But the evolution of a whole new stem type and concord class ('feminine') from a single form is not easy to trace in detail.

263. SINGULAR CASES (see table opposite).

1. Nom.sg. PIE **-eH₂*, the bare stem, whence G -ᾱ, -η (**54-5**). The long vowel was retained in Sab., with regular rounding in word-final position as represented by O **-ú**, *-o*, U **-u**, *-o*, beside **-a**. In L the ending is *-ă*. The shortening of final **-ā* in L (cf. the nom./acc.pl neuter, **260.3**, and see **83.2**), but of no other final long vowel, is perplexing. Shortening rules do not normally single out specific vowels. Some think that the shortening in this

THE SINGULAR CASES OF *ā*-STEMS

	Mycenaean	Doric	Attic	Attic	Ionic	PItal.	Latin
Nom.	do-e-ra[1]	τῑμᾱ́	χώρᾱ	τῑμή	χώρη	-ā	via
Voc.		τῑμᾱ́	χώρᾱ	τῑμή	χώρη		via
	(Hom. νύμφα, Lesb. Δίκα)					-a	
Acc.	ta-ra-si-a[2]	τῑμᾱ́ν	χώρᾱν	τῑμήν	χώρην	-ā̆m	viam
Inst.		κρυφᾷ[3]					
Dat.	po-ti-ni-ja[4]	τῑμᾶι	χώρᾱι	τῑμῆι	χώρηι	-āy	viae
Abl.						-ād	viā(d)
Gen.	ko-to-na[6]	τῑμᾶς	χώρᾱς	τῑμῆς	χώρης	-ās	familiās
							viae[5]
Loc.		πάλαι[7]					viae

Note that ᾶι = ᾷ, ῆι = ῇ.

	Oscan	Umbrian	Vedic	PGmc.	Gothic	OE	OCS	Lith.
Nom.	**víú**	**mutu**[8]	priyā́[9]	-ō	giba[10]	giefu[10]	žena[11]	mergà[12]
Voc.		tursa[13]					ženo	
			iḷe[14]	-ō	giba	giefu		mergà
Acc.	**víam**	**tuta**[15]	priyā́m	$-ō^n$	giba	giefe	ženǫ	mer̃gą
Inst.			jihvā́[16]					mergà
			jihváyā[16]				ženojǫ	
Dat.	**deívaí**[17]	**tute**	śivā́yāi[18]	-ōy	gibai	giefe	ženě	mer̃gai
Abl.	toutad	**tuta**	kanā́yās[19]					
Gen.	eituas[20]	**tutas**	kanā́yās	-ōz	gibos	giefe	ženy	mergõs
Loc.	**víaí**	tote	návāyām[21]	-ōy	gibai	giefe	ženě	mergojè

1. 'Slave' (= G δούλη; no satisfactory etymology).
2. 'Allocation by weight' (?) (*talansiān*).
3. 'Secretly, in private'.
4. There seem to be no examples of an *ā*-stem dat.sg. in Myc.; this form, 'to the mistress' (*potniyāi*), is from the devī type (**268–9**).
5. OL *viāī.*
6. 'Arable land' (or 'land under cultivation') (*ktoinās*). —The gen.sg. is well-attested as a case, but most of the actual words are of uncertain meaning.)
7. Hom. 'recently; customarily of late'; Att. 'in olden times'.
8. 'Fine, penalty'; alternates with **muta**; cf. L *multum* < *mulctum.*
9. 'Dear'.
10. 'Gift'.
11. 'Woman'.
12. 'Girl'.
13. Name of a goddess.
14. 'Libation'.
15. 'City'.
16. 'With the tongue'; the inst. in *-ā́* is Vedic only.
17. 'Goddess'.
18. 'Gracious'. There are two instances in the RV of this ending in plain *-āi.*
19. 'Girl'.
20. 'Money'.
21. 'New'.

---

form started in iambic words (**84**); it prevailed, unlike other similar developments, because of the support for *-ă* afforded by acc.sg. *-ăm.* (This explanation is perhaps less cogent than it looks at first sight, as it cannot account for the identical development of the neuter pl.)

a. The absence of a marker for the nom.sg. is unusual in PIE, where bare stems serve as nom.sg. chiefly in pronoun and neuter paradigms. Elsewhere it is seen only in the devī-inflection (268-9), another feminine type.

2. Voc.sg. PIE *-eH_2, endingless and originally homophonous—except for accent (257.2)—with the nom.sg. In vocatives ending in a vowel plus laryngeal, however, the laryngeal drops without lengthening the preceding vowel. The lengthening of most short vowels before a word-final laryngeal comes from sequences in which a following word begins with a consonant (as the great majority do), which creates the closed-syllable environment in which a laryngeal lengthens a vowel. But in PIE, as in directly observable languages—IE and non-IE alike—vocative nouns were phonologically as well as syntactically separate from the clauses they occur in, with the result that the *-H_2 just dropped from *-eH_2, leaving an altered but short vowel, as in G (Hom.) *νύμφᾰ* 'O maid', Sapph. *Δίκᾰ* 'O Dikē'; Ved. *devi*[1] 'O goddess'; U *tursa* (name of a goddess; NB *-a* in the voc.sg. in contrast to the *-o* of the nom.); OCS *ženo* 'O woman' (cf. nom.sg. *žena*). The G feminines mostly use the nom.sg. form for the voc. (cf. 267.3), as is the case in L too —where an orig. *-*ă* undisturbed would probably have given L ×-*e* (71.4).

3. Acc.sg. PIE *-eH_2m > G -*ᾱν*, -*ην* with the regular change of final *-*m* (236.2). The tonic form (-*ᾶν*, -*ῆν*) is evidence against the expected PIE construct *-$eH_2\mathring{m}$, because *-$\acute{e}H_2\mathring{m}$ should have given ×-*ᾶν* (if not ×-*ᾶ*). Cf. the gen.sg. (7, below).

PItal. *-*am* shows shortening of the vowel before final -*m* (83.1). But PItal. *-*ăm* would have given L ×-*em* (71.4), and O actually has a long vowel in **paam** = L *quăm*. An Ital. acc.sg. in *-*ām* is easily explained by paradigmatic leveling; subsequently in L it underwent the shortening of long vowels in final syllables before all cons. except -*s* (83.3).

a. The absence of any evidence in any IE language for *-$eH_2\mathring{m}$ is paralleled in the devī stem acc.sg. *-iH_2m. There is, by contrast, what might qualify as evidence for *-$uH\mathring{m}$ in the cons. stems mentioned in 318. But in those stems it is unknown which *H is involved.

4. Inst.sg. The details of the ancestral form are indeterminate. The case as such is not a member of G and Ital. paradigms, but some adverbs have been traced to it, such as G *κρυφᾶ*, -*ῆ* 'in secret' ("by means of secrecy'), perh. L *quā* 'in what manner' (indistinguishable from the ablative, and often declared to be such).

5. Dat.sg. PIE *-eH_2-*ey*, hence PG and PItal. *-*āy*: G -*ᾱι*, -*ηι* (-*ᾳ*, -*ῃ*; see 64), L -*ae*. Ending-accented forms in G in -*ᾶι*, -*ῆι* point to *-$\acute{e}H_2ey$. Note that the L shortening of the diphthong must have postdated the development of final short diphthongs to -*ī* (75.4).

a. Phonologically speaking, there is a puzzling lack of parallelism between the

---

[1] There is a complication in the voc. of the InIr. senā type; this is from the devī type (268-9) whose nom./voc.sg. *-iH_2 develops straightforwardly.

development of L *-ae* < *-*āy* and L *-ō* < *-*ōy* in the *o*-stems (63.3). But in OL inscriptions there are in fact a number of examples, mostly from outside of Rome, of a dative in *-ā* (presumably), such as DIANA and FERONIA, which may represent a development parallel to *-ō* from *-*ōy*. But this makes the standard L development more mysterious than ever.

6. Abl.sg. L *-ā* is from *-ād*, frequent in early inscriptions (SENTENTIAD for example). This *-ād* was formed after the analogy of the *-ōd* of the second decl. as part of a general Italic innovation, mentioned above (259.7), whereby distinctive abl.sg. endings on the model of the *o*-stems were created for all vowel stems, namely *-ād*, *-īd*, *-ūd*; whence with the loss of final *-d* (237.4) the usual *-ā*, *-ī*, *-ū* and (in Sab.) *-ē*. The loss of the final cons. is shown to be late not only by epigraphic evidence, but also by relative chronology: it must have occurred in U after the rounding of final long *-*ā* (83.3b), and after the shortening of original *-*ā* in L (83.2)—but prior to the shortening of vowels in final syllables before all cons. except *-s* in L.

a. This account is the orthodox one. But as mentioned in **259.7b**, the abl. of BS *o*-stems (Lith. *vil̃ko*, OCS *vlĭka*) points to PIE *-*āt*, not *-*ōt*. An analogical origin for *-*ā*- in the *o*-stem paradigm is unlikely, and the BS evidence raises the possibility that Ital. *-ād* is the *o*-stem ending itself, not an imitation of the *o*-stem ending. If this is so, it would not change the usual history of the form in InIr. and Gmc., where the vowel quality is immaterial; in Ital. alone the incongruous *-*ā(d)* was remodeled as *-*ō(d)*. This sorting out of endings *-*ād* and *-*ōd* could be what provided the catalyst for the unique Italic manufacture of a complete set of abl.sg. endings in *-V̄d*.

7. Gen.sg. PIE *-*es*, *-*os*, and *-*s* are all attested forms of the gen.sg. marker and all three would yield much the same results in the historically attested IE languages when added to the stem *-eH_2-. Most authorities assume a full grade form, and G ending-accented forms in -ᾶς, Att.-Ion. -ῆς, are easiest to explain if one starts from *-$\acute{e}H_2os$ (48) or *-$\acute{e}H_2es$.

The ending is attested unchanged, apart from regular phonetic developments, in InIr., Gmc., Celt., G, and Ital. It is retained in Sab., but in L it occurs only in a few forms in inscriptions and early authors, as MOLTAS 'multae' and Enn. *viās*. But it survived in fossilized phrases, of which *pater familiās* 'head of the household' is doubtless the best known, and also in several adverbs like *aliās* 'at another time/place'.

The usual L ending in *-ae* is a purely L creation. Its makeup is revealed in its OL manifestations like Plaut. *fīliāī* gen.sg. 'daughter': *-ī* imported from the *o*-stems (**259.8B**) was added to the stem in *-ā-*. (This would have happened most readily in the masc. *ā*-stems like *pīrāta* 'pirate' and *agricola* 'farmer', but they are too unimportant to be credited as the catalyst.)

Strangely, there are no valid proportions for the transplanting process. Presumably the first step was the appreciation of *-os*, *-om* and the rest as case endings on a par with *-ī*, rather than stem *-o-* plus case endings *-s*, *-m* and so on. Nevertheless, a proportion like *lupōrom* : *lupī* :: *viārom* : *viāī* works only if the Romans perceived the forms as *lup-* + *-ōrum* but *viā-* + *-rum*, which hardly seems likely.

Note that at the outset, the gen.sg. *-āī* was distinct from the *-āi* of the nom.pl. (265.1) and dat.sg. (item 5, above). It is so scanned often in Plaut. but subsequently the three endings fell together.[1]

8. Loc.sg. PIE **-eH₂i* would give *-ăy* early in the history of most IE groups, but there is little trace of such a form. InIr. *-āyām*, Lith. *-oje* point to **-eH₂i-* plus some additional element beginning with a vowel, whence **-eH₂y-* > **-āy-V-*, but further details are obscure. The length of O **-aí** cannot be determined, but L *-ae* must continue **-āy* for the reason given in 5, above. The most probable explanation is analogy with the other *-ā-* stem-vowels.

In G there are some forms in -ᾰι as in Θηβαι-γενής 'born in Thebes', πάλαι adv. 'lately; in olden times'. This looks like the expected reflex of PIE **-eH₂i*. A competing theory takes it to be analogical to *o*-stem loc. -οι, but as the noun to which πάλαι was built was lost from the language in prehistoric times, πάλαι at any rate is more easily explained as a relic than as a new coinage.

a. The paradigmatic status of the loc. in Ital. is ambiguous. In O the existence of loc. phrases (such as **mefíaí víaí** 'in the middle of the street') might mean—but hardly proves—that the loc. was still a paradigmatic case in O, and, hence, in PItal. Being able to examine a language directly does not always settle such matters definitively: in L there are numerous forms (most notably place names) in *-ae* meaning 'at' or 'in', for example *Rōmai*, *-ae*; but these are special to some degree, and the ancients were probably stating their genuine intuitions when they identify them as datives with a special meaning.

264. THE PLURAL CASES OF *ā*-STEMS

	Mycenaean		Greek	PItal.	Latin	Oscan
Nom.	a-ni-ja[1]			-ās	OL viās	**aasas**[2]
			τῑμαί[3]		viae	
Acc.	a₃-ka-sa-ma[4]	*Dor.*	τῑμάνς, -ᾱς, -ας	-āns	viās	**víass**
		Att.-Ion.	τῑμᾱ́ς			
		Lesb.	δίκαις			
Inst.	a-ni-ja-pi	*most dial.*	τῑμᾱ͂ις[5]	-āys	viīs[5]	**diumpaís**[6]
Loc.	do-ka-ma-i[7]	*Ion.*	τῑμῇσι[5]			
Gen.	ko-to-na-o	*Dor.*	τῑμᾱ́ων, -ᾶν	-āsōm[8]	viārum	egmazum[9]
		Att.	τῑμῶν			
		Ion.	τῑμέων, -ῶν			

Notes to the table are on page 271

[1] The form -AES found in some epitaphs of Republican date, mostly from outside Rome, has several possible explanations. One traces it to G influence, either regular L *-ae* (perhaps pronounced [ɛ:]) embellished with *-s* in imitation of the G ending -ης, or else that it is the G ending itself, imaginatively misspelled. Another suggests the conflation of competing *-ās* and *-ae*, though the forms occur rather too late for *-ās* to be a factor.

	Umbrian	Vedic	PGmc.	Gothic	OE	PBS	OCS	Lith.
Nom.	**urtas**[10]	priyā́s[11]	-ōz	gibos	giefa	-ās	ženy	meȓgos
Acc.	**vitlaf**[12]	priyā́s	-ōz	gibos	giefe	-ā(n)s	ženy	mergàs
Inst.	**tekuries**[13]	māyā́bhis[14]	-ōmi	gibom	giefum	-āmīs	ženami	meȓgomis
Dat./Abl.		aghnyā́bhyas[15]	-ōmu	gibom	giefum	-āmos	ženamŭ	meȓgoms
Gen.	**urnasiaru**[16]	divyā́nām[17]	-ōaⁿ?	gibo	giefa	-un	ženŭ	meȓgų
Loc.		priyā́su				-āsu	ženaxŭ	meȓgose

1. 'Reins'; it cannot be told whether the ending matches G ἡνίαι (265.1) or is the original form, namely *hāniyās*.
2. 'Altars'.
3. All dialects.
4. 'Spearheads' (*aiksmans*; cf. Hom. αἰχμή).
5. The 'dat./abl.' of the grammars.
6. ? that is, *dumpais* 'to the water-sprites' (L *lumpīs*).
7. There are several words of unknown meaning which however are manifestly dat.pl. in *-a-i*.
8. Originally a pronominal ending; cf. Ved. *tā́sām* 'of them (fem.)'.
9. 'Of things'.
10. 'Standing up' fem.; cf. *ortom* nom.sg.neut.
11. There are only some 20 Vedic instances of nom.pl. *-āsas*; cf. the masculine *a*-stem nom.pl. in *-āsas* (260.1d).
12. 'Calves' fem. = L *vitulās*.
13. Festival of the Decuriae; U **-ies** < **-yāys*, cf. dat.sg.
14. 'With supernatural powers'.
15. 'Cows' (verbatim 'not to be killed').
16. Meaning not known, beyond the likelihood that it has something to do with water-vessels.
17. Adj. 'heavenly'.

---

265. PLURAL CASES.

1. Nom.pl. PIE *$\textit{-eH}_2\textit{-es}$ whence *-ās* is attested in most IE languages, including Sab. and OL, but in both G and L the inherited form was replaced: in G by -ᾰι, in L by **-āy*. In both languages the starting-point is obviously the masc. *o*-stem ending, G *-οι*, L **-oy* (later *-ī*)(260.1); but the details are vexing. In fact, the forms would be easier to understand had they been G ˣ-ᾱι and L ˣ*-ăy* instead of the other way round. (In any case, the same puzzling short stem vowel in G must be assumed for the nom.du. masc., 266, 267.4.) But the L diphthong had to be long originally, or else it would have become ˣ*-ī* per 75.4. There are few instances of inherited *-ās* in OL: QVAS 'quae', HASC(E) 'hae', RELIQVIAS. These, and the few literary instances of *-ās*, are mistakenly described by the Roman grammarians as *accusativus pro nominativo*.

The G and L innovations are necessarily independent, as shown by the survival of the ancestral formation in the Italic languages and the difference of length in the G and L endings.

2. Acc.pl. All forms of G and Ital. go back to **-ans* < **-āns* < *$\textit{-eH}_2\textit{ms}$ (Osthoff's Law, 63.2; also 257.14). The absence of evidence for *$\textit{-eH}_2\textit{m̥s}$ rather than *$\textit{-eH}_2\textit{ms}$ is puzzling. PG **-ans*, preserved in Cret. and Argive, gives the usual Att.-Ion. -ᾱς, Lesb. -αις, in some dialects -ας (228.4). O **-ass**, U *-af*, L *-ās* all are from **-ans* or **-āns*, like O **-úss**, U *-u(f)*, L *-ōs* < **-ons* (260.2, and cf. 237.5).

3. Dat.(-abl.)pl. G -αις (< ?-ᾱις) is formed after the analogy of -οις; Myc. *-a-i* agrees, ambiguity and all. The same innovation is seen in Ital. *-*āys* after -*oys* (**260.4**): O -*ais*, **-aís**, OL -*eis*, -*īs* (**75.2**), U -*es* (later -*er*). An original loc. in -ᾱσι, Att.-Ion. -ησι (cf. Ved. -*āsu*), with intervocalic -*s*- retained by analogy with -σι in cons. stems and *r*- and *n*-stems (**172a**), and instr. -οις (*-*ōys*, **260.4**), serves as the dat. in early Att. inscriptions, as ΔΙΚΕΣΙ (that is δίκησι) 'for amends' and ΤΑΜΙΑΣΙ (ταμίᾱσι) 'for dispensers', and persists in loc. adverbs like Ἀθήνησι 'at Athens' and θύρᾱσι 'out of doors'. From this, with -ι- imported from -οισι, comes early Att. -ησι, -ᾱισι (in a few inscriptions), Ion. -ησι. —Lesb. -ᾰισι is directly modeled on -οισι.

a. In Att. inscriptions, -αις is the latest form in chronological sequence, prevailing only after about 420 BC. Most other dialects have it from the earliest times.

b. L *deābus*, *fīliābus*, and a few other similar forms are not inherited; they are latter-day creations which distinguish fem. and masc. forms in the few words where homophony between *o*- and *ā*-stem endings was genuinely inconvenient.

4. Gen.pl. PIE *-*eH₂ōm*/*-*eH₂ŏm* would give, at least fleetingly, *-*aōm*/*-*aam* in the early histories of the IE branches (if it was not remodeled as *-*āŏm* on the basis of the prevailing -*ā*- stem-marker). Some such form apparently underlies Go. *gibo* 'of gifts', whose final vowel is the reflex of no ordinary long vowel (cf. the acc.sg. *giba* < PGmc. *-*ōⁿ* < PIE *-*eH₂m*). With the loss of intervocalic *-*s*- in PG, the PIE pronom. ending *-*eH₂sōm* (Ved. -*āsām*) became *-*āhōm* next to presumed nominal *-*āŏm*. The conventional explanation of the resulting remodeling is that the pronoun ending was taken over by the nouns, but the actual change is probably better viewed as an obliteration of the differences between two nearly-identical forms having identical functions. G -ᾱων, showing loss of intervocalic -*h*- from *-*s*- (**172**), is the earliest actual G form and the source of all the others. It occurs in Myc., Homer (where it must be Aeol., beside the Ion. -εων mentioned below), Thess., and Boeot. It early contracted to -ᾶν in most dialects; but in Att.-Ion. -ᾱων > -ήων, whence -έων, -ῶν, Att. -ῶν (**54**, **79.3**, **86.3**).

In Ital. the transfer of the pronoun ending to the nouns was more straightforward, at least if took place at a point when the noun form was still something like *-*aom* or (with -*ā*- imported from other case forms) *-*āom*; very similar, that is, to prn. *-*āsom*. Thus O -*azum*, U **-aru**, L -*ārum* (**71.6**, **173**).

a. The ending -*um* occurs in a few *ā*-stem nouns in L: some G names such as *Aeneadum* (cf. G -ων); in weights and measures like *amphorum*, *drachmum*; and in masc. forms like *agricolum* 'of farmers' and *Trōiugenum* gen.pl. 'born in Troy'. The latter two types follow the analogy of the conservative *o*-stem forms mentioned in **260.5**.

266. Dual cases. The only ᾱ-stem dual in Homer is the nom./acc./voc. in -ᾱ, and significantly it is virtually limited to the masculine *ā*-stems. Thanks to Myc. evidence this ending is now known to continue *-ᾰε

(267.4), which explains why it is not -η in Att.-Ion. like the nom.sg. The other cases were invented by analogy with the *o*-stem forms (261), so -αιιν, -αιν like -οιιν, -οιν. This is of a piece with the creation of nom.pl. -αι after masc. -οι.[1]

In feminine articles and some of the other pronominals such endings (τᾰ́, ταῖν) occur in most periods but are rare, the *o*-stem formations (τώ, τοῖν) being normal. Pronoun inflection is usually archaic vis-à-vis nouns, and anyway analogical replacement of original (but unattested) fem. forms by masculines would be unfathomable—though most authorities assert just such a replacement. The proper assumption surely is that the G articles are more original than the fem. noun inflection. This is confirmed by the inflection of fem. *ā*-stem dual NOUNS in Myc., which are indistinguishable from *o*-stem duals: *to-pe-zo* nom.du. (*torpeȷ̆ō*) 'two tables'; *ko-to-no* acc.du. (*ktoinō*) 'two parcels of land'; *wa-na-so-i* dat.du. (? *wana(k)(t)soiin*) 'for the two mistresses' (stem **wanakt-iH₂*-). The PIE sources of such forms are enigmatic, unless it is simply the case that in PIE there was no distinctive dual for the eH_2-stems. The expected nom.du. would be either *-eH_2H_1 or *-$eH_2(H_2)e$; the plausibility of the former could be better judged if we knew more about the phonetics of laryngeals; the latter from an early date would have been homophonous with the nom.sg.

267. THE GREEK MASCULINE ᾱ-STEMS are mainly of two kinds: agent nouns in -τᾱς/-της and adj. compounds built to -ᾱ/-η stems, like χρῡσοκόμης 'golden-haired' (namely Apollo). In Hom. the nouns in -της are likewise compounds for the most part, such as περικτίτης 'neighbor', where the ultimate formation appears to have been adjectival (here, 'dwelling around' or the like). From complexes like περικτίτης the abstraction by back formation of a simplex κτίτης 'inhabitant' was a straightforward matter, and such forms are tolerably common already in Myc., including *ki-ti-ta* 'κτιτᾱ(ς)' specifically. The same underlying formation, *-teH_2, may be manifest in L *monēta* (an appellation of Juno and particularly associated with her major individual temple in Rome) if the correct interpretation of the word is 'warner' or 'admonisher' or the like. The functional specialization of the type as an agent noun is partly the result of its coincidental similarity to inherited -τηρ, -τωρ. Why the formation would show an early and striking partiality for masc. *ā*-stem inflection, rather than (say) masc. ×-τος, fem. ×-τᾱ, is however an enigma.

The masculine ᾱ-stems differ from the fem. ᾱ-stems in three endings (four, apparently, in Myc.). While two of these are assimilations of the basic

---

[1] A proportional analogy along the lines of λύκω : λύκοιιν : λύκοι :: ἱππότᾱ : ἱππόταιιν : *X* leads right to pl. ἱππόται, short diphthong (265.1) and all; but chronology does not allow it—the pl. in -αι greatly predates the first appearance of du. -αι(ι)ν.

type to the forms of the *o*-stems, one, the voc.sg., is actually archaic compared to the more innovative form of the fem. paradigm (**263.2**). But a unifying theme underlies this apparent mixture of remodeled and conservative forms: the DEGREE OF DIFFERENCE between the ᾱ-stem (feminine) endings and the corresponding masculine *o*-stem ones. Thanks to the overall convergence of *o*-stems and ᾱ-stems, the nom.sg. and gen.sg. were the only ᾱ-stem cases which were not closely parallel to *o*-stem forms already:

	o-*stem*	ā-*stem* *masculine*	ā-*stem* *feminine*
Nom.sg.	-os	-ās	-ā
Voc.	-e	-a	-ā (*earlier* -a)
Acc.	-on		-ān
Gen.	-oyo	-āyo	-ās
Dat.	-ōy		-āy
Nom.pl.	-oy		-ay
Acc.	-ons		-āns
Gen.	-ōn		-āōn
Dat.	-oys		-ays

(Note that the original voc. -ᾰ fits (as it were) better with the *o*-stem ending -ε than the remodeled fem. voc. in -ᾱ does.)

1. Nom.sg. -ᾱς, -ης, with -ς imported from m. -ος. Owing to the writing system, it is not possible to tell whether final -*s* is a Myc. trait as well; see **b**, below.

a. The Homeric forms in -τᾰ, as ἱππότα (ἱππότης) 'horseman', μητίετα 'counselor, all-wise' (an epithet of Zeus), and εὐρύ-οπα 'far-seeing', occurring as epithets with another noun, are probably stereotyped vocatives used in apposition with nominatives. Cf. L *Iuppiter* nom.sg. which is a voc. in origin (**327**; a probable G example of a divine vocativus pro nominativo is Ποσειδῶν 'Poseidon'; see **304.2b**).

b. There are scattered dialectal examples of masculines in nom.sg. -ᾱ, that is, identical to the usual feminines.

2. Gen.sg. Inherited -ᾱς (**263.7**) was replaced by -ᾱο, with -*o* taken over from the final of the *o*-stem gen., -*οιο*, -*οο*. This was long explained as early G *-*yo* abstracted from masc. *-*o-yo* and grafted onto the stem-vowel -*ā*-, whence *-*āyo* > -ᾱο. However, Myc. has only -*a-o* in the masc. *ā*-stems, not at all parallel to the -*o-jo* of the *o*-stems: *su-qo-ta-o* gen.sg. (*sūg^w otāo*) 'swineherd'. This admits of various explanations. The simplest retrieves the traditional account by adding the surmise that intervocalic -*y*- dropped earlier after long vowels than after short ones, disrupting the parallelism of orig. -*oyo* and *-*āyo*. Some evidence seems to support this, as Myc. *a-e-ri-qo* (*āeri-k^wh os*, a man's name, containing **āyeri*- 'early', as in Hom. ἠέριος 'early', Av. *ayarə* n. 'day'). Another possibility is that the singular was influenced by the form of the plural, that is *-*āhōn*, as for example *e-re-ta-o* gen.pl. (*eretāhōn*) 'of rowers'. The survival of uncontracted -ᾱο, -ηο in

Homer is better in accord with Myc. *-āho* than with *-āo*; cf. the Hom. contraction of du. -αε to -ᾱ. But this is indirect evidence indeed.

Whatever its earlier history, this -ᾱο, as an Aeol. feature, occurs in Homer along with the Ion. manifestation -εω (*-ηο), the latter also found in several dialects; it contracted to -ᾱ in Dor. In Ion., -ηο > -εω > -ω (54, 79.3, 86.3). Att. -ου in place of expected -ω is another instance of the elimination of trifling differences in isofunctional forms: before [o:] > [u:] (76), Ion. -ω [ɔ:] and *o*-stem gen.sg. -ου [o:] differed only by a degree of tongue height, a difference which was effaced in favor of [o:].

There are scattered dial. examples of masculine gen.sg. in -ᾱς.

3. Voc.sg. Words in -τᾱς, -της and some others (mostly national names like Πέρσης 'Persian' and compounds like παιδοτρίβης 'trainer of boys') have -ᾰ, the original voc. which is rare in feminines (**263.2**). But the ending -ᾱ, -η, of the feminines (etymologically the nom.sg.) also occurs in the masculines.

4. Nom.du. In literary G the dual of the masc. and fem. *ā*-stems are the same (**266**). Myc. however attests several forms like *e-qe-ta-e* nom.du. (*hek^{w}etae*, as it were ἑπεταε) 'two "followers"' (the title of some sort of official). This appears to be the same as the *-e* of the consonant stem nom./acc.du. If this form is the source of Hom. -ᾱ nom./acc./voc.du., it must continue -ᾰε, not $^×$-ᾱε (which would have given $^×$-η), with the same short stem vowel as in the nom.pl. It provides a straightforward explanation for two hitherto puzzling facts: that duals looking like innovations based on a feminine type first appear on MASC. stems (**266**), and they were at first limited to one case-form.

THE PROTO-INDO-EUROPEAN *devī* INFLECTION

268. GREEK TYPE WITH NOM.SG. IN -ᾰ. The PIE devī inflection (**251a**) is a derivative feminine stem which forms both nouns and adjectives, and generally speaking it had the same function as the senā type (**251a**, **262-6**). In Vedic the two formations occur side by side as feminine derivatives from *a*-stems (that is, PIE *o*-stems) in both nouns and adjectives; but in other categories we find specialization: the devī type forms the feminine stem to athem. stems, such as pres. and aor. pples. (**559.2a**), perf. pples. (**561-2**), *u*-stem adjectives (**340**), and agent nouns in *-tar-*. Thus Ved. *bhárantī* f. 'carrying' (*bhárant-*); *vidúṣī* f. 'knowing' (*vidvás-*); *urvī́* f. 'broad' (*urú-*); and *nayitrī́-* f. 'leader' (*nayitár-* m., written here as scanned, for textual *netrī́-*, *netár-*; root *nī-*). Similar distributions are found in other languages, for example Lith. *vežanti* f. 'traveling'. In Gmc., where the type is gone as such, it is nevertheless visible just below the surface in the pres.pple.fem. stem: Go. *-andein-*, that is PGmc. **-anđī-* < PIE **-ont-íH₂-* but with the devī stem papered over as an *n*-stem. A word which escaped this remodeling because its form was no longer transparent is Go. *frijondi* f. 'friend', an *iō*-stem in

Gothic terms but originally a fem. present participle of the devī type. (From this and one or two other forms, it appears that *jō-/iō*-stem feminines would have been the regular expression of the devī type in Germanic, outside of the pres.pple.)

The devī stem was either *-iH_2- or *-yeH_2- (traditionally written *-ī-/-yā-), depending on case and number. The details of the distribution of the two grades are uncertain, owing to discrepancies between languages; and because some of the evidence is unexpected, it would be incautious to extrapolate from other stem-types.

An example of inconsistent evidence is the ending of the accusative singular. Ved. *-īm* and G *-*yan* point to *-iH_2m (unless *-*yan* is a remarking of *-*ya* < *-$iH_2\mathring{m}$); but Go. *-ja*, as in *mauja* acc.sg. of *mawi* 'girl', and Lith. *-ią̄* in *marčią̄* acc.sg. 'daughter-in-law' point instead to *-yeH_2m (not *-$yeH_2\mathring{m}$, NB). An example of an unexpected form is the nom.pl. *-iH_2-*s*, instead of *-iH_2-*es* or *-yeH_2-*es*. But *-īs* is the only form of the nom.pl. in the RV; it is matched by Av. *-īš* and corroborated by OIr. *-i*ᴴ. As this is the only example of zero grade of the nom.pl. affix, and as zero grade of an affix is unexpected on the zero grade of a stem, authorities are chary of taking this as evidence for the ending *-*s*. But whereas the creation of an ending *-*īs* by analogy can easily be managed in PInIr. (the relationship between the nom. sg., acc.sg., and nom.pl. of the two types: *-ā* : *-ī* :: *-ām* : *-īm* :: *-ās* : *X*, where *X* = *-īs*), it cannot be accounted for thus in PIE, or for that matter in Celtic.

Among the differing opinions on the original distribution of grades in the stem, the view endorsed here is that zero grade of the stem was found in the nom.sg. *-iH_2 (endingless, like the senā type); acc.sg. *-iH_2m (and like the senā type pointing to *-*m* rather than *-$\mathring{m}$); voc.sg. *-iH_2; and in some other cases that do not bear on the G paradigm, such as the inst.sg. Full grade was found in dat.sg. *-yeH_2-*ey* (> PG *-*yāi*, Ved. *-yāi*), and gen.sg. *-yeH_2-*os* (> PG *-*yās*, Ved. *-yās*).

Whatever the orig. nom.pl. was, *-iH_2-*(e)s* or *-yeH_2-*es*, it was remodeled in G on the pattern of the pronouns (265.1). As a result, owing to the accident that PIE *iH_2 > PG **ya*, with the subsequent absorption of the **y* by the G palatalizations (195-207), the devī paradigm in PG came to differ from the senā type only in the forms where *-*yă*- < *-iH_2- was distinct from -ᾱ- < *-eH_2-: the nom., acc., and voc. sg. Of these, only the distinctive nom.sg. persists into literary G, and it is natural that the resulting paradigm would be treated as a subvariety of the first decl. ('nouns in -ᾰ') even though it is unrelated to the senā type historically.

a. In traditional G grammar, 'adjectives of the first and second decl.' have feminines of the senā type; what are called 'adjectives of the first and third decl.', that is, feminine stems to participles and *u*-stem adjectives, have feminines of the devī type, like the corresponding formations in Vedic.

269. In addition to forming adjectives, the G type in -ᾰ is found in fem. nouns formed from stems or roots ending in a consonant. Formally, their disguised unity is brought out when one recognizes that the -ᾰ is from *-*ya*, and, though only rarely preceded by an actual -ι- (as in *ψάλτρια*

f. 'harper'), they are preceded by consonants which reflect old clusters with *-*y*-: -λλ- from *-*ly*-(204); -σσ-/-ττ- from voiceless dorsal or apical + *-*y*- (199); -σ- from *-*(n)ty*- (196, 199); -ζ- from voiced dorsal or apical + *-*y*- (200-1); -αιν- from *-*any*- (203); -ῡρ- from *-*ury*- (203); and so on.

a. Some words which never had *-*ya* have been drawn into this type, as τόλμα 'courage', μέριμνα 'solicitude', δίαιτα 'mode of life'. All words actually derived from *-*ya* inevitably had a heavy penult, hence the analogical extension was most natural in forms with that property. In some cases these creations are Att. only, even late Att., as κνῖσα 'nidor' (Hom. κνῖση), πεῖνα 'hunger' (earlier πείνη).

The type is also secondary in abstracts in -εια (such as ἀλήθεια 'truth'), where Ion. has forms like ἀληθείη < *-*esyā*.

b. In two PIE nouns, the fem. derivative was *-niH_2-: *$reH_1\acute{g}$-niH_2- 'queen' (cf. *$reH_1\acute{g}$- 'king'), and *pot-niH_2- 'mistress' (cf. **potis* 'master'). The latter is attested in G πότνια, Ved. *pátnī*-. For *$reH_1\acute{g}$-niH_1-, see 270.4 below.

270. THE DEVĪ TYPE IN LATIN. The fate of the devī type in Italic as a whole is obscure, thanks in part to the scantiness of attested feminine derivatives in Sab. In L, at any rate, the type disappeared as a distinct paradigm, for the most part merging with the *i*-stems (306-7) but leaving a number of telltale remnants.

1. The clearest L reflex of the devī type qua type is the feminine of the agent noun, -*trīc*-, as in *genetrīx*, -*trīcis* 'mother' (*genitor*). Cf. Ved. *jánitrī*- 'mother' (*jánitar*- m.). Direct as the ancestry of -*trī*- is agreed to be, the L -*c*- is a puzzle which has resisted satisfactorily explanation.

2. The PIE pres.pple. (originally a consonant stem) and *u*-stem adjectives are remodeled as *i*-stems in L: **bherent*- 'carrying' has L *ferentium* gen. pl., *ferentīs* acc.pl.; **tn̥nu*- 'thin' > L *tenuis*. It happens that these are the very form classes which in PIE built feminine stems of the devī type.

The exact process by which devī-inflection was converted to an ordinary *i*-stem, which spread to all three genders, is unclear; but some such theory is supported by the phrase *Laurentis terra* quoted from Ennius. The third syllable must scan as heavy, whereas in Ennian versification a short vowel before word-final -*s* scans as light even before a following consonant. As the word is an adjective modifying a fem. noun, the inference is that we are dealing here with *Laurentīs*, a form intermediate between the devī nom. in -*ī* and the classical nom. in -*ns* (that is, *-*ntīs*, 306.1).

Also significant is what FAILED to happen in the L adj. system: the comparative adjectives in *-*is*-/*-*yos*- are *s*-stem adjectives, but unlike most cons. stem adjectives they did NOT form a distinct feminine stem of the devī type in PIE; and they are the only consonant-stem adjective type which were not remade as *i*-stems in L. The correlation between PIE feminine adjectives in devī and L *i*-stem adjectives from consonant-stem adjectives is therefore complete.

3. The fem. counterpart of L *avus* 'grandfather' is *avia*, inexplicable on purely L terms but easily unriddled as a modification of an original devī form **avī*. Similar formations, but attested only in OL, are *nepōtia* and *neptia*

'niece; granddaughter', ultimately from **nept-iH₁-*, cf. G ἀνεψιά (simplex **nepot-* 'nephew, grandson', L *nepōt-*, Ved. *nápāt-*). L *neptis* 'niece, granddaughter', an ordinary *i*-stem, has the same source.

a. The Ved. cognate *naptī́-* belongs to the vr̥kīs paradigm, in fact, a different fem. type; in this word it apparently supplanted the original devī stem.

4. L *rēgīna* 'queen' is cognate with OIr. *rígain* /r'īγəν'/ (fem. of *rí*). (Late Ved. *rājñī́-*, though it is invariably mentioned in this connection, is certainly an Indic formation derived directly from *rā́jan-*, itself not a direct cognate of the Celt. and L forms. It is formally and functionally superimposable on G ἀρηγών.) The details present a number of difficulties, and so several—largely speculative—explanations of the L form have been proposed. Of these the one endorsed here runs as follows. PIE **reH₁ǵ-niH₂-* > PItal. **rēgnī-*, which was remodeled first as **rēgnīā-* (like **awīā* 'grandmother', 3, above), further to **rēgnīnā-* (a clear model being **galnīnā* 'hen' to **galnos* 'cock'), whence *rēgīna* by a combination of dissimilation and attraction to the base-shape of *rēg-* 'king', *rēgius* 'royal', and so on, and such forms as *gallus* vs. *gallīna.*

CONSONANT STEMS

271. The case endings proper are virtually the same for all kinds of cons. stems, but some details depend upon characteristics of the stem, and we distinguish different classes according to whether the stem ends in a stop, in a liquid or nasal (mostly *r*-stems and *n*-stems, respectively), or in -*s*-. Some widely-attested nouns that were ordinary consonant stems in PIE have undergone obscuring changes and merit individual treatment (323-9).

The case endings as they apply to cons. stems in general will be given in connection with the stems in stops. Details peculiar to individual stem types will be mentioned as they come up.

272. ACCENT AND GRADATION. There were originally several systems of accentual shift between stem and ending, with vowel gradation (125) to match. These were substantially obscured by leveling even in the parent speech, as in the *s*-stems, but were maintained in monosyllabic stems and in the *r*- and *n*-stems, thought to be most faithfully reflected in Vedic.

A somewhat speculative scheme has recently gained currency, though it has been around for several generations. The theory sorts root/stem/ending alternations into four accentual patterns. The theory can be grasped through its terminology:

1. ACROSTATIC ('stationary on the beginning'): accent on the first syllable only. The root has only full grades, while the ablauting endings had zero grade (the gen.sg. for example, 257.4). The best-attested example of this type, though it was much altered in most daughter languages, is the PIE word for 'cow', **gʷow-* (324). Attested in fragments, but clear enough in general outline, is the ancient paradigm of the word for 'house': **dōm*

nom.sg. (< ***doms*), **dōm* acc.sg. (< ***domm*), **dems* gen.sg., **dem* loc., **démes* or **dómes* nom.pl., and so on.

2. PROTEROKINETIC ('earlier-mobile'): the accent moves between the first syllable and the stem. As in the acrostatic type, ablauting endings were in zero grade. The type is clearly seen in the ablauting *u*-stem neuters and their analogs, as **doru* 'tree, wood', gen. **drews* (that is, **dór-u*, **dr-éw-s*); **nóm-n̥* 'name', gen. **n̥m-én-s*; *g^w*én-*H_2 'woman', gen. *g^w*n-é*H_2*-s*. All of these were neuter, though there is some reason for thinking that *H_2*ewi-* 'bird' was a masc. proterokinetic: *H_2*ew-i-s*, gen. *H_2*w-ey-s*. See also 311a.

In these examples, as in most such, the 'root' cannot be identified apart from these forms. And while the TYPE is clear, the paradigms are difficult to work out beyond a case or two, having been much leveled in the daughter languages.

a. Some think that ALL *i*- and *u*-stem inflection (304.2a, 312) was originally proterokinetic, as: ***mén-ti-s* 'thought', gen. ***mn̥-téy-s*; ***méntus* 'advice', gen. ***mn̥-téw-s*, and so on. But there is no actual evidence for tonic kinesis in these paradigms, and it is not easy to imagine the means for getting from a single proterokinetic pattern to the attested patterns, with fixed root ablaut grade, stem-only ablaut alternation, and fixed accent: **mn̥tís*, **mn̥téys*, and the rest, vs. **méntus*, **méntews*, and so on.

3. HYSTEROKINETIC ('later-mobile'): the accent moves between the stem and the ending. Ablauting endings were in full grade. Certain kinship terms, and most *r*- and *n*-stems (279-87), went like this: nom. ***p-*$H̥_2$*tér-s* (**p*$H̥_2$*tēr*) 'father', gen. **p-*$H̥_2$*tr-ós*, acc. **p-*$H̥_2$*tér-m̥*, and so on. The type is much better preserved than the other three, which means that our understanding of the distribution of ablaut grades of both stem and ending is the most complete for this type; it is this pattern that is outlined in 273, below.

4. AMPHIKINETIC ('both ends mobile'): the accent moves between the first syllable (root) and the case-markers.

There is little evidence for such a pattern, actually, which seems to be posited mainly to account for paradigms such as G μήτηρ, μητρός. But all of the presumed reflexes of the type show more or less sharp departure from the ancestral paradigm (***má*H_2*tr̥s*, gen. ***m̥*H_2*trós*, and so on). Some scholars, therefore, assume that the case-forms with full grade (tonic accent) of the first syllable likewise had full grade of the stem: **légōn* 'gatherer', **légonm̥* acc., **lognés* gen. But even if such paradigms occurred in the parent language they can hardly be aboriginal. Perhaps the best evidence for the amphikinetic pattern is indirect, namely the attestations of **yen*$H̥_2$*tr-* 'husband's brother's wife' (Hom. εἰνατέρες, L *ianitrix*—for **ieniter*—OLith. *gentė* ~ *žentė*) vs. gen. **yn̥*H_2*tros*, dat. **yn̥*H_2*trey* (as leveled in Skt. *yā̆tar-*, a typical hysterokinetic noun). But the evidence is confined to the ablaut grades; there is no evidence for accentuation, one way or the other.[1]

273. For hysterokinetic masculines and feminines, the strong cases—that is, cases built to full or lengthened grade STEMS—were as follows (see tables 274 and 283 for inflection):

---

[1] Ved. *yā̆tar-*, found in the handbooks, seems to be either imaginary or a confusion with *yā̆tar-* 'a going'; the kinship term is not attested in accented texts.

Lengthened grade: nom.sg. The long vowel is likely to be from compensatory lengthening (126.1), involving the consonant clusters created by the nom.sg. marker *-*s*; these however were usually restored by analogy. That is, ***pots* 'foot' > ***pōs* → **pōts*.

Full grade: acc.sg.; nom. and acc. du.; voc.sg., du., and pl.; and loc.sg.

The lack of symmetry in the accusative forms—InIr. has zero grade stems here—has been held to be secondary. If so, then the basic pattern is simple: all nominatives, vocatives, and accusatives were built to full grade stems.

In the gradation of *r*- and *n*-stems the loc.sg. shows both full and zero grades, depending on the language: Ved. *pitári* 'father' and *mūrdhán(i)* 'head' exhibit full grade, but G πατρί, ἀρνί 'lamb' are zero grade. (L abl.sg. *patre*, *carne* 'meat' could be either old zero grades or syncopated full grades, **patere* and the like.) The Skt. loc.sg. type *mūrdhni*, often quoted in this connection, is strictly post-Vedic and surely secondary; presumably forms similar to G πατρί are secondary too.

Zero grade: the remaining cases (incl. the nom./acc.n.) were 'weak', that is with accent on the ending and zero grade of the stem.

There is no reason to doubt that this originally applied even to stems containing no potentially syllabic elements, like **ped*-/**pod*- 'foot', thus gen. **pdós*. Unsurprisingly, such forms have been largely eliminated from attested paradigms (116.1).

The one feature of this pattern that has remained in G and L is the lengthened grade in the nom.sg. The other cases have been leveled in various ways (a process still under way in Homer). But in monosyllabic stems not even this is much evident, apart from a few nouns, such as L *pēs*~*pĕd*- and G πούς ~ ποδ- (and the vowel of πούς is a puzzle, 116.1). Both G and L (especially L) show a tendency to generalize the lengthened grade originally proper to the nom.sg., thus G φώρ, φωρός 'thief' = L *fūr, fūris*; L *vōx, vōcis* 'voice, word'; *nepōs, nepōtis* 'nephew, grandson'. (Gmc. shows a similar tendency; but such leveling is rare or unknown in the other branches.)

In masc. and fem. *r*-, *n*-, and *s*-stems likewise the one constant is the long-vowel nom.sg.: G -ηρ, -ωρ, L -*er*, -*or* (from *-*ēr*, *-*ōr*, 83.3); G -ων, -ην (from *-ω, *-η, 282), L -*ō*; G -ως (αἰδώς '(self-)respect') and -ης (εὐμενής 'well-disposed', cf. μένος n. 'intention'), L -*ōs*, -*or* (the former in monosyllables like *flōs* 'flower', but polysyllabic *s*-stems like *honōs* 'worth' were leveled to *-*ōr*, 299, whence by shortening before final -*r*, the attested -*or*, -*er*).

The accent shift in G πούς, ποδός, πατήρ, πατρός is the same as in Vedic, except for the acc.pl., so πόδας in contrast to Ved. *padás*. The Indic shape is a secondary development from something on the order of original **pắdas* < **pódm̥s* (the same etymon as for G πόδας). See 274, note 11.

The kinship terms show the effects of much leveling in both accent and stem-grade. G θυγάτηρ 'daughter' for *θυγατήρ (Ved. *duhitár*-) shows the influence of μᾱ́τηρ 'mother', but cf. undisturbed θυγατρ-ός gen.sg. In the gradation of the G kinship terms generally, the inherited strong grade of the nom.pl. πατέρες (= Ved. *pitáras*) and the acc.pl. πατέρας was for some reason extended to the gen.pl. πατέρων; the original form is seen in Hom. πατρῶν. A similar remodeling of the gen.sg. (Hom. πατέρος and the like) was less successful (284A.1).

In the majority of the *r*- and *n*-stems, the old gradation has been reduced by the leveling of the whole paradigm to one grade (284-5).

ROOT NOUNS AND STEMS ENDING IN A STOP

274. TABLE OF ROOT-NOUN INFLECTION.

		PIE	Mycenaean	Greek	Latin	Sanskrit
Singular						
	Nom.	pōts (**pōs)	ti-ri-po[1]	πούς[2]	pēs	pā́t
	Acc.	pódm̥		πόδα	pedem[3]	pā́dam
	Dat.	pdéy	po-de[4]		pedī[3]	padé
	Gen.	pdós	ko-ru-to[6]	ποδός	rēgus[5]	padás ?
		pdés			pedis	padás ?
	Loc.	péd, pedí		ποδί	pede ?	padí
	Inst.	pdéH$_1$	po-ni-ke[7]		pede ?	padā́
Plural						
	Nom.	pódes	to-ra-ke[10]	πόδες	pedēs[9]	pā́das
	Acc.	pódm̥s		πόδας	pedēs	padás[11]
	Dat.	?			pedibus[9]	padbhyás
	Gen.	pdō̃m		ποδῶν	pedum	padā́m
	Loc.	ptsú	pi-we-ri-si[12]	ποσί[13]		patsú
	Inst.	pdbhi ?	po-ni-ki-pi[8]			padbhís

1. 'Tripod'. It is unknown whether this is equal to Hom. τρίπος or reflects a more original form in **-ō(t)s*.
2. This vowel is enigmatic. See 116.1 for 'Doric πώς'.
3. These could be either cons. stem or *i*-stem forms (308).
4. *Podei*, showing that the genuine PIE dat. sg., distinct from the loc.sg., survived into PG.
5. 'Of the king' (276.7).
6. 'Of a helmet' = κόρυθος (κόρυς).
7. *P^{h}oinīkē* 'with purple'.
8. *P^{h}oinīk^{h}p^{h}i.*
9. These are evidently *i*-stem forms; but see 277.4a.
10. 'Breastplates' = θώρᾱκες (θώρᾱξ).
11. A replacement of original **pā́das* < **pódm̥s*. **Pā́das* itself is not quotable, but the TYPE is attested in RV *ā́pas* acc.pl. 'waters' (6×; but the remodeled *apás* is very much more frequent).
12. A word of uncertain meaning but aligning with *pi-we-ri-di*, which is evidently a loc.(dat.)sg.
13. Hom. ποσσί, πόδεσσι (277.6a).

275. ROOT NOUNS AS A MORPHOLOGICAL TYPE IN PIE. Root nouns have the case markers added directly to a root; if the root vowel ablauted as shown in 274, this was largely eliminated in both G and L. Some, like **suH-* 'pig', seem not to have ablauted in the first place. A large number of root nouns embody verb roots, but not all; examples of nominal roots are **ǵhwer-* 'wild animal', **mūs-* (**muHs-*?) 'mouse', **bhruH-* 'eyebrow', **ḱerd-* 'heart', and **g^{w}ow-* 'cow' (324).

Many such matters are not open and shut, however. It is a matter of debate whether **pod-* 'foot' is at bottom a verbal or nominal root. PIE **dont-* 'tooth' looks like a root noun, but some scholars take it to be a pres.pple. from **ed-* 'eat' (with the inference that the original meaning of **ed-* was something like 'chew').[1]

Given the multitude and variety of root nouns, it is remarkable that only one root adj. has been certainly identified, **meǵ*H_2*-* 'big' (343); and on the basis of the array of derived stems from this root in attested languages, some scholars suspect that it was in the beginning actually a noun rather than an adjective.

Functionally, root stems fall into three major categories.

1. Nomina actionis (feminine) based on verb roots, 'the act of doing (or being) so-and-so':
G ὄψ, ὀπός 'voice', L *vōx*, vōcis, Ved. *vā́k, vācás* 'speech; voice' (root **wekʷ-* 'speak').
G φλόξ, φλογός 'flame' (root **bhleg-*, cf. φλέγω).
L *lūx, lūcis* 'light', Ved. *rúk, rucā́* instr. (root **lewk-* 'shine').
L *lēx, lēgis* 'law' (root **leg-* 'gather').
G νύξ, νυκτός f. 'night', Ved. *nák* 'night', *naktám* adv. (old acc.) 'at night' originally *'dusk' < PIE **nekʷ-* 'get dark, become evening'. (L *nox, noctis* like most fem. root nouns was taken into the *i*-stems.)

2. Nomina agentis (simplex usually masculine; feminines by derivation) based on verb roots, 'one who does (or is) so-and-so':
G κλώψ, κλωπός 'thief' (root **ḱlep-*, cf. κλέπτω 'steal').
G Ζεύς, Δι(ϝ)ός *'daytime sky', L *Iuppiter, Iovis*, Ved. *dyā́us, divás* (*'bright one', root **dyew-* 'be bright').
L *dux, ducis* 'leader' (root **dewk-* 'draw, lead'; cf. *dūcō*).
L *rēx, rēgis* 'king', OIr. *rí*, gen. *ríg* < **rīks*, **rīgos* (root **re*H_1*ǵ-* 'be efficacious'; G ἀρήγω 'assist (successfully)').

3. Nominal roots—nouns not based on verbal roots (all genders):
G θήρ, θηρός m. 'wild beast' (**ǵhwer-*; 160).
G θρίξ, τριχός f. 'hair'.
L *pix, picis* f. 'pitch' (cf. G πίσσα/πίττα < **pikya*).
G ἅλς, ἁλός m. 'salt', f. 'sea', L *sāl, salis* m. and n. 'salt'.
Hom. κῆρ n. 'heart', L *cor, cordis*, Ved. *hā́rdi* (PIE **ḱēr* nom.sg. < ***ḱerd*, 126.1, 276.4a; gen. **ḱr̥dós*).
G μῦς 'mouse', L *mūs, mūris* : Ved. *mū́ṣ-*, Av. *mūš*, OE *mús* pl. *mýs*. (Moved to other form classes in Arm. *mukn*, OCS *myšĭ*, NHG *Maus* pl. *Mäuse*.)
G χήν, χηνός 'goose' (Dor. χᾶν), OE *gós* < **ǵhans-*, pl. *gés* (Ved. *haṃsá-* is an

---

[1] Even **mūs-*, as securely a nominal form as could be wished, has been connected with the Skt. root *muṣ-* 'steal'. But in addition to the questionable semantics, there is no way to connect **mūs-* (or **muHs-*) and **mūs-*.

o-stem; OHG *gans* is an *i*-stem, as is Lith. *žąsìs*—but with a remnant of root-noun inflection in gen.pl. *žąsų̃*. L *ānser*, obviously cognate, has an enlargement of disputed origin).

Root inflection is particularly common in the second part of compounds, and not a few root-nouns are only attested as such:

G *σύζυξ*, *σύζυγος* 'spouse', L *coniux*, *-iugis* (cf. Ved. *sayúj-* 'companion, comrade' < **sm̥-yug-*); root **yewg-* 'join'.

G *χέρνιψ*, *χέρνιβος* 'lustral water' (lit. 'hand-wash', like NE *eyewash*), cf. *νίζω*; root **neygʷ-*.

L *index*, *indicis* m.f. 'informer; sign', *iūdex*, *iūdicis* m. 'judge' (cf. *dīcō*, G *δείκνῡμι*); root **deyḱ-* 'point out'.

L *auspex*, *-spicis* m. 'observer of omens' (**H₂ewi-speḱ-* lit. 'bird-watcher'); *auceps*, *-cipis* 'fowler' (**H₂ewi-kap-* 'bird-catcher').

a. It has been suggested that the masc. nomina agentis (Type 2, above) are in origin back-formations from such compounds. Reasonable suspicion that some nomina agentis have that history is not the same thing as proof that they all do, however, and ancient-looking intransitives like **dyew-* 'be bright', as a root-noun 'sky, sky god', can hardly be so explained.

b. Root nouns are the most elemental noun type and must have been numerous in the remote history of the parent language. But they are a relic class in all attested IE languages. OE for instance has some 15 root-nouns, and OIr. fewer still, compared to the dozens of G. Commonly, a root noun in a given language will have close cognates belonging to other stem classes. So Hom. *κῆρ* 'heart', L *cor, cordis*—root nouns—align with G *καρδίᾱ*, OIr. *cride* < **ḱr̥dyom*, Go. *hairto* (*n*-stem), Lith. *širdìs* (*i*-stem). Several other instances are noted under 1-3, above. In such cases it is safe to assume that the root inflection is original.

276. SINGULAR CASES.

1. Nom.sg. PIE **-s*. The ending is seen in G *θρίξ* 'hair', *γῦψ* 'vulture', L *rēx* 'king', *urbs* /urps/ 'city'. For its treatment after a stem-final apical stop (and similarly for *-σι* in the dat.pl.), as in G *πούς*, L *pēs* 'foot', see **215**.

a. G *χθών* 'earth' < **dhǵhōms* does not show the regular outcome of **-ns* (< **-ms*) as seen in *εἵς* 'one' < **hens* < **sems*. *Χθών* was in effect refashioned into an ordinary *n*-stem (see **228.6**). G *χήν* 'goose' < *χᾱ́ν* < **kʰăns*, in which the **-s* belongs to the stem, likewise shows the effect of analogy, but a different one (**286.5d**).

b. Many monosyllabic L nom.sg. forms like *mōns* 'mountain', *pars* 'part', *mēns* 'mind' are not cons. stems but *i*-stems (for the most part *ti*-stems) with syncope; see **309**. The true nature of a formation can be determined by the gen.pl.: *montium*, *partium* vs. cons. stem *pedum*. Etymology can also be useful; for example, there is an exact match of form and function between OE *mynd*, Ved. *matí-*, and Lith. *mintìs*, pointing unambiguously to a PIE nomen actionis **mn̥tí-*, which goes bail for a Latin **mentis*. A number of L nouns lacking the confirming evidence of outside cognates probably have a history like that of *mēns*, for example *lēns*, *lentis* 'lentil', *crux*, *crucis* 'cross'. Some words have inconsistent inflection, so gen.pl. both *fraudum* and *fraudium* to *fraus* 'deceit' (**147.1a**).

2. Voc.sg. The original PIE voc.sg. was the bare stem, but in G for the most part and in L everywhere the nom.sg. serves also as voc.sg.

The few G words that retain the inherited endingless voc.sg. forms are altered by the regular loss of stem-final stop(s) (236.1): παῖ 'boy' stem πα(ϝ)ιδ-, γύναι 'woman' stem γυναίκ-, Hom. ἄνα 'lord' stem (ϝ)άνακτ-. So also regularly from stems in -ντ-, as γέρον 'old man'; and -ιδ-, as ἐλπί 'hope' (but the latter types do not have the archaic detail of the recessive accent of παῖ and γύναι, 257.2).

In some classes of consonant stems the voc. is distinguished from the nom. in both grade and accent, as πάτερ (nom. πατήρ), Σώκρατες (nom. Σωκράτης).

3. Acc.sg. PIE *-m̥, hence regularly G -α, L *-em* (99).

a. Conventional wisdom holds that *-m̥ would give InIr. *-a*, as (apparently) in the morphologically isolated Ved. *dáśa* '10' < **déḱm̥(t)*. If that is correct, the InIr. acc.sg. cons. stem ending *-am* in Ved. *pā́dam* has its *-m* on the analogy of vowel stems. (In fact, however, it is probably the regular outcome of final *-m̥; see 389.10.) Indubitably analogical is G -αν for -α, occasional in the dialects and frequent in late inscriptions.

b. L *-em*, being the outcome of **-im* as well as *-m̥ (71.1), is one of the points of tangency which led to the partial conflation of *i*-stems and cons. stems in L (308).

c. Hitt. *-an* is conventionally explained as imported from the thematic class (PIE *o*-stems, 259.3). But the them. type is insignificant in Hitt. and an unlikely source for remodeled endings. Perhaps Hitt. *-an* is the regular outcome of *-m̥. Some have proposed as much; but the acc.pl. in *-uš* is usually taken as preserving the regular outcome of *-m̥s (277.2), and the 1sg.pret. ending *-un*, as in *e-šu-un* 'I was', apparently continues *-m̥. Alternative explanations of both of these last have been offered, but none has gained general acceptance.

4. Nom./acc.sg.neut. As in all PIE noun types apart from *o*-stems and the pronouns, these cases were the bare stem without ending. So L *cor* (*cordis*) 'heart' < **kord* < **ḱr̥d* (see **a**, below); *lac* (*lactis*) 'milk' < **lakt*, G γάλα < **galakt* (γάλακτος)—ultimately *$dl̥H_2ekt$ or so; G μέλι (μέλιτος) 'honey' < **melit*.

a. The long vowel seen in Ved. *hā́rdi* nom.sg. 'heart', Hom. κῆρ (for *κῆρ), OPr. *seyr* /sēr/, Hitt. ŠÀ-*ir* (gen. *ka-ar-ta-aš*), all 'heart', is not in origin a lengthened grade of the root in the nom.sg., which would be anomalous in a neuter. Rather it is a compensatory phenomenon of PIE date, namely **ḱēr* < ***ḱerd*, an ordinary *e*-grade form of the root also attested in Germanic (with a different stem type), as seen in OE *heorte*. When Indic restored the final *-d* to PInIr. **ź́hār*, the impossibility of word-final clusters in Indic necessitated a prop-vowel as well, thus **źhārdə*.[1] Arm. *sirt* has a similar history. The Italic etymon, a uniform stem **ḱr̥d-*, shows leveling of the zero grade of the oblique cases into the nom./acc. (L *cord-* is of course ambiguous; but while there is no unambiguous evidence pointing to *o*-grade of this root, there is plenty confirming zero grade.)

5. Dat.sg. PIE **-ey* (257.7), O **-eí**, OL *-ei*, *-e* (that is, *-ẹ̄*, 57.2a): HERCOLE(I), MARTEI, IVNONE, whence the usual *-ī* (75.1).

Before the decipherment of Myc., the replacement of the PIE dat. **-ey*

---

[1] Ved *hārd-/hr̥d-* and Av. *zərəd-* reflect **ǵherd-* rather than the **ḱerd-* universally attested elsewhere.

by the loc. ending *-*i* was thought to be PG. But both endings survived into early G, as shown by Myc. cons. stem dat.sg. like *po-de* 'to the foot', *ka-ru-ke* 'to the herald', *po-me-ne* 'to the shepherd', as if *ποδει, κᾱρυκει, ποιμενει*. In the later-attested dialects we find in this function only -*ι*, the loc.sg. (= Ved. *padí*), but with no trace of the *e*-grade of original PIE **pedí*.

a. A similar encroachment of the loc. on the inherited dat. is seen in Hitt.: in older texts, dat.sg. -*a* (and a few times even -*ai*, both < *-*ōy*) is distinct from loc. -*i*; in later texts the old dat. is obsolete except for *i*-stems, and as in G the erstwhile loc. performs both dat. and loc. functions.

6. Abl.sg. OL cons. stem formations in -*īd* (COVENTIONID 'assembly', AIRID 'bronze', BOVID 'cow') show the *i*-stem version of the Pan-Ital. abl. (263.6 and **b**, below). This cannot underlie the L ending in -*e*, however, which is the PIE loc.sg. *-*i* with regular change to -*e* in final position (71.1). The same form occurs in specifically locative expressions like *rūre* 'in the country', *Carthāgine* 'at Carthage' (beside competing forms in -*ī*, like *rūrī*, on the analogy of *o*-stem forms like *domī* 'at home' and *humī* 'on the ground').

a. This is the usual explanation of the L abl. in -*e*. It is functionally strange, however, as the basic uses of the loc. and abl. have little or nothing to do with one another. The instr. would be a far likelier source for the abl., functionally. The PIE instr. in *-*eH₁* as seen in Ved. *padā́*, Myc. *po-ni-ke* 'with purple' would probably have given L -*ē* rather than -*e*, but there are three possible explanations (none of them compelling) for L -*e* from the PIE inst. (1) Vowels do shorten in final position in L on occasion (83.2). (2) Postvocalic laryngeals in final position have unpredictable outcomes; they usually lengthen the preceding vowel, as in 1sg. -*ō* < *-*oH₂*, but sometimes simply drop. Lengthening would in fact be the expected reflex here, but *-*eH₁* > PItal. *-*e* is not out of the question. (3) The zero grade form of the inst. ending is otherwise a peculiarity of *i*- and *u*-stems, but such a zero grade (PIE *-*H̥₁* > PItal. *-*a*) would give L -*e* regularly (71.4). If any of these possibilities is valid, then the L loc. -*e* and abl. -*e* would have different etymologies.

b. The parent language did not have a distinction between gen. and abl. in the singular apart from some pronouns and the *o*-stems (257.5); but all three Italic languages, in keeping with their tendency to manufacture ablative endings on the plan of the *o*-stems, have different forms for the two cases in cons. stems, but this is achieved in the various languages by different means. O **-úd**, **-ud**, -*ud* is the *o*-stem ending taken over entire. U -*e* is less straightforward; it is usually taken to be the same as L -*e*, with the same range of uncertainties about its ultimate source, plus the additional detail that in U the ending might be either -*ē* or -*ĕ*, whereas the quantity of L -*e* is known.

7. Gen.sg. PIE *-*es* and *-*os* are obviously ablaut grades, but the original distribution in PIE has been rendered unrecoverable by leveling: *e*-grade is seen in Ital., Gmc., and BS; the *o*-grade in Celt., Ital., and G; and InIr. -*as* is ambiguous. Although Ital. has both, *-*es* prevails in L (seen unaltered in a few old inscriptions, SALVTES, VENERES, APOLONES), whence the usual -*is* (71.3); *-*os* is seen occasionally in OL and even L inscriptions, as DIOVOS 'of Jupiter', REGVS 'of the king', NOMINVS 'of name'. The ending *-*es*

is attested in G, if it is attested at all, only in adverbs such as Hom. σῆτες, Att. τῆτες 'this year' < *$\acute{k}$yeH₂-wet-es (199c).

a. In Sab. the *i*-stem ending **-eís** eliminated the inherited cons. stem forms. Such an ending would have given L *-īs*, but it is found neither in the consonant stems nor in the *i*-stems; for both, *-is* serves. Such leveling in forms that differ only in vowel length is general in language, and very common in L. But in L, except for this instance it is invariably the long vowel alternative that ousts a short vowel competitor. This fact alone is grounds for doubting that the EXPECTED *i*-stem ending, **-eis*, was really a participant in the evolution of L *-is*: see 306.6.

277. PLURAL CASES.

1. Nom.pl. PIE **-es* > G -ες, O *-s* (syncopated), for example **meddíss** (an Oscan official) from **meddikes*, **humuns** 'men' from **homōnes*. In L this ending, which would have yielded ˣ*-is*, was replaced by the *-ēs* of the *i*-stems (307.1). There is no certain evidence for the original ending of the cons. stems, as OL *-es*, epig. -E(S), might stand for either *-ĕs* or *-ēs*.

2. Acc.pl. PIE **-m̥s*, whence regularly (99) G -ας, Ital. **-ens*, whence ultimately L *-ēs* (226.1) O **-s**, and U **-f** (237.5).

3. Nom./acc.pl.neut. PIE **-H̥₂* > Ved. *-i*, G -α (102). This suffix would have given PItal. **-a*, L ˣ*-e*. The Ital. cons. stem nom./acc.pl. **-ā* (whence L *-a*) is the *o*-stem ending (260.3).

a. The decads *trīgintā* '30', *quadrāgintā* '40', and so on are thought by some to have the nom./acc.pl. ending **-ā* retained unchanged, in contrast to cons. stem *-ă* < **-H̥₂*; for the correct view see 391.

4. Dat.pl. Perhaps PIE **-bhos* (see 257.8 for the endings in **-bh-*), PItal. **-fos*; in Sab. this syncopated early, first to O **-fs** (uniquely attested in an early inscr.), then to the usual form *-ss*, *-s*, U *-s*. Early L *-bos* (per 143), then *-bus* (per 71.6). InIr. forms (Ved. *padbhyás* dat.pl. 'feet') and Myc. (*po-pi* 'with feet') indicate that the ending was originally added directly to the stem, as if L ˣ*pedbus*; but in Italic this arrangement is everywhere modified. In O it is replaced by the *i*-stem form **-ifos* (307.4), as in the unique *-ifs*, later *-is*, as O *ligis* = L *legibus*. But U replaces the inherited athematic ending with the *u*-stem form, as in U **fratrus** < ˣ*frātrufos* 'for/from/by brothers'. This diversity suggests that the Indic type, or something like it, lasted into PItal.

a. L *-ibus* is usually stated without qualification to be an *i*-stem import, but in fact it could continue either **-ifos* (like O) or **-ufos* (like U). Indeed, the cons. stem gen.pl. in *-uom*, well-attested epigraphically (333.3a), might tend to confirm **-ufos*.

SC de Bacch. SENATORBVS, once next to usual SENATORIBVS, is agreed to be a spelling mistake (missing letters are nothing unusual in this inscription).

5. Gen.pl. PIE **-ŏ̄m* (257.15) > G -ων, PItal. **-ŏm* (83.1) whence Sab. *-um*, *-om*, OL *-om*, L *-um* (71.6).

6. OTHER PLURAL CASES. G -σι is in origin the loc.pl. answering to Ved. *-su* (257.12). For -σιν see 240. Italic has no remnant of such an ending.

Myc. attests *-pi*, that is -φι, as inst.pl.: *po-pi* 'with feet'.

a. Beside the usual forms like φύλαξι 'to the guards', ποσ(σ)ί 'to/on feet' (*ποδ-σι, **215**), forms in -εσσι are characteristic of the Aeolic dialects and are frequent in Homer, as πόδεσσι, κύνεσσι, ἄνδρεσσι, βόεσσι 'to feet, dogs, men, cows' (also with simplification of the -σσ-, **232.1**, as αἴγεσι 'to goats'). This looks like the *s*-stem dat.pl., as βέλεσσι 'to javelins', and this formation is often mentioned in discussions of the πόδεσσι type. But there is no parallelism here. The real source is the *o*-stems, in which the dat.pl. looks like the nom.pl. plus -σι: λύκοι, λύκοισι. Applied to the consonant stem nom.pl. like πόδες, the same relationship (fanciful though it is) would yield πόδεσσι, accent and all.

278. DUAL CASES. Nom./acc./voc. G has -ε for all genders and for all classes of the third declension, including ι- and υ-stems. This might represent either PIE **-e* or **-H₁* (**257.16**). But there is no clear evidence from the other IE languages, in which the endings have been imported from other stem-classes: Ved. has *-ā(u)* (the *o*-stem form) in the masc. and fem., and *-ī*—which may be the genuine cons.-stem form—in the neut.; Slavic has the *i*-stem form in the masc. and fem., and the *o*-stem form in the neut.

r-STEMS AND *n*-STEMS

279. In PIE there were consonant stems ending with *-r-* (paradigms given in **283**). Masc. and fem. nouns thus formed are attested in all varieties of IE. Neut. inflection is more fugitive. In Indic, the reflex of the nomen agentis suffix **-tor* builds a kind of future participle (**555**); a few neut. forms are actually attested, but not before the Brāhmaṇas. In Hitt., with a more original state of affairs, there are neuter *r*-stem nouns as well, and a few primary adjectives. Parallel stems in *-n-* (see **283** and **285**) formed nouns in all three genders, and (at most) one or two primary adjectives.

In G and L, the PIE neut. *r*-stems have disappeared as a type; G has one *n*-stem primary adjective, ἄρσην, Att. ἄρρην (**warsen-*) 'male' (= Ved. *vṛ̥ṣan-* 'vigorous, macho'); but bahuvrīhi compounds formed from both *r*- and *n*-stem nouns are abundant, like σώφρων 'sane, of sound mind' < σαϝο- 'sound' and φρήν 'diaphragm').[1]

The *r*-stems included one or two items that look like root nouns, such as **(H₂)ner-* 'man' (G ἀνήρ, ἀνδρός, Ved. *nár-*, O **niir**), and a few more that look like primary derivatives, though the 'root' in question is obscure, as in **swesor-* f. 'sister' (L *soror*, Ved. *svásar-*) and **day(H)wer-* m. 'husband's brother' (G δᾱήρ, L *levir*, Ved. *devár-*). Most *r*-stem nouns are built with the suffixes **-tor-* 'agent' and **-H₂ter-* 'kinsman'.

The *n*-stems likewise included a few items that look like root nouns, such as **ḱwon-* m. 'dog' (G κυών, Ved. *śvan-*). Derivative forms were built

---

[1] The abundant Germanic *n*-stem adjectives, the so-called weak adjectives, were in fact specifically marked for the semantic feature of definiteness and were a precursor of the definite article in effect. In origin they are accretions, of a pronominal element with various original adjective inflections, and are not in any way continuations of the PIE *n*-stem adjectives (if there really was such a category).

not only with plain *-*on*-, forming among other things agent nouns, but also with larger suffixes like *-*mon*- and *-*won*-.

PIE *r*- and *n*-stems are traditionally treated together because they went nearly alike as regards endings and gradation of stem. The main difference is the treatment of the nom.sg., a difference which was effaced in most IE languages (282).

280. Both stems came in two types: those with *o*-grade for the full grade of the stem, and those with *e*-grade.

These two types were unevenly represented in the parent speech. Among the *n*-stems, those with full grade in *-*on*- preponderated. (The cases taking full grade are detailed in 273.) However, even in this type, on the evidence of Indic -*ăn(i)*, whose short stem-vowel points to *e*-grade, the loc.sg. was *-*en(i)* (283, 257.11).

By contrast, there were very few *en*-stems. The most certainly attested is **ukʷsen*- 'ox', whose structure is vouchsafed by InIr. and Gmc. forms. Vedic full grade stems such as RV *ukṣáṇam* acc.sg., *ukṣáṇas* nom.pl., with -*ăn*- pointing to *-*en*-, contrast with the prevailing *n*-stem type in -*ān*- from *-*on*- by Brugmann's Law (36.4).[1] In Germanic, the OE inflection of *oxa* nom.sg. 'ox' < **ukʷsē*, *exen* nom.pl. < **uχ⁽ʷ⁾siniz* < **ukʷsenes* also reveals an *en*-stem; cf. the usual OE *n*-stem nom.pl. *guman* 'men', nom.sg. *guma*, with suffix -*an* and unchanging root vowel. (OE *exen* is regular from **öxen*, some kind of analogical replacement of **üxen*; *exen* was further leveled to *oxen* at an early date.)

Lith. too has evidence, albeit unclear, of an earlier *en*-stem type, limited to the formative *-*men*- in a few OLith. nom. forms like *gilmė/gelmė* 'depth'. Though no actual paradigm *gilmė*, *gilmen*- is attested parallel to the usual mixed type (*piemuõ* 'shepherd', stem *piemen*-), the old nom.sgs., taken together with the remodeled stem-forms like *gilmenà* 'depth', point to the prior existence of just such a type. Nevertheless, the only lexical correspondence between the OLith. *men*-stems and the five or six G nouns in -μήν is the tentative identification of an earlier **limė*/**limen*- in certain Baltic place names, aligning with G λιμήν 'harbor'. (The remaining G items are πυθμήν 'bottom', ποιμήν 'shepherd', ὑμήν 'membrane', and ἀτμήν 'slave'). And strangely the G nouns are all masc., the Lith. nouns all (evidently) fem.

Rare as it seemingly was in PIE, the *en*-type proliferates in G. It follows that few G forms can be securely traced to a PIE *en*-stem, perhaps in fact only one: G (ϝ)ἀρσήν 'male'. The original *en*-stem is corroborated by Ved. *vṛ̥ṣaṇam* acc.sg. (in the RV the regular *n*-stem type, *vṛ̥ṣāṇam*, is rare and late). A possible second example is λιμήν 'harbor', mentioned above. The remaining cognates are uninformative: ποιμήν 'shepherd', Lith. *piemuõ*,

---

[1] Already in the RV the dominant -*ān*- pattern has started to encroach on the 'ox' type: in the RV there were only four nouns that inflected like 'ox'; for this particular noun, the most conservative, there is a single instance (in a late hymn) of *ukṣāṇam*—the type that thereafter prevailed in Skt., even for these words.

piemen-; but that is merely the usual paradigm for *n*-stems in Lith. Put differently, since Lith. attests very little that looks like a distinction between stems with *o*-vocalism vs. *e*-vocalism, a stem like *piemen*- has no more bearing on specifically εν-stems in G than a stem like Lith. *akmen*- (nom. *akmuõ*) 'stone' has on the G ον-stem ἄκμον-.

The evolution of a tolerably numerous form class from a few original forms is not unusual. A parallel example is the expansion of NHG nouns, typically but not exclusively neut., forming the plural with -*er* together with umlaut of the root vowel, for example *Buch Bücher* 'book' and *Mann Männer* 'man'. This inflection continues that of the PIE *s*-stem neuters, a form-class which had shrunk to something like three nouns in West Germanic (reflected in NHG *Lamm* 'lamb', *Kalb* 'calf', and *Ei* 'egg') prior to its vigorous efflorescence in High German.

a. Some scholars imagine a single original paradigm along the lines of the Lith. *n*-stems, with assorted full grades in *e* or *o* depending on the case, and trace the two types evident in G, L, Celtic, and Gmc. to leveling. Given the agreement among most IE languages as to the details of the stem types, such leveling must have taken place in PIE. Evidence in favor of an aboriginal unity is at best suggestive. And even in Lith., there is a distinction between *e*-grade and *o*-grade types in the *r*-stems which parallels the usual reconstruction of *n*-stem patterns.

A more plausible suggestion, but still speculative, is that the close parallelism of *r*- and *n*-stems reflects a common ORIGIN, namely *r*/*n*-stems (**290-2**). This view gets some support from the emergence in Hitt. of *r*/*n*-stems -*tar*/-*nn*-, -*mar*/-*mn*-, -*war*/-*un*-, neatly echoing the familiar IE stems in *-*t*^{e}/*or*-, *-*m*^{e}/*on*-, *-*w*^{e}/*on*-. But even in Hitt. there already are separate *r*- and *n*-stems.

281. The details of the *r*-stems are somewhat different. Here too the bulk of evidence is for *or*-stems, though old-looking *er*-stems are well attested: the kinship terms in *-H_2*ter*- were certainly *e*-types (apart from *or*-stem derivatives attested in G such as ἀπάτωρ 'fatherless' from πατήρ 'father', **129a**). So too **day(H)wer*- 'husband's brother'; but kinship terms were not necessarily *er*-stems, as proved by **swesor*- 'sister'. —Agent nouns in *-*t*^{e}/*or*-[1] seem to have come in both *e*- and *o*-types, though the evidence for *o*-grade is considerably more general than for *e*-grade. InIr. and Ital. have evidence solely for *o*-grade; in Hitt., -*tara*- is ambiguous as to grade, but the parallel -*talla*- points to *o*-grade; OCS on the other hand attests only *-*tel*-. In G there are both types, which correlate suggestively with accent: δοτήρ, -τῆρος vs. δώτωρ, -τορος both 'giver' as if from **d*$\underset{\circ}{H}_3$-*tér*- vs. **déH*$_3$-*tor*- (**129**). The neatness of this pattern is spoiled however by numerous forms such as δωτήρ.

a. In the RV there is a distinction between stem-accented forms in -*tár*-, which were agent nouns just as in G and L; and paradigmatically identical forms, usually root-

---

[1] More exactly, the agent suffix is attested in a total of four forms: *-*ter*-, *-*tor*-, *-*tel*-, and *-*tol*-. G and L attest only the *r*-forms, BS attests the *l*-forms, Hittite attests both, and of course InIr. is ambiguous (**175.3**). The suffix is unattested in Gmc. and Celt. The agent suffix builds a devī-feminine in *-*t(e)r*-*i*H_2-.

accented, which were participles (a function which agrees with OCS forms in *-telĭ*). Here there is no correlation between the grade of the root and the location of the tonic accent, however; and Brugmann's Law (in nom.pl. *-tāras* for example) throughout indicates that both formations were built with full-grade **-tor-*.

b. In G, the masc. ᾱ-stem formation in -της which first competes with -τηρ, -τωρ and eventually all but supplants them (so δότης for earlier δοτήρ) is unconnected with them historically (see **267**).

c. Lith. distinguishes between *o-* and *e-*vocalism in *r-*stems, but only in the nom.sg.; so *sesuõ* 'sister', stem *seser-* vs. *duktė̃* 'daughter', stem *dukter-*. Cf. L *soror, sorōrem* (= Ved. *svásā, svásāram*, but the long vowels of the oblique stems are not inherited; **284B.3**) vs. G θυγάτηρ, θυγατέρα (= Ved. *duhitā́, duhitáram*).

282. NOMINATIVE SINGULAR. In the parent language the chief divergence between the inflectional patterns of *r*-stems and *n*-stems was in the nom.sg. m.f. This difference arose from the action of pre-PIE sound laws acting on nom.sg.m.f. forms of normal type, ***maH₂ters* 'mother' and ***ḱwons* 'dog', whence PIE **maH₂tēr* (**126.1**) but **ḱwō* (**237.6**). This distribution is preserved in Celtic, Germanic (in part), and Italic (in part).

Elsewhere the close parallelism of the *r-* and *n*-stem inflection led to leveling, though differently in different languages. In G the stem-final *n* of *n*-stems was restored to the nom.sg.: **maH₂tem̥* : **maH₂tēr* :: **ḱwonm̥* : *X*, where *X* = **ḱwōn* (thus G κύων, ϝαρσην 'male' < **wr̥sē*; similarly Arm.). Contrariwise, in InIr. and the Baltic Assemblage the *-r* was deleted from the *r*-stems, thus Ved. nom. *mātā́* 'mother', *dātā́* 'giver' like *n*-stems *śvā́* 'dog' and *tákṣā* 'carpenter'; Lith. *mótė* 'woman', OCS *mati* 'mother'.

a. A similar phonological development in pre-PIE resulted in a morphologically opaque nom./acc.pl. for the neuter *n*-stems: ***nomonH₂* 'names' (or more likely **n̥monH₂*) > PIE **nomōn* or **n̥mōn*, PInIr. **nāmān*, whence (with apparently regular loss of *-n*) Ved. *nā́mā*,[1] Av. *nāma̧n*; the remodeled nom./acc.pl. in *-āni*, with *-i* < **-H̥₂* (imported from other cons. stem neuters), is already the dominant type in the RV, and soon thereafter the inherited type in *-ā* disappears altogether.

However, in G, with the restoration of -ν to the nom.sg. of *n*-stems, the PIE nom. pl.n. in **-ōn* was identical to the remodeled m. or f. nom.sg., and on occasion such n. plurals in **-ōn* seem to have been reinterpreted as m.f. singulars. (Cf. the reanalysis of neut.pl. nouns as fem.sg. in Romance languages: It. *opera* 'work', *foglia* 'leaf'.) Such a reinterpretation explains the nouns of **286.5**, below.

b. There are some words in both G and L, particularly G, which have stems ending in *-r-* or *-n-* but without gradation and with nom.sg. in *-s*. Some of these appear to be non-IE words, such as G μάρτυς 'witness' < *μαρτυρς (cf. Cret. μαιτυρς), and μάκᾱρ 'blessed' (cf. Dor. μάκαρς). Others are indubitably IE, as μέλᾱς 'black' and τάλᾱς 'suffering' (from *-ανς, **228.4**), but the details of their G and PreG history are uncertain. It has been suggested that they are reworkings of original *μέλανο- and *τάλαντ-, respectively, but these are just surmises. Others are more transparently remodelings of ordinary *n*-stems, such as κτείς (**pktens*) 'comb', κτενός next to the L *n*-stem *pecten* (**289b**).

---

[1] All but six of the numerous occurrences of nom.pl.neut. *n*-stems transmitted as *-a* in the RV are to be read *-ā*.

Finally, there is a whole class of G nouns in -ῖς (*-ῖνς), -ῖνος, for example δελφῖς 'dolphin'. The majority of words thus formed are of uncertain etymology. (A more *n*-stem-like nom.sg. in -ῖν does in fact occur—δελφῖν—but later than -ῖς.)

There is less of this in L; the chief, perhaps only, example is *sanguīs* (*-*ins*) 'blood', *sanguinis*, whose original *n*-stem status is indicated by OL *sanguen* n. (Enn.).

c. A significant difference between O and U is that Oscan has nom.sg. **-f**, as in **tríbarakkiuf** 'building'. This is manifestly from *-*ns*, that is, the restored stem-consonant further enlarged with a nom.sg. -*s*. Umbrian, like L, appears to retain the inherited *n*-stem nom.sg. as in **tribřiśu** 'threesome'; however, it is possible that these forms are actually the same as the O forms and have only lost a final *-*f*.

Hitt. too has added the usual ending -*š* to the nom.sg., as *ḫa-a-ra-aš* 'eagle' (gen. *ḫa-(a-)ra-na-aš*), but it is unclear whether this represents something like the O restoration of *-*ns*, or is just a retouching of the original *-*ō*, as both would give the same outcome in Hitt.

283. GRADATION OF THE STEM. The PIE paradigms were as follows, taking *maH_2ter- 'mother' and *ḱ*won*- 'dog' as models:

	Singular		*Plural*	
Nom.	maH$_2$tēr	ḱwō	maH$_2$teres	ḱwones
Acc.	maH$_2$term̥	ḱwonm̥	maH$_2$term̥s	ḱwonm̥s
Voc.	maH$_2$ter	ḱwon	maH$_2$teres	ḱwones
neut.	n̥-maH$_2$tr̥	nomn̥	n̥-maH$_2$torH$_2$	nomōn (?*n̥mōn)
Inst.	maH$_2$treH$_1$	ḱuneH$_1$	maH$_2$tr̥bhis, -mis	ḱwn̥bhis *etc.*
Dat.	maH$_2$trey	ḱuney	maH$_2$tr̥bhos *etc.*	ḱwn̥bhos *etc.*
Abl.	maH$_2$tr̥s?		"	"
	maH$_2$tros?	ḱunos		
Gen.	"	"	maH$_2$trŏm	ḱunŏm
Loc.	maH$_2$ter(i)	ḱwen(i)	maH$_2$tr̥su	ḱwn̥su

1. The neuter forms are exemplified by a bahuvrīhi, 'motherless'. For the form of the nom./acc.pl. see **282a**.
2. The marker of the loc.sg., *-*i*, was optional in *r*- and *n*-stems.

The only peculiarity in this array, apart from the nom. forms treated above (**282**), is the abl./gen.sg. of the *r*-stems. Ved. -*ur* points to *-*r̥s*, with zero grade of both stem and ending. The gen.sg. of Av. kinship nouns ends in -*rō*, matching G -ρος, L -*ris*, but Av. *nərəš* 'man's' aligns with the Indic *r*-stem gen.sg. An inflected form with no full grades is unexpected. That is an argument in favor of the validity of the reconstruction—it is much easier to explain the replacement of a peculiar form by the more normal-looking forms of G μητρός and L *mātris* than it is to argue that an unremarkable *maH_2tros or the like was remade as something like *maH_2*tr̥s*. Significantly, furthermore, though the usual Germanic forms agree with G and L, the Indo-Iranian forms are corroborated by early and dialectal forms in OE: *feadur* gen.sg. (Vespasian Psalter), *uuldur-fadur* gen.sg. 'glory-father' (Caedmon's Hymn): these point to PGmc. *-*ur(z)* < PIE *-*r̥s*.

Evidence for *e*-grade in the loc.sg. is afforded by Ved. -*ăni*, -*ări* (*o*-grade would have given ×-*āni*, ×-*āri*), Go. dat.sg. -*in* < *-*eni*, and by paradigmatically isolated forms in G, such as *αἰέν* poet. 'forever' < *H_2eywen*, cf. *αἰών* 'period, lifetime'; all derived from *H_2eyu-* n. 'lifetime'; and infin. -*εν* (552A.1).

284. THE STEM TYPES OF GREEK AND LATIN. The array of G and L *r*- and *n*-stem inflectional subtypes is secondary, derived from the single type of **283** (counting the *o*-types and *e*-types together) via partial or complete leveling of stem grades.

r-STEMS

A. GREEK. In Greek the *r*-stems survive as non-neuter nouns only, apart from bahuvrīhis such as *ἀμήτωρ* 'motherless' from *μήτηρ*. Apparent exceptions to this observation, like neut. *ὕδωρ* 'water', continue old *r/n*-stems, **290-2**.

There are five *r*-stem types. (These 'types' do not represent a standard classification, like the numbering of declensions in the classical languages; they are for convenience only.)

1. The most conservative type, in that it preserves some of the original patterning: *πατήρ, πατρός, πατέρα, πατέρες, πατράσι*; but the full grades of *πατέρων* gen.pl. and *πατέρας* acc.pl. are innovations. In Hom. we find conservative forms like *πατρῶν* gen.pl. side by side with innovations not found in Att., like gen.sg. *πατέρος*.

This type is virtually confined to three nouns, *πατήρ* 'father', *μᾱ́τηρ* 'mother', and *θυγάτηρ* 'daughter'. *Δᾱήρ* (**δαιϝήρ*) 'husband's brother' is a special case: in Att., it belongs to type 2, below, but in Homer textual *δαερῶν* gen.pl. has to be disyllabic, presumably **δαιϝρῶν*—that is, the original type 1 alternation is intact.[1]

2. Nom.sg. in -*ηρ*; -*ερ*- before oblique endings with vowels, thus *αἰθήρ* 'upper air', *αἰθέρος*; *γαστήρ* 'stomach', *γαστέρος*; *ἀήρ* 'mist'; Att. *δᾱήρ* 'husband's brother'; *ἀστήρ* 'star'. The zero grade still occurs in the dat.pl., so *ἄστρασι* < *-*r̥su* (**172a**, **257.12**).

3. As type 2, but with -*ο*- generalized outside of the nom.sg. The type is found both in primary nouns, such as *δώτωρ, δώτορος* 'giver', and in derived forms, such as *ἀμήτωρ, ἀμήτορος* 'motherless', *προπάτωρ, προπάτορος* 'forefather'. (This is the only *or*-stem type.)

4. With the -*η*- of the nom.sg. generalized through the whole paradigm, thus agent nouns like *σωτήρ* 'savior', *σωτῆρος* (-*ερ* only in the voc.sg., which also has recessive accent (**257.2**): *σῶτερ*).

5. With zero grade generalized to all cases and numbers outside of the nom.sg., thus *ἀνήρ* 'man', *ἄνδρα, ἀνδρός*. (But Homer still has inherited

---

1 G *φρᾱ́τηρ* 'member of a phratry' (= L *frāter*, OE *brōþor*, Ved. *bhrā́tar-* all 'brother'), must originally have belonged to this type. It became a type 2 and evolved a by-form, *φρᾱ́τωρ* (type 3) from compounds like Homeric *ἀφρήτωρ* 'bound by no social ties'.

ἀνέρες nom.pl. next to novel ἄνδρες, as well as full-grade innovations like ἀνέρος gen.sg. next to inherited ἀνδρός.)

B. LATIN. Latin *r*-stems fall into three classes.

1. Kinship terms in *-ter*, a small, closed class (three items in classical Latin: *māter, pater, frāter*). The original *ē*-grade was preserved in the nom. sg.—at least until **-tēr* > L *-ter*, 83.3; zero grade elsewhere: *patrī* dat. (old), *patrem* acc.sg. (new, for **paterem*), and so on. The replacement of full grades by zero grades, as in *patrem*, is by leveling.

2. A short list of words of often obscure etymology with a uniform, usually short-vowel, stem throughout: masc. *later* 'brick, tile', *carcer, -eris* 'prison', *gibber* 'hunch-back', *augur* 'soothsayer'. Neut. *cicer* 'chick-pea'; *iubar, -āris* 'brilliant light'.

3. The remaining type, which includes the only productive *r*-stems in L, has generalized the *-ō-* of the nom.sg. through the whole paradigm. Thus **sorōr* (Ved. *svásā*) 'sister' *sorōris*, and the agent noun suffix in **āctōr, āctōris* 'driver' (*agō*). (Note that the *-ā-* of Ved. *svásāram* acc. is from Brugmann's Law, 36.4, and only coincidentally agrees with L *sorōr-*.) —Since long vowels shorten in final syllables before any consonant but *-s* (83.3), in the literary period the nom.sg., which was the point of departure for the long vowel oblique stem in the first place, ends up as the ONLY form in the paradigm with a short vowel: *sorŏr, āctŏr.*

a. Note that *arbor, arbŏris* 'tree', and many of the nouns in *-or, -ōris*, are historically *s*-stems, 299.

b. Dat./abl.pl. *sorōribus* and *patribus* look like *i*-stem forms in place of expected **sorurbus* and **paturbus* < **-orbos* < **-r̥bhos*. But the parallel forms in U point to *u*-stem influence (U **fratrus** < **frātrufs* < **frātrufos*, 277.4), which raises the possibility that L *-ibus* is likewise from PItal. **-ufos*, with regular development of *i* < **u* (66.4 and 69; 277.4a).

c. The evolution of the stem-forms, whatever the exact mechanisms, was dialectal rather than pan-Italic: Sab. *r*-stems show a mixture of forms which are in part more conservative and in part more innovative than the L details. Thus the U nom.pl. *frater* < **frāters* < **frāteres* continues the original grade of the stem for the case, unlike L *frātrēs* (the syncope of the vowel of the U ending shows it was the original cons. stem ending **-ĕs*, not the *i*-stem ending *-ēs* of literary L, 307.1). On the other hand, a novel full grade is seen in O **patereí** dat.sg. 'father' (a divine title), several times attested, next to U **iuvepatre** dat.sg. 'Jupiter' (also several times attested), with what might be either the more original zero grade or the result of syncope.

d. RV *devā́ram* acc.sg. 'husband's brother' agrees with other evidence (such as G δαήρ, -έρος) in pointing to an ordinary *r*-stem noun which however was unusual in having full grade in **e*, as **-or̥m* would have given Ved. *ˣ-āram*. The inflection of the L cognate, **laever* 'husband's brother', is not recorded; indeed the word itself barely is, being mentioned only in Paul.Fest. and in the Pandects of Justinian (6th century) in the late and corrupt form *levir* (*l* < **d*, 151).

n-STEMS.

285. The *n*-stems of G and L include neuter as well as masc. and fem. nouns. The few primary *n*-stem adjectives of PIE have been eliminated in

L, and survive in G in the unique form ἄρσην (Att. ἄρρην) 'masculine, male'. In G there are also the usual bahuvrīhi compounds like ἀκῡ́μων 'barren' from κῦμα, -ατος n. 'fruit'. (The latter type makes neuter nom./acc.sg. with full grade, ἀκῦμον, rather than with the original zero grade.)

MASCULINE AND FEMININE *n*-STEMS.

286. GREEK. The Greek *n*-stems fall into five types which parallel the five *r*-stem types (284A), if only vaguely.

1. Nom. in -ων; -ον in the voc.sg.; otherwise with generalized zero grade: κύων 'dog', voc.sg. κύον, gen. κυνός, dat. κυνί, acc. κύνα, nom.pl. κύνες. The nom. κύων is itself a remodeling of something like *π(π)ών < **ḱwō* (160); acc.sg. κύνα (via **kwuna*) is superimposable on Ved. *śvā́nam*; both are regular from **ḱwónm̥* (Cowgill's Law, 44; Brugmann's Law, 36.4). Cf. RV *śvā́*, gen. *śúnas*, acc. *śvānam*, and later Skt. *śvani* loc., *śvānas* nom.pl.

a. On the evidence of δράκαινα 'dragoness', the masc. δράκων, -οντος is a remodeling of an earlier *n*-stem, **dr̥ḱ-on-* 'seeing one' or the like (an example of an *on*-stem agent noun, a type obsolete in G).

2. As type 1, but with *e*-vocalism: nom. (ϝ)αρην 'lamb' (attested epigraphically only), the remaining forms ἀρνός, ἀρνί, and so on.

3. Masc. and fem. nouns with nom.sg. -(μ)ην, oblique forms in -(μ)εν-. There were evidently only a few ancient *en*-stems, as noted above (280), and of them only one survives in G: ἄρσην 'male', ἄρσενος (cf. Ved. *vŕ̥ṣan-*). For the most part, forms in other languages cognate to these nouns point to *o*-grades or show discrepancies of form or meaning. Thus G ποιμήν 'shepherd' = Lith. *piemuõ*, which goes exactly like *akmuõ* 'stone' (G ἄκμων); G ἀδήν f.m. 'gland' matches L *inguen, -inis* 'groin' (PIE **n̥gʷen-*) but the latter is neuter (289).

4. As type 3 but with *o*-vocalism: nom.sg. masc. and fem. in -(μ)ων, remaining forms in -(μ)ον-, like δαίμων, -μονος 'spirit'.

a. The original zero grade still is seen in φρασί (replaced by the usual φρεσί after φρένες 'seat of emotions/intellect'). An indirect trace of the original zero grade in types 3 and 4 is seen in dat.pl. ποιμέσι, δαίμοσι which replace *ποιμασι, *δαιμασι (-α- < **n̥*). Note that this is not the substitution of the actual full grade stem, -μον- and -μεν-, which would have resulted in quite different forms, namely ˣποιμείσι, ˣδαίμουσι; rather, it entails a replacement of original -α- by -ο- or -ε- in accord with the vowel of the other cases.

5. Masc. and fem. nouns with -(μ)ων- throughout, thus ἀγών, ἀγῶνος 'assembly'. This type, which is tolerably common, is easily taken as the result of leveling in which the -ω- of the nom.sg. is generalized. Doubtless some are just that, such as Ἀπόλλων, -ωνος; but it has been pointed out that much of the class has fairly consistent semantics, namely collectives, and assemblages or sets of things: ἀγών itself; κυκε(ι)ών 'potion, specif. any mixed drink'; χαλκεών 'smithy'; μυών 'muscles, musculature'; and χειμών 'winter' (cf. χεῖμα neut. *n*-stem 'frost'). Most of the oldest such forms are

equally intelligible whether taken as singular collectives or as plurals. These are in origin old plurals in fact, thus *χειμών* < **ǵheymōn* < ***ǵhey-monH₂* neut. 'winters', reinterpreted as singulars (**282a**).

a. The old zero grade is seen in a few feminines in *-iH_2: *Λάκαινα* f. as if from **lakanya* < **lakn̥iH₂* 'a Laconian woman';[1] cf. masc. *Λάκων, Λάκωνος*.

b. The so-called apocopated accusative, as in Ἀπόλλω, Ποσειδῶ, in place of usual -*ωνα*, is not apocopated at all: the shape is imported entire from the comparative adj. (354.4).

c. Nom. and fem. nouns with a frozen -*ην*- in all forms, thus *κηφήν, κηφῆνος* 'drone' (the bee), Ἕλλην, Ἕλληνος 'Hellene, Greek', are the fewest in number. These are sometimes taken as the *e*-grade equivalent of type *5*, but are probably unconnected to *n*-stems proper. In the first place, as *καφάν* (Hesych.; presumably *κᾱφᾱ́ν*) and Dor. Ἕλλᾱν, Ἕλλᾱνος reveal, these are for the most part *ᾱν*-stems, not *ην*-stems. Second, the words as a group are of very obscure history.

d. G *μήν, μηνός* m. 'month' continues a form **mēns*- in which **s* is part of the stem (cf. L *mēnsis*, Lesb. *μηννος* gen.sg.). The most conservative form is Ion. *μείς* < **μενς* < **μηνς* (via Osthoff's Law, 63.2). Att. *μήν* is therefore reminiscent of *χήν, χηνός* 'goose', the nom.sg. in both nouns being back-formed from the oblique stem, though the course of events is quite different in the two: gen.sg. *χηνός* < *χᾱνός* < **χᾰνσός* < PIE **ǵhans-os*, 228.1; cf. L *ānser*, NHG *Gans*. (The acc.pl. *χένας* is in turn a remodeling of **χῆνας* < **χανσας* on the basis of forms like *ἀρσένας*.)

287. LATIN. The Latin m. and f. *n*-stems fall into three types, which are not particularly parallel to the G types, above.

1. The least altered L *n*-stem is the unique *carō, carnis* f. 'meat' (etymologically *'a cut', apparently from the root **(s)ker*-, though the vocalism of L *carn*- is difficult, 97). The apparent zero grade of the suffix throughout the paradigm, even in place of the full grades originally proper to the acc. sg. and nom.pl., is commonly said to be the result of leveling; but in view of the especial readiness of vowels to drop in L after *r* (74.6), it is more likely that the stem *carn*- continues syncopated full grades (as type 2, below). Cf. U **karu** 'piece, part', dat.sg. **karne**.

2. is the converse of the *carō* type, that is with full grade generalized in place of zero grade. This large group includes a few primary nouns and a number of more or less productive complex derivatives. The primary nouns, *cardō, -inis* f. 'hinge', *homō, -inis* m. 'man', are predominantly fem.; and exclusively so are the numerous and variously productive composite affixes *-tūdō, -tūdinis*; *-āgō, -āginis*; *-ūgō*; *-īgō*, and others.

a. The stem in *-in*- could of course continue either *-*en*- or *-*on*- (66.2-3). Where there is any evidence on the point, it suggests original *on*-stem inflection in accord with the evidence of other IE languages. So for example O **humuns** nom.pl. and the obsolete L *hemōnem* acc.sg. (Fest.—usually so interpreted, but perhaps rather *hemŏnem*?) point to

---

[1] The genuine zero grade formation, **lakniH₂*, would have given ˣΛάκνια, like *πότνια* 'mistress' < **potniH₂*, 49.2, **269b**. Similarly *δράκαινα* 'dragoness' (**286.1a**), which cannot directly continue **dr̥kniH₂*.

original *o*-grade. Similarly the vanished full grades of type 3, below: *carbunculus* 'little coal; gem' attests a stem **carbŏn-* no longer evident in the noun paradigm (*carbō, -ōnis*) itself.

b. At least two old *n*-stem nouns in L acquired new nom.sg. forms that obscure their original nature: *iuvenis, -enis* 'a youth; young' looks like an ordinary *i*-stem, but cognates such as Ved. *yúvā*, acc. *yúvānam* reveal an original *on*-stem in its makeup; and *sanguīs* (*-*ins*) 'blood' by its stem *-inis* reveals a prior incarnation as an *n*-stem—apparently originally neuter, **289**, but the exact history is uncertain; see also **282b**.

3. The majority of non-neuter L *n*-stems have generalized *-ō-*, the vowel originally proper to the nom.sg. alone, thus *crābrō, -ōnis* 'hornet', *carbō, -ōnis* 'charcoal', *caupō, -ōnis* 'shopkeeper', *ligō, -ōnis* 'hoe'. This form class is large, and productive enough to include a fair number of loanwords from diverse sources (*sīpō* 'siphon' from G σίφων; *sāpō* 'soap, pomade' from a Germanic source; *pavō* 'peacock' from an eastern source).

a. The nouns in simple *-ōn-* are almost all masc.; the few feminines are mostly names—*Iūnō*, and loan words from the G Σαπφώ class (322) such as *Gorgō* (Γοργώ). A few fem. *n*-stem nouns are seen in sublimated forms, for example the deity *Bellōna*. The two main fem. classes in this type are morphological complexes: (1) the vigorously productive affix *-tiōn-*, which is historically an agglutination of the *ōn*-stem and fem. *ti*-stem nomina actionis: *ratiō* (*reor*) 'reckoning', *mentiō* 'mention', *nātiō* 'birth, race', *āctiō* 'motion', and also *-ātiō, -ītiō*, and so on. (This formation is abundant also in Celtic.) (2) A large but closed class of verbal abstracts in *-iō*: *legiō* 'legion' (*'levy', from *legō*), *regiō* 'line, direction' (from *regō*).

b. There are no clear examples of an original *en*-stem in L. Apparent specimens have various histories, only partly transparent. The rare *liēn, liēnis* 'spleen' (probably *-ĕ-* on the evidence of Plaut. *liĕnōsus* 'splenetic') is morphologically unique, and is thought to owe some of its details of form to the influence G σπλήν, -ηνός of the same meaning; but the latter is a post-Homeric word of obscure history and structure. (Some think this σπλήν actually continues **splēnkʰ*, that is, it was not originally an *n*-stem at all.) L *flāmen, -inis* 'priest' is a neuter noun in origin, perhaps akin to Ved. *bráhman-* n. 'worship', and an instance of a word for an office becoming a personal noun (a commonplace; cf. NE *magistrate, counsel*, and *justice*).[1] *Pecten, -inis* m. 'comb' looks like a neut., but its only close cognate, G κτείς (*πκτενς) is also masc. An original *en*-stem nom.sg. would have been ˣ*p(e)ctē*, so if the attested *pecten* is a genuine *en*-stem the form of the nominative itself is not inherited, **289b**. L *oscen* 'an augural bird', *tibīcen* 'flute-player' (71.4), and several similar forms are compounds of the root *can-* 'sing' with regular weakening (**68**).

NEUTER *n*-STEMS.

288. GREEK. The PIE neuter *n*-stems underlie the G stems in -α(τ)- and -μα(τ)-, exemplified by ὄνομα 'name', gen. ὀνόματος. In these nouns, a new stem in -(μ)ατ- replaces the original *n*-stem. Although this shape prevails already in Myc., the innovation must have been relatively late, as revealed by transparent derivatives which were built to the original *n*-stem.

---

[1] The functionally closer *brahmán-* m. 'priest' is an *on*-stem and cannot be directly superimposed on L *flāmen*. In any case, L tolerated neuter personal nouns, such as *scortum* 'prostitute' (of either sex).

An example above, **285**, is the *n*-stem bahuvrīhi ἀκῦμων 'barren', based on κῦμα, -ατος, a neut. noun without an -ν- anywhere in the source paradigm as attested. Similarly, from ὄνομα 'name': Hom. νώνυμνος 'inglorious, nameless' (**108**), and ὀνομαίνω 'call by name' < **nomn̥-yoH₂* (a derivative from a *t*-stem ὄνοματ- would have been ˣὀνομάσσω/-άττω). Furthermore, in the dat.pl. Homer has only -ασι < *-*n̥su* (cf. Ved. -*asu*, **172a**), never ˣ-ασσι as if from *-*at-si*. But Myc. already attests the familiar type: *pe-ma* nom./acc. 'seed' (σπερμα), *e-ka-ma-te* inst.sg. 'support' (*ekʰmatē̆*, root **seǵh*-) and, with *o* < **n̥* (**100d**), *a-mo* nom./acc.sg. 'wheel' (cf. G ἅρμα 'chariot'—though strange to say the Myc. word, which is tolerably common, is never spelled with a_2-; **26.6a**), *a-mo-te* nom./acc.du., *a-mo-ta* nom./acc.pl. Given Hom. -ασι, above, Myc. *a-mo-si* dat.pl. cannot be interpreted with confidence but probably stands for *harmosi* < -*n̥su* rather than for *harmotsi*. The parallel interpretation of *e-ka-ma-pi* inst.pl. would be *ekʰmapʰi*.

The source of this -τ- is uncertain. All the usual explanations have grave weaknesses (**291.1a**). One ingredient in the development might have been stems in *-*nt*-, namely the pres. and aor. pple., in the original athematic inflection in which -ντ- < *-*nt*- alternated with *-ατ- < *-*n̥t*-. But it is hard to progress beyond a vague likelihood to that effect, and the supposed model paradigm has itself been everywhere replaced (G has no pple. stems analogous to Ved. *júhvat* nom.sg.m. 'invoking' < **ǵhe-ǵhw-n̥t-s*). A different (and slightly more cogent) point of departure might be two similar suffixes in PIE: a primary *n*-stem *-*mon*-, forming both nomina agentis (masc.) and nomina actionis (neut.), mostly the latter; and a secondary derivative *-*mᵉ/ont*-, forming possessive adjectives which are frequently nominalized as neut. nouns; cf. the L abstracts in -*mentum*. The very common G type of χεῦμα, -ματος 'a pouring, a stream', was to begin with χεῦμα, *χεῦμνος—that is, *t*-less like RV *hóman*- 'a pouring; an oblation', root **ǵhew*-. Such a nom.sg. is identical to the nom./acc.sg.neut. -μα < *-*mn̥t*, gen. -ματος < *-*mn̥tos*. Evidence that such forms might interact is provided by pairs like L *strāmen*, *strāmina* 'bed of straw, litter', and the virtually synonymous *strāmentum*, -*menta*; cf. G στρώματα.

In sum, to put it informally, ALL neuters in G whose inflection was a little bit peculiar were converted to the τ-stem type which (seemingly) started in the *n*-stems: see **293**.

a. As it happens there does exist a flawless analogical proportion—μέλι : ὄνομα :: μέλιτος : *X*, where *X* = ὀνόματος. But it is hardly likely that the inflection of the word for 'honey' had anything to do with the rise of the G τ-stem neuters.

289. LATIN. Neuter *n*-stem nouns have a nom./acc.sg. in -*en* < *-*n̥*; the remaining forms are built to a stem in -*in*-: *nōmen*, *nōminis* 'name'. This type includes many derivatives in -*men*, -*minis* and only a very few primary nouns (*nōmen*, *inguen* 'bulge, groin', *unguen* 'salve', and *glūten* 'glue').

Straightforward descriptively, this pattern is hard to relate to the facts of the parent language. Hysterokinetic neuter *n*-stems[1] had full grade stems only in the nom.du. and pl. (*-*oniH₁* and *-*onH₂*, respectively—neither evidently reflected in Ital.), and the loc.sg. Therefore the standard L stem shape—*strāminis, strāminī, strāmina*—must be no less secondary than the enigmatic G stem in -ατ- (**288**, above); and so it is perhaps pointless to worry about whether the ambiguous (**66**) -*in*- continues *e*- or *o*-grade. On the basis of the evidence in other languages, most of the neut. *n*-stems were in fact *on*-stems, but a few may have been *en*-stems. For example, *inguen, -inis* n. is identical to *nōmen* from the L standpoint, but if G ἀδήν, -ένος f. (later m.) 'gland' can be taken at face value, it implies that the L stem was etymologically **n̥gʷen*-. Similarly, on the evidence of OIr. *anme* gen. sg. 'name' < **n̥mens*, *imbe* gen.sg. 'butter' < **(H₃)n̥gʷens*, both L *nōmen* and *unguen* are old proterokinetic *en*-stems. Whatever the truth of that, it is hardly compelling to trace the L *strāmen, -minis* type to the influence of these three nouns.

In the alternative, it might be supposed that -*minis*, -*minī* are regular phonological developments of *-*mnes*, *-*mney* by anaptyxis. L does of course have -*mn*- sequences, but only (a) in words of obscure etymology (like *Vertumnus*, a god's name, and *autumnus*) and (b) from **pn*, as *somnus* 'sleep' < **swepnos*.

a. A disguised neut. *n*-stem is *fel, fellis* 'gall', the obl. stem < **fel-n*-. But the history of the inflection is uncertain in the details. The usual explanation is the reciprocal contamination of the original paradigm and that of *mel*, **meles* 'honey', whence obl. *mellis* like *fellis* and nom. *fel* like *mel*. In fact, of course, as remarked above, zero grade of the stem (**ǵhelnes* gen.sg.) is exactly what one would expect, and this may therefore be a conservative rather than innovative paradigm, only the nom.sg. *fel* requiring some manipulation, and for that the appeal to *mel(l)* < **meld* < **melit* (**237.7-8**) may be thinkable.

b. L *pecten, -inis* m. 'comb', G κτείς, κτενός m. 'comb', though ordinary cons. stems in appearance, are probably remnants of an original *r/n*-stem. neut. as there is no PIE *n*-stem suffix *-*ten*-.

NEUTER *r/n*-STEMS

290. In a number of IE languages we find neuter nouns which end in -*r* (in InIr. also -*r̥t*, -*r̥k*) in the nom./acc.sg., in some derivatives, and sometimes in the nom./acc.pl., but which build the other cases (and some derivatives) to a stem in -*n*-. Hence the term '*r/n*-stems'. This mode of inflection is attested only very fragmentarily within the familiar IE languages, but the type is obviously both ancient and important. For one thing, the lexicon involved belongs to the most basic stratum of vocabulary —body parts and words like 'water', 'fire', 'blood', and 'day'. For another, though any given language has only a handful of such items, there is little lexical agreement from language to language, so that even though the type is attested only in scraps, the sum of words pointing to *r/n*-inflection is considerable.

The original, unaltered, mode of inflection is scantily attested within the familiar IE languages: L *femur, feminis* 'thigh' (remodeled *femoris* also occurs); U **utur** acc. 'water', **une** abl. < **udni* or **udneH₁*; or Ved. *ū́dhar* nom./acc. 'udder', *ū́dhnas* gen. Less obvious, though in fact relatively untampered-

---

[1] As contrasted with the proterokinetic **nom-n̥*, **n̥m-en-s*, **272.2**.

with, is the G type ὕδωρ, ὕδατος 'water' and ἧπαρ, ἥπατος 'liver', in which the stem -ατ- somehow continues *-n̥- (**288**).

More abundant are conflated and dismembered paradigms. Conflation, that is the incorporation of both stems in the same form, is seen in the oblique stem of L *iter* 'road, way' (*itineris*), or of *iecur* 'liver' (*iocineris*; later *iecineris*). Dismembered paradigms take two forms: (1) Closely cognate forms in different languages, like ON *vatn* (gen. *vats*) 'water' and Go. *wato* (an ordinary neut. *n*-stem), next to WGmc forms like OE *wæter* and OHG *uuaz(z)ar*, which collectively attest the survival of *r/n* inflection for 'water' as late as PGmc. (2) The disintegration of an inherited paradigm into different paradigms in one and the same language, based on the two stems; thus G πῖων m.n. 'fat, rich' (an ordinary *n*-stem) but πῖειρα f. < *$piHweriH_2$. In Indic this is a regular feature of the verbal adjective in *-van-*, a common type: the masc. and neut. go like ordinary *n*-stems, but the feminine stem is *-var-ī-*: to *yaj-* 'worship', RV *yájvan-* m.n. 'worshipping', fem. *yájvarī-*.

The atrophy of the *r/n*-stem class was an ancient and continuing process, and dismemberment of a given paradigm can have taken place at any time. This opens the door to a variety of speculations. Some authorities, for example, see in L *dōnum* 'gift', Ved. *dā́na-*, OIr. *dán*, and G δῶρον, evidence for an aboriginal *r/n*-stem noun differently remodeled as neut. *o*-stems. L *manus* 'hand', G μάρη (Pind.) have been similarly explained. Again, the stems for 'sleep'—**swepno-* (L *somnus* m., Ved. *svápna-* m., OE *swefn* n. and perhaps G ὕπνος); **supno-* (OCS *sŭnŭ*, perh. G ὕπνος), where *-*no-* is affixed to inexplicably different grades of the root **swep-*, taken together with L *sopor* m. 'deep sleep'[1] and Hitt. *šu-up-pár-ri-ya-* 'sleep'—might be explained as breakup products of an original *r/n*-stem (say, ***swépr̥* nom., ***supnós* gen.; denom. **supr̥-y*^{e}*/o-*). But the prevailingly masc. gender of the nouns in *-*no-* is inconsistent with this view, and L *sopor* is easily taken as an ordinary *ōs*-stem (**299**; cf. its formal and semantic yokefellows *torpor, rigor, languor*). Obviously, such analyses are on a very different footing from, say, the Gmc. 'water' words or G πῖων/πῖειρα.

a. HETITICA. Notwithstanding the confident assumption that *r/n* stems were once more prominent, the abundance of the type in Hittite is nothing short of astonishing. It is found in a number of productive affixes such as *-war, -un-* (cf. Skt. *-van-/varī-*, above); *-ššar, -šn-*; *-mar, -mn-*; and nomina actionis in *-tar, -nn-* (< *-*ter*, *-*tn-*) as in *a-ku-wa-tar* 'a drinking', *a-ku-wa-an-na-aš* gen. (cf. *e-ku-uz-zi* 'drinks'); or *aq-qa-tar*, gen. *ag-ga-an-na-aš* 'death' (cf. *a-ki* 'dies'). Particularly striking is *i-tar* 'a going; road', directly superimposable on L *iter*, above.

In addition to such derived forms, there are primary nouns, some familiar from the well-known IE languages, but some unfamiliar:

Hitt. *(ú-)wa-a-tar* 'water', gen. *ú-i-te-na-aš* (whose nom.pl. *ú-i-da-a-ar* superimposes on G ὕδωρ morphologically).

Hitt. *pa-aḫ-ḫur* 'fire' (old; later once as *pa-aḫ-ḫu-wa-ar*), dat. *pa-ḫu-ni* (old), *pa-ḫu-e-ni* (in the later language); cf. G πῦρ, πυρός (-ῠ-); U **pir** (< *-*ū-*), loc. *purome* (which points to *-ŭ-*). Germanic has a dismembered paradigm: OIc. *fúrr*, OE *fȳr*, next to Go. *fon*, gen.

[1] L *sopor* would then continue an original neut.pl., **swepōr* or the like (cf. **291.2b**); note that OE *swefn* is commonly found in the pl. with the same sense as the sg.

funins. OPr. *panno* shows *-n-* (as do a number of possible derivatives, like NHG *Funke* 'flash, spark').

Hitt. *e-eš-ḫar* 'blood', gen. *(e-)eš-ḫa-na-aš* (/esḫnas/); cf. Ved. *ásr̥k*, gen. *asnás*, G ἔαρ (?=ἔᾱρ; from ἦἄρ, 79.3), OL *assyr* (i.e., *aser*; Paul.Fest.), Latv. *asins*, Toch. A *ysār* (and conceivably, though any such history for the word is highly speculative, OL *sanguen* n. (**282b**, **287.2b**), L *sanguīs*).

Next to these there are a number of ancient-looking Hitt. forms without evident *r*/*n* cognates elsewhere: *me-ḫur* gen. *me-(e-)ḫu-na-aš* 'time', *še-e-ḫur* gen. *še-e-ḫu-na-aš* 'urine', and *pa-an-ku-ur* gen. *pa-an-ku-na-aš* 'family'.[1]

b. It has been suggested that G adverbs in -α, such as θαμά 'often', κάρτα 'very', and πύκα 'strongly' reflect *-n̥, namely the zero grade *n*-stem of the *r*/*n*-stem type. They are traced to compounds via metanalysis, exactly as Fr. *très* 'very' was abstracted from compounds in **tra(n)s-* 'surpassingly-'. A weakness in this explanation is that the source compounds have been lost, though G has compounds of appropriate TYPE, as in Hom. ἀγα-κλεής 'much-famed' < **m̥ǵH̥₂-*, δασύ-μαλλος 'thick-fleeced' < **dn̥su-*. (And after all the original Romance compounds in **tras-* have also been lost.) If this explanation of at least some of the hitherto much-debated G adverbia in -α is correct, it additionally explains the occurrence of thematic adjectives in -νο-, rather than -ο-, beside the adverbs, as θαμ(ι)νός 'frequent', πυκ(ι)νός 'compact'.

291. There were two types of *r*/*n*-stem, differing in the form of the nom./acc.sg.; sometimes the evidence a particular stem is uniform, but there is often disagreement among the languages. And much is unclear about the distribution of ablaut grades in the 'root' and suffix in oblique cases.

1. Nom./acc. *-r̥.

PIE **yekʷr̥* 'liver', thus Ved. *yakŕ̥t*, *yaknás*; G ἧπαρ, ἥπατος; L *iecur*, *iocineris*. L *femur*, *feminis* 'thigh' has no outside connections, but is obviously ancient.

Other words in this category are PIE **ḱokʷr*/*n-* 'excrement' (Ved. *śákr̥t*, cf. G κόπρος); PIE **piHwr̥* 'fat' (Ved. *pī́van-* m.n., *pī́varī-* f. = G πῑ́ων, πῑ́ειρα, also NB πῖ(ϝ)αρ n. indecl. 'cream, fat'); and PIE **esH₂r*/*n-* 'blood' (**290a**), though OL *aser* points rather to Type 2, below.

a. The *-t*, *-k* seen in some InIr. reflexes is thought by many to be secondary. On the other hand an original *-r̥k, *-r̥t would give the G and L forms just as well as plain *-r̥, and some see the G oblique stem -ατος < *-n̥tos evidence for original *-r̥t as the source of the *-t- in *-n̥t-. A serious difficulty with this idea, however, is that the migration of the *-t- alone, rather than the creation of a new oblique stem in *-r̥t- (ˣ-αρτ-), is hard to account for.

b. There are many problems of detail with the 'liver' words. The accent of Ved. *yakŕ̥t* is unexpected; the length of the first syllable of ἧπαρ is an enigma. The vocalism of the L oblique stem *iocin-* has not been satisfactorily explained (it is certainly neither a case of assimilation nor a vulgarism, though *iocur*, with its importation of the oblique stem vocalism into the nom., is censured in the App.Prob.). —Some have proposed a

---

[1] Probably PIE **ponkʷr̥*; cf. Hitt. *pa-an-ku-uš* 'assembly', and L *cunctus* 'the whole', **141a**. —Hitt. *me-ḫur* may in fact be related to PIE **mē-* (**meH₁*) 'measure', but not on the basis of graphic *-ḫ-*. In Hitt., the sequence *-eḫu-* does not point to a PIE laryngeal; rather the *-ḫ-* is a purely graphic element, like *-h-* in L *ahēnus* (**159**).

connection between these forms and the Gmc. *liver* words, via Gmc. *ƀ < *kʷ, confiming incidentally the Indic accent (139, 154.3).

2. Nom./acc. *-*er* (? that is, *-*ér*).

PIE **ewH̥dher*, **uHdher* 'udder' (the root vowel in different ablaut grades, obscure in detail): G οὖθαρ, οὔθατος, Ved. *ū́dhar*, *ū́dhnas*. (L *ūber*, *ūberis*, and also the Gmc. 'udder' words, have generalized the *r*-stem.)[1]

PIE *-*ter*, *-*tn*- (L provides the evidence for *e*-grade specifically) forming nomina actionis, as in Hitt. *aq-qa-tar* 'death' quoted above, *ap-pa-a-tar*, *-an-na-aš* 'a taking' (*e-ip-zi* 'takes'). Thus Hitt. *i-tar*, L *iter* 'way', conflated stem *itineris*, from the root **ey*-/**i*- 'go'.

The *-*er* type does not survive as such in G; on the evidence of οὖθαρ, οὔθατος, reflecting a word whose nom.sg. clearly ended in *-*er*, type 2 paradigms were all remodeled as type 1 in G.

a. In Hittite *-*er* and *-*r̥* both give *-ar*. In *pa-aḫ-ḫu-ur* 'fire', *-ur* reflects *-*wr̥*. The same explanation can be supposed for the others with nom./acc. in *-ur* with the *n*-stem in *-un-*: *me-ḫur* 'time', *pa-an-ku-ur* 'family' (*-*kʷr̥*, in this case), *še-e-ḫur* 'urine', gens. *me-(e-)ḫu-na-aš*, *pa-an-ku-na-aš*, *še-e-ḫu-na-aš*.

b. G ὕδωρ, U **utur** 'water' is often treated as a third type, namely with nom./acc.sg. in *-*ōr*. But the discovery of the Hitt. distinction between *wa-a-tar* (also *ú-i-ta-ar*) nom./acc.sg. and *ú-i-da-a-ar* nom./acc.pl. suggests that this *-*ōr*, while genuine, is a form of the nom./acc. PLURAL (lit. 'waters'). It is parallel with the *n*-stem pl. in *-ōn* < **-*on*H_2, and therefore is ultimately probably **-*or*H_2. The only other G form like this is σκῶρ/σκώρ, σκατός 'feces', usually explained as a back-formation from ordinary (but unattested) *r*-stem compounds of the type *μῦσκωρ, *βουσκωρ 'mouse-, cow-droppings', parallel to L *mūscerda*, *sucerda* (*-ū-*?). But it is more likely just an old plural, parallel to ὕδωρ. (Many words of similar meanings are pl.tant.: *droppings*, *feces*, *dregs*, *lees*.)

Neut. plural in *-*ōr* was not limited to *r/n*-stems: the best explanation of the ending of L *quattuor* 'four' and Go. *fidwor*, both of which must continue *-*ōr*, is an archaic neut.pl., otherwise unattested (unless it is latent in Ved. *catvā́ri* nom./acc.n.pl., if orig. **catvā́r* = *quattuor* but re-marked with the usual Ved. nom./acc.n.pl. cons. stem ending *-i* < *-$H̥_2$). The peculiar shape of L *aequor* 'level surface' may have a similar history.[2]

292. PREHISTORY OF *r/n*-INFLECTION. In InIr. there are a number of genuinely heteroclitic neut. nouns which inflect with a stem in *-n-* but which build the nom./acc. with something other than *-r*. Thus RV *śíras* 'horn', *śīrṣṇás* gen.; here an *n*-stem paradigm is appended to the *s*-stem of the nom./acc.sg. Ved. *ásthi* 'bone', AV *asthnás* gen., and *ákṣi* 'eye', abl. *akṣṇás*

---

[1] The original paradigm was something on the order of **uHdhér*, **éwH̥dhnos*. Some such paradigm survived into PGmc., as NHG *Euter* points to full grade next to zero elsewhere in Gmc., as in OE *úder* (NE *udder*). The prehistory of G οὖθαρ is ambiguous. Early *ἐοθ- < **ewotʰ*- < **ew*$H̥_3$*dh*- would do the trick for Att. Those who hold that *H_3*u*- would give Pan-G οὐ- directly might think instead of *H_3*udh*-, perh. a metathesis of the **u*$H_{(3)}$*dh*- seen in Gmc. and InIr.

[2] *Aequor* is commonly taken as an old *s*-stem, like *fulgur* 'lightning' and *rōbur* 'oak' (297), with the *-o-* preserved after *-qu-* (71.6c). In the case of *fulgur* and *rōbur*, however, there is evidence for the original *-s-*; in the case of *aequor* there is none.

are root/*n*-stems, NOT '*i*/*n*-stems' (as they are usually called): the nom./acc. sg. is actually endingless. The Indic *-i* has two different sources. In *ásthi* < $*H_3estH_1$ it reflects $*\text{-}\mathring{H}_1$. The history of *ákṣi* 'eye' is different: the nom./acc. is from endingless $*H_3\acute{e}k^ws$ with a prop-vowel after the consonant cluster, as in *hā́rdi* 'heart' < **ḱērd*. In endingless nouns where no prop-vowel was necessary, as in *dós* '(fore)arm', AV *doṣáṇī* nom./acc.du., none developed.

The question is whether the *r*/*n*-stems were heteroclitic like these. Some authorities say so. However, there are two data which suggest that the **r* and the **n* might have developed in pre-PIE by phonological split (whose details are long past reconstructing) rather than by morphological accretion. The data are:

1. ENDINGS OF THE 3PL. VERBS. Some PIE verb-types had 3rd sg. endings in **-t(i)* (active) and **-to(r)* (middle), with 3rd pl. endings in **-nt(i)* and **-nto(r)*. Others, most familiarly the 'perfect' (stative) but also some pres. and aor. types, had a *t*-less 3rd sg. ending as **-e* or **-o(r)* (426, 436.3, 514.1). In these the 3pl. was also *t*-less, **-r(i)* and **-ro(r)*; that is, it appears that there were two forms of the 3rd.pl.: one built with **r*, when followed by a vowel or nothing; and one built with **n*, when followed by **t*. This looks very much like an alternation between **r* and **n*.

2. ROOTS. At least two PIE roots show alternation between root-final **l* and **n*: $*H_2el\text{-}/H_2en\text{-}$ 'other' and $*suH_2el\text{-}/*suH_2en\text{-}$ 'sun'. Now, heteroclisis in roots is not a realistic analysis, and this supports the idea that *r*/*n*-stem neuters were not heteroclitic either.

293. GREEK *τ*-STEM FORMS IN OTHER NEUTERS. From its presumed beginnings in connection with *n*- and *r*/*n*-stem neuters (**288**, **290-2**), an oblique stem in *-τ-* spread to a wide range of neuter nouns which originally had one or another quite different inflection. This took place especially in Attic, and spread even further in the later *κοινή*.

By way of secondary *τ*-stem neut. inflection Hom. has *οὖς*, *οὔατος* (Att. *ὠτός*) 'ear'; Ion. *κάρη* nom./acc.n. 'head' (poet.; elaborated from *κάρ* < $*\acute{k}\mathring{r}H_2$, like *κρῑθή* f. 'barley' next to *κρῖ* n.), gen. *κρᾱ́ατος* (**krāsat-* < $*\acute{k}\mathring{r}H_2s\mathring{n}\text{-}t\text{-}$; cf. Ved. obl. stem *śīrṣṇ-*), contracted *κρᾶτος*; there are also conflations like *κάρητος* and *καρήατος*. Additionally, there were patterns like *γόνυ* 'knee', *γούνατος* (**gonwatos*) and *δόρυ* 'tree', *δούρατος* (**dorwatos*), Att. *γόνατος*, *δόρατος* (190.1). Originally these nouns were ablauting (proterokinetic) *u*-stems, of a type (311) lost in both G and L: **ǵonu* nom./acc., **ǵnew-s* gen. They had already been remodeled once as simple consonant stems, *γόνυ*, *γουνός* (from **gonwos*) 'knee', and *δόρυ*, *δουρός* (from **dorwos*) 'tree, shaft'. —The underlying formation provides no possible source for the *-α-*, here, which indicates that *-ατ-* had become a unit.

Att. *πέρας*, *πέρατος* 'end, boundary' (without clear cognates in other languages) must be an *r*/*n*-stem in origin, as shown by Hom. *πεῖραρ*, *πείρατος* (**perwar*, **perwatos*) and the derivative *ἀπείρων* 'boundless'; *πέρας* (Pindar *πεῖρας*) was back formed from obl. *πέρατος*, after the analogy of other neuters in *-ας*, *-ατος* (following).

Old *s*-stems like *τέρας* 'prodigy; monster' and *κέρας* 'horn', which have only *ʃ*-stem inflection in Hom. (τέραα nom.pl., κέραος gen.sg.), become Att. τέρατος, κέρᾱτος (the -ᾱ- of the latter from *κερα-ατος), like γόνατος.[1] Similarly φῶς n., φωτός '(day)light' (Hom. φάος, φάει); and Att. κρέας, κρέως (*κρέαος) 'meat', but later κρέατος.

a. T-stem inflection is found in a few masc. nouns, such as γέλως m. 'laughter', ἔρως m. 'love'. These were originally *ʃ*-stems like αἰδώς f. 'self-respect', **299**; the original -σ- is in evidence in γελαστός 'laughable', ἐραστός 'beloved'. For these, τ-forms compete with *ʃ*-stem inflection even in Homer. In Hom. already there are a few τ-forms for χρώς m. 'body, skin' (χρωτός gen., χρωτ' acc. beside usual χροός, χρόα); but none yet for ἱδρώς m. 'sweat' (Att. ἱδρῶτος gen.).

294. There are no productive types of stems ending in *m* or *l*. There were however a few nouns (root-formations in point of fact, **275**) ending in such consonants.

1. In G, there are disguised reflexes of what originally were three *m*-stems; ν has replaced the original *m* by leveling in all three, though with some differences in detail:

G χιών, χιόνος 'snow' and χθών, -ονός 'earth'. G χιών (cf. L *hiems*, below) continues an ancient root noun with an original paradigm based on three stems, **ǵhyōm(s)* nom.sg., **ǵhyom*-, and **ǵhim*-, parallel to **dyēws* nom. sg., **dyew*-, and **diw*- 'sky/day' (**325-6**); to both, likewise, were built thematic adjectives with a different full grade: **ǵheym-o*-, **deyw-o*-. Bits of the original paradigm are seen in Av. *zyå* nom.sg. 'winter', *zyąm* acc., *zimō* gen.sg.

χθών, χθονός 'earth' is from something like **dhǵhōms* nom., **dhǵhmos*.[2]

Both nouns became *n*-stems in every detail; the original **m* is seen only in derivatives: χειμερινός 'wintry'; χαμαί 'on the ground' and χθαμαλός 'near the ground'; cf. *o*-grade in L *humus* 'ground', *e*- or (probable) zero grade in Ved. *kṣamā́* 'on the ground'. Exactly how this restructuring as *n*-stems happened is not clear; nom.sg. *-*ōms* > *-*ōns* (> *-*ŏns* by Osthoff's Law) would not give PG *-*ōn* by regular sound laws; and outside of the nom.sg. and dat.pl., all the oblique forms, PG **čoma* acc. (**198**), **k^himos* gen., and so on, would have had -μ-. (The remodeling includes the leveling of original σ-/τ-, depending on dialect, from **k^hy*-; **199c**.) The restructuring of *χθωνς, *χθ(ο)μος, though less extreme, is no less mysterious.

For εἷς m. 'one' < **hens* (presumably < **hēns* via Osthoff's Law (**63.2**), starting from **hēn* < **sēm* < ***sems* like **dōm* nom. 'house' < ***doms*), μία f. < **smiH₂*, ἕν n. < **sem* the remodeling was different, though no less drastic; despite the strange appearance of the paradigm, its history is much clearer than that of χιών and χθών. Nom.sg.m. εἷς is the regular development of

---

[1] In Att. the military phrase ἐπὶ κέρως (-αος) 'in a column' is the only relic of the original inflection.

[2] Cf. Hitt. *te-(e-)kán* nom., *ták-na-(a-)aš* gen. The Hitt. noun is neut., and inflects differently from the familiar stem: **dhéǵhm̥* nom./acc., **dhǵhmés* gen.

**hens* (< **hēns* with restored *-*s*), likewise neut. ἕν < **hem*. The replacement of **hemos* gen., **hema* masc.acc. by attested ἑνός, ἑνά is relatively straightforward. Though very early and general, it was not PG, as is now revealed by Myc. *e-me* dat. (*hemei*). The original **m*, preserved because formally remote, is also to be seen in μία f. < **smiH₂*, and because semantically remote in ὁμός 'the same'; cf. L *semel* 'once'.

The nom.sgs. are usually assumed to be the point of departure, but in fact it would be remarkable for that case to be the basis for this kind of remodeling. The problem is to find the true key. One possibility is the acc., given that **ǵhyomm̥*, **dhǵhomm̥*, **semm̥* raise questions of what might be called realization. One might speculate that these developed regularly (as it were) to *-*nm̥*, whence PG **čona*, **kʰtʰona*, **hena*. (Indic has a parallel development of inherited *-*m̥m*- to -*anm*-, as in *jaganma* 'we went' < **gʷe-gʷm̥-me*.) From such a beginning the replacement of paradigmatic *-μ- by -ν- would be a straightforward matter. This theory would be in effect proved by a Myc. form like **e-na* acc. 'one' contemporaneous with *e-me* dat.

There is only one *m*-stem in L, namely *hiems*, *hiemis* 'winter' < PIE **ǵhyom*-. The unvarying L stem continues a single grade of the original stem, **ǵhyom*-, whence *χ*iom*- (disyllabic by **193**, *hiem*- by **66.3**). The nom.sg. is based on this stem (a late creation, thus the unexampled sequence -*ms*). The zero grade is apparently preserved in *bīmus* 'two years [old]', lit. 'two-wintered' < **bi-him*- < **dwi-ǵhim*- (**389.2Aa**). The secondary full grade stem seen in Brāh. *hémani* 'in winter', G χεῖμα 'frost; winter', χειμερινός 'wintry' is not attested in L, unless *bīmus* actually continues **dwi-ǵheym-o*-.

2. There is only one λ-stem in G, namely ἅλς, ἁλός m. 'salt', f. 'sea', superimposable on L *sāl*, *salis* 'salt' (the vowel of *sāl* is an enigma). The details of *mel* n. *mellis* 'honey' are usually traced to *fel*, *fellis* 'gall' (itself actually an *n*-stem, **289a**); but the nearly universal evidence elsewhere is for a stem **melit*- (G μέλι, -τος, Go. *miliþ*, Hitt. *mi-li-it*), and L probably somehow continues the same etymon (via **meld*- or the like; **237.8**).

Sōl 'sun' is an old *l*/*n*- stem (**292.2**; for vocalism **88.3c**).

Vigil 'watchman' and *pugil* 'boxer' have -*il* (*l*-exilis, **176a**) < *-*ill* < *-*ils* (cf. *facul* 'easily' with word-final *l*-pinguis) and cons.-stem inflection (so *vigilum* gen.pl., not -*ium*). These are manifestly *l*-stems from the L point of view, but genuinely ancient cons. stems seem unlikely, and the usual surmise is that the forms come from *li*-stems in -*(g)ilis* < *-*(g)lis* (per **92**), despite lack of evidence for *i*-stem inflection.

Exsul 'an exile' is of uncertain etymology (the verb *exsulāre* 'live in exile' is a denominative). The spelling -*xs*-, which is never found epigraphically, is based on some imagined etymology (both *solum* 'ground' and *saliō* 'leap' are suggested by ancient authorities). The etymology of *cōnsul* 'consul' is much discussed; among the contenders is **kom-sod*- with *l* for *d* (**151**), lit. 'throne-mate' (*solium*). *Praesul* 'dancer' is supposed to be from **prae-sal*-, cf. *saliō* 'leap, dance'. The failure of **s* to become *r* (**173**) might result from its position between two liquids (**173a**); more of a problem is that no verb ˣ*praesiliō* or the like is attested. And what, exactly, a 'fore-dancer' might be is unobvious.

s-STEMS

295. In PIE there was a heterogeneous group of nouns and adjectives built to stems ending in *-s-*. These include the so-called comparative suffix **-yos-* (treated in 349-54) and the marker of the stative (perfect) participle, **-wos-* (treated in 561-2). Here we will treat a few root forms, the much larger group of derived *s*-stem nouns, and the adjectives based on them. The two or three primary *s*-stem adjectives seen in Vedic do not correspond to anything in G and L.

296. NEUTER NOUNS. Where the derivation is transparent, neut. *s*-stem nouns were built to the tonic *e*-grades of verb roots. The stem had the form **-os* in the (endingless) nom./acc.sg., **-ōs* < ***-os*H_2 in the nom./acc.pl; the stem of the remaining cases and numbers was an invariant **-es-*. Thus, from the root **ǵen*H_1- 'beget', the inflection of **ǵén*H_1*os* 'race, type' went as follows:

	Singular	*Plural*
Nom./Acc.	ǵénH_1os	ǵénH_1ōs < **-osH_2
Inst.	ǵénH_1eseH_1	ǵénH_1esbhis, -mĭ̄s
Dat.	ǵénH_1esey	ǵénH_1esbh-, -m-
Abl.	ǵénH_1esos, -es	"
Gen.	"	ǵénH_1esŏ̄m
Loc.	ǵénH_1es(i)	ǵénH_1esu (**ǵénH_1essu)

Forms as they occur:

		Mycenaean	Homer	Attic	Latin	Vedic	OCS
Singular	Nom./Acc.	te-me-no[1]	γένος	γένος	genus	vácas[2]	slovo[3]
	Gen.		γένεος	γένους	generis	vácasas	slovese
	Dat.	e-re-e[4]			generī	vácase	slovesi
	Loc.	we-te-i[5]	γένεϊ	γένει	genere	mánasi[6]	slovese[7]
Plural	Nom./Acc.	pa-we-a$_2$[8]	γένεα	γένη	genera	vácāṃsi	slovesa
	Inst.	pa-we-pi			generibus	vácobhis[9]	
	Gen.	pa-we-o	γενέων	γενῶν	generum	védasām[10]	slovesŭ
	Loc.	pa-we-si	γένεσ(σ)ι			rájassu[11]	slovesĭxŭ[12]

*In G the uncontracted forms occur in Homer and elsewhere; Attic has only the contracted forms. For the loss of intervocalic *-s- in G and its change to -r- in L, see 172-3.*

1. 'Piece of land' (τέμενος).
2. 'Word, speech' (ἔπος, ϝεπος; PIE root **wekʷ-*).
3. 'Word' (PIE root **ḱlew-* 'hear').
4. 'To Helos' (/helehei/; placename).
5. 'Year' (/wetehi/; ἔτος, ϝετος; Myc. *we-to* /wetos/).
6. 'Mind' (PIE root **men-*).
7. Not from **ḱlewesi*; rather, the bare stem **ḱlewes* with particle *-e*.
8. *Pʰarweha* 'pieces of cloth' (φᾶρος). For *-a$_2$*, see under nom.pl., below.
9. Regular sandhi from **vacas-bhis*.
10. 'Knowledge'.
11. 'Skies', showing the effect of recombination of stem *rájas-* and ending *-su*. The original loc.pl., with truncation of the long consonant, is seen in *apásu* 'active'. The

(notes to the table are continued on page 306)

form in the later language is *vacaḥsu*, in which the ending is treated by the sandhi rules as if it were a separate word.
II. Ending with -*ĭ*- imported from *i*-stems.

---

297. 1. Nom./acc.sg. Scholars have long maintained that the nom./acc. form -*os*, albeit of securely PIE date, is secondary; presumably the zero grade nom./acc. of the type **krewH̥₂s*, **298** (morphologically **krewH̥₂-s*), is a relic of a more original state of affairs.

Additional evidence comes from data pointing to zero grade *-*is* as the original form of the nom./acc.n. comparative suffix (**351**), as seen in ancient-looking forms like L *magis* 'rather', next to the paradigmatic nom./acc.sg.n. *maiius* < *-*yos*.

There is an undoubted zero-grade nom./acc.sg. of an ordinary *s*-stem in RV *yós* 'welfare, contentment' < **(H₂)yew-s*.[1] The form is found only in the RV, in two stereotyped phrases *śáṃ yóḥ* (earlier) and *śáṃ ca yóś ca* (later), both something like 'happiness and well-being'. Some have seen in this *yós* a precise cognate of L *iūs*, *iūris* n. 'law; right'; semantics are a problem, but the meaning of the latter perh. continues an earlier *'fitness, rightness, meetness', as still seen in the ancient collocation *iūs est* 'it is right'. (The *i*-stem details of the L paradigm, as in *iūria* nom.pl., are secondary.) OL IOVESTOD (L *iūstō*) '(by) right' proves the existence of an oblique stem *-*es*-, but that was not in question in any case.

A more problematic example is L *aes, aeris* n. 'copper'; see **88d**.

a. L *far, farris* n. 'spelt' is from **fars*, **fars-es*; the likely explanation is that both of these stems are syncopated from **faros* **fares*- in view of the particularly ready syncope of short vowels after -*r*- (**74.6**), for example *ager* 'field' < **agros*, *fert* 'carries' < **feret* (**485**).

b. There are a very few neuter *s*-stems in L in which the -*s* of the nom./acc.sg. has been replaced by -*r* after the analogy of the other cases, parallel to the regular treatment of the masculines and feminines (**299**). The certain examples are *rōbur, -oris* 'oak' (early *rōbus*, and cf. *rōbustus*); and *fulgur, -uris* 'lightning' (arch. *fulgus* quoted by Paul.Fest.). On the evidence of Go. *atisk*- 'seed-corn', L *ador, -ōris* n. 'spelt' (a ritual word) would be a remodeling of an old *s*-stem. (The stem *adōr*-, unexpected for a neut., may point to an original nom./acc.pl. in *-*ōs*.) For *aequor, -ŏris* n. 'flat surface', often mentioned in this connection, there is no evidence for the original stem class. —The remaining neuter *r*-stems in L are old *r/n*-stems (**290–2**), *ūber, -eris* 'udder', and the much-remade *vēr vēris* 'spring(time)' (orig. **wesr̥* **wesnes*; cf. *vernus* 'vernal' < **wesinos*, G ἔαρ, ἔαρος; ἐαρινός). *Aequor* may belong among these.

2. Dat. and loc.sg. OCS has indirect evidence (**296** note 6) for an endingless loc.sg., Hitt. actually attests a few (*ne-pí-iš* 'to/in the sky'); Ved. and Av. have evidence only for *-*es-i*. L *penes* prep. 'in one's power' (orig. ?? *'in the pantry') is often mentioned as an endingless loc., but an original **penes*, or for that matter an original **penesi* with apocope, would have given L ˣ*penis* (cf. *legis* 'you gather' < **legesi*; *cordis* gen. 'heart' < **kr̥des*). See also **257.II**.

---

[1] A second Indic example might be Ved. *ákṣi* n. 'eye' if from **H₃ekʷs*; the -*i* is a prop-vowel (**292**). The cognate noun in OCS is an ordinary *s*-stem.

The overtly marked loc.sg. in *-*esi* is the likeliest candidate for the etymon of the L infinitive ending in -*se*, -*(e)re* (553.1).

In literary G the only ending of the dat.sg. is -ι, representing the original loc.sg. (seen—apparently—in the L abl. -*e*; **276.6a**). Mycenaean has forms pointing to both -*ei* (dat.) and -*i* (loc.), apparently used interchangeably; the latter is already in the ascendancy.

3. Nom.pl. The aboriginal formation would have been the stem plus *-H_2, yielding PIE *-*ōs* (or, less likely, *-*ēs*). In G, L, and OCS this has been remodeled as *-*esă̄*, namely the oblique stem with the usual cons. stem nom./acc.pl. ending (-ᾰ in G, *-*ā* in Ital. and OCS; see **260.3**). The inherited ending is preserved unchanged in Av. -*å* < *-*ās*, as in *vačå* 'words'; and possibly is latent in OE forms like *lombor* 'lambs', *calfur* 'calves' nom./acc.pl., which point to a composite form, PreGmc. *-*ōza*. (The outcome of PreGmc. *-*eza* (= G -εα) would be ˣ*lembir*) Ved. -*āṃsi* in place of *-*ās* is an analogical development characteristic of the neuter nom./acc.pl. in Indic (389.3, fn.) parallel to PreGmc. *-*ōza*, above.

The Myc. writing of the nom./acc.pl. with -a_2 rather than -*a*, especially frequent in tablets from Pylos, is thought to stand for -*ha* (< *-*sa*); if this is the correct interpretation, then the other case forms were presumably parallel: *wetehi*, *wetehei*, and so on.

4. In the dat.pl. Homer has -εεσσι in addition to -εσ(σ)ι (**277.6a**); this arises by analogy with other consonant stems: ποδῶν : γενέων :: πόδεσσι : *X*, where *X* = γενέεσσι.

5. In L, the stem vowel in -*er*- is ambiguous; G, InIr., OCS, Hitt., and Gmc. all point to *-*es*-, however, which must be the source of L -*er*-. However, beside the type *genus generis* there is the type *corpus, corporis* 'body'. This is a purely L development—as just stated, either **genos*- or **genes*- would give *gener*- (**66.2-3**). The *corporis* type is a by-blow of the remarkable restoration of -*ŏ*- in medial syllables mentioned in **67**. Here it is not a restoration, however, but a misinterpretation of the obl. stem **corper*- as a weakened form of **corpor*-, on the basis of the nom./acc. **corpos*. The original vocalism sometimes survives in derivatives: next to *tempus*, -*oris* 'time' are found *temperī* adv. 'at the right time' and *tempestās* 'storm'. The ETYMOLOGICAL grade of the -*er*- is ambiguous, of course, but at all events it is the original (or expected) vowel. *Tempestās* is definitely from *-*es*-; a remodeled stem or an original *o*-grade would have given ˣ*tempustās*, like *rōbustus* 'oaken' < **rōbosto*-. (L *rōbustus* and the like show incidentally that the remodeled -*os*- stem can also be found in derivatives).

298. GREEK NEUTERS IN -ας, as γέρας 'honor, prerogative', gen. γέραος (Att. γέρως), Myc. *ke-ra-a* nom.pl. 'horns', invite comparison with Ved. *is*-stems (*kravís*- 'raw flesh' = κρέ(ϝ)ας 'flesh, meat'). The idea is that the unvarying stems, G *-*as*- and Ved. -*is*-, reflect an original, unvarying *-$\underset{\circ}{H}_2$*s*-. There are at most a dozen forms like this in the RV, and about the same number of old-looking forms in G. In at least a few of these there is independent evidence for a laryngeal. Ved. *kravi-* is attested in compounds (*á-kravi-hasta-* 'having bloodless hands') and *krū-rá-* 'bloody, raw, wounded' (L *crūdus*, 235.2) can be gathered together as **krewH̥-*/**kruH-*. For **ḱerH-* in G κέρας, κέραος 'horn': the Ved. paradigm *śíras* nom./acc.n. 'head', gen. *śīrṣṇás* is manifestly **ḱr̥Hos* nom./acc., **ḱr̥Hs-n-* obl. A different *n*-stem is seen in OLith. *širšuo* (for **širšruo*) and L *crābrō, -ōnis* 'hornet' (225.2), both from **ḱr̥Hs-ron-*; cf. L *cerebrum* 'brain' < **kerabrom* < **kerasro-* < **ḱerH̥s-ro-*.

However, note that an Indic stem in *-is-* is ambiguous, as it might just as well reflect PIE **-is-*; and in fact the analogous Iranian neuters in *-iš-*, such as *saiθiš-* (a kind of weapon), are unlikely to reflect **-H̥s-*. Furthermore, in InIr. there is a wholly parallel form class in *-us-*, for example RV *cákṣus-* n. 'eye; vision' (also adj. 'seeing'), which can only reflect **-us-*. (Given its adjectival function, it is thinkable that the form-class is ultimately based on the perfect pple., 561-2). *Is-* and *us-*stems stems are found in G and L as well, albeit uniquely: κόνις f.m. 'dust, ashes' (= L *cinis* f., *-eris* < **kenis*). But these have the wrong gender and are in other ways too enigmatic to be considered independent evidence for the InIr. *is*-stem type. (The single *us*-stem δελφύς, -ύος f. 'womb' is fractionally more useful: in form it closely resembles Av. *gərəbuš* n. 'whelp'.) It is probable therefore that only some of the Vedic *is*-stems correspond formally to G ασ-stems. (See 297.1.)

a. Hom. γέρᾰ, κρέᾰ are of doubtful explanation, and even of doubtful interpretation: some take them as apocopated forms of the nom./acc.pl., beside the regular formation as seen in τέραα; others take them as collectives (so κρέα 'flesh in general' vs. κρέας 'piece of meat'). The two analyses are not necessarily incompatible.

b. Some neuters in -ας have gen. -εος like the neuters in -ος, instead of normal -αος: Hom. οὖδας 'the ground', οὔδεος. A special type of *s*-stem is unlikely to be the explanation, as in Hom. in particular and in Ion. in general there are a variety of instances of εο, εω for expected αο, αω, for example Ion. ὁρέω = Att., Dor. ὁράω 'see'. Furthermore, there is much hesitation: κνέφας 'darkness', dat. κνέφᾰι (< *-αει, with the original dat.??; 257.7), but also κνέφεϊ (as if from **-esi*) and Att. gen.sg. κνέφους (*-εος). All these phenomena are better, if still somewhat tepidly, explained as incorrect distractions from ambiguous contracted forms.

299. MASCULINE AND FEMININE *s*-STEM NOUNS. These are less widespread than the neuter type (296), being found among the IE languages only in InIr. and G, where they are rare; and in L, where they abound. The nom. sg. is the bare stem with lengthened grade, **-ōs* and **-ēs* (from original ***-oss* and ***-ess*, with nom. **-s*). The remaining cases, including the acc.sg. and the nom./acc.pl., are formed to a non-ablauting stem with the usual endings: **-os-m̥*, **-os-es*, **-os-m̥s*. There are no formal distinctions between masc. and fem.

There are only seven such nouns in the Rigveda: two masc. nouns (*rakṣás-* 'demon' and *vedhás-* m. 'ordainer', both of somewhat dim etymology. Indeed, bafflingly, evidence suggests that the latter was remodeled from a karmadhāraya in *dhā-* 'put, fix', the model for which innovation is anything but obvious); one fem. (*uṣás*- 'dawn', solidly PIE); one proper noun; and three primary adjectives. Much more numerous are bahuvrīhi compounds whose second element is an *s*-stem noun, such as *nṛ-máṇās* 'mindful of men' and *vásu-śravās* 'famous for wealth'. (The *is*- and *us*-stems (298) likewise make bahuvrīhis, but with the nom.sg.m.f. homophonous with the neut.: *viśvátaś-cakṣus* nom.sg.m. 'having eyes on all sides' and *á-havis* nom.sg.m. 'not offering oblations'.) The masc. nouns and all the adjectives build all cases to a stem in *-ăs-*, that is, they agree with the G bahuvrīhi type (300) in having *e*-grade of the stem. Some of the nouns are probably back formations from such compounds. The solitary stem in Ved. showing evidence for *o*-grade, at least in certain case-forms, is also the only one showing secure outside connections, which incidentally confirm the stem grade: *uṣā́s* nom.sg.f. 'dawn' (= Att. ἕως, and cf. L *aurōra*). Thus acc.sg. *uṣā́sam*, nom.pl. *uṣā́sas*. (PIE **-os-*), but dat.sg. *uṣáse* < ? **-es-*.

G has even fewer such nouns: ἕως 'dawn' (Lesb. αὔως, Ion. ἠώς, that is **āwsōs* < **H₂ewsōs/*H₂usos*; G **āw-* for *aw-* is unexplained); αἰδώς 'self-respect'; and some others with remnants of *s*-stem inflection beside competing types, for example γέλως 'laughter': Hom. γέλω acc. < -οα next to γέλον (eventually remade as a *τ*-stem γέλωτον, 293). The nom.sg. reflects lengthened grade **-ōs*, the other cases **-os-*: αἰδῶ acc. < -όα < **-osm̥*, αἰδοῦς gen. < -όος < **-osos*, αἰδοῖ dat. < -όϊ < **-osi*.

In L, by contrast, the TYPE is commonplace, though genuinely old-looking forms are not numerous; and the morphology was much altered by both phonological and analogical changes. First, in all case forms apart from the nom.sg., there was the regular change of **-s-* to *-r-* between vowels (173). Second, as is typical in situations where long and short vowels alternated in L, the long vowel of the nom.sg. was generalized through the paradigm (with three exceptions—*arbor*, *-oris* 'tree', *mulier*, *-eris* 'woman', and *Cerēs*, *-eris* 'Ceres'). Finally, the *s/r* stem alternation was leveled in favor of the oblique stem, along the lines of say *sorōrem* : *sorōr* :: *colōrem* : *X*, where *X* = *colōr*. Early-attested *honōs*, *-ōris* 'worth', *arbōs*, *-ŏris* 'tree', *colōs* 'color', *odōs* 'smell' later are *honor*, *arbor*, *color*, *odor*. The leveled nom.sg. is usual from Plautus on, but the older forms in *-ōs* appear occasionally even in later writers and inscriptions, and *honōs* in particular never really became obsolete.

Subsequently in the nom.sg. *-ōr* > *-or*, 83.3. As in the *r*-stems, these developments paradoxically result in a paradigm where the one form with a short stem vowel is the only form whose stem vowel was etymologically long.

As a result of these developments, *s*-stems became indistinguishable from inherited *r*-stems (284B) like *soror* 'sister' and the agent nouns in *-tor*. Only derivative forms give away the true makeup of these nouns: *honestus* 'worthy', *arbustus* 'having groves'.

The *s*-stem type is productive in L; noteworthy is the pairing of nouns in *-or* with adjectives in *-idus*: thus *timidus*, *timor*; *īnsipidus*, *sapor*; *candidus*, *candor*; and so on.

a. L has two *s*-stem nouns with stem vowel in *e*: *mulier* (**-ēr*), *-eris* 'woman', with the usual nom.sg. leveling; and *Cerēs Cereris* 'Ceres', without it. Neither has generalized the *-ē-* of the nom. sg., in contrast to the regular leveling of *-ō-* throughout the *os*-stems.

The usual interpretation of *mulier* may have to be abandoned in light of MVLIAR[

deed—not so much as a single word can be read with confidence—which weakens its importance, but a (? non-IE) stem **muliar-* would give L *mulier, mulieris* regularly. It would not however give *muliebris* 'womanly', which presupposes an original **-sr-* (**225.2**), and is unlikely to be a fabrication. On the other hand, a stem **mulias* would give all of the L forms (*muliebris* included, **66.1**, **71.4**), but hardly the Corcolle MVLIAR, if it is correctly dated (see **173**).

L *tellūs, -ūris* f. 'earth' (poet.) is evidently an *s*-stem, but is a word of obscure formation.

b. The L cognate of Ved. *uṣā́s* 'dawn' and G ἕως is *aurōra* < **awsōsā*, both 'dawn' and the name of a deity. In form it is parallel to *Flōra* from *flōs*. Perhaps there was once a parallel distinction between **awsōs* 'daybreak' and **awsōsā* 'goddess of the dawn'.

300. *s*-STEM ADJECTIVES. In G and InIr., *s*-stem nouns freely formed adjectival bahuvrīhi compounds, for example **H₁su-men-es-* 'well-disposed' and **dus-men-es-* 'ill-disposed', based on **men-es-* 'mind'. In InIr. there are also two or three primary *s*-stem adjectives, like *apás-* 'active' (cf. *ápas-* n. 'work', L *opus*). The inflection of the adj. differed from the neuter nouns only in the nom./acc.m.f.:

	PIE	Homeric	Attic	Vedic
Nom.	*H_1sumenēs	εὐμενής	-ής	sumánās
Acc.	*H_1sumenesm̥	εὐμενέα	-ῆ	sumánasam
neut.	*H_1sumenes	εὐμενές	-ές	sumánas
Gen.	*H_1sumenesos	εὐμενέος	-οῦς	sumánasas
etc.				

The stem vowel was mostly *-*e*-, as in the sample paradigm. Indic has no evidence for *o*-grades in bahuvrīhis (thus RV *sumánăsas* nom.pl.), which therefore parallel the G formation εὐμενής, Myc. *e-u-me-ne* (man's name). This Myc. form exemplifies an abundant type in G: nouns derived FROM bahuvrīhis. Many of these are names: Σωκράτης (from σάϝο- 'safe', κράτος n. 'strength'), Δημοσθένης (from δῆμο- 'land, people', σθένος 'might'). These names, in late Att. and the κοινή, may have acc.sg. in -ην after the analogy of 1st decl. names in -ης, so Σωκράτην after Θουκυδίδην—a process one might think virtually inevitable once the real acc.sg. Σωκράτεα had become Σωκράτη by regular Attic contraction (**86.4**), and helped along by such proportions as ἀγαθός : ἀγαθόν :: Σωκράτης : *X*, where *X* = Σωκράτην. See also **320.2-3**.

a. Given the abundance of *s*-stem nouns in L, evidence for bahuvrīhi compounds in L is strangely meager—indeed, elusive. The candidates are *dēgener* (?< *-*ĕr*), *-eris* 'unworthy of one's race' (with leveling) and *pūbēs, -eris* 'downy; (post-)pubescent, ephebic' (without leveling), supposedly back-formed from *impūbēs* 'beardless, prepubescent'; but both words admit of other interpretations and much about *(im)pūbēs* in particular suggests a long history of contamination and remodeling.

301. MISCELLANEOUS *s*-STEMS. In some dozen monosyllabic nouns in L like *flōs flōris* 'flower', *mōs mōris* 'custom', *mūs mūris* 'mouse', *glīs glīris* 'dormouse', the stem ends in *-s-*; but these are root-nouns rather than *s*-

stems as such. In these monosyllabic forms, the nom.sg. *-s* is never leveled to *-r*, such as is the rule for polysllabic masc. and fem. *s*-stems.

G μῦς 'mouse' is cognate with L *mūs*, OE *mús*, and Ved. *mūṣ-*, whose details (nom.pl. *mūrēs*, *mýs* < **mūsiz*, and *mūṣas*, respectively) indicate a PIE stem **mūs-* or **muHs-*; but the G details, such as acc.sg. μῦν, show that in G the paradigm had been reinterpreted as a sort of *ū*-stem (or *uH*-stem, 317-8), like ὗς, ὑός, ὗν 'pig', ὀφρῦς, -ύος, -ῦν 'brow'. The shortening of vowels before a vowel in, for example, the gen.sg. μυός < *μῡός < **mūhos* prepared the way for such a reinterpretation.

L *vīs* f. 'force, power', *vim* acc. (< **vīm*), *vī* abl., *vīrēs* nom.pl., *vīrium* gen.pl.; and *spēs* f. 'hope', *speī* gen., *spem* (**spēm*), *spērēs* nom./acc.pl., were originally root-nouns whose root ended in a vowel, at least in Italic times (NB that *spēs* is mostly a fifth declension noun, 330-1). Cf. Hom. *(ϝ)ῑ́ς* f. 'strength', *(ϝ)ῖν*; and *(ϝ)ῖφι* 'stoutly, mightily', and see 49.1. The intermixture of *s*- and *i*-stem forms is a secondary development. That is, the *-s* of *vīs* and *spēs*, actually the nom.sg. ending, was subject to reinterpretation as part of the stem, hence *vīrēs* and *spērēs* parallel to *mūrēs* 'mice'.

i-STEMS

302. In PIE, *i*-stems formed nouns of all genders, and adjectives. Adjectives and nouns inflected alike, and the genders differed only as regards the details characteristic of the neuter, namely no ending in the nom./acc.sg., and the special endings of the nom./acc.du. (257.16) and pl. The neuter *i*-stem nouns, however, are few in the IE languages that have any at all; and it is not possible to trace any specific lexical items to PIE with confidence.

The attested relationship—*attested* is the operative word, here—between stem and ending in PIE was as follows, taking **mn̥-ti-* 'thought' for the singular and **tri-* 'three' for the pl. Note particularly the ablaut gradation in the stem:

	Singular	*Plural (masc.)*
Nom.	mn̥ti-s	trey-es
Voc.	mn̥tey	trey-es
Acc.	mn̥ti-m	tri-ms
neut.	n̥-mn̥ti	tri-H_2
Inst.	mn̥ty-eH_1	tri-bh-
Dat.	mn̥tey-ey	tri-bh-
Gen.	mn̥toy-s	triyō̆m (**tr̥yō̆m)
Loc.	mn̥tēy (**-ey-i)	tri-su

The nom./acc.n.sg. is here exemplified by a bahuvrīhi 'without thought, insensate'. See 305 and 389.3 for further details of the original inflection of **trey-/tri-*.

The *i*-stems originally were parallel point for point with the *u*-stems (312-4): **i*, **ey* correspond to **u*, **ew*. But in both G and L all parallelism was lost when the *i*- and *u*-stems evolved in divergent directions. The evolution of the *i*-stems in G and L differ so radically, in fact, that it is infeasible to discuss them together; the G forms will be presented in 304–5, the L forms in 306–7.

303. TABLE OF *i*-STEM DECLENSION.

		Vedic	Latin	Oscan	Gothic	OCS
Singular	Nom.	agnís[1]	turris[2]	**aídil**[3]	ansts[4]	kostĭ[5]
	Voc.	ágne	turris		juggalaud[6]	kosti
	Acc.	agním	turrim	**slagím**[7]	anst	kostĭ
	neut.	su-astí[8]	mare[9]	U uerfale[10]		svobodĭ[11]
	Inst.	pát(i)yā[12] agnínā				kostĭjǫ
	Dat.	agnáye	turrī			kosti
	Abl./Gen.	agnés	turris	aeteis[13]	anstais	kosti
	Loc.	agnā́(u)	turrī, -e	**fuutreí**[14]	anstai[15]	kosti
Plural	Nom.	agnáyas	turrēs	**trís**[16]	sauleis[17]	kosti
	Acc.	sūrī́n̐(s)[18]	turrīs	U **trif**[16]	waurtins[19]	kosti
	neut.	śúcī[20]	tria[16]	U **triia**, trio-per	þrija[16]	tri[16]
	Inst.	agníbhis			waurtim	kostemi[23]
	Dat./Abl.	agníbhyas	turribus	**luisarifs**[21]		kostemŭ
	Gen.	agnīnā́m	turrium	[a]**íttíúm**	daile[22]	kostĭjĭ
	Loc.	agníṣu				kostexŭ[23]

The Vedic forms are the masc. *i*-stems; the fem. *i*-stems are given in notes 12 and 18.

1. 'Fire' m. (PIE **n̥gni*-). The inflection of the masc. and fem. *i*-stems in Vedic diverged in a few details (see notes 12 and 18, below.)

2. 'Tower', a loanword from G but (or rather, and) unusually faithful to distinctive *i*-stems forms (306–7).

3. 'Aedile'; for ***aídils** < **aydīlis*.

4. 'Joy, grace'.

5. 'Bone', fem. (In OCS the masc. declension is less conservative than the fem.) Cf. L *costa* 'rib; side'.

6. 'O youth' m., a compound whose second element is *laudi* f. 'form(ation), shape', Av. *raoδi*-.

7. 'Boundary, limit'.

8. 'Prosperity, well-being', *ti*-stem nomen actionis from *as*- 'be'.

9. 'Sea'.

10. 'Templum'.

11. 'Free'.

12. 'Lord'. In the later language the inst.sg. masc. ends only in *-inā*, imported from the *n*-stems; the fem. in *-yā*. In the RV, *-(i)yā* is still found in two otherwise ordinary masc. *i*-stems. —A Rigvedic peculiarity of the feminines is a competing inst.sg. in *-ī̆*, also ancient, reflecting **-i-H₁*.

13. 'Piece'; the gen.pl. [a]**íttíúm** (below) shows the O doubling of consonants before *y* (cf. 185.4).

14. 'Mother' (epithet of a goddess); the Sab. dat. continues the old loc.

15. The ending *-ai* (< **-ēy*) is found in the fem. only; the masc. ending *-a* was imported from the *a*-stems.

16. 'Three'.

17. 'Columns', nom.sg. *sauls*; PIE **-eyes* > **-eyis* > **-iyis* > **-iis* > PGmc. **-īs*, in Go. spelled *-eis* (30.1). The variant *-es* exemplifies the sporadic substitution of *-e-* for *-ei-* in the mss.

18. 'Bright, glorious'. The fem. *i*-stems make a different acc.pl., *-īs*, patterned on the *ā*-stem form *-ās* (264).
19. 'Roots' pl.tant., PIE **wr̥Hd-*; cf. L *rādīx*.
20. 'Bright, glorious'.
21. Meaning uncertain, perhaps 'player', like L *lūsor* (an *s*-stem). This is the only attestation of the ending *-fs* < **-fos* or **-fis*, which is everywhere else shown as *-s(s)*.
22. 'Of pieces'; nom.sg. *dails**.
23. The forms in *-ĭmĭ*, *-ĭxŭ* as met with in handbooks are not found in texts.

GREEK

304. THE *i*-STEMS IN GREEK. As seen in the table below, the inflection of *i*-stems within the history of G underwent thorough remodeling—in two diametrically opposed ways. Prehistorically there had also been a major innovation, namely the spread of **-ēy-* at the expense of the inherited full-grade form of the stem, **-ey-*.

		Proto-Greek	Homeric & other dial.		Attic
Singular	Nom.	polis	πόλις		πόλις
	Voc.	poli	πόλι		πόλι
	Acc.	polin	πόλιν		πόλιν
	Dat.	polēyi	πόληϊ	πόλι, -ῑ	πόλῃ
			πόλεϊ, -ει		πόλει
	Gen.	polēyos	πόληος	πόλιος	πόλεως
Plural	Nom.	polēyes	πόληες	πόλιες	πόλεις (? < -ēyes)
	Acc.	polins	πόλινς (? -ῑς)		πόλεις (spurious diphthong < *-ens*, 228.4)
			πόλεις (? -ῑς)		
		polēyas	πόληας		
		poliyas	πόλιας		
	Dat.	polisi	πόλισι		πόλεσι
	Gen.	poliyōn	πολίων		πόλεων

1. In most dialects, including Homer, the type becomes a sort of consonant stem, with an invariant stem in -ι- to which the usual consonant stem endings are added—apart from the accusatives, which preserved the inherited endings. This stem is a generalization of the -ι- of such cases as -ιων gen.pl., -ισι dat.pl., at the expense of original -ε- (< **-ey-*) along such lines as ποδῶν : πόδες :: πολίων : *X*, where *X* = πόλιες nom.pl., in place of original *πόλεες < **-eyes*.

a. INFLECTION OF **H₃ewis* 'SHEEP'. G has two ι-stems inflected with quasi-consonant-stem endings: Hom. ὄϊς 'sheep' < **H₃ewis*, but ὄϊν < **H₃ewim* (gen. ὄϊος analogical for οἰος < **H₃ewyos*, and in general the paradigm much subject to remodeling in all dialects); cf. Ved. *ávis*, gen. *ávyas*. Vedic *-yas* acc.pl. < **-ym̥s*, because unexpected, looks more original than G οἶς (ὄϊς), ογινς. (The other noun, φθόϊς 'a kind of cake', is of unknown etymology.) —In the RV, next to 'sheep' there is one additional member of the class, the adj. *arí-* 'strange' (as noun, 'stranger, outsider, enemy'), and a stray form or two from *páti-* 'lord, master', which otherwise is an ordinary *i*-stem. Much effort has been devoted to tracing the 'sheep' type and the regular *i*-stem type to a common origin. That is debatable, and in any case the *H_3*ewis** type played no role in the evolution of the G πόλις, -ιος type. See 306.6.

2. In Att.-Ion. a very different kind of generalization is seen, or more exactly two successive generalizations. In the first stage the stem in **-ēy-* replaced the inherited full-grade stem. In PIE the long vowel stem is seen only in the loc.sg. **-ēy* (descriptively endingless but probably a development of Pre-PIE ***-ĕyi*). The first step was the importation of the usual dat. (orig. loc.) ending *-ι*: **-ēy* → **-ēyi*. From here, **-ē(y)-* spread to πόληος and the rest, on the basis of such proportions as ποδί : ποδός :: πόληϊ : *X*, where *X* = πόληος. This sort of formation is seen as such in Homer.

In Attic, phonological developments alter this paradigm, leading to a second round of generalizations, whereby -ε- replaces both the secondary stem in -η- and inherited -ι- before a vowel. This -ε- arose from -η- in two ways. One was quantitative metathesis (79.3), as in πόληος > -εως;[1] and the other was the shortening of -η- before vowel to -ε- (79.3), whence -ηες > -εες (-εις) nom.pl. (The form -εες could be an inheritance directly from **-eyes*, but that is possible only if remodeled **-ēyes* and conservative **-eyes* persisted side by side in PG.) Original -ι- was replaced by the newly-developed ε-stem in πόλεσι dat.pl., likewise in πολέων for πολίων gen.pl., and *πολενς acc.pl. for orig. πολινς, yielding -εις (spur. diphth.) per regular sound law (228.4). The dat.sg. -ει (Hom. also -εϊ) looks like the new stem -ε- with the usual ending -ι, though its appearance so early as Hom. makes that explanation suspect. Hom. -εϊ would be easier to explain as a reflex of the orig. dat. *-εει < PIE **-eyey* (Ved. *agnáye*), now that Myc. evidence reveals that the PIE dative survived into PG side by side with the locative **-i* that underlies the usual G dat.sg. But as it happens Myc. provides no information on this point regarding *i*-stems specifically. In any case, this -ει replaces inherited (locative) -ηι, attested in Att. inscriptions down to the 4th century BC.

The same substitution of ε for ι extends to the dual forms πόλει (spurious diphthong, that is, *-εε) and πολέοιν.

a. It must be recognized that tracing the Attic inflection to the loc.sg. in **-ēy* is, as an explanation, more satisfactory formally than functionally; the loc.sg. is hard to see as pivotal in any paradigmatic sense. Alternative explanations suffer from other inadequacies, however. For example, a recent theory holds that originally there were two PIE types of *i*-stem inflection that were very different from both the **mn̥tis* and **H_3ewis* paradigms as presented here, but gave birth to both of them:

	Type A *(Proterokinetic, 272.2)*	Type B *(? Amphikinetic, 272.4)*
Nom.	**mént-ēy-s	**H_3éw-i-s
Acc.	**mént-i-m	**H_3w-éy-m̥
Gen.	**mn̥t-éy-s	**H_3w-y-ós

[1] Poet. -εος gen.sg. can be explained by several different analogical processes.

In its favor, this scheme parcels out accent and grade in accord with PIE norms, unlike the usual reconstruction; and it allows one to trace the G stem in -ηι- to the nom.sg., not to the loc. But neither G nor any other IE language actually attests a nom.sg. **-ēys* in ordinary *i*-stem inflection;[1] and it is not clear how the nom.sg. can be the fulcrum of a major restructuring while itself being routed by the **H₃ewis* type. In any case, the surviving *i*-stem inflections, which in this view are a sort of Chinese menu selection of items from Column A and Column B, exhibit too much agreement in detail in InIr., Gmc., Ital., and BS to be independent innovations. Accordingly, even if this theory is accepted, the necessary leveling to get to the usual reconstruction must have been complete in the parent language.

b. A distinctive voc.sg., endingless, with full grade of the stem, is attested in InIr. and BS. In G, the form in -ι is analogical—though to what is unclear (βασιλεῦ to βασιλεύς?, 320). The expected full-grade form is perhaps sublimated in Ποσει-δάων (Hom.) 'Poseidon', Att. Ποσειδῶν (Myc. *po-se-da-o*; other dial. attest Ποτοι-, Ποτῑ-, Ποτει-, among others), if that is in origin a vocative epithet, **potei dā̆hōn* 'O lord of [some gen.pl. noun]', reassessed as a nom. like L *Iuppiter* (327).

305. The original inflection of the plural is better seen in the forms of 'three': nom.pl. Cret. τρεες, Thera τρης, Att. τρεῖς, all from PIE **tréyes* (Ved. *tráyas*, L *trēs*, OIr. *tríᴴ*, OCS *trĭje*); gen.pl. τριῶν (L *trium*) even in Att.; dat.pl. τρισί (Ved. *triṣú*) even in Att.; acc.pl. **trins* whence τρῖς (for *τρί̄ς; circumflex from the nom.sg.). —Cret. τριινς acc.pl. is said to be based on case forms like τριων. There are no valid proportional analogies, however, that will produce a form with the stem-vowel twice over, in effect. Presumably the basis of τριινς was the abnormality (from the G point of view) of an inflection in which the acc.pl. was a syllable shorter than the nom.; a disyllabic τριινς, with a stem τρι- abstracted from other cases such as τρισι and τριων was therefore a sort of prosodic contamination rather than any more fastidious analogical relationship.

The nom./acc.pl.neut. τρία reflects **triH₂*, directly superimposable on Ved. *trī́*, OCS *tri*. The apparently identical L *tria* has a different evolution (307.3).

LATIN

306. In Italic the *i*-stems prosper. The nouns occur in all genders (though neuters are few), and the inventory of *i*-stem adjectives (342) is enormously enlarged by the transfer of *u*-stem and most consonant stems adjectives to that class. Endings proper to *i*-stem inflection furthermore invade other stem types, details of the spread differing somewhat in the various languages.

1. Nom.sg. PIE **-is*, L *-is* is unchanged in most words, but syncope with anaptyxis of **-ris* after consonant is regular, so *imber* 'rainstorm' from **imbris*, like *ager* 'field' from **agros* (74.4). Likewise in adjectives like *ācer* m.

---

[1] Except, possibly, the L *i*-stems in *-ēs*: 306.1a and 322.1b.

'sharp' (*ācris* f., *ācre* n.; see **342**). Syncope is also regular after *-nd-*, *-nt-*, and *-rt-*: *frōns* (*frondi-*) 'leaf', *gēns* (*genti-*) 'clan', *mōns* (*monti-*) 'hill', *pars* (*parti-*) 'part' (**309**). But in other environments the vowel survives: *hostis* 'enemy', *sitis* 'thirst', *apis* 'bee', *piscis* 'fish', *collis* 'hill'.

a. There are a score or so nouns, some rare, with nom.sg. in *-ēs*. Of these, three go like cons. stems: *sēdēs* 'seat' gen.pl. *sēdum*; so also *caedum* (*caedēs* 'slaughter'), and *vātēs* 'seer' (the only masc. in the class), though Cicero has *vātium*. The rest, *aedēs* 'room' gen.pl. *aedium*, *clādēs* 'destruction', *prolēs*, and so on, are like *i*-stem nouns in all regards apart from the nom.sg., and on the evidence of the App.Prob., which proscribes *caedis*, *prolis*, and some others as well as *vātis*, as a class they were liable to remodeling into ordinary *i*-stems.

The history of these nouns is unknown. The closest lexical match in another language is OIr. *fáith* /fāθ'/ 'prophet', corresponding to L *vātēs*, but it is an ordinary *i*-stem.

All this suggests that cons. stem inflection, or anyhow the gen.pl. in *-um*, is secondary in the three nouns that have it. See further under diphthongal stems (**322.1b**).

2. Voc.sg. PIE *-^{e}/*oy* as in Ved. *ágne* 'O fire' was replaced by the nom.

3. Acc.sg. PIE *-*im*. In L the majority of *i*-stem nouns and all *i*-stem adjectives form the acc.sg. in *-em*, homophonous with the cons. stem ending < PIE *-*m̥* (G -α, PCelt. *-*an*). The few nouns with acc.sg. in *-im* also form the abl.sg. (q.v.) in *-ī*, a form otherwise uncommon in nouns. The interpretation of these facts is disputed. The obvious (and standard) view is that *-em* < *-*m̥* is proper to the consonant type, and *-im* is the regular reflex of the *i*-stem type. However, the evidence of *quem* acc.sg.m. 'whom' < **kʷim* (*quis*) indicates that *-em* < *-*im* is a regular phonological development. The arguments pro and con are rehearsed in **71.1a**; in addition to them, note that a regular development of *-*im* to *-em* provides a salient point of tangency between the original consonant stems and *i*-stems. (In the standard view, such tangency—necessary to account for the convergence of *i*- and cons.-stem inflection (**308**)—is implausibly limited to a single form, the dat.sg.)

4. Nom./acc.n. PIE *-*i*, that is, the bare stem, L *-e* (**71.1**) in *mare* 'sea', *rēte* 'net'. Polysyllabic neut. NOUNS apocopate the final vowel, so *animal*, *exemplar* 'copy' < *-*āli*, *-*āri* (**74.1**, **.6**, **83.3**). For the different treatment of adjectives, see **342**.

5. Dat.sg. PIE *-*eyey* (Ved. *agnáye*) > *-*eey* > *-*ēy* > *-ei*, *-ẹ̄* whence L *-ī*; from *-ei* on, this ending is homophonous with the original cons. stem dat.sg. (**257.7**), and is one of the points of tangency between cons.-stem and *i*-stem inflection which led to further convergence of the two types (**308**).

6. Gen.sg. PIE *-*oys* (*o*-grade guaranteed by Go. *-ais*, all other attestations being ambiguous), Osc. *-eis* (extended to cons. stems and *o*-stems). This would have given OL *-*eis*, L *-īs*; but already in OL the ending had been completely displaced by *-es* (L *-is*). This latter looks like the cons. stem ending, and is usually so explained. But this is surprising, as the early trend otherwise—where it is unambiguous—is for *i*-stem endings to dis-

place cons.-stem endings. (The clear instances of cons. stem encroachment on *i*-stem forms, such as the abl. *-e* and acc.pl. *-ēs*, happened later, within the historical period.) Moreover, when Latin eliminates differences in vowel length in isofunctional forms, it otherwise invariably favors the long competitor (as in the nom.pl. *-ēs* ousting cons. stem **-es*). Oddest of all is the complete lack of attestation of the expected *i*-stem ending **-eis*, **-īs*. All these riddles are solved if the L *i*-stem gen.sg. *-es*, *-is* actually continues **-yes*, the type of ending seen in G *οἶος* 'sheep', Ved. *ávyas* < **H_3ewyos* (304.1a). And if that is so, it would provide another point of functionally important (if accidental) identity between the original inflection of *i*- and cons. stems. Now, the insignificant 'sheep' type cannot be the whole explanation; vital for the L replacement of **-eys* by **-yes* would have been the inherited gen.pl. in **-yom*.

The development of *-is* from **-yes* might be questioned, but is exactly paralleled by the development of the third conj. verbs, in which **-yesi* 2sg. does in fact become *-ĭs*, as in *capis* from **kapyesi*; 481. Moreover, this interpretation of the *i*-stem gen.sg. gets additional support from a common form of the *u*-stem gen. in OL, 314.8

7. Abl.sg. There are two endings. The one proper to *i*-stems is Ital. **-īd*, formed after the analogy of **-ōd* (259.7): O **-id** (presumably *-īd*, cf. acc. *-ĭm* written **-ím**), OL *-īd*, -ID, whence literary *-ī*. This is characteristic of certain nouns, including most neuters, and is regular for adjectives. But in the majority of nouns the *-e* of the consonant stems (276.6) is usual.

a. OL *-īd* happens not to be attested in any *i*-stem noun surviving in literary L; but it is tolerably well attested in what are properly cons. stems, for example OPID (*ops*) and IN COVENTIONID (SC de Bacch.).

307. PLURAL CASES.

1. Nom.pl. PIE **-eyes* (Ved. *-ayas*, G *-εες*, *-εις*), whence **-ees*, L *-ēs* (192). This ending spreads to the cons. stems and completely displaces their proper ending **-es*.

a. Nom.pl. *-īs*, cited by Varro, is found occasionally in Plaut. and epigraphically. Since the latter are found alongside -EIS, the ending is to be explained as a syncopated form of *-eyes*. The occurrences of the ending in literature are considerably commoner than often stated, as they are routinely eliminated from standard text editions. Their survival must be explained by the acc.pl. *-īs* (below), as parallel to the homophony between nom. and acc. *-ēs* in the cons. stems.

2. Acc.pl. PIE ***-ims*, **-ins* (G dial. *-ινς*), L. *-īs* (226.3). This remained the usual form down to the Augustan period, when the *-ēs* of the cons. stems became increasingly frequent and eventually prevailed; in poetic style *-īs* lasted longer.

3. Nom./acc.pl.neut. PIE **-iH_2* would give Ital. **-ī*. To this was added the *o*-stem nom./acc.n. ending *-ā* (260.3), **trīā*, whence **triā* (85) > *tria* (83.2). Similar remodelings underlie U *trio-per* 'thrice' (260.3), early OIr. *tre* < **tria*, Go. *þrija*, and so on.

4. Dat./abl.pl. PIE *-*i-bh-*, whence Ital. *-*ifos*, O **-ifs** (once, early; presumably ***-ífs**, but written in a signary that does not include the signs for **í** and **ú**), **-íss**, **-is**, early L -*ibos*, usual -*ibus*.

5. Gen.pl. *-*y̆ōm*, L -*ium* (83.1, 71.6, 193): *collium* (*collis*), *marium* (*mare*), *frontium* (*frōns*). In the imparisyllaba *i*-stems like *frōns*, this case is the only dependable point of contrast between cons. stem and *i*-stem inflection.

308. THE PARTIAL FUSION OF CONSONANT STEMS AND *i*-STEMS IN LATIN consists of the following:

The *i*-stems furnished the nom.pl. -*ēs* and -*īs* and (at least in part) the dat./abl.pl. -*ibus*.

Identical in both classes from an early period: the dat.sg. -*ī*, acc.sg. -*em*, and probably the gen.sg. -*is* (-*es*).

Later, in fact within the attested history of L, the cons. stem endings encroached upon those of the *i*-stems as follows: first, abl.sg. -*e* tended to replace -*ī*; acc.pl. -*ēs* competed with -*īs*.

The fusion of cons. stems and *i*-stems had begun in the PItal. period, but was carried further in L than in Sab. (where the forms of the nom.pl. remained distinct). In L the differences between the two types were progressively reduced. The *i*-stems are distinctive in the nom.sg. of the so-called 3rd decl. parisyllaba (see 309), like *collis* nom., *hostis* 'enemy' and *avis* 'bird'; more consistently in the gen.pl. -*ium* and in the nom./acc.pl. -*ia* of the neuters. It is upon such a basis that we still call forms like *pēs* and *cor* cons. stems (gen.pl. *pedum*, nom.pl. *corda*), but forms like *mōns* and *animal* *i*-stems (gen.pl. *montium*, nom.pl. *animālia*).

309. LATIN 'MIXED STEMS'. Roman grammarians thought of such differences in detail as the genitive plurals like *animalium* vs. *capitum* as a matter of different ENDINGS rather than of a different makeup of historical STEMS. In their scheme, 3rd decl. nouns were classed as parisyllaba—those with the same number of syllables in the principal parts (nom. and gen.sg.), as *collis collis*, *hostis hostis*; and imparisyllaba—those like *rēx rēgis*, *flōs flōris*, *arbor arboris*, *iter itineris*. The gen.pl. 'ending' of parisyllaba was -*ium*, of imparisyllaba, -*um*.

The customary designation for nouns like *mōns* (gen.pl. *montium*), *gēns*, *pars*, *nox*, *urbs*, and the like is that they are 'mixed stems'—not in the sense that ALL nouns of the third declension are a historical mixture, but because they are so to say imparisyllaba with parisyllaba endings.

The majority of these are revealed by comparative evidence and other considerations to be *i*-stems, more accurately *ti*-stems (Ved. -*tis*, G -σις), with syncope in the nom.sg. (306.1): *mors* < **morts* (215) < **mortis* < **m̥rtis* (Av. *mərəti-*, Lith. *mirtìs*); *gēns* < **gents* < **gentis* < *ǵn̥tis* (? anit), and so on, in contrast to aboriginal **pēts* 'foot' (Ved. *pā́t*), **reH₁ks* (Ved. *rā́ṭ* f. 'strength'). Some words of this type, like *urbs*, have obscure etymologies; others, however, like *dēns* 'tooth', gen.pl. *dentium*, were certainly cons. stems to begin with: NB unambiguously cons. stem inflection in G ὀδούς, -όντος, Ved. *dán* nom.sg., *dántam* acc. (and even in L, gen.pl. *dentum* is quoted by Varro). In the case of *nox* 'night', *noctium*, G has a cons. stem (νύξ, νυκτός) but other languages show a mixture of cons. stem details and inflection according to other types, prominently including *i*-stem inflection (so Ved. *nák* nom.sg. < **nakts*, and *náktam* 'by night', next to *nákti*-; the Lith. gen.pl. *naktų̃* next to nom. *naktìs*, OCS *noštĭ*; OHG *naht* dat./gen. (usual), next to occasional *i*-stem forms like *nahti* dat./gen.). But there was in any case a pan-IE tendency to move inherited root nouns into other stem types, and some of the agreements on *i*-stem inflection scattered about in the IE languages, as seen in the 'night' words, are coincidence rather than common heritage.

A few root-nouns ending in -*s* have gen.pl. -*ium*, as *mūrium* (*mūs*) 'mouse', *mārium* (*mās*) 'the male', *glīrium* (*glīs*) 'dormouse'. So also *assium* (*as*) 'whole; a denomination of coin'; *ossium* (*os*) 'bone'. But for some of these (as for no small number of nouns) evidence as to the USUAL gen.pl. form is insufficient.

The opposite relation to that noted in imparisyllaba *i*-stems like *gēns* 'clan', gen.pl. *gentium* is seen in a few nouns like *canis* 'dog', apparently a parisyllabum *i*-stem but with gen.pl. *canum*. Lists of nouns with secondary nom.sg. in -*is* provided by ancient grammarians suggest that there was at some point in the history of L a vogue for such remodelings (**327b**; nom.sg. *bovis* for usu. *bōs*, **324**). Some are original cons. stems, as *canis* (cf. G κύων, Ved. *śvā́*—that is, assuming that L *canis* belongs here at all), *iuvenis* 'young' (cf. Ved. *yúvan*-), *mēnsis* 'month' (cf. G μήν, gen. μενός, Lesb. μῆννος from stem **mēns*-); for such nouns the gen.pl. -*um* is inherited. Cf. the complete transition to *i*-stem inflection for *nāvis* 'boat', **328**). From *senex* 'old (man)' (for **sē*, *senis*, with the original *n*-stem nom.sg. replaced by a form embellished with a *k*-suffix) the rest of the declension follows that of its antonym *iuvenis* (gen.pl. *senum*, *iuvenum*). The gen.pl. *volucrum* to *volucris* 'flying (creature)' is presumably due to some specific, but unknown, analogy.

a. Varro's mention of gen.pls. in -*tātium* hardly pertains to anything ancient: the plural of abstract nouns is unlikely to preserve old and unusual forms.

u-STEMS AND *ū*-STEMS.

310. In PIE, nouns and adjectives were built to an ablauting *u*-stem exactly parallel to the *i*-stems (**302-3**), that is, having *u* or *w* where the *i*-stems have *i* or *y*, respectively. Thus nom.sg. *-*us* like *-*is*, nom.pl. *-*ewes* like *-*eyes*, and so on. But in both G and L the *i*- and *u*-stem paradigms sharply diverged: in L, sound laws were the main cause; in G, the *i*-stems apart from τρεῖς 'three' were radically remodeled (**304**) along lines largely unparalleled by anything in the *u*-stem paradigm. To be sure, a certain parallelism is found in Att., where there was a shared tendency for -ε- to spread as a stem vowel, especially in the du. and pl.; thus -εων gen., -εις (< -ενς) acc., -εσι dat. are endings found in both stem types, replacing both -υων, -υνς, -υσι in the *u*-stems and -ιων, -ινς, -ισι in the *i*-stems. Note however that the *i*-stem development in question is Attic only, whereas in the *u*-stems the spread of -εϝ- is at least Att.-Ion. (The situation in the other dialects is imperfectly known.)

In Italic, *u*-stem adjectives, an important class in PIE and G, are obliterated: all inflect instead as *i*-stems, remodeled by adding the *i*-stem marker to the inherited stem (270.2).[1] Nouns however survive, and make up the sizable form class known in L as the fourth declension.

Greek is the mirror image of Italic: *u*-stem adjectives persist as a well-defined (albeit closed) form-class, while it is the *u*-stem nouns which almost disappear. A nearly complete inventory, all masc. and neut., is: πῆχυς 'fore-arm', πέλεκυς 'axe', πρέσβυς 'old man' (orig. an adj.), and ἄστυ n. 'city'; and also υἱύς 'son' (cf. usual υἱός) is found in Attic inscriptions, Homer, and several dialects. A number of nouns like δάκρυ 'tear' survive in defective paradigms (336).

The majority of G nouns follow an inflection based, mainly, on the PIE *uH*-stems (317-8; nom. -ῡς, gen.sg. -υος, and so on), a type etymologically unrelated to *u*-stems proper, being actually a kind of consonant stem. The class is made up in part of derivative nouns built with a suffix *-*uH*- (the Skt. *tanū́s* type) and in part of root nouns like **suH-s* 'pig', **suH-m̥* acc.sg. Some of the endings of this type in G continue *u*-stem forms, such as the dat.pl. -ῠσι (rather than ˣ-ῡσι) and the alternative nom. and acc. endings in -ῠς, -ῠν (317). Fluctuation between the two types is seen in the Attic inflection of ἔγχελῠς 'eel', for example (gen.sg. -έως, nom.pl. -εις) vs. ἐγχέλῡς (gen.sg. -υος, nom.pl. -υες). Items like this are the only fem. ῠ-stems.

Two underived *ū*-stems are the only representatives of the type in L: *sūs* 'pig' and *grūs* 'crane'. (PIE **swek̂ruH*- f. 'husband's mother' is continued in L *socrus*, an ordinary *u*-stem; cf. Ved. *śvaśrū́s*, and NB the parallel shift to an ordinary *i*-stem of PIE **neptiH₂*- 'niece', L *neptis*, 270.3.)

311. PROTEROKINETIC *u*-STEMS (272.2). In PIE there was a second class of *u*-stem noun, neut. only, with ablaut affecting both the root (which is usually not a verbal root) and the stem. There are two subtypes: those like **doru*- 'tree' and **ĝonu*- 'knee' with *o*-grade, and those like **H₂eyu*- 'age' and **pek̂u*- 'movable property' with *e*-grade. As is typical with differences between the two full grades in PIE, there is no explanation for the distinction. Furthermore there are some inconsistencies, as the *e*-grade in L *genū̆* 'knee' and Hitt. *gi-e-nu*, next to *o*-grade elsewhere (G γόνυ, Ved. *jā́nu*).

Even in conservative IE languages this class was much attacked by leveling and remodeling, such that even though the nouns in question were hardly rare, little beyond what is given here is known about the paradigms. The most certain forms are nom./acc., as in **doru* 'tree, wood', and the gen./abl.sg., as in **drew-s* (Ved. *dā́ru*, gen. *drós*); **pek̂u* nom.acc. 'wealth, movable property', **pk̂ew-s* gen. (Av. *pasu*, *-fšaoš*). The combining form was

[1] It cannot be told whether the starting point was the zero grade, as in Skt. *svādvī́*-, or the full grade, as in G ἡδεῖα: PItal. **tənwī*- and **tənewī*- would turn out the same in L.

the zero grade **dru*-, **pḱu*-, thus Ved. *dru-ṣád-* 'tree-sitting' (of birds), *kṣu-mánt-* 'wealthy' (**pśu-mánt-* lit. 'having cattle', = Av. *fšūmant-*). *Paśu-mánt-* of the same meaning is an ordinary example of recomposition.

Already in the RV, more straightforward inflection competes with the inherited one, so gen. *druṇás* 'of wood' is found next to inherited *drós*; *páśu-* is recast as an ordinary *u*-stem (and became masc. besides); *mádhu-* 'sweet (drink)' develops an array of secondary forms (*mádhunas*, *mádhvas*, and *mádhos* all gen.sg., none being the original form); and so on.

In G some of these items survived in defective paradigms, as μέθυ, nom./acc. only, 'wine'. Others have been remodeled as if they were *w*-stems, thus δορυ, δορϝος gen., δορϝα nom./acc.pl., in Hom. δούρος, δούρα, Att. δόρος, δόρα (190.1). In L the items in question were reassigned to other stem-classes. *Pecū* and *genū* were accommodated as ordinary *u*-stems, still neut.; but other stem-types are seen in *pecus*, *-ŭdis* 'a head of cattle', also *pecus*, *-oris* 'cattle, livestock'. *Genus*, *-ūs* 'knee', an ordinary *u*-stem, is fem.

a. OTHER PROTEROKINETIC STEMS. PIE **nomn̥* 'name' (the basis of L *nōmen*, G ὄνομα, Go. *namo*, Ved. *nā́man-*), gen. **n̥men-s* attested in OIr. *anme* gen.sg. of *ainm*, and in the stem-form of OCS *imę*. PIE **gʷenH̥₂* n. 'woman', gen. **gʷneH₂-s*; stem much remade in all daughter languages into one or another feminine type (G γυνή, the Go. *n*-stem *qino*). The most crucial data here are from Old Irish: *bé*ᴺ < **gʷenH̥₂*, a poetic (and legal) term which is usually neut., as befits its form-class;[1] gen. *mná*ᴴ < *gʷneH₂s*. (The usual OIr. nom., *ben*ᴸ f., is from a remodeled stem, PCelt. **benā* or the like.)

PIE **H₂ewi-* 'bird', gen. **H₂wey-s* may belong here, but possibly was masc. to begin with. (Still, it is important to remember that the all-important attestation of **gʷenH₂-* as a neuter hangs by a thread.)

312. PROTO-INDO-EUROPEAN *u*-STEM DECLENSION.

	Singular	*Plural*
Nom.	suHnu-s *'son'*	suHnew-es
Voc.	suHnow	suHnew-es
Acc.	suHnu-m	suHnu-ms
neut.	pl̥H₁u *'much'*	pl̥H₁u-H₂
Inst.	suHnw-eH₁	suHnu-bh-
Dat.	suHnew-ey	"
Gen.	suHnow-s	suHn(e)w-ōm
Loc.	suHnēw (**-ew-i)	sunHu-su

Parallel to the two types of *i*-stems mentioned in 304.2a, it has recently been suggested that the real PIE *u*-stem paradigms were as follows:

---

[1] The *-*H₂*- in **gʷenH₂*- has no necessary connection with the feminine marker *-*H₂*- of *eH₂*-stems (262-7), devī stems (268-70), and other fem. types. Of course, other proterokinetic nouns appear to terminate in what look like stem-forming elements in other paradigms (*-*u*/*ew*-, *-*n̥*/*en*-), so the *-*H₂*- in **gʷenH₂*- might likewise be a morphological element. But the relationship of the 'stem' of **gʷenH₂*- to the feminine 'long vowel' stems, or to the nom./acc.pl. marker of the neuter gender, is unclear.

	Type A	Type B
Nom.	**dhérs-ēw-s 'brave'	**néḱ-u-s 'corpse'
Acc.	**dhérs-u-m	**n̥ḱ-éw-m̥
Gen.	**dhr̥s-éw-s	**n̥ḱ-w-ós

The same reservations apply here as before.

313. TABLE OF SINGULAR _u_-STEM FORMS.

	Vedic	Greek	Italic[a]	Gothic	OCS	Lith.
Nom.	sūnús[1]	ἡδύς[2]	tribus[3]	sunus[1]	synŭ[1]	sūnùs[1]
Voc.	sūno	ἡδύ		sunau	synu	sūnaũ
Acc.	sūnúm	ἡδύν	tribum	sunu	synŭ	sū́nų
			U **trifu**[3]			
neut.	vásu[4]	δάκρυ[5]	genū[6]	faihu[7]		
Inst.	Av. vohu		tribū ?			
			U **mani**[8]			
Dat.	sūnáve		tribuī		synovi	sū́nui
			tribū ?			
Abl./Gen.	pitvás[9]	υἷος[1]	SENATVOS[10]			
			O castrous[11]			
	śátros[12]		tribūs ?	sunaus	synu	sūnaũs
		ἡδέος	tribūs ?			
		πήχεως[13]				
Loc.	sūnávi	ἡδέϊ, -εῖ	U **manuve**[14]			
	āyā́u[15]		tribū ?	sun(a)u	synu	sūnujè

_a._ Unmarked forms are Latin.

1. 'Son', PIE *_suH-nu-_, root *_sewH-_ 'bear, beget'; cf. related *_suH-yu-_ in G υἱύς (-ός).
2. 'Sweet', PIE *$sweH_2du$-.
3. 'Tribe' (one of the ethnic divisions of the Roman populace). U **trifu**, evidently cognate, seems to mean 'populace' or 'citizenry'.
4. 'Wealth', the neut.sg. of 'good(s)', PIE *_wesu-_.
5. 'Tear', PIE *_daḱru._
6. 'Knee', PIE *_ǵonu_; see 311.
7. 'Money', PIE *_peḱu_ 'wealth, movable property'. One of two, possibly three, neuter _u_-stems in Go.
8. 'With the hand (?) By force (?)' Cf. L _manus._ (PItal. *_ū_ > U _i._)
9. 'Draught, swig'.
10. 'Senate'; the usual form of the gen.sg. in the SC de Bacch.
11. O 'head'(?) (meaning conjectural).
12. 'Enemy'.
13. 'Arm'.
14. Loc. **manuv** with an enclitic particle **-e** (occasionally **-en**) 'in'.
15. 'Lively', PIE *H_2oyu-, cf. G αἰεί, L _in aevum_ 'for ever'.

---

314. SINGULAR CASES.

1. Nom.sg. PIE *_-us_, G -υς, L _-us._

2. Voc.sg. PIE *_-ow._ Endingless, full grade of the suffix, revealed by Go. _-au_ as specifically _o_-grade. All attestations of a special ending agree except for G -υ, which is the result of analogy (voc. = nom. minus -ς); cf. πόλι (304). Certain names in -εύς provide indirect evidence for an earlier voc.sg. in *_-ew_; 320.4. In L the nom. form is used.

3. Acc.sg. PIE *-*um*, G -*υν*, L -*um*. The type seen in Hom. *εὐρέα* 'wide' is one seventh as common as the *εὐρύν* type. It is a metrically convenient invention based on the acc.pl. *εὐρέας*, q.v., itself secondary. Hom. *υἷα* is thought by some to be an ancient detail, namely the expected *-*wm̥* (cons. stem inflection) for the usual *-*um*. It is more likely to be the same kind of analogy, namely a back formation from the acc.pl.

4. Nom./acc.n. PIE *-*u*, G -*υ*. L has -*ū* in the few quotable forms from poetry (*genū*, *cornū*, and a few others). Since original *-*ŭ* would most likely have given L ˣ-*e* (71.7), the occurrence of -*ū* in poetic texts is unlikely to be artificial, as some have suggested. (What kind of artifice, in any case?) A more attractive suggestion is that L -*ū* is an old dual, in view of the meaning of the commonest neut. *u*-stem nouns—both 'horns' and 'knees' would have been practically du.tant. But this idea is problematic in light of the likeliest form of the du. ending, -*uī* or the like < *-*w*-*iH₁* (as in RV *urvī́* nom./acc.du.n. 'broad').

5. Inst.sg. PIE *-*w*-*eH₁*? *-*u*-*H₁*? —Ved. retains no example of the hoped-for inst. in -*ū*, in any gender; cf. the *i*-stems (303 note 12). However, such a formation does show up in Av. *vohu* 'good(s)' (the lexical match of Ved. *vásu*-). This ending could be one of the sources of the L abl. in -*ū*, but that might as well continue the loc.sg. or the characteristic Ital. abl. in *-*ūd*. The same uncertainty applies to U **mani** < *-*ū*. In Myc. there are one or two forms that look like *u*-stem instrumentals in -*e*, such as *ka-ru-we*, but the matter is unclear because the words themselves are uninterpretable.

6. Dat.sg. PIE *-*ew*-*ey*, whence regularly Ved. *sūnáve*, OCS *synovi*, and OL -*uei*, L -*uī* (*-*ewey* > *-*owey* 42 > -*uei* 66.5). The form -*uei* is attested directly in OL SENATVEI, a form also found in the playwrights.

Another OL form, in -*ū* (cf. U dat.sg. **trifu**, *trifo*), is well-attested in inscriptions and the early playwrights but apparently was always non-standard. It is nevertheless probably the real etymon of the 'ablative' supine in -*tū* (553), in such collocations as *facile factū* 'easy to do', *miserum memorātū* 'sad to relate', *mīrābile dictū* 'marvelous to say' (by a forced analysis the 'ablative of limitation'). This -*ū* has been traced to: (1) *-*ew* or *-*ow*, presumably loc. though it is hard to tell, as the forms are not paralleled by anything in cognate languages; (2) a contraction of -*uī*;[1] and (3) the loc.sg. in *-*ēw*. But none of these explanations is wholly satisfactory, and in fact dat. -*ū* is most likely to be nothing but an analogical creation based on the -*ī* dat.sg. of *i*-stems.

a. Myc. *i-je-we* (*huyyewei*) 'to the son' (?) and the place name *ko-tu-we* 'to Gortyn' (?) seem to attest the original dat. ending for G.

---

[1] Such a contraction would be unparalleled in L, but this explanation has the compensating virtue of allowing the form in -*tū* to be immediately cognate with the Ved. infin. in -*tave*, easily the most abundant of the chorus of infinitive formations in the RV (551).

7. Abl.sg. Ital. *-*ūd*, formed after the analogy of *o*-stem -*ōd* (259.7), early L -*ūd* (MAGISTRATVD, SC de Bacch.), whence L -*ū*. (See also loc.sg., below.)

8. Gen.sg. PIE *-*ows* (*o*-grade seen unambiguously in Go. -*aus*; all other reflexes have an unidentifiable full grade), OL once SENATOVS, L -*ūs*.

There are a number of competing forms for the *u*-stem gen.sg. in the prior stages of L.

Early L SENATVOS—the usual form in the SC de Bacch.—and parallel forms *fructuis* (Varro) and *senātuis* (for the most part only known from grammarians, but also occurring in Terence), continue *-*wos*, *-*wes* parallel to the *i*-stem gen. *-*yes* > *-*is* (306.6).[1]

In OL the USUAL gen.sg., however, is *senātī*, with -*ī* imported from the *o*-stems. It has been urged that this gen.sg. -*ī* is a peculiarity of *senātus* specifically (and not a *u*-stem form generally), derived from its stereotyped collocation with *populī*. But the ending is in fact attested in a half dozen or so other words in the early playwrights (*quaestī* 'of profit', *tumultī* 'of uproar', and so on).

Finally, several grammarians report a gen.sg. in -*ū* for neuter *u*-stems. This is probably only a misinterpretation of compounds like *cornūbūbulum* 'a steer with horns' as genitive phrases.

G -εος, regular in adjectives (as ἡδέος) and also, except in Att., in the few nouns left in this type (Hom. υἱέος, ἄστεος, Cret. υιεος; disguised in Boeot. ϝαστιος), is from -εϝος. This is a wholly manufactured form, whose ingredients are the usual gen.sg. -ος added to -εϝ-, the latter in place of original *-οϝ- after the analogy of other case forms, such as dat.sg. -εϝι, nom.pl. -εϝες.

There is no attestation of *-η(ϝ)ος, so Att. ἄστεως, πήχεως, πρέσβεως may be in effect imported whole from the *i*-stem type πόλεως (304.4, 79.3).

The neuters γόνυ, δόρυ have Hom. γουνός, δουρός from **gonwos*, **dorwos* (like Ved. *paśvás*, *mádhvas* 311), and the other cases are similarly formed, as δουρί from **dorwi*, δοῦρα from **dorwa* (for the τ-stem forms, as γούνατος, Att. γόνατος, see 293). Of the same type is Hom. υἷος from **huwyos* whence also dat.sg. υἷι, acc.sg. υἷα.

9. Loc.sg. PIE *-*ēw* must be an analogical replacement of *-*ĕwi* on the pattern of *i*-stem *-*ēy*, if the latter is correctly explained as the reflex of earlier **-*eyi*. We do in fact find forms that could reflect original *-*ewi*: Ved. *sūnávi* (occurring eight times in seven stems), G -ε(ϝ)ϊ, as in G dat.sg. πήχει, ἡδεῖ < **hwādewi*. The analogical importation of loc. -*i* to an ending *-*ēw* should produce Ved. ˣ-*āvi*, G ˣ-η(ϝ)ϊ, which are nowhere attested. —It is possible that *-*ēw* underlies the L dat. -*ū* (as mentioned in 6, above); and note that *-*ewi* would produce the same result.

---

[1] The occasionally-encountered late form in -*uus* is not a direct reflex of -*uos*, but a false archaism for classical -*ūs*.

315. TABLE OF PLURAL *u*-STEM FORMS.

	Vedic	Greek	Italic[a]	Gothic	OCS	Lith.
Nom.	mádhvas[1]					
	sūnávas	ἡδέις	tribūs	þaurnjus[2]	synove	sū́nūs
		ηδεες[3]				
Acc.	paśvás[4]	υἷας				
		πήχεας				
	śatrū́ñ(s)[5]	υἱύνς	tribūs	þaurnuns	syny	sū́nus
			U **manf**			
neut.	purū́[6]	δάκρυα	genua			
			U **berva**[7]			
		ἡδέα				
	purú					
	purū́ṇi					
Inst.	sūnúbhis			þaurnum	synomi[9]	sūnumìs
Dat./Abl.	aśatrúbhyas[8]		tribubus		synomŭ[9]	
			U **berus**			
Gen.	śatrū́ṇām	υἱῶν	tribuum	þaurniwe	synovŭ	sūnų̄
	(Av. pasvąm[9])					
Loc.	paśúnu	ἡδέσι			synoxŭ[10]	sūnuosè

a. Unmarked forms are Latin

1. 'Sweet' m., PIE *medhu-; the only example in the RV of a *u*-stem nom.pl. with zero grade of stem.
2. 'Thorns', PIE *$t\mathring{r}nu$-.
3. Dial. form.
4. Masc. 'cattle', namely cows viewed as property. (*Páśu* n. < PIE **peḱu* occurs once in the RV; cf. 313 note 7.)
5. The ending in *-ū̃n(s)* < **-*ums* is masc. only; the f. ending is *-ūs*. A parallel gender-marked difference is seen in the *i*-stems (303 note 18).
6. 'Many' (G πολύ); forms in *-ŭ* also occur but are less frequent than the type in *-ū*, and mainly occur when the word is the last word in the line. (In the later language both types disappear in favor of remodeled *purūṇi*.)
7. 'Spits, skewers' (= L *verua*; PItal. *g^w*erwā*).
8. 'Without adversary', an epithet of Indra (simplex *śátru-* 'enemy').
9. 'Cattle' n. (= Ved. *páśu*, note 4).
10. The forms in *-ŭmi*, *-ŭmŭ*, and *-ŭxŭ* as met with in handbooks are not found in texts.

---

316. PLURAL CASES.

1. Nom.pl. PIE *-*ew-es*: Ved. *sūnávas*, OCS *synove*; Go. *þaurnjus* < *-*iws* < *-*iwis*, G -εϝες (now quotable from Myc.: *pa-ke-we* (*pak*^{h}*ewes*) 'thick'); the resulting -εες is uncontracted in most dialects, but gives Att. -εις.

L *-ūs* is a problem, as *-*ewes* should have given ˣ-*uis*, parallel to dat. -*uī* (314.6). Early syncope of the final vowel would give the attested form (*-*ewes* > PItal. *-*owes* > *-*ous* > -*ūs*); but for some reason, that is not generally regarded as likely. Some think instead that -*ūs* is the ending of the acc.pl., imported into the nom. by analogy to the cons. stem -*ēs*, which serves as both nom. and acc.pl. An occurrence of the nom.pl. in O, or in an early L inscription (showing whether the spelling was -ovs or -vs), would settle the matter.

2. Acc.pl. PIE **-*ums*, *-*uns*, G -υνς, -ῡς (**228.4**), L -*ūs* (**226.3**). G -υνς occurs in Cret., Arg. υἱύνς, whence the -ῡς of the majority of *u*-stem (and, secondarily, *ū*-stem) nouns (**317-8**, below). Otherwise it was replaced, at least in Att.-Ion., by a form with -ε- based on the nom., thus -ενς (whence Att. -εις); or, based on the cons. stems, -εϝας (Hom. πελέκεας 'axes', πολέας 'many'). Hom. υἷας, the usual form in Hom., points to **súHiwm̥s*, parallel to Ved. *paśvás* 'cattle' (at that period about as frequent as *paśū́n*, which later ousted -*vas* altogether).

L *manūs* < *-*uns*; O **manf** < **manuf* < **manuns* (**237.5**).

3. Nom./acc.pl.n. PIE *-uH_2 is seen in Vedic: *purū́* 'full'. As mentioned in **50.2**, some think that *-uH_2 gives G -υα (-ϝα) by regular sound law, so G **gonwa* 'knees' would be a direct reflex of the ancestral formation. This theory has two points in its favor. First, it provides a natural starting point for the wholesale revision of γονυ-, δορυ- as *w*-stems. Second, if original *-*ū* < *-uH_2 were embellished with a marker of the nom./acc.pl.n. -α, the result should have been -υα, not -ϝα, as in fact it is in the *ū*-stem paradigm (**317**).

Eventually, this -ϝα was everywhere replaced in Att.-Ion. Already in Hom., adjectives and most nouns have -ε(ϝ)α instead, after the analogy of m.f. -ε(ϝ)ες, thus Hom. ἄστεα, Att. ἄστη 'towns'; Att.-Ion. ἡδέα is regularly uncontracted (but late epigr. Dor. ημιση 'halves'). Alternatively, the old δορϝα, γονϝα (**311**) were reshaped as δόρατα (δούρατα), γόνατα (γούνατα) **293**.

In Ital., the *o*-stem ending *-*ā* was added to the inherited *-*ū* < *-uH_2, whence L *cornua* < **kornūā*, like *tria* < **trīā*. (U *castruo*, **kastruvu** directly attest the original length of the final vowel.)

4. Dat./abl.pl. PIE *-*u-bhi*-. Myc. attests *ka-ru-pi* (of uncertain meaning, and not necessarily a *ŭ*-stem rather than a *ū*-stem). U **berus** < **berufs* comes from either **berufis* or **berufos* (PItal. *g^w*eru*-). The normal L ending is -*ibus*, attested in both OL inscr. and early literary sources. Attestations of -*ubus* are scarce but indubitable. Here there is a complication of phonetic factors (as exemplified by *optumus/optimus*, **69**), though -*ibus* would have been the eventual outcome. Significantly, in literary L -*ubus* seems to be most frequent in situations of potential homophony: dat.pl. *arcibus* to *arx* 'citadel, castle', but *arcubus* to *arcus* 'bow'. Otherwise the ending is attested in *specubus* 'caves' and *lacubus* 'lakes, tanks' beside usual *specibus*, *lacibus*; and occasionally in other words. On the other hand, though *tribubus* is endorsed by grammarians as the only correct form and is uniform in our literary texts, an inscription has TREBIBOS.

G -υσι representing the PIE loc. (cf. Ved. -*uṣu*) was retained in the words which passed over to the *ū*-stem type (**317-8**), as δακρύσι; but in the paradigm more closely continuing the PIE *u*-stems the ending was replaced by -εσι, as ἡδέσι, πήχεσι.

Hom. *υἱάσι* (also Cret.) shows the influence of the *r*-stem kinship terms (as in *πατράσι*, 284A.1).

5. Gen.pl. The PIE form is uncertain. PIE *-*wōm* is indicated in Av. *pasvąm* 'of cattle'. On the other hand, a full grade stem *-*ew*- is seemingly attested in BS, and is unambiguous in Go. -*iwe*. Either etymon would give L -*uom*, -*uum*. The full grade stem, being unexpected, is for that reason likely to be original. Furthermore, the problem with taking it to be analogical is that there is no obvious model for it except in G, where there was a wholesale spread of -ε- in *i*- and *u*-stems alike.

L -*uom* kept -*o*- much later than the gen.pl. in the other declensions because of the preceding -*u*- (71.6c). A monosyllabic form -*um* occurs long before the change of -*uom* to -*uum* and therefore cannot be a contraction of the latter. Its source is *mīlle passu(o)m* 'thousand paces', which shows the influence of the gen.pl. -*um* of other words denoting measures and coins, as *iūgerum*, *amphŏrum*, *nummum* (260.5); once established, it passed from *passum* to other *u*-stems, as *currum*.

G -*υων*, found in words which follow the *ū*-stem type (317-8), as *δακρύων*, continues *-*uHōm*, not *-*wōm*. The regular *u*-stem type has -*ε(ϝ)ων*, with -ε- generalized as in the *i*-stems, for example *ἡδέων* (Att. *πήχεων* with accent in imitation of gen.sg. *πήχεως*); this later contracts to -*ῶν*, -*ων*, but such forms are disparaged by grammarians.

ū-STEMS

317. The Greek inflection with gen.sg. -*υος* is based upon that of PIE *uH*-stems, which are directly represented by *σῦς* 'pig', *ὀφρῦς* 'brow', and some others.

	Singular		*Plural*	
	Greek	Vedic	Greek	Vedic
Nom.	ὀφρῦς (βότρυς)	sū́s[1]	ὀφρύες	vibhúas[2]
Voc.	ὀφρῦ (βότρυ)			
Acc.	ὀφρῦν (βότρυν)	asúam[3]	ὀφρύας ὀφρῦς	bhúvas[4]
neut.	δάκρυ		δάκρυα	
Gen.	ὀφρύος	bhuvás	ὀφρύων	yātu-jū́nām[5]
Loc.	ὀφρύι	bhuví	ὀφρύσι	prasū́ṣu[6]

The Vedic distinction between monosyllabic stems like *bhuvás* 'world' vs. polysyllabic stems like *vibhvàs* 'omnipresent' (read: *vibhúvas*) is purely a matter of spelling. In this table 'restored' readings—that is, syllabifications determined by the meter to be different from the spelling of the received text—are given without the semivowel—*vibhúas*—to distinguish them from textual -*uv*-, as in *bhúvas*.

1. 'Pig', PIE **suHs*, G *σῦς*, L *sūs*.
2. 'Omnipresent' (from *bhū*- 'world').
3. 'Barren' (root *sū*- 'beget').
4. 'Worlds'.
5. 'Possessed by a yatu' (a kind of demon); root *jū*- 'incite, drive'. Cf. the *ā*-stem gen. pl. -*ānām* (260 note 3; 257.15).
6. 'Fruitful, productive' (root *sū*-).

The majority of inherited *u*-stem NOUNS also follow this type, regardless of their etymology. The rule is that if they are barytone they retain the short -υ- in the nom., acc., and voc.sg. (βότρυς 'bunch of grapes', στάχυς 'ear of grain', δάκρυ n. 'tear'), while those accented on the last syllable usually have -ῦς (as in Hom. βρωτῦς 'meat'; this particular noun was originally a **tŭ*-stem). There is some fluctuation, with the στάχῡς type occurring next to usual στάχῠς.

318. From the PIE point of view, these were actually consonant stems: to an unvarying affix *-*uH*- (arguably *-uH_2- specifically, as the class seems to be basically feminine, though there is no real evidence one way or the other for the index of the laryngeal) were added the usual cons. stem endings: *-*s* nom., *-*m̥* acc., *-*os* gen. and so on.

The inflection of ὀφρῦς agrees with that of Ved. *ū*-stems. Discrepancies are: acc.sg. ὀφρῦν, not ὀφρύα (which does occur but is rare) matching Ved. -*u(v)am.* Acc.pl. ὀφρύας, like Ved. -*uvas*, occasionally in Homer; but the regular Hom. form is ὀφρῦς from -υνς (the *u*-stem form). Dat.pl. ὀφρύσι is the *u*-stem form in place of expected ×-ῡσι parallel to Ved. -*ūṣu.*

In L the *ū*-stem type is represented by two isolated stems, *sūs* 'pig' and *grūs* 'crane'. The acc. *suem* shows the expected ending; the expected acc. sg. was remodeled after the nom.sg. in e.g. U *sim* (< **sūm*) and G σῦν. The dat./abl.pl. is regularly *suibus* with the usual *i*-stem form, but occasionally *sūbus* or *sŭbus* (-*ŭ*- from the cases where it is regular, *suis*, *suem* and so on).

DIPHTHONGAL STEMS

319. GREEK NOUNS IN -εύς (informally, the βασιλεύς type). Prominent in this class are denominative nouns of occupation: ἱππεύς 'knight, horseman', (ἵππος), φονεύς 'murderer' (φόνος 'murder'), φορεύς 'bearer' (φόρος 'tribute, payment', orig. *'a carrying'), γραμματεύς 'secretary (γράμμα 'letter'), χαλκεύς 'smith' (χαλκός 'copper'). Some are instruments rather than human agents, as τομεύς 'knife' (**tem*- 'cut'), ὀχεύς '(carrying) strap, bar' (**weǵh*- 'carry, fetch'). The majority of these are derived from *o*-stem nomina actionis, and that is thought to be the original state of affairs.

A few are in competition with older types of agent formation, as Hom. τροφεύς next to τροφός, both 'bringer-up, rearer' (τρέφω), the latter belonging to an ancient type of *o*-stem nomen agentis with the verb root in *o*-grade and the accent on the stem; τροφεύς is presumably based on *τρόφος 'a bringing-up' (an equally ancient type of *o*-grade *o*-stem nomen actionis, with the accent on the root—though this particular form is not attested).

A number denote place of origin (ὁ Θηβαιεύς 'the Theban', an epithet of Zeus; Μεγαρεύς 'a Megarian'; Ἐρετριεύς 'an Eretrian'). The stem is also typical of hypocoristic or otherwise truncated forms, as Ἀνδρεύς for Ἀνδροκλέης, or Νικεύς for Νικόδημος. It is prominent among Homeric names which are vaguely Indo-European-looking but of vexed explanation (such as Ἀχιλλεύς, Ἀτρεύς, Ὀδυσσεύς). Finally there are etymological puzzles, which include the type-word βασιλεύς 'king'; -*si*- points to *-*ti*-, and Myc. *qa-si-re-u* (and derivatives) 'foreman'—or some such petty official—reveals that β- comes from

*g^w-, but beyond that the explanation of the word has been much discussed with little result.

The βασιλεύς type is the most abundant diphthongal stem in G by far, but has no evident parallels in cognate languages.[1] As a result, there have been many different suggestions about its origins, some of them taking the stem as is, others proposing one or another ancient compound in which the second element (or a piece of it) had been reinterpreted as a stem.

Descriptively, the stem has an unvarying *-*ēw*-, to which the usual cons. stem endings are added. Myc. *qa-si-re-u* nom.sg. (= βασιλεύς) and *i-je-re-wo* gen.sg. 'priest' (= ἱερῆος), proves that Att.-Ion. -η- is original and not from *-*ā*- by 54. It is at least possible that the stem is an ablaut alternative of the *ōw*-stems (321); and the notion that the stem ultimately continues an ablauting suffix of more familiar type receives a little support from the form of the voc.sg. in -εῦ, and perhaps also from proper nouns with alternative endings in -εϝ- (320.5) and the fem. derivatives in -ειᾰ (320.4), though both of these have other, probably better, explanations.

Assuming a uniform stem in *-*ēw*-, the Homeric paradigm (320) was reshaped by two sound laws—the loss of -*w*- and Osthoff's Law (63.2); the Attic paradigm (320) embodies two more, quantitative metathesis and the shortening of long vowels before a vowel (79.3); the 'mild' Ionic dialects show the effects of the last only.

A recent suggestion takes the type to be a derivative of *o*-stems nouns by means of the ablauting suffix *-*ew*-/*-*u*- of the *u*-stems (312). The combining form of the *o*-stem would have been *e*-grade, as in for example the fem. derivatives in *-*e*-H_2- (262-6) and denominative verbs of the οἰκέω type (**woyke-y*^{e}/*o*- to *woykos*; 468.2A). The result would have been *g^w*hone-w-s* nom. 'murderer', *g^w*one-w-m̥* acc., *g^w*honēws* gen.sg., *g^w*honēwes* nom.pl. (the last two from full grade *-*e-ew*-), and so on. Just as they are, these forms fit well with the familiar paradigm. The necessarily analogical origin for certain details like acc. -ηϝα in place of *-εϝα and -ηϝος gen.sg. for *-ευς is a trifling complication; and the close association of the formation with the *o*-stems is not only explained but exploited to advantage.

A serious problem, however, is that *u*-stems do not otherwise form personal nouns in IE languages. (The Ved. agent nouns of the type *gr̥bhú*- 'beggar', *bhindú*- 'destroyer' are merely nominalized adjectives, based on the *u*-stem verbal adjectives that abound in InIr., such as *dakṣú*- 'burning', *vavakṣú*- 'calling aloud'.) Nearly as troubling is the complete lack of evidence in IE languages for *u*-stem elaborations based upon already marked noun stems, thematic or otherwise. Finally, there is the minor reproach that it provides no insight into the association of the affix with the names of Homeric heroes.

---

[1] Hitt. *ḫé-e-uš* 'rain', *ḫé-e-ú-un* acc., *ḫé-e-u-wa-aš* gen., is often quoted in this connection; but it has been satisfactorily argued that the -*u*- is an affix, and furthermore that the underlying structure must be something like **ḫey-au-*/**ḫey-u-*.

320. TABLE OF THE βασιλεύς INFLECTION.

		Proto-Greek	Homer	Attic	Ionic
Singular	Nom.	g^watilews	βασιλεύς		
	Gen.	g^watilēwos	βασιλῆος	-έως	-έος
	Dat.	g^watilēwi	βασιλῆϊ	-εῖ	-εῖ
	Acc.	g^watilēwa	βασιλῆα	-έᾱ	-έα
	Voc.	g^watilew	βασιλεῦ		

		Proto-Greek	Homer	Attic	Ionic
Plural	Nom.	g^watilēwes	βασιλῆες	-ῆες, -ῆς, -εῖς	-εῖς
	Gen.	g^watilēwōn	βασιλήων	-έων	-έων
	Dat.	g^watilewhi	βασιλεῦσι		
	Acc.	g^watilēwas	βασιλῆας	-έᾱς, -ῆς, -εῖς	-έας

Note: This table embodies the standard theory mentioned above, namely, a non-alternating stem in *-*ēw*- shortened to *-*ew*- in the nom.sg. per Osthoff's Law (63.2).

1. In Attic the nom.pl. -ῆς (from -ῆες) is the prevailing form till about 350 BC. The later -εῖς is from -έες, an analogical creation with stem -έ- back-formed from gen.pl. -έων, acc.pl. -έᾱς. The nom.pl. forms were also used for the acc.pl. after the analogy of the *i*- and *u*-stems, in which -εις served in both functions (304.2, 316.1-2). So occasionally -ῆς, and regularly -εῖς, as acc.pl. from about the end of the 4th century.

2. The acc.sg. -ῆ from -ῆα is early in some dialects (and is found twice in the Iliad); and it occurs in the κοινή.

3. A nom.sg. -ης, acc. -ην is regular in Arcadian (as in φονης) and in proper nouns occurs elsewhere. Such a variant form of Ὀδυσσεύς was Ωλιξης (Ουλιξης), from which L *Ulixēs*. The source of the monophthong is disputed, the opinion of most authorities being that it cannot be the result of regular sound change, and it is therefore accounted for by the following analogy: first, -ευς, -ην arose on the pattern of Ζεύς, (*)Ζῆν (325-6); then, -ευς was leveled to -ης on the basis of the acc. But if the influence of the paradigm of Ζεύς was enough to cause the convergence in the first place, it should have been worked to preserve the nom. in -εύς.

An account which avoids the contradictions of the Ζεύς explanation and additionally accounts well for the dialect distribution of the new type, which is not found in dialects with quantitative metathesis, is as follows. PG *-*ē*-, after the loss of the *-*w*-, shortened before a vowel (79.3) in certain endings: -έα acc., -έος gen., -έϊ dat. These were now identical to the corresponding endings of m.f. *es*-stem adjectives (300: εὐμενής 'well-disposed'), εὐμενέα, -έος, -έϊ < *-*eha*, *-*ehos*, *-*ehi*. This led to the replacement of nom. -εύς by -ής, after εὐμενής. Acc. -ην then arose on the basis of the nom./acc. pattern of the vowel stems generally: -ος/-ον, -ᾱς/-ᾱν, -ης/-ην. (On the other hand, some have seen in Arc. -ην an archaism, namely PIE *-*ēm* < **-*ĕ̄wm* like **dyēm* < ***dyewm* (324-5); but this is unlikely.)

4. Voc.sg. -εῦ cannot be derived from *-ēw. It is probably therefore an inherited form as such. First, the voc.sg. of the *i*- and *u*-stems, which seem to have been created in G from the nom.sg. by dropping the -ς, must have had some kind of model to start from, and the βασιλεύς type, if inherited, would provide the pattern. Additional evidence for the antiquity of a stem in *-ĕw- might be provided by the fem. derivatives in -εια, as in βασίλειᾰ 'queen, princess', if they reflect *-ewiH_2 rather than *-ēwiH_2. (But the real story here may be the action of Osthoff's Law (63.2) on PG *-ēwya < *-ēwiH_2.)

5. Proper nouns in -ευς sometimes show forms differing from those given above, as Hom. Τῡδεύς, Τῡδέος, Τῡδέϊ, and Τῡδέα (Τῡδῆ). Such forms point to a stem -εϝ- in contrast to the usual generalized -ηϝ-. However, epigraphic ΤΥΔΥΣ nom.sg. is thought not to reflect earlier -ευς, still less -ηυς, and rather to imply that the names in -εύς, gen. -έος are a modification of ordinary *u*-stems. The peculiar treatment of proper nouns among the *u*-stems might be traced to the prominence (relatively speaking) of the voc. case in the paradigms of names as compared to common nouns. This would have been *Τῦδευ, a form no longer found in actual *u*-stems, and only coincidentally identical—in the usual view—to the voc.sg. of the βασιλεύς type.

6. Myc. confirms the broad outlines of this paradigm. It clearly preserves the formal distinction, lost in literary G, between the orig. dat.sg. in *-*ey* and the loc. in *-*i*: *ka-na-pe-we* dat. 'fuller' (*knap^hēwei*, cf. κναφεύς) vs. *ka-ke-wi* loc. 'smith' (*k^halkēwi* to χαλκεύς). As in the literary dialects the majority of the Myc. words are occupations and personal names, with a few ethnic terms and *qa-si-re-u* (= βασιλεύς).

321. GREEK NOUNS IN -ως (informally, the ἥρως type). This class contains a handful of forms: ἥρως 'hero', ἅλως 'threshing floor', πάτρως 'father's brother', and remnants of others.[1] The stem appears to be a constant *-ōw-, parallel to *-ēw- in βασιλεύς (319), but the nature of the evidence is different. First, the type seems to have no namable function, though generalization on the basis of such a small number of nouns would be difficult in any case. Second, forms with -ϝ- are not quotable; that too may just follow from the diminutiveness of the class (which is not certainly attested in Myc.). In any case etymological -ϝ- is probably guaranteed by derivatives like μητρυιᾱ́ 'step-mother'.[2] Similarly L *patruus* 'father's brother' and Skt. *pitṛvya-* (late, but cf. RV *abhrātṛvyá-* 'having no rival', based on *bhrā́tṛvya-* lit. 'father's brother's son') point to a constituent *-w-. Besides, in contrast to the ευ-stems (319), there are cognate forms in other languages though not very revealing ones. Hitt. has a declension with stem in -*a-(a-)u*-. Primary nouns are few, in fact limited to *ḫar-na-a-uš* 'birth-chair' (acc. *ḫar-na-ú-un*, dat./loc. *ḫar-na-a-u-i*). However, *u*-stem adjectives functioning as

---

[1] G γάλως (γάλοως) 'husband's sister', often considered a member of this paradigm, has a problematic history; see 3a, below.

[2] Based on G μήτρως 'mother's brother'. This is a G coinage, on the pattern of inherited πάτρως, but obviously an early one.

nouns inflect thus in oblique cases: *(a-)aš-šu-u-wa-aš* gen.sg. 'good' adj.; the same case as an noun being *(a-)aš-ša-wa-aš*.

The inflection in Homer:

	Singular	*Plural*
Nom./voc.	ἥρως	ἥρωες
Gen.	ἥρωος	ἡρώων
Dat.	ἥρωϊ, ἥρωι	ἡρώεσσι
Acc.	ἥρωα	ἥρωας

In Attic, there was a tendency for the details of this paradigm to become tangled up in the 'Attic inflection' of *o*-stems (259.1a); this accounts for the Att. gen.sg. -ω (normal from the 3rd century), acc.sg. -ων, nom.pl. ἅλῳ (Aristotle), and so on.

1. Nom./voc.sg. -ως (ἥρως) might be the direct reflex of *-*ōws*, but is much more likely to be analogical for *-ους (genuine diphthong, the expected outcome of Osthoff's Law, 63.2; cf. βοῦς 'cow' < **g*ʷ*ōws*, 324, below). A proportional analogy with cons. stems as the fulcrum can be constructed for such an innovation (say, φύλακα : φύλαξ :: ἥρωα : *X*, where *X* = ἥρως). But paradigmatic leveling of the small and nonfunctional difference between two phonetically adjacent long vowels (the expected nom.sg. -ους and the -ω- of the rest of the paradigm) would be unremarkable. Cf. gen.sg. -ου of the masc. ᾱ-stem type in place of expected -ω (267.2).

2. The voc. -ως must be a replacement, either of *-ου < *-*ow* (the bare stem, like the -ευ of the βασιλεύς type, 320.4), or of *-ω (= nom.sg. minus -ς). But why either of these two endings would have been vulnerable to remodeling as -ως is unclear.

3. The Att. acc.sg. -ω < -ωα is normal from the 4th century; similarly nom./acc.pl. -ως < -ωες/-ωας.

a. Hom. γάλοως 'husband's [unmarried] sister', nom.pl. γαλόῳ. As attested in Hom. it plainly does not belong in the ἥρως class; it appears rather to be most immediately based on an ordinary *o*-stem (the position of the accent in γάλοως points to a secondary lengthening of the final syllable, such as by quantitative metathesis, 79.3, though that as we shall see is probably not the explanation here). Some say that the stem in -ω[ϝ]ο- is a remodeling of an original that went like πάτρως, though a fem. *o*-stem would be a strange choice for 'clarificatory restructuring' in this instance. A different tack is suggested by Hesych. γέλαρος· ἀδελφοῦ γυνή; this is plainly a blunder[1] for *γέλαϝος (187a), and implies that the sequence -οω- is an incorrect distraction of *γαλω- < **galawo-* (cf. the factitive denominatives in -όω, 468.3). All this points to an original *o*-stem of ordinary type, **galawos* < PIE ? **ǵl̥H₂ewo-*, with nom.sg. γάλ(ο)ως in place of *γάλοος, *γάλους, influenced by the analogy of the πάτρως type. L *glōs* (98, trivially remodeled—by the time of its worrisomely late attestation—as an *s*-stem) and OCS **zŭly* (*ū*-stem, gen. *zŭlŭve*) are more or less consistent with this analysis. But inconsistencies between the various attestations remain.

---

[1] The word is moreover characterized as Phrygian, but the tags in Hesych. are untrustworthy; cf. his 'Etruscan' forms that are plain Latin, for example σπίνα ἄλβα.

322. GREEK NOUNS IN -ώ, gen. -όος (informally, the Σαπφώ type). This feminine-only class includes many names, Σαπφώ, Γοργώ, Καλυψώ, and so on; and, like the masc. nouns in -εύς (319), the type occurs in pet-names, such as Ἀφρώ for Ἀφροδίτη, Εἰδώ for Εἰδοθέα. There are a fair number of words for female beings: κερδώ 'wily one; fox', καμῑνώ 'furnace-woman'; and a few abstract nouns: φειδώ 'a sparing; thrift', πειθώ 'persuasion', χρεώ 'want; longing'.

The nom.sg. is -ώ; the remaining cases with one exception have consonant stem endings appended to -ό- (prior to contraction): -όος/-οῦς; -όϊ/-οῖ; -όα/-ῶ. The exception is the voc.sg. in -οῖ. In the absence of any more direct evidence from Myc. (where examples of the type are not apparent), epigraphy, or the glossaries, these forms suggest a stem in *-ō̆y-, reminiscent of those in *-ēw- (319) and *-ōw- (321) but differing from them in showing a long vowel in the nom.sg. only, and (more significantly) in lacking the usual nom.sg. ending -ς. Furthermore, a clear analogue of this type is found in another IE language, Vedic, and there are some less clear ones elsewhere:

1. In Ved. there is a unique noun, *sákhay-* 'friend', which from the perspective of IE looks like a typical *r-* or *n*-stem (279-89), with *y as the final cons. instead of *-r- or *-n-. That is, in PIE terms, we seem to have a stem alternating between *-ō-, *-oy-, and *-y/i-, just like the alternations of say *-ō-, *-on-, and *-n/n̥-. Likewise obvious are the parallels with the Σαπφώ type. A Vedic *n*-stem, *rā́jan-* 'king', is provided for comparison.

Singular	Nom.	sákhā	Σαπφώ[1]	rā́jā
	Voc.	sákhe (*-ay)	Σαπφοῖ	rā́jan
	Acc.	sákhāyam	Σαπφόα	rā́jānam
	Inst.	sákh(i)yā		rā́jñā
	Dat.	sákhye		rā́jñe
Plural	Nom.	sákhāyas		rā́jānas
	Inst.	sákhibhis		rā́jabhis (*-n̥bhi-) *etc.*

(Ved. *-āy-* and *-ān-* are via Brugmann's Law, 36.4.)

The two obvious discrepancies between *sákhay-* and Σαπφώ are the position of the accent and the fact that the Ved. form is masc. whereas all the G forms are fem. This among other considerations has led some to doubt that the two types are in fact related, with the corollary that the Σαπφώ class is not an inherited type at all.

---

[1] The nom.sg. -ωι attested both in early inscriptions and by grammarians is not the welcome datum it might be, as it might be influenced by the voc. Furthermore, a number of the examples are actually from inscriptions written -OI in signaries lacking omega (24.2), and might therefore stand for either -οι or -ωι. On the other hand, a few very early inscriptions show unambiguous -ω.

a. When borrowed into L, G nouns of this type are treated as *n*-stems; but the similarity between the Σαπφώ and the *n*-stem types was not lost on native speakers of Greek themselves: in dialects and inscriptions there are transfers to *n*-stem inflection, as Γοργων nom., -ονος gen.; and yet more extreme remodelings like Γοργονη nom.

b. Speculatively, the score of L feminines with nom.sg. in -*ēs* (*vātēs* 'seer' is the only masc.), mostly otherwise ordinary *i*-stems (306–7), may reflect a parallel type in *-*ēy*-. The L cognate of *sákhay*- is not one of these; it is *socius*, an ordinary *yo*-stem, like OE *secg* poet. 'fellow', OS *segg*. The closest formal parallel to these is Ved. *sakhyá*- n. (read *sakhiyá*-) 'friendship', and perh. the etymon of L *socius*, OE *secg* and so on was in fact an adjective, *'friendly'. Some such shift in function seems to underlie L *amīcus* 'friend', OIr. *carat* 'friend', and the Gmc. words of which NE *friend* is an instance.

2. Hittite has the richest material parallel to the Vedic and G types, namely nouns (in both genders) built to a stem in -*ai*- throughout: nom. *ḫur-ta-a-iš* c. 'curse', *ḫa-aš-ta-a-i* n. 'bone'. The (optional) spellings with plene -*a*- are found only in the nom. in the common-gender nouns, and in the nom./acc. of the neut. Thus only *ḫu-ur-ta-in* acc., *ḫa-aš-ta-i* dat., and so on. The Hitt. -*s* is secondary (in Hitt. all common gender nouns end with -*s* in the nom.sg., including *n*-stems, where the -*s* is certainly secondary, **282**, especially **c**).

323. Monosyllabic diphthongal stems. These nouns, few in number, have idiosyncratic inflection which paradoxically is both highly conservative and much subject to analogical innovation. The ones in G are βοῦς 'cow' (**324**), Ζεύς (*'sky' **325–7**), and ναῦς 'ship' (**328**). From the point of view of PIE inflection all were straightforward, albeit belonging to three different form classes.

In L these three are joined by one more, L *rēs* 'thing' (**329**).

324. PIE **gʷow*-, G βοῦς 'cow', L *bōs* (an Italic loanword, **155**, **162**). The PIE paradigm was evidently 'acrostatic' (see below); the acc.sg. and pl.—and by analogy, the nom.sg.—were built to a stem **gʷōw*-; the remaining paradigm was built to stems **gʷów*-/**gʷéw*-:

	PIE	PG	Ved.	PIE	PG	Ved.
	Singular			*Plural*		
Nom.	gʷōws	gʷows	gā́us	gʷówes	gʷowes	gā́vas
Acc.	gʷōm	gʷōn	gā́m	gʷōms	gʷōs	gā́s
Dat.	gʷéwey	gʷowey	gáve	gʷéwbh-	gʷowpʰi	góbhyas
Gen.	gʷews	gʷowos	gós	gʷéwōm	gʷowōn	gávām
Loc.	gʷéwi	gʷowi	gávi	gʷéwsu	gʷowhi	góṣu

The Pre-PIE paradigm had the same stem in the nom. and acc.: nom. sg. ***gʷows*, acc. ***gʷowm*. Note the sequence **-*wm*, which could not have occurred in 'classical' PIE, whose phonotactics would require **gʷowm̥*. Conceivably the real shape was indeed ***gʷowm̥*, as some authorities hold; but **gʷowm* accords better with the next development, namely, the loss of the *-*w*- with compensatory lengthening, thus PIE **gʷōm*; similarly, acc.pl.

*g^w*ōms*, rather than expected **g^w*owms* or **g^w*owm̥s*, whence Ved. *gā́s*, Av. *gå*, Dor. βῶς. Since a long vowel in the nom.sg. was already a trait of many consonant stems, such as **pH̥₂tḗr* 'father' < ***pH̥₂ters* (282), the acc.sg. *g^w*ōm* led to the introduction of a long vowel into the nom.sg., *g^w*ōws*, which via Osthoff's Law (63.2) gives G βοῦς (the circumflex is secondary, 244, end), as well as L *bōs*, Ved. *gā́us*. Acc.sg. *g^w*ōm* gives G βῶν, attested in Doric.[1]

In all dialects of G the nom. and acc. continued to interact, so that in Att.-Ion. the acc. βῶν was replaced by βοῦν (early; βῶν is found—once—in Hom. in the meaning 'shield') patterned on the nom.; in Dor., contrariwise, the inherited nom. was replaced by βῶς patterned on the acc.

Regarding the PIE paradigm, we are plainly not here dealing with a root noun of the **p^e/od-* 'foot' or **dyew-* 'sky/day' varieties (such as, that is, *g^w*ōws* nom., *g^w*ōm* acc., *g^w*wós* gen., *g^w*wéy* dat., *g^w*usú* loc.pl.).

Some authorities redesign the reconstruction as *g^w*eH₃u-*: nom. *g^w*eH₃u-s*, gen. *g^w*H₃ew-s*, and so on, that is a proterokinetic (272.2) inflection like **doru* 'tree, wood', gen. **drew-s*. This would explain both the ubiquitous *o*-vocalism and the absence of palatalization phenomena in InIr.; but it raises as many problems as it solves. For example, the nom. *gā́us* occurs 22 times in the RV in all periods and is never disyllabic, unlike disyllabic *nā́us* 'ship' < **neH₂us*, 328. More troubling, the acc.sg. should have been *g^w*eH₃wm̥*, PInIr. ˣ*gāvam*, G ˣβω(ϝ)α; and the loc.sg. should have been *g^w*eH₃wi*, PInIr. ˣ*gāvi*, G ˣβω(ϝ)ι. But no such forms occur, and it is hard to see how such well-integrated forms could have vanished without a trace.

The correct explanation is that we have here an ACROSTATIC paradigm (272.1). The salient features of this paradigm are tonic accent on the root throughout, with *o*-grade in the nom. and acc. and *e*-grade in at least some other cases; case endings that ablaut (the most securely attested is the gen. sg.) take the zero grade. There is a lack of evidence regarding the distribution of *e*/*o*-ablaut of the stem, beyond the testimony of G δεσ- in δεσπότης < **dems* gen. 'house' (per 228.3), and the telltale -*ă*- in Ved. *gáve* dat., *gávi* loc. On the basis of Ved. *gávām* gen.pl. we also infer *g^w*éwōm*.[2]

If L *bōs* were a native word, it would confirm *g^w*ōws*, because *-*ows* would have given *-*ūs*. But PItal. **ow* gives Sab. *ō*, and in any case in a dialect borrowing we are not dealing with diachronic developments proper to L, and that applies to the paradigm as a whole: loan-words do not as a rule

[1] The theory sanctified by time is that the loss of **w* in acc. *g^w*ōm* was specifically traceable to the long vocalism of original **g^w*ōwm*, which presupposes nom. *g^w*ōws* as the source of the long vowel. The explanation endorsed here reverses the direction of influence.

[2] This *gávām* occurs about 50 times thus in the RV, scanned as transmitted. But once, in an early hymn, it apparently scans *gā́vām*. It is easier to find an anological model for the creation of *gávām* than for *gā́vām*; but in view of the trifling headway of such analogies elsewhere in the paradigm—the gen.sg. *gṓs*, which is very frequent, may perhaps only three times be read **gávas*—it is likeliest that *gávām* is the genuine form of the gen.pl.

retain morphological features of the source, beyond trivial details of the English *fungus, fungi* sort (and then in a technical lexicon only. When words of this kind become everyday vocabulary, as in *medium/media* and *data*, the niceties of loan-morphology quickly erode). The very ordinary-looking consonant-stem inflection of L *bōs, bovis*, apart from the unique nom.sg., is therefore without value as evidence for the earlier history of the paradigm.

L *bovem* acc. is analogical for **bōm* or the like (= U **bum**), on the basis of oblique forms like gen. *bovis* (*pedis* : *pedem* :: *bovis* : *X*). Nom. *bovis*, cited by Varro, is likewise analogical. Vedic preserves the PIE state of affairs: nom. *gā́us*, acc. *gā́m* (which like Av. *gąm* is occasionally scanned as a disyllable), acc.pl. *gā́s* (rarely disyllabic). The disyllabic scansions are innovations.

The remaining cases in G and L are built straightforwardly to reflexes of a stem **gʷow-* (indistinguishable in Italic from the reflexes of **gʷew-*). This is the same sort of leveling that introduced uniform stems for *r-* and *n*-stems (284, 286-7). L *bovēs* and G βόας acc.pl. are equally remote from PIE **gʷōms*. (Some think that Dor. βῶς acc.pl. is the innovation, but there are no models for such an analogy and the Dor. form is fully in accord with expectations.)

On the evidence of Av. *gə̄uš* abl./gen. and the very frequent Rigvedic *gós*, the inherited form had full grade of the stem but with zero grade, **-s*, of the gen.sg. ending. G βο(ϝ)ός, L *bovis* are analogical. (If **gʷowos* had been the form to begin with, the rationale for Indo-Iranian **gaws* would be unfathomable.)

Of the various forms of the G dat.pl., the least altered is βουσί (= Ved. *góṣu*); βούεσσι is an innovation of the πόδεσσι stripe (277.6a). Βόεσσι and βοσίν imitate πόδεσσι and ποσ(σ)ί(ν), formed on some such model as πόδες : βό(ϝ)ες :: πόδεσσι : *X*, where *X* = βό(ϝ)εσσι. Similarly βό(ϝ)α, βό(ϝ)ας after the consonant stem forms seen in πόδα, πόδας.

a. The rare L *bōbus* (for *būbus* < **gʷowbh-*) fits with the original paradigm as reconstructed, but a loanword would not transmit details of an archaic and therefore idiosyncratic paradigm. Therefore *-ō-* must be from the nom.sg., along such analogical lines as *arcus* 'bow' : *arcubus* :: *bōs* : *X*.

b. Att. χοῦς, -οός 'gallon' inflects like βοῦς but was originally an *o*-stem **kʰowos* (cf. χέ(ϝ)ω 'pour', root **ǵhew-*), identical to χόος (χοῦς), gen. χόου (χοῦ) 'heap (of dirt)'. In Hellenistic G there are similar forms for νοῦς (νόος) 'mind', πλοῦς (πλόος) 'voyage', and others.

c. Avestan has no forms in *ǰ-*. The significance of this is that whereas Indic levels root-initial alternations resulting from the interaction of the Law of Palatals (153d) with ablaut, Av. is more conservative: for example PIE **gʷem-tu-* 'a going; course' appears in Ved. in the leveled form *gántu-*, but Av. retains the PInIr. shape *ǰantu-*; from the same root Av. has aor. (injunctive, 416) *-ǰə̄n* 3sg., *gəmən* 3pl., cf. Ved. aor. *(á)gan, (á)gman* (*gmán*) respectively.

Avestan and Vedic agree in the lack of evidence for the customary zero grade formations: full grade is securely attested even in such forms such as Ved. *góbhis* instr.pl. (=

Av. *gaobīš*) and *góṣu* loc.pl., namely in cases where zero grade is (where possible) otherwise the strict rule.

325. G Ζεύς, L *Iuppiter*, *Iovis* reflect a PIE paradigm built to an ablauting stem **dyew-*, **diw-*/**dyu-* 'blue sky, day' (zero grade **diw-* before vowel, **dyu-* before consonant). A secondary full grade is seen in the thematized stem **deyw-o-*. In the root noun, the ablaut scheme was hysterokinetic: full grade in the nom. and acc. of all numbers, and the loc.sg.; zero grade elsewhere. In the daughter languages this pattern was obscured by sound laws and leveling.

The origin of the special forms **dyēws* nom.sg. and **dyēm* acc. sg. is the same as for **gʷōws*, **gʷōm*, above: original ***dyewm* (or *-*wm̥*) became **dyēm* by a purely phonological development, on the basis of which **dyēws* replaced original ***dyěws* by analogy.

	PIE	Greek	Vedic
Nom.	dyḗws	Ζεύς	dyā́us
Voc.	dyew	Ζεῦ	dyāus
Acc.	dyḗm	(*)Ζήν[1]	dyā́m,[2] dívam
Dat.	diw-éy	Δι(ϝ)ει[3]	divé[4]
Abl.	diw-ós		divás[5]
Gen.	diw-ós	Δι(ϝ)ός	divás[6]
Loc.	dyéw-i	*Ζέϝι[7]	dyávi[8]
		Δι(ϝ)ί	diví

A note on Hitt.: Though the precise explanation of the form is uncertain—[ǰiu-]? [dziu-]? —Hitt. *ši-ú(-na)-* 'god' is thought to be cognate. (The usual form for the noun, to oversimplify somewhat, is a derived *a*-stem, *ši-ú-na-aš*; a more archaic form is seen in possessed nouns in the older language, *ši-i-uš-mi-iš* 'my god'.)

1. This form MAY be attested in Homer 8 times (326), next to Ζῆνα (the normal form) and 11 instances of the obviously analogical Δί(ϝ)α.
2. The usual Vedic form; *dívam* is much less frequent, and found prevailingly in late passages.
3. Attested in Ion. (Corinth) Δι(ϝ)ει, Myc. *di-we*, and in compounds like Cyp. διϝει-φιλος 'dear to Zeus'.
4. A post-Vedic *dyave* also occurs.
5. This is the usual form; it is both frequent and early. A secondary *dyós* (after regular *gós*, 324) occurs twice; the peculiar *dyā́us* occurs once, in a late passage; the inspiration for the analogy is unobvious.
6. The usual form; extremely frequent. *Dyós* (as if **dyew-s*) occurs six times. It is not likely to be old, even though a parallel form occurs in Av. *dyaoš*.
7. Not attested. The grade of Δι(ϝ)ι, Διί, and Δῖ if not in fact inherited (see note 8), was influenced by the orig. dat.
8. RV *diví* which agrees with G Δι(ϝ)ί is much more frequent than *dyávi*; nor does *dyávi* mainly occur in antique passages. But if *e*-grade is de rigueur in a loc. sg. *diví* and Διϝί must be innovations.

---

326. GREEK. Nom.sg. **dyēws* > Ved. *dyā́us* 'sky; day', and presumably G Ζεύς (per Osthoff's Law, 63.2), Corinth. Δευς, Lesb. Σδεῦς. Although PIE **dyěws* would account for most data except InIr., the plene vowel (31) in

Old Hitt. *ši-i-uš-mi-iš* 'my god' may confirm an ancestral long vowel. The long diphthong in the nom.sg. is here explained (324) as analogical to the acc.sg., whether in PIE or later.

Voc.sg. **dyew*, G Ζεῦ. (The inherited voc., which would have been **dyo*, is lost in Indic, having been displaced by a form homophonous with the nominative; in any case the voc. occurs but once in the entire RV.)

Acc.sg. **dyēm* underlies Ved. *dyā́m*, G *Ζήν, Ζῆν (uncertainly attested, but it is the expected form and its prior existence is indispensable for explaining the form Ζῆνα; see below).

In G there were wholesale levelings, with results so different from dialect to dialect that the PG starting-point must have been a paradigm little changed from PIE. One basis for leveling was the stem-form **diw-*, the weak grade, as Δι(ϝ)ός gen. (whose form is ancient), Δι(ϝ)ί dat. (that is, loc., where it presumably is not), and Δί(ϝ)α acc. (manifestly a G coinage). These forms, minus the -ϝ-, are the standard ones for Attic. The extension of the weak grade to acc. Δία (11× in Homer) in place of original *Ζῆν(α) (Ved. *dyā́m*) is parallel to the creation of ἄνδρα. El. Ζῑ (next to El. Δῑ) 'Διί' imported the Ζ- of the nom./voc.

In Hom. and various dialects another set of cases was created on a new stem Ζην-, originally the acc. *Ζήν < PIE **dyēm*. The latter is apparently attested some eight times in Homer, Θ 206 for example; but as in all such passages the next word begins with a vowel, the reading is ambiguous. But once remodeled Ζῆνα (Cret. Δηνα) appeared, the remaining two cases built to the same stem (Ζηνός, Ζηνί) followed easily.

In much the same way τίς, *τίν < **kʷis*, **kʷim* 'who' was remodeled as τίνα, with subsequent τίνος gen., τίνι dat. (378). (Expected τίν, like Ζῆν—326—is but uncertainly attested.)

The inspiration for Ζῆνα and τίνα is the oddity of the inherited forms compared to the pattern otherwise universal in the large and important class of nouns with monosyllabic nom.sg.: φλέψ, φλεβά 'vein', θρίξ, τριχά 'hair', θῑς, θῑνά 'heap', a pattern paralleled in consonant stems in general, as φύλαξ, φύλακα. Compared to these, the inherited acc.sg. **kʷis*, **kʷin* and **ǰeus*, **ǰēn* would stop too soon, so to say, as well as differ morphologically from the acc.sg. of all other nouns with monosyllabic nom.sg. Both peculiarities are eliminated by the addition of the usual cons. stem acc.sg. marker -α to the inherited acc. (Note that this history is different from the development of the stem seen in ἕνα acc. 'one', for which see 294.1.)

327. LATIN. The original paradigm split into two almost completely distinct ones: *diēs* 'day' (very rarely 'Jupiter') and *Iuppiter*, *Iovis* 'Jupiter' (but the meaning 'day, sky' in the expression *sub iove* 'alfresco').

The original nom. **dyews*, whether or not by Osthoff's Law from **dyēws* (326), is not part of the L paradigm for 'day'. The paradigmatic nom. sg. *diēs* is back-formed from the acc. **diēm*. This form is an especially appropriate fulcrum for remodeling in view of the L usage known as *accusative of duration of time*, and in fact it appears to be the basis for the entire 'day' paradigm. (The usual form, *diem*, is from **diēm* by **83.1**.)

The original nom.sg. survives in L entombed in two fossilized expressions, one in the sense of 'Jupiter' and one as 'day': *mediusfidius* (*mē diūs fidius*) an asseverative oath—something like 's'welp me god'—and *nudiustertius* (*nū diūs tertius*) 'day before yesterday', lit. 'the third day now'; similar phrases, as *nudius decimus* 'nine days ago', are innovations based on this. (The form is often erroneously *dīus*, contaminated by *dī(v)us*.)

Regarding the treatment of the initial cons., it is clear that **dy* > L [(y)y] (**194**), as in *Iovis* < **dyewes* gen.sg., so the nom. and acc.sg. should be ˣ*iēs* and ˣ*iēm* (monosyllabic). The survival of the *d-* has been traced to positional alternants, **diyēs* and the like, via Lindeman's Law (**181**), but it is more likely to be simple analogy to, or contamination by, **dīwo-* < **deyw-o-*, derivatives in **diw-*, and the oblique cases of **dyew-* (before they were remodeled out of existence in L).

In PIE the word is often combined with **pH̥₂ter-* 'father': G Ζεῦ πάτερ, Ved. *dyā́uḥ pitā́*; in Ital. this combination became stereotypic: U **iupater** (also dat.sg. **iuve patre**), L *Iūpiter* voc. (**61**, **66.1**), then *Iuppiter* (**234**). This vocative form serves for the nominative. The status of *Diēspiter* nom. is uncertain; it may be a genuinely ancient form, but by common consent the other cases in the paradigm (acc. *Diēspitrem* for example) are held to be secondary.

The other forms of the Jove paradigm are from **dyew-*, whence (**61**, **194**) early L DIOVOS, DIOVEI and the like, usual *Iovis*, *Iovī* (Osc. **diúveí**, **iuveí**, Umb. **iuve**), *Iovem*, dat. *Iove* < loc. **dyewi*. The expected zero grade of the stem is found only in compounds such as *trīduō* (**tris-diwōd*) 'in three days'.

a. The earliest inscriptions with initial DI- in Ital. are possibly accurate indications of contemporary pronunciation; but from say the 3rd century BC it is certainly an artificial spelling, which persisted after the *d-* ceased being pronounced in ordinary speech. This is proved by inscriptions with pseudoarchaic DI- in divine names which never had had a **d-* (*Iānus* and *Iūturna*), and the occurrence of IVNONE and DIOVIS in the same (short) inscription.

b. Nominative *Iovis* (Enn.), *Diovis* (Varro) are secondary creations based on *i*-stems (among a number such forms quoted by the grammarians). A different innovation is indicated by an inscription of uncertain date from Praeneste which includes IOVOS. It is one of eleven labels on the figures of deities; the other ten are unambiguously nom., and this is surely nominative too.

c. L *dĭū* 'by day; for a long time' is either an endingless loc. **dyew* or, more likely, an apocopated reflex of **dyewi* (and therefore a doublet of *Iove*, much like *prōvidentia* next to *prūdentia* **61.2a**). The *-ī-* of *dīū*, in place of well-attested *dĭū*, is imported from *dīvus*, below.

d. L *dīvus* 'divine; god', and the phrase *sub dīvō* 'outdoors, alfresco' (lit. 'under the sky') are from the thematic stem **deyw-o-*, which also split into two distinct paradigms, *deus* 'god' and *dīvus* 'divine'; see **183a**.

e. L *Diālis* 'of or pertaining to Jupiter', chiefly in the collocation *flāmen Diālis* 'priest of Jupiter', is a derivative of **dyew-* of a type common in L religious terminology (*Vestālis* and the like); but exactly what originally preceded *-ālis* is obscure.

328. PIE *neH_2u- 'boat' was a non-ablauting cons. stem:

	PIE	PG	Ved.	PIE	PG	Ved.
		Singular			*Plural*	
Nom.	neH_2us	naus	nā́us	neH_2wes	nāwes	nā́vas
Acc.	neH_2wm̥	nāwa	nā́vam	neH_2wm̥s	nāwas	
Dat.	neH_2wey	nāwey		neH_2ubh-	naup^h^i	nāubhís
Gen.	neH_2wos	nāwos	nāvás	neH_2wō̃m	nāwōn	
Loc.	neH_2wi	nāwi	nāví	neH_2usu	nawhi, -si	

The chief potential for complication here is the alternation between *u and *w (fully automatic, according to whether a syllabic follows), which interacts with the rules governing the development of laryngeals: *-eH_2u- becomes in effect *-*au*- whereas *-eH_2w- becomes *-*āw*-.

In Ved. the paradigm reveals that *neH_2us originally became PInIr. ***naüs**—that is, it is still disyllabic in its single Rigvedic occurrence. This ***naüs*** eventually contracts to a long diphthong (Skt. ***nā́us***), in curious contrast to the development of *-*aï*-, which becomes either -*e*- (as in ***préṣṭha***- 'dearest', still scanned ***práïṣṭha***- in early Vedic) or -***ayi***- (as in ***rayí***-, **329**) rather than -*āi*-; likewise presumably ***nāubhis*** inst.pl. (regrettably not attested in the RV) < *neH_2ubhis = G ναῦφι.

In G the original paradigm would have been something like that shown above. There is no way of telling whether nom. ναῦς is the straight reflex of *neH_2us or the Osthoff outcome (**63.2**) of **nāws* (with -*ā*- imported from the cases with -*w*-). Such leveling is seen in Hom. νηῦς nom. and νηυσί dat.pl., in which the -η- proper to the *w*-cases has been introduced into the diphthongal cases. The original diphthong from *neH_2u- remains in ναῦφι 'from aboard ship', ναύτης 'sailor'. Gen. sg. *neH_2wos > **nāwos*, whence Dor. νᾱός, Hom. νηός, Att. νεώς (**79.3**; cf. Ved. *nāvás*). So in other cases, stem νᾱ(ϝ)-, Hom. νη-, Att. νη- in νηί, νῆες or shortened in νεῶν. Att. ναῦν acc.sg. is secondary, but on what pattern is unclear. The original state of affairs is found in Hom. νῆα (= Ved. *nā́vam*), νῆας pl. (Ved. form not quotable, but given by the grammarians as *nā́vas*).

In L the word became a commonplace *i*-stem, *nāvis, -is*; a number of the original case forms (acc. *nāvem*, dat. *nāvei*) would have been ambiguous as to form class, and as mentioned in **309** a miscellany of nouns which had peculiar inflection in L acquired a more or less impermanent nom.sg. in -*is*. But for this word the absorption into the *i*-stems was complete.

329. PIE *reH_1i- '(valuable) object' is not attested in G, but is found in Ved. and L. The original paradigm was like that of *neH_2u- 'boat' (**328**):

	PIE	Vedic	Latin
Nom.	*$reH_1$is	rayís[1]	rēs
Acc.	*reH_1im? -ym̥?	rayím[2]	rem
Dat.	*reH_1yey	rāyé	rei
Gen.	*reH_1yos	rāyás	rē̆ī

1. From **răĭs*; Skt. *rā́s*, often quoted in this connection, is a late, analogical form. It bears a merely coincidental resemblance to L *rēs*.

2. The normal form in the RV; once in a late hymn—and unique in all of Indic—is found *rā́m* acc.sg. Although it is standard to align this with L *rem*, in fact it is analogical, patterned on *gā́m* 'cow' (above) by some such proportion as *gā́vas* nom.pl.: *rā́yas* :: *gā́m* : *X*, where *X* = *rā́m*. The acc.sg. form prescribed by the grammarians is *rā́yam*; it is not found at all in the Vedas.

Nom.sg. L *rēs* is necessarily analogical—the PIE nom.sg. **reH₁is* undisturbed would have given PItal. **reis* whence L *ˣrīs* (57)—but the exact history of the L nom.sg. form is uncertain. It might reflect a form **rēys*, created on the basis of other case-forms in **rēy-* < **reH₁y-*. It might be based on acc. **rēm* (below), like the creation of *diēs* 'day' after **diēm* acc. (327). Of course, disyllabic **reïs* would have become *rēs* regularly (**88.3**), like *sōl* 'sun' from disyllabic **suol* (**88.3c**), though it is unlikely that **-eï-* < **-eHi-* could have lasted long enough to do so.

Acc.sg. The correct account of the history of L *rem* (**rēm*) depends on what the PIE form of the acc.sg. was. The phonologically simplest derivation would start from **reH₁ym̥*, not unambiguously attested elsewhere; from this, **rē(y)em* > L **rēm*, *rem*. On the other hand, as in the case of the nom.sg., above, regular phonological development from **reH₁im* via **reïm* (= Ved. *rayím*) is remotely thinkable. See 330 (5th decl.) following.

THE LATIN FIFTH DECLENSION

330. The history of the L fifth declension is obscure, and has long been a topic of much discussion. There is nothing similar in the other IE languages. Lith. *iē*-stems (*žẽmė* 'land' gen.sg. *žẽmės*), which look somewhat similar, have been shown to be largely, if not wholly, *iyā*-stems in origin. Elsewhere there are a few isolated nouns in *-ē* which are probably verb stems used substantively, proper to compounds of the type seen in Ved. *śraddhā́-* 'faith' (a compound of root *dhā-* 'put', PIE **dheH₁-*) which inflects as an ordinary *ā*-stem. G χρή 'necessity' and ἀπόχρη 'sufficiency; enough' are 3sg. verb-forms which underwent reinterpretation in such expressions as ἀπόχρη τινί 'is sufficient for someone' > 'enough [for someone]'.

In reality, the 'fifth declension' is a historical accident—a collection of nouns of heterogeneous ancestry which converged (in a none too orderly fashion) on a type. This explains the difficulty of finding analogues in other languages, including, most particularly, the other Italic languages; and also the variability in morphological detail from noun to noun and from period to period.

The nouns in the fifth declension are all feminine with the exception of *diēs* 'day' and its derivative *merīdiēs* 'noon/south'; and the great bulk of them are abstracts in *-iēs*. The three exceptions are: *rēs*, whose history is given above (329); and *spēs* 'hope' and *fidēs* 'faith', whose histories are considerably more uncertain. In OL there were some fifth decl. forms unknown later, such as *plēbēs* (classical *plēbs*, but NB the adj. *plēbēius*). G names in -ευς (*Achillēs*) and -ης (*Themistoclēs*) early inflect as fifth declension nouns, later as third.

a. The question of whether Sabellian has such a form class bears on the question of the validity of an Italic Branch of IE (17-8): the type qua type is not inherited from PIE, so its presence in both Sab. and L would be evidence for a period of common development. (On the other hand, the absence of the type in Sab. would have no bearing on the question of common descent.) The few possible Sab. attestations are cited in the literature as follows. (1) The U *iouie* acc.pl. (twice), *ioues* dat.pl. (once); meaning uncertain, but apparently 'young [? soldiers]'. But if we are dealing with reflexes of **yewH-* 'young', these forms are ultimately from a comparative **yewHyos-* or **yewHyes-* (Ved. *yávīyas-*, OIr. *oa*). They either show leached semantics, 'young' < *'younger' parallel to the commonplace development of 'new' (the normal meaning of RV *návīyas-*) from *'newer, rather new'; or else they are literally 'younger' or 'lesser'. The latter reading is easily allowed by the contexts, in which the term invariably contrasts with *ner-* 'leaders? nobles?' perhaps simply 'men'. (2) The forms of U **ri** abl. and **ri** dat.sg. accord well with the L correspondents *rē* < **rēd* and *rēī*, but these forms in both U and L can be traced more or less directly to details of the original **reH₁i-* paradigm, with no implications for a special form class like the L fifth declension.

Manifestly, there is no case for a Sabellian analogue to the L fifth declension.

b. L *famēs* is said to have 3rd as well as 5th decl. forms. But metrics confirm that the abl. *fame* has -*ē* rather than -*ĕ*, and the only seeming 3rd decl. forms apart from grammarians' mention is Plaut. *famis* nom.sg. next to his usual *famēs*. (Whether this *famis* persisted or was reinvented, it is found also in the Appendix Probi.)

331. INFLECTION.

1. Gen.sg. There are several forms for the ending. The oldest is -*ēs* (*-*ēes*) known through citations by ancient authorities from early poetry (*diēs*) and scattered instances in literature (such as Lucr. *rabiēs* 'madness') where they are often edited out of our standard editions. Its similarity to the inherited gen.sg. of the *ā*-stems, namely -*ās*, led to its replacement by -*ēī* at the same time that -*ās* was remodeled as -*āī* (263.7). In OL this remodeled ending always has two heavy syllables. These prosodics persisted after -*i*-, thus in later periods regularly *diēī*, *faciēī*. After consonants, however, the ending became -*ěī* by 85. The persistence of -*iēī* is mysterious, as the shortening of a vowel before another vowel should have affected -*iēī* and -*ēī* alike. —In another trend altogether, and parallel to the development of -*āī* to -*ae* (263.7), the ending monophthongized to -*ei* [ey], whence eventually by 57 -*ī*, so *fidei*, *fidē* (that is, -*ẹ̄*), *fidī* not only in the early playwrights but also in Ovid and Horace, among others, and epigraphically (DII, DIE). This development, being parallel to -*āī* > -*ae*, is the expected one, and probably represents the colloquial pronunciation; the disyllabic ending, with its unexpected distinction between -*ěī* and -*iēī*, is possibly an artifact of schoolmasterly prescriptivism.

2. Dat.sg. The early monosyllabic -*ei*, that is, -*ẹ̄y*, is not the expected outcome of *-*ē*-*ey* of whatever age. A long diphthong like *-*ēy* should have

lost the glide, whence *-*ē*. The regular form, -*ei*, is therefore a L creation modeled on the *ā*-stem form -*āi*, also monosyllabic. (The prosodics of this -*ei* are revealed by orthographic hesitation in OL between -*ei*, -*i*, and -*e*.) There is some reason for thinking that in late Republican times the diphthongal pronunciation was most persistent in the monosyllable *rei*, even as *fidei*, *diei* (so written) were being pronounced *fidī*, *diī*. Eventually the dat.sg. fell completely together with the gen.sg. (above), and Roman grammarians prescribe the same distinction between -*eī* vs. -*iēī* for the dat.

3. Acc.sg. L -*em* < *-*ēm*.

4. Abl.sg. L -*ē*, U -i are commonly traced to *-*ēd*, formed after the analogy of -*ād*, -*ōd*, but the lack of quotable forms actually showing -*d* is peculiar. It is therefore more than ordinarily thinkable that we are here dealing with the old instr. -*ē* < *-*eH*$_n$, particularly in the case of *rē* and *diē*. The former would follow directly from **rēē* < **reH*$_1$*yeH*$_1$ (= Ved. *rāyā*); and note that for 'day' the PIE inst. seems to have had adverbial significance 'by day; for a day' (as in the very frequent Ved. *dívā*, with original stem grade).

5. PLURAL CASES. Neither abstract nouns nor personal names readily occur in the plural—Cicero goes so far as to deny that *spērum* and *speciēbus* are possible forms (but see **a**, below)—so plural formations in this class are practically confined to *rēs* and *diēs*.

Nom.pl. PIE **reH*$_1$*yes* (Ved. *rā́yas*) would give attested *rēs*, and **dyewes* would give *diēs* homophonous with the nom.sg. (The old **eH*$_2$-stem ending, -*ās* is unlikely to have played any role in this: the patterns are not really parallel, and NB the failure of nom.pl. *rēs*, *diēs* to join with the *ā*-stem remodeling of -*ās* as -*āi* (265.1) in contrast to the treatment of the gen.sg., 1, above.)

The remaining cases are built to the stems *rē*-, *diē*-: gen.pl. -*ērum* (*-*ē*-*som*) like -*ārum* (*-*ā*-*som*), acc.pl. -*ēs* like -*ās* (? or earlier, as *-*ēns* like *-*āns*). The dat./abl. form -*ēbus* has no straightforward source: imitation of specific forms like *būbus* 'cows' is unlikely to be the whole story, or even much of it; nor can the forms be traced directly from any ancestral form. The obviousness of the stems *rē*-, *diē*- and the readiness with which L coined such forms as *deābus* and *filiābus* (265.3**b**) are part of the answer.

a. For an abstract noun, L *spēs* forms plurals pretty freely, not unlike G ἐλπίδες, and such forms were possibly inspired by the G. This is stated as fact by some authorities, but NE *hopes*, first attested only in the 17th century, is most unlikely to owe its genesis to imitation of any classical forms; the L development could have been as spontaneous as the English. Early attestations vacillate between nom.pl. *spēs* and *spērēs*; Varro quotes *spēribus* abl.pl. as well.

Nouns in other declensions occasionally have fifth declension pl. endings, as *sordērum* (Plt.; *sordēs* 'filth' 3rd decl.) and *boverum* (*bōs*), *regerum* (*rēx*) (presumably -*ērum*; quantity not recoverable from the citations by the grammarians).

332. NOUNS OF VARIABLE DECLENSION, or heteroclites (ἑτερόκλιτα lit. 'differently bent'), have various histories. They may represent a mixture of

two inherited stems, as L *domus* 'house' which is found following both the *u*-stem and *o*-stems declensions. Such matters are usually proper to the study of lexicon, though this particular heteroclisis may be ancient (there is a parallel discrepancy in the declensions of the cognate nouns, which are *u*-stem in OCS *domŭ*—and indirectly in Ved. *dámūnas-* 'dear to the house' —but *o*-stem in G *δόμος*, Ved. *dáma-*).

A more general source of heteroclisis is the partial interpenetration of what were once two or more distinct paradigms. The starting point for such confluence is of course a form or forms common to different paradigms. Being dependent upon specific details, such conflations are different in different languages even when they are descended from a common ancestor:

In L, as discussed in 308, the *i*- and cons. stems partially merge; in G it is the *ŭ*- and *ū*-stems; in Skt. the devī and vr̥kīs types progress from being almost totally unalike to differing only in the nom.sg.; in Go. the *i*-stems and *a*-stems (the PIE *o*-stems) nearly merge, and many root nouns have *u*-stem forms. In G, too, neologisms like *Σωκράτην* acc. (300) are based on *Θουκυδίδην* as a result of their common nom.sg. -*ης*; in L there were a number of interchanges between *o*-, *u*-, and *s*-stem forms, as a result of the common nom.sg. -*us* (333.1–2).

Sometimes a difference in meaning grows up around competing forms, so *pecus*, -*udis* n. typically a single animal ('head') next to collective *pecus*, -*oris* n. 'cattle, livestock, herd'. (Neither formation is old; both replace inherited *pecu* n.) In the most extreme cases, leveling turns a single original form into several more or less unrelated paradigms, as *diēs*, -*ēī* 'day' vs. *Iuppiter*, *Iovis* 'Jupiter' (327).

a. Some authorities assume that *r*/*n*-stems of the *femur*, *feminis* 'thigh' type (290) arose by some pre-PIE heteroclisis. The view endorsed here (292) is that the interchange of **r* and **n* is more likely to have been purely phonological in origin. It is in fact possible that the familiar *r*- and *n*-stem paradigms, or some of them, grew out of *r*/*n*-stem inflection by leveling. Cf. the case of the Italian heteroclites mentioned in 334, such as *filo* sg. 'thread', *fila* pl. (for expected *fili*); these APPEAR to be a composite (heteroclitic) paradigm but in reality they are conservative reflexes of earlier *fīlum*, *fīla*: what has changed is the overall noun system.

333. Among the many examples of heteroclitic forms in G and L the following may be noticed here:

1. Interchange between *o*- and *u*-stem forms in L. Beside *domus*, mentioned above, several names of trees fluctuate thus, as *fāgus* 'beech' and *laurus* 'laurel', which are basically *o*-stems but also have an acc.pl. -*ūs*; conversely *quercus* 'oak' is prevailingly *u*-stem but gen.pl. *quercōrum* is also attested. In early L, *u*-stem nouns in -*tus* (a large class) have a gen.sg. -*ī* (314.8).

2. Interchange between *o*-stems and neut *s*-stems. G *σκότος* 'darkness', gen.sg. *σκότου* or *σκότους*, and so in the other cases. L *vulgus*, -*ī* 'the people'; *pelagus*, -*ī* (lw. from G *πέλαγος* n. *s*-stem) 'ocean'; *vīrus*, -*ī* (cognate with G

ʼἰός, -ου) 'slime; poison' are ordinary *o*-stems except for their acc.sg. in *-us* (= nom.sg.) as if they were *s*-stem neuters.

3. Interchange between *o*-stems and cons. stems. Mainly in neuters, where the nom./acc.pl. form was ambiguous. L *vās* 'vessel', *vāsis* but pl. *vāsa, -ōrum.* L *iūgerum* (a land measure), *-ī* but pl. *iūgera, iūgerum* (which last is of course itself ambiguous, owing to the persistence in measures of the old *o*-stem gen.pl. in *-um,* as *nummum* 'of coins' (260.5) and may have contributed to the use of 3rd decl. endings in the rest of the pl., so *iūgeribus*). There are examples, chiefly epigraphic, of *-ibus* for *-īs* (VETRANIBVS, PENATIBVS). Contrariwise, the *o*-stem gen.pl. in *-ōrum* is widely attested in cons. stems: FRATRORVM, PARENTORVM, MENSORVM, MVLIERORVM (!). Such forms are virtually limited to inscriptions.

a. Chiefly in inscriptions, the *u*-stem gen.pl. *-uum* is also well attested in cons. stems, as FRATRVVM, -OM (very frequent), MENSVOM, VIRTVTVOM.

4. For L, cf. also the interchange between the first and fifth decl. as *māteria* vs. *māteriēs*; between the third and fifth in some of the nouns in *-es,* as *plēbs* vs. *plēbēs* (Varro); between *i*-stems and cons. stems in *canis* 'dog', gen.pl. *canum,* and so on (309).

5. For G cf. also the mixture of *τ*-stem forms with others in neuters (293), also in γέλως 'husband's sister' (321a); the *o*- and *υ*-stem forms in υἱός, υἱύς 'son'; the diphthongal inflection of Att. χοῦς 'gallon'(324b); and so on.

334. NOUNS OF VARIABLE GENDER. Many nouns have different gender in singular and plural, with or without a distinction in sense. G ὁ σῖτος 'grain', pl. τὰ σῖτα; ὁ δεσμός 'bond; halter', pl. τὰ δεσμά and οἱ δεσμοί; τὸ στάδιον a measure of length, pl. τὰ στάδια and οἱ στάδιοι. L *locus* m. 'place; citation', pl. *loca* n. 'places', *locī* m. 'citations, passages in authors'; *iocus* 'jest', pl. either *ioca* or *iocī*; *frēnum* 'bridle', pl. either *frēna* or *frēnī.*

Probably owing to the coincidence in form between the nom./acc.n.pl. in *-a* and the nom./acc.fem. in *-a* (with the loss of *-m*), in late VL, many neut. plurals turned into singular feminines of the first declension, such as *gaudia* (L *gaudium* 'delight') whence It. *gioia,* Fr. *joie*; similarly *opera* 'work(s)', *ligna* '(pieces of) wood', *folia* 'leaves' (It. *opera, legna* 'firewood', *foglia* 'leaf, leaves'; cf. *foglio* 'sheet of paper'). In some cases a collective meaning promoted the reassignment, though that is hard to see in the case of *gaudia* for one.

In the classical languages some gender variations were routinized, as in the typical use of a neuter noun for a fruit beside a similarly formed but feminine noun for the name of the plant: G ἄπιον 'a pear', ἄπιος f. 'pear tree'; σῦκον 'a fig', συκῆ (συκέη) 'fig tree'; L *mōrum* 'a mulberry', *mōrus* f. 'mulberry tree'; *cerasum* 'a cherry', *cerasus* f.'cherry tree'.

The tendencies described in the preceding sections were important forces in the evolution of the Romance languages. *U*-stems and neuter *o*-stems generally coalesce with masculine *o*-stems in Romance. But in It. some original neut.pl. forms persist in minor paradigms that the school grammars call 'masculine nouns that are feminine [singular!]

in the plural', so *uovo* m. 'egg' pl. *uova* (Lat. *ovum*, *-a*). In some cases the conservative pl. competes with the regular one, as *fila* and *fili*, both pl. of *filo* 'thread' (L *fīlum*). In some instances there are differences in meaning: to *corno* 'horn' (regular from L *cornu*), pl. *corna* (of an animal), vs. the innovative *corni* (the musical instruments); *braccio* 'arm' (L *brāchium*), pl. *braccia* (the body parts), vs. *bracci* (of rivers; wings of a building or an army). Indirect evidence of a period of paradigmatic confusion in early Romance is the remarkable fact that most of the nouns exhibiting these properties in It. were actually masc. to start with, such that the pl. in *-a* is a secondary development rather than inherited: so *mura* 'walls of a city' vs. *muri* 'walls' (in general) to sg. *muro* < L *mūrus*.

335. INDECLINABLE AND DEFECTIVE NOUNS. Indeclinable nouns are words which are syntactically noun-like but which do not have the usual morphological apparatus of nouns. In an IE language in which morphological traits are the primary definers of form classes, such a notion verges on a contradiction in terms, and on the face of it uninflected nouns in G and L are aberrant.

Among the indeclinable nouns are the names of the letters in both G and L, as G ἄλφα, βῆτα; L *ā*, *bē*, and the rest. (The *τ*-inflection of G letter names, as σίγματος gen. sg., formed after analogy of the ὄνομα type, is a late development.) Similarly, many numbers are uninflected (L *sex*, G ἕξ 'six'). Some of these formerly had inflection but lost it (PIE 'four' inflected for gender and case, as it does in G, but L *quattuor* is indeclinable).

Most foreign names and words are somehow accommodated in the inflectional systems of L and G, but Egyptian words are undeclined in Herodotus, and in the Septuagint the names transliterated from Hebrew are indeclinable (though in later texts the usual endings start to appear); the same is true of such exotica as the names of Egyptian months and of Semitic weights and measures. In L there are only a few such, for example *abba* 'father'.

A basically different type are the indeclinables that have a syntactic basis—words that are stuck (so to say) in a given case. So L *frūgī* 'useful, worthy', apparently a dat. of *frūx*, *frūgis* 'fruit; virtue', is effectively an adjective as the result of reinterpretation of some (unknown) phrase. L *fās* and *nefās* are virtually limited to expressions where a nom. or acc. would be expected anyway (most commonly *fās est* 'it is right'). And of course, in a sense all the infinitives of G and L are indeclinable nouns; see 551-3.

Hom. nom./acc. δῶ = δῶμα 'house' (in Hes., pl. δῶ = δώματα), κρῖ = κρῖθή 'barley', look like abbreviated forms (and as such were imitated by later writers); that is hardly likely to be the real explanation, but their actual source is uncertain.

In extreme instances the 'indeclinable noun' is in fact a fossilized phrase. So G χρεών (mostly nom./acc. but also τοῦ χρεών) 'need, necessity', which is from χρεὼ ὄν lit. 'it being a need', parallel to ἄδηλον ὄν 'it being uncertain'.

a. The various inflected forms of a word incidentally reveal much about its make-up, and hence its history; accordingly, a commonplace trait of indeclinables is a certain degree of opacity. For example, L *fās* looks like an *s*-stem, a root noun in the nom.sg.

This interpretation fits with derivatives (*nefārius* 'impious', *nefăstus* 'unholy'); and perhaps the lack of oblique forms is just a result of limited syntactic contexts. However, other interpretations are possible. The most interesting theory takes the form to be the active infinitive corresponding to *fārī* 'declare', that is, from something like PItal. **fāsi* with apocope of the final vowel predating rhotacism. Such an origin would neatly explain why the word does not inflect—it is already in a case, the loc.sg. (553.1).

336. Among the so-called *defective* nouns are many for which the lack of a quotable example of a particular case form is merely accidental—indeed, innumerable nouns in both G and L are not attested in all possible cases and numbers. The isolated G *νίφα* acc. 'snow' (Hesiod) is distinctive only because it is an extreme example of the same phenomenon: this acc.sg. is attested once, and is the sole relic of *νίψ**, *νίφος**, the inherited word for 'snow' corresponding to L *nix*, *nivis* (and, shifted to the thematic class, Go. *snaiws*, OE *snáw*, NE *snow*), but displaced by *χιών*, *χιόνος*. It is a stray relic, not a defective noun.

Nouns that are plural (or dual) only, such as G *(τὰ) ἔναρα* 'spoils', L *tenebrae* 'darkness', might be thought of as defective in a sense. More clearly defective are nouns in which one or more case is in a real sense missing. Sometimes the occurring forms are paradigmatically isolated, as G *μέθυ* n. 'wine, mead', which once had a full inflection on the evidence of cognate languages (and what is perh. the gen.sg. is seen in Myc. *me-tu-wo*); but in literary G it is known only in the nom./acc.sg. Sometimes the missing parts are 'filled out' by formations built to a different stem or perhaps totally unrelated. This kind of complementary defectiveness, known as *suppletion*, is much more evident in pronouns and verbs, but does occasionally occur in nouns. Thus for a long time the the proper nom.sg. *ἀρήν* 'lamb' implied by gen. *ἀρνός*, acc. *ἀρνά* and so on was unknown—*ἀμνός*, which has a full paradigm of its own, usually serves as the nom. to *ἀρνός*; but ΑΡΗΝ eventually turned up in a 5th century Attic inscription, and then ϜΑΡΗΝ was found in an earlier Cretan one. (This situation is typical: the missing items of a noun paradigm have usually been lost, as opposed to never having existed.[1]) The stem of *μέγας* m. 'big' is found in compounds (*μεγακήτης* 'cavernous') but in inflection only in *μέγας*, *μέγαν* acc.sg.m., and *μέγα* nom./acc.n.; the remaining forms are built to a derivative *μεγαλο-*, *μεγαλᾱ-* (-η-) (343 and 341).

G *εἷς* m., *μία* f., *ἕν* n. 'one' and Ζεύς, Διός raise an interesting question of definition. They LOOK like suppletive paradigms, but in both cases the oddity results from the action of regular sound laws upon what historically speaking is a regularly-constituted paradigm (294.1, 326). A definition of

[1] The case is otherwise with suppletive verbs: part of the explanation for compilations like G *φέρω*, *οἴσω*, *ἤνεγκα* and L *ferō*, *tulī*, *lātus* is that PIE **bher-* 'carry' (for one example among dozens) did not in fact form a perfect or aorist stem ab origine.

suppletion based descriptive rather than historical criteria would class such paradigms as suppletive.

a. A tolerably large class of words are isolated case forms spoken of figuratively as 'frozen' or 'fossilized' cases which are not however functionally members of the noun lexicon. Rather they are adverbs or prepositions. Thus G *χαμαί* 'on the ground', *λάθρᾱ* 'secretly', *σῖγᾰ* 'silently', L *nātū* 'by birth', *sponte* 'of free will, voluntarily', *forte* 'by chance', *palam* 'openly', are all nouns for which other case forms are unknown or rare. (Contrast *causā* 'for the sake of', a specialized use of a case, but in addition the whole paradigm is in regular use.) These are similar to the restriction of NE *sake* to the phrases *for the sake of* and *for (someone's) sake*, whereas OE *sacu* was, and its cognate NHG *Sache* still is, simply a noun with a full set of cases and numbers, and open-ended contexts. The matter of frozen cases belongs mainly to etymology, that is, the history of the vocabulary. It does however have much interest for the historian, since such forms sometimes preserve otherwise unattested or poorly attested stems or endings, such as the instrumental endings (or what are thought to be instrumental endings, 257.9) in G *ἁμαρτῇ* 'at once', *ἄφνω* 'unawares; of a sudden'; the archaic gen.sg. in *δεσπότης* 'master' < **dems* 'of the house'; and so on.

STEM FORMATION AND DECLENSION OF ADJECTIVES

337. The principal type of adjective—*o*- and *ā*-stems—is the same in G and L, but otherwise the adjective systems of the two languages evolved very differently from their common beginnings. G retains *u*-stem adjectives, which were lost in L; *i*-stem adjectives are abundant in L but rare in G. The PIE cons. stem adjectives (for example, the so-called comparative adjectives, 348-50) developed differently in L and G. Bahuvrīhi (possessive compound) adjectives are common in G, but in L are practically limited to privative compounds like *inermis* 'unarmed' (*arma*), and numericals like *trifaux* 'three-throated'.

338. *o*- AND *eH₂*-STEM ADJECTIVES. In the commonest type of adjective the masc. and neut. are formed from an *o*-stem (258-61), the fem. from an *eH₂*-stem (262-6), as G *σοφός* m. 'skilled', *σοφή* f., *σοφόν* n.; L *bonus* m. 'good', *bona* f., *bonum* n.

The inflection is the same as for nouns, including such details as the G division of *η*-stems and *ᾱ*-stems (262), and the L treatment of stems in *-*ro*- (74.4): *ruber* 'red', *līber* 'free', exactly like the nouns *ager* 'field' and *puer* 'boy', respectively; that is with nom.sg.m. -*er* from *-*(e)ros*. But G adjectives in -*ιος* like *ἄξιος* 'worth' ('equivalent to') have the accent of the nom.pl.f. and gen.pl.f. aligned with that of the corresponding masc. forms: *ἄξιαι*, *ἀξίων*, in contrast to nouns, for example *οἰκίᾱ* 'house': *οἰκίαι*, *οἰκιῶν*; and L adjectives in -*ius* have gen.sg. -*iī* and voc.sg. -*ie* instead of the nouns' -*ī* (see 259.8Ba and 259.2).

339. GREEK ADJECTIVES OF TWO ENDINGS is the traditional term for what are more accurately adjectives of ONE STEM, that is where the *o*-stem paradigm serves for the fem. as well as the masc.: ἄλογος m. and f., ἄλογον n. 'without speech; non-rational'. This type is especially characteristic of adjective compounds built to *o*-stems: governing compounds like *παιδο-τρόφος* 'boy-rearing; a mother' (cf. *τροφός* 'feeding, nurturing') and possessive (bahuvrīhi) compounds like the privative ἄ-λογος, above; but it probably does not owe its origin to such formations. Rather, it is an archaism, and an archaism unparalleled in any other IE group—even in Ital., which alone among IE groups agrees with G in having *o*-stem nouns of fem. gender. The existence of fem. *o*-stem nouns, on the one hand, and the easy association between transparent derivatives like ἄλογος and the source noun (in this case λόγος), on the other, no doubt contributed to the survival of the ancient type especially in such formations. As to the antiquity of uncompounded adjectives of this type, like *φρόνιμος* m.f. 'sensible', ῞ῑλεως 'kindly, affable' (< ῞ῑλᾱος, like λεώς, 259.1a), and *μάχλος* 'hot' (lustful), little can be said in general; some are doubtless ancient, others are equally doubtless secondary.

The *o*-stem adjective compounds built from fem. eH_2-stems, like ἄδικος m.f. 'wrong-doing' (*δίκη* 'law; right'), are not secondary, either, as a type. The PIE norm is for adjective compounds based on eH_2-stem nouns to inflect as *o*-stems (this in fact is one of the pieces of evidence that eH_2-stems are historically derived from *o*-stems). Thus in Indic of all periods, adjective compounds built to nouns like *senā-* f. 'army' are in every way indistinguishable from compounds built to nouns like *deva-* m. 'god': *vīra-senas* m. 'having an army wholly of heroes' (*vīra-*), just like *a-devas* 'impious'. In the history of G, as well, compounds built from *o*-stem and eH_2-stem nouns would have been alike in all regards, including archaic traits like *o*-stem feminines both from *eH_2-stems and original *o*-stems.

a. Some adjectives fluctuate between fem. forms in -ος and in -ᾱ/-η. This is especially typical of adjectives in -ιος, -αιος, but is not limited to them (so *κοινός* f. 'common, shared' ~ *κοινή*).

340. GREEK *υ*-STEM ADJECTIVES. The G adjectives like ἡδύς and γλυκύς, both 'sweet', represent an inherited type which is common in Hittite and Indo-Iranian, and preserved as a distinct type also in Lith., Celt., and Go. In PIE the typical formation was stem-accented and built to the zero grade of an often non-verbal root, and denoted elemental physical properties (sweet, wide, strong, high). In most branches where the type is lost the lexical items in question were transferred to the dominant -*o*-/-eH_2-stem type (West and North Gmc., OCS). In Italic, however, the original *u*-stem adjectives have mostly become *i*-stems, by ADDING *i*-stem endings to the original stem marker. This stem formation started in the feminines, which in PIE were usually inflected after the devī paradigm (268)—the devī suffix being added to the zero grade of the *u*-stem. When the devī type was submerged into the ordinary *i*-stems in Ital. (270) the result was the creation of *ui*-stem

adjectives, in effect: L *suāvis* 'sweet, pleasant' from **swādwi-* (Ved. *svādú-* m.n., *svādvī́-* f. < **sweH₂dwiH₂-*; G ἡδύς); L *gravis* 'heavy' (Ved. *gurú-* m.n., post-Vedic *gurvī-* f. < **gʷr̥wiH₂-*; G βαρύς, Go. *kaurus*; see **96**).

The G declension of the masc. and neut. has already been discussed in connection with the nouns (**312-6**). The fem. is formed, like that of most consonant stems, with the suffix **-yă/-yā-* (the devī type, **268**), corresponding to Ved. feminines in *-ī-/-yā-*. There are two differences between Indic and G. First, in Vedic the fem. of *u*-stem adjectives is formed in three different ways. One type agrees with the noun paradigm in inflecting the masc. and fem. alike (or nearly so), for example *cā́ru-* m.n.f. 'dear'. There are relatively few such. The second type forms the fem. in *-ū-*, that is, the m.n. stem with the addition of the fem. marker **-H₂-*; the result inflects as a kind of consonant stem, known informally as the tanūs type (**317**). In addition to a few primary formations like *tanū́-* f. 'thin' (**tn̥nu-H₂-*), the large class of mostly deverbative modifiers in *-yu-* build the fem. stem thus.

The third type includes the majority of *u*-stem adjectives. It is formed with the devī suffix, as in G and (originally) L: *svādvī́-*, *urvī́-* 'wide', *pr̥thivī́-* 'broad'. (Some stems form the fem. in more than one way, so that while the Rigveda has only *tanū́-*, later Vedas have also *tanú-* f.; and eventually, in Classical Skt., *tanvī-* appears.)

The second difference between Indic and G is that in Indic the feminines of the devī type add the fem. marker to the zero grade of the *u*-stem, whereas in G the stem is in the *e*-grade, thus G ἡδεῖα f. < **hwādewya* < **sweH₂dewiH₂* vs. Ved. *svādvī́* < **sweH₂dwiH₂*. This discrepancy can be reconciled only speculatively. Some authorities, pointing out that in G -εϝ- spreads at the expense of zero grade in *u*-stem endings generally (**314.8**, **316.3**), take the G **-ew-ya* type to be an innovation of the same sort as acc. pl. -εας < **-ewas* ← **-ums*. (In this connection, note that feminine adjectives of the type χαρίεσσα (**346**) MUST have a sort of counterfeit full grade, which necessarily was manufactured within the history of G.) But there is another possibility here. The devī marker ablauted from case to case (**268**), which implies complementary ablaut elsewhere in the form. Presented with ablaut discrepancies between G and InIr. in these formations, the most elegant explanation (nevertheless speculative) would be the reconstruction of an original paradigm ***-éw-iH₂* nom., ***-éw-iH₂m* acc., ***-u-yéH₂-s* gen., ***-éw-iH₂-eH₁* instr., ***-u-yéH₂i* dat., and the rest, from which both the G and InIr. uniform stems were leveled.

341. THE DECLENSION OF πολύς 'much, many' is a composite. One ingredient is an ordinary *u*-stem **pl̥H₁u-* (seen in Ved. *purú-* and, with full grade of the root, Go. *filu*; for the vocalism of the first syllable in G, see **106.2a**). The paradigm is quasi-suppletive: in Attic this stem is limited to πολύς nom.sg.m., πολύν acc.sg.m., and πολύ n. The remaining forms in most dialects are from the stems πολλο-/πολλᾱ-. The distribution of stems came to be exactly that of *μέγας, μεγάλη* (343) except for the adverbial forms *μεγάλως/μεγαλωστί* vs. *πολλάκι(ς)*.

Of the many surmises made about the history of the stem *πολλ-*, the most generally accepted hold that the formations of *μεγαλο-* and *πολλο-* are at bottom the same: the usual explanation is that **πολυ-λο-* (patterned after *μεγα-λο-*) syncopated to *πολλο-*. In support of this notion is the implied difference in chronology of the two forms: though both are abundant in Hom. as adjectives, the primogeniture of *μεγάλο-* is shown by its occurrence in one or two compounds from the earliest period (first in competition with *ἀγα-*, 343, later with *μεγα-*), whereas *πολλο-* offered only the feeblest competition with the inherited combining form *πολυ-*.

This theory has its weaknesses. The rarity of syncope (80) in G is part of the problem. In addition, it has been shown that in the texts themselves there is no particular association between the two forms, such as a tendency for the two adjectives either to collocate or to serve in what linguists call a substitution class. And finally, if there had been enough association between the paradigms of *πολύς* and *μέγας* to lead to the CREATION of parallel stems in the first place, such association should also have worked to PRESERVE the parallelism.

Curiously, the inflection of Rigvedic *purú-* is defective in ways similar to the G: although it is exceedingly frequent, it is in effect limited to the nom./acc. neuter (sg. and pl.).[1] But unlike G, there is a full complement of cases for the regularly-formed feminine stem *pūrvī́-* (**pl̥H*$_1$*w-íH*$_2$*-*), so this paucity of case forms is not the result of chance gaps in attestation of one or another case—an unlikely theory anyway for a stem so copiously attested. (The balance of the m. and n. cases are handled by the stems *bhū́yas-* and *bhū́ri-*.) Whatever the explanation for this, it encouraged some authorities to think that the fem. stem **pl̥H*$_1$*w-íH*$_2$*-* is the source of G *πολλο-/-η-*, that is, **polwya-* > **πολλα-*, whence *πολλᾱ-* and, by back formation, the *o*-stem *πολλο-*. Such an explanation was more attractive before the development of laryngeal theory (though not without its problems even then): in current thinking, a construct like **pl̥H*$_1$*w-íH*$_2$ would give ˣ*plēwya* (**106.2**) whence ˣ*πληια*, ˣ*πληα*, ˣ*πλεᾱ*—remote indeed from the attested stems. (If the theory mentioned in **106.2a** is valid, the outcomes would have started from something like PG ˣ*poliwya*, closer to but still remote from the attested forms.)

The best explanation ventured so far starts with an ordinary thematic (that is, thematized) paradigm, **πολεϝ-ο-*, **πολεϝ-ᾱ-*. The key development is synizesis of the full grade stem vowel after the loss of *-ϝ-*, as discussed in **195a**; this was followed by the gemination of the preceding *-λ-* (233). Significantly, in Hom. the adv. *πολλάκι(ς)* accounts for over half of the

[1] Though the circumscribed distribution of the *u*-stem therefore must date from a very early period, the process was still going on in recorded history: in the Rigveda there is a form or two in addition to those named, and a few additional cases built to the *u*-stem are seen in Homer, namely *πολέες* nom.pl., *πολέων* gen.pl., *πολέεσσι* dat.pl., *πολέας* acc.pl.

total number of forms in πολλ-, and, also significantly, the presumed source, *πολέ(ϝ)ακι(ς), is metrically impossible in hexameter. Many of the thematic forms, such as the gen.sg. πολέϝοιο, would also have been either impossible or awkward, which may be some part of the explanation for the success of πολλό-, πολλᾱ́-. (Possibly πολλο- is an anachronistic redactional substitution for Homer's *πολγο-.)

342. *i*-STEM ADJECTIVES. In L *i*-stem adjectives are numerous, while in G and even InIr. they are rare. Manifestly, the abundance of *i*-stem adjectives in L is in part a consequence of their occurrence wherever fem. adjective stems were formed with the devī-suffix (270.2); but often the L forms correspond to *o*-stem adjectives elsewhere, as *similis* 'like', G ὁμαλός 'even, equal; level'; *humilis* 'low', χθαμαλός 'near (on) the ground'. The importance of *i*-stem adjectives in Hitt. has demanded a rethinking of the question, however; perhaps the withering of *i*-stem adjectives is a shared innovation in G and InIr. (which share many important innovations).

The L declension is very nearly that of the *i*-stem nouns (306-7), differing in two details: in the adjectives the abl.sg. is regularly (as opposed to occasionally) -*ī*, and the stem-vowel of the nom./acc.sg.n. never apocopates as in the nouns (306.4: *animal*, *exemplar*) so neut. adjectives like *familiāre*, and the neut. adj. *vectīgāle* 'taxable' next to noun *vectīgal* 'impost, tax'.

The normal type has a single paradigm for the masc. and fem., as *gravis* m.f. 'heavy', with a gender-distinctive form only for the nom./acc.n.: sg. *grave* < *-*i* (71.1), pl. *gravia*. The type with different masc. and fem. endings in the nom.sg., like *ācer* m. 'sharp', but *ācris* f., is a development from the normal type, as follows. A regular sound law (74.3) would give masc. AND fem. *ācer* from **ākris* via **ākers*. Beside this there was a restored *ācris*, likewise epicene in OL; it was reconstituted on the pattern of other *i*-stems. In the *o*-stems, however, syncopated forms like *ruber* 'red' < *-*ros* (74.4), are masc.-only (cf. *rubra* f., *rubrum* n.), and this provided the basis for the specialization of *i*-stems in -*er* as masculine-only. In a similar way, polysyllabic neut. adjectives like *facile* and *simile* had the final vowel restored (or conserved) by analogy to forms like *ācre*, where it was phonologically regular.

a. In G, primary *i*-stem adjectives are very few in number, as ἴδρις 'experienced, knowing' (root ϝιδ-), τρόφις 'well-fed, large' (root τρεφ-). Adjectival compounds whose second member is an *i*-stem noun originally inflected as *i*-stems, and keep the *i*-stem inflection in most dialects, as ἄπολις 'cityless; outlaw', neut. ἄπολι, gen. ἀπόλεως, and so on. In Att. such forms were remodeled as δ-stems (like ἔρις, ἔριδος 'strife'), so there we find ἄπολις, gen. ἀπόλιδος, and so on.

The most frequently-occurring *i*-stem modifier, and the most conservative morphologically, is τρεῖς 'three' (= Ved. *tráyas*, L *trēs*); see 304.

b. In InIr., *a*-stem adjectives (the reflexes of PIE *o*-stems) are exclusively masc. and neut., unlike G; but also unlike G, the specifically fem. stems that fill out the paradigm are formed either as *ā*-stems (corresponding to the G and L *ā*-stems) or as devī stems, so Ved. *áruṇī-* f. 'red' to *aruṇá-* m.n. Since it is evident that devī-class feminine stems led to the remodeling in L of *u*-stem adjectives and pres.pples. as *i*-stems (270.2), one might wonder if Ital. *i*-stem adjectives corresponding to ordinary *o/ā*-stem adjectives in other languages started out as paradigms of the InIr. *-a/ī-* type. However, for this to be more than a possibility, in the absence of actual heteroclisis (**similus* m., *similis* f.) there should be some degree of lexical match between the Ital. forms in question and the InIr. forms, and this alignment is absent.

CONSONANT STEM ADJECTIVES

Stem formation and inflection of the consonant stem verbal adjectives, namely the stative pple. in *-wos- *and the eventive pple. in* *-nt-, *are discussed in 554-62; for comparative adjectives in* *-yos- *see 349-54.*

343. ROOT ADJECTIVE. The declension of G μέγας 'big' continues the only primary root adjective of PIE, **meǵH̥*$_2$-. Thus **meǵH̥*$_2$*-s* nom.sg.m.f., **meǵH̥*$_2$ nom./acc.n. by regular sound laws yield G μέγας (m. only), μέγα n. (= Ved. *máhi*). The expected *μέγα acc.sg.m. < **meǵH*$_2$*m̥* is replaced by or remodeled as μέγαν, while all the other forms are from the elaborated stem μεγα-λο-, μεγα-λᾱ-. Ved. too shows enlarged stems—a number of them in fact (*mahánt-*, *mahás-*, *mahá-*, *mahiṣá-*)—and other peculiarities, such as no nom.sg.m. built directly to the root; but neither Ved. nor any other IE language has forms which correspond to G μεγαλο-, for which various explanations have been attempted.

The zero grade, **m̥ǵH̥*$_2$-, is preserved in the G combining-form ἀγα- 'much, greatly-', as Hom. ἀγακλε(ϝ)ής 'greatly-famed'; such formations are the rule in Hom., which has only a single compound in μεγα- (Od.), and but a few forms built to μεγαλο-.

344. *s*-STEM ADJECTIVES. In G there are two sorts of *s*-stem adjectives: stative (perfect) pples., 561-2; and adjective compounds of *s*-stem nouns, of the type εὐμενής m.f., εὐμενές n. 'well-intentioned' built to μένος 'intent' (300). The comparative degree of adjectives, originally an *s*-stem type (349-51), has lost all traces of distinctively *s*-stem morphology in G through remodeling (354); and the only remnant of the original morphology in the L comparatives (352-3) is the nom./acc.sg.n. in *-ius* < **-yos*. L has lost the category of stative pple. altogether (apart from an embalmed form or two, 561) and has few or no examples of the type seen in εὐμενής (300a).

L *vetus, -eris* 'old' is (apparently) an old neut. noun, as in G ϝετος 'year'. How a noun becomes an adjective of a different form class in a highly inflected language is a much-discussed puzzle. The usual suggestions presume some kind of back-formation from, or interference with, complexes like *vetustās* 'age' and *veterānus* 'old' (originally of livestock). But the details of such a remodeling are difficult and its motivation is questionable, and *vetus* has remained unexplained to date.

A similar-looking matter but easier to explain is L *ūber* 'abundant'. Though it appears to be the neut. *r*-stem noun *ūber* 'udder' (291.2) used without formal change as an adjective, it is in fact an ordinary *i*-stem adjective < **ūbers* < **owθris* (61, 147.2) < **ow(H)dh-ri-*, semantically (though not formally) aligned with OHG *ōtag* 'rich', OE *éadig* 'prosperous' < PGmc. **auđ-ōka-*.

L *celer* 'swift' (and derivatives) may be an old *s*-stem, on the evidence of *celeber, -ris* 'thronged, crowded; celebrated' (and derivatives) if *-br-* continues *-*sr-* (225.2). (The semantics work if the starting-point was 'rapidly repeated, frequent'; but most good-looking cognates mean simply 'swift', from which the meaning 'throng' is an unlikely derivative.)

a. G compounds (incl. many proper nouns) in -κλέϝης '-famed' (based on κλέϝος n. 'fame') make up a special formal category, not because of anything special in their makeup but because of the loss of both the intervocalic *-*w*- and *-*s*- (182, 172), with subsequent contractions (86) or shortening (79.3). Cyp. -κλεϝης, -κλεϝεος is the least altered, and agrees with the Hom. forms in -κλῆα acc., -κλῆος gen., which are in any case often to be scanned as -κλέ(ϝ)εα, -κλέ(ϝ)εος. Dialect forms, for all their variety, are for the most part phonologically regular: Dor. -κλῆς (*-κλέϝης) nom., -κλέα (< -κλέα < -κλεεα) acc. Att. -κλῆς < -κλέης nom.; -κλέᾱ < -κλέεα acc. (55); -κλέους < -κλέεος gen.; -κλεῖ < -κλέεϊ dat.; -κλεῖς < -κλέεες (*-*kleweses*) nom.pl. The last two show the regular loss of -ε- before another -ε- (particularly typical of three-vowel sequences), a phenomenon sometimes called *hyphaeresis*. Cf. **dewei* 'lacks' and **deyei* 'binds' which both become first *δεει then Att. δεῖ (86.1).

345. *n*-STEM ADJECTIVES IN GREEK, type σώφρων (σαϝό-φρων) 'of sound mind'. The only difference from the noun declension (288) is in the neut. -ον (pl. -ονα), based on -ων m.f. after the analogy of εὐμενής m.f., εὐμενές n. (pl. -έα) 'gracious' and the like. The original forms would have been something like *σώφρα sg. < *-*n̥*, as in ὄνομα (288), *σώφρων pl. < *-*ōn* < **-*onH₂* (282a). Likewise analogical are the forms to the ντ-stem adjectives and participles: χαρίεν (χαρίεντος) 'graceful' and ἄγον 'driving' (ἄγοντ-), and so on. The orig. nom./acc.n. was endingless, like these, but they were probably built to zero grade of the stem (L *ferēns* < **bhern̥t*, 237.5, Skt. *bharat*); the corresponding G *ἄγα would have been an obvious target for analogical remodeling. A similar replacement of the original neuter form by the form of the stem appearing in the oblique cases occurs in the primary ν-stem adjectives, such as τέρεν n. 'smooth'. The similar-looking forms to consonant stems which merely happen to end in -ν-, as μέλαν 'black' (masc. μέλᾱς < *μελανς), are probably original.

a. Beside the numerous epicene adjectives in -ων, -ονος, there are a few ν-stem adjectives with a separate fem. stem formed with the devī suffix (268): τέρην m., τέρεινᾰ (**terenya*) f., τέρεν n. 'smooth'. This may be ancient. Less clear is the antiquity of the cons. stem formations like μέλᾱς (< -ανς) m., μέλαινᾰ (**melanya*) f., μέλαν n. 'black'.

Like τέρην is ἄρρην 'masculine', neut. ἄρρεν (only seemingly oxymoronic: NB the grammatical terms ἄρρεν ὄνομα 'masculine noun', ἄρρεν γένος 'masculine gender'; less obviously τὸ ἄρρεν 'the male'). The fem. chances not to occur.

346. THE GREEK TYPE χαρίεις m. 'graceful', χαρίεσσα f., χαρίεν n. These are possessive adjectives, etymologically, formed from noun-stems (which are not always independently attested) with the suffix *-*went*-. This PIE hysterokinetic (272.3) suffix is seen in Ved. *prajā́vant-*, *prajā́vat-* 'having progeny' (*prajā́-*). Forms with -ϝ- are attested in Myc., and a few are quotable from inscriptions, as Boeot. χαριϝετταν and Dor. (Corcyran) στονοϝεσαν 'wretched' lit. 'full of sighs'.

In G the strong grade -ϝεντ-, originally proper only to certain cases (**273**), is generalized throughout the masc. and neut., as gen.sg. -ϝεντος (cf. zero grade in Ved. *prajā́vatas*). The nom.sg.masc. in -(ϝ)εις is the regular development from *-*wḗnts*, itself however a leveling of original PIE *-*wēn* or the like < **-*wents*; cf. Ved. *prajā́vān* (see also the inflection of the eventive pple., **554-9**). The nom./acc.sg.n. in -ϝεν < *-*went* is an innovation, cf. Ved. *prajā́vat* nom./acc.n. with zero grade *-*wn̥t*.

The fem. stem in G (as in Indic) is formed with the devī suffix. Original *-*went-ya*, however, would have given ˣ-εῖσα as in the pple. τιθεῖσα f. 'putting'. G -εσσα is rather from *-*wečča*, which however confirms the prior existence of *-*wat-ya* < *-*wn̥t-iH₂* corresponding to Ved. *prajā́vatī* f.: the source of the -ε- is the stem in -ϝεντ-, which spread at the expense of *-*wat-*.[1] Note however that -ϝεντ- as such was not generalized: we have here rather a vowel adjustment postdating the G palatalizations (**195-207**) which had distorted the shape of the fem. suffix to *-*wačča*. (Had the stem been *-*went-ya* to begin with, the loss of the -ν- would be incomprehensible.) What looks like the familiar G shape is seen already in Myc., as in *to-qi-de-we-sa* (of vessels) 'having twists' or the like (*tork*ʷ*idwessa*).

From the Att. perspective, this class of adjectives is almost wholly poetical, hence they commonly appear with the non-Att. -σσ- (**199b**) in the fem. and without contraction, so μελιτόεις 'honeyed', τῑμήεις 'full of esteem', στονόεις 'full of sighs'. But some gave rise to nouns in common use, which assume the proper Att. form (-ττ- rather than -σσ-, contraction of -οε- to -ου-): names of cakes like μελιτοῦττα (cf. μελιτόεσσα, above), πλακοῦς, -οῦντος m., and οἰνοῦττα f.; and place names like Ῥαμνοῦς.

a. In the familiar dialects, derivatives in -ϝεντ- based on consonant stems are formed with a linking vowel -ο- (of uncertain origin), as in μελιτόϝεντ- from μελιτ- 'honey'. In Ved. however the suffix is added to the stem of the noun directly, as in *pad-vánt-* 'having feet' (rather than wings, say). The G arrangement had always been taken to be the innovation in any case, and now Myc. agrees with Ved., thus *te-mi-dwe* nom.sg. n., *te-mi-dwe-ta* nom.pl.n., *te-mi-de-we-te* nom.du.n. = *te-mi-dwe-te*, all from *temidwent-* (meaning uncertain—always used of wheels). These data shed light on the unexpected -ῐ- of Hom. φοινῐκόεντα 'purple, crimson', traditionally explained as poetic license for φοινῑ́κοεντα (cf. φοῖνιξ, -ῑκος 'purple' (noun) and a large number of allied forms, all with -ῑ-). These forms mostly occur in line-final position, where conservatism rather than innovation is the norm and deformations metri causa are out of place. The Myc. evidence now provides the real key, namely that the textual form is a replacement (with prosodic tampering) of original φοινῑ́κϝεντα.

347. THE LATIN ADJECTIVES OF ONE ENDING (present participles and adjectives like *duplex*, *audāx*, *ferōx*).

The L present participle has no distinct fem. form, in contrast to G, Ved. Gmc., and so on. This is explained by the history of *i-* and consonant stems in L. Old devī nom.sg.f. **ferentī* (= Ved. *bhárantī*) were remade as *i-*

---

[1] Cf. the replacement of -α- < *n̥ by a pseudo-full-grade in *n*-stems, **286.4a**.

stems (270.2), so **ferentis*; whence by regular syncope (306.1) *ferēns*, homophonous with masc. *ferēns* < **ferents*. Something similar underlies cons.-stem types like *duplex* 'twofold', whose fem. continues **duo-plekĭs* (though here the syncope of -*ĭ*- is analogical to the pples.).

The remarkable feature of these L adjectives is the NEUT. nom./acc.sg. in -*s*, as *amāns*, *duplex* 'twofold', *audāx* 'bold', for which the explanation is disputed. There seems to be agreement that whatever the correct explanation is, it is the same for *ferēns* and *audāx*. In 237.5 the view was endorsed that neut. *ferēns* shows the regular phonetic development of final *-*nt*, the expected form for the case (557); from the participles, the pattern spread to the *audāx* type.

a. A different explanation which has enjoyed wide acceptance starts from RV compound adjectives in which overtly masc. forms are also used for the nom.sg.neut.: *dvipā́t* 'biped' nom.sg.masc. AND neut. < **dwi-pōts*, much like the L *duplex* type. These are held to vouchsafe the ancestral use of nom.sg. -*s* in bahuvrīhi compounds modifying neut. nouns. The crucial phenomenon in the RV, however, is found only in three forms, all compounds of the element -*pad*- '-footed': *dvipā́t* 'bipedal', *tripā́t* 'having three feet' (of a man), and *cátuṣpāt* 'quadrupedal'. Now, the forms expected for neuters, *dvipát* and *cátuṣpat*, actually occur, as frequently as the seemingly masc. forms and in hymns of the same age. Second, in all other similar formations, which are fairly numerous, the masc. and the neut. would have been homophonous in any case, not because of their morphological makeup but because of Indic sound laws which simplify final consonant clusters. For example, determinative compounds in -*vit* nom. (some 28 different formations to two roots, 'find' and 'know') reflect both *-*wits* m. and *-*wid* n. The gender ambiguity of a nom.sg. in -*vit* nom.sg.m.n. is a purely Indic phenomenon, and the is the MODEL for the use of the distinctively masc. -*pā́t* (one of the few that is) in compounds for the nom./acc.n.

b. The distribution of *i*- and cons. stem forms in L adjectives has lost any connection with gender. The *i*-stem form of the gen.pl., -*ium*, is regular for ordinary adjectives like *gravis*, though in early L it is still sometimes -*um* in participles, as Plaut. *amantum*. The nom./acc.pl.n. is regularly -*ia*. In the abl.sg. there was fluctuation between -*e* and -*ī*, with a tendency to prefer the latter.

Comparison of Adjectives

348. Adjectives in PIE as discussed in 337-47 are in what is called the *positive degree*: they express the generic force of the adjective without semantic coloration such as emphasis, attenuation, contrast, pejoration, and so on. There were several adjective stems in PIE, however, which did qualify the force of an adjective. As the daughter languages developed, one or another of these formations evolved into the 'comparative and superlative degrees' of adjectives familiar from the principal languages of Europe.

One such suffix was *-*yos*- (349-51), an INTENSIVE marker signifying 'very; rather; to a marked degree'. This yields the L comparative, and is one of the ingredients in the G comparative. It is also the basis of the L and G superlative. Another stem, *-(*t*)*ero*- (355-6), was PARTICULARIZING and by implcation ANTONYMIC: 'the hot one (not the cold one)'; 'our (own)'.

This function explains the distinction between **H_2en-tero-* 'the other (of two); a different one' and **H_2el-yo-* 'another, some other', and the prominence of the suffix in the possessive pronouns (L *noster*, G *ἡμέτερος* 'our [own]'), for example, and in the expression of such notions as **deksitero-* 'the one on the right'.

Various other modifications of adjectival force are handled morphologically in one or another of the IE languages, such as the Celtic equative (OIr. *dénithir* 'as swift' to *dían* 'swift') and the English attenuative (*biggish*). But most such modifications are handled in IE languages syntactically, as in English *very big, as big as, too big.*

349. THE PIE INTENSIVE MARKER **-yos-* was a primary suffix, that is, it was added directly to the root (which was in full grade) rather than to the stem of the adjective. So to a *u*-stem like **sweH$_2$du-* 'sweet' the intensive/comparative would have been **sweH$_2$d-yos-* rather than ×*sweH$_2$duyos-* or the like. This accords with the view that the original meaning of the suffix was different from our notion of a paradigmatic comparative, which should be a derivative of the generic itself (as is clearly the case in NE *damnedest* and L *difficilior*). Thus Vedic *átavyas-*, a form with both the intensive suffix and the privative prefix, means 'not very strong' (from *tavyás-* 'very strong') rather than 'very unstrong; very weak'. That is, it is a privative based on an intensive, not the other way around like the NE comparative *untidier.*

MORPHOLOGICAL COMPOSITES (**-isto-*, **-ison-*, and the like). Several formations were made up of combinations of **-is-* (the zero grade of **-yos-*) with some other adjectival element. The two oldest, on the basis of their distribution in the IE family, are **-is-to-* (InIr., G, and Gmc.), and **-is-on-* (G and Gmc.). A third, **-is-m̥mo-*, is found only in Ital. and Celt., and appears to be an innovation peculiar to those two groups.

The first of these, **-isto-*, forms what is traditionally known as the superlative ('most sweet'). Semantically it is better taken as more like Fr. *le plus*, that is, a comparative with a particularizing marker, so that **sweH$_2$d-yos-* 'very sweet', **sweH$_2$d-is-to-* 'the very sweet' are like Fr. *plus doux* 'sweeter', *le plus doux* 'sweetest'.[1] This complex underlies the superlative seen in G ἥδιστος 'sweetest' (ἡδύς; ἡδίων), τάχιστος 'shortest' (ταχύς; θᾱ́σσων). The same formation is seen in Ved. *svā́diṣṭha-* 'sweetest', *náviṣṭha-* 'newest, most recent',[2] and also forms the basis of the Gmc. superlative, as OE *scyrtest* 'shortest' (*sceort*, comparative *scyrtra*), Go. *spedists* 'last' (*spediza* 'later').

The complex **-is-on-* is less widely attested but is important in the histories of G and Gmc., which as a rule do not share innovations. In G it was in competition with the original formation in plain **-yos-* and the two paradigms were eventually conflated (354). It has been suggested that **-on-*

---

[1] NG has evolved the same system: *ομορφότερη* (or *πιό όμορφη*) 'prettier', *η ομορφότερη* (or *η πιό όμορφη*) 'the prettiest'.

[2] The aspirated *-th-* of Indic is unexpected and unexplained.

originally acted as a nominalizer (indefinite, in contrast to *-*to*-): **sweH₂d-yos-* 'very sweet', **sweH₂d-is-on-* 'a very sweet one'.

The composite *-*is-m̥mo-* is the basis for the productive superlative in Italic and Celtic, the only two IE groups where it is found. It appears to be a conflation of two earlier types of absolutive forms, *-*isto-* (above) and *-*(t)m̥mo-* (356).

In the process of converting these varied ingredients into a regular system of paradigmatic comparative and superlative degrees, both G and L ended up with a number of different formations with the same function, somewhat like the English hesitations between *kindest* and *most kind.*

a. In early IE languages, such adjectives could be made directly to verbal roots: Ved. *pányas-* 'more wonderful, very wonderful', root *pan-* 'to marvel'; *tápiṣṭha-* 'excessively burning', root *tap-* 'burn'; and—apparently—even nouns, though the matter is ambiguous: RV *yódhīyas-* 'more of a warrior' is apparently based on *yodhá-* 'warrior, hero', but might perhaps instead be *'more belligerent', that is, built directly to the root *yudh-* 'fight'.

b. Emphatic or intensive force may attenuate or vanish: NE *near, rather,* and *less* are all etymologically comparatives. But this evolution seems to be particularly characteristic of certain notions: 'very new; rather new', 'rather young', 'very dear', for example, routinely fade to generic force. Even in the RV, *návyas-* and *návīyas-* are little more than synonyms of *náva-* 'new'; *préyas-* (that is, *práïyas-*) is as much merely 'dear' as 'very dear'.

Contrariwise, some words not formally comparatives are (or become) functionally comparative, as L *minus,* NE *worse.*

350. The suffix *-*yos-* added to a root *X* originally meant '*X* to a pronounced degree; very *X*'. This is essentially the force of the affix in InIr. Pragmatically, of course, a statement like *Fruit is sweet, but honey is very sweet* is equivalent to *Fruit is sweet, but honey is sweeter,* and that is the basis for the evolution of the paradigmatic comparative of L and (more complexly) G. As befits independent developments, there are differences in detail: in L but not in G there is the alternative force 'too *X*, excessively *X*'—a meaning which follows easily from *'very *X*', but cannot readily be got directly from the notion 'more *X*'.

The affix was added to the *e*-grade of the root (if there was one) regardless of the grade or stem of the generic adj. Thus to Ved. *dīrghá-* 'long' (*o*-stem, root in zero grade), *drā́ghīyas-* 'very long; longer': PIE **dl̥H₁gh-ó-* but **dléH₁gh-yos-*. To Hom. κρατύς 'strong' (PIE **kr̥t-ú-*), κρέσσων (Ion.) 'stronger; better' (PIE **krét-yos-*). To L *magnus* 'big', (*no*-stem), *maiior* 'bigger; too big' (**mag-yos-*). Since the positive is itself full grade, there is no ablaut alternation in Ved. *návyas-* 'rather new' to *náva-* 'new' (**néw-o-*, **néw-yos-*).

However there was much leveling of the root grade: G βραδίων 'slower' for *βρεδίων or *βερδίων, with -ρα- imported from positive βραδύς (**gʷr̥du-*); vice versa L *brevis* 'short' with -*re*- from the comparative *brevior* (itself a composite: the -*v*- is from the positive degree. The ultimate etyma were **mr̥ǵhu-*, **mreǵhyōs*: the unaltered developments of these in L would have been **moruis*, **breiior*).

351. The PIE forms were as follows, taking **néw-yos-* 'very new' (generic **néw-o-*) as the model:

	Singular	*Plural*
Nom.m.f.	newyōs (< **-yoss)	newyoses
Acc.m.f.	newyosm̥	newyosm̥s
neut.	newis, newyos	newyōs (< **-yosH_2)
Dat.	newisey? newyesey?	newisbh-? newyesbh-?
Gen.	newisos? newyesos?	newisōm? newyesōm?
etc.		

In Ved. the fem. stem is built with the devī suffix (**268**), as *náv(ī)yasī-* f. The absence of any such forms in G, where a form like θάσσων 'shorter' is both masc. and fem., and the lack of *i*-stem inflection in L (*seniōrum* gen. pl., *breviōra* nom./acc.pl.n.), indicate that the devī feminines of InIr. were not inherited from PIE.

The existence of stem-forms in *-*yes*- is problematic. Isolated forms like L *māiestās* 'greatness, majesty' point to **magyes-*; but the only paradigmatic evidence is the lack of lengthening (per **36.4**) in Indic, as *návyase* dat., *návyasas* gen. This however is to be taken as secondary, under the influence of the inflection of *s*-stem bahuvrīhi adjectives (*sumánasas* gen. 'well-disposed'; **300**), where the shape is phonologically regular. In any case, the expected alternation would be not between *o*- and *e*-grades, but between full grade (generously attested as *o*-grade specifically) and zero grade. OCS, with its frozen stem in -*ĭš*-, suggests that the comparative suffix also made weak cases in zero grade, as very likely gen.sg. *-*is-os*; and certainly the affixes *-*is-to*- and *-*is-on*- are the zero grade of the comparative suffix plus an additional element (see **349**). Additional evidence comes from adverbial elements built to a zero grade stem in *-*is*-: L *magis* 'more, rather' < **mag-is*, like Go. *mais*, OE *má*, OHG *mēr* < PGmc. **ma-iz* 'more' (this **ma-* is enigmatic, but the morphology is clear), and Go. *minns* 'less' < **minn-iz*. These correspond to the nom./acc.neut. or the instrumental in Ved. *návyas* nom./acc.n. and *návyasā* inst., both 'anew', Ved. *bhū́yas* nom./acc.n. '(the) more'. Perhaps therefore *-*is* is actually the aboriginal form of the nom./acc.n., already in PIE largely but not quite wholly displaced by secondary *-*yos* as in *s*-stems generally (**297.1**).

352. THE COMPARATIVE IN LATIN. In L this formation agrees with the *s*-stem nouns (**296**) in retaining the original -*s* unaltered in but a single locale: the nom./acc. of the neut.: *maiius* < **magyos*. Also as in the *s*-stem nouns, in the masc. and fem. paradigm (**299**) the long vowel of the nom.sg. was generalized to the whole paradigm, with the same replacement of the nom.m.f. -*s* by -*r*, whence -*ior* < -*iōr* (**83.3**). That is, *melior*, *meliōris* has the same history as *honor*, *honōris*. However, the oblique stem -*iōr*- is found in the neuter as well, unlike the nouns: oblique *meliōr-* n. ≠ *gener-* or *tempŏr-* (**297.5**).

353. 1. The development of *-*y*- in the suffix follows the usual L rules, so for example disyllabic **senyōs* 'older' > trisyllabic *senior* (193). In a few forms the etymon is more or less obscured by regular sound laws. L *maiior* (*māior*) 'bigger' regularly from **mag-yōr-* per 194, with the same element **mag-* seen in *magnus* 'big' and *magis* 'rather'. L *peiior* (*pēior*) 'worse' contains the usual suffix but for the rest various etyma have been proposed (see 194, 358.3b).

2. *Prior* 'earlier' is an old comparative **pri-yos-*; several other formations are from the zero grade of this stem, **pri-is-*, namely *prīmus* 'first' (358.1 and further 398.1) and *prīstinus* 'former, early'.

3. *Minor*, *-ōris* m.f., *minus* n. 'less' inflects as a comparative in L, but it obviously lacks the expected *-*y*-. This has been explained variously. The simplest explanation traces the m.f. stem to a stem **minu-* 'less', not formally a comparative any more than NE *less*; to this stem was built a comparative **minuyōs*, but with the simplex *minus* incorporated in the paradigm as the neut. stem. Presumably original *minus* *m.*f. was to start with in competition with **minuyōs*, somewhat like NE *lesser* vs. *less*. The loss of intervocalic -*y*- (192) is straightforward; the loss of the *-*u*- before *-*ō̆*- parallels the development of L *sōl* 'sun' < **suol* (88.3c).

4. L *plūs* 'more' has a difficult history. The OL forms are: PLOVS (SC de Bacch.); PLEORES nom.pl. (Carmen Arvale); *ploeres* (Cic.); superlative PLOIRVME and PLOVRVMA—the former is the earlier—(Scipio epitaphs); *plisima* (*plī-* ?; Paul.Fest., quoting the Carmen Saliare); and *plūsima* (Varro). Cognate forms in other languages include G πλείων 'more', πλεῖστος 'most' (354d) = Av. *fraēšta-*; and Skt. *prāyas*. The last is only attested well after the Vedic period and with the wrong meaning ('for the most part; usually'); but its formal twin, Av. *frāyas-* 'more', puts **prāyas-* 'more' at least as far back as PInIr.

Given *pl̥H_1-u-* 'many, much' one expects an intensive **pleH_1-yos-*, and superlatives **pleH_1-is-to-* (G, Av.) and **pleH_1-is-m̥mo-* (L, Celt; 358). (The Indic outcome of the superlative, **prayiṣṭha-*, would have been homophonous with 'dearest'—one of the few instances when 'homophonic clash' would be genuinely inconvenient.) OL *plīsima* looks like the expected form, neither more nor less, apart from the detail that -*ī*- from *-*ei*- is anachronistic for a form still showing intervocalic *s*. (This would be more troubling in an epigraphic attestation, of course.) The comparative **pleH_1yōs* would have given Ital. **plē(y)ōs*, *-*(y)ōses*, whence L **plē̆ōs*, *plē̆ōres*. This state is attested as such in the Carmen Arvale. A HIGHLY speculative entering wedge for the remodeling the paradigm eventually underwent would have been the neut. and adverbial **plē(y)os*: if the latter very early became **plē̆(y)us*—not via sound law but by contamination with *u*-stem *minus* (when it was still masc. and fem.) 'less' (3, above)—the development of *-*eu*- > -*ou*- > -*ū*- would take care of itself. Epigraphic PLEORES and the like suggest that inherited oblique *pleōres* (directly from **pleH*$_1$*yos-* but with the usual L generalization of the long vowel in the stem) survived unaltered until fairly late. The forms in *-oi-* and the like for expected **pleisemos* are peculiar, and of doubtful explanation. They would however regularly give *plūs*, *plūrēs* and *plūrimus*—the regular forms of the classical period, which ironically are therefore the hardest to account for exactly. (Cf. *-issimo-*, 358.3.)

354. THE GREEK COMPARATIVES result from the partial conflation of two quite different formations. One is the intensive type seen in L *-iōr*, *-ius*, Ved. *-yān* (**-yām̥s*), *-yas* (349-53). The other is a composite, **-is-on-*, an *on-*stem based on the zero grade of the first type. The latter is the basis of the comparative of Gmc. also. (NE *harder*, Go. *hardiza*). The original paradigms, using **sweH*$_2$*d-* 'sweet' as a model, would have gone:

	**-yos-*	PG	**-is-on-*	PG
Nom.sg.	*sweH$_2$dyōs	*hwāǰǰōs	*sweH$_2$disō	*hwādihō
Acc.	*sweH$_2$dyosm̥	*hwāǰǰoha	*sweH$_2$disonm̥	*hwādihona
neut.	*sweH$_2$dyos	*hwāǰǰos	*sweH$_2$disn̥	*hwādiha
Gen.	*sweH$_2$disos	*hwādihos	*sweH$_2$disnos	*hwādisnos
Loc.	*sweH$_2$dyes(i)	*hwāǰǰehi	*sweH$_2$diseni	*hwādis(e)ni
Nom.pl.	*sweH$_2$dyoses	*hwāǰǰohes	*sweH$_2$disones	*hwādihones
Loc.pl.	*sweH$_2$dissu	*hwādis(s)i	*sweH$_2$disn̥su	*hwādihasi[1]

1. Loc.pl. **-asi* is regular from **-n̥si*; cf. δασύς 'thick' < **dn̥su-* (172a).

Whence the late prehistoric Greek types:

	**-yos-*	**-is-on-*
Nom.sg.	hwāzōs	hwādiōn
Acc.	hwāzoa, -ō	hwādiona
neut.	hwāzos	hwādion
Gen.	hwādios	hwādisnos (> Att.-Ion. -ῑνος)
Loc.	hwādii	hwādisni (> " " -ῑνι)
Nom.pl.	hwādoes	hwādiones
Loc.pl.	hwādis(s)i	hwādios(s)i

The partial conflation of these two types, together with some leveling, had the following results:

	(based on **-yos-*)	(based on **-is-on-*)
Nom.sg.	βάσσων 'deeper'	ἡδίων (-ῑ́ων) 'sweeter'
Acc.	βάσσω, -ονα	ἡδίονα, -ίω (-ῑ́ονα, -ῑ́ω)
neut.	βάσσον	ἡδίον (-ῑ́ον)
Gen.	βάσσονος	ἡδίονος (-ῑ́ονος)
Dat.	βάσσονι	ἡδίονι (-ῑ́ονι)
Nom.pl.	βάσσους, -ονες	ἡδίονες, -ίους (-ῑ́ονες, -ῑ́ους)
Dat.pl.	βάσσοσ(σ)ι	ἡδίοσ(σ)ι (-ῑ́οσ(σ)ι)
etc.		

Summary:

1. The nom.sg. of all types is -ων.

2. A few forms reflect the unvarnished **-yos-* type, namely with with palatalization (198-207) of the root-final consonant, as in βάσσων 'deeper' (βαθύς), ἐλᾱ́σσων 'smaller' (ἐλαχύς), Ion. μέζων 'bigger' (μέγας), Ion. κρέσσων 'stronger; better' (κρατύς), θᾱ́σσων 'shorter' (ταχύς), μᾶλλον adv. 'more' (μάλα 'very'), μάσσων 'longer' (μακρός). NB here Myc. *ka-zo-e* n.pl.m. 'inferior', that is *kaččohes* < **kakyoses*, which does not superimpose on Hom. κακίων (Att. κακῑ́ων).

3. The stem of the -ι(h)ον-/-ῑν- type was generalized, usually as -ῐ́ον-, but sometimes—chiefly in Att.—as -ῑ́ον- (from the case-forms in -ῑν- reflecting original **-isn-*, 227.2). Thus ἡδῑ́ων (-ῐ́ων) 'sweeter' (ἡδύς), βραδῑ́ων 'slower' (βραδύς), κακῑ́ων (-ῐ́ων) 'worse' (κακός). Occasionally, earlier forms belonging to the *s*-stem type are attested, like Myc. *ka-zo-e*, above. (In inscriptions, glossaries, and many mss the length of the -ι- is of course unrecoverable.)

4. Even in the prevailing -ῑ̆ων type, original *s*-stem forms are seen in acc.sg.m.f. -ω (-ῑ̆ω) < **-(y)oha* < **-yosm̥*; nom./acc.pl.n. -(ῑ̆)ω < -οα < **-yosH̥₂*; nom.pl.m.f. -ους (Att.-Ion), -ως (Dor.) < -οες < **-yoses*; acc.pl.m.f. -ους, -ως (Dor.) in place of *-ως < -οας < **-yosm̥s*. The ν-stem endings (acc.sg. ἡδῑ́ονα) are favored in poetry and formal prose. Both types of endings occur on the 'wrong' stem, so βάσσονα on the one hand and ἡδῑ́ω on the other.

The dat.pl. in -(ι)οσ(σ)ι is curiously remote from both **-is(s)i* and the *n*-stem type (cf. 286.4a). The typical cons. stem form -(ι)ονεσσι is late and secondary.

a. Some forms showing palatalization are necessarily secondary, though ancient, as μέζων 'bigger', Myc. *me-zo* nom.sg., *me-zo-e* nom.pl. These cannot directly continue PIE **meǵH̥₂yos-* or **meǵH₂-iyos-*; PreG **megyos-* was a neologism manufactured from μέγα(ς). (In the alternative they may be taken as evidence that the **H₂* of **meǵH₂*, usually assumed to be part of the root, is actually affixal.)

b. Myc. shows no trace of the **-is-on-* type in unambiguous forms, so nom.pl.m.f. *ka-zo-e* (*kaččohes*) for Att. κακῑ́ονες; nom.acc.pl.n. *me-zo-a₂* (*mejǰoha*); nom.du.m.n. *me-zo-e* (*mejǰohe*), cf. μέζονε, Att. μείζονε. The nom.sg. *me-zo* could be either *mejǰōs* or *mejǰōn*, but in view of the absence of *n*-stem forms in unambiguous cases it is more likely to be the former. The *n*-stem complex has however been identified in Myc. patronymics of the type *ma-so-ni-jo* (*maččonyos*) < *makyon-yo-*, which would fit with the idea that *-ison-* was a nominalization: **sweH₂dyos-* 'very sweet', **sweH₂dison-* 'the very sweet one'.

An interesting datum confirms the secondary nature of the G comparatives in **-ison-*. G ἀρείων 'better' and ἄριστος 'best' are built to a root **H₂erH₁-*. The superlative is a straightforward reflex of original **H₂erH₁-isto-*, but a matching form of any great age in **-ison-* would have given ˣἀρίων, not ἀρείων. The original formation, that is to say, must have been **areyoh-* < **H₂erH̥₁-yos-* (cf. ἀρετή 'excellence' < **H₂erH̥₁-t-* or **H₂erH₁-et-*). Attested ἀρείων < **are-ihon-* therefore vouchsafes a preexisting stem **areyoh-*. (G ἀρέσκω 'am pleasing' is obviously related somehow—but **H₂r̥H₁-sḱ-* would not result in such a form; and **H₂erH̥₁-sḱ-*, which would, has the wrong grade for a *sḱe/o*-present, 456.3.)

c. The lengthened vowel of the root syllable in ἐλᾱ́σσων, θᾱ́σσων, Att. ἐλᾱ́ττων, θᾱ́ττων (ᾱ shown by the accent of the neut. θᾶττων) is difficult to explain. Regular, but isolated, is ᾶσσον adv. 'nearer' built to ἄγχι 'tight, near, close' (cf. L *angustus*), that is *H_2enǵhyos- > *ank^{h}yos- > *anččos- (199) > *anssos- > āsso- (228.2). The later (chiefly but not exclusively Att.) forms with long vowel in place of the earlier short: μείζων 'bigger', κρείττων 'better', ὀλείζων 'fewer', and others (spurious diphthongs), are analogical, based on some sort of perception that the comparative degree is built to a root with a long vowel. The role of analogy is proved by the vocalism of ὀλείζων, originally the full grade of ὀλίγος and therefore including a genuine diphthong; later the form is ὀλε̄γος (a spurious diphthong). The exact model for the innovation is somewhat speculative—μείζων?—but it is clear that contamination did take place. Further, showing analogical shortening, is ἄσσον 'nearer' for regular ᾶσσον (by contamination with μᾱ́σσων 'longer, greater'?).

Similarly, for ἐλᾱ́σσων the full grade of ἐλαχ-/ἐλαφ- (*$l̥ng^wh$-) is *ἐλεγχ-, not *ἐλαγχ-. That is, a genuine etymon *elank^{hw}- is impossible. Such a form could only have arisen by contamination: the vocalism of positive *elak^{hw}*- combined with the consonantism of *elenk^{hw}-. The result would of course have become ἐλᾱ́σσων; similar formations, however, fail to show any such development: so πᾱ́σσων 'thicker' (παχύς = Ved. *bahú*- < *bhn̥ǵh-, cf. *baṃhiṣṭha*- 'most thick'), and βᾱ́σσων 'deeper' (βαθύς; cf. βένθος 'depth'). Of course, where analogy is concerned it is normal that not all eligible forms undergo the remodeling, and it is perhaps significant that the earliest clear case of what must be purely analogical lengthening involves -ᾱ-, to wit Hom. μᾶλλον 'more', replacing *μέλλον (cf. L *melior*). The Att. developments would seem to be a further elaboration of the analogical process.

The details of the positive degree generally spread at the expense of other shapes in G: early *s*-stem nouns βένθος, (Aeol.) θέρσος, and so on, with etymologically correct *e*-grade, were replaced by βάθος, θάρσος.

d. G πλείων 'more' (Att. πλέων), Hom. πλέες nom.pl., πλέας (also Cret. πλιες and some others), πλεῖστος 'most, very large', the G cognates of L *plūs, plūrimus* (353.4), are ultimately from PIE *$pleH_1$-yōs, *$pleH_1$-is(-to)-, PG *plēyōs, *pleis(-to)-. It is uncertain whether any detectable remains of the expected *πλεων paradigm survive (that is, with -η- before a vowel (79.3) shortened to -ε-); when the comparative paradigm shifted to the *-ison- type, it took on the shape of the superlative πλεισ- < *$pleH_1$is-, perhaps with some help from ἀρεισ- 'better' (**a**, above), whose resemblance to πλεισ- is accidental.

e. It seems to be widely assumed that G -ῑων and Ved. -*īyas*- (a type unknown in Avestan) are Sievers' alternants (178) in *-*iy*-.

This is incorrect. We have already seen the history of the G forms (354.3). In the RV the basic -*yas*- is limited to twelve stems. Nearly three times as many formations are built to -*īyas*-, including forms in competition with the above, for example *návīyas*- 'quite new; new' and *távīyas*- 'very strong' next to *návyas*-, *távyas*-. Eventually the longer form of the suffix ousts the other entirely, with the partial exception of *sanyas*- 'older'. Indic -*īyas*- started in connection with heavy bases (121-3) such as *terH̥yos- (RV *tárīyas*- 'more easily passing through'. The -*ī*- is regular before -*y*-). This explanation accounts for the absence of any such formation in Avestan, where syllabic laryngeals in medial syllables drop. Thus the apparently parallel Ind. and G formations in -*īyas*- and -ῑων respectively are unrelated, as the former results from a detail of Indic phonology (*i* < *H̥) and the latter is wholly traceable to the G complex *-ῐον-/*-ῑν- < *-is-on-/*-isn-.

355. CONTRASTIVE *-*(t)ero*-. An altogether different kind of derivation was the contrastive suffix *-*tero*- (occasionally *-*ero*-). To begin with, these were typical of adverbs and pronouns; unlike *-*yos*- the suffix was affixed to stems rather than to the root directly. The original force of the suffix was contrastive and particularizing rather than intensive, and the implied contrast was not between two adjectives in *-*(t)ero*-, or between an adjective in *-*(t)ero*- and its generic (as is the case with most true comparatives), but between the contrastive formation and a generic adjective of different meaning. In other words, something δεξίτερος 'right(-hand)' was not 'further to the right'—that is, more δεξιός than δεξιός—but rather something that was (emphatically) non-σκαιός 'left(-hand)'. Similarly the specific contrast of ἀριστερός 'left' would be with δεξιός.

Some extensions of the basic idea are easy to penetrate, as **k*ʷ*o-tero*- 'which (of two)?' next to **k*ʷ*o*- 'which' (in general); and, as mentioned above, **H₂en-tero*- 'the other' in contrast to **H₂el-yo*- '(an)other'. Ved. (late) *aśvatará*- 'mule' is lit. 'the horsy one', in contrast to 'ass'.

Some require more thought: L *mātertera* 'maternal aunt; mother's sister' is often explained as 'quasi-mother' or the like, which is wrong; if anyone in that society was a quasi-mother it was the *amita* 'paternal aunt'. 'Quasi-AUNT' would be closer to it. The formation in *-tera* implies a specific opposition—'the mother one' vs. *amita* 'aunt par excellence' (the generic term, as corroborated by its survival in Romance).

In these senses the suffixes are attested in G, L, Indic, and elsewhere. The contrastive force is lost in some forms, which therefore have generic meaning, as in G ἡμέτερος 'our', L *noster*, and OIr. *náthar* du. 'of us two' (371), or the Hom. phrase θηλύτεραι γυναῖκες 'delicate women' (unless of course this still has some such force as 'by-contrast-delicate women').

G δεξίτερος 'right', L *dexter*.

G πότερος 'which of two'; Ved. *katará*-, OE *hwæþer* (which corroborates the G accent).

L *alter* 'the other', Go. *anþar*, OE *óþer*; Ved. *anyatará*-. Cf. L *alius*, G ἄλλος 'another'.

The form without *-t-* is limited to derivatives of relational forms, as seen in G ὕπερος 'pestle', Ved. *upári* 'upper', L *superus*.

The original state of affairs, albeit in relic form, is preserved in L. In Indic and G, the function of the affix graduates to the paradigmatic comparative: G δηλό-τερος (δῆλος 'conspicuous'), γλυκύ-τερος (γλυκύς 'sweet'), μελάν-τερος (μέλᾱς 'black'), ἀληθέσ-τερος (ἀληθής 'true'), χαριέσ-τερος (χαρίεις 'graceful'). In some cases the affix is based on a noun, as in βασιλεύτερος 'more king'.

356. ABSOLUTIVES IN *-(T)M̥MO-. Correlative with the suffixes in *-*(t)ero*-, and like them built to stems rather than directly to roots, was another pair of suffixes: *-*tm̥mo*- and *-*m̥mo*-, the latter like *-*ero*- somewhat rare. The function of these in the protolanguage is harder to pin down, but seems to have been one of extreme (or unsurpassable) particularity—something like the familiar superlatives of modern European languages, in fact.

The syllabic nasal is remarkable. Sievers' Law (178), in the unlikely event that it even applied to such matters, cannot be the explanation: most PIE adjective stems ended in vowels, so an appeal to leveling from the relatively few forms where the suffix was preceded by a consonant and was therefore **-tm̥mo-* per Sievers' Law is implausible; and in any case that explanation cannot account for the *t*-less **-m̥mo-*. The latter, furthermore, is probably the original form of the suffix, having acquired its *-t-* from **-tero-* via the following proportion: **upero-* : **upm̥mo-* :: **entero-* : *X*, where *X* = **entm̥mo-*. Note that Gmc. still has **enm̥mo-* as in Go. *innuma* 'innermost'. (The long *-nn-* is a puzzle.) An original **-(t)m̥Ho-* solves the phonological problem, but there is no reason otherwise to suppose the presence of a laryngeal. A complex of two separate elements, **-m̥-* and **-mo-*, is indefensible morphologically. Without prejudice to the verities of reconstruction, we will continue to write **-(t)m̥mo-*.

In Italic there are a handful of forms built this way. Each is typically paired with a contrastive in *-tero-* on the one hand and an antonym on the other: *extimus* 'outermost' (cf. *exterus* 'an outsider', with the typical force of the **-tero-* suffix); *intimus* 'innermost' (*intero-* not attested as such but evident in *interior*). Similarly *citimus* 'nearest', *ultimus* 'farthest', and so on. The same apparently holds for Sab., so O **últiumam** = L *ultimam*, U *hondomu* 'from the lowest' (cf. U *hondra* = L *īnfrā*). Gmc. has parallel forms, like Go. *fruma* 'first' and *innuma* 'the innermost'; and also some others where the original form has been papered over with the usual superlative affix, as in *hindumists* 'hindmost'. The forms are few in number, and in meaning refer exclusively to orientation, as in L. (This is the source, via metanalysis, of the NE affix *-most* in *topmost, uppermost, northernmost,* and so on.)

In G and Indic, however, the type effloresces pari passu with the spread of **-tero-* as a paradigmatic comparative. On both formal and functional grounds the G and Indic developments appear to be independent. In Indic the reflex is *-tama-*, a straightforward product of the sound laws, whereas in G the expected suffix **-ταμο-* was replaced by *-τατο-*, usually explained as contamination by *-ιστο-*. Such a heaping up of suffixes is not uncommon, but usually it is found in particular words rather than in a whole class, for example L *interior* with **-tero-* and **-yos-* on the same stem, or G ʼἀσσοτέρω 'closer', ʼἀσσοτάτω adv. (built to comparative ἆσσον < **ankʰ-yon*, 354).

Functionally, too, in the RV the suffix is still close to the parent language, with inherited relational forms like *uttamá-* 'uppermost' and a few intensives, not true superlatives, derived from adjectives: *puru-táma-* 'abundant, very much, very often'; *rayíntama-* 'very rich'. At this stage, moreover, it actually forms more derivatives from nouns than from adjectives by a ratio of about two to one: *mātṛ́-tama-* (of the waters) 'very motherly' or perhaps 'best of mothers'; and it is even added to participles (*sáhant-tama-* 'most conquering'). In the later Vedas the importance of both *-tara-* and *-tama-* considerably increases, and by the Epic period they have evolved into paradigmatic comparative and superlative suffixes. It is possible of course that the paradigmatic use of these things actually occurred much earlier, and that the pattern of Vedic attestation is a matter of diction, the new-fangled use of *-tara-/-tama-* as simple comparative/superlative being too colloquial for poetic and ritual purposes but eventually supplanting *-(ī)yas-/-iṣṭha-* even in the literary language.

357. DETAILS OF THE GREEK FORMATIONS IN -τερος AND -τατος.

1. From *o*-stem adjectives there are two types, *-ότερος/-ότατος* following a heavy syllable, and *-ώτερος/-ώτατος* following a light: *σοφώτερος*, *-ώτατος* (*σοφός* 'skilled'), *νεώτερος* 'younger', *-ώτατος* 'youngest, most recent' (*νέος* 'new, young') but *μῑκρότερος* (*μῑκρός* 'small'), *κουφότερος* (*κοῦφος* 'nimble'), *πικρότερος* (*πικρός* 'sharp'). Only apparently exceptional are *στενότερος* (*στενός* 'narrow'), *κενότερος* (*κενός* 'empty'), since these are from earlier **στενϝο-*, **κενϝο-*. (In poetry there are occasional genuine deviations from the general rule.)

Some authorities explain the innovation as metrical lengthening in a string of light syllables. But there is no obvious reason why only forms built to *o*-stems underwent lengthening (there is no ˣ*γλυκῡτερος* in place of earlier *γλυκῠτερος*, for example.), not to mention numerous unaltered forms of the same shape elsewhere in the language, like *φερόμενος* midd. pple. Others therefore think that formations based on directional adverbs in *-ω* (**269.6a**) were the starting point, for example *ἀνώτερος* 'higher' (*ἄνω* 'upwards'), such formations then spreading as a result of their prosodic advantages. Such models were very few, however; and given the untidy nature of analogical remodeling, it is surprising—if this is the correct account of the form—that this process did not lead to at least a few established formations in *-ώτερος* following a heavy syllable.

2. From regular forms like *ἀληθέσ-τερος* and *χαριέσ-τερος* (**355**), secondary suffixes *-έστερος*, *-έστατος* evolved by metanalysis. These were transplanted to adjectives in *-ων* and to some in *-ο(ϝ)ος* (*-ους*) (including all in *-νο(ϝ)ος* (*-νους*)); and to some others. Thus *εὐδαιμονέστερος*, *εὐδαιμονέστατος* (*εὐδαίμων* 'fortunate, blessed'); *ἁπλούστερος* (*ἁπλο-έστερος*: *ἁπλόος* 'single'); *εὐνούστερος* (*εὔνους* < *εὔνο(ϝ)ος* 'friendly'); poet. *ἀφθονέστατος* next to usual *ἀφθονώτερος* (*ἄφθονος* 'without envy').

3. From several adjectives in *-αιος* and some others we have formations without expected *-ο-*, as *-αίτερος* (Hom. *γεραίτερος* for regular *γεραιότερος* from *γεραιός* 'old'); exceptionally *μεσαίτερος*, *-αίτατος* from *μέσος* 'middle'. This type started in certain forms in which adverbs in *-ᾰι* occurred next to adjectives in *-αιος*, like *παλαίτερος* (for *παλαιότερος*) 'old; ancient', where what is actually the comparative to *παλαιός* is formed as if based on *πάλαι* 'lately; anciently, long ago'.

4. Another metanalogical creation is *-ίστερος*, *-ίστατος*, resegmented from forms like *ἀχαρίσ-τερος* 'very ungracious' (*ἀχαριδ-*, **212**). Most such forms are derogatory: *κλεπτίστερος* 'thievingest' (*κλέπτης* 'thief'), *λαλίστερος* 'garrulous' (*λάλος* 'talkative').

358. The Latin superlative. The L superlative—apparently pan-Italic, but barely attested outside of L—agrees with Celtic: instead of the **-is-to-* complex shared by Gmc., G, and Indic, it combined the comparative suffix **-is-* with the **-m̥mo-* of the **-(t)ero-/*-(t)m̥mo-* set. (The original suffix **-(t)m̥mo-* also occurs in Italic, but in relics only; see 355.) The sound-laws yielded first **-isamo-* (Celt. and Sab.), **-isemo-* (L). The results in L were various, thanks to sound laws, contractions, and so on.

1. L *prīmus* 'first' < **prīsmos* < **prīsemos* < **pri-ism̥mo-* (cf. *prior* compar. < **pri-yōs*). Similarly *plūrimus* 'most' (see 353.4).

2. The same suffix underlies the forms in *-errimus* and *-illimus*, built originally to stems in *-ro-* and *-lo-*, respectively: thus to **polkro-* 'lovely' something like **polkrisemo-* > **polkrsemo-* (74.3) > **polkersimo-* (66.2) > *pulc(h)errimus* (223.3). Similarly *pigerrimus*, *integerrimus*. *Miserrimus* 'most wretched' < **miser-isemo-* shows the loss of the vowel in *-ri-* before an apical (74.3), which takes precedence over the Exon's Law syncope (74.5), thus intermediate **misersemo-*.

Whether superlatives to *ri-* and *li*-stems can be so arrived at depends on judgment: possibly forms like **fakliisemos*, **ākriisemos* would have become **faklisemos*, **ākrisemos* by the regular action of Exon's Law; but some might feel, with reason, that such forms would be more likely to have developed like *prīmus* in the absence of some analogical remodeling which yielded **faklisemos* and **ākrisemos*.[1] Much remodeling must underlie the similar-looking formations built to erstwhile *s*-stems: *veterrimus* 'oldest' cannot readily continue **wetusisemo-*; the development of *suprēmus* (3a, below) means that **wetusisemo-* would have given ˣ*vessēmus*. *Mātūrrimē* adv. 'most timely' (*mātūrus*), however, directly continues **mātūrisemo-*, with syncope of **-ri-* (74.3).

3. The most usual L type, as in *clārissimus* 'clearest', *gravissimus* 'heaviest', is also the most difficult. It is unparalleled in either Sab. or Celtic. It is pertinent that the expected development of **-(o)ism̥mos*, namely **-erimus*, is in fact nowhere at all to be found. The only explanation for both of these facts seems to be that *-issimus-* is an example of *expressive lengthening* of the **-s-*. Now, 'expressive' change has been invoked frivolously over the years, and is little more than a gong announcing the lack of a real explanation. But in this case for once it is not far-fetched. The superlative adjective has a distinct, and salient, semantic 'push', an emphasis which is often moreover conscious, like the emphatic aspirated stops in French in place of the otherwise plain articulation of such consonants. Besides, one might suppose that the prosodics of the specific form *pessimus* 'worst', and of the prominent types in *-errimus* and *-illimus* would inevitably contribute to the ultimate success of the ending *-(i)ssimus*.

a. There are a few L forms which might be traced to **-sm̥mo-* rather than **-ism̥mo-*,

---

[1] Formations with nom.sg. in *-ris* and *-bilis*, however, all form superlatives of the productive type (*illustrissimus*, *nōbilissimus*, and so on).

and they are so explained by many. But inasmuch as all can be just as easily traced to **-ism̥mo-*, and furthermore as all the forms in question formed comparatives with the usual suffix **-yos-/*-is-* from which **-ism̥mo-* is derived, Occam's Razor eliminates **-sm̥mo-*. So *maxumus/maximus* (**69**), given *magis* 'more', must have developed as follows: **magism̥mo-* > **magisemo-* > **maksemo-* per Exon's Law (**74.5**); likewise *proximus* 'closest' < **proksemo-* < **prokʷisemo-* (or **propsemo-* < **propisemo-*? cf. *prope* 'near', *propius* 'nearer'). Similarly *oxime* (*ōx-*? known only from Paul.Fest.) for usual *ōcissimē* 'most speedily': PItal. **ōkism̥mēd* would in fact give *ōximē* by regular processes. Similarly *clārimum* < **clārrimum* (**232.2**) < **klārisemo-*.

It is significant that the three odd-looking superlatives *suprēmus*, *extrēmus*, and *postrēmus* occur beside ordinary comparatives in *-ior*, and must be traced therefore to **-(t)erism̥mo-*: original **(s)uperisemo-*, for example, would regularly give **superezemo-* (**37a**: **iz* > **ez*, as in *serō* 'sow' < **sisō*). In such a string of light syllables, via extrapolation from Exon's Law, we would expect the the fourth as well as the second short vowel to syncopate, giving **suprezmo-*, whence regularly *suprēmo-*. Similarly with the others.

b. The etymology of *pessimus* 'worst' is uncertain. The scheme outlined above would yield the form starting from either **pet-* or **ped-* plus either **-ism̥mo-* or **-tm̥mo-*: the first via an Exon's Law syncope to **petsemo-*, the second via **212** treating a sequence of apical stops. The deciding evidence must be the antonym *optumus/optimus* (**69**) 'best': in L, superlatives in *-(t)imus-* always form antonymic pairs (*extimus/intimus*, for example), and they denote physical orientation. *Optimus* is therefore odd on two counts. The formal oddity is eliminated if we recognize *pessimus* as the other half of the pair, namely **ped/t-tm̥mo-*. The semantic problem is solved if the root of *pessimus* is recognized as **ped-* 'foot', which further implies that *op-* is etymologically something like 'head' or 'top' (which would point to taking G ἐπί 'on' to be the loc.sg. of a root noun, like ἀντί 'facing', **406.1**).

c. The special force of 'very', as seen in L superlatives, is merely a development out of the superlative sense—unlike the secondary sense of 'too' in the L comparative (**350**), which must be inherited. Cf. the NE distinction between *most* modifying definite and indefinite nouns: *the most amusing story* vs. *a most amusing story* (where *most* means no more than 'very').

359. SUPPLETIVE (COMPOSITE) COMPARISON. In G and L, as in many languages, several of the commonest adjectives form the comparative and superlative suppletively, that is, from stems formally unrelated to the positive (and, in a few cases, to one another). So in NE *bad*, *worse*, *worst* (formerly the comparative and superlative to *ill*); *good*, *better*, *best* (< *betst*). Additionally, sometimes different denotations of a semantically complex positive form different comparatives, as NE *little*, *less* (of quantity) next to *little*, *littler* (of size).

G ἀγαθός 'good', ἀμείνων, ἄριστος.
G ἀγαθός 'noble', βελτίων, βέλτιστος.
G κακός 'inferior', χείρων, χείριστος (but κακός 'bad', κακίων, κάκιστος).
L *bonus*, *melior*, *optimus*.
L *malus*, *peior*, *pessimus*.
L *multus*, *plūs*, *plūrimus*.

PRONOUNS

Personal Pronouns

360. The personal pronouns in the IE languages show a bewildering variety of forms. The similarities are obvious, but the precise paradigms of the parent speech are very difficult to reconstruct. Even a full-blown grammar of PIE would be all but overwhelmed by a discussion of everything at stake. What are given as PIE forms here, therefore, are not always explained or defended, and are to be taken as points of departure for certain sets of correspondences, with more or less extensive remodeling that can be only briefly outlined.

A single example of the complexities involved will drive this point home, and may be interesting per se:—

G ἐγώ and L *ego* 'I' may be unproblematically combined in the (pre-laryngeal) PIE etymon **eǵō̆*. But **-ō̆* does not accord either with Go. *ik*, which like all the Germanic forms requires a short final vowel originally; or with OCS *azŭ*, which reflects a final **-oC*; and still further off-target are Ved. *ahám*, Av. *azəm*, (OP *adam*), all of which imply a PIE **eǵhóm*. Hom. ἐγών bears an obvious resemblance to these but cannot be superimposed on the InIr. forms; the most straightforward explanation for the form, and for the unexpected accentuation of ἐγώ, would be that both G forms are conflations of expected *ἔγω and *ἐγόν (= Ved. *ahám*). Other forms are Latv. *es*, Lith. *àš* (OLith. *eš*; Lith. *a* < *e* is unremarkable), with devoicing in final position and with no evidence for anything at all following the **ǵ*.

With the laryngeal theory, it became possible to gather up some of the cited forms under **éǵoH* (G and L) and **eǵH-óm* (G, OCS, InIr.), the latter derived from the former by a tonic particle (emphatic? deictic?). Such an **eǵHom* would also do for the literary Gmc. languages (Go. *ik*, OE *ic*, OHG *ih*; cf. Go. *haurn*, OE *horn* < PGmc. **hurna*^{n} < **ḱr̥nom*). But the golden horn of Gallehus has *ek* and *horna* acc. 'horn' in the same inscription: PGmc. **eka*^{n} < **eǵHom* should have given archaic ˣ*eka*, just like archaic *horna* < PGmc. **hurna*^{n} < **ḱr̥Hnom*. So the Gmc. pronoun is perhaps from **éǵoH* after all, if the final laryngeal was lost without lengthening.

But problems remain. A form like **éǵoH* has too many full grades to be a genuinely ancient form (especially if the **H* is specifically **H*$_3$, and the etymon is **éǵeH*$_3$), so perhaps our attested forms are ALL more or less compilations of some sort. The astute proposal has been made that the etymon of the classical (and Germanic?) forms represents the innovation: that **éǵom* (not **eǵHom*[1]) is composed of **om* '1st person', seen in the verb endings **-mi*, **-m̥*, and in the oblique stems of the 1st person pronoun (as seen in 363), plus an atonic deictic element seen elsewhere in such elements as G γε, γα, Go. *mik* acc. 'me' < **me-ge* (or **me-ga*), *þuk* acc. 'thee' < **te-ge* (*-ga*), Venetic EGO/MEGO. Indic **aǰham* (whence *ahám*) in place of expected **aǰam* is then to be explained as contamination by dat. **maǰhi* (367.3; the ancestor of *máhya*). The **eǵō̆* of the classical languages in this view is a remodeling, presumably independent, of a reanalyzed **éǵom* on the pattern of the domi-

---

[1] Or maybe **eǵHom* after all: on the basis of the oblique G stem ἐμ- (367.2) it has recently been argued that the obl. 1sg. stem was **H*$_1$*me-*, not **me-*: thus **eǵ-H*$_1$*om*.

nant 1sg. verb ending *-ō*. Evidence for the originality of the InIr. and OCS forms might be further provided by L *egŏmet* (emphatic; ? < **eǵom eti* 'I moreover; I for my part').

Even this elegant analysis leaves loose ends. It envisions a surprising position of the particle in PIE **eǵ-om*: in PIE, **ǵe*, **ǵa*, like deictic particles in general, typically follow the modified element—seemingly, in clause-initial position were obliged to (Wackernagel's Law, 87 fn.)—as is the case with G γε, PGmc. **mek*, **þek*, and the usual analysis of Ved. *ahám*. Moreover, an analysis which does away with suppletion is not (for once) attractive per se: suppletion, particularly in the nom. forms of PIE pronouns, is the rule (361, 374.1). Nor under this analysis is PGmc. **ek* 'I' instead of ˣ*eka* any less puzzling than before, though one possibility for rescue is the surmise of an early remodeling after **mek* and **þek*. Older Hitt. *ú-uk*, later *ú-ug-ga* are not conspicuously in harmony with the analysis. Finally, a pronominal particle *-*ōm* is in any case otherwise needed for Ved. *idám* 'it' (= L *id* plus *-*óm*), *iyám* 'she' (**iH₂-óm*), and for Gmc. *-*ōm* in **þatā* 'that', **hitā* 'it', **hʷatā* 'what', seen in Go *þata*, *hita*, OE *hwæt*.

Note that in a general sense the number and kind of things left unexplained by either analysis is about the same; only the details differ.

361. PECULIARITIES OF PERSONAL PRONOUNS. The personal pronouns are distinctive in several ways.

First, they are reconstructable for the first and second persons only. The third person paradigms differ importantly from group to group and are specialized deictics, not really personal pronouns at all in the sense that the 1st and 2nd persons are, or in the sense that 3rd person pronouns are in languages like English or French. The parent language presumably had a 3rd person paradigm (366.2)—it is indispensible in fact, in oblique cases—but it has not been identified to general satisfaction.

Second, they are undifferentiated for gender. (Tocharian is remarkable for having gender-specific 1st person pronouns, an alien development influenced by neighboring languages.)

Third, in each paradigm the stem for the nominative is different from the stem for the oblique forms. Suppletion is a feature of PIE pronouns in general, but the lack of integration of the forms of the personal pronouns in particular into a proper paradigm follows from the lack of functional integration: since the subject functions '1sg.', '2pl.', and so on, are carried by the verb, the so-called nom. of a personal pronoun is not a SUBJECT CASE but rather an emphatic or topicalizing PARTICLE, like Fr. *moi* 'as for me'.

Fourth, the roots for the du. and pl. forms appear to be unrelated to the roots for the singular, though a common root for the oblique forms of the 1sg. and 1du./pl. has been defended (366.6).

362. The following reconstruction of the PIE personal pronouns endorses one of several quite different analyses, all more or less schematic, which have been recently framed by important scholars. No matter how the forms are analyzed, they show a system of inflection which is unlike the nouns in some ways. The case-marked forms fall into two subdivisions. The earliest stratum is represented by certain case forms which appear to

be the most ancient—accusative and genitive, and the enclitics generally—probably predating the usual PIE noun inflections. A somewhat later stratum consists of a set of case-marked forms resembling the nominal declension but very different in detail. For example, in the dual and plural paradigms (in this analysis) the markers for cases and number (*-H_1- 'du.' and *-*s*- 'pl.') are separate and distinct, the case-markers most closely resembling items of SINGULAR noun inflection (cf. 366.3).

The final peculiarity of these paradigms is the presence of atonic (enclitic) vs. tonic forms for certain basic cases, pretty systematic in the protolanguage but diverging in the daughters and much subject to leveling and contamination. Indo-Iranian, OCS, and Hittite best attest the enclitic/tonic distinction, but the history of both G and L pronouns is clarified by reference to the earlier system.

363. TABLES OF PERSONAL PRONOUN FORMS. The personal pronouns of the most archaic IE languages are as follows. (Full discussion will be found in 366–70.) In these tables only selected forms, typically the oldest, are list-

1ST PERSON SINGULAR

	Vedic	Avestan	OCS	G	OL	Go.	(Old) Hitt.
Nom.	ahám	azəm	azŭ	ἐγώ	ego	ik	ú-uk
				Hom. ἐγών			
Acc.	mā́m	mąm		ἐμέ	mēd	mik	am-mu-uk
encl.	mā	mā	mę	με			-mu
Gen.	máma	mana	mene	ἐμεῖο	meī	meina	am-me-el
				ἐμός	meus		
encl.	me	mē		μευ	mīs		-mi-iš
Abl.	mát	maṯ			mēd		am-me-e-da-az
Dat.	máhya(m)	maibyā	mĭnĕ	ἐμοί	mihī	mis	am-mu-uk
encl.	me		mi	μοι			-mu

2ND PERSON SINGULAR

	Vedic	Avestan	OCS	G	OL	Go.	(Old) Hitt.
Nom.	(*tū)	tū	ty	σύ	tū	þu	zi-ik
	tuvám	tvə̄m		Hom. τύνη			
Acc.	tvā́m	θwąm		σέ	tēd	þuk	tu-uk
encl.	tvā	θwā	tę	σε			-ta, -d-du
Gen.	táva	tava	tebe	σεῖο	tuī	þeina	tu(-e)-el
					tīs		
				σός	tuus		
encl.	te	tē		σευ			-ti-iš
Abl.	tvát	θwāṯ			tēd		tu-e-da-az
Dat.	túbhya(m)	taibyā	tebě	σοί	tibī	þus	tu-uk, tu-ga
encl.	te		ti	σοι			-ta, -d-du
				(τοι)			

ed. In many cases attested pronoun systems have undergone changes during the historical period, or retain a few antique relics in the earliest records. So, for example, in OCS generally genitives are used as accusatives; this secondary development within OCS is not noticed in these tables.

The Vedic forms shown with *-(m)* regularly have the final consonant in the later language; in the RV they often occur without it, and even when it is present in the RV text as received the meter sometimes points to an originally *m*-less form.

Ved. *tuvám* nom. is always written *tvám* and often so scans. In later portions of the text at least a few instances of monosyllabic *tvám* might be the normal result of a sound law (which yields postvedic Skt. *tvam*). In earlier passages, where it is particularly common in line-initial position, it is a replacement of **tū*. Contrariwise, *tvā́m* acc. (always so written) often must scan *tuvā́m*. Since this reading is unetymological and more frequent in later hymns than early ones it is unlikely to continue anything old.

On the basis of the preceding, we reconstruct the PIE singular forms as something along the following lines:

		First Person	*Second Person*
'Nom.'		eǵoH	tī̆ (tū̆)
Acc.	*enclitic*	me	te
	tonic	**m-mé (> *mé)	t-wé
Gen.	*enclitic*	mos (*adj.*)	tos (*adj.*)
	tonic	mé-me	té-we
Dat.	*enclitic*	mey, ?moy	tey, toy
	tonic	mébhi	tébhi
Abl.		**mm-ét (> *mét)	tw-ét

364. TABLES OF THE PLURAL PRONOUNS.

1ST PERSON PLURAL

	Vedic	Avestan	OCS	G	OL	Go.	(Old) Hitt.
Nom.	vayám	vaēm	my OPr. mai Lith. mes	ἡμεῖς/ ἄμμες	nōs	weis	ú-e-eš
Acc.	asmā́n	ahma		ἡμέας/ ἄμμε	nōs	uns(is)	an-za-a-aš
encl.	nas	nå	ny				-na-aš
Gen.	asmā́kam	ahmākəm	nasŭ	ἡμέων	nostrī, nostrum	unsara	an-zi-el
encl.	nas	nə̄					
Abl.	asmát	ahmat̰			nōbīs		an-zi-ta-az
Dat.	asmé asmábhya(m)	 ahmaibyā	namŭ	ἡμῖν/ ἄμμι(ν)	nōbīs	uns(is)	-na-aš
encl.	nas	nə̄	ny				-na-aš

2ND PERSON PLURAL

	Vedic	Avestan	OCS	G	OL	Go.	(Old) Hitt.
Nom.		yūš	vy	ὑμεῖς/ ὔμμες	vōs	jus	šu-me(-e)-eš
	yūyám	yūžəm					
Acc.	yuṣmā́n			ὑμέας/ ὔμμε	vōs	izwis	šu-ma(-a)-aš
encl.	vas	vå	vy				-š-ma-aš
Gen.	yuṣmā́kam	yušmākəm	vasŭ	ὑμέων	vostrī	izwara	šu-me-en-za-an
encl.	vas	və̄					
Abl.	yuṣmát	yušmaṯ			vōbīs		
Dat.	yuṣmé		vamŭ	ὑμῖν/	vōbīs	izwis	šu-ma(-a)-aš
	yuṣmábhya(m)	yušmaibyā		ὔμμι(ν)			
encl.	vas	və̄	vy				-š-ma-aš

On the basis of the preceding, we reconstruct the PIE plural forms along the following lines:

		First Person	Second Person
'Nom.'		we-i	yūs (?yuHs)
Acc.	tonic	n̥smé	usmé
	enclitic	nŏ̄s	wŏ̄s
Gen.	tonic	n̥sóm	usóm
	enclitic	nŏ̄s	wŏ̄s
Dat.	tonic	n̥sm-éy	usm-éy
	enclitic	nŏ̄s	wŏ̄s
Abl.		n̥sm-ét	usm-ét

365. FIRST AND SECOND PERSONS DUAL

		First Person			Second Person		
		Vedic	OCS	Greek	Vedic	OCS	Greek
'Nom.'		āvám	vě	νῶϊ, νώ	yuvám	va	σφώ, σφῶϊ
	(RV vā́m once)						
Acc.		āvā́m	na	νῶϊ, νώ	yuvā́m	va	σφώ, σφῶϊ
encl.		nāu				vām	
	(Av. nā)						

Reconstructed PIE:		First Person	Second Person
'Nom.'		weH₁	yuH₁ (?yūH₁)
Acc.	tonic	n̥H₁-wé	uH₁-wé
	enclitic	nŏ̄H₁	wŏ̄H₁

366. GLOTTOGONIC NOTES.

1. The paradigm of the reflexive *se- is parallel to that of 2sg. *te-, differing only in lacking a 'subject' form, naturally. Otherwise: *s-wé tonic objective, *se enclitic; sé-we tonic gen., *sos encl.; and so on.

2. In the most archaic IE languages the reflexive pronouns reflecting

*se- served for all persons and genders. The G forms of this stem partly retain their reflexive force in Homer, but are generally used for simple reference to the third person, and in L, too, often refer to entities other than the subject of the verb. Some have seen this as evidence that *se- was originally simply a third person pronoun, the missing analog of the PIE first and second person stems. This is reasonable; PIE MUST have had some sort of third person pronoun predating the assortment of deictics that take over that function in the daughter languages.[1] However, the semantics of emphatic (or high-focus), reflexive, and ordinary pronouns are diachronically fairly unstable; three humdrum examples among the countless attested are: the weakening of reflexives to more or less ordinary pronouns seen in colloquial English, as in a sentence like *It was addressed to Fred and myself*; L *ipse* (377.6) is used of all persons and numbers; and Fr. *son, sa* 'his, her' (generic 3sg.) is from L *suus* (refl.).

3. The tonic elements *-*wé* and *-*mé* seen in several cases do not exactly agree with any nominal element. They look like (nascent) stem-formants, not case-markers: the addition of 'singular' case-markers like **n̥-s-m-et* 1pl.abl. appears to be the beginnings of the rather different system seen in the usual noun inflection (in which in the present example the abl. *-*t* is limited to the singular).

4. The tonic acc. has this element *-*wé*, *-*mé* added to the zero grade of the pronoun; the resulting ***mmé* (? < ****memé*) is for all practical purposes PIE **mé*. With the addition of tonic endings, the element is itself in zero grade: **twét* abl.sg. is morphologically **t-w-ét*.

5. Where morphological boundaries can be readily seen, the atonic cases are added to zero grade of the stem, as in **n̥smi* (***m̥-s-m-i*) 1pl.loc., where *-*i* is the case ending proper; dat. **moy*, **toy*, **n̥smey* are ambiguous, but are presumably to be analyzed the same way: ending *-*oy*, *-*ey* added to zero grade **m-*, **t-*, **n̥sm-*.

6. The 1du. and 1pl. in **n̥H_1-* (366.7) and **n̥s-* probably continue earlier ***m̥H_1-*, ***m̥s-*, with the same element as seen in the 1sg. oblique stem. This surmise might be making too much of what could be a chance resemblance, except that there is reason to think that genuinely ancient ***n̥s-* would have developed differently; NB the change of **-*ons* nom.sg. of the *n*-stems (282) to *-*ō*, in contrast to acc.pl. *-*ons* < **-*oms* (257.14). If this is the correct

[1] In this view, the 'missing' nominative singulars of the paradigm would be found in **se* m., **seH_2* f., of the deictic paradigm discussed in 376.1. The development of deictic force by one case of a deixis-neutral item is easy in a language where the neutral expression of a nominative 3rd person subject anaphor would have been in the verb ending. An overt nom. 3rd person pronoun, that is to say, would necessarily have had a marked meaning (emphasis, contrast and such), which might lead to their alienation from the neutral (oblique-only) paradigm.

interpretation, the change of *m̥- to *n̥- was very early, as its results were generalized though the whole paradigm, even to the enclitic *nŏ̄s (L nōs, Ved. nas, Hitt. -na-aš), which would then be a replacement of *mŏ̄s. But the verb endings *-me(dhH̥₂), *-mos(dhH̥₂) (427) were unaffected.

7. RV vā̆m 1du. is from PInIr. *vā-ám; later āvám has ā- imported from the oblique stem. —The development of the du. pronouns in Gmc. is easier to defend if the marker of the du. is reconstructed as *-H_3- (257.16c, 370a). The outcomes in all other languages are the same if *-H_3- is substituted for *-H_1- in these etyma.

8. Hitt. zi-ik nom. 'thou', tu-uk acc., reveal that the nom. *tŭ̄ of the familiar IE languages is a remodeling of original *tĭ̄, a root which may or may not be connected historically with obl. *t-; but once the complexes *twé and *téwe came to be perceived as manifestations of a root *tw-, the original *tĭ̄ was remodeled as *tŭ̄.

a. There have been a variety of attempts to trace the Anatolian 2sg.nom. pronoun, Hitt. zi-ik and Palaic ti, to PIE *twe- or *tū. None can be called successful, and in fact the evidence of Hitt. that the 2sg. pronoun was suppletive like all the other pronouns of PIE should be welcome news.

367. SINGULAR.

1. Nom.Sg.

1st. person. PIE *eǵoH, G ἐγώ, L ego with iambic shortening (84). Cf. Go. ik, OE ic /ič/, Northumbrian ih, NE I. See 360 for full discussion of the evidence and the reconstruction.

2nd. person. G σῠ̆ (in most dialects), Dor. τύ, L tū. See 366.7, above. The σ- of G σύ is after the analogy of other cases where it comes regularly from *tw- (190.4), for example acc. σέ (σε) < *twé (4, below). The -νη of Hom. and Dor. τῦνη is probably an emphatic particle; it reminds one of the RV 2pl. marker -(ta)-nā (428) though as that is pl. only its relevance is doubtful. What is clearer is that the interplay between ἐγών and τῦνη resulted in hybrids like ἐγώνη (unless it was simply formed from ἐγώ the same way) and Boeot. τυν nom. Go. þu, OE þŭ̄ (long tonic, short atonic, the former underlying early NE thou), OCS ty. Ved. tuvám (written tvám) < *tū-óm, either with the same added element as in 1sg. ahám, or as some think (360) original in ahám and imported from it. Remarkably, the form is very commonly monosyllabic in the RV, which is easily explained as the redactional replacement of earlier *tŭ̄ with tvám (tū̆ freely occurs, but only as an adverb 'pray!, do!, then'; in the RV it is usually found with 2sg. imperative verbs, but even there its original function as a form of address had been reinterpreted as an asseverative.) Av. has both tū and tvə̄m, the latter disyllabic.

2. Gen.sg. The aboriginal tonic form *méme is preserved only in Indic (Ved. máma); in Av. (mana) and BS the second -m- dissimilates, and in BS becomes the stem for a number of other cases. In G (and Arm.) the devel-

opment is to **eme*, which may be a case of dissimilation but may rather show the influence of nom. **eǵ-*.[1] This was further remodeled in G with the usual pronominal gen.sg. ending **-syo* (**259.8A**): so Hom. ἐμεῖο (**eme-syo*); as if from **twe*, σεῖο 2sg. (**twesyo*, for expected **tewesyo*); as if from **swe*, εἷο refl. (**swesyo*, for expected **sewesyo*; the stems **tewe-* and **sewe-* are in fact attested in dial. gen.sg. forms, below). The use of the acc. as the basis for **twesyo* and **swesyo* must have something to do with the homophony of gen. **eme* and acc. **eme* in G. The 1st. person gen.sg. corresponding to **twesyo*, that is, built to the acc. encl. stem is actually seen in Att. μου (enclitic) < *μεο < *μειο < **mesyo*. The influence of ἐγώ certainly promoted the dominance of the types with initial ἐ-, whatever their precise source. —From the same forms the sound laws variously produce ἐμέο, ἐμεῦ, Att. ἐμοῦ; σέο, σεῦ, Att. σοῦ (enclitic σεο, σευ, σου); ἕο, εὗ, Att. οὗ, (enclitic ἑο, εὑ, οὑ).

G ἐμέθεν, σέθεν, ἕθεν have the same adverbial ending as ἄλλο-θεν 'from elsewhere', added to gen. **eme* and acc. **twe*, **swe*.

In the Dor. forms ἐμέος, ἐμεῦς; τέος, τεῦς; and Locr. ϝεος, the starting points are genitives **téwe*, **séwe*, in all probability first as **tewes*, **hewes* with the addition of genitival *-s*, but when all **-es* in the gen.sg. were ousted by *-os*, the pronouns were remodeled too as **tewos*, **(h)ewos*; the 1sg. was presumably **emewos*, based on these.

A remodeling very similar to what happened in Doric accounts for the Italic forms: from **tewe* and **sewe* were created regularly inflected adjectives: nom. **tewos*, **sewos*, gen. **tewī*, **sewī*, whence via the usual Italic and L sound laws, OL *tovos*, *sovos*, later *tuus*, *suus* (O **tuvai**, U *touer*, O **suvam**). But expected 1sg. **memos* is not seen. Attested *meus* etc. might be **memos* with loss of the the second *-m-*. More likely than the loss of an *-m-* without a trace, however, would have been **mewos*, whether a remodeling of **memos* in imitation of **tewos*, **sewos*, or via some sort of dissimilation similar to *f* . . . *m-* < **m* . . . *m-* (**223.4**). But then the form should be ×*muus*, like *tuus*, *suus*. Any would-be explanation is ad-hoc. **Mewos* might be salvaged as the etymon via some sort of dissimilatory loss of the **-w-*. Or perhaps the starting point was **mey*, the enclit. dat. (used as possessive), whence **meyos*. Formally this is straightforward, except that the only unambiguous attestation of the starting form (G μοι) has *o*-grade (Ved. *me*, Av. *mē*, OCS *mi* are all ambiguous outright; Gmc. **mis*, **þis* might be more readily traced to **mey*, **tey* than **moy*, **toy*, but the forms are difficult in detail either way). Functionally there is the discrepancy of the employment of the tonic possessive as the basis for **tewos* and **sewos* but the atonic dat. (possessive) for **meyos*.

L *meī*, *tuī*, *suī* are in origin the gen.sg.m. (**259.8B**) of the possessives

---

[1] Some see in G ἐμε- a prothetic vowel (**89**) on original **me-*, which may be true; but analogical forces alone readily account for the ἐ-. In a latter-day variation of this theory, it has been argued that the PIE 1sg. stem was actually *H_1*me-* (**360**, fn.; **90**).

meus, tuus, suus. Early L has also, but rarely, *mīs, tīs*, perh. by adding gen. *-s* to enclitic **moy*, **toy* (or even more easily from **mey*, **tey*, if such existed; see above), as seen in Ved. gen.dat. *me, te*, G dat. μοι, σοι, OCS *mi, ti.*

a. In Hitt., the genitive personal prn. is chiefly found as the object of postpositions governing the genitive. It is used as a possessive only in the later language, and then not commonly. The older mode of expressing possession is an enclitic pronominal adjective, agreeing with the possessed noun in gender, number, and case. In earlier or archaic texts, both noun and enclitic inflect fully; later there is a tendency for the noun to appear in a sort of frozen nom.sg., the enclitic alone inflecting. Nothing exactly like this is evident in other IE languages, but G 'short' possessives (Hom., Att.-Ion. σός 'thy', ὅς 'own') and the OCS possessive adjectives *mojĭ, tvojĭ, svojĭ* (all persons; *tvojĭ* and *svojĭ* imported their *-v-* from other forms) continue the old category. Ved. *me, te* Av. *mē, tē* (genitive, atonic) appear to be datives, traced by some authorities to the dative of possession (a construction extinct in InIr., but its loss might in fact explain how original datives came to be reinterpreted as gen. in InIr.). Of course, in the pl. the enclitics **nas* and **vas* (368) served as both dat. and gen. in PInIr., which perhaps led to the use of orig. dat. **may*, **tay* as gen. in the corresponding singular. —G ἐμός appears to be in a sense the reflex of both **(m)éme* and **mos*: whether the ἐ- on the reflex of the latter is best regarded as a prothetic vowel or a contamination from ἐγώ, ἐμεῖο, and the like, is a matter of personal choice.

b. A gen. **méne*, with the second **-m-* dissimilated, forms the basis for other tonic oblique cases of the BS 1sg. prn. In the 2sg. there is a similar reworking of oblique cases, but with a dialect division: in East Baltic the parallel gen. **téwe* is the basis of the new forms; but in West Baltic and Slavic the orig. dat. **tébhi* is the basis.

3. Dat.sg. The tonic form **mébhi* is lost in G; tonic ἐμοί, σοί are restressed enclitics. Next to these are the more conservative enclitic μοι (= Ved. gen.dat. *me*) and σοι. The latter might be the regular development of **twoy*, but the σ- of nom. σύ (for τύ) must come from σέ < **twe*, and that could be the source of the σ- of σοι < **toy* (the properly *w*-less form) as well. (Definitely *w*-less is the Att. particle τοι 'see here, mark you', if it is the encl. dat. < **toy*, Ved. *te*, unaltered by the leveling that altered the paradigmatic dat. σοι.) Dor. τοί, τοι present a similar ambiguity: since **tw* > Dor. τ, there is no way of knowing whether the precursor of τοι was unchanged from PG or first modified to *τϝοι after τϝε. At all events there is no direct attestation of *τϝοι, as there is of τϝε acc. (190.4). 'Refl.' οἷ, οἱ, in many dialects ϝοι, is from **swoy*, a replacement of orig. **soy* (as also in Ved. *svayám* 'self'). This is not a development of PG date, however, as the form not uncommonly scans in Hom. with no ϝ-; Av. *he, šē* are likewise without *-*w*-, as **sw*- would give Av. x^v-, not *h*-. Hom. also has ἑοῖ < **sewoy* modeled after the gen.

Dor. also has dat.sg. ἐμίν, τίν, ϝιν, with the same shape as in the dat.pl. (for example Hom. ἄμμιν). However, it would be remarkable for a sg. pronoun to be remodeled in the image of a pl. one. Some have therefore thought of InIr. loc. singular forms **asmi* 'him/it', **kasmi* 'whom/what' **yasmi* rel. (Ved. *asmín, kasmín, yásmin*—but in a large proportion of passages the meter runs better without the *-n*, and cf. Av. *ahmi, kahmi*). Such forms are to be sure functionally very much more plausible as a source, but they are hardly attested in G: Gortyn inscr. OTIMI, which might be such a form, has been explained as ὄ-τῑμι (*-τισμι remodeled from *-τεσμι or *-ποσμι on the basis of the τίς paradigm); but this explanation is disputed.

L *mihi, tibi, sibi* with iambic shortening (84) from *mihī, tibī, sibī,* from *meǵhey, *tebhey, *sebhey.* Cf. U *mehe, tefe,* O **tfei** (that is, /tefei/), **sífeí**, OPr. *tebbei, sebbei,* OCS *tebě, sebě.* Beside *mihī* also *mī,* like *nīl* for *nihil* (159, 88.1). The weakening of the first-syllable vowels to *-i-* is mentioned in 41.2.

a. In both Ital. and BS, dat. forms originally in *-*bhi* (the ending seen in G ναῦφι, 257.8), were slightly retouched as *-*bhey* and *-*mey* to make them look more like proper dative forms. Anything so obvious cannot be assumed to be a shared innovation. In Indic there was also remodeling, the *-am* either imported from *ahám* and *tuvám* or having a common origin with them. The etymon **meǵhi* for **mébhi* in the 1sg. is attested in Ital. and Indic but not in Iranian, as witness Av. *maibyā.* The likeliest explanation is dissimilation. It is not an ancient development; if it were PInIr. or earlier, the Av. form *maibyā* has to be explained as an importation from 2sg. *taibyā,* and one does not expect to see 2nd person forms influencing 1st person forms. (If such an influence were so salient, it should have militated against the replacement of **mebhi* in the first place.) In fact, the similarity between Ital **meχey* and Indic *máhyam* may be only skin deep: *-bh-* occasionally becomes Indic *-h-* (140.3), a development all the more reasonable here as a dissimilation from the initial *m-*, together with the influence of nom. *ahám.* Indic *túbhya(m)* for **tábhya(m)* is a case of contamination.

The above-recited derivation (360) of Indic *ahám* nom. from **eǵom* assumes the reverse development: **maźhi(-am)*—from **mabhi(am)* by dissimilation—then by contamination **aźham,* whence regularly Ved. *ahám* and *mahyá(m).*

4. Acc.sg. In PIE the tonic form had the same element as the tonic gen., *-*me* or *-*we*; in this case it bears the tonic accent and the pronoun stem itself is in zero grade: ***m-mé* (presently **mé*), **t-wé,* **s-wé.* The enclitic forms consisted of the full grade of the bare stem, **me,* **te,* **se.* In Indo-Iranian this contrast was remodeled: the old atonic underwent vowel lengthening (apparently regular in monosyllables), so encl. *mā, tvā,* the latter with *-v-* imported from tonic *tvā́m.* (The refl. prn. **swe-* disappears in Indic apart from stray forms like *svayam* 'by itself', and is attested only in two stray cases in Av.) New tonic forms were created by the usual addition of *-ám* to the original tonic forms, hence *mā́m* and *tvā́m* < **ma-ám,* **tva-ám.* Both are not uncommonly disyllabic in the RV, but the disyllabic readings are actually commoner in later hymns than in earlier ones, and in any case disyllabic *tvā́m* is usually ambiguous as to whether *tuvā́m* (in imitation of nom. *tuvám* < **tūám*) or *tvaám* is to be read. Both readings are probably to some extent artificial, like *merimaid* for *mermaid* in the old song. The monosyllabic scansion of Av. *θwąm* accords with the development of *θw* < **tw.* The long vowel of Indic *mā, tvā* encl. is secondary; that of Av. *mā, θwā* is purely graphic.

G ἐμέ, με; σέ, σε, Dor. τέ (Dor. also τύ, nom. used as acc.), Hesych. τϝέ (190.4); ἕ, ἑ (dial. ϝε), Hom. ἐ[ϝ]έ (to ἑ as ἐμέ is to με). These point to **me,*

**twe, *swe,* in effect the tonic forms, though as before in G the evidence is mixed and ambiguous—there are many instances of Hom. ἕ, ἑ(έ) without ϝ-, and there is the possibility that the etymon of Att.-Ion. σέ, **twe,* is not the inherited **twe* but a replacement of **te.* (Dor. τέ is ambiguous; and though τϝέ is actually attested, that does not prove that no **te* existed as well.)

L *mē, tē, sē* look like Ved. *mā, tvā* but are revealed by OL inscriptions to continue earlier MED, TED, SED, and by scansion in the early playwrights these are seen to have been more specifically *mēd, tēd, sēd.* (Note that L *tē* and *sē* have not necessarily lost **-w-*, as is commonly stated; they probably continue the enclitic pronouns, which never had it.)

The source of the *-d* is unobvious. Some kind of particle such as is necessary for Germanic **mek, *þek, *sek* (**me-gé* or **-gá*, etc.) is likely—they are a common feature of the personal pronouns—but the element involved is obscure.

5. Abl.sg. L *mē, tē, sē* are from OL *mēd, tēd, sēd,* with the same ablative ending *-d* as in nouns and other pronouns. Cf. Ved. *mát, tvát,* Av. *mat̰, θwat̰,* whose short vowels, being unexpected, are likely to be faithful to the original state of affairs. The significance of the long vowels in L is ambiguous: they may be from lengthening in monosyllables, but are more likely to be importations from the otherwise ubiquitous long vowel in the abl. ending of various noun classes (257.5). The lack of *-v-* in contrast to InIr. **twat* is likewise ambiguous, being either from leveling or the result of atonic reduction. Both may have played a role.

368. PLURAL. The oblique stems of the 1st and 2nd person plural pronouns were composed of **n-* (? originally ***m-*) and **u-*, respectively. These roots, in several different ablaut grades, were directly followed by the plural marker **-s-*. For some enclitic cases, that is all there is to the stem; other cases additionally have the element **-m-/*-mé* already encountered in the singular. The case markers are often the same as for the singular.

PIE **no-s* and **wo-s* were one form of the enclitic acc., and are reflected as such in Ved. *nas, vas,* and Hitt. *-na-aš.* The same forms serve as gen. and dat. enclitics in InIr. They are also the basis for the L possessives *noster* and *vester* (early *voster,* 46.1), built with the contrastive adjective suffix **-tero-* (355).

PIE **nōs, *wōs* were alternative forms of the enclitic acc.; they are attested in L *nōs, vōs,* Av. *nå, vå,* and OCS *ny, vy.* The reason for the difference in vowel length is unknown.

Zero grade **n̥-s-* and **u-s-* are found in such forms as tonic acc. **n̥s-mé, *us-mé*; dat. **n̥sm-éy, *usm-éy*; abl. **n̥sm-ét, *usm-ét.* (The 1st person forms underlie Go. *uns,* NHG *uns,* OE *ús,* NE *us.*)

In L and G there was extensive remodeling, but in opposite directions; the only agreement is the complete loss in both branches of the PIE nom. forms, that is, forms cognate to NE *we* and *ye* (but not *you*, which is unrelated to *ye*).

The Italic picture apart from L is a mystery: not a single 1st or 2nd pl. form—verb or pronoun—is attested in Sabellian.

369. A. Greek. The Greek and most of the InIr. plural forms are made up of the weak grades reflecting **n̥-s-*, **u-s-*.

Acc. **n̥s-mé*, **us-mé*, historically the tonic forms, parallel to sg. ***m-mé*, **t-wé*, give PInIr. **asma*, **ušma*, the former seen unaltered in Av. *ahma* (the 2pl. is not attested). Ved. *asmā̃n* and *yuṣmā̃n* are from **asma-ám*, **ušma-ám*, that is, the PInIr. forms with the usual particle *-ám*. The oblique 2nd pl. forms of InIr. have *y-* from the nom. form, *yūyám*, which is built to a root unattested in G and L but seen in NE *ye*, Go. *jus*. Ved. *yūyám* is ultimately from **yūs*—seen in Lith. *jū́s*, Go. *jus*, Av. *yūš* and *yūžəm*—plus the usual particle *-ám*; expected but aberrant **yūrám* (corresponding to Av. *yūžəm*) was replaced by *yūyám* under the influence of 1pl. *vayám*. The change of **-m* to *-n* in Ved. *asmā̃n* and *yuṣmā̃n* looks like dissimilation.

PG **asme* and **usme* are seen as such in Lesb. ἄμμε, ὔμμε and Dor. ῾ᾱμέ, ῾ῡμέ (the rough breathing in the former imported from the latter, where it is regular before initial ῠ-). Att.-Ion. ἡμέας, ῾ῡμέας show regular η- < ᾱ- and the same rough breathing from the 2pl., and have added the noun case ending -ας, whence by contraction Att. ἡμᾶς, ῾ῡμᾶς, encl. ἥμᾱς, ῞ῡμᾱς (with puzzling ᾱ < εα instead of usual η, perhaps per **86.6**).

Strangely, the PIE nom. forms were lost. In their place we find neologisms more or less transparently based on the acc. With the addition of -ς to the acc. forms, as in Lesb. ἄμμες, ὔμμες and Dor. ῾ᾱμές, ῾ῡμές, the results look exactly like ordinary cons. stem nom.pl. nouns in -ες although there is no strict proportional analogy for the innovation. Att.-Ion. ἡμεῖς, ῾ῡμεῖς are easier to account for, being based on acc.pl. ἡμέας, ῾ῡμέας after the analogy of nom.pl. -εῖς (-έες) to -έας in σ- and υ-stems.

For the gen., Lesb. ἀμμέων, Dor. ῾ᾱμέων, Ion. ἡμέων, Att. ἡμῶν; ῾ῡμέων ῾ῡμῶν; encl. ἥμων, ῞ῡμων, all show the usual ending -ων added to the original acc.

Dat. Lesb. ἄμμι(ν), ὔμμι(ν), Dor. ῾ᾱμίν, ῾ῡμίν (encl. ἆμιν, ὖμιν), Att.-Ion. ἡμῖν, ῾ῡμῖν (encl. ἧμῐν, ὗμῐν, Hom. also ἥμῑν, ὕμῑν). The likeliest source for these forms would be the PIE loc.pl. forms, as that is the source for the dat. pl. of other G paradigms; the PIE loc.pl. forms, however, are uncertain. A reasonable surmise would be **n̥sméy*, **usméy*, homophonous with the dat.pl. but accidentally so—the dat. formation being structurally **-m-éy* and the loc. being **-mé-i*. If this is so, we would expect the early coinage of a new and unambiguous loc. in **-mi* based partly on the loc.sg. of cons. stem nouns in **-i* and partly on the singular pronominal loc.sg. **tosmi*, **kʷosmi* (unrelated to the pl. personal forms and only coincidentally similar): **n̥smi* and **usmi* (already PIE). These are seen as such in some of the G forms. The -ῑ- of the Att.-Ion. tonic forms is secondary, as revealed by encl. ἧμιν, ὗμιν. The explanation for the long vowel is unclear, but they were the only form of the pl. pron. in Att. with a short vowel in the 'ending', and prosodic leveling is a fairly common phenomenon.

B. LATIN. In L, as in G, the special PIE noms. disappear, as does much else: all attested forms can be traced to the enclitic acc.pl. in **nō̆s*, **wō̆s*. Nom./acc. *nōs*, *vōs* were originally acc. only, as in Av. *nå*, *vå*. These forms were well-suited for the purpose, because all other acc.pl.m.f. endings in L consist of a long vowel plus *-s*. The use of *nōs*, *vōs* as nominatives is secondary, fostered by the formal identity of nom. and acc.pl. in the nouns; in literary L this homophony was limited to cons. stems, but in earlier periods it was true of *o-* and *ā*-stems as well, prior to the remodeling of their nom. pl. (260, 265.1).

Gen.pl. *nostrum*, *vestrum* (early *vostrum*, 46.1) are in origin gen.pl. forms of the possessives *noster*, *vester*. (The contrastive affix **-tero-* (355) was added to the enclit. gen. **nos*, **wos*; **nosterom* and **wosterom* predate the creation of the *o*-stem gen.pl. **-ōsom*, 260.5.) *Nostrī* and *vestrī*, used for the objective genitive, are the gen.sg. forms of the same, and parallel to gen.sg. *meī*, *tuī*.

Dat.pl. *nōbīs*, *vōbīs* (OL *nōbeis*, *vōbeis*) are remodelings of **n̥smey*, **usmey* (= Ved. *asmé*, *yuṣmé*) on the basis of encl. **nos*, **wos*, first as something like **nosmey*, **wosmey*, whence **nōmey*, **wōmey* (225.1); these were then replaced by **nōbey*, **wōbey* (or perh. earlier as **nōfey*, **wōfey*). The addition of *-s* probably owes more to the pronominal and *o*-stem dat.pl. as seen in *illīs* < *-eys* < **-oys* < **-ōys* (82, 75.2) than it does to the nominal endings in *-ibus*. The crucial intermediate forms with *-m-* are unattested, but are paralleled by OCS dat. *namŭ*, *vamŭ*, inst. *nami*, *vami* < **nōs-m-*, **wōs-m-* based on **nōs*, **wōs*; cf. enclit. *ny*, *vy* < **nōs*, **wōs*, and dat. *tomŭ* 'that' < **tŏsmoy*, Ved. *tásmāi*, Go. *þamma*; 374.7.

a. For L, enclit. **nōsmey*, **wōsmey* would work as well as **nŏsmey*, **wosmey* but the short vowel forms are required for the gen. and are therefore the likeliest basis of the whole pl. paradigm.

370. THE GREEK DUAL. The nom./acc. du. of the first person, νώ, agrees with Ved. encl. *nāu* (**nā*), Av. *nā*, which continue the acc. enclit. **nō̆-H₁* parallel to pl. **nō̆-s*. Much as in the history of L *nōs* and *vōs* (368), it has replaced the original nom. **wéH₁* seen in Ved. *vām* < **vāám*, OCS *vě*. The Homeric form νῶϊ from νωϝ-ι is obscure in detail, but the starting point has some connection with forms in **n̥H₁-w-*, such as the tonic acc. **n̥H₁wé* (which underlies Ved. acc. *āvām* < *āva-ám*). This would have given PG **nēwé*, and similarly other cases. The replacement of **nēw-* by *nōw-* on the basis of enclitic **nō* is easy to understand, and the result is attested as such in Cor. νωε acc., less directly in Hom. νῶϊν gen./dat.

a. The G forms could be got directly if the prn. du. marker were **H₃* rather than

*H_1 (366.7, and see 257.16c), as *$n̥H_3$ > G νω (107.1); and moreover this accords with the prevailing *o*-vocalism of the dual forms. Such an *-H_3 would serve as the du. marker for *o*-stems—the noun form class most similar to the pronouns over all; and for that matter likewise for the *i*- and *u*-stem duals. In that case the cons. stem duals would then be just what they look like, namely *-*e*. But the PLURAL pronouns have pervasive *o*-vocalism too (presumably nothing more than *o*-grade), and the idea that the pl. might influence details of the du. is hardly a daring hypothesis. Besides, OCS *vě* nom.du. would come from **we*-H_1 straightforwardly.

b. The σφ- forms of the 2du. and 3pl. (and the reflexive) are very obscure. An interesting suggestion traces them to an adj. **sǵhu*- 'powerful' (root **seǵh*- 'have in one's power, prevail', G ἔχω, Ved. *sah*-), and there are pronominal forms (mostly 2pl.) in a variety of other IE languages that are at least arguably parallel. The thought is that the forms are in origin polite/deferential forms of address. The semantics are good, and the strange absence of specifically polite forms of address from the known PIE lexicon would be partially repaired. But Myc. *pe-i* effectively forestalls any reconstruction tracing the labial stop to an underlying dorsal.

c. In some IE languages the dual forms are as transparent as the G ones are opaque: OE *wit* 1du., *git* /yit/ 2du. (vowel imported from the 1st person), Lith. *vèdu*, *jùdu* are manifestly **we-duwo* 'we two', **yu-duwo* 'you two'. These are often treated as latter-day remodelings of the expected forms, but the short vowel in the stem militates against an underlying **wē*, **yū* < **we*H_1, **yu*H_1 (the original du. forms) and points instead to a genuinely ancient nom. form.

POSSESSIVE PRONOUNS

371. These have already been mentioned in several places; it will be useful to gather the facts together here.

'Possessive pronouns' are ordinary adjectives formed from the stems of the personal pronouns by the addition of thematic inflection (-*o*-/-*e*H_2-) or with the contrastive suffix *-*tero*-/-*tere*H_2- (355). The contrastive function of such adjectives is obvious, but the reason for the prominence of the contrastive affix in the plural is not.[1]

1. G ἐμός, ἐμέος have a mixed ancestry, continuing the old gen. **méme*; the enclitic possessives attested as such in Hitt. (-*mi-iš* nom., -*mi-in*, -*ma-an* acc., and so on); and yet other ingredients. See 367.2. L *meus* is presumably from **meyos* elaborated from the enclitic gen.dat., but the only unambiguous attestations of such point to **moy*, not **mey*: OCS *mojĭ* 'my', G μοι dat. Contamination from acc. *mē̆* with help from possessive adj. **tewos*, **sewos* is likelier than a special *e*-grade etymon.

2. G σός is either from **twos* like OCS *tvojĭ* or possibly, more conservatively, from **tos* (with σ- for expected τ- imported from acc. σέ < **twé*; 190.4), directly attested in the Hitt. *e*-grade encl. -*ti-iš* nom., -*ti-in* acc., and so on. G τεός is from **tewos*, a neologism based on the gen. **téwe*. The same innovation (which may well be of late PIE date) gives Ital. **towos*, U *touer* 'tui', OL *tovos* (rare), whence usual *tuus* with vowel weakening in enclisis (66.5 per 41.2).

---

[1] It must be a potent one: a close parallel is to be seen in modern Spanish *nosotros* and *vosotros*, literally 'we-others' and 'you-others', where exactly the same kind of contrast is seen in the 1pl. and 2pl. (this time of the pronouns proper).

3. G ὅς is either from **swos* like OCS *svojĭ* or, more conservatively, from **sos*; significantly, many Homeric attestations lack evidence for ϝ-. Such a form is directly attested in the Hitt. *e*-grade encl. *-ši-iš* nom., *-ši-in* acc. (also *-ša-an*). G ἑός is from **sewos*, based on gen. **séwe*. The same innovation (which like **tewos* may well be as early as late PIE) gives Ital. **sowos*, O **súvad** abl., OL *sovos* (rare), whence the usual *suus* with weakening as in *tuus* (2, above).

a. This stem (like the corresponding substantive pronoun) was originally a reflexive with reference to all persons and numbers, as in Skt. and in the BS languages. There are traces of this wider use in Homer, where ὅς sometimes means 'my own' or 'your own' (for example Λ 142 and ι 28).

b. The rare OL forms like *sīs* and *sās* (to be distinguished from the similar forms of a demonstrative pronoun *so-*, 377.7), are obscure and have been explained variously. One uncertainty is whether the forms have somehow lost **w*, or never had one (as, for instance, *sē* and *tē* probably never did).

4. G ἡμέτερος and ʽᾱμός are both based on the source of all the G plural forms, the old tonic acc. **asme* < **n̥smé*. Differently, L *noster* < **nosteros* is built to the gen. encl. **nos*.

5. G ʽῡμέτερος and ʽῡμός, like the above, are based on the tonic acc. **usmé*, and L *vester* (earlier *voster*, from **wosteros*) is built to the original gen. enclitic **wos*.

6. G σφέτερος is analogical to ἡμέτερος and the like, on the basis of the stem in σφεῖς.

Greek Reflexive Pronouns

372. The usual G reflexive pronouns are combinations of the personal pronouns with the intensive αὐτός 'same, self' (itself of obscure and disputed origin). In Hom. they are still uncompounded, as ἐμοὶ αὐτῶι, σοὶ αὐτῶι, ἑοὶ αὐτῶι. The later Ionic forms in Hdt., such as ἐμεωυτοῦ, started with the dat.sg. ἑωυτῶι from *ἑοαυτῶι from ἑοῖ αὐτῶι.

The Att. forms, ἐμαυτοῦ, σεαυτοῦ or σαυτοῦ, ἑαυτοῦ or αὑτοῦ, would seem to be most simply explained as starting from the acc. sg. forms ἐμ'αὐτόν, σὲ αὐτόν, ἓ αὐτόν. But if instead they are properly ἐμᾱυτοῦ and so on, to which some late forms like ἑᾶτοῦ point, they will rather have started with the dat.sg. ἑοῖ αὐτῶι like the Ion. forms, corresponding to the latter in the same phonetic relation as Att. ʽᾱνήρ to Ion. ὡνήρ (both from ὁ ἀνήρ).

a. The dialects have various expressions for the reflexive: (1) the personal pronouns with αὐτός, as in Homer; (2) αὐτός alone as sometimes in Homer; (3) reduplicative expressions such as αὐτὸς αὐτός, reduced to αὐτοσαυτός, further reduced to αὐσαυτός and the like. The last, which is still transparent, is nevertheless much altered, and a lesson in how rapidly a pronominal compound can become barely recognizable if not outright unetymologizable.

Greek Reciprocal Pronouns

373. The stem ἀλλᾱλο- (Att.-Ion. ἀλληλο-) 'one another', occurring only in oblique cases of the du. and pl., are developments from phrases, *ἄλλος ἄλλον, *ἄλλοι ἄλλους, and so on, parallel to L *alter alterum*, *aliī aliōs*, Indic **anyás anyám*, containing a nominative and an accusative (or some other oblique case). Dissimilation accounts well enough for the shortening

of the second *-λλ-; the -ᾱ- is surprising, however, and much discussed. It could arise automatically only in certain feminine and neuter forms, such as *ἄλλᾱ ἄλλᾱν (*ἀλλᾶλλᾱν). But feminines were certainly less common than masculines, and neuter plurals in any such function were rare absolutely. One possibility is that the intermediate forms were something like *ἀλλ'αλλον, with the ending of the first element truncated (as in κατ'ἔχω 'hold back') rather than contracted. If the result was felt as a compound, the lengthening of the -α- could be a case of Wackernagel's Law (87), as in στρατᾱγός (στρατηγός) < *στρατο-αγ-. Finally, there may be a connection between the shortening of the -λλ- and the lengthening of the -α-: unlike L, G had no system of trading off length between a vowel and a following consonant, but such a trade-off is a very general feature of language change (it is the underlying principle of compensatory lengthening). The total effect would have been several rather weak forces all pushing in the direction of ἀλλᾶλος.

DEMONSTRATIVE, INTERROGATIVE, INDEFINITE, AND RELATIVE PRONOUNS

374. DIFFERENCES BETWEEN NOMINAL AND PRONOMINAL DECLENSION. Compared to the personal pronouns (360–71), the other pronouns agree more nearly with nouns and adjectives overall, but nevertheless present a number of peculiarities. Some of these are typical of the whole class; others are found only in certain paradigms. They are as follows:

1. SUPPLETION. Many pronouns, some would say all true pronouns, are characterized by being built from more than one stem in the same paradigm. This is radical in the personal pronouns: **egóH* (nom.sg.), **m-* (oblique); **we-* (nom.pl.), **n-* (oblique). It is similarly radical in the deictic **so* (nom.sg.m.), **seH₂* (nom.sg.f.), **to-* (elsewhere); but it is no less salient in say the interrog. *k^w*i-* (nom. and acc. all numbers), *k^w*e-* (elsewhere). As the latter examples show, the distributional details vary, but the common thread is a distinctive root or stem for the nom.

In attested IE languages, suppletion in pronouns is general not only because it is their patrimony but also as the result of subsequent conflation of different paradigms, as in NE *he* vs. *they*; and the appearance of suppletion can result from sound changes, as NE *it* (from *hit*) next to *he*, *his*, and —in one analysis (which is disputed)—NE *she*, dial. *sho*, if from the OE nom.sg.fem. *héo*. Similarly traceable to one original stem are G τί-ς < *k^w*is* next to τίν-α acc. (remade from *τίν), further ποῦ 'where' < *k^w*osyo* the old gen.sg.; L and *is* and *id* next to *ea*, *eum* (377.1).

Suppletion can be used as a criterion for deciding what was and was not a pronoun in PIE; so *H_2*elyos* 'other', *H_2*enteros* 'the other', **solwos* 'all, whole', **oynos* 'one' have uniform stems and therefore are not true pronouns. More interestingly *k^w*os* 'which' (380), obviously related to *k^w*i-*/*k^w*e-* 'who(ever)' (379–80), is best regarded as an ordinary thematic adjective, like *H_2elyos, though the pronominal and adjectival paradigms were subject to confusion in the IE languages.

2. NOMINATIVE/ACCUSATIVE NEUTER. The PIE ending was *-*d*, in contrast to *-*m* (*o*-stem nouns) and no ending at all (everywhere else). In G, where a final stop was lost, the pronouns in appearance come to match the dominant nominal pattern of an endingless nom./acc.sg. (in contradistinction to the *o*-stems; so τὸ ζυγόν): τό, αὐτό, τοῦτο, ἐκεῖνο, τί. In L the sound mostly survives, as in *id*, *illud* (*-*od*), *quod*, *quid*; in *hoc* < **hod-ce* the lost consonant is close to the surface in Plt. *hocc* (377.3); HOCE in the SC de Bacch. is presumably for *hocce*. Cf. Ved. *tát* 'that', *yát* 'which', *ít* 'just, only' (perh. = L *id*), *cit* indef. (encl., thus *kás* 'who', *káś cit* 'whoever'; formally *cit* = L *quid*, G τί); with added particle, Ved. *idám* (= L *idem*), Go. *ita* (**id*-), *þata* (**tod*-); the Gmc. reflexes indicate PIE **d*, not **t*.

a. Some notions are functionally much like pronouns but at the same time are like ordinary adjectives or nouns, such as 'one', 'some', 'all', 'other', 'few', 'several', and so on. In PIE these are simply adjectives, as mentioned above, but in the daughter languages many acquire traits of pronominal inflection. So G ἄλλο nom./acc.n. 'other' = L *aliud*, and in L also the pronominal gen. *alīus*; but otherwise in both languages the words inflect like ordinary adjectives. Indic goes much further in such matters than G and L, inflecting 'all', 'other', 'yonder', and a number of others almost wholly as pronouns—the single surviving specifically noun trait being the ONE place where G and L agree on a pronominal importation: the neut. -*am*, as *sárvam* nom./acc.n. 'all', *anyám* 'other', and the like. This 'pronominalization' was still taking place within the recorded history of the language: the oldest texts preserve substantial remnants of nominal inflection in such words, which a little later disappear entirely except for -*am*.[1]

3. NOMINATIVE SINGULAR MASCULINE IN -*o*. An ancient type of pronominal paradigm has no nom.sg. ending *-*s* for the nom.sg.m.: G ὁ, Ved. *sá*, Go. *sa*, all point to a PIE **so* without the usual case ending. Similarly L *iste* < **esto* (377.5).

4. NOMINATIVE IN *-*i*. Very anciently this seems to have marked the subject form of both sg. and pl. pronouns, but it is best attested in plurals and seems to have been early (that is, already in PIE times) taken as a saliently plural marker, as in items 5 and 6, below.

Singular: L *quī* nom.sg.m. rel.prn. from *quoi* (QOI in the Duenos inscription, 19; cf. also O **pui**). The phonological development is that of an atonic form (*quoi*, *quei*, *quī*). G shows no examples of the sg. type, but it has been argued that the paradigm of G ἄλλος, L *alius* is not formed from a root *H_2el- with the familiar adj. affix *-*yo*-, but is the thematic vowel *-^{e}/*o*- added to the original nom. *H_2el-i.

Nom.sg.f. By analogy, but by what appears to have been a very early analogy or one arising independently in many places, a nom.sg. in *-*āi* (?

[1] Conversely, nom./acc. forms like *anyát* appear in the RV beside the commoner *anyám*.

*-eH_2i) is found for some nom.sg.fem. forms: L *haec* (**hai-ce*), *quae*, O **pai**, OPr. *quai*, *stai*, Av. $\chi^v a\bar{e}$ (**swāi*), *θwōi* (**twāi*).

a. A different analysis takes OL QOI, L *quae* nom.sg.f., nom.acc.n., O **pui**, from **kʷo-ī*, **kʷā-ī*, that is, as (relatively) late conglomerations of the originally endingless nom. with a deictic element *-ī*, also attested in G as in *οὑτοσ-ί* 'this-here', *νυνί* 'right now'; Ved. *īm* (occasionally simply *ī*) may or may not be related to the G element. But this analysis leaves unexplained the adhesion of this element to nom. forms only.

5. PLURAL IN *-*i* (cf. 4, above): The pronominal nom.pl.m. in *-*oy*, that is *-*o-i*, is attested widely. In G and L it escapes from the prn. paradigms and replaces orig. nom.pl. *-*ōs* (**-*oes*) of the *o*-stem nouns (**260.1**; in Sab. the reverse happened, and the noun ending ousted the old prn. ending). It is seen as such in G *οἱ* (original *τοί* is preserved in Dor.). In L, although obscured by the regular development of diphthongs (**75.2**), it is reflected in *hī*, *illī*, *istī*, *quī* rel. Corroborative evidence comes from Hitt. *a-pí-e* 'those', *ki-e* 'these', *ku-e* 'who' (that is, something like *apē̆*, *kē̆*, *kwē̆* with -*ē̆* < *-*oy*), Ved. *té*, Go. *þai*, OCS *ti*, Lith. *tiẽ*.

The neut.pl. in *-*ǎy*, as in L *haec* (**hai-ce*), *quae*, OPr. *kai* 'what', are most closely paralleled in Hitt., where the nom./acc.pl. forms of neuter pronouns are homophonous with the nom.pl.comm. (*a-pí-e*, *ki-e*, *ku-e* cited above, are also neut.). Like the nom.sg.f., these forms in *-e-H_2-i must rest upon some (ancient) analogy.

6. The same *i*-element (or what appears to be the same) spread to case-marked forms, as in the gen.pl.m.n. *-*oysōm* (Ved. *téṣām*), inst.pl. **toybh-* (Ved. *tébhis*), loc.pl. **toysu* (Ved. *téṣu*). (In various languages, details of this inflection spread to *o*-stem nouns; the last form may have been transplanted into *o*-stem nouns even in the parent speech, **257.12**.) Such forms are similar to the personal pronouns (**364–5**) in having what appears to be a number marker between the stem and the case marker.

7. A series of forms contain an element *-*sm(o)*- between the root and the ending, as **tosmōy* dat. (Ved. *tásmāi*, Go. *þamma*), **tosmi* loc. (Ved. *tásmin*, Av. *tahmi*—in many Vedic passages, significantly, though it is never so written, **tásmi* makes better meter). This occurs only in singular forms, and therefore cannot have any connection even by contamination with the plurals **n̥smé* 'us' and **usmé* 'you', nor with Hitt. *šu-me-(e-)eš* nom.pl. 'you', encl. -*š-ma-aš* 'you; to you; them; to them'. It has been suggested that this *-*sm*- is the zero grade of **sem-* 'one', and in colloquial English *one* is often appended redundantly to *that* (*We could always use that one table in the laundry room*). —The forms containing *-*sm*- are not attested in either L or G, though some dialect forms, and entries in Hesychius, appear to show the expected forms; in the latter group is *τέμμαι· τίνι* 'to whom', which is superimposable on Av. *čahmāi*.

a. The case is otherwise in Sab. U *esmei*, **esmik** (both apparently dat.), *esme* loc., from a deictic paradigm, likewise South Picenian *esmen* loc., and U **pusme** '(to) whom', are generally interpreted as examples of *-*sm*- forms in Ital. Neither notion is likely to be correct. The pronouns of Sab. are poorly understood, but as the forms in *esm*- mean 'this (one)', they presumably belong to the paradigm *eks*-, *ess*-, and reflect **ekssmey* and the like. Since original *-*sm*- should lose the *s* (as in **nuvime** 'newest' via syncope < *-*isamo*- < *-*ism̥mo*-, 389.9a), so **pusme** must be a restoration of the *s* imported from *esm*-.

375. THE LATIN GENITIVE AND DATIVE SINGULAR.

1. Genitive sg. The origin of the two unisex pronominal types (*eius*, *huius*, *cuius*—really *eiius* and so on, **194c**—on the one hand, and *illīus*, *istīus*, *ipsīus* on the other) is disputed. The elements of the correct explanation are nevertheless clear. At bottom these are old genitives in *-*esyo* and *-*osyo*, fem. *-*esyeH₂s*, *-*osyeH₂s*. The *e*-grade version was original in the interrogative pronoun (379), as OCS *česo* 'whose', Go. *hʷis*, and Av. *čahyā*; in the interrogative adj. 'whose' and the demonstrative **to*- (376.1) the form was *-*osyo*. There was leveling in most languages: Gmc. **þes* is based on **hwes* and conversely Ved. *kásya* 'of whom' is from the adj. paradigm. L *cuius* like the Ved. reflects just such a levelled **kʷosyo*, originally proper to the interrogative adj. At some very early period, prior to changes in vowels in final syllables and to the ouster of gen. *-*os* by *-*es* in L (276.7), they were remarked with the usual gen.sg. *-*s*: **kʷosyo* > **koyyo* → **koyyos* > *cuius*. Genitives in -*īus*, like *illīus*, are regular phonological developments of the same *-*osyos* (via *-*eyyos*) in posttonic syllables. Contributing to the process of remarking doubtless were the fem.gen.sg. in *-*esyeH₂s*, *-*osyeH₂s* (Ved. *tásyās*, *kásyās*, *asyā́s*; Go. *þizos*, *hʷizos*, *izos*), which should have given OL ˣ-*eiiās*, ˣ-*oyyās*. The loss of a contrast in a pronominal system is unusual, so the disappearance of ˣ*eiās*, ˣ*huiās* and the like from L morphology is unexpected. The easiest explanation is that masc.neut. forms like *eiios* and *quoiios* were reinterpreted as consonant stems with gen.sg. -*os*, appropriate for all genders. The basic correctness of this scenario is confirmed by the new dat. *quoiei* (*quoi*, L *cui*), which is easiest to explain as a back formation from a *quoios* that had been taken to be a stem *quoi(i)*- with a gen. suffix -*os*.

a. A variety of alternative explanations have been suggested for these forms. One of them starts from the similarity between L *cuius* (OL QVOIOS, CVIIVS) and G ποῖος, -ᾱ, -ον adj. 'what kind of' (functionally equivalent to L *quālis*). The L would therefore be frozen nom.sg.m. from an original adj. of ordinary kind. The discrepancy in meaning between ποῖος and *cuius* is one drawback for this idea; another is the unlikelihood that an adjective's transparent form-function relationship in a highly inflected language could be thus lost sight of. (Indeed, *cuius*, -*a*, -*um* 'whose' seems to have developed later, starting from the ambiguity of, say, OL *quoios servos* 'whose servant?' lit. 'the servant of whom?', whence *quoia serva*.)

An alternative explanation for -*īus* is that it is a remodeling of original *-*ī*, that is, the usual L gen.sg. -*ī* seen in *o*-stem nouns. There seems to be no pattern to support such an analogy; and indeed the form/function relationship of the supposed starting point was clearer than in the result of the supposed remodeling.

b. In early poetry *quoios*, *eius*, *huius* must sometimes be read as two short syllables or perhaps as one long. There are grounds for taking the latter reading as correct, that is, monosyllabic *quois, huis,* just as *illīus* must sometimes be read *illīs*. All these are ordinary cases of syncope.

From *illī(u)s modī, istī(u)s modī* arose further *illīmodī, istīmodī* 'of that kind; such', with regular loss of *-s-* before *-m-* (225.1); and in imitation of these some other forms in *-ī*, as *istī formae.*

2. Dative sg. The ending looks exactly like the loc.sg. *-ei* of *o*-stems, but is in fact probably the athemat. dat. in **-ei.* This served for the masc. and neut. dat.sg. of pronouns in Sab. (O *altrei* 'altero', *piei* 'cui') and in L was fem. as well. As to the question of whether unisex L *cui, illī, huic* or the occasional OL forms like *eae, istae* are the innovation, the latter are more likely to be: there are plenty of models for the creation of a distinctive fem. in *-ae*, whereas had such a form been a regular part of the ancestral paradigm to begin with it is unlikely that it would be lost.

Datives of *is, hic, quī* go back to *eiiei, *hoiiei, quoiei*, back-formed from —or formed in parallel with—the genitives of the **eiios* type resegmented as **eii-os* (as 1, above). The form *eiiei* is not attested as such, but is confidently inferrable from epig. EIEI and by what is to be read as *ēī* (or *ēę̄*, 57.2a) in early poetry, where, however, monosyllabic *ei* is already more common. This latter is the regular form of the classical period, parallel to the monosyllabic *huic* and *cui*; *eī* (with *-ī* imported from *illī*) is not attested before Ovid. Early attestations of *huic* are mostly just that, but are sometimes spelled HOIC, HOICE; Plautine *hūīc* (< **hoiiei-ce*) is very rare, but being found in self-consciously solemn contexts it is certainly both genuine and old. Early QVOI is common (it is the regular spelling of inscriptions before 50 BC) for *cui*, and the latter is often attested as scanning ⏑–, that is, *quoiei* (actually so attested epigraphically) in the early playwrights; there is no certain instance of expected **cūī.* In post-Augustan scansion (Juvenal, Martial) disyllabic *cuī, huīc* reappear.

Greek Demonstrative Pronouns

376. 1. The greek definite article, ὁ, ἡ (ἁ), τό is in origin a demonstrative pronoun. In Hom. it still has demonstrative force to a large extent, and although also used as an article it is not an obligatory marker of a noun with definite reference (as it is in Attic), except with proper nouns. The scantiness of the attestation of the form in Myc. suggests the same thing: if Myc. had had a syntax similar to Attic, the form would have been abundant. When it does occur in Myc. (384.1), it seems to be a demonstrative anaphor, virtually a relative pronoun (as the form became in Gmc., such as OE *þe*, NE *that*).

It has no formal or functional counterpart in L, but it corresponds with impressive fidelity in detail to pronominals in Indo-Iranian (thus Ved. *sá, sā́, tát*) and Germanic (thus Go. *sa, so, þata* (**tod-ōm*), OE *se, seo, þæt*) all from PIE **so, *seH₂, *tod.* The original inflection:

	Singular			Plural		
	m.	n.	f.	m.	n.	f.
Nom.	so[1]	tod	seH_2, siH_2	toy	teH_2	teH_2s
Acc.	tom	tod	teH_2m	toms	teH_2	teH_2ms
Dat.	tosmey		$tosyeH_2ey$	toybh-		teH_2bh-
Abl.	tosmōt		$tosyeH_2s$	"		"
Gen.	tosyo		"	toysōm		teH_2sōm
Loc.	tosmi		?	toysu		teH_2su

The makeup of this paradigm is unique: a stem **s*^{e}/*o*- occurs in just two forms (nom.sg.m.f., respectively **so* and **seH₂* or **siH₂*), and all other forms are built to an unrelated stem **to*-, **teH₂*- (and **tosm*-, **tosy*-). This state of affairs is preserved in early Germanic languages, InIr., Toch., and most of the WG dialects, which accordingly have nom.pl. τοί, ταί (cf. Go. *þai*, *þos*; Ved. *té*, *tā́s*). Such forms are found in Hom. as well, but they were replaced in Att.-Ion. and elsewhere by οἱ, αἱ after the analogy of the sg. ὁ, ἡ (ἁ). This is unique in the IE languages: elsewhere the aberrant nom.sg. m. and f. forms were the ones that were eliminated (so in OCS, Lith., sporadically in late OE, and in the modern Gmc. languages).[2]

a. For the gen.sg., G τοῖο, τόο, τοῦ point to **tosyo*; Go. *þis*, OHG *thes*, *des*, OE *þæs* are traditionally held to point to **teso* (but probably wrongly; see **259.8A**). The Gmc. forms, with *-*esyo* in place of expected *-*osyo*, are imported from interrog. **kʷesyo* (379-80), whereas the **kʷosyo* indicated by L *cuius* and Ved. *kásya* are either from **tosyo* or from adjectival **kʷosyo* (379).

b. A fem. **siH₂* is attested in G ῑ̔, a Sophoclean hapax corresponding to OIr. *sí*, Go. *si*, NHG *sie*. (Thus the usual view; but one would expect G *ἴα from **siH₂*; cf. **389.1Aa**.) Some scholars have wondered with reason whether many instances of Homeric ἡ might not be redactional replacements of original ῑ̔. —Parenthetically, note that this echoes the InIr. vacillation between senā and devī fem. derivatives to thematic adjectives (**251a**).

c. These stems are extinct in L except for obscure formations (377.7), but individual cases survive in adverbs and conjunctions such as *tum* (**tom*) and *tunc* (**tom-ke*) both 'then', like Av. *təm*.

2. G ὅδε, ἥδε, τόδε 'this' is formed from the preceding by the addition of the particle -δε. Similarly ὁδί, ἡδί, τοδί 'this here', with a different particle, -δί. The dialects have parallel forms, but with other particles, as Thess. ονε, Arc. ονι, Arc.-Cyp. ονυ.

3. G οὗτος, αὕτη, τοῦτο 'this' (weakly deictic) is manifestly a composite,

---

[1] Note that the nom.sg.m. has no marker for case. In Skt., and occasionally already in the RV, original *sá* is fitted with the usual nom.sg.m. marker -*s*. The G paradigm right down to modern times has retained the endingless form.

See also **366.2**, footnote.

[2] In point of fact a loc. *sásmin* occurs in the RV nine times (next to about twenty occurrences of *tásmin*). The hymns are middle to late, and the forms are manifestly analogical; but it is a mystery why the loc.sg. should have been uniquely singled out for a transplanted stem in *s*-.

one of whose ingredients is etymologically the same as the G article. Beyond that, the details of the original paradigm and of its more or less extensive remodeling are speculative. The communis opinio is that a particle *u of asseverative or deictic meaning is the starting point.

A full grade, *ᵉ/ow, is attested in InIr. In one view, the original G state of affairs was more or less like InIr., namely the ὁ, ἁ, τό paradigm with particle -ευ, -αυ, or -ου (depending on what the full grade was); thus *ωὑ, *ᾱὑ, *τωυ. A more familiar version of this analysis supposes a particle *u, clearly wrong for InIr. but possible for G, whence *οὑ, *αὑ, *τou; but with the addition of the -το, long diphthongs would have fallen together with short ones anyway (63.2), so PreG *tōwto > τουτο. OCS kŭto 'who' and čĭto 'what' vouchsafe a deictic particle *to. (The heaping up of deictic elements is not exceptional in pronouns; cf. Fr. ce, ceci, celui, celui ci.) Since the nom./acc.sg.n. looked—more or less by chance—like a reiteration of το separated by an -υ-, other forms were created accordingly: *αὐτο as αὖτᾱ, *τουτο nom.pl. as τουτοι, and so on; and then, in a reverse trend, the eventual limitation of the original pronoun to a single form (as in Att.-Ion. οὖτοι with οὑ- imported from the sg.). A different view, both more complicated in absolute terms as well as starting from the less probable hypothesis of complexes of ὁ, ἁ, το plus zero-grade -υ, takes the Dor. type τοῦτοι, ταῦται as the starting point of a new G paradigm: inherited *του (*toy-u) nom.pl.m. and *ταυ (*tās-u), which thanks to the action of sound laws no longer were much like their functional yokefellows, were fitted out with a more clearly case- and number-marked reiteration of the basic pronoun, as *του-τοι, *ταυ-ται; and from this sort of thing the whole paradigm arose.

Neither scenario, candidly, leads very easily to the attested paradigm; both should have yielded a much more highly inflected pattern: ˣτόνυτον acc., ˣτώτου (< *toyo-u-toyo), and so on. It is however often the case that in reiterative inflection in IE languages the first component is reduced through a combination of phonetic and structural pressures to a 'stem' more or less appropriate to the function,[1] here οὐ- 'masc.nom.', του- 'neut.nom.; masc. neut.obl.', αὐ- 'fem.nom.', ταυ- 'fem.obl.' Some dialects have οὐ- or του- throughout, as (h)ουτα (Boeot.) or τουτα (West Ion.) corresponding to Att. ταῦτα nom./acc.pl.n.

4. G ἐκεῖνος 'that (over there)' includes a prefixed pronominal particle ἐ- like that in L e-quidem 'truly', OL ENOS 'nos' (Carmen Arvale), O e-tanto 'tanta'. The point of departure is a paradigm seen in Ep. κεῖνος, in dialects also κῆνος, from *κε-ενος; the deictic particle is cognate to that in L ce-do 'gimme', huius-ce, ecce 'look here; here is', while the second part is a demonstrative stem akin to Indic ana- 'this' (post-Ved. instr. anena, but NB anā́, the original instrumental, still in the RV but only in the special function 'for, since'), OCS onŭ 'that yonder', and, as a conjunction, L enim. Dor.

---

[1] Such a reduction seems to be the basis for Gmc. n-stem ('weak') adjectives, and the BS 'long' adjectives; in Hitt. the duple inflection of a noun and its enclitic possessive adjective within recorded history lost the inflection of the noun form (367.2a); and a similar withering of a once inflected stem seems to underlie the L verb formations in -b-, as amā-bō, amā-bam; 501.3, 498.

τῆνος corresponds in use, but is of different origin, derived from or otherwise related to Hom. τῇ 'there'.

a. Outside of G the deixis of *e-, and even more of *$\acute{k}^{e}/_{o}$-, *ḱi-, is HITHER-directed, as in the L forms mentioned: *equidem* is for example characteristic of 1sg. asseverations; *cis* 'on this side of'; Gmc. pronouns in *h- (for example Go. *himma daga* 'today', NE *hither* and *here*); Hitt. *ka-a-aš* 'this'; and so on. On the other hand, deixis is mutable, indeed highly mutable when markers are heaped up (as they are in the case of G ἐκεῖνος); altogether typical is NHG *heraus*, usually 'come out' but not infrequently 'go out'. And Fr. *ceci* 'this here' and *cela* 'that there' derive their specific deixis not from the inherited deictic marker in the first syllable but from the locative elements *ci* 'here' and *là* 'there'. This phenomenon contributes to the difficulty of sorting out the histories of pronominal systems.

5. G ὁ δεῖνα 'such a one' is of disputed origin. Its mixture of undeclined and declined forms (ὁ δεῖνα nom.m. but both τοῦ δεῖνος and τοῦ δεῖνα gen.) is consistent with some kind of composite formation albeit with much restructuring. A reasonable analysis traces it to the paradigm of ὅδε (item 2, above), e.g. an acc.sg. τόνδε ἕνα, whence τονδεῖνα, resegmented as τὸν δεῖνα, whence by back-formation ὁ δεῖνα, τὸ δεῖνα, ἡ δεῖνα.

LATIN DEMONSTRATIVE PRONOUNS

377. 1. *Is, ea, id* 'that' (weakly deictic); 'he, she, it' (anaphoric). The PIE paradigm which this continues was, like *so/*to- (376.1), suppletive. The components were *i- (nom./acc. all numbers and genders), which inflected as an ordinary *i*-stem, apart from building a fem. stem in *iH_2-; and *e-, the latter occurring with pre-desinential enlargements: *e-sm-, *e-sy-, and *e-y- parallel to *to-sm-, *to-sy-, *to-y-. The overall paradigm is therefore parallel to that of the interrog. pronoun (379-80). The original PIE inflection was as follows (the *i-root forms are enclosed in a box):

	Singular			*Plural*		
	m.	n.	f.	m.	n.	f.
Nom.	is	id	iH_2	eyes	iH_2	iH_2es
Acc.	im	id	iH_2m	ins	iH_2	iH_2ms
Dat.	esmey		$esyeH_2ey$	eybh-		
Abl.	esmod		$esyeH_2s$	"		
Gen.	esyo		"	eysom		
Loc.	esmi		?	eysu		

For the f.pl., the nom. and acc. forms as actually attested point to something like *iyās, *iyā(n)s, to use non-laryngeal notation, as if the forms in question had been remade as *iH_2eH_2es, *iH_2eH_2ms with the fem. marker *H_2 twice, introduced into the inflection a second time in imitation of pronominal and nominal fem. forms in *-$eH_2(e)s$. Such remodeling could have taken place in the parent language or at any time in the development of the paradigm in the daughter languages, as PItal. *$\bar{\imath}\bar{a}$.

The L forms *is, id*, and an early acc.sg. *im* (often *em*, which is probably the regular phonetic development, 71.1) are straightforward, and correspond to O *iz-ic*, **id-ik**, Go. *is* 'he', *ita* 'it', *ina* acc.m., Ved. *id-ám* nom./acc.n., *im-ám* acc.m. (with particle *-ám*, 360). The orig. nom./acc.pl.n. was as usual remodeled with the addition of the thematic ending, so PItal. **iā* (= Go. *ija*), whence **ia* like *tria* nom./acc.pl.n. 'three' (= Go. *þrija*; 389.3). Similarly the feminines were remodeled as, at first, something like **iās* nom.acc.pl., later **iās*. It is unclear whether the unmodified acc.sg.f. would have been **īm* or **iem*; it is likely that the nom. and acc.f. were remade prehistorically as **iā* and **iām* after the nominal *senā* inflection (262-6). (The similarly remodeled acc.sg.m. *ium* is actually attested.) In any case, all OL forms with prevocalic syllabic *i-* were then remodeled as *e(y)-*, on the basis of the gen.sg. *eiius* < **esyo*, nom.pl. **ēs* < **eyes*, and dat.pl. **eibos* (*ībus*); thus *ea* ← **iā* nom.sg.f., *eās* ← **iās* nom.pl.f., and so on. On the basis of these forms, which are apparently thematic but in reality imitations of thematic forms, were created new *eum* acc.m. (replacing both original *im/em* and the first remodeling *ium*), *eōrum eārum* gen.pl., and so on. The nom.pl.m. **ēs* < **eyes* (= Go. *eis*) was remodeled as **ēoy* or **ĕoy* (the results would be the same) along with thematic nouns (260.1), whence OL *eī*. Similarly dat.pl. **eyōys* (the old inst.pl.) > OL *eīs*. In the classical period these are contracted to *ī*, *īs* (often spelled *iī*, *iīs*). In later poets *eī*, *eīs* appear again, by analogy; cf. the corresponding forms of *deus* (183a).

a. In InIr. reflexes of this paradigm there is also a third stem, nom.sg. **so*, **seH₂*, from the deictic seen in 376.1, but enlarged with the particle **ow* (376.3). It functions only as the nom.sg.m.f. (Ved. *asáu*), and appears to be secondary.

2. *Īdem*, *eadem*, *idem* 'the same' are formed from the preceding with the addition of a particle *-dem*. This is not inherited as such, but results from resegmentation of *idem* nom./acc.n., properly *id-em* (and directly superimposable on Ved. *idám*, above). Paul.Fest. reports *emem*, with the same *-em*, as a precursor of *eundem* acc.sg.m.

Thus far the standard account. But the formal and functional components of *idem* (*id-em*) are unambiguous, and therefore there is no way that *-d-* could have been reassigned to the second element. We must look elsewhere for a catalyst, and it is to be found in the abl.sg. *eōdem*, *eādem*, properly *eōd-em*, *eād-em*: once the simplex forms had become *eō*, *eā*, the enlarged forms would appear to contain an added element *-dem*, which would easily lend itself to some such perception as being the allomorph of *-em* appropriate for forms ending in vowels, whence *eadem* nom.sg.f. and so on; and finally, the *-dem* would be added everywhere, so *eundem* for *emem* and the like.

The similarities between the paradigms of *is*, *ea*, *id* and *īdem*, *eadem*, *idem* were close enough for recomposition to undo most of the obscuring effects of sound laws, which explains acc.pl. *eōsdem*, *eāsdem* in which the *-s-* should have been lost (225.1). Only the nom.sg. *īdem* < *is-dem* (actually quoted from Enn. by Cic.) and *idem* n. (for expected **iddem* like *quiddam*), and forms showing superficial alterations like *eundem* for **eumdem*, remained untampered with.

a. If this analysis is correct, it means that *tamen* 'however, nevertheless' < **tam-em* and *tandem* 'at length' < **tam-dem* (*[more of] the same') are doublets. —Once created, the 'identity-marker' *-dem* spread to a variety of forms which can hardly be very ancient, *totidem* 'just as many', *tantundem* 'just so much', *ibīdem* 'in the same place', and so on.

b. O shows an element **-om* in a few forms, as **pidum** 'any(thing)' (**píd** 'what', 161), and some authorities attempt to derive L *idem* from the same element. Desirable as this might be, there are serious phonological difficulties, as the development of *-om* to L *-um*, not *-em*, seems certain (71.6).

3. *Hic, haec, hoc* 'this here'. There are no certain cognates in the other languages apart from particles of emphasis or focus like Ved. *gha* 'at least; indeed' and OCS *-go*; but on the basis of PIE deictics overall, certain limited surmises suggest themselves. The facts of L are easiest to explain on the basis of typically suppletive stems **ǵhi-* (as in *hic*) and **ǵho-*/*$\acute{g}heH_2$-. (OL HEC ἅπ.λεγ., often mentioned in this connection, merely shows the well-attested hesitation between E and I in OL—apparent in this very inscription, which has also HIC and a nom.sg. in -ES.) The particle *-ce* (usually apocopated to *-c*) is permanently attached to singular forms except for the genitive, and to the nom./acc.pl.n. *haec*. In the beginning it was an optional element, and remains so for many forms, as *huius-ce, hōs-ce, hīs-ce*, beside usual *huius* and so on; and an earlier, wider, distribution is revealed by such forms as *hōrunc* and *hārunc*. The etymon for this *-ce* could be either **ḱi* or **ḱe* (71.1); both occur.

In early poetry the nom.sg.m. *hic* is always a light syllable before a word beginning with a vowel, but later is more often heavy, namely *hicc* (as stated by the grammarians and sometimes so written). This prosody is traceable to contamination by the nom./acc.n. *hocc* (*hoc*) where it is etymological, representing **hocce* < **hod-ce*.

Acc.sg.m. *hunc*, early *honc*, from **hom-ce*, as acc.sg.f. *hanc* from **ham-ce*. Abl.sg. *hōc, hāc* from **hōd-ce*, **hād-ce*. For *huius* gen.sg. and *huic* dat.sg. see 375; for *haec* nom./acc.pl.n. see 374.5.

a. Messapian ΖΙΣ has been interpreted as a dat./inst.pl. deictic reflecting **ǵhōys*; if so, it is directly superimposable on L *hīs*.

4. *Ille, illa, illud* 'that', attested as such from Plt. on; earlier forms like *olle* and *olla* are attested epigraphically and quoted by grammarians and others from ancient laws. This is perhaps from a stem **ol-no-*, *-nā-*, the source of OCS *lani* 'last year' < **olney* or **alney* (lit. 'in that', with some understood noun), and of L *ultrā* (**oltrād*) 'on the other side of' and *ōlim* 'formerly; in those days' (*ō* unexplained; perh. < **ŏllim*, but see 232.3; and NB U **ulu** 'to that place' = L *illūc*, whose **u-** (never **ú-**) likewise points to **ō-*).

The element **ol-* 'that (yonder)' is usually taken as the *o*-grade of **al-*

'other' (or better *H_2*el-, *H_2*ol-). The semantics are satisfactory (cf. NE *other* as antonym of 'this' in *the other side* vs. *this side*). However, according to the view endorsed here (48), *H_2*ol- and *H_2*el- should have had the same outcome. Zero grade, *$H_2\textit{l̥}$-, would be phonologically impeccable. But this formation is in fact the only evidence for either *o-* or zero grade (OCS *lani* cited above is ambiguous); the real question is which grade, if either, is EXPECTED. The second part of the complex looks like the ordinary adj. suffix in **-no-* (which takes *o*-grade in **oy-no-* 'one'), but given the readiness of pronouns to clump together it might be some form of the deictic **eno-* encountered above in connection with G ἐκεῖνος (376.4). If that is the correct analysis, then the *-e* of *olle, ille* is from **-o* (374.3), just as in *iste.* (If the formation was originally an ordinary adj. like *ūnus* < **oy-no-*, then endingless *ille* is analogical.) But much about this formation remains uncertain.

The change in the initial vowel from *olle* to *ille* has no parallel. Since in the usual view proclisis alone would give ˣ*elle*, some further influence must be found. The usual explanation is that the pronunciation was influenced by *is* (1, above) and *iste* (5, below). This is possible; however, the palatalizing effect of the *l* exilis (176a) is perhaps enough to do the trick without contamination.

a. In the Romance languages, with the solitary exception of Sardo, the *ille* paradigm lost specific deixis and became the definite article, such as Fr. *le, la,* Sp. *el, la,* and Romanian *-l.* (The same kind of semantic weakening had turned ὁ, ἡ, τό into a definite article in G centuries earlier, and the cognate paradigm into NHG *der,* NE *the.*) In Sardo, uniquely, the source of the definite article is *iste* (5, below).

5. Iste, ista, istud 'that' (or 'that of yours', with specifically 'thou'-deixis). A similar form is known from Sab. (for example U **estu** 'istum'), but otherwise almost everything about this paradigm is a puzzle. It is unclear whether L or Sab. has innovated here: an original **es-* might well have been altered by the influence of *is, id* in L; but since a number of pronominals in Sab. begin with *e-* (**eks- ek-**, *ess-* 'this', **essuf** 'same'), perhaps instead they influenced original **is-*. Furthermore, although the stem is manifestly a composite, authorities are divided over whether we are looking at a pronoun **is-* (**es-*) plus a particle **to* (or **te*), or the deictic pronoun **to-* (G το-, Ved. *ta-*) plus a particle **is-* (**es-*). Perhaps both elements were inflected pronouns. Such forms as *eāste* acc.pl.f. point to the first analysis, but they would have arisen in L whenever a speaker took *iste* to consist of *is* (as in *is, ea, id*) plus *-te.*

6. *Ipse, ipsa, ipsum* 'selfsame; exactly; very'; sometimes reflexive. The starting point of the familiar paradigm is nom.sg.m. **is-pse*, that is, a member of the usual *is, ea, id* paradigm plus an element **-pse.*[1] Once this **ispse*

---

1 One theory takes the source to be the acc.sg.m.f. forms, such as **eompse* < **eom-se* (226.2) ← **inse* < **im-se.* Evidence for the element **-s^e/o* is very slender, which is to say

had become *ipse*, which obscured its morphological makeup, the way was open for reinterpretation of the form as parallel to *ille* and *iste*: accordingly there arose *ipsa* for Plautine *eapse*, *ipsum* for *eumpse*, *ipsam* for *eampse*, and so on. As can be seen, the remodeling process took place well within recorded history. It seems odd that a single morphological ambiguity could precipitate the complete upheaval of a paradigm which was otherwise unambiguous, but that seems to be the case. —During the transitional period there should have been forms with both parts inflected, though there are only a few such (and the readings in question are no more than probable), for example *eumpsum*. A remnant of the original paradigm survives in L *reāpse* 'truly, in fact' < *rē-eāpse* lit. 'by/with/from the thing itself' (*e* < *ē* per 85).

7\. The rare OL *sum, sam, sōs, sapsa* (Enn., quoted by Festus), *sumpse* acc. sg.m. (Plt.), and some conjunctions and adverbs like *sī* 'if' (*sei*) and *sīc* 'thus' (*sei-ce*), are based on the originally nom.-only stems **so*, **sā*, PIE **so*, **seH₂* seen in G ὁ, ἡ, Ved. *sá*, *sā́* (376.1).

INTERROGATIVE, INDEFINITE, AND RELATIVE PRONOUNS

378\. THE GREEK INTERROGATIVE-INDEFINITE, τίς, τί; τὶς, τὶ; the L interrogative-indefinite *quis*, *quid*; and the L relative *quī*, *quae*, *quod*, represent a PIE interrogative-indefinite paradigm built from the stems **kʷi-* and **kʷe-*. In these functions these two stems are found in all the IE languages. A stem *kʷo-*, in effect an *o*-stem adjective and the basis of the relative pronoun of L, was originally distinct from the above but in most languages there was some conflation of the two stems. An additional stem **kʷu-* occurs only in adverbs and conjunctions.

Among the familiar IE languages, Italic has two peculiarities. One is the reduplicated indefinite pronoun, L *quisquis*, *quaequae*, *quidquid* (recomposed from *quicquid*); O **pispis**, *pitpit* (the last quoted by Festus). The other peculiarity is the use of the same stem (but vid. inf.) for both relative and interrog.-indef. pronouns. Until the discovery of Hitt. and Toch., it was assumed that Italic had innovated in both these regards, in part because what looks like a similar innovation is found in Indic: the later language—but not Vedic—has forms like *yo yas*, *yā yā*, *yad yat* 'whoever, whatever' (and correlative *tat tat*, in effect 'thatsoever' or the like). If Indic could invent such a formation, the reasoning went, so could Italic.

However, Hitt. has both traits fully developed: Hitt. *ku-iš ku-iš* (always written as two words) 'whoever'; and the relative and interrog. pronouns are the same. The latter detail, with a difference, is found in Toch. as well;

---

better than evidence for *-*pse* (which is nonexistent). It is nevertheless not easy to accept the spread of the element from these two forms (cf. 528 re -[*w*]*ish*). Still, on the other side, NB the effect of the single form *ipse* on the paradigm, below.

and the syntax of these two groups provides clues to the transition from indefinite to relative. In Hitt. and Toch. the 'antecedent' of the relative pronoun occurs inside the 'relative clause' itself, modified by the pronoun (which agrees with it in number, gender, and case); what is normally thought of as the main clause contains only a resumptive pronoun, or no marker at all. Typical Hitt. is: *...ku-ú-ša-ta-ma ku-it pid-da-a-it, na-aš-kán ša-me-en-zi* '...but he forfeits the bride-price which she had received', lit. 'she received which bride-price, he relinquishes [it]' (verbatim, 'bride-price-but what she received, and-he-loc. relinquishes'). Here it is easy to see that what is translated here as a relative clause differs very little in force from an indefinite pronoun modifying a noun ('whatever bride-price she received').[1] —In Toch., specifically relative function is marked by a particle *ne* which appears to be enclitic on the 'antecedent'.

In both these groups the 'relative clause' precedes the main clause, a trait characteristic also of InIr. In Indic, as in modern IE languages, the relative pronoun is in the subordinate clause and the antecedent is in the main clause, e.g. *yáḥ sunvatáḥ sákhā, tásmā índrāya gāyata* 'Sing to Indra, who is the friend of the soma-presser' (lit. 'who [is] presser's friend, to that Indra sing [pl.]'). But even in Indic, though its significance was unobvious before the discovery of Hitt. and Toch., the more archaic syntax is widely found: so Ved. *yáṃ yajñám paribhū́r ási, sá íd devéṣu gacchati* 'the offering that you (Indra) protect surely goes to the gods' (verbatim 'which offering you are surrounding, that surely to the gods goes').

Some uses of relative pronouns in L are reminiscent of this syntax, though a noun modified by a relative pronoun and occurring in the same clause with it is usually emphatic or clarificatory, as in Cicero's *causam dīcit eā lēge, quā lēge senātōrēs sōlī tenentur* 'he is making his defense under this law, by which law senators alone are bound'.

a. Though the distribution of the relative function of $^*k^w$- is best in accord with that of a relic feature, it is remarkable that the interrog. and indef. functions persisted in EVERY SINGLE IE branch while the rel. function was usually lost, being expressed instead by various other stems.

These other formations are as follows. InIr. and literary G use a stem **yo-* (usually explained as a thematic derivative of the anaphoric stem **i-*, **ey-*, 377.1), which in BS and Germanic is found in demonstrative function. The only scrap of it in L is (perhaps) *iam* 'now, already', like *tam* and *quam* an old acc.sg.f. OCS uses the demonstrative with a particle *-že* as a relative prn. (*jĭže, eže, jaže*). Myc. has few relative clauses—possibly none; the evidence such as it is indicates the use of **to-* rather than **yo-* as a relative marker (as is also seen in other G dialects, 384.2). The history of the Celtic relative marker(s) is obscure, though there is good evidence that at least one of them was an element **yo-*.

---

1 In Hitt. there is in fact a difference between a specific and an indefinite 'antecedent', depending on whether the interrog./indef./rel. precedes or follows the noun it modifies; when it precedes it has the (emphatic) force 'what(so)ever'.

(The principal relativizing particle, however, was evidently a deictic in *s- which, in a familiar arrangement, is the same as the root of the Celt. def.art.) Proto-Germanic has no reconstructable relative syntax at all. Each of the three main branches of Gmc. uses a different marker, and as PGmc. did not greatly predate the attested Gmc. languages this has been taken to mean that it actually had no relative pronoun.

b. It has been suggested that the puzzling dual function of *k^wi-/*k^we- as both interrogative and relative can be explained if it was aboriginally neither, but a marker of a discourse category called *focus*. That is, a more faithful translation of the Hitt. sentence above might be 'She received this, you know, bride-price . . . ; well, he forfeits it'. In this interpretation the interrog. was in effect a focus-marker without a noun, such that **k^wid esti* was not so much 'What is it?' as 'As for this [thing] . . . ; it's a—?'.

379. PIE **k^wi-*/**k^we-* INTERROGATIVE AND **k^wo-* ADJECTIVE/RELATIVE. On the evidence of L and Av.—especially the earlier parts of the Avesta—in PIE there were two related paradigms which were widely confused. First, there was an interrog./indef. PRONOUN which had two suppletive stems parallel to those of the anaphor **i-*/**e-* (377.1), **k^wi-* in the nom. and acc. of all genders, **k^we-* elsewhere. It had no distinctively feminine forms, which fits with the pragmatic needs of discourse in questions. (Indeed, grammatical gender is a positive nuisance in interrogatives, and it is likely that the actual distinction betweem **$k^w$is* vs. **k^wid* was 'human' vs. 'non-human'.)

Next to this there was a derivative stem in **k^wo-* m.n., **k^weH$_2$-* f., which built pronominal ADJECTIVES, 'which' and the like. The latter stem builds derivatives like **k^wo-tero-* 'which of two', and ordinary adjectives (*what man would dare*). It is from the latter function, as shown above (378), that the RELATIVE pronoun evolves. The two overlap functionally, most obviously in the genitive: *whose* or *which cow* (adj.) vs. *the cow of whom* (prn.); and in most groups the two paradigms more or less coalesced. Such is the case in Hitt., G, Gmc., and Indic. In OCS the ancient human/non-human distinction is extended beyond the nom./acc. (*kŭto* nom., *kogo* gen., *komu* dat., instr. *cěmĭ* (**k^woy-m-*) all regardless of gender 'who?'; *čĭto, česo, če(so)mu*, inst. *čimĭ* (**k^wey-m-*) 'what?', all three genders). In Avestan, such forms as *čahmāi* dat. and *čahyā* gen., from **k^we-*, are pronouns, interrog. and indef.; *kahmāi, kahyā* by contrast, from **k^wo-*, are adjectival. In Indic. the only remnant of the earlier distinction is the indefinite marker *cit*. L has restructured the original system too, but in a different way (383).

380. TABLE OF PIE INTERROGATIVE/INDEFINITE FORMS

Pronominal Stems:

	Singular		*Plural*	
	m.f.	n.	m.f.	n.
Nom.	$k^w$is	k^wid	k^weyes	k^wiH$_2$
Acc.	k^wim	"	k^wims	"
Dat.	k^wesmey		k^weybh-	
Gen.	k^wesyo		k^weysom	
Loc.	k^wesmi		k^weysu	

Adjectival Stems:

	m.	n.	f.	m.	n.	f.
Nom.	k^wos	k^wod	k^weH_2	k^woy	k^weH_2	k^weH_2(e)s
Acc.	k^wom	k^wod	k^weH_2m	k^woms	k^weH_2	k^weH_2ms
Dat.	k^wosmey					
Gen.	k^wosyo					

The gen.sg. *k^w*esyo* survives in Gmc. (for example Go. *h^w^is*) and as a relic in Hom. *τέο* (Att. *τοῦ*). No **τεῖο* gen.sg. (= Av. *čahyā*, from *k^w*esyo*) is attested in Hom. parallel to *τοῖο* < **tosyo* or like *ἐμεῖο* beside *ἐμέο*. This is probably accidental. Hitt. shows what look like *e*-grade forms throughout the paradigm, though many details of Hitt. pron. formations are unlike those reconstructed above on the basis of InIr. and European evidence: gen. *ku-e-el*, dat. *ku-e-da-(a-)ni*, abl. *ku-e-iz(-za)*. (But *e*-grades, or what look like *e*-grades, are typical of oblique stems of Hitt. pronouns generally: *a-pa-a-aš* 'that', but *a-pí-e-el*, *a-pí-e-da-ni*; *ka-a-aš* 'this', but *ki-(e-)el*, *ki-e-da-ni*; *da-ma-a-(i-)iš* 'other', but gen. *da-me-(e-)el*, *da-me-e-da-ni*.)

*K^w*e*- is indicated in the non-human forms of OCS, and the interrog./indef. pronouns of Av., as noted above (379). Apart from *cit*, Ved. has a uniform *k*- but with a mixture of *i*- and *e/eH₂/o*-stems: *kás* nom.sg.m.f., which is the regular Indic form and matches Av. *kō*, but also *kís* 'why' (= Av. *čiš*, L *quis*, G *τίς* all 'who'; the original meaning survives in Ved. in the derivative *ná-kis* 'no one'); *kím* nom./acc.n., also as an adv. 'why?' (= L *quem* (71.1) and G *τινά* ← **τιν* < *k^w*im*). These Indic instances of *k*- are the results of leveling.

PIE *k^w*osyo* is the form of the gen.sg. expected in an *o*-stem, which *k^w*o*- 'which' manifestly is. The degree to which *k^w*o*- was an ordinary *o*-stem has however been obscured by leveling and contamination. L *quod* and RV *kát* are specifically pronominal types, as is much of the rest of the paradigm in InIr.: *kásmāi* dat. like *tásmāi*, *kásmin* loc. like *tásmin*, and so on. On the other side of the coin, OL *quom* (> *cum*, the conjunction) and even more suggestively Indic *kím* neut. 'what' point to the erstwhile presence of ordinary nominal *k^w*om* as the neut. form.

381. Not only has leveling confused the paradigm of the stems in *k^w-, but the original makeup of the many non-paradigmatic forms—conjunctions, adverbs, locatives, and so on, derived from the same elements—can hardly even be guessed at, so diverse are the attested forms. A study of such matters is more the business of etymology than comparative grammar, but for reference a few items are given here. (For the phonetic changes of the initial consonant, see 154 and 161.)

1. Adjectival stem *k^w*o*-. G *πο*- in adverbs and other derivatives, as *ποῦ* (Ion. *κοῦ*) 'where?', *πόθεν* 'from where?', *πότερος* (Ion. *κότερος*) 'which of two' (355), *πότε* (Ion. *κότε*, Dor. *πόκα*) 'when?' < *k^w*ok*^{w}*e*, *ποῖος* 'what kind of?'; *e*-grade forms throughout G in -*τε* 'and' (if encl. -k^w*e* really has anything to do with the interrog. stem) and in Dor. *πεῖ* 'where?' (cf. Att. *ποῖ* 'whither?').

L *quī* (from *quoi*, 374.4) 'who', *quod* 'because', *quoque* 'also' (cf. G πότε, above), *cum* 'since, as' (OL *quom*, cf. Av. *kəm*, Go. *hʷan*), *-que* 'and' (= G -τε, Ved. *ca*, Av. *ča*, Go. *-uh*), *quō* 'whither', Hitt. *ku-wa-at* 'why?'. What looks like lengthened grade, for which the reason is not evident, is seen in L *cūr* < *quōr* (52.3a) 'why?' (the *-r is genuine; the same suffix on prn. stems is also seen widely in Gmc., as in NE *where, there, here*; and in Ved. *tárhi* 'then', *kárhi* 'when?').

2. Interrog. stem *k^wi-. Interrog. Ved. *kís* (only 'why?'; similarly Skt. *kím*), indef. particle Ved. *cit* (indecl.), Av. *čiṯ*, Go. *hʷi-leiks* lit. 'what-form' (transl. G ποῖος) = OE *hwilc* /hwilč/ > NE *which*. In G and InIr. also indefinitizing: G ἄνθρωπός τις 'some man; any man' Ved. *rā́jā cit* 'any king', Av. *čiṯ*; both G and Indic are atonic, and the InIr. particles, historically identical to G τι, L *quid*, are indeclinable.

3. Stem *k^wu- in adverbs and conjunctions. Ved. *kútra* 'whither?', *kútas* 'from where?', *kúha* 'where?' (< *k^wudhe on the evidence of Av. *kudā* and OCS *kŭde*. G ὅπυι in some dialects for ὅποι (Ion. ὅκοι) 'whither?'. L *ubī* 'where', *ut(i)* 'where; so that, as', *unde* 'whence', *uspiam* 'anywhere' are well-explained as metanalyses of the negatives *nĕcub(e)i* (*k^wudhe-i),[1] *necut(e)i (*k^wuta-i), *nĕcundi. Several facts of the language facilitated this resegmentation: the apocope of *neque* 'and not' to *nec*, such that the negative forms were resegmented as *nĕc-* plus *ut(i)*, *undi, and so on; and more specifically *ibī* 'there' would have promoted the perception of *nĕcubī* as *nĕc-ubī*. The presumed earlier state of affairs is attested in compounds *alicubi* 'anywhere', *alicunde* 'from anywhere', *sīcubi* 'if anywhere', and *sīcut(ī)* 'just as'. Corroborative evidence comes from Sab. forms like O **puf**, U *pufe* 'ubi', O **puz** 'ut(i)'. Some such explanation may also account for L *uter* (*uteros) 'which (of two)', though the details are obscure. Its meaning agrees with that of Ved. *katará-*, G πότερος, Go. *hʷaþar*, O **pútereípíd** 'from each (of two)'; but all these point to *k^wotero- rather than *k^wu-, and there are no L corroborations of an earlier stop such as is afforded by *alicubi*.

It has been objected that a reconstruction *k^wu- is suspect on its face if not actually absurd. One must agree. Would-be alternative explanations, however, of the etyma of L *ubī* and some others are at best no worse than the usual reconstruction.

382. THE INTERROGATIVE PRONOUN IN GREEK. G τίς, τί (*k^wid; cf. οὐτιδανός 'of no account' lit. 'nothingly', show original -τιδ-). The paradigm was radically remodeled at an early date. Most of the case forms are from a secondary stem τιν-, as τίνος gen., τίνι dat., τίνα acc. (also nom.acc.pl.n.). This is obviously the acc.sg.m. *τίν < *k^wim; its elaboration with the cons. stem ending -α is like that of Ζῆνα 'Zeus' from (*)Ζῆν. Why such accusatives were tagged with an additional acc. ending is discussed in 326.

To the original *i*-stem belong τίς, τί, and the peculiar-looking but actually regular Hom. ἄσσα, Att. ἄττα nom./acc.pl.n. 'some', based on *k^wya < *k^wiH_2 (49.2, 199). The ἄ- admits of various explanations, such as metanalysis of expressions like πολλά σσα 'several' as πολλ' ἄσσα. (For ἄσσα see 384.3.) The dat.pl. τίσι is the result of leveling, and replaces expected ×ποίσι or ×τείσι (cf. Hdt. τέοισι, below).

The gen.sg. Hom. and Ion. τέο, τεῦ, Att. τοῦ (in competition with τινός), is from PIE *k^wesyo. On the basis of this gen.sg. τέο were formed dat.

1 This equation is set aside by some authorities in favor of a comparison with Hitt. *ku-wa-pí* (presumably /kʷabi/) 'where, when' < *k^wo-bhi.

sg. *τέωι*, *τῶι*, with the usual *o*-stem endings (**259.6**), and Hom. gen.pl. *τέων*, Hdt. dat.pl. *τέοισι*.

Owing to the genre of the texts themselves—ledgers, in essence—no interrog. forms are attested in Myc.; it is less obvious why there seem to be no indef. forms either.

383. THE DECLENSION OF LATIN *quī* AND *quis*. The differentiation of rel. *quī*, *quae*, *quod* (with *o*/*ā*-stem forms) and interrog./indef. *quis*, *quid* (*i*-stems), while it is not an absolute one, is seen also in the corresponding Sab. forms. In the same vein NB OL *quēs* nom.pl. interrog./indef. (genuinely ancient, from **kʷeyes*) contrasts with rel. *quei* (from PIE **kʷoy*, like demonst. **toy*, **374.5**) as in SEI QVES ESENT QVEI SIBEI DEICERENT in SC de Bacch., and *sīquēs hominēs sunt quōs* in Cato. (OL *quīs* dat./abl.pl. is modeled on forms like *hīs* and is nothing antique.)

In the other case forms, as the result of levelings from the inherited patterns given in **380**, there is no trace of such differentiation in the distribution of *o*-stem and *i*-stem forms. Note that the rel. prn. has a fem. stem *quā-* in *quam*, *quārum*, and so on (but no ˣ*quābus*), whereas the epicene inflection was preserved in the interrog. and indef. Nevertheless, *quae*, normally rel., is sometimes used for the interrog., and for the indefinite use the usual form is the conservative *qua* next to occasional *quae*. Similarly, the nom./acc.n.pl. indef. is usually *qua*, occasionally *quae*.

384. THE GREEK RELATIVE AND INDEFINITE PRONOUNS.

1. In Aeolic, Hdt., Arc.-Cyp., West G, sometimes in Hom., and even in Att. poetry, the definite article (**376.1**) is also a relative marker: *αἰχμὴ σιδηρέη τὴν φοβέαι* 'the iron point that you dread' (Hdt.). Myc. evidence on the point is scanty and obscure. But the use of a deictic as a rel. pronoun is a commonplace: it is seen also in West Gmc. languages, and NB rel. **yo-*/**yeH₂-* (2, next).

2. ὅς, ἥ (ἅ), ὅ, the usual Att. and Hom. forms, correspond exactly to the InIr. rel. exemplified by Ved. *yás*, *yā́*, *yád*. This is apparently a demonstrative pronoun in origin, but its demonstrative force is completely absent in both G and InIr. (see **378a**).

3. ὅστις, ἥτις, ὅτι 'any(one)' is a combination of rel. ὅς and the indef., with declension of both parts, as gen.sg. *οὗτινος*, *ἧστινος*, and so on. There is another set of forms with only the second part declined, and usually with the shorter forms of *τίς* in the oblique cases. Thus Hom. *ὅτις*, *ὅττεο*, *ὅτεωι*, *ὅτινα*, *ὅτεων*, *ὁτέοισι*, *ὅτινας*; Att. *ὅτου*, *ὅτωι* and, rarely, *ὅτων*, *ὅτοις*. The withering of the inflection of the first component is typical of doubly-inflected elements (see **367.2a**). —Hom. (Aeol.) *ὅττι* nom./acc.n. is from **yot kʷid*, a form predating the loss of the final **-d*, whence *-ττ-* in Hom. *ὅττεο*, Lesb. *ὅττινας*, and others, though the exact explanation for the importation of *-ττ-* into some cases but not others is unknown. It is unclear as well

whether forms such as ὅππῃ for ὅπῃ 'in what way, whereby' directly reflect ancient *$yot\ k^w\bar{a}$ (with frozen *yot-) or are analogical creations of a later date. —Ion. ἅσσα 'ἅτινα' nom./acc.pl.n. is regular for original *$yeH_2\ k^w iH_2$.

a. The derivation of ὅτ(τ)ι from *$swot\ k^w id$, given by some, rests on a single form, the Locr. hapax FOTI, which is at variance with all other evidence and is probably just an error for HOTI.

385. PRONOUN COMPLEXES. G and L have complex forms consisting of the interrogative, indefinite, and relative pronoun stems combined in various ways, as G ὅστις 'whoever', above. G -τε properly 'and' is added to a large array of particles and pronouns, especially rel. pronouns, though without any apparent change in meaning, in contrast to the large difference between L *quis* 'who' and *quisque* 'each, every' (and identically between Hitt. *ku-iš* and *ku-iš-ša*; see below). More distinctive is G πότε (Ion. κότε, Dor. πόκα) 'when', πώ-ποτε 'ever yet' (mostly in the neg.), formally but not functionally equivalent to L *quoque* 'also'.

G ἕκαστος 'each, every(one)' is thought to be ἑκασ- plus τις, τεο, τωι (382). The first part appears to be the same as ἑκάς adv. 'separate, away, afar', itself of difficult explanation but apparently including *swe- 'self, own'. The hypothetical composite *ἕκαστις was drawn into the o-stems by its chance similarity with superlatives in -ιστος (349); the points of entry were ambiguous forms like ἑκαστωι dat. Later came the coinage of ἑκάτερος 'each (of two)' modeled on πότερος 'which of two' (355).

L *quispiam, quaepiam, quodpiam* 'any, anyone, anything' (neut. also *quidpiam* or *quippiam*) may continue *-pe-yām*, with the ancestor of *iam* superimposed on *-pe* as in *quippe* < **quidpe* 'certainly'. L *quisquam, quaequam, quicquam* (*quidquam*) has much the same force, but like NE *any* is peculiar to denials and questions. L *quisque, quaeque, quicque* (*quidque*) 'each, every'. Ved. *káś ca* m.f., *kác ca* n. and Hitt. *ku-iš-ki* (*-ka, -ku*), *ku-it-ki* may correspond formally to L *quisque*—the apparent loss of the labial element in the clitic in Hitt. is a problem—but functionally are closer to *quisquam.* (Hitt. *ku-iš-ša, ku-i-da* 'each' is however descriptively *ku-iš, ku-it* plus enclitic *-(y)a* 'and'; that is, descriptively though not etymologically it is the same as L *quisque.*) L *-que* with generalizing force is found on a number of forms: *ubīque* 'everywhere', *undique* 'from all sides', *uterque* 'whichever of two'. L *quisquis, quaequae, quicquid* 'whoever, any(-one)' has meanings which partially overlap simple *quis.* The reduplicated form is found also in Sab. and in Hitt. Such a thing in G is attested only once, Arg. τιστις. L *quīcumque* 'whoever' is composed of the ordinary rel. prn. and *-cumque* < **-quomque* (cf. *quisque*); it forms indefinites: *ubicumque* 'wherever' (whose *-ĭ-*, **84**, proves the lateness of the formation; cf. the details of the earlier-formed *ubīque*, above), *quōcumque* 'whithersoever', *quīvīscumque* 'whosoever you will' (*quīvīs* 'anyone you please'), *utercumque* 'whichever of two', and so on.

NUMERALS

Properties of Number Systems

386. PIE had words for 1 - 10 (388-9) and 'both' (**389.2B**). The only recoverable form for 'half' is found in bahuvrīhi compounds (**389.1Bc**). For the teens (11 - 19, 390) there were additive combinations, with hesitation between phrases and compounds. The decads (391) were formed by what looks like derivation, but the formations were actually compounds originally. The hundreds (394-5) were phrases, as were the intervening numbers (such as 23, 59, or 120). There is evidence for one or more term for 1,000 (396), but for no higher number.

The system is obviously decimal/centesimal. Some have seen in the appearance here and there of terms for dozens, scores, and sixties what they call traces of a sexagesimal system. But such terms do not necessarily point to an earlier system: the English terms *dozen* and *score*, for example, are themselves both quite recent in the history of the language, not relics of anything ancient. The striking French deviations from a decimal scheme (as in *soixante-douze* '72', *quatre-vingts-quinze* '95'—verbatim 'sixty-twelve' and 'four-twenties-fifteen') are wholly post-classical in their evolution, and provide no evidence for some earlier system.

Of the digits the first, third, and fourth were certainly declined; the rest were indeclinable, with the qualified exception of 'two'.

From the beginning of IE studies attempts have been made to discover metaphors and metonymies behind the words for numbers. So for example **newn̥* 'nine' (389.9) was held to be based on **new(o)-* 'new', on the theory that before the term was coined the highest number was 'eight'. PIE **dek̑m̥t* 'ten' (389.10) was taken as **d(w)e-* 'two' (**389.2Aa**) and the zero grade of **k̑emt-* 'hand', whose *o*-grade is seen in the pan-Gmc. *hand* words (which is the only attestation among the IE languages of the element in question with the meaning 'hand'). Hands and fingers in terms for numbers are certainly found in languages, so this interpretation is more convincing than the 'nine' = 'new number' business, which is fantastical. Among the most persuasive of these suggestions is the connection of **penkʷe* 'five' (389.5) with **ponkʷ-to-*, **ponkʷu-* 'all, whole' (L *cūnctus*, Hitt. *pa-an-ku-uš*, **141a**), that is 'five' = 'the whole [hand]'.

Although they are entertaining to ponder, such etymologies assume a degree of naïveté on the part of the speakers of PIE which was more imaginable when PIE was taken to be something like Original Human Language, whose speakers would be driven to epistemology when faced with a high-tech concept such as 'nine'. Besides, given the time-depths, we have only vague resemblances not testable hypotheses, which makes it practically impossible to decide between chance similarities and genuine history.

387. CONTAMINATION. *Compact series* such as counting, names of days or months, or letters of the alphabet, commonly show the influence of one form on another. Thus PRom. **octembrem* in place of L *Octōber*, on the basis of flanking **septembrem* and **novembrem*. As such influences are practically confined to ADJACENT MEMBERS OF A SEQUENCE, it is idle to look to NE *seven* as a possible source for the unexpected *-v-* of *five* (which should rime with *life*: OE *fīf, līf*). On the other hand, although non-adjacent *December* is not the cause of the creation of **octembrem*, above, it is not quite irrelevant either: a sequence or SET of like forms in a string (*November, December*) is a particularly potent catalyst for remodeling.

In PIE the difference in form between a cardinal number and the ordinal derived from it was merely a matter of ablaut (397), but thanks to sound changes the forms often diverged more or less. (A notable example of this is Av. *čaθwārō* nom.m. 'four' next to *tūirya-* 'fourth'.) This divergence set the stage for analogical disturbances, as an important factor in the development of counting systems is interplay between cardinal and ordinal numbers. It may seem obvious that ordinal numbers are subject to remodeling on the pattern of the cardinals from which they are derived semantically and formally: NE *tenth* built to *ten* supplanted inherited (that is, phonologically regular) *tithe*; similarly Fr. *dixième* '10th' vis-à-vis regular *dîme*. And it is equally obvious that the forms of ordinals would influence one another, as NE (phonologically regular but non-standard) *fift, twelft* and the like remodeled as *fifth, twelfth*, on the basis of the usual form of the suffix, *-th*. What is less obvious but nevertheless richly attested is the converse: the details of cardinals can be influenced by the forms of the ordinals, as when expected L **quĭnque* 'five' becomes *quīnque* under the influence of *quīn(c)tus* 'fifth' (81.2). Sometimes such influence is extensive, as in the history of Baltic and Slavic, where the whole cardinal system has been remade on the basis of the ordinals.

A final complication is that the combining forms, the teens, or the decads each constitute systems within which interactions occur ('30' is in a sense adjacent to '20' and '40') without necessarily influencing the forms of the other systems. So G *διᾱκόσιοι* '200' is based on *τριᾱκόσιοι* '300', but there is no corresponding influence of 'three' on 'two', 'thirteen' on 'twelve', or 'thirty' on 'twenty'.

As a result of these factors, even in discussing the elemental words for the cardinal units it will be necessary to refer to other numerals in the series, and to details of the combining forms, the ordinals, the teens, and the decads.

a. PIE and many daughter languages freely formed compounds having a numeral as the first element. These were bahuvrīhi adjectives, *number-X* 'having so-and-so many *X*'s'. Such numerical compounds are among the very few bahuvrīhis still found in English, as *two-shoes, one-horse, five-pound*.

CARDINAL NUMBERS

388. THE UNITS AND ONE HUNDRED.

	Vedic	Avestan	Greek	Latin	Gothic	Lith.	OIr.
1	éka-	aēva-	εἷς *m.*	ūnus	ains	víenas	óen
			ἕν *n.*				
			μία *f.*				
2	dvā́(u)	dva	δύο	duo	twais	dù	dáu
3	tráyas *m.*	θrayō	τρεῖς *m.f.*	trēs *m.f.*	þreis*	trȳs	trí *m.*
	trī́ *n.*		τρία	tria	þrija		tre *n.*
	tisrás *f.*	tisrō					téoir *f.*
4	catvā́ras *m.*	čaθwārō	τέτταρες	quattuor	fidwor	keturì	ceth(a)ir *m.*
	catasrás *f.*	čataŋrō					cethéoir *f.*
5	páñca	panča	πέντε	quīnque	fimf	penkì	cóic
6	ṣáṭ	χšvaš	ἕξ	sex	saihs	šešì	sé
7	saptá	hapta	ἑπτά	septem	sibun	septynì	secht
8	aṣṭā́(u)	ašta	ὀκτώ	octō	ahtau	aštuonì	ocht
9	náva	nava	ἐννέα	novem	niun	devynì	nóen
10	dáśa	dasa	δέκα	decem	taihun	dešimtis	deich
100	śatám	satəm	ἑκατόν	centum	hund*	šim̃tas	cét

1. The G forms for '4' and '5' show a great deal of dialect variation.
2. The BS forms have all been influenced by details of the ordinal forms. —The contemporary Lith. form corresponding to OLith. *dešimtis* is *dẽšimt*.
3. The OIr. forms are pronounced /oyν/, /daw/ (later /dō/), /tρī/, /tρe/, /tēə̯ρ'/, /k'eθəρ'/, /k'eθēə̯ρ'/, /kōg'/, /s'ē/, /s'eχt/, /oχt/, /noyν/, /deχ'/, /k'ēd/.

389.1. ONE. PIE had two roots usually translated 'one': **oy*- and **sem*- (294.1). This state of affairs has been variously accounted for. The opinion endorsed here takes PIE **oy*- as denoting singularity and uniqueness, and unity in a counting sense, namely in the sense that nine is 'one more' than eight. This kind of 'one' is briefly called 'one-alone'; the implications of isolation or uniqueness are overt in such derivatives as G *οἶος* 'alone, solitary' and *οἴνη* 'one-spot' (on dice). Compound adjectives would have the sense of 'having (only) one such-and-such' (a unicorn, for example). PIE **sem*- was 'one-together', that is, several things taken as a whole, or considered a unit for some purpose (as when several people 'speak with one voice'), or several things are regarded as interchangeable in some way (cf. NE *one and the same*). Accordingly the term shades into notions like 'same' and, adverbially, 'at the same time' (for example Ved. *sa-dyás* 'on the same day') and, in compounds, 'having one (= the same) such-and-such', for example G ἁ-τάλαντος 'having the same weight'.[1]

---

[1] In Indic, eventually, such compounds lose the force of sameness, becoming just another kind of possessive adjective ('having such-and-such'), as in *sa-pakṣa-* 'having wings'. A different, simultaneous, semantic evolution produces a type meaning 'together with such-and-such', as in *sa-pattra-* 'feathers and all'.

Most IE languages, including G and L, have reflexes of both of these elements; as might be expected most use formations based on **oy-* for numerical unity. But G, Arm., and Toch. use reflexes of **sem-* instead.

a. The principal competing view of PIE 'one' is that **sem-* is the original root in all senses, and **oy(no)-* is a later innovation. In favor of this view are two good arguments. First, **sem-* is an underived form with an archaic type of root inflection (294.1), and an abundance of derivatives and combining forms of ancient type; whereas **oyno-* is a derived form—one of several such, in fact (see A, below). Second, the geographical distribution of **sem-* is characteristic of relics, as it occurs in two widely separated areas (G/Arm. and Toch.) while **oyno-* is found in a large and continuous area. It might be added that no IE language is actually attested with two semantically differentiated words for 'one'—these particular two or any other—and that might indicate that **sem-* and **oyno-* were substantially synonymous ab origine.

A. PIE **oy-*, an ablaut grade of the pronoun root **i-* 'it', 377.1, occurred with various suffixes well known as adjective-forming elements: **oy-no-*, **oy-wo-*, and possibly **oy-ko-*. The first of these underlies most IE words for 'one', including L *ūnus* (58), OL OINOS, *oenus*, U **unu** : OIr. *oin* (*óen*), OPr. *ains*, OCS *ino-* (in compounds, *inorogŭ* 'unicorn' for example) and PGmc. **ainaz*, whence Go. *ains*, OE *án*, OHG *ein*. This formation is represented by G *οἴνη* (*οἶνος*) 'ace' (on dice).

The formation **oywo-* is reflected as G *οἶος* 'solitary, alone; only', Cyp. *οιϝος*. (Att. *οἶος* occurs, but was largely displaced by *μόνος*.) It underlies the Iranian number seen in Av. *aēva-*, OP *aiva-*, though a different formation, **oyko-*,[1] underlies Indic *éka-*.

a. The Hom. fem. *ἴα* 'one', *ἴαν* acc. but *ἰῆς* gen., *ἰῆι* dat. (Aeol.), once also *ἰός*, reflect **i-H₂-*, based directly on the pronominal stem **i-*; cf. Cret. *ιος* = *ἐκεῖνος*, and L *is*, *ea* (**iā*), *id* (377.1). This lends weight to the idea that the **oy-* of **oyno-* is one and the same with **i-* 'he, she, it'.

b. COMBINING FORMS. The stems **oyno-*, **oywo-*, **oyko-* were used without change as the first elements of compounds. So L *oenigenōs* (Paul.Fest.) 'only-begotten; only'; *ūniversus*, and others.

G *οἰνο-* in this sense does not occur, even in fossil forms (*οἰοβώτας* 'feeding alone' contains *οἰϝο-* 'alone', and is not based on the system of numerals).

Other IE languages: Ved. *éka-pad-* 'one-footed' (apparently a kind of storm), *eka-rā́j-* 'autocratic, ruling alone' and (more figuratively) *eka-vīrá-* 'incomparable hero' lit. 'one-hero'. OCS *ino-*, as mentioned above, is more conservative than the cardinal. Go. *ainabaur* and *ainaha* both translate G *μονογενής* 'only-born' and are perhaps merely calques; more genuine, certainly more ancient, are *ainfalþs* 'simple, single' and *ainlibim* dat.pl. 'eleven' (*'one-left')—note the syncope of the stem-vowel of the combining-form **aina-*. Similarly

[1] Indic **ayka-* is an isolated form, occurring outside of Indic neither as a counting form nor with some derived sense, like G *οἶος*. The terms for 'one', in fact, are one of the defining traits of the Indic vs. the Iranian branches of InIr. One interpretation is that **ayka-* was the InIr. form, and a significant innovation; Iranian **aywa-* is an innovation. It is noteworthy that modern Iranian forms for 'one' such as Farsi *yak* are also innovations, this time apparently a borrowing from Turkic.

OHG *einfalt* 'single', *einlif* 'II', OE *ánfeald, en(d)le(o)fan,* as well as in extended senses, for example OE *ánpæþ* 'a path requiring single-file', NHG *Einbahn* 'one-way street'.

B. PIE **sem-* (with gradation) underlies the G numeral for unity. The *e*-grade is reflected in G εἷς, Dor. ἧς, Cret. ἐνς all regular from **sems* nom.m.; neut. ἕν < **sem.* (For the original m.n. inflection and its evolution see **294.1.**) The fem. stem μία is the regular development of the regularly-formed **sm-iH₂*, with the devī suffix (**268**) on the zero grade of the stem.

In L the root is seen only in derivatives: *semel* 'once' (**99**, and **b** below), *simul* (OL SEMOL) 'at the same time as', *semper* 'always', *singulī* 'one each'; cf. Go. *simle* 'formerly' (for the semantics cf. NE *once* in the same sense).

The *o*-grade *o*-stem derivative **somo-* is widely attested in the meaning 'same', as in Ved. *samá-*, Av. *hama-*, G ὁμός, OE *sama,* NE *same.* (The InIr. forms point to **somH-o-*, as otherwise the reflex would have been ˣ*sāma-* per **36.4.** See note a, next.)

a. G *(h)*αμο- in ἀμόθεν 'from somewhere', ἀμῆ 'somehow', οὐδ-αμός 'no one' (and many similar forms): Ved. *sama-* encl. 'some', Av. *hama-*, PGmc. **sumaz* (OE *sum,* Go. *sums*), all point to **sm̥mo-* or the like, an improbable shape. Possibly we are dealing here with the original PIE word for 'pair', namely the du. **semH₁*, thematized as **sm̥H₁o-* adj. 'a couple' with subsequent semantic development exactly as in NHG *ein Paar* 'some (few)', NE *a couple (of)* commonly for 'a few'. G ἅμα 'at once; at the same time' belongs here somehow, but the details are difficult; the accent suggests assimilation (**91**) < **héma.* The form may then be the original acc.sg.

b. COMBINING FORMS. 1. Zero grade **sm̥-* > G ἁ-, psilotic ἀ-, Ved. *sa-*, Av. *ha-* in bahuvrīhi compounds originally meaning 'having the same...', as ἄλοχος 'having the same bed' (that is, 'spouse'); cf. Ved. *sa-* in *sa-jātá-* 'related by birth' (lit. 'of the same stock'). See also fn. to 2, next.

2. The *o*-grade, **som-*, forms similar compounds in InIr., as Ved. *sam-mātár-* 'born of the same mother', though from the very beginning these often mean 'with' or 'having' or 'together', as *sam-bháraṇa-* 'a bringing-together', *sam-údra-* 'ocean', lit. 'meeting/gathering of water' (cf. G ὕδωρ), *saṃ-hotrá-* 'collective offering'.[1] It may be connected with G συν- 'with, having'; the development of -υ- < *-ο- is in accord with **44**, but σ- < **s-* is not expected (170). Hom. and Early Att. ξυν- (and Myc. *ku-su-*) are assumed to be the ancestor of συν-, though σ- < ξ- is also unexpected. Perh. G *(κ)*συν- is a conflation of two originally different elements.

3. The meaning 'one' in such compounds is overt in **sm̥-ǵheslo-* 'one-thousand' > Ved. *sahásra-* (396), and in Ved. *sakŕ̥t*, Av. *hakərəṯ* 'once'; G ἅπαξ 'once' (**404.1**); and L *semel* 'once' (**sm̥-mēlom* 'one time'). For G ἑκατόν '100' see **389.10**.

c. HALF. PIE **sēmi-* 'half' must be unrelated to **sem-*. It is attested only in compounds: G ἡμίβιος, L *sēmivīvus* 'half-dead': Ved. *á-sāmi-* 'whole' (lit. 'not-half'), Brāh. *sāmí-cita-* 'half piled up', OE *sám-cwic* 'half-dead'. In the first element of a compound zero grade of the vowel is expected, but full grade is thinkable; the unvarying long vowel points to **seH₁mi-*. It remains confined to compounds in G; L *sēmis* 'half' (sometimes spe-

---

[1] Very commonly *sam-* has a completive force, reminiscent of the synonymous but etymologically unrelated L *com-*, thus *pr̥cch-* 'ask' but *sam-pr̥cch-* 'find out by asking'; *han-* 'strike (dead)', *saṃ-han-* 'smash to bits'.

cifically 'half-pound') is a L creation whose shape is somehow based on *bis* 'twice'. It is indeclinable to begin with; its declined forms, as *sēmissis, sēmissem*, are late. A syncopated form, *sēs-* < **sēms-* < **sēmis-*, underlies *sēsqui-* 'one and a half' and *sēstertius* 'two and a half'.[1] *Sēmuncia* 'half ounce' (*uncia* 'ounce') shows truncation of the first element before a vowel; *sēmodius* 'half-bushel' (or so) is from *sēmimodius* by haplology.

389.2. Two.

A. The PIE lexical item 'two' would have been used in counting, mainly: the dual inflection of nouns would have been used to refer to two named things. The evidence for the counting form is as follows. G δύο, Hom. also δύω 'two', L *duo*, U **tuva** acc.n., RV *duvá-*, Av. *dva* (two syllables[2]), OCS *dŭva*, Latv. *divi*, Alb. *dy*, all point to **duwo-*; contrariwise, G δίς 'twice', L *bis*, RV *dvís*, Av. *biš*, point to **dwis*. The Rigveda has *dvá-* and *duvís* alongside *duvá-* and *dvís*. However, the long form *duvá-* greatly preponderates over the short form *dvá-*[3] and is also found in the compound *duvā́daśa* 'twelve'. (Trisyllabic *dvā́daśa* is found only in two very late passages and merely shows the regular late Vedic syncope of *-u-* before *-v-*). On the basis of the remaining evidence, RV *duvís* shows contamination by *duvá-*.

Other branches—Celtic, Germanic, and Armenian—syllabify 'two' and 'twice' the same. This is certainly the result of purely phonological developments in the case of Celtic (which shows no trace of Sievers' Law) and, though different in detail, also for Germanic (as indicated by PGmc. **swīnaz* 'swine' < **suwīno-* < **suHīno-* 'porcine'). The same is probably the case in Armenian, though leveling is a possibility there. Lith., unlike Latv. and OCS, points to **dw-* throughout.

In sum, the PIE shape for the cardinal was **duwo*, that of the combining form was **dwi-*, and the best interpretation of the conflicting evidence for the word for 'twelve' is that it began **dwo-*. All other numerals have *e*-grade in the simplex forms, so the truly original form for 'two' must have been something like ***dewo*, combining form ***du-*. Under the influence of **tri-* (389.3a), a new combining form **dwi-* replaced **du-* everywhere except in 'twelve'. No ***dewo* is reflected anywhere; the source of simplex **duwo* is less certain than the fact of its existence.

This **duwo* (whence Hom. δύο) was originally indeclinable (like the numbers above 'four'). When construed with nouns they inflected as PLURAL. This distribution is still tolerably clear in Hom., where there is a sec-

---

[1] Verbatim 'and half' and 'half-third', respectively.

[2] The form *baē* fem. and neut. quoted in the literature as if < **dw-* is actually from an unrelated stem, *ubay-* 'both'. —Note that the Vedic readings of the type *duvá-* are recovered by metrical analysis; the text always writes *dvá-* and the like.

[3] Of the items showing such alternative forms in the RV (179-81), this is the only one in which the long form (*duvá-*) preponderates. In all others the short form is at least twice as frequent as the long one.

ondary distinction according to case (δύο with pl. in nom./acc., δυοῖν with du. in dat./gen.). Unsurprisingly, however, the numeral 'two' was drawn into inflectional patterns in various languages. Most frequently it was treated as a dual for obvious reasons. So in G δύω (Hom.), δυοῖν, and Ved. _duvā́_, later _duvā́u_ (always written _dvā́(u)_) though even in InIr. there are intimations of the original uninflected form in Av. _dva_ (disyllabic). In L too there are scraps of the original indecl. morphology, as in an abl. expression like _duo verbīs_ (as late as Novius), neut. _duo talenta_ (Plt.), and in collocations with decads (invariant _vīgintī duo_ '22', for example). The earliest-attested inflected form is the acc.pl. _duōs_, and this may in fact have been the starting point. A new paradigm closely resembling the _o/ā_-stem plurals quickly developed: _duōrum_ gen. (earlier _duum_, frozen in _duumvirī_ ← _duum virum_ sc. _comitium_ or some similar noun, '[committee] of two men'), _duae_ nom.f., _duās_ acc. —In other languages various other accommodations were made, such as the largely pronominal (pl.) inflection of Germanic. In G dialects and late Att. the inflection becomes pl., as δυῶν gen., δυοῖς dat., δύας acc. —In NG δυό, which is indeclinable, the wheel has come full circle; the souvenir of its adventures is the shifted accent (though the classicizing δύο also occurs).

a. Combining forms. An early form of 'twelve' was probably _*dwo-dekm̥t_, but its reflexes were always subject to influence by the independent form for 'two'. G _*dwōdeka_[1] (whence δώδεκα), whose shape is at odds with the simplex form δύο/δύω, can only have been inherited—unless it is the result of syncope. In purely Indic terms, the primogeniture of _duvā́daśa_, the usual form in the RV, vis-à-vis later _dvā́daśa_, showing the regular syncope of _-uv-_, is suggested by _ékādaśa_ '11', whose long vowel has been imported from '12'. Such influence would have been unlikely if '12' had been trisyllabic. (Contrariwise, the prosody of _*ékadaśa_ '11' may have contributed to the replacement of aboriginal _*dvá-daśa_ by _*duvā́daśa_.)

The ordinary combining form was _*dwi-_, hence G δι-, L _bi-_, Ved. _dvi-_, Av. _bi-_, Gmc. _*twi-_: Ved. _dvi-pád-_ 'having two feet', OE _twi-féte_, G δί-πους, L _bipēs_, OL _duicensus_ ('dicebatur cum altero, id est, cum filio census') Paul.Fest., Lith. _dvìgubas_ 'twofold'. This is the same element seen in the adverb _*dwis_ 'twice', G δίς, L _bis_ (_duis_ Paul.Fest.), Ved. _dvís_, Av. _biš_. The _*-i-_ was imported (in PIE times) from _*tri-_, _*tris_ 'three-, thrice', perh. with some help from _*wi-_ (in '20', q.v.). Hitt. alone, and unclearly, seems to indicate the earlier form: _ta-a-(i-)ú-ga-aš_ 'two-year-old' (of animals) next to _i-ú-ga-aš_ 'yearling' reveals an element _ta-a-_, seen also in _da-a-an_ indecl. 'second'. (The lack of any trace of a _w_ is unexpected.[2])

In Italic the prefix is also attested as _du-_, L _duplex_ 'double', (cf. G δίπλαξ), _ducentī_ '200', U _dupla_ 'two each', _dupursus_ 'bipedibus'. There is no wholly satisfactory explanation

---

1 With secondary -ω-; _*dwoH_$_1$- with an overt marker of the dual would be impossible as the first element of a compound.

2 Some have seen in Hitt. _da-ma-a(-i)-_ '(an)other' the same element. If that is correct, these forms and PIE _*dekm̥t_ '10' (386) may point to _*de-/*do-_, not _*d(u)w-_, as the truly aboriginal stem for two, such that _*dwo_ is some kind of elaboration. A minor problem: in better-understood languages, elements for 'other' are certainly used for 'second' (especially 'of two'), but the use of 'second' to mean 'other' is less to be taken for granted.

for this *du-*. The usual assumption is that it is somehow based on the simplex, though *dŭ-* < **duo-* presents many problems.

b. Some authorities, concerned about G δύο, -ω vs. δι-, trace the latter to a *w*-less etymon **di-*, and in fact actual evidence in G for δϝι- is not to be found. Occam's Razor nevertheless favors the etymon clearly attested outside of G, **dwi-*. Some nevertheless see in L *dis-* 'apart, away' (cf. NE *in two*) independent evidence for a *w*-less form; formal and semantic parallels are afforded by a WGmc. prefix (OE *tó-* in *tó-drífan* 'drive apart', OHG *ze-uuerfan* 'throw away'). Semantically the connection is reasonable, but the loss of -*w*- is a problem whether one dates it as late as Germanic and Italic or pushes it back to PIE. —The association of the meaning 'away, apart' with the *w*-less forms, specifically, is both striking and inexplicable.

c. The element **wi-* seen in the PIE form for '20', orig. ***wi-dḱomt-* whence **wīḱomt-* (391), bears a resemblance to **d(u)wo*, even more to **dwi-*, but it is unclear whether the resemblance is coincidental or significant. If coincidental, it implies (yet) another root for 'two', lost except in '20', and, perhaps, in InIr. **wi-* 'apart, away' (*'in two'). In Skt., where it is enormously frequent, this element is limited to bound forms such as *vi-caranti* 'they move in different directions'. In Vedic it still occurs as a preposition, with the meaning 'through, between'. The preverbal function is reminiscent of L *dis-*; the prepositional, of G διά 'through'—which latter has also been traced to **d(w)i-* 'two'. For those who see laryngeals behind all G prothetic vowels, G εἴκοσι '20' < *ἐϝίκοσι < **ewīkoti* implies **H₁wi-* rather than **wi-*, which, if valid, would diminish the possibility of any ultimate connection with **dwi-*. There is in any case the question of why **dwi-* would sometimes lose its *-*w*- (L *dis-*), at other times its **d-*.

Some see the same **wi-* in PIE **widheweH₂-*, **widhewo-* 'widow(er)', attested far more widely than the element **wi-* itself.

In the case of such short forms, chance similarity is as likely as any other explanation. Those who assume a connection, however, propose two possible sources for the *d*-less form for '20'. First, the counting sequence ***déḱm̥t, dwidḱomt-* . . .'ten, twenty . . .' might lead to the absorption of the **d-* into the preceding *-*t*. Alternatively, it might be a dissimilation from ***dwi-dḱomt-*. How convincing these theories are is a matter of opinion; but it is evident that they hardly can account for the loss of ***d-* in the etymon of InIr. **wi-* 'apart, between'.

d. Toch. A *wu* m., *we* f., Toch. B *wi* m.f. 'two' do not confirm the etymon discussed in **c**, above. Rather, **dw* > *w* is a regular development in Toch., as seen also in Toch. A *wiyo* m. *wiyoss* f. 'frightened' perf.pple. to a root **dwey-* (G δείδω, 190.3); and in Toch. B *śwerppewä* 'quadruped' which includes *-*ped-wo-*.

B. TERMS FOR 'BOTH' ('all two'; always definite whether or not overtly so marked) have a number of similar but irreconcilable forms in IE languages.

1. Ved. *ubhá-* (du.tant.), *ubháya-* adj. 'of both kinds' (sg. and pl.; never du.), Av. *uwa-*, *baya-*.

2. G ἄμφω (indecl. in Hom.; du. and pl. later), eventually displaced altogether by ἀμφότεροι;[1] L *ambō* indecl. (used with fem. nouns in Plt., and

---

[1] Cf. the G coinage ἕτερος 'one of two'. The reason for the contrastive marker *-*tero-* (355) in ἀμφότεροι is not clear. Perhaps the enlarged form was originally contrastive ('both, not just the one'); but on the basis of πότερος 'which of two', -τερο- could have come to be felt as a sort of dual.

neut., like *duo,* at all periods). It is mostly attested with an inflection like *duo,* except that *ambōs* acc. remained stylistically marked: a few Latin authors, such as Ovid and Tacitus, always use it; many more hesitate between the two; some, notably Terence, Horace, Cicero, and Caesar, never use *ambōs.* —The only cognate of this particular formation outside of the classical languages is Toch. A *āmpi.*

3. OCS *oba* (inflects exactly like *dŭva* 'two'), Lith. *abù.*

4. Gmc. **bai* apparently went just like **twai* 'two', namely inflected for the most part as a pl. pronoun. So Go. *bai,* cf. *þai* nom.pl. 'those' = G *οἱ,* Ved. *té;* OE *bá* (fem. and neut.; the masc. *bégen* is like *twégen* m. 'two'). In Gmc. the form so often occurred with the definite article—which followed —that the sequence coalesced into NE *both,* NHG *beide.* Go. *bajoþs,* which inflects as a SINGULAR cons. stem, may have a similar origin though the details are difficult.

C. It has been remarked that all of the forms in 2B, above, bear a resemblance to **H_2m̥bhi* 'on both sides of, around' seen in G *ἀμφί,* L *ambi-, amb-, am-, an-* (only in compounds), Gaul. *ambi-,* OHG *umbi,* OE *ymb,* and perhaps Ved. *abhí* 'toward, into, over' (whose form is more appropriate than its meaning). All point to a zero grade except G and L (Gaul. is ambiguous), and some have suggested that *ἀμ-* and *am-* are the proper reflex of initial **H_2m̥-* (100a) rather than a full grade **H_2em-*; others that *ἀμφί* is a remodeling of inherited **ἀφί* after *ἀντί* 'facing'. Such an etymon, **H_2m̥bhi,* looks like the loc.sg. of a root noun **H_2embh-*, cf. **H_2enti* 'in front of' lit. 'in face' (406.1). But a loc.sg. should have been full grade, and the distribution of the specific form **H_2embho-* around the periphery of IE territory, namely in G, L, Toch., and perhaps Celt., points to its antiquity; the remaining forms are not so much evidence as problems to be solved.

a. PIE **H_2m̥bhi-* has been etymologized quite differently, as ***H_2n̥t-bhi,* that is, a case-form in **-bhi* of **H_2ent-* 'face' (406.1). This is formally elegant, but it is unclear where, exactly, the sense of BOTHNESS comes from.

389.3. THREE. PIE *tréyes* m., *triH_2* n. inflected as an ordinary *i*-stem plurals (302-3). The fem., however, was **tisres* < ***tri-sr-*, a consonant stem consisting of root **tri-* and a feminine marker **-sr-* seen also in the fem. of 'four' and attested only in Celt. (OIr. *téoir* /tēə̯ρ'/) and InIr. (Ved. *tisrás* nom./acc., *tisṛ́ṣu* loc., *tisṛ́bhis* instr.; Av. *tisrō* nom.); the InIr. and Celt. forms are precisely superimposable. The distribution of **tisr-*, together with its formal oddity, proves its authenticity. In all other IE branches the weird fem. stem was lost, and a single paradigm (orig. masc.) served as both masc. and fem., as is the norm with *i*-stem nouns and adjectives.

G *τρεῖς* and L *trēs* reflect **tréyes* (= Ved. *tráyas,* Av. *θrayō,* OCS *trije,* OIr. *trí*^{H}, O **trís**). Acc. OL *trīs* < **trins,* like G **trins,* Ved. *trīn.* —This is one of the few clearly-attested numbers we have in Hitt., where most numbers are written in digits and the few that are not are problematic; but Hitt. *te-ri-ya-aš* gen. 'three', can confidently be taken as /triyas/ or the like.

G τρία n. is regular from **triH₂* (**49.2**), which also gives Ved. *trī́* and OCS *tri.* L *tria* and U **triia**, superficially similar, reflect a PItal. remodeling of **trī* < **triH₂* through the addition of the usual nom.pl. **-ā* imported from *o*-stem neuters (**260.3**). Go. *þrija* and OIr. (archaic) *tre* have a similar history, and so the remodeling of the *i*-stem nom./acc.neut.pl. as *-īā* may be a shared 'western' innovation. (Skt. *trī́ṇi*—the only form in the later language but already found in Vedic—is likewise a remodeling under the influence of what came to be the pattern in Indic for nom./acc.pl.n.[1])

a. COMBINING FORMS. G τρι- (τριπλόος, -πλοῦς 'threefold') is the zero grade of the stem. L *tri-* is regular before labials and dorsals; before apicals the regular shape is *ter-* (**74.3**) as in *ter* 'thrice' < *terr* (so scanned in Plt.) < **ters* < **tris* = G τρίς, Ved. *trís*; *ternī* 'three each'; *tertius* 'third' (cf. U *tertim* 'for the third time', L *tertium*); *terdeciē(n)s* 'thirteen times'; and covertly in *testis* 'witness' < **ter-st-* < **tri-stH₂-* lit. 'third standing [by]' (cf. O **trstus** 'witness', and, with full grade of the verbal root, in L *testāmentum* < **ter-stā-* < **tri-steH₂-*; cf. O **trístaamentud**). Otherwise *tricornis* 'having three horns', *tripudium* a kind of dance. The rarest form, *tre-*, in L *trecentī* '300' and *trepondō* indecl. 'three pounds', though evidently old, has an obscure history.

b. PIE **trey-/*tri-* looks like a stem-forming element **-ey-/-i-* added to **tr-*. The only evidence for such a primitive is Myc. *to-pe-zo*, G τράπεζα 'table'. The first syllable is traditionally traced to **kʷtwr̥-* (a combining-form of '4', q.v.) via **kʷtwra-*. But the word cannot have any original connection with 'four', as the article in question until a later period had three legs[2] (four-legged furniture is practical only on perfectly even floors), and the forms reconstruct straightforwardly to **tr̥-ped-iH₂* with the '3' primitive. It is the kind of term which furthermore may convincingly be posited for a very early period of PIE material culture.

389.4. FOUR. PIE **kʷetwór-* (? **kʷétwor-*), zero grade **kʷetwr̥-* (before cons.), **kʷetur-* (before vowels). So **kʷetwores* m.; **kʷetwōr* n. < ***kʷetworH₂*; loc. **kʷetwr̥su*, gen. **kʷeturōm*. As in the case of 'three', above, the extraordinary feminine stem **kʷetesr-* (cons. stem) is attested only in Celtic and InIr., thus OIr. *cethéoir* /keθēə̯ρ'/, Ved. *cátasras*, Av. *čataŋrō.* Thanks to Indic sound laws, Ved. *catur-*, which is the combining form as well as the zero grade of the inflected m. and n. stem (inst. *catúrbhis* for example), could be the regular outcome of either **kʷetwr̥-* or **kʷetur-*. But the latter is unambiguous prevocalically in Av. *čaturąm* gen.pl., and in the Rigveda too the forms normally occur in places where a heavy first syllable (presumably **čatwur-*) is implausible.

---

1 The pattern: all nom./acc.pl. neuters contain (1) a long vowel, (2) a nasal, and (3) suffixal *-i*. Whatever ingredient was lacking in the historically correct form—which is sometimes attested in the earliest texts—was supplied, such as *trī́ṇi* for *trī́*; the *a*-stem form *-āni* for original *-ā*; *s*-stem *-āṃsi* for original **-ās*, **297.3**.

2 'Table-shaped' (trapezoid) reflects this peculiarity, as for stability's sake their tops were narrower at the one-leg end.

Ved. *catvā́ras* nom.m. < *k^wetwóres* (-*ā*- < *-*ŏ*- via 36.4) = OIr. *ceth(a)ir* /k′eθəρ′/. G forms are: Myc. *qe-to-ro-we* (k^w*etrowes*?—apparently nom.sg. neut.), Hom. τέσσαρες, πίσυρες, Ion. τέσσερες, Att. τέτταρες, Boeot. πέτταρες, Lesb. πέσ(σ)υρες, Dor. τέτορες (-τ- regular in Dor. < -τϝ-). Of these, Dor. τέτορες, Hom. πίσυρες and Lesb. πέσ(σ)υρες (specifically the -(σ)συρες parts) are the least disturbed of the attested forms, being the regular reflexes of *(*k^we)twores* (154.1, 164A, 44, 190.4) like Ved. *catvā́ras*, Av. *čaθwārō̆*. The more usual forms reflect *k^w*eččares* with -*ar*- generalized from zero grade formations (for example dat.pl. τέσσαρσι). Ion. τέσσερες is presumably a modification of τέσσαρες, traceable to the multiple influences of **treyes* 'three', *u*-stem forms in -εϝες (and similar nom.pl. types), perhaps with some help from assimilation.

L *quattuor* indecl. continues *k^w*etwōr* nom./acc.n < **k^w*etworH*$_2$. The -*ttu*- is explained in 185.4. The same form is seen in Ved. *catvā́ri* (see 389.3 fn., 291.2b), and in Gmc., as in Go. *fidwor* (for *f*- see 155). Gmc. and Indic agree, in contrast to the G forms, in having the accent on a non-*e*-grade syllable; *k^w*étwōr* as in G would have given Go. ×*fiþwor*.

In both G and L there are many puzzling details about these forms. Myc. *qe-to-ro-we* 'having four handles' apparently continues *k^w*etr̥*-; the loss of the **w*, perhaps by dissimilation, can have taken place at any time. Metathesis with all parts preserved, i.e. of *-*wr̥*- to *-*ru*-, is seen in Av. *čaθru*-, Gaul. *petru*-, L *quadru*-, and possibly in G τρυφάλεια (a, below). This does not necessarily mean it is inherited: **luk*^{w}*os* for **wl̥k*^{w}*os* 'wolf', though reflected in both G λύκος and L *lupus*, is hardly a shared innovation. Hom. πίσυρες has an inexplicable first vowel (and a surprising reflex of *k^w-, 154.1, 161; perhaps it shows the influence of πέντε); the -*a*- of L *quattuor*, *quadru*-, and the rest, is no less mysterious. Such vowels are the traditional redoubts of schwa secundum or reduced grade vowels (124); but an unexpected vowel in PIE is a poor way to explain an unexpected vowel in G or L.

The change of *-*t*- to -*d*- in L *quadru*- is more than unexplained: it is inconsistent with the seeminlgy regular development of **dr* to *tr* (223.5).

a. COMBINING FORMS. The PIE combining form was *k^w*(e)twr̥*- (before cons.), *k^w*(e)tur*- (before vow.), though in a number of the most conservative IE branches, the two forms would merge: Ved. *catur*-, Go. *fidurfalþs* 'fourfold' (< **fidwur*- < *k^w*etwr̥*-), Lith. *keturkójis* 'four-footed'. The expected forms would have had zero grade throughout, as *k^w*twr̥*-, *k^w*tur*-, *k^w*tru*-; but these are nowhere unambiguously attested. The best candidate is G τρυφάλεια, a kind of Homeric helmet, from *k^w*tru*-, if properly explained as 'having four φάλοι' (bosses or crests or some such thing). Its obscurity makes this interpretation uncertain, but the selfsame obscurity would account for the survival of unaltered *(π)τρυ- in the first place.

G τετρα- is straightforwardly from *k^w*etwr̥*- (154.1, 95.1). L *quadru*- (in *quadrupēs* 'four footed' and also, presumably though ambiguously, in such forms as *quadrifāriam* adv. 'fourfold'), points to *k^w*etru*-, a modified shape also seen in Av., Ital., and perhaps indirectly in Myc. *qe-to-ro-we* (see above). The antiquity of the metathesized forms is uncertain.

b. How the fem. **kʷetesr-* (InIr.), **kʷetisr-* (Celt.) relates to **kʷetwor-* is not as apparent as the relationship of **tisr-* to **tri-* 'three' (389.3). The loss of the first **r* is straightforward, but the absence of **w/u* is not. Of course, in terms of PIE morpheme structure **kʷetwor-* contains too many consonants to be a genuine primitive in any case, and the fem. stem might be evidence for an elemental 'four' in ***kʷet-* or ***kʷetu-*.

389.5. FIVE. PIE **pénkʷe* > G πέντε, πεμπα- (in πεμπάζω 'count on the fingers', πεμπώβολον 'five-pronged fork'), Aeol. πέμπε, Ved. *páñca*, Av. *panča*, OIr. *cóic* /kōg′/, W *pimp*, Gaul. ΠΕΜΠΕ-, all by regular sound laws. The Ital. and Celt. forms show the replacement of **p* by **kʷ* before a **kʷ* (141a). The expected L form would be ˣ*quĭnque* per (41.1); -*ī*- for expected -*ĭ*- is imported from the ordinal *quīn(c)tus*. Sab. **pomp-* 'five' though unattested as such is guaranteed by the given names O **púntiis** and ΠΟΜΠΤΙΕΣ 'Quintius' (the L given name *Pontius* is an Italic borrowing), and O **púmperiaís** dat.pl. (a festival). The reason for development of **e* to -*o*- (-**ú**-) is uncertain, but may have something to do with the strongly labial environment; cf. the rounding in NHG *fünf*, OHG *funf* (? [ü]) from the orig. PGmc. **fimf*, seen in Go. *fimf*, OE *fīf*. (PGmc. -*f* < **kʷ*, 155.)

a. COMBINING FORMS. In compounds there are a few G forms in πεντε-, as in πεντετάλαντος 'worth five talents', none of great antiquity. Most compounds have πεντα- after τετρα- (original) and ἑξα- (secondary, as next, note **a**).

389.6. SIX. Several different etyma for 'six' represented in the IE languages are reconstructed as follows: (a) **sweḱs* in G ἕξ (dial. ϝέξ), Gaul. *suexos*, W *chwech*, OIr. *sé* (lenition to *f*- shows underlying **sw*-). (b) **seḱs* in Ved. *ṣáṣ* nom. (-*ṣ* is a secondary development; the stem and combining form *ṣaṭ-* has the original shape, being the direct development of **saṭṣ* < **saśs*, with *ṣ*- by assimilation); more straightforward developments yield L *sex*, Gmc. **sehs* (Go. *saihs*, OE *s(i)ex*), Lith. *šešì*, and OCS *šestĭ*. (c) A third form, PIE **ksweḱs*, is indicated by Av. *xšvaš*; but that may be from **sw-* after all (the sporadic development of **ksw*- for expected **sw*- in word-initial position is seen in other InIr. words). (d) OPr. *uschts* '6th' and Arm. *vec̣* point to an *s*-less etymon, **weḱs*. (In fact this etymon could account for the G forms too, per 188.) This is probably the original state, and paradoxical as it may seem, this also accounts for the discrepancy between forms pointing to **sw*- vs. **s*-: in both, the initial **s*- was secondary (imported from 'seven'). When it was just added the result was **sweḱs*, but when it replaced the original cons. the result was **seḱs*.

a. COMBINING FORMS. In compounds G has a few examples of the original shape, which appears as G ἑξ-, ἑκ- (ἑκκαίδεκα '16'), and ἑσ- (Boeot. εσκηδεκατος '16th') as shaped by sound laws and leveling; see also 398.6. But the usual form is ἑξα-, which was modeled on ἑπτα-: ἑξάπεδος 'six feet long'. L *sēdecim* '16' and *sēnī* 'six each' show the regular development of *-*ksd*- and *-*ksn*- (231.1). In most forms, however, the shape *sex*- has been restored by recomposition, as *sexcentī* '600' and even *sexdecim*.

389.7. SEVEN. PIE **septḿ̥* > Ved. *saptá*, Av. *hapta*, G ἑπτά, L *septem*, OIr.

secht, W *saith*. An oddity here is the accent on the zero grade syllable instead of the *e*-grade, the influence of neighboring 'eight' (389.8). PGmc. **seƀun* (Go. and OHG *sibun*, OE *seofon*) is unexpected on two counts: first, word-final *-*un* < *-*m̥* means that in PreGmc. a consonant must have followed; second, there is no trace of the *-*pt*- seen in all cognates outside of Gmc. The likeliest source of the implied etymon, **sepḿ̥t*, can be traced to the ordinal (398.7). OCS *sedmĭ* likewise shows the influence of the ordinal **septmo*-.

a. THE COMBINING FORM **septm̥*- (? for ***sptm̥*-) is reflected in G ἑπτα- and L *septem*-. The latter shows trifling assimilatory traits in forms like *septendecim* '17' and *septentriōnēs* 'ursa minor' (lit. 'seven threshing oxen'; see also 490.2a), and even these are often *septem*- at least in writing.

389.8. EIGHT. For the PIE word for 'eight' the evidence of the daughter languages is clear in its general outlines but polyambiguous in detail, which allows for various reconstructions of the etymon.

Traditionally, the etymon was taken to be **oḱtō*, possibly a simplex but commonly (if improbably) regarded as a nom./acc.du. PIE **oḱtō*, functional ambiguity and all, is still one of the possibilities. But as the word both begins and ends with vowels, there are a number of ways laryngeals can be added. So for example **oḱtoH₁* (overtly marked as a dual); **oḱteH₃* or **H₃eḱteH₃* (simplexes); or the latter with one or more *o*-grades along with the laryngeals—**H₁oḱteH₃*, **H₃oḱteH₃*, **H₃eḱtoH₁*, and several other combinations.

Since all the numerals from '3' through '10' (and also **sem*- 'one') have *e*-grade, the correct choice among the alternatives must be **H₃eḱt*-. But the correct continuation of the form is less evident. The reconstruction of a dual ending is improbable, given the opacity of the preceding part—the usual explanations of what is dual about 'eight' are fantastic—and is nothing more than a coincidence of form in the IE languages most relied-upon for evidence on the point, and even there the evidence has not been carefully read. The dual ending which is uniformly -*āu* in classical Skt. is in competetion with -*ā* in the Rigveda, and occurs only one-seventh as often as this -*ā*. The Rigvedic ratio of *aṣṭā́* to *aṣṭā́u*, however, is 1:3, which is remarkably unlike the statistics for the du. formation in -*ā(u)*.

A quite different reconstruction has the most to recommend it. The crucial data are Go. *ahtau*, which cannot reflect *-*ō* or *-*eH₃*; and the ordinal **H₃eḱtowos* (398.8). These point to an original **H₃eḱtów* (Go., InIr.) which alternated with **H₃eḱtō* (as seen in InIr., G, and L) under conditions not yet determined. Two points: the tonic accent in this reconstruction is on the 'wrong' syllable, and the form has too many consonants to be a genuine primitive. (See however 398.8a for yet another reconstruction.)

G ὀκτώ and L *octō* are straightforward given these assumptions, as is Ved. *aṣṭā́*, -*ā́u*. Elean *hoπτω* shows contamination by ἑπτά.

a. COMBINING FORMS. Most combining forms contain *-ō-* or its reflexes. This might reflect the influence of the cardinal, but if old, is further evidence that the numeral was not a dual: a case- and number-marked element as the first member of a bahuvrīhi is unthinkable.

G has ὀκτω-, but ὀκτα- is more frequent. The latter is obviously based on ἑπτα-, but ὀκτω- is not necessarily any more ancient. L usually has *octō-* as in *octōdecim* '18'; but *octūplus* 'eightfold' and perh. *octussis* (probably *-ū-*) 'eight *asses*' < **oktowassis* with syncope of the third vowel (61.2a) point to an earlier **oktow-* as proposed above. Ved. usually has *aṣṭā-*; the normal form later, *aṣṭa-*, is after *sapta-*.

b. For those who trace all prothetic vowels in G to laryngeals (90), G ἐννέα 'nine' (9, below), Arm. *inn*, next to initial *n-* in all other IE groups, points to PIE **H₁newn̥*. If this is so , it is possible (remotely) that the baffling final of 'eight' reflects a phonological development originally peculiar to the counting sequence *. . . *H₃eḱtow‿H₁newn̥* . . . .

389.9. NINE. PIE **néwn̥* (or, for those who trace G prothetic vowels to laryngeals, **H₁néwn̥*) straightforwardly gives Ved. *náva* and Go. *niun* (< **niwun*; there is evidence that *niun* was disyllabic). OE *nigon* [niɣon], OS *nigun* attest a PGmc. hesitation between **gw* and **w*, cf. OE *wearm* < **gʷhormos*, and *snáw* < **snoygʷhos*, with **w* for expected PGmc. **gʷ* < PIE **gʷh*. —As in the case of 'seven', above, Gmc. forms presuppose a consonant after the nasal.

G ἐννέα, the form in all dialects,[1] has usually been explained as a conflation of two forms: the first is expected **newa* or **enewa* (*e-* prothetic, 89; cf. Arm. *inn*) < **(H₁)néwn̥*; and the second ingredient is **enwa* < **(H₁)enwn̥*, with a different full grade. The competition between **(e)newa* and **enwa*, by this account, resulted in PG **enwewa*, whence ἐννέα. There are two large difficulties with this explanation. Ablaut of the stem is not expected in a form with no inflectional morphology at all (apart from the ordinal, 397, 398.9, and even in that form all PIE languages point to full grade **newn̥-o-* in place of the presumably original ***nun-o-*). Still less expected is Schwebeablaut (114.2), as in **werǵ-* 'work' next to original **wreǵ-*. Besides, **nw* would not give Att. *-νν-* in any case (190.1); the correct outcome of PG **enwa-* is evident in some conservative forms such as 'ninefold': Att. ἐνάκις, Ion. εἰνάκις < **enwa-*.

Apparently, then, ἐννέ(ϝ)α is a modification of expected **enewa*. Etyma in **enw-* (rather than **enew-*) are attested in the adv. ἐνάκις mentioned just above, in the ordinal ἔνατος, Ion. εἴνατος < **enwatos*, and in the unique Hom. ἐννήκοντα '90' < ? **enwnakont-* < **(e)nwn̥̄komt-* (next to ἐνενήκοντα < **enewna-* < **(H₁)newn̥̄-*). Some say that such instances of **enw-* arose by syncope, others say they are inherited, still others attribute disyllabic **enwa-* to the influence of ἑπτα-, ὀκτα-, and δεκα-. How the forms arose, however, is immaterial. Once they had come into being, bringing **enewa* into PRO-

[1] Myc. *e-ne-wo* (*o* < **n̥*, 100d) is at most a qualified exception, as there is no way of telling whether this represents *enewo* or *ennewo*.

sodic alignment with *enwatos would mean a first syllable *ἐν-*, such that **e-ne-* was reshaped as **en-ne-*. Also important in the process were *ἑπτά* 'seven' and *ὀκτώ* 'eight', which are partially similar to one another prosodically and, once the prothetic vowel is added, to expected 'nine' also: they all begin with atonic vowels and have a tonic second syllable. Prosodically, **enewa* would agree with the rhythm of *ἑπτά* and *ὀκτώ* better if it had a consonant sequence before the tonic vowel: *ἑπ-τά, ὀκ-τώ, ἐν-νέϝα*. (For an exact parallel note the lengthened *-t-* in NE *thirteen* and *fourteen* in the usual pronunciation of many English speakers, a prosodic assimilation to *fifteen* and *sixteen*, among others.)

L *novem* for expected **noven* shows the influence of *decem*. The original shape of the word is preserved in the ordinal *nōnus* < **nowenos* (**61.2a**) < **newn̥os*.

a. A note on the reconstruction of PIE 'nine'. In most IE languages *-*n̥* and *-*m̥* would have identical outcomes. Evidence for the correct choice between **newn̥* and **newm̥* comes from derived forms, and is in fact equivocal.

Evidence for *-*n̥*: L *nōnus* '9th' < **nowenos*, as above, and also from OCS *devętĭ*, Lith. *devynì*. The latter two show the BS importation of *d-* from 'ten'. The OCS form confirms *-*nt-* in contradistinction to the reflex of *-*mt-* seen in OCS *sŭto* < **śəmto-* < **k̑m̥tom*, cf. Lith. *šim̃tas*. (For the OCS development, cf. OCS *sŭvęzati* 'to tie together' < **sm̥-* next to *sǫsědŭ* 'neighbor' < **som-*.)

Evidence for *-*m̥*: original *-*m-* might be preserved in Gaul. NOMET[OS], OIr. *nómad* '9th' (PCelt. **nawametos* for **nawamos* < **newm̥mos*); if so, L *nōnus* would be derivable from **nowemos* via dissimilation. U **nuvime**, usually interpreted as '9th', would be a welcome datum here; its -i- is unexpected, however (weakening of short vowels medially is a L trait, not Sab.; cf. U **maletu** = L *molitus*). In fact, in the context of the word in question, which is about soldiers, it is rather a superlative 'newest' (the opposite of 'veterans')(358). Toch. A *nmuka*, B *ñumka* '90', while obscure in detail, indubitably show *-m-* from somewhere. Finally, the remodeling of the ordinals in InIr. is a fraction easier if one starts from **newm̥-* rather than **newn̥-*, such that Ved. *navamá-* is inherited rather than a replacement of **navaná-*. (The usual explanation, that it was contaminated by *saptamá-* and *aṣṭamá-*, is satisfactory, and some such influence is required in any case for *aṣṭamá-* and *daśamá-*.)

Most of the evidence for *-*m̥*, however, can be explained the same way as the *-m* of L *novem*, namely as contamination by adjacent ordinals (NB Gaul. DECAMETOS '10th' next to **nawametos* '9th'), though in the case of Toch. even the possibility of such an explanation is uncertain. On the other hand the BS evidence is hard to explain by anything other than inherited **n̥*.

389.10. Ten. The PIE form is traditionally reconstructed **dek̑m̥*, but **dék̑m̥t* is implied by the ordinal **d(e)k̑m̥t-ó-* (**398.10**) and the decad element **-*dk̑omt* (**391**). In several languages the final *-*t* of the cardinal would have been lost per sound law: G *δέκα* and L *decem* would result from either reconstruction. Arm. *tasn* and PGmc. **tehun* (Go. *taihun*) however require some final cons. to account for the survival of the nasal—an original **dek̑m̥* would have given PGmc. ˣ*tehuⁿ*, Go. ˣ*taihu*, OE ˣ*tieh*. On the other hand the PInIr. reflex of **dek̑m̥t* would have been **daśat*, whereas Ved. *dáśa*, Av.

dasa point to PInIr. **daśa*. This **daśa* can be explained, however, as back-formed from the (inherited) ordinal **daśatá-* < **dekm̥t-ó-*, after it was metan-alyzed into **daśa-ta-* (as if it contained the commonplace adj. suffix *-*to*-), whence **daśa*. After **daśa* had been created, inherited **daśata-* was replaced by **daśama-*, 398.10.

OLith. *dešimtis*, OCS *desętĭ* are based on the ordinal (the secondary nature of Lith. *dẽšimt* is patent in the -*t*, as a genuinely original word-final stop would have been lost.) OIr. *deich* nasalizes the initial of a following word, but that is not significant: *ocht* 'eight' does the same thing and it cannot have had a final nasal originally; and if *ocht* could have imported nasalization from adjacent numbers ('seven' and 'nine' in this case), *deich* from original **dekm̥t* can have done the same thing.

390. THE TEENS. The numbers 11-19 were originally phrases, typically asyndetic, which tended to metamorphose into compounds by phonological developments. The basic form was '*n* ten' meaning '*n* plus ten'; but in most IE languages and probably in the parent language as well there were variations with an overt conjunction ('*n* and ten' or 'ten and *n*').

Very commonly, and so perhaps inherited from the parent language, the higher teens are formed subtractively. This was optional to start with, but sometimes this method supplanted the additive formation, as happened in L *duo-*, *un-dēvīgintī* '18, 19'. The process can go a step further: in Skt. a common expression for '19' is *ūnaviṃśatis* lit. 'twenty lacking', which makes no sense. It is clipped from the straightforward *ekonaviṃśatis* 'one-deficient twenty'.

Yet other methods for expressing teens arise sporadically, of the sort seen in W *deunaw* 'twice nine', *un ar bymtheg* 'one and fifteen'; or 'one left over, two left over [scil. ten]' for '11, 12' seen in Gmc. and Balt. (Go. *ainlif**, *twalif*; Lith. *vienúolika*, *dvýlika*).

G ἕνδεκα, δώδεκα, dial. also δυώδεκα, δυόδεκα (both influenced by simplex δύω, δύο), δέκα δύο; τρεῖς καὶ δέκα, τρεισκαίδεκα (τριακαίδεκα), τρισκαίδεκα indecl., or (especially when the head precedes) δέκα τρεῖς. The last two teens are optionally expressed as δυοῖν (~ἑνὸς) δέοντα εἴκοσι lit. 'twenty lacking two (~one)'.

The L forms are more altered. L *ūndecim* (71.2, 82b) would pass for the reflex of **oinodecem* with syncope of -*o*- via Exon's Law (74.5). Such a compound however, if ancient, would have meant 'having a single ten', so the etymon of *ūndecim* was probably a phrase of the usual asyndetic type, **oynom dekm̥t*, which coalesced into a single word (237.1).[1]

Similarly *duodecim* (NB -*ŏ*-), *trēdecim* (**treyesd-*, 225.1), *quattuordecim*, *quīndecim* (ultimately **quinque decem*, probably), *sēdecim* (**seksd-*, 231.1), *septendecim*. All show -*decim* for expected *-*dicem* (71.2), a metathesis traceable to the influence of simplex *decem*—though it is odd, if that is really the explanation, that the influence did not take the form of adjusting *-*dicem* to ˣ-*decem*.

[1] Just such a process results in NE *eleven*, *twelve*.

The last two teens are actually attested as _octodecim_ (? _-ō-_) and _novendecim_, but the usual forms are subtractive: _duodēvīgintī_, _undēvīgintī_ (_ŭn-_, rather than _ūn-_, perh. from _ŭndecim_, **82b**). These are similar to the G _δέοντα εἴκοσι_ phrases mentioned above, and are sometimes traced to the G model specifically; but differences in detail make it unlikely that the G phrases were the inspiration for the L ones, or even very important.

Syndetic phrases are occasionally met with instead, as epigraphic DECEM ET VNA, DECEM ET TRIBVS, DECEM ET SEPTEM; but DVODECIM occurs beside these in the same inscription. The inverted form for '12' is usually _decem duo_ rather than _decem et duo_; cf. U _desenduf_ acc. (_*dekem-duōns_).

391. The decads. Historically the decads were compounds made up of the units plus an element which is superficially _*-ḱomt_. If the denominator ended in a syllabic, as most do, it is lengthened: so _*trīḱomt_, _*k_^{w}_etwr̥̄ḱomt_, _*penk_^{w}_ēḱomt_, _*septm̥̄ḱomt_. It is obvious that some consonant preceding the _*-ḱ-_ had been lost, with compensatory lengthening of the preceding syllabic. (In _*sweḱsḱomt_ '60' the consonant was lost without effect.) The consonant in question must be _*-d-_, since the second element of the compound is transparently 'ten'. Transparent are _**tri-dḱomt_, _**k_^{w}_etwr̥-dḱomt_, _**penk_^{w}_e-dḱomt_, _**(s)weḱs-dḱomt_, _**septm̥-dḱomt_, _**oḱto(w)-dḱomt_, and _**_(H_1)_newn̥-dḱomt_. On the basis of these, the less transparent _*wīḱm̥t-_ '20' may confidently be traced to an earlier _**wi-dḱomt_. (The inconsistent ablaut grades of the denominator cannot be original. Probably they were originally all zero grade, but with the exception of '30' and perhaps '20' they were remodeled after the units.)

Already in PIE there were some analogical disturbances as well as some morphological retouching. The expected form for '20', _*wīḱomt-_, is nowhere attested, having been replaced by _*wīḱm̥t-_ under the influence of _*deḱm̥t_. (This is another datum in favor of _*deḱm̥t_, as an original _*deḱm̥_ without the final _*-t_ would have been unlikely to interact with _**wīḱomt-_.) This zero-grade shape spread further in InIr., whence Ved. _triṃśát-_, _catvāriṃśát-_ (with details imported from _viṃśatí-_ '20', itself secondary for _*vīśatī_, cf. Av. _vīsaiti_), and _pañcāśát-_. (Skt. _saptatí-_ and _navatí-_ show the same, with however the addition of _-í_.) In Gmc. also the zero grade vocalism of '10' and '20' spread, hence forms like Go. _sibuntehund_ '70' for _×sibuntehand_.

As late as PGmc., the formation of decads was in flux. The last phase was a program of replacing words for the decads with phrases, 'four tens' and the like, as Go. _fidwor tigjus_[1] '40'. But this is actually a second round of innovation: in the earliest texts the higher decads are formed in a more conservative—but nevertheless distinctively Germanic—manner. The details of the forms disagree from branch to branch, which indicates independent development. So in the recent prehistory of Gothic a form _*fimfēhund_ must be assumed for '50' (though it is everywhere already replaced by a phrase in the attested

[1] The source of NE _-ty_, NHG _-zig_. —Go. _tigjus_ is the nom.pl. of a _u_-stem, _tigu-_ (a Gmc. or Go. creation, though a fanciful PIE _*deḱú-_ is often mentioned in the literature).

languages), whence on the proportion **fimf* : **fimfēhund* :: **sehs* : *X*, the form **sehsēhund* '60' was created, and in this turn led to the touching-up of **seftunhund* as **seftunēhund* '70'. Under the combined influence of *taihun* '10' and cardinal *sibun* '7', the last was remodeled as *sibuntehund*, which is the form actually occurring in Go., and on the proportion *sibun* : *sibuntehund* :: *ahtau* : *X* provided the pattern for Go. *ahtautehund* '80' in place of expected **ahtauhund*. In WGmc. the pivotal form was not '50' but **ahtōhund* '80', whence **sebuntōhund* '70'; these are represented in earliest OHG by the truncated set *sibunzo, ahtozo*; and in OE, with wholesale metanalysis of the counting-series, as *hundseofontig, hundeahtatig* (that is, each *hund-* belongs etymologically to the PRECEDING decad. The same phenomenon underlies the early OHG forms). The OE forms additionally have the usual decad marker *-tig*, imported from the lower numbers.

A source of discussion over the years has been the termination of the decads. L *vīgintī* looks like a nom./acc.neut.du. in **-iH₁*, but G εἴκοσι and Ved. *viṃśatí-* (a SINGULAR fem. *i*-stem noun) do not agree. OIr. *fiche* /fiχ'e/ and its Celtic cognates are ambiguous. The G and InIr. forms can be imagined to show the loss of a word-final laryngeal without other effect, as in the voc.sg. of G *ā*-stems (263.2), though the failure of **-iH₁* to become **-ye* (49.2), as in ὄσσε nom.du.n. 'eyes' < **H₃ekʷiH₁*, is a serious problem.

Similarly obscure is the termination of L *-gintā* of *triāgintā, quattuorgintā*, and the rest (where the preservation of *-ā* in final syllable would be a puzzle per se, 83.2), next to the *-ᾰ* of G -κοντᾰ, and assorted InIr. decads in *-ĭ* (*saptatí-* for example), which are fem. *i*-stems.

Despite the great differences in detail, Go. and OE confirm that the PGmc. form ended in an obstruent, **-d*, which must have been followed by a short vowel in PIE.

The most economical explanation of all these facts is PIE **-ḱomtH̥₂* (**-ḱm̥tH̥₂*). The **-H̥₂* gives Skt. *-i* and G *-ᾰ* automatically, and likewise the Gmc. forms, and is consistent with OIr. *tricho, cethorcho*, and the rest (postconsonantal word-final laryngeals dropped without a trace in PCelt.). The only surprise is L *-ā*. The replacement of expected *-ă* < **-ā* started in forms like *septuāgintā* and *nōnāgintā*, that is, with *-ā-* at the end of the denominator; *-gintā* is in effect brought into 'agreement' with the denominator. Perhaps the similar pattern in *vīgintī* was a factor, but that form is rather too remote in the series to have exerted strong influence.

a. The PIE element **-H̥₂* on the decads 30-90 looks like and is usually taken to be the marker of the nom./acc.n.pl., perhaps inspired by the nom./acc.du.neut. ending **-iH₁* on '20': if '20' is overtly marked (or seems to be overtly marked) as a neut. dual, marking the higher decads with the corresponding neut.pl. marker seems like a simple innovation. The feminine gender of the InIr. decads, however, might suggest instead that **-H₂* is here the same as the fem. element in **-eH₂-* (262) and **-iH₂-* (268), and that the termination of '20' is not **-iH₁* the marker of the neuter du., but **-i(H)* the marker of the FEMININE du. (as in Ved. *śípre* nom./acc.f.du. 'both cheeks', stem *śíprā-*).

According to one opinion, however, this **-H̥₂* on the decads is a phantom, and the real explanation for the G *-ᾰ*, InIr. *-ĭ*, the unknown (but necessary) short vowel at the end of the Gmc. forms, and perh. for (presumed) Ital. **-ă*, is that they are prop-vowels after the consonant cluster **-mt*. There are several problems with this view. First, **-mt* seems to have been a permitted final in PIE (as in aor. **e-gʷemt* 3sg.); that is, it did not require propping. Second, a final vowel is necessary in these forms in at least four branches, whereas InIr. is the only IE group in which prop-vowels are certainly attested. Last, and weightiest, when sound laws knap consonants off the ends of words, speakers are rarely if ever aware of the process UNLESS ALTERNATION RESULTS. This latter is seen in the case of early PIE ***ḱerd* 'heart' ***ḱr̥dos* gen.: when regular phonological developments produced nom. **ḱēr*, the oblique forms provided grounds for reinstalling the **-d* of the nom.sg. Whether such a reinstallment took place in G cannot be told, as **ḱēr* and **ḱērd* would develop identically. In Ved. *hā́rdi*, however, we have a genuine instance of a restored final cons. with a prop-vowel of the sort proposed for **trīḱomtə*. But the situations are completely different. In the case of decad **-ḱomt*, similarities with **deḱm̥t* were slight enough to begin with, and in the developments of the various branches, reflexes of **deḱm̥t* as well would have been losing their final obstruents. In other words, any tendency for the final **-t* of the decads to drop, in PIE or at any point along the development of the branches, must have proceeded undisturbed by any analogical influence.

b. Note the semantics of the decads: **trīḱomt* for example is the number which marks the END of the third decad, or a tally of three tens. Most number systems work this way. However, it is arguable that we have come to think of *thirty*, say, as the FIRST of a group of ten numbers called collectively *the thirties*.[1] Some numbering systems actually work the way the modern (mis)perception seems to—that is, the name of the decad refers to the beginning rather than the end of the set of ten: in such a terminology, the lexical equivalent to our *thirty-four* would stand for the number '24' lit. 'four in the third decad'. This kind of thing is called *Oberstufenzählung*.

392. GREEK. PIE **wīḱm̥tiH₁* '20'. Dor. (also Boeot., Thess.) ϝικατι (ϝῑ-) '20' is the most conservative G reflex, directly continuing **wīḱm̥tiH₁* except for the detail of the final **-iH₁* mentioned above (though of course for some of the dial. forms the length of the final -ι is not known). Att.-Ion. (also Hom.) εἴκοσι shows the influence of the decads in -κοντα (an ancient influence: once **-ti* had become -σι per 148, **ewikasi* would have been too different from **-konta* to be affected by it). The initial εἰ- < **ewī́-* includes a prothetic vowel. Hom. ἐείκοσι is a redactional fantasy for tetrasyllabic ἐ(ϝ)ίκοσι.

**Trīkonta* '30' was replaced by τριᾱ́κοντα (Ion. τριή-) after **kʷetwrākonta* '40' < **kʷetwr̥̄ḱomtH̥₂*, which itself was subsequently influenced by the simplex τέτταρες, whence τετταρᾰ́κοντα. Some try to trace Dor. τετρώκοντα to **kʷetwr̥̄ḱomtH̥₂* directly; but some think instead of Ved. *catvārim̐śát-*, and hold that the Dor. form is a metathesis of **kʷet(w)ōrkonta*. The latter explanation, while appealing, suffers from the weakness that ˣτετ(ϝ)ωρ- 'four' is not actually attested anywhere in G.

---

[1] At intervals, newspapers print attempts by the tidy-minded to point out that midnight of December 31 of the year 1999 is NOT the expiring moment of the millennium, as the year 2000 is not the first year of the 21st century, but the last year of the 20th. It is nevertheless safe to predict that the major focus of philosophical and spiritual interest will be on the last days of the year 1999.

G πεντήκοντα (Dor. -η-) '50' is regular from **penkʷēkomtH̥₂*. G ἑξήκοντα '60' replaced original **h(ϝ)εσκοντα* < **swekskomtH̥₂* (230.3). Restoration of canonic ἑξ- by itself (say, ˣἕξκοντα) was scarcely possible for G phonotactics; the rescuing -η- comes from the flanking decads, πεντήκοντα and (Att.-Ion.) ἑβδομήκοντα < **hebdmākonta* < **septm̥̄kontH̥₂*.

The voicing of **-pt-* > -βδ- in G ἑβδομήκοντα is probably from the sequence **heptmā-* < **septm̥̄-*, at least in part (see also 398.7). Nevertheless, in most instances of apical stop + nasal in G, nothing of the sort happens: πότνια 'mistress', πότμος 'destiny'. The *-o-* of this form and the ordinal (q.v.) is either epenthetic or else original in the ordinal and imported from there. Epigraphic *hεβδεμηκοντα* (Heracl.; attested more than once) and ordinal *εβδεμαιον* (Epidaurus) favor a third scenario: original -ε- by epenthesis, converted to *-o-* (influenced by 'eighth', 398.8) in the ordinal and then imported into ἑβδομήκοντα.

G ὀγδοήκοντα replaces expected ὀγδώκοντα, which is attested in Dor. and Ion. The -οη- for -ωη- could be a purely phonological development of -ωη- per 79.3, or it could be a result of two analogical influences: ἑβδομήκοντα on the one hand and ordinal *ογδοϝος* on the other (398.8).

Hom. ἐννήκοντα and Att. ἐνενήκοντα have both been traced to **enewnā-* < **newn̥̄-*, the former with syncope. It has also—more plausibly—been taken at face value to reflect **enwnā-* < either **(H₁)enwn̥̄-* or **H₁n̥wn̥̄-*.

a. Aeolic and Doric forms attest -η- even in ἑβδομήκοντα and ἐνενήκοντα where the inherited vowel was certainly -ᾱ- to begin with. The source of this -η- is '50', PG **penkʷēkonta* < PIE **penkʷēkomtH̥₂*.

393. LATIN. The L forms taken as a whole present three special developments. One, the *-ā* of the decads from '30' up, has been discussed above (391).

The easier to explain of the remaining two (but none too easy) is the vowel *-i-* in *-gintī* '20' for *-en-* from **-m̥-* (*-ḱm̥tH*), and, in the *-gintā* of '30-90', for expected *-u-* from **-o-* before a nasal in medial syllable (**-ḱomtH*). It is the result of assimilation to the preceding vowel in the first two decads, *vīgintī* and *trīgintā*, whence it spread to the higher decads. (This explanation is plausible but not compelling.)

The voicing of expected *-c-* to *-g-* is even less confidently explicable. One theory traces it to the clusters **-r̥̄ḱ-* ('40'), **-m̥̄ḱ-* ('70') and **-n̥̄ḱ-* ('90'), on the assumtion that a long syllabic resonant might be reasonably expected to voice a following voiceless stop. There is no confirming evidence of such a thing, in L or any other IE language; but if that is actually the explanation, then from the three forms where the *-g-* is regular it ousted **vīcintī* and the others. Indeed, such a development might have been pan-IE, but everywhere was levelled in favor of the voiceless version, but except in L in favor of the voiced stop. (Leveling seems definitely to be an agent in the L details; as remarked below, in the discussion of ordinals

(399a) and hundreds (395), the distribution of *-g-* is different from the cardinals.)

Vīgintī '20' is from **wīk̑m̥t(-iH)* per the phonological and analogical developments discussed above. The persistence of earlier **wīkentī* is indicated by the forms of the distributive (*vīcēnī*, not ˣ*vīgīnī*) and the ordinal (*vīcē(n)-simus*, not ˣ*vīgē(n)simus* or ˣ*vīgī(n)simus*).

Trīgintā '30' and *octōgintā* '80' are (or appear to be; see '70', below) purely phonological reflexes of their etyma, apart from the *-g-* and *-ā* (discussed above).[1] In addition, *nōnāgintā* '90' for **nūnāgintā* < **nownā-* < **newn̥-* shows only the minor disturbance of *-ō-* in place of *-ū-*, imported from the ordinal *nōnus*, where it is regular (61.2a, 398.9), perhaps with some help from cardinal *novem*.

Septuāgintā '70' reflects **septmāginta* < **septm̥-*. The likeliest source for the remodeling of this form is '80', which may therefore be less conservative in fact than it appears to be: once **septmāginta* developed an anaptyctic vowel between the *-pt-* and the *-m-*, it would have closely resembled **oktowāginta*, if that was in fact the form (*-ā-* from **sept(o)māginta*); whence **septowāginta* by contamination. This develops undisturbed to attested *septuāgintā*, but the simplex *octō* derailed the development of '80' to *octōgintā* in place of **octuāgintā*.

Quadrāgintā continues **kʷetwr̥k̑omtH̥₂* in accord with the usual developments, but with the enigmatic *-a-* characteristic of all 'four'-words in L, and the voicing of expected *-tr-* to *-dr-* (also seen in *quadrīgae* 'a harness of four horses', *quadrāre* 'to make square', combining form *quadru-*, 223.5a).

The next two decads, *quīnquāgintā* and *sexāgintā*, have imported the *-ā-* from other forms (it is not known which of the two was created first).

394. HUNDRED AND THE HUNDREDS. PIE **k̑m̥tóm* '100' is obviously related to PIE **dek̑m̥t* '10' and therefore to the terms for the decad series discussed in 391-3, but the exact nature of the relationship is disputed. According to one view, the word should be understood in terms of the decads, the tenth of which would have been ***dék̑m̥t(d)k̑omtH₂*, or even ***dék̑m̥k̑omtH₂*. (Just such a construct, 'tenth decad', is actually seen in Go. *taihuntehund* and OE *hundtéontig*, but however interesting these are as parallels, they are neologisms based on the decads and nothing ancient.) In any case, while getting from the presumed compound to **k̑m̥tóm* may not be phonologically impossible, it involves much fiddling with the form via dissimilations and other ad hoc appeals, and at a very early date—the IE reflexes point to a uniform **k̑m̥tóm*.[2] On the other hand, perhaps the proper reconstruction is

---

[1] Original **trīk-* is conserved in *trīcēsimus* '30th' and *trīcēnī* '30 each'.

[2] In fact the etymon must have been something like **dek̑m̥tˢtk̑ómt(H)* per 212, from which the emergence of **k̑m̥tóm* would be even more of a feat.

**dk̑m̥tóm*, namely the expected form for the ordinal of **dek̑m̥t* (zero grade of all syllables and the thematic suffix *-*ó*-, 397). If that is so, it would be a clipped phrase (rather than a clipped compound), whose elided noun head can only be surmised.

A third possibility: some think that the formation is a gen.pl. in *-*om*. Fourthly, it might be a nominalized adjective, presumably the ordinal mentioned above, of a type commonplace in IE languages. (This pregnant use of an ordinal would be similar to the use of ordinals in NE and many other languages to refer to fractions: if *tenth* can conventionally mean 'one (or more) of ten equal parts', it just as easily can mean 'the decad after the ninth'.)

Whatever the prior history of the form, PIE **(d)k̑m̥tóm* directly yields L *centum*, Ved. *śatám*, Av. *satəm*, Lith. *šim̃tas* (remodeled as a masc. *o*-stem), OCS *sŭto* (an ordinary neut. *o*-stem), OIr. *cét* /k'ēd/, Toch. A *känt*, OE, OHG *hund* and, pl.tant., Go. *hunda*.

In Germanic, the term seems to have acquired the meaning of '120' ('long hundred'), such that an unambiguous term for ordinary '100' had to be manufactured. In Go., the original form occurs only in phrases like *twaim hundam* dat.pl. '200', and in compounds like *hundafaþs* transl. κεντυρίων (lw. from L *centuriō*). Similarly OHG *zwei hunt*, OE *twá hund*. Even in these expressions there was evidently the possibility of confusion: a Gothic glossator added the word *taihuntewjam* 'tens-wise' to the expression *fimf hundam* dat.pl. (I Cor. 15.6), apparently feeling that it was unclear that *hund** here was to be understood as 100 rather than 120. Seemingly always unambiguous were Go. *taihuntehund* lit. 'tenty' (like *ahtautehund*, *niuntehund*);[1] and the analogous OE *hundtéontig* (like *hundeahtig* '80' and *hundnigontig* '90').

G ἑκατόν presents a special problem. It has long been understood as a contamination, by ἑν- 'one', of *ἁ-κατόν < **sm̥-k̑m̥tóm* 'one-hundred', formed like Ved. *sahásra*- 'one-thousand' (396). All of the (slightly different) versions of this explanation suffer from two rarely-mentioned weaknesses. First, if the form has any antiquity at all it should have been **sm̥̄k̑m̥tóm* < ***sm̥dk̑m̥tóm*, with a very different outcome in G (×μᾱκατόν or ×μηκατόν). Second, if ἁ- were to be modified by the influence of ἑν-, the likely result would have been ×ἑγκατόν, not ἑκατόν. (The usual explanation is like imagining that *tithe* 'tenth' could be replaced by NE /teð/, that is, with the vowel, and only the vowel, imported from *ten*.) On the other hand, G ἕτερος 'one of two', necessarily a late form, indicates that somehow a nasalless ἑ- could be an allomorph of ἑν-.

395. HUNDREDS. It does not appear that the expressions for '200', '300', and the rest, were fixed in PIE, certainly not as fixed as the decads or even the teens. Among the options was a kind of bahuvrīhi ('four-hundreded', like 'four-footed') with stems variously formed according to morphological types productive in late PIE. These underlie the G and L formations.

---

[1] Go. *taihuntaihund*, though occurring three times to once for *taihuntehund*, is thought to be a folk-etymological distortion of the latter.

The hundreds in Att.-Ion. are adjectives formed with an element -*κόσιοι*, more conservatively -*κάσιοι* and, a still more conservative version, Dor. -*κάτιοι*, all ultimately from **-ḱm̥tiyo-*.[1] The change of -*τ*- to -*σ*- is regular (148); -*ο*- for expected -*α*- is usually traced to the decads in -*κοντα*, which is plausible since the decads are obviously the source for some of the denominators: *τριᾱ-* (Ion. *τριη-*). Although the element **ḱm̥tiyo-* must ultimately reflect ***dḱm̥t-*, there is little evidence for the kind of vowel lengthening seen in the decads (391), which is consistent with the idea that the hundreds are a later formation entirely. Given *τριᾱκόσιοι*, it is safe to assume that *πεντηκόσιοι* is likewise imported from the decads. Otherwise the usual combining forms are used, *τετρα-*, *ἑξα-*, *ἑπτα-*, *ἐν(ϝ)α-*, though with hesitation in some forms (*ὀκτω-* next to *ὀκτα-*, *πεντα-* next to *πεντη-*; but no ˣ*πεντε-*). The most distinctive form, *διᾱκόσιοι* '200' (Ion. *διηκόσιοι*), in place of expected **δικόσιοι* or **δυοκόσιοι*, continues no ancient etymon: it was modeled on adjacent *τριᾱκόσιοι*.

The formation in L is similar as far as the termination, but with a different stem: *-centī, -ae, -a* < **-ḱm̥to-*. These are usually adjectives; rarely, instead, they are neut. sg. nouns (as in *ducentum*) in genitival construction with another noun. In those forms where the first part of the compound ended in a nasal, the form is *-gentī*: *quīngentī, septingentī, nōngentī*. As this cannot well be phonological, the influence of the decads must somehow be the source, which may be taken as evidence in favor of the view hesitantly urged above (391, end) to the effect that the decad forms in *-gintā* started in just such formations and spread throughout the decads. The distribution of *-g-* in the hundreds, in this view, is therefore closer to the original, except that *quīngentī* is secondary for **quīnquecentī* or **quīn(c)centī*, but early enough to provide the model for *quadringentī* with its intrusive *-n-*; likewise *octingentī* from *septingentī*, in place of **octōcentī*.

Some details of the denominators are of uncertain explanation. The mere fact that *du-* rather than *duo-* is attested in some other formations (*duplex* 'twofold' and *dubius* 'of two minds', for example) does not make *ducentī* any easier to explain. *Tre-* in *trecentī* has been mentioned above (389.3a). *Sescentī* is straightforward from **sexcentī* per 231.1. *Quīngentī, septingentī*, and *octingentī* are discussed above. *Nōngentī* is straightforwardly from **nowen-* < **newn̥-* via 61.2a.

396. THOUSAND. PIE **ǵheslo-* is attested in Ved. *sahásra-*, Av. *hazaŋrəm* < **sm̥-ǵheslo-* lit. 'one thousand' (a neut. noun) but used in InIr. for higher thousands as well. This element, with a different stem, is reflected in a number of G dial. forms: Lesb., Thess. *χελλιοι*, Lac. *χηλιοι*, Ion., Boeot.

[1] Or perhaps better **-ḱm̥tiHo-*, as **-ḱm̥tiyo-* has the wrong Sievers alternant for the suffix; 178).

χειλιοι, all regular (227.2) from PG *k^h*esliyo-*. Att. χῑλιοι is one of a small number of forms with unexplained -ῑ- for expected -ει- (76d).

The termination of the G forms does not match that of the InIr. counting forms; it aligns with Ved. *sahasríya-* 'having a thousand; thousand-fold', which may be the original force of *k^h*esliyo-*. On the other hand, the stem for '1000' and for the hundreds in -κατιοι, -κοσιοι (395) is the same; the latter may have influenced the former, or they may both be from the same source as Ved. *sahasríya-*.

L *mīlle*, remarkable to say, may be connected with the foregoing. Two analyses have been proposed, both leave a number of loose ends. First, the form is a phrase with 'one' modifying a feminine abstract: **smiH*$_2$ *ǵhsliH*$_2$ (**smiH*$_2$ = G μία), whence **smīkslī*. But this would regularly give L ˣ*mīlī*, not *mīlle* (for *-*ksl*- > -*l*- cf. **tekslā* > *tēla* 'cloth', 231.1). The -*ll*- is a stubborn problem, but the -*ĕ* can be explained as back-formed from pl. *mīlia*, on the pattern *maria* : *mare*. The second hypothesis starts with **smiH*$_2$ *ǵhesli* (any final short vowel would do), which would have given first **mī hēli*, from which **mīle* would be the expected form, seen in the pl. *mīlia*. But the -*ll*- of *mīlle* is a problem for this theory too; so is the inflection in the pl. as a neuter, as both theories start out with an overtly fem. formation.

a. Higher numbers. G μῡριοι '10,000'; μῡριάς, -άδος 'a number of 10,000'; combining forms μῡρι- and μῡριό-. These also have the meaning of any immense number, and that is probably the original sense. The stem-forms are obviously based on the morphology of actual numbers, but that does not prove that they were numbers to begin with (NB NE *umpteen* 'a medium-sized number', *jillion* 'a huge number'). Various other IE languages have specific words for '10,000', with little agreement among them. The closest match in form and function is between the G forms and a poetic OIr. form, *múr* 'great number, multitude'.

Ordinal Numbers

397. The PIE ordinals, except those for 'first' and 'second' (398.1-2), are derived from the cardinals. As in the case of the decads (391), the scheme was a simple one; but the relationship between the forms was disturbed by the action of sound laws, the analogy of the cardinals, and the analogy of adjacent ordinals, as remarked in 387.

The ordinal stems were as follows, with the cardinal stems given in parentheses for comparison: ****tr̥y-ó-* (**trey-*), ***k*^{w}*tur-ó-* (**k*^{w}*etwor-*), ***pn̥k*^{w}*-ó-* (**penk*^{w}*e*), ***(s)uks-ó-* (**(s)weks*), ****sptm-ó-* (**septm̥*), ****H*$_3$*ktw-ó-* (**H*$_3$*ektow*), ****nun-ó-* (**newn̥*), ***dkm̥t-ó-* (**dekm̥t*); the decads ***wi-dkm̥t-ó-*, ***tri-dkm̥t-ó-*, and so on.

As is evident, PIE ordinals were *o*/*eH*$_2$-stem adjectives with a tonic stem-vowel and all else in the zero grade. The forms in this list marked with *** are nowhere reflected as such. Expected ****tr̥yó-* was replaced by **triyó-* already in the parent language, on the analogy of the **tri-*, **trey-*

seen in all other 'three' formations.[1] The influence of the cardinals on '7th', '8th', and '9th' was likewise early, pervasive, and obvious in effect. However, because the results would be pretty much the same whether ****sptmós* for example was replaced by **septmós* in early PIE, late PIE, or at almost any point in the histories of the individual daughter languages, the date of the RECONSTRUCTABLE full-grade forms **sept(m̥)mós*, **H*$_3$*éktuwós* (**oktuwós*), **newn̥nós* is indeterminate. The replacement of PIE ***dḱm̥tós* by **deḱm̥tós* is the same kind of leveling, but this remodeling was almost certainly of PIE date, being prompted by the emergence of the specialized sense '100' for the original ordinal **dḱm̥tóm*, which remained unaltered (394).

Of far-reaching consequence were two metanalyses. Already by late PIE, **triy-ó-* had been metanalyzed into **tri-yó-*. This is revealed by the remodeling of adjacent ***k*^{w}*turó-* as **k*^{w}*turyó-*. Similarly, **deḱm̥t-ó-* was metanalyzed as **deḱm̥-tó-*, that is, the affix was reinterpreted as **-tó-*, which like **-yó-* was a common adjective formant. (Similarly **wīḱm̥-tó-*, **trīḱm̥-tó-*, and so on.)

Now, metanalysis normally hinges on some structural ambiguity, as in **triyó-*, where **tri-* could be taken as a root; in the case of **deḱm̥tós*, next to cardinal **déḱm̥t*, the assignment of the **-t-* to the root rather than to the suffix was at all times transparent and unambiguous. But **-tó-* was a PIE element of clear form and appropriate meaning, which moreover was generously productive in late PIE, and in such an environment a structural reassignment is sometimes possible even in the absence of any real ambiguity. This is the explanation for NE *cherry*: throughout the history of English, *a ripe cherries, a bowl of cherrieses* should have always been as unambiguous as *one lens, two lenses* is today; but the existence of a clearly-defined element *-s* 'pl.' led to the reinterpretation of *cherries* as pl. anyway.

Note that the relocation of a morpheme boundary is in and of itself invisible; as in the case of the resegmentation **tri-yó-*, above, the replacement of PIE **deḱm̥t-ó-* by **deḱm̥-tó-* is revealed only when some new form is created—in this case, **penk*^{w}*-to-* 'fifth'.

At that point the system of ordinals looked like this: **triyo-*, **k*^{w}*tur(i)-yo-*, **penk*^{w}*to-*, **(s)ukso-*, **sept(m̥)mo-*, **H*$_3$*eḱt(u)wo-*, **new(n̥)no-*, **deḱm̥to-*. These, prior to undergoing additional contamination and remodeling, are the etyma of the ordinal number systems of the IE languages.

---

[1] Some would trace **tr̥yo-* ~ **triyo-* to the effects of Edgerton's Law (179). But **triyo-* would have been the form which occurred only after a word ending in a short vowel, while **tr̥yo-* occurred elsewhere, accounting for at least four-fifths of the total. The argument might be made that Edgerton's Law provided the raw materials, and that although the alternant **triyo-* was much less common, it prevailed for the reasons given above.

And note that according to Lindeman's widely-accepted refinement of Edgerton's Law (181), **tr̥yo-* would not have alternated at all.

a. It is a commonplace of IE studies that the formations of the superlative (or rather absolutive, **356**) and of the ordinals were somehow related. However, according to the view espoused here, this is due to a chance resemblance between certain ordinal forms such as Ved. *saptamá-* '7th' (in which both the *-t-* and the *-m-* belong etymologically to the element '7') and the quite unrelated affix *-tamá-* < *-*tm̥mo-* of forms like Ved. *uttamá-* 'uppermost' (**356**). In any case, despite vague claims in the literature to the contrary, there is no SEMANTIC tangency between the two functions. The notion 'first' (**398.1**) is a trifling exception to this fact.

398.1. FIRST is not (necessarily) a number at all but a contrastive relationship; it has as much in common with 'last' as with specific designations like '3rd' or '10th'. Accordingly, in very many languages words for 'first' are not based on a numeral. Furthermore, the notion '1st' is not a primitive, and many languages discriminate between first of all vs. first of two (OE *forma* and *ǽrest*, respectively), or make other distinctions. Words for '1st' are commonly derived from elements whose root meaning is 'in front' (*first*), 'on top' (*chief*), notions of beginning (OE *ǽrest* and NHG *erst*, related to NE *early*), and others. Many such notions, unlike the remaining ordinals—see **397a**—do have, or acquire, superlative morphology.

The most basic PIE words are built to **preH₃-* 'forth; in front of [and facing (or going) away]' (G πρό, L *prō*, Ved. *prá*); the two most widespread formations are **pr̥H₃-wo-*, and **pr̥H₃-mo-* (which may include the most ancient form of the particularizing suffix *-*mo-*, earlier than the usual *-*m̥mo-*, **356**).

PIE **pr̥H₃-mo-* > Lith. *pìrmas*, PGmc. **furmōn-* (OE *forma*; Go. *fruma* with metathesis). What looks like a full grade, **proH₃mo-*, is seen in U **prumum**, *promom*; but full grade in a *mo*-adjective is contrary to expectation, and perhaps inherited PItal. **prāmom* < **pr̥̄mo-* was remodeled on the basis of **prō*. Such a **prāmo-* is perh. also hidden in L *prandium*, below.

PIE **pr̥H₃-wo-* > OCS *prĭvŭ*, Ved. *pū́rva-*, *pūrvyá-* (scanned *pūrviyá-*).

The usual Indic form for '1st', Ved. *prathamá-*, is in all respects a superlative adj.; already in late Vedic it had replaced *pū́rva-* (and *pūrviyá-*, which though often still 'first' in the RV, was already more usually 'former, earlier'). Similarly in Germanic: in late PGmc. **furmista-* and **furista-*, formed after the morphology of superlatives, were in competition with earlier **furmōn-*. This is the state of affairs in Go. and OE; in the latter language, the original superlative *forma* eventually acquired the force 'former, earlier', exactly as happened in Indic.

G πρῶτος is a much-discussed form, not in connection with the ordinal system but as a phonological crux. It is most simply traced directly to **pr̥H₃-to-*, and that may be the whole explanation. But such a stem is unattested elsewhere, and Dor., Boeot. πρᾶτος cannot be so explained. Preferably, both πρᾶτος and πρῶτος would have much the same history, and it would be best of all if they could be connected with cognates in other IE languages. That source is at hand in **pr̥H₃-wo-* (= Ved. *pū́rva-*), which would give, first, **prōwos*; by contamination with **hupatos* (ὕπατος) 'highest, uppermost', this was elaborated into **prōwotos*, the etymon of G πρῶτος. The etymon of Dor. πρᾶτος, **pro(w)atos*, has undergone two additional modifications: a closer approach to **hupatos*, and contamination of original **prō-* by the commonplace πρό. The vowel contraction is as in ἁπλᾶ 'single' < ἁπλόα nom./acc.n.pl.; see **86.6**.

But against the theory of an early **prōwatos* is Homeric scansion, which allows *πρόϝατος in place of some textual πρῶτος but never seems to require *πρώϝατος. All these considerations can be gathered up under a Proto-Greek replacement of **prōwatos* by **prowatos* on the basis of πρό; then πρῶτος and πρᾶτος would merely represent two different kinds of contraction.

Note that the correct interpretation depends on one's views of the G reflexes of long syllabic resonants (**104-8**). For those who take G **prāwos* to be the expected outcome of **pr̥H₃wos* or **pr̥̄wos*, the form πρᾶτος is the conservative one and πρῶτος would reflect a remodeled **prowatos*, but this time with ordinary contraction.

Some scholars do not accept πρᾶτος as a possible contraction from **prowatos* (**86.6**). In accord with the view of G phonology espoused here (**106.1**) the etymon would have to be **pr̥H₂wo-* rather than **pr̥H₃wo-*, whence **prāwotos*, Dor. πρᾶτος. Since the outcome in the other dialects should have been the same, Att.-Ion. πρῶτος must in that case have its origin in a sort of echo of πρό, either via a remodeled **prowatos* or later *προατος directly patterned on ὕπατος. This question cannot be resolved by an appeal to principle.

L *prīmus* is likewise an innovation, one which jettisons **pr̥H₃wo-* and **pr̥H₃mo-* altogether in favor of a new creation: **pri-isemos* > **prīsemos* > **prīsmos* (cf. Paelig. PRISMV) > *prīmus*. This is, in Latin terms, an ordinary superlative **358.1**, functionally like such (formally different) innovations as Ved. *prathamá-* and PGmc. *furmista-*. That is to say, despite superficial appearances, it has no direct historical connection with *pìrmas*, U **prumum**, OE *forma*, and the like.

The first element for this and similar formations in L is usually given as PIE **pri-*, somehow related to **pr̥H₃-*. But such an element is hardly attested, and it is surprising that such a shadowy element would surface in a formation like this. The most similar forms in other languages, formally and functionally, point rather to **pr̥H-i-* (? **pr̥H₃-i-*): PCelt. **ari-* 'facing', OIc. *fyr*, OHG *furi* 'before'. That is, L **pri-* is better traced to **pr̥Hi-*, a case of L *-r-* from prevocalic *-r̥-* (**96**). Whatever its previous history, it is seen elsewhere in L *prior* 'earlier, former', *prae* 'in front of', and perhaps G παραί (though the latter is more likely to be an elaboration of παρά 'next to, beside'). —Earlier Ital. **prāmos* < **pr̥H₃mos*, as in the BS and Gmc. forms above, is perhaps to be found in L *prandium* 'lunch', but originally 'breakfast' (cf. *prandēre* denom. 'to breakfast') < **prāmdeyom* (**82**) < **prāmo-deyom* 'first eating' (**ed-*); cf. G ˝ἄριστον 'breakfast' (**212**).

398.2. SECOND. Languages commonly distinguish between '2nd of two; other' and '2nd in a series', as Fr. *second* and *deuxième*, respectively. In many languages figurative notions like 'following' are used rather than formations based on counting-forms; numeral-based ordinals for '2nd' in IE languages are late and secondary, as NHG *zweite* (first attested at the end of the 15th century; in OHG only *ander*), and Fr. *deuxième* (cf. L *alter*, *secundus*). A PIE term for '2nd' can nevertheless be recovered at least for the western groups, namely *H_2*en-tero*- ('the other (of two)', 355); examples below.

G δεύτερος, however, is neither of these types. It is unrelated to δύο, to which it bears a purely chance resemblance. There is a standard etymology for it, less cogent than is usually conceded: it is traces to δεύομαι 'am wanting; am inferior'. The supposed semantic development rests on the marked tendency for words originally 'second [in rank]' to acquire connotations of outright inferiority (as in NE *second-rate*). That is, we first suppose that for a time the inherited G form for 'second', whatever it was, was partly synonymous with δεύτερος in that they shared the meaning 'inferior'. The final step—acquisition of the rest of the meaning ('the ordinal coming between first and third')—is semantically remarkable, and suspect. (It is hard to imagine replacing *second* in the English sentence *The second time he called I was in the shower* with, say, *factory reject*.) But no better explanation has been proposed, and perhaps the large (if accidental) resemblance between δεύτερος and δύο would be enough to suck δεύτερος into the ordinals.

The ordinary L term for 'second' was *alter*, which may be a direct inheritance from the parent language (apart from *al*- for original **an*-, **292.2**); OIr. *aile*, the ordinary word for 'other' (directly comparable to L *alius*) is occasionally used for '2nd'; OHG *ander*, Go. *anþar*, OE *óþer* 'other; second' (the latter meaning fossilized in NE *every other* and in *the other day* *'day before yesterday'); Lith. *añtras* only 'another', but definite *antràsis* 'the other; second'. L *alter* was early joined by *secundus*, the pres.pple. of *sequor* lit. 'following' (567), which is the basic word for 'second' in Romance, and was borrowed into English.

L *iterum* 'a second time; secondly' (denom. *iterāre* 'do a second time') is from the prn. stem **i*- and the contrastive suffix **-tero*- (355); **i*- seems to have meant '(the) one' (389.1A), and the semantics can be accounted for if the original force was something like 'once more'. (The sense 'repeatedly' is a later development.)

398.3. THIRD. Although (late) PIE **triyo*- '3rd' influenced the form for '4th' (397), as it develops in the daughter languages it is commonly itself influenced by the *t*-suffix characteristic of the higher ordinals. This usually resulted in a conflation, **trit(i)yo*- or **tretiyo*-; the obvious source of the raw materials is '4th', q.v. **Trit(i)yo*- underlies L *tertius*, U *tertiu* adv. (*ter*- < **tri*-, 74.3) and PGmc. **þri-đjōn*- as in Go. *þridja*, OE *þridde*, OHG *drittio*. The Gmc. form is ambiguous, however, and might instead reflect the **tretiyo*- unambiguously seen in OCS *tretĭjĭ*. G τρίτος, by contrast, appears to be a wholly new formation, employing the combining form (**389.3a**) and patterned after τέταρτος, τέτρατος '4th' (themselves secondary formations; q.v.).

Ved. *tṛtī́ya*- is apparently a replacement of PInIr. **tritī́ya*-, whose existence would be necessary to account for the form of *dvitī́ya*- '2nd' even if it were not actually attested in Av. *θrit̰ya-* (read *θritiya-*). But how such a thing might have happened, especially given the transparency of the original form and the oddity of its replacement, is very unclear. (OPr. *tirts* is not direct evidence for any such etymon, as it is only a copy of '4th' in *kettwirts* < *-wr̥tos.)

398.4. FOURTH. The original form was presumably **k^wturó-, as mentioned above (397). The earliest form reachable by the comparative method, *k^wtur(i)yo-, showing the influence of '3rd', was possibly of PIE date: Ved. *turī̆ya-*, Av. *tūirya-* (that is, *tū̆riya-), and perh. Hitt. *du-ya-na-al-li-* 'man of the 4th rank' (according to some; the meaning is disputed). Av. *āχtūirīm*, to be read *ā-χturiyam '(up) to the 4th [time]', provides evidence for *k^wt- rather than plain *t-; the reading of the -χ- has recently been challenged, however. Commonly the original form, whatever it was, was replaced by *k^wetwr̥to- on the pattern of *penk^{w}to-. (This is not a modification but a fresh creation, just as NE *tenth* was not a modification of *tithe* but was built afresh from *ten*.) More or less directly this yields G τέταρτος, τέτρατος (the former based on the latter; it is earlier attested, but genuinely antique *k^wetwar- should have given ˣτεσ(σ)αρ-, 190.4); OCS *četvrŭtŭ(jĭ)*; and Skt. *caturthá-*, first found in the AV and soon becoming the usual form though never supplanting *tur(ī)ya-*.

L *quārtus* reconstructs to *k^wewr̥tos or the like, exactly the form required for the Gmc. numeral as well. The loss of the first *-t- in the original *k^wetwr̥tos by dissimilation is unremarkable, but not so much a matter of course that it can be supposed to have occurred independently in two adjacent language groups. It is better viewed as a shared innovation. In the two branches this form develops pari passu with the cardinal, so PGmc. *fewurþōn- > OE *féorþa*, OHG *fiordo*, and ON *fiórði*; the Go. form is unattested. (The known Gmc. forms unaccountably imply PIE *k^wewŕ̥tos rather than *k^wewr̥tós.) The L outcome *quārtus* < *k^wa(w)ortos (183, 88.3) < *k^wewr̥tos has the usual puzzling *-a-* of all the 'four' words; Falisc. QVORTA (fem. given name, like L *Quārta*), apparently attests the expected *quowor- < *k^wewr̥-.

a. In a different analysis, L *quārtus* has been traced to Ital. *k^wartos*, a remodeling of *turtos, itself remade from original *turos < *k^wturos, with *tur- replaced by *k^war- on the basis of *quattuor* and *quadru-*. This resourceful explanation does not however account for the long vowel of *quārtus*, which is vouchsafed epigraphically; and grafting productive *-to- onto a morphologically obscure stem like *tur- (*k^wtur-) is not too likely. (Morphological remodeling usually has a clarifying purpose; in the case of *turos '4th' next to cardinal *k^watwōr, there is in effect nothing to clarify—though arguably *k^winktos '5th' by itself could have engendered *turtos.)

398.5. FIFTH. Expected **pn̥k^{w}ó- was replaced in times PIE by *penk^{w}tó-. (Evidence for a stage *pn̥k^{w}tó- is discerned by some authorities—see **b**, below.) The *-t- was imported from the ordinal *d(e)ḱm̥t-ó- '10th'; the full grade from the cardinal *penk^{w}e. The resulting composite is attested in most IE languages with few changes not chargeable to sound laws: Av. *pan̰tahva-* (*paŋχta-) 'fifth part', Lith. *peñktas*, OCS *pętŭ*, PGmc. *femftōn- (Go. *fimfta-*,

OHG *fimfto*, OE *fīfta*), G πέμπτος (accentuation after πέντε), L *quīn(c)tus* (with *qu-* < **p-* per **141a**, lengthened vowel per **81.2**).

a. The Sab. form for '5th', **pom(p)tos*, is confidently recoverable from proper nouns like O **púntiis**, ΠΟΜΠΤΙΕΣ, Paelig. *ponties*, all equivalent to L *Quīn(c)tius*.

b. RV *pakthá-* is often cited as a reflex of **pn̥kʷtó-* (*-th-* for *-t-* is secondary) but it is a proper noun, and '5th' is only a possibility for its etymology. It appears to align with Av. puχδa- '5th', whose vowel however is a problem. The usual Skt. ordinal is *pañcamá-*, which is straightforwardly analogical (*sapta* : *saptama-* :: *pañca* : *X*). —OHG *funfto*, a rare variant of usual *finfto*, *fimfto*, is not an independent attestation of **pn̥kʷto-*, as it probably stands for [fünfto] with the secondary rounding of *-i-* manifest in NHG *fünf*, ord. *fünfte*.

398.6. SIXTH. Orig. PIE ***(s)uḱsó-* is thought to be indirectly attested in OPr. *uschts* (below). More typically the form was remade as **sweḱsto-*, **sweḱto-* (see below), the ending from **penkʷto-* and the full grade (as well as **s-*) from the cardinal, so Ved. *ṣaṣṭhá-*, Av. *xštva-* (with metathesis; a curious form altogether), G ἑκτός, L *sextus*, Go. *saihsta*, OHG *seh(s)to*, OE *siexta*. G ἑκτός rather than ˣἑχθός < **sweḱsto-* (**230.2a**) raises the possibility that the cluster **-ḱst-* was simplified to **-ḱt-* already in PIE times, and that the *-s-* seen in L *sextus* and Go. *saihsta* was reimported from the cardinal—with the subsequent loss in L of the *-k-*, as indicated by the L name *Sestius* (if, as is likely, originally '6th'), and the reimportation of *-k-* into *sextus*; see **209**. A parallel Sab. **sestos* is inferrable from U **sestentasiaru**, if that in fact means something like 'bimonthly'. OPr. *uschts* retains the zero grade of the root and the archaic *s*-less form of the stem, but has *-t-* from '5th'.

398.7. SEVENTH. The PIE form is disputed. Original ****sptmó-* is nowhere attested, but OCS *sedmŭ* (and, indirectly, OCS *osmŭ* '8th' < **oḱtmo-*), OLith. *sẽkmas*, OPr. *sep(t)mas* all point to a lightly retouched ***septmos*. This reconstruction has been dismissed as impossible because it violates a widely-accepted elaboration of Sievers' Law (**178**), but it is better viewed as evidence that the law does not apply. There is no better explanation for the BS forms than inheritance, since PBS **septmas* would be incomprehensible as a replacement of an inherited **septimas* (cf. PBS cardinal **septim*).

To take PIE **septmos* for granted, in most IE languages the cardinal **septm̥* influenced the prosody of the ordinal, which accordingly became **septm̥mos*. This is attested as such in Ved. *saptamá-* and L *septumus*, later *septimus*. G confirms the proto-form **septmos*, as such a consonant sequence is the only hope of accounting for the voicing of **-pt-* to -βδ- in ἕβδομος, ἕβδεμος < *ἕβδμος. (For a different explanation of the -βδ-, see **389.8a**, below). It is a moot point as to whether the vowel between the stops and the *-m-* was anaptyctic or analogical, influenced by ὄγδοϝος '8th'.

a. Some authorities suppose **sebdmos* or **sebdm̥mos*, that is, with voiced stops already in PIE, as they appear in both OCS and G. But there is no evidence otherwise suggesting that a voiceless stop followed by a nasal became voiced in PIE, except, possibly, at word boundaries (so **bhered me* 'he carried me')—a different matter altogether. In fact, even in

G, in which there is voicing of SOME stops before some nasals at least (219), it is surprising to see such a process taking place in a sequence of voiceless stops: they should be more resistant to interresonant voicing than a single stop. Doubts and all, this analysis is superior to that mentioned in **389.8a**, below.

b. PGmc. *_seƀundōn-_ (the ordinals, usually definite, are only attested as _n_-stems) either reflects a metathesis of *_septm̥mo-_, or even of *_septmo-_, to *_sepm̥to-_; or else it is a dissimilation of *_septm̥to-_ to *_sepm̥to-_. Already in PGmc. the _t_-less ordinal had influenced the form of the cardinal, PGmc. *_seƀun_ as if from *_sepḿ̥t_. The origin of the *_-to-_ suffix, if it is not an artifact of metathesis, is *_penk^wtos_ '5th', *_swekstos_ '6th', and so on.

398.8. EIGHTH. The ambiguities of the etymon of the cardinal (**389.8**) apply to the ordinal as well. Given the likeliest form of the cardinal as *_H_3eḱtow_, the ordinal would have been *_H_3ḱtuwó-_ (per Sievers' Law, 178). Such a form would be highly subject to retouching as *_H_3eḱtowo-_ by the influence of the cardinal. G ὄγδο(ϝ)ος might reflect either of these.[1] L _octāvus_ (Italic details indirectly confirmed by the O name **úhtavis**) continues *_-tōwos_ (? PItal. ? PIE); for _-āw-_ < *_-ōw-_ see **46.2**. A single etymon *_H_3eḱtōwos_ would therefore cover both the G and L forms, but there is no reason to suppose that such an obvious remodeling was early rather than later and independent. If in fact ἕβδομος '7th' gets its form from '8th' (**a**, below), that points to ογδὄϝος, as ογδōϝος would be less likely to influence *_heptamos_.[2] (Ital. *_oktŏwos_ could easily have become *_oktōwos_ after the cardinal.)

'8th' is often influenced by '7th', whence PInIr. *_aśtamá-_ (Ved. _aṣṭamá-_, Av. _aštəma-_) after PInIr. *_saptamá-_ (and so on: _navamá-_ '9th', _daśamá-_ '10th'). OCS _osmŭ_, OPr. _asman_ acc., Lith. _ãšmas_ continue *_oś(t)mo-_, remade after *_septmo-_ '7th'; such a remaking implies earlier *_ośtwo-_, as, if the point of departure had been *_ośtowo-_ or the like, the results would have been ×_ośtomo-_ rather than *_ośtmo-_.

In G the influence of '7th' took the remarkable shape of replacing the -κτ- of the simplex with -γδ-.

a. The relationship between the ordinals '7th, 8th' in Greek, and between them and the cardinals, has been explained differently. Among the varieties of laryngeal theory are those which hold that *_H_3_ was specifically VOICED, as revealed by its voicing of a preceding voiceless stop (**451B** fn.). If so, if PIE '8' is reconstructed as *_H_3eḱtéH_3_ or even *_H_3eḱté H_3w_, the ordinal *_H_3(e)ḱtH_3o(w)-_ (more exactly *_H_3(e)ǵdH_3o(w)-_) would give G ὀγδο- directly. In this scenario it is ἕβδομος '7th' whose voiced stops are secondary, in imitation of the -γδ- of '8th'. Apart from considerations of the phonetic features of laryngeals and the plausibility of a shape like *_H_3eḱtéH_3w_ (both per se and in regard to the attested forms), if *_-ǵd-_ was present from the beginning it is surprising that its attestation is limited to G, and particularly puzzling are the facts of OCS: there we find voicing in '7th', where it would be analogical, but not in '8th'.

398.9. NINTH. The starting-point was **_nunó-_ (or **_numó-_, if the numeral

[1] The Gmc. and Baltic (as exemplified by Go. _ahtuda_, Lith. _ãšmas_) also might continue original *_H_3ḱt-_. Like Italic, the OCS form—see below—requires something like *_H_3eḱt-_.

[2] The one attestation with -ϝ- is in an alphabet that uses one sign for _o_ and _ω_.

was **néwm̥*; 389.9a. Those who wish to may add **H_1-* to the beginning of all these forms). This was replaced already in PIE by **newn̥nó-* —an impossible shape according to Sievers' Law (cf. 389.7)—modeled on the cardinal **newn̥*. It appears to be attested as such in L *nōnus*, but in most languages it was contaminated by **deḱm̥tós* '10th' or its avatars; thus G **enwatos* (Hom. εἴνατος, Att. ἔνατος), syncopated from **enewatos* < **newn̥tos* by prosodic analogy to the trisyllabic forms on either side of it in the series. Similar morphology is reflected in Gmc. **newundōn-*, Lith. *deviñtas*, OCS *devętŭ* (*d-* from '10'; OPr. *newints* '9th' vouchsafes original **n-* for BS). In other languages it was influenced by **septm̥mos*, whose shape spread upward in the series, so Ved. *saptamá-*, *aṣṭamá-*, *navamá-*, *daśamá-*.

398.10. TENTH. Quasi-original **deḱm̥tó-* (397) is reflected in G δέκατος except for the accentuation, which comes from the cardinal, as it does in Gmc. **tehundōn-* (Go. *taihunda*, OE *téoþa*, OHG *zehanto*); further Lith. *dešim̃tas*, OCS *desętŭ* (for **desŭtŭ* < **deḱm̥tos* after *devętŭ*). In InIr., as already noted, the set 7th-10th was remodeled with *-amá-* based on '7th'; when inherited cardinal **daśat* had been replaced by **daśa* (389.10), the original ordinal **daśata-* was remodeled on the proportion **sapta* : **aśtā* : **nawa* : **daśa* :: **saptama-* : **aśtama-* : **nawama-* : *X*, where *X* = **daśama-* (Ved. *daśamá-*, Av. *dasəma-*). The outwardly similar Ital. **dekemo-*, **dekamo-* (L *decumus*, later *decimus*; cf. *decumānus* 'tithe', which is apparently the sense of O **dekmanniúís** dat.pl.) is a parallel innovation, postdating the loss of **-t* in **dekem* < **deḱm̥t* '10', via some such proportion as **nowen* : **nowenos* : : **dekem* : *X*, where *X* = **dekemos*.

399. HIGHER NUMBERS. The decad ordinals were ***wīḱm̥tó-*, ***trīḱm̥tó-*, and so forth, exactly as the units—cardinal forms with zero grade throughout and the thematic stem **-ó-* (397). With the metanalysis of **deḱm̥t-ó-* into **deḱm̥-tó-* (397), the suffix **-tó-* spread to them as well: **wīḱm̥t-tó-*, **trīḱm̥t-tó-*, and the rest. This was certainly early, as the forms show the effects of the PIE rules governing clusters of apical stops (212): **-ḱm̥t^{s}tó-*. These are directly attested in G εἰκοστός, τριᾱκοστός, and so on; the Att.-Ion. *-o-* has been imported from the cardinals (more conservative details in Boeot. ϝῑκαστος). L *vīcēsimus*, *trīcēsimus*, and so on[1] have been influenced by '10th' a second time, being remodelings of earlier **vīcēnssos*, **trīkēnssos* (212), and so on, via the addition of the affix of *decimus*.

a. The persistence of the voiceless stop in *vīcē(n)simus* and *trīcē(n)simus* (*vīgēsimus*, *trīgēsimus* also occur), in contrast to the uniform *-g-* in the cardinals *vīgintī* and *trīgintā*, and the unvarying *-gē(n)simus* for *quadrāgēsimus* and the higher numbers, supports the idea that *-g-* for *-k-* arose in some particular form or forms somewhere in the higher members of the series, and spread to the others (393).

---

[1] These are usual forms; *-ensimus* is attested in inscriptions and legal documents, 226.1.

Numerical Derivatives

400. Multiplicatives. The term *multiplicative* is commonly applied to forms like G τριπλοῦς (τριπλόος), L *triplex*, NE *threefold* or *triple*. In their use they cover a variety of relations to the numeral, only some of which have distinctive formal types. In origin they are possessive compounds of words meaning 'fold', 'ply', and the like, and originally meant 'consisting of three of the same thing'—'three' here and in the following discussion will serve as the type-example—is seen in L *triplex mūrus* 'triple wall', that is, a series of three walls, or NE *triple play*. For this kind of use there may be formally distinct types known as *collectives*, like NE *threesome*. An early figurative development was to 'having three components', as L *triplex mundus* 'the threefold world' of sky, land, and sea. Hence also 'of three kinds', a use shading off from the preceding, but one for which special formal types might develop, as LL *trīfārius*, NHG *dreierlei*. Furthermore, a group of three may be viewed as a single thing taken three times, such as 'three times as much or as many' in L *duplex centuriōnī, triplex equitī* 'double [pay] to the centurion, triple [pay] to the knight'. This is the proportional use, for which there may also be distinctive formal types sometimes called *proportionals*. So Att. τριπλάσιος, though τριπλοῦς is used in the same sense in most dialects and sometimes in Attic; L *triplus* (properly; though *triplex* as in the example is also so used).

401. Multiplicatives proper. The common multiplicatives of G, Ital., and the Gmc. languages are compounds, the second part of which contains the root **pel-* 'fold' or one of several roots perh. derived from it: **pleḱ-* (cf. G πλέκω, L *plicō*) and **pelt-* (cf. Go. *falþan*, OE *fealdan*), all 'fold'.

G τριπλόος (-πλοῦς; Locr. also διπλειōι), L *triplus*, U *tripler* (with a different meaning, 'three each').

L *triplex*; Hom. τρίπλαξ 'with three bands', δίπλαξ 'with two folds'.

Att. τριπλάσιος 'thrice as many' (the proportional use) is derived from *τρίπλατος, like ἀμβρόσιος 'ambrosial' (*'immortal') from ἄμβροτος; cf. poet. τρίπαλτος 'threefold' < **tri-pl̥to-* (the morpheme division of the last part is uncertain). With the same meaning τριπλασίων, whose comparative form is thought to result from its use with ἤ 'than, as'.

Cf. Go. *ainfalþs*, OE *þrífeald*, NE *threefold* (the last is not a direct inheritance; the undisturbed reflex would have been **thriffled*).

a. Other, less common, G types are:

τριφάσιος (Hdt.) 'of three kinds' (also collective) < **tri-pʰa-t-* (? φαίνω 'show; appear').

τρίπτυχος 'threefold', from πτυχ-, 'fold'.

διφυής, δίφυιος 'of two parts, kinds' (also proportional)—only attested in μονο-, δι-, πεντα-, and δεκα-; from φῡ- 'be' (cf. φύσις 'nature'). Cf. El. διφυιος = Att. διπλάσιος; δεκάφυια ζωάγρια 'tenfold rewards' (Callimachus).

τρισσός 'threefold', Att. τριττός < **trikʰyo-*, cf. adv. τρίχα 'threefold'; similarly Ion.

τριξός < *trik^h^t^h^yo- (τριχθά 'in three'). Mostly collective 'consisting of three'; in Hellenistic times frequent for 'in three copies' (cf. NE *in triplicate*).

b. L *bifāriam, trifāriam* 'in two (three) parts' are adverbs; *multifāriam* 'in many places'. The adjectives of the type *trifārius* derived from them do not occur till the 2nd century AD, and the specialized sense 'of three kinds' (as in NE *multifarious*) belongs mainly to medieval Latin.

c. G numerical adjectives of the type τριταῖος 'on the third day' have a curious syntax: though in effect adverbs, they are morphologically adjectives modifying the subject of a verb. Of events τριταῖος means 'lasting three days' (and hence pregnantly 'a tertian fever').

402. THE LATIN DISTRIBUTIVES. The distributives *bīnī, ternī*, 'two, three each' are in origin collectives. That is, their earliest use is in two non-distributive senses: first, as the (real) enmeration of pluralia tantum (as in *bīna castra* 'two encampments')[1]. This includes the enumeration of nouns whose meaning is saliently different in the pl. and is therefore a kind of pl. tant.: *bīnae litterae* 'two epistles' vs. *duae litterae* 'two letters (of the alphabet)'. Second, the terms were used of sets, most often pairs (*bīnī bovēs* 'a span of oxen'). Their distributive force grew from contexts in which the distributive notion was already expressed otherwise—as in fact it continued to be. Thus where G (like NE) uses the simple cardinals with a distributive word or phrase, as ἑκάστωι δύο 'two (for) each', L used the collectives, as *ūnīcuique bīnī* lit. 'two together for each'. This use of collectives became fixed, with the result that they themselves absorbed distributive force (*bīnī imperātōrēs* 'two consuls each [year]').

Formally, they are related to certain collective forms in Gmc. and BS with the suffix **-no-*. Thus *bīnī* < **dwis-no-* (cf. *bis* 'twice' < **dwis*); *trīnī* (preferred in the collective use) is either directly from **tris-no-* or in imitation of *bīnī*, while *ternī* is evidently formed anew from *ter(r)-* (< **tris*, 389.3a, 404.3); *quaternī* is modeled on *ternī*, like *quater* 'four times' (404.4) on *ter* 'thrice'; *quatrīnī*, quoted by grammarians, is based on *trīnī*. *Sēnī* 'sixsome' is regular from **seksno-* (231.1). This last was the model for **k^w^ink^(w)^sno-*, whence regularly *quīnī*.

The remaining units admit of more than one explanation. One scenario takes **deksno-* 'tensome' as the next to be coined, on the basis of **k^w^inksno-*, whence regularly *dēnī*, which provided the model for the others: *decem* : *dēnī* :: *septem* : *X* :: *octō* : *Y* :: *novem* : *Z*, where *X* = *septēnī*,[2] *Y* = *octōnī*, *Z* = *novēnī*. Alternatively, **seksno-* inspired **septensno-* as well as **k^w^inksno-*, whence *septēnī* coeval with *sēnī*, while *octōnī* and *novēnī* followed later by the same kind of proportional analogy as above. The problem with this scheme is that 'ten each' should have been ˣ*decēnī*.

In any case, once *-ēnī* had acquired the force of a distributive marker

[1] The exception is distributive *singulī*: for enumeration of pl.tant. the usual numeral is used, resulting in such odd-looking phrases as *unae bīgae* 'one two-horse team'.

[2] The outcome of a rigorous proportion, **sēnī*, is ineligible for obvious reasons.

it was transplanted to the decads, hundreds, and '1000': *dekem* : *dēnī* :: **wīkentī* : *X* (*X* = *vīcēnī* '20 each'); *trecentī* : *Y* (*Y* = *trecēnī* '300 each'), and the rest.

No proportion underlies *mīllēnī*, however; here -*ēnī* was simply grafted on to *mīlle*, and in fact some such crude process may underlie the decads and hundreds.

The exact inspiration for *centum* : *centēnī* is not evident. It is most closely paralleled by *septem* : *septēnī*, but there can be no direct connection.

a. Different from the above is L *singulī* 'one each'. Its special status is underscored by the different treatment of unity in enumerating pluria tantum, in which a plural of *ūnus* is used: 'one encampment' is *ūna castra*, not ˣ*singula castra*.

Singulī obviously contains **sem*- 'one' (389.1B), but the morphology of the remainder of the word is obscure and has been variously explained—not, to date, convincingly.

403. COLLECTIVES. As previously noted (400), multiplicatives may function as collectives, but there are other forms that are collectives primarily, as G τρισσός and the like (401a), likewise Hom. δοιοί 'twofold, twin', and—in origin—the L distributives (402).

The collective notion may also be expressed in prepositional phrases, as G ἀνὰ τρεῖς 'by threes'. Such phrases are commonly called distributive, but where the meaning is simply 'by threes, in groups of three', they are obviously collectives. Of course, the same phrase can be used both for the collective and for the true distributive sense, as when G ἀνὰ τρεῖς is, according to context, either 'by threes' or 'three apiece'.

True collective nouns, that is meaning 'group of three, triad' occur in the IE languages in considerable variety, often in specialized applications. They are accordingly more a matter of lexicon and diction than of a paradigm-like array: NE *quartet*, *sextet* in music but *foursome* in golf or cards, *tetrad* in biology, *octave* in music and church calendars, *decade* of years, and so on.

The principal series in G and L are:

G τριάς, -άδος. This type started in forms like ἑπτάς, δεκάς, with -α- from *-m̥-. Cf. Skt. *daśát*- 'decad'. By analogy also G μονάς, -άδος 'unit, monad' from μόνος 'single, solitary'.

L *terniō*, -*iōnis*, formed from *ternī*; it is not clear whether this is from **ternī-ōn*- directly (85), or was created de novo on the type *legiō*, -*iōnis*.

Other, more specialized, terms are:

G τριττῦς lit. 'the number three', hence specifically 'sacrifice of three animals', and (at Athens) a division of the tribe; πεντηκοστῦς 'body of fifty men', χῑλιοστῦς 'body of a thousand men'.

L *decuria*, *centuria* 'a body of ten (a hundred) men', U *dequrier* 'decuriis'. Cf. O **pumperias** 'quincuriae', OIr. *cóicer* /kōg′əρ/ 'group of five men', Lith. *penkerì* 'set of five', and some similar formations in Toch. There are a number of explanations for these forms, the most convincing starting with a derivative noun based on 'four', **kʷetwerom* or the like, from which the sequence *-*erom*, or elaborated as *-*eryeH₂*, spread first to **penkʷerom* 'group of five' (displacing the original ***penkʷom* built just like **kʷetwerom*) and then to the remaining (low) numbers. Higher numbers like L *centuria* are later than the others—an early coinage would have yielded L ˣ*degmeria* (220) or ˣ*decenteria*, depending on exactly when it was made, rather than *decuria*.

404. NUMERAL ADVERBS. The most distinctive class and the one to which the term *numer(ic)al adverb* is often applied specifically is made up of words for '*n* many times'.

There is little agreement among IE languages in their forms for 'once', and partly for that reason there is much obscure about them.

1. G ἅπαξ 'singly' includes ἁ- < PIE **sm̥*-; the remainder of the formation is obscure; the most convincing explanation takes it to be a syncope of *ἁ-πακυς < **sm̥-pn̥kʷu*- lit. 'alone' (< *'all-one'), cf. Hitt. *pa-an-ku-uš* 'whole', L *cūnctus*.

L *semel* likewise is from **sm̥*- (an *e*-grade would yield the same form, but is unlikely in a compound). The remaining details are multiply ambiguous; of the many suggestions made about its history the most convincing is **sm̥-meH₁lom* n. lit. 'one time'. PIE **meH₁-lo*- n. '(point in) time' (root **meH₁*- 'measure') is attested in Go. *mel* 'time', OE *mǽl*, ON *mál*, and OHG *māl* 'occasion, (meal)time'; L -*ĕ*- < *-*ē*- before final -*l* (83.3); *sem*- < **sm̥m*- just as **tn̥nu*- > L *tenuis* 'thin'. Cf. *nihil* 'nothing' < **ne hilom* (41.2).

2. PIE **dwis* 'twice' (? ← ***dwos* after **tris* 'thrice') regularly gives G δίς, L *bis*, Ved. *dvís* (rarely scanned *duvís*), Av. *biš* < **dw*-, MHG *zwir*.

3. PIE **tris* 'thrice' > G τρίς, L *ter* (*terr* still in Plautine scansion) < **ters*, 74.3, 223.3 : Ved. *trís*, Av. *θriš*, elaborated in ON *þrisvar*, OHG *driror*, OE *þréowa*.

4. G τετράκις 'four times', πεντάκις, and so on (also -άκι and -άκιν). The denominator is just the combining form; the source of the -ακις, -ακι(ν) is obscure, though the Hitt. numeral adverbs, which end in -*an-ki* (so *3-an-ki* 'thrice'), point to *-*n̥ki*.

L *quater* 'four times' may be from **quatrus*, superimposable on Av. *čaθruš* and very similar to (late) Ved. *catúr* which on the evidence of the *r*-stem gen.sg. of the type *mātur* 'mother' < *-*tr̥s* (283.2) could be either the reflex of **kʷetwr̥s* or **kʷeturs*, or a metathesis of **kʷetrus* (? an old kind of gen., as in **tris*). Since L has such a shape, in effect, in the combining form *quadru*-, its presence here is believable. Some therefore take *quater* to be the regular development of **quatrus*, like *ager* 'field' from **agros*; but -*er* from *-*rus* is difficult.[1] At least as likely is a purely L modification (of whatever was in-herited) on the model of *ter(r)*. It is even possible that *quater* was made up out of whole cloth on the basis of *ter(r)*.

---

[1] Particularly difficult for this theory is *socrus* 'husband's mother' < **swékrus*; cf. *o*-stem *socer*, -*erī* < **swékuros* 'husband's father'. And on the basis of the cardinal *quattuor*, one might expect that **kʷat(t)ru*- would have given **quatter* (185.4).

5. L *quīnquiē(n)s*, *sexiē(n)s*, and so on, like *totiē(n)s* 'so many', *quotiē(n)s* 'how many', formed with *-*ient* (PIE *-*yn̥t*-, cf. Ved. *kíyant*- 'how much'); 237.5.

a. In late times these adverbs came to be replaced by phrases analogous to NE *three times* (now usual for *thrice*; *twice* and *once* are still vital). So Hellenistic τρεῖς καιρούς, NG τρείς φορές (cf. NG φορά 'time, occasion', and ancient πίνειν κατὰ φοράν 'drink at one gulp'), LL *tribus vicibus* and its Romance reflexes such as Fr. *trois fois*, and similar formations (such as It. *tre volte* 'three times').

b. Among other numeral adverbs are: G τρίχα or τριχθά 'in three parts or ways', τετραχθά, πένταχα, and so on; hence also τριχῆι, τρισσῶς, and the rest, that is, adverbs built from numerical adjectives the same way adverbs are built to ordinary adjectives, as κακῶς 'badly, wickedly' to κακός 'bad, wicked'.

PREPOSITIONS

405. A discussion of prepositions and their uses belongs to lexicon and syntax. But it may be noted here that a number of the G and L prepositions are historically related, even though in some cases their meanings have widely diverged.

The parent language seems to have had fewer such elements than the daughters. Relationships between nouns were expressed by case markers, and nuances of verb-object relations were expressed though preverbs marking the verbs themselves. The latter were not necessarily literally attached to the verb, though, and especially when separated from the verb by intervening words might shade into something very much like our prepositions.

The difference between preverbs and prepositions may be easily grasped in English. In the phrase *look up*, *up* is a preposition in a sentence like *Edwin looked up the chimney*; it is a particle (in effect, a preverb except that in English it follows the verb) in a sentence like *Edwin looked up the address*. It appears that the PIE forms directly ancestral to our prepositions were mainly like what is seen in *look up (the address)*, that is, elements which altered the meaning of the action or state expressed by the verb. Such elements came to be reinterpreted as relating to the noun they are apparently in construction with.

In the daughter languages there was another, completely different, kind of relational element: a noun in a certain case in construction with another noun. The specific instances are typical enough as a rule, but unlike the preverb-derived elements, mentioned above, which show a high degree of similarity from one language to another, they do not (with a striking exception or two) have cognate forms in different languages. These are forms whose equivalent in English are prepositional phrases like *because*, *in back*, *on top*, *for the sake*, *in spite*, *among*, *away*. (NE *because*, *among*, and *away* are prepositional phrases which have coalesced into words.) If English were an inflectional language, we would say that the first five of these expressions 'take the genitive' (*because of*), the last 'takes the ablative' (*away from*).

Of this type are G *χάριν* 'for the pleasure (of)' (*χάρις* 'grace, favor'), *δίκην* 'in the manner (of)' (*δίκη* 'custom'); L *cōram* 'in the presence of' (*co-ōs-* 'mouth, face'), *circum* 'around' (*circus*). Forms of this type can be reconstructed for the parent language too, such as *H_2*enti* 'in from of' (*H_2*ent-* 'face', **406.1**).

The histories of 'prepositions' present special difficulties. Even when relatedness seems obvious, there may be many differences in detail. Sometimes these were differences in the ancestral forms themselves, such as ablaut grades or case markers. But the specific phonological developments they show sometimes deviate enigmatically from the usual correspondence sets, as in L *sub*, G *ὑπό* (**406.8**). Perhaps these are actually regular, and seem deviant only because they are proper to a few forms. A strong caveat, however, should be entered against assuming that similar forms with similar functions are related, as the risk of chance resemblance is highest for short words of vague meaning (and of unpredictable form, to boot). Where time-depths are relatively small, it is possible to be confident about what is and is not related, and so we know for a certainty that NE *with* and the synonymous NHG *mit* are unrelated despite their similarity. As appearances suggest, NE *to* (and also *too*), Du. *toe* (atonic *te*), NHG *zu* are all cognate; but appearances suggest the same thing for Go. *du*, and yet it is unrelated to the others. See also **406.8**.

One final comment about the semantic vagueness mentioned above: this class of forms is highly mutable semantically. That is, originally cognate forms might develop widely divergent meanings and be recognizeable as cognate only with difficulty. Note that even English and German, languages much more recently derived from a common source than G and L, have such discrepant semantics as NE *up* vs. NHG *auf* 'on, to, towards, at' (the earlier force survives in adverbial senses and in many compound verbs such as *aufspringen* 'jump up'); and NE *with* vs. NHG *wider* 'against' (here too the earlier force is attested in OE, and survives in compounds like *withhold* and *withstand*).

406. The following is a sample of G and L forms traceable to the parent language.

1. PIE *H_2*enti* 'in front and facing', loc.sg. of a root-noun 'face' > G *ἀντί*, L *ante* : Ved. *ánti* 'near, in the presence of'. The noun, and other derivatives, was lost in IE languages but survives in Hitt. *ḫa-an-za* /hants/ 'front' and various Hitt. derivatives.

2. PIE **pro* (or **preH₃*) 'in front and facing away' > G *πρό*, L *prō* : Ved. *prá*, Av. *frā*, OIr. *ro-*, Go. *fra-*. The latter two are preverbs only, and likewise preverbal is the zero grade, **pr̥-*, seen in L *portendō* 'predict; presage' and *porrigō* 'reach out' (*regō*).

For such a short and widely-attested element, the degree of ambiguity in the make-up of the proto-form (or forms) is remarkable. The usual reconstruction is **preH₃-* as mentioned above, but the failure of a long vowel to develop uniformly is troubling, especially in verb complexes. Differently, there is a certain amount of evidence pointing instead to **proH₂*, such as the resulting ease of tracing G *παραί*, L *prae*, OIr. *a(i)r*ᴸ 'before, on account of', and Go. *faura* to **pr̥H₂-ey*. But L *por-* cannot have any laryngeal at all.

3. PIE **en* (or **eni*) 'in, on' > G *ἐν(ί)*, *εἰς* (see below), L *in* : Ved. only in *ánīka-* 'face' < **eni-H₃kʷo-* (the second element means 'eye'; see **117.2**), Go. *in*, OIr. *in* (both from **eni*); G dial. also *ἰν*. G *ἐν* was originally used

with acc. and dat., just as L *in* with acc. and abl., and this double use of ἐν persisted in several dialects. But in others ἐν with the acc. was replaced by an elaborated form, ἐνς (-ς imported from its antonym ἐξ), whence (by 228.4) ἐς or εἰς.

4. PIE *éks 'out of' > G ἐξ, ἐγ-, ἐκ- (dial. ἐς), L *ex*, *ē* (before certain consonants) : OIr. *ess-*; Lith. *iš*, OCS *iz*, *is* (the *i-* in these forms is problematic); the element is not found in InIr. or Gmc.

On the basis of G ἔσχατος 'outermost; last' the etymon is sometimes given as *éǵhs; this would give ἐξ, and *éǵhs-ko- would give *ékskho-, whence ἐσχ- per 230.3.[1] A likelier explanation of ἔσχατος is that it represents a purely Att. development of *ἔξατος, different from sporadic σφυχή for ψυχή, Σχενοκλῆς for Ξενοκλῆς, only in having somehow become standard.

5. PIE **ep-* 'on', **op-* 'behind/back'. Formally these look like ablaut alternants. G ἐπί 'on', Hom. ὄπι-θε(ν) 'behind', Att. ὄπισθε(ν) (formed on the pattern of πρόσθε(ν)) 'back', L *ob* 'next to, near' (OL); 'against' (classical; cf. the polysemy of NE *against*). The explanation for the voicing is conjectural; of course many words officially spelled *ob-*, like *obtineō*, were actually pronounced *op-* on the evidence of inscriptions, and orthographic *-p-* was preserved in a few derivationally opaque preverbal reflexes (*operiō* 'cover' < **op-wer-*) : Ved. *ápi*, Av. *aipi*, OIr. *iar*ᴺ (**epi-r-om*), Lith. *ap-* (*api-* before labials), Hitt. *ap-pa* 'back, again'. Zero grade perh. in L *po-*, preserved in a couple of verb paradigms (*positus*), and OCS *po-*.

Some see in these forms various cases of an otherwise lost root-noun meaning literally 'back'. The 'on' sense may have something to do with pack animals or riding (it has recently been proved that in the likely region of the Indo-European homeland horses were ridden astride for a good millennium before the invention of wheeled vehicles). This may be the etymon of the element *op-* seen in L *optumus*, *-imus* 'best; (?)*tops' (358.3b).

Unrelated are G ἀπό, L *ab*, Ved. *ápa*, because too different in both form (evidently including *H_2) and meaning ('away').

6. PIE **peri-* (possibly at bottom related to **preH*$_3$, **proH*$_2$); basic meaning of 'away' whence often 'through': G περί, L *per* : Ved. *pári*, Av. *pairi*, OIr. *ir*, Lith. *per̃*; in Gmc. only as preverbs and in elaborated forms like Go. *fairra* 'far (from)'. In composition, the element often has an intensive meaning: Ved. *pári-bhūti-* 'overwhelming power', G περιγλαγής 'full of milk', L *percōmis* 'very friendly', Lith. *per̃didis* 'too big', OCS *prěslavĭnŭ* 'exceedingly splendid'. This is probably not an ancient detail, as the independent development of the same semantics is widely seen, as in NE *thorough(ly)* (a doublet of *through*, being respectively the tonic and atonic reflexes of OE *þurh*).

---

[1] This *-*kskh-* is earlier than, and different from, the development of voiceless aspirated stops in G consonant clusters containing **s*, 230.2-3.

7. PIE **uperi* 'above, over' > G ὑπέρ, L *super*. The G reflex could continue **su-* like the L, but Ved. *upári*, OIr. *for* (**wori* < **uori* < **upori*), Go. *ufar*, NE *over*, all point unambiguously to an *s*-less form. The source of the Italic *s-* is obscure, as it also is in *sub* and *sine*.

8. PIE **upo* 'down (on); below' > G ὑπό, L *sub*, *subs-* (the second *-s-* secondary). As with *super/ὑπέρ* above, G and Ital. on their own would point to **supo*, but the remainder of the evidence indicates **upo* instead: Ved. *úpa*, Av. *upa*, OIr. *fo* (**wo* < **uo* < **upo*), Go. *uf*, OHG *oba*. (NE *of/off* and NHG *auf* 'on', despite appearances, are unrelated to these.)

9. PIE **me* 'with' has been identified in combinations: **me-ta* > G μετά 'among; next to' : Go. *miþ*, OE *miþ*, ON *meþr* 'with'; cf. NHG *mit*. It has been suggested that **me-ǵhsri* > G μέχρι(ς), and zero grade **m̥-ǵhsri* > G ἄχρι(ς), both 'up to, as far as', contain the loc.sg. of the old word for 'hand', **ǵhesr-* (G χείρ, Hitt. *ki-eš-šar*). The element is not preserved in L, unless (as some think) ***me-dhi* 'with, among' is the ultimate etymon of the widely-attested adj. **medhyos* 'middle', G μέσ(σ)ος, L *medius*.

10. PIE **ad* (? **H_2ed*) 'to' > L *ad*, also *atque* (**ad-que*): U **ař-**, O *az* /ats/ like *eks* 'out', cf. G ἐνς, εἰς, 3, above, OE *æt*, Go. *at*, OHG *az* (lost in NHG). Not preserved in G.

Some old prepositions/preverbs are attested in the classical languages only in the weakened sense of a conjunction or adverb. For example PIE **eti* 'beyond' is attested as a prep. and preverb in Ved. *áti* 'beyond', Av. *aiti-*. But in western IE it weakened to a conjunction via some such sense as 'beyond that; moreover': G ἔτι 'yet, still', L *et* 'and' (in competition with and eventually ousting inherited *-que*), Go. *iþ* (always clause-initial) 'but; and', Gaul. *eti* 'also'.

CONJUGATION

Survey of the PIE Verb System

407. Verb systems generally considered. The verb system of most languages is a complicated affair. This has nothing to do with elaborate paradigms, but with functional categories however they are marked. The formal categories of a language in fact cannot be depended upon to mark functional categories straightforwardly. First, functional categories are commonly combined in various ways: in PIE you could not specify a subject's person without also specifying number, and vice-versa. Second, functional categories are often expressed by formally inconsistent means.

A few examples from English will make these points clearly, since English is usually regarded as elementary in these regards compared to the luxuriance of G, L, and Skt. But the relationships between form and function in English are anything but elementary, as we shall see, and have little congruence with the terminology of the school grammars.

In English the *present tense* is usually regarded as self-explanatory; in the words of a dictionary, s.v. *present*: '*Gramm.* Denoting, or pertaining to, time that now is; as the *present tense*'. To the contrary: the 'present tense' of English turns out to have very little in the way of reference to 'time that now is'. The four principal functions of the NE 'present tense' are: (1) it is used of future events; (2) it is used of reiterated or habitual events; (3) it is used of a state, which has no tense; (4) it is used with a special class of verbs known as performatives, such as *say, declare, promise.*

Examples of (1) are: *Alice* LEAVES *in a week*; *When Megan* CALLS *tell her I'm on my way*; *Unless someone* TELLS *him he will never find out.* This future force is a relic, albeit a robust one, of an earlier period in the history of all Germanic languages, when there were formally only two tense categories: 'past' (officially known as *preterite*) and 'non-past' (the so-called *present*, which included the future and some unreal events). For most future events English now uses overtly marked verb forms (*might, must, will, may*, and so on)—at least in independent clauses: the invariable use of 'present tense' verbs in future temporal clauses introduced by *when, unless*, and *if* is an instance of the general truth that the morphosyntax of subordinate clauses tends to be more conservative than that of independent clauses.

Type (2) is exemplified by *Bruce* DRINKS *at least six cups of coffee a day*; *Wayne* IS *always the last to leave.* Such sentences explicitly state that something both has taken place and will take place; they are silent about what Bruce and Wayne are doing hic-et-nunc.

Examples of Type (3) are: *It* COMES *with a set of blades*; *Lucy* IS *unreasonable*; *Elliott* OWNS *an antique Rolls-Royce.* These predications all refer to (tenseless) states, which are admittedly valid at present but that is incidental to their real meaning.[1]

---

[1] The assertion that stative predications lack tense may require some discussion. *Jane's family owned most of downtown Altoona* may well look like the past tense of *Jane's family owns most of downtown Altoona* but semantically the meaning of the second sentence includes the

Type (4) would include such remarks as *Bruce SAYS that he drinks too much coffee*, or *I THINK he's right.* Note that if the first sentence refers to any actual event it was something that happened (possibly more than once) in the past. And note that *Bruce said that he drinks too much coffee* is an aorist of an ordinary eventive verb, not the past tense of the first (performative) example.

So much, then, for the notion of a 'simple present' in English; it turns out to be a formal category only, whose nomenclature conceals more than it reveals about the English verb CATEGORIES.

An additional problem in dealing with a verb system either descriptively or historically is that it might be sensitive to some functional contrast in a formally unobvious way. PIE, as we shall see, verbs denoting events and states had important formal distinctions. In English, although there is no such morphological uproar—the distinction is not even mentioned in most school grammars—eventive and stative verbs nevertheless belong to different categories. The contrast is handled differently in different tenses—a commonplace occurrence, incidentally, which is another source of confusion when talking about verb systems. The main contrast is found in the distinction between states (tenseless) and such events as are taking place as the speaker is talking—the true present tense. For this latter we use the so-called present progressive, in contrast to the misnamed simple present: *Alice IS WRITING a letter*, *The tenor IS STRANGLING the soprano*, *Leigh IS TAKING a shower* are examples of genuine hic-et-nunc events. Contrast the states in *Alice KNOWS The Iliad by heart*, *The tenor HAS an excellent voice* and *Leigh IS TAKING Korean.* Note that in English, stative verbs do occur in the present progressive; these have the specific meaning 'TEMPORARY state': compare the force of *Tom HAS a good time at parties* and *Tom IS HAVING a good time (at this party)*; or *Lucy IS unreasonable* and *Lucy IS BEING unreasonable.*

In verb systems there is one additional source of confusion: a verb may exhibit the morphosyntactic properties of inappropriate categories, or be defective for a category. In English, *be* has all the earmarks of a stative verb as outlined above. In PIE and its daughters, however, the verb 'be' (**H₁es-*) in its inflectional makeup belongs wholly to the EVENTIVE type. In NE, *sleep*, which is semantically stative, behaves like an eventive: *Alice IS SLEEPING* rather than ˣ*Alice SLEEPS* would be the appropriate answer to a question like *What is Alice doing?*

And note one example of how the morphosyntax gets in the way of the tense system, with complicating effect: the past tense of *David is late* is *David was late*; but the past tense of *David might be late* is not ˣ*David might was late*, because modals are followed

---

meaning of the first sentence: in English at least, the past tense of a stative verb identifies the state as having terminated, and is here synonymous with *Jane's family no longer owns most of downtown Altoona*, whose verb form is in the (so-called) present tense. —In English the verb *be* is a partial exception to this generalization. It is often an ordinary stative, as in *David is lovable*; but it also readily takes punctual predicates, as *Her response was evasive*, an example of a genuine past-tense statement. Note that *We would have gotten here sooner, but Alice was late [on that occasion]* is not the past tense of *Alice is late [as a matter of habit].*

only by tenseless forms; instead we have *David might have been late.* That is, the auxiliary *have*, when used with modals and infinitives, means '(simple) past tense of the main verb'.

408. This discussion only touches the surface of what is generally thought to be the simple (if not primitive) verb system of modern English. It makes it easy to see that there might be disagreement about the correct analysis of the categories of living languages, for which much information is available (native-speaker reactions, for example, or discussions of nuance). The analysis of dead languages is much more uncertain; and even dead languages are much easier to analyze than a reconstructed one.[1]

It is now generally recognized that the categories of the PIE verb system were different from what have been usually presented, but there is rather less agreement as to the correct analysis. Indeed, the correct analysis of the L and G verb systems themselves (always remembering that the Homeric and Attic systems are fundamentally different), is neither self-evident nor settled by convention. Even the most superficial questions, like what do G negative constructions with *οὐ(κ)* have in common against those with *μή*, are far easier to ask than answer. Regarding the PIE verb system, the framework given here is little more than a sketch regarding which there is room for reasonable disagreement.

409. The G and L verb systems could not have evolved more differently from their common starting-point if that had been some conscious purpose. Accordingly, little can be learned from a direct comparison of the two verb systems; one must trace the evolution of each, independently, from the common source. However, traditional handbooks give little idea of the basic plan of that common source mainly because they tend to take Indic or (Attic) Greek as windows on the ancient system, but more particularly because such handbooks are more at home with forms than with functions. (The hazards of a form-driven approach are manifest in the English 'present tense', as discussed in 407.)

It might be objected that in a historical morphology forms are all that can really be agreed upon. But the formal facts of a paradigm are capable of explaining only some of the changes that paradigms undergo—and verb systems are much subject to remodeling both formally and functionally, as is easily seen in the large differences between the Latin and, say, French verb systems. The key to many formal changes is function. For example, the appending of *-ī* to the 1sg. ending of the perfect in L, so *tulī* 'I carried' < **tetola-i*, is incomprehensible without an appeal to function (530.1)—and to the correct function, moreover. Alternatively, the suggestion (544) that the L imperf. subj. marker **-sē-* is some kind of aorist element because it contains **-s-* does not hold water: it ignores

---

[1] Even for some well-attested ancient languages the categories of the verb system are poorly understood. The use of 'tenses' in Vedic is unlikely to have been as haphazard as it seems; much about the distribution of stems and endings in Hittite is murky, and the force of certain particles is elusive; and even the basic verb categories of Sumerian have resisted analysis to date.

the differences between the functions of the L imperf. and the IE aorist (both to start with and also as the aorist evolved in L).

410. STATIVE VS. EVENTIVE VERBS.[1] The inflection of PIE verbs was divided along functional lines into two types, which might be called *stative* and *eventive*. The former denoted states, for example 'know', 'remember', 'be afraid', 'prevail', 'hate', 'be dead', 'be aware'. (In PIE, as in many other languages, many of the notions rendered in English with *be* and some predicate are expressed by primary verbs.) The other, much larger, class includes things that happen, arrive at conclusions, bring about or undergo changes, and so on: 'learn', 'fly', 'throw', 'get full', 'look for', 'find', 'kill', 'break', 'die'.

In PIE the two types differed in how their stems were formed, what endings were used, and in their functional categories (the nuances traditionally known as *voice*, for example (414), contrast in the eventives but not in the statives). The statives make up the system known as the PIE *perfect tense*, though it was in fact neither perfective nor a tense (509-14). The eventives comprise everything else, namely the present and imperfect tenses, and the aorist (also not a tense, but so called; 413). Which class a verb belonged to was largely determined by its meaning—but not wholly: 'be', as mentioned above, inflects like an eventive verb in PIE, as do verbs with stative meanings like 'lie', 'stand', and 'sit'. (This non-stative morphology of verbs of basically—fundamentally—stative semantics is further evidence for the possibility touched on in the footnote below, namely that in the system which underlay the one described here for PIE, the 'stative' form-category earlier had some different function.) And of course a given basic NOTION may assume different functional roles, such as *make hot*, *become hot*, and *be hot*, signalled by characteristic morphology; see also 413a. Finally, figurative senses blur such distinctions (*speak* is literal/eventive, but in *This gesture speaks well for his sensitivity*, the verb is figurative/stative), as do derivational processes—all causatives are eventive, for example, including those built to statives: 'understand' is stative; 'teach' (= 'cause to understand') is eventive.

411. PERSON. Morphologically, PIE verbs relate to other elements of a sentence in only one way: they were marked via suffix in accord with whether the subject of the verb was the SPEAKER, the SPOKEN-TO, or OTHER (familiarly *first*, *second*, and *third person*, respectively). The PIE verb is anaes-

---

[1] The scheme presented here fits the facts of the familiar IE languages better than Hittite. Indeed, it is probable that the proper relationship between the (IE) system given here and the Anatolian system can be understood only if they are both traced to a yet earlier system which was rather different. A discussion of that matter would take us too far afield, and however poorly it accommodates Anatolian, the system presented here, or something like it, will do well for the attested IE languages.

thetic to the gender of the subject, social status, proximity, definiteness, and other categories which are found in various languages; nor, unlike many highly-inflected languages, does the verb provide any information about direct or indirect objects.

412. NUMBER. Like the nouns, the verb had a dual as well as a singular and plural. The semantics are straightforward except for one point: the FIRST PERSONS DU. AND PL. do not mean (or very rarely mean) two speakers or a multitude of speakers. Rather they mean the usual—singular—speaker together with one or more other persons.

Very many languages distinguish between 'speaker + other(s) including the spoken-to' and 'speaker + other(s), NOT including the spoken-to', and so have two sets of forms, usually known as *inclusive* and *exclusive*. PIE has a single category for 'speaker + other(s)', but perhaps the inconsistent distribution of **m*- and **w*- among the dual and plural paradigms of endings and pronouns alike can be explained by supposing a pre-PIE system in which the **w*-forms were 1pl. inclusive and the **m*-forms were 1pl. exclusive, the two stems having been parcelled out among a later-arising dual/plural and nominative/oblique contrast along functional lines.

EVENTIVE VERBS

Eventive Verb Categories

413. THE EVENTIVE VERBS of PIE were subdivided into two form/function categories (albeit all but unmarked by formal differences), namely they were either *punctual* or *durative*. (Other terms are encountered for the same concepts.) The distinction hinges on whether the action or event is conceived of as requiring an elapse of time; the membership of a verb in one category or the other is therefore a matter of the meaning of the verb itself: 'look for' or 'travel' or 'carve' are inherently durative; 'find' or 'arrive' or 'stab' are inherently punctual.

However, durative events can be conceived of as POINTS in future or past time (*Alice traveled in Europe last year*, punctual in contradistinction to the durative *Alice was traveling in Europe when she met her husband*), and punctual notions readily can be used in transferred (figurative) senses which are durative: *I'm finding that Howard is possessive* is an ordinary kind of sentence, whereas *I'm finding a cat under the bed* is so odd as to be unprocessable.[1]

---

1 Figurative uses retain most of the sense of the basic punctual verb but add some nuance: the punctual essence of 'break' is latent in *is breaking*, which has the sense of 'is approaching a punctual event more or less palpably'. In English some punctuals used as duratives have future force, as *I'm giving you five more minutes* or *He's taking the 12:15 train.* Such figurative types are not language universals. In G, for instance, the use of an aorist (that is, punctual) formation for an inherently durative notion often has the special force of 'begin to'—the *ingressive aorist*—which is unlike anything found in English.

A linguistic consequence of the real-world distinction between durative and punctual events is that although we may speak of a durative event as taking place as we talk about it, we cannot readily refer to a punctual event that way. Punctual events are pretty much necessarily referred to as having already happened or as not having happened yet, or as being habitual (which is in effect the two together; the 'gnomic aorist' of G is in this category). Note that 'has not happened yet' includes not only the simple future, but also imperatives and an array of notions collectively known as *modal* (conditionals, optatives, desideratives, conatives, debitives, precatives, and so on).

This then is the basis for the distinction, formally and functionally, between the PIE *aorist*—usually called a tense, but not in fact any such thing—and the *present/imperfect.* The PIE aorist comprised the punctuals, and as PIE had no generic future tense formation, the forms in question referred chiefly to past events. However, punctual stems occur readily in the several kinds of 'yet to happen' inflections that PIE did have, most significantly the imperative (hardly appropriate for a true 'past tense'), and also in the subjunctive and optative.

The present/imperfects—another term for the duratives—had two genuine tenses: *imperfect* ('was occurring in the past', with no information as to whether or not the action has ceased), and *present* (everything else, including future; linguists call this category *non-past,* a term which has regrettably not gained acceptance in Indo-Europeanist circles).

Thus, to use English once again as a laboratory specimen, the verb *walk* (durative) forms the simple present *is walking* and the imperfect *was walking*; it also forms an aorist *walked.* The punctual *arrive* in its literal sense forms only the aorist *arrived*; the so-called present *arrives* is in fact never present-time but only future (*The train arrives at 3:05*) or habitual (*The 3:05 always arrives late*); and the forms appropriate to the present/imperfect system, *is arriving* and *was arriving,* have the elaborated meanings (per the footnote on p. 446) of 'is/was closely approaching the moment of arrival'.

In PIE, the person and participle markers for the aorist and the present/imperfect formations were the same, except of course that 'primary' person endings, being markers of hic-et-nunc present time, did not occur in the aorist. Only the stems have differences, and even here several of the most basic stem-formations occur in both types. That means that the aorist of a punctual verb and the imperfect of a durative one might be formed identically. What makes _*e-dheg^{w}h-t_ 'was burning' an imperfect but _*e-g^{w}em-t_ 'arrived' an aorist is not the morphology, which is identical, but the existence of a root-present _*dheg^{w}h-ti_ 'is burning' on the one hand and the absence of any corresponding _×g^{w}emti_ on the other. Instead of the latter we find the present tense _*g^{w}m̥-ske-ti_ and _*g^{w}m̥-ye-ti_ (each with its own imperfect, _*e-g^{w}m̥-sḱe-t_ and _*e-g^{w}m̥-ye-t_). Moreover, to the root _*dheg^{w}h-_ there is an overtly-marked aorist, _*e-dhē̆g^{w}h-s-t._

CHARACTERIZED VS. UNCHARACTERIZED STEMS. These examples exemplify another important trait of the aorist vis-à-vis the present/imperfect: the most basic formations (root inflection, **447-8**, and stems with a linking vowel between root and ending, **449**) convey the inherent meaning of the root, whereas derived functions will have more elaborate ('characterized') morphology—reduplication, infixation, and so on. In the samples given here, the root *dheg*^{w}*h-* makes a root present/imperfect, in keeping with its durative sense ('is/was burning'), but also builds a derived punctual past tense ('burned') with the overtly aoristic ('characterized') stem-marker *-s-* (**459**). Contrariwise, the root **g*^{w}*em-* has a root aorist, in keeping with its punctual meaning ('arrive' or 'depart'—it is not clear which, but both are punctual), and builds a figurative present/imperfect stem ('is on the way; is going/coming') with a characterized stem in **-sḱ*^{e}*/o-* (**456.3**).

This morphological trait (characterized = derived/figurative) incidentally reveals mismatches between form and function in PIE on the punctual/durative axis, as well as on the stative/eventive axis as mentioned in **410**: for example, on the basis of its punctual meaning the root **g*^{w}*hen-* 'strike dead, slay' should be an aoristic verb, but in fact it makes a root present (**g*^{w}*hen-ti* 3sg. pres. > Ved. *hánti*, Hitt. *ku-(e-)en-zi*) and seemingly had no aorist at all.

a. Many notions are of course versatile as to state vs. action, and as to duration. For example a root 'fill' in a language like PIE might equally well be a state ('is full') or an event; as an event, it might equally well be a process ('approach fullness'; durative) or a point reached ('got full; made full'). The attested morphology indicates that the PIE root **pleH*$_1$*-* was inherently eventive and aoristic: primitive **e-pleH*$_1$*-t(o)* (root aor.: Ved. *aprāt* 'made full', Hom. πλῆτο 'got full') vs. a characterized (derived) pres. **pl̥-ne-H*$_1$*-ti* 'fills', imperf. **e-pl̥-ne-H*$_1$*-t* (Ved. *pr̥ṇā́ti*).

Verbs which might be either transitive or intransitive, but with the detail that the transitive object stands as intransitive subject (like English *fill*, *break*, *burn*, *cook*) are known in some grammatical traditions as *middle verbs*. In PIE morphosyntax, it appears that such roots were inherently intransitive; the transitive agnates were formed by characterized stems. See also **414b**.

414. VOICE. The endings of eventive stems conveyed a nuance traditionally called *active* voice and *middle* (less aptly, *medio-passive*) voice. The latter is represented by the Hitt., Toch., G, Celtic, and InIr. middle; the same or similar endings are found in the passive paradigms of InIr., G, Celt., and Go.; and in the L deponent/passive. In PIE itself there was no true passive, that is, a type of morphosyntax with the direct (or indirect) object as the subject of the verb, with an agent in an oblique case. In the several IE languages that have them, the forms used to express the passive are different and grew up independently.

The middle was used for actions in which the subject was intimately concerned—what one did to oneself (the reflexive middle); for oneself; with one's own possessions; what one felt oneself, and so on. Thus both Ved.

yájati act. and *yájate* midd. mean 'worships, venerates, performs a rite': the active forms would be used of a priest, or of a deity cast in the role of mediator; the middle would be used of the worshipper himself. The distinction is easily observed from G usage as well. In both G and InIr., however, the contrast between active and middle is often subtle if not altogether absent.

a. In some forms the middle developed a special sense, for example **sekʷetor* orig. *'keeps in sight' (root **sekʷ-* 'see, view') but already in PIE with the sense 'follows'—perhaps specifically a hunting term—whence G ἕπεται, L *sequitur*, Ved. *sacate*, OIr. *sechithir* all 'follows'. This verb is incidentally an example of a whole type, the so-called deponent verbs, that is, verbs which occur only in the middle voice. They are found in all IE languages that preserve the active/middle distinction in more than remnants, but L is peculiar in that the old middle function (in ossified form) is confined to deponents, and the middle forms that contrast with actives are only PASSIVE, a distinctly different category.

b. The middle had an important additional use in PIE in connection with the so-called middle verbs mentioned in **413a**, namely those verbs in which the grammatical subject is the undergoer rather than the agent. The most basic formation was typically in the middle voice, as befit the involvement, as it were, of the subject in the action. By contrast, the derived (characterized) transitive forms were active or middle as the occasion demanded.

415. Mood. The *moods* of the eventive verbs in PIE are traditionally listed as *indicative*, *subjunctive*, *optative*, and *imperative*, as seen in Greek and Indo-Iranian. Evidence suggests (533) that the *irreales moods* (subjunctive and optative) were limited to eventive verbs, and possibly the same was true of the imperative also; but in daughter languages stative irreales formations patterned on the eventives early grew up. The functions of the subjunctive and optative are best observed from Homeric usage, which agrees in its main lines with that of the Vedas. In Italic and Germanic the old optative becomes the all-purpose irreales mood, familiarly known as the *subjunctive* (but unrelated to the PIE, G, and InIr. mood of that name, an unfortunate terminological confusion). The PIE subjunctive is lost in Gmc. altogether, but in Italic it becomes the *future tense*. In classical Skt. like Gmc. the subjunctive disappears (except for the first person, in a special use[1]), the optative remaining as the sole irreales paradigm. In G, contrariwise, the use of the optative is on the wane in the Hellenistic period, being infrequent in the New Testament, and a few centuries later it disappeared.[2] In the

---

[1] The grammars call the forms imperative, but functionally they are more in the nature of inviting a command: *nahyāni* was therefore not something like 'tie, O self' but rather as in colloquial English 'How about I tie it?' or 'Maybe I should tie it . . . ?', both of which even in English are in fact more subjunctive than imperative in feel.

[2] The process was helped along by phonological developments: a good many pivotal forms, for example φέροις and φέρῃς, φέροι and φέρῃ, had become homophonous by the 5th or 6th century AD.

modern Germanic languages—English included, despite reports to the contrary[1]—the subjunctive (PIE optative) is alive and well.

In Hitt. there are the usual imperatives, but no trace of any special morphology for irreales forms. This has been much commented upon; but the PIE subjunctive obviously evolved late in the history of PIE, and the opt. originally was structurally very different from its appearance in the familiar classical languages (see 533).

416. The injunctive (or conjunctive) mood. In Vedic and in the earliest Avestan, and likewise in Homer, there are verbs that have the form of augmentless (441) imperfects and aorists. As these sometimes have irreales force and are particularly notable as the verb form occurring in negative imperatives (introduced by a particle, Ved. *mā́*, G *μή*), for a long time they have been supposed to constitute a separate formal/functional irreales category, known as the *injunctive* (or *conjunctive*) *mood.* Some scholars, while doubting the existence of a distinct functional category on a par with the subjunctive and optative, use *injunctive* or *conjunctive* as a short expression for 'augmentless past indicative forms with irreales force'.

The facts are significantly otherwise: we have here verbs marked for person and voice only, and lacking any mark for mood or tense. The misidentification of the forms as past tense comes in part from failing to recognize that the PIE secondary person endings are the generic endings (419-21). Verbs unmarked for tense and mood play a specific role in PIE syntax: on the evidence of Homeric and Vedic, in a sequence of verb forms having the same tense or mood only the first verb was marked fully for such categories; subsequent verbs, as long as the categories remained unchanged, were marked for person and voice only. There are two other uses for tenseless-moodless forms: in negative imperatives, tense and mood are obviously inapplicable; and sometimes tense and mood are simply left unspecified, for example in the Vedas in ritual mantras.

In Vedic the distribution is particularly clear:

dadāti . . . *carat* 'gives (3sg.pres.act.indic.) . . . wanders (3sg.act.)';
pibā . . . *sadaḥ* 'drink (2sg.pres.act.imper.) . . . sit (2sg.act.)';
śr̥ṇavaḥ . . . *dhāt* 'may you listen (2sg.pres.act.subj.) . . . may [the sacrifice] bestow (3sg.act.)';
pári no vr̥jyāḥ . . . *pári gāt* 'may [the spear] miss us (3sg.act. precative) . . . may [his malevolence] pass by (3sg.act.)';
apacat . . . *pibat* '[Agni] cooked (3sg.imperf.act.indic.) . . . [Indra] drank (3sg.act.)'.

[1] It is commonly stated that the subjunctive is extinct in English 'or nearly so'. It is true that there are few forms that are distinctively subjunctive, but too firm an insistence on the extinction of subjunctive as a category means analyzing a sentence like *Suppose I came early—would that be a help?* as using a past tense verb to refer to a future event. This palpable absurdity is easily avoided if we recognize here a (tenseless) subjunctive rather than a past indicative.

The assumption that a Vedic-type pattern historically underlies Homeric syntax explains a number of seemingly unrelated facts. For example, it has long been remarked that the augment is omitted (as it is usually put) most often in narratives; its omission is less frequent in speeches, and very rare in proverbs and gnomic utterances. But it is exactly in narratives that sequences of verbs sharing tense and mood are most common, and, at the other extreme, gnomes and proverbs are by their nature independent of the discourse in which they crop up. There is no denying that Homeric syntax is much less consistent than Vedic in the handling of these reduced forms. That may be the result of changing syntax, but subsequent redaction is partly to blame, as editors sought to normalize the text by inserting augments wherever the meter allowed it.

A similar kind of syntax is evident in Old Irish: in a sequence of conditional predications only the first verb is in the subjunctive and the rest are in the indicative. This may be all that is left of the old rule; but as the bulk of OIr. attestation consists of disconnected glosses, it would not in any case reveal much about discourse. Enough remains to make it clear that the syntax of G and Vedic is not a shared innovation, but an inheritance from PIE.

a. THE HISTORICAL PRESENT. It has been convincingly argued that the *historical present*—the use of present tense verbs in narrative—is an outgrowth of the PIE system of reduced verb marking in sequences discussed above. This accounts for the total absence of the historical present from Homer, a text dating from a time when the role of forms unmarked for tense and mood was still well-defined. When such a system was becoming obsolete, the obvious way to rationalize something like λεῖπε 3sg.inj. was to add an augment and make it into an unambiguous imperfect. But it could just as easily be worked into the emerging tense system by turning it into λείπει, an unambiguous present. Evidence in favor of this interpretation is that in early IE texts, unlike our own concept of the device, the 'historical present' is typically introduced by a regular past-tense form: ἔλαβον δὲ καὶ τὸ φρούριον καὶ τοὺς φύλακας ἐκβάλλουσιν is good Greek but 'They captured the fort and drive out the garrison' is inconceivable English. Conversely, in ancient IE languages the lengthy sequences of historical present verbs that occur in present-day languages are unknown. It is not clear whether the L historical present is a domestic product with a history similar to G, or an imitation of G.

417. TENSE. The relative time of an action may be marked in various ways, by adverbs ('already') and conjunctions ('and then...') as well as by specific verb forms. In PIE only the durative eventive verbs had distinctive forms marking relative time of the action: 'right now' (sometimes known by the tag *hic et nunc*), and 'at that time' (with or without the additional nuance of 'still'). These two categories are familiarly known as the *present* and *imperfect tenses*, respectively.

As remarked in 413, PIE did not have any future tense as such, but of course a variety of utterances in all languages refer to events that are neither past nor hic-et-nunc. These include commands, expectations, wishes, possibilities, and conditions. The term 'future tense' is usually reserved for such expressions as convey the unshaded conviction of the speaker that an event will take place. In PIE what is known as the present tense probably filled that function, as it continued to do in the early Gmc. languages. In addition, the subjunctive and the imperative all refer to actions which will take place in the future if they take place at all. Likewise PIE had secondary (derived) verb stems with conditional, hortatory, and desiderative force, all necessarily future; in Indic, G, and Ital. the optative stems were worked into the overall paradigmatic scheme of tenses and stems, and in InIr. and G the desiderative formation evolved into the generic future tense. (Exactly the same thing happened in English: the OE etymon of the usual marker of the unshaded future, *will*, meant '[would] want to'. Put differently, *will* is etymologically a desiderative, and optative to boot.)

As for verb forms referring particularly to anterior events, there were two. Their formations are similar in many details; they were marked with generic ('secondary') person-endings, and in G, Arm., and InIr. were embellished with a prefix known as the augment: the *imperfect* is the anterior tense of durative verbs (and as such is the only true tense in the whole system). The *aorist* often refers to an anterior punctual event, or to a durative event as the point of beginning (*ingressive aorist*); the point of completion (*resultative aorist*); or, more generally, a past durative action viewed in summary. Exactly the same thing is seen in the simple past of durative verbs in English and other modern European languages—English for example lacks the ingressive aorist, but *Wagner wrote an average of five letters a day* is a resultative; and *George V reigned for 26 years*; *Einstein played the violin* are aoristic summaries of durative eventives.

It is important to remember that anterior reference is not the essential function of the aorist, from the PIE point of view; the aorist freely names potential or otherwise future events when it occurs in moods (subjunctive, optative, imperative).

The tense values assumed for the parent speech are substantially those observed in Homeric. In L the aorist and the PIE perfect (actually stative; 410, 509) merge formally and functionally to form a completive past, and apart from the distinction in use between imperfect and perfect, which still survives in the Romance languages, the L tenses are purely temporal. In general the tendency in most of the IE languages has been to use the simple tenses for distinctions of time, leaving the *aspect* of the action—punctual vs. durative, completed vs. uncompleted, habitual vs. incidental, intentional vs. inadvertent, and so on—either unexpressed or expressed by different means. In the Slavic languages there is a system of aspects, embodied in two parallel conjugations known as 'imperfective' and 'perfective'; the function of the latter has much in common with certain values (but by no means all) of the old aorist.

There were no tenses of RELATIVE TIME, that is, with reference to time other than that of the speaker, like the L pluperfect and future perfect; nor past and future forms of the true (present) perfect, like the G pluperfect and future perfect. As indicated before, such nuances could all be expressed —but not through verb morphology.

418. NON-FINITE FORMS. The parent speech formed active and middle participles to eventive STEMS. Thus, since they are built to the same stem, the present and imperfect tenses do not form separate participles; but every primary and secondary stem—causative, desiderative, and the rest—might have its own participle:

1. Active participles, formed with the suffix **-ont-/-n̥t-*, whose formation is discussed in detail in 554-6. This is very widely attested in IE languages, including Hitt.; its absence from Celtic, where it is attested only in non-verbal forms (for example *car(a)e*^{H} /kaρe/ 'friend'), is striking.

2. Middle participles, formed with the suffixes **-meno-*, **-mno-* (560), simple thematics. They are much less widely attested than the active participles, being wholly absent in Celtic, Slavic, and Germanic, and the formation is found in Italic and Anatolian only in fugitive and disputed remnants.

a. Infinitives (551-3) did not exist as such in PIE, nor gerunds. Nomina actionis based on roots belonging to a number of different stems could enter into a variety of relationships with other nouns (as in NE *his departure for France* or *the expectation of arrival* and so on). But as in the case of English nomina actionis, as exemplified by *reject, rejection*; *expect, expectation*; *respect, respect*; *conflict, cónflict*, and so on, there was to begin with no paradigmatic system.

PERSONAL ENDINGS OF THE EVENTIVE VERB

419. The personal endings that are common to several verb categories are for convenience discussed in advance of the treatment of tense stem formations in G and L.

The two sets of endings traditionally known as *primary* and *secondary* are so called from their distribution (clearest in InIr., G, and Hitt., but discernable in Gmc. and Ital.). Primary endings occur in the present and future indicative; secondary endings occur in the preterital tenses and the optative, with fluctuation in the subjunctive. The terms themselves indicate that the primary endings were imagined by G grammarians to be somehow basic, the secondary endings somehow derived from them or otherwise subordinate. Unhappily, this is backwards: the 'secondary' endings of traditional grammar are in fact BASIC, what linguists call *primary*; and the 'primary' endings are DERIVED FROM the 'secondary' (basic) forms by the addition of one or another present-time marker. That is, they are what linguists would normally call *secondary*.

It may strike a speaker of a modern European language as perplexing that the forms proper to the present indicative would be derived from forms proper to past action or unreal action, but that is the situation not only in PIE but in a large number of the world's languages. A correct appreciation of the relationship of the two sets of endings explains why the optative is marked with 'past tense endings': the endings in question were not specifically past tense, rather they are the GENERIC or UNMARKED endings. It also explains their role in the so-called injunctive forms, **416**, which are not past tense forms but tenseless ones.

420. TABLE OF THE ACTIVE PERSONAL ENDINGS

A. *Secondary*

	PIE	Ved.	Av.	Hitt.	G	OL	Go.	OCS	Lith.
1sg.	-m	-m	-m	-nun	-ν	-m	-∅		-u
	-m̥	-am	-am	-un	-α		-u	-ŭ	-mi
2	-s	-s	-s	-š	-ς	-s	-s	-∅	-si
3	-t	-t	-t	-t	-∅	-d	-∅	-∅	-∅
1du.	-wĕ̄	-vā̆	-va	—	—	—	-u, -wa	-vě	-va
2	-tom	-tam	?	—	-τον	—	-ts	-ta	-ta
3	-tām	-tām	-təm	—	-τᾱν	—	—	-te, -ta	—
1pl.	-mĕ̄	-mā̆	-ma	-wen	-μεν	*-mos	-m(a)	-mŭ	-me
2	-te	-ta(na)	-ta	-ten	-τε	*-tes?	-þ	-te	-te
3	-nt	-n(t)	-n		-ν	-nt	-n(a)	[+ nas]	—
	-n̥t	-at	-at						
	-r̥	-ur							
	-ēr			-er		-ēre			

B. *Primary*

	PIE	Ved.	Av.	Hitt.	G	OL	Go.	OCS	Lith.
1sg.	-oH_2	-āmi	-ā(mi)		-ω	-ō	-a	-ǫ	-u
	-mi	-mi	-mi	-mi	-μι	-m	-m	-mĭ	-mi
2	-si	-si, -ṣi	-hi, -ši	-ši	-ς	-s	-s	-si, -šĭ	-si
					-εις				
3	-ti	-ti	-ti	-zi	-τι	-t	-t/þ	-tŭ	
	-i				-ι			-∅	-∅
1du.	-wos	-vas	-vaihi	—	—	—	-os	-vě	-va
2	-tH_1es	-thas	?	—	-τον	—	-ts	-ta	-ta
3	-tes	-tas	-tō	—	-τον	—	—	-te, -ta	—
1pl.	-mos	-mas(i)	-maihi	-weni	-μες	*-mos	-m	-mŭ	-me
2	-te	-tha(na)	-θa	-teni	-τε	*-tes?	-þ	-te	-te
3	-nti	-nti	-nti	-(a)nzi	-ντι	-nt	-nd	-[+ nas]tŭ	—
	-n̥ti	-ati	-aiti		*-ατι				

A dash in a column means that the CATEGORY is missing in the language; for example, there is no 3rd person dual in Go. (two subjects construe with a 3pl. verb). A zero (∅) means that the category is morphologically unmarked ('endingless'). A question mark means that the form is presumed to have existed, but is unattested.

The two rows of forms for the 1sg endings are for thematic and athematic, in that order.

The notation [+ nas] in the OCS column means that the ending includes different preceding vowels which are always nasalized.

The 3pl. forms are explained in the text.

421. Most of the primary endings consist of the secondary ending plus a following element. This is *-*i* for the singular endings and the 3pl. In the case of the 1pl., *-*s* is added to the *o*-grade of an element which is *-*me* in thematic stems, *-*mé* in athematic ones. Evidence for the 1du. is scanty, but indicates 1du. *-*we*, *-*wos*, parallel to the 1pl. The marker *-*s* does not mark 'plural'—it is found on several duals; it marks rather 'real present' or the like.

There is no formal distinction between primary and secondary endings of the 2pl.

The makeup of neither the 2,3du. secondary nor the corresponding primary endings is confidently known. The 2,3du. primary appear to be derived with the same *-*s* as the 1du. and 1pl., though most of the morphology is unexplained. As will be seen (432-3, 435-8), in the MIDDLE the primary endings are differently derived from the secondary, but agree in certain broad ways.

422. THEMATIC present and imperfect indicative active. Illustrative sample paradigms:

Present:

	PIE	Vedic	G	L	Go.	OCS	Hittite
sg.							
1	bheroH$_2$[1]	bhárāmi[1] (Av. spasyā[5])	φέρω[1]	legō[2]	baira[1]	nesǫ[3]	pí-eš-ki-mi[4]
2	bheresi	váhasi[6]	φέρεις	legis	bairis	neseši	pí-iš-ki-ši
3	bhereti	bhárati		legit	bairiþ	nesetŭ	pí-eš-ki-iz-zi
	bherei		φέρει			nese	
du.							
1	bherowos	cárāvas[7] (AV)			bairos	nesevě	
2	bheretH$_1$es	bhárathas	φέρετον		bairats	neseta	
3	bheretes	váhatas	φέρετον			nesete, -ta	
pl.							
1	bheromos	bharāmasi cárāmas	φέρομεν φέρομες	legimus	bairam	nesemŭ	pí-eš-ga-u-e-ni
2	bherete	bháratha vádathana[8]	φέρετε	legitis	bairiþ	nesete	pí-eš-kit$_9$-te-ni
3	bheronti	bháranti	φέρουσι Dor. φέροντι	legunt	bairand	nesǫtŭ	pí-eš-kán-zi

1. 'Carry', PIE **bher-*.
2. 'Gather', PIE **leg-*; for the L reflex of **bhereti* see (485).
3. 'Carry', PIE **H₁nek-*.
4. Iterative-frequentative 'am giving', something like /peskimi/ < **payskemi*, the -*šk*- derivative of *pa-a-i* 'gives'.
5. 'I see', like L *speciō*, an example of the inherited type in Av. (where also -*aimi*, corresponding to the Indic form, is common).
6. 'Convey', PIE **weǵh-*.
7. 'We two wander'; PIE **kʷel-*.
8. 'You speak', PIE **wed-* or **H₂wed-*.

		PIE	Vedic	Greek	Hittite
Imperfect	1*sg.*	ebherom	abharam	ἔφερον	ak-ku-uš-ki-nu-un[1]
	2	ebheres	ábharas	ἔφερες	i-ya-aš, i-ya-at[2]
	3	ebheret	abharat	ἔφερε?	pí-eš-ki-it
		ebhere		ἔφερε?	
	1*du.*	ebherowe	vr̥heva[3]		
	2	ebheretom	ábhavatam	ἐφέρετον	
	3	ebheretām	ábhavatām	ἐφερέτην	
				ἐφερέτᾱν	
	1*pl.*	ebherome	ábharāma	ἐφέρομεν	i-ya-u-en
	2	ebherete	ábhavata	ἐφέρετε	pí-eš-kit$_9$-tin
	3	ebheront	ábharan	ἔφερον	pí-eš-kir

There is no trace of the PIE Imperfect in Latin; see **498**.

1. 'I was drinking', /ak^{w}skinun/ or the like.
2. 'You went'. The ending *-š* is inherited.
3. (With preverb *vi-*) 'may we two tear to bits', 1du.opt. of *vr̥hati.* (This is the only 1du. thematic verb form in the RV with a secondary ending.)

423. ATHEMATIC present and imperfect indicative active. Examples:

A. Root inflection: **ey-* 'go'

		PIE	Vedic	Greek	Latin	Hittite[1]
Present:	1*sg.*	éymi	émi	εἶμι	eō	e-ip-mi
	2	éysi	éṣi	εἶ	īs	e-ip-ši, e-ip-ti
	3	éyti	éti	εἶσι	it	e-ip-zi
					OL īt	
	1*pl.*	imós	imás(i)	ἴμεν	īmus	ip-pu-u-e-ni
	2	ité	ithá	ἴτε	ītis	e-ip-te-(e-)ni
	3	yonti	yanti?		eunt	ap-pa-(a-)an-zi
		yenti	yánti?			
				ἴᾱσι		
				ἶσι (rare)		
Imperfect:[2]	1*sg.*	eeym̥	ā́yam	ἦια, ἤιειν		e-ip-pu-(u-)un
	2	eeys	ā́is (AV)	ἤιεισθα, ἤιεις		e-ip-ta
	3	eeyt	ā́it	ἦιε (Hom.)		e-ip-ta
				ἦιει(ν) (Att.)		
	1*pl.*	eyme	atakṣma[3]	ἦιμεν		e-ip-pu-en[4]
	2	eyte	ā́itana	ἦιτε		e-ip-tin
	3	eyent	ā́yan?			
		eyont	āyan?	ἤι(ε)σαν *etc.*		
		eyēr				e-ip-pí-ir

1. Athem. verb *ep-/ap-* 'take'. (The Hitt. verb corresponding to Ved. *émi* is a stem *i-ya-* which is furthermore deponent.) The distribution of grades (*e*-grade in all forms except the 3pl. as well as some non-finite forms, such as the pple. *ap-pa-an-za*) is the most typical of several patterns. PIE **eH₁p-*/**H₁p-*; cf. Ved. *āp-*, G ἅπτω (perhaps), L *apīscor.*
2. No Latin forms reflect the PIE imperf.
3. 'We fashioned' (pres. *tákṣati* 3pl.). The form for 'we went', *ā́ima*, occurs in the later language.
4. Once *a-ap-pu-en.*

B. Reduplicated inflection: *dhe-dheH$_1$- 'put'

		PIE	Vedic	Greek
Present:	1*sg.*	dhedheH$_1$mi	dádhāmi	τίθημι[1]
	2	dhedheH$_1$si	dádhāsi	τίθης
	3	dhedheH$_1$ti	dádhāti	τίθητι (Dor.)
				τίθησι (Att.-Ion.)
	1*pl.*	dhedhH̥$_1$mos	dadhmási[2]	τίθεμεν, -μες
	2	dhedhH̥$_1$te	dhatthá[2]	τίθετε
	3	dhedhH$_1$n̥ti	dádhati[3]	τίθεντι (Dor.)
				τιθέᾱσι (Att.)
Imperfect:	1*sg.*	edhedheH$_1$m	adadhām	ἐτίθην
	2	edhedheH$_1$s	ádadhās	ἐτίθης (Hom.), ἐτίθεις
	3	edhedheH$_1$t	ádadhāt	ἐτίθη (Hom.), ἐτίθει
	1*pl.*	edhedhH̥$_1$me	*Note 4*	ἐτίθεμεν
	2	edhedhH̥$_1$te	ádatta	ἐτίθετε
	3	edhedhH$_1$r̥[5]	adadhur	
		edhedhH$_1$n̥t?		ἔτιθεν (Dor.)
				ἐτίθεσαν (Att.-Ion.)

1. With change of the reduplicating vowel to -ι-, **443.2A**.
2. The Indic deletion of *-i-* < *-H̥- in the reduplicated presents is an innovation already well under way in the RV; the expected development is seen in, say, *dadhidhvé* 2pl.midd. In the perfect, contrariwise, the ending *-ima*, originally found in seṭ roots, is generalized. Note that this criss-cross leveling is found in the form in which the ending LEAST distinguishes the redup. present from the perf.: inherited *dadhima* 1pl. could be either (augmentless) imperf. or perf. After the levelings, *dadhima* became unambiguously perf., *dadhma* unambiguously imperf. (In non-laryngeal roots the ambiguities remained: *juhuma* 'pour' could be either imperf. or perf.)
3. Zero grade is typical for the 3pl. of the reduplicated class but is occasionally found in other classes, as *tákṣati* 'they fashion' (**423A** note 3).
4. The 1pl. imperf. of the reduplicated class is not attested in the RV. For this paradigm it would be *adadhma*.
5. The 3pl. imperf. *-ur* is usually taken as an innovation, but see **429**. —The RV attests one nasal form, *abibhran* 'they were carrying' (pres. *bíbhrati*) instead of the expected *abibhrat**.

C. *new*-suffix: *r̥-new- (or *H$_3$r̥-new-) 'rise'

Present	PIE	Vedic	Greek	Hittite
1*sg.*	r̥newmi	r̥n̥omi	ὄρνῡμι	ar-nu-mi
2	r̥newsi	tanoṣi[1]	ὄρνῡς	ar-nu-ši, -ut-ti
3	r̥newti	r̥n̥oti	ὄρνῡσι	ar-nu-(uz-)zi
1*pl.*	r̥numos	tanmasi[2]	ὄρνυμεν	ar-nu-um-me-ni[3]
2	r̥nute	aśnutha[4]	ὄρνυτε	ar-nu-ut-te-ni
3	r̥nwenti	r̥n̥vánti?	Dor. -νυντι, Att. -νύᾱσι	
	r̥nwonti	r̥n̥vanti?	Hom. -νυουσι	(a-)ar-nu-(wa-)an-zi
		r̥n̥vati?		

The notes and the paradigms of the imperfect are on the following page.

Imperfect:	PIE	Vedic		Greek	Hittite
1*sg.*	r̥newm̥[5]	kr̥ṇavam[6]		ὤρνῡν	ar-nu-nu-un
2	r̥news	ákr̥ṇos		ὤρνῡς	pa-aḫ-ḫa-aš-ša-nu-ut[7]
3	r̥newt	ákr̥ṇot		ὤρνῡ	ar-nu-ut
			Hom.	ὤρνυε	
1*pl.*	r̥nume	*Note 8*		ὤρνυμεν	wa-aḫ-nu-um-me-en[9]
2	r̥nute	akr̥ṇuta		ὤρνυτε	
		akr̥ṇota(na)[10]			ar-nu-ut-tin
3	r̥nwent	ákr̥ṇvan?			
	r̥nwont	ákr̥ṇvan?	Hom.	ὤρνυον	ar-nu-e-ir
			Att.-Ion.	ὤρνυσαν	
				ὤρνυν	

1. 'Stretch', PIE *_tn̥-new-si_, root *_ten-_.
2. The expected endings *_-umasi_ act., *_-umahe_ midd. do not occur; the _u_-less endings are probably by analogy with redup. _dadhmasi_ (**423B** note 2).
3. After _-u-_ the ending _-men(i)_ in place of usual _-wen(i)_ is regular in Hitt. The significance of the highly consistent double consonant writing (_-um-me-ni_, as here) is unclear.
4. 'Attain' < *_H$_1$n̥k-nu-_, root *_H$_1$neḱ-_.
5. The forms are quoted here without the augment. (The history of the augmented forms in the daughter languages can be framed only in terms of specific reconstructions: the developments which start from *_e-H$_3$r̥-new-_ will be quite different from those which start from *_e-r-new-_ or *_e-r̥-new-_.
6. There are remarkably few Rigvedic imperfects built to this stem class, even to well-attested present stems. The only nearly complete paradigm is to this verb, _kr̥ṇóti_ 'makes', PIE *_k^{w}er-_, which has no cognates in G or L.
7. That is, /pahsnut/ 'you protected'.
8. There are no 1pl. forms in the RV; if it occurred, the 1pl. would probably be _ákr̥ṇuma_*.
9. 'We turned' (transitive).
10. The full grade stem in a pl. form is remarkable.

ENDINGS

424. FIRST PERSON SINGULAR. *Secondary ending:* *_-m_ after vowels, *_-m̥_ after cons.; L _-m_, G _-ν_, _-α_. In Hom. ἦα 'I was' imperf. < *_e-H$_1$esm̥_) and in G generally in the aor., as ἔλῡσα. In Ved. _ā́sam_ athem. 'I was', for example, there is the question of whether _-am_ rather than _-a_ is regular from *_-m̥_ in final position, or imported from thematic imperfects like _abharam_ 'I carried' < *_e-bher-o-m_, and aorists like _avocam_ 'I said' < *_e-we-wk^w-o-m_. (A regular development seems more likely. If the spread of _-m_ was analogical, it is hard to understand how it could have passed over the perf. 1sg. in _-a_ < *_-H$_2$e_.) G ἐτίθην 'I put' < *_-dheH$_1$-m̥_, like the acc. of _eH$_2$_-stems (**263.3a**), shows no evidence of a syllabic nasal, though some laryngealists would trace -θην to PG *_-t^{h}e-en_, with *_-en_ < *_-H$_1$m̥_ (**100a**).

Primary ending: *_-mi_ in athematic forms; *_-oH$_2$_ (traditionally *_-ō_) in thematic, where *_-o-_ is the thematic vowel, _-H$_2$_ the person marker. So G εἰμί, τίθημι but φέρω, λέγω. In InIr. the _-mi_ was extended to the thematic type, being added to the original ending in *-ā* < **-oH₂*. This process is complete in the earliest known Indic, but still in progress in Avestan, where *-ā* and *-āmi* occur side by side. In OCS and Lith. the old primary ending is found in very few verbs, such as OCS *esmĭ* 'I am', *damĭ* 'I give' (where the ending is conservative) and *věmĭ* 'I know' < **woydmi* (an eventive ending on a stative stem; *vědě*, a more conservative form, is also attested, **512**). The nasal vowel originally proper to the secondary paradigms, PIE **-om*, was generalized to the thematic presents, exemplified by *nesǫ*; this presupposes **-ō-m* (cf. the *ā*-stem acc.sg. *ženǫ* **262**) which reveals its thematic primary-ending basis. In Gmc. the only remnant of the athematic ending is in the verb 'be', PGmc. **emm* < **H₁esmi* (Go. *im*, OE *eom*, less directly OHG *bim*) 'I am'. In L *-mi* is not unambiguously represented but it is probably seen in *sum* (**492**), where it shows the usual loss of primary *-i* (**74.2**). Some feel that the *-m* of *sum* is the secondary ending, though in view of the general L tendency to replace secondary endings with primary ones, such an interpretation is no more likely than necessary. In *inquam* 'indeed', by contrast, we might have the secondary ending appropriate to the optative, the form being etymologically **en-skʷ-ām* 'I might say', root **sekʷ-*. For iambic shortening in *volo* 'wish', *nescio* 'not know' (influenced by *scĭŏ*), and the spread of short *-o*, see **84**.

a. The primary ending in the G them. opt., as in φέροιμι, is not a reflex of the original formation with its secondary ending, **-oy(H₁)m̥*; neither is the rare -οιν (as in τρέφοιν Eur.), nor even the epigraphic -OIA (Arc. εξελαυνοια 'I would drive out', arguably the single most famous verb form in G). The usual form, -οιμι, is an importation of the primary ending bodily; -οιν and -οια are genuine secondary forms of the ending, but added to a stem whose form is influenced by 2sg. -οις, 3sg. -οι. The unaltered reflex of the etymon would have been **-oya*, later **-oa*, and finally *φέρω homophonous with the indicative. See also **541**, especially **b**.

425. SECOND PERSON SINGULAR. *Secondary *-s* is unambiguously attested in Ved. *ábharas* 'you carried', *adās* aor. 'you gave', G imperf. ἔφερες, ἐδείκνῡς, ἐδίδως. Likewise L *erās*, historically an opt., **539.3** (cf. Go. *nimais* opt. 'may you take' < **-oys*, **539.2**). In Hitt. this ending is seen only in thematic preterites (as in *da-aš-ki-eš* 'you used to take'), and not regularly even there. Usually the Hitt. 2sg.pret. is indistinguishable from the 3sg.pret., as in *pí-eš-ki-it* 'you/he used to give', and this is uniformly the case in the athematic type: *e-eš-ta* (/est/; the *-a* is a dummy, **31**) 'you were', just like *e-eš-ta* 'he was'.

The *primary endings* are attested in Hitt. *-ši*, InIr. **-si* (Ved. *-si*, *-ṣi*, Av. *-hi*, *-ši*), and Lith. *-si*. OCS *-ši* is enigmatic, as the vowel points to **-ī* or a diphthong. The Gmc. ending (as in Go. *-s*) is ambiguous, but on the evidence of the unambiguous 3rd persons, q.v., it is economical to assume that the regular Gmc. loss of final short vowels resulted in homophony between the primary and secondary forms.

The WGmc. form *-st* (for example OE *þú berist* 'thou bearest') arose early but became general only within the historical period. It is usually explained as a metanalysis of the enclitic pronoun as in **beristū* 'you carry' (next to **þū beris*), but metanalysis requires structural ambiguity and there is none in **beristū*. The 2sg. ending *-st* was phonologically regular in the statives whose roots ended in apical stops, **þū waist* 'you know', **þū mōst* 'you may'; in THESE forms the enclitics **waistū*, **mōstū* were ambiguous, and from here they spread.

The expected forms in G would have lost the *-*s*- intervocalically, leading first to *φερει < *-*esi* and *δεικνῡι (or *-νευι < *-*newsi*), *τιθηι, *διδωι, and so on. In all cases the sibilant has been restored, reimported from the secondary endings where it survived because it was final. There is a discrepancy between the thematic and athematic types in the way this remodeling was carried out. The -ς was simply added to the inherited form in the thematic type, thus *φερει → φέρεις (a genuine diphthong, as revealed in Aeolic), but the secondary shape was taken over whole in the athematic types: -ῡς, -ης, -ως rather than ˣ-ῡις, ˣ-ηις, ˣ-ωις. This paradox is resolved under 3sg., **426**.

Ital. -*s*, on the unambiguous evidence from the *i*-less forms of Sab. in the 3rd persons, is from *-*si*, with loss of the final *-*i*. This loss is seen even in very short forms, like *es* 'you are' (Plautine scansion guarantees *ess*) < **essi* and *vel* 'or' < **well* < **wels* < **welsi* 'you wish'.

a. An original 2sg. primary form continues unaltered in Att.-Ion. εἶ 'you are' < **esi* (= Ved. *ási*, Av. *ahi*); it incidentally shows the PIE treatment of long consonants (apart from a sequence of two apicals, 212) arising in morpheme sequences. But an odd shape is always liable to therapeutic recomposition, which is exactly what leads to Hom. ἐσσί. Ironically, this form, a product of analogical remodeling, preserves the only instance of unaltered 2sg. *-*si* in G. (It must date from a very early period, prior to the regular G phonetic changes in **s*, 172, 227.2. And that also means that ἐσσί and ἐ(*h*)ί existed side by side for a surprisingly long time.)

b. Homeric forms like διδοῖς 'you give' could be coinages in imitation of φέρεις, or they could be the Osthoff reflex (63.2) of **didōys* ← **didō(h)i* < **didōsi* (if **didōys* took shape early enough). Either way, they hint that a 2sg. like **didōy* was in the air. —The loss of -*s*- between vowels obviously created special problems in the 2sg., as is revealed by other neologisms in Hom.: διδοῖσθα 'you give' and, slightly differently arrived-at, τίθησθα 'you put' and φῆσθα 'you say'; the ending -σθα is imported from the perf., 514.2. Somewhat later there is still evidence of flux, as attested by such forms as ἀμέλγες 'you milk' and συρίσδες 'you whistle' (Theocritus). These seem to be licensed by the same patterns that led to δίδως, τίθης, and the like, though taking shape much later.

426. Third person singular. The *secondary* *-*t* is attested as such in InIr.[1] and Hitt. In most IE languages, a final stop is lost: Go. *bairai* 'would carry', OCS *moli* aor. 'begged' (cf. pres. *bairiþ*, *molitŭ*). G is in this group

[1] Ved. *ā́s* 'was' 3sg. imperf., and similar athem. imperfects, lose the *-*t* through the regular truncation of consonants—any consonants—in a word-final cluster.

(**236.1**): ἔφερε, Hom. ἐδίδω, ἐδείκνῡ, as well as ἦς 'he was' < *e-H_1s-t. This ἦς, preserved in most dial., was replaced in Att.-Ion. by ἦν, originally the 3pl. (**493B**). It is possible that the thematic forms, or some of them anyway, were *t*-less to start with in G (below), such that the thematic and athematic types merely became more alike when for example **edidōt* > ἐδίδω. In Ital., final *-*t* became *-*d* which in U dropped altogether. So O **kúmbened** perf., **fakiiad** pres.subj.; U **dede**, O **deded** perf. 'gave', U **kuraia** subj. 'let him take care of' (cf. U **tiśit** 'it is proper' = L *decet*); OL SIED subj., FECED perf. (originally aor.). (The Praenestine FHE⁝FHAKED would be an example if it were not a forger's creation, **19**.) Subsequent to the very oldest epigraphic attestations, in all tenses and moods in L the primary ending -*t* < *-*ti* displaced inherited -*d* < *-*t*.

The *primary ending* *-*ti* is attested as such in InIr.; in Hitt., the stop was affricated before the vowel, hence *ku-en-zi* /gwentsi/ 'he slays' < *g^w*henti* (= Ved. *hánti*), *e-eš-zi* /estsi/ 'he is' < *H_1*esti* (**31**). Even though the final vowel is lost in Gmc. and Ital., some such underlying form neatly accounts for the distinction between Go. *bairiþ* 'carries' and *bairai* 'would carry' (PGmc. **beriþ* and **berai*, respectively, < PIE **bhereti* and **bheroyt*) and Ital. primary -*t* vs. secondary -*d*. OCS -*tŭ* is unexpected for *-*tĭ*.

T-LESS THIRD PERSON SINGULAR ENDINGS. OCS -*tŭ* (above) is a fixed part of the paradigm only in the athem. stems (which are few), while in thematic paradigms it is optional—though present about three quarters of the time. In Baltic, the stop is found in thematic inflection only in a small number of Old Lith. forms (since lost), and uniquely in modern Latv. *iêt* 'goes'. This suggests that OCS and the Baltic languages were evolving in different directions from a system in which endingless thematics were commoner than they are in OCS.

In Greek, *-*ti* is attested as expected in the athem. types, thus ἐστί 'is', φησί 'speaks', δίδωσι 'gives', τίθησι 'puts' (Dor. φᾱτί and φᾱσί, δίδωτι, τίθητι), all straightforwardly (**148.3**) from PIE *H_1*esti*, **bheH*$_2$*ti*, **dedeH*$_3$*ti*, **dhedheH*$_1$*ti*. The outcomes for the thematic forms, as usually reconstructed, should have been like this:

	PIE		Proto-Greek		Greek	
	primary	*secondary*	*primary*	*secondary*	*primary*	*secondary*
2sg.	*bheresi	*ebheres	*p^herehi	*ep^heres	ˣφερει	ἐφερες
3sg.	*bhereti	*ebheret	*p^hereti	*ep^here	ˣφερεσι	ἐφερε
				Actually attested:	φερεις	ἐφερες
					φερει	ἐφερε

Now, φέρει obviously does not reflect PIE **bhereti*. The explanation which has been standard for generations is that φέρει results from analogy, namely the interplay between primary and secondary forms of the 2nd. and 3rd. persons. The 2sg. primary looks like the secondary plus -ι-, so: ἔφερες :

φέρεις :: ἔφερε : *X*, where *X* = φέρει. Although it is an impeccable proportion, there are three weaknesses in this view. First, the pivotal form φέρεις is itself the result of an analogy, and the usually-cited pattern form for that analogy, τίθης 2sg. pres., is not only ITSELF analogical but is not easy to account for. Second (a stronger objection), in analogical restructurings of verbs it is prevailingly the 3sg. forms that are pivotal. And last, a very serious objection, it is incomprehensible that the athematic types, which inherited exactly the same pattern, failed to undergo the same remodeling of either the 2sg. or the 3sg.

A likelier explanation is that the 3sg. athematic and thematic types were in fact different from an early period, that is, that G started with a system similar to that in BS: primary **-ti* in athematic paradigms, but *t*-less **-i* (at least optionally) in thematic ones:

	PIE		Proto-Greek	
	primary	*secondary*	*primary*	*secondary*
2sg.	*bheresi	*ebheres	*pʰerehi	*epʰeres
3sg.	*bherey	*ebhere(t?)	*pʰerei	*epʰere

Such an analysis has four benefits. First, motivation: with the loss of **h* in 2sg. **-ehi* < **-esi*, the 3sg. and 2sg. primary forms were homophonous, reason enough for touching up the endings. Second, an appeal to analogical remodeling is necessary for only a single form (2sg. prim. -εις). Third, it provides a flawless analogical source entirely within the thematic system for this remodeling: the solution for *X*, given ἐφερε : φερει :: ἐφερες : *X*, would be φέρεις. The trouble with assuming instead that the inherited primary **pʰerei* < **bheresi* was simply 'refreshed' with the *-s* of the secondary ending is that such a process cuts the ground from under the fourth and most important point: if φερει was the original form of the 3sg. primary and the basis for the thematic 2sg. primary, the reason why the thematic and athematic 2sg. developed differently is easy to see—ἐδιδω : διδωτι :: ἐδιδως : *X* is not a proportion; there is, in effect, no solution for *X* except possibly ˣδιδωστι. (Exactly how, in the athematic types, the secondary 2sg. ending pure and simple came to be used in primary paradigms remains unclear. There are proportions that work formally, as ἐφερει (3sg.imperf.) : φερεις (2sg.pres.) :: ἐδιδω : *X*, where *X* = διδως. But influence by the 3sg. secondary on the 2sg. primary seems functionally improbable for Greek.)

a. The evidence for the original distribution of *t*-less 3rd person forms is conflicting. BS as seen above points to a division along thematic/athematic lines, sharper in Baltic than in OCS, and that accords with the G evidence (if only vaguely). But it is unlikely that ALL thematic verbs were thus *t*-less, however, as if that were the case the *t*-less inflection must surely be more generally attested.

Ved. attests *t*-less 3sg. forms built to some fifteen stems, but only in the MIDDLE; and, confusingly, they are exclusively ATHEMATIC: *duhé* 'gives milk' < **dhugh-oy*, *śáye* 'is lying down' < **k̂ey-oy*. (The imperf. *áśayat*, apparently but inappropriately act., is actually a papering-over of midd. **áśaya* < **e-k̑ey-o*, see 436.3). There appear to be *t*-less middles in Sab. as well, for example U *ferar* (? < **fera-or* 3sg. subj.).

Hitt. has only *-zi* and *-t* in the active, but parallel to InIr. has middle forms in both *-ta(ri)* and *-a(ri)*: *ar-ta(-ri)* 'he takes his stand', *u-wa-it-ta(-ri)* 'he appears', but *e-ša(-ri)* 'he sits', *ne-i-ya(-a-ri)* 'he turns'. In the middle, G has only forms WITH *-τ-*, as *κεῖται* (= Av. *saēte* and Skt. *śéte*—Vedic, but not yet in the RV, which has only *śáye*). Hitt. agrees with G rather than the RV: *ki-it-ta(-ri)* 'is lying down'. In fact, there is not a single instance of lexical agreement between InIr. and Hitt. on *t*-less 3rd person forms. Nothing emerges from this hubbub except the fact of the existence of *t*-less 3sg. forms.

427. FIRST PERSON PLURAL. 1pl. verbs, common in normal discourse, are rare in most kinds of ancient text—epitaphs, chronicles, epics, tax receipts, and so on. There are no attestations at all in Sab., or in Myc.; and in the RV there are fewer than 130 1pl. verbs altogether. Accordingly, the early history of this form is less well charted than most other endings.

The distinction between the primary and secondary endings in the 1sg. is not paralleled in the plural. But there has been much leveling in the daughter languages, so that any theory of the original distribution is necessarily based on some subset of the available facts. The view endorsed here is that the secondary ending was **-me*, the primary was **-mos*, *o*-grade of the former and with **-s* as the marker of primariness which is seen in several du. forms as well. Latin, with its tendency to generalize the primary endings, has only *-mus* < **-mos*. The uniform *-mŭ* of OCS has the same explanation. The leveling in favor of *-me* in Lith. is easy to explain, as it is partly due to the attraction of the 2pl., which is **-te* for both primary and secondary (428), and the same influence was probably at work in the history of G. (It is a cause for wonder that the influence of **-te* was not more general.) OIr. forms of the 1pl. are many and problematical, but the primary ending /-μi/ (in, say, *mór-m(a)i* 'we magnify') has a neutral *-m-* rather than a palatalized one, indicating **-mo-*; Toch. *-mäs* likewise reflects **-mos*. Germanic appears to have generalized the secondary ending along the same lines as Lith.: PIE **bherome* would give Go. *bairam* as attested, whereas **bheromos* or **bheromes* should give ˣ*bairams*.

InIr. preserves the original distinction between secondary *-ma* and primary *-mas*, with two peculiarities. First, in the RV there are a number of instances, no more than 5 percent of the total, where the eventive ending scans *-mā*. This occurs more frequently in later texts than in earlier; it is an import from stative *-mā* (514.1) and a pseudoarchaism. Second, in PInIr. the already primary **-mas* was optionally embellished with the primary marker **-i* of the sg. endings and the 3pl., thus **-masi*. The reflex of this, *-maihi*, is the only form of the 1pl. primary ending in Av. In the RV, however, both *-masi* and *-mas* occur; *-masi* greatly preponderates—the ratio is six to one—but by the AV *-masi* makes up less than half the total, and by Epic Skt. there is no trace of the once dominant *-masi*.

No G dialect distinguishes between primary and secondary endings in the 1pl. The uniform ending is -μες in Dor. and WG, -μεν elsewhere. The former appears to be a composite of the primary and secondary forms (though some authorities trace it directly to a PIE prim. *-*mes*). The -ν of -μεν has usually been assumed to be a case of ν-movable (240) attached to *-με = Ved. -*ma*. But in fact the -ν is not particularly movable, and is better taken as part of the ending ab origine. Latterly, Hitt. has shed some light on this: Hitt. 1pl.prim. -*weni*, sec. -*wen* appears to be the same kind of thing as G -μεν; the additional element will be discussed together with the 2pl. endings, 428. (The Hitt. variants -*meni* and -*men* occur after *u*, and are a development from **w* rather than inherited.) Parenthetically, the Hitt. forms of the 1pl. middle (437.1), -*waštat(i)*, suggest that the regular active forms of Hitt., -*wen*/-*weni* replace endings more like the InIr. paradigm, namely *-*we* secondary, *-*waš* primary.

a. Another opinion traces G -μεν and the Ved. alternative -*mā* to PIE *-*mem*, originally the secondary ending, with the same *-*m* as seen in some secondary endings of the dual. The development of *-*mem* to Ved. -*mā* is questionable; note that the *-*m* of the duals survives unchanged. (Its loss in -*mā* is tepidly explained as somehow dissimilatory.) Taking -*mā* as a relic accords ill with the pattern of attestation mentioned above. Besides, tracing Ved. -*mā* to prim. *-*mem* does not shed any light on why it is chiefly characteristic of stative forms (513, 514.1), where the contrast between primary and secondary endings was nonexistent.

428. SECOND PERSON PLURAL. The InIr. distinction between primary *-*tha* and secondary *-*ta* (Ved. -*tha* and -*ta*, Av. -*θa*, -*ta*) is thought not to be original, but to have been imported from the du. where, however, the facts are not much clearer. Much more ancient is the occasional addition in Vedic of an element -*na* (so written, but evidently to be scanned -*nā*). The enlarged form makes up about one fifth of the total; with one (very late) exception it is found only in athematic paradigms.

Before the discovery of Hitt., the enlarged forms of Indic were a mere curiosity, but Hitt. 2pl. -*ten* pret., -*teni* pres., is the same formation. The details are obscure: Hitt. pret. -*ten* 2pl., -*wen* 1pl. might always have been vowelless, or have lost a final short vowel by apocope; pres. -*teni* and -*weni* could come either from *-*tene-i*, *-*wene-i* (or *-*teno-i*, *-*weno-i*), or—least likely—from *-*teni*, *-*weni*; all would be the secondary ending, whichever that actually was, enlarged by the primary marker -*i*, which spread widely in the Hitt. present tense beyond its original situs.

To sum up, the most archaic Indic attests an optional element -*nā̆*, limited to the 2pl. (both primary and secondary) of athematic stems; G attests a nasal element, limited to the 1pl. and optional in the sense that some dialect groups have only -μεν (all stem types) while others have only -μες. Hitt. attests an obligatory element, pres. *-*nV*, pret. -*n*, found on both 1pl. and 2pl. verbs of all conjugations. These facts are not notably coherent, but it is hard to understand how the 1pl. could have had two different primary forms ab origine. Even Hitt., via 1pl.midd. -*wašta* (437.1), corroborates a 1pl.prim. in *-*s*. Hitt. also shows that it is possible for the element to spread from the 2pl. to the 1pl., though its attestation in G ONLY in the 1pl. is troubling. So is the truncation of *-*νε* to -*ν*.

Of the explanations that have been offered for the history of Latin -*tis* 2pl., there are two chief contenders.

(1) The ending is the old 2du., *-*tH₁es*, PItal. *-*tes*, relocated in the system as a plural. The reassignment of a dual to plural function is unremarkable; it has happened wholesale in the case of modern Icelandic. The chief weakness with the explanation is that one might expect such a reassignment in the 1st person; or in both 1st and 2nd; but not in the 2nd person alone.

(2) The formation dates to a time after the loss of the final vowel in the 2sg. primary but before the weakening of short vowels in medial and final syllables (65–75); an analogical interplay arose between indicative and imperative as follows: *lege* : *leges* :: *legete* : *X*, where *X* = *legetes* (coincidentally identical in form with the old 2du.). The action of later sound laws results in the usual forms *legis*, *legite* imper., and *legitis*.

The second explanation has won general acceptance, but it suffers from a number of weaknesses. One problem is the dubiousness of the very idea of an imperative providing the fulcrum for the remodeling of an indicative. The strongest reason, though, for taking (1) as the correct history is that the 2pl. ending of OIr. also points to *-*tes*;[1] this is unlikely to be an independent development, and if that view is correct, would qualify as a shared Italo-Celtic innovation—which must considerably predate the loss of final vowels in Italic.

429. THIRD PERSON PLURAL. In both PIE and the daughter languages there is more complexity in the history of the 3pl. than in all the rest of the endings together.

ENDINGS IN **r* VS. **nt*. In the parent language there were two sorts of 3pl. ending: those in *-*r* and, more widely reflected, those in *-*nt(-)*. It is commonly stated that the *r*-forms are proper to the stative (perfect) paradigm (514.4), as in L *meminēre* 'they remember' (root **men-*) and Ved. *mamrur* 'they are dead' (PIE root **mer-*). A better way of looking at the distribution is that the 3pl. forms in *-*nt* correlate with 3sg. forms with *-*t*, whereas the *t*-less 3pl. forms (that is, the ones in -*r*) correlate with *t*-less 3sg. In the stative, all 3rd person forms were uniformly *t*-less, in contrast to the jumble of competing inflections in the eventives (426, 430); this may account for the clearest survival of the *r*-forms in the stative paradigm, though even there it was subject to encroachment by the *nt*-types and their reflexes. The

[1] The OIr. absolute form *beirthe*[H*] 'you [pl.] carry' points to an earlier **bereteēh* from **beretes-es*. The conjunct form ·*berid* is ambiguous: it could continue *-*tĕ̄(s)*. Of the four possibilities, *-*tes* is the likeliest choice, as that matches the ending of the absolute before the final particle.

lack of any intrinsic connection between the *r*-forms and the stative (perfect) paradigm is revealed by such Indic forms as Ved. *śére* 'they are lying down' < **k̑ey-roy*, which same verb significantly also makes a *t*-less 3sg., Ved. *śáye* < **k̑ey-oy*; Ved. *aduhran* imperf. 'they gave milk' (a remodeling of **aduhra* < **e-dhugh-ro*); cf. *t*-less 3sg.pres. *duhé* < **dhugh-oy*).

a. Possibly pertinent here, but ambiguous, is the curious distribution of 3pl. endings in the Skt. root imperfect and root aorist. In the RV this is a mix of *-an* and *-ur* with a vaguely regular distribution: roots ending in vowels (from the InIr. point of view) take *-ur*, the others, *-an*: aor. *ádhur* 'they put' but *gman* 'they went'. This *-ur* is usually stated to be an importation from the perfect. The functions of the aor. and imperf. were from the beginning different from the perf., however, likewise formally different in the remainder of the paradigms, so that influence of the one on the other would be itself more a puzzle than an explanation. Nor does this theory account for the gravitation of such person markers to root formations specifically. (The appearance of *-ur* in the imperf. of reduplicated presents, as *adadhur* 'they put', is a little easier to connect with the perf., on the grounds that they both have a reduplicated stem.)

A similar perplexity lies at the heart of the usual description of the Hitt. facts. In Hitt. there are two classes of verbs, differing in the endings of the singular only. In the singular, the *ḫi*-verb endings are related to the stative inflection of the IE languages (513), those of the *mi*-verbs to the present/imperfect type of PIE. But the plural endings of both verb types are the same; and there we find 3pl. *-anzi* in the present, obviously PIE **-onti* or **-n̥ti*; and in the pret., *-r*, variously written but suggesting *-ēr*. This state of affairs is traditionally explained as the generalization of the 3pl. ending of the *mi*-type throughout the present tense, and the contrary generalization of the 3pl. ending of the *ḫi*-type throughout the pret.

However, in all other regards it is obvious that the *mi*-type endings have spread at the expense of what probably were the original *ḫi*-types: the first and second persons in the pl. are obviously the *mi*-type, the 1sg. pret. of the *ḫi*-class in *-ḫun* is obviously the grafting of the *mi*-type ending *-un* onto the *ḫi*-ending; and so on. The reverse influence, namely the replacement of a *mi*-type ending by a *ḫi*-type, would be odd anywhere and particularly so in the pret. tense, as it seems likely that the paradigm ancestral to the PIE stative (perfect 'tense') and the Hitt. *ḫi*-class HAD no preterital tense.

It is therefore reasonable to take Hitt. *-er* (*-ēr*) as a reflex of a *mi*-type (eventive) ending ab origine, correlative with the *r*'s of Ved. *aduhran* 3pl.aor. 'give milk' and *ádr̥śran* 3pl.aor. 'saw', also the root aor. and root imperf., rather than with the ending of the stative (perfect) verbs.

The **-nt* endings generally spread at the expense of the *r*-endings, ousting the latter completely in G as well as Gmc., BS, and Celt. In G, in the process, a number of by-forms arose (430, 437.3).

b. As discussed in **292**, and implicit in much of the discussion here, the 3pl. forms in **-r* and **-nt* are probably at bottom one and the same ending.

430. 1. Thematic. The secondary ending was **-nt*, with *o*-grade of the theme, so **-o-nt*. This is directly reflected in OCS *něsǫ* aor., and G ἔφερον imperf. It is unattested in Gmc., where there are no thematic secondary inflections, and in L, where the primary *-ont*, *-unt* is everywhere found. That the latter is a special feature of L is indicated by Sab. forms distinguishing between prim. *-nt* < **-nti* and secondary *-(n)s* < **-nt*: U *furfant* (meaning uncertain, but plainly 3pl. pres.) vs. O *deicans* 'may they say', O **patensíns** 'panderent'.

The primary ending was formed by the addition of *-*i*, so *-*o-nti*. The primary ending is thought to underlie OCS *nesǫtŭ* 'they carry', with the same unexplained -*ŭ* as in the 3sg.; it is clearly seen in Gmc. (Go. *bairand*), in G (Dor. φέροντι, Arc. φέρονσι, Lesb. φέροισι, Att.-Ion. φέρουσι), and in L (*ferunt*; -ONT is still found in early inscriptions.[1]).

InIr. attests sec. *-*an(t)*, prim. *-*anti*, which contains no information about the grade of the stem vowel. Hitt. -*anzi*, as in *ak-ku-uš-kán-zi* 'they are drinking', appears to reflect *-*onti*; the same shape occurs in athematic types. There is no trace of the corresponding sec. ending (**429a**).

2. ATHEMATIC *-*ent*, *-*enti*. (Note that here the vowel is a part of the ending.) PIE *H_1*s-énti* 'they are', Ved. *sánti*, O **se(n)t**, U *sent*. In Gmc., Go. *sind*, OE *sind(on)* and the rest attest *e*-grade, but atonic (**245**); the reflex of *H_1*sénti* would have been Go. ˣ*sinþ*, OE ˣ*síþ*, and so on. OCS *sętŭ* is the form in a single text (but several present-day Slavic languages have forms presupposing such an etymon); the usual form is *sǫtŭ*, like L *sunt*, OL *sont*. Hitt. *a-ša-an-zi* (and other athematic forms in -*anzi*) evidently point the same way, as do a few G athem. forms, as κάμνουσι 'they toil'. The usual view is that *-*ent(i)* is the inherited form, and that *-*onti* in athem. formations is imported from the thematic paradigm. Against this view are the OCS facts: with the solitary exception of *sǫtŭ*, the few remaining athem. verbs have the expected -*ętŭ* (*dadętŭ* 'they give', *ědętŭ* 'they eat', and secondarily, *vědętŭ* 'they know'). The verb 'be' should be the last of these verbs, not the first, to show an inherited peculiarity encroached on by a common pattern.

There can be little doubt, then, that both full grades occurred in the parent language. Their proper distribution is a puzzle, however. A common suggestion is that they represent the tonic and atonic forms of the ending. But one would expect *e*-grade to correlate with tonic accent (**sénti* vs. atonic **sonti*), and the only branch affording information about both accent and grade—Germanic—reflects a **senti* which is atonic. (The forms are given above.)

Developments in G pose many problems. See **491-6** for a discussion of the forms of the verb 'be' in particular; for now it is enough to say that at least the ending *-*enti* is certain in Myc. *e-e-si*, Dor. ἐντί, and Att.-Ion. εἰσί. For Hom. ἔασι, see below, 5.

Secondary athematic endings in G proliferated. The reflexes of **e-*H_1*s-ent* 'they were' (Ved. *ā́san*; see **493**) are most straightforward: G ἦεν, ἦν < **ēhen* imperf. (**493B**), used as 3sg. in Att.-Ion. but originally 3pl. (as ἦν

[1] The reading *tremonti* in a quotation from the Carmen Saliare is open to doubt: such final *-*i* must have been lost in the PItal. period if not earlier.

remains regularly in the Doric dialects). Att.-Ion. ἦσαν has -σαν from the σ-aorist.

This is the only G present/imperfect showing this form of the endings which, if we judge by the situation in InIr., originally belonged to all the athematic present classes except the reduplicating. The root aor. ending *-_ent_ may be seen in G in roots ending with a laryngeal, section 4 below.

OL _sient_ 'may they be' probably starts from *_H_1s-iH_1-ent_, which would regularly give *_siēns_ (237.5); like all secondary endings, it was touched up with the primary -_nt_. The regular development of _sient_ would be first *_sīnt_, whence regularly _sĭnt_.

3. ATHEMATIC *-_n̥t_, *-_n̥ti_. This form was regular after a consonant when the ending was unaccented in the tonic form of the verb, in contrast to the accented -_énti_. In Ved. it is found chiefly in the reduplicating class, as _júhvati_ 'they pour', _dádati_ 'they give', _dádhati_ 'they put', from *_ǵhéǵhwn̥ti_, *_dédH_3n̥ti_, *_dhédhH_1n̥ti_, with the accent on the reduplication. (In the RV a very few root presents are thus formed, as _tákṣati_ 'they fashion'.) As mentioned under the discussion of the present participle (559), the attested forms of G, as seen most conservatively in Dor. τίθεντι, δίδοντι, admit of various interpretations. The more traditional one, as only slightly reformulated in light of the laryngeal theory, assumes that the regular development of the above would have been ˣτίθατι, ˣδίδατι (Att.-Ion. ˣ-ασι), from *_dhedhH_1n̥ti_ and so on, with secondary forms ˣἔτιθα, ˣἔδιδα, from *_edhedhH_1n̥t_ and so on. The stems τιθε-, διδο-, and the like would however have been regular in the du. and 1,2pl., in both the pres. and the aor.: τίθεμεν, δίδοτε < *_dhedhH̥$_1$mos_, *_dedH̥$_3$ter_; ἔθετε, ἔδοτε < *_edhH̥$_1$te_, *_edH̥$_3$te_; and the 3pl. -ατι is assumed to have been replaced by -αντι, -εντι, and -οντι under the influence of the other persons (for the vowels) and the thematic stems (for the -ν-). Some laryngealists take -εντι, -αντι, -οντι directly from *-_H_1-n̥ti_, *-_H_2-n̥ti_ *-_H_3-n̥ti_, via regular sound laws (100a). The expected -ᾰσι (not -ᾱσι, NB; item 5 below), is actually attested in scattered perfect forms, as Arc. εσλελοιπασι 'they leave out', Hom. πεφύκασι 'are by nature'; and NB particularly ανατεθηκατι 'they dedicate' (Rhodes). These do not settle the question one way or the other as they are from stop stems (*_loyk^w_-) or are kappatic perfects (in effect the same thing, but secondary).

PIE *-_n̥t_ is indirectly represented by -(σ)αν of the aorist (see below, item 5). Otherwise, its expected outcome was -α, at least according to the view that all *-_n̥t_ had the same reflex whether or not preceded by a laryngeal; as this was hardly an ending at all, it was very much liable to being touched up so as to be more saliently 3pl.

There is no trace of either *-_n̥ti_ or *-_n̥t_ in Italic.

4. In G all the ACTIVE ATHEMATIC PRESENTS except εἰμί are from roots or present stems ending in a laryngeal or a vowel, and whatever the prehistory (3, above), the earliest known 3pl. forms had the regular endings -ντι,

-ν, like the thematic forms. So Dor. φαντί 'they say', τίθεντι, δίδοντι. (Not quotable are *δείκνυντι 'they point' and *ἵντι 'they go'.) Corresponding to these are Att.-Ion. φᾱσί and Ion. τιθεῖσι, διδοῦσι, δεικνῦσι, and the rare ἶσι. But Att. has τιθέᾱσι and the like, for which below, 5.

The corresponding secondary ἔτιθεν, ἔδιδον, ἔθεν, ἔδον are the usual forms in most dialects outside of Att.-Ion., and some occur in Homer, as ἔσταν, ἔφαν, ἔβαν. The aorist forms are regular outcomes of expected **e-dhH₁ent*, **edH₃ent*, **estH₂ent*, **ebhH₂ent*, **eg*^w^*H₂ent* (the last is not built to the root of βαίνω, PIE **g*^w^*em-*, but rather **g*^w^*eH₂-* seen also in InIr. and BS, for instance Ved. aor. *gāt* 'goes; went'). In Att.-Ion. these were replaced by ἐτίθεσαν, ἔθεσαν, and the like, with -σαν taken over from the σ-aorist.

a. The form ἶσι (**inti*) looks like evidence in favor of the view that τίθεντι (τιθεῖσι) and the like are secondary creations rather than direct phonological developments from *-H_1-*n̥ti* and the like, as it cannot itself be anything but an analogical creation on the basis ἴμεν, ἴτε, and so on. The PIE 3pl. of **ey-* was **yenti*, as in Ved. *yánti*, Hitt. *pa-a-an-zi* 'they go' < **pa-yanti*; and even if by some unlikely freak the formation actually had zero grade of the ending, **yn̥ti*, this could not give G *ἵντι, either. In a similar way, G *δεικνυντι cannot continue anything ancient. Still the question remains unsettled as to whether *ἵντι and *δεικνυντι took shape pari passu with τίθεντι, δίδοντι and so on, in the same round of analogical remodeling; or whether τίθεντι and the others are the simple result of sound laws, and *ἵντι, *-νυντι are later innovations based on that pattern.

5. G -αντι (-ᾱσι), -αν. According to traditional views, these cannot directly represent any of the PIE varieties of the endings, but have grown up and become productive, among a sizable field of competing formations, wholly within G. According to more recent views, as reviewed above, these are the regular outcome of *-*n̥t(i)* after roots ending in *-H_2- (and parenthetically of aor. *-H_2-*ent(i)* as in φαντι 'they say' < **bhH₂-enti* and ἔβαν 'they went' < **e-g*^w^*H₂-ent*). For those holding this view, the endings -αν, -αντι, -ᾱσι, may simply be taken as original in such forms and transplanted from there.

A different explanation starts with the vestigial ('undercharacterized') *-*a* < *-*n̥t* of the redup. imperf. (and possibly also the *-*ar* < *-*r̥* of the perfect (stative), 514.4, and the root imperf. and aor., **429a**). Whichever the starting point was, it was first remodeled as -αν, parallel to thematic -ον. In several dialects this -αν spread to other aorist types at the expense of -ν, so Boeot. and Locr. ανεθεαν 'they dedicated', Arc. συνεθεαν 'they constructed'—much as in Att.-Ion. the full -σαν spread to ἔθεσαν 'they put', and so on.

In the perfect the old *-ατι, -ασι (see above, 3) was generally replaced by -αντι (whence Att.-Ion. -ᾱσι), partly because of secondary -αν but even more importantly after the analogy of the present eventive ending -οντι (whence Att.-Ion. -ουσι).

The spread of -ᾱσι to present forms occurs only in Att.-Ion. and is mostly Attic at that. Hom. has ἔᾱσι (beside εἰσί) and ἴᾱσι (to εἶμι); in Att.

not only ἴᾱσι, but also τιθέᾱσι, διδόᾱσι, ἱστᾶσι (*ἱστάᾱσι), δεικνύᾱσι, and so on.

431. DUAL. The G secondary endings -τον 2du., -τᾱν (Att.-Ion. -την) 3du. correspond to the Ved. secondary endings *-tam*, *-tām*. The former is manifestly **-tom*, the latter is more enigmatic. PIE **-tām*, as traditionally reconstructed, is (if of PIE date) secondary somehow.

There is no trace in G of the original primary endings, which on the basis of the Ved. primary endings *-thas* 2du., *-tas* 3du.; OCS *-ta* 2du., *-te* 3du.; and Go. *-ts* 2du., would have been *-τες < *$-tH_1es$* 2du., and *-τες from **-tes* 3du. The secondary -τον is used instead, for the third as well as the second person. Even in the secondary tenses the distribution of -τον, -την (-τᾱν) is not fully maintained: sometimes -τον is 3du. in Hom., or -την is 2du. in Att.[1]

PERSONAL ENDINGS OF THE MIDDLE

432. TABLE OF MIDDLE PERSONAL ENDINGS.

		Ved.	Av.	Hitt.	G	L	Go.
				Secondary			
sg.	1	-i	-i	-ḫa(ḫa)t(i)	-μην (Dor. -μᾱν)	-ar	
		-a					
	2	-thās	-sa	-tat(i)	-σο	-re	
	3	-ta	-ta	-tat(i)	-το	-tur	
				-at(i)			
du.	1	-vahi	-vadi				
	2	-āthām			-(σ)θον		
		-ithām					
	3	-ātām			-(σ)θᾱν		
		-itām					
pl.	1	-mahi	-madi	-waštat	-με(σ)θα	-mur	
	2	-dhvam	-δvəm	-tumat	-(σ)θε	-minī	
	3	-nta	-nta	-antat(i)	-ντο	-ntur	
		-ata	-ata				
		-ra(te)					
				Primary			
sg.	1	-i	-i				
		-e	-ē	-ḫa(ḫa)(ri)	-μαι	-r	-da
	2	-se, -ṣe	-hē, -šē	-ta(ri), -tati	-σαι, -σοι	-re	-za
	3	-te	-tē	-ta(ri)	-ται, -τοι	-tur	-da
		-e		-a(ri)			

---

[1] InIr. is ambiguous as to the grade of the 3du. The spread of -τον in G is easier to explain if the ending was *-τος to begin with, rather than *-τες; but OCS *-te* speaks in favor of **-tes*, G *-τες. The ambiguities of Myc. orthography make its few pertinent forms unhelpful: even if *e-to* is in fact 'they two are' rather than some other verb or some other tense, it could equally well stand for either *estos* or *eston*.

		Vedic	Avestan	Hittite	Greek	Latin	Gothic
du.	1	-vahe					
	2	-āthe -ithe			-(σ)θον		
	3	-āte -ite			-(σ)θον		
pl.	1	-mahe	-madē	-wašta(ri) -waštati	-με(σ)θα	-mur	-nda
	2	-dhve	-δvē	-tuma(ri)	-(σ)θε	-minī	-nda
	3	-nte -ate -re	-ntē -atē -āirē	-nta(ri)	-νται, -ντοι	-ntur	-nda

Evidence for the PIE middle system also comes from Old Irish but as is often the case OIr. is chiefly a source of puzzles to be solved; for example, OIr. deponents (verbs of middle form but active meaning, just as in G and L) and true passives have MOSTLY the same endings, but there are some enigmatic differences. For another problem, referring to the paradigm below, how could PIE **-e-tH₂or* 2sg. and **-e-tor* 3sg. result in such different shapes?

The forms of the OIr. deponent *·suidigedar* 'places' (thematic, conjunct):

1*sg.*	·suidigur	1*pl.*	·suidigmer
2	·suidigther, -der	2	·suidigid, -th
3	·suidigedar	3	·suidigetar

433. TABLE OF THE PIE MIDDLE ENDINGS. Forms in parentheses are more than ordinarily conjectural.

	Secondary	Primary
1*sg.*	-H_2o	-H_2or
2	-tH_2o	-tH_2or
3	-o -to	-or -tor
1*du.*	(-wedh$\mathring{H}_2$)	(-wosdh$\mathring{H}_2$)
2	(-teH_1)	(-HtoH_1)
3	(-tē)	(-Htē)
1*pl.*	-medh$\mathring{H}_2$	-mosdh$\mathring{H}_2$
2	-dhwo	-dhwo
3	-(ē)ro -nto -n̥to	(-(ē)ror) -ntor -n̥tor

434. EXAMPLES OF PRESENT AND IMPERFECT INDICATIVE MIDDLE INFLECTION.

	Vedic	Greek	Latin	Hittite	Gothic
Present:					
1*sg.*	bháre	φέρομαι	sequor[1]	e-eš-ḫa-ḫa-ri[2]	haitada[3]
2	vahase[4]	φέρεαι, -ηι	sequere, -ris	e-eš-ta-ri	haitaza
3	bhárate	φέρεται -τοι (Arc.-Cyp.)	sequitur	e-ša((a-)ri)	haitada

The notes to this table are on page 472

	Vedic	Greek	Latin	Hittite	Gothic
1pl.	bharāmahe	φερόμε(σ)θα	sequimur	e-šu-wa-aš-ta(-ti)	haitanda
2	bháradhve	φέρεσθε	sequiminī	i-ya-ad-du-ma[5]	haitanda
3	bhárante	φέρονται	sequontur	e-ša-an-da(-ri)	haitanda
Imperfect:					
1sg.	ájuṣe[6] (AV)	ἐφερόμην	_Note 7_	e-eš-ḫa-(ḫa-)-at[8]	
2	árocathās[9]	ἐφέρεο, -ου		i-ya-at-ta-at	
3	árocata	ἐφέρετο		e-ša-at, e-eš-ta-at	
1pl.	_Note 10_	ἐφερόμε(σ)θα		e-šu-wa-aš-ta-ti	
2	ajuṣadhvam	ἐφέρεσθε		e-eš-tum-ma-at	
3	ájuṣanta	ἐφέροντο		e-ša-an-ta-at	

1. 'Follow', PIE *_sek_^{w}_-_ (414a); deponent in L as in G, Ved., and OIr.
2. 'Am sitting', evidently PIE *_eH_$_1$_s-_; deponent in Hitt. as in G ἧσται, Ved. _ā́ste._ (Hitt. spelling of _e-eš-_ before cons. vis-à-vis _e-šu-_, _e-ša-_ can have no bearing on inherited vowel length.)
3. 'Is named, is called'; the same formation is seen in Gmc. (OE _(ic) hátte_ for example); the root is Pan-Gmc. but of unknown prior history.
4. 'Convey', PIE *_weǵh-_.
5. 'Walk', stem _i-ya-_, presumably related to PIE *_ey-_.
6. 'Taste', PIE *_ǵews-_ as in G γεύω 'give a taste of', L _dēgūnō_ 'taste', _gustus, -ūs_ '(a) taste'. (No 1sg. thematic imperf.midd. occurs in the RV.)
7. No L paradigm, the imperf. included, is related to the PIE preterital forms reflected in InIr., G, and Hitt.; see 498.
8. The pret. of Hitt. has alternative forms in _-ti_, which look like (but can hardly be —435c) the primary marker added to the pret. marker: _e-eš-ḫa-ti_ 1sg., _e-ša-ti_ 3sg., _e-šu-wa-aš-ta-ti_ 1pl., _ki-id-du-ma-ti_ 'you lay down' 2pl., _ki-ya-an-ta-ti_ 'they lay down' 3pl.
9. 'Shine', root _ruc-_, PIE *_lewk-_.
10. No 1pl. them. midd. imperf. is found in the Vedas. The form if it occurred would probably be _ábharāmahi_*.

---

435. ANALYSIS OF THE MIDDLE ENDINGS. Most of the PIE middle endings of the eventive verbs (432-3) are derived from the active endings (420-1). But the different persons and numbers are derived differently, and the 2nd person endings of all numbers are unrelated to the active ones.

In the active endings which form the primary with *_-i_, the middle is formed by adding *_-o_, usually tonic, to the active form; the typical athematic stem is in zero grade, thus *_ǵheǵhutór_ 'pours' (Ved. _juhuté_; cf. act. *_ǵheǵhéwti_, Ved. _juhóti_), *_yungH_$_2$_ór_ 'I join' (Ved. _yuñjé_, cf. act. *_yunégmi_, Ved. _yunájmi_). In the athematic formations of the Narten type (128.3a), the middle marker was atonic: *_wéstor_ 'gets dressed' (Ved. _váste_), *_éH_$_1$_stor_ 'is sitting' (Ved. _ā́ste_).

In those forms in which the middle is marked by *_-o_ added to the generic person marker, the present (primary) endings have a final *_-r_. Thus for example act.sec. *_-t_, prim. *_-t-i_; midd. sec. *_-t-o_, prim. *_-to-r_ (see 433). This marker is preserved in languages found around the edge of the IE territory: Celtic, Italic, Tocharian, and Anatolian. Indeed, the marker _-r_ spreads into non-present or non-indicative categories in Celtic and Italic, and completely new endings have been created, as quite generally for the 1pl. (OIr. *-mir*, L *-mur*, Toch. *-mtär*, Hitt. *-waštari*). In the central IE area, the functionless distinction between the two primary markers—**-r* in the middle, **-i* in the active—was eliminated; the **-r* of the middle endings was replaced by the active **-i* (or rather, **-y*). InIr., G, and Gmc. are included in this area.

a. Prior to the discovery of Toch. and Hitt., the assumption had been that the *r*-medio-passives of Italic and Celtic were an innovation, one that defined Italo-Celtic as a distinct subgroup in the IE family. Taken as an innovation the type is highly mysterious, in the sense that there is no satisfactory way to derive it from PIE ingredients. This added weight to its importance as a subgroup-defining trait, since independent innovation was out of the question. But with the discovery of similar forms in other groups, at the periphery of the IE area and widely separated, a new explanation was required: the *r*-forms are conservative, not innovative. The LOSS of the *r*-forms in the center of the IE speech area was the innovation. This at last explained why such forms in Italic and Celtic were so hard to explain as innovations—if an ending had always been there, it would naturally be next to impossible to find a 'source' for it. However, one of the main supports for an Italo-Celtic subgroup was knocked out.

b. THEMATIC FORMATIONS. In thematic stems, the theme vowels of G (-εαι), Ved. (*-āse*), and OIr., follow the same **-^{e}/o-* pattern of alternation as in the active; but Go. *-aza* 2sg., *-ada* 3sg., Hitt. *-at-ta-ri*, and Toch. point to a uniform thematic vowel **-o-*. This is unexpected. But it is easier to explain the **-^{e}/o-* as leveled on the active pattern, than it is to account for the loss of a pervasive pattern of alternation. (L *-eris* 2sg. indic., *-ere* indic. and imperat., and possibly also *-itur* 3sg., are ambiguous.) Nevertheless, in this book the conventional reconstruction has been followed, as **sek^{w}etor*, even though the better arguments favor a uniform theme vowel **-o-*, as **sek^{w}otH$_2$or*, **sek^{w}otor* and so on.

c. HETITICA. While Hitt. has proved indispensable for a correct understanding of the middle endings, its forms are not without their puzzles. Chief among them is the element *-t* or *-ti* which is most typical in the preterite, but in the later language is fairly frequent in the pres. as well. The consonant is never written double (31), a typical spelling being *ne-ya-at-ta-ti* 2sg. 'you lead'. (Note the typical double writing of *t* in the person marker proper.)

Nor is it apparent what functional distinction, if any, underpins the alternative endings with and without final *-(r)i*, for example *-tat* and *-tati* (3sg. pret.), *-ta* and *-tari* (3sg. pres.). If the two pairs of endings were parallel, we would expect pres. **-tar* ~ *-tari*; the inference is that the *r*-less endings of the present tense have lost the word-final *-r*. But final *-r* is preserved in the *r/n*-stems (290-2); if there were a tendency for such a sound to drop, it is odd that it would be attested in isolated forms but lost in the verbs, where it was in alternation with endings preserving the *-r-* nonfinally. Nevertheless there are parallels for this kind of thing, notably the **-i* of primary verb endings which is lost in Ital. and Celt. even while the selfsame sound in other functions, or in isolated forms, generally survived (71.1).

It appears that within Hitt. itself pairs like *-ta* and *-tari* were reinterpreted at face value; that is, the latter was taken as the former with an added *-ri*. Evidence for this is the addition of *-ri* to *-wašta* 1pl. and *-tuma* 2pl. (which alternate with *-waštari*, *-tumari*). These forms never had a final *-r* to lose. Unexplained by any such means, however, is the use of forms in *-ti* (with what looks like a primary marker) with PRETERITE meaning, which occurs in the most archaic Hitt. and is therefore unlikely to result from confusion. Perhaps forms like *-ttati* 2sg.pres. and *-ttati* 2sg.pret. are mere look-alikes, whether homophonous or only written alike. (Cf. the case of the productive past tense and past participle of English, as in *he received, he was received,* which though now homophonous are in fact historically unrelated.)

d. It has been recently suggested that the PIE marker of the present tense in the middle endings was **-ri*, not **-r*. This would simplify the history of the Hitt. paradigms, and would pose no problems for Italic, where primary **-i* dropped early and generally in the primary active tenses. In Irish the absolute form presupposes, for one, 3sg. **-tori-es*, traditionally explained as having imported a final **-i* from the active type; an inherited **-tori* would simplify the explanation. The conjunct form, however, requires an original neutral vowel after the **-r-*, as PCelt. **sekʷītori* 'follows' should give ×*·seichthir* /s'eχ'θ'əρ'/ instead of *·sechethar* /s'eχ'əθəρ/. But the correct explanation of the Irish forms is uncertain anyway.

The usual idea (an independent remodeling of an original **-tor* with primary **-i*) dovetails in Hitt. with the manifest remarking of the *ḫi*-conjugation in exactly the same manner. An element **-ri*, on the other hand, provides a better explanation for why Hitt. *-ta-ri* alternated with *-ta* rather than with **-tar*, but an implication of the analysis—that Hitt. verb forms with and without a primary marker were ab origine isofunctional or nearly so—is unparalleled in the active paradigm.

436. I. FIRST PERSON SINGULAR. PIE *-H_2o sec. (see **48**) is inferrable from the prim. *-H_2or (L *-ar*, Hitt. *-ḫa(-ḫa)*, *-ḫa(-ḫa)-ri*[1]), which would be the sec. ending plus the present-marker **-r*. This is made up of the 1sg. marker *-H_2-, seen also in the stative and the thematic eventive, followed by the marker of the middle voice. Ved. points to the laryngeal: RV *tatane* 'stretch, extend' 1sg. vs. *tatne* 3sg., the former from *te-tn̥-H_2oy, the latter from **te-tn-oy*. (Being built to the perfect stem, neither can be truly ancient; but they apparently at least date from a period when PInIr. still had laryngeals.) Contrast *śáye* 'I am, he is lying down' where the reflexes of *ḱey-H_2or 1sg. and **ḱey-or* 3sg. are homophonous.

In InIr. and G, the **-r* was replaced by **-y*, the active primary marker (**421**), thus Ved. *bháre* directly. Expected G *-αι was further retouched as -μαι, with -μ- imported from the active athem. ending.

The secondary ending was almost everywhere remodeled. Hitt. *-ḫa(-ḫa)-t(i)* is the orig. **-ḫa(ḫa)* with the addition of the mysterious *-t*. In Ved. it is retained unaltered only in the opt.: athem. *-īya* < *-iH_1-H_2o, as seen in Ved. *íśīya* 'may I possess'; them. *-eya* < *-oy(H_1)H_2o, as in Ved. *saceya* 'may I follow'. In the preterite indicative, it was part of a general remodeling, in which the 1pl. (whose *-i* < *-$H̥_2$ has no connection with the primary tense marker) was pivotal:

PIE	1sg.	1pl.	> PInIr.		> Indic (Vedic)	
sec.	*-H_2o	*-medh$H̥_2$	*-a	*-madhi	-i	-mahi
prim.	*-H_2or	*-mosdh$H̥_2$	*-ai	*-madhi	-e	-mahe

[1] The significance of the spelling *-ḫa-ḫa-*, optional but very frequent, is enigmatic.

(These forms are for the athematic inflection; in thematic stems, the new sec. ending *-*i* combined with the thematic vowel (*-*a*-*i* > -*e*), making it homophonous with the primary. Similarly, the perf. ending -*a* < *-H_2e (514.1) acquired a middle counterpart -*e* < *-*a*-*i*.)

The secondary ending in G, -μην (Dor. -μᾱν), is without obvious parallel. The nucleus of the form is *-μα, whose vowel is from *-H_2o, and whose -μ- has the same origin as in -μαι. The remaining details are in the highest degree obscure.

Italic essentially agrees with Hittite, except for having extended the primary -*r* to the past and unreal tenses, once -*r* had been reanalyzed as a marker of the middle per se. The them. ending -*ōr* (so Plaut., later -*or*, **83.3**) is the expected outcome (**88.3**) of *-*oar* < *-*o*-H_2or. Expected **legā̆* < -*āa* < *-*e*H_2-H_2o subj. (originally opt., **498**) was remarked with 'middle -*r*', *legār* (Plaut. -*ār*, later -*ăr*). Similarly the 1sg. forms in other tenses, *legēbar*, *legerer*, and the like.

a. For the development of -α- and -*a*- from *H_2o, see **48**.

2. SECOND PERSON SINGULAR. Owing to its widespread replacement, the the original PIE ending can only tentatively be recovered. The etymon endorsed here is *-*t*H_2o sec., *-*t*H_2or prim., preserved as such in Hitt. -*ttat(i)* and -*tta(ri)*, respectively, with similar forms in OIr. In InIr. the original ending is found in the Indic secondary -*thās*, whose long vowel and -*s* are unexplained. (One would have expected rather Indic *-*tha*.)

In all other IE languages, including Iranian and the primary ending in Indic itself, the 2sg. has been replaced by a form based in part on the 2sg.act. ending, and in part on the 3sg.midd.:

	active		middle	
	secondary	*primary*	*secondary*	*primary*
3sg.	-t	-ti	-to	-tor, -toy
2sg.	-s	-si	-X	-Y

where *X* = sec. *-*so*, *Y* = prim. *-*soy*. So, in the primary forms, PInIr. *-*sai* > Ved. -*se* and -*ṣe* and Av. -*hē* and -*šē*; G *-*soy*, whence -οι, later -αι (-σοι, -σαι after cons.; see the 3sg. below), Go. -*za* < *-*soy*. Secondary *-*so* in G -ο, -σο (after cons.), Av. -*ŋha*, L -*re*.

L -*re* < *-*so* prevails in early L (Ter. has only -*re*, Plaut. has mostly -*re* but occasionally -*ris*) and also in Cicero except in the present indicative of passives. In the Augustan period -*ris* is the more usual form, with -*re* limited to the imperative.

This -*ris* is composed of -*re* and an -*s* imported from the active, with subsequent regular vowel weakening (**71.3**). The conflation of the two endings seems to have happened twice, independently. (See **b**, below.) In OL the ending -RIS is rare, but -RVS as in VTARVS 'utaris' is several times attested. The latter points to an extension of *-*so* to *-*sos* prior to the change of *-*o* to *-*e*, whence -RVS. The usual L form was retouched with 2sg. -*s* only after the final vowel had weakened to -*e* (71.1).

In G, The difference in the vocalism of prim. -*(σ)αι*, -*ται* vs. secondary -*(σ)ο*, -*το* is inexplicable in terms of PIE vowel alternation. L -*tur* from *-*tor* indicates that *-*toy*, rather than *-*tay*, underlies ambiguous InIr. -*te*, Hitt. -*ta(ri)*, Go. -*da*. Overall, since the system makes most sense if the secondary endings were basic and the primary endings were derived from them, the expected G endings would be -*(σ)οι* and -*τοι*, and in fact just such endings occur—albeit in a very limited attestation: Arc. *κειοι* 'you lie (down)' < **key-soy* (Att. *κεῖσαι*, Hom. *κεῖαι*). Similarly in the 3sg., Arc. *εσ(σ)ετοι* 'will be' (Att. *ἔσται*), Cyp. *κειτοι* (Att. *κεῖται*), and Myc. *e-u-ke-to* (euk^{h}etoi) 'takes a vow'. The usual view sees -*σαι*, -*ται* as the inherited forms, replaced by -*σοι*, -*τοι* in Arc. under the influence of the secondary endings. But the appearance of -*τοι* in Myc., together with the morphological clarity which results from basing *-*toy* (*-*tor*) on secondary *-*to*, must mean that -*(σ)αι*, -*ται* are the innovations. One source was the 1sg. -*μαι* (a remodeling of *-*αι*, ultimately from *-H_2*or*). Another would have been the original form of the 2sg. ending, PG *-*tai* ultimately from *-*t*H_2*or*—though of course that depends on how long it survived. It will be very interesting to see what the Myc. 2sg. turns out to be; the least changed form would be *-*tai*; but even *-*sai* or *-*hai* (with the more characteristic 2sg. marker) would provide a natural point of departure for the split of G dialects into the -*μαι*, -*(σ)αι*, -*ται* varieties and the -*μαι*, -*(σ)οι*, -*τοι* varieties.

a. In G the endings -*σαι* (-*σοι*) and -*σο* would remain unchanged only after certain consonants (so *γέγραψαι*, *ἐγέγραψο*), while after a vowel, with the regular loss of intervocalic **s* (172), they would appear as -*αι*, -*ο*. This distribution is more nearly maintained in Hom. than in Att., where there is an extensive analogical restoration of -*σαι*, -*σο*. Thus Att. has -*σαι*, -*σο* regularly in the pres. and imperf. indic. and pres. imper. of athematic verbs, as *τίθεσαι*, *ἐτίθεσο*, *τίθεσο* (but subj. *τιθῇ*, opt. *τιθεῖο*); likewise in the perf. and pluperf., as *δέδοσαι*, *ἐδέδοσο*. Hom. has such forms as *δίζηαι* 'you seek' and *κεῖαι* pres. 'you are lying', *ἐμάρναο* imperf. 'you fought', *βέβληαι* perf. 'you threw', beside others like the Att., as *παρίστασαι* 'you stand by', *παρίστασο*.

Even in Att., the forms resulting from the loss of intervocalic **s* prevail in the present and imperfect of the thematic verbs and in the aor. Thus: *φέρεαι* (*φέρῃ*); *ἐφέρεο* (*ἐφέρου*); *ἔθεο* (*ἔθου*); *ἐλύσαο* (*ἐλύσω*) (uncontracted forms usually in Hom., contraction the rule in Att.).

In the 2sg.pres.indic. the later Att. spelling -*ει* (< -*ῃ* < -*εαι*, 64) persisted in certain words, as *βούλει*, *οἴει*, *ὄψει* 'you wish; suppose; will see'.

In Hellenistic G -*σαι*, -*σο* spread from the athematic verbs to the contract verbs (cf. *ἀκροᾶσαι* NT 'you hearken') and eventually to all the thematic verbs. So NG *φέρεσαι*, *κάθεσαι*, and so on.

b. The L forms for all eventive paradigms are based on *-*so*, which answers to the secondary ending type. This is strange because in L it is generally the primary endings which oust the secondary ones. It is not obvious what an overtly marked primary form in L would have been: *-*soy* is out of the question, and *-*sor* is not likely, in part because had it ever existed it is hard to guess why anything so well-fitted to the overall scheme of L verb morphology would have been lost.

No 2sg. middle forms are attested in Sab., but the OL forms of the VTARVS type (vid. sup.) are attested in formerly Umbrian regions, and it has been suggested that the form might betray U influence.

3. THIRD PERSON SINGULAR. PIE **-o* and **-to* sec.; **-or* and **-tor* prim.

As mentioned above (426, esp. **a**), Ved. still has a number of *t*-less forms built to some 15 athematic stems of all types. These are all primary, with **-y* for original **-r*: *joṣe* 'is enjoying' and *śáye* 'is lying down' (root presents; cf. *t*-ful forms of the ending in the latter: G κεῖται, Av. *saēte* and Hitt. *ki-it-ta-ri*); *gr̥ṇé* 'is praised' (*n*-infix, root **gʷerH-*); and so on.

The corresponding secondary forms in **-a* were everywhere either replaced by the dominant *-ta* or else retouched with a final *-t*. The former cannot in principle be detected; a remodeled *-at* may be discerned when it is an active ending in an otherwise middle paradigm. (This remodeling took place very early. Even in the RV, the *-t* of a form like *áśayat* 3sg.imperf. is usually necessary for good meter, and the meter is never improved by omitting it.) As mentioned in 426, Hitt. and Sab. have similar alternative 3sg.midd. endings without *-t-*.

In G the endings are secondary -το, inherited unchanged, and primary -ται, a replacement of -τοι attested in dial. forms as outlined under 2**a**, above.

In L and Sab., with the exception of the *t*-less forms in the latter, the primary ending **-tor* was retained and ousted the secondary form, whence the L *-tur* of all tenses and moods. (The imperative in *-tor*, OL *-tōr*, is unrelated, 550.2.)

437. 1. FIRST PERSON PLURAL. The middle endings are the active endings with an added element **-dhH̥₂*, thus secondary **-me-dhH̥₂*, primary **-mos-dhH̥₂*. Most IE languages generalized one or the other, G alone retaining both -μεθα and (with altered vowel) -μεσθα, but not in the original distribution.[1] Ved. has sec. *-mahi*, prim. *-mahe* (as if the full grade of *-mahi*; the innovation is PInIr., so also in Av. *-maidi*, *-madē*); inherited **-masdhi* would have become Ved. ˣ*-mehi*, Av. ˣ*-mazdi*. Go. *-nda* too points to a generalization of **-medhH̥₂* > PreGmc. **-meda* → **-meday* prior to the loss of final short vowels, whence Go. *-nda* (< **-mda*) by syncope. Toch. *-mtär* apparently represents a similar formation, except that the primary marker grafted on is *-r*, as is appropriate for that system.

Contrariwise, the primary form is the basis for both Hitt. *-waštat* pret. and *-wašta(ri)*, *-waštati* pres.

---

[1] G -μεσθα is particularly frequent in hexameter poetry because a great many forms in -ομεθα, -νυμεθα and so on are metrically inconvenient or even impossible. Modern scholars have sometimes traced the form to the influence of 2pl. -σθε, by no means impossible but unnecessary in view of the Hitt. evidence.

In Ital. and Celt. the 1pl. was much more drastically remodeled. The general idea was a midd. form like the act. one but ending with *-r* in place of either primary **-s* or nothing: thus **-mor(i)* based on act. **-mos(i)*, or **-mer* based on **-me*. The former is attested in L *-mur*, the latter appears to be the Celtic etymon.

a. The failure of G to touch up -μεθα as primary ˣ-μεθαι is strange, but can be understood as part of the loss of the primary/secondary distinction for the first and second persons plural throughout the system.

2. SECOND PERSON PLURAL. The PIE ending was **-dhwe* or **-dhwo*, and as in the case of the 2pl.act. there was no distinction between prim. and sec. forms. Such an ending is attested once in the RV, *yájadhva* 'perform ye rites'—an imperative, but when they agree with the indicative endings at all, imperatives agree with secondary endings. The primary **-dhwa* was retouched with the proper midd. **-y* already in PInIr., just like the 1pl., whence the finite primary Ved. *-dhve*, Av. *-δvē*. Likewise PInIr. was **-dhwam* secondary, whose *-m* is reminiscent of the *-m* of the secondary dual endings, but is otherwise unexplained.

Evidence relating to the vocalism is meager, but an *o*-grade is likelier for several reasons. First, *o*-vocalism seems to be general in the middle endings. Further, **-dhwo* would yield Luv. *-tuwari* and Hitt. *-tuma(ri)*, pret. *-tumat* regularly. Go. *-nda* reflects **-da* < **-d(w)ay* < **-dhwo*, though the *-n-* is not self-explanatory.

When it is possible to do so, Hitt. scribes write the endings *-ttuma*, *-dduma*, which is unexpected; 31.

Much more difficult are the endings in the classical languages.

GREEK. The relationship of G -σθε to **-dhwo*[1] is a vexed question. Direct evidence for the development of **-dhw-* medially is virtually limited to one difficult form, G (ϝ)ὀρθός 'straight', Ved. *ūrdhvá-* 'upright'; here the **w* simply drops. G θύραι 'door', IF it is from **dhwor-* (44, rather than **dhur-*, 190.5), points to the same thing in initial position. The development of **tw* offers little illumination: depending on dialect it yields either τ (as in Dor.) or σ (as in σέ 'you' acc. < τϝε, 190.4, and Hom. πίσυρες 'four' < **kʷetwores*, 389.4). Most authorities, then, see -θε by itself as the proper development of **-dhwe*, and find some other source for the -σ-: metanalysis (not likely); the 2sg.perf. ending -σθα (514.2; less likely); or the influence of -μεσθα, dating from a period when -μεθα and -μεσθα were still secondary and primary, respectively, so -μεθα : -θε :: -μεσθα : *X*, where *X* = -σθε. This works, but the treatment of the pattern as the language developed subsequently is

[1] G -ε has various plausible explanations. The most likely is that the inherited ending in **-o* was contaminated by the vowel of act. **-te*. Less likely is that **-dhwe* is the PIE original (meaning that the forms pointing to **-dhwo* in the other languages were contaminated by other middles in **-o*). Least likely is the possibility that **-dhwe* and **-dhwo* are different ablaut grades.

puzzlingly inconsistent: the extinction of -μεσθα on the one hand, and of -θε on the other—simultaneously. If structural patterns are salient enough to bring certain forms into a system, they ought to be salient enough to maintain them.

LATIN. One of the enigmas of classical scholarship, ranking in mystery with what name Achilles took when he hid among the women, is the explanation of L *-minī*. The blank record of Sab. is keenly felt here, as the Latin form looks like nothing at all, or worse, bears a distracting resemblance to what are certainly unrelated elements in cognate languages. An idea dating back to the infancy of historical linguistics, for example, traced the form to the nom.pl. (masc.) of the middle pple., answering to G -μενοι (560). Another idea, almost as old, compares it to the Hom. and Lesb. middle infin. in -μεναι, Ved. *-mane*, imagined first to have been employed as an imperative which then took over indicative function. Both ideas suffer from a lack of motivation, unless we accept the absurdity that by some calamity pre-Latin had no form for the 2pl.midd. and so speakers resorted to makeshift periphrases to eke out their grunts and gestures.

The correct place to start looking for the history of *-minī* is PIE **-dhwo* itself. The chief problems are the source of the nasal, and of the final long vowel. Perhaps the starting point was **-dhwo-ne* with the same added element as in the active (428). The puzzle of the final vowel apart, this would give, first, PItal. **-þwone-*, then **-fone-* (147.2), then with syncope **-fne-* or **-bne-* (whether the development of **-b-* pre- or postdated the syncope is immaterial), then **-mne-* (219), and finally, with anaptyxis, *-mine-*, *-minī*. —A problem for this theory is the U 2pl. imperat.midd. **-mu**, *-mu*. The details are uncertain; but if this ending is somehow superimposable on L *-minī*, a derivation from **-dhwo(m)* is harder to support, as in Sab. it appears that PItal. **fn* does not assimilate as it does in L.

3. THIRD PERSON PLURAL. As in the active, evidence points to two sets of endings (429), secondary **-nto* (**-ento*, **-n̥to*) and **-ro*; primary **-ntor* (**-entor*, **-n̥tor*) and **-(ē)ror*. The endings with **-r-* rather than **-nt-* are attested only in InIr., where they are found in the same forms which have *t*-less 3sg.midd. endings. The marker **-y* replaces the middle primary marker **-r* in both types of endings, hence Ved. *śére* 'they are lying down' < **śay-ray* ← **ḱey-ror*, Av. *åŋhāire* 'they are sitting' < **āsāray* ← **eH$_1$s-ēror*, Ved. *sunvire* 'they press' (*nu*-present, 455) < **sunwr̥ray* ← **su-nu-ror*. In the secondary tenses, expected **-ra* < **-ro* has been everywhere papered over with the usual 3pl. ending, much as happened in the secondary 3sg. (436.3): for expected **aduhra* 'they milked' and **aśera* 'they were lying down', we have *aduhran* and *aśeran*.

L has only the primary *-ntor* type, class. *-ntur*, which was extended into all tenses and moods. (The imperat. *-ntor* is unrelated; 550.2.)

The G forms closely parallel the 3sg. as well, with primary *-νται* for *-ντοι* (← **-ntor*), and conservative secondary *-ντο* < **-nto*. G *-αται*, *-ατο*, like Ved. *-ate*, *-ata*, represent the form after consonants in athematic formations, PIE **-n̥to*, **-n̥tor*.

a. The forms *-αται*, *-ατο* occur in only a few indicative stems, as Hom. *εἵαται*, *εἵατο* (for *ἥαται*, *ἥατο*; cf. Ved. *ā́sate* 'they are sitting', *āsata* 3pl.imperf.), but they are regular in Hom. and Hdt. in the opt. and in the perf. and pluperf. Thus Hom. *γενοίατο*, *τετεύχαται*, *ἐτετεύχατο*, and, with extension to vowel stems, *βεβλήαται*, *βεβλήατο*. From forms like the last with vowel shortening come the later Ion. *-εαται*, *-εατο* in Hdt., as *κεκλέαται* and the like, and with further extension to the present even *τιθέαται* and the like.

438. DUAL. The G dual endings are obviously formed after the analogy of the active endings: *-σθον*, *-σθον* after *-τον*, *-τον*; and *-σθον*, *-σθᾱν* (Att.-Ion. *-σθην*) after *-τον*, *-τᾱν* (*-την*). The *-σθ-* is reminiscent of the 2pl.midd. *-σθε*, imper. *-σθω*, but why or how is an enigma. Nor are comparisons with Ved. *-āthām*/*-ithām* 2du.midd., and *-ātām*/*-itām* 3du.midd. especially revealing. The *-ā-*/*-i-* alternation in Ved. makes it look as though the endings actually began with a laryngeal, but a construct like **-HtHo-* is not immediately persuasive.

a. The G 1du. *-μεθον*, quotable only in three poetic forms, is merely stitched together from the pl. *-μεθα* and *-ον* imported from *-σθον*.

EVENTIVE STEMS

439. PIE EVENTIVE STEMS fall into two classes, *thematic* and *athematic*.

Thematic stems, to which the person endings are added, are invariant (tonic accent and all) apart from the *ᵉ/ₒ*-ablaut of the theme vowel.

The athematic paradigms add the person endings directly to a stem-final consonant (those stems that appear to consist of a long vowel or *ə, such as the opt. marker traditionally written **-yē-*, **539**, are now known to have contained laryngeals). Tonic accent typically was mobile: in the dominant pattern, it stood on the stem in the sg.act., but on the person endings in the du. and pl., and in all forms of the middle. The stems themselves alternate between the *e-* (tonic) and zero grade (**440**), in accord with the position of the accent.

The two types of stem also differ in at least one personal ending, that of the 1sg.act. primary (**424**).

THEMATIC STEMS. All thematic stems end in a (short) vowel coming immediately before the person endings:

	sg.	*du.*	*pl.*
1	o	o	o
2	e	e	e
3	e	e	o

(For evidence of a different pattern in the middle voice see **435b**.) This distribution is observed in G, apart from its missing 1du., and Gmc., apart from its missing 3du. In L the facts are similar, except that owing to the regular changes in medial and final syllables, the thematic vowel is represented by *i* or *u*. Only before *r* does *e* remain unchanged, as 2sg. *legeris*, though the point is moot since any short vowel would become *-e-* (**66**). In the 1pl. **-omos* would yield partly *-imus*, partly *-umus* (**69**); but the former, supported by 2pl. *-itis*, prevails except for the few verbs in which there is no 2pl. *-itis*. (So *sumus* 'are' and its derivatives; *volumus* 'wish' and its derivatives; and *quaesumus* 'ask'.) In BS the original distribution is disturbed, differently in Lith. and OCS—the former extending the range of *o*-grade (so for example 2pl. *vedate*), the latter that of the *e*-grade (so *-ete* 2pl. as inherited, but also *nesemŭ* 'we carry'). This indicates that the inherited alternation survived until a late date. In OIr. the pattern remains unchanged, but so altered by sound laws that unless one knew in advance what to look for, the history of the forms would not be discoverable. Even InIr., which merges **e* and **o*, preserves indirect evidence of the old state of affairs. First, in the 1du./pl., the theme-vowel **-o-* lengthens in accord with Brugmann's Law (**36.4**), thus Ved. *sacāvahe* 'we two follow' < **-o-wosdhH̥*$_2$, *páśyāmasi* 'we see' < **-o-mos*. This lengthening is sometimes ascribed to contamination by the 1sg. in *-āmi* (the original them. **-ā* embellished with the athem. ending *-mi*). Regular phonological development is however the correct explanation: in Av., *-āvaibi*, *-āmaibi* as predicted by Brugmann's Law occur, but the correct relationship between *-āmi* and orig. *-ā* is still evident, as the two occur side by side.

In InIr., the alternation of root-final palatalized and dorsal stops (**153d**) in thematic stems has been leveled, usually in favor of the palatalized alternant: **lewketi* 3sg. 'shines', **lewkonti* 3pl. presumably > PInIr. **raučati* and **raukanti*, whence Skt. *rocati*, *rocanti*.

a. The term 'thematic vowel' means any stem vowel, and so the perfect (**516**) is called 'alpha-thematic' in reference to the linking *-α-* that develops in G between the (original) stem and the endings. In PIE terms, however, taking the different full grades as the same element, there was only one vowel that formed stems.

The term 'thematic stem' is commonly used in two slightly different senses. (1) Any stem which includes such a vowel, as in the suffixes **-sḱ*^{e}*/o-* (**456.3**) and **-y*^{e}*/o-* (**456.1**). (2) Specifically, the stem which consists of the *-*^{e}*/o-* vowel per se. Thus when we speak of a quondam athematic inflection as having been 'thematized', we mean that the new stem consists of the theme vowel **-*^{e}*/o-* as stem per se (**449**). That is, one would not refer to **gʷhen-y*^{e}*/o-* 'strike, kill', or **pr̥ḱ-sḱ*^{e}*/o-* 'ask' as 'thematized' formations, though they are certainly 'thematic' ones.

b. Theorizing about the origins of the the PIE theme vowel, and more specifically about the alternation of grades, is an occupational disease of Indo-Europeanists. The observation that **o* occurs before resonants (**w* and the nasals), **e* elsewhere, long ago led to attempts to connect the origin and distribution of the alternation. When however **-oH*$_2$ as 1sg. took the place of the reconstruction **-ō*, the original generalization became harder to maintain; but on the evidence the urge to speculate about the origin of the theme vowel is undiminished.

A survey of theories of the PIE theme vowel would take us too far afield, but three very general observations are appropriate:

(1) If thematic inflection started in athematic inflections in which vowels 'grew' anaptyctically between the stem and the ending, as some have speculated, it is difficult to understand how or why any athematic paradigms could have survived. That is, if **legeti* 'gathers' is an automatic development of **legti* (**lekti*), how did **yunekti* 'joins' survive? (One might register particular surprise that the 3pl. would have sprouted a theme vowel at all, as anything like **legn̥ti* would have had an altogether normal PIE structure; yet *-*ont(i)* is the single best-attested thematic form of all, reflexes being found as such in all IE languages except Lith., and indirectly even there.)

(2) If the thematic types are somehow an organic development from athematic types, the fixed tonic accent and the lack of quantitative ablaut, which are properties of all thematic types, are not only unexplained but an embarrassment.

(3) Most theories of the ultimate origins of thematic inflection naturally take the simplest thematic type—root plus stem *-^{e}/*o*- (**legeti*)—as the most original. This reasonable opinion is undercut by Hitt., in which the simple thematic type is extremely rare (some would say nonexistent) but the characterized affixes *-*sḱ*^{e}/*o*- and *-*y*^{e}/*o*- abound. This indicates that the simple thematic type of the familiar IE languages is a secondary development, abstracted from such suffixes as *-*sḱ*^{e}/*o*- and *-*y*^{e}/*o*-, with their paradigmatically uniform root grade and columnar (non-mobile) accent.

c. To account for the L 3rd conj. in -*iō*, -*ĭmus* (480-1), and for certain details of OCS and Arm., some scholars espouse the idea of a 'semithematic' inflection, in which *-*yo*- alternates not with *-*ye*- but with *-*i*-. This suggestion has never found more than limited favor among Indo-Europeanists.

440. ATHEMATIC STEMS. Athematic forms show gradation of the stem, more exactly of the last vowel before the person endings. The grade correlates with the position of the tonic accent, and there is presumably a glottogonic connection, namely that zero grades result from the syncope of atonic vowels (125). The accent was on the last vowel of the stem (which in the case of indicative root presents was the only vowel) in the singular active, on the personal ending in the du. and pl. active, and apparently on the ending in all middles (but see **a**, below).

For a root verb, **wek*^{w}- 'speak' for example, the following synopsis of forms obtained:

		Active	Middle
Indicative	*1sg.*	*wék^{w}-mi	*uk^{w}-H$_{2}$ór
	1pl.	*uk^{w}-mós	*uk^{w}-mósdhH̥$_{2}$
Optative	*1sg.*	*uk^{w}-yéH$_{1}$-m̥	*uk^{w}-iH$_{1}$-H$_{2}$ó
	1pl.	*uk^{w}-iH$_{1}$-mé	*uk^{w}-iH$_{1}$-médhH̥$_{2}$

(The reduplicated presents provide the chief exception to this generalization; in Ved. the tonic accent is on the reduplicating syllable and, in accord with this, the 3pl. ending is in the zero grade: so *dádati* 'they give' < **dédH*$_{3}$*n̥ti* (root **deH*$_{3}$-). But the 1,2pl. have their usual forms, -*más(i)*, -*thá*.)

In L as in most IE languages there are only relics of athematic forms, which are therefore accounted irregular verbs. G and InIr. and, in a some-

what different way, Hitt., best preserve the athematic stem types as types: G εἶμι 'I go' but ἴμεν (= Ved. *émi, imási*; PIE root pres. **éy-mi, *i-mós*); G τίθημι but τίθεμεν (= Ved. *dadhāmi, dadhmási*; PIE reduplicated pres. **dhe-dhéH₁mi, *dhedhH̥₁mós*); also the following:
G ἵστᾱμι (Att. ἵστημι) 'stand' but ἵσταμεν (PIE **stistéH₂mi, *stistH̥₂mós*; InIr. has a thematized formation here, **sti-stH₂-ᵉ/ₒ-*);
G δάμνᾱμι (Att. δάμνημι) 'tame' but δάμναμεν (root **demH₂-*, PIE *n*-infix pres. **dm̥-né-H₂-mi, *dm̥-n-H̥₂-mós*);
G δείκνῡμι 'point out' but δείκνῠμεν (PIE *nu*-suffix type **dik̑-néw-mi, *dik̑-nu-mós*), and so on.

So too the athem. opt. suffix (**-yéH₁-/-iH₁-*): G εἴην but εἶμεν (PIE **H₁s-yéH₁-m̥, *H₁s-iH₁-mé*; see **496.1**); τιθείην < **dhedhH̥₁yéH₁m̥* but τιθεῖμεν (etymon open to different interpretations depending on one's views of the sound laws: **dhe-dhH₁-iH₁-mé* might yield **titʰeyemen* or **titʰeīmen* directly, either of which would give the attested form; or **titʰīmen* or **titʰyemen* which would have been remodeled with weak stem τιθε-). These patterns were extended very generally through the language, so that forms like πίμπλημι, πίμπλαμεν 'fill' does not—cannot—reflect any PIE etymon directly. In a genuinely antique formation, in the case of this verb root, the zero grade **pl̥H₁* would have ended up in G homophonous with the full grade, namely -πλη- (**106.2**).

a. NOTES ON THE GRADATION OF ATHEMATIC STEMS.

1. Certain old-looking middles have full grade of the root, thus Ved. *śáye* 'is lying down' Av. *saēte*, G κεῖται. This is a distinct PIE type, known informally as Narten stems. They have tonic accent on the (full-grade) root in the middle voice. The evidence is strong for such a view (see **128.3a**); but it nevertheless only replaces an attested puzzle with one of an earlier date.

2. In G and InIr, athematic monosyllabic stems in *-eH-* commonly appear without gradation WITHIN A SINGLE TENSE. Thus Ved. *yā́ti* 3sg. 'goes', as expected, but also such forms as otherwise would take zero grade of the root: *yāthá(na)* 2pl., *yāmas* 1pl., *yāyām* 1sg.opt., *yāhí* imper., and so on. This is certainly secondary (4 below). In G such forms are ἄημι 'blow' (cf. Ved. *vā́ti* 'blows', with full grade in imper. *vāhi*, 3du. *vātas*); and aorists like ἔδρᾱν 'ran off', ἔβην (-ᾱ-) 'went', ἔβλην threw', ἔγνων 'was aware of', ἔδῡν 'sank, went into'. These all have a long vowel throughout, except for regular shortening before -ντ- (**63.2**), as in the pple. (ἀέντες, γνόντες, and the like) and the old 3pl. forms like ἔβᾰν, ἔγνον, ἔδῠν. There are a few relics of the original alternation, as ἔθεμεν, ἔδομεν (but ἔστημεν).

3. In L some few forms of the first and second conj. may belong here, as *nō* 'swim, float', *nās, nat, nāmus* (cf. Ved. *snā́ti* 'bathes', *snāmas* 1pl.), or *pleō* 'fill', *plēs, plet, plēmus* (cf. Ved. *prā́si* 2sg.). The L forms could however come from *yᵉ/ₒ*-stems, of a type that was enormously productive in Ital. (**456.1Ba**): **snāyō, *snāyesi, *snāyomos* and **plēyō, *plēyeti, *plēyomos* would yield identical results.

4. It is likely that non-ablauting full-grade athem. stems (imperat. *yāhí* rather than **īhí*, and so on) are the result of leveling, and continue nothing ancient. They nevertheless have been accepted by some scholars as original for the type. But the same freezing of ablaut in the full grade affects the athem. opt. in Indic (and also in Attic, **540**), so Ved. *syā́ma* 'may we be' and *syā́tha* 2pl., just like the sg. stem *syā-*. Here however, thanks to OL

singular/plural stem alternation (*siem* 1sg. but *sīmus* 1pl.), among other data, there can be no question about whether or not the stem originally alternated or not. A paradigm like *vā́ti* 'blows', *ūhí 'blow!', or *drā́si* 'you are running', 2pl. *dūrthá, might exist for a long time; but it is no wonder when such things are eliminated. Less self-evident is the early disappearance of plural forms like *īmási in favor of *yāmási*, and of pple. *īta- in favor of *yātá-*, since in some Indic paradigms there was a thriving -*ā*-/-*ī*- alternation, as in the so-called *nā*-stems: *pr̥ṇā́ti* 'fills', *pr̥ṇītas* 3du.

5. Evidence suggests that the root *ǵneH$_3$- 'know' did not ablaut, except late and by analogy. Similarly *bhū- (or *bhuH-) 'be(come)' had no full grade, hence unaltering ἔφῡν 1sg. In G, however, some apparently non-alternating stems may be the artifacts of sound laws: *dreH$_2$- as in *edreH$_2$t 3sg. and *dr̥H$_2$- as in *edr̥H$_2$me 1pl. would both yield G δρᾱ-, as seen definitively in the pres. διδρᾱ́σκω 'run off' < *di-dr̥H$_2$sḱ^e/o-.[1]

441. THE AUGMENT is a prefixal *e- added to past-tense eventive verbs (imperfects and aorists). In PIE it was seemingly a particle, whose quondam independence is reflected in the G rule that the accent cannot precede it, just as it cannot precede the last of two preverbs, so that παρ-έσχε 'kept in readiness' is parallel to παρ-έν-θες 'you put in beside'. Its original function is unknown, but a hint is provided by Old Ionic prose, in which the augment was regularly absent from imperfects built with -σκω. As such verbs referred not to specific events but to habitual or generalized matters, like NE *used to*, **456.3**, one may speculate that the original function of the augment was some kind of specifier, the anterior analog of the hic-et-nunc 'primary' markers (**419**). And like the elements distinguishing the primary endings, it was omitted in sequences of verb forms of the same tense and mood. Thus in Homeric Greek, Avestan, and Vedic Sanskrit, augmentless aorists and imperfects occur. In classical G, as in classical Skt., with the abandonment of the old system of reduced verb marking, the augment became fixed, and augmentless forms belong only to poetic usage. (See **416** for a discussion of these forms.)

The augment is attested in G, Indo-Iranian, and (in the tense called the aorist) Armenian.[2] In the remainder of the IE languages there is no trace of it, despite the great antiquity of a form like L *fēcī*. The question

---

[1] Note that ἔβην (ἔβᾱν) 'went' and ἔδρᾱν 'ran off' are not built to the same roots as βαίνω and δράσκω, respectively. InIr. (among others) attests two roots, *gam-* (PIE *g^{w}em-) and *gā-* (PIE *g^{w}eH-), of similar meaning ('go (away)' and 'approach', respectively) but very different morphology, apart from both being aoristic (punctual). These seem to have been gathered into a single covertly suppletive paradigm in G, just like many other, more obvious, suppletive aggregates.

[2] Phrygian is usually mentioned among the languages having the augment. This would not be surprising, in view of the extent of general similarity between G and Phygian; but there seems to be only one, doubtful, example of it. —Among modern IE languages, the augment is found in the imperf. and aor. of NG. It has been identified in Yaghnobi, a minority language of Iran, but its existence there has been questioned.

therefore is: did the augmentless languages all lose it, or did they never have it to begin with? The geographical pattern of distribution, taken together with the large number of innovations shared by G, Indo-Iranian, and Armenian, points to innovation. The prestige of G and InIr. in IE linguistics, however, has fostered acceptance of the augment as a feature of the parent language.

a. In verb complexes the normal position of the augment is after the preverb, as Skt. *abhyagacchat* (*abhigacchati* 'apprach'), G συνέλεγον (συλλέγω 'collect'), ἐξέβαλλον (ἐκ-βάλλω 'throw out'), and so on. But in G some were treated like simple verbs: ἐ-καθήμην from κάθ-ημαι (κάτ-ἧμαι) 'sit (still)' (ἧμαι); with temporal augment (442) ἠμφίεσα from ἀμφιέννῡμι 'put round' (ἕννῡμι 'clothe', PIE **wes-*), and ἠπιστάμην from ἐπίσταμαι 'understand' (ἵστημι < PIE *$steH_2$-).

442. THE GREEK TEMPORAL (QUANTITATIVE) AUGMENT. In G the ordinary prefix ἐ- is called the 'syllabic augment'; it reflects the original type, so ἔφερε is directly comparable to Ved. *ábharat* 3sg.imperf. Another type of augment in G is called the 'temporal augment', and is found in G alone. It entailed the lengthening of a word-initial vowel. It arose by imitation of paradigms in which the usual augment *e-* contracted with the initial vowel of the root (or a laryngeal) to make the corresponding long vowel. Thus from PIE *H_1*es-* 'be' the forms with the augment, **e-*H_1*es-* and **e-*H_1*s-* alike, contracted to **ēs-*, as in Ved. *ā́sam*, Hom. ἦα imperf. The ε : η relation observed in such inherited forms—if in fact the verb 'be' was not the principal source—was extended to all verb-initial vowels, hence α : ᾱ (Att. α : η), ο : ω, ι : ῑ, υ : ῡ.

1. The syllabic augment is sometimes ἠ- instead of ἐ-. Most of the examples are from roots beginning with ϝ-. In Vedic, a long augment *ā-* also occurs with tolerable certainty in forms built to six roots, all beginning with resonants: *naś-* 'attain', *ric-* 'leave' (PIE *$leyk^w$-), *var-* 'cover' (PIE **wer-*) and *var-* 'choose' (PIE **wel-*), *vṛj-* 'turn', and *vyadh-* 'wound'. For example, *ā́var* 2,3sg. 'you, he (un)covered'. Where there are no objections to doing so, it is possible to take these as evidence for a root-initial laryngeal, the augment being an ordinary **e-* lengthened in the usual way by the following laryngeal. The Skt. root *naś-* is an example of a form with clear evidence for an initial laryngeal, PIE *H_1*ne(n)ḱ-*, whence not only aor. *ā́naṭ* 2,3sg. < **e-*H_1*neḱs*, **e-*H_1*neḱt* but also perf. *ānáṃśa* 3sg. < *H_1*e-*H_1*nonḱ-e*. Similar evidence is provided by G ἤνεγκα, which serves as an aorist to φέρω. The form is superimposable (apart from the augment) on RV *naṃśi* 1sg.midd., that is from PIE **(e-)*H_1*nenḱ-*. (Further evidence for the initial laryngeal includes the inf. *parīṇáśe* 'to attain', with lengthening of the last vowel of the preverb *pari-*.)

This however is the only clear case. Typical of the rest is RV imperf. *ā́riṇak* 2sg. (*n*-infix, like L *linquit* and G -λιμπάνω), aor. *ā́rek*, both to the root *ric-* 'leave over'; this exhausts the evidence for an initial laryngeal in the PIE root *$(H)leyk^w$-. None of the many G forms— -λιμπάνω, ἔλιπον, λείπω, and so on—point in that direction. And the remaining Vedic forms showing such a phenomenon, few in number in any case, have little in the way of clear G cognates.[1]

Nor are G forms with η- augment limited to forms with evidence for an initial laryngeal; in fact it is found in forms where a laryngeal is inconceivable: Hom ᾔείδει plpf. < **ē-weyd-* 'know' (PIE **weyd-* 'know' certainly did not have a laryngeal before the **w*. The pluperfect is not an ancient formation in any case).

Some Att. forms with ἐ-, ἑ- are apparently examples of temporal augment which have been disguised by quantitative metathesis: ἐᾱ́γην pass. aor. from **ēwăgēn* (ᾰ̓́γνῡμι 'break, shatter'); ἑώρων impf. < **ēworōn*, (ὁράω 'see'), ἑᾱ́λων aor. < **ēwalon* (ἁλίσκομαι 'am caught'). But in fact the histories of all these forms are obscure in detail; ἄγνῡμι has no satisfactory etymology at all; ϝορ- (PIE **wer-* 'pay attention') is well-attested but has no hint of an initial laryngeal in G or anywhere else. (Everything would be taken care of by an etymon **swor-*, a possible alternative root-shape (**168d**) but not unambiguously attested elsewhere.) Finally, **wal-*, though it agrees in form with an assortment of words of vaguely appropriate meaning (L *vellō* 'pluck', Hitt. *walḫ-* 'fight'), affords no evidence for a laryngeal apart from a barely possible Hitt. *ḫu-ul-la-a-i* 'smites'. —The later Att. ἠβουλόμην (βούλομαι 'wish, intend'), ἤμελλον (μέλλω 'intend'), ἠδυνάμην (δύναμαι 'suffice, am equal to') are obviously secondary, perh. especially in view of the semantics specifically traceable to ἤθελον 'wished'—the imperf. of ἐθέλω, mistaken as the imperf. of θέλω.

2. Verbs which originally began with **s-*, **y-*, **w-* and **sw-* regularly (and properly) had the temporal augment, and if contraction took place this followed the rules of G contraction according to dialect (**86**). Thus from ἔχω (**hekʰō* < **seǵh-*) 'have', imperf. **ehekʰon*, Att. εἶχον, in some dialects ἦχον (cf. forms like ἦν 'I was' with η- in all dialects, that is, with ancient **ēs-* < **e-H₁(e)s-*). Similarly εἷρπον (ἕρπω 'creep' < **serp-*); εἱπόμην (ἕπομαι 'follow' < PG **hekʷ-* < **sekʷ-*); ἐωνούμην (ὠνέομαι 'buy' < **wosnos* 'price'); and Cret. εϝαδε, Ion ἕαδε (ἁνδάνω 'please' < **hwandanō* < **swad-*). The rough breathing in εἷρπον and the rest may be due to the analogy of the present, or have arisen like that of εὕω 'burn' < **euhō* (**172c**).

But some verbs take the temporal augment purely after the analogy of those with original vowel initial. So ἷζον (ἵζω 'seat' < **si-sd-*, root **sed-*); ὥρκισα (ὁρκίζω 'exact an oath'); Att. ᾤκουν (οἰκέω, ϝοικέω 'inhabit'); imperf. ἡλισκόμην and aor. ἥλων beside ἑᾱ́λων (ἁλίσκομαι, ϝαλίσκομαι 'am caught', above, item 1).

---

[1] A typical example: PIE **H₁wer-* 'cover' (Ved. *var-*) might be reflected in G εὐρώς, -ῶτος 'mold, mildew'. (Well, it covers things.) On the formal side, this connection depends upon the validity of the disputed sound law that takes εὐ-, αὐ-, οὐ- to be the regular G reflexes of PIE **H₁u-*, **H₂u-*, **H₃u-*, 100a. The root **wer-* is securely attested but this one questionable cognate is the only form pointing to an initial laryngeal.

443. REDUPLICATION. Reduplication in IE languages is the copying of all or part of a root to form a prefix. It is tempting to think that it originated in the doubling of a form to indicate repetition (as in NE *hoppity-hop*) or emphasis, though reduplication has such a variety of functions in the grammars of known languages, IE and otherwise, that such guesses must be seen as naive.

The roles of reduplication in IE morphology will be taken up under the stem types (451 and 459; and in the stative, 512); here the subject is solely the form.

1. The fullest form of reduplication, which reiterates the whole root, appears in the InIr. intensives, as Ved. *dardarīti* (*dar-* 'split, flay'), *carkarmi* 1sg. (*kar-* 'praise'), and in G πορ-φῦρω (a verb of uncertain meaning having to do with the motion of the sea), παμ-φαίνω 'shine splendidly', and L *murmurō* 'buzz'.

2. The following forms of reduplication probably started out like the preceding, but have been reduced to a single consonant or two followed by a vowel:

A. PRESENT/IMPERFECT AND AORIST REDUPLICATION. The root-initial consonant(s) followed by a vowel which, outside of InIr., is always *i*, so G ἵ-στημι (ἵστᾱμι: from **sti-steH$_2$-* with simplification of the initial cluster) 'stand', τί-θημι 'put', δί-δωμι 'give', γί-γνομαι 'am born', δι-δάσκω 'teach', ἵζω (**si-sd-*) 'seat'; L *sistō* 'stand' (trans.: also from **sti-stH$_2$-*, with a different simplification), *gignō* 'beget', *sīdō* (**si-sd-*) 'sit down', *serō* (**si-sH$_1$-*) 'sow'.

Reduplicating aorists were probably not numerous in PIE. A tolerably certain one is **e-we-wk^w-* (root **wek^w-* 'speak'): Ved. *ávocat* = G εἶπε (61.1a).

In InIr. the vowel of the reduplicating syllable varies. It is often *-i-* as in the other languages (*jígharti* 'moistens', *bíbharti* 'carries', *síṣakti* 'follows'). When the root contains a *-u-*, however, it is *-u-*, so *yuyoti* 'separates', (root *yu-*), *juhóti* 'pours' (root *hu-*); *aśuśruvur* 3pl.aor. 'made to hear' (root *śru-*). This is obviously an innovation; but the status of *a-*reduplication in InIr. is less obvious. Some authorities take forms like *dádāti* 'gives' (G δίδωμι), *rárate* 3pl. 'give over' (RV imper. *rirīhi*), *dádhāti* 'puts' (G τίθημι) as the same phenomenon as *yuyoti*, namely replacement of earlier *i*-reduplication (as in G) by a vowel matching the root. But against such a view, most roots with *a*-vocalism HAVE *i*-reduplication in the pres./imperf. (such as *mimā-* 'measure', *sisar-* 'run', *śiśā-* 'sharpen'). What is significant about this is its contrast with the perf. paradigm, where there is a virtually complete adjustment of the reduplication vowel to agree with the details of the root. These facts indicate that both *i-* and *e*-reduplication originally occurred in the pres. Now Hitt. has provided an abundance of eventives with *e*-reduplication, such as *me-im-ma-i* 'he says' and *ú-e-wa-ak-ki* 'begs' (cf. *ú-e-ik-zi* 'asks'). It is obvious that in the histories of G and L the few pres. stem forms with *e*-reduplication were eliminated in favor of a uniform contrast between a present-tense-only *i*-reduplication and perf.-only *e*-reduplication.

B. STATIVE (PERFECT) REDUPLICATION. Originally this was with the vowel **e* only, as in G δέδορκα 'saw', λέλοιπα 'saved', L *cecinī* 'sang', *pepulī* 'beat', *tetigī* 'touched', Go. *faifalþ* 'folded', *h^{w}aih^{w}op* 'boasted'. In InIr. and L (523), however, as a result of analogy the vowel of the reduplication almost entirely came to agree with the vocalism of the root, so L *cucurrī* 'ran', Ved. *śuśru-* 'hear', *viviś-* 'enter'; additionally, Indic adjusts the reduplication vowel when the root begins with a glide, as *uvac-* 'say' (**vu-vac-*), *iyaj-* 'perform a rite' (**yi-yaj-*).

In G a type peculiar to the perfect stem develops, the so-called Attic Reduplication, as in *ὄρωρα* 'stir myself' (root *ὀρ-*). This formation is discussed in 444.

3. Consonants. In the present and perfect reduplication, if the root begins with a single consonant this is copied in the reduplication, as above: Ved. *dadárśa*, G *δέδορκα* 'saw' (root **derḱ-*). (The dissimilation of aspirates—Grassmann's Law (138)—accounts for Ved. *dádhāti* 'puts', *juhóti* 'pours', G *τίθημι*, *κέχυκα*.)

When a root began with **s-* followed by a stop, both consonants were reduplicated. Direct evidence is provided by Gmc. (Go. *skaiskaiþ* 'cut', *gastaistald* 'procured'), Ved. (*paspaśé* 'sees': root *spaś-* seen in *spáśa-* 'spy'), and L (*spopondī* 'pledged', OL *scicidī* 'split'). Indirect evidence is provided by inconsistencies from language to language and form to form: from the selfsame root **steH₂-* come not only L *sistō*, G *ἵστημι*, and Av. *hi-štaiti*, but also Ved. *tíṣṭhati*; and L perfs. *stitī*, *stetī*. The most economical explanation is that these are all products of an original **sti-steH₂-*/**ste-stoH₂-*.

When the root begins with any other sequence of two or more consonants, only the first is copied, as in Ved. *jagrábha* 'I seized' (root *gra(b)h-*), G *βέβρῑθα* 'am weighed down' (*βρῑ́θω*).

Note that a large number of forms like *βέβληται* 'put (on)' and *τετμηώς* 'cutting' have a different explanation. In these, the consonant clusters are not originally root-initial, but arise from the action of sound laws (104–7) on **g^we-g^wl̥H₁-* and **te-tm̥H₂-*, built to roots **g^welH₁-* and **temH₂-*.

444. Attic reduplication is found in roots beginning (descriptively) with a short vowel; the reduplicated stem copies the short vowel and the following consonant, and the original root-initial vowel appears long, as *ὄρωρα* 'stir myself' to *ὄρ-νῡμι*. The type is not paralleled in any other IE language, but must be old within G on the basis of the vowels *-ω-* and *-η-* rather than *-ου-* and *-ει-* serving as the long equivalents of *-ο-*, *-ε-* (76).

The usual explanation of these stems appeals to intensive reduplication (443.1) as the model. Intensive reduplication copies the whole root, as in Ved. *várvarti* 'covers' (root *var-*). From such a basis, Attic Reduplication resulted from loss of the final consonant of the reduplication, with compensatory lengthening, with forms like *ὄρωρα* analogical to the resulting pattern. The demerits of the theory are three. The least of them is the unlikelihood that intensive and stative morphology could thus interact. A much graver demerit is that it fails to explain why such formations are peculiar to stems or roots beginning with a short vowel, with no parallel forms like ˣ*λῖλοιπα* < **lik^wloik^wa*. In fact, the great majority of the attested forms, like ὄρωρα, above, ὀμώμοκα 'swear an oath', ἀκήκοα 'heard', ἐνήνοχα 'carried' cannot be traced directly to any such process, but must themselves be analogical. Finally, the very basis for the explanation is untenable by current views of G historical phonology: a construct like *(e)nek̑-nok̑- was thinkable before the advent of the laryngeal theory, but a reconstruction in accord with current views, *H_1nek̑-H_1nok̑-, would give PG ×enekenok-.

A more promising explanation traces the characteristic shape of Attic Reduplication to roots beginning with a cluster of a laryngeal followed by a consonant, with the full consonant cluster appearing in the reduplicating syllable. That is, to a root like *H_1lewdh- 'run' (whose laryngeal is posited, it must be admitted, mostly in the service of this explanation) the reduplicating syllable was not *H_1e- but *H_1le-. The resulting shape, *H_1le-H_1lowdh-/*H_1le-H_1ludh-, gave G *elēlout^h-/elēlut^h- directly. From such forms it spread to others where it can hardly be original: ἐδηδώς 'having eaten' (*H_1e-H_1od-, *H_1e-H_1d-); ὄδωδα 'smelled' (*H_3eH_3(o)d-); and ὄρωρα.

But this theory demands reduplication of a type unparalleled by initial clusters of a more directly observable kind, namely obstruent plus resonant. Unlike reduplication of the *ste-st- type, for which there is good evidence, there is no evidence at all for reduplication of the *pre-pr- or *sle-sl- type, which would seem to be apter parallels for the proposed *Hle-Hl- type.

It seems significant that the forms eligible for this type of reduplication are defined by their shape IN GREEK, rather than in PIE. So for example ὀδ- 'smell', ἐδ- 'eat' show Attic Reduplication despite not having the right PIE shape (according to the theory just mentioned). Even more telling, there are some PIE roots which should have Attic Reduplication, by reason of their word-initial laryngeal, but do not: to αἴρω 'take up' < ἀείρω < *aweryō < *H_2wer- the perf. stem should have been *H_2we-H_2wor- or *H_2we-H_2wr-. The former would give early ×ἀήορα (or ×ἀήορκα), the latter ×ἄαυρα (or ×ἄαυρκα). Instead what we find is ἦρκα, ἦρμαι.

The correct explanation does depend on root-initial laryngeals, in fact, but probably starts from roots like *H_3er- 'rise', *H_3ed- 'smell' rather than roots like *H_1leudh-, and relies on the ordinary type of reduplication: both *H_3e-H_3or- and *H_3e-H_3r- should have given G *ὦρα; both *H_3e-H_3od- and *H_3e-H_3d- should have given G *ὦδα; so too, though much less certainly, *ēdwōs 'having eaten' < *H_1e-H_1d-wos-. But such forms would not look like reduplicated stems at all (from the G standpoint they look like augmented forms). Nevertheless, the expected shapes *ὠρ- *ὠδ-, *ἠδ- are the source of the otherwise strange presence of long vowels in the root in Attic Reduplication. The creation of new forms ὄρ-ωρα, ὄδ-ωδα, ἐδ-ηδώς resembles the 'internal reduplication' seen in the aorists of a few verbs which, significantly, share the trait of beginning with short vowels: to ἐρῡ́κω 'keep in check' Homeric aor. ἐρύκακον (next to ἔρυξα). The ruling idea in both types seems to be the procurement of consonantal reduplication by hook or crook.

445. SPECIAL GREEK DEVELOPMENTS.

1. Alternation between reflexes of labiovelars (154, 161-3) in reduplication is nearly always leveled, as βέβαμεν for *δεβα- < *g^we-g^wa- (βαίνω), aor. ἔπεφνον 'slew' < *e-g^whe-g^whn- (θείνω; 164A.1).

2. For roots beginning with *s-, *w-, and *y-, odd-looking but historically regular shapes result from regular changes:

Many such perfects have ἐ- rather than reduplication. This type started with perfects from roots beginning with σ- plus consonant (στ-, σπ-, σκ- but including ζ-, and ῥ- < *sr-): ἔσταλμαι (στέλλω 'equip'), ἔσπαρμαι (σπείρω 'sow'), ἐρρύηκα (ῥέω 'flow' < *srew-), in which the initial *s- of the (reduced) reduplication became *h*-, and the resulting ἐ- fell together with the usual form of the augment ἐ-. From such the ἐ- spread to words beginning with other combinations: so 'ἐ-reduplication' is the rule not only to roots beginning with σπ-, στ-, and σκ- but also ζ-, ξ-, ψ-; πτ-, γν-, and in part from those beginning with ῥ- (so always in Att.), γλ-, βλ-, and γρ-. There is hesitation in some verbs (γλύφω 'carve', βλαστάνω 'sprout'); and a dialectal difference is seen in Ion. ἔκτημαι = Att. κέκτημαι (κτάομαι 'procure, obtain'); Cret., El. εγραμμαι = Att. γέγραμμαι (γράφω).

3. The perfects εἴληφα (λαμβάνω 'take') and εἵμαρται (μείρομαι 'get one's share') come regularly from *he-slap^h- (*se-slabh-; but see 517.2), *se-smr̥- (227.2). From these the ει- spread to roots that never began with *s: εἴληχα (λαγχάνω 'obtain by lot'), and συν-είλοχα, συν-είλεγμαι (συλλέγω 'gather'; and note that λέγω 'say', originally the selfsame verb, has regular morphology).

a. In εἴρηκα (ἐρέω 'say'), εἰρύαται 3pl. 'draw', and εἴλῡμαι 'am covered' we are dealing with a genuine diphthong, the result of dissimilation from *we-wr-, *we-wl- like εἶπον < *eweik^w- < *ewewk^w- (61.1a).

4. In verbs beginning with ζ- < *y-, the reduplication in ἐ- (as in ἔζευγμαι, perf. midd. to ζεύγνῡμι) must have some such history as *ǰeyowg- → *ǰeǰowg- > *sdesdowg- (201) > *sesdowg- > *hesdowg- (→ *hesdewg-) > ἐζευγ-. There is nowhere any trace of laryngeals in any of these developments.

But in verbs beginning with ζ- < *dy-, the original (and regular) reduplication was διζ-, as in Hom. δίζημαι 'seek' < *didyā- (< *di-diH_2-, 49.2); but to ζητέω (ζᾱτ-) from the same root—the formation is apparently an intensive built from an unattested pple. *ζᾱτός—the later perf. is ἐζήτηκα, by analogy to the foregoing.

a. The perf. ἔφθιται to φθίνω 'decay' is remarkable. One can understand that expected *πτέφθιται may have been vulnerable to replacement, but the apparent results of the remodeling are unanticipated.

b. In 206 it was argued that the change of *s- to PG *h- must have predated the Second Greek Palatalization. The different reduplication of initial ζ- depending on its source in Pre-G *y- or *dy-, *gy- seems to accord with that view. That is, the reduplication of ζ- from *y- seems to predate the change of *s- to *h-, that of ζ- from stop + *-y- seems to postdate it.

EVENTIVE STEM FORMATIONS

446. The parent speech had a number of present/imperfect formations, and a much smaller array of aorist formations. It is probable that each of these originally had some function. Some of these are becoming more clear, but we have to take some of the stem-formations merely as formal types.

Synopsis of eventive stems FROM THE PROTO-INDO-EUROPEAN POINT OF VIEW:

1. Uncharacterized 447-9
    - Root inflection (pres./imperf. and aor.) 447-8
    - Simple thematic (pres./imperf. and aor.) 449
2. Characterized 450-8
    - I. Present/imperfect *and* aorist.
        - Reduplicated (pres./imperf.) 451A-B; (aor.) 451C
        - Stative in *-eH_1- (pres./imperf. and aor.; denominative) 452
    - II. Present/imperfect *only*.
        - *n*-infix 453-4
        - *new*-suffix 455
        - Characterized thematic stems 456
            1. *-y^e/o-
            2. *-ey^e/o-, *-eH_2y^e/o-
            3. *-$\acute{s}k^e/o$-
        - Desiderative *-H_1s^e/o- 457
            - A. *i*-reduplication
            - B. unreduplicated
            - C. *-H_1sy^e/o-
        - Miscellany 458.
    - III. Aorist *only*.
        - Athematic *-*s*- 459
    - IV. Denominative *-y^e/o- 460-2

In a given IE language some stem types will remain productive, while others disappear or are represented by a relic class or maybe a stray form or two. By phonetic changes one type may give rise to several; or conversely distinct stem types may merge in one. New types arise and become productive.

The results are so diverse that classifications tailored to the specifics of the various branches of the IE family are unavoidable. This is an obstacle to straightforward comparison of the systems Greek and Latin, or even of details within the systems: the classification of L verbs under the four conjugations based on the infinitive, for example, is passably suited to the facts of L, but it would be quite unsuitable for G and for the parent language, in both of which there is little or nothing of 'conjugations' in the L sense.

For these reasons, the scheme followed here will cover the same ground twice. First, there will be a survey of the important PIE stem classes (447-62), with remarks about their fates in IE languages, including G and L. Then the stem-classes of G and L be considered, separately perforce but keyed by cross-references to the earlier general discussion.

UNCHARACTERIZED EVENTIVE STEMS

447. ROOT INFLECTION. (Durative and punctual.) In root present and aorist stems the person endings are added directly to the root. This is the most basic formation of all, giving the raw force of the verb root. Therefore it is diagnostic of whether a given root was originally punctual, in which case the root formation is an aorist contrasting with one or more characterized presents; or durative, in which case the root formation was a present/imperfect, and the aorist is characterized. Such a test is pretty reliable because the root class was a relic class in all of the daughter languages. A rough tally of root present/imperfect stems, exclusive of compounds, is as follows:

Hittite:	60	
Vedic:	130	
Classical Skt.:	50	
Germanic:	1	('be')
Greek:	9	(all ending in vowels except ἐσ- 'be')
Latin:	4	(*sum, volō, dō, eō,* all of which have some thematic forms)

The root ablaut:

Full (*e*-)grade: the singular of the indic. active (in which the tonic accent was on the root); throughout the subjunctive.

Zero grade: all du. and pl. forms; all middle forms. In these the tonic accent was on a suffix or the personal endings. Zero grade also in the optative, which was built with the affix **-yéH₁-/-iH₁-* (539).

a. Narten Roots have fixed, root-accented, full grades in all forms—not only in the active but in the middle voice, most conpicuously in deponents (**128.3a, 440a.1**).

b. In Ved. and G root aorists the full grade in the active occurs throughout the du. and in the 1,2pl. Some authorities wonder if this might be an old feature, but it is more likely that it developed independently in InIr. and G from an earlier system with ablaut more in accord with the general pattern.

448. Some examples of *present indicative active* root inflection.

HITTITE:	*kuen-/kun-* 'kill'	*ep-/ap-* 'take'	*eš-/aš-* 'be'	*ed-/ad-* 'eat'
1	ku-e-mi (!)	e-ip-mi	e-eš-mi	e-it-mi
2	ku-e-ši, ku-en-ti	e-ip-ši		
3	ku(-e)-en-zi	e-ip-zi	e-eš-zi	e(-iz)-za-az-zi
1		ip-pu-u-e-ni		a-tu-e-ni
2		e-ip-te(-e)-ni		az-za-aš-te-ni
3	ku-na-an-zi	ap-pa(-a)-an-zi	a-ša-an-zi	a-da-an-zi

Hitt. *ku-en-ti* 2sg. has the ending proper to the *ḫi*-conj. (A certain amount of hesitation between the two conjugations is found in Hitt., the bulk of it involving the 2sg.) Regarding *e(-iz)-za-az-zi* and *az-za-aš-te-ni*, see **212**.

VEDIC:		*han-/ghn-* 'kill'	*e-/i-* 'go'	*as-/s-* 'be'	*ad-* 'eat'
	1	hanmi	émi	ásmi	admi
	2	háṃsi	éṣi	ási (!)	átsi
	3	hánti	éti	ásti	átti
	1	hanmas	imási	smás(i)	
	2	hanthá	ithá	sthá(na)	
	3	ghnánti	yánti	sánti	adanti

GREEK:		φη-[1] 'say'	ει- 'go'	εσ- 'be'
	1	φημί	εἶμι[3]	εἰμί,[4] dial. ἔμμι
	2	φῄς[2]	εἶ	εἶ, εἶς, ἐσσί
	3	φησί	εἶσι	ἐστί
	1	φαμέν	ἴμεν	ἐσμέν, εἰμέν
	2	φατέ	ἴτε	ἐστέ
	3	φασί	ἴᾱσι	εἰσί,[4] Dor. ἐντί
				Myc. e-e-si

1. Dor. φᾱ-. This verb and εἰμί 'am' are the only G verbs with the PIE enclitic accentuation, sometimes written φημὶ, εἰμὶ.
2. φῄς ← *p^hēi < *p^hāsi. 3. Genuine diphthong. 4. Spurious diphthong.

LATIN:		*īre* 'to go'	*dare* 'to give'	*velle* 'to want'
	1	eō	dō	volō
	2	īs	dās	vīs
	3	it, OL īt	dat	vult
	1	īmus	damus	volumus
	2	ītis	datis	vultis
	3	eunt	dant	volunt

The details of the L paradigms will be discussed in **486** (*eō*), **488** (*dō*), and **484** (*volō*).

In GERMANIC the one surviving root present is 'be' (**491-3**); all the Gmc. groups have innovated in various ways; the PGmc. paradigm was manifestly different from any of these:

	Gothic	OHG	OE	ON
1	im	bim	eom	em
2	is	bist	eart, earþ	est (ert)
3	ist	ist	is	(er)
1	sijum	birum	sind(on)	erom
2	sijuþ	birut	"	eroþ
3	sind	sint	"	ero

The OE 2sg. *earþ* is limited to Mercian, where it is not the common form. It is the only form in all of Gmc. with the expected form of the stative 2sg. ending *-þ*.

449. SIMPLE THEMATIC INFLECTION was in competition with and tended to replace the root type. It is formed with tonic root in *e*-grade; the only stem-feature is the theme vowel *-^{e}/$_o$- (**439**).

This or that IE language attests simple thematic pres./imperf. stems with roots in zero grade, but that is a later type which arose independently: so RV *dvéṣṭi* 3sg., *dviṣánti* 3pl. 'hate' attests a root inflection, **dwéys-ti*, **dwis-énti*; the stem seen in *dviṣati* 3sg. is first attested in the Sūtras and manifestly is a thematization starting from the structurally ambiguous 3pl. *dviṣanti*. Similarly G γραφ- 'scratch, write': all the G formations, noun and verb alike, appear to continue a stuck zero grade **ǵr̥bh-* whose full grade **ǵerbh-* —if it is not a Germanic creation—is attested in OE *ceorfan* for example (NE *carve* is a borrowing from the cognate Scand. form). In any case, the division into full-grade and zero-grade stems has no importance for the classification of G and L presents.

The simple thematic type is virtually non-existent in Hitt. In later PIE, however, it was a productive ('open') class, and, as with all productive types, there is no way of identifying which verbs thus inflected in PIE.[1] This class remained productive in InIr., but in G, L, and other daughter languages such as Gmc., the simple thematic presents themselves become a closed (relic) class (see 479.1).

THEMATIC AORISTS, like thematic presents, were the rival of and successor to the root formation, but the similarity ends there. First, thematic aorists are typically built to the zero grade of the root rather than the *e*-grade; typical are G ἔλιπον (**leykʷ-*), Ved. *ávidat* 'found' (**weyd-*). Second, their rise is later than the thematic present/imperfects, with the result that there is little lexical agreement from language to language: **ewidom* 'I found', seen in Ved. *ávidam*, G εἶδον, and at most one or two others, exhaust the list of agreements between these two usually highly congruent languages. Furthermore, though the innovation was a vigorous one, there are notably fewer thematic aorists in the RV than simple thematic presents. (More than 300 roots form simple thematic pres./imperf., next to 130 building root presents. But next to the approximately 60 roots that make thematic aorists there are 80 root aorists; and as a large percentage of the thematic aorist stems are attested in only a form or two, the different importance of the two types is not fully revealed by these two numbers.)

CHARACTERIZED EVENTIVE STEMS

450. At least in the beginning, all characterized stems were formed only to roots: two stem-affixes did not occur together. This was a purely abstract structural principle, like the principle that limits modal auxiliaries in NE verb-phrases to one only. Pragmatically speaking, there is no objection to such combinations as causative + desiderative (make someone wish

---

[1] That is, simulacra of **sekʷ-ᵉ/ₒ-* midd. 'follow' are attested in Celt., Ital., G, Lith., and InIr. A hypothesis of independent innovation is just as plausible as a hypothesis of common inheritance, since thematic stems are a productive type.

to do something) or the reverse (wish to make someone do something); habitual + causative (always make someone do something); and so on. The combining of such stem elements does eventually become routine in IE languages, but it was very limited in the earliest texts: in all of the Rigveda there are but two examples of a future to a causative (the future marker in Skt. continues what was originally a characterized stem, with desiderative force, 457C, cf. 500). Later, futures to causatives are commonplace.

a. There is in Rigvedic a similarly extreme rarity of MODES built to characterized stems of any kind (533), the optative being exceptionally scarce: there are four optative causatives in the entire RV, half-a-dozen optative denominatives. Similarly for the athematic characterized stems: there are no optatives at all for the intensive, there is a single opt. built to an *n*-infix present, and another unique form to a *nā*-present (historically the *n*-infix type, 453C, 454A.2). Although the optative markers, both athem. *-*yeH*$_1$-/-*iH*$_1$- and thematic *-*oy(H*$_1$*)*-, are not generally treated as derivational affixes in grammars of PIE, their distribution in Rigvedic verb morphology indicates that they were originally a deverbative element in the same set with affixes like *-*sḱ*^{e}/$_o$- 'habitual' (456.3), *-*eH*$_1$- 'stative' (452), *-*éy*^{e}/$_o$- 'causative' (456.2), and the rest, discussed below. See 533.

451. REDUPLICATED STEMS.

A. ATHEMATIC PRESENT/IMPERFECT. The position taken here is that the reduplicating prefix of eventive stems was built with either *e* or *i*, and that apart from InIr. the latter was generalized (443.2A). The root has *e*-grade in the singular act.indic., zero grade elsewhere. The location of the tonic accent is peculiar in Vedic: with the exception of one verb, it falls on the reduplicating syllable in the forms which take full grade of the root. This state of affairs must be secondary. (In the 3pl., unlike the du. and the other pl. forms, the accent is not on the ending but on the reduplication, and both root and ending are in the zero grade: *dádhati* 'they put' < **dhé-dhH*$_1$*n̥ti*, *júhvati* 'they pour' < **ǵhé-ǵhwn̥ti*, *sáścati* 'they follow' < **sé-sk*^{w}*n̥ti*. The other forms are more typical: *juhūmási* 'we call' < **ǵhe-ǵhuH-mós*, *juhuyā́t* 3sg.opt. 'may he pour' < **ǵhe-ǵhu-yéH*$_1$*-t*.) The single paradigm in Ved. with the accent in the expected place—on the full grade of the root—is *juhómi* 1sg. 'I pour', *juhóti* 3sg. Hitt. has many reduplicated present stems, but in the *mi*-conjugation (which corresponds most closely to the eventives) it seems not to be a class per se, and the reduplication is often of the full sort seen in InIr. intensives (Ved. *bharibhrati* 3pl. 'they carry hither and thither'), but no specific semantic flavor, 'intensive' or anything else, can be discovered from the texts themselves. There are no redup. pres. stems in BS, Gmc., or Celt.

In G the type is represented by a tiny but prominent relic class. Reduplicated stems are built to half a dozen roots whose full grade ends in a long vowel (that is, full grade + laryngeal). The central forms are τίθημι 'put' (Ved. *dádhāmi*, PIE **dhedheH*$_1$*mi*); δίδωμι 'give' (Ved. *dádāmi*, PIE **dedeH*$_3$*mi*); ἵστημι, Dor. ἵστᾱμι 'stand' (PIE **stisteH*$_2$*mi*); and ἵημι 'cast, send' (PIE **yiyeH*$_1$*mi*?; cf. L *iaciō*, *iēcī*, like *faciō*, *fēcī*; but for this company the G form is unusually isolated). The remaining G forms are peripheral, or at least of opaque history, such as ὀνίνημι 'assist, gratify'.

A number more have been thematized, such as γίγνομαι 'am born' (cf. L *gignō* 'beget'), μίμνω 'stay, stand fast' (cf. Ved. *pári mamanyāt* 3sg. opt. < **me-mn̥-yeH₁-*).

The type has been completely absorbed into the thematic (3rd conj.) class in L; the basis is the zero grade of the stem: *sistō* 'set up' < **sti-stH₂-* (G ἵστημι, Ved. *tíṣṭhati*—the latter thematized); *sīdō* 'sit down' < **si-sd-* (G ἵζω, Ved. *sī́dati*); *serō* 'sow' < **si-sH₁-*; *reddō* 'give back' < **rededō* < **-de-dH₃-*.

B. THEMATIC PRESENT/IMPERFECT. Even in InIr., where the original athematic type is not only at home but enjoyed a certain productivity, a number of quondam reduplicated pres./imperf. stems were thematized (*tíṣṭhati*, above). The process seems to have started anciently, though there is only one such stem that can be confidently postulated for the parent language: **pib(H₃)eti* 'drinks', as seen in Ved. *píbati* (next to root aor. *ápāt*), L *bibō* with assimilation (cf. Falisc. PIPAFO fut.), OIr. *ibid.* This is based on **poH₃-y-* seen in G πῑ́νω 'drink', πῶθι 'drink!', πῶμα 'a drink', L *pōtus* 'drunk' (in both senses of the word). Without the aberrant voicing of the medial stop, it would not be possible to date this form to PIE times so confidently.[1] A second thematization, **si-sd-ᵉ/ₒ-* 'sit' is attested in L *sīdō*, G ἵζω, Ved. *sī́dati*, and may be inherited.

C. AORIST. Reduplicated aorist stems are virtually limited to InIr. and G, where they generally function as the aorist to causative formations in **-éyᵉ/ₒ-* (456.2). This seems an unlikely coincidence, and is usually taken as inherited. Nevertheless, there is little lexical agreement between the two groups; indeed, the only form which can be confidently viewed as inherited does not have causative force in either InIr. or G: Ved. *ávocam* 'I said' = G εἶπον both from **e-we-wkʷ-o-m* (see 61.1a).[2] In the RV some 10 formations out of 90 are athematic, such as *síṣvap* 2sg. 'you put to sleep' (caus. pres. *svāpaya-*); there is nothing which distinguishes the athematics as archaic. In G, there are no athematic reduplicated aorists.

A redup. aor. formation has been discerned in L *tetigī* 'touched'. By itself, it is formally indistinguishable from a reduplicated perfect; but the meaning is inappropriate for a perfect (410, 509), and G τεταγών, -όντος 'having grabbed', if it is an aor. participle (as an isolated form, its paradigmatic relationships are debatable), would favor such an interpretation.

---

[1] The form is traced by many to **pi-pH₃-*, and is taken as evidence —virtually the only evidence—that **H₃* was distinctively voiced. The form has been identified as hypocoristic by others, however, an alternative if ad hoc explanation for the voicing.

[2] The Hindu grammarians give *avīvacat* (unattested textually) as the aor. to the causative; this form is in accord with the usual Indic redup. aor., with such secondary features as the lengthened vowel in the reduplication and the full grade of the root.

452. STATIVE STEMS IN **-eH*$_1$*-*/**-H̥*$_1$*-*. This is well-attested in L, Celt., Gmc., and BS, and marginally in Av. and early Hitt. It has two functions: making stative (or durative) forms out of aoristic roots, and stative denominatives. In L for example the ancient lexical contrast between the punctual (aoristic) roots for 'sit (down)', **sed-*, and the durative counterpart **ēs-* (**eH*$_1$*s-?*) 'is sitting' was lost. In place of the latter, the aoristic root occurs with a stem in **-eH*$_1$*-* (and probably with a further thematic suffix, **-y*^{e}*/o-*, whose presence is hidden in Ital. by the action of sound laws): **si-sd-* 'sit down' > L *sīdō*, vs. **sed-eH*$_1$*-y*^{e}*/o-* 'is seated' > L *sedeō*; cf. OCS *sěděti*, Lith. *sėdė́ti* (root **sēd-* is secondary). This type underlies the Class III weak verbs of Germanic (for example Go. *habaiþ* 'has', where however the suffix appears to be in zero grade, PGmc. **ha-ƀ-ayiþ* < **kap-H̥*$_1$*-ye-ti*, cf. L *habet* < **ghabh-eH*$_1$*-ye-ti*), though L attests zero grade of the stem in perf. *habuī* < **hab-a-wai* < **ghabh-H̥*$_1$*-*. In L there are a number of pairwise durative and punctual verbs, the durative member formed with this stem: *capiō* 'take' vs. *habeō* 'have' (etymology above); *sīdō* vs. *sedeō* (etymologies above); *pendō* 'suspend' vs. *pendeō* 'am hanging'; OL *vegeō* 'quicken, enliven' < caus. **woǵ-ey*^{e}*/o-* vs. *vigeō* (*-i-* unexpected) < **weǵ-eH*$_1$*-* 'am vigorous'; disguised by the effects of sound laws: *sistō* 'set up' vs. *stō* 'stand' < Ital. **staēy*^{e}*/o-* < **stH̥*$_2$*-eH*$_1$*-y*^{e}*/o-*, 475.5 (the two present stems share a pple. *stătus*). Others, like *taceō* 'am silent' (cf. Go. *þahaidedun* 'they were quiet' < **tak-H̥*$_1$*-y*^{e}*/o-*) correspond to no eventive. (All other verbs of this class are in the L 2nd conj. (477.2), but *stō* was transformed by sound laws into a slightly aberrant 1st conj.)

In G the deverbative type may be attested in the pair πεινῇ 'is hungry' (*πεινήει), διψῇ 'is thirsty' (*διψήει), though the point is blunted by the obscurity of the roots themselves. On the other hand, the denominative type is abundant in the pres./imperf. system, as seen in verbs like θαμβέω 'am astounded' (θάμβος 'astonishment'), ῥῑγέω 'am cold' (ῥῖγος 'frost'), and ἀλγέω 'feel pain' (ἄλγος). These are formally indistinguishable from ordinary denominative stems (462), but a typical denominative to ἄλγος 'pain' should mean 'cause pain' rather than 'feel pain', and so on. Additional reason for suspecting a stative stem in -η- in these forms is the formal and lexical match with L statives *frīgeō* 'am (stiff with) cold' and *algeō* 'am cold'. A few OIr. forms are easiest to explain thus, as *·ruidi* /ruδʹi/ 'is red' < PCelt. **rudīt* < **rudhēti* < **rudh-eH*$_1$*-*. And Old Hitt. provides such forms as *na-ak-ke-e-iz-zi* 'is important' (cf. *na-ak-ki-* 'heavy') and *mar-še-e-er* 'were false' (cf. *mar-ša-* 'false').

AORIST. In G the **-eH*$_1$*-* statives are generously attested in aor. formations. This type is confined to G, and may be an innovation. In fact, an aor. of a (derived) stative may seem like an impossibility, since 'stative' and 'aorist' are to a degree contrary notions. The point of entry appears to have been the proper aoristic notion 'arrive at a state'; thus to μίγνῡμι 'mix', ἐμίγην < **mig-eH*$_1$*-* 'got mixed' (opt. μιγ-ε-ίην < **-H̥*$_1$*-yeH*$_1$*-m̥*); to μαίνομαι 'rage, am furious' aor. ἐμάνην 'was driven mad, went mad'; ἐχάρην 'became happy' (χαίρω); ἐσάπη 'became rotten' (σήπω); and ἐφύην (a late formation) simply 'became'. —This affix has been mentioned as an ingredient in the passive aor. marker -θη- (508.2), though there are many problems with this as with all other explanations.

Not all forms resembling these belong here: ἔβλην 'threw', for example, is secondary; the genuinely old form is ἔβλητο < *e-g^wl̥H_1-to, an ordinary root-aor.

a. A characterized athematic stem should have been built to the zero grade of the root, and the athematic stem-element should have alternated between tonic *-éH_1- (in the sg.) and atonic *-H_1- (du., pl.). No IE language directly attests such a state of affairs for this marker, but the attested remnants of the stem formation are not inconsistent with such a history. BS generalized the zero grade in the present stems, the full grade in the non-present stems (including the infin.). The Germanic Class III weak verbs, mostly stative and frequently denominative, are built with a stem element *-ai-/*-ā-, straightforwardly from *-H̥$_1$-ye- and *-H̥$_1$-yo-, respectively (via *-ayi-, *-aya-), that is, zero grade of the original stem—as in BS—plus the thematic affix *-y^e/o- (456.1Ba). The history of the G stem formations seems to be tangled up in the history of the denominatives in -αω and is in several ways obscure; it will be discussed below (468.1). The loss of alternation in G parallels the athem. opt. suffix (540) and root aorists (507.1). And finally, in a mirror image of the BS generalization, L has the full grade in the pres. stem and the tenses derived from it (*monēbam* and the rest), namely *-eH_1-, probably with a thematic tag *-y^e/o- as in Gmc.; and the short vowel in the perf. -*uī* (528a) continues *-a-wai (66.5) < *-H̥$_1$-.

453. Nasal infix stems. This type was formed by the ablauting affix *-*né*-/*-*n*- inserted before the last consonant of the root. The root itself is in zero grade; the affix ablauts like a root present: full grade (tonic) in the sg.act.indic., zero grade elsewhere, that is, when the tonic accent is on a suffix. Thus, to the root *$leyk^w$- 'leave', the stem-forms are *li-né-k^w-, atonic *li-n-k^w-.

There are constraints on the possible shapes of roots which form *n*-infix stems: the final consonant is always either a stop or a laryngeal, except for *w in one root (*ḱlew*- 'hear': pres. **ḱl̥-né-w-ti*, **ḱl̥-n-w-énti*); and all roots contain a non-initial resonant. Thus roots like **yewg*- 'join', *mel*H*- 'grind', *pleH_1- 'fill', *k^wreyH_2- 'buy', and *sterH_3- 'spread' form *n*-infix presents. Roots like **ed*- (or *H_1ed-) 'eat', **sed*- 'sit', *wek^w- 'speak', and **ḱey*- 'lie down' do not, seemingly cannot, form such stems. There are attestations, particularly from InIr., for such stems built to roots of a shape like **ghrebhH*- 'seize' (Ved. *gr̥bhṇā́ti*) and *metH_2- 'stir vigorously' (Ved. *ámathnāt* 3sg.impf.). But these may well be secondary imitations of routine *n*-infix stems to disyllabic roots (121-3) like *demH_2- 'tame'.

Note that the zero grades of *n*-infix stems violate the rules (93.2) that otherwise govern syllabicity in sequences of resonants. According to those rules, **ḱlnuenti* 'they hear' should be syllabified ˣ*ḱln̥wenti*, likewise ˣpln̥H_1enti, ˣ*iwn̥genti*. However, the *n of the *n*-infix is never syllabic; the distribution of syllabicity in adjacent resonants follows from that given: **ḱl̥nwenti*, *pl̥nH_1enti, **yungenti*.

Interestingly, many of the best attested *n*-infix stems are built to roots also attested in a shorter form which additionally has a variety of 'root extensions'; so for instance **yew-*, **yew-H-*, and **yew-g-*, all mean basically 'join, link'; to **yewg-* is built the *n*-infix stem **yunég-*/**yung-* 'yoke, harness' attested in InIr. (Ved. *yunákti*), L *iungō*, Lith. *jùngiu*, and, a little mixed up, in G ζεύγνῡμι. Similarly **mel-*, **melH-*, **meld-*, and **meldh-* (not all reconstructable with equal confidence) seem to have the general meaning 'grind; crush; soften'. From the second of these, Ved. *mṛṇā́ti* 'grinds' and G μύλλω (thematized) attest an *n*-infix stem **ml̥néH-*/**ml̥nH-*. This suggests the origin of the 'infix', namely that a complex segmented as **yu-ne-g-* consisted of a sequence of two suffixes and zero grade of a basic root **yew-*. These 'root extensions' remain speculative, having resisted all functional explanation. Furthermore, no matter how it arose, once the infixing pattern was established it might at any time be extended to roots of suitable shape which were not built up of a nuclear root plus extensions.

Functionally, *n*-infix stems formed transitive verbs from basically intransitive roots. In Hitt., where there is no clear representative of the type, there are a handful of verbs of causative force built with an infix *-nin-*, as *ḫar-ni-in-ki-ir* 'they destroyed' next to *ḫar-ki-e-ir* 'they perished'. (In Hitt. the usual causative stem is built with a suffix *-nu-*, 455.) In Baltic the formation is more or less productive as a causative stem. One can imagine such a force in the remote history of say G δάμνημι (Dor. δάμνᾱμι) if the simplex root **demH₂-* could safely be thought to have meant 'become tame, be tame' such that **dm̥néH₂-* was 'cause to be tame', in effect 'tame (trans.)'; but such matters are speculative.

a. Since PIE root shapes include those with a resonant before a final stop or laryngeal, such as **serp-* 'creep', it is to be expected that such a resonant was sometimes a nasal, and so it is: **sweng-* 'twist', **H₃engʷ-* 'anoint', **ǵenH₁-* 'be born', and others. This promoted the possibility that a nasal infix might become reinterpreted as a fixed part of the root, and in all IE groups there are cases of just that. For example, L *iungō, iūnxī, iūnctus* 'join', whose *-n-* is proper to *iungō* alone (cf. Ved. *yunájmi*, and NB such *n*-less derivatives as L *iuxtā* 'next to', *iugum* 'yoke').

b. Many roots casually described in the technical literature as containing an *n*-infix cannot really be so explained. For example, Ved. *vand-* 'praise; honor, venerate' is usually taken as an *n*-infix form of *vad-* 'speak', PIE **wed-*; but genuine *n*-infixation in a root of such a shape is impossible. Now, if instead we reconstruct a root **H₂wed-* on the basis of G ἀείδω 'sing' < αϝειδω (< **H₂we-wd-*? 445.3a), we have a shape eligible for infixation; but note that neither the full grade **H₂uned-* nor the zero grade **H₂und-* would give the attested form of the Indic root. G ἀνδάνω 'please' cannot continue an *n*-infix of **sweH₂d-* 'sweet'. Gmc. roots of the type seen in NE *drink* and *bring*, which are much commoner in Gmc. than in PIE (they make up the bulk of the Class III strong verbs), have been called *n*-infix formations in origin; but the Gmc. type can be related to the *n*-infix type only with great difficulty.

c. The '*nā*-suffix' stems of G and InIr. are in fact *n*-infix stems of ordinary type, built to roots which ended in a laryngeal. Thus to a root **pleH₁-* 'get full', *n*-infix stems **pl̥néH₁-*/**pl̥nH₁-* yield Ved. *pṛṇā́ti* 'fills', *pṛṇītá* 3sg.midd.; the root **demH₂-* 'be tame' would make *n*-infix stems **dm̥néH₂-*/**dm̥nH₂-*, whence G δάμνημι (Dor. δάμνᾱμι) 'tame'.

454. A. GREEK. There are four distinct types of G stem derived from the PIE *n*-infix stem: two athematic, two thematic.

1. In roots ending in a stop, the infix is always in the zero grade, and in addition to the infix there is a thematic suffix in -$\alpha\nu^{\epsilon}/_{o}$-: Lesb. *(ἀπυ)λιμπάνω* 'leave' (displaced in Att.-Ion. by λείπω; cf. Ved. *riṇákti*, L *linquit*); *μανθάνω* (aor. ἔμαθον) 'find out, learn', *πυνθάνομαι* 'learn about' (aor. ἐπυθόμην).

a. Where the nasal tag comes from is unclear; see 466. It is found also in non-infixed stems (ἁμαρτάνω 'miss, go wrong', χανδάνω 'hold' ← *χαδάνω, the -ν- imported from other paradigmatic forms such as perf. κέχανδα). The μανθάνω type remained marginally productive, whence Att. λαμβάνω in place of Hom. λάζομαι < *$s\d{l}g^{w}$-y^{e}/o-.

2. In roots originally ending with the laryngeal *H_2, the result of infixation is a G type that appears to entail a suffix -νη-/νᾰ- (Dor. -νᾱ-/-νᾰ-): δάμνημι, -ᾱμι, δάμναμεν < **dm̥néH₂mi*, **dm̥nH̥₂mós*; cf. ἄδμητος < ἄδμᾱτος 'untamed' < **n̥-dm̥H₂-to-*; aor. ἐδάμασα < **e-demH̥₂-*. This is the same type as Ved. *pr̥ṇā́ti*, *pr̥ṇītá*, above.

3. As type 2, but built to roots originally ending in *H_3. By Cowgill's Law (44), the resulting stems in *-*nō-/-no-* became *-*nō-/-nu-*. When this alternation was leveled to -νῡ-/-νῠ-, the type fell together with the G development of the PIE *new*-suffix (472). Thus PIE **sterH₃-* 'strew, spread' in στόρνῡμι < **str̥neH₃-*; cf. στρωτός 'laid, strewn' < **str̥H₃-tó-*, ἐστόρεσα (< *ἐστέροσα) and ἔστρωσα aor., Ved. *ástr̥ṇāt* imperf., L *sternō*, *strātus*, perf. *strāvī* (originally an aorist).

Other forms likely to belong to this class are θόρνυμαι 'copulate' (more originally as θάρνυμαι; cf. θρῴσκω 'leap' < **dhr̥H₃-sk^e/o-*); and ὄλλῡμι 'slay' (L *ab-oleō* 'destroy'; PIE **(H₁)elH₃-*). To these may be added ὄμνῡμι 'swear' (Ved. *amīṣi* 2sg.—root-inflection—'you injure'; but the semantics require ingenuity: PIE **H₂emH₃-*[1] 'force'? 'menace'?).

4. Some inherited *n*-infix formations were thematized. Related to type 1, above: κυνέω 'kiss' < **ku-ne-s-*, root **kews-* (no satisfactory outside connections but the G evidence is clear: Hom. ἔκυσσα aor., κύσω fut.). Related to type 2, above: κάμνω 'toil, am weary' (κεκμηώς perf.pple. < **kekm̥H₂wōs*), τάμνω 'cut (off)' (Att. τέμνω with ε imported from aor. ἔτεμον). Parallel developments are seen in Skt.; for example *mr̥ṇati* 'crushes' is a new 3sg. backformed from the ambiguous 3pl. *mr̥ṇanti*.

a. In some forms the nasal formation is disguised by assimilation, as βάλλω 'throw' < **g^w aln^e/o-* < **g^w l̥-ne-H₁-* (no satisfactory outside connections, but Hom. ἔβλητο aor., Arc. εδελε aor., derivative βέλεμνον 'javelin' and other forms reveal all the details of the underlying root).

B. LATIN. All *n*-infix present stems were thematized, based on the zero grade of the stem. In some the nasal is in the pres./imperf. stem only: *tangō* 'touch', perf. *tetigī*, pple. *tāctus*; derivatives *intāctus* 'untouched', *integer* 'entire, whole', *tăctus*, *-ūs* 'a touch'. But in most paradigms the nasal spread

---

[1] The *o*-vocalism of the G form is secondary, as it is in all forms built this way, such as στόρνῡμι/ἐστόρεσα, above. In any case, a root **H₃emH₃-* is hardly possible.

into other principal parts. All combinations are observed: perf. only (*fingō* 'model', *fīnxī*, but *fictus*); participle only (*pungō* 'stab', *pūnctus*, but *pupugī*); and both (*iungō, iūnxī, iūnctus*). The nasal spreads to certain derivatives as well, so *pūnctum* 'small hole, dot' but no *-n-* in *pugiō* 'dagger'.

As in G and Indic there are disguised *n*-infix presents in L:
PIE **tl̥neH₂-/*tl̥nH₂-*, root **telH₂-*: *tollō* 'lift'; cf. *(sub)lātus* < **tlātos* < **tl̥H₂-to-*.
PIE **str̥neH₃-/*str̥nH₃-*: *sternō* (for **stornō*, after *cernō*? If **str̥n-* was replaced by **strin-* in PItal., then regularly L *stern-*); cf. perf. (originally aor.) *strāvī*, pple. *strātus* < **str̥H₃-to-* (G στόρνῡμι).
PIE **ḱrineH₁-/*ḱrinH₁-* 'sort, sift': *cernō* < **krinō* (74.3); cf. perf. (original aor.) *crēvī* < **kreya-* < **ḱreyH̥₁-*; pple. *crētus* a remodeling of **crītus*, unless it is manufactured whole from *crēvī*. (Cf. L *certus* 'separated; decided' < **kritos*, like G κριτός 'select(ed)' from an aniṭ form of the root.)
PIE **sey(H)-* 'place', **sinH-*: *sinō*, cf. perf. (orig. aor.) *sīvī*, aniṭ pple. *situs*. More disguised still is *pōnō* < **posnō* < **po-sinō*.
L *contemnō* 'despise' < *'cut off' < **tm̥nH-* (cf. G τάμνω, τέμνω).

a. Not all forms with a medial nasal have the nasal infix, and not a few forms are uncertain. In the former category are *prandeō* 'take breakfast; dine' (see 398.1 'first' for the etymology); *pandō* 'extend' < **patnō* (222.2); *dē-fendō* 'repel' < **gʷhen-yō* (218) or **-gʷhen-d(h)ō*; *unguō* 'anoint' < root **H₃engʷ-*, cf. *unguen* 'salve', Ved. *áñjas-* 'salve', *áñjasā* 'speedily' (*'like oil'); though if that is so, Ved. *anákti* 'anoints' is a back formation from forms like *añjmas* 1pl., *añjanti* 3pl., and *aṅgdhí* imper., which look like *n*-infix forms. —L *frangō* 'break' appears to be a conflation of two well-attested and synonymous roots, **bhreǵ-* and **bheng-*.[1]

455. Suffix **-néw-/*-nu-*, athematic, with the usual distribution of full grade of the affix (440). For years it seemed obvious that the source of the formation was a metanalysis of PIE **ḱl̥néw-/*ḱl̥nu-* 'hear', an ordinary *n*-infix formation to a root **ḱlew-*. There is nothing inherently unlikely about a formal type springing from a single item, but in fact the traditional explanation was always dubious: no root **ḱel-* 'hear' is independently attested, and the relationship between the infix and the root in **ḱl̥néw-* was unambiguous. In any case the usual explanation became untenable with the discovery of Hitt., where the *new*-type is copiously attested, indeed productive; the ordinary *n*-infix type is all but nonexistent; and the root *ḱlew-* is not attested in any form. (In other IE languages it is a notably tenacious root.) In Hitt. the suffix forms both deverbatives (causatives) and denominatives (factitives), so *ḫu-iš-nu-zi* 'causes to live' (*ḫu-i-iš-zi* 'is alive, lives'), and *e-eš-ḫar-nu-ut* imperat. 'make bloody' (*e-eš-ḫar* 'blood'). The same de-

[1] The latter is usually attested with an **n*. Ved. *bhanákti*, an *n*-infix stem, is secondary, like *anákti*: all other nominal and verbal forms are better served by a root **bheng-*, and besides **bheg-* is not a shape eligible for an *n*-infix. (The point of departure was an ambiguous form like 3pl. *bhanganti**.) OIr., unlike Indic, attests a variety of *n*-less forms, so next to *bongid* /bon'g'əθ'/ 'breaks' are a number of verbal nouns like *taibech*. (Perf. *bigsa* is ambiguous.)

verbative causative force is seen in Baltic; and it is detectable elsewhere in some formations that appear to be old, notably G ὄρνῡμι 'stir up, incite' and Hitt. *ar-nu-uz-zi* 'moves; brings'; cf. intrans. L *orior* '(a)rise, move'. (Ved. *r̥ṇóti* agrees in form with G and Hitt., but agrees in meaning with L *orior*. The affix builds stems to some 45 roots in the Vedas, where it seems to have no semantic kernel at all.)

In G the suffix is common, and occurs in obvious neologisms like δείκνῡμι 'point out' as well as in ancient forms like ὄρνῡμι. The original alternation is however to be seen only in remnants, having been replaced by an alternation of length alone, -νῡ-/-νῠ-, so δείκνῡμι, δείκνῠμεν. There is no semantic flavor traceable to the affix. (No verb form belonging to this stem has been recognized in Myc.)

A few verbs, οἰχνέω 'go, come' (cf. οἴχομαι 'am gone') for example, look like thematizations of original **-neumi* as **-newō*. A different kind of thematization is also seen, one based on the zero grade **-nw-*^{e}/*o*-, and the same thing is attested in some Vedic stems, as *hinva* (thematic) imperative 'urge on!' next to *hinuhi*, imperat. formed to the stem of *hinóti* 'urges, impells'. In G this accounts for τῑ́νω (so Hom.), Att. τῐ́νω 'pay', where the etymon **tinwō* would account for the cited forms. Supporting this interpretation are: Eurip. τινύμεναι and Hom. τείνυται 'exacts retribution'; the *n*-less forms of the balance of the paradigm (aor. ἔτῑσα for ἔτεισα, cf. Cyp. πεισαι); and the cognate formation in Ved. *cinóti*.

New-stems are best regarded as not attested in Latin. Two verbs are sometimes cited: *sternuō* 'sneeze' and *minuō* 'lessen'. The former is often said to be connected with G πτάρνυμαι 'sneeze', but the connection is necessarily tenuous: a PIE etymon **pstr̥-new-* has only the slightest chance of ever having existed, not least because the affix seems to have formed transitive verbs—particularly, not incidentally. The cluster **pst-* might give L *st-* but is unlikely to have given G πτ- rather than, say, φθ-. But this is all beside the point: in principle, colorful words like 'sneeze' are not suitable data for rigorous diachronic arguments.

L *minuō* is better taken as a denominative in **-y*^{e}/*o*- to *minū-* (as in *minūtus* 'tiny', homophonous with the pple. of *minuō*).

456. DURATIVE THEMATIC STEMS.

1. PIE **-y*^{e}/*o*-. This suffix is prominent in late PIE verb morphology, and is so various in function that it is perhaps not a single suffix. It forms both primary stems (that is, to roots directly), and secondary stems (denominative and deverbative). It does not show the effects of Sievers' Law (178), so RV *médyantu* 'may they be stout', not ˣ*médiyantu* < **masd-y*^{e}/*o*-; *mathyámānas* 'being shaken' passive pple. < **mn̥tH*$_2$*y*^{e}/*o*-. Sound laws (chiefly the second G palatalization, 198-207) often obscure the shape of the stem in G, but occasionally also in L, as L *tendō* = G τείνω 'stretch' < **ten-yoH*$_2$ (218; cf. early pple. *tentus*).

A. The most basic kind of formation has zero grade of the root and tonic accent on the suffix; these verbs are intransitive and often deponent. Examples are **g^w m̥yéti* 'comes, goes' > G βαίνω, L *veniō*; **mr̥yétor* 'dies' > L *moritur*, Ved. *mriyase* 2sg., Av. *miryeite*; **mn̥y^e/o-* 'think' > G μαίνομαι 'rave' (cf. Ved. *mányate* 'thinks' and OIr. *do·moiniur* /mon'əρ^w/ 'I believe'). This type is the source of the passive in Skt., so *bharati*, *-te* 'carries', pass. *bhriyate* 'is carried'. As such it remains (as originally) prevailingly formed to roots; so the passive of *yunákti* *n*-infix 'joins' is *yujyáte*, of *śr̥ṇóti* 'hears' is *śrūyáte*, of *juhóti* 'pours' is *hūyáte*.[1] It is however generalized to some characterized stems, as *pr̥cchyáte* 'is asked' (stem **pr̥k-sḱ^e/o-*, 3, below), evidence that the stem has been reanalyzed as a root.

a. The Skt. *dī́vyati* type (Class 4 according to native grammarians) is as above but with the accent on the root. The whole type is presumed to be a secondary development within Skt.

B. A different type has full grade of the root with tonic accent, and mainly transitive meaning, as **spéḱyoH₂* 'see' > G σκέπτομαι (with metathesis), L *speciō*, *-spiciō*, Ved. *páśyati*; PIE **teny^e/o-* (position of accent unattested) 'stretch', G τείνω, L *tendō*. The type is unlikely to be genuinely old. A very large percentage of the forms are, like **speḱ-y^e/o-*, above, and **pek^w-y^e/o-* 'ripen; cook', built to roots which would be awkward in zero grade. That consideration does not apply of course to **teny^e/o-* 'stretch', but that form is strictly speaking attested only in G: if L *tendō* is a *y^e/o*-present at all, it could in fact come from more typical **tn̥-y^e/o-* (and its prevailingly intrans. semantics fit such a history). The existence of an apparently earlier stem type (Hom. τάνυται = Ved. *tanute* < **tn̥-nu-*) further attests to the lateness of τείνω. Another indication of the lateness of the type is the G hesitation between different grades, as in the case of **werǵ-y^e/o-* and **wr̥ǵ-y^e/o-*, the former giving ἔρδω, the latter ῥέζω (a modification of **wrajǰō* < **wr̥gyō*, 201, corresponding to unremodeled Myc. *wo-ze* (*worǰei*) and PGmc. **wurkijiþ*). —Similarly isolated and probably late is L **-veriō* in *op-eriō* 'cover', *ap-eriō* 'uncover' < **-wer-y^e/o-* (parallel Lith. *ùžveriu* 'I close' and Ved. *vriyáte* pass. 'is closed' do not indicate antiquity, as they belong to productive types).

a. In various daughter languages, the **-y^e/o-* affix is used to convert originally athematic inflections of all types into thematic ones, for example the stative complex **-eH₁-y^e/o-* of Ital., Gmc., and BS (452), or the fut. (orig. desiderative) stem *-iṣya-* of Skt. (457C). The process went so far in L that all verb types apart from the simple thematics and a handful of irregular verbs appear to have been so formed, a state of affairs which was later disguised by the loss of intervocalic **-y-*.

2. PIE CAUSATIVE AND ITERATIVE STEMS. Two elements, **-ey^e/o-* and **-eH₂y^e/o-*, form verb stems with well-defined semantics. (They look like

[1] Lengthening of *u* before *y* is common in Indic; *-riy-* is regular from **-r̥y-*.

*-y^e/o- added to other elements.) These verbs have either causative force or iterative/frequentative force. The point of tangency between these two clear-cut functions is an enigma.[1]

A. PIE *-$\acute{e}y^e/o$-. The root in most forms is in the *o*-grade, though some old-looking forms have zero grade instead. The type is conspicuous in InIr., and prominent in Gmc. So to InIr. *sad-* 'sit' (Ved. pres. *sī́dati* < *si-sd-$^e/o$- and an assortment of aorists): caus. *sādayante* 3pl. 'they set', -*ā*- < **o* via Brugmann's Law, 36.4; Go. *satjiþ* 'sets', OCS *saditŭ* 'plants', both from **sod-eyeti*. One or two plausible cases have been noticed in Hitt., *lu-uk-ki-iz-zi* 'sets fire to' < **lowkeyeti* like L *lūcēre* 'ignite, kindle' (477.3), and *wa-aš-ši-ya-zi* 'clothes' if < *wos-ey^e/o- like Ved. *vāsayati* (but many forms are unambiguously simple thematics, so *wa-aš-ša-an-zi* 3pl. next to *wa-aš-ši-ya-an-zi*), and see 128.3a.

In G and L the type is differentiated from denominatives chiefly by function; formally there is only the *o*-grade of the root, and that is also of course encountered in denominative verbs built to *o*-grade *o*-stem nouns, 460-1:

G φοβέω 'frighten; put to flight' beside φέβομαι 'am afraid'. But φοβέω might be a denominative from φόβος 'flight, panic' instead.

G σοβέω 'shoo away' (say, birds) beside σέβομαι 'am in awe' is more clearly causative: it is based on an earlier meaning of the root—'avoid' or the like, still seen in Ved. *tyaj-* 'leave, get out of the way' < *$tyeg^w$-; and furthermore there is no noun ˣσόβος or ˣσοβή.

The type is not productive in L, but is preserved in a number of forms:

L *moneō* 'remind, warn' (*'cause to think') < *mon-ey^e/o-.

L *torreō* 'dry' trans. < *$tors$-ey^e/o- (Brāh. *tarṣáyati* is the same formation); cf. zero grade *tṛ́ṣyant-* 'thirsting', also OHG *dursten*, OE *þyrsten* < **þurs-tV-ji/a-* 'be dry, be thirsty', typical denominatives, 460-1; and *e*-grade in *terra* '[*dry] land', *testa* 'pottery' < *-*rst*-, 231.3.

This formation in its iterative-frequentative meaning is less ambiguously attested in G, owing to its distinctive semantics:

G φορέω 'carry around; wear (clothes)' (φέρω 'carry').

Hom. ποτέομαι 'fly this way and that; be on the wing' (πέτομαι); cf. Ved. *patáyati* with the intensive meaning 'fly along rapidly'.

It is commonly stated that there are no instances of the iterative function in L, but L *mulgeō* 'milk', the expected development of *$mol\acute{g}$-$\acute{e}y^e/o$-, is certainly not stative and seems not to be denominative. Milking is an iterative process if there ever was one, especially if the original meaning of the roots **melǵ-*, **merǵ-* was 'stroke'. Proposals to

---

[1] In a parallel case, PIE *-$s\acute{k}^e/o$- (item 3, below) mostly has functions clearly connected to an originally iterative meaning, while in Toch. it makes causatives. But two examples of the same enigma are no more illuminating than one.

include other forms here—*mordeō* 'bite', *tondeō* 'cut, shear', *sorbeō* 'suck up, guzzle'—are not so much based on their meaning as faute de mieux.

B. PIE **-eH*$_2$*y*^{e}*/o-*, like **-éy*^{e}*/o-*, is added to the *o*-grade of the root, and is even more difficult to segregate from denominatives built to thematic stems. Additionally, iterative-frequentative semantics readily shade off into intensive semantics, and most of the L formations apparently traceable directly or indirectly to this formation are better described as intensive. L *domāre* 'tame; subdue' like OHG *zamōn*—in contrast to Ved. *damáyant-* pple., which reflects rather **domH*$_2$*-éy*^{e}*/o-* (type A above)—and *vorāre* 'to eat greedily' (iter.-freq.) are identifiable as such chiefly because there are no nouns eligible as the basis for denominative formations. The similar-looking *dōnāre* 'to make a gift of' is obviously based on *dōnum*. Others, like *occupāre* 'take possession of' (simplex *capere*), developed within the history of L—for one thing, they chiefly occur in forms with preverbs, as in the example—but probably ultimately continue the PIE **-H*$_2$*y*^{e}*/o-* TYPE. Some clear examples of causatives per se have a long vowel in the root, a puzzling feature: *sēdāre* 'to set, make settle' (*sedēre* 'to be sitting'), *plācāre* 'to soothe, appease' (*placēre* 'to be pleasing').

a. L *domuī, domitus* from **doma-* < **demH̥*$_2$*-* imply that *domāre* is to be traced to original **doma-y*^{e}*/o-* < **demH̥*$_2$*-y*^{e}*/o-* (475.6) instead of the account given above. Perhaps the two formations were conflated.

b. Some authorities have wondered whether the denominative and causative/iterative types might not be ultimately one and the same. Against this idea is the observation that deverbatives as a rule have predictable meanings, whereas denominatives as a rule have from the outset decidedly specific meanings which cannot be anticipated because they never cover the full range of meanings of the base noun. L *lūnāre* (from *lūna* 'moon') 'to bend into a crescent shape' is a typical denominative: its meaning is at the same time unsurprising and essentially unpredictable, and is just one meaning of the many thinkable. (Verbs derived from adjectives are, curiously, much more predictable in meaning.)

The causatives in **-ey*^{e}*/o-* and **-eH*$_2$*y*^{e}*/o-* are typical deverbatives in that they have predictable meanings. Where the meaning of a given form is less transparent, this is the result of later semantic development, as L *moneo* 'warn', whose etymological link to *meminī* 'remember' via causative semantics is obvious enough. L *spondeō* 'pledge, promise' is unrelated to anything in L, but thanks to G *σπένδω* 'pour an oblation', *σπονδή* 'a drink-offering', Hitt. *ši-pa-an-ti* '*σπένδει*', is seen to be an outbirth of *'have an oblation poured', pregnantly *'perform a rite [in connection with vows]' whence 'vow, pledge' without any reminiscence of the rite itself. Similarly L *foveō* 'cherish' is a fossilized caus., *'keep warm' (**dhog*^{w}*h-ey*^{e}*/o-*; cf. Ved. *dáhanti* 'are hot').

3. PIE **-sḱ*^{e}*/o-* (iterative/durative). This stem is built to the zero grade of the root, with accent on the thematic vowel. Thus PIE **g*^{w}*m̥-sḱ*^{é}*/ó-* 'be going, be coming' (root **g*^{w}*em-*, cf. Go. *qiman*, NE *come*): Ved. *gácchati* (accent secondary), Av. *jasaiti* (*j-* imported from the aor.), G *βάσκε* imperat. 'get going' (either away from or toward the speaker, depending on context). PIE **pr̥ḱ-sḱ*^{é}*/ó-* 'ask' or perhaps better 'inquire into' (root **preḱ-*, cf. L *procus* 'suitor'): Ved. *pr̥cchā́mi*, L *poscō* (**-rksk-* **231.3**). PIE **r̥-sḱ*^{é}*/ó-* (or **H*$_1$*r̥-sḱ*^{é}*/ó-*, on

account of the G) > Ved. *r̥cchánti* 'they arrive', Hitt. *ar-aš-ki-iz-zi* /arskitsi/ 'comes', G ἔρχομαι.

Ved. *gácchati*, L *poscō*, and G ἔρχομαι result from phonological developments which, though regular, disguise the component parts of the formation.

The function of the stem is not self-evident. In Vedic the thirteen stems in *-cchá-* share no semantic color at all. In Av. the same thing is true of the present stems, though significantly an element *-sa-*, which is probably the same, forms a past tense with habitual force. In Toch. the formation seems to be causative. In Hitt. the stem is freely productive, added to virtually any simplex stem, usually with iterative meaning but sometimes durative depending on the semantics of the underlying stem: *pí-en-ni-iš-ki-iz-zi* dur. 'is driving' (*pí-en-na-a-i* 'drives'), but *(-zi-ik) ḫa-aš-ki-it* iter. 'kept having children'. In the past tense it often has the meaning of NE *used to*, so *ap-pí-iš-ke-ir* 'they used to take' (in the revision of the law code, the usual way of mentioning former penalties) vs. *e-ip-pí-ir* 'they took'.[1]

In classical G the matter of function is as opaque as in Indic; but in Homeric, Herodotean, and Ionic forms generally, something formally similar to Hittite but functionally similar to Avestan (and some Hitt. usage) is found: -σκ$^{\epsilon}/_{o}$-, affixed to a variety of stems, has the sense of 'was accustomed to': Hom. μαχέσκετο imperf. 'used to fight' (μάχομαι); ἴδεσκε 3sg. 'was accustomed to see' (ἰδέω); δόσκον aor. 'was accustomed to give' (δίδωμι); καλέσκετο 'used to call himself', and many others. In a few forms the affix seems to appear twice, that is, it is added to a stem originally built with the same affix (though the base stems are often etymologically difficult): βόσκω 'feed (an animal)', βοσκέσκοντο 'they were accustomed to being fed'. Large numbers of Hom. forms in -σκ- are uniquely attested, which is what one would expect of a freely productive type, used opportunistically.

In two cases, εἰμί and φημί, the formation developed almost a plain imperfect sense in contrast to the aoristic flavor of the genuine imperfect form: Hom. ἔσκον and φάσκον next to ἦν and φῆν, ἔφην.

In L the ancient forms, like *poscō* 'ask', have no apparent semantic coloration, but the type (as modified; see **c**) is productive as an ingressive, especially from adjectives: *albēscō* 'whiten', *grandēscō* 'become great'; but also from nouns, as *ignēscō* 'kindle' (*ignis*). Some have unexpected meanings, as *miserēscō* 'have pity for', rather than *'become wretched'. There are deverbatives as well, as *calēscō* 'get hot' (*calēre* 'to be hot'), which might be the ultimate source of the complex *-ēscō*, namely stative *-ē-* (452) plus *-sc$^{e}/_{o}$-*.

---

[1] Although meaning largely determines whether a given verb is a frequentative or a durative depends, sometimes the selfsame item will have either force depending on context: *The phone was ringing but she kept (on) washing her hair* vs. *John kept washing the colored and white clothes together, so that everything turned pink.*

There are many verbs of miscellaneous relationship, formally and functionally, to the base form.

These various functions in the IE languages might be traced to an iterative/durative origin. The tendency for iteratives to coalesce into past-habitual has been noticed above. Even some of the oldest forms of L and G, in which no special semantic color is evident, can be understood in this light: *$\acute{g}neH_3$-$s\acute{k}^e/o$- orig. 'come to know, come to understand' (that is, by degrees); *$g^w\text{m̥}$-$s\acute{k}^e/o$- 'come to being on the way, set out'. The development of the L ingressive is usually traced to the agency of a single form, *crēscō* 'grow'; but a Hitt. formation (see **c**, below) has been interpreted as evidence that the complex *-ēscō* (that is, *-eH_1-$s\acute{k}^e/o$-) was inherited from the parent language. An inherited iterative function underlying the L *-ēscō* type is thinkable: if *calēscō* once meant 'keep getting warm', it would be a small step from there to 'become warm'. But this is highly speculative, and most such verbs in L resist even that much explanation.

a. The requirement of zero grade for the root bestows particular significance on G γιγνώσκω 'know', L *nōscō*, Av. *xšnāsāitiy* opt. 'would understand', collectively pointing to PIE *$\acute{g}neH_3$-$s\acute{k}^e/o$-, with full grade of the root.

b. In Hitt. and G no small number of verbs formed with this stem have reduplication as well. (The only such form in L seems to be *discō* 'teach, train' < *di-dk̂-$s\acute{k}^e/o$-, root *dek̂- 'be fitting, conform to societal values'.) Such forms in G are notably often transitive, as γιγνώσκω, διδάσκω 'teach', βιβρώσκω 'devour', μιμνήσκω 'remind'. According to some authorities, reduplicated stems in *-$s\acute{k}^e/o$- are not an ancient type but arose from a sort of contamination of reduplicating and $s\acute{k}^e/o$-presents, so for example *ĝi-$\acute{g}neH_3$-ti next to *$\acute{g}neH_3$-sk̂e-ti were conflated in *ĝi-$\acute{g}neH_3$-sk̂e-ti. The weakness of this theory is that many—most—PIE roots built an assortment of present stems, and it is not obvious why these two should have been singled out for conflation, and not, say, *n*-infix presents.

c. In L there are actually three similar affixes, *-ēscō*, *-īscō*, and *-āscō*. Of these, *-ēscō* is the commonest, and is presumed to be the starting point for the other two. This *-ēscō* is usually explained as arising by metanalysis from forms like *quiēscō* where the long vowel probably belonged to the stem-like element before the suffix. However, evidence from Hitt. suggests rather that *-ēscō* is in essence inherited from PIE. Denominative stative formations in *-e-* occur in Old Hitt., usually written with plene vowels that might mean that the vowel is long (31). It has been somewhat speculatively argued that the well-known Hitt. ingressive ('inchoative') marker *-eš-* is in effect equivalent to L *-ēsc-*. The functional alignment is straightforward, but formally there are problems, chiefly that *-sk̂- > Hitt. *-šk-* in the usual form of the suffix. And it is noteworthy that the vowel of *-eš-* is never written plene, implying that this formation was originally *-H̥_1-s(k̂)-, that is, it followed the rule that *-sk̂- was added to zero grade of the stem. That means that the only specifically L innovation here was to replace *-H̥_1-$s\acute{k}^e/o$- with *-eH_1-$s\acute{k}^e/o$-, which might be taken together with the L generalization of the full grade of the stative element in the present (452).

G also has a by-form -ισκω. The length of the -ι- is unknown.

457. DESIDERATIVE IN *-$(H_1)s^e/o$-, *-$(H_1)sy^e/o$-. These are compilations: of *-H_1s-, the desiderative marker proper, plus a thematic affix. Straightforwardly desiderative force is evident only in InIr. In most branches the formations are future tenses. The semantic connection between desiderative and future is elementary; note that NE *will*, currently in effect the marker of future tense, is etymologically '(would) want to', namely a desiderative.

Three different formations are attested.

A. With _i_-reduplication and zero grade of the root. The shape *-_Hs_-$^e/_o$- is attested unambiguously in Indic desideratives of the type _jíghāṃsati_ 'wishes to slay' < *_ǰhighā-sa-_ < *_g^whi-g^whn̥-Hs_$^e/_o$-, root *_g^when-_). The suffix type without the laryngeal is equally unambiguous for roots ending in stops, as _īpsa-_ < *_H_1i-H_1p-s_$^e/_o$- 'wish to obtain' (_āp-_), _bí-bhit-sa-_ 'wish to split' (_bhid-_, cf. L _findō_) and, with simplification of consonant clusters, _śíkṣa-_ 'wish to be able' (for *_śíśkṣa-_, root _śac-_), _bhíkṣa-_ 'wish to share; beg' (for *_bhípkṣa-_, root _bhaj-_). This is the same affix as the former, with some as yet unexplored loss of the laryngeal between a stop and *-_s_-. Support for such a view comes from the oldest Indic texts showing the same phenomenon where the presence of an underlying laryngeal in the root itself cannot be questioned, as _dhítsa-_ 'wish to put' and _dítsa-_ 'wish to give' from roots *_dheH_1-_ and *_deH_3-_ respectively, such that _dhits-_ for example must at the very least reflect *_dhi-dhH_1-s-_ if not in fact *_dhi-dhH_1-Hs-_.

The selfsame type is attested in OIr. as one kind of future stem, the so-called _é_-future, whose appearance is much altered by Goidelic sound changes: exactly superimposable on Ved. _jígāṃsati_, above, is OIr. _génaid_ /g'ēnəδ'/ 'will injure' < *_geγnaheθ_ < PCelt. *_g^wig^wnāset-es_[1] < *_g^whig^whn̥-Hse-_. OIr. like Ved. shows no evidence of a laryngeal in forms built to roots ending with stops.

a. Indic desideratives of the type _śiśariṣa-_ (root _śar-_ 'crush'), that is with a connecting vowel -_i_- as if from *-_H̥_-, are not found in the RV, though they occur in the later Vedas; the earliest is _pipatiṣa-_ 'wishes to fly' (AV).

B. With no reduplication and _e_-grade of the root. This is the type of the G future. The varieties of the suffix match the two types given in A. In G terms, it is marked with *-_es_$^e/_o$- < *-_H̥$_1$s_$^e/_o$- after nasals and liquids but *-_s_$^e/_o$- elsewhere: πείσομαι 'will be persuaded'< *_p^hent^h-s_$^e/_o$-, δείξω 'will show' < *_deik-s_$^e/_o$-; but Hom. μενέω 'will remain' < *_menehō_ < *_men-H̥$_1$s_$^e/_o$- (Att. μενῶ). This is best taken as showing the loss of the *-_H_1_- between a stop and the *-_s_-. However, some authorities take the μενέω type in G to be a generalization from seṭ roots, as in ἐρέω 'will say' < *_werH̥$_1$-s_$^e/_o$-. A serious defect with this reasonable-sounding explanation is that *-_H_2_- seems to have been much more frequent than *-_H_1_- after resonants at the ends of roots, and so it is peculiar that *-_es_$^e/_o$- and not *-_as_$^e/_o$- should have become the general affix. That problem disappears if the *-_H_1_- is taken to be part of the affix itself.

Note that δείξω (δείκνῡμι 'point out'), φανέω, -ῶ (φαίνω 'appear'),

---

[1] OIr. absolute verb forms had some kind of enclitic tag. This underwent the ablative effects of the sound laws which attacked final segments of words, leaving the person marker in a recognizeable form. The conjunct (tagless) equivalent of absolute _génaid_ is the less revealing ·_géna_ < *_g^wig^wnāss_ < *_g^whig^whn̥Hst._

βαλέω, -ῶ (βάλλω < *g^w*aln-* 'throw') reveal that the future was formed on the root directly rather than on the present stem.

L has what appear to be two stray examples of this formation (479.8), *vīsō* 'visit' (< **wīss-* < **weyd-s-* *'wish to see') and *quaesō* 'beg' (*k^w*ayssō*; 232.2); cf. *quaerō* < *k^w*aysō*. Both seem to agree with the evidence elsewhere for *-*s*^{e}/*o*- rather than *-*Hs*^{e}/*o*- after an obstruent, though it is easy to make too much of two forms whose connection with the desiderative is speculative in any case.

Almost as obscure are the OL *s*-futures attested in a remnant or two, as *faxitur* 'will be done', *capsō* 'will take' (Plaut.). The type was general in PItal., as it seems to be the basis for the Sab. futures such as U **ferest** 'will carry' < *-*eset*, and in -*ast*, **-ast** < *-*āset* (U **prupehast** 'he will propitiate'). These have been quite differently explained as originating in the subjunctive of *s*-aorists (502)—a more convincing theory, as the subj. was the source of Ital. futures otherwise.

a. OIr. has six *s*-future stems with *e*-grade of an unreduplicated root (in contrast to the *génaid* type, above), like the G type; for example *seiss* /s′es′s′/ 'will sit' < **sesset* < **sed-s-* (cf. G. εἴσομαι < **hess*^{e}/*o*- < **sed-(H₁)s-*).

C. InIr. and Baltic have a FUTURE in *-*(H)sy*^{e}/*o*- which appears to be the element *-*H₁s*- enlarged with a different thematic affix. In contrast to the desiderative (A, above), even in the oldest Indic texts the form -*iṣya*- < *-*H̥sy*^{e}/*o*- is prominent, and with the passage of time becomes even more general (so Epic *vahiṣyati* 'will carry' in place of Ved. *vakṣyá*-). The customary explanation for this -*iṣya*- is that it results from metanalysis of formations built to seṭ roots, so *jani-ṣyá*- 'will beget' < **ǵenH̥₁-sy*^{e}/*o*- metanalyzed as *jan-iṣya*-. However, though just such metanalyses are patent in Indic, especially as time went on, in this case it leaves unexplained an important fact: in the earliest text, the -*iṣya*- affix is limited to roots ending in resonants—that is, the same distribution as in A and B (*vakṣyá*- as above, *kartsya*- 'will cut', root *kr̥t*-; *dhakṣyá*- 'will burn', root *dah*-; but *kariṣyá*- 'will do', root *kr̥*-, *maniṣyá*- 'will think', root *man*-). But already in the RV the distribution is not quite sound, as there are instances of -*sya*- after semivowels and one after a nasal: *kraṃsyá*- 'will stride' (to a seṭ root in fact, cf. Ved. *krāṃtá*- pple.).

As a demonstration of the importance of date of attestation, already by the time of the AV the crucial facts of the original distribution have yielded to generalization of the -*iṣya*- alternant, so *naśiṣya*- 'will disappear', *vadiṣya*- 'will speak', and so on; and in short order -*iṣya*- becomes the normal form of the future marker after any cons.

458. OTHER PRESENT CLASSES. Noteworthy in this survey of stem types is the lack of overall congruence between the various IE branches: a stem formation abundantly attested in one branch might be rare or even missing altogether in some others. It follows that a PIE stem-forming element might theoretically become rare in ALL known IE groups, and scholars have suggested one or another element as just such a poorly-attested ancestral present-stem type.

1. An *s*-suffix, seemingly unrelated to the desiderative **H₁s* (457), is

seen in Hitt. *pa-aš-* 'take a sip; drink' (PIE root **peH₃-y-*; is this the aoristic, that is punctual, **s* (459) of the familiar IE branches?); G αὐξάνω 'strengthen', Ved. *vakṣáyati*, Go. *wahsjan*, NE *wax* (cf. *s*-less L *augeō* 'make grow', Go. *aukan*, PIE **(H₂)weg-*); G ἀλέξω 'ward off' (aor. ἀλαλκεῖν, PIE **H₂lek-?*).

2. A *dh*-suffix in G πλήθω 'become full', cf. πίμπλημι, and perh. in L *tendō*, *(de)fendō* < **tn̥-dh-*, **gʷhn̥-dh-* (or full grades)—if they do not instead reflect **-d-* (next) or **-y-* suffixes.

3. A *d*-suffix, surmised mostly from L forms: *tendō* 'stretch' (G τείνω, L *tentus* pple.); L *sallō* 'salt' (*salsus* pple. < **sald-to-*, 212); *pellō* 'strike, knock' (*d*-less *pepulī* perf., *pulsus* pple. < ? **pl̥d-to-*).

L *sallō*, *salsus* without doubt continues **sald-*; but Gmc. NOUNS attest a form **sald-* 'salt' (the gloss is an example), and a basic noun like 'salt' could hardly be deverbative. Much more likely the L verb is a denominative, **sald-yᵉ/ₒ-* (194). It is customary to cite L *clādēs* 'harm, injury' and in support of **-d-* in L *percellō* 'beat down', perf. *perculī*. If it is related at all, *clādēs* must continue something like **kl̥Hd-*. No such root is possible for any of the verb forms, but a root-form **kelH-* would license an *n*-infix pres.: **kl̥nH-* > L *percellō*[1] which would also do for *perculī* (cf. *tollō*, *(sus)tulī*). That leaves the laryngealless *perculsus* to be explained. Regarding *pellō*, the old iterative *pultāre* 'pound on' (Plaut.) indicates that the usual pple. *pulsus* is secondary for **pul-to-*, but at the same time cancels the evidential value of *pulsus* for an etymological **-ld-* in *pellō*.

Perhaps the least tendentious evidence for a present stem in **-d-* (or **-dh-*) is afforded by *tendō*, with *tentus* establishing the secondary nature of *tēnsus*. But *tendō* has an alternative explanation (218).

Overall, the quality of the evidence for a *d*-present is on a par with taking NE *lend*, *astound*, and *plead* (cf. *d*-less *loan*, *astonishment*, and *plea*) as evidence for a verb-forming suffix *-d* in English. In any case it is not always obvious how to distinguish between these 'present tense suffixes' and root extensions, as in **ǵhewd-* 'pour' (needed for Gmc. and Ital.) next to **ǵhew-* (InIr., G; see 453).

PUNCTUAL (AORIST) STEMS

459. The only stem-formation which is uniquely aoristic is an athematic stem consisting of an element **-s-* directly affixed to the root. Perhaps because of its distinctiveness it enjoyed considerable productivity in the daughter languages. There is little lexical agreement from one IE language to another as to which aorist stems are thus built, suggesting that the period of productivity came late in the history of PIE; and there is no certain trace of the element in Hitt.

Evidence for the shape of the root in *s*-aorists is conflicting. In Indic the root vowel is in lengthened grade in the active indicative; in the middle, it is zero grade (though some roots ending in **y* and **w* have full grade instead). The subj. takes full grade. So to *hr̥-* 'fetch', *ahārṣam* 1sg.act., *ahr̥ṣata* 3pl.mid.; to *dr̥-* 'split', *dárṣat* 3sg.subj.; to *ji-* 'conquer', *ajāiṣam* 1sg.act., *jéṣat*

---

1 *Percellō* < **koll-* < **kl̥n-ᵉ/ₒ-* is the expected development of a short vowel in medial syllable before *ll*.

3sg.subj.; to _diś-_ 'point out', _ádiṣṭa_ 3sg.midd. (regular from _*adikṣṭa_; the _-s-_ of the stem is overt in forms like _ádikṣi_ 1sg.midd.). In G the root is normally in the same grade as the present stem, so δείκνῡμι, ἔδειξα; γράφω, ἔγραψα; but there are exceptions like τῑ́νω/τίνω 'pay', ἔτεισα (cf. ἔτῑσα). L and OCS evidence bears on only part of the question, as neither language builds middles to the reflexes of the aorist, but as far as it goes their evidence agrees with Indic: L _vehō, vēxī_; OCS _vezǫ, věsŭ_, PIE _*weǵhō_, _*wēǵh-s-_ 'convey' (cf. Ved. _ávāṭ_ 2sg. < _*avāśss_ < _*ewēḱss_ < _*ewēǵhss_). Over the years the trend of scholarly opinion has wavered back and forth between taking G as the best evidence for the parent language, or taking InIr., OCS, and L as the more conservative. The latter view is supported by G evidence of an inferential nature: G γηράσκω 'grow old', ἐγήρα aor. 'am [gotten] old' appear to be from an ordinary root _ǵer-_ 'age' (G γέρων 'old man'); the _s_-aorist from such a root, if _*eǵērsm̥_, would have given G ἐγήρα (_*eǵersm̥_ would have given either ˣἔγειρα or ˣἔγερρα, **229**), from which the other forms were created. (Later remodelings of the _s_-aor. would naturally pass over the form, as it is not recognizable.)

Finally, inherited lengthened grade in _s_-aorists is easy to explain, not as ablaut but as compensatory lengthening which was original in the 2sg. and 3sg.: _**eǵerss_, _**eǵerst_ whence _**eǵēr_ (or _**eǵērs_), from which came _*eǵērsme_, _eǵērste_, and so on, by leveling, and also reconstituted _*eǵērss_, _*eǵērst_. Cf. the development of PIE _*ḱēr_ nom.sg. 'heart' < _**ḱerd_ (**126.1**, **276.4a**), and the nom.sg. of _s_-stems in _*-ēs_ and _*-ōs_ of _s_-stems (_**-ess_, _*-oss_, **299**).

DENOMINATIVE STEMS

460. DENOMINATIVE *-_y_^{e}/_o_-STEMS. The usual formation of denominatives is by the addition of the suffix *-_y_^{e}/_o_- to the stem of the noun. The formation is most transparent in Ved., where the _-ya-_ (usually in fact _-yá-_) is everywhere preserved, while in G and L and other IE languages it is disguised by the loss of intervocalic _-y-_, contraction, and other phonetic changes. Note that in PIE the _o_-stems do not appear as such; most appear in the _e_-grade, while many others make denominative verbs to a stem *-_eH_$_{2}$- which does not otherwise appear in nominal paradigms.

A table of forms is given on page 512.

461. FUNCTIONS OF DENOMINATIVES. Most denominatives fall into broad functional categories, such as factitive (_to enslave, to shred, to steady_); ingressive (inchoative) (_to age_; not a common type in NE, but abundant in L); agentives (_to dog, to shepherd, to doctor_ 'to do what a dog/shepherd/doctor does [in some specific regard]'); instrumentives (_to force_ 'to employ force'; _to rope_; these include the numerous denominatives meaning 'to use _X_ in the usual way', as _to bandage, to paint, to phone, to wedge_); locatives (_to center, to list_), ablatives (_to seed, to gut, to skin_), and others. But in any given lexicon there are in addition an infinity of miscellaneous relationships: _to sand_ 'to rub wood smooth'; *to bag* 'to catch game or anything figuratively similar'; *to hoof* 'to dance'; *to wing* 'to wound slightly'; *to blanket* 'to cover thickly' (but never with literal bedclothes). Many have semantics so extreme as to be unguessable, as *to corn* 'to preserve in brine'; *to table* 'to put off indefinitely',

Stems	Vedic	Greek	Latin[1]
-o-	*devá-* 'god'	οἶκος 'abode'	*dēnsus* 'thick'
-ey^e/o-	*devayá-* 'be pious'[2]	οἰκέω 'inhabit'	*dēnseō* (?) (II) 'make thick'[3]
-o-	*amítra-* 'enemy'	φοῖβος 'bright'	*pugnus* 'fist'
-eH$_2$y^e/o-	*amitrāyá-* 'be hostile'	φοιβάω 'cleanse'	*pugnō* (I) 'fight'[4]
-eH$_2$-	*pŕ̥tanā-* 'battle'	τῑμή 'honor'	*cūra* 'care'
-eH$_2$y^e/o-	*pr̥tanāyá-* 'do battle'	τῑμάω 'honor'	*cūrō* (I) 'care for'
-i-	*sákhay-* 'friend'	μῆνις 'rage'	*fīnis* 'boundary'
-iy^e/o-	*sakhīyá-*[5] 'desire friendship'	μηνίω 'am angry'	*fīniō* (IV) 'limit'
-u-	*gātú-* '(open) way'	μέθυ 'wine'	*metus* 'fear'
-uy^e/o-	*gātuyá-* 'obtain free progress'	μεθύω 'am in wine'	*metuō* (III) 'fear'
-s-	*rájas-* 'dust'	τέλος 'end, goal'	*fulgur* 'lightning'
-sy^e/o-	*rajasyá-* 'turn to dust'	τελείω, -έω 'complete'	*fulgurit* (IV)
-n-	*ukṣán-* 'bull'	ὄνομα 'name'	— *(Note 6)*
-n̥y^e/o-	*ukṣaṇyá-* 'wish for bulls'	ὀνομαίνω 'call by name'	
-d- *(etc.)*	*(Note 7)*	ἐλπίς, -ίδος 'hope'	*custōs, -ōdis* 'guard'
-dy^e/o- *(etc.)*		ἐλπίζω 'hope for'	*custōdiō* (IV) 'guard'
-eH$_1$- *all stems*[8]	(**rudhro-* 'red')		*ruber*
			rubeō (II) 'am red'
	(**srīgos-* 'frost')	ῥῖγος	*frīgus*
		ῥῑγέω	*frīgeō* (II)
	(**dhr̥su-* 'bold')	θρασύς	
		θαρσέω	

G denominatives seemingly from *-*oy^e/o-* based on *o*-stem nouns, as δουλῶ 'enslave' to δοῦλος 'slave', are not included in the table. They are not an inherited type; indeed, there is reason to doubt whether the type actually existed. See **468.3**.

1. The roman numerals refer to the L conjugation classes.
2. More lit. 'yearn for the god(s)'. This denom. type, common in Skt., is unknown in G and L.
3. See **477.2** fn. Factitive denominatives of this stem type are prominent in other IE languages. The great bulk of L factitives are first conjugation verbs, **475.1**; but see **462.2**.
4. L *pugna* 'fight' is a back-formation from the verb, not the basis for it.
5. Lengthening of *-i-* before an affix beginning with *-y-* is normal in Ved.
6. There are no denominatives in *-*y^e/o-* built to *n*-stems in L.
7. In contrast to their abundance in G, Indic denominatives built to consonant bases other than the major stem-forming categories (*n*-stems for example) are rare: the whole of the RV has only two such stems, *bhiṣajyá-* 'heal' and *iṣudhya-* 'implore'. Both are peculiar.
8. Athematic suffix; added to bare root.

to skirt 'to move around the edge of something, especially so as to avoid being met or otherwise detected'; *to snowball* 'to increase rapidly', *to neck* 'to exchange amorous caresses'.

Even the general categories are language-specific. Ved. for example has denominatives meaning 'wish for, crave such-and-such', like *avasyá-* 'seek help' (to *ávas-* 'support'), and *ukṣaṇyá-* 'wish for bulls'; no such type is seen in G, L, or NE, whereas the ablative type (*to bone, to gut*) familiar from NE is unknown in Ved., and the once-commonplace ingressive type has become a small closed class in NE.

A particular denominative affix will sometimes have a particular function, as the factitive **-(i)j*$^{i}/_{a}$- in Gmc., the factitive *be-* of NE (*belittle, begrime*), the agentive -εύω of G (πυκτεύω 'play the boxer, spar' < πύκτης 'boxer'), or the ingressive *-ēscō* of L (479.5). Even in such classes there are always verbs whose meaning does not fit, as the non-factitive sense of *bemoan*, the non-ingressive sense of L *miserēscō* 'have pity for, commiserate', the non-factitive sense of L *nāvō* 'do energetically' (*nāvus* 'diligent, energetic'), or the non-agentive sense of G παιδεύω 'rear a child; train, educate' (παῖς 'child').

462. 1. Denominatives in greek. Greek denominatives in -άω, -έω, and -όω share the property of having a short stem vowel in the pres./imperf. stems and a long vowel in the fut. (-ᾱσω, -ησω, -ωσω) and aor. (-ᾱσα, -ησα, -ωσα). The -άω type originally had -ᾱ- throughout; the original properties of the -όω type are unknown (it may not actually be a type, 468.3). The history of the -έω type depends on whether one is speaking of the statives in **-eH*$_r$- (452) or the denominatives in **-y*$^{e}/_{o}$- (460.1) built to *o*-stems. The latter certainly had a short -ε- in all forms, which originally must have included only the pres. and imperf. Though its distribution and formation has everywhere been disturbed (see 452), comparative evidence for the stative points to an originally athematic stem with the usual alternation between **-eH*$_r$- and -*H̥*$_r$-. The shortening of -ᾱ́ω to -ᾰ́ω was extremely early, since it must predate the Att.-Ion. change of ᾱ to η—which is to say, much too early to be explained by the purely phonological shortening of a long vowel before another vowel, a development which postdates the Att.-Ion. fronting (79.3a)

The usual explanation, then, is that **-āyō, *-āye(h)i(s), *-āyei* and so on simply assimilated to the prosody of **-eyō, *-eye(h)i(s), *-eyei*, and that conversely when aorists and futures were being manufactured, the pattern *-ăyō* : *-āsa* : *-āsō* of the ᾱ-stems was captured by the *-eyō* type, whence -ησα and -ησω. This hypothesis is reasonable, but leaves the Aeolic athem. inflection (469.1) of the denominative verbs unexplained. Therefore, a group of theories which have enjoyed a certain vogue assume that one or another of the denominative types may have been athematic in PG. On the basis of the athem. Hitt. factitives in *-aḫḫ-* (*dan-na-at-ta-aḫ-ḫu-un* 'I emptied', *šu-up-pí-*

ya-aḫ-mi 'I make clean' to *dan-na-at-ta-* 'empty', *šu-up-pí-* 'clean'), the ancestor of the -άω type is usually nominated as having been **-āmi*, **-āhi* and so on. Similarly, the stative in **-eH₁-* might have been athematic to begin with, and therefore possibly the 'Aeolic' -ημι is more conservative than the familiar -έω.

But for all its charm this theory does not account for the details well. Original paradigms of the type **-āmi* (or later -ημι) have no point of formal tangency with the inflection of **-eyō*. Given the prehistoric paradigms laid out on the following page, it is not at all evident how the thematic and athematic types could have converged on a single type.

Once some sort of PRELIMINARY remodeling took place—however that was accomplished, say, the creation of the thematics **pʰileyomen*, **pʰileyete*, **pʰileyonti* in place of the inherited plurals—the door would have been open to further analogizing along the lines of **pʰileyonti* : **pʰilēti* :: **woikeyonti* : *X*, where *X* = **woikēti*, in the prehistory of Aeol. and Arc.-Cyp., with the subsequent loss of the thematic type altogether; while in Att.-Ion the current flowed in the opposite direction, something like **woikeyonti* : **woikeyei* :: **pʰileyonti* : *Y*, where *Y* = **pʰileyei*. But such a scheme requires a period when athem. and them. inflection, or even a mixed type, persisted together—for which there is no actual evidence; and it accounts only with difficulty for the parallel development of the νεϝᾰ- type.

	stative in **-eH₁-*	denom. in **-yᵉ/ₒ-*	? denom. in *-eH₂-*
1sg.	pʰilēmi	woikeyō	newāmi
2	pʰilēhi	woikeyehi	newāhi
3	pʰilēti	woikeyei	newāti
1pl.	pʰilemen (**-H̥₁-*)	woikeyomen	newamen (**-H̥₂-*)
2	pʰilete "	woikeyete	newate "
3	pʰilenti (**-H₁-enti*)	woikeyonti	newanti (**-H₂-enti*)
Aor.	epʰilēsa	?	newāsa
Fut.	pʰilēhō	?? woikeyehō	newāhō

Starting with a stative stem **pʰile-yᵉ/ₒ-* < **-H̥₁-yᵉ/ₒ-* (as attested in Gmc.) is no solution, as the paradigms of the φιλέω and οἰκέω types would simply have been identical from the outset in that case.

a. Inflection of the -ᾱω, -ηω, -ωω type, found in Lesb. and elsewhere, admits of several explanations, all plausible, none certain—thematization of -ᾱμι, -ημι, -ωμι; leveling from the aor. and fut.; and so on.

2. DENOMINATIVES IN LATIN. The PIE type, which remained productive, is mostly found in the L 4th conj. (so *fīnīre* 'finish' to *fīnis* 'end', *fulgurīre* 'to lighten', and so on). The chief feature of the denom. in L was the efflorescence of the 1st conj. type in *-ā-* < **-ā-yᵉ/ₒ-*. This type originally was typical of *ā*-stem nouns (as in all IE languages) and of some *o*-stem base forms (which ditto), and of a factitive de-adjectival formation with clear parallels in other IE languages—of especial note the Hitt. formation in *-aḫ-ḫ-*: L *novāre* 'to renew' (like G νεάω also pregnantly 'to plow anew'; to put land back into cultivation'), Hitt. *ne-wa-aḫ-ḫu-un* 1sg.pret. But it spreads far beyond these functional foundations in L, where it forms denominatives

based on all manner of stems, as *levāre* 'raise; mitigate' (*levis* 'light'), *laudāre* (*laus, laudis* 'praise'), *nōmināre* 'to name' (*nōmen*). Intransitive denominatives in L are often deponent, as *laetārī* 'to be happy', though there are many exceptions to this generalization (for example deponent *partīrī* 'to divide'; active *lascīvīre* 'be sportive, wanton, insolent'; and the virtually synonymous *cruciāre* and *cruciārī* 'torment').

THE PRESENT CLASSES IN GREEK

THE THEMATIC CLASSES

463. SIMPLE THEMATIC (449). The great majority are from roots of the *e*-series and in the *e*-grade. Thus φέρω 'carry', λέγω 'gather', μένω 'remain', λείπω 'leave (over)', φεύγω 'flee', τρέπω 'turn'. Of the same type, but altered in appearance by loss of -ϝ- are ῥέω 'flow' from **hrewō* (**srewoH₂*), πλέω 'float; sail' from **plewō*. Laryngeal effects have obscured the kinship with this group of ἄγω 'drive' (**H_2eǵoH_2*) and perh. αἴθω 'kindle' (?**H_2eydhoH_2*).

Other grades (or roots of other series) are seen in γράφω 'scratch', γλύφω 'carve', and λήγω 'abate, cease'.

a. Athematic stems were often converted into thematic stems, such as the following erstwhile reduplicated presents: γίγνομαι 'am born', μίμνω 'stand fast', πῑ́πτω 'fall down' (ῑ by contamination with ῥῑ́πτω 'toss, throw'?), ἴσχω 'restrain' (**hiskʰō* < **si-sǵh-*, cf. ἔχω 'hold' < **seǵh-*), τίκτω 'beget' (< **titkō* 235.1).

464. THE IOTA CLASSES. Greek presents a great variety of superficially distinct present stem-classes which in fact are all traceable to a single original formal type, the *-y^e/o*-stems. A number of functional types are represented here: primary (a diverse group, 456.1); denominative verbs (460, 462.1, the largest group); and **-y^e/o-* elaborations of earlier (athematic) verb stems. The diversity in stem-forms, detailed in 465, is the result of the various phonetic changes of the second palatalization (198–207).

465. 1. Tau-class. These started in verbs in -πτω, the regular outcome of PG **py* and **p^{h}y* (202). So σκέπτομαι 'look carefully' (from **skep-y^e/o-*, a metathesis of the root seen in L *-spiciō*, Ved. *páśyati*), κόπτω 'beat' (but the etymon **kopyō* is no more than probable), and κρύπτω 'hide' (also only probably from **krup^{h}yō*; cf. κρυφαῖος 'hidden, secret'). With the help of ambiguous forms such as aorists in -ψα, a stem -τω was abstracted from these forms; its association with roots and pseudo-roots ending in labials was extended to include labials from **k^w* as well, so that to fut. πέψω, aor. ἔπεψα, a new pres. πέπτω 'cook, ripen' arose beside πέσσω/πέττω, the real reflexes of **pek^w-y^e/o-* (Ved. *pácyate*)(199).

a. In Hom. or pre-Hom. times such forms were limited to labial environments, but eventually the suffix -τω spread to stems with aorists in -ξα as well, so NG δείχτω 'point out' (aor. ἔδειξα). In later G and NG, furthermore, -πτω itself becomes a productive verb termination. (The beginnings of this are seen in Hellenistic G, for example δύπτω for δύω 'enter; set'.)

2. Presents in -σσω (Attic -ττω). From stems or verb roots ending in any voiceless dorsal or apical (*k, *k^h, *k^w, *k^{wh}, *t, *t^h).
φυλάσσω, -ττω 'keep watch' from *p^h*ulak-yō*; cf. φύλαξ, φύλακος 'guard'.
ὀρύσσω, -ττω 'dig' from **oruk*^{h}*-yō*; cf. ὀρυχή 'a digging'.
πέσσω, -ττω 'cook, ripen' from **pek*^{w}*-yō*; cf. aor. ἔπεψα, Ved. *pakvá-* 'cooked; ripe'.
ἐλασσόω, -ττόω (468.3) 'lessen; detract from'; cf. ἐλαχύς 'small', ἐλαφρός 'light; nimble', PIE **l̥ng*^{w}*h-*.
ἐρέσσω, -ττω 'row'. (The exact source of ἐρετ- is unclear; it has been suggested that ἐρε-τμόν (**erH*$_1$*-tmo-*) 'oar' was metanalyzed as ἐρετ-μόν. Since G had a number of transparent deverbatives in -μό- metanalysis would be reasonable; but *-*tmo-*, though paralleled by such well-attested noun-deriving elements as *-*sneH*$_2$-, *-*tro-*, *-*smeH*$_2$-, is itself so rare in G—perhaps one other form—that it is hard to be confident that its -τ- really belongs to the affix.)

a. Stems in *-*g-yō* and *-*g*^{w}*-yō* become -ζω, as in 3, below. However, some stems in -γ- have presents in -σσω/-ττω, as ἀλλάσσω, -ττω 'change; exchange', cf. ἀλλαγή '(ex)-change' (ἄλλος 'other'); τάσσω, -ττω 'put in order', cf. ταγ-οῦχος 'holding command'. The point of departure for the new forms must have been the futures and aorists in -ξω, -ξα, perf.midd. in -κται, for example fut. ἀλλάξω, aor. ἤλλαξα; fut. τάξω, aor. ἔταξα; so fut. φυλάξω : ἀλλάξω :: φυλάσσω : *X*, where *X* = ἀλλάσσω. In some cases presents of both types are attested, as Att. σφάττω 'slay' in contrast to the conservative Ion. σφάζω (fut. σφάξω, aor. ἔσφαξα) from **sp*^{h}*ag-yō* (cf. σφαγή 'slaughter').

3. Presents in -ζω. From stems or verb roots ending in *g, *g^w, or *d (**200-1**).
ἁρπάζω 'snatch away' from **harpag-yō*; cf. ἁρπαγή 'seizure; booty', Ion. (Hom.) ἥρπαξε 3sg.aor. (extra-Greek connections obscure).
νίζω 'wash' from **nig*^{w}*-yō*; cf. fut. νίψω and χέρ-νιβα acc.sg. 'water for hand-washing' (PIE **neyg*^{w}*-*).
ἐλπίζω 'hope' from **elpid-yō*; cf. ἐλπίς, -ίδος 'hope'.

The great majority of these, like the last, are from stems ending in -δ- or analogical extensions of such. The enormously productive suffixes -άζω and -ίζω, starting from denominatives in *-*ad-yō* *-*id-yō*, form denominatives from stems of all kinds to the number of several thousands.

In general, -άζω is built from first decl. stems, -ίζω from other stems. Thus δικάζω 'decide, judge' (δίκη 'custom; right; judgment'), ἀγοράζω 'market; loiter' (ἀγορᾱ́ 'market-place'), θαυμάζω 'wonder, admire' (θαῦμα 'a wonder, a marvel'); ὑβρίζω 'act extravagantly or outrageously' (ὕβρις, an ι-stem, 'insolence'), ἑλληνίζω 'speak Greek' (Ἕλλην, Dor. -ᾱν 'a Greek'), νομίζω 'own, use' (νόμος 'use, custom'), τειχίζω 'build a wall' (τεῖχος 'wall').

a. In the future and aorist the difference between dorsal and apical stems normally shows itself: -ξ- from *-*g-* or *-*g*^{w}*-* + *-*s-*, vs. Att. -σ- from -δ-σ-; but owing to the shared shape of the present stem there is sometimes confusion. Thus from ἁρπάζω the appropriate aor. ἥρπαξα is found in Ion., next to Att. ἥρπασα.

As for the great mass of derivatives in -ά́ζω, -ίζω, which are not strictly speaking derived from either *-_g_$^{(w)}$_yō_ or *-_dyō_, there is in principle no such thing as an incorrect formation. At any rate, in Att.-Ion. they generally follow the treatment of apical stems, as Att. ἐδίκασα, ἐνόμισα. But Hom. has πτολεμίξω as the fut. of πτολεμίζω 'wage war', and in Doric forms like ἐδίκαξα are the usual ones.

4. Presents in -λλω. By regular sound law from stems and verb roots ending in -λ- (**204**).
στέλλω 'put in order' from *_stel-yō_ (cf. στολή 'equipment; raiment').
ἀγγέλλω 'bear a message' (cf. ἄγγελος 'messenger'; without satisfactory etymology but evidently containing a single -λ-).

a. For βάλλω 'throw', often classed here, see **466**, below.

5. Presents in -αίνω and -αίρω. These result by regular sound law (**203**, **203.2**) from stems and verb roots ending in -αν- or -αμ-, and -αρ- (from *-_n̥_-, *-_m̥_-, *-_r̥_-, **96-7**, **99-100**).
μαίνομαι 'rage' < *_man-y_^{e}/_o_- < *_m̥n-y_^{e}/_o_- (root *_men-_).
βαίνω 'go' < *_g_^{w}_an-yō_ < *_g_^{w}_m̥-y_^{e}/_o_-.
χαίρω 'rejoice' < *_k_^{h}_ar-yō_ (cf. χάρις 'grace').

From denominatives like μελαίνω 'blacken' (μέλας, μέλανος 'black'), ποιμαίνω 'am a shepherd' (from the zero grade stem of ποιμήν 'shepherd'), and especially from forms like ὀνομαίνω 'name' < *_nomn̥-y_^{e}/_o_- whose G cognates have no overt nasal (ὄνομα, ὀνόματος), the -αίνω was resegmented as a suffix per se, as in λευκαίνω 'whiten' (λευκός 'white') and θερμαίνω 'warm' (θερμός 'warm').

6. Presents in -είνω, -είρω (spurious diphthongs), -ῑ́νω, -ῑ́ρω, -ῡ́νω, -ῡ́ρω come by regular sound law from stems ending in -εν-, -ερ-, -ιν-, -ιρ-, -υν-, -υρ- (**203.1**). Other forms in the paradigm, or closely related forms, reveal a root with a short monophthong:
τείνω 'stretch' < *_ten-yō_ (cf. τόνος 'a stretching'; L _tendō_).
φθείρω 'destroy' < *_p_^{h}_t_^{h}_er-yō_ (cf. φθαρτικός 'destructive').
κρῑ́νω 'pick out, discern' < *_krĭn-yō_ (see **a**, below).
οἰκτῑ́ρω 'pity' < *_oiktĭr-yō_ (cf. οἰκτιρμός 'pity').
πλῡ́νω 'wash' < *_plŭn-yō_ (cf. πλυνός 'a tank or trough for washing clothes').
μαρτῡ́ρομαι '(call to) witness' < *_martŭr-yomai_ (Aeol. μάρτυρ 'witness').

Like πλῡ́νω though hardly based upon it is the productive stem -ῡ́νω, mostly built to υ-stems. There is no genuine derivational history here; like the gravitation of -άζω to the historically unrelated ᾱ- (η-) stems, 3, above, the association of ῠ-stems with denom. -ῡ́νω seems to be based on mere similarity. So βαρῡ́νω as if ×_g_^{w}_arun-yō_ 'weigh down' (βαρύς 'heavy'); ἡδῡ́νω 'sweeten, flavor' (ἡδύς 'sweet'); παχῡ́νω 'thicken, fatten' (παχύς 'thick'); but also λεπτῡ́νω 'pulverize' (λεπτός 'fine (of dust, for example); delicate').

a. G κρῑ́νω and κλῑ́νω 'make slope' have special histories. PIE *_kreyH-_ 'sort, separate, sift' is a heavy base (full grade in L _crēvī_ < *_kreawai_ < *_kreyH̥-_ perf. of _cernō_), though some forms, like G κρῐτός 'picked out', seem not to point to a final laryngeal.

Like L *cernō* < **kri-n-H-*, G κρῖνω is a thematized *n*-infix stem (453-4, 466). PIE **ḱley-* 'lean' has no reflexes indicating a laryngeal (typical is RV *śritá-* pple. of *śráya-* 'lean'). Av. has a *nu*-suffix pres. (*srinav-*), and the Gmc. *lean* words as well as L *clīnō* point to some kind of *n*-suffix. There are formal difficulties of various kinds (such as L *clīnāre* 'to lean' for expected **clĭnere*), but PG **klinyō* seems to be an elaboration of a present stem of this kind. Eventually κριν-, κλιν- were abstracted as pseudo-roots which spread to other tenses, aor. ἔκρῖνα (*ἔκρινσα), similarly ἔκλῖνα; but a more conservative appreciation of the 'root' is evident in perf. κέκριται, κέκλιται (even though not particularly antique forms); and hesitation is seen in some forms, as aor.pass. ἐκρίθην and ἐκρίνθην.

b. G ἐλαύνω (aor. ἔλασ(σ)α) 'drive' is commonly regarded as an aberrant *n*-affix formation from a root **elH*$_2$- (or **H*$_1$*elH*$_2$-). But ἐλαύνω can be explained as a denominative based on an *r/n*-stem **elH̥*$_2$*-wr̥*, **elH*$_2$*-un-* 'haste'; cf. the bare root seen in non-pres./imperf. stems, in Hom. ἐλάω (**ela-yō* < **elH̥*$_2$-) and ἐλατήρ 'driver' (**elH̥*$_2$*tēr*), and in scattered dialect forms such as Cos ελατω imperat. The ἐλαύνω that ousted ἐλάω has been explained as a denominative, **elaun-yō*, to the *r/n*-stem **elawar*, **elaunos*. But the only evidence for an *r/n*-form is Gaul. *Elaver*, the name of a short, swift-flowing river (Fr. *Allier*), and perhaps a singularly archaic denominative built to the stem form in *-*un*- is improbable.

7. Presents in -αίω (*-*awyō*), -εύω (*-*ewyō*), as καίω 'kindle' (**kaw-yō*; cf. aor. ἔκαυσα), κλαίω 'wail' (**klaw-yō*, cf. aor. ἔκλαυσα). For Att. forms like κᾱ́ω and κλᾱ́ω see 207.

Parallel stems in *-*ew-yō* underlie G verbs in -εύω. The normal phonetic development would have yielded *-ειω (cf. ἡδεῖα f. 'sweet' < **hwādew-ya*, 205, and καίω above), and this is the actual form in Elean (φυγαδειω = Att. φυγαδεύω 'drive out'). But elsewhere it was replaced by -εύω, whose -ευ- was imported from fut. -ευσω.

a. The -εύω type started as a denominative based on nouns in -ευς, as ἱππεύω 'ride on horseback' to ἱππεύς 'horseman', and the transparency of this connection contributed to the success of the stem in -ευ- in supplanting regular -ει-. Like -πτω, -αίνω, and -ῡνω (1, 5, and 6, above), the complex -εύω was subsequently reinterpreted as an affix per se, becoming productive quite independently of nouns in -ευς.

8. Stems in vowels. Denominatives in -ιω and -υω, as μηνίω 'am furious' (μῆνις), μεθύω 'am in wine' (μέθυ), for which see 460-1; and the great majority of contract verbs in -άω, -έω, -όω (468). Similarly some primary verbs in -υω, as φύω 'beget' (correct etymology thanks to Lesb. φυίω, which indicates **bhu-y*^{e}/*o*-). Whether λύω 'loosen' and others belonged to this or to the simple thematic class is impossible to determine.

These stems generally show -ῠω in Hom., but -ῡω in Att. This implies a morphology more elaborate than a simple theme vowel, but the known behavior of *-*y*- does not explain Att. -ῡω.

466. THEMATIZATIONS OF *n*-INFIX PRESENTS (453-4). Presents in -νω, as κάμ-νω 'labor' (root **ḱemH*$_2$-: original pres. **ḱm̥-ne-H*$_2$-; **ḱm̥H*$_2$*-t-* in ἀκμής, -ῆτος 'tireless'; cf. Dor. κμᾱτός); τέμ-νω 'cut' (replacement of Hom. τάμνω, like κάμνω from **tm̥-ne-H*$_2$-, perh. also seen—the semantics are troublesome—in ORu. *tĭnu* 'strike'; **tm̥H*$_2$*tos* in τμητός 'cut', Dor. τμᾱ-; **temH̥*$_2$- in τέμαχος 'slice of meat').

A disguised example of the class is βάλλω 'throw' < *g^w*alnō* ← *g^w*alnē-mi* (*g^w*l̥-ne-H*$_1$-). There are no satisfactory extra-Greek cognates, but it is clear from the forms within G that the root was *g^w*elH*$_1$- (**162**, end).

Superficially similar formations, but not of PIE date, are πί-νω 'drink' and δάκ-νω 'bite' (cf. aor. ἔδακον; PIE **dn̥ḱ-*? Neither G nor other attestations point to a laryngeal, so for example RV *dáṃṣṭra-* 'fang' < **denḱ-tro-*). Such formations became possible once the true relationship of stem and root in forms like κάμνω was lost sight of. (The same thing happened in Indic, where *-nā-* became a mildly productive stem-forming element.)

Likewise mere look-alikes are τίνω 'honor', φθάνω 'outstrip', φθίνω 'decay' (Hom. τῑνω, φθᾱνω, φθῑνω) from **tinwō*. These are early-thematized verbs of the *nu*-suffix class (**455**); later thematizations of this type resulted in more transparent formations like δεικνύω (δείκνῡμι) and Hom. τανύουσι.

Presents in -άνω, as αὐξάνω 'enlarge', ἁμαρτάνω 'fail', αἰσθάνομαι 'perceive', are unlike anything in other IE languages. Descriptively they seem to have a suffix in *-*n̥n*^{e}/*o*-, which will not do. It might be explained as (a) the ordinary reflex of *-*n*^{e}/*o*- after a heavy syllable, per Sievers' Law (**178**); (b) the reflex of *-*n̥H*-^{e}/*o*-; (c) the reflex of *-*Hn*-^{e}/*o*- (that is *-*Hn̥*-^{e}/*o*- since via Sievers' Law, **178**, all such forms by definition have the semivowel after a heavy syllable). Sievers' Law is a weak explanation—there is no evidence from other, more certain, formations that it applied with any rigor to nasals. No suffix *-*Hn*- is suggested by cognate forms in other languages in any case. An etymon *-*n̥H*- would be an expected (alternative) result of the thematization of *n*-infix stems built to heavy (*CVRH-) bases, like τάμνω. (The difficulty is explaining an element -ανω next to the vowelless shape seen in τάμνω.) Some such history is consistent with the general rule that present/imperfect stems in -άνω, -άνομαι have root aorists, since nasal infixation is one of the ways that pres./imperf. stems are formed to basically aoristic roots (**413**). Convincing evidence for this would however require a stem in -άνω built to a heavy base with an undoubted *n*-infix present attested either earlier in G or in some other language, but none of the attested forms qualifies.

Even in the absence of such, there is at least a suggestive datum: stems in -άνω, -άνομαι have a marked affinity for roots with *n*-infixation, as λανθάνω 'escape notice', ἁνδάνω 'please', πυνθάνομαι 'learn'. The standard practice is to compare these to what appear to be componentially similar forms in Lith., like *bundù* and *bùdinu*, as if πυνθάνομαι were somehow a conflation of G *πύνθομαι and *πυθάνομαι. The Baltic forms are however irrelevant; both are productive stem types: *bundù* is inchoative ('wake up' or the like); *budin-*, the causative, is the stem of the whole causative paradigm, not just of the present. Nevertheless, the regular combination of original *n*-infix presents and the -άνω/-άνομαι stem extension, enigmatic as it is, cannot be accidental.

The key is in the conflicting patterns, morphological and prosodic both, which arose with the loss of laryngeals and the resulting disintegration of what had been a single inherited type. There are no precisely correct proportional analogies, but not long after the loss of laryngeals the paradigms would have looked something like this:

Root:	*leyk^w- *leave*	*Root:*	*tem(a)- *cut*
Root Aor.	*eleyk^w-/*elik^w-		*etema-/*etmā-/*etam-
n-*infix 3sg.*	*linek^{w}ti		*tamnāti
3pl.	*link^{w}onti		*tamanonti (*in place of inherited* *tamnonti < *tm̥nH$_2$onti? *Or the regular development?*)

The aorists and other forms serve to keep the stem-forming nature of the nasal forms salient. The pattern **tamnāti* : **linek^{w}ti* :: **tamanonti* : **link^{w}onti* would lead to remodeling the last as **link^{w}anonti*.

The process is similar to the untidy, essentially prosodic, analogy which led to the creation of 3pl. *danunt* in OL for *dant* 'they give', *-īnunt* for *-eunt* 'they go' (in compounds only; **486**), and of Hitt. *-nun* (in place of **-n*) 1sg.pret. for verb stems ending in vowels.[1] Once **link^{w}anonti* became established, it would be the starting-point for a wholesale remodeling of the stem as a thematic, whence **link^{w}anō*, **link^{w}anehi* and so on. The element -άνω/-άνομαι itself was productive as a stem-formation quite apart from original *n*-infix stems, but to a degree the whole ensemble was productive; thus Att. λαμβάνω (aor. ἔλαβον) 'take' for Hom. λάζομαι (**slag^w-y^e/o-*, aor. ἔλλαβε 3sg.), which appears to be the more original pres.-stem from the root **slag^w-*.

a. For G ἐλαύνω (aor. ἔλασ(σ)α) 'drive', see **465.6b**.

467. σκ$^e/_o$-CLASSES (**456.3**, q.v. also for the function of this suffix).

1. Primary formations, zero grade of root, as βάσκω* (only in imper. βάσκε 'get moving'—both 'go!' and also 'come!'), ἀρέσκω 'make amends'.

2. With reduplication: γιγνώσκω 'become aware', βιβρώσκω 'eat'. (As remarked in **456.3b**, the type is widely attested.)

3. With consonant changes: λάσκω 'crash' from *λακ-σκω (aor. ἔλακον); πάσχω 'suffer' from *παθ-σκω; μίσγω 'mix' from *μιγ-σκω (midd.aor. ἐμίγην, pres. μίγνῡμι; cf. μίγα adv. 'mixed with', and L *misceō*).

a. G -ισκω (or -ῑσκω, the length of the vowel is unattested) became a productive suffix, much like L *-īscō*, as εὑρίσκω 'discover', ἁλίσκομαι 'am captured', στερίσκω 'deprive', and even to roots in long vowels, θνῃίσκω (Dor. θνᾱ́σκω) 'am dying', μιμνῃίσκω 'remind', θρῴισκω 'leap'. The source of the elaborated form of the affix is uncertain.

4. Thematic stems form stems in -εσκω, as φερέσκω to φέρω 'carry', Hom. θέλγεσκε 3sg. to θέλγω 'charm'. The same is seen in **-y^e/o-* stems, as Ion. χαίρεσκον to χαίρω 'am glad' < **k^{h}ar-y^e/o-*, but they are infrequent, and often have unexpected vocalism such as the -α- of Ion. κρύπτασκε to κρύπτω 'hide' < **krup^h-y^e/o-*.

---

[1] Sound laws would result in the pattern *e-eš-mi* : *e-šu-un* :: *a-ar-nu-mi* : **a-ar-nu-un*; the elaboration of the last form to *a-ar-nu-nu-un* is purely prosodic, like the doubly-marked nom.pl. of *o*-stems (as in Ved. *dévāsas*), **260.1d**.

More commonplace are such forms to verbs in -έω, both causative/intensive like ποθέω 'yearn for, regret' (Hom. ποθέεσκον) and stative like φιλέω 'love' (Hom. φιλέεσκε). As the type was originally built from roots, the φερέσκω and φιλέεσκε shapes are analogical, but the model is uncertain. Forms like ἀρέσκω 'make good, make up', where the -ε- probably continues $^*H_1$, are not prominent; besides, in this case the crucial form for the analogy, *ἄρω, is missing.

a. A peculiarity of the forms in -σκ- built to denominatives is that the normal formations in -έεσκ-, -άασκ- are limited to metrically light roots, as in the examples here. The forms based on heavy roots are like Hom. πωλέσκετο 'used to barter' (πωλέω). The impossibility of forms like πωλεέσκετο in dactylic meter explains why they are not found in poetry, but that hardly can explain the ORIGIN of πωλέσκετο and the like.

THE CONTRACT VERBS

468. The bulk of the contract verbs are denominatives (460-1). They are traditionally grouped into three etymological types:

1. -άω/-άομαι.

A. The majority are derived from actual ā-stems, as τῑμάω 'honor' (τῑμή), νῑκάω 'win' (νῑκή 'victory'), σῑγάω 'am silent' (σῑγή 'silence').

B. Some of the remainder are derivatives of o-stem nouns and adjectives, a PIE type of factitive formation: νεάω 'renew' < **new-eH₂(-yᵉ/ₒ)-*, cf. L *novāre*, Hitt. *ne-wa-aḫ-*.

C. There are a few primary verbs, as δράω 'accomplish' (stem δρᾱ-, cf. aor. ἔδρᾱσα); and some of obscure history like σπάω 'draw (a sword)' (aor. ἔσπασ(σ)α, perf. ἔσπασμαι; it is unclear whether the verb stem is σπα- or σπασ-, or what the outside connections are); χαλάω 'slacken' (even more obscure); and so on.

For the shortening of the -ᾱ- in the pres./imperf. stem, see **462**.

Forms like περάασκε 3sg. 'went through', inf. περαᾶν, are false distractions of περᾶσκε, περᾶν, whose real etyma are more like *περάεσκε, *περαεῖν (see -όω stems, below).

2. -έω/-έομαι. There are five principal sources of these verbs.

A. Denominatives of ancient type built to o-stem nouns, with the stem in the *e*-grade: οἰκέω 'inhabit' (οἶκος 'house'), μετρέω 'measure' (μέτρον); but also to other stem types, as φωνέω 'speak out' (φωνή 'voice'), μαρτυρέω 'call to witness' (μάρτυς).

B. Denominatives built to σ-stems, as τελέω 'complete' from earlier τελείω (**teles-yō*; τέλος, τέλεσ- 'goal'). Here the aor. ἐτέλεσσα reveals the original stem, but for the most part the distinction is one of etymology only, as such derivatives usually merge with those from o-stems: μῑσέω 'hate' aor. ἐμῑ́σησα (μῖσος, -ους 'hatred') just like μετρέω, aor. ἐμέτρησα.

C. Old statives in -η- (**-eH₁-*; **452**), as φιλέω 'love' (φίλος), ἀλγέω 'feel pain' (ἄλγος), θαμβέω 'am amazed' (θάμβος); here the fut. ἀλγήσω and aor. ἐθάμβησα preserve the original vowel length; in the μετρέω, ἐμέτρησα pattern (type A, above), the pres./imperf. stem has the original vowel length and the -η- of the aor. and fut. is analogical.

A single stative δοκέι 'seems (good)', has an aor. without the -η- imported from the denominatives and statives, namely ἔδοξε.

D. Causative/frequentative formations in *-*éy*^{e}/*o*- (**456.2A**), as σοβέω 'shoo away, put to flight' (σέβομαι), φορέω 'carry about, wear' (φέρω). These have completely coalesced with the denominative type (A), meaning alone being the (not always decisive) basis for deciding whether a given form is denominative or causative/frequentative.

E. Primary verbs in -έω, mostly presents of the simple thematic class in origin, with the loss of intervocalic *-*w*- (**189**), *-*y*- (**192**), or *-*s*- (**172**), as ῥέω 'flow' (**brewō* < **srew*-^{e}/*o*-), πλέω 'float' (**plewō* < **plew*-^{e}/*o*-); ζέω 'boil' (**ǰehō* < **yes*-; Ved. *yas*-, NE *yeast*), τρέω 'flee from' (**trehō*; Ved. *trásanti* 3pl. 'are in dread'; with preverbs, 'flee'); δέω 'bind' < **de-yō* < **dH̥₁-y*^{e}/*o*-, cf. pple. δετός < **dH̥₁-to*- and Ved. *á-saṃ-dita*- 'unfettered', and Hom. δίδημι).

3. -όω/-όομαι. One such formation is aboriginal, being a primary formation from a verb root: ἀρόω 'plow' < **H₂erH̥₃-y*^{e}/*o*- (cf. ἄροτρον 'plow' **H₂erH̥₃trom*). Otherwise, the stem type is a purely G entity. As the type develops in the literary language it has the appearance of a denominative based on *o*-stems, but built directly to the unaltered noun stem (unlike the inherited types, **460** and 2A, above). Functionally, some have instrumentive force, as στεφανόω 'crown', but most are factitive, as δηλόω 'make clear' (δῆλος 'visible'), δουλόω 'enslave' (δοῦλος 'slave'; cf. δουλεύω 'am a slave')—note that ἀρόω is neither, another indication that its resemblance to the type is coincidental. Both of these functions are quite natural for a denominative type, but the seemingly self-evident makeup of the forms—a new type formed to *o*-stems parallel to -άω from ᾱ-stems—is not consistent with three remarkable facts. In Hom., the genuine denominatives in -έω and -άω occur mostly in the pres./imperf., by a wide margin; but in the same text, and by an even wider margin, the stems in -όω occur chiefly in the aor. Another peculiarity: despite its predominantly preterital use, the type never occurs with iterative -σκ- in Hom. (**456.3**). Finally, there is not a single epigraphic attestation of uncontracted -*o*-.

The origin of the formation must have something to do with the non-pres. forms with stem in -ω-. What the history of that might be is still unexplained, but what is clear is that pres./imperf. contract stem in -ῶ(μαι) is secondary and analogical to the other denominative classes, and the notion of '-όω presents' is a grammarians' invention. As mentioned in **86.6a**, editorial creations like κραιαίνω 'accomplish' reveal the lengths that redactors would go to to bring the text into line with the meter; -όω is a trifling venture by comparison.

469. INFLECTION OF THE CONTRACT VERBS.

1. Thematic (Att.-Ion.) inflection. This type involves, descriptively, a thematic element -$^{e}/_{o}$- after a preceding -ε-, -ᾰ-, or -ο-. There is great divergence among the dialects in the matter of contracted and uncontracted forms of the vowel sequences which result from a lost yod, and they differ also in the results of contraction (**86**). Since this follows from the late date of the contraction, the details depend on innovations peculiar to the individual dialects.

In general, uncontracted forms are most frequent in Ionic, while Attic stands at the other extreme, with almost complete contraction. (In modern G, contracted and uncontracted forms exist side by side; the latter are not survivals of the ancient uncontracted forms, but are innovations, via distraction. Through the years the ratio between contracted and distracted forms has varied; the distracted forms are said to be preferred nowadays.)

Uncontracted forms are most frequent from verbs in -έω, less frequent from those in -άω and rare for those in -όω. This is in part a matter of phonetics, more similar vowels tending to contract more readily than less similar vowels, so (even in Att.) δέω 'need' (**dewō*, cf. Lesb. δεύω) and δέομεν but δεῖς, δεῖ < δέεις, δέει. But the comparative rarity of uncontracted forms in -όω in texts and their complete absence from epigraphy is due to the fact that they are only inkhorn spellings to begin with (**468.3**).

There is considerable variation in Homeric usage, where we find both φιλέει and φιλεῖ, φιλέοντες and φιλεῦντες; for these the uncontracted forms are usual, but some forms hardly ever contract—φιλέουσι, φιλέοι, φιλέωμεν, and some others (though these are sometimes to be read φιλγώμεν, with synizesis); with other stem vowels we find ὑλάει, ὕλαον and the like, or more frequently forms like ὁρόω, ὁράασθαι (with distraction), beside contracted ὁρᾶι, νῑκᾶι, ἐνῑ́κων.

In Att., contraction is the rule. Only a few disyllabic presents in -έω < *-*ewō*, such as πλέω 'float' and δέω 'need', have uncontracted forms; and even then, as noted above, contraction of -εε- occurs.

2. 'Aeolic' (athematic) inflection (**462.1**). In Lesb., Thess., Arc., and Cyp., the verb types corresponding to the contract verbs of the familiar literary dialects have prevailingly athematic inflection. Thus in Alcaeus and Sappho κάλημι, ἐπαίνεντες (= Att. ἐπαινοῦντες), Thess. στραταγεντος (= Att. στρατηγοῦντος), Arc. ποίενσι (like τίθενσι).

3. There are a few contract verbs which differ from the usual type in that they come from -ηω (that is, -ᾱ́ω), and -ωω, and consequently show different results of contraction. Thus χρῶ (χρᾱ́ω) 'utter an oracle', 3sg. χρῆι; διψῶ (Hom. διψᾱ́ω) 'am thirsty', πεινῶ (Hom. πεινᾱ́ω) 'am hungry', inf. διψῆν, πεινῆν; ψῶ (ψᾱ́ω) 'touch', σμῶ (σμᾱ́ω) 'anoint', κνῶ (κνᾱ́ω) 'scrape, scratch', infin. ψῆν, and so on; χρῶμαι 'use', 3sg. χρῆται, inf. χρῆσθαι, from χρέωμαι

(< *χρήομαι < χρᾱ́ομαι); ῥῑγῶν 'shiver' (also ῥῑγοῦν), ἱδρῶ 'sweat', Hom. ἱδρώω, from stems ῥῑγωσ-, ἱδρωσ-. (The inflection of ἱδρώων 'sweating' < *hidrōh- is responsible for that of ῥῑγώων 'shivering with cold'; the original inflection of the latter was based on a stem *hrigē-, a stative in *-eH_1-: so ῥῑγέω, Hom. fut. ῥῑγήσειν. There is no reason to think that a stem *hrigōh- actually existed.)

a. Att. ζῶ 'am alive', 3sg. ζῇ, 3pl. ζῶσι, inf. ζῆν, as if from *ζήω, *ζήει, and so on, has traditionally been traced to *g^wyē-. This is an impossibility if *$g^w iH_3$- is the correct reconstruction of the root. But even Hom. ζώω, ζώει are only tentatively explicable. Only the zero grade *$g^w iH_3$- is securely attested in IE languages. The most widely attested formation is an adj. *$g^w iH_3$-wo- 'alive' (L *vīvus*, Ved. *jīvá-*, Lith. *gývas*, Go. *qius**) whose G reflex, ζωός 'alive', has gone unrecognized until recently (49.3). Hom. ζώω is probably the same development (denom. *$g^w iH_3$-$y^e/_o$-, whence *jōyō > ζώω), though unlike ζωός this etymon is not supported by an array of clear cognates. The Att. inflection is however a wholly novel formation: formally it has been absorbed into the inflectional type of ψῶ and κνῶ, though there is no obvious functional reason why such words would have influenced it.

THE ATHEMATIC CLASSES

470. ROOT CLASS (447). Here belong εἰμί 'am' (491-6), εἶμι 'go' (in Att. a fut. tantum apart from compounds; see a, below), φημί (φᾱμί), 'say', ἠμί 'I say', ἄημι 'blow' (*ἀϝη- < *H_2weH_1-, 90), ἧμαι 'am seated' (*ēs- or *eH_1s-, 51), κεῖμαι 'am lying down', ἐπί-στα-μαι 'understand' (< *-stH̥_2-, zero grade of *$steH_2$- 'stand' as in ἵστᾱμι, ἵστημι). These are mostly relics of the once very large class of root stems, though ἠμί has a disputed and doubtful etymology, and a root inflection of *$steH_2$- must be secondary (either imported from the aor., where it belongs, or the result of some process like haplology of an originally redup. **epi-s(t)ista(m)ai*).

Middle forms are attested only from roots originally ending in a laryngeal, at least apparently—many etymologies are doubtful: ἄγα-μαι 'wonder at' (etymology uncertain, but the -α- has been traced to *-H̥_2-); κρέμαμαι 'hang' (etymology also uncertain, but cf. *n*-infix κρήμνημι, with secondary full grade of the root); δέατο 'seemed' (**deya-* < *$deyH_2$-, cf. Ved. *dī-* 'shine', perf. tant.); ἔραμαι 'love, lust after' (doubtful outside connections; most often compared to Ved. *arí-* 'attached to, faithful', though the latter has an ordinary *-*y*- and the whole form has been differently explained both formally and functionally); πέτα-μαι 'fly' (cf. Ved. seṭ forms like *patitá-* pple., and intens. *pătáyanti* 'they fly along', though the majority of the Indic forms are aniṭ or ambiguous); δύνα-μαι 'am able' (perh. originally *δύ-να-μαι, an *n*-infix present, but reinterpreted as a root, whence aor. ἐδυνήθην, fut. δυνήσομαι. Its etymology is very doubtful, the surmise of an orig. *n*-infix being based on the recognition that a root **dewn-* is impossible, whereas **dewH-* would be a routine root shape and furthermore apt for *n*-infixation); δίε-μαι 'flee' (unless this is a back formation from them. δίεται; no clear etymology in any case); ῑ̔́εμαι 'am sent forth' < *yi-yH̥_1- ? (root *yeH_1-);

ὄνο-μαι 'blame' (no clear cognates; a root *H_3enH_3- is unlikely in any case, though an assimilation from original *ἔνομαι or *ἄνομαι is a possibility).

For inflection, see **448**.

a. The imperfect of εἶμι 'go' (**423A**) shows a great variety of forms, some of which are not certainly explained. Leveling analogy is responsible for much of it, most obviously in the restoration of lost intervocalic *-*y*- on the basis of preconsonantal -*y*- as in 1pl. ἤιμεν, such that ἠι- < *e-ey- becomes an invariant stem. PIE *ēyṃ 1sg. imperf. (cf. Ved. *āyam*) gave early G *ēya, from which *ἠα would have been regular; but the reimportation of -*y*- resulted in ἤια. Similarly 2sg. ἤισθα, 3sg. ἤιει(ν), 3pl. ἤισαν, which closely resemble and may have been influenced by the anterior tense (the pluperfect, formally) of οἶδα 'know', namely ᾔδησθα, ᾔδεισθα, ᾔδει(ν), ᾔδεσαν, respectively, as also the later 1sg. ἤιειν like ᾔδειν.

Hom. 1sg. ἤϊα, 3sg. ἤϊε are a special problem. Some think they are deformations of original *ἤεα, *ἤεε which were themselves analogical creations based on ᾔδεα, ᾔδεε. In view of the likely influence of οἶδα elsewhere in the paradigm such influence here would be thinkable, but the expected forms would have been rather *ἤιεα, *ἤιεε; in any case, whether starting from *ἤιεα or *ἤεα it is hard to understand why either would have undergone SUBSEQUENT deformation. It is therefore more likely that ἤϊα and the like are exactly what they look like: results of the importation of -ι- from zero grade forms—that is, the vowel /i/ not the glide—like ἴμεν, ἴτε, augmentless impf. ἴτην 3du., ἴσαν 3pl. Similarly the thematized 1sg. ἤϊον, next to Hom. ἤιομεν 1pl. (a thematized version of the usual secondary stem in ἠι-).

The subj., opt., and imperat. forms are all formed from the zero grade of the root, as ἴω, ἴοιμι, ἴθι. As the subjunctive formation calls for full grade of the root (**128.1**), the zero grade is secondary. The expected full grade is attested in dialect forms (εἴω for example); and perh. Hom. ἴομεν, when scanned ī-, is a redactional anachronism for original *εἴομεν.

471. REDUPLICATING CLASS (**451**). Straightforward, including the effects of Grassmann's Law (**138**), are τί-θη-μι 'put' (*$dheH_1$-, cf. Ved. *dádhāti*); ἵ-στη-μι, ἵστᾱμι 'stand' (*sistā- < *$stisteH_2$-, root *$steH_2$-, cf. Ved. *tíṣṭhati*, thematized); δί-δω-μι 'give' (*deH_3-, cf. Ved. *dádāti*); ἵ-η-μι 'send, throw' (*yiyē-, root *yeH_1-); κί-χρη-μι 'resort to'; βί-βη-μι* 'stride' (as attested in the pple. βιβᾱ́ς), and others. With less obvious reduplication, δί-ζη-μαι 'look for' (-η- < -ᾱ-) perhaps < *di-diH_2-, **49.2**; good outside connections are lacking, but G ζῆλος 'goal' and ζητέω (Dor. ζᾱτέω) 'seek' appear to be related. With what looks like inner reduplication (**444**), ὀνί-νη-μι 'benefit' (verb stem ὀνᾱ-, cf. fut. ὀνήσω, < *neH_2- or *H_3neH_2-; doubtful outside connections).

With inserted nasal πί-μ-πλη-μι 'fill' trans. (NB imperat. πίπλη), πί-μ-πρημι 'burn', Dor. κί-γ-κρημι (= Att. κίχρημι). These last are reminiscent of the *n*-infix type of λαμβάνω 'seize', but in the latter the puzzle is the nasal tag (**454.1**, **466**) not the infix. The route by which a pseudo-infix found its way into the reduplicating syllable is unobvious.

a. For a note on the formation of the imperf. of these stems in G, see **497a**.

472. THE νυ-CLASS. From the G point of view, these are verbs with a stem formed with -νῡ- in the act.sg.indic. and -νῠ- elsewhere. There are two different sources for such forms, which are manifested in G as three types.

1. PIE *-*néw-*/*-*nu-* (455) was a suffix ablauting in accord with the usual distribution of full and zero grades (440); also in accord with the usual patterns of characterized athematic formations, it was built to the zero grade of the root. The ablaut of the suffix is modified in G to an alternation of length only. The most original formation is seen in ὄρνῡμι (ὄρνῠμεν) 'arise', directly superimposable on Ved. *ṛṇoti* < **r̥-new-ti* (or **H_3r̥-new-ti*; the former, if Hitt. *ar-nu-uz-zi* 'brings' is cognate). Similar but secondary are δείκνῡμι 'point', ζεύγνῡμι 'join', whose full grade roots reveal them to be post-PIE formations.

a. The original full grade of the affix is only indirectly attested in G, in the thematized verbs in -νεύω such as θαρνεύω 'leap' (cf. orig. athem. θάρνυσθαι) and, with loss of -ϝ-, Hom. δῑνέω 'drive or spin around' next to δῑνεύω.

2. The type in -ννῡμι, -ννῠμεν is the result of adding the same suffix *-*new-* to roots ending in *-*s*-, though the details of the formation result from a zig-zag interaction between sound laws and analogy: taking ἕννῡμι, ἕννῠμεν 'dress' (PIE **wes-*; cf. Ved. *váste*) as an example, the form **wes-nu-* would have given, first, εἰνῡ- (227.2), a stage actually attested in Ion. εἴνῡμι. Subsequently in most forms the -σ- was restored on the basis of such forms as the aor. ἕσσα; and this **hesnū̆-* then became *hennū̆-* in accord with the rules for the development of SECONDARY -σν- (227.2c). Among verbs of this sort, unremodeled forms are commonest in the paradigm of ἕννῡμι/εἴνῡμι, as is fitting for the most basic verb in this class, and in addition this verb has relatively few forms in which -σ- is regularly preserved. More uniformly attested are σβέννῡμι 'quench' (cf. σβεστός), and ζώννῡμι 'gird' (cf. ζωστός). In any case, the conglomerate -ννῡμι was subsequently transplanted to roots of various shapes, though typically ending in a vowel, as στρώ-ννῡμι, στορέ-ννῡμι both 'spread, scatter' (byforms of στόρνῡμι, 3, below; cf. aor. ἐ-στόρε-σα; metathesis for **stero-* < **sterH̥₃-*), κορέ-ννῡμι 'satiate' (though this may in fact continue **kores-*), κεράννῡμι 'mix', πετά-ννῡμι 'spread (open)', and many others.

3. Of completely different origin are ὄμνῡμι 'swear an oath', στόρνῡμι 'spread, scatter', and ὄλλῡμι (-λλ- < *-*ln*-) 'destroy'. These are in origin *n*-infix presents (454A.3) built to roots ending in **H_3*; so to **sterH₃-* 'spread, scatter': **str̥-ne-H_3-*/**str̥-n-H̥₃-*. The zero grade of the stem would have been, first, *-*no-* and then by Cowgill's Law (44) -νυ-, and then the *-νω-/-νυ- type and the *-νευ-/-νυ- types converged on the attested -νῡ-/-νυ- type (1, above).

a. Θαρνεύω 'leap', mentioned above, seems to reveal how the capture of the original *-νω-/-νυ- type by the -νευ- type took place: first the full grade suffix *-*nō-* was replaced by -*new-*, since θαρνεύω presupposes *θαρνευμι in place of *θαρνωμι, created on the basis of ambiguous θαρνυ- < **tʰarno-* (cf. θάρνυσθαι). The outside connections of the root are not as clear as one would like, but θρώσκω, Att. θρῴσκω < **dhr̥H₃*-, θοροῦμαι (that is, θορέομαι, with the usual metathesis from *θερο-), and other forms, point unambiguously to **dherH₃*-.

But this is mildly surprising. In the absence of θαρνεύω, one would have supposed that the capture of *-*nō*-/-*nu*- took place after the remodeling of original *-*new*-/-*nu*- to -νῡ-/-νῠ-. Possibly some stems followed one route, some the other.

473. THE νη- (νᾱ-)CLASS. Descriptively a suffix in G, this is historically an *n*-infix type built to roots ending in *-H_2- preceded by a consonant, as shown in 453 (and cf. 121-3). In Att.-Ion. the original -νᾱ-/-νᾰ- alternation becomes -νη-/-να- in accord with the sound laws, 54: δάμνημι 'subdue' (root **demH₂*-), πέρνημι 'export (for sale)', (root **perH₂*-?; related to **pro* 'forth'?), πίτνημι 'spread out' (a conservative form of πετάννῡμι, mentioned above), σκίδνημι 'disperse' (the later form σκεδάννῡμι is more usual), κίρνημι 'add water to wine' (more usually κεράω and κεράννῡμι), μάρναμαι 'fight; quarrel', πίλναμαι 'approach'. Most of these are found in poetry or in the dialects, and the class is not productive in any attested variety of G.

a. Several common thematic stems started out in this class, κάμνω 'toil' and τάμνω (later reshaped as τέμνω) 'cut' (466).

b. The -ι- that seems to take the place of normal -ε- in many of these roots (while the expected vowel does appear in the aor. stem: ἐπέτασσα, ἐσκέδασσα, ἐκέρασσα, ἐπέλασσα) has no satisfactory explanation. The development of -ι- in Hom. πίσυρες from **kʷetwores* 'four', is comparable only in being an enigma too; there is no guarantee that it is the same phenomenon. Since *n*-infix formations take the zero grade of the root, the original forms of these roots would have been **sḱd-ne-H₂*-, **pt-ne-H₂*-, and the like and some scholars have proposed a reduced grade (schwa secundum) in such stems. Such clusters might be the ideal spot to find syllabics which are intermediate between a full vowel and no vowel at all; but apart from the usual objections to that concept (124) roots of the shape **skedH₂*- and **petH₂*- would not be typical shapes for *n*-infix stems in PIE (though there are some similar ones, 453): most *n*-infix stems are made to roots with a potentially syllabic consonant before the infix. And such an explanatory strategy actually creates problems for κίρνημι and πίλναμαι, because there is no reason for a reduced vowel in a shape like **ḱr̥-ne-H₂*-.

THE PRESENT CLASSES IN LATIN

474. THE LATIN CONJUGATIONS. The familiar classification of L verbs in four conjugations is based on the infinitive only. Except for most of the verbs in the first conjugation there is no uniformity in the perfect stem or the participle within a given conjugation. Perfects in -*vī* or -*uī*, reduplicated perfects (with and without the reduplication intact), and root aorists occur in all four conjugations; and perfect stems based on the *s*-aorists occur in all but the first.

Verbs of the first, second, and fourth conj. reflect *-*y*ᵉ/*o*- stems (456, 460), often added to some earlier stem. Those of the third conjugation represent the thematic presents, both simple and formed with other thematic suffixes, including some (the *capiō* subvariety) in *-*y*ᵉ/*o*- (479.6; 481).

The peculiarities of the 'irregular verbs' (482-96) are mostly relics of athematic inflection.

FIRST CONJUGATION

475. The Italic 1st conj. comprises the most productive type of denominative, together with a few primary verbs (including some causative/frequentatives, 456.2B). In addition to the types described below, there are a good number of composite *ā*-stems which arose by metanalysis, as *-igāre*, *-īcāre*, *-ināre*, and the like.

1. The great mass are denominatives answering to G *-άω* and reflecting the PIE **-eH₂-yᵉ/o-* type (460), and originally based upon *o*-stems and *eH₂*-stems, as *dōnō* 'make a present of' (*dōnum*), *pugnō* 'fight' (*pugnus* 'fist'), *cūrō* 'take care of' (*cūra*). The numerous de-adjectivals are prevailingly factitive, as *novō* 'renew' (*novus*), *sōlō* 'make solitary' (*sōlus*). Already in the earliest known stages of L, such forms are freely based on stems of all kinds, not just *o*- and *ā*-stems: *levō* 'raise up' (*levis*, *i*-stem), *laudō* 'praise' (*laus*, *laudis*), *nōminō* 'name' (*nōmen*), *generō* 'beget' (*genus, -eris*).

2. The inherited caus./frequent. (intensive) type (456.2B) is not always easy to distinguish from the preceding, but evidently includes *vorō* 'eat up' (intens.; $g^{w}orH_3$-eH_2-y^{e}/o-, cf. G *βόρα* 'food'); *sēdō* 'to set' (caus., cf. *sedere*); and *occupō* 'take possession of' (intens., **ob-cap-*; cf. *capere*).

a. Some of these verbs have a lengthened form of the root vowel, as in *sēdō, cōnor*; and a majority have preverbs, as in *occupāre*. The only certain thing about the lengthening is that it is unconnected with the long root vowels of Vedic causatives (*tān-aya-* 'make taut', *vās-áya-* 'cause to stay'); these result from a sound law (36.4) affecting *o*-grade vowels in open syllables (**ton-éye-*, **wos-éye-*).

3. From the standpoint of L, more prominent are the frequentative or intensive verbs in *-tō, -sō, -ĭtō*, and *-titō*, denoting repeated or energetic action. In origin they are denominatives formed from the stem of the perf. pass.pple. of the simple verb. Thus *dictō* from *dictus* (*dīcō*); *versō* from *versus* (*vertō*); *habitō* from *habitus* (*habeō*). In a few cases this formation attests to the previous existence of an unattested participle, as *pultō* 'beat on' from **poltos*, the original pple. of *pellō* 'strike' ousted by *pulsus*. In a further development, secondary verbs in *-(i)tāre* came to be formed from the pres. stem directly: so from *agō*, *agitō* 'drive about', not ˣ*āctō* from *āctus* (like *tractō* 'drag along' from *tractus*); *haesitō* 'stick fast' (**haess-itā-*, cf. *haereō*). The expected form for 1st conj. verbs, **-ātāre*, is nowhere to be found: *rogitō*, not ˣ*rogātō*, 'inquire eagerly' (*rogāre*). The exact source of this form, and the explanation for its ubiquity in the *ā*-stem conjugation, are unknown. To be sure, in those 1st conj. stems derived from seṭ roots (type 6, below), as *domō*, *domitus* < **domH̥₂-to-*, the formation seen in *domitāre* 'tame, break' would be regular. But such forms are too few and insignificant to be a realistic explanation for the uniform *-itāre* of the *ā*-stem deverbatives.

Some frequentatives lost distinctive force and new frequentatives in

-tō were formed from them, the so-called double frequentatives. Thus *cantō* has the same force as *canō* (and in the vernacular displaced it, hence It. *cantare*, Fr. *chanter*), and from it was formed *cantitō*; similarly *dictitō* from *dictō*, and so on. As in the case of *-itāre*, however, some such forms in *-titāre* appear to be based on primary present stems, as no frequentatives, faded or otherwise, are attested; for example *ēmptitō* 'buy up' (*emō* 'buy'), *scrīptitō* 'write frequently' (*scrībō*). It is noteworthy that many of these forms have regularly-formed derivatives in *-t-* (*-s-*), as *ēmptor* 'purchaser, *ēmptiō* 'purchase', *scrīptor* 'writer', and the like, which would have made coinages like *scrīptitō* easy on the basis of such proportions as *dūcō* : *dūctor* (: *ductō*) : *ductitō* :: *emō* : *ēmptor* (: —) : *X*, where *X* = *ēmptitō*, even in the absence of the term ×*ēmptō*.

4. Root presents. Monosyllabic stems ending in *-ā* (**-eH₂-*), such as *fārī* 'to say' (G φημί, φᾱμί), *nāre* 'to swim' (*sneH₂-*, Ved. *snā́ti* 'bathes'), *hiāre* 'to yawn', and *flāre* 'to blow', belonged to the IE root class (447), but there is no overt evidence in L of their quondam root inflection such as there is for *dare* 'to give' (488) with its archaic pl. *dămus*, *dătis*. In all likelihood, therefore, *nō*, *nāmus* continue a stem enlarged with the usual **-yᵉ/ₒ-* element, **snāyō*, **snāyomos* < **sneH₂-*. (**SneH₂-* and **sn̥H₂-* would give the same Ital. outcome, but there is no actual evidence, in L or anywhere else, for a zero grade form of this root, as NB Ved. *snātá-* 'bathed'—though that could be a remodeling of expected **sātá-*.) Short vowel forms like intens. *nătāre* 'be swimming in, overflow' must be secondary, somehow based on legitimate forms like *făteor* 'admit'; cf. *fātus* pple. of *fārī*.

5. The inflection of *stō*, *stāmus* coincides completely with type 4 from the L point of view, but crucial forms in other languages reveal something else: U *stahu*, O **staít** 3sg., **stahínt** 3pl., and OCS *stoěti*[1] infin. point to a stem **stăē-*. This is obviously **sta-* < **stH̥₂-* enlarged with the stative affix **-eH₁-* (452). This formation is parallel to, and probably coeval with, its semantic yokefellow **sed-eH₁-* 'be sitting', L *sedeō*, OCS *sěděti*. (The same stative formation for this verb is attested also in Germanic and Celtic.) U *stahu* (/stāō/) 1sg. reflects **stăēyō*; O **staít, stahínt** continue **staēti*, **staēnti*, that is, **staēyeti*, **staēyonti*. Now, the usual expression of *ē*-statives in L is the 2nd conj. (477.2). This stem **staē-* is treated differently because the vowel sequence peculiar to this form resulted in its submergence in the *ā*-conj. Whether the stem was further enlarged with the usual **-yᵉ/ₒ-* affix cannot be told directly from L, where the outcome would be the same either way. But as all other *ē*-statives are so derived, and in Germanic likewise (452a), and OHG *stēn* 'to stand' specifically can be taken as a reflex of **staj-* < **stH₂-H̥₁yᵉ/ₒ-*, it is likely that the Pre-Latin etyma were **staēyō*, **staēyesi*,

---

1 That is, /stojeti/. The usual transliteration *stojati* exhibits the regular backing of *ě* to *a* after palatal cons.

staēyomos*, **staēyonti* whence L *stō*, *stās*, *stāmus*, *stant* via regular vowel contraction (88.3**) and the usual remodeling of the 1sg. (**476**).

6. There are several primary verbs built to roots which originally ended in *-H_2- preceded by a consonant, as **demH_2*- 'tame', **sekH_2*- 'cut', **yewH_2*- 'help'. The distinctive history of these verbs shows up in the non-present forms: the perf. in *-uī* (for usual *-āvī*) points to **-wa(i)* preceded by a short vowel; and likewise the pple. in *-itus*[1] and the agent nouns in *-itor*. So **dematos* > *domitus*; agent noun **demH̥₂tōr* > *domitor*. The pres. stem was a *-*y*^{e}/*o*- form built to the root, as **demH̥₂-y*^{e}/*o*-. The resulting **domay*^{e}/*o*-, after *y*-loss and vowel contraction, would automatically become identical to the usual 1st conj. forms. (For the change of **dem*- to *dom*-, see **42.6**.) Historically speaking, therefore, verbs like *domāre* belong with the *capiō* and *veniō* types (**479.6**, **480-1**), and owe their ultimate form to the action of sound laws.

a. Verbs built to roots ending originally in *-H_3- were assimilated to the 1st conj. pattern completely, as *lavāre* < **lewH_3*- (cf. G λοετρόν 'bathhouse' with metathesis from **lewo*-, **235.1**), *arāre* 'to plow' < **H_2erH_3*- (cf. G ἄροτρον). In the latter, the remodeling of the tool-noun **arātrum* 'plow' as *arātrum* also shows the influence of the usual 1st conj. type. It is likely that some roots in *-H_2- were likewise absorbed into the dominant patterns without a trace, and it is not significant that there are no certain examples of pples. in *-itus* (or supines in *-itum*) built to roots in *-H_1- or *-H_3-.

476. INFLECTION. The usual explanation of 1sg. *-ō* is contraction from **-āō* < **-āyō* except for the few verbs under 6, above, with *-ō* < **-ăyō*. As argued in **88.3**, however, the contraction of *-ā̆*- with any following non-high vowel was actually *-ā*-, which means that *-ō* here must be analogical—an analogy of very early date, to be sure. In Sab., in the few such forms attested, the vowels are uncontracted, as in U *suboca(u)u* 'invoco'; and, remoter but still pertinent, U *stahu* = L *stō* (**475.5**). This is taken as an archaism, but might instead be distraction. Possibly, in fact, L *-ō* did not simply replace **-ā*, but was rather the product of a sequence of events: **spēsāyō* 'I expect' > **spēzāō* > **spērā* → **spērāō* (or **spērăō*), with this last contracting (under different rules) to *spērō*.

The *-ā*- of the other persons (shortened before *-t* and *-nt*, **82**) is the regular development of Ital. *-*āy*^{e}/*o*-. (As mentioned in **475.4**, it might be the vowel of the bare root in a few primary verbs like *nā*- 'swim', but in such roots it is more likely to be the regular contraction of **-ā̆ye*- and **-ā̆yo*- after the loss of *-*y*- per **192**.)

SECOND CONJUGATION

477. The 2nd conj. comprises verbs with stems ending in *-ē*-, namely

[1] The unique *sectus* is presumably syncopated from **secitus*, whereas *iūtus* is regular from **yuHtos* (perf. *iūvī* < **yowa-wai* < **y*^{e}/*owH̥*-).

statives in *-ē-* (452) and roots in *-eH$_1$-*. Both probably include the stem element **-y^e/o-*. A few verbs continue causative/frequentatives in **-ey^e/o-* (456.2). Finally, there are a very few denominatives of the Ved. *devayá-* 'be pious', G μετρέω 'measure' type.

1. VERBS FROM ROOTS in **-eH$_1$-*, as **pleH$_1$-* 'fill', only surviving in compounds like *compleō* 'fill up' (cf. G aor. πλῆτο, Ved. *aprāt*); *neō* 'spin' (pple. *nētus*; cf. Hom. νῆμα 'thread' = L (epigr.) *nēmen**, MIr. *snúm*, root **sneH$_1$-*); and *fleō* 'weep' (cf. OCS *blějǫ* 'bleat'). The perf. in *-ēvī* apparently reflects full grade, **pleH$_1$-*, which is wrong for the perf. and right for the (root) aor., and at least some of these roots were certainly aoristic to begin with. Though it is likely, therefore, that the stem was originally **plē-ye-ti* if not already **pleH$_1$yeti*, there is no way to tell for certain.

2. STATIVES formed with **-eH$_1$-*, apparently enlarged with thematic **-y^e/o-*, as *videō, habeō, taceō, sedeō, iaceō.* These are both deverbative and denominative. (See 452.)

This large class in L includes a number of stative verbs paired with eventives built to the same or very similar roots: *sedeō* 'am sitting', *sīdō* (**si-sd-*) 'sit down'; *habeō* 'have', *capiō* 'take' (chiming roots **ghabh-* and **kap-*, respectively); *pendeō* 'am suspended', *pendō* 'suspend, weigh (out)'.

Examples of denominatives include one built to the adj. **lewkos* 'bright' (lost in L, but seen in G λευκός): **lewk-eH$_1$-y^e/o-* > L *lūcēre* 'to be bright, shine'. Cf. the factitive **lewke-y^e/o-* in OL *lūcēre* 'to ignite, light' (the two verbs became homophonous by the action of sound laws).

The prevailingly intransitive force of these verbs is often remarked on. Perhaps by count most stative verbs are intransitive, but there is no intrinsic connection between intransitivity and stativeness, and many basic stative notions are transitive: *know, hate, love, remember, fear,* and so on.

a. As remarked in 475.5, historically and functionally *stō, stāre* 'stand' < **staē-y^e/o-* belongs here.

b. Forms such as *albeō* 'am white' (*albus*), *caleō* 'am hot' (no immediate source attested in L; remotely *calidus, calor*), *claudeō* 'limp, am lame' (*claudus* 'lame'), and many others, look like denominatives in *-e-y^e/o-*, and are often so analyzed. But in fact these are stative formations in **-eH$_1$-(y^e/o)-*, described above. The ordinary denominative type in *-e-y^e/o-*, abundant in G, as μογέω 'toil' (μόγος) and κροτέω 'make rattle' (κρότος 'clatter'), is barely attested in L, possibly in OL *lūcēre* 'to ignite'.[1] But thanks to L sound laws, the factitive, stative, and causative formations had become homophonous, which resulted in the early loss of the factitive type and the dwindling of the 2nd conj. causative (3, below). Of the three functions, the only one that remained vital in L was the stative.

3. CAUSATIVE/FREQUENTATIVES, with *o*-grade of the root and a suffix *-éy^e/o-* (456.2). These are mostly causatives, at least etymologically: *moneō* 'warn' (cf. *meminī* 'remember'), *torreō* 'make dry' (cf. Brāh. *tarṣáyati*, caus. of

---

[1] The isolated factitive *dēnseō* 'make thick' (Lucretius) apparently derived from *dēnsus* is best taken as a nonce-form in place of usual *dēnsō, -āre.*

tṛ́ṣyati 'is thirsty'), *doceō* 'teach' (cf. *decet* 'is fitting'), *noceō* 'injure' (cf. *necō -āre* 'slay'; *nocēre* and *necāre* taken together imply an unattested primary verb **necō* 'suffer grievously, die'). From the L point of view, this is a relic class, much like the quondam NE causatives *set, fell, drench, ret,* and *wend.* Frequentatives are few, certainly *mulgeō* 'milk' (root **melǵ-* 'stroke, wipe'), maybe *tondeō* 'shave, shear'; one or two others are sometimes mentioned, but with less probability.

478. INFLECTION. Of the three principal components of the L 2nd conj., the first two were originally athematic, the last thematic. It is usually assumed that the general rout of athematic inflection in L involved the enlargement of athematic stems with *-$y^e/_o$-. It is not clear how, exactly, a form like **flōsēmi* 'bloom' turned into **flōsēō*, **nēmi* 'I spin [thread]' into **nēō.* It might have been a replacement of endings without remodeling of the stem as such. It is hardly evidence in favor of this view that 3pl. **nēyonti* and **flōsēyonti* should have become ˣ*neunt*, ˣ*flōreunt* rather than *nent, flōrent* (88.3), since the incontrovertably thematic formations of the causative do not have a 3pl. in *-eunt*, either. Analogical influence might explain the replacement of **moneont* 'they warn' by *monĕ̄nt*, but it is hard to get beyond the vague proposition that however the caus. 3pl. *-*ĕyonti* made it to L *-ent*, the verbs in *-*ēyonti* did likewise. Analogical patterns are certainly available—in particular, the pattern of the 1st conj. in *-ās, -āt, -āmos, -ātes, -ānt* might be enough to account for the replacement of *-*ĕ̄ont* by *-*ĕ̄nt* (and, though the facts are not quite parallel, the replacement of 1pl. *-*ĕ̄omos* by *-*ēmos*).

In any case, with the loss of intervocalic *-*y*- (as in the 1st conj.) and subsequent vowel contraction a number of originally different formations became identical: the *-ē-* of *-ēs, -ēt* (Plt.), *-ēmus* could reflect *-*eH₁ye-*, *-*eye-*, *-*eH₁-*, and so on. 1sg. *-*ēō* and *-eō* from any source would fall together as *-eō.* The 1pl. *-ēmus* and 3pl. *-ent* < *-*ēnt* would directly continue *-*eH₁mos* and *-*ēnti* (wherever the latter might have come from), but replace expected *-*eomus* (88.3) < *-*ĕ̄omos* and *-*eunt* < *-*ĕ̄yont* from stems built with *-$y^e/_o$-.

THIRD CONJUGATION

479. 1. SIMPLE THEMATIC class (449). This was the most productive type of late PIE verb formation; but in L the $y^e/_o$-stems became the productive type, the simple thematics being a closed, relic class. But because simple thematics are fairly numerous in L, and include much basic vocabulary, their threatened status is not immediately obvious. Examples are *legō* 'gather', *tegō* 'cover', *dīcō* 'point out, say', *dūcō* 'lead, conduct', *gerō* 'carry on', and *agō* 'impel'; deponent *ūtor* 'use, enjoy', *sequor* 'follow', and many others.

2. ROOT-PRESENTS (447) to roots originally ending in a laryngeal, namely **melH-* 'grind', **wemH₁-* 'vomit', and a collection of compounds

based on the zero grade of _*dheH$_1$-_ 'put'. (Two more, _sonere_ and _tonere_, are known in classical L only as 1st conj. forms.) From _*melH̥si_, _*melH̥ti_ and _*wemH̥$_1$si_, _*wemH̥$_1$ti_ would come, first, _*molas_, _*molat_, _*womas_, _*womat_ (cf. Ved. _vámiti_), and by regular vowel weakening, attested _molit_, _molis_. The selfsame stems _*mola-_, _*woma-_ underlie perf. _moluī_, _vomuī_ < _*-a-wai_ (528), and pple. _molitus_, _vomitus_ < _*-a-tos_ with leveled full grade (_nātus_ 'born' (pres. _nāscor_) shows the original _*ĝn̥H$_1$tos_ type with the root in zero grade). The same process underlies the compounds of _*dheH$_1$-_, such as _condō_ 'put together, found', _condis_, _condit_ < _*-θō_, _*-θas_, _*-θat_ < _*-dhH̥$_1$-_, pple. _conditus_. (See **488Ba**.) Apart from the elimination of ablaut alternation, the convergence of these original root-presents on the simple thematic type in L was probably a purely phonological process. There is no actual proof that none of these forms underwent a true morphological thematization at some point, but strong evidence in favor of the interpretation endorsed here is provided by the development of _*deH$_3$-_ 'give' in L (488): that is, the history of a form like _reddimus_ 'we give back' is surely one with the history of _damus_, and probably one with the history of _molimus_ and _vomimus_.

3. REDUPLICATING CLASS (451). There was at least one of these already in the parent language, which is reflected in L _bibō_ 'drink' (**451B**); but in L as in other IE languages a number of the original reduplicating athematic class were shifted to the thematic type by the addition of the thematic endings to the zero grade of the athematic stem: _sistō_ (cf. Ved. _tíṣṭhati_; PIE _*sti-stH$_2$-_), _gignō_ 'beget', _serō_ 'sow' (_*si-sH$_1$-_), _sīdō_ 'sit down' (_si-sd-_ = Ved. _sī́dati_, G ἵζω, both thematized too), _reddit_ (< _*red(e)dat(i)_ < _*de-dH̥$_3$-_; cf. O _didest_ 'dabit'). As with type 2, above, the thematization process started with purely phonological developments: as 1pl. _*sistamos_ (_*stistH̥$_2$mos_) > _*sistemos_ > _sistumos_, _-imus_, 2pl. _*sistetes_ (PIE _*stistH̥$_2$tHes_) > _sistitis_, which therefore became identical to thematic inflection. Early analogical creations like _*sistăs_, _*sistăt_, if they existed, would likewise give the attested forms straightaway.

4. NASAL INFIX CLASS (453). This is a relic class in L, but contains a fair number of forms belonging to the most basic vocabulary. It falls into two descriptively different types, both representing the plural stem of the PIE athematic _n_-infix type.

A. Roots ending in stops: _rumpō_ 'break' (_ruptus_; cf. AV _lumpáti_ 'breaks, injures'), _linquō_ 'leave' (G -λιμπάνω, Ved. _riṇákti_; cf. L _reliquiae_ 'relics'), _findō_ 'split' (_fissum_ 'cleft', Ved. _bhinátti_), _fundō_ 'pour, melt' (_fūdī_, also OE _géotan_ 'pour'), _tangō_ 'touch' (_integer_ '*untouched, entire'). The nasal is extended to the perf. in _fingō_ 'model' (_fīnxī_, but _fictus_), _stringō_ 'draw together' (_strīnxī_, but _strictus_). The nasal infix transplanted to the pple. but not to the perf. is seen in _pungō_ 'stab' (_pupugī_, _pūnctus_) and _tundō_ 'pummel' (_tutudī_, _tūnsus_). The nasal is extended to the whole paradigm in _iungō_ 'join' (_iūnxī_, _iūnctus_) and _plangō_ 'strike resoundingly'.

a. These last are to be distinguished from verbs in which the nasal belongs to the root, such as *pendō* 'suspend'. The distinction is usually clear from forms outside of the verb paradigm: *iugum* 'yoke', *iūgis, -e* 'joined'; *plāga* 'a blow' (unless that is a borrowing from G). For *pendō*, although connections with other IE forms are very uncertain, *pondus* 'weight' indicates the *-n-* belongs to the root itself.

Evidence from other languages may provide the only basis for interpreting the L *-n-* (for *plangō*, if *plāga* is in fact a borrowing, we have G πληγή 'a blow', OE *flócan* 'clap, applaud'); but it is always welcome as confirmation of what may be already evident in L (so Ved. *yunájmi* 1sg. 'join', *riṇákti* 'leaves', *bhinátti* 'splits').

Tendō 'stretch' continues a root *ten- which is well attested (L *tenuis* 'thin', G τείνω 'stretch', etc.); here it is the *-d-* which needs explaining (218, 458.3).

In the case of *cingō*, all derivatives are like *cīnctus, -ūs* 'a girding', and the evidence (which is very weak) in related languages points to *-n- as an integral part of the root.

More certain is the root *H$_3$engʷ- 'anoint', the likely etymon of L *unguō* 'anoint'; cf. Ved. *áñjas-* n. 'salve', L *unguen*, OHG *anc(h)o* 'butter', OPr. *anctan*; the zero grade in OIr. *imb* 'butter' (*H$_3$n̥gʷon-) could give L *unguō* as well, 100b.

B. Roots ending in laryngeals. Here belong *spernō* 'reject' (*sprēvī, sprētum* are analogical: Ved. *sphuránt-*, Lith. *spìrti* 'to kick' confirm a root *sperH-); *cernō* 'sort, sift' (< *krinō < *kri-n-H- per 74.3; *crēvī* < *kreyaway; cf. aniṭ *krey- in *crībrum* 'sieve' < *kreydhrom,[1] *certus* 'separated' = G κριτός < *kritos). The first principal part of *sinō* 'allow', orig. 'put' points to an *n*-infix, which means something like *seyH-; but *sīvī, situs*—not ˣ*sēvī*, ˣ*sītus*—are both apparently aniṭ. (Evidence is extremely slight; possibly two different roots have been conflated.)

A similar discrepancy is seen in *linō* 'smear', pple. *litus* either seṭ or remodeled. The likeliest cognates are unreassuringly diverse semantically: Ved. *riṇā́ti* 'melts, flows'; Hesych. ἀλίνω (-ῑνω, if from *-ĭnyō, 203.1) 'anoint'? (Cf. G λῑτός 'smooth'?) Clearer is *temnō* 'shun' (*'cut off') < *tm̥nH- = Hom. τάμνω, and perh.—the semantics are troubling—Lith. *tinù* 'sharpen a heavy blade (of a scythe, for example) by pounding', ORuss. *tĭnu* 'strike' < *timnō < *tm̥nH-. (G τμῆσις 'a cutting', Dor. τμᾱτός pple. confirm *temH$_2$-.) With unaltered perf. and pple., L *sternō* 'strew, spread' (for *stornō < *str̥-n-H-), perf. *strāvī*, pple. *strātus* < *str̥H-; cf. G στόρνῡμι (472.3).

Here also belong some forms in *-ll-* < *-ln- (223.1), as *tollō* 'lift (up)' (*tl̥-n-H$_2$-; root *telH$_2$- directly revealed in G τελαμών 'carrying-strap', *tl̥H$_2$- in Dor. τλᾱ́μων 'suffering'; cf. L *(sub-)lātus* < *tl̥H-to-). But most L verbs in *-ll-* are of ambiguous makeup. L *pellō* 'strike' is perhaps from *pl̥nH- with remodeling of the pres. stem *pallō; cf. OIr. *ad·ella* < *ad alnāt < *-pl̥-ne-H$_2$-ti 'seeks' (= L *appellat* in form and function), but clear evidence for a root-final laryngeal is otherwise scanty and the old pple. *poltos implied by the intensive *pultāre* 'beat on' points to aniṭ *pl̥-to-. (The pple. *pulsus* is analogical, like *tēnsus* for original *tentus* 'stretched'.)

---

1 L *crībrum*, OE *hríd(d)er* and its Gmc. cognates could as well reflect *kriH-dhro- (also for Gmc. *kriH-tró-); however OIr. *críathar* points unambiguously to *kreytro-.

As with types 2 and 3, above, the submergence of these types into the 3rd conj. was a process as much phonological as morphological. The development of a uniform preconsonantal stem in *-*na*- (ultimately from the plural persons in *-*nH̥*-) would have meant, **tolnasi*, **tolnati*, **tolnamos*, whence by regular development **tolles*, **tollet*, **tollemos* and finally *tollis*, *tollit*, *tollumus*.

5. *scō*-CLASS (**456.3**). The long-vowel forms in -*ēscō* and -*īscō* (a few in -*āscō*, see **456.3c**), with inchoative force, are productive in L; and, with attenuation of their function, they remain productive right into Proto-Romance. The inherited forms without the long vowel are a small relic class; they do not share any semantic properties. This group includes *nōscō* 'understand' (**ǵneH₃-sḱ^{e}/o*-, with irregular full grade of root also seen in Ved. *jñātá*-, L *(g)nōtus*). With components disguised by the action of sound laws, *discō* 'learn' (**di-dḱ-sḱ^{e}/o*-, root **deḱ*-; cf. perf. *didicī*); *poscō* 'ask' (**porkskō* < **pr̥ḱ-sḱ^{e}/o*-, cf. Ved. *pr̥cchāmi*); *posc*- was reinterpreted as a root whence perf. *poposcī* and extra-verbal derivatives like **posculum*/**postulum* 'query' (**porsktlom*) inferred on the basis of denom. *postulāre*.

The aberrant 2nd conj. *misceō*, *mixuī*, *mixtus* 'mix' is evidently remade from presumed **miscō* < **mig-sḱ^{e}/o*-.

6. *y^{e}/o*-CLASS (**456.1**). Presents of the type *capiō*, *capĭs*, *capĭmus*, inf. *capere*; these belong historically with the primary verbs of the 4th conj. (**480-1**) like *veniō*, *venīs*, *venīmus*, *venīre* and will be discussed there. They are classed in the 3rd conj. because of their inf. (which was the Roman basis for classification). Such agreement is secondary; see **480-1**.

Some verbs in -*uō* form a cryptic subvariety of this type, as *suō* 'sew' < **sūō* < **syuH-y^{e}/o*- (**193a**; cf. Go. *siujiþ*); similarly *struō* 'pile up, build' and *ruō* 'fall with a crash' (?**ghruH*-; **158a**), *fluō* 'flow'. Here also *solvō* 'loosen, untie' from **se-luō* < **se-lūō* < *-*luH-y^{e}/o*- (cf. G λύω) and *volvō* 'rotate' from **weluō* < **weluyō* (cf. G ἐλύω), though the details, such as the source of the long vowel in *volūmen* 'roll', are obscure.

Another subvariety includes denominatives from *u*-stems: *minuō* 'diminish' (cf. *minus*, **353.3**), *statuō* 'put in place, set up' (*status*, -*ūs*), *metuō* 'be afraid' (*metus*, -*ūs*).

7. PRESENTS IN -*tō*. Thus *pectō* 'comb' (cf. G πέκω and πέκτω); *plectō* 'braid, plait' (cf. G πλέκω); *flectō*, *nectō*. These have the appearance of containing a present suffix *-*t^{e}/o*-, but there is little evidence elsewhere for any such PIE stem, once it is recognized that G presents in -πτω continue *-*p-y^{e}/o*- (**202**). But elsewhere we do find *t*-extensions of the root, that is, an elaboration of a shorter root and occurring in all tenses and derivatives (like **yewg*- and **yewH*- next to **yew*-, all 'join'). So OE *fleohtan*, OHG *flehtan* like L *plectō*, and many others in Gmc.; and for L *pectō* cf. *pecten* 'comb', G κτείς, **289b**. *Plect*- and *pect*- can be assumed to underlie perf. *plexī*, *pexī* < **p(l)ekt-s*-; and unless pples. *plexus* and *pexus* are analogical (which they well might be), they too require forms with *-*t*-: **plekt-to*-, **pekt-to*- (**212**).

8. Two verbs in L can be interpreted as thematized survivors of the PIE desiderative formation in *-(H_1)s- (457): L *vīsō* < **wīss-* < **weid-s-* 'visit' (*'wish to see'); and *quaesō* 'beg' < *quaessō*; cf. *quaerō* < *k^ways-*, and also derived forms like *quaestor*. In the latter the desiderative sense is attenuated, as both the basic and derived forms have essentially the same meaning, 'seek (to obtain)'. (A third form is sometimes mentioned in this connection: *haesō* 'adhere' next to *haereō* (stative, 477.2); but it is unobvious where the desiderative force is.)

FOURTH CONJUGATION AND THIRD CONJUGATION VERBS IN *-iō*

480. The 4th. conj. comprises primary verbs with presents of the $y^e/_o$-class, and denominatives built with the same suffix. But the 4th conj. is not the manifestation of all such stems: as remarked in the preceding discussions, a large number of $y^e/_o$-stem verbs—mainly secondary formations, stem enlargements, and so on—end up in the first three conjugations purely by the agency of sound laws.

1. PRIMARY VERBS WITH $y^e/_o$-PRESENTS (456.1).

3rd. conj.: *capiō* 'take', *faciō* 'do', *iaciō* 'throw', *rapiō* 'seize', *sapiō* 'taste', *fugiō* 'flee', *fodiō* 'dig', and *(cōn)spiciō* 'see'. Less obviously, *āiō* (*ăiiō*) 'say' < **agyō* belongs here.

4th. conj.: *veniō* 'come', *saliō* 'leap', *operiō* 'shut' and *aperiō* 'open' (stem **wer-*$y^e/_o$-), *reperiō* 'encounter', *vinciō* 'bind, fetter' (outside connections very doubtful, but NB pple. *vīnctus*, and *vinculum* 'bond' < **wenktlom*), and *farciō* 'stuff'.

There is some fluctuation between the two types. For some reason this is most evident in deponent paradigms: *morior* 'die' (*morī*, *moritur*, but early L *morīrī* and *morīmur*), *orior* 'rise' (*oritur* but *orīrī*), and *potiō* 'to put in the power of someone, enslave' (*potitur*, but *potīrī*).

2. DENOMINATIVES, originally from *i*-stems and cons.-stems (460-1), but by analogy from other stems too. Thus *fīniō* 'limit' (*fīnis*), *partior* 'divide' (*pars*, *parti-*); *custōdiō* 'guard' (*custōs*, *custōd-*); but also *serviō* 'serve; be subject to' (*servus*, an *o*-stem).

481. SPLIT BETWEEN THE *capiō* AND *veniō* TYPES. The 1sg. *-iō* is from *-*yō* (193) or, in the denominatives of *i*-stems, from *-*i-yō*; likewise the 3pl. *-iunt* from *-*(i-)yonti*. Thanks to sound laws the two types coalesce completely. The *-ī-* seen in *-īs*, *-īmus*, *-ītis*, and presumably in *-it* (regularly shortened), is the straightforward development of *-*ie-* or *-*ii-* from *-*iye-* and *-*iyi-* (the details depend on the trifling question of whether the loss of the *-y-* and the contraction of the vowels pre- or postdated the weakening of **e* to *i*, 66.2).

To refine the traditional Roman basis for the classification of verbs, the difference between the 4th conj. and the *capiō* subtype of the 3rd conj.

is that the stem-vowel is morphophonemically *-ī-* in the former and *-ĭ-* in the latter. When the usual endings are added, normal L sound changes are all that is needed to produce the paradigmatic forms:

*wenī-si *infin.*	venīre	*kapĭ-si	capere
*wenī-ō	veniō	*kapĭ-ō	capiō
*wenī-s	venīs	*kapĭ-s	capis
*wenī-t	venit	*kapĭ-t	capit
*wenī-mos	venīmus	*kapĭ-mos	capimus
*wenī-tes	venītis	*kapĭ-tes	capitis
*wenī-ont	veniunt	*kapĭ-ont	capiunt

The task for the historian is to determine whether these were different formations from the beginning, or evolved from a common source. As seen above, the inflection of the *ī*-stems can easily be traced to a variety of yod stem in *-*iy*^{e}/*o*-. The *capiō* type is harder to explain. The hypothesis of a semi-thematic type, with *-*yo*- for the persons with the *o*-grade of the thematic vowel but *-*i*- only for those forms aligning with the *e*-grade stem of simple thematics, has won a certain respect but has never been generally accepted. A more plausible hypothesis is that the *-ĭ-* of *capis*, *capimus*, and *capitis* is from *-*y*^{e}/*o*-. This theory requires answers to two questions: is the development *-*yes*, *-*yet* > *-is*, *-it* and the like phonologically defensible? And, secondly, Why was the affix *-*ye*- in some PItal. stems but *-*iye*- in others?

As for the first question, there are a number of other formations that are well explained by just such a development: *-is*, the gen.sg. of both *i*- and cons.-stem nouns < *-*yes* or *-*yos* (306.6); and *velim* 'I would like' 1sg. subj. (opt.) < **welyem* (484.1).

The first step in answering the second question is to identify the forms proper to the ORIGINAL distribution, but in the case of the *ī*-stems that is a nearly hopeless task because the 4th conj. is a productive class. The only hope therefore rests with the *capiō* type, which has all the appearance of being a relic class. Relic or not, a number of the *capiō* verbs are only secondarily in the *-*y*^{e}/*o*- class, on the evidence of cognate forms in other languages, for example G φεύγω 'flee' next to L *fŭgiō*. (Note that original **fugyoH*$_2$ must have given ˣ*fuiiō*, like *aiiō* < **agyō*. Similarly **fodyoH*$_2$ 'dig' has an unexpected root-grade for a *y*^{e}/*o*-stem, and furthermore it would have become ˣ*foiiō*. Either *fugiō* and *fodiō* were coined after the change of **gy* and **dy* (194), or the stops were restored by analogy.) L *faciō* is an Italic invention (**488Ba**).

It has been observed that a majority of the *capiō* type end in stops, and a majority of the *veniō* type end in liquids and nasals, or a consonant cluster, or are polysyllabic. (The detail about consonant clusters is reminiscent of Sievers' Law, 178, but only glancingly, as the other factors can have nothing to do with it.) The list of environments in which **-ye-* > **-iye-* do not make a natural class, however, and are better taken as what is left over after the *capiō* type split off. If the *veniō* type is the normal reflex of the parent inflection, where does the *capiō* type come from? With this in mind, iambic shortening (84) in the 2sg. and 3sg. may have been a factor in the spread of the *-i-* type. Iambic shortening neatly accounts for the contrast between simplex *pariō* 'bring forth, bear' (*pari-*) and the compounds *reperiō* 'reveal', *comperiō* 'find out, discover' (*-perī-*), the etymological meaning of *pariō* being 'open'.[1] Of course there are many exceptions, such as the *recipiō*, *percipiō* family, all belonging to the *capiō* type; and *veniō* itself should by rights be a *capiō* verb. These may be ascribable to analogy.

In Sab. even more than in L the *-ī-* type prevails, though the imperatives O *factud* and U **fe(i)tu** from **fakĭtōd* appear to be evidence for at least one member of the *-i-* type, as a long vowel would not syncopate.

LATIN IRREGULAR VERBS

482. The irregular verbs of L grammars are so designated because in large or small ways they do not conform to any of the four conjugations (elastic as that classification is). The usual reason for this is the survival of athematic forms of the root class, such as *est* 'is'; or of the athem.opt. in *-ī-* (in L terms, the pres.subj.). Some of the irregular paradigms however are suppletive, that is, the full complement of inflected forms is made up from several partially defective paradigms, as *sum, fuī,* or *ferō, tulī.* Lesser oddities, such as the apparently aniṭ root in pple. *litus* 'smeared' vs. the presumably seṭ form of the same root as seen in pres. *linō*, are not traditionally classed as irregularities, as they are lost amid the general chaos of the 3rd conj. principal parts. Also, verbs like *taedet* 'makes disgusted with', *piget* 'is irksome', and *pluit* 'it is raining', whose finite forms are limited to the 3rd pers., are not generally reckoned as irregular.

483. POSSUM 'am able'. The present system evolved from phrases consisting of *potis* 'master' and the ENCLITIC forms of *sum* 'am' (**492**), as *possum* from *potis sum* with the loss of the final *-s* and syncope (in ordinary phrases this is regular in the playwrights) and assimilation of *-ts-* to *-ss-* (**215**), similarly *potest* from *potis'st* (via **potist*). In OL the uncompounded forms are still in use, either as *potis* (the morphophonemic spelling) or *pote* (closer to actual pronunciation). This is historically a nom.sg.m. but even in our earliest records is used indeclinably, so *potis sunt* 'they can'. (Appearances may be deceiving here, however: L *potis* would also be the outcome of earlier **potyes*—see **306.6**—if that was the nom.pl. form in the phrase **potyes sonti.*)

---

[1] A precise semantic parallel is afforded by Hitt. *ḫa-a-ši* usually 'opens', but with the refl. particle *-za*, 'gives birth, begets' (used of both sexes).

The imperf. subj. _possem,_ stem _possē-,_ in place of the rare _potessem,_ is due to the influence of pres. _possum_ indic., _possim_ subj.; so also the infinitive _posse_ in place of _potesse_ (both occur in OL). The early language also attests a few passive forms like _potestur._

To _potis est_ the perf. should be _*potis fuī,_ and some scholars have flirted with the idea of such an etymon for perf. _potuī._ But this requires problematic phonetic developments. The usual interpretation is to take the form as what it looks like, namely the perf. of a pres. _*poteō_ as actually attested in the pple. _potēns_ used as an adjective; the stem seems to be guaranteed for Italic thanks to its appearance in O as **pútíad** (as if _*poteat_) 'possit'. (PRom. has a verb _*potēre,_ usually taken to be a Romance back-formation from _potuī_ and _potēns,_ but it could be that the full paradigm remained current in the form of speech underlying Romance even while it had been lost from classical L.)

484. VOLŌ, VELLE AND COMPOUNDS.

1. VOLŌ 'wish'. This reflects an original root-inflection (447) of which substantial details remain. The _e_-grade of the root—see **42.5** for the L sound laws—ousted all other forms. A normally-ablauting paradigm would have included a number of forms highly vulnerable to leveling, as the 3pl. _*lent_ < _*wlenti_ or 1pl.subj. _*līmus_ < _*wl-i_H_1_-_. On the other hand it has been suggested that we have here a Narten root (**128.3a, 440a.1**) with full grade of the root throughout. This is a much more economical theory, and a corroborating detail is that the opt. forms built to this root in Gmc. have the full grade (Goth. _wiljau,_ OE _wille_ < _*wel-ye_H_1_-_). Since Gmc. is conservative in such matters, this is strong support for the theory of a Narten root.

1sg. _volō_ (from _*welō,_ **42.5**) is a thematized replacement of _*welmi_ (cf. Lith. _pa-vélmi_ 'allow'); thematic forms are also seen in _volumus_ 1pl. (replacing _*volmos_ < Narten _*wel-mos;_ for _u_ see **69**) and probably _volunt_ for _*volent_ (< Narten _*welenti_). Athematic 3sg. _vult,_ earlier _volt_ (**45.1**) is from _*welti_ (**42.5**; cf. Lith. _pa-vélt_); similarly 2pl. _vultis,_ earlier _voltis,_ ultimately from _*wel-t_H_1_es._

The 2sg. _vīs_ is a much-debated form. The original paradigmatic form, _*welsi,_ by sound laws became _vel,_ earlier _vell_ (cf. inf. _velle_ < _*welsi,_ **223.1**); this is known only as the conjunction _vel_ 'or (instead)', whose semantic development was probably helped along by the fortuitous resemblance between _vel_ and inherited _-ve_ 'or'. The usual theory traces the replacement form, _vīs,_ to a completely different root, _*wey_H_1_-,_ which has an athematic inflection in Ved. (_vémi, véṣi, véti_).[1]

There is nothing suspect about the idea of such a verb having a para-

[1] The regular outcome of _*wey_$\mathring{H}_1$_si_ > _*weyas_ > _*weas_ should be L ˣ_vēs,_ not _vīs._ This may not be an insuperable problem, if syncope of _*weyas_ to _*weys_ could have taken place prior to the loss of intervocalic _*-y-._ But such a syncope would be very unlikely.

digm suppletive for a single form, and the particular explanation here might be supported by OL *veis* (cited by Priscian). But there are two real problems with the theory.

First, the root **weyH₁*- is not certainly known in L otherwise, with the possible exception of a couple of ancient-looking forms such as *invītus* 'unwilling'.

The second and larger problem is the likely meaning of the root **weyH₁*- itself, as Ved. *vémi* (the principal evidence for L *vīs*) seems to have had nothing to do with 'wish, desire'. Such a gloss might do for some Vedic passages—see below—but in the RV the essence of the semantics is very different: 'go to, carry to, approach'. This often has implications of eagerness (hence shading to 'grasp' or 'make a grab for', even 'attack'); in fact, according to the native grammarians, the root supplies the perf. for *aj*- 'drive'! Furthermore, compounds with root *vī*- (which are limited to the Vedic period) point toward a basic meaning quite remote from 'prefer, wish': *devă̄-vī*- 'gratifying the gods', *parṇa-vī*- 'carried by wings', *pada-vī́*- 'leader, guide' (lit. 'foot-carrying'), and *pratī-vī́*- adj. 'receiving gladly'; as noun, 'acceptance'. Finally, in Ved., even those occurrences which might fairly be rendered 'desire(d)' always have connotations of affection or sexual heat, rather than preference. The case is the same with the other likely cognates of the form, in which energy or vehemence (rather than choice) is the salient trait, as in L *vīs* 'force', G *ῑ̔́εμαι* 'hasten; am eager', *ῑ̔́ς* 'strength; muscle'. In fact, even L *invītus* 'unwilling', mentioned above as evidence for a root **weyH*- 'wish', is as well explained semantically—and much better explained morphologically—as **en-wiH-to*- 'forced'.[1]

One should ask, given the development of inherited **welsi* to **well*, what the LIKELY next step would have been; and the answer clearly is: the recomposition of a new 2sg. **wells*. This would probably have become **wels* in short order, but by definition this development would postdate the sound law which turned original **ls* into *ll*. Secondary *ls* remains in *fulsit* 'it lightened' and *alsus* 'suffering from cold', but both of these have *l* pinguis < **lks*, and **wels* < **wells* would have had *l* exilis (176a), probably the only case in the language of an *l* exilis before a consonant. There are no parallels for the suggestion that **wels* [weʎs] > *weis* > *vīs*—but there are no cogent objections to it, either, such as there are to the root **weyH₁*-.

Pres.subj. *velīmus* 1pl. < **wel-ī*- and imperf.subj. *vellem* < **wel-sē*- are examples of athematic morphology. Since the paradigm is so conservative otherwise, the *e*-grade of the root is most easily explained by assuming we are dealing with a Narten formation (vid.sup.). Futhermore, given that the 1sg.opt. must have been the most frequent and basic form of the verb, it is

[1] In German, one antonym of *freiwillig* is *mit Gewalt*.

likely that velim is not analogical at all, but reflects *weliem (whether or not via *welīm; cf. 306.6) < *wel-iH$_1$-m̥. For infin. velle < *wel-si see 553.1.

For sī vīs 'if you will; please' the contracted sīs (cf. 184.3) is common. In imitation of this arose also sultis (presumably via *soltis) beside sī vultis.

2. NŌLŌ 'am unwilling' is from *ne wel-, that is, it includes the PIE sentence-negating particle *ne. As a proclitic (cf. nesciō and nequeō), this should have become *no- per the relevant sound law (42.1); and then the *-w- would have been lost between like vowels (184.3), thus: *newelti > *nowelti > *nowolt > *nōlt.

However, this is plainly not the course of history, as it is precisely in nōn vult 3sg. that the w- survives, and moreover Plautine nevīs, nevolt confirm the survival of original *ne as such (whether unchanged or restored is immaterial). The key is that in the present tense the coalescence of particle and stem takes place in all—and only—the forms remodeled as thematics: *newelō, *newelomos, and *newelont (cf. volō, volumus, volunt). What these have in common against the uncontracted forms is the light second syllable. The 1pl. *newelomos would have been subject to Exon's Law (74.5), whence *newlomos. Syncope of *newelō and *newelont, though covered by no rule, would have been typical of the promiscuous loss of medial short vowels in L (73-4). The resulting *newl- smoothed to nōl-. This is also the explanation for the perf. nōluī < *newel-Vw- (where V = any vowel) and pres.subj. *newolim (<*-yem); but inf. nōlle < *newelsi and imperf. nōllem < *newelsē- with heavy second syllables indicate that the contracted type could spread beyond its original environment.

3. MĀLŌ 'had rather; prefer' is from māvolō (183, 88.3), from earlier *magwolō < *mag-wel- (160); or else (according to some authorities) from *maks-wol- < *magis 'rather'.[1] The early language has māvolō, māvelim, though more commonly mālō and mālim, and regularly mālllem. Generally the pattern has assimilated to that of nōlō, so uncontracted māvīs, māvolt, māvoltis.

485. FERŌ, FERRE 'carry'. Pres. fers, fert, fertis, fertō, ferre have the appearance of an athematic inflection, like Hom. φέρτε pl.imperat. and Ved. bhárti beside the usual bhárati. Yet the present of this root is normally thematic in the IE languages geographically closest to L, and in L the pres. subj. feram tellingly belongs to the thematic type (in contrast to sim and velim). Hence, since vowel syncope is so common after -r- (cf. vir, ager, ācer, 74.3-4, .6), the forms in question are syncopated from earlier *feres, *feret, infin. *feresi. (If the virtually regular syncope of vowels after -r- predated the change of s > r in gerō, geris that would explain why there is no syncope in such verbs, as ferō seems to be the only 3rd conj. simple thematic with original root-final *r.)

1 Parallel to sēvirī 'committee of six' < *seks wiroy and tēla 'cloth' < *tekslā.

An irregularity of different stripe is in a sense inherited. The PIE root **bher-* was pres./imperf. only, forming no aor. or perf. From the PIE point of view there is nothing unusual about such a state of affairs; the *paradigm* in the L or Gmc. sense was not a property of the PIE system. As such paradigms consolidated, however, only the very highest-frequency verbs might be expected to retain a PIE-style suite of forms in a suppletive relationship. Greek was conservative in such matters, remarkably so in Homer but even much later maintaining many suppletive paradigms. (A handful survive into NG, as τρώγω aor. έφαγα 'eat', λέγω aor. είπα 'say', βλέπω aor. είδα 'see'.) The verb 'be' in the familiar IE languages is the very type of this phenomenon, but the verb 'carry' is not far behind. In several IE languages, that is, including OIr. and G as well as L, the root **bher-* forms only the present-system. In L the perf. is supplied by *tulī*, earlier *tetulī* (the reduplication was first lost in compounds), this from **tetolH₂-* or **tetl̥H₂-* from the root of *tollō* (**b**, below). From the same root comes pple. *lātus* < **tlātos* < **tl̥H₂-to-*.

a. The reduplicated form *tetulī* is actually attested, both as such and in *rettulī*, but as the root **telH₂-* was essentially aoristic to start with, and as one of the root aor. stems would have been L **tul-* < **tol-* < **tl̥H₂-* (like *fidī* 'I split'), it is possible that L *tulī* has a dual ancestry (523-4).

b. The characterized present belonging to the aor. root **telH₂-* is seen in L *tollō* 'lift (up), carry off', historically an *n*-infix (**tl̥nH₂-*, 479.4B). Its paradigm is filled out by a compound in *sub(s)-*: *sustulī, sublātus*.

486. Eō, īre 'go'. Ablauting pres./imperf. root **ey-/*i-* is one of the best-attested PIE verbs: Ved. (*émi, imás*, 3pl. *yánti*), G εἶμι, and many others. As in G (423A, 470a), the full grade **ey-* was generalized in L. The zero grade is certainly attested only in derivatives, as *exitus, -ūs* 'a going out', *iter, itineris* 'way, road'.

Between vowels, however, the **-y-* dropped (192), hence *eō, eunt*, and the subj. stem *eā-*. Athematic *īs* < **eysi*, early *īt* < **eyti*, pl. *īmus* (in contrast to the original zero grade seen in G ἴμεν and Ved. *imás*), *ītis*; even in the 3pl. the stem form *ī-* is attested in *red-īnunt* 'they return'. Similarly with *ī-* < **ey-*, imperf. *ībam*, fut. *ībō*, imper. *ī, ītō, īte*, imperf.subj. *īrem*, inf. *īre*.

Pres.subj. *eam, eās* is of the thematic type. This is not surprising: the original type, parallel to *sim* and *velim*, would have been in part identical with the indicative forms, as in 1pl. *īmus*. Once an unambiguous form of the type *eāmus* was coined, the remainder of the paradigm would follow quickly

The perf.—*iī, iistī*, and so on—is a puzzle. (The forms like *īvī*, though attested early, are rare to begin with and plainly are not original.) Nothing among the possible starting-points, **e-oy-H₂e* 1sg., **e-y-me* 1pl. will result in the attested forms. Of course, the root did not form a perf. stem in PIE in the first place, and the L forms in all probability are confections based directly on the stem **ey-* (**ī-*) with perfect endings attached, and subsequent prevocalic shortening.

487. EDŌ, EDERE 'eat'. The pres. tense built to the root *ed- (or, less likely, *H_1ed-) is an ordinary root pres. in Hitt. (*e-it-mi* 1sg., *a-tu-e-ni* 1pl.); similarly in Vedic, apart from the peculiarity that the root has no zero grade, so 3pl. *adanti* rather than ×danti (unproblematically attributable to leveling, though some see a Narten root here; **440a.1**). The L paradigm shows the typical Latin mixture of thematic and athematic forms, but with the unusual detail that where *ed- was immediately followed by a *t or an *s, the result is a stem *ēs-*:[1] *ēs* 2sg. < *etsi, *ēst* 3sg. < *etsti (**212**), *ēstis* 2pl., ditto imperatives *ēs, ēstō, ēste*; likewise the imperf.subj. *ēssem*, inf. *ēsse*, 3sg. midd. *ēstur*. The long vowel is seen also in derivatives like pple. *ēsus* 'eaten', *comēstus* 'eaten up' (whose *-t-* is an additional puzzle). The thematic type forms are *edō, edimus, edunt*, with a short vowel in the root. Similarly the pres.subj. is of the athem. type, *edim, edīs*. (Forms based on the thematic type, *edam, edās*, are late, and later still come 3rd conj. indicative forms of the type *edis, edit*, which underlie the Romance reflexes.)

The source of the long vowel in *ēst* and similar forms is a much-discussed problem. Some authorities have thought of a root *ēd-, seen also in Lith. *ėd-* and OCS *-ěd-* (in forms like *vŭzěsti* 'eat up'), though a lengthened grade is uncalled-for and an etymon *eH_1d- is not possible. Differently, to the theory mentioned in **128.3a**, which explains why in some roots there are full grades where zero grades are expected, there is a controversial corollary which posits a type of root with lengthened grade where full-grade ablaut is expected, alternating with full grade in the categories where zero grade is normally found. But in that case both Vedic and Hitt. have considerably rebuilt the inherited pattern; and if such a pattern really was an ingredient in the L paradigm, it is perplexing that we do not have ×ēdō and ×ēdimus preserved as well. (The shape *ēd-* does occur, but only in the perf. *ēdī*, which is either from ancient *e-od-, *H_1e-H_1(o)d- or was created out of whole cloth after other long vowel perfects like *vēnī* 'came', **525**.)

Some have tried to find significance in the fact that the forms built to *ēs-* would have been homophonous with the verb 'be' if they had a short vowel. It is hard to see how that could have presented a problem in communication, however; certainly the homophony between NHG *ist* 'is' and *ißt* 'eats' seems not to cause present-day Germans any inconvenience. In any case, spontaneous change in pronunciation to avoid troublesome homophony, once upon a time very freely invoked, is currently thought to be far from common.

Another problem is the development of *-st-* < *-dt- (**212b**). In the case of 3sg. *ēst*, that is easily explained as leveling from expected *ēss. On the other hand, the salient pattern of roots in *-t-* or *-d-* forming a past participle with *-ss-* (**212**; cf. *findō, fissus*) makes leveling a less likely explanation for *comēstus*, and the mismatch between simplex *ēsus* and derivative *comēstus* (next to *comēsus*) deepens the mystery.

488. DŌ, DARE 'give'.

A. From the Latin point of view, the irregularity lies in the short *-ă-*

---

[1] The length is a hidden quantity, and the inflection was too much altered in Romance languages for any evidence from that quarter. What evidence there is for *ēs-*, though scanty, is nevertheless accepted by all authorities.

of most of the forms, as *damus, datis*; *dabam*; *darem*; *dare*; *datus*, by which they differ from those of *stāre* and the first conj. in general. From the historical point of view, on the contrary, the irregularity lies in the *-ā-* of 2sg. *dās* indic., *dā* imperat.

The PIE root was *$^*deH_3$-/$^*dH_3$-*, which built a root aorist and a reduplicated present, as **de-deH$_3$-ti* 3sg. (Ved. *dádāti*, G δίδωσι), 1pl. **de-dH̥$_3$-mos* (Ved. *dadmasi*, G δίδομεν). Remnants of the latter are indicated in L *re-ddō* 'give back', and in Sab. forms like O *didest* fut. The perf. *dedī* is of the reduplicating type. The only remnants in L of the root aor. are the imperatives *cedo* < **kedō* < **ḱe-deH$_3$* (the bare root evidently) and pl. *cette* < **kedate* < *ḱe-dH̥$_3$te* (= G δότε, **102**). Even in face of these two forms, the complete ouster of reflexes of **deH$_3$-* by those of **dH̥$_3$-* is no great mystery. Full grade forms do well in monosyllabic stems like **wel-* and **ey-*, but in the *n*-infix presents and the other reduplicating presents (such as *serō* and *sīdō*), the plural (zero grade) stem is always the basis of the new L paradigms. Still, it has been surmised that imper. *dā* and 2sg. *dās* might be remodelings of more original **(di)dō* and **(di)dōs* and, if that is true, likewise 3sg. *dat* might reflect **dāt*, the parallel remodeling of **(di)dōt*. A simpler explanation is that *dă-* was generalized from its original sites such as the plural persons and the infinitive, and that the resulting **dăs*, **dă* then became *dās* and *dā* by regular developments involving monosyllables. In support of this notion is the 3rd conj. inflection of compounds like *reddō*, with *-ddis*, *-ddit* pointing to **-dedas*, **-dedat*. 1sg. **-(de)dō* can be explained in a number of ways; the simplest would be an early remodeling of **dedōmi* in the course of the wholesale loss of the athem. 1sg. ending, which would yield a form suitable for a 1sg. even though etymologically unconnected with the marker *-ō*. No such construct as **dă(y)ō*, or **dōyō* (like OCS *dają*), is necessary, but cannot be ruled out.

Inf. *dăre* points to **dasi*, which in fact is often stated to be the etymon; but the genuine form would have been **deH$_3$esi* (**553.1**), whence *$^\times$dōre*. Such a form might have existed, of course; but the infin. was most probably coined in the first place at a significantly later date, that is, after original **sed-esi, -eti* had been metanalyzed as **sede-si, -ti*, as seems to be the correct history of *velle, esse* from **welsi*, **H$_1$essi*. Considerably more straightforward is pple. *datus* from **dH̥$_3$-to-* (**102, 565**).

3pl. *danunt* is the most frequent of the 3pl. forms in *-nunt* which occur sporadically in OL. Some have speculated that **dan* < **dant* was 'refreshed' as *danunt*; but there is no reason to suppose that the *-t* of *dant* was ever lost. This leads to the opposite surmise, that the starting point was a twice-marked **dantont*, with dissimilatory simplification of the medial cluster.

An entirely different line of reasoning is the suggestion that *sinō* 'put', pple. *situs* (**454B**) might have interacted with *dō* in an OL proportion like *sitos* : *datos* :: *sinont* : *X*, where *X* = *danont*. The semantics of the two verbs make mutual influence credible, but it is incomprehensible that the 3pl. alone would have been thus influenced, as ×*danō* 1sg., ×*danis* 2sg. solve the proportion as neatly as *danont*.

The real explanation is certainly prosodic analogy (see **466**, end), though the details are difficult.

a. Though the ending *-nunt* is scantily attested apart from *danunt* it must have been a feature of colloquial Roman speech, as it is the basis for the It. 3pl. ending *-ano*, *-ono*.

b. OL and Sab. attest various non-indicative forms built to a stem that looks like **duwī-* or **dowī-*, so Falisc. DOVIAD 'det', Plaut. *duīs*, *duit*, *duint*, U imper. **purtuvitu**. An OL inscription of uncertain date (3rd or 2nd century BC) contains CEDVES and CEDVAS, which look like 2sg. verbs formed like *cedo*, above and 377.3. But there are difficulties of interpretation. Similar-looking things are found in Plaut. forms like *perduint* and *crēduīs*, but these are probably reflexes of **dheH₁-* (**Ba**, below), and therefore unrelated.

There are two basic plans of attack for explaining these forms: tracing them to a different form of the (same) root, or treating the glide as arising within the history of Ital. (According to both types of theory, forms like *perduint* are analogical.) A root by-form **deH₃w-* is ad hoc, and its supposed attestation is bizarre: only in the inf. in Ved. *dāváne* and G δοῦναι (Cyp. *to-ve-na-i*) < **dōwenai*; only in the pret. in Lith. (*daviaũ*); and only in modal forms in Ital. The G and Lith. forms have likely sources within the histories of the individual languages, which leaves the Ital. forms too isolated to think in terms of an inherited by-form of the root. The source of the glide in Italic is however unobvious.

B. As a result of regular sound laws, many forms of the compounds of *dō* would have turned into what look like 3rd conj. forms, so *addere*, *reddere* < *-*dedăsi*; *addendus* < *-*dandos*, imperf. subj. *adderem* < *-*dăsēm*, and so on. From such a basis the convergence on the 3rd conj. was made complete by the coinage of new forms like fut. *addēs*, *addet*, imperf. *addēbam*. Scattered future tense forms attest the original state of affairs, for example Plaut. *reddibō* (aligning with simplex *dabō*), epigr. REDDEBIT (-*ĕ*-).

a. In a number of identically-inflected forms, such as *condō* 'found' (*condidī*) and *abdō* 'put away, hide', the root is PIE **dheH₁-* 'put', rather than **deH₃-*; the zero grades **dhH̥₁-* and **dH̥₃-* in non-initial position have identical outcomes in L. The simplex is *faciō*, a PItal. innovation as indicated by O **fakiiad**, U **faśia**. This starts from PItal. **θēk-* of the aor. seen in L *fēcī*, superimposable on G ἔθηκα, which occasioned the reworking of the pple. **θatos* < **dhH̥₁-to-* (continued unaltered, apart from sound laws, in *conditus*) into **θaktos*. The pres. **θakyō* was created on the basis of some such analogy as **spektos* : **spekyō* :: **θaktos* : *X*. (The pivotal role of the pple. derives from its function as the passive of *θēk-*.) What earlier pres. was displaced by this **θakyō* can only be surmised.

Compounds of later date are revealed by their phonology (root-initial *f-*, not *d-*), their inflection (that of *faciō*), and their more transparent meanings: early *condō*, *-dere*, *condidī*, *conditus* 'establish, found'; later *cōnficiō*, *cōnfēcī*, *cōnfectus* 'put together, finish'.

489. FĪŌ, FIERĪ. The passive of *faciō* is transparent in the perf. system (*factus est* and so on) but the pres. system is supplied by an active form with an inflection reminiscent of the *veniō* type. Uniquely however it has -*ī*- before a vowel—*fīō*, *fīunt*; *fīēbam*; *fīam*. The infinitive *fierī*, then, is exceptional for two reasons: it is actually passive in morphology, and it has *fĭ-* rather than *fī-* (though act. *fīere* is also attested). The subj. is *fierem*, though times *fī-* in early L. The *-ie-* of the infin. and subj., regardless of the length of the first vowel, departs from the inflection of *veniō* (*venīre, venīrem*). The *-ī-* of *fīō* and *fīunt* is probably an importation from forms like *fīs* 2sg. and *fīmus* 1pl. The exceptional treatment of *fīō* and *fīunt*—no such analogy is seen in the paradigms of *veniō* and *moneō*—and also the persistence of *-ī-* despite the general rule shortening long vowels followed by a vowel (**85**), may be attributed to the fact that this was the only verb in *-iō* with tonic accent on the *-ī́-*. But this leaves *fierī, fierem* unaccounted for: the expected *fīerī, fīerem* do occur, but only in OL, and even there the forms in *fī-* are the usual ones. Of course, the sample is skewed: most information about the quantity of vowels comes from verse, and most classical verse is in dactylic hexameter where forms like *fīerēs, fīerēmus* could not be used. That is, if such forms in *fī-* were common, even the norm, we would know about it only if a Roman grammarian happened to mention it.

The formation might be easier to explain if we knew its etymology with greater certainty. The usual explanation is that the active inflection points away from an underlying passive (*fītur* and *fīēbantur* are quotable, but are innovations). In the RV, furthermore, aor. *(á-)bhūt* usually means 'became' (or 'becomes') rather than 'was', and the occasional use of *fuit* as the passive of *fēcit*, rather than the usual *factus est*, are taken as evidence that PIE aoristic root **bhū-* (or **bhuH-*) is the etymon of *fīō*. However, the details remain problematic. What is needed is something like **bhiy^{e}/o-*, but what that might be in either formal or functional relationship to a root **bhū-* or **bhuH-* is hard to see. The reconstructions usually encountered (**bhwī-* or **bhwiy^{e}/o-*) are little more than guesswork.

490. QUOTATIVE VERBS.

1. ĀIŌ, that is *aiiō*, is from **agyō*, PIE **H̥gyoH₂*. Cf. *adagium* 'proverb' (evidence is lacking regarding the length of the medial *-a-*: there is no morphological justification for *-ā-*, but survival of *-ă-* would be very odd, 66, ditto the preservation of *gi* < **gy*; on the other hand, *-ă-* is needed for *prōdigium* 'an event contrary to the laws of nature'[1]). For the phonological development, and the hesitation between *-āi-* and *-aii-*, cf. *māior, maiior* from **magyōs* (**194**). Its early inflection was that of the 4th conj.: *aīs, aīt*, and *aibam* (**aībam*) like *audībam* (beside *aiēbam* like *audiēbam*). Later *ais, ait* sometimes in two syllables but usually in one, though always with the old spelling (never ˣ*aes*, ˣ*aet*).

2. INQUAM, INQUIT continue the root **sek^{w}-*, which underlies NE *say*, NHG *sagen*. The root is homophonous with—probably ultimately the same

[1] The likely history of the word (**pro-adagium* via **88.3**) accords well with its meaning: a *prōdigium*, like the ringing of a telephone, was not itself a message but only a sign that the pax deorum had been or was about to be broken. Information about what was actually amiss would have to come from some other source.

root as—*sek^{w}- 'see, notice', and that was probably the original force. (In NE, for example, the verb *note*—especially in the past tense—is a synonym of *say*. And present-day solecisms of the type *the Attorney General sighted no specific statute* hint that 'see' and 'quote' are possible synonyms.) At all events, apart from its attestation in Gmc., it occurs with the sense 'say' or 'tell' only in fragments. These include L *inquam* 'to be sure, of course' < *in-sk^{w}-$\bar{a}$- (orig. opt., like NE *I might say* 'it is my opinion'), but most of the forms are of the simple thematic type, as *inquis, inquit, inquimus*, imperative *inque*, and so on; but some, as *inquiunt* and *inquiēbat*, follow the verbs in *-iō*, perhaps influenced by *āiunt*. There is continuing (if minor) debate over whether **insqu-* continues a genuine zero grade or is a syncopation of **in-sequ-*. Syncope is not really plausible, given Plaut. *īnsece* 'go on' (encouraging someone to continue with a story, say) = G ἔννεπε—if syncope would occur anywhere, it would be here; and Hom. ἐνίσπε(ς) imper., ἔνισπον aor. 'tell, relate, describe' establish that we are dealing with an old ablauting (root) present. The apparent zero grade of *inquis* and *inquit* is better taken as the form of the stem proper to the pl., just as in other thematized athematic formations (*sistit* 479.3, *iungit* 479.4); but in this particular case the zero-grade stem would be given especial support by the extremely common **insquām* 'I might say; indeed; of course' (> *inquam*), whose zero grade is correct for the formation. On the other side of the question, it may reasonably be countered that quotative verbs are often little more than particles, which are subject to the radical reductions typical of enclitics. In that case, the survival of the root vowel in *īnseque* imperat. may result from some particular influence, such as fanciful association with *īnsequor* 'follow'.

a. The phonological derivation of *inqu-* from *$ensk^{w}$- continues to be regarded as problematic. On the one hand, *ns* before voiceless stop seems to persist, as in *īnscius* 'ignorant'—though in this and other examples recomposition is a realistic possibility (which is not the case with *inqu-* < *$ensk^{w}$-). On the other hand, forms like *tranquillus* 'calm' and *septentriōnēs* 'Ursa minor' are held to support the development in *inquam*. But the etymologies of both *tranquillus* and *septentriōnēs* are disputed; the pertinence of the latter depends on discarding the excellent traditional **septem triōn-* 'seven threshing-oxen' in favor of **septem striōn-* 'seven stars'. (Among other difficulties, Ptolemy catalogues eight stars in the constellation in question, which accords better with the traditional image of seven objects circling about the stella polaris.)

The Verb 'be' in Greek and Latin

491. Because of its extreme idiosyncracy in both G and L, it is worthwhile to present an account of the whole paradigm of the verb 'be' separately; discussions of some of the components will also be found elsewhere, under the appropriate headings.

In PIE—unlike G, L, and most attested IE languages—there was very little out of the ordinary about the verb 'be'. The odder traits of the verb in G and L are the result, paradoxically, of the extreme conservatism of these forms. For example the OL subj. *siem* 1sg., *sīmus* 1pl., *sient* 3pl., unique to this verb, is actually the sole survivor in L of what was once the normal way of forming the optative stem to roots (**539.1**).

The two primary roots at stake both inflected as EVENTIVE verbs (**410**): *H_1es-*, which inflected as a present/imperfect; and **bhū-* (or **bhuH-*), which was aoristic. It is peculiar enough that these inherently stative verbs ('be, exist') inflect as eventives; more peculiar still is the existence of an aoristic paradigm, as the basic semantics of the verb would seem to preclude the very idea of a punctual eventive. The explanation seems to be that the original meaning of punctual (aorist) **bhū-* was 'become', that is, 'come into existence'. (This hints that the G 'ingressive aorist', **417**, is an archaic trait, not a G innovation.)

492. The inflection of *H_1es-* in PIE was an ordinary root-present as follows:

1sg.	*H_1ésmi	*1pl.*	*H_1smés
2	*H_1ési	2	*H_1sté
3	*H_1ésti	3	*H_1sénti

2sg. *H_1ési* for *H_1és-si*, which is attested as such in Ved. *ási*, Av. *ahi*, Lith. *esi*, and Hom. εἶ, is the only noteworthy detail in this array, and is in fact regular. It shows the truncation (shortening) of a sequence of two identical consonants. Such truncation was normal for PIE, except in the case of two apical stops (**212**).

	PIE	Vedic	G	L	Go.	Lith.[1]	Hitt.
1sg.	*H_1ésmi	ásmi	εἰμί	sum	im	esmì	e-eš-mi
			Lesb. ἔμμι				
2	*H_1ési	ási	εἶ	es	is	esì	
			εἶς				
			ἐσσί	OL ess			
3	*H_1ésti	ásti	ἐστί	est	ist	ẽsti	e-eš-zi
1pl.	*H_1smós	smási		sumus	sijum	esme	
		smás	εἰμέν				
			ἐσμέν				
2	*H_1sté	sthá(na)	ἐστέ	estis	sijuþ	este	
3	*H_1sonti	sánti		sunt		OCS sǫtŭ	a-ša-an-zi
	*H_1senti	santi	εἰσί		sind	OCS sętŭ	
			Dor. ἐντί				
			Myc. e-e-si				

GREEK. In G these forms are inherited largely unchanged, though some later underwent transparent remodeling. In the 2sg. the most conservative form is Hom. εἶ < *esi*, which was twice modified, once by tacking on the usual person marker -ς, just like thematic φέρεις (**425**), and once—very

[1] Early texts only; the pl. forms are found with various contradictory tone marks.

anciently—through recombination of the root **es-* (abstracted from 3sg. ἐστί) with the usual athem. ending **-si*, whence ἐσσί. The same recombination of the root is seen in ἐσμέν, beside the more original εἰμέν < PG **esmen* (except that this recombination must be much later, and here the likeliest source of the root was the 2pl. **este*). As is often the case in G, the only real problem in this paradigm is the 3pl. Prior to the discovery of Myc., the G forms were usually explained as cognate to Gmc. forms of the type of Go. *sind*, that is, from PreG **senti*, with ἐ- for expected ἑ- via analogy. Myc. *e-e-si* makes it clear however that the PG form of the 3pl. was actually **ehenti*, the regular outcome of **H₁senti*. But: PG **ehenti* ought to give G ˣεἱσί, like εὕω < **euhō* 'kindle'. We are therefore still dependent on leveling analogy to explain the loss of rough breathing (or its failure to develop in the first place). Note that a reconstruction **ehenti* sheds no light on Dor. ἐντί, as one would have expected **(h)ēντι* or the like. (Getting from here to the attested form is in effect TOO easy—a number of different histories are readily imaginable, with no way of deciding between them.)

LATIN. Despite appearances, none of the forms shown with the exception of *sunt* are directly inherited, no matter how simple a development like **esti* > *est* looks on its face. They are the end results of a process of enclitic reduction (see **245** on the enclitic status of verbs), still evident in Plautine *factust, factast, factumst* for classical *factus est, facta est, factum est* 'became'. This means that classical *es, est,* and *estis* are actually restressed enclitics: the *e-* is not inherited from PIE but is a sort of prop-vowel. The development of **somos* 1pl. from **mos* (the regular reflex of **H₁smos*, **225.1c**) probably started with a proportion like **legont* : **sont* :: **legomos* : *X*, where *X* = **somos*.[1] Whatever the reason, all L athematics which ended in consonants evolve thematic type 1pl. forms, so *sumus, volumus* but *īmus, damus*. —The exact history of 1sg. **som* (O **súm**) is less clear. Varro cites *esum* as the (or a) former pronunciation. It is very unlikely that such a form is ancestral to *sum*; rather **esom* is based on **som*, created at the same time that (enclitic) *-ss* and *-st* were evolving into restressed *ess* and *est*—not by the same process, of course, but by imitation. The development **esmi* > encl. **-sm̥* > **som* must have taken place prior to the loss of **s* before **m* as in *cōmis* 'kind' (relatively late; COSMIS in the Duenos inscr.). The vowel, in place of expected **sem*, is likewise presumably owing to the influence of

---

[1] The change of **som-* to *sum-* is best explained via non-initial syllable vowel weakening rules (65-75) as applied to the enclitic **somus*. In favor of this, parallel cases of vowel weakening which can only be explained by enclitic prosody are attested in inscriptions, as SECVTI SIMVS 'we followed'.

Those inclined to do so can trace **somos* directly to **semos* < **H₁sm̥mos*, that is, the 'regular' Edgerton/Lindeman syllabification (181) of **H₁smos*; the form would be the unique instance of a syllabic nasal in the 1pl.

**somos*; that matter might be clearer if we knew the Sab. shape of the 1pl. form. —L *estis* is problematic in that there seems to be no evidence at all for a pronunciation **stes* (or **stis*) parallel to encl. *-ss*, *-st*, yet the most likely explanation for its source is of the type *-ss* : *ess* :: **stes* : *X*, where *X* = *estis*. Importation of full grade **es-* from the sg. is unlikely to have singled out the 2pl.

a. Both G and L have *-*sḱ*^{e}/*o*- stems (456.3) built to this root: Hom. ἔσκον (once), ἔσκε (often) 'used to be' < **H*$_1$*s-sḱ*^{e}/*o*-, are in effect the true imperfect of εἰμί in contrast to the quasi-aoristic ἦν. By contrast L *escit*, *escunt* (Paul.Fest.; *escit* also Lucretius); seem to mean 'will be' < *'is coming to be'. (But although Festus explicitly states that *escit* = *erit*, in the passages he quotes from the Twelve Tables the sense apperas to be the simple present—though a case could be made for the semantic nuance 'happens to be' vs. generic 'is'.) The G forms may reflect correctly-formed **H̥*$_1$*s-sḱ*^{e}/*o*-, with zero grade of the root; the L forms in *es-* must be analogical.

493. The imperfect. There is no historical connection between the G and L paradigms called the imperfect.

Greek. A. The closest relatives of the G forms are found in InIr., and to some extent in Hitt.:

	Vedic		Greek			Hittite
	imperf.	*perf.*	*Homer*	*Attic*	*Other*	
1*sg.*	ā́sam	ā́sa	ἦα, ἔᾱ, ἦν	(old) ἦ; ἦν		e-šu-un
			ἔην, ἤην, ἔον		ἔον (Aeol.)	
2	*ā́s*	ā́sitha	ἔησθα, ἦσθα	ἦσθα		e-eš-ta
	ā́sīs		ἦς (Ion.)			
3	ās	ā́sa	ἦ(ε)ν	ἦν	ἦς	(e-)eš-ta
	āsīt		ἔην, ἤην			
1*pl.*	*ā́sma*	āsimá	ἦμεν			e-šu-(u-)en
2	*ā́sta*	*āsá*	ἦστε, ἦτε			e-eš-tin
3	ā́san	āsúr	ἔσαν	ἦσαν	ἦν (Dor.)	e-šir
					ἔον (Aeol.)	e-še-ir

(The four Indic forms in *italics* are Vedic but not attested in the Rigveda.)

The singular stem **ēs-*, Indic *ās-*, is straightforwardly from **e-H*$_1$*es-*. In the plural (and dual, not shown), however, both languages unexpectedly show what appears to be the stem of the singular. Actually it is the regular interaction of the augment with the following laryngeal in the expected shape **e-H*$_1$*s-*.

The immemorial explanation for the uniform stems was leveling, evidently already of PIE date (since it is unlikely that such an innovation would have taken place independently). The earliness of such a development, and in such a basic paradigm—the last place, not the first, where such an innovation should make an appearance—make the account implausible, and the straightforward explanation afforded by a reconstruction **e-H*$_1$*s-* for the du. and pl. imperf. stem is therefore welcome.

B. Endings in greek. PIE had no perfect paradigm to this root, such that the Vedic perf. (table, above) is an innovation based on the model of inherited perfects. On the evidence of several G forms, it appears that G too had contrived a perf. paradigm, which however by the time of Homer had already coalesced with the imperf., partly for functional reasons and partly because the two paradigms would have had forms in common anyway. Once the typical leveling of grades in the perf. is taken into account, the forms ἦα 1sg., ἦμεν, ἦστε and ἦστον 2du., would have been homophonous in the two paradigms. Att. ἦν 1sg. is ἦ (contracted from ἦα or—more likely —ἔᾱ) touched up with the thematic -ν. Hom. and Aeol. ἔον is a thematic form as such; it would be the regular reflex of *H_1*esom* though it is unlikely any such form existed in the parent language. Hom. ἔᾱ is from ἦα by quantitative metathesis.

The unaltered imperf. 2sg. ἦς, a form actually attested in Ion., was displaced in Hom. and Att. by the more distinctively marked perf. ἦσθα (cf. Ved. *ā́sitha*).

PIE 3sg. **e*H_1*est* would have given the same ἦς (directly superimposable on Ved. *ā́s*), once again actually attested in a large number of dialects but replaced in Attic-Ionic. The replacement—Hom. and Att. ἦν—is contracted from ἦεν (with stable -ν) still seen in Hom.; this is the original 3pl. < **e*H_1*sent*, retained in that function in the Dor. 3pl. ἦν. How a reassignment of 3pl. to 3sg. can take place is hard to fathom on any functional grounds; a formal explanation is however workable: an original (unattested) perf. *ἦε would, with ν-movable, have been homophonous with inherited imperf. 3pl. ἦεν (with fixed -ν). When clearly-marked 3pl. forms like ἦσαν started to become current, ambiguous ἦεν was free, as it were, to be exclusively 3sg.

1pl. ἦμεν and 2pl. ἦστε are straightforward; as mentioned above, the imperf. and perf. forms would have been homophonous in G. The 2pl. ἦστε was the only imperf./perf. form where the root-final -σ- was not lost by the agency of sound laws; Hom. ἦτε is a coinage revealing that a stem ἦ- had been abstracted from the (regular) σ-less forms of other persons, helped by metanalysis of 2sg. ἦσθα as ἦ-σθα and the correct perception of the 3pl. as ἦ-σαν. The upshot is that the imperf. tended to generalize forms of the root without -σ-, while in the pres. system forms of the root WITH -σ- were favored.

3pl. ἦσαν has -σαν imported from the *s*-aorist (504-5). Hom. ἔσαν is in effect an augmentless form, and could either be an artificial back formation from ἦσαν or an indirect continuation of *ἔεν, the phonologically regular reflex of *H_1*sent*.

Such forms as ἔησθα, ἤην, ἔην (? perhaps to be restored to *ἦεν) are regarded as artificial literary creations.

a. Middle inflection of the imperf. is occasionally met with in late G, though the imperat. ἔσσο is attested in Homer and Sappho, and of course the future is regularly middle (500a). Along such lines OL attests only *potestur* (Plaut.), *poteratur* (Fest.). —Hindu grammarians expressly allow for a middle inflection of *ásmi*, but no forms are quotable from texts.

C. Latin. In L there is no trace of the PIE imperfect, in this or any other paradigm (498). That function is filled by a stem in *-ā-*, (? *-eH_2-) an element which is historically a modal of some sort (539.3). In most verbs, as explained in 498, this element is found in the affix *-bā-*. In the verb 'be' alone the same element is added directly to the root of the present tense: *esām, *esās, *esāt. With the action of regular sound laws (173, 83.3) these become *eram, erās, erat*.

494. Perfect. No perfect was formed to the roots *H_1es- and *bhū- (*bhuH-) in PIE. As mentioned above, there are reasons for supposing that a perf. paradigm once existed in G, not inherited but created on the usual patterns of stem-formation and inflection. But if so it was lost as a distinct paradigm in preliterary times. (The Ved. perfect is hardly vigorous: the Rigveda, with its several thousand forms from this root alone, has in all only 25 instances of the perf. stem.)

In L the perf. of *sum* is *fuī, fuistī, fuit*, based on the root aor. of the root *bhū-. This formation is seen in a less altered form in Ved. *ábhūt* (injunct. *bhū́t*), G ἔφῡ, (φῡ), and OCS *by*. The same root ultimately underlies NE *be* (a finite stem in OE *béom, bist, biþ*). The stem *fŭ-* is from *fū-* by shortening before a vowel (85); forms such as *fūimus* and *fūit* are actually attested in OL. The perf. indicative stems are formed and inflected in the usual way (531): *fuisset, fuerit*, and so on. Early L attests a subj. *fuat*, in effect an aorist opt. in *-ā-* (539.3) built to this stem; however *fŭ-* early was generalized, as indicated by pple. *fŭtūrus*, imperf. subj. *forem* < *fŭsēm (**38b**). A similar back-formation led to G φῠ́σις 'form, nature', φῠτόν 'a plant' ('that which has grown' if you will) and φῠτεύω 'plant, produce, beget'.

a. Cf. the L future affix *-bō, -bi-* and the imperf. *-bā-*; see 501.3 and 498.

495. Future: greek. Formed to *H_1es- in G in the usual way (500.1), with one proviso: the 3sg. usually syncopates the thematic vowel, so ἔσται. Hom. has also ἔσ(σ)εται and the 'Doric fut.' is ἐσ(σ)εῖται < ἐσσεε-. The normal inflection is in the middle: ἔσ(σ)ομαι, ἔσ(σ)εαι (Att. ἔσῃ).

Latin. Like all L futures, the future of *sum* is the PIE subjunctive, as attested unaltered in Ved. *ásas(i), ásat(i)*, Hom. ἔω, ἔῃς, ἔῃ (ἔῃσι). From *esō, *esesi, *eseti come the L future forms *erō, eris, erit* via the usual phonological processes (74.2, 71.3, 173).

496. Optative, imperative, infinitive.

1. Optative. The PIE paradigm, to stems *H_1s-yéH_1-, *H_1s-iH_1- was a normal athematic optative (539.1): zero grade of the root, to which is added the opt. affix *-yéH_1- in the singular active and *-iH_1- elsewhere, and with generic ('secondary') endings (419-20): *H_1syéH_1m̥, *H_1syéH_1s, *H_1syéH_1t, *H_1siH_1mé, *H_1siH_1té, *H_1siH_1ént (or *H_1siH_1ont). It is preserved as such in

Ved. *syā́m, syā́t,* where it is original, but even so early as the RV the singular stem had been generalized to the du. and pl. (so *syā́ma* 1pl.) and the singular stem seemingly influenced the prosody of *syúr* 3pl., which only twice scans *siyúr* as expected from *H_1siH_1-. Hom. εἴην, εἴης, εἴτην 3du., εἶμεν, εἶτε, εἶεν are the most original forms, continuing **eh-yē-*; thematic-type forms like ἔοι(ς) are based on obvious patterns, and εἴησαν 3pl. εἰήτην 3du. (typical of the opt. of reduplicating μι-verbs) show the same kind of generalization as seen in RV *syā́ma.*

This formation underlies what is traditionally known as the L subjunctive. The earliest attested paradigm in L is OL *siem, siēs, siet* (epig. SIED, **426**), *sīmus, sītis, sient.* This preserves the original distribution exactly, with 3pl. *sient* (← **siens*) < *siH_1ent resembling the singular stem *siē-* < *$syeH_1$- by accident. In classical Latin, the stem *sī-* is generalized, so, with the usual shortening rules (**82-3**), *sim, sīs, sit, sīmus, sītis, sint.*

a. The 1,2pl. is an implausible basis for a generalized stem; in G and InIr., significantly, leveling in such forms always took the shape of extending the SINGULAR stem into the plural. Perhaps then the actual history of the L development has more to do with phonology than usually recognized: the eventual outcome of *sient* in any case, likewise **welient,* would probably have been **sīnt, *velīnt,* like *vīta* 'life' < **wietā* < **wiotā* < *$g^wiH_3eteH_2$ (**68**). From there the first new form must have been 3sg. **sīt,* patterned on **sīnt,* and so from there to **sīm, sīs.*

b. The relative fewness of Vedic forms in *siy-* (and their dates—*siyā́ma,* the most frequent, is found mostly in late parts of the RV and is commoner still in the AV) are surprising if the genuine etymon is *H_1syeH_1-, as in all positions Edgerton's Law (**179**) would have required *H_1siyeH_1-. The early and general replacement of original *siyúr* < *H_1siH_1- is a particular difficulty, as it should not have alternated at all in terms of any theory. The L development (*siē-* in two syllables from **syē-*) is purely phonological, like *medius* (three syllables) from **meθyo-* (**193**).

c. The G stem εἰ- in εἶμεν < **ehī-* < *H_1s-iH_1- is one of the strongest pieces of evidence that *-iH_1- > G -ῑ- rather than -ιε-, at least medially; see **49.1**.

2. IMPERATIVE: GREEK. G ἴσθι is an enigma. An athematic stem should form the 2sg. imper. with zero grade of the stem and the affix **-dhi* (so Ved. *śrudhí* 'hear!'). For the root *H_1es- this would be *H_1sdhi (if not *$\mathring{H}_1sdhi$), and exactly that form is attested in Gāth. *zdī.* The undisturbed outcome would have been G *ἔσθι. The question of how attested ἴσθι arose has no answer, but even so that is an easier question than WHY *ἔσθι would have been vulnerable to replacement at all. (Tracing the ι- to schwa secundum (**124**) was no explanation even before laryngeals, and is unthinkable for a root *H_1es-.)

LATIN. The L imperatives are straightforward. The sg. *es* looks like the bare root (**547.1**); it might actually be **ess,* the 2sg. indicative, instead, but the form chances not to occur in revealing metrical passages in OL. The other forms, *este, estō(te), suntō,* and so on, are all formed normally within the L system (**548**).

3. INFINITIVE. The G infinitives (εἶναι, ἔμμεναι, ἔμμεν, ἔμεναι) are formed in the usual way (**552**). The same thing is true of the L infin. *esse,*

except that it appears to be formed athematically, namely **es-si*, a distinction it shares with *velle*, *nōlle* < **welsi* (553.1; regarding *ferre* see 485.)

The Durative Eventive Preterite (Imperfect)

497. The Greek imperfect agrees with Indo-Iranian and Anatolian and reflects the PIE imperfect. This was an anterior tense marking uncompleted, continuous, or iterative action, and was formed from the present stem with generic ('secondary') endings (419-20), with or without the augment, which finally became fixed in G as in Indo-Iranian and Armenian. Thus G ἔφερον = Ved. *ábharam* 'I was carrying'. In stem-types shared by the present/imperfect and the aorist paradigms, the formation itself is ambiguous. That is, what makes ἔφερον an imperfect and ἔλιπον an aorist is the relationship of the formation in question to the other forms in the paradigm—specifically, there is a present φέρω, whereas there is no present ˣλίπω.[1] A formation built to a present-only stem type, such as ἐμάνθανον, can of course only be an imperfect to μανθάνω.

Imperf. paradigms are given in 422-3; for further discussion of the augment, see 441-2.

a. The impf. of τίθημι, ἵημι, and δίδωμι have some forms that follow the analogy of the contract verbs. Thus 1sg. ἐτίθην, ἵην, but 2sg. ἐτίθεις, ἵεις, 3sg. ἐτίθει, ἵει (ει = ē̜); from δίδωμι all three persons of the singular are cited, ἐδίδουν, ἐδίδους, ἐδίδου (replacing -ων, -ως, -ω), but ἐδίδουν seems not to be quotable from any text. 1sg. ἐτίθουν is quotable, but only from very late sources. These replace the inherited imperf. paradigms for stems, attested in Homer, which agree in every particular with those seen in Ved. and Av.: ἐτίθην, ἐτίθης, ἐτίθη = Ved. *adadhām*, *ádadhās*, *ádadhāt*; similarly ἐδίδω = Ved. *ádadāt*.

498. In Italic, as in Germanic and Celtic, there is no trace of this formation. In Italic the tense with the corresponding function (and name) is formed with an element in *-ā-* (539.3). This is historically the same as the *ā*-subjunctive (*sīdāmus* 'let us sit', 543), and was presumably therefore some kind of optative. Now, past-tense conditionals often have past-habitual semantics, as is the case in present-day English (*Except during blizzards, even in winter he* WOULD WALK *to work.*). The element *-ā-* with preterital force was added directly to the stem/root in only one verb, the verb 'be' (493c).

In all other forms, the tense sign is L *-bā-* (with regular shortening in *-bam*, *-ba(n)t*, 83), from Ital. **-fā-*, a formation which seems to have spread even further in Sab., as in O **fufans** 'they were', functionally but not formally equivalent to the more conservative L *erant*. This affix is somehow from **bhŭā-*. This possibly (but not likely) is attested in the rare L *fuat*,

---

[1] For a parallel, what makes *drank* a past tense is not its SIMILARITY to other past tenses like *sank*—a 'similarity' fully shared by *thank*, *crank*, *spank*, and other non-past-tense forms —but its relationship to *drink*.

which is typically found in negative imperatives, *nē fuās*, *nē fuat*. In enclitic position it reduced to *-*fā*-. What exactly preceded the *-*bhŭā*- originally is more obscure still, and has been much debated. As attested, 1st, 2nd, and some 4th conj. forms look like stems (*amā*-, *manē*-; and in early L *venī*- is commoner than *veniē*-); but in the 3rd and some 4th conj. forms, the partials *legē*-, *capiē*-, *veniē*- correspond to no other stem. Even without the difficulties raised by the 3rd and 4th conj. types, the one possibility that can be eliminated out of hand is the notion that an inflected form of **fū*- was grafted onto a stem directly. Rather, it is to be taken for granted that the imperfect (and mutatis mutandis the future of the 1st and 2nd conj.) are in origin PHRASAL VERBS, that is some kind of verbal noun or adjective in construction with an inflected form of the verb **fū*-. The fusing of the two into a single inflected stem was like the development of the Romance future from PRom. infinitive + **habyo* (so **cantáre hábyo* > Fr. *chanterai*, It. *cantarò*). Among the known verbals of L, the likeliest candidate for the original stem is the pres. pple. But phrases which coalesce into single phonological words undergo changes for which there are no testable hypotheses; that is, if the starting points of the L imperfect were in fact phrases of the type **amānts fŭām* (pl. **amāntēs fŭāmos*) or **amāntsbhwām* or something of the sort, they would have been the only structures in the language remotely like this, and so whatever sequence of phonological and analogical changes actually took place would be not only complex but also sui generis. The best hope of definitively unriddling the history of the formation would be the discovery of intermediate, and therefore less changed, forms.

a. The element -*bā*- is added directly to the root in *dăbam* 'I was giving' and *ībam* 'I was going'—to the zero grade of the former and the full grade of the latter (which had spread throughout the whole paradigm as an invariant stem, **486**).

b. The Italic imperf. -*ā*- is often compared to Baltic formations in -*ā*-. The latter however are simple pasts, without the 'infectum' function of Italic (stative, iterative, or uncompleted). Moreover, the BS formation, whatever its antecedents, was formed to the zero grade of the root, while this element takes the full grade. Besides, it is evident that the Italic and Celtic *-*ā*- is isofunctional with the ending *-*oy*- seen in all other IE languages—Baltic included—namely it is the optative of thematic stems (539.3); it is not credible that Baltic could have both *-*oy*- and *-*ā*-. Given the formal and functional mismatch, it is best to regard the Baltic formation and the Italic and Celtic opt./imperf. in *-*ā*- as basically unrelated.

c. The Italo-Celtic 'preterital -*ā*-' is limited to **bhā*- in Sab., but L and Celt. (Middle Welsh *oed* < **esāt*) also formed **esā*-. Several theories trace preterital -*ā*- to aorist formations. One reconstructs a root aor. **bh(w)ā*- < **bhweH$_2$*- (a regularized replacement of the inherited **bhuH$_{(2)}$*- seen in G and Vedic). From this, **esā*- was formed by analogy. Another theory postulates, as an Ital.-Celt. innovation, the addition of an aor. marker *-*H$_2$*- (evidence for which is immaterial here) to the subj. (= fut.) stem **H$_1$ese*-, so **esā*-. The result was functionally a conditional ('past of the future'). But the central role of the aorist in both these theories is a serious problem. The otherwise invariable resting-place of inherited aorist features is the L perfect (completed action), which is hard to see as a source for an essentially infectum formation (actions incomplete, continuing, habitual).

THE FUTURE

499. As discussed in 417, what is called the *future tense* might better be called the *simple future* or the like. Other ways of talking about events that have not yet taken place include promises, commands, and what collectively might be called modals: conditionals, conatives, purposives, necessitatives, precatives, desideratives, and others. PIE had special forms for some of these, but no simple future tense. The so-called present tense—more accurately the non-past tense—served also for ordinary future events, as it continued to do to some extent in G, as εἶμι which, like its English gloss 'I am going (to) . . .', often refers to the future.

GREEK

500. In a number of IE languages, the PIE desiderative (457) is the basis for a simple future. This is the source of two different-looking but originally identical G formations: the σ-future and the 'liquid futures' in -έω.

1. The original desiderative formation was formed directly from the root, by means of the desiderative element *-H_1s-, which inflected athematically. When the root ended in a voiceless stop, the marker seems to have lost its laryngeal already in PIE, and furthermore was remodeled as one or another type of thematic stem in most IE groups. It directly underlies futures like G δείξω < **deyḱs*^{e}/*o*- < ***deyḱ*-H_1*s*- and πέψω < **pek*^{w}*s*^{e}/*o*- < ***pek*^{w}-H_1*s*-. The -σ^ε/$_o$- was transplanted from these formations to build the futures of secondary stems like παιδεύσω and τῑμήσω (παιδεύω, τῑμάω) and also to stems ending (from the G point of view) in vowels, as δώσω 'will give' (δίδωμι), λῡ́σω 'will loosen' (λύω).

a. Many G futures to active present and aorist verbs are in the middle voice, as Hom. λοέσσομαι 'will wash' to pres. λούω (λοέω), fut. λούσω occurring only later. This is even true of the fut. of εἰμί: ἔσ(σ)ομαι, ἔσ(σ)εαι, ἔσ(σε)ται. This is in accord with the theory that the G future is historically a desiderative: if our understanding of the function of the middle voice in PIE (414) is accurate, most forms of the desiderative should by rights be in the middle voice, and that is the traditional explanation for the future middles of G. But while this explanation makes sense on its own terms, it receives unexpectedly little support: in the RV, which likewise cannibalized the old desiderative for a paradigmatic future, future middles are downright rare. Middles are more evident in the desiderative formation itself, though fewer than half of the desiderative verb forms are middle.

b. A theory once more widely endorsed than it is nowadays traces the G future to a short-vowel subjunctive of the σ-aorist. The form and meaning accord tolerably well, but these similarities are accidental. Roots of certain shapes reveal the formal distinction clearly, as **ten*- 'stretch (out)' (pres. **ten-y*^{e}/*o*- > G τείνω) forms the aor. **(e)ten-s*- whence G ἔτεινα (228.1), but fut. **ten*-$\mathring{H}_1$*s*- > **teneh*^{e}/*o*- whence τενέω, τενῶ.

c. The consonant changes, the interchange of -ξω and -σω from verbs in -ζω, the retention of the -σ- in δώσω, λῡ́σω, are parallel to the situation in the σ-aorist and are discussed in 465.3a, 504–5.

2. LIQUID FUTURES. The future of most verb roots ending in a resonant (ρ, λ, μ, ν), whether or not they were followed by a laryngeal in PIE, is formed with *-es^e/o- < *-H_1s- (**102**) which, with regular loss of the *-*s*- (**172**), becomes *-e^e/o-, -έω, Att. -ῶ, as τενέω, τενῶ 'will stretch' (τείνω, **ten*-), βαλέω, βαλῶ—analogical for regular *δελέω, -ῶ (**164A.1**)—'will throw' (βάλλω; root *$g^w elH_1$-).

3. THE ATTIC FUTURE. The Attic future is the nickname for a future like the preceding, but formed from a greater variety of verb stems, corresponding to futures in -σω in other dialects (which accounts for the tag 'Attic', though in fact such forms occur in Homer and elsewhere).

These may all be regarded as analogical extensions of the type of βαλῶ (item 2, above) which is general G. Thus τελῶ 'will complete' (pres. τελέω, stem τελεσ-; τελῶ also Hom., beside τελέσ(σ)ω); ἐλῶ (ἐλάσω, Hom. ἐλάσσω, also Hom. ἐλάω; pres. ἐλαύνω, **465.6b**); σκεδῶ 'will scatter' from -άω (pres. σκίδνημι and σκεδάννῡμι, aor. ἐσκέδασα; so from all in -αννῡμι and some in -εννῡμι); κομιῶ 'will take care of' (elsewhere κομίσω; pres. κομίζω; so from most in -ιζω).

4. THE DORIC FUTURE in -σέω/-σέομαι is the regular form in the West Greek dialects, as Delph. κλεψεω. But some forms of this type occur also in Att.-Ion. Thus Hom. ἐσσεῖται 'will be' (beside ἔσσεται, ἔσεται, ἔσται); πεσέονται 'will fall', Att. πεσοῦμαι (pres. πίπτω); πλευσοῦμαι beside πλεύσομαι 'will float'; φευξοῦμαι beside φεύξομαι 'will flee'. The Att.-Ion. examples are always in the middle voice.

This type appears to be a blend of those in -σω and -εω, and that may be all there is to it. The blending might however be of much earlier ingredients, namely the thematized suffix *-H_1s-$^e/o$- seen in G and the differently thematized *-H_1s-y^e/o- seen in BS and InIr (**457C**), whence *-H_1sey^e/o-.

a. Some authorities separate Hom. πεσέονται, Att. πεσοῦμαι from this type and trace it instead to *πετέομαι (an Attic future). But there is nothing against the derivation from *πετσέομαι, since for metrical reasons -σσ- could not stand in the quotable Homeric forms. The aor. forms, as in ἔπεσον, can have no other history than *ἔπεσσον < *ἐπετσ-, and whatever the explanation is for the shortening of the -σσ- in the aor., it presumably would be valid for the fut. too.

LATIN

501. In L the simple future is for the most part the reflex of the PIE subjunctive (**534**, **537**), which originally referred to a future event whose likelihood is shaded by some doubt or other condition.

1. The clearest formation is the unique future formation of the verb 'be', consisting of the non-ablauting *e*-grade of the root with a thematic vowel, that is, *H_1esoH_2, *$H_1eses(i)$, *$H_1eset(i)$, whence L *erō*, *eris*, *erit* by regular sound changes (**74.2**, **71.3**, **173**) and formally superimposable on Ved. *ásā-(ni)*, *ásas(i)*, *ásat(i)*.

2. It is only slightly less clear in the 3rd and 4th conj. which, being thematic, show the 'long vowel' subjunctive, which is the contraction of the marker of the subjunctive with the thematic vowel: **-(y)e-es(i)*, **-(y)e-et(i)* > **-(y)ēs(i)*, **-(y)ēt(i)*. From this come not only L *legēs*, *leget* (< **-ēt*) but the G subj. φέρῃς, φέρῃ (and the less remodeled φέρωμεν, φέρητε).

The 1sg. ending would have been *-ō*, as in *erō* and *-bō*. In the 3rd and 4th conjugations this would have been homophonous with the present, and that fact must underlie the replacement of the regular ending by one which was formally distinct. The exact source of *-am*, earlier *-ām*, is however a mystery.

3. The 1st and 2nd conjugations (475-8) form the future with an element *-b-* with the endings of *erō*. This is at bottom the same formation as the imperfect in **-bā-* (498) and, like that formation, is partly transparent and partly opaque. Obviously the root is **bhū-*, as in *fuī*, and in Falisc. PIPAFO 'I will drink'. The details of the inflection are uncertain, however. If the form was conservative, the subj. would have been formed with the zero grade, a unique feature of this root: **bhuHet(i)*, **bhuHes(i)*, **bhuHome* (or **bhuw-*), as reflected in Ved. *bhúvas*, *bhúvat*; and presumably its development was parallel to the imperfect in **fŭā-* (498). What stood before the finite verb in **fuw^e/o-* and **fuwā-* was presumably identical.

a. In early L there are instances of this in the 4th conj. as well, as in *dormībō.*

502. ITALIC *s*-FUTURES. Early L *faxō* 'will do', *capsō* 'will take', though commonly called future perfects, are simple futures functionally. Formations like the two examples are mainly from the 3rd conj.; the corresponding formation for the 1st conj. is seen in *indicāssō*, subj. *negāssim*, and so on; and 2nd conj. forms in *prohibēssīs* (common in prayers), *habēssit*; the 4th conj. in *ambīssit.* It is tempting to classify the *faxō* type in particular with the G futures in **-(H$_1$)s^e/o-* (500) and the seemingly identical formation in Sab., but the subjunctives (that is, optatives, 543) in *faxim* (*faxīs*), *axim*, *ausim* suggest rather that these are in origin subjunctives of *s*-aorists. If this interpretation is correct, they must belong to a period of development prior to the L coalescence of the original aor. and perf. into the perf. tense (522-31). The aor./perf. amalgam differs from the *faxō* type in a number of important ways: (1) the stem formation itself (*faxō* and the like must be much later than the extremely antique root aor. *fēcī* which prevailed in the original function); (2) special mediopassive forms never developed in the L perfect—so periphrastic *factus est*—but did in the case of *faxitur* and the like; and (3) there is a different formation for the infinitive, as in *impetrāssere* (cf. *fēcisse*).

In the forms in *-āssō*, *-ēssō*, *-īssō* the precise source of the *-ss-* is uncertain, and much discussed. It is probably a L development, that is, it continues no inherited type. Most likely such formations were suggested by the proportion seen in the subjunctive (old opt.): **deixēm* : *deixīm* :: **amāssēm* : *X*, that is, they are based on paradigms with similarly-formed stems in the *s*-aor.-type perf. and in the *faxō*-type future. (*Amāssem* for *amāvissem* is the short form of the perf.subj.; **529**.)

a. In Plautine L such forms are commonplace. Their disappearance thereafter (except in a fossilized expression or two, as *haud ausim* 'I wouldn't dare') has been interpreted as pointing to a subliterary or colloquial status for the formation. But this is unlikely: the forms lasted longest in the most formal and solemn kinds of texts, namely laws and ritual formulae, which is the last place where one would expect to find breezy colloquialisms.

THE PUNCTUAL EVENTIVE (AORIST)

503. The only distinctively aorist stem in PIE was the *s*-aorist, formed by the addition of *-*s*- and athematic secondary endings (**419-31**). In G there is no gradation of the root syllable, which if not in the *e*-grade has the same grade as the present. There is evidence however that the G *s*-aorist originally ablauted in a fashion more like the Vedic paradigms (**459**).

The other types of aorist are formally indistinguishable from imperfects; see **413** and **497** regarding what 'makes' a given stem imperfect or aorist. So ἔγραφον is the imperfect of γράφω, while identically formed ἔτραπον is the aor. to τρέπω (imperf. ἔτρεπον); ἔφην is imperf. (φημί; aor. ἔφησα), while identically formed ἔβην is aor. (βαίνω); and so on. The same thing is true of Vedic: *ápāt* 'protected' is the imperf. to *pā́ti* pres., but identically formed *ádhāt* 'put' is an aor. (*dádhāti* pres.). Of course, a form like ἔλιπον, even if nothing else were known about it, would be much more likely to be an aor. than an imperf. The reason for this is not formal but statistical: zero grade of the root is very much more common in thematic aorists than in thematic presents.

It appears that pres. stems were occasionally back-formed from ambiguous aorists, or forms marked for person only (**416**) that formally resembled aorists. The root **leykʷ*- 'leave', an aoristic root, originally formed a characterized pres. (*n*-infix, **454A.1**: Lesb. -λιμπάνω, Ved. *riṇákti*, and L *linquō*) and a root aor., **eleykʷm̥*, **elikʷme*. The former stem is attested in L *līquī* perf., the latter in the Ved. inj. *riktam* 2du. G ἔλιπον aor. is an innovation, a thematic stem based on the pl. stem of the old root aor. (**449**); the usual present in G, λείπω, is historically the aorist stem, the transfer probably beginning in forms marked for person only which were not specifically aor. (they were simply unmarked for the durative/punctual distinction, **416**).

A similar development accounts for λήθω 'escape notice' (next to old λανθάνω), back-formed from ἔληθον, properly an aor. but somehow reinterpreted as an imperf. The lack of good outside connections makes the matter hard to judge with confidence, however. Similar transfers in Indic are fewer in number owing to the early loss of the aor.: for example, the pres.

cayate 'notices' (aoristic root *ci-*, PIE *k^w*ey-*) is in origin the subj. of root-aor. *ácet*, and displaces the earlier redup. pres. *cikéṣi* (AV), imperf. *áciket* (RV).

In Ital., as in Gmc. and Celt., the aorist was lost as a distinct tense. The three groups differ however in the fate of the aor. vis-à-vis other tenses. In L the aor. stems that survived are a component of the perfect system (522–31) and will be discussed in that connection.

The Greek Sigmatic Aorist

504. The G sigmatic aorist represents the PIE *s*-aorist, but with an important innovation. Originally the formation was athematic, as 1sg. **-s-m̥*, 2sg. **-s-s*, 3sg. **-s-t*. Albeit obscured by the action of sound laws affecting word-final consonant clusters, this is still the state of affairs in InIr.: to the root *hā-* 'leave', Ved. *áhās* 2sg. (**-ss*), *ahās* 3sg. (**-st*); to the root *bhī-* 'be frightened', 1pl. *ábhāiṣma*, 3pl. *abhāiṣur*; cf. *mā bhāis* 'do not be afraid'; to the root *nī-* 'lead', 2pl. *anāiṣṭa*. For G, parallel forms would be ἐλῡ(σ)α (< **-sm̥*), ×ἔλῡς (< **-ss*), ×ἔλῡς (< **-st*), ×ἔλῡ(σ)μεν, ×ἔλῡστε, ×ἔλῡ(σ)α (< **-n̥t*). Once the 3pl. was remade as ἔλῡσαν after them. -ον (like the imperfects of athematic stems, 430.1), the -σα- spread to all the indicative forms except 3sg. -σε, with -ε imported from the thematic aor. and the perf.; and further to the optative, the imperative (except 2sg. -σον), and participle (though this may partly reflect a PIE **-sn̥t-*, 556)—in fact, to virtually the whole aorist system except the subj.

The only straightforward proportion was something like ἔφερον : ἔλῡσαν :: ἐφέρομεν : *X*, where *X* = ἐλῡ́σαμεν. Exactly how -σα- spread beyond that point is less obvious. Original *ἔλῡστε 2pl. would have been inconsistent with flanking ἐλῡ́σαμεν and ἔλῡσαν, of course. However obscure the means, the motive for reworking the 2sg. and 3sg. is clear: as a result of sound laws they were not only homophonous but unmarked for person altogether. (The likeliest shape for the 3sg. consistent with this remodeling, ×ἔλῡσα, is not found. It was probably uttered from time to time, but its homophony with the 1sg. would have been a disadvantage.)

505. 1. From roots or verb stems ending in a cons. the usual results of the combinations with -σ- are observed. Thus (213–5) ἔγραψα 'scratched, wrote', ἔδειξα 'pointed out', ἔπεισα 'persuaded' < **e-peit^h-sa*. For -ξα and -σα from verbs in -ζω, see 465.3. For roots and stems ending in resonants, the results are those of ORIGINAL **-ns-*, **-ls-* (228.1, 229): ἔφηνα 'made to appear' < **e-p^{h}an-sa*, ἔστειλα 'set in order' < **e-stel-sa*, ἔφθειρα 'destroyed' < **e-p^{h}t^{h}er-sa*. But ὦρσα 'stirred up' (ὄρνῡμι) shows what looks like the more typical Attic treatment (229.1), and NB ἔκελσα 'ran aground'. Both of the latter are however secondary forms in the first place: the present stems being characterized (ὄρνῡμι < **r̥-new-* or **H$_3$r̥-new-*), κέλλω < **kel-n-H-*, *n*-infix), the original should have been of the root or thematic types (so in fact Ved. root-aor. *ārta* 3sg. midd.). In G the fut. and σ-aor. routinely have similar details in their stems, so here too fut. κέλσω, a patently secondary form (instead of ˣκελέω, 500.2-3). A genuinely old σ-aor. would have been ˣἐκέλεσα < *e-kelH̥₁-s-, like ἤμεσα 'vomited' < *e-wemH̥₁-.

2. From verb stems ending in a vowel the retention of the intervocalic -σ- (172**b**) is due to the analogy of forms like ἔγραψα.

The great majority of verb stems ending in a vowel have a long vowel before -σα, as ἔλῡσα 'loosed', ἐτῑ́μησα (Dor. ἐτῑ́μᾱσα) 'honored', ἐφίλησα 'loved', ἐδήλωσε 'was clear'. In some this is the true form of the verb stem, as in the case of denominatives in -άω (468.1) and statives in -έω (452, 468.2), where the short vowel in the present is secondary. But it is largely due to analogical extension, especially in causative/frequentatives (456.2) and some types of denominative (462.1). Many other verbs, though not aboriginally inflected as *s*-aorists, had long vowels (or syllabic plus laryngeal, 103-9) from the beginning, as φῡ- 'become', δρᾱ- 'run off' (< *dr̥H₂- or *dreH₂-), πλη- 'fill' (< *pl̥H₁- or *pleH₁-), γνω- 'understand' (< *ǵneH₃-).

3. Those that have a short vowel before -σα are from stems ending in -σ-, as ἐτέλεσα 'completed' (Hom. ἐτέλεσσα, pres. τελείω < *teleh-yō), ἔζεσα 'boiled', ἔτρεσα 'flee', and ἔσβεσα 'quenched'; or else from roots ending in a short vowel from *H̥, as Hom. ἔμεσσα (εμέω 'vomit', *wemH̥₁-), ἐδάμασα 'subdued' (by assimilation for *δεμα- < *demH̥₂-), ἐστόρεσα 'scattered' (by metathesis for *ἐστεροσα < *sterH̥₃-). The Homeric forms in -σσα, parallel to forms in -σα which are themselves commonly attested in Homer as well, are usually explained as imported from forms like ἐτέλεσσα. (It is noteworthy and puzzling, however, if that explanation is the correct one, that no similar importation of the parallel type of fut. τελέσσω took place into other fut. formations.)

In some verbs there is fluctuation, as, from αἰνέω 'tell; extol', Hom. ᾔνησα but Att. ᾔνεσα (the same discrepancy in the fut. αἰνήσω, αἰνέσω; and cf. Aeol. αἴνημι pres.). All of these forms are secondary to begin with, being based on a pseudo-root αἰν(ε)- abstracted from the old pres. *H₂i-ne-H₁-/*H₂i-n-H̥₁- to a root evidently *H₂eyH₁-, though there are few if any satisfactory cognates.

THE GREEK UNSIGMATIC OR SECOND AORIST

506. THEMATIC. Most of these belong to the type which has the weak grade of the root and the accent originally on the thematic vowel (449, 503). Thus ἔλιπον, ἔφυγον, ἔτραπον, ἔδρακον, ἔσχον (ἔχω), ἐπτόμην (πέτομαι), ἑσπόμην (ἕπω), ἔλαβον (λαμβάνω). A few have the *e*-grade, as ἔτεκον (τίκτω), ἐγενόμην (γίγνομαι), ἔτεμον (τέμνω) beside ἔταμον. The accent proper to the former type is preserved in the infin. and pple., as λιπεῖν, λιπών, and is extended to the others, as τεκεῖν, τεκών (for *τέκειν, τέκων). That is, it becomes a characteristic of the aor.

A few have reduplication, as ἤγαγον (ἄγω), Hom. ἐκέκλετο (κέλομαι 'urge on'), λέλαθον (λανθάνω 'cause to forget'). Of the same origin is εἶπον 'said' (Hom. ἔειπον) < *eweikʷon (ϝειπ- attested in many dial., as Cret. 3pl.

subj. ϝειποντι, with -ō-) < **e-weik^w- < *e-we-wk^w-* (61.1a) superimposable on Ved. *ávocam* (root *vac-*). Ved. agrees with G in assigning distinctively causative sense to such formations, as seen above. A coincidence may seem implausible, but a theory of common inheritance has to explain why there is no such causative force in G εἶπον, Ved. *ávocam*, the only redup. aorist stem which is likely to be inherited.

507. Athematic. 1. These are mostly forms of the root class without gradation but with shortening of the vowel in the 3rd pl., as ἔβλην 'threw' (**e-g^wleH₁-*), ἔβην 'went' (**e-g^weH₂-*), ἔγνων 'understood' (**egneH₃-*), 3pl. Hom. ἔβαν, Dor. ἔγνον (429). This pattern is paralleled in Vedic, which however shows it also in formations where it is not found in G: *ádāma* 'we gave', *ádhāma* 'we put', unlike G ἔδομεν and ἔθεμεν (3, below). (Whether paradigms with full grade in all but the 3pl. are inherited or the result of leveling is still being debated.)

2. In G, the so-called η-aorists are in origin imperfects to present stems built with the stative suffix **-eH₁-* (452), as ἐσάπη 'was/became rotten' (pres. σήπω), though in the later language these lose salient stative force (so Att. ἐμίγην 'mixed', which is nothing more than the aor. to pres. μίγνῡμι). A disguised form of this formation is Hom. ἔστην (Dor. ἔστᾱν), ἔστημεν, ἔστητε, from **e-stH₂-eH₁-* 'was standing'—whose form uncharacteristically parts company with the paradigms of δίδωμι (ἔδωκα, ἔδομεν) and τίθημι (ἔθηκα, ἔθεμεν) (3, below). The development of στᾱ- < **stH₂-eH₁-*, in which the preceding laryngeal colors the vowel and the following one lengthens it, is paralleled in ἐβίων 'got out alive' (Hom.), later 'was alive', from **e-g^wiH₃-eH₁-*.[1]

3. The aorists of τίθημι, ἵημι, and δίδωμι are peculiar in having their singular stem built with -κ-: ἔθηκα, ἧκα (ἔηκα), ἔδωκα. The antiquity of this formation is very strongly supported by L *fēcī* 'did' and *iēcī* 'threw' (*faciō*, *iaciō* being secondary elaborations based on these; but only the former actually has *k*-less stems as well, like *condō* 'put together, found'). But it is otherwise unattested and its status in the parent language is obscure.

4. The alpha-thematic aorists developed from root aorists along the same lines that -σα- became the sigmatic aor. marker: **eǵhewm̥* 'I poured' > ἔχε(ϝ)α by regular sound laws, but ἔχεας 2sg., ἔχεε 3sg. replaced original *ἔχευς, *ἔχευ (cf. conservative middle χύτο). Hom. ἔχευα beside ἔχεα indirectly confirms the quondam existence of *ἔχευ 3sg; it is obviously a leveling in the opposite direction from the leveling that eventually prevailed. Like ἔχεα is Hom. ἔκηα 'kindled' < **ekāwa* (pres. καίω < **kawhyō*, fut. καύσω) and like ἔχευα are ἄλευαι imperat. 'avoid' (ἀλέομαι), ἔσσευα 'chased'

---

[1] G ἐβίων is usually taken as a root aor.; but as the root in question was not aoristic it should not have had a root aorist.

(σεύω < ? *$k^{(w)}$*yew*-). Arc. απυδοας (functionally equivalent to ἀποδούς pres. pple. 'making restitution') has been taken among other things to point to an unattested aor. **edowa* 'I gave' (cf. L *duim*, **488Ab**). It is better taken as based on a 3pl. *ἔδοαν, with -αν transplanted to vowel stems from its original site in consonant paradigms, as is seen here and there in dial. (for example Boeot. εθεαν for original ἔθεν 'they put').

a. Att. ἤνεγκα 'I carried' has over the years been explained in various ways. Given the functional gulf between perf. and aor. in early G, it is implausible to suppose (as many have) that the form is in origin a perf. In fact, the Vedic root aor. to this root is precisely superimposable on the G stem, both pointing to **e-H₁nenḱ-* (root **H₁nenḱ-*). In Vedic the stems of the root aor. and the perf. do fall together, thanks to sound laws, so 1sg. **H₁e-H₁nonḱ-* perf. and **e-H₁nenḱ-* aor. both become *ānaṃś-*, which does not look much like either a perf. or an aor. Formal confusion is a general risk in this remarkable paradigm: Ved. aor. *ānaṃśúr* 3pl. is commonly misclassified as a perf., when in fact the real perf. would have been *ānaśúr**; cf. the perf. middle *ānaśé*. In some varieties of G, including later Att., the stem was thematized, whence 1sg. ἤνεγκον and others (but 2sg. only ἤνεγκας).

Adding to the confusion, most dialects have a form ἤνεικα, which is unrelated to ἤνεγκα. It is made up of preverb **en-* with root **seyk-* 'reach (for)' seen elsewhere in G in ῞ἵκω, Dor. εἵκω (probably the same form originally, **76d**) 'reach, come to', ἵκτωρ, ἱκτήρ (ῐ) 'suppliant'. The replacement of earlier ἤνεγκα by ἤνεικα resulted from the coincidental similarity of form and function. Conflated forms, which would be expected even in the absence of direct evidence, happen actually to be attested, as epigraphic Att. ηνειγκαν 3pl.

b. εἶπα beside εἶπον 'I said', rare in Hom. (εἶπας, εἴπατε) but frequent in Att., Ion., and other dial. (cf. Cret. προϝειπατω, Lac. προϝειπαhας) is hardly to be explained as an inherited by-form, as the reduplicated aor. was thematic already in PIE. It seems rather to be formed after the analogy of other aorists in -α-. But no explanation has been found for why the α-thematic forms are early and widespread in this particular verb. In later times, of course, such a shift is frequent, as ἦλθα for ἦλθον 'I came', similarly εὗρα 'I discovered' (for εὗρον), ἔφαγα 'I devoured' (for ἔφαγον), and this is the source of the normal type of non-sigmatic aor. in NG, as έφυγα, έφυγαν 'I, they fled' (classical ἔφυγον).

508. THE GREEK AORIST PASSIVE. Early G agrees with InIr. in using middle forms of the usual aor. stems with passive force, as Hom. βλῆτο sometimes 'was thrown'. This use is encroached upon by specific formations, the G aor. passives in -ην and -θην—both with the ACTIVE secondary endings, and in Hom. often with an active meaning as well.

The inflection of both types is the same as that of ἔβλην, with -η- throughout except for the regular shortening to -ε- before -ντ-, as in the participle and the old 3pl. -εν: Hom. ἄγεν 'they were shattered' (ἄγνῡμι) and κόσμηθεν 'they were arranged' (κοσμέω), beside -ησαν as in Att.

1. The type in -ην has been variously explained, most commonly as stemming originally from active athem. aorists which happen to end in -η-, for example ἔβλην (actually attested in the active in Hom. ξυμβλήτην 'threw together', infin. συμβλήμεναι), midd. βλῆτο (< **gʷl̥H₁-to*). Such stems very commonly had intransitive force, and frequently appear beside *y*ᵉ/ₒ-presents which are likewise largely intrans. The transition to passive func-

tion involved the same kind of semantic reassessment as the development of the Indic *-yáte* type into the passive (456.1).

This explanation can be improved by appealing not to aor. roots that happen to end in -η- but more particularly to STATIVE STEMS with the element -η- < *-*eH₁*- (452, 468.2). Many of the Homeric forms that are not manifestly active make just as good sense as stative or passive: ἐάγη 'broke/ was broken', ἐκάη 'burned/was burned', μίγη 'mingled/was mingled', ἐχάρην 'rejoiced/was glad', φάνη 'appeared'. (The glosses 'was so-and-so' here are not to be understood as passives, as in *Washington was burned by the British in the War of 1812*, but as statives as in *The coffee was cold and the oatmeal was burned.*) The special circumstance that led to the development of true passive force for these old statives may have been the the formally similar (but probably unrelated) -θη- passives (next).

2. The type in -θην is much commoner than the preceding in Att. (and unlike the η-formations, is characteristically passive already in Hom.). Occasionally both types occur from the same verb, as Hom. μιγήμεναι and μιχθήμεναι 'to mingle'; ἐφάνην 'appeared' and ἐφάνθην 'was'; ἐγράφην 'was written', later ἐγράφθην. In what look like older formations, the root is in zero grade (so ἐτάθην 'was strained' < **e-tn̥-*); later, stems typically agree with the σ-aor.; indeed, the aoristic sigma is sometimes even imported into the passive formation, as ἐπετάσθην after ἐπέτασα, σ-aorist to πετάννῡμι 'spread out'. The latter process was fertilized by passive aorists to *s*-stem denominatives, as ἐτελέσθη '[a rite] was performed' (τελέω < **teleh-yō*).

The element -θη- itself is of enigmatic origin.

STATIVE VERBS

509. THE PIE STATIVE was formally different from the eventive (present/imperfect and aorist) types in most person endings, in the formation of the finite stem, and the participle.

This is the paradigm traditionally known as the PERFECT TENSE. In fact it was neither perfective (completive) nor a tense: it was instead STATIVE, and tenseless (407 fn.). To begin with it was a formation limited to roots that were semantically appropriate, though not exhaustively: as mentioned in 410, roots with such palpably stative meanings as 'sit', 'lie', and 'be' were inflected in PIE as eventives.

Unlike the interplay between punctual and durative senses of roots, most eventives are hard to see in a stative light (it is doubtful that 'be in the state of killing' or 'be in the state of eating' even make sense). But inherently stative notions can be recast as eventives, as in 'have/take', 'know/ find out', 'be dead/die'. And of course what amount to derivational categories entail an eventive based on an inherently stative notion:

ingressive (and punctual): 'die' ('be dead'); 'get full' ('be full');

causative/factitive: 'make full' ('be full'); 'bring to mind' ('have in mind').

Not all opportunities along such lines are taken advantage of: although many languages derive 'kill' from 'be dead', for example, IE languages as a rule do not.

For purely functional reasons, the eventive verb categories of voice and tense were not applicable to the statives, except perhaps with some idiomatic force. A state is neither middle nor active, for two connected reasons: the grammatical subject of a stative verb is not an agent, and a state has no outcome. 'Is dead for his own benefit' is pragmatically marginal. Tense contrasts, for the reasons described in 407, are either impossible for states or irrelevant.

Another eventive category is not applicable to the PIE stative: in InIr. there is an extreme rarity of perfect optatives in the earliest texts. In the Rigveda, with its several hundred instances of the perf. *véda* alone, there are in all only 14 optatives formed to perfect stems; and of these, all but four are in the first and tenth books or are otherwise in late passages. This suggests that the stative did not originally form optatives. There is no thinkable pragmatic basis for this; conditions and exhortations are perfectly at home in states—*If I were rich . . .*, *If I knew . . .*, *Let us be content . . .* are all pragmatically normal. The explanation therefore must be morphological: what is traditionally known as the optative marker was in fact a deverbative affix proper to the eventive system—a primary eventive affix correlative with the nasal infix, iterative **-sḱ^e/o-*, and caus./intens. **-éy^e/o-* (450-8). Thus like those suffixes it would not be found in the stative paradigm. (See also 533, 538.)

Imperatives are less obviously utilitarian for stative notions, but have some use (*Be mindful of . . .*, or Sir Epicure Mammon's advice, *Be rich!*). Old-looking imperatives, though few in number, are in fact attested.

Once the stative system was captured by the tense system of various daughter languages, it usually acquired such attributes of eventive verbs as voice and mood. There are some notable exceptions, such as the failure of perfect passive FORMS to develop in Italic, though of course the FUNCTION 'passive of the perfect' did arise as expected (530a).

In Homer still, and also in the Rigveda (though less commonly), the perfect indicates the state of the subject. (A fuller definition—'PRESENT state of the subject'—is a misconception; 407 fn.) Thus πέποιθα 'am persuaded', in contrast to πείθω 'persuade' (but much like the eventive πείθομαι in meaning); τέθνηκε 'is dead'; ἕστηκε 'is standing'. In later G the perfect is for the most part a past tense, and one formed to a great many verbs for which stative force is out of the question. But certain forms retain the ancient stative sense, such as πέποιθα above, οἶδα 'I know', and μέμονα 'I yearn for'.

Similarly in L there are three 'perfects of present meaning', so called, (*ōdī* 'I hate', *meminī* 'I remember', and *(g)nōvī* 'I understand'). The fewness of these relics of the earlier system is presumably due to the comparatively shallow time depth of our Italic texts. But the importation of details of the primary endings into the perf. in prehistoric Italic (530) indicates that as the tense system evolved, at some stage the old perfect was aligned with the present system. In G and Indic too, when middle paradigms were invented for the perf., they were formed with PRIMARY endings, that is the endings characteristic of real present (hic-et-nunc) tenses: πέπεισμαι 'am persuaded', Ved. *babhre* 3sg. 'carries, carried'.

In Germanic, where the perfect paradigm became the preterite tense, some fourteen stems nevertheless remain stative and in effect tenseless, though traditionally termed 'preterite-presents' (that is, verbs which like L *meminī* and G μέμονα inflect like a past tense but have stative meaning), such as **lais-* 'understand', **kann-* 'know how', **ōg-* 'fear', **wait-* 'know', **skal-* 'be obliged', and **mag-* 'be able'.

These are the source of the modal auxiliaries of English, German, and the other Germanic languages, still characterized by oddities of inflection such as a lack of a 3sg. *-s*, as *he can, may, shall*, and so on. Some verbs that belonged here originally have shifted to ordinary inflection, as *dare* and *own*; others have simply been lost, as 'fear' and 'understand' (except as entombed in derivatives like *learn*). The verb *will*, which currently is a modal auxiliary, was originally an ordinary verb. NHG *wissen* 'know' retains some of the preterital inflection of the preterite-presents *ich weiß* 1sg. and 3sg., *wir wissen* 1pl.; and uniquely, it remains a main verb.

In Hitt., the paradigm known as the *ḫi*-verbs aligns with the PIE stative convincingly on the formal level: *o*-grade of root and, in the singular, the characteristic stative endings. But there is no functional similarity—both the *ḫi*-verbs and the Hitt. congener of the eventive paradigm ('*mi*-verbs') are both ordinary presents. Nor is there any lexical agreement, that is, agreement on which roots occur in which paradigm. So for example **dheH₁-* 'put', which in IE is the type and model of the aoristic/eventive root, in Hitt. inflects as a *ḫi*-verb.

510. ERRONEOUS VIEWS OF THE PIE STATIVE. As the functional nature of the PIE stative has become clear, three long-held views have become untenable. They nevertheless are still repeated, and so merit discussion here.

1. *The meaning of the perfect was '(present) state resulting from previous action or experience'.* This is supported by such examples as 'was persuaded' = 'trusts', 'has seen' = 'knows', or 'has died' = 'is dead'. But the fact is that MOST predications, whether events or states, and however expressed in a language, can be analyzed—if one is determined to do so—as 'resulting from previous action or experience'. On the other hand, consider such PIE statives as 'is brave (dares)', 'hates', 'yearns for', 'owns/has', 'prevails'; these are all perfectly stative ideas, but entail no obvious (and certainly no necessary) precedent action or experience. 'Fears', 'understands', and 'is able' are more amenable to such a conception but hardly support the analysis even so, because they can be the result of any number of previous experiences.

2. In earlier technical literature, and occasionally even these days, attention is drawn to *pervasive similarities between the endings of the middle (eventive) and of the perfect*, on which basis some ancient unity (or point of tangency) between the two categories of verb is to be inferred. In reality, most of the endings of the perf. (513-4) align with the eventive ACTIVE endings, as the 3sg. **-e* (perf.) which bears the same relationship to the *t*-less 3sg. eventives (it is in effect the full grade thereof) that the 1sg. **-H_2e* bears to the eventive them. **-H_2*. Between the forms of the eventive middle and the stative there is no similarity at all in the 1pl. (stative **-me*, eventive **-medhH_2*, **-mosdhH_2*) and 2pl. (stative **-e*, eventive **-dhwo*)(437.2). Here too the stative endings are actually most similar to the ACTIVE eventives **-me*, **-te* (the stative **-e* being the *t*-less equivalent of the latter). In sum, out of the nine person endings there is only a single point of noteworthy similarity between the two paradigms: the 2sg. (middle **-tH_2o*, primary **-tH_2or*, 436.2; cf. perf. **-(s)tH_2e*, 514.2).

a. Functionally there is a trifling (and uninteresting) point of tangency between some eventive middles and the old stative. Some mostly intransitive middles are very similar in feel to perfects, πείθομαι and πέποιθα being virtual synonyms in some contexts. This is a convergence upon functional common ground, however, and not a point of departure.

3. Despite the immense (and obvious) antiquity of transitive statives like **woyde* 'knows' and **memone* 'has in mind', it is nevertheless repeated by respected authorities that *the meaning of the perfect in Homer and the Vedas was typically intransitive.*

511. In the later-attested IE languages, the reflex of the PIE perfect is prevailingly an anterior (preterite) tense. It is the basis for the 'strong', that is, ablauting, preterites of Gmc., like NE *drank*, *bore*, and *sat*, and is one of the ingredients in the L perfect tense. In G from the 5th century BC on, the perf. functions much like NE phrasal verbs with auxiliary *have* (that is, action completed in the past but with implication of a continuing effect or state). The further step, the use of the tense as a simple past tense, the 'historical perfect' or the 'narrative perfect', is sometimes observed in Attic writers, and becomes common in the Hellenistic period.[1] This amounted to a loss of a functional contrast between the perf. and the aor., which proved fatal for the perf.; in any case it disappeared except for a few survivals passing as aorist forms (the aor. being the preterital completive tense of NG, much like the NE simple past). Its earlier function was reincarnated in periphrastic expressions like έχω γράψας or έχω γεγραμμένον 'I have written'.

---

[1] A similar shift of the perfect to the role of a simple past has recently taken place in colloquial French, where for example the difference between *j'ai vu* and *je vis* is no longer parallel to *I have seen* and *I saw*, but is rather one of casual vs. formal style.

In post-Vedic Skt. likewise, the perfect took on the role of the simple past, with the same result as in G except that here it was aorist that became extinct. Another difference between G and Skt. is that in the latter the perf. was more or less in competition with the imperfect and freely interchangeable with it; it was never as common as the imperf., however, in part because not all roots formed a perfect stem, even in later Skt.[1]

Much as in L and early Gmc., in post-Vedic Skt. there are remnants of the earlier state of affairs: in the Brāhmaṇas, a number of perfect stems still had present or stative force: *dādhāra* 'is secure', *dīdāya* 'shines', *bibhāya* 'fears'. By the Epic period, they have dwindled to two, *veda* 'knows' and *āha* 'says'. (The last is hardly a stative notion. The explanation seems to be that the form originally meant something like 'regards; holds the opinion', but cognates outside InIr. are doubtful.)

FORMATION OF THE STATIVE

512. STEM. The stem of the stative was formed with the *o*-grade of the root in the sg., and zero grade in the du. and pl. The root was prefixed by a reduplicating element made up of the initial consonant of the root followed by the vowel *-*e*-. For the details of the consonants in the reduplication, see **443.2B–3**.

The stem **woyd*-/**wid*- 'know', which is very widely attested in IE languages, is without the reduplicated prefix in all of them. Thus G οἶδα, Ved. *véda*, OCS *vědě*, Go. *wait*, all from **woyd*-H_2*e*. The lack of reduplication in this stem is however apparently not unique. In the Rigveda five additional stems have what look like perfect inflection (on the basis of the person endings) without reduplication, for a total of eight attestations. The significance of this is uncertain, as several of them are in hymns improbably late for a truly archaic feature. Decidedly better attested in the RV are unreduplicated participles, or what look like perfect participles, notably *dāśvás*- 'worshipping' (which occurs well over a hundred times), and some others. On the basis of their palpably eventive meanings, however ('conquering', 'worshipping', 'oppressing'), most of these cannot be taken as ancient perfects. The unique *jānúṣas* gen.sg. 'knowing' is right semantically, but is (a) irregularly formed even apart from the question of reduplication, and (b) occurs in a very late hymn. The well-attested *mīḷh(u)vás*- 'bountiful' is semantically appropriate, but the formation is enigmatic: there is no contemporary verbal root ˣ*mīḷh*-/*mīḍh*-, though it has satisfactory cognates pointing to a PIE nominal **mizdh*- 'prize' or the like. (The traditional derivation of the form—from *mih*- 'piss', not obviously a stative notion—seems far-fetched.)

Glottogonically, there are two options for reduplication in the stative stem: either **woyd*-/**wid*- shows that there was a class of PIE perfects that

---

[1] According to native grammarians, the perfect was used to narrate events not witnessed by the speaker, the imperfect was for events in which the speaker had participated personally. Such a distinction is known in natural language; but no Indic text of any period exhibits the contrast claimed by the grammarians.

never had reduplication; or, in the alternative, that that stem once had it like all the others, but lost it. The discovery that Hitt. has a paradigm (the *ḫi*-verbs) agreeing very well with the IE stative in the matter of endings and ablaut grade of the root, but without reduplication as a regular or even characteristic feature of the stem, has tipped the balance of evidence in favor of the relic status of unreduplicated **woyd-*. But in truth, even before the discovery of Hitt., the Gmc. 'preterite-present' verbs—properly appraised—had pointed in the same direction: these either never had reduplication or else lost it, but as they are obviously among the most basic vocabulary, and in all regards the most conservative perfect formations in the language, it is much likelier that they never had it.[1] Nor is there evidence that L *(g)nōvī* has lost reduplication. But there is a stronger argument still: the unlikelihood—the virtual impossibility—that an item like 'know' would be in the vanguard of innovation. That verb, in fact, has one of the most conservative paradigms in IE languages, even rivaling the verb 'be' when it comes to retaining inherited details of inflection that differ from the regular paradigms of the language.

Nevertheless, the participle to this paradigm has been interpreted as evidence for just such a lost reduplication. G εἰδώς and possibly Go. *weitwods* 'witness' point to **weyd-wos-*. But no full grade is called for in the pple., still less *e*-grade. The mystery is explained if one postulates aboriginal ***we-wid-wos-*, with dissimilatory loss of the medial *-*w*- yielding **weydwos-*. The form is in every detail the expected one, and the early loss of the middle of three *w*'s is easy to understand. The best interpretation of these contradictory data is that a newfangled (which is to say more normally formed) participle ***wewidwos-* was added to the archaic non-reduplicating finite paradigm seen in **woyd-H_2e*, **wid-me*, and the rest. Both G and InIr. indicate that the pple. is less resistant to change than the finite forms: in both languages the finite forms are aberrant because conservative, however much tinkered-with in detail (such as G ἴσμεν for ἴδμεν); but in one or the other language—it is immaterial whether Ved. *vidvás-* or Hom. εἰδώς is the innovation—the stem-form of the participle was remodeled.

a. It has been suggested that G and InIr. represent an evolutionary extreme rather than a mirror of prehistory, that to begin with verbs formed the perfect with EITHER *o*-grade of the root, as in **woyde*, the Gmc. pret.-pres., and the Hitt. forms; OR ELSE with reduplication. But stems with both features are copiously attested in the IE languages apart from Hitt.

b. It is noteworthy that among L perfects with reduplicated stems those to roots in -*a*- (such as *pepercī*, root *parc-*; *tetigī*, root *tag-*; *cecidī*, root *cad-*) are unusually prominent, presumably because these roots had no distinctive *o*-grade.

---

[1] For most of the pret.-pres. roots it is not possible to tell about previously existing reduplication, but for those corresponding to the Strong Class IV and V verbs, the plural (weak grade) stems are significant: if they were formerly reduplicated stems, **skal-* 'must', **man-* 'intend', **mag-* 'be able', and **(ga)nah-* 'suffice' should have had the pl. stems ×*skēl-*, ×*mēn-*, ×*mēg-*, and ×*(ga)nēg-*, like **bēr(um)* '(we) carried', **sēt(um)* '(we) sat' (525.6a).

513. Endings. The endings were added directly to the (reduplicated) root. The inflection is therefore generally analogous to the eventive athematic types.

The discussion of the endings will be based on the following evidence:

	Vedic	Greek (Homer)	Gothic	Hittite	
				present	*preterite*
1*sg.*	véda[1]	*(ϝ)οἶδα*	wait	a-ar-ḫi[2]	(a-)ar-aḫ-ḫu-un
2	véttha	*(ϝ)οἶσθα*	waist	a-ar-ti	ša-ak-ta[3]
3	véda	*(ϝ)οἶδε*	wait	a-ri	a-ar-aš, a-ar-ta
1*pl.*	vidmá[1]	*(ϝ)ἴδμεν*	witum	e-ir-u-e-ni	e-ru-u-en
2	vidá[1]	*(ϝ)ἴστε*	wituþ	e-ir-te-ni	ir-te-in
3	vidúr	*((ϝ)ἴσ(σ)ᾱσι)*	witun	a-ra-an-zi	e-ri-(e-)ir

1. The final vowels of these three endings usually scan long in the RV, but are rarely so written (514.1).
2. 'Arrive'. The root **woyd-* 'know' is not attested in Hitt.
3. 'You knew', /sakt/? /sakst/?; cf. pres. *ša-ak-ḫi, ša-ak-ti, ša-ak-ki.*

A note on the hittite forms.
The Hitt. present endings have been disguised by the addition of the primary marker **-i* imported from the eventive type (the Hitt. *mi*-verbs). The resulting diphthongs in **-ḫai*, **-t(ḫ)ai*, **-ei*) became *-i*. The preterite endings of the 2sg. and 3sg. are puzzling. In vowel stems the ending is often written *-aš-ta* and the like, often *-aš*, but never ×*-at*. One interpretation is that the actual ending was *-st*, impossible to write as such and particularly inconvenient in the case of consonant stems like *ar-* and *šak-*. If that is correct, *a-ar-aš* and *a-ar-ta* both are orthographic compromises for /arst/ or the like. (Such an ending for the 2sg. is not unwelcome—see 514.2—but in the 3sg. it is an enigma.)

---

514. Endings.

1. The endings easy to reconstruct are 1sg. *$-H_2e$, 3sg. **-e*, 1pl. **-me*. These follow the usual sound laws in the attested languages. But in the Rigveda the great majority of 1pl. perf. forms are found in lines that scan better if the ending is *-mā* rather than *-mă* as transmitted. Similarly, though in slightly lesser degree, the 1sg. ending often scans *-ā*. The 2pl. is likewise usually *-ā*, but as the 2pl. is not common it is harder to be sure of its statistics. (None of these except *-mā*—which is rare—are written as such in the text, but their scansion is unmistakable.) The explanation for these long vowels is unknown, beyond the certainty that they are not artificialities, as (1) the eventive secondary ending *-ma* shows a similar scansion so rarely that it must be imitative rather than inherited (427), and (2) there is little evidence for scansion in *-ā* in the otherwise homophonous 3sg.

L *-ī* < Lat.-Falisc. **-ai* has a history parallel to Hitt. *-ḫi* (513 note), namely it is the inherited ending **-a* embellished with primary **-i*, whence *-ī* by 75.4; see 530.1.

2. The second persons are more difficult. First, the 2sg. ending, Ved.

-tha, Av. *-θa*, G *-(σ)θα*, has traditionally provided one of the best pieces of evidence for a PIE aspirated series of voiceless stops (131), in accordance with which it has often been reconstructed as **-tha*. More likely is some such shape as *$-tH_2e$, the *H_2 accounting at once for the *a*-vocalism guaranteed by G and for the aspirated stop of PInIr. That reconstruction, however, leaves the G *-θ-* unaccounted for. (A development of G *-θ-* from *tH_2 has been entertained, but is contradicted by much evidence, such as the clear case of G πλατύς rather than ×πλαθύς 'wide' < *$p\c{l}tH_2u$-; cf. Ved. *pṛthú-*.) Another suggestion is that the shape *-θα* next to regular *-τα arose to begin with in formations to roots ending in aspirated stops per Bartholomae's Law (211). But this idea is contrary to the usual treatment of aspirated Bartholomae alternants of endings in G, which are for the most part eliminated (if they ever existed in the first place): γραπτός 'written' for expected *γραφθός, and no trace of Bartholomae 3sg. *-θαι/-θο for -ται/-το.

Possibly the ending was at least sometimes *$-stH_2e$ (? with the eventive **-s-*) rather than *$-tH_2e$. In any case the ending in G is actually attested only as *-σθα*, never unambiguously as *-θα*: so even after vowels, βάλοισθα aor.opt. (βάλλω 'throw'), ἔφησθα imperf. to φημί 'say'. The usual view is that this *-σθα* was transplanted bodily from οἶσθα and ἦσθα, where it is regular. Toch. has some 2sg. pret. in *-st*, however, as does Hitt.: the Hitt. pres. *-ti* points to *$-tH_2e(-i)$, but the pret. *-st*, if that is the correct interpretation (see notes to table 513, above), is evidence for *$-stH_2e$. (There are some clear instances of just *-ta* in Hitt., however, as in *da-(a-)at-ta* 'you took', stem *da-a-*.) L *-istī* is ambiguous as to detail, as there are several possible sources (either etymological or by way of analogy) for the *-is-*, but it nevertheless shows a shape like that of G, Toch., and the Hitt. pret. Indic is ambiguous; at least, the great majority of forms would have lost an original *-s-* between consonants anyway, and the remainder could be analogical. Gmc. evidence points to an *s*-less form.

G *-(σ)θα* (limited to this paradigm and a few others like the imperf. ἦσθα 'was', **493A**, and some Homeric oddities, **425b**) is impossible to derive from *$-tH_2e$, or nearly so; but it could be arrived at from PreG **-sta* < *$-stH_2e$, via the development seen in ἑφθός 'boiled' < **-pst-* (pres. ἕψω): all roots ending in a labial or dorsal stop would have had *-θα* (next to *-στα* after vowels or apical stops), and some such development was likely after liquids as well, though the evidence is poor. The expected outcomes, *-στα and *-θα, were leveled to *-σθα* and *-θα.

All this is uncomfortably speculative. But as the new ending *-ας* all but obliterated the inherited 2sg. perf. ending, it thereby also obliterated evidence for early details of distribution.

3. The 2pl. in all but one IE group is identical to the eventive ending, just like the 1pl. In InIr., however, the ending is *-á*, probably PIE **-é*. The parallelism of the 2pl. and 3sg. endings is striking: both involve otherwise identical endings with and without a **-t-* (**426**). The occurrence of all three *t*-less forms in the same paradigm (3sg. *-e*, 2pl. **-e*, and 3pl. (see 4, below, and **429**)) is significant. Nor is the nearly universal replacement of the

poorly-characterized 2pl. *-*e* any wonder. Poorness of characterization is no drawback in a marker for the 3sg., where *t*-less forms both in the stative and the eventive paradigms were much more persistent.

4. The ending of the 3pl. was evidently *-*r*, namely the *t*-less equivalent of *-*nt* (429). The Hitt. ending of the pret., which is often written -*e-ir* or -*i-e-ir* or with some other combination of plene vowels (31), may have been -*ēr*, and if so aligns with L -*ēre* (< *-*ēr-i*, 530.6). A datum of uncertain significance is the unique Avestan *åŋhāire* 'they are sitting' (PInIr. **āsārai*), which apparently continues a shape *-*ēroy*, a remodeling of original *-*ēror*, 437.3. Although this is found in a present eventive formation, it is in a way a validation of the reconstruction of 3pl. *-*ēr*. The proper distribution and function of this ending remain unexplained, and a genuine long vowel is unexpected. The usual InIr. perf. endings (Ved. -*úr* and Av. -*ərə*, -*arə*) point instead to *-*r̥*, which is however very odd for a tonic ending. There is no direct trace of either one in G, but the importation of the eventive ending in the shape -*αντι* rather than -*οντι* is fractionally easier to explain if the starting point (or one ingredient) was an inherited *-*αρ* < *-*r̥*.

THE GREEK PERFECT SYSTEM

515. The G perfect paradigm which most faithfully reflects the PIE formation as to gradation of the root syllable (as seen in InIr. and Gmc.), and in adding the endings directly to the root, is *οἶδα* 'know'. The regular G treatment of two apical stops (212) accounts for 2pl. *ἴστε* and possibly for the 2sg. *οἶσθα*, though the latter may actually continue **woyd-stH₂e* rather than **woyd-tH₂e* (514.2). The Att. 1pl. *ἴσμεν*, for the more original *ἴδμεν* as in Hom., shows the influence of *ἴστε*. But the 3pl. *ἴσᾱσι* is a new formation. It is from **wid-santi* (cf. the parallel Att. *εἴξᾱσι*, 3pl. of *ἔοικα* 'am like'), whence Hom. *ἰσσᾱσι* beside *ἴσᾱσι*, Dor. *ἴσαντι*. The starting point is 3pl. **wid-san*, Hom. *ἴσαν*, which has -*σαν* from the *σ*-aor.

In Dor., *ἴσαντι* is the basis for other novel forms: 1pl. *ἴσᾱμι* and so on after the analogy of athematic eventives in -*ᾱ*-, as *ἵσταντι* : *ἵστᾱμι* :: *ἴσαντι* : *X*, where *X* = *ἴσᾱμι*.

Unetymological *e*-grade tended to spread in the perf. (see below), and even in the conservative realm of *οἶδα* the *e*-grade stem appears in subj. *εἰδῶ* (Hom. *εἰδέω*, 1pl. *εἴδομεν*), fut. *εἴσομαι*, infin. *εἰδέναι* (Att.); these forms, root grade and all, were of course manufactured within the history of G on patterns provided by the eventive verbs. The same thing applies to the pluperf. *ᾔδη* (Hom. *ᾔδεα*), 3sg. *ῃείδει* < **ἠϝειδεε* with *η*-augment (442). The opt. *εἰδείην* is in this category too, but unexpected in detail—assuming it was created in the mold of the PIE the athem. opt., which was built to the zero grade of the root (128.3); but since the expected form would have been *(*ϝ*)*ἰζην* < **wiǰǰēn* < **widyeH₁m* the substitution of a more intelligible analogical creation is no cause for wonder.

The history of the pple. εἰδώς has been variously treated, including taking it to be what it looks like, PIE **weyd-*. But this is the least likely explanation. As mooted above (512, end) it might be ultimately from ***we-widwōs*. If that is the genuine etymon, then it is Hom. ἰδυῖα f. < **widus-iH₂* and Ved. *vidvás-* m.n., *vidúṣī* f. that are the innovations. (Since zero grade is proper for the perf.pple., the pattern for replacing something like Ved. **vedvás-* by *vidvás-* would have been obvious, whereas there is no pattern at all for substituting an *e*-grade for an original zero grade.) The Homeric infinitives, ἴδμεν and ἴδμεναι, and εἰδέναι are none of them inherited (551-2).

516. THE SECOND PERFECT (of the type λέλοιπα) is so called in the school grammars because it is second in frequency to the first (or kappatic) perfect, but historically it is the direct descendent of the PIE perf. As compared with οἶδα and the perfect paradigms of InIr., OIr., and Gmc., it shows two important innovations: First, the old gradation is given up, with the usual result that the *o*-grade of the singular was generalized in all the active forms. Second, the root syllable is followed by -α- in all the indicative forms with the exception of the 3sg. -ε. This is like the spread of -α- in the σ-aor. (504). Here the source of the -α- is to be found in the early 3pl. -ατι < *-*n̥ti*, and in forms like ἕσταμεν and τέθναμεν, where the -α- reflects root-final *-*H̥₂*-. Then the old 3pl. -ατι was mostly touched up as -αντι (that is, recast as theme-vowel -α- plus the usual 3pl. desinence -ντι), whence Att.-Ion. -ᾱσι. (There was a similar leveling in Skt., such that the endings *-ima*, *-it(h)a*, and *-iva*, originally proper to seṭ formations, eventually become general. In the RV this process is well under way but had progressed only to the point that in aniṭ formations endings with the *-i-* occurred after heavy stems, so *ūcimá* < **wu-wc-* 'we said', *sedima* < **sa-sd-* 'we sat', *jaghnimá* 'we slew'; but *yuyujma* 'we yoke', and *vidmá* 'we know').

Most roots of the *e*-series regularly show the *o*-grade, as λέλοιπα 'left', πέποιθα 'am persuaded; trust', γέγονα 'am born, come into being', τέτροφα 'become firm', but roots containing -ευ- were treated differently. For them, the perf. is normally based on the *e*-grade, thus πέφευγα 'fled'; the only *o*-grade perf. is Hom. εἰλήλουθα 'went' (cf. fut. ἐλεύσομαι) beside ἐλήλυθα with weak grade as in Att. The reason for this special treatment is unknown.

A disguised *o*-grade form is Hom. δείδω 'I fear'—not the pres. stem it appears to be but the regular outcome of **dedwoya* (192, 190.3, 86.3) beside competing δείδια (δέδϝια, Att. δέδια), a zero-grade stem generalized from, say, 1pl. δείδιμεν (actually δέδϝιμεν; in Hom., the -ει- is a representation, probably purely artificial, of the heavy first syllable of orig. δεδϝ-; 190.3).

A parallel gradation, with η : ω < **eH₁* : **oH₁*, is seen in ἔρρωγα 'broke (out)' (ῥήγνῡμι), Hom. εἴωθα 'am accustomed', and (with κ-type) Dor. ἔωκα 'sent' (ἵημι).

Roots which have gradation between α and ᾱ (Att.-Ion. η) show the latter in the perf., as ἔᾱγα 'is broken' (ἄγνῡμι), πέφηνα 'appeared' (φαίνω

< *p^h*anyō*), Hom. ἕᾱδε 'is pleasing' (ἀνδάνω). This is best taken as analogical, though some scholars have entertained the idea that *-*o*H_2- might at least sometimes result in -ᾱ- directly—an idea not without its appeal. But analogy must in any case be the explanation for such formations built to roots with no laryngeals in their etymological makeup.

Many G verbs show no gradation of the root in the perf., as γέγραφα 'wrote'.

a. There are many scattered traces, mainly in Hom., of the earlier system exemplified by the inflection of οἶδα—gradation of the root, endings added directly to the root, or both. Such are the so-called μι-forms of the perf. or pluperf.: ἔοιγμεν (= ἐοίκαμεν), ἐΐκτην (= ἐοικάτην: ἔοικα 'am like' < **we-woyk-*); infin. γεγάμεν; pple. γεγαώς (γέγονα 'am born, come into existence'). Of course, neither γέγαμεν nor *γεγαϝώς is inherited: a root **ǵenH₁-* would have given ˣγέγνημεν, ˣγεγνηϝώς.[1] Rather they are patterned on μέμαμεν (for typical ˣμεμόναμεν), μεμάᾱσι, μεμαώς (μέμονα 'yearn for').

Further examples: εἰλήλουθμεν (εἰλήλουθα 'went'); ἐπέπιθμεν (πέποιθα 'am persuaded'), δείδιμεν, Att. δέδιμεν (δείδω 'am afraid', root **dwey-*, mentioned above).

Sometimes there is gradation of the root in the pple., with weak grade in the fem. Thus εἰδώς, ἰδυῖα 'knowing'; μεμηκώς, μεμακυῖα 'bleating'; ἀρηρώς, ἀραρυῖα 'being arranged' (ἀραρίσκω).

517. THE ASPIRATED PERFECT, as for example Att. κέκοφα (κόπτω 'strike'). This is mainly Attic, though some examples occur in other dialects. It is unknown in Hom. in the act. (so Hom. κεκοπώς 'striking') but does occur in some 3pl. midd. forms, as τετράφαται (τρέπω 'turn'), ἔρχαται 'they were fenced in' (εἴργω), ὀρωρέχαται 'reached out' (ὀρέγω); and that has long been taken as the starting-point for the type. However, as we shall see, there are cogent reasons for regarding the Homeric middles and the Attic perfects as unrelated developments, the former exclusively Ionic and the latter exclusively Attic, or nearly so. The one is wholly middle, the other exclusively active; and there is next to no lexical agreement.

1. The Ionic (Homeric) middles are easy to account for as resulting from morphophonemic ambiguity. Note the perfect middle forms of roots ending in stops of the three manners of articulation:

τρῖβω:	1sg.	τέτριμμαι	2sg.	τέτριψαι	3sg.	τέτριπται	2pl.	τέτριφθε
κόπτω:		κέκομμαι		κέκοψαι		κέκοπται		κέκοφθε
γράφω:		γέγραμμαι		γέγραψαι		γέγραπται		γέγραφθε

(see 220, 213, 210), and similarly pples. τετριμμένος, κεκομμένος, γεγραμμένος. There are similar series from roots ending in dorsal stops.

That is, apart from 3pls. such as τετρίβαται, roots ending in all three labial stops have identical forms in the perf.midd.; likewise roots ending in

[1] There is the (slim) possibility that γέγαμεν and the like, and some similar Ved. forms, are actually from an aniṭ form of the root, **ǵen-*. See 123.3.

any dorsal stop, or any apical stop. In some roots ending in a labial or a dorsal stop, the leveling common to all the other forms was extended to the 3pl.; thus novel *τετρίφαται* and *κεκόφαται* in imitation of *γέγραφαται*.

The choice of the aspirated consonant (rather than ×*γεγράβαται* or ×*γεγράπαται*) is not self-explanatory; it is usually traced to the 2pl. in -*φθε*, -*χθε*. It is not evident, however, why the 2pl. rather than (say) the 1pl. should have been the model.

This is the situation in Hom., so *τετράφαται* (perf. of both *τρέπω* and *τρέφω*), and by other similar forms in Hdt. and Thuc.

2. The source of the distinctively Attic forms, which are active only and mostly formed to different roots from the Homeric type, is less clear. The task of the usual accounts is to explain a shift from 3pl. middle to exclusively active inflection, with the complete loss of the starting point in the process. But such a shift is very difficult to motivate, and the two types are best taken as historically unrelated whether or not the following account is deemed sufficient.

The best suggestion to date for the origin of the Attic type starts with *εἴληφα* (the perf. of *λαμβάνω*/*λάζομαι* 'sieze') as the key. This is explained as a reflex of PIE **labh*- (G *λάφῡρον* 'booty', Ved. *árabdha* aor.midd. < **e-lebh-to*); that is, a root unrelated to *λαμβ-*/*λαζ-* < **hlag*^{w}- < **slag*^{w}-. Once **g*^{w} > *β* (a stage attested in Aiginetan ΛΗΑΒΟΝ, that is *hλαβōν*), **lap*^{h}- became **hlap*^{h}- by contamination with **hlab*- (< **hlag*^{w}-), whence perf. **he-slap*^{h}*a* > *εἴληφα*. The -*ᾱ*- is secondary, as it is in *κλάζω*/*κέκληκα* 'screech', and others.[1] The rest is straightforward: from this paradigm, once its suppletive makeup had been lost sight of, arose things like *τέτροφα* (*τρέπω* 'turn'), *κέκοφα* (*κόπτω* 'strike'), *τέτρῐφα* (*τρῑβω* 'rub'), *πέπομφα* (*πέμπω* 'lead'), *δέδειχα* (*δείκνῡμι* 'point out'), and even to the perfects of denominative formations (460-1), as *πεφύλαχα* (*φυλάττω* 'guard'). The type, rare in the early Att. writers, spread from word to word without ever becoming universal.

This explanation has its weaknesses, chiefly that the pivotal *εἴληφα* depends upon two contaminations for its final form. (Neither is implausible, however, and the more important of the two—the remodeling of **lap*^{h}- as **hlap*^{h}- after *hlab*- ~ *hlag*^{w}-, is straightforward.) Nor is it helpful that both roots are poorly attested: **slag*^{w}- is without certain reflexes outside G; **labh*- is well-attested in InIr. but in G itself is only doubtfully identifiable in *λάφῡρον*.

Tracing the aspirated perf. of Att. to a single form is NOT among the weaknesses of the theory, however; in fact it is the likeliest course of events. The only subject worthy of debate is whether the starting point identified here is the correct one.

a. 'DELTA-PERFECTS'. The Ionic (middle) type of aspirated perf. is not found to roots ending in apical stops. Of course, the manners of articulation of apicals were still different in the early period before endings beginning with -*μ*- (cf. *κεκαδμένος* 'surpassing' (*καίνυμαι*), *κεκορυθμένος* 'fitted out, armed'); and so there was no ambiguity conducive to ana-

---

[1] The pattern of *λάμβανω*/*εἴληφα* is also responsible for the replacement of *λέλογχα*, the earlier perf. of *λαγχάνω* 'obtain by lot', by *εἴληχα*.

logical leveling in the 3rd pl. like that in Hom. τετράφαται. (This is strong evidence for the validity of the usual view of the origin of the Ionic type.)

There was on the other hand a curious extension of 3pl. -δαται, -δατο, from verb stems ending in -δ-, such as Hom. ἐρηρέδαται, ἐρηρέδατο (properly ἐρηριδ-, pres. ἐρείδω 'make lean against'), to stems originally ending in vowels (including -α- < *$\mathring{n}$): Hom. ἐρράδαται, ἐρράδατο (ῥαίνομαι 'sprinkle'), ἀκηχέδαται (1sg. ἀκάχημαι 'am grieved', pres. ἄχομαι), ἐληλέδατο (3sg. ἐλήλατο; pres. ἐλαύνω 'drive').

518. THE κ-PERFECT, as seen in τέθηκα (the FIRST PERFECT of the school grammars), embodies a stem type peculiar to G. Its inception must belong to prehistoric G, for it is already established, within limits, in Hom. and in the earliest records of other dialects. (No instance has yet been identified in Myc., which in view of the paucity of verb forms in the texts is no wonder.) Yet certain stages of its growth are observable in the historical period.

In Hom. the formation is found in some 20 roots, all ending in long vowels (from the G standpoint), and in all of them the κ-stem is virtually limited to the SINGULAR stems which actually contain the long vowel, so ἕστηκα 1sg. 'I stand' but ἕσταμεν 1pl., ἕσταθι 2sg. imper.; βέβηκας 'you go', βέβηκε but βεβάᾱσι 3pl., βεβάμεν infin., βεβαώς pple. Thus similarly even in Att. ἕστηκα but ἕσταμεν; δέδοικα 'I fear' replaces original δείδω (Hom., 516), but δέδιμεν 1pl. corresponds to Hom. δείδιμεν. Occasionally in Hom. the stem is found in the 3pl., for example ἑστήκᾱσιν, and in participles. Later the formation, by now more accurately a κα-perfect, spreads to other stems ending in a long vowel, then to stems ending in any vowel (including denominatives), and finally to stems ending in consonants, and to all persons and numbers.

The *e*-grade of ἕστηκα (that is, **hestā-* < **ste-steH$_2$-*) and βέβηκα (*$g^weg^w\bar{a}$- < *g^we-g^weH_2-) would be out of order for a genuine perf., and has reinforced the conventional wisdom that the kappatic aorist formation (as seen in ἔδωκε 507.3) is the source of the perfect type. The functional links between the aorist and the perfect are weak, however; some would say nonexistent, especially at the early date when the kappatic perfects must have taken root. And even on the formal side there is a major obstacle: among Homeric kappatic perfects no forms at all are to be found that correspond to the kappatic aorists—there are only three of the latter altogether in any case: ἕηκα, ἔθηκα, and ἔδωκα.

Many other suggestions have been made for the source of the -κ-: a hiatus-filler, a root-extension, and so on. Fresh possibilities arrived on the coat-tails of the laryngeals, such as the theory that the -κ- developed in the 1sg. when a root-final laryngeal was followed by the ending *-H_2e: *ste-$stoH_2$-H_2e > *ἕστοκα (with allowances for the root vowel and details of the reduplication). From this starting point the -κ- spread to other persons. In general, this suggestion has not met with much favor.

It is pertinent to start with the observation that the 1sg. and 3sg. perfects of long-vowel roots would have been a formal problem in G, becoming something like **hestō* (**hestā*?), **dedō*, and so on; and if, next to one of the roots suffering this fate, there was a synonymous and formally similar root which ended in some consonant, like *g^wem- next to *g^weH_2- 'go', the perf. formations based on it would have enjoyed a considerable advantage of structural clarity over those based on the usual roots. Just such a root, in the form of **stek-* next to *steH_2- 'stand', seems to be attested, as in Skt. *stákati* (known only from grammatical sources, regrettably) whose meaning is given as 'strikes against',[1] Av. *staχta-* 'strong', U **stakaz** 'established', possibly the Gmc. 'steel' words (OHG *stahal* and cognates) which appear to align with Av. *staχra-* 'severe' (of cold). 1,3sg. perfs. built to this root, **hestoka* and **hestoke*, would have had much to recommend them over ambiguous **hestō* (? **hestā*) and one can easily imagine the spread of such a shape. But these starting-points are formally remote from attested ἕστᾱκα, ἕστηκα, which can have been reached only by much remodeling.

In sum, all suggestions made to date fall short of cogency.

a. The pivotal role of long-vowel roots is revealed by the generalization, occasionally, of -ηκα rather than just -κα to new stems, as νενέμηκα (νέμω 'deal out'), Hom. τετύχηκε (τυγχάνω 'hit'), μεμάθηκα (μανθάνω 'perceive'), and similarly λελάβηκα (λαμβάνω 'grasp') in several dialects.

b. Where κ-perfects and the older type persist side by side, the older form generally retains the original (stative) sense while the kappatic form functions as the anterior tense, so πέπεικα 'have persuaded' (back-formed from metanalyzed πεί-σω, ἔπει-σα rather than directly to πειθ-) next to original πέποιθα 'am persuaded, trust'; διέφθαρκα pret. 'have destroyed' next to original διέφθορα 'is in ruins'; πέφαγκα 'have made appear' vs. πέφηνα 'seem, am apparent'.

519. PERFECT MIDDLE. A middle stative could have had at best idiomatic value in PIE, and in most IE languages preserving the stative inflection in one or another guise (Hitt., Celt., Gmc., and Ital.) the inherited perf. FORMS remained active-only. Middle forms were however created in InIr. and G, with the rise of the perf. as a kind of past tense. In both groups the innovation was carried out in a straightforward way: the (eventive) middle endings—primary endings, note—were added to the weak grade of the stem, as in athematic eventive paradigms. (In Skt. the only deviations from this program were the 3sg. *-e* < **-a-i*, on the pattern of the eventive **-ta* : **-tai*; and the 3pl., where (to ignore certain details) the midd. ending *-re* from *-r̥ is based on the *t*-less eventive inflection preserved in *duhé* 3sg., *duhré* 3pl., **426**, esp. **a.**) Though an innovation, the formation in G must be of some age, as it retains a number of traits lost in the successive remodelings of the basic ('active') perfects: the endings are added directly to the root, and the original zero grade thereof often contrasts with the leveled *o*-grade of the active. Thus τέτραμμαι (τρέπω 'turn'; cf. τέτροφα, later τέτραφα); τέθραμμαι (τρέφω 'nourish'; cf. τέτροφα); ἔφθαρμαι in contrast to ἔφθο-

[1] Perhaps a misunderstanding for 'is resistant, is hard'.

ρα (φθείρω 'perish'); and so ἔσπαρμαι (σπείρω 'sow', perf. ἔσπαρκα), ἔσταλμαι (στέλλω 'equip', perf. ἔσταλκα), τέταται (τείνω 'stretch', perf. τέτακα), κέχυται (χέω 'pour', perf. κέχυκα), ἔσσυμαι (σεύω 'set on'), πέπυσμαι (πυνθάνομαι 'find out'). But often the grade of the pres. stem is followed, as λέλειμμαι (λείπω 'leave'), πέπεισμαι (πείθω 'persuade'), ἔρρηγμαι (ῥήγνῡμι 'break'), cf. λέλοιπα, πέποιθα, ἔρρωγα; and many cases are like λέλεγμαι (λέγω 'say'), in other words to roots which show no paradigmatic gradation.

a. It is one thing to say 'the middle perfect formation in G escaped the successive remodelings of the active', but quite another to explain how it happened—or even COULD have happened. When such newfangled forms as **leloykʷamen* (λελοίπαμεν) were competing with and supplanting **likʷmen* it is profoundly mystifying that **le-likʷmetʰa* (λελίμμεθα) did not pari passu become ˣλελοιπάμεθα or the like.

b. The numerous consonant changes before the endings are partly in accordance with the regular phonetic processes (213, 219-21, and so on), but partly are due to analogical leveling. Important among the latter is the analogical extension of the -σ- which is regular in the 3sg. from stems ending in an apical stop or -σ-, as πέπεισται (πείθω 'persuade'), τετέλεσται (τελέω < **telehyō* 'complete'), to the forms with μ-endings: πέπεισμαι, τετέλεσμαι, and from these even to some stems ending in -ν-, as πέφασμαι (φαίνω 'make appear'; cf. 3sg. πέφανται). Even the remarkably conservative ἴδμεν (Hom.) 'we know' gave way to Att. ἴσμεν. This development is not easy to understand.

The shapes -σμαι, -σμεθα were also extended to roots ending in a vowel, as τέτεισμαι (τῑ́νω 'pay what is due', fut. τείσω, 500.1), ἔγνωσμαι (γιγνώσκω 'understand'), and so on. These arose out of the competition between forms like ἔζωσμαι, ἔζωσται and ἔζωμαι, ἔζωται (ζώννῡμι, root ζωσ- 'belt') which show leveling in opposite directions starting from regular ἔζωμαι (< *ἐζωσμαι), 3sg. ἔζωσται.

520. Pluperfect. This is a wholly G innovation. It is plainly based on the inherited perf., but its history is obscure in detail. Some old du. and pl. forms like Hom. ἐπέπιθμεν, (ϝ)ἐ(ϝ)ίκτην (ἔοικα 'am like'), βέβασαν are simply forms of the perf. stem with augment or with secondary endings; and in the pluperfect middle (ἤϊκτο 'was like') these are the only characteristics. But in the active the earliest forms of the sg., namely 1sg. -εα, 2sg. -εας, 3sg. -εε (-ει), as in Hom. ἤιδεα, ἤιδεε 'knew', πεποίθεα, ἐπεποίθει 'was persuaded', contain an element -ε- before the usual endings of the perf. This scheme (-ε- before the usual perf. endings) is also the norm in the du. and pl. forms, as ἐλελοίπεμεν, and in the perf. infin. λελοιπέναι. The source of this -ε- is obscure. The derivation of Hom. ἤιδεα from a hypothetical **eweydeha* and the further comparison of this to the L pluperf. *-eram* (from **-isā-*, 531.1), will not do. Apart from the **-s-*, which is wholly hypothetical in the case of G, there is no point of similarity. A different theory traces -εα, -εας, -εε to *-ηα, *-ηας, *-ηε, with regular shortening before vowels and the subsequent spread of -ε- to preconsonantal forms. This -η- is variously explained. Some think it is a modal marker of some kind, and so the formation would be formally somehow related to the enigmatic L *ē*-subj. (1st conj., 543.2, imperf., and pluperf. subj. in **-sē-*, 531.4), and semantically analogous to the L anterior tenses in *-ā-* (498); some think it is the PIE stative element *-eH_1- (452, 468.2C). A stative stem based on an already stative stem might possibly have a meaning of the 'used to be' type. Evidence for -η- is seen mainly in Hom. forms in the paradigm of οἶδα: ἠείδεις, ᾔδησθα both 2sg., ᾔδη 3sg., fut. εἰδήσω, all apparently *-*weydē*-. This is often compared to L *vidē*- 'see', and if the comparison is correct, lends some weight to the opinion that the pluperf. is at bottom a kind of secondary stative.

The regular contraction of the old sg. forms gives -η, -ης, -ει, and these, with du. -ετον, -ετην, pl. -εμεν, -ετε, -εσαν, are the standard Att. forms of the best period. In later Att. the -ει of the 3sg. was transplanted to other persons, as 2sg. -εις (doubtless the first to change), recharacterized 1sg. -ειν, du. -ειτον, -ειτην, pl. -ειμεν, -ειτε, and eventually even -εισαν.

521. FUTURE PERFECT. This is a G innovation, and is simply a future in -σω from the perf. stem. It is rare in the active, mainly ἑστήξω and τεθνήξω from perfects with stative meaning (ἕστηκα, τέθνηκα). Middle forms are usual for eventives, as λελείψομαι, γεγράψομαι, and so on.

THE LATIN PERFECT SYSTEM

522. The development of the L tense known as the perfect followed a course altogether unlike G. The greatest difference was manifested from the outset, namely the L tense is a conflation of the PIE aorist and stative; its function was basically aoristic/completive. A single set of personal endings evolved, but a souvenir of the mixed ancestry of the category was the variety of stem types, partly stative and partly aorist in origin (sometimes ambiguous as to which). The commonest type, however—the *vī*-perfect—is a specifically L development of obscure history.

The merging of the aor. and perf. belongs to the Ital. period, but the evolution of the 'completed past' tense in Italic languages followed diverging paths: O and U show several stem types which are unknown in L, and conversely nothing corresponding to the L *vī*-perfects is seen in Sab.

a. In Gmc. too the distinction between the aor. and the perf. disappeared prehistorically, but with very different consequences. The perf. assumed the role of preterite in the conservative verb type, the so-called strong verbs, as NE *sing/sang*, *bear/bore*, and *ride/rode*. Though a large class, it was nevertheless from the beginning of history closed; as in the Italic languages, the open form-class is a past tense paradigm of obscure origin, the celebrated 'dental preterite' (as NE *rip/ripped* and *hate/hated*). Some have seen traces of aoristic person endings in the dental preterite type.

b. It is remarkable how obscure the formations of preterital tenses in the IE languages are. The enigmatic *vī*-perfects of L and the *nky*-perf. of U are in a large company: a number of the Celt. past paradigms are no more than hazily explicable; the Gmc. dental preterites and the G kappatic perf. (518) are puzzles; the preterital marker of the mediopassive in Hitt., -*t(i)*, is an enigma, and preterital stems of Toch. have no satisfactory explanation.

523. REDUPLICATED STEMS. These directly represent the IE reduplicated

stative. For the consonant of the reduplication in general, and for the type of *stetī, spopondī* in particular, see **443.3**.

The original vowel of the reduplication is preserved in *dedī* (*dō* 'give'), *stetī* (*stō* 'stand'), *pepulī* (*pellō* 'strike'), *tetendī* (*tendō* 'stretch'), *cecinī* (*canō* 'sing'), and others; but it is replaced by the vowel of the root syllable wherever this is *i, u,* or *o* in both the pres. and perf., as in *didicī* (*discō*),[1] *cucurrī* (*currō* 'run'), *pupugī* (*pungō* 'stab'), *momordī* (*mordeō* 'bite'), *spopondī* (*spondeō* 'pledge'), and so on.

As in Indic reduplication (**443.2B**), this cannot be a matter of phonetic assimilation, but is an analogical extension of the relation observed in cases like *tetendī* 'stretched' (root **ten-*), *fefellī* 'sucked' (pres. *fellāre*)—a pattern that was very common prior to the weakening of short vowels in medial syllables (so **pepelai* for later *pepulī*). On this pattern arose *momordī* to *mordeō* in place of *memordī, cucurrī* to *currō* in place of *cecurrī*, and the rest. (These forms with the orig. *e*-reduplication, and some others, are quoted by grammarians; *peposcī* (*poscō* 'ask') is also attested epigraphically.)

The loss of reduplication, in compounds particularly, is due to syncope, generally in accord with Exon's Law (**74.5**). In the few cases where the prefix ends in a short vowel the resulting long consonant would remain, as *re-ttulī* 'carried back' (simplex *tetulī*), *re-pperī* 'discovered' (simplex *peperī* to *pariō*). But after a long vowel or a consonant the long consonant is simplified, so that nothing really is left of the reduplication: *attendī* 'attended to' (**ādttendī*, cf. simplex *tetendī*), *occīdī* 'felled' (**obccaidī*, cf. *cecīdī*), and others. A few perfects of compounds regularly retain the reduplication of the simplex, as those in *-didī* (= *dedī*), *-stitī* (= *stetī*), *-didicī, -poposcī*, and *-cucurrī* (beside *-currī*).

There is little trace of the original gradation. With rare exceptions, such as the cited *totondī* for *tetendī*, the vowel of the root syllable is the same as in the pres., albeit altered by regular weakening as in *cecinī* (*canō*), *cecīdī* (*caedō*), *pepulī* (*pellō*), and so on. Details of the pres. stem consonantism are also sometimes imported into the perf.: manifestly in the case of *poposcī*, for example; probably (**218**) in the case of *tetendī*; and so on.

524. In some verbs the loss of reduplication in compounds led to the use of an unreduplicated perf. in the simplex. Thus *tetulī* (frequent in Plaut.) was gradually replaced by *tulī, scicidī* by *scidī* (late).

It is hard to know how far to press this explanation. The facts are tolerably clear in the case of *tulī*, but much less so for many others, as *fidī* 'split', *fūdī* 'poured', *vertī* 'turned', *līquī* 'left', *vīcī* 'overcame', *vīdī* 'saw', *vēnī* 'came', which from the earliest period appear thus only, without reduplica-

[1] Note that the 'root vowel' *-i-* of *discō* is historically the vowel of the reduplicated present **di-dḱ-sk-* 'learn'.

tion in simplexes OR compounds. It therefore seems likely that many or most of these are actually reflexes of old root and thematic aorists—particularly in the case of demonstrably aoristic roots, that is, those with characterized present stems such as *n*-infix presents like *findō* 'split' (cf. Ved. *bhinátti* pres., *bhét* 3sg. aor.), *fundō* 'pour', and *linquō* 'leave' (Ved. *riṇákti* pres., *riktam* 2du. aor.). These would not have had stative stems in PIE in any case. It is in principle impossible to tell which is the actual history of a given form like *līquī*. The most that one can say is that the survival of an indisputable aorist stem like *fēcī* (*faciō*), not to mention the vigorous spread of the stem-forming suffix of *s*-aorists, prove beyond argument that specifically aor. stems survived into the early history of L. To this must be added the observation that forms like *līquī* and *fūdī* have exactly the shape that the reflex of a root aor. would be expected to have.

a. In principle it is possible that what looks like a L reduplicated perfect might actually continue a reduplicated aorist. The evidence is exceedingly slender, however, the best being a surmise that L *tetigī* 'touched' to an *n*-infix pres. (*tangō*) is superimposable on G *τεταγών, -όντος* 'having grabbed', a form isolated from any paradigm in G. But the root in question is unattested in IE apart from L and the formally difficult OE *þaccian* 'pat', OHG *thacolōn* 'caress'. The *n*-infix pres.—very improbable to a root **tag*-—would imply a root aor. rather than a reduplicated one, and just such a root aor. formation has been seen in the ancestry of the OL subj. *tagam, tagit*.

525. LONG VOWEL PERFECTS have several origins.

1. Some appear to have a long vowel in the perf. stem as the result of the contraction of the reduplication syllable **e*- with the root-initial vowel. Thus *ēgī* < **eagai* (*agō* 'drive'; 88.3), *ēdī* < **eodai* (*edō* 'eat'), *ēmī* < **eomai* (*emō* 'buy'). This type cannot be too ancient; none of these would have formed perfect stems to begin with, and *agō* poses a special problem: *H_2*e*-H_2*ǵ*- (or more likely *H_2*e*-H_2*eǵ*-, as the root seems not to have ablauted; 127, 117.1) would have resulted in L ˣ*āgī*. Had such a form existed, it is not credible that it would have been replaced by *ēgī*; this implies a post-laryngeal **e-ag*-. Cf. *ōdī* 'hate', regrettably of obscure etymology but credibly from something like *H_3*e*-H_3*od(h)*-.

2. At least one has a long vowel from compensatory lengthening (225.1): *sēdī* < **se-sd*- (*sedeō* 'sit'; the same phenomenon in pres. *sīdō* < **si-sd*- with a different reduplicating vowel).

3. Stems (or roots) in -*v*- lose the root-final glide with subsequent contraction: **kawa-wai* > **kaawei* > *cāvī* (*căveō* 'am on guard'), **mowawai* > **moawei* > *mōvī* (*moveō* 'move'), **lawawai* > **laawei* > *lāvī* (*lavō* 'wash'), **wowawai* > **woawei* > *vōvī* (*voveō* 'vow'). That is, these are members of the *vī*-perf. class, more exactly members of the -*uī* type of *vomuī* < **womawai* (66.5)(root **wemH̥*$_1$- 'vomit'), but converted by sound-laws into stems which differ from the pres. stems only in the length of the vowel.

4. A number of stems to roots with diphthongs have zero grade in the

pres. and full grade (of aor. origin) in the perf.; as a result of sound laws affecting diphthongs, the perf. stem comes to differ from the pres. stem only in the length of the vowel, as *fundō, fūdī* < **ǵhewd-* 'pour'; *vincō, vīcī* < **weyḱ-* 'defeat'; *videō, vīdī* < **weyd-* 'see'; *fugiō, fūgī* < **bhewg-* or **bhowg-* 'flee'.

5. A few inherit a long vowel from the parent language, most demonstrably *fēcī* 'did' < **dheH₁-k-* like G ἔθηκα. Perhaps *frēgī* (*frangō* 'break') and *pēgī* (*pangō* 'fit together') belong here too, though they are more likely to be analogical (say, *āctus* : *ēgī* :: *frāctus* : *X*).

6. The preceding developments resulted in a goodly number of roots of diverse shape which had a long vowel in the perf. stem and a short vowel in the pres.; and on such a pattern additional long-vowel perfects were created de novo. For example, the long vowel of *vēnī* 'I came' (*veniō*, root **g^{w}em-*, an aoristic root), can have no morphological or phonological source; but a straightforward analogical source is at hand in *fugiō fūgī, sedeō sēdī*, and many others. Similarly *fōdī* (*fodiō* 'dig'), *scābī* (*scabō* 'scratch'), *lēgī* (*legō* 'gather'), and probably *frēgī, pēgī* mentioned above.

a. It is traditional to compare the L long vowel perfects with similar-looking things in InIr., Gmc., and Celt. However, in those languages what looks like a long ROOT vowel is in fact the lengthened vowel of the reduplicated PREFIX (exactly as in L *sēdī* < **se-sd-*, 2, above). The Indic phenomena were early recognized as such. As in L, the ultimate source was phonological, involving two different sound laws: **sa-sd-* (the zero grade stem of **sa-sad-* 'sit') > *sed-*; **ya-ym-* (zero grade of *yayam-* 'reach') > *yem-*; **ya-yt-* (zero grade of *yat-* 'stretch') > *yet-*. So ordinary 3sg. *sasā́da, yayā́ma* but 3pl. *sedúr, yemúr*, and 3sg. midd. *yete*. Much of the spread of this pattern occurred within recorded history: to *papā́ta* 'flew' the weak grade stems *papt-* and *pet-* occur side by side in the RV. In post-Vedic Skt. the matter achieved the status of a rule: an 'unreduplicated weak stem in *-e-*' is the norm for roots which would have been non-syllabic in the weak stem, so *pet-* and *ten-* in place of *pa-pt-* and *ta-tn-*. (But this principle does not apply when the reduplication syllable is altered by palatalization (so *ja-gm-*, not ×*jem-* or ×*gem-*.)

The Gmc. 'long vowel perfects' were much more recently recognized as secondary. They are found chiefly in two classes of Gmc. perfects (traditionally, Classes IV and V); what these have in common is being the two types where the verb root would have been nonsyllabic in the pl. So from sg. **bhe-bhor-* 'carried' and **se-sod-* 'sat' come, with loss of reduplication typical of Gmc. preterites, PGmc. **bar-* and **sat-*. From pl. stem **bhe-bhr-* and **se-sd-*, however, come PGmc. **bēr-* and **sēt-*, in which the surviving vowel is etymologically the vowel of the reduplicating syllable, not of the root at all. There is an important difference between the Gmc. developments and those of Indic (*sed-*) and L (*sēd-*): in the latter two we are dealing with the action of specific sound laws operating on consonant clusters, whereas the development of Gmc. **bēr-*, **sēt-* (and dozens of others) was a dissimilatory process.

526. PERFECTS IN *-sī*. These are based on the PIE *s*-aorist. Since the type was productive in late PIE (459), it follows that there is very little agreement as to actual forms in G, L, and InIr. Where we do find lexical agreement, as in L *dīxī* = G ἔδειξα; L *clepsī* = G ἔκλεψα; *vēxit* 'conveyed' = Ved. *ávāṭ*, OCS *věsŭ* (1sg.), it is impossible to know whether we are dealing with independent innovation or inheritance of common forms.

Productive as it was in L, the formation remained confined to primary verbs built to roots ending in a stop, *s*, or a nasal. For the cons. changes in the resulting clusters, see **225-6**, **213-5**, and **232**. —Surprisingly, given its prominence in L, the type is represented in Sab. only in a few forms, which are disputed.

1. Forms in *-psī* come from roots ending in any labial stop, as *scrīpsī* (*scrībō* 'write'), *clepsī* (*clepō* 'steal'). So also from roots ending in *m*, with anaptyctic *p*, as *sūmpsī* (*sūmō* 'take'), *tēmpsī* (*temnō* 'despise').

2. Forms in *-xī* are from roots ending in any dorsal obstruent, as *dīxī* (*dīcō* 'say'), *coxī* (*coquō* 'cook, ripen'), *auxī* (*augeō* 'increase'), *iūnxī* (*iungō* 'join'), *īnstīnxī* (*īnstinguō* 'incite'). The underlying obstruent has sometimes been lost in other stems through sound laws, so for example the perf. *vĕ̄xī* to *vehō* < **weχ-* < **weǵh-* 'convey'; *cōnīxī* to *cōnīveō* < **kneygʷh-*, **231.4**, **163** 'close the eyes'; *fīxī* to early L *fīvō* < **dheygʷ-* 'fasten' (the later *fīgō* was back-formed from *fīxī*).

a. After the analogy of the relation between *fīxī* and *fīvō*, or the like, there arose similar forms from roots which did not end in a dorsal: *vīxī* to *vīvō* 'live' and *strūxī* to *struō* 'pile up'. But *fluō* 'flow', *flūxī* could be directly from **bhlewgʷ-*, as seen in early L *cōn-flugēs* (Fest.) 'place where several streams empty'. (A parallel form of the root, **bhlew-*, is seen in G φλέ(ϝ)ω 'teem'. See also **225.2b**.)

b. There are some cryptic members of this class, whose root-final dorsal obstruent was lost in the groups **-lks-* or **-rks-* (**231.2**), as *fulsit* (*fulget* 'lightens'), *fulsī* (*fulciō* 'prop up'). As a result, these look like type 3, next.

3. Forms in *-ssī*, *-sī* (the latter after a diphthong, long vowel, or consonant, **232.2**) are mostly from roots ending in an apical obstruent, as *-cussī* (*-cutiō* < *quatiō*, *quassī* 'shake') and *clausī* (*claudō* 'shut'). So *iussī*, OL *iousit* (*iubeō* 'command', OL *ioube-*, root **yewdh-*, **147.2**; see also **527** below). Others are from roots ending in *n*, as *mānsī* (*maneō* 'remain'); or in *s* (which becomes *r* in the present), as *gessī* (*gerō* < **gesō* 'do'), *ussī* (*ūrō* < **ewsō* 'burn, flame'), *hausī*, early *haussī* (*hauriō* 'draw' < **aws-* or **H_2ews-*; spurious *h-* as in *humerus*, **159**). Accordingly, *pressī* from *premō* 'press' must be from a root **pres-* different from **prem-*. A similar set is seen in **tres-*/**ters-* 'shake' in Ved. *tras-*, G τρέω (Hom. aor. τρέσσαι), L *terreō*, next to **tremH-* in L *tremō*, Lith. *trìmti*.

527. The vowel of the root syllable is usually the same as in the present, apart from the regular lengthening before *-ns-* or *-nx-* (**81.2**). But there are some differences. *Ussī* (*ūrō* 'burn') has what looks like a zero grade, but it probably continues **ūssī*, adjusted to agree with the (inherited) vocalism of the pple. *ustus*;[1] *cessī*, which is from **ke-st-s-*, is actually the same forma-

[1] The perf. and the pple. in effect belong to the same paradigm (to *ussĭ̄t* act. the corresponding passive is *ustus est*), and there is great deal of mutual influence between the two stems.

tion as *cēdō* 'go' from **ke-zd-* consisting of deictic *ce-* as in *cedo* 'give me'; and root *sed-* 'sit'. For semantics cf. NE *set out* 'depart' and G ὁδός 'road, way' < **sod-*.

The opposite relation, long vowel in the perfect beside short vowel in the present, appears in two classes of forms:

Those with *-ī-*, *-ū-* from a diphthong, in contrast to zero grade in the present. Thus *dīvīsī* (*dīvidō*), *strūxī*, *flūxī* (*struō*, *fluō*, 526.2; the *-ŭ-* in the pres. stem might well be the result of shortening, 85). A secondary specimen of this type is seen in *mittō* 'send', perf. *mīsī* < **mīss-* < **mīt-s-*; the perplexing present in *mitt-* is almost certainly from **mītō* via 234. More complex is *iubeō*, *iussī*, pres. once epig. IOVBEATIS, perf. 3sg. *ious(s)it*, *iūssit*. The usual *iussī* is doubtless, like *ussī* above, influenced by the pple. *iussus*.[1]

Those with *-ē-* or *-ā-*, such as *rēxī* (*regō* 'arrange, order'), *tēxī* (*tegō* 'cover'), and *trāxī* (*trahō* 'drag'), are commonly traced to lengthened grades, and such a grade is at least arguably an original feature of the *s*-aorist (459). But long vowels in the perf. manifestly proliferated in L, so these may be no more inherited than the root vowels of *lēgī* and *vēnī*. That long vowels were not a regular feature of *s*-perfects is established by the short vowels of *gessī* 'did', *pressī* 'pressed', *quassī* 'shook', *illexī* 'enticed' (< **-ă-*: NB *illiciō* < **laciō*, **laxī*). On the other hand, this question is complicated by the fact that these forms have (regular) short vowels in the pple. (*gestus* and so on), and so an original **gēssī* might have been influenced by the vocalism of *gestus*, just as **ūssī* was remodeled as *ussī* under the influence of *ŭstus*.

a. Several of the perfects in *-sī* are secondary beside older formations of other types. Thus *pānxī* beside *pepigī* (*pangō* 'fit together'), *parsī* beside *pepercī* (*parcō* 'am sparing'), *-pūnxī* beside *pupugī* (*pungō* 'stab'), *sūmpsī* (*sūmō* 'take') beside simplex *ēmī* (*emō* 'buy; *take'), and an old *surēmī*.

b. Forms like *dīxtī*, *dīxem*, *dīxe* beside *dīxistī*, *dīxissem*, *dīxisse* must be via haplology of *-sis-*; if it were only a matter of short-vowel syncope, we would expect similar forms from other than *s*-perfects, as ×*lēxtī* ~ *lēgistī*, which we do not find.

528. PERFECTS IN *-vī* OR *-uī*. These are a type peculiar to L—they are not even Italic. It is characteristic of (a) derivative stems (denominatives, causatives); (b) seṭ roots (for example *domuī* 'tamed' < **domawai* < **demH̥-*); (c) a small class of roots ending in a long vowel, typically from **VH* and often where one would expect a root aorist: *flēvī* (*fleō* 'cry'), *(com)plēvī* 'filled up' (*-pleō*), *crēvī* (perf. of both *crēscō* 'grow' and *cernō* 'sort'), *sprēvī* (*spernō* 'reject'), *sēvī* (*serō* 'sow'), *sīvī* (*sinō* 'put'), *scīvī* (*sciō* 'know'), *trīvī* (*terō* 'rub'), *pāvī* (*pāscō* 'nourish'), *strāvī* (*sternō* 'strew'), *nōvī* (*-gnōvī* 'I understand', pres. *(-g)nōscō*), *-lēvī* (in compounds like *dēleō* 'erase').

---

[1] IOVBEATIS is often called an error, but in fact if the formation is the causative of **yewdh-* 'fight, do battle', stem **yowdh-eye/o-*, then OL *ioube-*, L **iūbeō* is exactly what is expected. Several means for the shortening of the vowel in L *iūbeō* can be surmised.

What these have in common is that without the *-v-* they would have a hiatus between the root and the personal endings, all of which in L begin with vowels. Any element that could be pressed into service as a hiatus-filler for such stems would have spread rapidly. For the most part, that is what historians have searched for to explain the L *-v-*. It is hard to imagine that any possibility has been overlooked: root extensions (as mentioned in 453) in **-w-*, metanalysis of roots ending in **-w-* (like **sprew-*), and, inevitably, laryngeals. But all these suggestions are more or less desperate.

An alternative possibility is that the element was a morpheme to start with: a tense marker like the aor. **-s-*; something originally part of a particular personal ending; or some kind of particle. For example, some have wondered if the formation might not have begun with the perf. pple. in **-wos-* (561-2), which is however all but unattested in L—quite apart from the extreme difficulty of grafting personal endings onto a participle. (If the person markers of the forms in *-vī* resembled, say, remnants of the verb 'be', then a theory of an old periphrastic inflection fused into an inflected stem would be a realistic possibility.) An old idea notes that Indic long vowel roots like *dhā-* 'put' and *pā-* 'drink' make the 1sg. and 3sg. form in *-āu*, as *dadhā́u*, *papā́u* (for expected **dadhā́* from both **dhe-dhoH₁-H₂e* and **dhe-dhoH₁-e*). The necessary point of tangency, however, say OL **gnōwai*, **plēwai*, involves reflexes of AORISTS, not statives, and there is nothing in the Indic aor. system remotely like the *dadhāu* type. (In any case, the long-vowel perfects in *-āu* are a purely Indic development, being unknown in Iranian, so *daδa* 3sg. 'put' = Ved. *dadhā́u*; and the RV actually still has a single form—in a strangely late hymn—with original *-ā*: the unique *paprā* 'fills'.

According to one view, the origin of the *vī*-perfects is traceable to the perf. of 'be': **fūe(i)t* 'was' was evidently pronounced at least optionally as **fūwe(i)t*, as in OL occasionally so written (FVVIT). A similar kind of thing is seen in OE verbs like *bláwan* 'bloom', *blówan* 'blow', where the *-w-* to begin with was just a transition between the root and the ending, which hints that the same thing might account for *(g)nōvī* 'understand' (cf. *ōvum* 'egg' < **ōom*, 46.2). (The similar-looking development of It. *vedova*, *Genova* from L *vidua* 'widow', *Genua* is not a true parallel, as in those two words the /w/ was present from the outset, but was simply not written; see 66.5.) The difficulty with such an explanation is that a [w] occurring this way as a transition between a rounded vowel and an unrounded one would have had so little salience. By way of comparison, in NE one would hardly expect a new suffix *-wish* to arise from a misdivision of *bluish*, giving rise to ˣ*greywish*, ˣ*boywish*, and so on. In any case, neither this nor any other suggestion has won any but the most limited acceptance.

a. The perf. in *-uī* is only a variety of *-vī*, being formed from stems ending in a short vowel (cf. the usual corresponding pple. in *-i-tus*), that is **-uvī* < **-e-wai* < **-awai* with the same weakening as in *ēluō* and *dēnuō* (66.5). According to some, this is the source of the perf. stem in *-uī* when the root itself ends with *-v-*, as in *mōvī* < **movuī* < **mowawai*; a different (and better) explanation is given in 525.3.

b. *-Uī* and *-sī* are conflated in *messuī* (*metō* 'reap') for **messī*, due to the influence of early *seruī* (*serō* 'sow'). Similarly *nexuī* (*nectō* 'knot, weave, tie') for early *nexī*, after *texuī* (*texō* 'weave') where the *-s-* is part of the root (235.1a).

c. The exact history of the caus. perfects like *monuī* is uncertain. Outside of the present (456.2) a stem in **-i-* seems to be attested in Vedic, which may match the L type of *monitus*, though the medial vowel of the L is of course ambiguous (66). The etymon of *monuī*, therefore, if **mon-i-w-*, was perhaps directly modeled on the pple. **monito-*, and in no sense an inherited formation.

529. THE SHORTER FORMS OF THE *-vī* PERFECT. Some of the apparently contracted forms are the result of actual contraction, while others arose by analogy. Where **-v-* stood between like vowels it should have been regularly lost (184.3), but as a morphological TYPE was involved, the underlying form was always available to speakers, as *dīvitis* beside *dītis*. (The same thing was of course at stake in the history of *mōvī*, *lāvi*, and the like (525.3), but there the long form was lost altogether because the short form happened to conform to the important general type of *sedeō*, *sēdī* and *veniō*, *vēnī*; 525.) Such parallel forms as *audīvistī/audīstī*, *audīvissem/audīssem*, *audīvisse/audīsse*, *dēlēvĕrunt/dēlērunt*, *dēlēveram/dēlēram*, led to others created on the same pattern, like *nōstī* (*nōvistī*), *nōrunt* (*nōvĕrunt*), *nōsse* (*nōvisse*), and those of the 1st conj. which are naturally the most frequent (*amāstī*, *amārunt*, *amāram* next to *amāvistī*, *amāvĕrunt*, *amāveram*).

In the 4th conj. the contracted forms remain restricted to those which had the sequence *-īvi-*: thus *-īstī*, *-īt*, and so on. There are no forms in ˣ*-īrunt*, ˣ*-īram*, and the like parallel to *amārunt*, *amāram*; but rather we find *audiĕrunt*, *audieram*, *audierō*, *audierim* (to which one should probably add *audiī*). These are probably not from forms with earlier *-v-*, but arose after the analogy of *iī* (*eō*)(486).

The shorter forms, especially those of the first conjugation, are quotable from OL (CONIOVRASE, short for *coniūrāvisse* 'to have sworn an oath', SC de Bacch.) and in the classical period are actually more common than the full forms. But the details of relative frequency and shifting status are too involved to be presented here.

530. ENDINGS. Although the inherited stative was not a tense, in the history of Ital. it came to be a component of the tense system. All but three forms were reinterpreted as a past completed ('perfectum') tense, and as mentioned above eventually merged, formally and functionally, with the old aorist.

Before this happened, however, it was manifestly taken as a kind of present tense. A souvenir of the early association with present tense meaning is found in the forms of several personal endings: as described below, those persons which in eventive pres. tense verbs were originally marked with suffix *-*i* (all the singulars, and the 3pl.) are so marked in the Ital. perf. as well. This innovation must therefore be of considerable antiquity, as it reaches back to a time in the history of L when the primary marker *-*i* was still pronounced (that is, *-*onti* 3pl. for later -*ont*). Hitt. shows an analogous development: 1sg. -*ḫḫi* < *-*ḫai*, earlier *-*ḫa* (*-H_2e); 2sg. -*tti* < *-*t(ḫ)ai*, earlier *-*tḫa* (*-*t*H_2e); 3sg. -*i* < *-*ei*, earlier *-*e*. The survival of the primary marker *-*i* in the perf. endings even as it was lost in the source paradigms is the result of the shape of the endings, such that most of them formed a diphthong with the vowel of the original ending. The exception is the 3pl., apparently *-*ēri* (6, below).

a. The category of voice did not apply to a stative. The forms were therefore neither active nor middle, but in their forms the PIE endings on balance most resemble the eventive active, and came to be so categorized in the various IE daughters, which created distinctively middle endings in contrast to the inherited perfect endings (thus InIr. and G). L however did not create middle inflections for the perf. stem; instead, the inflection of the perfect for voice is in effect suppletive, the past-completed passive being expressed by a phrase made up of the past participle and the present (!) tense of the verb 'be', as *scrīptus est* 'was written' to *scrīpsit* 'wrote'. By analogy, a similar formation is used for deponent verbs, as *secūtus est* 'followed', the perf. of *sequitur*.

1. 1sg. -*ī*, early -*ei* (epigr. FECEI for example), is from a 1sg. in -*ai*, seemingly once attested as such in Falisc. PE⁝PARAI̩ = *peperī* 'gave birth'—in which, regrettably, the reading of the last letter is uncertain. Etymologically this is PItal. *-*a* < PIE *-H_2e (G -α; the laryngeal is vouchsafed by the short vowel in the root of the 1sg.: *jagama* 'set out' < *$g^{w}e$-$g^{w}om$-H_2e next to 3sg. *jagāma* < *$g^{w}e$-$g^{w}om$-*e* via 36.4). This was remodeled as *-*ay* with the addition of the primary (pres.) tense marker -*i* (as in *-*mi*, *-*si*, *-*ti*, *-*nti* in the eventives, 424-6, 429). Such a remodeling is intelligible only if the formation in question was in some sense on the same functional plane as presents or ambiguous somehow.—An identical remodeling is seen in the Hitt. ending -*ḫi*, as shown above, and in OCS *vědě* 1sg. 'know' < **woyday*, a rare byform. (The usual form, *věmĭ*, has the hic-et-nunc ending *-*mi* imported outright.)

a. A standard view, still repeated, that the Lat.-Falisc. *-*ay* is either a middle ending or a remodeling in the image of one. But this is impossible. First, the Italic middle endings like *-*tor* are faithful reflexes of the original type, whereas such things as G -ται, Ved. -*te* (which most resemble the Lat.-Falisc. 1sg. perf. in *-*ay*) are the innovations (433-8). That is, if the 1sg. had in fact been influenced by the middle, the result must have been $^{\times}$-*ar*, not *-*ay*. Second, and more fundamental, the notion that there ever was any particular connection between forms (or the functions) of the stative and the eventive middle in the first place is erroneous (510.2).

2. 2sg. -*istī*, early -*istei* (514.2). The original form of the ending was *-*ta* (or *-*sta*, see below); like the 1sg. it was marked as present with *-*i*, whence *-*(s)tai* > OL -*(s)tei* > -*(s)tī*. The -*is*- (as also in the 2pl. -*istis*) has so far resisted satisfactory explanation. It is usually taken as some kind of *s*-aor.

stem, though this would only account for the *-s-* and not the *-i-*. (Indic *-iṣ* and *-siṣ-* aorist stems, despite appearances, are irrelevant. In their case the *-i-* is ultimately from laryngeals.) The possibility of an inherited 2sg. including an **-s-* (**-stH₂e*, Ital. **-sta*; 514.2) is a further source of uncertainty. An idea occasionally encountered is that the attested ending is a composite of the inherited (thematic or thematized) aor. **-es* and perf. **-ta(i)*, an appealing suggestion except that the result of such a grafting would almost certainly have been ˣ*-estī*, not *-istī*—unless the attested shape reflects some ancient confusion between **-estai* and the completely unrelated element **-is-* seen in modal stems (531).

3. 3sg. The earliest forms have -ED, as epig. FECED, like O **deded**, with the secondary ending *-d* < **-t* (237.3), originally proper to thematic (or thematized) aorists. Owing to the scantiness of records during the critical period, it is unclear how this *-ed* and the proper ending of the perf., **-e*, interacted. That the latter survived is revealed by the form of the ending in the playwrights, *-īt* (epig. also -EIT), which is to say **-ey* embellished with the primary ending *-t*. This *-ey* is already a composite: perf. **-e* (= G -ε, Ved. *-a*) with the addition of the primary marker, like 1sg. **-ai* and 2sg. **-(s)tai*.

It is possible that the old aor. ending *-ed* survived long enough to be remodeled in the usual way as **-et*, whence *-it*; the classical L *-ĭt* would however be the expected reflex of earlier *-īt* in any case.

a. The OL ending -ED, O **-ed**, U **-e**, is one of the few points of tangency between the endings of the pret. in L and in Sab. The endings of the latter (at least the 1sg. *-um* and 3pl. *-ens*, the only ones we know about) are the endings of the aor., with no remnant of the PIE stative type.

4. 1pl. *-imus*, *-umus* is indistinguishable from the primary thematic ending, and thus in apparent functional agreement with the hic-et-nunc **-i* tacked on to all three singular persons and the 3pl.; but it is so only by inference, as the same transplantation of the primary ending **-mos* was made into all tenses and moods.

The only question is the source of the linking vowel. The inherited endings of the aor. and the perf. would have differed little in any case, and remodeling on the pattern of the primary thematic 1pl.—which shows up everywhere except *damus* and (perhaps) *īmus*—is the simplest explanation. There are of course a number of other possible sources for a short vowel before the *-mus*, even in athematic inflection (as is the case for example with **deda-* < **dedH̥₃-*, whence *dedumus/dedimus* 'we gave').

5. 2pl. *-istis* for **-(i)te*, with the usual form of the 2pl. (514.2), but additionally refashioned on the plan of 2sg. *-istī*.

6. 3pl. L has three forms, *-ēre*, *-ērunt*, and *-ĕrunt*.

A. The earliest of these appears to be *-ēre*, that is, **-ēr-i*, the old ending plus primary **-i*. As mentioned in 513.3, a 3pl. **-ēr*, in contrast to the **-r̥* of Indic and, perhaps, G (**429a**), is indicated by Hitt. evidence, albeit debatable, and Avestan *å̄ŋhāire* 'they are sitting' (PInIr. **āsārai*).

a. It is widely repeated that L *-ēre* continues **-ēro* with a middle marker (435). The phonology is unimpeachable, but the rationale for expecting perfect endings to exhibit formal details of the middle—either imported or ab origine—is specious (510.2). In this case it is also incoherent, as it imagines converting the 1-3sg. endings into PRIMARY middles but the 3pl. ending into a SECONDARY middle.

But now the Lapis Satricanus provides STETERAI 'they set up', 3pl. perf. of *sistō*. This cannot, or probably cannot, underlie L *-ēre* (it would give ˣ*-ērī*). It appears to show a different kind of remodeling, with *-ai* imported from 1sg. *-ai*, 2sg. *-(s)tai* (? replacing **-ēri*). But it clearly indicates a remarking of the 3pl. not as a secondary but as a primary form. (The objections to taking the ending as middle are as before.)

B. L *-ērunt* is transparently *-ēre* with the primary eventive ending *-unt* grafted on, as part of the process of the generalization of primary endings in L. (Roman authorities assumed, reasonably but incorrectly, that *-ēre* was a shortened form of *-ērunt*.)

L *-ēre* and *-ērunt* continued in use side by side. The former is more characteristic of poetry, though the actual incidence of the two forms differs markedly from one corpus to another. The most extreme imbalance is seen in hexameter versification, where *-ēre* is four times more frequent than *-ērunt*. This plainly has to do with usefulness of the form in hexameter—for L poetry generally the ratio is more like three to one. Its abundance in hexameter verse led to the gradual evolution of a general association between *-ēre* and poetic style. In Plaut. *-ērunt* is twice as common as *-ēre*, in Terence the two forms are nearly equal. The distribution in Plaut. is probably a reasonably faithful mirror of the contemporary spoken style.

C. L *-ĕrunt* has a disputed history. It could have arisen from *-ērunt* by paradigmatic leveling (the long vowel of *-ērunt* was aberrant in terms of L morphology). It is usually, and better, taken to be a completely unrelated formation, one based on the element **-is-* seen elsewhere in the L perf. system (531) as well as in the endings *-istī* and *-istis*. This would make *-ĕrunt* a direct survival of the old aor., like epig. -ED 3sg., with of course the usual importation of the primary form of the ending. If this explanation is correct, *-ĕrunt* is older than *-ērunt*, and may have been the catalyst for the latter. Indeed, it has been suggested that *-ĕrunt* was in Cicero's day the ordinary conversational form of cultivated and vulgar Latin alike. For one thing, it is well-attested in Romance (OFr. *distrent* 'they said', It. *dissero*, both < **dísseront* < **dīksĕrunt*). It must be old, and had been sanctioned in poetry from the earliest times in such forms as *stetĕrunt*—that is, notably, in any verb whose prosodic details made both *-ēre* and *-ērunt* metrically impossible in hexameter.

Such a rationale will not account for *dedĕrunt*, also early attested. It might easily be analogical, but a totally different explanation traces such forms (and *-ĕrunt* generally) to a retouching of **steta-ro* < **ste-st$\underset{\circ}{H}_2$-*, **deda-ro* < **de-d$\underset{\circ}{H}_3$-* with subsequent metanalysis of the forms as containing the ending **-aro* rather than **-ro*. The loss without a trace of the unenlarged form **-ēre* is a drawback to this view, as the **-ēro* certainly was very successful. Note however that this theory crucially depends upon the reconstruction of L *-re* as

*-*ro*: loss of the ending in prehistory implies that its remodeling into *-*ront* must have been very early, which rules out original *-*ri* as endorsed above. But see 510.2 regarding the notion that there were significant points of agreement between the stative and middle; and 6A, above.

531. OTHER TENSE AND MOOD STEMS OF THE LATIN PERFECT SYSTEM are all based upon a combination of the L perf. stem, whichever that happens to be, with an element *-*is*-, of wholly obscure origin but most commonly imagined to be related somehow to the *s*-aorist. (The impossibility of any connection with the Indic -*iṣ*- and -*siṣ*- aorist stems is discussed in 530.2.) To this *-*is*- were added elements which are partly of obscure origin and are partly recognizable as modal markers which function much as they do in the pres./imperf. system (543-4).

1. PLUPERFECT INDICATIVE. Functionally the past of the perfect, in effect, like NE *had gone*. L -*eram*, -*erās*, -*erat* from *-*is*- together with *-*ā*-, the opt. formation which functions as an anterior tense marker in -*bā*- (498) and *erā*- 'was' (493C). (The vowel of -*er*- is of course ambiguous per se, but its historical value can be surmised from the pluperfect in *-*issē*-, 4, below.)

2. FUTURE PERFECT. 'Action completed in the future', formed, like the usual future, from what had been the PIE subj. (534), so *-*is*-$^{e}/_{o}$-, whence -*erō*, -*eris*, -*erit*, -*erimus*.

3. PERFECT SUBJUNCTIVE. Formed, like the athematic opt. (539.1), from -*ī*- < PIE *-*iH*$_1$-, zero grade of the opt. marker *-*yeH*$_1$- seen in OL *siem*, *siēs*, *siet*. So *-*is*-*ī*- plus endings, whence by regular sound laws -*erim*, -*erīs*, -*erit*, -*erīmus*.

These are the forms that prevail in early L, but in later periods there is much confusion between this paradigm and the forms of the future perfect, with either -*erīmus* or -*erĭmus* (for example) serving both functions. The pivot for the confusion was the 3sg., which as a result of the sound laws was -*erĭt* for both paradigms in the classical period.

4. PLUPERFECT SUBJUNCTIVE. Descriptively, the stem in *-*is*- with an additional element *-*sē*- of profoundly obscure origin; so *-*is*-*sē*-, whence -*issem*, -*issēs*, -*isset*. —The same *-*sē*- is found in the imperf. subj. (544).

MOODS IN PROTO-INDO-EUROPEAN

532. SURVEY OF THE MOOD MARKERS.

		Subjunctive	Optative
A. Athematic	PIE	e/o	yeH$_1$/iH$_1$
	Vedic	a	yā/ī
	Gothic		ī
	G	ε/ο (*later* η/ω)	ιη/ι
	L	(*see Note*) ā	iē/ī

B. Thematic	PIE	ē/ō (ee/oo)	oy (? oyH_1)
	Vedic	ā	e
	Gothic		ai
	G	η/ω	οι
	L	*(see Note)*	ā, ē

Note: The L reflexes of the PIE subjunctive are the basis for the L future (501, also 531.2); the L 'subjunctive' of traditional grammar reflects as a rule the PIE OPTATIVE.

533. HISTORY OF THE MOODS. It is common to say that the mood markers of PIE are limited to finite forms, and occur between the verb stem and the person ending. However, the use of moods in the Rigveda is constrained in ways not compassed in that statement: in the earliest Indic, subjunctives formed to secondary stems (frequentatives, causatives, desideratives, intensives, 456-7) are notably few in number; and optatives based on such stems are genuinely rare. This rarity is especially apparent in the case of the causative/frequentative formations in *-áya-* (456.2): for all of this very numerous class—there are some 150 stems in the RV—a mere four optative forms are found. Among the hundred-odd denominative stems there are a total of eight optatives; there are 18 optative forms to stems in *-ya-* (for example *paśyema* 'may we see'); and not a single one to the passives in *-yá-*. In contrast, optatives are formed by the dozens to the 130 or so root-present stems; for example, a single, moderately common thematic stem, *saca-* 'follow', has 15 optative forms—half the tally of all characterized thematic stems together.

This cannot be a pragmatic matter. In discourse, the combination of modal force with notions like causation and iteration should be routine. In particular, the yoking of some kind of qualifying mood with the notion of desire is both natural and commonplace. In Fr., for example, the indicative of *vouler* 'want' is practically confined to the cruder sorts of dialogue. In Gmc., the paradigm for 'want' was in effect stuck in the optative, so Go. *wiljau* 'I want' was etymologically *'I would want'; the paradigms of NE *will* and NHG *willen* are reflexes of this opt.tant. paradigm. Notwithstanding, in the RV there are only six optative forms to desiderative stems, and a like number of subjunctives.

Nor is the scarcity of optatives in the RV a peculiarity of secondary (deverbative and denominative) stems: they are rare in ALL characterized stems: though some 70 roots build *n*-infix presents (this includes *nā*-presents, 453c), there are only two optative forms to such stems in the whole text. The reduplicating class includes stems (some of them very frequent) built to some 50 roots, among which 11 optative forms are found.

Finally, in the RV, opt. and subj. forms are exceedingly rare in the perfect (509 fn.).

The simplest way to explain this rarity of moods, especially the opt., in the stative paradigm and in secondary and characterized eventive verb stems, is to suppose that the subj. and opt. markers were actually eventive stem-derivatives, exactly like **-sḱ*^{e}/*o-* and the *n*-infix. They thus would no more have occurred on a causative stem than a desiderative marker would have, or a desiderative would have been built to an *n*-infix stem rather than directly to the root. From the glottogonic point of view, then, an account of PIE moods would most fittingly be included among the specifically eventive stem-building elements discussed in 450-8. The traditional description can be at least excused in light of the early growth of the moods, in most IE languages, into a fully-deployed adjunct of the evolving tense-system, freely occurring in connection with all stems.

a. The state of affairs which obtained in (late) PIE is reminiscent of the NE use of modal auxiliaries: by a rule of grammar no more than one modal occurs in a verb phrase, and the modal must be finite (that is, it will never occur in a complement to a verb such as *keep (on)* or *want*). These constraints have nothing to do with pragmatics, as combinations like 'obligation in the future' and 'conditional efficacy' are not only theoretically possible, they routinely occur in conversation—but they must be expressed somehow using no more than one (finite) modal. Hence such locutions as *will have to, might be able to,* and *want to be able to.* Some non-standard NE dialects have cut the Gordian knot, creating *might could* and the like. One speculates that in PIE an optative built to a causative would have struck speakers somewhat the way *might could* strikes speakers of other dialects of English.

b. Treating the opt. and subj. markers as PIE characterized stem-forming elements on a par with the desiderative, causative, stative, and the rest, provides insight into the total absence of these formations from Hitt., which has caused much probably futile comment. If they are simply derivative stems, then their absence from Hitt. is on the same footing as the absence of the desiderative stems (457), which—correctly—occasions little comment.

SUBJUNCTIVE

534. FUNCTION. The PIE subjunctive seems to have referred to a future event anticipated with some slight reservation on the part of the speaker —the equivalent of 'I suppose' or 'in that case'. In Vedic the subj., whether to a pres. or aor. stem, is most often a simple future, occasionally something little different from an imperative. More saliently conditional, doubtful, or wished-for future events are typically in the opt. mood. The distinction may be pondered in the following passage from the AV: *iyám agne nā́rī pátiṃ vedeṣṭa; . . . súvānā putrā́n̐ máhiṣī bhavāti; gatvā́ pátiṃ subhágā ví rājatu* 'may this noble lady, O Fire, find a husband; giving birth to sons, she will become powerful; having attained a husband, let her rule in happiness'.[1] Its only feebly modal force explains how the subj. could be transformed into a simple future tense in L (501-2) and some Celt. types. The mood is very

---

[1] If distinction there is. In truth, it is hard to tell whether we are dealing with a finely-nuanced distinction between *vedeṣṭa*, opt. 'may she find', *bhavāti* subj. 'she will [presumably] become', and *rājatu* 3sg.imper. 'let her rule'; or with practically interchangeable parts.

common in the RV and the AV, outnumbering the opt. by a factor of three or four. However, it virtually disappears in the later language, only the 1sg. *-āni* surviving as the so-called 1sg. imperative. Its functions otherwise are assumed by the fut. in *-(i)ṣya-* (457C). In G, by contrast, the modal flavor seems to have increased with time, thereby encroaching on the function of the opt., with the result that the opt. forms eventually disappeared.

FORMATION. *Stem.* In PIE the subj. was formed from the unvarying *e*-grade of the root with what appears to have been the ordinary thematic vowel. Thus to **H_1es-* 'be' the subjunctive would have been **H_1esoH₂*, **H_1eses(i)*, **H_1eset(i)*, **H_1esome*, **H_1esete*, **H_1esont*. (This becomes L *erō, eris, erit* —the future tense.) The same relationship apparently obtains with subjunctives built to the thematic indicatives: the result of adding the subjunctive marker to the regular theme vowel was a long vowel, so **bherōH₁* (**-ooH₂*? **-eoH₂*?), **bherēs(i)*, **bherēt(i)*, **bherōme*, **bherēte*, **bherōnt*.

Endings. The endings of the subj. are a mixture of primary and secondary in the RV, but in the 2sg. and 3sg. only. If there was a functional distinction between the primary and secondary endings, it has not yet been discovered. The secondary endings greatly preponderate in athematic formations, while the frequency of the two is more nearly even in the thematic stems. It is unclear why the stem type should have any bearing on such a thing.

In PIE a distinction in them. stems between 1sg. indicat. **-oH₂* and subj. **-ōH₂* was possible, but in all IE languages these would have fallen together. They both gave *-ā* in PInIr., a homophony which was corrected in Indic when the indicative ending was remodeled as *-āmi* (424). The usual Indic form of the 1sg. subj. is *-āni*; the *-ni* is of uncertain origin. The original 1sg. subj. *-ā* is found only 13 times in the RV, but is well attested in Av.

In G the primary endings prevail. It appears that the same was true of Ital.; in L, of course, primary endings eventually displaced secondary endings everywhere, but in Sab., which better retained the distinction between primary and secondary endings, the futures continue primary endings: U **furent** < **fūsenti* 'they will be'.

The subj. is a common formation at all periods in the history of G, occurring freely with all stems except the fut., and is retained virtually unchanged apart from pronunciation in Modern Greek.

535. THE GREEK SUBJUNCTIVE FROM ATHEMATIC STEMS. The original type is that with ε/ο, corresponding to Ved. *ásas(i), ásat(i)* (= L *eris, erit* 'will be'), but this was widely replaced by the more distinctive η/ω originally proper to the thematic stems (534, 536). Many old 'short-vowel subj.' forms occur in Hom. and various dialects, especially in the σ-aor. Thus, in Hom. ἴομεν (cf. indicat. ἴμεν 'we go'), φθίεται (ἔφθιτο 'perished'), ἅλεται (ἆλτο 'leapt'), εἴδομεν (ἴδμεν 'know'), πεποίθομεν (πεποίθαμεν 'are persuaded'); and σ-aor.

βήσομεν (*βαίνω* 'go'), *ἀμείψεται* (*ἀμείβω* 'change'), *ἀλγήσετε* (*ἀλγέω* 'feel pain'); in inscriptions, Ion. *ποιησει* subj. (*ποιέω* 'make'), Cret. *αδικησει* (*ἀδικέω* 'do wrong'). (The 3sg. ending -*σει* was doubtless Homeric also, but once redactionally altered to the metrically identical -*σηι*, it cannot be detected).

So also from stems ending in a long vowel, as Hom. *γνώομεν* 'know', *στήομεν* (*στείομεν*) 'stand', *θήομεν* (*θείομεν*) 'put', whence with quantitative metathesis (79.3), Hom. *στέωμεν*, *θέωμεν*, Att. *στῶμεν*, *θῶμεν*. So also in aor. pass. -*θή-ομεν* > Ion. -*θέωμεν*, Att. -*θῶμεν*.

Attic has thematic type formations in *δύνωμαι* 'would be able', *ἐπίστωμαι* 'would understand', *κρέμωμαι* 'would be suspended'.

a. A different formation, with long vowel corresponding to a short vowel in the indicative, occurs in some dialects, as Mess. *τιθηντι* beside indicat. *τιθεντι*, Cret. *δυνᾱμαι* beside indicat. *δύναμαι*. These are analogic extensions of the patterns in thematic verbs as in indicat. *φέρομεν*, subj. *φέρωμεν*.

536. The greek subjunctive from thematic stems was formed with *η/ω* corresponding to *ε/ο* of the indicative. 2sg. -*ῃς*, 3sg. -*ῃ* are patterned on the indicat. -*εις*, -*ει* (425-6), parallel to the relation of 2pl. -*ητε* to -*ετε*. In Hom. there are also forms of the sg. with *μι*-endings, as *ἐθέλωμι* 'I would wish', *ἐθέλῃσθα* (cf. *τίθησθα*, **425b**), *ἐθέλῃσι*. In the 3pl. -*ωντι* (Att. -*ωσι*) and midd. -*ωνται*, the -*ω*- is preserved by the analogy of -*ωμεν*, -*ωμεθα* and so does not show the usual shortening before -*ντ*- (63.2).

a. There is no unambiguous evidence for original 3sg. -*η* from *-*ēt* (= Ved. -*āt*): the dialect forms in -*η* (Arc. *εχη* to *ἔχει* 'has', Thess. *θελη* to *θέλει* 'wishes') may continue such, but may stand for the usual -*ῃ*.

537. The latin future (the PIE subjunctive in Latin). As mentioned in 501, the PIE subjunctive is the basis for the Italic future. This is most straightforward in formations based on the verb 'be', thus *erit* 'will be' < **H₁eseti*; and -*bit* (as for example *amābit* 'will love') from some subjunctive form of **bhŭ̄*- (501.3). These correspond then to the G short vowel subjunctives.

Elsewhere, that is in the thematic 3rd and 4th conj., the marker was originally *-*ē*-, shortened in some environments by the usual rules to -*ĕ*- (83.1, .3 so *legēs*, *legēmus* but *leget*, *legent*; cf. U **furent** 'they will be'). These correspond to the long vowel subj. of G and Ved. Conventional wisdom reconstructs the original paradigm of the thematic subj. with alternation in the stem-marker between *-*ē*- and *-*ō*-, as seen in G. In that case the unvarying stem in *-*ē*-, a pan-Italic feature, would be the result of leveling. The PIE distribution of grades in the long vowel subj. is however uncertain, and in fact the usual view has a serious weakness. If the stem originally alternated along the lines attested by G, it would fit so well with the thematic pattern that its ouster in Italic in favor of a uniform *-*ē*- would be comprehensible only if some powerful influence could be found. No such influence is evident, and therefore the likelier explanation is that the Ital.

system is the conservative one, and that the *ē/ō* alternation was introduced in G on the analogy of the thematic vowel.

An unexplained detail of the L system is the 1sg. *-am*. Of course, if the inherited 1sg.subj. was *-ō*, homophonous with the present, that would explain its ouster by some unambiguous form. On the other hand, the orig. 1sg. might have been **-ē*. This is not necessarily inherited; it would be the result of a sacrifice of a saliently 1sg. form (**-ō*) for a saliently future one. Just such a form might be seen in the curious early 1sg. forms quoted by grammarians (*dice, facie, recipie*). One would have expected rather **-ēm* (that is **-ĕm*, 83.1), and the forms quoted could in fact stand for **dicĕm* and so on, given the fragility of final *-m* in L (237.1). Either way, the source of *-am* is obscure.

a. The imperf. and perf. subj. marker **-sē-* (544) is often traced to this formation; but as it has a different distribution and a different function it is best regarded as having a different origin as well. If the two types were originally one, moreover, the replacement of 'original' **legēm* (like **legerēm* or **essēm*) by *-am* would be hard to fathom.

OPTATIVE

538. As remarked in 533, the evidence from the earliest InIr. texts suggests that the optative was not a mood correlative with the indicative and derived from inflected stems, but was itself an eventive stem per se, formed directly from the root like all stem-forming elements; and only in the evolution of the IE daughter languages did it become freely derivable from STEMS, including (though in some groups only) the stative (perfect) stems.

Note that the use of 'secondary endings' in the optative (and the absence, in G and InIr., of the augment, 441) implies no affinity with anterior tenses (the imperf. and aor.): the optative, being a conditional or irreales form, was neither real present (as marked by primary endings) nor real past (as marked by the augment). Its closest formal/functional yokefellow, in the sense of being marked with generic person endings, would have been the so-called injunctive (416). This is, once again, a grammatical rather than a pragmatic limitation: overtly preterital conditionals, like NE *would have (written)*, are not only semantically coherent, they are widespread, and L for example did develop tense-marked optatives, as did Gmc.

539. STEM FORMATIONS OF THE OPTATIVE.

1. The clearest is an athematic element **-yéH*$_1$*-/*-iH*$_1$*-*, affixed to zero grade of the root and ablauting exactly in accord with the distribution of other athem. stems: *e*-grade in the singular active, zero grade in all other forms. In what appears to be an innovation shared (like so many others) between G and InIr., this marker was generalized to characterized athematic stems: **H*$_1$*és-ti* : **H*$_1$*s-yéH*$_1$*-t* :: **yunékti* : *X*, where *X* = **yungyéH*$_1$*t*. In InIr. this alternation was reconfigured as a matter of voice contrast: the full grade stem *-yā-* was generalized throughout the active (with the partial exception

of 3pl. *-yur*), leaving the zero grade *-ī-* as the opt. marker of the middle, in effect. A similar thing happens in Attic. In L *-ī-* < **-iH₁-* spreads at the expense of *-iē̆-*: *sīm, sīs, sīt* (later *sim, sit*) take the place of earlier *siem, siēs, siet*. Similarly L *velīs, velit* (= Go. *wileis* 2sg., *wili* 3sg.).

2. In thematic stems, G, Gmc., Baltic, and InIr. attest an element **-oy-* in place of the theme vowel, so indicat. **bheresi*, **bhereti*, **bheromos*; opt. **bheroys*, **bheroyt*, **bheroyme*: G φέροι (indicat. φέρει); Skt. *bharet* (indicat. *bharati*); Go. *bairai* (indicat. *bairiþ*). Some authorities theorize that this **-oy-* is a concatenation of the theme vowel **-o-* with the zero grade of the just-discussed athem. opt. marker **-iH₁-*. Against this attractive idea, however, is the absence of evidence for **H* in this formation: it should in fact have been **-oyH̥₁-* rather than **-oyH₁-*, with the laryngeal therefore readily detectable. Both G and Ved. would be expected to show at least occasional evidence for an additional syllable, such as G ˣ*-οιε* or Ved. scansion ˣ*-aït* for textual *-et*; but neither do. (See **541b** below, however.) A bigger problem is that the theme vowel in a derivative should be **-e-*, not **-o-*, as in derivatives of nominal thematic stems (**460, 468.2A, 319a**).

a. The 1sg. **bheroym̥*, unlike final **-m* after laryngeals, clearly shows its syllabic character: Ved. *śíkṣeyam* 'I would learn', Go. *-au* < **-ayuⁿ*, G dial. -ΟΙΑ (541).

3. Celt. and Ital. have a different opt. marker, namely **-ā-* in place of the theme vowel. This is seen in the L pres. subj. of the 2nd, 3rd, and 4th conj. (*habeās, -at*; *legās, -at*; *capiat*; *veniat*). It is also found in the formation of the imperf. INDICATIVE of ATHEMATIC stems (*erat* < **esāt* 'was'; *-bā-* < **fŭā-*; **498**). The possible relationship of this formation to **-oy-* and **-yeH₁-* has been much discussed, with particular attention to something like *-ā-* < **-oa-* < **-oya-* < **-oyH̥₁-*. Such an explanation might work for Celt., in which the loss of intervocalic *-y-* was very early—prior even to the Celt. loss of **p*—but must have resulted in Ital. ˣ*-ō-* rather than *-ā-* (**88.3**).

540. THE GREEK OPTATIVE FROM ATHEMATIC STEMS is formed with -ιη-/-ι- (that is, *-ī-) from **-yeH₁-*/**-iH₁-* (**539.1**). Thus, to 'be', εἴην < **esyēn*, εἶμεν < **ehīmen*, εἶεν < **ehyen* (**H₁s-iH₁-ent*); cf. Ved. *syā́-* < **H₁syeH₁-* = early L *siem, siēs, siet*. Long-vowel roots have been variously analyzed; the predicted forms would be **dhe-dhH̥₁-yeH₁-*, **sti-stH̥₂-yeH₁-*, **de-dH̥₃-yeH₁-*, and the like, whence *τιθέην, *ἱστάην, *διδόην. In the attested forms, τιθείην, ἱσταίην, διδοίην (and likewise aor. θείη < *θέη < **dhH̥₁-yeH₁-t*), with the inspiration of sg. εἴην, the -ι- was imported from the pl. stems, τιθεῖμεν, τιθεῖτε, and so on. But the explanation of these pl. stems (τιθεῖ-, ἱσταῖ-, διδοῖ-) will vary depending on one's understanding of the sound laws. Some think the development of -θει-, -σται-, and -δοι- from **-dhH₁iH₁-*, **-stH₂iH₁-*, and **-dH₃iH₁-* is phonetically regular. Others, that the expected stems would have been *τιθῑ-, *ἱστῑ-, and *διδῑ-, which were remodeled according to the usual root-forms -θε-, -στα-, -δο-.

The inherited distribution of full grade of the suffix in the sg. act. and zero grade of the suffix in the du. and pl. and all middles is maintained in Hom. with only one exception, aor. *σταίησαν* 3pl. for regular *σταῖεν*. But in Att. the singular stem form is often carried over into the pl., as *εἴημεν* 'we may be', *εἴητε*, less often *εἴησαν*; and *θείημεν*, *δοίημεν*, and so on.

CONTRACT VERBS. On the analogy of *διδοίην*, *διδοῖμεν* were formed *φιλοίην* 'I may love', *μισθοίην* 'I may hire out' on the basis of the pl. forms (*φιλοῖμεν*/*φιλέοιμεν*, *μισθοῖμεν*), and further *τῑμῴην* 'I may esteem' (**τῑμα-οιην*). For the sg. of contract verbs this is the usual Att. type, though forms in *-οῖμι*, *-οῖς*, and especially *-οῖ* also occur. In Hom. there are only two examples of this: *φιλοίη* 'would love', *φοροίη* 'would wear'. Among the Attic details is *σχοίην*, based on pl. *σχοῖμεν* (*ἔχω* 'have').

Conversely, sometimes athem. verbs take on thematic features: 3sg. midd. *τιθοῖτο*, *θοῖτο* for *τιθεῖτο*, *θεῖτο* after *φιλοῖτο*.

Presents in *-νῡμι* regularly follow the thematic type, as *δεικνύοιμι*. But there are a few forms with *-ῡ-* (< **-νῐ̄-*), as Hom. 3sg. *δαινῦτο*, 3pl. *δαινῦατο*.

541. THE GREEK OPTATIVE FROM THEMATIC STEMS was formed with *-οι-* in place of the theme vowel (539.2), as *φέροις*, *φέροι* = Skt. *bhares*, *bharet*, Go. *bairais*, *bairai*.

The most archaic attested 1sg. form, *-οια* < **-oym̥* (more in note **b** below), was hypothesized by August Schleicher well before an attestation actually appeared in Arc. *εξελαυνοια* 'I would drive out'. This ending was replaced by *-οιμι*, as *φέροιμι*, with the substitution of the familiar athem. ending of *εἰμί*, though it remains more than slightly strange that the remodeling was not rather to ˣ*φέροιν* or ˣ*φέροιην* or the like, after *τιθέιην*. (An ending in *-οιν* is attested, but very much later—Euripides—than *-οιμι*.) The 3pl. *φέροιεν* is parallel to *εἶεν* with *-εν* from **-ent* (430.2). In 3pl. midd. Hom *γενοίατο*, but Att. *φέροιντο*, like *-νται* for earlier *-αται* (437.3).

a. 3pl. *-εν* is traceable to **-ent* only in athem. *εἶεν* and the like (*H_1*s-i*H_1*-ent*, cf. L *sient*); them. *φέροιεν* 3pl. is a remodeling of something like **pʰeroya* < **bheroyn̥t*. Ved. has *-(i)yur* in both, and Go. *sijaina* 'may they be' and *bairaina* are themselves manifestly remodeled in several (mysterious) ways.

b. The apparent retention of intervocalic *-y-* in *-οια*, *-οιεν*, *-οια(ν)το*, is easily explained as due to the analogy of the *-οι-* which is salient in other forms. Something very similar is seen in Skt. *bhareyam* (for expected **bharāyam* < **bheroym̥*) and 3pl. *bhareyur*. In these forms, where the endings begin with a vowel, it is almost as if the **-y-* appears twice: **bheroyym̥* and the like, and some scholars have suggested that that is the actual prehistorical shape. Before the advent of laryngeal theory, such a suggestion was arbitrary; nowadays however the idea has renewed vigor, as G *-οια*, Ved. *-eyam* might be the regular reflexes of **-y*H_1*-*.[1] If so, that would make things easy, but the attested forms of both

---

[1] The expected outcome of say **-oy*H_1*m̥* in G would depend on the tenets of the particular laryngealist, but the possibilities would include **-οα* (just as from **-oym̥*) and **-οεν* < **-oyem*. In Indic, **-oy*H_1*m̥* would have given **-ayam*.

languages would be unlike everything known or reasonably surmised about the usual behavior of laryngeals. In fact the analogical replacement of G *-οα by -οια and of Indic *-*āyam* by -*eyam*, and similarly in the 3pl., would be of such a commonplace variety that no special explanation is called for.

542. GREEK OPTATIVES OF THE σ-AORIST. The usual type, λῡ́σαιμι, λῡ́σαις, λῡ́σαι, is obviously formed from the stem -σα- (after its spread at the expense of -σ-, 504) by analogy with the thematic forms φέροιμι, λίποιμι. The only exact proportional analogy would be in the 1pl., as φέρομεν : (ἐ)λῡ́σαμεν :: φέροιμι : *X*, where *X* = λῡ́σαιμι. From there the analogy would have spread from person to person step-wise, φέροιμι : φέροις :: λῡ́σαιμι : *X*, where *X* = λῡ́σαις. Of course, the history of the formation might have less to do with exact analogical proportions than with the general spread of alpha-thematic stems in certain G tenses.

An earlier type is represented by the forms in -ειας, -ειε, -ειαν, which are common in Hom. and in Att., with traces in other dialects. (The remaining persons, 1sg. -εια, 1pl. -ειμεν, 2pl. -ειτε are quoted by grammarians.) The source of this type is much disputed, but it looks like a formation in *-*sey*- parallel to the usual them. *-*oy*-. The 1sg. -εια would then be parallel to -οια (541), and from this the -ειας, -ειε would be formed with the endings of the indicative. However, what this *-*sey*- might have been is unknown, as it has neither recognizeable cognates in other IE languages nor a credible source in the history of G. (Some have entertained the idea that *-*s-iH*$_1$- > *-*siy*- whence *-*sey*-; but this is inconsistent with the usual (reasonable) explanation of 3pl. -ιαν as in Cret. (δια)λυσιαν, namely that it is ultimately < *-*siyn̥t*.)

543. THE SUBJUNCTIVE OF LATIN GRAMMAR is etymologically the PIE optative, though not all details are straightforward. The distribution of mood signs, all of which are long vowels with regular shortening before -*m*, -*t*, -*nt*, and -*r*, is as follows:

1. The western PIE opt. *-*ā*- (539.3) in the 2nd, 3rd, and 4th conj. Apart from lingering uncertainty about the history and function of this element in PIE, its evolution in L as a marker of the 'subjunctive' is a simple matter.

2. The vowel *-*ē*- of the 1st conj. is enigmatic. The underlying PItal. stem has commonly been reconstructed as *-*ā-yē*-. This does not make sense morphologically: *-*yē*- could be an opt. marker, but then its etymon combined only certainly with roots; possibly in Italic (as in Indo-Iranian) the suffix spread to athematic stems. And although the reconstruction *-*āyē*- fits the facts of Sab. well enough—O *deiuaid* 'may he swear', **sakahíter** 'may it be dedicated'—the same cannot be said for L: the vowel resulting from the contraction of these constructs should have been -*ā*-, not -*ē*- (88.3). This would of course have been homophonous with the indicative. Furthermore, since the *ā*-conjugation in Ital. is actually an ordinary thematic type at

bottom (PItal. *-*āyō*, *-*āyesi*, *-*āyeti*, 475-6), just like much of the 2nd and 3rd and all of the 4th conj., it is curious that some special *ē*-formation would be limited to just this one.

Similarly problematic is the imperf. (544) and pluperf. (531.4) subj. element *-*sē*-, which looks as though it should be somehow related. But it is ultimately an athem. formation (see 3, below, and 544), and it is difficult to accept the idea of the distribution of the same element *-*ē*- now in thematic, now in athematic formations.

a. Descriptively, the relationship between indicat. and subj. (opt.) in L is one of *polarity*: indicat. stems in -*ĕ̄*- form the subj. in -*ā*-, indicat. stems in -*ā*- form the subj. in -*ē*-. Polar relationships are not uncommon in the morphology of languages, but an unanswered question is whether polarity is ever the goal of an innovation or only the effect of something else (with the polarity principle at most inspiring a tidying-up of the imperfections of a not-quite-polar pattern). It is at least barely thinkable that as vowel contraction was rendering the indicat. and subj. paradigms of the *ā*-conjugation homophonous, the subj. in -*ē*- might have been created out of thin air as a sort of therapeutic polarity. Another, less fanciful, possibility is that at some point *-*ā*(*y*)*ēs*, *-*ā*(*y*)*ēt*, and so on, metathesized to *-*ē*(*y*)*ās*, *-*ē*(*y*)*āt* under the influence of other optatives, such as **kapyās*, **wenyās*, and especially **monēyās*; sound laws would automatically result in attested *amēs*, *amet*, *amēmus*

b. Long-vowel conditionals or 'conjunctives' occur in various IE languages, but typically in a manner too fragmentary to analyze. The Skt. imperatives (hortatory) 1du. -*āva*, 1pl. -*āma* might, for example, continue the element *-*ē*- or *-*eH₁*- seen in L, but might just as well be the usual subj. forms—athem. *-*ome* and them. *-*ōme* having the same outcome.

3. -*ī*- < *-*iH₁*-, zero grade of the athem. opt. marker, is evident in the subj. of several root stem verbs: *sim*, *velim* (but see 484.1, end), *edim*; and in the perf.subj. < *-*is*-*ī*- of all conjugations—evidence, if evidence were needed, that the element *-*is*-, whatever its origins, formed an athematic stem.

a. The only trace of the old gradation -*yē*-/-*ī*- is in the early L *siem*, *siēs*, *siet*, *sīmus*, *sītis*, *sient*. Even early L has also *sīm*, *sīs*, *sīt* with generalized -*ī*-.

The 3pl. *sient* is not from **syē*-. It reflects either **H₁s-iH₁-ent*, as in G εἶεν, or else **H₁s-iH₁-n̥t*, implied by Ved. *syúr*. Both would give **siens*, whence *sient* by the usual spread of primary endings in place of secondary ones. Later *sint* is from **sīnt*, which could be either analogical or by regular contraction (68) from *sient*.

544. THE IMPERFECT SUBJUNCTIVE. The imperf. subj. is formed with *-*sē*-: to athem. stems **essē*- (*essem*, *essēs*), **velsē*- (*vellem*, *vellēs*); to vowel stems, with rhotacism, **amāsē*- (*amārem*, *amārēs*), **habēsē*- (*habērem*, *habērēs*); and so on, in all four conjugations, and also in the pluperf. subj. (531.4). The 1st conj. *ă*-stems from laryngeals (475.6) have been absorbed into the *ā*-stem type, so *domārem*, the one exception being *dărem* 'I would have given'. Sab. seems to attest a similar formation, though the only forms identified are O **fusíd** corresponding formally to the OL imperf. subj. *foret* < **fusēt* (38b), **h]errins** 'they would have taken', and **patensíns** 'they would have opened'. Note that the imperf. subj. to *ferō* (*ferrem*, *ferrēs*) is no ancient stem **fersē*-, but a regular syncopation of **feresē*-.

The ultimate origins of this *-*sē*- have been much discussed, with little result. The usual view was touched on above, namely that this is an *ē*-optative (as seen in the *ā*-stem 'subjunctive') built to an *s*-aorist. The difficulties with supposing that the same mood-marker might be added to thematic and athematic stems has already been noted. An additional objection is that originally the aor. opt., like the 'pres.' opt., was actually tenseless, which raises the question of how it could have become both preterital and modal (as remarked above, **498**, modals do become preterital, but preterital INDICATIVE). A third difficulty, and the most serious one, is the inappropriateness in the first place of any aoristic component in the makeup of the Ital. imperfect, whose explicit 'infectum' semantics—incomplete, continuing, or iterated action—are the exact antithesis of the proper function of the aor., whose indisputable forms in fact end up in the L COMPLETIVE anterior tense, the perfect (**522**). Other suggestions have been made, most notably that the form is an *ē*-optative (? < *-*yeH*$_1$-) of the desiderative (**457**). The semantics of the last are appropriate, being to begin with something like NE *would*; but *-*syeH*$_1$- should give L ˣ-*iiē*- (cf. *cuiius* < **k*^{w}*osyo*), not -*rē*-.

For the perf. and pluperf. subj. see **531**.

IMPERATIVE

545. The classification of the imperative as a MOOD, correlative with subj., opt., and indicat., is obviously an analysis faute de mieux. But no straightforward alternative analysis suggests itself.

Since the imperative is a kind of future, it is perhaps reminiscent of opt. and subj., moods; but probably it has most in common FUNCTIONALLY with the desiderative (**457**). The main differences are the roles: in the desiderative, desire is ascribed at will to any person, who is also the one to undertake the action, whereas in imperatives the desire for a (future) action is only on the part of the speaker, and the action itself is always on the part of someone else: 'I want you to build a fire' is not a possible expression via the IE desiderative.

What sets the IE imperatives most sharply apart from the moods (and the desiderative also) is morphology: they have no special stem marker, instead having special person-markers. In the 2pl. active there is no difference in form between the imperative and indicative endings (and in fact most of the special endings are lost in L). Of course, the expression of desire for a future action on the part of a speaker can be couched in a variety of ways, some of them using actual mood paradigms, as in the hortatory forms familiar from the classical languages, or else the sentence complement structure of NE *let's*, or else syntactic particles (as in G *μή*), and circumlocutions for various purposes, differing according to such variables as politeness, intimacy, and so on (*Why don't we sit down* or *How about sitting down* or *Perhaps you would like to sit down*, and so on).

a. Since a literal command given to oneself would be at best a special use of the usual 2sg. imperat., there is no real 1sg. or pl. imperat. The so-called 1sg. imperat. of certain languages usually turns out to be one of two things: either a form of opt. of the *I should drop dead if I'm lying* type; or a request for a command (such requests are expressed in no fixed way in NE, but *What if I give Edna a lift?* or *How about I give Edna a lift?* would be typical).

The speaker's desire for future action involving the speaker together with others eventually acquires special endings in some IE languages, such as Skt. *-āva* du., *-āma* pl., or special locutions like the NE *let's* + supine, or the NHG inversion of pronoun and verb (*trinken wir* 'let's drink'), but is usually just some kind of non-indicative 1pl. form like the G and L hortatory subj. (historically an opt. in the case of L).

b. As the imperative invariably deals with a future event, it is obvious that a present imperative, and still more a past-tense imperative, would be contradictions in terms. The mere occurrence of imperative forms to aorists and (albeit much less commonly) perfects is therefore weighty evidence that their preterital function in various IE languages is a secondary development.

546. TABLE OF ENDINGS.

	Active		Middle
	athematic	*thematic*	
2sg.	-∅	-∅	-so
	-dhi		
3sg.	-tu	-tu	-to
	-u		
2pl.	-te	-te	-dhwo
3pl.	-entu	-ntu	-nto

547. SECOND SINGULAR ACTIVE.

1. The bare stem, the commonest and most primitive type. So universally from thematic stems, PIE **bhere*, **spekye*, **gʷm̥ske*: G φέρε, στέλλε (465.4), βάσκε; Ved. *bhára*, *páśya*, *gáccha*, L *lege* (= G λέγε), *posce* (= Ved. *pr̥ccha*, PIE **pr̥ḱsḱe*). So also Go. *bair* (with regular loss of final short vowel), OIr. *beir* /beρ'/ < PCelt. **bere*; Hitt. *u-uš-ki* 'see'.

The L *-ā*, *-ē*, *-ī* of the 1st, 2nd, and 4th conj. are likewise the bare stem, but presumably *-ā* reflects **-āe* < **-āye*; *-ē* reflects **-ĕe* < **-ĕye*; and so on. The *-e* of the *capiō* type (*cape*, OL *face*) continues earlier **-i*, a reduction of expected **-ye* and additional evidence in favor of the idea (481) that **-yesi*, **-yeti*, **-yemos* in the same stems became *-is*, *-it*, *-imus*. 4th conj. *-ī* < **-iye* shows the same development as *-īs* < **-iyes* and the other finite endings.

For the athem. stems, IE languages fall into two general types. In G and InIr., the most usual form of the 2sg. athem. imperat. was marked with a special ending (PIE **-dhi*, 3 below); and in Hitt. and Ital., the bare stem is used, just as in the thematic types. Endingless imperative forms built to athematic stems are also found in Vedic, but only as a comparatively infrequent alternative 2sg. form in the *nu*-suffix class; so *śr̥ṇú* 'hear', *tanu* 'stretch' and some half-dozen more; very much more frequent are *śr̥ṇuhí*, *tanuhi* <

*-*dhi*.[1] The endingless variety corresponds to G δείκνῡ, except for the grade of the stem. Perhaps the peculiar status of *nu*-stems among athematics has some connection with the fact that they are the only athematic stems which in PIE ended in a vowel, which makes them like the bare stem of the thematic types. Corresponding to G ἵστη, Dor. ἄνασστᾱ, Indic has only forms in -*(d)hí*.

L *es* 'be' does not correspond to Ved. *edhi*, G ἴσθι; nor does *ī* 'go' (*ei* in *abei*, Plaut.) match Ved. *ihí*, G ἴθι, Hitt. *i-it*.

An endingless root aor. imperat. is fossilized in L *cedo* < **cedō* < **ḱe-deH₃* 'give here'.

G τίθει, δίδου reflect *τιθε-ε, *διδο-ε with a shape in imitation of the thematic imperatives—the -ε in the pattern form is actually the theme vowel and not an ending, of course, but its appearance in a complex like *διδοε in place of *διδοθι shows it had been reinterpreted.

a. L *dīc* 'say', *dūc* 'lead', *fac* 'do', *fer* 'carry' are not the bare roots they look like, but reflect regular OL *dīce*, *dūce*, *face*, and **fere* with apocope. These are usually stated to owe their special status to their extreme frequency. Of course, *dūc* is hardly in the same category with the others, but more to the point, commonness does not cause peculiar pronunciations—rather it helps phonologically regular but descriptively peculiar forms resist the effects of leveling analogies.

In fact, the explanation for the L apocopated imperatives seems to be phonological. *Dīc* and *dūc* happen to be the only primary 3rd conj. verbs with roots ending in -*c*-. (*Faciō* does not quite fit here.) The loss of short vowels after -*r*- is a regular feature of L (74.6); and *fer*- happens to be the only primary 3rd. conj. verb ending in original -*r*-. The dropping of vowels after -*r*- was early, which accords with the lack of attestation of **fere*: in contrast to the others, *fer* is already uniform in the playwrights, additional evidence that the loss of *-*e* in these four forms involved separate developments.

2. G forms with secondary ending -ς and zero grade of the root. This G innovation is limited to certain root aor. forms: θές, δός, ἕς, σχές, in place of earlier *τεθι (or *θῆ), *δοθι (or *δῶ), *ἑθι, *σχε. Some scholars have entertained the idea of a development of -ς from -θι (item 3, next)—or rather *-*tʰy*—parallel to πρός < προτί (**148-9**), which is certainly possible, but a back formation founded on the ambiguous 2pl. forms θέτε, δότε is more likely.

Various IE languages use INDICATIVE 2sg. forms as imperatives, either routinely (as in Go. *ni ogs* 'don't be afraid') or sporadically (as in Vedic).

3. PIE *-*dhi*, Ved. -*dhi*, -*hi* (a weakening of -*dhi*), Av. -δī, -*dī*, OCS -*dĭ*, G -θι. It is unattested in the remaining groups except possibly Hitt. It was

---

[1] In the AV the ratio of imperatives in -*nu* to those in -*nuhi* has already changed significantly in favor of the endingless type. In the later language a pattern unlike anything foreshadowed in the RV became established: *nu*-stem imperatives to roots ending in vowels are endingless, to those ending in consonants take -*hi*. Thus *sunu* 'press', *śṛṇu* 'hear', but *āpnuhi* 'get' and *dhṛṣṇuhi* 'dare'.

formed only to athem. stems—eventive and stative alike—which originally were in zero grade. So ἴσθι, ϝισθι 'know' (**wid-dhi*) = Skt. *viddhi*, though a late form; the two are superimposable on OCS *věždĭ*, apart from the grade of the root. G ἴθι 'go' = Ved. *ihí*; φαθί 'speak'; ὄρνυθι 'rise', corresponding to the Ved. *hinuhi* 'drive' type. Indic introduced the full grade into long-vowel root imperatives, so Ved. *pāhí* 'protect', *vāhí* 'blow' in place of expected **pihí*, **vihí*. The same is found in most G imperatives of parallel makeup: στῆθι, δίδωθι; these might be viewed as original, but such a view is undercut by forms like κλῦθι 'hear' which are necessarily analogical, and the others are probably analogical too. G γνῶθι 'know', however, is likely to be from PIE **ǵneH₃-dhi* with irregular full grade.

This remains the regular ending of the aor. passive in -ηθι, as φάνηθι, or, with dissimilation of aspirates (138), λύθητι. For G ἴσθι 'be' see 496.2.

a. Hitt. has a 2sg. imperat. in *-t* in one form—*i-it* 'go'—and in the *nu*-stems, as *pár-ku-nu-ut* 'make pure', *(a-)ar-n-ut* 'bring'. It is tempting to see in this a reflex of **-dhi*, though it is disconcerting that apart from the isolated *i-it* 'go' it is limited to the very form class for which the ending was originally optional in Indic (1, above).

b. A number of Vedic imperatives have unobvious forms. Ved. *edhi* 'be' is actually the regular outcome of **azdhi*, with analogical full grade of the root (Gāth. *zdī* preserves the original form). Ved. *jahí* 'slay' is the regular but descriptively strange imper. to *hánti*: **gʷhn̥-dhí* > **ghadhi* (→ **jhadhi*, in keeping with the usual leveling of the effects of palatalization of root-initial consonants) > **jadhí* (Grassmann's Law, 138) > *jahí*; a precise cognate is preserved in Av. *jaiδi*. Ved. *dehí* 'give' and *dhehí* 'put' are traditionally traced to **dazdhi*, **dhazdhi*, originally **dedᶻdhi*, **dhedhᶻdhi*, respectively, with the usual sibilant between two apicals (212). This account is incorrect, however, for two large reasons. First, such sibilants in Indic disappear (NB *viddhi* 'know', above, next to G ἴσθι, both < **widᶻdhi*). Second, the putative etyma would not have had an apical-apical sequence in the first place, as they must have been **dedH̥₃dhi* and **dhedhH̥₁dhi*, respectively. Of course, the shape of the imperative as built to the reduplicated stem is beside the point, as the aboriginal imperative forms must have been root aorists (as in L *cedo*, Av. *dāiδī*, and OLith. *duodi*) rather than pres., that is, something like **di(d)hí*, **dhi(d)hí*. Why these were remade as bogus full grades *dehi*, *dhehí* is the question.

c. OCS *daždĭ* 'give' is a late form and not traceable DIRECTLY to **dedH₃dhi* or anything of the kind, though the element **-dhi* is beyond question an ingredient. The original state of affairs is preserved in OLith. *duodi* (= Av. *dāiδī*), and the OCS form is probably a remodeling of earlier **dadĭ* on the basis of regular *věždĭ* 'know' and *jaždĭ* 'eat' < **ēdᶻdhi*.

4. The rare πίει (πῖνω 'drink'), ἄγει 'drive', δίδοι 'give' are probably nothing more than the zero grade stem forms with an added -ι. This, in all likelihood, is only the primary marker. (If Hitt. *i-it* 'go' and the imperatives to *nu*-stems in *-nu-ut* are cognate with **-dhi*, either the Hitt. forms have lost the final **-i*, a realistic possibility, or else it never had it; in that case the **-dhi* of InIr., BS, and G might include the primary marker, which is much less realistic.)

5. The -ον in the σ-aor. (λῦσον, δεῖξον) is of obscure origin.

548. PIE **-tōt*. G -τω, L *-tō* (early *-tōd*), Osc. *-tud* (presumably /tōd/),

U *-tu*, Indic (mostly Vedic) *-tāt*. In Indic, commonly though not invariably, the form is used of an event following another event, implying 'and then' or 'next'. This is the general force of the affix in L too, and is the basis for a commonly held theory of its origins: an abl.sg. of the pronoun **to-* (376.1), lit. 'from that' or 'after that', appended to the imperative proper: so originally **lege tōt* 'after that, gather', which eventually coalesced into a single word, **legetōt*. This idea is however seriously embarrassed by a formal problem, namely the form of the abl.sg. of **to-* in PIE is **tosmōt*, as in Ved. *tásmāt*, 376.1.)

In earliest Ved. the main (in some opinions, the sole) function of the formation is a 2sg. Only later, and feebly at that, its use is extended to other persons and numbers.

In G, however, the inherited *-τω* is limited to 3sg. Transparently based on it were the 3du. *-των*; and the 3pl., which had four distinct formations, namely:

-των, with added secondary ending, as Att.-Ion. *ἔστων*.

-ντω, created from 3sg. *-τω* by obvious analogy. Found in Doric, Northwest Greek, and other dialects.

-ντων, with double marking (not a distinct type, really, but a combination of the two preceding types), in Att.-Ion. and several other dialects: *φερόντων*, *τιθέντων* and the like.

-τωσαν, with the *σ*-aor. ending *-σαν*: late Att. *φερέτωσαν*, *ἔστωσαν*.

In L, *-tō* serves as 2sg. and 3sg. of the future imperative (so-called in the school grammars—a better term would be *sequential imperative*, as all imperatives are 'future imperatives'), and the plurals are based on it: *-tōte* with *-te* imported from the usual 2pl. imperat.; 3pl. *-ntō*, by an obvious analogy exactly parallel to G dial. *-ντω*. —A form of great age is *mementō*, which serves as the ordinary imperative of *meminī* 'remember'.

a. It is probable that the vagaries of person and number seen in the various daughters are attributable to the parent language. The starting points were 2sg. *bhere tōt*, 2pl. **bherete tōt*, 3sg. **bheret tōt*, 3pl. **bheront tōt*. The first three forms would all have turned into **bheretōt*, the last into **bherontōt*. Apart from its elegance, such an analysis has three considerations in its favor: the unlikelihood that an adverbial particle (unlike a person-marker proper) would have been limited to one person and number in a system, or not to begin with anyway;[1] the lack of agreement between Ved., G and L as to the function of the formation (and its functional diversity in L); and the use of the same ending in L for active and middle forms (550.2). For the reason touched on above, however, the association of the element with an ablative pronoun is very difficult to maintain.

549. 1. The 2pl. imperative is (apart from the formations in **-tōt*, above) the same as the indicative. The ending **-te* is thus simultaneously primary,

[1] The strict limitation of **-dhi* (547.3) to the 2sg. is one reason why its suggested origin as a particle is unconvincing.

secondary, and imperative. So Ved. *bhárata* 'carry', *śṛṇutá* 'hear', *itá* 'go', *hatá* 'slay'; Go. *bairiþ*; OCS *nesěte* 'carry' (only the last is distinct from indicat. *nesete*). The classical languages agree completely: G φέρετε, δείκνυτε, θέτε, δότε; L *legete, manēte, portāte, venīte, īte* 'go'. The only L irregularities are *dăte* 'give' (which at all events fits the usual scheme in that it is identical to the indicative) and the same form in the makeup of *cette* < **ke-date* < **ḱe-dH̥₃te* aor. 'give here', the pl. of *cedo* (above). U **etatu**, *etato*, however, point to PItal. *-*tā*. This is best taken as etymologically the dual ending seen in OCS -*ta*, Lith. -*ta*, though not otherwise corroborated. If this interpretation is correct, it supports the view that the L 2pl. indicat. -*tis* (428) is etymologically a dual.

a. Not a few 2pl. forms in the RV have full grade of the stem: *éta* next to *itá*, above, cf. 2pl. indicat. *itha*; *stota* 'praise', cf. 2sg *stuhí*; *sunutá* and *sunotá* 2pl. 'press'; aor. *śruta* and *śróta* 2pl. 'hear'. The restored full grade is typical of long-vowel roots, so pres. *pātá* 'protect', aor. *dāta* 'give', *dhāta* 'put'. None of these are likely to be ancient, but the explanation is unobvious (and for that reason some authorities do take them to be inherited).

2. PIE had 3sg. and 3pl. endings *-*tu* and *-*ntu* respectively. A *t*-less *-*u* next to more general *-*tu* would be in accord with the overall pattern of personal endings containing *-*t*- (426, 514.3). However, the *t*-less ending is found only in Hitt. in the *ḫi*-conj., and to some extent even there competes with -*tu* as *a-ku* 'may he die' next to *ak-du*, *ša-ak-ku* 'may he know' next to *ša-a-ak-du*, and it may be secondary rather than inherited.

a. The lack of evidence for a *t*-less *-*ru* (below), the 3pl. correlative of *-*u*, accords with the suspicion that the 3sg. -*u* is an analogical creation on the basis of the *t*-less 3sg. indicat. The usual endings are well-attested in Hitt., and are also seen in Ved.: *gacchatu* 'may he go', *ástu* 'may he be', *yunáktu* 'may he yoke', *śṛṇótu* 'may he hear', *mamáttu* 'may he be exhilarated' (perf.; root *mad*-), *dātu* 'may he give' and *dhātu* 'may he put' (aorists). Similarly 3pl. *gacchantu, santu, yuñjántu*. Something similar may underlie the Go. *bairadau* 3sg., *bairandau* 3pl. types, which however show the replacement of expected -*u* by -*au* of uncertain origin, but possibly imported from the 1sg. opt. (*bairau* 'may I carry') where it is regular, 539.2a.

Parallel to 3sg. *-*tu*/*-*u* one would expect 3pl. *-*ntu*/*-*ru*, but the last is nowhere attested.

550. THE MIDDLE IMPERATIVE.

1. *Second person*. In the 2sg. both G and L (in the pres.) reflect the PIE ending *-*so*, which in both languages had also displaced the ancestral form of the indicative (436.2), as G τίθεσο, φέρου (**bhereso*), L *sequere* (71.5). Ved. -*sva* is the same ending at bottom, but with -*v*- imported from somewhere; there are several good possibilities—the reflexive prn. *sva*- and the 2pl. ending -*dhva(m)*, below.

The original 2pl. ending *-*dhwo*, identical to the secondary indicative ending, is reflected in the unique RV *yajadhva*. OIr. *suidigid* /suδ′əγ′əθ′/ 'place' 2pl. midd.imperat. might contain such an ending, but the form is multiply ambiguous. Hitt. -*tum-ma-at* is identical with the pret. ending;

except for the mysterious final stop it is evidently equivalent to Ved. *-dhva*. In G and L, the 2pl. imperative endings are identical to the secondary endings of the indicative (437.2), whatever their histories: G -σθε, L *-minī*, and the G 2du. -σθον.

a. In early L, next to indicat. *-minī* 2pl. an imperative *-minō* arose, as in *fruiminō* 'enjoy, use'. Its function as a 3sg. as well as 2sg., as well as its ending, point to *-tō* (548) as the inspiration for the new form, but the details are obscure: *este* act. vs. *estō* midd. is only approximately like *-minī/-minō*. The proportion would however be exact if etymological **-mine* were one of the points of reckoning; and in fact just such a **-mine* may have been a stage in the history of *-minī* (437.2).

2. *Third person.* The 3rd person imperat. endings of the middle in PIE were evidently identical to the secondary indicative, so **-to*, **-nto*. In L these were perhaps conflated with the active **-(n)tōd* (548); at all events, the endings *-tō*, *-ntō* served as middle endings in OL, such as *utito* 'use' 2sg., *obsequito* 'may he honor' 3sg. (Cato), *utunto* 3pl. These all presumably were *-ō*; evidence for the length of the final vowel is provided by the more usual endings *-tor*, *-ntor*, which are manifestly *-(n)tō* with the addition of the *-r* of the middle endings (originally the primary tense marker, but by this point reinterpreted as a marker of the middle) with regular shortening before *-r* (83.3).

In G likewise there was a proliferation of analogical creations, which however took a totally different direction from the L analogues: on the pattern of the relation of midd. -σθε to act. -τε were created -σθω to act. -τω 3sg., -σθων to act. -των 3pl. and du.

As in the active (548), there are various 3pl. forms:

-σθων (the commonest type) parallel to act. -των in Att.-Ion. ἔστων: so φερέσθων and the like.

-(ν)σθω, parallel to act. -ντω, in Arg. ποιγραψανσθο (-ō), Epid. φεροσθο (both ο as ō).

-(ν)σθων, parallel to act. -ντων in early Att. επιμελοσθον (written in a signary in which neither -ου- (-ō-) nor -ω- are distinguished from -ο-).

-σθωσαν, parallel to act. -τωσαν, in late Att.

NON-FINITE FORMS

INFINITIVES

551. The infinitive is in origin a case form of a verbal noun which has become a fixture of the verb system, substituting under certain circumstances for a finite (person-marked) verb. While the use of verbal nouns as absolutes in this way may have begun in the parent speech, no particular set of forms was standard. By contrast, in most attested IE languages, including Sanskrit (from the Epic period on), G, and L, the range of infinitive forms and the formal relationships they bear to finite stems are to a large extent predictable.

But the systems seen in these languages are only the end points of an evolution which is no more than well underway in the Rigveda, which therefore provides a window on history. In the absence of the Vedic information we would simply have said that the regular Skt. infin. in *-tum* (as seen in *gantum* 'to go' and *janitum* 'to beget') and the L supine in *-tum* continued a PIE form of absolute verbal noun. More or less simple statements could be made about all other infinitive forms, the only hint of a more complex story being the lack of agreement from group to group.

The evidence provided by the Rigveda makes it unnecessary to speculate on why this is: its 700-odd forms that may be confidently taken as infinitives are made from a variety of noun stems and cases, amounting to thirty-five different types in all. Not all formations are equally frequent. One is unique (*i-tyā́i* 'to go', the dat. of a stem in *-tyā-*); some occur fewer than five times (such as *-vane*, the dat. of the otherwise common noun suffix *-van-*, is found to only four roots). Much more frequent are root nouns, *s*-stems, *n*-stems, and *tu*-stems, the acc. of the last (*-tum*) being the type that ultimately prevailed. The cases employed are likewise very unevenly distributed. 85 percent of infinitives in the RV are dative (a case that is relatively rare in declension); 9 percent are accusative; most of the remainder are genitive/ablative. There are but 14 instances of the locative, and no certain instances of the instrumental. But within the Vedic period itself the use of the dative declines steeply from its Rigvedic preeminence, and by the post-Vedic period the accusative, no more than a tenth as frequent as the dat. in the RV, became universal. It is a lesson of the highest importance that the ultimately triumphant formation—full grade of the root with *-tum*—is found on a mere five roots in the RV: the evolution of the paradigmatic post-Vedic infin. was an untidy process whose earlier stages provide no hint either as to the direction of the evolution or its final goal.

The Vedic situation is echoed in Old Irish, in which there is also no paradigmatic infinitive. Rather, to each verb there is a verbal noun; all genders are found, and virtually all stems. There are even suppletive relations, as to *fichid* 'fights', infin. *gal*.

In both Vedic and OIr. the verbal absolutes are built to ROOTS rather than to stems, though in the RV a few stem-traits occur (which disappear again, in the further evolution of the infin.). In both groups infinitive formations sport the same range of preverbs as the finite forms. As with the nomina actionis of English, there were to begin with no distinctions of voice or tense, modality, iterativeness, or anything else associated with the inflected stems (including the distinction between events and states).

In most IE languages this system changes in several basic ways. First, the verbal absolute system is boiled down to a small number of forms, which furthermore may acquire traits of tense and voice (as in G and L), though not necessarily (thus Skt. and Gmc.); and with the exception of

Indo-Iranian, the forms early come to be built to STEMS rather than to the roots underlying the stems (including, as in the case of the L type *legere*, 553.1, perceived as built to stems even when historically root-formed).

Given that these developments for the most part precede the historical period, and given the range of choices as to both stem class and case, there can be no surprise at the lack of agreement between G and L, or even between L and Sab.; indeed, even within G there is much diversity among dialects.

552. THE GREEK INFINITIVES. Infinitives in G have voice and tense, and are fully incorporated in the stem system. The case-markings of G infinitives are either an endingless loc., or a dat. in -αι. The latter is historically proper to only two forms, -σαι and its middle offshoot -σθαι, but early became identified as the infinitive tag par excellence and was transplanted to a number of other formations.

A. ACTIVE.

1. *From thematic stems.* Att.-Ion. -ειν (spurious diphth., 76: in some dial. -ην; contract verb -ᾶν < *-*āyehen* in contrast to 3sg. -ᾶι < *-*āye-i*). The familiar -ειν is a contraction of -εεν, still indicated in Myc. *e-ke-e* (*(h)ek*[h]*ehen*) 'to have' (G ἔχειν). It is clear that the *-*en* component is an endingless *n*-stem loc., like Ved. *kṣāman* 'on the earth'; but the whole complex must have been *-*e-sen*, *-*e-wen*, or *-*e-yen*. The last option can be eliminated: there is no evidence for an element *-*yen*-, which in any case would not give Myc. *e-ke-e*. The same Myc. form rules out *-*wen*- (for which there is fairly rich evidence outside of G). This leaves *-*sen*, for which there is also cognate evidence such as Hitt. *r*/*n*-stem deverbatives like *pár-ḫi-eš-šar* (dat. *pár-ḫi-eš-ni*) 'haste' to *pár-aḫ-zi*/*pár-ḫi-zi* (that is, /parhtsi/) 'drives'; and RV forms in -*sani* loc. (which include several of the very few infinitives built to present stems instead of roots, for example *gr̥ṇīṣáṇi* 'to sing', cf. *gr̥ṇā́ti* 'sings').

The insignificant role of the loc. in RV infinitives undercuts the view that these are locatives; but at the same time the recorded history of the infin. in Indic teaches a valuable lesson: the importance of a given formation at a given period is no predictor of subsequent developments.

a. The them. ending -εν of many dialects, as φέρεν, ἄγεν, is to be explained as the result of the following developments: first, abstraction of -εν from them. -εεν, which was transplanted to athem. stems (which originally formed a quite different infin.; 2, below); then this -εν was reimported into the thematics where they started. The essential correctness of this scenario is indicated by infinitives in simple -εν even to verbs in -εω (that is, *-ηω), as Arg. πωλεν = Att. πώλειν 'close a deal'.

2. *From athematic stems.* Att.-Ion. (also Arc.-Cyp.) -ναι, -εναι, and -ϝεναι. Thus τιθέναι (τίθημι), διδόναι (δίδωμι), perf. εἰδέναι (οἶδα), aor. θεῖναι (*θε-εναι), δοῦναι (*δοεναι), Cyp. δοϝεναι. This last, like Ved. *dāváne* 'to give', is to be analyzed as δο-ϝεναι. To εἰμί, Att.-Ion. εἶναι, Arc. ηναι may be from either **ehenai* or **esnai*.

These are not distinct formations but are the preceding forms elaborated with -αι imported from aor. -σαι, midd. -σθαι (below).

Similarly Hom., Lesb. -μεναι next to Hom. (and many dial.) -μεν. The former is reminiscent of the uncommon Ved. infin. in *-mane* (and the even rarer *-vane*), but the price of connecting -μεναι and *-mane* is the necessity of positing a dat.sg. ending **-ay* for the parent language (257.7), a weighty claim which such a slender basis cannot support. Others have taken -εναι to an underlying fem. **-eneH₂-*; such a stem, though nowhere attested as an infinitive, is twice attested in the RV forming abstracts of apparently suitable meaning from roots (*hasanā́-* 'jest', root *has-* 'laugh'; and perhaps—the meaning is uncertain—*vanā́nā-* 'desire', root *van-* 'wish, desire').[1] It is much more likely, however, that -μεν like -εν continues an endingless loc., and -μεναι like -(ϝ)εναι is an embellishment of the inherited form with the 'infinitival -αι' (see B, below).

3. Aor. εἶπαι (εἶπον 'said'), χεῦαι (ἔχευα 'poured') and the like are modeled on the type πέμψαι 'to lead' and δεῖξαι 'to point out', in which metanalysis took the -σ- of -σαι as the aor. stem. and -αι as the marker of the infinitive, which was thereupon transplanted to other types of stems. (The origin of the σ-aor. -σαι is discussed below.)

B. THE MIDDLE INFINITIVE IN -(ε)σθαι is uniform for all formations, apart from some minor details. It is possibly related to Rigvedic *-adhyāi*, which forms infinitives—but only active—to some 35 roots; it is a purely Rigvedic formation which had dropped out of sight by the Atharvaveda. Its etymon, whatever its ultimate history (there is no known noun-forming element *-(a)dhyā-*), would give G -(ε)σ(σ)αι; apart from the matters raised in note a, below, this is essentially the so-called σ-aor. infin., as λοέσσαι 'to wash', δεῖξαι 'to point out'. Its role results from reassessment of the form, which to begin with probably had no connection with *s*-aorists: in the RV it is built directly to roots. Such formations would have included **pʰeressai* 'to carry' (= RV *bhára̍dhyāi*), **hekʷessai* 'to follow' (= RV *sacádhyāi*), and **keyessai* 'to lie' (= RV *śayádhyāi*). It is noteworthy that in such formations as these, that is for which there were no σ-aor. forms to capture the infin. in -σσαι, they remained present tense, albeit slightly remodeled.

How or why an originally neutral formation becomes specifically middle or passive is unclear. It has been suggested that in this case accidental associations like κεῖται/*κεγεσσαι led to a reassessment of the formation as distinctively middle. But no exact source is really necessary,[2] and in any

---

[1] Furthermore, the infin. in Gmc. reflects **-onom*, an acc.sg. The corresponding fem. would have been **-oneH₂-*, which is not too different from **-eneH₂-*.

[2] As an example of the mutability of voice in verbals, note that the English pres.pple. to transitive verbs was originally—and now once again is—distinctively active; but for several hundred years expressions like *dinner is preparing* or *when the grave was covering*

case the actual attested form -σθαι (as in φέρεσθαι, κεῖσθαι) needs further manipulation such as contamination by the middle finite endings in -σθ- (437.2).

a. The equation of RV *-dhyāi* and G -σ(θ)αι, though widely endorsed, has a number of large formal problems. G -αι does not match Indic *-āi*; and the importation of -θ- from person markers into an infinitive marker is only barely believable.

In any case, a number of transparent analogical adjustments are evident in the details of the -σθαι formations. Athem. ἔσεσθαι, which serves as the future infin. of εἰμί, actually has the same structure as φέρεσθαι: the ending, originally -εσθαι, was added to roots; forms like παιδεύεσθαι presume a reanalysis of the φερ-εσθαι type as φερε-σθαι. Such a -σθαι is a component of ἵστασθαι, τίθεσθαι, δίδοσθαι (that is, ἵστα-σθαι and so on), and was added to the fut. stem ἐσ(σ)ε-.

b. Some scholars derive Ved. *-adhyāi* from **-n̥dh-* and see the latter in the L gerund in *-(e)ndī* (567-8). Such analysis cuts the ground from under the Vedic/Greek comparison endorsed (unenthusiastically) here.

553. THE LATIN INFINITIVE AND SUPINE.

1. THE ACTIVE INFINITIVE ENDING in L is *-re* in most verbs (thus *amāre, habēre, legere, audīre, dare*, also *ferre*), but *-le* in *velle, nōlle*, and *-se* in *esse* and the perf.infin. *-isse*. All these taken together reveal that the consonant was originally **-s-*. The final vowel is ambiguous, but **-si* would fit all the phonological facts and has a familiar structure: the loc.sg. of a neut. *s*-stem (297.2). This has no match elsewhere, however: the G infin. in -ειν is a loc., but to a different stem, and Ved. *s*-stem infinitives are only dative.

True *s*-stems are of course built to roots (*e*-grade), and the shape of the loc.sg. would be **-esi*, parallel to the formation seen in Ved. *car-áse* 'to fare', *jīv-áse* 'to live', *bhár-ase* 'to carry'. Such formations as PIE **leg-es-i, *weǵh-es-i, *H_2eǵ-es-i* would all of their own accord become L *legere, vehere, agere*, and such 3rd conj. forms are inherited without change. Early in the history of L, however, **legesi* and other forms of the simple thematic type were metanalyzed into **lege-si*; the suffix **-si* thus abstracted, being (apparently) added to a stem, spread to other stems. This probably started with the characterized thematics, **spekyesi* (*specere*), **kapyesi* (*capere*), **weniyesi* (*venīre*). At an early time, of course, most L paradigms were thus built, that is with the **-y^e/o-* element (474-81): **habēyesi* (*habēre*), **worāyesi* (*vorāre*), **moneyesi* (*monēre*).

The only genuinely vowelless forms were in fact presumably among the last to be coined: **dăsi, *welsi, *essi*, and perf. **-issi*. These, which can only have been coined after **leg-esi* was metanalyzed as **lege-si*, have the

---

were the equivalent of present-day *is being prepared, was being covered*, and in fact the first appearance of the now-obligatory construction was attacked as inelegant (or worse) and, above all, unnecessary. In contemporary English note the (formally unmarked) passive force of infinitive complements to a particular class of adjectives in expressions like *hard to swallow, easy to please, difficult to repair*.

misleading appearance of something primitive; the *legere* type is the genuinely primitive formation. The pseudo-root-formations are presumably the result of some such proportion as **leget* : **legesi* :: **welt* : *X*, where *X* = infin. **welsi*. Such coinages must predate rhotacism (173) to account for *esse* and perf. *-isse*.)

Infinitives to set roots like *domāre* (*domitus*) probably were something like **demH₂esi* to begin with, whence **domasi*, which if allowed to evolve undisturbed would have become ˣ*domere*, indistinguishable from a 3rd conj. form. (Forms like *vomere* 'to vomit' < **wemH₁-esi* presumably have just such a history.) The touching-up of **domă(si)* as **domayesi* at some point prior to the weakening of medial vowels would have been an obvious innovation, but by no means the only possible one.

a. There are a few cases of the loss of the final *-*i* : epig. TANGER, OL *biber dare*.

2. THE PRESENT INFINITIVE PASSIVE. As with act. *-ere*, above, the 3rd. conj. shows the most conservative formation. Consisting of an ending in *-ī* attached directly to the root, it closely resembles the most common of the Ved. types (built to some 60 roots in the RV), namely the dat.sg. of a root-noun: *yujé* 'to yoke' < **yug-ey*, *rucé* 'to shine' < **luk-ey*, *ajé* 'to drive' < **H₂eg-ey*; thus also L *legī*, *agī*.

The two formations are not an exact match: the Vedic type takes atonic zero grade of the root, except for roots that would have been non-syllabic in the zero grade (like *sad-* 'sit'); these have (tonic) full grade, as *-sáde*. Additionally, most of this type are formed to compound verbs, as *āsáde* 'to sit near', *niṣáde* 'to sit down'; no simplex *sáde** 'to sit' actually occurs. There is no evidence for such a distribution in the history of L, but then the development of the L infin. system is fully complete at the dawn of written records, and even in the conservative 3rd conj. the formation is built to stems which only by happenstance continue the original forms built to roots, as *legī* to *legō*, which is either old or of an old type, whereas *iungī* to *iungō* is quite unlike Ved. *yujé* next to pres. *yunákti*. As for the development of specifically medio-passive force, cf. footnote 2 on p. 609.

The infin. in *-rī* of the remaining conjugations is usually taken as this ending *-ī* grafted onto the usual (active) infinitive. But there are no analogical proportions for such a spread, and, more troubling still, such a view leaves unexplained the failure of 3rd conj. infinitives to show the same grafting, as ˣ*legerī*, ˣ*sequerī*.[1] Therefore, instead of tracing the medio-passive infin. to a remodeling of originally active infinitives, a likelier history is that 'infinitival *-r-*' (or *-*s*-) was INSERTED into the original form of the medio-passive infinitive. As the root-based verb system evolved into a

[1] L *ferrī* 'to be carried' for **ferī* is not derived from *ferre* in this manner; rather, original **ferī* was remodeled on the basis of *ferre*.

stem-based one, the inherited system of infinitives would have evolved pari passu. On the basis of **legetor* (3sg.) : **legei* (infin.) new forms were coined: to **amāyetor*, infin. **amāyei*; to **dator*, **daei*; to **moneyetor*, **moneyei*; to **oriyetor*, **oriyei*; to **moryetor*, **moryei*. With loss of intervocalic **-y-* and smoothing, these became **amāī*, **daī*, **moneī*, **oriī*, and **moriī*, respectively. In the *capiō* type, the ending and stem coalesced (*orī*, *morī*), becoming indistinguishable from the simple thematics like *legī*. The rest were assimilated into the pattern of the actives by the insertion of *-s-* (or *-r-*, depending on the chronology) between the stem and the ending: **amāī* → **amāsī* or **amārī*, **monēī* → **monēsī* or **monērī* (cf. the actives in **-āsi*, **-ēsi*). Note that this evolution explains why the thematics like *legī* and *morī* were unaltered: they were unalterable, there being no between (as it were) for the insertion of the consonant.

a. The type of OL *laudārier*, *dīcier*, GNOSCIER (SC de Bacch.), frequent in Plaut., appear to be formed from the usual *-(r)ī* with the addition of *-er* and regular shortening of the vowel (83.3). But while one could readily understand the addition of an *-r* or *-or* after the analogy of finite passive forms, an *-er* is difficult to explain. Of course, given that **-ir(-)* > *-er(-)* (66.4) some such development as **-īr* (or earlier **-eyr*) to *-ier* is thinkable. Alternatively, apocopated *fīer* 'to be made, to become' (for *fīere*) has been suggested as the model. But the true explanation remains in doubt.

b. Active *dari* 'to give' is quoted by Varro; passive *dasi* 'dari', by Paul.Fest. If the first is genuine, it indicates that *-s-* > *-r-* intervocalically prior to the lowering of *-i* to *-e* in final position. That is acceptable, since rhotacism is thought to have been pretty early—early enough for L *aurum* to be borrowed with an *-r-* in Celt. (so OIr. *ór*), which probably dates the change to before 387 BC and the Gaulish invasion of Italy. *Dasi* is a genuine puzzle, as any form with *-s-* would predate the change of *-ei* to *-ī*. Perhaps *dasi* is an error for **dasei*, or a pseudoarchaism.

3. PERIPHRASTIC INFINITIVES. The remaining infinitive formations of classical L are periphrastic. In OL, however, *-tūrum* fut.act. is more common than *-tūrum esse*; and because it serves for fem. as well as masc. and neut., and for pl. as well as sg., it is thought by some to be the infinitive itself, a fusion of the supine in *-tū* (item 4, below) plus **erom* < **esom* = O *ezum* 'esse'. This idea neatly accounts for several facts at a stroke, but means that the participle in *-tūrus* must be a formation of different history which merely by chance looks like the infin. (An alternative explanation—which disregards the chronology of attestation—takes *-tūrum* without *esse* to be a back formation based on the alternation between *dictum esse* and *dictum*, next.)

The perf.pass.infin. of the type *dictum esse* 'to have been said' likewise often, in OL especially, occurs without *esse*. This can with some confidence be taken as the supine rather than the pple.[1] The redundant *esse* in that

[1] The voice of the supine is ambiguous in any case. The stereotyped 'ablative' supines like *horribile audītū* and *mīrābile dictū* might with reason be rendered 'horrible to BE heard;

case would be on the analogy of the finite perf. passive of the type *dictum est* 'was said'.

The fut.pass. *-tūrum īrī* is based on an active *-tum īre* (the supine with *eō*, as in Plaut. *eō questum* 'I'm going to cry'), which was made passive by coining *īrī* (otherwise unknown) on the basis of *īre*.

4. THE SUPINE is formed with the same suffix *-tu-* that appears in nomina actionis like *cantus* 'song' and *adventus* 'arrival'. Acc.sg. *-tum* corresponds to the formation which from inconsequential beginnings (551) eventually became the paradigmatic infinitive of Sanskrit. The supine in *-tū*, traditionally described as abl., is more likely to be dat. (314.6; as we have seen (551), in the RV the dat. is the favorite case for infinitives of all stem types, including specifically *-tave*, built to some 30 roots). The question would be settled by an epigraphic example early enough to show whether the form is *-*tūd* or *-*tou*. The overtly dat. supine *-tuī* (which is very rare) is probably secondary.

a. Sab. shares *tu*-stem verbal nouns with InIr. and L. Otherwise the Sab. infinitive is *-om*, reminiscent of a Vedic infinitive type consisting of the acc.sg. of a root noun, of which some dozen formations are attested in the RV. In the Sab. equivalent of the L 3rd conj., the infinitive is formed to the root, much as in L (1, above). In the 1st conj., the termination is *-aum*, presumably < *-*āyom*, parallel to the hypothetical L passive *-*āī* mentioned in 2, above.

PARTICIPLES

554. THE ACTIVE EVENTIVE PARTICIPLES IN *-nt-*. In PIE this participle was formed from the STEM, by means of the suffix *-*ont-*/*-*n̥t-*. That is, in contrast to such verbals as the infin. and verbals in *-*to-* and *-*no-*, which were originally built directly to the root, there might be a distinct pple. in *-nt-* to every pres./imperf. or aor. stem, including denominatives. The often-repeated statement that the pple. was built to a TENSE stem is however not exactly correct. A contrast between a pres. and an imperf. pple. was never possible—not because the distinction is irrelevant but because the two tenses were built to the same stem.

The original meaning of the affix was essentially that of the NE participle in *-ing*: functionally, the noun modified by the pple. corresponds to the noun that would stand in subject relation to a finite verb. If formed to a transitive verb, a participle would construe with a noun object exactly as a finite verb would (*Lincoln Freeing the Slaves was a favorite theme for lithographs*, or *Beware of Greeks bearing gifts*).

This description applies to all the IE languages which have such a participle—which is to say, all apart from Celt.—except for Hitt. There, interestingly, *-nt-* participles

---

remarkable to BE said', as what is horrible, remarkable, and so on, is the logical object of the verb not its subject.

CONSTRUE ONLY WITH SUBJECT-NOUNS AT THE CLAUSE LEVEL. This means that to transitive verbs the participles are necessarily PASSIVE in force, as otherwise they would be construing with both subj. and obj. nouns. Examples: to *eš-* 'be', *a-ša-an-za* /asants/ (31) 'being'; to *ḫa-ar-k-* 'perish', *ḫar-ka-an-za* /hargants/ 'perishing'; but to *ḫar-ni-in-k-* 'destroy', *ḫar-ni-in-ka-an-za* /harningants/ 'being destroyed'; to *e-ip-* 'seize', *ap-pa-an-za* /apants/ 'being taken'; to *ku-en-* 'kill', *ku-na-an-za* /g^{w}nants/ 'being killed'.

The passive sense of the Hitt. forms is usually described as having anterior force to boot, unlike the intransitives, thus 'having been destroyed' rather then 'being destroyed'. But there is very little pragmatic difference between present and anterior here: 'my uncle being killed in battle' or 'the letter being written' are more or less the same as 'my uncle having been killed in battle' or 'the letter having been written'. —There are two interesting exceptions to the passive force of Hitt. transitives, *a-da-an-za* 'eating' and *a-ku-wa-an-za* 'drinking', a semantic matched set. Cf. the unusual active force of L *pōtus* and *cēnātus*, 564.

555. PARTICIPLES AS NOMINA AGENTIS. Semantically, present participles and agent nouns have much in common: a 'dancing [one]' and a 'dancer' are functionally very similar. In a variety of IE languages, verbals in *-*ont-* routinely have some agentive role, as in Ved. *saścánt-* 'pursuer, enemy' (root *sac-* 'follow'), next to *sáścant-* 'assisting'; *sravánt-* 'stream' (lit. 'flow-er', root *sru-* 'flow'), next to *srávant-* 'flowing'. As these examples show, there is a consistent formal difference between the pple. and the agentive formation, namely the position of the accent. In Indic this distinction is paralleled in the *-tar-* derivatives. These are mostly thought of as agent nouns (as they are in cognate formations, G -τηρ, -τωρ, L *-tōr-*), but in Ved. they are also participles, with the same accentual details as in *-ant-*: *dā́tar-* 'giving' vs. *dātár-* 'giver'. Note also the relation between accent and function in *o*-grade *o*-stem nouns, which formed ending-accented agent nouns in contrast to root-accented action nouns: G τρόχος 'course' (*'a run') vs. τροχός 'wheel' (*'runner').

The agentive use of stems in *-*ont-* is not alive in G and L, but is discernable etymologically in a few forms: G γέρων 'old man', τένων 'tendon, sinew', L *parentēs* 'mother and father' (not formed directly from *pariō* 'beget', NB), and *cliēns* 'dependent; hanger-on'.

a. In Gmc., where there is no trace of the agent formation in *-*t*^{e}/*or-*, the majority of agent nouns are either *n*-stems (the type of ἀρηγών 'rescuer' to ἀρήγω, an obsolete type in G) or indistinguishable from the pres. pple., as Go. *nasjands* 'savior' (transl. σωτήρ, the epithet of Christ), *gibands* 'giver', OHG *uuīgant* 'warrior'.

Although the formation is completely absent as a participle in Celt., in OIr. there are a few nouns which correspond formally, as *car(a)e* /kaρe/ 'friend' < **karonts* (or *-*n̥ts*), gen. *carat* /kaρəd/ < **karontos*; *cano* 'poet', gen. *canat* both < **kanont-* etym. *'singer'. (There are several stem types, seemingly representing various kinds of leveling from the pattern described in 556.)

556. STEM ABLAUT. The full grade of the suffix *-*ont-* alternated with the zero grade *-*n̥t-* in the usual hysterokinetic way (full grade in nom./acc., zero grade in most other cases, 272.3, 273); the nom.sg. presents a spe-

cial problem, about which more below (558). The ablaut of the suffix was the same for thematic and athematic types, that is, a complex like **bheront-* 'carrying' is to be segmented **bher-ont-*,[1] in contradistinction to the segmentation of the similar-looking thematic 3pl. **bher-o-nti.* This indicates once upon a time the affix was in fact originally added to roots rather than stems, just like the verbal nouns.

The only difference between athematic and thematic types is that in the athem. classes the marker was affixed to the zero grade of the finite stem. In such formations the accent moved between the full-grade suffix and the ending in accord with the usual hysterokinetic pattern (272.3, 273), with the stem in zero grade in the latter: **H_1s-ónt-m̥* acc.sg., **H_1s-n̥t-ós* gen. sg. 'being' (**H_1es-*); **d-ónt-m̥*, **d-n̥t-ós* 'eating', (**ed-*); **yung-ónt-m̥*, **yung-n̥t-ós* 'joining' (**yuneg-*); **dhedhH_1-ónt-m̥*, **dhedhH_1-n̥t-ós* 'putting' (**dhedheH_1-*). In the forms corresponding to the simple thematic presents, the accent was always on the root (which was full grade throughout) even as the suffix alternated as in the athematic types: **bhér-ont-m̥*, **bhér-n̥t-os* 'carrying'. In derived tonic thematics (built to zero grade of the root) the accent and grade of the affix seem to have been fixed: **g^w^m̥-sḱ-ónt-m̥*, **g^w^m̥-sḱ-ónt-os* 'going'.

The similarity of form between the pple. in **-ont-* and the 3pl. verb ending (430) is almost certainly coincidental, though it is unnerving to find such a bulky coincidence. At the same time, coincidences of similar bulk can be found elsewhere in morphology, for example the PIE kinship affix in **-ter-* (actually *-H_2*ter-*) and the agentive suffix **-ter-*.

557. TABLE OF FORMS OF THE PRESENT PARTICIPLE.

	PIE	Vedic	Greek	Latin	
Nom.sg.	H_1sōn[1]	sán[1]	φέρων[2]	ferēns[2]	sōns[3]
Acc.	H_1sóntm̥	sántam	φέροντα	ferentem	sontem
neut.	H_1sn̥t	sát	φέρον	ferēns	
Dat.	H_1sn̥téy	saté	φέροντι[4]	ferentī	sontī
Gen.	H_1sn̥tós	satás	φέροντος	ferentis	sontis
Nom.pl.	H_1sóntes	sántas	φέροντες	ferentēs	sontēs
Acc.	H_1sóntn̥s	satás	φέροντας	ferentīs	sontēs
neut.	H_1sóntH_2	sā́nti[5]	φέροντα	ferentia[7]	
Inst.	H_1sn̥dbhís	sadbhís*	—	ferentibus	sontibus
Gen.	H_1sn̥tṓm	satā́m	φερόντων	ferentium[7]	sontum

Notes to the table will be found on page 616.

---

[1] A pattern **bheront-*/**bhern̥t-* cannot include a thematic vowel; thematic stems by definition do not show quantitative ablaut, so the alternation must be between **-ont-* and **-n̥t-*, not between **bhero-* and **bher-*.

Notes to the table on page 615.

1. 'Being'.
2. 'Carrying'.
3. 'Guilty'; poetical. Forms derived from the pres. pple. of 'be' in IE languages, if they mean anything other than the obvious, mean 'true, valid' in some ritual or legal sense (so Ved. *satyá-* < *H_1*sn̥t-yo-*, a technical term in religion); and ON *sunnr* means both 'valid' and (legally) 'guilty'.
4. Etymologically the loc.
5. The sole occurrence of a neut.pl. nom./acc. pres.pple. in the RV stands in the text as *sā́nti*, with unexpected *-ā-*. The oldest RV commentary (the Padapāṭha) 'explains' the form as *sánti*. The one other example of this type is not a participle but is formed to an identical stem: *íyānti* nom./acc.pl.n. 'so many'. These are appears to be the result of an Indic analogy (389.3, fn.) which apart from these two forms did not affect *nt*-stems. (It is unobvious how or why the antecedent forms with *-ă-* were still available to the compilers of the Padapāṭha.)
6. Gen.pl. *-ntum* is attested occasionally in Plaut., *amantum* e.g.; and because many regularly-formed gen.pl. forms in *-ntium* would be awkward in hexameter, *-ntum* was always in demand as a poetic alternative even in later periods. Neut.pl. in *-nta* are very much rarer.

---

558. THE ORIGINAL NOMINATIVE SINGULAR **-ōn* (***-onts*) is preserved as such only in G φέρων. The remaining IE languages reveal a recomposed form **-onts*: L *sōns*, Ved. *sán*, Go. *gibands* 'giving', and OCS *nesŭ* 'carrying' (< BS **-on(s)*).

Much leveling has taken place in most IE groups. The original distribution of ablaut grades is best preserved in Ved., apart from the introduction of the zero grade into the acc.pl.—an Indic innovation in cons. stems generally—and also into the loc.sg. Most other IE languages generalized the *o*-grade throughout the stem, so G -οντ- (apart from the nom.sg.m.), Gmc. *-and-*, OCS *-ǫt-*, Hitt. *-ant-* (though the Hitt. shape would be the outcome of **-ont-* and **-n̥t-* alike).

559. 1. In ITALIC, uniquely, it was the zero grade of the stem that was generalized in the participles: **bhern̥tey* dat. > Ital. **ferentey*, **legn̥tes* gen. > **legentes* by regular sound laws, and the resulting stems *ferent-*, *legent-* ousted all *o*-grade forms apart from the isolated *sōns*, and *eunt-* (below). So also O *praesentid* abl. 'praesenti', U **zeřef** 'sedens'. Traces of the original *o*-grade can be found in *voluntāt-* 'will, wish', which enshrines **welont-*; cf. *volēns.*

a. The antiquity of the oblique stem *eunt-* (*eō* 'go') is debated. There is no reason why it should not be a relic, as it is the kind of vocabulary where one expects to find the most conservative forms. It is not wholly conservative, however; *eunt-* < **eont-* < **eyont-* shows the full grade of the root, as do all paradigmatic forms of *eō* in L (with the exception of the supine *itum* and related stems). The grade of *iēns* nom.sg. is ambiguous, but its history is probably on the order of **eyents* > **eents* > **ēn(t)s* → **īēns* (with the now general form of the root, *ī-*, reintroduced), finally *iēns* with regular vowel shortening (85). Such an analysis leaves unexplained the central puzzle: that the only surviving zero grade stem of this pple., *iēns*, is in the case which originally had lengthened grade. A plausible if tepid explanation might be that the surviving paradigm is a conflation of two competing patterns of leveling—one, which in a sense won out, being **eyont-* (the *o*-grade stem as in *sōns*); the other, with the generalization more usual in the participle system as a whole, somehow surviving only in the nom.sg.

b. In the two L words which were participles etymologically, different outcomes are seen. The evolution of L *dent-* 'tooth' follows that of the living participles, whereas *H_1sont-/*H_1sn̥t-* '*being; guilty' generalized *o*-grade.

c. A number of L deponent verbs have what amount to present active participles formed with **-ondos*: *secundus* 'following' (whence 'second' and also 'according to'), *oriundus* 'arising', *lābundus* 'sliding', and some others. See 568.

2. In GREEK, descriptively, stems which end in a short vowel simply add the suffix -ντ- to the stem: τιθέντ- 'putting', ἱστάντ- 'standing', διδόντ- 'giving'. These formations are probably not superimposable on Ved. *dádhat-*, *tíṣṭhat-*, *dádat-*, whose etyma, PIE **dhedhH_1-n̥t-*, **stistH_2-n̥t-*, **dedH_3-n̥t-*, would have given G ˣτιθατ-, ˣἱστατ-, ˣδιδατ-. The attested G stems, despite their straightforward appearance, are the result of considerable remodeling, including a nom.sg. representing recomposed **-nts*: **tit^{h}ents* > **tit^{h}ens* (215) > τιθείς (228.4), and similarly in the aor. θείς. These nom.sg. forms give away the secondary nature of the whole athematic formation.[1]

Verbs in -νῡ-/-νῠ- build two types of pple. More conservative is the type ζευγνύων 'yoking'; the Attic version, ζευγνῦς, -ύντος, has been remodeled exactly like τιθείς, -έντος, though whether starting with actual *-ῠντς or just in imitation of the pattern (-εις/-εντ-, -ους/-οντ-) is unknown.

a. THE FEMININE STEM. Case endings added to the bare stem formed the masc. and neut. The fem. was built with the devī suffix (268), thus Ved. *bháranti*, G φέρουσα, and—a secondary trace of the formation—the inflection of L pres. participles (apart from *sōns*) as *i*-stems outside of the nom./acc.n.sg. (270.2). The Vedic devī feminine formations hesitate between full and zero grade of the pple. affix; the usual rule is that root-accented thematic presents take full grade (as *bháranti*), while athematic formations take the zero grade (as *yatī́-*, *yuñjatī́-*). G generalized the full grade *-ontiH_2*, with zero grades only in remnants such as Dor. ἔασσα f. 'being' < **H_1sn̥tiH_2*, like Myc. *a-pe-a-sa* < *H_2ep-H_1sn̥t-iH_2* nom.sg.f. '(being) missing'. Att. ἐών m. directly reflects **H_1sṓn*; the usual forms, ὤν, ὄντος; οὖσα, are attributed to aphaeresis, but look like assimilations to the usual thematic forms.

b. NEUTER. G -ον (also -εν, -αν) is from **-ont*, the bare stem with full grade per leveling. L *-ēns* nom./acc.neut. is at bottom the same, but is from **-ent* < **-n̥t* (= Ved. *-at*). See 237.5.

c. Some laryngealists hold that G -εν-, -αν-, -ον- are the phonologically regular outcomes of **-H_1n̥-*, **-H_2n̥-*, and **-H_3n̥-* (and similarly other syllabic resonants). If so, τιθέντ- would be the regular reflex of **dhedhH_1n̥t-*. This would simplify the history of the G pple., but it creates problems elsewhere. For example, the pivotal role of -α(τι) in the evolution of the G 3pl. (430) is incomprehensible if it was from the outset in competition with **-en(ti)*, **-an(ti)*, and **-on(ti)* which are considerably more straightforward from the

---

[1] Prior to the advent of the laryngeal theory (117-20, 165-7), it was possible to think of these things differently, namely as slight remodelings—along the lines of the retouching of the suffix **-wat-* as *-wet-* (346)—of original *διδαντ- *τιθαντ- < **didənt-*, **dhidhənt-* and the like. Constructs like **didH_3nt-* and **dhidhH_1nt-*, in place of **didH_3n̥t-* and the like, are untenable, however.

structural point of view. Besides, the analogical processes accounting for τιθέντ- are of the most elementary sort.

d. Dor. (Heracl.) ℎεντες nom.pl. 'being' is traditionally described as from *H_1s-ent-. At the PIE level, this is an impossible form of the suffix; at the G level, it is in addition a nearly impossible one for the root (*H_1(e)sent- should have given ˣehent-). Descriptively, the form appears to have been influenced by the 3pl., on some such proportion as *p^heronti : *p^heront- :: *ehenti : X, where X = pple. *ehent-, and then sharing the later development of 3pl. *ehenti to Dor. ἔντι—however that actually happened (492).

e. As the G nom.sg. -ων was shared with one class of *n*-stems (286.1), there were occasional transfers of the latter into the former, as in λέων, -οντος 'lion', whose original stem is revealed by the fem. λέαινα and by L *leō, leōnis*; and similarly for δράκων, δράκοντ- 'dragon' (fem. δράκαινα), and θεράπων, θεράποντ- 'attendant' (fem. θεράπαινα).

560. THE MIDDLE PARTICIPLE. PIE *-*meno*- and *-*mno*- (gradation is inexplicable in a thematic stem) formed middle participles to eventive stems. Indic has only -*māna*- built to thematic verb stems, -*āna*- to athematic stems (more about the vowel length, below), but Av. has -*mna*-, for example *barəmna*- 'carrying' corresponding to Ved. *bháramāṇa*-. The zero grade is probably confirmed by Anatolian forms such as Luv. *kesama*- 'combed' < *-*mna*-, but the explanation for the differing grades is unknown.

The form for G eventive stems is -μενος with regressive accent, so G φερόμενος 'carrying', δεικνύμενος 'pointing out', ἑπόμενος 'following'; aor. θέμενος 'putting', δειξάμενος. The perf. middle is similarly formed but with a different accent (-μένος) and of course a reduplicated base, as λελυμένος 'loosing', γεγραμμένος 'writing'. The latter is a part of the general G importation of eventive categories into the stative.

a. No such paradigm is preserved in either L or Sab., where the ordinary active form serves as a middle (so to deponent verbs: *cōnant*- to *cōnor* 'try', *orient*- to *orior* 'rise', *ūtent*- to *ūtor* 'use'). Fossil forms have been detected in L *fēmina* 'woman' < **fē-yo-menā* *'suckling [one]' < **dheH₁i*- 'give suck' med.tant.; and *alumnus, -na* 'nurseling, child' (*'the being-nurtured one', from *alō*). Their semantic symmetry tells in favor of the analysis. By contrast, most other words of similar shape in the language, such as *autumnus* 'autumn' and *Vertumnus* (a deity), are obscure.

b. Indic forms would be most simply accounted for by *-*e-mono*- (in contrast to *-*o-meno*- for G): Ved. *pátyamāna*- 'being master, reigning' (pres. *pátyate* mid.), *nr̥támāna*- 'dancing' aor. (*nr̥tur* 3pl.). Descriptively, this looks like metathesis, which is in a sense true, but the key is the InIr. athem. ending, -*āna*-. This -*āna*- actually continues two different endings. The athematic EVENTIVE middle was originally *-*ana*- < *-*m̥no*-; the STATIVE (perf.) middle was -*āna*- < *-*ono*-, the same element seen in the Gmc. pple.: PGmc. **buranarⁿ* '[having been] carried' (OE *boren*, Go. *bauran*), **wurdanaⁿ* 'become, *turned' (OE *worden*, Go. *waurdan*). In the beginning therefore Indic had thematic **bharāmaṇas* 'carrying' (= G φερόμενος), athem. **dadanas* 'taking' (midd. of *dadant*- 'giving'), and perf. **čikitānas* 'seeing'. As a first step, the functionless distinction between perf. -*ānas* and the athem. eventive middle *-*anas* was eliminated in favor of -*ānas*. Finally, them. *-*āmanas* was contaminated by these two, to become -*amānas*.

561. THE STATIVE (PERFECT) PARTICIPLE. The only non-finite form of the perfect in PIE was the participle in *-*wŏs*-/*-*us*- m.n., *-*us-iH₂*- f., built to the zero grade of the reduplicated stem. Like all stative forms it originally had no voice, but in the daughter languages which introduced attributes of the eventive verbs into the perfect paradigm the inherited pple. stem became specifically active, and next to it were created special middle participles, formed differently in different languages: Ved. *dadṛśānā-* < *-*ono-* 'seeing' (for oneself, presumably) is a novel creation, whereas Hom. κεκορημένος 'having one's fill' is just the middle eventive pple. entire. See **560b**.

The IE groups preserving the perf.pple. are InIr., G, OCS, and Lith. Remains of the formation have been identified in several other groups, however, such as Go. *weitwods* 'witness' (lit. 'knowing [one]', though the *-d-*, reflecting either **t* or **dh*, is unexpected); and OIr. *fíathu*, same meaning (inflecting as an *n*-stem, a shift that can be explained).[1] Go. *berusjos* pl.tant. 'parents' is descriptively a *ja*-stem (PIE *-*yo*-); but underpinning the formation is PGmc. **bērus-*, ultimately **bhe-bhr-us-* (**525.6a**), the zero grade of the perf. pple. **bhebhr̥-wos-* 'bearing'.

Of the L words which might encyst the formation the only persuasive one is *memor, -ŏris* 'mindful' if from **memnor-* < **me-mn-us-* (zero grade of **me-mn̥-wos-*) from which **memōr* was created by back-formation.

562. The participle was formed directly from the zero grade of the perfect stem, thus **wid-wos-* 'knowing' (**woyd-e* 'knows', root **weyd-*); the G form probably continues ***wewid-wos-* (**512**):

	PIE	Vedic	Avestan	Greek	Mycenaean
Nom.sg.	-wōs	vidvā̃n[1,2]	vīδvå[1]	(ϝ)εἰδ(ϝ)ώς[1]	
Voc.	-wos	cikitvas[3]			
Acc.	-wosm̥	vidvā̃ṃsam[2]	-vīδvåŋhəm	(ϝ)εἰδ(ϝ)ότα	
neut.	-wos	tatanvát[4]	?-vat̰	(ϝ)εἰδ(ϝ)ός	
Gen.	-usos	vidúṣas	vīdušō	(ϝ)εἰδ(ϝ)ότος	
Dat.	-usey	vidúṣe	vīdušē		
Nom.pl.	-woses	vidvā̃ṃsas[2]	vīδ våŋhō	(ϝ)εἰδ(ϝ)ότες	ke-ke-tu-wo-e[5]
Gen.	-usom	vidúṣām	viδušąm	(ϝ)εἰδ(ϝ)ότων	
Nom.sg.*f.*	-usiH₂	vidúṣī		(ϝ)ιδυῖα[6]	a-ra-ru-ja[7]

1. 'Knowing', masc.
2. The nasalized strong stem in *-vāṃs-* is an Indic innovation; the similar-looking Avestan *-åŋhəm* is not similar in fact, as it merely shows the normal development of *-s-* between low vowels, a phenomenon unconnected with the Indic innovation.
3. 'Noticing', root **kʷeyt-*.
4. 'Extending far', root **ten-*.
5. Verb not certainly identified, though the form is clear.
6. PG **widuhya*.
7. 'Fitted with' (= G ἄρᾱρα, perfect of ἀραρίσκω).

In both InIr. and the familiar forms of G, the original paradigm has been much altered. In the beginning the inflection was straightforward, with the distribution of full grade (which is always *-*o*-) and zero grade in the suffix in the usual hysterokinetic pattern (272.3, 273). (The lengthening of

[1] For the apparent *e*-grade of the root in these forms see **512**.

the *o*-grade stem vowel in the acc.sg.m. in Ved. and Av. is per sound law, 36.4.) In Av., the main innovations were sound laws, disruptive though they were. The only exception would be the doubtfully-attested nom./acc.n.sg. in *-vaṯ*. (See also **a**, below.) In Indic the paradigm became thoroughly confused with the inflection of the (stative) denominative adjectives in *-vant-*, which are enormously common, for example *ámavant-* 'impetuous' (*áma-* 'impetuosity') and *íḷāvant-* 'refreshing' (*íḷā-* 'refreshment, vital spirit').

The evidence for the grade of the perf. stem preceding the suffix is conflicting. As seen above, InIr. has only zero grade, which is in agreement with fragmentary evidence like Go. *berujos*. In later types of G, the stem is based on the finite perf., which apart from οἶδα does not alternate and is typically in full grade. The verb 'know' alternates in Hom., not only in the finite forms but in the pple., where it shows full grade (*e*-grade, apparently, but see below) in the masc. and neut., and zero grade in the fem. (Later the fem. was remodeled after the masc. as εἰδυῖα.)

According to some, the full grade of the stem, as in PG **weidwōs*, Go. *weitwods*, and OIr. *fíathu*, was the original type (with perhaps the fem. stem in zero grade). According to others, the suffix was added to a uniform zero grade, say **wid-wos-* m., **wid-us-iH₂-* f. 'knowing', such that G ϝειδϝως m. is as much an innovation as the later εἰδυῖα f. According to still others, the stem itself alternated from case to case, say **wéydwōs* (***-woss*) nom.sg., **wéydwosm̥* acc., but **widuséy* dat., from which InIr. and G leveled in different directions. (Such a pattern of alternation makes a funny kind of sense, but is paralleled only in equally speculative reconstructions.) But PIE **weydwos-* has been best explained as something quite different from what it looks like (namely, ***we-wid-wos-*; see 512). An unambiguous Myc. attestation would perhaps settle the matter. For now the most that can be said is that the name *wi-do-wo-i-jo*, if it is based on **widwōs*, points to a stem more in agreement with Ved. *vidvā́n* than with (ϝ)εἰδ(ϝ)ώς.

a. The presence of a *-t-* in various forms of G, Ved., and (apparently) Go. *weitwod-* has led some to posit a distinctive PIE paradigm with alternation between **s* and **t* in addition to the usual ablaut. Something similar has been seen in **mēnot-*/**mēn(e)s-* 'moon', **nepot-*/**nepos-* 'nephew/grandson'. As has long been remarked, however, the lack of accord between the DETAILS of the G and Indic paradigms is complete: as is evident in the table above, their paradigms do not agree on a single form containing *-t-*. In fact, Indic and Iranian disagree among themselves, as in the inst.pl. (Ved. *-vad-bhis*, Av. *-ūž-bīš*) and loc.pl. (Ved. *-vatsu*, Av. *-ušu*). Indic *-t-*'s in such forms are secondary developments altogether, in part phonological, in part the result of extensive contamination of the paradigm by that of the suffix *-vant-*, most clearly evident perhaps in the voc. *vidvan*, as if from **-vant*, which is first seen in the AV; it eventually replaces the orig. Ved. voc. form *-vas* < **-wos* (RV *cikitvas* 'O observant [one]'—a common epithet of Fire). The rise of *-τ-* forms in the G paradigm is quite unlike this; and the absence of *t*-forms from Myc. is merely confirmation of an already well-formed suspicion that the familiar G paradigm is not inherited. Its history is less clear than the Indic development, but probably was part of the spread of *-τ-* in neuter paradigms, so to begin with (ϝ)εἰδότα nom./acc.n.pl. for original **weydwoha* (a formation attested as such in Myc. *te-tu-ko-wo-a₂* 'wrought') and spreading from there. Those who endorse a stem in **-wot-* seem to think it was limited to the nom./voc.masc./neut, where of course it would have been lost already in PG in the sg.: any leveling of the **-t-* would therefore have to have been in the prehistory of G. (And in Indic it is exactly in those forms, with the lone exception of nom./acc.sg.n. *-vat*, that forms in *-t-* are NOT found.)

b. In the Aeol. dialects the inherited perf.pple. was replaced by the thematic *ντ*-type, as Lesb. *κατεληλύθοντος* 'going down', Thess. *πεφειρᾱκοντες* (*τεθηρακ-*) 'hunting', Boeot. *ϝεϝῡκονομειοντων* 'managing a household'. Such forms are among the specifically Aeol. traits of Homer, for example *κεκλήγοντες* for usual *κεκληγώς* (perf. of *κλάζω* 'screech').

c. The model of the *u*-stem fem. adj., for example *ἡδεῖα* (340) explains the appearance of a fem. perf. pple. in *-εῖα* in competition with inherited *-υῖα*.

d. Sound laws on occasion result in odd-looking forms which are in fact old and conservative, so Hom. *κεκμηώς* 'weary' < **kekmāwōs* < **ḱe-ḱm̥H₂-wos-* (*κάμνω*), *τεθνηώς* '[being] dead' < *$t^{(h)}et^{h}$*nāwōs*.

563. THE LATIN FUTURE ACTIVE PARTICIPLE IN *-tūrus*. This obscure suffix is thought by some to be related to adjectives like *mātūrus* 'ripe', and feminines like *nātūra* 'natural order', *cultūra* 'husbandry'; but others, with more reason, think of desiderative verbs like *parturiō* 'am in labor, desire to bring forth', *canturiō* 'wish to sing'. But this sheds little light on the matter, as the history of desideratives in *-turiō*, in turn, is largely unexplained: it appears to be a combination of the suffix *-tu-* (as in the supine) with *-ro-*, *-rā-* (cf. 569.2), giving *-turo-* as indicated by *partŭriō*, as well as *-tūro-*. The reconstruction **-ro-* rather than **-so-* is based mainly on the consideration that **partusyō* should have given ×*partūiō* (×*partuiiō*) rather than the attested forms in *-uriō* (194); just what **-ro-* actually was, or why it would agglutinate with a nomen actionis, is unknown. Nor has the development of *-tūrus* from *-tŭrus* been explained.

Miscellaneous adjectives in *-ŭ̄ros* are sometimes hopefully cited in this connection: G *γλαφῠρός* 'hollow(ed)', cf. *γλάφω*; *ἰσχῡρός* 'strong' (*ἰσχῠ̄ς* 'strength'); L *figūra* 'form, shape' (*'having been shaped', from *fingō*). But as they are prevailingly of passive meaning, they are unlikely to have anything to do with the case.

564. VERBALS IN **-tó-* (the Latin passive participle and the G verbal adjective in *-το-*). These are formally identical with the Ved. pple. in *-tá-* and the Gmc. passive participles to weak (dental preterite) verbs, as Go. *fulliþs* = NE *filled*, *lagiþs* = NE *laid*. They reflect a PIE verbal adj. formed with *-tó-*, originally built directly to the zero grade root, with the consequence that the formation was insensible to the distinctions of the various finite stems—inchoative, causative, and others. This is essentially the state of G morphology. In the RV the only departures from this are formations built, apparently, to zero grade of the causative stem, so *coditá-* 'having been set in motion' (*cod-áya-*). In the later language, derivatives from de-

nominatives are common, and likewise from desiderative stems (so *bhikṣita-* 'having begged', root *bhaj-* 'share'; *bibhitsita-* 'having desired to split', root *bhid-*); but it progresses no further. In Gmc. the formation is found to all weak stems, so Go. *nasiþs* 'saved' (*nasjan*), *salboþs* 'anointed' (*salbon*), *trauaiþs* 'believed' (*trauan*); and in present-day Gmc. languages there is no limitation (so NE *concertized, disoriented, positioned, whitened, pigeon-holed*). In L the distribution of the form falls between these two extremes, with stem-based forms typical in the 1st, 2nd, and 4th conj. (*-ātus, -ētus/-itus, -ītus*), but with some root-based forms (certainly *domitus* 'tamed' < **domH̥₂-*, possibly *ortus* 'risen'—this might well be syncopated from **oritus*); in the more conservative 3rd conj. the formation is prevailingly root-based, regardless of the details of the pres. stem (*capiō, captus* 'seized'; *serō, satus* 'sown'; *nāscor, nātus* 'born').

Functionally, the derivative made a verbal adjective which construed with nouns that would stand in object relation to a transitive finite verb. Nouns that would have been in subject relation are either absent or are marked with some case other than nom. or acc. There was in effect no tense to start with, but as such forms refer to states, they inevitably imply something like the completed past tense (once such a category became established in IE languages). This is largely the situation in L, where the force is prevailingly passive, and where, consequently, the supine rather than the pple. must be quoted for the fourth principal part of most intransitive verbs (so *itum* 'to go', *ventum* 'to come'). A significant class of exceptions are intransitive deponent verbs, which have such a participle as a necessary component of the perf. paradigm: *ortus est* '[the sun] rose', *gressa est* 'she entered', *orsum est* 'it began'. There is a miscellany of additional exceptions, as *iūrātus* 'having sworn', and the pair *pōtus* 'having drunk' and *cēnātus* 'having dined' (cf. the exceptions to the generally passive force of the Hitt. pple., 554). A few seem to have present-tense meaning, as *circumspectus* 'cautious' (*'looking around') and *īnfēnsus* 'hostile' (*'attacking'). In Ved., the passive force is characteristic of transitives, but the formation occurs freely with intransitives, much as in Gmc.: Ved. *gatá-* '[having] gone' (*gam-*), *taptá-* 'hot', *uktá-* 'having spoken' (*vac-*).

The G adjectives in -τό- are in part like the Indic, so trans./pass. γραπτός 'marked with letters' (γράφω), γνωτός 'understood' (γιγνώσκω), δρατός 'flayed' (δέρω) next to intrans./act. ῥυτός 'flowing' (ῥέ(ϝ)ω), ἔμετος 'vomiting' (**wemH̥₁-to-*). However, the Indic and G cases are not comparable. Such intransitives are routine in Indic, not so in G, and the semantics do not match: Ved. *srutá-*, formally identical to ῥυτός, means 'having flowed', not 'flowing'; *vamitá-* 'made to vomit', not 'vomiting'. There are however a few Vedic formations of the ῥυτός type: *drugdhá-*, for instance, means 'hurtful, malicious', not 'having been hurt'.

Much commoner in G than the ῥυτός type, though chiefly post-Hom., is a function unlike any in the other IE groups, namely possibility or necessity; for trans. verbs the force is passive: φυκτός 'to be shunned' (φεύγω), ἄϊστος, ἄ(ϝ)ιστος 'not to be seen' (ϝιδ-), φατός 'utterable' (φημί), βρωτός 'to be eaten' (βιβρώσκω), βατός and ἰτός 'passable' (βαίνω, εἶμι), βροτός '[mortal] man' (lit. *'to die' < *mr̥tós), ὁρᾱτός 'visible, to be seen'. This type of meaning is similar to the post-Hom. affix -τεος in G (γραπτέος 'to be described', δεικτέος 'to be shown'), which is thought on the basis of form and meaning to be from *-tewo- and therefore ultimately based on an infinitive like Ved. -tave, a history which fits the semantics well even if the whereabouts of the form during the Homeric period is a disquieting problem.

565. The original pattern of accented suffix with zero grade of the root is the norm in Vedic, in G too, and L agrees insofar as root grade; thus G κλυτός = L *inclutus* (*inclitus*) 'famous' (Ved. *śrutá-* 'heard'), G στατός 'placed' = L *status* (Ved. *sthitá-*), L *dictus* 'said' (Ved. *diṣṭá-* 'pointed'), L *ductus* 'led', *ustus* 'burnt'; from roots ending in laryngeals, G τλητός 'patient, enduring' (Dor. τλᾱτός) = L *lātus* 'having carried' < *$tl̥H_2$-tó- (106.2). Early-attested exceptions independently corroborated, like Ved. *jñātá-* 'having been understood' = G γνωτός = L *nōtus* < *ǵneH_3-to-*, are rare and significant. (L *agnitus* 'perceived', to *agnōscō*, is secondary.)

Ambiguous forms like *tentus* 'stretched' (*tendō*) are therefore surely reflexes of the zero grade, **tn̥-to-*. Later instances of unambiguous full grade forms are the result of leveling: G φευκτός 'to be shunned' for Hom. φυκτός, above; G γευστός 'tasted' is contradicted by Ved. *juṣṭá-* and, indirectly, by L *gustāre*, an intensive (475.3) based on **gustos*; ζευκτός 'harnessed'; L *scrīptus* 'written'. Most of the tampering with the vowel of the pple. in L was patterned on the perf. act. stem, so *fūsus* for **fussus* 'poured' after *fūdī*; *ēsus* 'eaten' after *ēdī*; but *ūsus* 'used' for **issus* is after pres. *ūtor*. (For *āctus* 'done', *tāctus* 'touched', *lēctus* 'gathered' see Lachmann's Rule, 81.3.) Occasionally the *n*-infix of the pres. stem was carried into the *to*-form, as *iūnctus* (*iungō* 'join'), *pūnctus* (*pungō* 'stab').

FIRST CONJ. Regularly *-ātus*, whose prior history is unknown in detail (*-āyeto-? *-āito-? *-āto-?). *Dătus* 'given' directly reflects *$dH̥_3$-to-* (= Ved. *ditá-*). Forms like *domitus* 'tamed' with perf. in *-uī* < *-awai (66.5) likewise continue PItal. *-ătos < *-H̥-to-, where the *-H- is part of the root.

SECOND CONJ. The *-ĭ-* of the stem *-itus* tells us nothing (66), but comparative evidence suggests that it has more than one ancestor. For causative/frequentatives such as *monitus* 'warned', the match with Ved. *-itá-* suggests an inherited formation in *-i-to- in which the *-i- is the zero grade of the caus. stem (456.2). For statives like *habitus* (*habēre* 'have') or *tacitus* (*tacēre* 'to be silent') the pple. must include zero grade of the suffix *-eH_1-, namely *-ato- from *-$H̥_1$-to-.

THIRD CONJ. forms, whether of the *legō* or *capiō* type, build the pple.

from the root. So *captus* 'seized' (*capiō*, y^e/o-stem); *fissus* 'split' and *strātus* 'scattered' (*findō* and *sternō*, respectively, both *n*-infix). This is so even for apparent exceptions like *molitus* 'ground' < **molato-* < **molH̥₁-*, and *genitus* (*gignō* 'beget'), which continues **genato-* < **ǵenH̥₁-to-*.

These last two examples, and any other similar form ending in a resonant, such as *vomitus*, are not of course original in every detail; the unaltered forms would have had a reflex of a long resonant, that is, *genitus* must replace an original **nāto-* (which actually occurs as the pple. of *nāscor* < **ǵn̥H₁-sk^e/o-* 'am born'); and instead of *molitus*, the regular form would have been *ˣblātus* or the like < **ml̥Hto-*. Cf. *lātus* 'carried' < *tlātos* < **tl̥H₂-to-*. The remodeling must have been very early, as a later recomposition would hardly show the root-final laryngeal (*ˣgentus*, *ˣmultus*).

Presents in *-scō* build participles variously. *Adultus* 'grown up' to *adolēscō*, and *crētus* 'sprung from' to *crēscō*, are built to roots. Secondary forms in *-ētus* to presents in *-ēscō* are based on *crētus* and make up a large group (479.5); still more secondary is *-ītus* after *-īscō* (such as *ascītus* 'imported, foreign' to *ascīscō* 'admit; import').

FOURTH CONJ. forms are partly based on roots (*sānctus* 'inviolate' to *sancīre*; *sepultus* 'interred' to *sepelīre*), but many are in *-ītus*, as *fīnītus* 'finished', *custōdītus* 'guarded', *polītus* 'polished'. The source of *-ī-* here is uncertain. It is probably enough to evoke analogy with the 1st conj. type: *-āvī* : *-ātus* :: *-īvī* : *X*, where *X* = *-ītus*. Denominatives especially (such as *fīnītus*, *mūnītus*) are reminiscent of *-ūtus* in denominative formations from *u*-stems (*tribūtus*, *statūtus* from *tribuō* 'allot', *statuō* 'place, set up'). *Volūtus*, *solūtus* (*volvō*, *solvō*) are from **welu-*, **solŭ-* < **se-luH₃-*. The last would give *-ūtus* directly; *secūtus* (*sequor* 'follow') and *locūtus* (*loquor* 'talk') are analogical, on the basis of *solvitur* : *sequitur* :: *solūtus* : *X*. This type, whatever the precise model, effloresced in Romance, which has many forms pointing to such neologisms as **habūtus* 'had'.

a. The pple. of *morior* is the unique *mortuus*, a form closely paralleled in form and meaning in OCS *mrĭtvŭ*, both from **mr̥twos*. It is found in the perf. *mortuus est* 'he died', but as a pple. has stative meaning, 'dead'.

566. ROOTS ENDING IN CONSONANTS. In forms from roots ending in a consonant the usual changes in consonant groups (210-2, 216, 230-2) are observed. Thus from roots ending in an apical stop, G πιστός (πείθω), L *fissus* (*findō*), *claussus*, *clausus* (*claudō*); in a dorsal, G θηκτός 'whetted, sharpened' (θήγω 'sharpen'). The chief discrepancy is that in G, as is the case with the agent suff. -τηρ/-τωρ and many others, the effects of Bartholomae's Law (211) are nowhere to be seen; instead, uniform -τος is added to roots ending in an aspirate, with deaspiration of the root-final stop, as γλυπτός 'carved' (γλύφω). In L too the outcome of **-to-* preceded by the reflexes of voiced aspirates behave like plain stops: *vectus* 'carried' (*vehō*; root **weǵh-*), *iussus* 'ordered' (*iubeō*; root **yewdh-*), *fictus* 'fashioned' (*fingō*; root **dheyǵh-*).

One difference between G and L is that the EXPECTED outcome in G is obvious (*γραφθός), whereas the regular outcome of something like **weǵdhos* (**weǵh-to-*) in L is uncertain; 211. One of the possibilities is that the outcomes that we see are regular, especially if L *lectus* 'bed' < **legh-to-* is what it appears to be (211). However, they are usually regarded as products of analogical disturbances, because *rēgula* 'rule' < **reǵdhlo-*, *tēgula* 'roofing tile' < **tegdhlo-*, *coāgulum* 'rennet' < *H_2*eǵdhlo-*, and *crēdō* 'believe' < **krezd-* < **ḱred-dheH₁-* (lit. 'place the heart') probably show something closer to the real outcomes (81.6). But these examples leave it unclear whether the regular outcome, if not *vectus*, would have been **vegdus* or **vēgus* or what. If *crēdō* 'believe' is correctly explained as **ḱred-dheH₁-* (a big 'if'), then the expected outcome of **yudh-to-* 'ordered' would have been **iūdus*, not *iussus*.

From forms like πιστός 'to be trusted', ζωστός 'belted' (cf. Av. *yāsta-*) in paradigms where -σ- was otherwise not much in evidence (πείθω, ζώννῡμι), the shape -στός spread to stems ending in a vowel, as γνωστός (Hom. γνωτός 'understood'), just as in the aor.pass. (508) and perf.midd. (519).

In L the great majority of the forms in *-sus* are derived from roots ending in an apical stop. From these, *-sus* spread by analogy to others. In verbs having an *s*-perf. this was especially favored by pairs like *clausī*, *clausus* (*claudō* 'close'), whence *fīxus* 'fixed' (*fīgō*, *fīxī*), *flūxus* 'flowing' (*fluō*, *flūxī*), *mulsus* 'milked' (*mulgeō*, *mulsī*), *mānsus* 'awaited' (*maneō* 'remain', *mānsī*). But it is also seen in others whose analogical sources are less apparent, as *cēnsus* 'appraised' for expected **cēn(s)tūs* (*cēnseō*, *cēnsuī*), cf. O *ancensto* = L *incēnsa* 'unregistered'; *lāpsus* 'fallen, slipped' (*lābor*) was back-formed from perf. *lāpsī*; *pulsus* 'beaten' (*pellō*; early L. *pultāre* 'beat on' discloses expected **pultus*); *falsus* (*fallō* 'make slip, lead astray'). If *percellō*, *perculsus* reflects **keldō*, **kl̥d-to-* (458.3) it would provide the pattern for *pulsus*, *falsus*.

567. THE LATIN GERUNDIVE AND GERUND. The *gerundive* is a formation peculiar to Italic. It occurs in Sab. (with *-nn-* from **-nd-*), as in O **úpsannam** 'operandam' ('faciendam'), U *pihaner* 'piandae'.

In L there are similar forms in *-ndo-* with adjectival-participial value, as *oriundus* 'rising', *volvendus* 'rolling' (*volvenda diēs* 'time rolling on'), *lābundus* 'slipping', and similarly in *secundus* 'following' (*sequor*), *rotundus* lit. 'rolling' (apparently from an unattested **rotor*, *-ī*; cf. *rota* 'wheel'). In this use it seems to be proper to deponent formations.

In L the gerundive to transitive verbs (active and deponent alike) developed a peculiar syntax. Though it has active force, it construes with the logical OBJECT, which object gives the impression of agreeing with the gerundive rather than the other way round: *cupiditās bellī gerendī* 'desire of waging war'. (This appears to be the syntax of the Sab. forms as well, an agreement so detailed that some authorities have wondered if it is the result of borrowing.) Given the generally passive force of the formation elsewhere, not to mention its clearly ancient connection with deponent paradigms mentioned above, a more etymological calque of the phrase is presumably 'desire of war being waged'.

The other use of the gerundive is obligation or necessity, the so-called 'future passive participle' or 'participle of necessity', as in the celebrated *Carthāgō dēlenda est* 'Carthage must be destroyed', and, in the negative, the equally familiar *dē gustibus nōn est disputandum* 'matters of taste are not to be debated'. The so-called future force, which is nowhere to be seen in the old-looking forms like *secundus*, is probably a misperception: the nub of the semantics is necessity, and of course 'must' and 'ought' and the like are merely special kinds of future. A virtually identical development is seen in Skt. gerundives in *-ya-*, Ved. *-ia-* (with a variety of different elements preceding the marker proper). These are remarkably like the L gerundive in use, and perhaps also in history (see below).

The L *gerund*, a neut. noun, is formed the same way, except that it lacks the nom. case, and the acc. occurs only as the object of a preposition. Thus it is in complementary distribution with the infinitive, which syntactically (not etymologically!) is solely in subj. and obj. relation to verbs. But there are at least a dozen examples like Afranius's *optandum uxorem*, where the parsing choice is between a (neut.) gerund in the nom. case or a transitive gerundive, and is more likely to be the former.

a. In late L the gerund, in absolute form (originally the abl.), came to be used as a kind of indeclinable present participle. It is the source of the present pple. in the Romance languages (It., Sp. *amando*, Fr. *amant*—the spelling of the latter influenced by L pples. in *-nt-*; the genuine pres.pple. in *-nt-* is preserved unchanged only in isolated forms like It. *oriente* 'east', *costante* 'faithful'). This development is easiest to account for if there had been all along a colloquial use of formations of the *secundus* type that went well beyond anything attested in the literary language.

568. Since the history of both of these forms is obscure, it is not easy to answer even such basic questions as whether they are historically the same form, and, if they are, which use is the more original.

Scholars have usually regarded the answer to the first question ('yes') as too obvious to warrant discussion, but that is hasty. There are many instances of chance similarity in affixes. The homophonous L supine *-tum* and the neut. of the pple. in *-tum* are unrelated formations; the same is true of the homophonous pple. and dental preterite in NE (*thought*, *wanted*, *met*). Even closer to the question at hand, the NE participle/gerund (*going*, *coming*) represents the confluence of two different etyma: action nouns, *leornung* 'learning', *gewemming* 'polluting', *grḗting* 'greeting'; and the true participles, *leorniende*, *wemmende*, *grḗtende*. (The latter may live on directly in colloquial *goin'*, *comin'*.)

There are a number of plausible choices for the ancestor of a form in *-nd-*, some of them on the basis of function better suited for the ancestor of a noun, others for the ancestor of an adjectival type. It is therefore thinkable that the gerund and gerundive do in fact have different ancestors; and the *secundus* type is not necessarily the same as either, historically.

On the assumption that the two structures were originally one, however, most scholars hold the view that the gerund is original, an infinitive-like verbal noun originally only transitive (and therefore in effect active, though not actually integrated into the voice system). The gerund is certainly in use in OL. The explanation of how the gerundive was born from the gerund lies in a potentially ambiguous phrase like *lūminis tuendī (causā)* 'for [the sake of] tending to the lamp', in which to begin with *lūminis* was in construction with *tuendī*, which in turn was in construction with something else in the sentence (such as *causā*). When this was reinterpreted as a sequence of two gen.sg. in agreement, novel forms like *lūminem tuendum, lūcis tuendae, lūcem tuendam*, and so on, would be created, with the birth of a new syntagm as well as a new paradigm. However, this view overlooks the obvious antiquity of *secundus* and *oriundus*, which cannot readily spring from prior gerunds.

It is less easy to come up with a course of development of the gerund from the gerundive. And if the *secundus* type is independent of the other two, we are dealing here with three separate origins rather than one or two.

The serious possibilities—the giddy ones are passed over in silence—for the ancestry of L forms in *-nd-* are as follows.

1. PIE **-n̥dh-* as seen in the Ved. infiin. *-adhyāi*. This idea labors under the difficulty of deriving *-und-* from **-n̥dh-*, and furthermore cuts the ground from under the more appealing association of Ved. infin. *-adhyāi* with the G middle infin. in -(ε)σθαι (552B), that is, with Indic *-a-* < **-e-*, not **-n̥-*.

2. PIE gerundives in **-n-iyo-* (?**-n-iHo-*), whence Ved. forms in *-enia-* (next to others in *-ia-* such as *-tavía-*). This possibility depends upon the validity of the sound law **-ny-* > *-nd-*, as in **tn̥yoH₂* > **tenyō* > *tendō* (218), which is not universally accepted. Besides, it would be more suitable as an etymon for the gerundive, than for either the gerund or the *secundus* type.

3. PIE **-tr̥* nom./acc., **-tn-* oblique, an ancient *r/n*-stem (290-2) verbal noun freely productive in Hitt. The oblique stem would give L *-nd-* on the evidence of development seen in *pandō* < **patnō* (222.2) 'extend' (cf. stative *pateō* 'lie extended'). A verbal noun would be a plausible etymon for the L gerund, with the welcome detail that it is after all the oblique stem; this might explain the peculiar absence of a nom. in the L paradigm. (The expected nom., something like **geritur, *faciētur*, and the like, would so little resemble the obl. *gerendī, *faciēndī* that their loss as such is no surprise.)

4. The middle pple. in **-o-meno-* (560), with dissimilation to **-o-medo-* with syncope (**-omdo-*) and assimilation (*-undo-*). The necessary dissimilation is reminiscent of L *crūdus* from **crūrus* (151b), It. *rado* < PRom. **rarum*. The merits of this audacious suggestion are its (relative) straightforwardness and the direct explanation it provides for both the form and meaning of the old-looking deponent participles like *secundus* and *oriundus* (567). But the dissimilation of **-n-* to *-d-* is not especially plausible in view of the apparent stability of *-m . . . n-* sequences (*homin-* 'man', *femin-* 'thigh', *lūmin-* 'light', *nūmin-* 'divine will', a dozen or more forms in *min-* (*minimus*), and so on). It is impossible, admittedly, to raise cogent objections to what is ex hypothese a sporadic type of change, and perhaps significant here is an apparent case of *-d-* < **-n-* in epigraphic MADIB (*manibus*) 'to the Manes'. —This explanation would be buttressed if the gerundive was ab origine passive in force;

but a middle pple. could be transitive (as in *secundus*) and develop the passive force only later, as the majority seem to feel. (Altogether, this etymology is appealing for the *secundus* type alone.)

569. VARIA. There were in PIE a multitude of verbal derivatives which might qualify as participles, gerunds, or verbal nouns or adjectives, but which are not so classified. The blurred line between participial and agentive function in the case of *-t^e/*or*- has been noted above (**555**). The following are a few more such pseudo-participles; fuller discussions of these and a large number of other types may be found in specialized handbooks.

1. Pple. **-nó-*: built directly to the zero grade of the root, just like **-tó-* (**564**), and often in competition with it. So in Ved., some roots take *-tá-*, some *-ná-*. The element may—but probably does not—underlie the pple. in **-ono-* which becomes Ved. *-āna-* and functions as the past pple. to the Gmc. strong verbs as still seen in NE *given, taken, known* (**560b**). It is seen in scattered forms in G and L, though typically built to full grade of the root, as G τέμενος (*τεμανος < **temH̥₂-no-*) 'piece of land cut off', σεμνός 'revered' (σέβομαι), L *plēnus* 'full' (that is 'filled'; cf. Ved. *pūrṇá-*, with more usual zero grade). Isolated forms might belong here such as λῆνος, L *lāna* 'wool', Ved. *ū́rṇā-* (though the position of the accent is unexpected). PIE **deH₃-no-* n. 'gift', L *dōnum*, OIr. *dán*, Ved. *dā́na-*, might be a nominalized example, though it is sometimes explained as a thematization of an *r/n*-stem (**290**, end). A pres. meaning is seen in G λιχανός 'licking' (also 'forefinger') (λείχω).

2. Verbal adj. in **-ró-* built to zero grade of the root. In InIr. it is only intransitive: Ved. *rudrá-* 'gleaming', *namrá-* 'bowing', *ugrá-* 'burgeoning'. A few are semantically parallel to **-tó-/*-nó-*, as *chidrá-* 'torn apart' (root **sḱeyd-*). Outside of InIr. it is attested with both trans. and intrans. force (though unlike true participles, not actually construing with an object): G πικρός 'sharp' (*'pricking'), λυγρός 'hurtful'; with *e*-grade of root: νεκρός 'dead', λεπρός 'scabby', lit. 'peeling' (λέπω 'peel'). L *cārus* 'dear' (*'loving'), *gnārus* 'knowing'. But perhaps L *cārus* was *'being loved', like Ved. *chidrá-* and NB L *integer* < **n̥-tagros* 'whole' (*'untouched').

3. Gerundival elements in **-eto-*, in Ved. mainly to full grade, in G mainly to zero grade of the root: ἄσχετος 'not to be held in' (= Av. *azgata-*); μενετός 'inclined to wait, patient'; ἑρπετόν 'quadruped; snake' (nominalized from *ἑρπετός 'going, walking'; cf. Lesb. ὄρπετον from expected **sr̥p-etó-*). These align with Ved. forms in *-ata-*, as *darś-atá-* 'visible', *yaj-atá-* 'to be worshipped', *anyá-vr-ata-* 'worshiping another' (root *vr̥-* 'desire'). The same element may be seen in the pair θάνατος 'death', βίοτος 'life', with the vowel colored by the laryngeals (*g^w*hn̥H₂-eto-*, *g^w*iH₃-eto-*).

This element is not certainly attested in L, though *monēta* (an epithet of Juno) if 'admonisher' or the like would pass as an example, albeit built to a stem rather than a root (unless earlier **monĕtā* was contaminated by *monē-*). Another possibility is pples. like *molitus* 'ground' if < **moletos* < **melH*$_1$*-eto-*, though the meaning does not fit well with the clearer examples.

Some have seen the element **-eto-* in the Latin class of stative deverbatives in *-idus*, as in *calidus* 'hot' (*calēre*), *lūcidus* 'full of light' (*lūcēre*); these do not correspond to any evident formation in other languages, and agree pretty well with the semantics of **-eto-*. However, although intervocalic voicing is commonplace in Western Romance languages, the appearance of **-edo-* < **-eto-* in prehistoric L would be remarkable.

❦

THE TYPE USED IN THIS BOOK is Monotype's version of *Janson*, one of a generation of 17th century interpretations of Garamond created in Holland. The name by which it has been known for three hundred years is an error of attribution: the actual creator of the face was Miklós Kis, a Hungarian typographer active in Holland. In a departure from the usual practice of the period, Kis also designed the complementary italic fonts, which are no less remarkable than the roman.

Among the qualities that Janson is admired for are traits which would seem to be as incompatible as they are desirable, which helps explain the high esteem in which the face is held: it has fine color on the page but at the same time is open and legible; it is graceful without weakness; and it is sober without stiffness. According to Alistair Johnston, it is one of 'the greatest half-dozen types in the history of letterpress printing'.

INDEXES

Greek
Latin
Albanian
Armenian
Avestan and Old Persian
Baltic
Celtic
Gothic
Hittite
Mycenaean
Old Church Slavic
Old English
Old High German and Old Saxon
Old Norse
Oscan
Sanskrit
Tocharian
Umbrian

Greek

Alphabetization is anaesthetic to material in parentheses and digamma *(ϝ)*.
For iota subscript, see **64**.

ἀ-, ἀν- *priv.* 108
ἁ-, ἀ- 'one-' 389.1Bb.1
ἀγα- *pref.* 341, 343
Ἀγαθθώ 234c
ἀγαθός 234c, 359
ἀγακλεής 290b, 343
ἄγαμαι 470
ἀγάννιφος (Hom.) 171
ἄγγελος 465.4
ἀγγέλλω 465.4
ἄγει *3sg.* 117
ἄγει *imperat.* 547.4
ἄγεν (Hom.) 508
ἅγιος 220
ἀγκοίναι (Hom.) 203.2
ἀγκών 203.2
ἅγμα 220
ἁγνός 220
ἄγνῡμι 442.1, 516
ἄγον *n.* 345
ἀγορᾱ́ 465.3
ἀγοράζω 465.3
ἀγός 117.1
ἀγρός 47, 188
ἄγχι 354.4c
ἀγχόνη 66.3
ἄγω 47, 48 *fn.*, 117.1, 463
ἀγωγή 117.1
ἀγών 286.5
ἀδάματος 107.1
ἄδαστος 212
ἀδελφεός 162
ἀδελφός 162, 170a
ἀδήν 100b, 162, 286.3, 289
αδικησι (Cret.) 535
ἄδικος 339
ἄδμητος 107.1, 123.4, 454A.2
ʽᾱδύς (Dor.) 53
ʼᾱεί 207
ἀείδω 61.1a, 90, 453b
ἀείρω 444
ᾱϝέλιος (Aeol.) 88.3c
ἀ(ϝ)έξω 39
ἄζομαι 200
ἄημι 440a.2, 470
ʼᾱήρ 54, 284A.2
ἄ(ϝ)ησι (Att.-Ion.) 90
Ἀθηνᾱ́ᾱ 207
Ἀθήναζε 201, 227.1, 228.3
Ἀθηναίᾱ, Ἀθηνᾶ 207
Ἀθήνησι 265.3
ἀθρόος, ἁθρόος 170a
αἰδώς 273, 293a, 299
αἰ(ϝ)εί, ʼᾱεί 60, 117.1, 207, 313.15
αἰέν (poet.) 283
αἰθήρ 284A.2
αἶθος 147.3
αἴθω 60, 117.1, 147.3, 463
αἴλουρος 251
αἰνέσω, Hom. -ήσω 505.3
αἰνέω 505.3
αἴρω 444
αἰσθάνομαι 466
ἀϊστός, ἀϝιστός 564
Αἰσχίνους *gen.* 54
αἰτέω 64
αἰχμή 230.2a, 264.4
αἰ(ϝ)ών 117.1, 283
ἀκάχημαι (Hom.) 517.2a
ἀκήκοα 444
ἀκηχέδαται (Hom.) 517.2a
ἀκμή 'point' 117.1, 220
ἀκμής 'tireless' 466
ἄκμων 280, 286.3
Ἀκράγᾱς 246
ἄκρις 48
ἀκρο- 48
ἄκτιτος 100d
ἀκῡμων 285, 288
ἀλαλκεῖν 458.1
ἀλγέω 452, 468.2
ἀλγήσετε (Hom.) 535
ἀλγήσω 468.2
ἄλγος 452
Ἀλέξανδρος 74.4
ἀλέξω 458.1
ἀλέομαι *imperat.* 507.4
ἄλεται (Hom.) 535
ἄλευαι 507.4
ἀλήθεια (Hom.) 206, 206a, 269a
ἀληθεΐᾰ 206a
ἀληθείη (Ion.) 269a
ἀληθέστερος 355, 357.2
ἀληθής 206
ἀλίνω (Hesych.) 479.4B
ἁλίσκομαι, ϝα- 442.1, .2, 467.3a
Ἄλκιππος 174
ἀλλαγή 465.2a
ἀλλάξω 465.2a
ἀλλάσσω 465.2a
ἀλληλο-, ἀλλᾱλο- 373
ἄλλο 71.6
ἄλλοθεν 367.2
ἄλλος 35, 193, 204, 355, 374.4, 465.2a
ἄλογος 108
ἀλοσύδνη 222.2

ἔπεψα 199, 465.1, .2
ἐπί 47, 358.3b, 406.5
ἔπιθον 115.2
ἐπὶ κέρως 293 *fn.*
επιμελοσθον (early Att.) 550.2
ἐπισ(σ)είω 190.4
ἐπίσταμαι 441a, 470
ἐπίστωμαι 535
ἐπλέχθην 208, 210
ἕπομαι 115.1, 160, 161, 164A.1, 170, 414a, 442.2
ἑπόμενος 560
ἔπος, ϝέπος 108, 116.2, 164A.1, 164B.2, 182, 296
ἑπτά 24.2, 170, 174.3, 388, 389.7
ἑπτα- 389.7a
ἑπτάς 403
ἐπτόμην 115.1, 506
ἐπυθόμην 115.3, 454A.1
ἔραμαι 470
ἐργασία 148.2
ἐργάτης 148.2
ἔργον, ϝέργον 230.2
ἔρδω 230.2, 456.1B
ἔρεβος 89
ἐρείδω 517.2a
ϝεϝρēμενα (Arg.) 190.6
ἐρέσσω 199, 465.2
ἐρέτης 199
ἐρετμόν 87, 199, 465.2
Ἐρετριεύς 319
ἐρέω (Ion.) 190.6, 445.3a, 457B
ἐρηρέδαται, -ατο (Hom.) 517.2a
ἔρις 342a
ἔρξω 230.2
ἑρπετόν 569.3
ἕρπω 442.2
ἐρράγην 190.7
ἐρράδαται, -ατο (Hom.) 517.2a
ἔρρεον 171
ἔρρηγμαι 519
ἐρρήθη 190.7
ἐρρύηκα *perf.* 445.2
ἔρρυθμος 224.1a
ἔρρωγα 516, 519
ἔρση 90
ἐρυθρός 38, 89, 147.2, 176
ἐρύκακον (Hom.) *aor.* 444
ἐρῦκω 444
ἔρυξα 444
ἔρχαται (εἴργω) (Hom.) 517
ἔρχεται 100a
ἔρχομαι 80, 100a, 456.3
ἔρως 293a
ἐς (= ἐξ) 230.3a, 406.4
ἕς *imperat.* (ἵημι) 547.2
ἑσ- 'six-' (Boeot.) 389.6a
ἐσάπη 507.2
ἐσάπην 452
ἔσβεσα 505.3
ἔσεσθαι *infin.* 552Ba
ἔσ(σ)εται 500.4
ἐσκέδασα 473b, 500.3
εσκηδεκατος (Boeot.) 389.6a
ἔσκον, ἔσκε 456.3, 492a
εσλελοιπασαι (Arc.) *3pl.* 430.3
ἐσμέν, εἰμέν 227.2b
ἔσ(σ)ομαι, ἐσόμεθα 80, 495, 500.1a
ἐσπάρθαι 230.2
ἔσπαρκα 519
ἔσπαρμαι *perf.* 445.2, 519
ἔσπασ(σ)α 468.1
ἔσπασμαι *perf.* 468.1
ἑσπέρᾱ 188
ἕσπερος 188
ἑσπόμην 115.1, 506
ἔσσαι 128.3a, 227.2c
ἐσσεῖται (Hom.) 495, 500.4
εσσετοι (Arc.) *3sg.* 436.2
ἔσσευα (Hom.) 507.4
ἐσσί (Hom.) *2sg.* 425a
ἔσσυμαι 519
ἔσται 80, 436.2, 495, 500.1a
ἐστάλθαι 230.2
ἔσταλκα 115.5, 519
ἔσταλμαι *perf.* 445.2, 519
ἕσταμεν (Hom.) 516, 518
ἔστειλα 229.2, 505.1
ἔστελλα (Lesb., Thess.) 229.2
ἕστηκα 518
ἑστήκᾱσιν (Hom.) 518
ἕστηκε 509
ἔστην, -ᾱν 507.2
ἑστήξω 521
ἐστί 31, 148.1, 169
ἑστίᾱ, Ἑστίᾱ 188
ἔστιχον 115.2
ἔστο 128.3a
ἐστόρεσα 109 *fn.*, 454A.3, 472.2, 505.3
ἔστρωσα (Hom.) 454A.3
ἔσφαξα 465.2a
ἔσχατος 406.4
ἔσχον 170a, 506
ἕσ(σ)ω 188
ἐτάθην 508.2
ἐτάλασσα (Hom.) 109, 123.2
εταλον (Cos) 41.2
ἔταμον 506
ἔταξα 465.2a
ἐτέθην 138.2
ἔτεινα 500.1b
ἔτεισα 459
ἔτεκον 506
ἐτέλεσ(σ)α 468.2, 505.3
ἐτελέσθη 508.2
ἔτεμον 454A.4, 506
ἕτερος 389.2B.2 *fn.*, 394
ἐτετεύχατο (Hom.) *3pl.* 437.3a
ἔτι 73.1, 148.1a, 406.10
ἐτίθει, -εις 497a
ἐτίθην, -ης, -η 497a
ἐτίμησα, -ᾱσα 505.2
ἔτῑσα, ἔτεισα 455, 459
ἑτοῖμος, ἕτοιμος 244
ἔτος, ϝέτος, ἔτος 41.2, 174.3, 296, 344
ἔτραπον 503, 506
ἔτρεπον 503
ἔτρεσα 505.3
ἐτρῑ́φθεν 210
ἐτύθην 138.2
εὐ- 86.2, 162
εὐδαιμονέστερος, -τατος 357.2
εὐθῦ́νω, εὐθῡνῶ 203.1
ϝεϝῡκονομειοντων (Boeot.) *perf.pple.* 562b
εὐμενής 273, 300, 344
εὐνούστερος 357.2
εὐπάτωρ 52.1
εὗρα (= εὗρον) 507.4b
εὐράγη (Lesb.) 190.7
εὑρίσκω 467.3a
εὖρος 39
εὐρύοπα (Hom.) 267.1a
εὐρύς 39
εὐρώς 442.1 *fn.*
εὕω 61, 172c
ἔφαγα 507.4b
ἐφᾱνα (Dor.) 228.1
ἐφάνην (Hom.) 508.2
ἐφάνθην 138.1, 508.2
ἔφην 456.3, 503
ἔφηνα 56, 228.1, .5, 505.1
ἔφησα 503
ἔφησθα (Hom.) 514.2
ἐφθάρην 76c
ἔφθαρμαι 519

LATIN

Alphabetization is anaesthetic to material in parenthesis.
The letters *u* and *v* are alphabetized together.

ALBANIAN

ARMENIAN

Avestan and Old Persian

OP adam 360
aēva- 388, 389.1A
ahi 425a, 492
ahma *1pl.* 369A
ahmi *dat.sg.* 367.3
aipi 406.5
aiti- 406.10
OP aiva- 389.1A
åŋhāire *3pl.* 437.3, 514.4
asman- 132
aspa- 160
āste 128.3a
ašta 388
āχtūirīm 116.1, 398.4
ayarə 267.2
azəm 360, 363
azgata- 569.3
aži- 163

baē 389.2A *fn.*
barāmi 52.2
barəmna- 560
baya- 389.2B
bi- 389.2Aa
biš 389.2A, .2Aa, 404.2

-ča 161, 381.1
čahmāi *dat.* 374.7, 379
čahyā *gen.* 375.1, 379, 380
čataŋrō 388. 389.4
čaturąm 389.4
čaθru- 389.4
čaθruš *adv.* 404.4
čaθwārō 387 *fn.*, 388, 389.4
čiš 380
čit̰ 381.1

daδa *perf.* 528
dāiδī 547.3b, .3c
dąm 257.11
dāŋ paiti- 257.4
dasa 156, 388, 389.10
dasəma- 398.10
daχša- 138
dažaiti 138
družaiti 147a
dva 388, 389.2A
dvaēθā 190.3
dvarə 257.11

frā 406.2
frabda- 111, 116.1
fraēšta- 353.4
fraγrīsəmnō 90
frāyas- 353.4
fšaoš *gen.* 311
fšūmant- 116.1, 311

gå *acc.pl.* 324
gąm 324
gaobīš 324c
gəmən *aor.* 324c
gərəbuš- 162, 298
gāš *gen./abl.* 324

ha- *pref.* 389.1Bb
ha, hā *prn.* 170
hačaitē 160
hakərət̰ 389.1Bb3
haoš- 62
hama- 389.1B, .1Ba
hapta 388, 389.7
hazaŋrəm 396
hē 367.3
hištaiti 443.3
huška- 117.1

jaiδi 547.3b
jantu- 324c
jasaiti 456.3
-jān *aor.* 324c

kaēnā- 161
kahmāi 379
kahmi 367.3
kahyā 379
kəm 381.1
kō 380
kudā 257.8 *fn.*, 381.3

mā 367.4
maibyā 367.3a
mana 367.2
mat̰ 367.5
mē 367.2, .2a
mərəti- 309
mərəzu- 223.4, 224.1
miryeite 456.1
mūš 275.3

nā *du.* 370
nå *pl.* 368, 369B
nāmąn *nom./acc.pl.* 282a
nava 388
nərəš 283

pairi 406.6
pairidaēza- 158
panča 141a, 161, 388, 389.5
paŋtahva- 398.5
pasu 311
pasvąm 316.5
ptā 102a
puθra- 223.2
puχδa- 398.5b

raoδi- 303.6
raoχšnā- 61, 230.2a, 231

saētē 128.3a, 426a, 436.3, 440a.1
saiθiš- 298
satəm 156, 388, 394
snaēža- 163
sōire 128.3a
spasyā 52.2
spasyeiti 168d
staχra- 518
staχta- 518

šē 367.3

tā 102a
tahmi *loc.* 374.7
taibyā 253
tē 367.2a
təm 376.1c
tisrō 388, 389.3
tū 363, 367.1
tūirya- 387 *fn.* 398.4
tvəm 363, 367.1

θrayō 261.2, 388, 389.3
θriš 404.3
θritya- 398.3
θwā 367.4
θwąm *acc.* 367.4
θwāt̰ 367.5
θwōi 374.4

upa 406.8

BALTIC

Unmarked forms are Lithuanian.

CELTIC

Unmarked forms are Old Irish

GOTHIC

Alphabetization is anaesthetic to prefixal *ga*-.

twalif 390

þahaidedun 452
þai 374.5, 376.1
þamma *dat.* 369B, 374.7
þata 236, 360, 374.2, 376.1
þaurnus 315
þeina 363
þis 376.1a
þizos 375.1
þos 376.1
þreis 388
þridja 398.3
þrija 303, 307.3, 377.1, 388, 389.3
þu, þuk 363, 360, 367.1
þulan 123.2
þus 363

uf 406.8
ufar 406.7
-uh 161, 381.1
unsara 364
uns(is) 364, 368

wahsjan 458
wait 512, 513
warmjan 163
wasti 188
wato 290
waurd 147.2
waurkeiþ 230.2
waurts 184.1, 303
weihs 58a, 156, 182
weis 364
weitwods 512, 561, 562
wiljau 484, 533
witum *1pl.* 36.6, 37, 513
wulfs 154.3, 161
wulla 104

HITTITE

The following letters are alphabetized together: *b* and *p* under *p*; *d* and *t* under *t*; *g*, *k*, and *q* under *k*; *i* and *e* under *e*; *w*, *ú*, and *u* under *u*. Plene vowels are disregarded for alphabetization purposes; doubly-written consonants are listed after singly-written ones.

a-i-iš 52.2
ag-ga-an-na-aš 290a
aq-qa-tar 290a, 291.2
a-ki 31, 290a
a-ku, ak-du 549.2
a-ku-wa-an-na-aš 290a
a-ku-wa-an-za *nom.* 554
a-ku-wa-tar 290a
ak-ku-uš-kán-zi 430.1
am-me-el 363
am-me-e-da-az 363
am-mu-uk 363
an-na(-i) 259
an-na-az, an-na-za 259
an-ni-iš *nom.pl.* 260
an-tu-uḫ-ša-aš *dat.pl.* 257.12
an-za-a-aš 364
an-zi-el 364
an-zi-ta-az 364
a-pa-a-aš 380
ap-pa 47, 406.5
ap-pa-an-na-aš 31, 291.2
ap-pa-an-za *nom.* 554
ap-pa-an-zi 119.1
ap-pa-a-tar 291.2
a-pí-e 260, 374.5
ap-pí-iš-ke-ir 456.3
a-ar- 513
a-ar-aš-ki-iz-zi 100a, 456.3
(a-)ar-nu- 423C, 455, 467 *fn.*, 472.1
(a-)ar-nu-ut 547.3a
ar-ta(-ri) 426a
a-ru-na 259.6a
a-ša-an-za *nom.* 554
a-ša-an-zi 430.2
a-aš-šu-uš 126.3
(a-)aš-šu-wa-aš, (a-)aš-ša-wa-aš *gen.* 321
a-da-an-na *supine* 259.6a
a-da-an-za *nom.* 31, 554
a-da-an-zi 31
a-da-tar 259.6a
a-tu-e-ni 487
at-ta-an 259
at-ta-aš *nom.sg.*, *gen.sg.* 259, 260.1
ad-da-aš *dat.pl.* 260
at-ti 259
at-te-eš 260, .1
ad-du-uš 260
az-za-aš-te-ni 212

É-ir, É-ni 257.11
e-ku-uz-zi 290a
e-ip- 103, 423A, 448, 554
e-ip-pí-ir 456.3
e-ip-mi 119.1
e-ip-zi 89b, 291.2
e-ir-u-e-ni 513
e-eš- 'be' 434, 448, 492, 493, 554
e-ša((-a)-ri) 'sit' 128.3a, 426a
(e-)eš-ḫa-na-aš 290a
e-eš-ḫar 290a, 455
e-eš-ḫar-nu-ut 455
e-eš-ta 425
e-šu-un 493
e-eš-zi 31, 169, 426, 492
e-it-mi 448, 487
e-iz-za-az-zi 212, 448

ḫa-an-za 406.1
ḫa-a-ra-aš, ḫa-(a-)ra-na-aš 282c
ḫa-ar-k- 554
ḫar-ka-an-za *nom.* 554
ḫar-ki-e-ir 453
ḫar-ki-iš 47
ḫar-na-a-uš 321
ḫar-ni-in-k- 554
ḫar-ni-in-ka-an-za *nom.* 554
ḫar-ni-in-ki-ir 453
ḫar-ta-ag-ga- 96, 235.1
ḫa-a-ši 481 *fn.*
(-zi-ik) ḫa-aš-ki-it 456.3
ḫa-aš-ta-(a-)i 102, 117.2a, 322.2
ḫa-wi- (Luv.) 117.2a, 182
ḫé-e-uš, -un 319 *fn.*
ḫu-iš-nu-zi, ḫu-iš-zi 455

MYCENAEAN

OLD CHURCH SLAVIC

OLD ENGLISH

æ is alphabetized between *a* and *b*.

Old High German and Old Saxon

k is alphabetized with *c*.

OLD NORSE AND OLD ICELANDIC

Old Norse forms are in roman type; *OIc. forms are in italic type.*

OSCAN

The letters *c* and **k** are alphabetized together

SANSKRIT

Alphabetical order as in Devanāgarī. Unmarked forms are Vedic.

TOCHARIAN

A āmpi 389.2B2
B arkwi 47
A känt 394
B nekcīye 113b
A nmuka 389.9a
A ñem 90B ñom 90
A ñu 90 *fn.*
B ñumka 389.9a
A smi- 171
B śwerppewä 389.2Ad
A tkaṃ, tkanis 235.1
B wi *m.f.* 389.2Ad
A wiyo *m.*, wiyoss *f.* 389.2Ad
A wu *m.*, we *f.* 389.2Ad
A ysār 290a

UMBRIAN

The letters *c* and **k** are alphabetized together.

ahesnes 88.3d, 225.1
alfer 143
ař- 406.10

berus 315, 316.4
berva 315
bum 324

karu, karne 287.1
castruo, **kastruvu** 316.3
kuraia 426

dede 426
dequrier 403
desenduf 390
dirsans 237.5
dupla, dupursus 389.2Aa

esme, esmei 374.7a
esmik 374.7a
esmen (SPic.) 374.7a
ess- 377.5
estu 377.5
etatu, etato 549.1

farsio 223.3
fašia 488Ba
ferar 426a
ferest 457B
fe(i)tu 481
frater 284B3c
fratrus 277.4, 284B.3b
furent 534, 537
furfant 430.1

hondomu 356
hondra 45.1

iouie 330a
iouies 330a
iuku 83.3b
iuvepatre 284B.3c
iupater, iuve (patre) 327

maletu 389.9a
manf 315, 316.2
mani 313, 314.5
manuve 313
mehe 367.3
mutu 83.3b, 260.3, 263

ner- 330a
nuvime 374.7a, 389.9a
nuvis 42.1a

onse 45.1

pelmner 231.2
pir 50.2b, 290a
promom 398.1
prumum 398.1
prupehast 457B
pufe 381.3
pufe 257.8 *fn.*
puntes 141a
púntiis 398.5a
purome 290a
purtuvitu 488Ab
pusme 374.7a

ri 330a

sahatam 34
sestentasiaru 398.6
sif 50.2b
sim 50.2b, 318
snata 225.1c
somo 219
stakaz 518
staflarem 147.2
stahmei 34
stahu 476
suboca(u)u 476

tekuries 264
tefe 367.3
tefre 259
tertim 389.3
tote 263
tertiu 398.3
tišit 426
tota 135
touer 367.2, 371.2
traha(f), traf 34, 97
trefi, trifu 50.2b
tribřišu 282c
trif 303
trifo 314.6
trifu 313, 314.6
triia 303, 389.3
triiuper 83.3b
trioper 303, 307.3
tripler 401
tursa 263
tuta, tutas, tute, 263, 263.2
SPic. **tútas** 135
tuva 389.2A

uerfale 303
ulu 377.4
une 290
unu 389.1A
urnasiaru 264
urtas 264
utur 290, 291.2b

vitlaf 264
vitluf 35, 41.2

zeřef 559.1